Contents

New Zealand

a Lonely Planet travel survival kit

Peter Turner
Jeff Williams
Nancy Keller
Tony Wheeler

New Zealand

8th edition

Published by

Lonely Planet Publications

Head Office: PO Box 617, Hawthorn, Vic 3122, Australia

Branches: 155 Filbert St, Suite 251, Oakland, CA 94607, USA
10 Barley Mow Passage, Chiswick, London W4 4PH, UK
71 bis rue du Cardinal Lemoine, 75005 Paris, France

Printed by

Colorcraft Ltd, Hong Kong

Photographs by

Vicki Beale
Trudi Canavan
Coastal Kayakers
DOC (Department of Conservation, New Zealand)
Dolphin Discoveries
Trust Bank, Royal Albatross Centre, Dunedin
Charlotte Hindle
Nancy Keller
Holger Leue
Richard Nebesky
NZ Tourism Board, Dunedin
Doc Ross
Ray Stamp
Richard Timbury
Peter Turner
David Wall
Tony Wheeler
Jeff Williams

First Published

December 1977

This Edition

June 1996

National Library of Australia Cataloguing in Publication Data

Turner, Peter
New Zealand

8th ed.
Includes index.
ISBN 0 86442 359 4.

1. New Zealand – Guidebooks. I. Williams, Jeff, 1954 Dec. 15-. II. Wheeler, Tony, 1946-. New Zealand. III. Title. (Series : Lonely Planet travel survival kit).

919.30437

Peter Turner

Peter Turner was born in Melbourne and after various forays around the world and a variety of occupations joined Lonely Planet in 1986 as an editor. Now a full-time travel writer, he works mostly in South-East Asia and has contributed to Lonely Planet books on *Malaysia, Singapore & Brunei*, *Indonesia*, *South-East Asia on a shoestring* and is the author of *Jakarta city guide* and *Singapore city guide*.

Jeff Williams

Jeff is a Kiwi, originally from Greymouth on New Zealand's wild West Coast. He lives in Melbourne, when not travelling, and tries to keep abreast of his toddler, Callum, and his enthusiasm and exploration.

When not working for LP he amuses himself walking, mountaineering, skiing and birdwatching on whichever continent will have him. He is the author or co-author of various other LP books including *Australia, Western Australia, South Africa, Lesotho & Swaziland, Outback Australia* and *Tramping in New Zealand*.

Nancy Keller

Nancy was born and raised in Northern California, and worked in the alternative press for several years, doing every aspect of newspaper work from editorial and reporting to delivering the papers. She returned to university to earn a master's degree in journalism, finally graduating in 1986 after many breaks for extended stays on the west coast of Mexico. Since then she's been travelling and writing in Mexico, Israel, Egypt, Europe, various South Pacific islands, New Zealand and Central America. She has worked on several LP books, including *Central America*, *Rarotonga & the Cook Islands*, *Mexico* and *California & Nevada*.

Tony Wheeler

Tony was born in England but grew up in Pakistan, the Bahamas and the USA. He returned to England to do a degree in engineering at Warwick University, worked as an automotive design engineer, returned to university to complete an MBA in London, then dropped out on the Asian overland trail with his wife, Maureen. Eventually settling down in Australia, they've been travelling, writing and publishing guidebooks ever since, having set up Lonely Planet Publications in the mid-1970s. Travel for the Wheelers is considerably enlivened by their daughter, Tashi, and their son, Kieran.

From Peter

Thanks to the New Zealand Tourism Board in Sydney and New Zealand, and to the many helpful information centres and tourism operators throughout New Zealand who gave generously of their time and expertise. Thanks also to the 'in-laws' – Doreen, Pat, Louise, Roy and John and everyone else for hospitality and help, and to Ann in Auckland for some great dining tips. Above all thanks to my wife, Lorraine, who first introduced me to New Zealand and the wonders of things Kiwi. Last but not least, a dedication to my daughters, Ruby and Madeleine, who loved New Zealand and got to see some of their second homeland.

From Jeff

There are so many people to thank for making my research trip to New Zealand so worthwhile. Thanks to Myra Williams, Linda & Winston Monk in Greymouth for unfailing hospitality; Rosemary & Bernard Green & kids in Runanga for proving that a family of seven is not an impossibility; Alison and Callum Hunter Williams at home; and co-author Peter Turner for company on the road and advice at home.

Thanks also to Gaynor Stanley of the New Zealand Tourism Board (Sydney); Michelle Kinney of Canterbury Tourism; Allanah James and Nicholas Cowie of Mt Cook Airlines for being the good sorts they are; the irrepressible Mary Anne Webber, ex of the Marlborough District Council; Andy Brinsley (and his partner Claire) for a great game of golf with a rodent at Millbrook; Helen Paterson of Fiordland Travel; white-water sledger Thierry Huet and fun yakker Eric Billoud (both Frogs); Graeme Kayak of Alpine River Guides; Brian & Lesley of Elm Lodge, Dunedin; the Coupers and Bob at the Southern Comfort, Invercargill; the staff of Surf Rafting Dunedin Ltd (especially Matt), yet again; Lesley Gray of Stewart Island Promotions; the Goomes family and son Tony Gomez for the Rakiura Track followed by paua and blue cod; Natalie and Smadar for being good companions in Central Otago; Rosco Baudin of Milford Sound Sea Kayaks for a great buzz in the 'Eighth Wonder'; Sue Newell of the Helicopter Line, Glentanner, and pilot Steve; Air Safaris, Tekapo, for the Grand Traverse; Glacier Helicopters, Franz Josef, for great photo opportunities; Icarus for melting his wings and turning Mount Cook to gold; Helen McConochie of Tourism Nelson; Erena Jarden of the Greymouth information centre; and the staff of The Villa, Picton, for letting me cook my fresh seafood.

In Wellington there were also many willing helpers. Alanah Joe of the Hub for bookings and info; the staff of the visitor information centre; Ferne McKenzie of DOC for sorting out photos of flora & fauna; and Pearl Hewson for info on DOC (thank goodness someone knows what the department is doing).

This Book

This book has had a varied history. Tony Wheeler did the 1st edition back in 1977 and the next two were updated by New Zealander Simon Hayman. The 4th edition was updated by Mary Covernton, Tony Wheeler updated the 5th edition with Robin Tinker who wrote the tramping section. The 6th edition was updated by Nancy Keller, who updated the 7th edition with Jeff Williams. Jeff Williams and Peter Turner updated this edition.

Thanks to the many travellers who took the time to write, giving us their opinions and comments. We've taken all suggestions on board and tried to accommodate as many as possible. A list of all your names is included on pages 708-9.

From the Publisher

This edition was edited by Lindsay Brown and Liz Filleul with editing and proofing assistance from Brigitte Barta, Paul Smitz, Adrienne Costanzo and Jane Marks. Ann Jeffree was responsible for the design, maps and illustrations with help from Jacqui Saunders, Indra Kilfoyle, Margaret Jung, Chris Klep and Tamsin Wilson. Thanks to Jane Hart and Adrienne Costanzo for their support and assistance in producing this edition.

Warning & Request

Things change – prices go up, schedules change, good places go bad and bad places go bankrupt – nothing stays the same. So if you find things better or worse, recently opened or long since closed, please write and tell us and help make the next edition better. Your letters will be used to help update future editions and, where possible, important changes will also be included in a Stop Press section in reprints.

We greatly appreciate all information that is sent to us by travellers. Back at Lonely Planet we employ a hard-working readers' letters team to sort through the many letters we receive. The best ones will be rewarded with a free copy of the next edition or another Lonely Planet guide if you prefer. We give away lots of books, but, unfortunately, not every letter/postcard receives one.

Map Legend

BOUNDARIES

- International Boundary
- Regional Boundary

ROUTES

- Freeway
- Highway
- Major Road
- Unsealed Road or Track
- City Road
- City Street
- Railway
- Underground Railway
- Tram
- Walking Track
- Walking Tour
- Ferry Route
- Cable Car or Chairlift

AREA FEATURES

- Parks
- Built-Up Area
- Pedestrian Mall
- Market
- Cemetery
- Glacier, Ice Cap
- Beach or Desert
- Mountain Ranges

HYDROGRAPHIC FEATURES

- Coastline
- River, Creek
- Intermittent River or Creek
- Rapids, Waterfalls
- Lake, Intermittent Lake
- Canal
- Swamp

SYMBOLS

- CAPITAL — National Capital
- Capital — Regional Capital
- CITY — Major City
- City — City
- Town — Town
- Village — Village
- Place to Stay, Place to Eat
- Cafe, Pub or Bar
- Post Office, Telephone
- Tourist Information, Bank
- Transport, Parking
- Museum, Youth Hostel
- Caravan Park, Camping Ground
- Church, Cathedral
- Mosque, Synagogue
- Marae, Embassy
- Medical Centre, Police Station
- Public Toilet, Petrol Station
- Airport, Airfield
- Swimming Pool, Gardens
- Shopping Centre, Fauna Park
- Winery or Vineyard, Golf Course
- A25 — One Way Street, Route Number
- Building of Interest, Monument
- Castle, Mine
- Cave, Hut or Chalet
- Mountain or Hill, Lookout
- Lighthouse, Shipwreck
- Pass, Spring
- Beach, Ski Field
- Archaeological Site or Ruins
- Ancient or City Wall
- Cliff or Escarpment, Tunnel
- Railway Station

Note: not all symbols displayed above appear in this book

Introduction

Fresh air, magnificent scenery and outdoor activities are the feature attractions of New Zealand. It's not a big country but for sheer variety it's hard to beat. As soon as you reach New Zealand, you quickly see that its reputation for being 'clean and green' is well deserved. Visitors who come expecting a pristine, green, well-organised little country are not disappointed.

New Zealand is like a microcosm of all the world's attractions. Here you can tramp on the sides of active volcanoes, or in remote, rugged patches of virgin rainforest, through thermal areas of geysers and boiling mud, or kauri forests with some of the largest and oldest trees on earth. You can swim with dolphins, watch whales, see glaciers descending into rainforests, fish for trout in cold, pristine streams and see fur seals and penguins swimming around the boat as you cruise on remote fiords. If you're adventurous you can go white-water rafting, cave rafting, rock and mountain climbing, tandem skydiving, skiing down long glaciers, and much more. And of course there's bungy jumping! Plus there are many chances to experience the fascinating Maori culture and the warmth of New Zealand's friendly people.

There are cities too, with some fascinating museums and a cultural life that's a lot more interesting than it was even just a few years ago. All the major cities have a great nightlife with live theatre, dancing and arty cafe scenes. Arts & crafts are popular and all the major cities have fine galleries.

Getting around is easy and cycling through the country is a popular way to

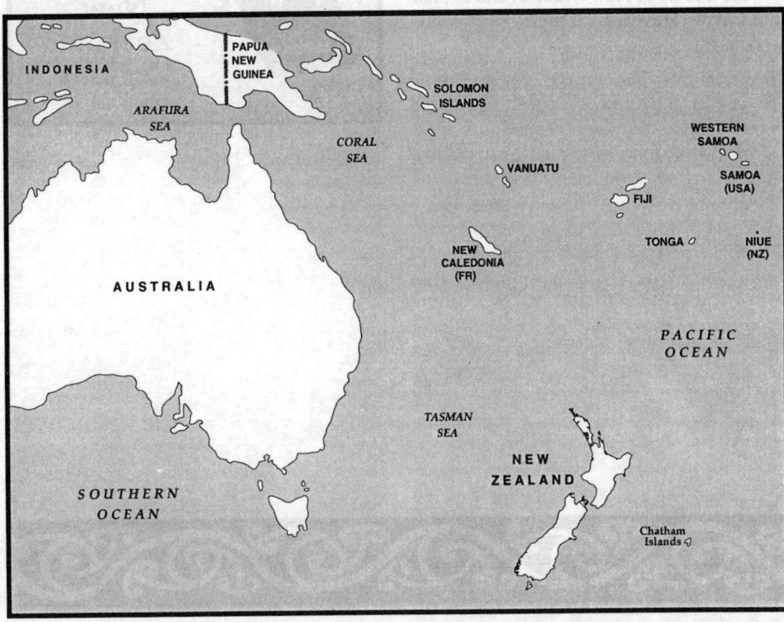

travel. Finding affordable accommodation is also easy, although it's a good idea to book ahead if you decide to go there in the high season. The food is fresh and there's plenty of it, and even the wine is excellent.

Travellers do have one consistent complaint about New Zealand, though. That is, that in their travel plans they haven't allowed themselves enough time in the country. Look at the map of the world and it doesn't appear as a big country. However, once you arrive in New Zealand, it soon becomes apparent how much there is to see and do.

If time is no object, we'd recommend allowing at least six weeks for a visit to New Zealand. Of course you can still enjoy the country if you have less time; you might pick just a few places or activities that especially captivate your interest and focus your trip around those. On the other hand, some travellers make a mad dash through the country, rushing from activity to activity, and have a great time.

This book will help to show you all there is to see and do in New Zealand, and to plan your travels. Have a great time. It's a beautiful country.

Organisation of this Book

The following map shows how we have divided the country:

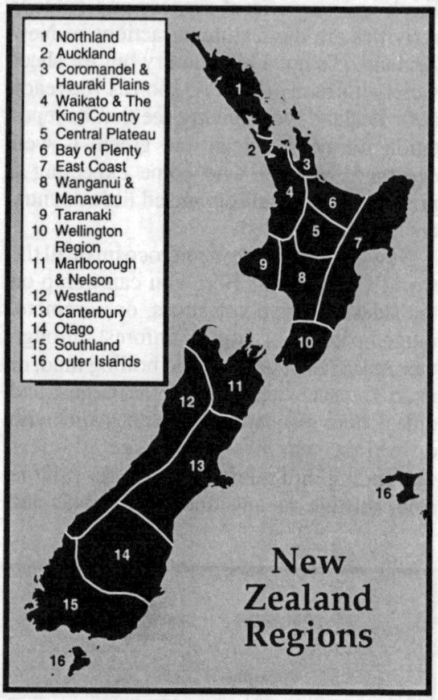

Facts about the Country

HISTORY

New Zealand's history has two distinct phases – the pre-European phase and the more recent history since the arrival of Europeans.

Pre-European History

The original inhabitants of New Zealand were known until fairly recently as Moriori, or moa hunters. Recent evidence indicates that Polynesians arrived in New Zealand in a series of migrations and that the people known as Moriori were in fact an early wave of these Polynesians and not a separate race from the Maori, who came later. Estimates are that these first Polynesians arrived in New Zealand over 1000 years ago, possibly around 800 AD or earlier.

The reason for the great voyage across the ocean in canoes remains unknown, but whether by accident or design, the first settlers found temperate islands far larger than any islands of the Pacific. They named it Aotearoa, or land of the long white cloud. Apart from bats, the land was devoid of mammals for hunting but the sea provided abundant food resources. Of the birdlife, the most spectacular was the huge flightless bird, the moa, standing up to 3.7 metres high.

This abundant food supply became the staple of early Polynesians, especially in the South Island, where the moa was hunted for its food and feathers until it became extinct. Agriculture was not well developed in this early 'Archaic' period of settlement, perhaps because of the colder climate. The agricultural societies based on imported Polynesian crops of *kumara* (sweet potato), taro and yams came later, and this second era of settlement is known as the 'Classic Maori' period.

Maori oral histories tell of the discovery of New Zealand by the navigator Kupe, ascribed to the year 950 AD, but differing tribes have differing legends explaining the settlement of New Zealand. Kupe sailed to Aotearoa from Hawaiki, the 'ancestral homeland' for many Polynesian peoples. Despite the similar names, Hawaiki is not Hawaii. The location of Hawaiki is unknown, though some experts believe it may have been an island in the Marquesas in what is now French Polynesia. The same legends tell of the Great Migration of around 1350, when a fleet of canoes left catastrophe-stricken Hawaiki for Aotearoa. The new immigrants from the great fleet soon established themselves in their adopted home, displacing or assimilating with the previous residents. This widely held 'history' is now believed to be the dubious adaptation of Maori legends by early Western historians, but it does point to a long period of migration from Polynesia.

Maori societies were tribal and revolved around the *iwi* (tribe) or *hapu* (sub-tribe). Ancestor worship was very important and long genealogies *(whakapapa)*, often stretching back to one of the canoe groups of the Great Migration, were committed to memory. The societies were hierarchical, and positions of leadership were largely hereditary.

The hapu were further divided into *whanau*, extended family groups that combined to form communal villages centred around the *marae*, sacred ground in front of the meeting house where the tribe's ancestral spirits resided. Here ceremonies were held and elders and others of authority addressed the community. Various local chiefs existed, all under the authority of the *ariki* or supreme chief of the entire tribe. At the bottom of the pecking order were the slaves taken from opposing tribes in battle.

Maori religion was complex with a variety of gods representing the sea, sky, mountains, war, agriculture etc. The priests or *tohunga* could communicate with the gods and knew the rituals associated with offerings, but they were also the scholars responsible for maintaining the history, genealogy, stories and songs of the tribe.

Essential to Maori religion and society were the notions of *mauri* (life force) and *wairua* (spirit) that reside in all things and *mana* (spiritual power or prestige). *Tapu* (taboo) applied to forbidden objects, such as sacred ground or a chief's possessions, but also to actions or even people proscribed by the tribe.

One of the best ways to promote the mana of a tribe was in battle, and the Maori had a highly developed warrior society. War had its own worship, sacrifices, rituals, dances and art forms. Tribes engaged in numerous battles over territory, for *utu* (revenge) or for other reasons, with the losers often becoming slaves or food. Eating an enemy not only delivered the ultimate insult but also took on the enemy's life force or power. The Maori built defensive villages or *pa*, which they retreated to when attacked. These fortresses were built on terraced hilltops with concentric defensive walls. If the outer wall was breached the defenders could retreat to the next fortified inner terrace.

Though remaining a Neolithic culture – it would have been difficult to get beyond that stage in New Zealand, since there are few metals apart from gold – the Maori evolved elaborate artistic traditions. Facing the marae ornate meeting houses were constructed featuring powerful wooden carvings depicting the ancestors, as well as woven flax wall panels and symbolic paintings.

The higher classes were decorated with intricate tattooing – the women with *moko* on the chin only, the high-ranking men not only with it over the entire face but over other parts of the body as well.

They made clothing from the fur of dogs, flax, feathers and other materials; warm fur cloaks decorated with feathers can still be seen in some NZ museums. Wood carving

Maori Legend – Creation of the Earth & Sky

In the beginning there was nothingness. Before the light, there was only darkness.

Rangi nui, the Sky, dwelt with Papa tu a nuku, the Earth. The two were united and bore many children. Papa's nakedness was covered with many things begotten from her union with Rangi – land, trees, animals of the sea, and many other created things – so that she would not be naked. But all lived in utter darkness.

Rangi (Sky-Father) and Papa (Earth-Mother) had six important children. They were Tawhiri matea, God of winds and storms; Tangaroa, God of the sea and of all things living in it; Tane mahuta, God of the forest and of all things that live in the forest; Haumia tiketike, God of wild plants that give food for humankind, including the fern root, berries and many others; Rongo ma Tane, God of cultivated food, including the kumara and all other plants cultivated for food by humankind; and Tu matauenga, the God of war.

After aeons and aeons of living in darkness, because their parents were joined together and no light had ever yet come between them, the children of Rangi and Papa could take it no longer; they wanted light. They debated what should they do. Eventually they decided that the thing to do was to separate their parents, so that light could enter the world.

They each tried, and failed, to separate Rangi and Papa. Finally it was Tane mahuta's turn to try, and he pushed and strained, his shoulders to the ground and his feet to the sky, and finally succeeded in forcing his parents apart. Light flooded into the world. Thus Tane mahuta became father of the day.

The two parents were grief stricken at having been separated. They have been separated ever since, but their love for one another has never faded. In the beginning, Rangi shed so many tears that much of the land that had been revealed to light became covered by sea. Finally some of their children turned Papa over onto her stomach, so that Rangi and Papa would not always be looking at one another and grieving. Rangi still cries for his wife, but not as much as before when there was a danger that all the land would be drowned because of his tears; his tears now are the drops of dew that form every night on Papa's back. The mists that form in the mornings in the valleys, and rise towards the heavens, are Papa's sighs of longing for her husband. ■

Maori Legend – Creation of New Zealand

A long time after the creation of the world – after Tane mahuta had created a woman out of red earth, breathed life into her nostrils, mated with her and had a daughter, who also became his wife and bore him other daughters, and after many other things had happened – the demigod Maui, who lived in Hawaiki, went out fishing with his brothers.

They went further and further out to sea. When they were a long way out, Maui took out his magic fish-hook (the jaw of his sorcerer grandmother), tied it to a strong rope, then dropped it over the side of the canoe. Soon he caught an immense fish and, struggling mightily, pulled it up.

This fish became the North Island of New Zealand, called by the ancient Maori Te ika a Maui (the fish of Maui) or sometimes 'Te ikaroa a Maui' (the big fish of Maui). The Mahia Peninsula, at the north end of Hawke Bay on the east coast of the North Island, was known as Te matau a Maui (the fish-hook of Maui), since it was the hook with which he caught the giant fish.

The South Island was known as Te waka a Maui or the 'canoe of Maui', in which he was sitting when he caught the fish. Kaikoura Peninsula, on the north-east coast of the South Island, was the seat of the canoe. Another name for the South Island was Te wai Pounamu (the water greenstone), since much greenstone (jade, or pounamu) was found in the rivers there.

Stewart Island, south of the South Island, was known as Te punga a Maui (the anchor of Maui). It was the anchor that held the canoe as Maui hauled in the giant fish. ■

became more and more refined, culminating in the period immediately preceding European intervention. They also made greenstone (jade) ornaments and war clubs, and beautifully carved war canoes, as well as a variety of household items. Expeditions were mounted to the South Island to find jade, but otherwise most of the tribes stayed on the much warmer North Island.

European Exploration

In 1642 Dutch explorer Abel van Tasman, who had just sailed around Australia from Batavia (modern-day Jakarta, Indonesia), sailed up the west coast of New Zealand but didn't stay long after his only attempt at landing resulted in several of his crew being killed and eaten. He christened the land Niuew Zeeland, after the Netherlands' province of Zeeland, and the European powers now knew of Aotearoa's existence.

The Dutch, after this first uncomfortable look, were none too keen to return and it was left alone until British navigator and explorer Captain James Cook sailed around New Zealand in the *Endeavour* in 1769.

Since Tasman had only sailed up the west coast, there had been speculation that this could be the west coast of the fabled great southern continent. In the logical European cosmology, it was thought that a large southern land must exist to balance the large land masses in the northern hemisphere.

Cook sailed right around the coast of New Zealand, on three voyages altogether, mapping as he went, and many places in New Zealand still bear the names that he gave them. Cook made a number of friendly contacts with the Maori, discovered that his Tahitian interpreter could communicate with them and was impressed with their bravery and spirit, and with the potential of this lightly populated land. Having concluded his sail around the coasts of both the North and South Islands and determined that this was not the large southern continent, he claimed the entire land for the British crown and continued on to Australia.

Another European, the French explorer Jean-François Marie de Surville, was sailing around New Zealand at the same time as Cook but the two never did bump into one another. They came very close, passing each other in a storm off the coast of the North Island, each unaware of the other's presence.

When the British started their antipodean colonising they opted for the larger and even more lightly populated Australia. New Zealand's first European settlers were temporary ones – sealers (who soon reduced the seal population to next to nothing) and then whalers (who did the same with the whales). They introduced diseases and prostitution, created such a demand for preserved heads that Maori chiefs started chopping off their slaves' heads to order (previously they'd only preserved the heads of warriors who had died in battle) and worst of all they brought in European firearms. When they exchanged greenstone *meres* (war clubs) for muskets, the Maori soon embarked on wholesale slaughter of one another. The Ngapuhi tribe from Northland, led by Hongi Hika, embraced the new technology and sent raiding parties throughout the central North Island as far south as Hawke Bay (East Coast) and Taranaki in the west.

By 1830 the Maori population was falling dramatically.

The *haka* (Maori war chant) is a traditional preparation for war

European Settlement

The first missionary, Samuel Marsden, brought Christianity to New Zealand in 1814, and other missionaries soon followed. The Bible was translated into Maori, and for the first time the Maori language was written down. By the middle of the 19th century tribal warfare had abated, cannibalism had been fairly well stamped out and the raging impact of European diseases were also curbed. But the Maori people now found themselves spiritually assaulted and much of their tradition and culture were irrevocably altered. Their numbers continued to decline.

During the early 19th century European (*Pakeha* in Maori) settlers were arriving in increasing numbers, some on settlement campaigns organised from Britain, and in the 1830s entrepreneurs from Australia raced to carve out holdings in the new land. Growing lawlessness from less savoury settlers and a deterioration in Maori-Pakeha relations resulted in petitions for British intervention.

The British were not too keen on further colonising – what with burning their fingers in America, fighting in Canada, and stretching their involvement in other places, not to mention having Australia to worry about. The need to establish law finally prompted them to dispatch James Busby as the British Resident in 1833. The fact that this was a very low-key effort is illustrated by poor Busby even having to pay his own fare from Australia and, once he'd set up shop in Kororareka (now called Russell) in Northland, his efforts to protect the settlers and keep law and order were made somewhat difficult by his having no forces, no arms and no authority. He was soon dubbed 'the man of war without guns'.

Treaty of Waitangi

In 1838 lawlessness was still a problem, unscrupulous 'purchases' of Maori land continued unabated and the threat of a French colonising effort at Akaroa in the South Island all stirred the British to seek annexation of New Zealand. Captain William

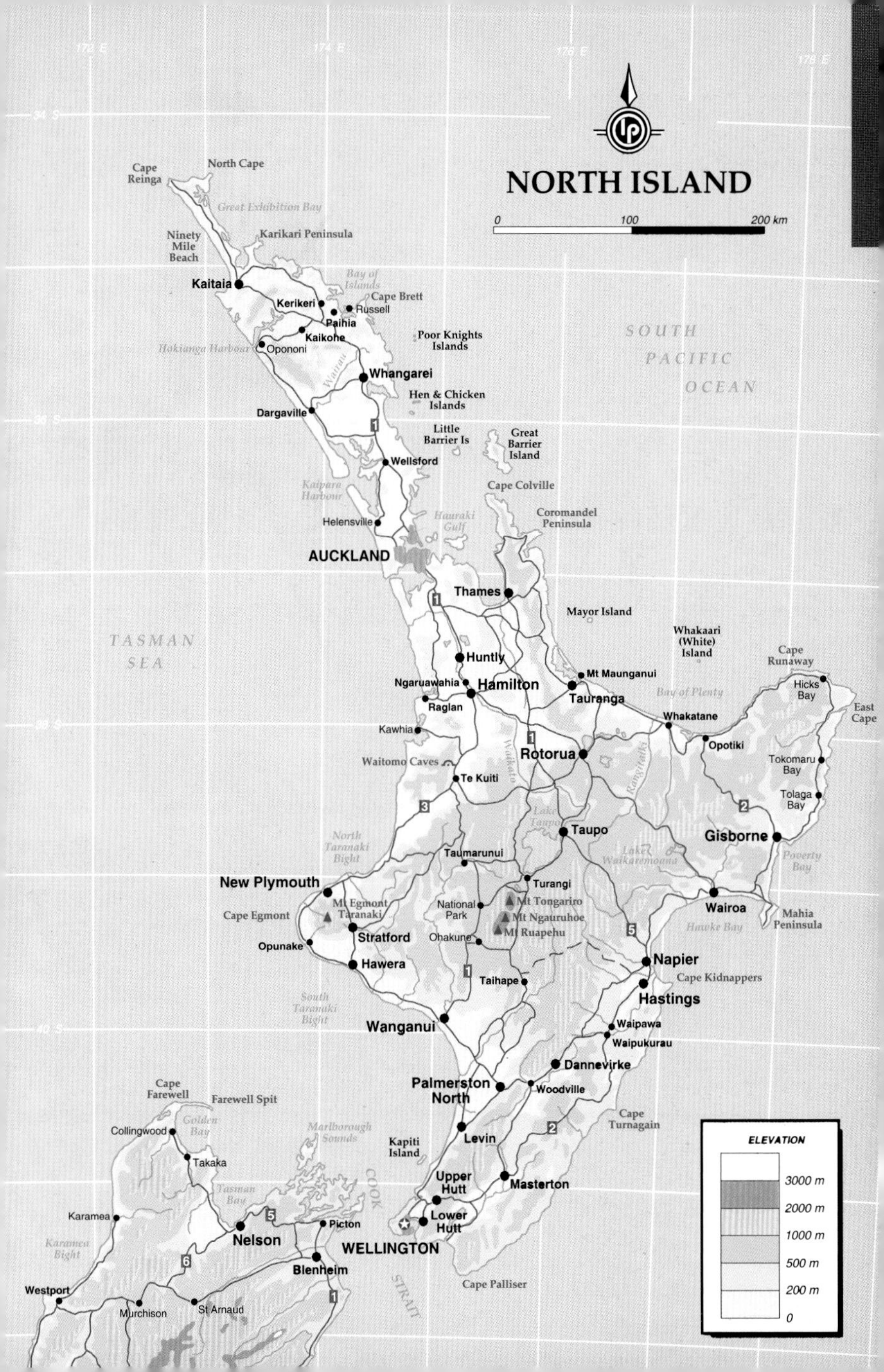

NORTH ISLAND
0
100
200 km
172 E
174 E
176 E
178 E
34 S
36 S
38 S
40 S
North Cape
Cape Reinga
Great Exhibition Bay
Ninety Mile Beach
Karikari Peninsula
Kaitaia
Bay of Islands
Cape Brett
Kerikeri
Russell
Paihia
Kaikohe
Hokianga Harbour
Opononi
Poor Knights Islands
Whangarei
Hen & Chicken Islands
Dargaville
Little Barrier Is
Great Barrier Island
Wellsford
Kaipara Harbour
Cape Colville
Coromandel Peninsula
Hauraki Gulf
Helensville
AUCKLAND
Thames
Mayor Island
SOUTH PACIFIC OCEAN
TASMAN SEA
Huntly
Whakaari (White) Island
Cape Runaway
Ngaruawahia
Hamilton
Mt Maunganui
Tauranga
Bay of Plenty
Hicks Bay
East Cape
Raglan
Whakatane
Kawhia
Opotiki
Rotorua
Waitomo Caves
Te Kuiti
Tokomaru Bay
Tolaga Bay
Lake Taupo
Taupo
Gisborne
North Taranaki Bight
Lake Waikaremoana
Poverty Bay
Taumarunui
New Plymouth
Turangi
Mt Egmont Taranaki
National Park
Mt Tongariro
Mt Ngauruhoe
Mt Ruapehu
Wairoa
Cape Egmont
Mahia Peninsula
Stratford
Ohakune
Hawke Bay
Opunake
Napier
Hawera
Cape Kidnappers
Taihape
Hastings
South Taranaki Bight
Wanganui
Waipawa
Waipukurau
Dannevirke
Palmerston North
Woodville
Cape Farewell
Farewell Spit
Golden Bay
Collingwood
Marlborough Sounds
Kapiti Island
Cape Turnagain
Levin
Takaka
Tasman Bay
COOK STRAIT
Upper Hutt
Masterton
Karamea
Lower Hutt
Picton
Nelson
WELLINGTON
Karamea Bight
Blenheim
Cape Palliser
Westport
Murchison
St Arnaud
ELEVATION
3000 m
2000 m
1000 m
500 m
200 m
0

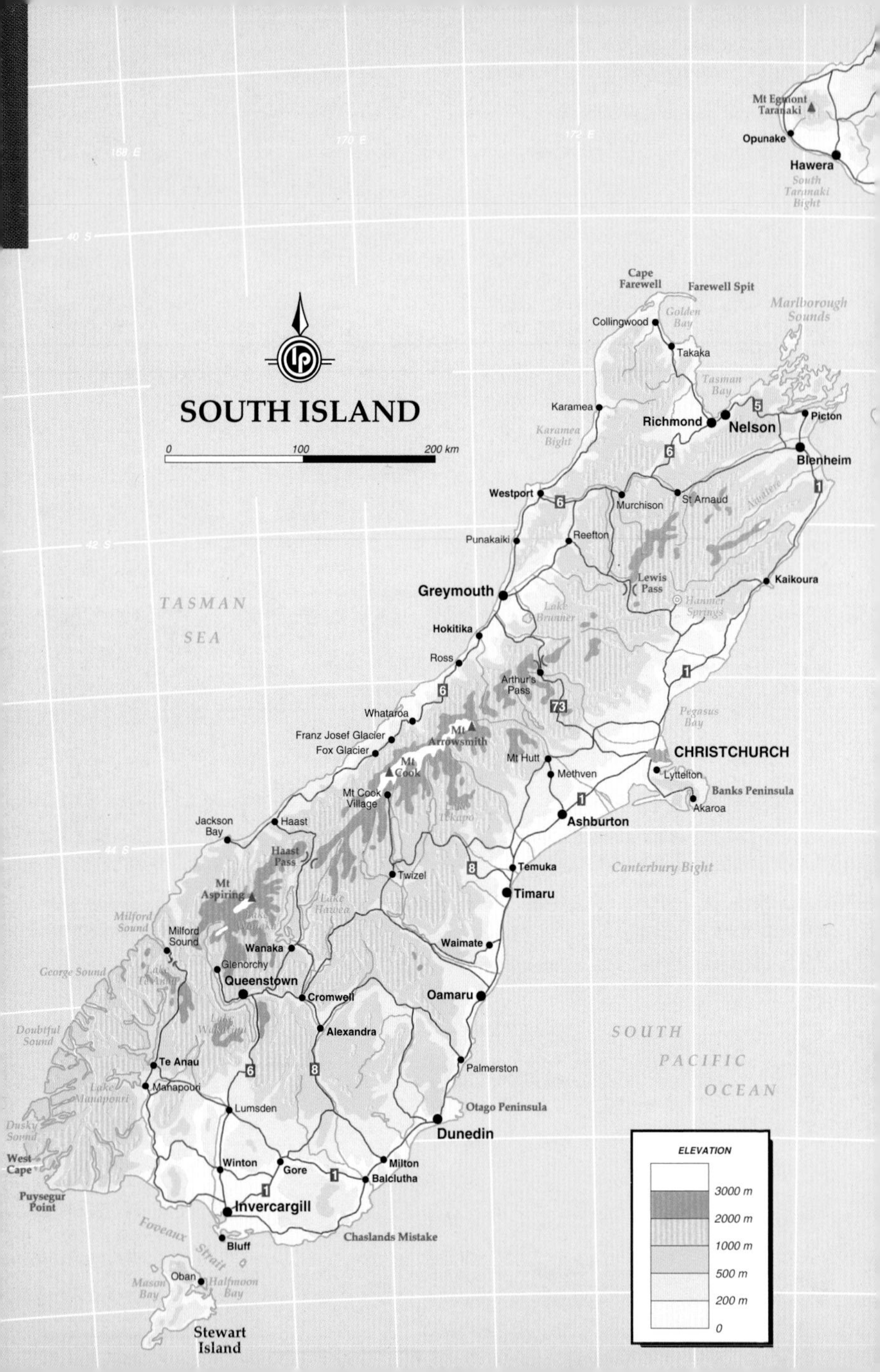
SOUTH ISLAND
0
100
200 km
168°E
170°E
172°E
40°S
42°S
44°S
Mt Egmont
Taranaki
Opunake
Hawera
South Taranaki Bight
Cape Farewell
Farewell Spit
Golden Bay
Marlborough Sounds
Collingwood
Takaka
Tasman Bay
Karamea
Richmond
Nelson
Picton
Karamea Bight
Blenheim
Westport
Murchison
St Arnaud
Punakaiki
Reefton
Lewis Pass
Kaikoura
Greymouth
Hanmer Springs
TASMAN SEA
Lake Brunner
Hokitika
Ross
Arthur's Pass
Whataroa
Pegasus Bay
Franz Josef Glacier
Fox Glacier
Mt Arrowsmith
Mt Cook
Mt Hutt
CHRISTCHURCH
Methven
Lyttelton
Mt Cook Village
Banks Peninsula
Akaroa
Lake Tekapo
Ashburton
Jackson Bay
Haast
Haast Pass
Temuka
Canterbury Bight
Twizel
Mt Aspiring
Timaru
Lake Hawea
Lake Wanaka
Milford Sound
Wanaka
Waimate
Glenorchy
George Sound
Lake Te Anau
Queenstown
Cromwell
Oamaru
Lake Wakatipu
Doubtful Sound
Alexandra
SOUTH PACIFIC OCEAN
Te Anau
Palmerston
Manapouri
Lake Manapouri
Lumsden
Otago Peninsula
Dusky Sound
Dunedin
West Cape
Winton
Gore
Milton
Balclutha
Puysegur Point
Invercargill
Foveaux Strait
Chaslands Mistake
Bluff
Mason Bay
Oban
Halfmoon Bay
Stewart Island
ELEVATION
3000 m
2000 m
1000 m
500 m
200 m
0

Hobson was sent to replace Busby and persuade the Maori chiefs to relinquish their sovereignty to the British crown.

A treaty was drawn up in 1840 within a few days of Hobson's arrival in New Zealand and on 5 February over 400 Maori gathered in front of Busby's residence at Waitangi in the Bay of Islands to hear the treaty read. The Maori chiefs had some objections, the treaty was amended, and they withdrew across the river to debate the issue throughout the night. The following day, 6 February 1840, with a truly British display of pomp and circumstance, the treaty was signed by Hobson and 45 Maori chiefs, mostly from the Bay of Islands region. Over the next seven months the treaty was carried throughout New Zealand by missionaries and officials, eventually being signed by over 500 Maori chiefs. Hobson proclaimed British sovereignty and established his capital at Kororareka but, a year later, moved it south to Auckland.

Though the treaty was short and seemed to be simple, it was a controversial document that remains hotly debated in modern-day New Zealand. Under the terms of the treaty, the chiefs ceded their sovereignty to the Queen of England, in exchange for the Queen's protection and the granting to Maori people of all the same rights, privileges and duties of citizenship as enjoyed by the citizens of England. The treaty guaranteed the Maori possession of their land, and stipulated that if the Maori wanted to sell their land it could only be sold to the crown. The Queen's agent would then sell the land to the settlers in an orderly and fair fashion.

The treaty seemed to promise benefits for both sides, but when settlers arrived and needed land and the Maori didn't want to sell, conflict inevitably resulted. The admirable idea that the government should act as a go-between in all Maori-Pakeha deals to ensure fairness on both sides fell apart when the government was too tightfisted to pay the price.

The Maori war canoe was once a fearsome sight to enemies

Maori Wars

The first visible revolt came when Hone Heke, the first chief to sign the Treaty of Waitangi, chopped down the flagpole at Kororareka, upon which flew the British flag. Despite new poles and more and more guards Hone Heke or his followers managed to chop the pole down four times, and on the last occasion it was covered with iron to foil further attempts. After his final destruction of the pole in 1845, he burnt down the town of Kororareka for good measure. In the skirmishes that followed, the British governor put a £100 reward on Hone Heke's head, to which he brilliantly responded by offering a matching £100 for the governor's head.

This was only one in a long series of skirmishes, battles, conflicts, disputes and arguments between the Maori and Pakeha. The original benign intent of the Treaty of Waitangi began to ebb under the pressure of ever-increasing numbers of European settlers. Many land sales were disputed, as local chiefs sold land which belonged to the whole tribe or sold land of other tribes in a new development of tribal conflict.

The government pressed on with developing the colony. The Constitution Act of 1852 divided the country into six provinces that administered local government and took over the responsibility for land purchases and sales. Alarmed Maori became increasingly reluctant to sell land. In the Waikato region, a number of tribal chiefs united to elect a Maori 'King' in 1859 and resisted land sales and Pakeha settlement in the Waikato/King Country right up until the 20th century.

Pressures between the Maori and Pakeha finally escalated into fully fledged wars. Known collectively as the Maori Wars, fighting took place in many parts of the country between 1860 and 1865. The most bitterly fought conflicts were in Taranaki. The force of arms eventually saw Imperial troops vanquish the Taranaki tribes, but later skirmishes erupted in the East Coast region with the rise of Hauhauism, a Maori religious movement that sought to oust the Europeans. Also around the East Coast, Te Kooti led raiding parties against European settlements until he finally retreated to the King Country in 1872.

Following the Maori Wars the government confiscated huge parcels of Maori land, and new legislation allowing private land sales resulted in the loss of the prime Maori land over the rest of the 19th century.

Late 19th Century

While development in the North Island languished because of the conflicts, the South Island prospered. First farming and then the discovery of gold saw the South Island become the main area of settlement. After 1870, the North Island economy began to recover but it remained the poorer cousin up until the 20th century. In 1876 the colonial government abolished the provincial governments and centralised power in Wellington, which had become the capital in 1865.

European settlement and influence grew, and New Zealand became an efficient agricultural country. Sheep farming, the backbone of modern New Zealand, flourished as refrigerated ships made it possible to sell NZ meat in Europe. New Zealand became what has been called 'an efficient offshore farm' in relation to England, exporting agricultural products, especially mutton, wool, sheepskins and dairy products, and importing manufactured goods.

Towards the end of the 19th century New Zealand went through a phase of sweeping social change that took it to the forefront of the world. Women were given the vote in 1893, 25 years before Britain or the USA, and more like 75 years ahead of Switzerland. An eminent leader at this time was Richard John 'King Dick' Seddon who, together with the Liberal Party, was responsible for many of the reforms. The range of far-sighted social reforms and pioneering legislation included old-age pensions, minimum wage structures, the establishment of arbitration courts and the introduction of child health services.

Meanwhile the Maori people floundered. New Zealand grew through immigration (a very selective immigration), but by 1900 the Maori population had dropped to an estimated 42,000 and was falling fast. The Maori were given the vote in 1867, but continued to lose the struggle to hold on to their culture and ancestral lands.

Early 20th Century

New Zealand had become a self-governing British colony in 1856, and a dominion in 1907. By the 1920s it controlled most of its own affairs, but it took until 1947 before it became a fully independent country.

Meanwhile New Zealand fought for the British in the Anglo-Boer war of 1899 to 1902, and in WWI. The Kiwi soldiers earned great reputations for skill and bravery, and they also suffered heavy losses of life with one in every three men aged between 20 and 40 killed or wounded in fighting for Britain in WWI. NZ troops again assisted in the European and Middle East arenas of WWII, but after 1941 when war was declared in the Pacific and New Zealand was directly threatened, a division was also established in the south-west Pacific.

The postwar years were good to New

Zealand, as the world rebuilt and prices for agricultural products were high. New Zealand had one of the highest per-capita incomes in the world, and a social welfare system the envy of many.

During the Korean War (1950-53), New Zealand again sent troops as part of a Commonwealth brigade. Australia, New Zealand and the USA signed the ANZUS defence pact providing mutual aid in the event of any attack. With the conceived threat of communism, New Zealand also joined the anti-communist SEATO (the South-East Asia Treaty Organisation).

New Zealand had become a member of the South Pacific Commission in 1947, a group responsible for promoting research in the region. During the 1960s and 70s an increased amount of NZ aid was directed to the Pacific countries and in 1971 New Zealand joined the South Pacific Forum, designed for Pacific governments to discuss common problems.

Recent History

New Zealand's economy prospered after WWII, but along with much of the rest of the world it took a nose-dive in the 1970s and 80s. The closure of much of its traditional European market for agricultural products, combined with the oil-crisis price hikes of many of its mineral and manufactured imports, saw a dramatic deterioration in the country's economy. Robert Muldoon's National government of the day sought to buy New Zealand's way out of trouble by running up large foreign debts and investing in ill-advised industrial development programmes.

In 1984 a Labour government was elected and, in a reversal of political roles, set about a radical restructuring of economy. The finance minister, Roger Douglas, instituted his programme of 'Rogernomics' that deregulated the financial system, lowered tariffs, reformed the tax system and eliminated agricultural subsidies. While the reforms produced some economic gains, it also resulted in growing unemployment that increasingly threatened Labour's chances of re-election. As the finance minister pressed on with privatisation of state industries and proposals of a flat income tax rate and deregulation of the labour market, Prime Minister David Lange decided enough was enough and sacked Roger Douglas. After the party reinstated Douglas, David Lange shocked the nation by resigning in 1989. Labour was in disarray, and the National Party led by Jim Bolger was swept to power in the 1990 elections.

The 1970s and 80s also saw a resurgence of Maori culture, as Maori leaders and activists pushed for social justice and highlighted Maori grievances. In 1975 the Treaty of Waitangi, which in 1877 had been ruled 'a simple nullity', was reconsidered. The Parliament passed the Treaty of Waitangi Act, establishing a Waitangi Tribunal to investigate Maori claims against the British Crown dating from 1975. In 1985 the act was amended to include claims dating all the way back to the original signing of the Treaty of Waitangi in 1840. Financial reparations were made to a number of Maori tribes whose lands were found to have been unjustly confiscated.

In 1983 Australia and New Zealand signed a Closer Economic Relations Trade Agreement, permitting free and unrestricted trade between the two countries. As it became increasingly aware of itself as a Pacific nation rather than an 'efficient offshore farm' for the UK, New Zealand's trade with the UK declined in proportion to its increased trade with Australia, the USA, Japan and the rest of Asia.

New Zealand took a strong stand on nuclear issues by refusing entry to nuclear-equipped US warships. In response the USA suspended its obligations to New Zealand within the ANZUS defence pact. Although this brave policy has caused more than a few problems for the Kiwis they have continued to stick by it.

New Zealand also became a leader in the Pacific in its opposition to nuclear testing by the French at Mururoa Atoll in French Polynesia. In 1985 the French government sent secret service agents to New Zealand to bomb and sink the Greenpeace ship *Rainbow Warrior* as it sat in Auckland Harbour, preparing to lead a flotilla to French Polynesia to protest against French nuclear testing. A Greenpeace photographer, Fernando Pereira, was killed in the bombing. Two French agents were caught, tried, found guilty and sentenced to 10-year terms, but after intense pressure from France, both were released into French custody, which resulted in a brief 'imprisonment' in luxury on a South Pacific island and then repatriation to France, with honours, well before their time was finished.

In 1995 the French recommenced nuclear testing in French Polynesia despite worldwide condemnation and New Zealand was again at the forefront of international protests.

In the 1990s the National government has pressed on with Labour's free-market economics, and more, with greater privatisation, cuts in welfare and deregulation of the labour market that emasculated unions. With little to show for a decade of economic pain, growing disparity of wealth and continuing unemployment, the government's majority in parliament was slashed in the 1993 elections and they managed to hold government by just one seat. Since then it appears that the economic reforms have finally started to benefit the country, and a buoyant economy in the mid-90s has significantly restored the National Party's popularity.

Perhaps the most significant event of the 90s, certainly the greatest cause for national celebration, was New Zealand's historic win of the America's Cup yachting race in 1995.

GEOGRAPHY

New Zealand stretches 1600 km from north to south It consists of two large islands around which are scattered a number of smaller islands, plus a few far-flung islands hundreds of km away. New Zealand's territorial jurisdiction extends to the islands of Chatham, Kermadec, Tokelau, Auckland, Antipodes, Snares, Solander and Bounty (most of them uninhabited) and to the Ross Dependency in Antarctica.

The North Island (115,000 sq km) and the South Island (151,000 sq km) are the two major land masses. Stewart Island, with an area of 1700 sq km, lies directly south of the South Island. The country is 10,400 km south-west of the USA, 1700 km south of Fiji and 2250 km east of Australia, its nearest large neighbour. Its western coastline faces the Tasman Sea, the part of the Pacific Ocean which separates New Zealand and Australia.

With a total land mass of 268,000 sq km, altogether New Zealand's land area is greater than that of the UK (244,800 sq km), smaller than that of Japan (377,800 sq km), and just a little smaller than that of Colorado in the USA (270,000 sq km). With only 3,540,000 people, and almost 70% of those living in the five major cities, that leaves a lot of wide open spaces. The coastline, with many bays, harbours and fiords, is very long relative to the land mass of the country.

A notable feature of New Zealand's geography is the country's great number of rivers. There's a lot of rainfall in New Zealand and all that rain has to go somewhere. The Waikato River in the North Island is New Zealand's longest river, measuring in at 425 km. Also in the North Island, the Whanganui River is the country's longest navigable river, which has made it an important waterway from historic times down to the present. New Zealand also has a number of beautiful lakes; Lake Taupo is the largest and lakes Waikaremoana and Wanaka are two of the most beautiful.

GEOLOGY

Both the North Island and South Island have some high mountains, formed by two distinct geological processes, both associated with the westward movement of the Pacific tectonic plate.

When one tectonic plate slides underneath another one, it forms what's called a subduction zone. The North Island of New Zealand is on the southern reaches of the subduction zone where the oceanic Pacific plate is sliding underneath the continental plate,

Maori Use of Plants

Perhaps the most important of the trees for the Maori was the mighty totara, large enough to be used to build war canoes. The hard, durable wood of the kowhai and the heavy wood of the maire *(Nestegis cunninghamii)* were used to make paddles, the matai was used for the carved canoe prows, the tough mangeao *(Litsea calicaris)* was used to make canoe bailers and the honeysuckle *(Knightia excelsa*; Maori: rewarewa) was used as firewood to burn out the interior of the canoe. Another wood used for boat building was the pukatea *(Laurelia novae-zelandiae)*. The maire was also used for war clubs, the matai for feather boxes and trays, the hard wood of the pigeonwood (*Hedycarya arborea*; Maori: porokaiwhiri) was considered the only wood suitable for *pahu* (wooden drums), and from the twigs of the celery pine (*Phyllocladus trichomanoides*; Maori: tanekaha) walking sticks and fish-hooks were fashioned.

Piupiu skirts were made from the lacebark (*Hoheria populnea*; Maori: hohere) and its tough fibre was used in basket work and as string. The bark of the kamahi was used to make a red permanent dye, the bark of the wineberry (*Aristotelia serrata*; Maori: makomako) a black dye and the inner bark of the tanekaha a red dye. The bark of the manuka, which peels off easily, was used as a crude brush and the dry berries of the nikau were used for necklaces.

The fruits, seeds and leaves of many native trees were put to a bewildering number of uses. The mealy matter of the hinau *(Elaeocarpus dentatus)* was cooked as a cake in the *umu* (steam oven), the berry fruit of the kahikatea was gathered and eaten, the poisonous berries of the karaka *(Cornocarpus laevigatus)* were made edible after three days of steam cooking, the leaves of the kohekohe *(Dysoxylum spectabile)* were used to impart a garlic taste to food, the berries of the tree fuschia were collected by children and made into jam, and the juice of the tutu *(Coriaria arborea)* was boiled with seaweed as a jelly.

The horopito was believed to have medicinal properties, nearly all the parts of the kawakawa *(Macropiper excelsum)* were used for their astringent and emollient properties, the buds of the upper shoots of the koromiko *(Hebe salicifolia)* were chewed to treat diarrhoea, the oil of the leaves of the ngaio *(Myoporum laetum)* was used as insect repellent, the leaves of the raukawa *(Pseudopanax edgerleyi)* were used for body oils, the gum from lemonwood (*Pittosporum eugenioides*; Maori: tarata) was used for scent and the seeds of the titoki *(Alectron excelsus)* were also used as a perfume and medicine.

The fragrant gum of the kohuhu *(Pittosporum tenuifolium)* was hung in sachets around the neck, charcoal from rimu was rubbed into *moko* (tattoo) incisions and the wood of the kaikomako *(Pennantia corymbosa)* was used as a firestick in conjunction with the mahoe *(Melicytus ramiflorus)* in the fire-making ceremony.

Ferns also had a variety of uses. The mokimoki *(Doodia caudata)* was wrapped around kumara in storehouses; the young shoots of the mauku had a taste similar to fresh asparagus; the upper part of the stem of the mamaku and rahurahu roots were staple food; fronds of the kiwikiwi *(Blechnum fluviatile)* were used in ceremonies; broken, overturned fronds of piupiu were used as markers in the forest; the tubers of the para were a delicacy; and ponga trunks were used as house posts. ■

resulting in volcanic activity which has created a number of large volcanoes and thermal areas, and some equally impressive volcanic depressions.

A rough 'line' of volcanoes, some of which are still active, extends from the steaming Whakaari (White) Island in the Bay of Plenty south past Mt Putauaki (Edgecumbe) and the highly active thermal areas in and around Rotorua and Lake Taupo. New Zealand's largest lake, Lake Taupo, was formed by a gigantic volcanic explosion in 186 AD, and still has thermal areas bubbling away nearby. South of Lake Taupo are the North Island's spectacularly large volcanoes Tongariro, Ruapehu, Ngauruhoe and the smaller Pihanga. Continuing south-west there's the lone volcanic cone of Mt Egmont/Taranaki. Port Nicholson, the bay Wellington is located on, is formed by a giant volcanic crater, now filled by the sea. Other parts of the North Island also have evidence of volcanic activity; in Auckland, for example, there are over 50 volcanic cones, including most of its famous 'hills' (One Tree Hill, Mt Eden etc) that rise up from the flatlands.

The North Island has some ranges of hills and mountains produced by folding and uplift, notably the Tararua and Ruahine ranges in the southern part of the North Island. In general, though, most of the high places of the North Island were formed by volcanic activity. In the centre there's a high plateau.

In the South Island the geological process is different. Here the two tectonic plates are smashing into each other, resulting in a process called 'crustal shortening'. This has caused the Southern Alps to rise as a spine extending along virtually the entire length of the South Island. Thrust faulting, folding and vertical slips all combine to create a rapid uplift of the Southern Alps – as much as 10 mm per year – and though the Southern Alps receive a lot of rainfall and hence a lot of erosion, their rapid rate of uplift is enough to keep pace and they are continuing to rise. Most of the east side of the South Island is a large plain known as the Canterbury Plains. Banks Peninsula, on the east coast, was formed by volcanic activity and joined to the mainland by alluvial deposits washed down from the Southern Alps.

CLIMATE

Lying between 34°S and 47°S, New Zealand is squarely in the 'roaring forties' latitude, meaning it has a prevailing and rather continual wind blowing over it from west to east all year round, ranging from gentle, freshening breezes to occasional raging gales in winter.

Coming across the Tasman Sea, this breeze is relatively warm and moisture-laden. When it hits New Zealand's mountains the wind is swept upwards, cools, and drops its moisture, resulting in a much higher rainfall on the west side of those high points than on the east side. When the wind comes up from the south, it's coming from Antarctica and is icy and cold; a southerly wind always means cold weather.

The North Island and the South Island, because of their different geological features, have two distinct patterns of rainfall. In the South Island, the Southern Alps, which make a north-to-south spine along most of the island, act as a barrier for the moisture-laden winds coming west across the Tasman Sea, creating a wet climate on the west side of the mountains and a dry climate on the east side: the annual rainfall is over 7500 mm per year on the west side but it's only about 330 mm a year on the east side, even though it's not so far away.

The South Island's geography also creates a wind pattern in which the prevailing wind, swept upwards, cooled and losing its moisture in the form of rain or snow, blows eastwards down onto the Canterbury Plains as a dry wind, gathering heat and speed as it blows downhill and across the Canterbury Plains towards the Pacific coast. In summer this wind can be very hot, dry and fierce. Called a katabatic or foehn wind, it is similar to other famous winds in the world including the Chinook wind formed by the Canadian and American Rockies. In the Grey River valley on the South Island's west coast there's another kind of downhill wind, locally called 'The Barber'.

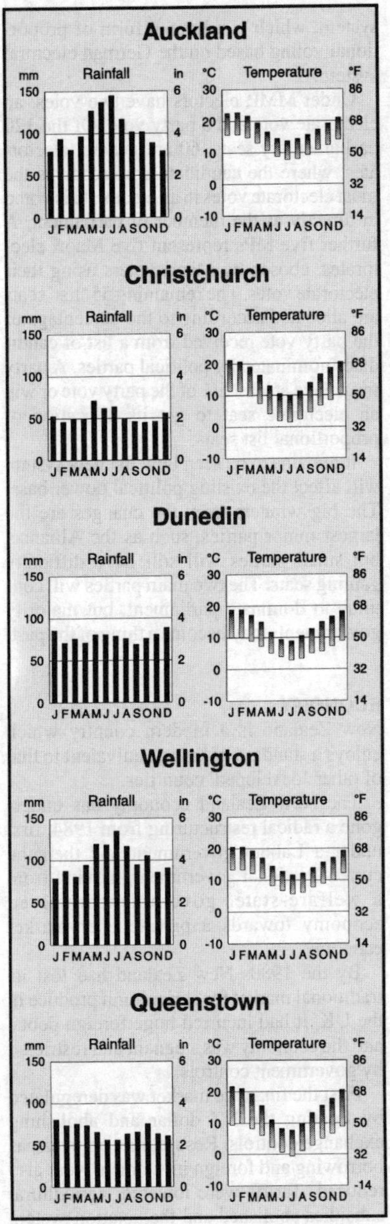

In the North Island, the west sides of the high volcanoes get a lot more rain than the east sides, though since there is not such a complete barrier as the Alps, the rain shadow is not so pronounced. Rainfall is more evenly distributed over the North Island, averaging around 1300 mm per year. In the North Island there's some rainfall throughout the year – typically there are rainy days alternating with fine days, all year round – and it's enough to keep the landscape always green.

It is a few degrees cooler in the South Island than the North Island, and of course it's colder in winter (June, July and August) than in summer (December, January and February). There are several regional variations – it's quite warm and pleasant up in the Northland region at any time of year, where it's almost always a few degrees warmer than the rest of the country. Higher altitudes are always considerably cooler, and it's usually windy in Wellington, which catches the winds whistling through the Cook Strait in a sort of wind tunnel from the Tasman Sea to the Pacific Ocean.

Snow is mostly seen in the mountains, though there can be snowfalls even at sea level in the South Island, particularly in the extreme south. Some of the plains and higher plateaus also receive snow in winter, notably the Canterbury Plains in the South Island and the high plateau around the Tongariro National Park in the North Island, especially on the 'desert' (east) side. Snow is seldom seen near sea level on the west coasts, and not at all in the far north.

One of the most important things travellers need to know about the New Zealand climate is that it's a maritime climate, as opposed to the continental climate typical of larger land masses. This means the weather can frequently change with amazing rapidity. We've alluded to this at many places throughout this book – it affects you in many ways when you're in New Zealand, and if you're going tramping at high altitudes, for example, the extreme changeability of the weather can be a life or death matter. So it is essential to equip yourself adequately for all kinds of unpredictable weather changes.

GOVERNMENT & POLITICS

The governmental structure of New Zealand is modelled on the British parliamentary system, elections being based on universal adult suffrage. The minimum voting age is 18 and candidates are elected by secret ballot. The maximum period between elections is three years, but the interval can be shorter for various reasons, and the government of the day can call an early election. Voting is not compulsory, although on average more than 80% of those eligible to vote do so.

The difference between the UK's Westminster system and the NZ model is that New Zealand has abolished the upper house and governs solely through the lower house. Known as the House of Representatives, it has 120 member's seats. The government runs on a party system. The party that wins a majority of seats in an election automatically becomes the government and its leader, the prime minister. The two main parties are the National (conservative) and Labour parties.

Like the UK, New Zealand is a constitutional monarchy. The traditional head of state, the reigning British king or queen, is represented by a resident governor-general, who is appointed for a five-year term. An independent judiciary makes up another tier of government.

The two-party system has traditionally made it difficult for other parties to gain much power. Nevertheless, in the 1993 election the Alliance party, composed of the Greens and other groups including Labour groups and former National Party MPs, gained 18% of the vote. Election results in 1993 were so close that the National Party was only voted in by a majority of one seat, ahead of the Labour Party, and the smaller Alliance and NZ First parties, which both had two seats.

After a referendum in 1993 to assess the public's ideas on a number of electoral reforms, New Zealanders voted overwhelmingly for proportional representation. The government has introduced the MMP (Mixed Member Proportional) electoral system, which is a limited form of proportional voting based on the German electoral system.

Under MMP, electors have two votes: an electorate vote and a party vote. Of the 120 parliamentary seats, 60 are general electorates, where the candidate who receives the most electorate votes in an electorate is voted in directly as the member of parliament. A further five MPs represent five Maori electorates, chosen by Maori voters using their electorate votes. The remaining 55 'list' seats are allocated according to the percentage of the party vote received from a list of candidates nominated by political parties. A party must have at least 5% of the party vote or win an electorate seat to get its allocation of proportional list seats.

It remains to be seen how the new system will affect the existing political power base. The big winners from the changes are the largest minor parties, such as the Alliance, but small parties will still have difficulty gaining seats. The two main parties will continue to dominate parliament, but majority governments may become a thing of the past.

ECONOMY

New Zealand is a modern country which enjoys a standard of living equivalent to that of other 'developed' countries.

The New Zealand economy has undergone a radical restructuring from 1984, first under a Labour government and then the current National government, moving from a welfare-state, government-involved economy towards a private open-market economy.

By the 1980s New Zealand had lost its traditional market for agricultural produce in the UK, it had incurred huge foreign debts, and the economy was stagnant and restricted by government controls.

First the financial market was deregulated by floating the NZ dollar and abolishing exchange controls. Restrictions on overseas borrowing and foreign investment were also reduced. Tariffs were lowered, agricultural subsidies abolished and the taxation system was reformed by introducing a goods and services tax (GST), while at the same time company and personal income taxes were lowered.

The initial changes resulted in a drop in the New Zealand dollar, an influx of foreign capital, even larger capital speculation, and an increase in private foreign debt. Inefficient, government-protected industries faced with foreign competition went to the wall. However, wealthier consumers had more money in their pockets, imported consumer items were cheaper, and economic confidence was high.

The bubble burst in 1987 with the worldwide stock market collapse, hitting New Zealand's speculation boom the hardest. Inflation and unemployment topped 10%, growth was non-existent and the country questioned the restructuring. The main engineer of the economic reforms, Labour's finance minister, Roger Douglas, pressed on with a programme of privatisation, selling off government enterprises and assets. Since then $12 billion dollars has been raised and helped reduce government debt.

With the economy in the doldrums and the country enduring all the pain but no gain from the economic reforms, Labour was booted out of office in 1990. The incoming National government continued with the free-market reforms, tackling the areas a Labour government never could. Welfare programmes were cut, including the abolition of the state-funded health insurance system, privatisation was increased and, most significantly, the labour market was deregulated. Individual workplace bargaining was introduced, undermining the once-strong unions.

The economy continued to languish in the early 1990s but recently has shown dramatic improvement. The government is running a budget surplus, and public debt, though still high at around $35 billion or 40% of GDP, has dropped from 50% of GDP in 1992. The economy is enjoying unprecedented growth of around 4%, inflation is under 2% and unemployment around 7%. New Zealand is receiving plaudits from around the world for its market reforms and business confidence is bursting.

The reforms have had a major effect on the New Zealand economy and society. Though still overwhelmingly reliant on agriculture for export income, New Zealand has made progress in its efforts to diversify its economy. Business efficiency and profit has increased in the manufacturing, finance and service industries. New Zealand also has a broader world outlook, in its trade and in general. Since 1960, when Britain bought over half of New Zealand's exports, New Zealand has shifted its focus elsewhere, especially to Asia. Australia is now New Zealand's single largest trading partner, accounting for 20% of all trade, but Asia takes 35% of exports, and the UK only 6%. New Zealand is also attracting greater investment from Asia, especially Japan and Singapore, and the Auckland property boom is spurred by Asian money.

The reforms have also had their downside. As the corporate philosophy engulfs New Zealand, the once-sacrosanct ideals of equality in society have taken a back seat. Income disparity has grown substantially. In the new user-pays New Zealand, social services have been cut back, or rather sold off to private enterprise resulting in higher charges and the axing of some non-profitable services. While the changes have created some bitterness, public opposition is noticeably muted in the current positive economic climate.

Tourism, service industries, manufacturing, small-scale industry and agriculture are all highly important in the NZ economy. In a recent count the sector of trade, restaurants and hotels accounted for the largest proportion of the gross domestic product (GDP), followed by the sector of financing, insurance, real estate and business services, followed by manufacturing, then agriculture, transport and storage, and then by food, beverages and tobacco, and a host of other smaller sectors.

With all the sheep, cattle and farms you see around New Zealand (New Zealand is reckoned to have around 68 million sheep and two million cattle) agriculture is not surprisingly an important part of the economy. In strictly dollar amounts it accounts for only about 10% of the entire GDP and employs about the same percentage of the total workforce, but 53% of all land in the country is devoted to pastureland, and agricultural products such as sheep, cattle, fish and forestry products are NZ's chief exports. Farming is a scientific proposition in New Zealand, with research constantly carried out and the most modern scientific farming methods used.

Principal exports are meat (with beef and veal bringing in slightly more revenue than lamb and mutton), dairy products, fish, forest products (primarily pine logs and timber products from non-native trees), fruits and vegetables (especially kiwi fruit, apples and pears) in that order. Main imports are machinery and mechanical appliances, electrical machinery and equipment, motor vehicles and a variety of manufactured goods.

Tourism is also a major source of foreign revenue. Tourist arrivals numbered 1.3 million in 1995 but the tourism industry is targeting three million by the year 2000.

POPULATION & PEOPLE

New Zealand's population of around 3.5 million is comprised of 78.3% New Zealand Pakeha, 13% New Zealand Maori and 5% Pacific Island Polynesian, while 1.3% are Chinese, 0.9% are Indian and 1.5% are 'Other'. Europeans are the only group declining, percentage-wise, while Maori, Polynesian, Chinese, Indian and 'Other' peoples are on the rise.

Many of the islands of the Pacific are currently experiencing a rapid population shift from remote and undeveloped islands to the 'big city' and Auckland is very much the big city of the South Pacific, with the greatest concentration of Polynesians on earth. It sometimes causes a great deal of argument, discussion and tension and much of it is not between the recent Pacific immigrants and the Pakeha population but between the islanders and the Maori, or among the various island groups themselves.

Asian migration is also increasing. As well as a sizeable Indian community, mostly from Fiji, New Zealand has been attracting migrants from East Asia, many of whom have migrated under New Zealand's recent immigration incentives to attract skilled people and especially finance to the country.

Over the last 15 years or so the economic situation has led to a mass exodus to Australia and further afield, though improving economic conditions has seen a slowing of emigration.

With only about 12.6 people per sq km, New Zealand is lightly populated by many countries' standards but it is much more densely populated than Australia with its stretches of empty country and 2.2 persons per sq km. The South Island once had a greater population than the North Island but now the South Island is the place to go for elbow room – the entire population of the South Island is barely more than that of Auckland. The nation's capital is Wellington but Auckland is the largest city. The five largest cities – the only ones in the country with populations over 100,000 – are:

City	*Population*
Auckland	1,002,000
Wellington	410,000
Christchurch	302,000
Dunedin	120,000
Hamilton	105,000

Altogether the population of the 15 largest 'urban areas' comes to nearly 70% of NZ's population – Auckland alone has 28% of the entire population. Despite its rural base, New Zealand is in fact very much an urban country.

EDUCATION

New Zealanders place a high value on education, and virtually the entire population is literate. By law, education is mandatory and free for all children between the ages of six and 15; in fact most children enter school by the age of five, and many also have attended preschools before that, all subsidised by the state. Correspondence school is available for children who live in remote places.

New Zealand has seven universities, a number of teachers' colleges and polytechnics and one agricultural college.

A new and growing facet of education in New Zealand is that it is gaining a reputation, especially in Asian countries, as a good place to learn English. There are numerous language schools throughout New Zealand (but most are in Auckland) and student visas are available which permit foreign students to study in New Zealand for up to four years.

ARTS

New Zealand has a multi-faceted arts scene, with both Maori and Pakeha engaged in all kinds of traditional and modern arts. Although there are distinct 'Maori arts' and 'Pakeha arts', in fact there is rarely a division in who practises which arts. There are Pakeha people who enjoy carving in bone and painting in traditionally Maori styles; Maori songs, poi dances, and a little bit of Maori language are taught in schools and all New Zealand children, regardless of background, learn them. Likewise, there are many Maori people who excel in the traditionally Pakeha arts – there are Maori in theatre, music and many European art forms. Dame Kiri Te Kanawa, a Maori, is one of the world's best known operatic divas, and there are many other examples.

New Zealand literature, especially, is an arena in which the Maori are making a strong mark – though the written word was not traditionally a part of Maori culture, NZ is experiencing a movement of dynamic Maori writing in fiction, non-fiction, poetry and every other written form.

Maori Arts

Maori arts are dramatic in many ways, and they include various arts that people of European backgrounds might not be familiar with.

Traditionally the Maori did not keep a written history; their history was kept in long, very specific and stylised songs and chants. As in many parts of the world where oral history has been practised, oratory, song and chant developed to a magnificent art in Maori culture. The many rituals associated with Maori protocol are also quite stylised – if you ever visit a marae and are greeted with the traditional *haka* (war chant) and *wero* (challenge), you will appreciate how artistic they are. The Maori arts of song and dance include some special features such as the *poi* dance and action songs. Martial arts, using a variety of traditional weapons and movements, are highly stylised and developed.

Other Maori arts include crafts such as wood, bone and jade carving, basketry and weaving, including a distinctive form of wall panelling known as *tukutuku*, which can be seen on marae and in Maori churches. Wood carvings, tukutuku wall panels and distinctive styles of painting (especially on the rafters and ceilings) can be seen in most Maori meeting houses. These traditional Maori arts are not used only on the marae, though – wood and bone carving, painting, basketry and various other arts are being used in both traditional and new ways, creating some vibrant artistic works.

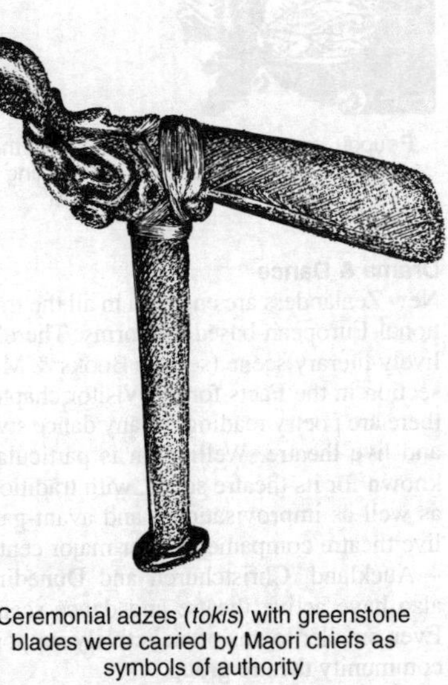

Ceremonial adzes (*tokis*) with greenstone blades were carried by Maori chiefs as symbols of authority

Poupou, carved wooden figures, adorn the walls of Te Hau-ki-Turanga, the meeting house in the National Museum

Drama & Dance

New Zealanders are engaged in all the traditional European-based art forms. There's a lively literary scene (see the Books & Maps section in the Facts for the Visitor chapter), there are poetry readings, many dance styles and live theatre. Wellington is particularly known for its theatre scene, with traditional as well as improvisational and avant-garde live theatre companies. Other major centres – Auckland, Christchurch and Dunedin – also have active theatre and dance scenes. Even smaller towns often actively support a community theatre group.

Music

As with theatre, so with music – the major centres have the liveliest music scenes but even smaller towns can have some interesting music on offer. Ruatoria, on the East Cape of the North Island, is not exactly New York City but it is the home town of Herbs, a popular and internationally known Maori reggae band.

There's plenty of opportunity for going out in the evening and hearing live music in the larger centres, with a choice of everything from a symphony concert, the ballet, or a rock, jazz or blues band, or even Irish music. Irish music – both the acoustic ballad minstrel variety and the rousing Irish dance band style – is very popular in New Zealand. In the larger centres you can hear Irish music any night of the week and Irish-style pubs are becoming very popular.

Rock New Zealand rock music doesn't begin and end in Dunedin, though over the last 10 years you could be forgiven for thinking so – it's true that in terms of innovative and alternative music, Dunedin is New Zealand's music capital. (See the Dunedin section in the Otago chapter for more details.)

In the 1970s and 80s, Split Enz was New Zealand's best known and most successful band. Originally a very unusual and eccentric group, their style became more mainstream in the 80s. Ridiculously enough, their completely apolitical song *Six Months in a Leaky Boat* was banned in England during the Falklands war of 1982.

Like many other New Zealand bands who achieved success, Split Enz based themselves in Australia and found themselves referred to as 'a great Australian band'. After the break-up of the band in the mid-80s, band member Neil Finn formed another successful 'Australian' band, Crowded House. (At least Crowded House *did* possess some Australian members.)

Bands from New Zealand have long been renowned not only for their 'alternative' feel but also for imaginative (sometimes surreal) names. Examples (all of which are or were quite good bands) include Sneaky Feelings, Straitjacket Fits, Look Blue Go Purple and the Jean-Paul Sartre Experience (who have recently modified their name to the JPS Experience). Possibly the prize example, however, are an outfit called The Great Unwashed, who later renamed themselves The Clean – signifying a major change in musical direction, perhaps?

Visual Arts

The larger centres have a variety of museums and art galleries where contemporary and traditional art can be seen, and even smaller towns often have a gallery which may combine both arts & crafts. You can find all the visual arts represented including painting, sculpture, ceramics and pottery, and a wide variety of handicrafts.

Literature

New Zealand has an active literary scene, with a number of modern authors and a few old classics. Probably the most internationally known New Zealand writer is still Katherine Mansfield (1888-1923), who was born and raised in New Zealand and later moved to England, where she spent most of her short adult life and did most of her writing (see the aside in the Wellington chapter). Mansfield's short stories can be found in many volumes, including *The Stories of Katherine Mansfield: Definitive Edition* edited by Antony Alpers.

Frank Sargeson (1903-82) is another classic New Zealand author. Within the country he is probably as well known as Mansfield, especially for his three-volume autobiography, his novels and many short stories, but since he lived all his life in New Zealand, his work did not become as widely known internationally.

For short stories see the *Oxford Book of New Zealand Short Stories* edited by Vincent O'Sullivan, and *Some Other Country: New Zealand's Best Short Stories* chosen by Marion McLeod & Bill Manhire. For a wide collection of fiction by New Zealand women, try *In Deadly Earnest* compiled by Trudie McNaughton.

For students of NZ literature there's the *Oxford History of New Zealand Literature in English* edited by Terry Sturm, or the *Penguin History of New Zealand Literature* by Patrick Evans.

Maurice Shadbolt is the author of several fine historical novels about New Zealand – so far he's published nine novels, four collections of short stories and several nonfiction books. His best known novel is probably *The Season of the Jew*, which won the NZ Wattie Book of the Year Award in 1987 and was chosen by the *NY Times* as one of the best books of that year. This book follows a dispossessed band of Maori who identify with the Jews of ancient Israel.

Janet Frame is another popular novelist, poet and short-story writer. Her three-volume autobiography *(To the Is-land, An Angel at my Table* and *Envoy from Mirror City)* was made famous by the film *An Angel at my Table* by acclaimed local director, Jane Campion. *Janet Frame: An Autobiography* is a fascinating insight to her life, and her many works are widely available.

Shonagh Koea is another popular author; her better-known works include *The Woman Who Never Went Home* (1987), *The Grandiflora Tree* (1989), *Staying Home and Being Rotten* (1992) and *Fifteen Rubies by Candlelight* (1993).

Other favourite New Zealand authors include Maurice Gee, whose novel *Going West* won the NZ Wattie Book Award in 1993; Fiona Kidman *(The Book of Secrets)*; Owen Marshall *(Tomorrow We Save the Orphans)*; Philip Temple *(Beak of the Moon)*; and Dame Ngaio Marsh (murder mysteries).

Children's Books This is a particularly fertile area of writing with many NZ writers achieving international success.

David Hill deals with the sensitive subject of children with disabilities in *See Ya, Simon*. Rural life is the setting for Jack Lasenby's *Uncle Trev* and *Harry Wakatipu*. Sports, especially sailing and swimming, are the impetus for Tessa Duder's *Alex* series, *Jellybean* and *Night Race to Kawau*; and the plight of the underdog is the substance of

William Taylor's novels, aimed at 11 and 12 year olds.

One of the most successful writers is Magaret Mahy, author of over 100 titles and winner of the international Carnegie Medal for *The Changeover* and *The Haunting*. And a favourite children's book (of LP writers' kids) is *The Terrible Taniwha of Timberditch* written by Joy Cowley and illustrated by Rodney McRae.

Poetry Poet James K Baxter, who died in 1972, is possibly the best known NZ poet. Others include RAK Mason, Allen Curnow, Denis Glover, Hone Tuwhare and the animated Sam Hunt. *Contemporary New Zealand Poetry Nga Kupu Titohu o Aotearoa* edited by Miriama Evans, Harvey McQueen & Ian Wedde is an excellent collection of NZ poetry, both in English and Maori. Wedde and McQueen also edited the comprehensive *The Penguin Book of New Zealand Verse*.

Contemporary Maori & Pacific Literature *Te Ao Marama – Contemporary Maori Writing* edited by Witi Ihimaera is a series, of which two books have been published so far. *Volume One: Te Whakahuatanga o te Ao – Reflections of Reality* (1992) is an anthology of written and oral Maori literature; *Volume Two: He Whakaatanga o te Ao – The Reality* (1993) examines the crucial issues affecting Maori people as seen by several prominent Maori authors. Witi Ihimaera is a prolific Maori author of novels and short stories. Some of his better known novels include *The Matriarch, Tangi* and *Pounamu, Pounamu*. His *Bulibasha* is a zany look at the life of Maori sheep-shearing gangs in the East Coast region of the North Island.

Keri Hulme, author of *The Bone People*, is one of New Zealand's favourite modern authors; she received international acclaim when *The Bone People* won the British Booker McConnell Prize for fiction in 1985. She has published several other novels and books of poetry.

Alan Duff is a controversial author who writes about Maori people in modern New Zealand society. He has written two novels and one non-fiction book, all of which have generated heated debate. His first novel, *Once Were Warriors*, has been made into the eponymous film receiving international acclaim; his second is *One Night Out Stealing*. In 1993 his non-fiction *Maori: The Crisis and the Challenge* sparked a rage of controversy.

Other significant Maori authors include novelists Apirana Taylor and Patricia Grace *(Potiki)*, and poet Hone Tuwhare.

With Auckland being the home of the largest concentrated population of Pacific islanders on earth, New Zealand also has some important Pacific Island authors. Albert Wendt, a Samoan author who is a professor of English at the University of Auckland, is one of the finest. His novels include *Leaves of the Banyan Tree* (1979), *Pouliuli* (1980), *Sons for the Return Home* (1987), *Ola* (1991) and *Black Rainbow* (1992); he has also published two poetry books and two collections of short stories.

The Shark that Ate the Sun: Ko e Ma go ne Kai e La by Niuean author John Puhiatau Pule is another excellent book by a Pacific author, writing about the Pacific islanders' experience in New Zealand.

Cinema

The history of New Zealand film doesn't really begin until the late 1970s when generous tax breaks were introduced to encourage local production. From some early stumbling attempts, notable feature films have survived the test of time and launched the careers of New Zealand directors and actors.

Sleeping Dogs (1977) is an accomplished psychological drama that was at the forefront of the new film industry, and which launched the careers of actor Sam Neill and director Roger Donaldson.

Bad Blood (1981) is a British/New Zealand production about the gun-toting psychosis of macho New Zealand, based on the true story of Stan Graham, a nutter oddly afforded hero status in NZ, who went berserk in a rural NZ town during WWII. *Smash Palace* (1981), about a marriage break-up and custody chase, was a local success.

Came a Hot Friday (1984), directed by Ian Mune, is one of New Zealand's better comedies.

Other films of note are *Utu* (1983) (Revenge), an amateurish but breakthrough Maori film, *Meet the Feebles*, a sick piece of splatter puppetry but not without innovation, and *The Quiet Earth* (1985), an end-of-the-world sci-fi movie done with wit and imagination. *Goodbye Pork Pie* (1980), an exuberant NZ road movie directed by Geoff Murphy, was a box office hit in New Zealand, as was the later *Footrot Flats*, starring New Zealand's favourite cartoon character, Dog.

New Zealand films moved into art-house cinemas with Vincent Ward's *Vigil* (1984), a brooding film about a girl's coming of age in the rain-drenched back blocks of New Zealand. It proved too ponderously artistic for many Kiwi film-goers but wowed them at Cannes. Ward's follow-up *The Navigator* (1988) is a strange modern/medieval hunt for the Holy Grail.

New Zealand's best known director, though Australian based and trained, is Jane Campion. Her greatest films explore New Zealand themes. *An Angel at My Table* (1990), based on Kiwi writer Janet Frame's autobiography, shows all the fine character development typical of her films. Campion's masterpiece, *The Piano* (1993), about the trials of a mute woman in New Zealand's pioneer days, received Cannes and Academy Award success. Suddenly the world noticed New Zealand's already accomplished movie industry. *Once Were Warriors* (1994), a brutal tale of modern urban Maori life, stunned movie-goers around the world. *Heavenly Creatures*, directed by Peter Jackson, also achieved critical acclaim. It is based on a famous case of matricide in the 1950s committed by two schoolgirls.

SOCIETY & CONDUCT

New Zealand culture is essentially European (Pakeha), transplanted by the British in these far off islands, but Maori culture has always been an integral part of New Zealand and is a strong and growing influence. While New Zealand is primarily bi-cultural, there is seen to be a growing need to be multi-cultural as the population changes.

Pakeha New Zealanders used to hold so strongly to their British traditions that they earned the tag of 'South Seas Poms'. While British culture is still a strong focus for many New Zealanders, a growing diversity of migrants and a wider global outlook has seen a distinct change in New Zealand society in recent years. Resurgent Maori culture and the new corporate philosophy have also helped to shape a new world view. New Zealand has always been independent and proud of its traditions, but more than ever the country is exploring its own identity.

Though the majority of New Zealand's population comes from English stock, other notable early influences came from the Croation Dalmations, who came to dig kauri gum in Northland. Scottish immigrants came in large numbers, and their influence is most notable in the far south, where Scottish games are held, the bagpipes still blow and a distinct Scottish brogue can be heard.

More recently, Polynesians have brought their cultures with them. In Auckland you can go to a Samoan rugby match on Saturday afternoon, go out dancing the *tamure* at a Cook Islands nightclub on Saturday night, and go to a Tongan-language church service on Sunday. The Indians and Chinese are New Zealand's other two major immigrant groups.

Through a common history and culture, based on the same British traditions, and a strong geographical link, New Zealand shares many cultural attributes with, and has long been influenced by, neighbouring Australia. Many New Zealanders have migrated to Australia, or at least travelled to and worked there, but Kiwis are keen to distance themselves from their brasher, patronising cousins across the Tasman.

In general, New Zealanders are intensely proud of their country. Aware of their small size, and relative insignificance on the world stage, national achievements, particularly world-beating sporting achievements, are greeted with great fanfare. New Zealand also values its independence, and is not afraid to take on the world, as it has done in its anti-nuclear stance, a policy so widely supported that not even conservative governments have been game to reverse it despite intense international pressure. In many other issues, such as the environment and race relations, New Zealand is also a world leader.

New Zealand Pakeha culture tends to place a high value on things like hard work, resourcefulness, honesty, fairness, independence and ruggedness – all the things a rugged pioneering culture would be expected to value. For the visitor, perhaps the most immediately obvious trait of all New Zealanders is their open friendliness.

Maori Culture & Race Relations

The Maori are the original Polynesian settlers of New Zealand, migrating from the islands of the South Pacific around 800 AD. As such, Maori language and culture is closely related to that of other Polynesian peoples. The ancestors of the Polynesians came from South-East Asia to the Pacific some 2500 years ago. The Austronesians, the common ancestors of South-East Asians and Polynesians, brought with them their animals and plants, though the existence of the kumara or sweet potato also shows that contact was made between Polynesia and South America. Polynesian languages show linguistic similarities to those of the Malay peoples, and other similarities exist in the arts and traditional religion.

The term Maori is one that has only applied to New Zealand Polynesians since the arrival of the Pakeha. Maori society was tribal, and the Maori referred to themselves in terms of their iwi (tribe), such as Ngati Kahu, or 'descendent of Kahu'. The tribes were headed by a supreme chief, but often of more relevance was the hapu (sub-tribe or clan), and the village structure based around family groups. Whakapapa (genealogy) determines everyone's place in the tribe and so ancestral and family ties are critically important. The marae, the sacred ground in front of the meeting house in a village, is the focus of Maori culture, the place where the tribe gathers. It is here that ancestors are as present as the current generations. (For a further discussion of traditional Maori culture, see Pre-European History at the start of this chapter.)

The history of the Maori parallels the decline of other indigenous peoples in colonised countries. The introduction of diseases and guns, which escalated tribal warfare, saw the decimation of the Maori population. Missionary activity, increasing foreign settlement and the appropriation of land all helped in the destruction of traditional Maori society.

The single most important event in the history of race relations in New Zealand was the signing of the Treaty of Waitangi in 1840. Though it signalled the annexation of New Zealand by Britain, its motives were at least partly humanitarian in a desire to stop lawlessness and the rampant grab for Maori land. In exchange for granting sovereignty over New Zealand to Britain, the Maori chiefs were promised full exclusive and undisturbed possession of their lands, forests, fisheries and other properties, and the same rights and privileges enjoyed by British subjects.

As settlement progressed, the terms of the treaty were increasingly ignored. Disputes over land resulted in the wars of the 1860s, which eventually broke the back of Maori resistance. Maori land was appropriated and the treaty, which was never ratified by a New Zealand parliament, was all but dead.

Despite romantic notions of the noble Maori people, partly inspired by the 'noble savage' sentiments fashionable in the 19th century, Pakeha remained largely separate from Maori society. Though intermarriage was common, for the most part the Maori retreated to the more isolated rural areas.

At the turn of the century when things looked their bleakest, the Maori began to organise and develop leaders skilled in Pakeha and Maori affairs. The setting aside of Maori seats in parliament gave the Maori a political voice. In the South Island the Ngai Tahu people petitioned parliament over land grievances. They also elected members of

Top Left: Jet-boating on the Shotover River near Queenstown (DW)
Top Right: Climbing in Mt Cook National Park (DW)
Bottom Left: Sea kayaking in mangrove forest, Bay of Islands (CK)
Bottom Right: Bungy jumping on Kawarau River, near Queenstown (DW)

Top: Milford Track, Southland (HL)
Bottom: Lighthouse, Castle Point, The Wairarapa (HL)

parliament specifically to lobby on these issues. The Young Maori Party, composed of Pakeha-educated Maori, pressed for greater education and health services for Maori communities.

Apirana Ngata was an inspiring Maori leader who became minister of Native Affairs in 1928, instituting Maori land development schemes and stressing the importance of Maori culture. Other Maori politicians lobbied the Labour Party, and when Labour achieved power in 1935, they introduced legislation guaranteeing equality in employment, and increased spending on health, housing and education. Though Maori were conspicuous on the rugby field and keen to sign up to defend the realm in times of war, up until WWII, the interaction of Pakeha and Maori communities remained minimal.

Despite disparities in education, wealth and power sharing, Maori people did enjoy greater acceptance and equality under the law than did the indigenous peoples of other European colonised countries. New Zealanders are proud of their record of racial harmony. In *Return to Paradise* James Michener tells of the outraged local reaction when WWII GIs stationed in New Zealand tried to treat the Maori like American Blacks.

The post-war economic boom years saw the greatest change in Maori society as Maori migrated to the cities with the promise of jobs. Urban Maori mixed with Pakeha as never before, as the government pursued the policies of assimilation fashionable at the time. But assimilation for the Maori meant the dominance of Pakeha culture and the destruction of their own. Though Maori culture survived, particularly in rural areas, Maori more than ever lost contact with their language and traditions.

In the late 1960s a new Maori voice arose and called for the revival in *Maoritanga* (Maori culture). Young activists combined with traditional leaders to provide a new direction, calling for the government to address Maori grievances. The contentious Treaty of Waitangi, always on the Maori agenda, came to the fore as never before. Increasing radicalism saw the Maori take to the streets and engage in land occupations. In the 1970s, historic land disputes involved the golf course in Raglan, Maori land appropriated during WWII for an airstrip, and Bastion Point in Auckland. The rise of black power groups and gangs such as the prominent Maori bikers, the Mongrel Mob, unsettled many in the Pakeha community.

The focus on Maori issues spurred the government to give the Maori language greater prominence in schools and the media, institute the Race Relations Act banning discrimination and introduce the Waitangi Tribunal in 1975 to investigate Maori land claims. Though some claims have resulted in the return of Maori land, the implications for private land ownership has seen claims delayed for many years.

In an attempt to extricate itself from the terms of the tribunal, in 1994 the government proposed a massive once and for all 'settlement envelope' of $1 billion to pay out all Maori land claims over the following 10 years. Though rejected by some Maori leaders, individual tribes have started to negotiate with the government and settlements have already been made.

Perhaps the greatest effect of the Maori revival has been the growing interest in Maoritanga. Maori language, literature, arts and culture are experiencing a flourishing renaissance. The Maori population is now overwhelmingly urban and largely integrated into Pakeha society, but the loss of traditional culture is being redressed as more and more Maori learn the language and return to the marae. Census figures show that 140,000 Maori, a quarter of all Maori, cannot name their iwi but with the great revival of Maori culture many are attempting to trace their whakapapa.

The marae is the main focus for Maoritanga and many Maori are re-establishing contact with the marae of their tribe. But even the maraes are subject to the winds of change. Traditional tribal leadership has evolved into today's trust boards, whose power base is the maraes in rural areas. The trust boards are coming under increasing

Marae Etiquette

Visitors to New Zealand will have several opportunities to witness fascinating aspects of Maori culture. Perhaps the best place to gain some understanding of Maoritanga is by visiting a marae. The marae is the open area in front of the *whare hui* (meeting house), but the term is often loosely used to describe the buildings as well. Either way it is a place which is sacred to the Maori and should be treated with great respect.

Some of the many customs and conventions of the marae include:

- That it is a place to stand *(Turangawaewae)*
- That it is a place of kinship *(Whanau-ngatanga)*, friendship *(Manaakitanga)*, love *(Aroha)*, spirituality *(Wairua)* and the life force *(Mauri)*
- Respect for elders *(Whakarongo kii nga kaumatua)*
- That it is a place where life and death merge, where the living *(te hunga ora)* give great honour to the dead *(te hunga mate)*
- The preservation and use of the Maori language *(Maori reo)*

A welcoming ritual *(Te Powhiri Ki Te Manuhiri)* is followed every time visitors *(manuhiri)* come onto the marae. They bring with them the memories of their dead. The hosts *(tangata whenua)* pay their respects to the deceased of the manuhiri, likewise the manuhiri to the tangata whenua. The ceremony removes the tapu and permits the manuhiri and tangata whenua to interact. The practice varies from marae to marae. Note that shoes must be removed before entering a whare hui.

Te Powhiri Ki Te Manuhiri may proceed as follows: a welcoming call *(karanga)* by women of the tangata whenua to the manuhiri. It could also include a ceremonial challenge *(taki or wero)*.The manuhiri reply to the karanga and proceed on to the marae. They pay their respects and sit where indicated, generally to the left (if facing outwards) of the whare hui.

Welcoming speeches *(mihi)* are given by the tangata whenua from the threshold *(Taumata Tapu)* in front of the meeting house. Each speech is generally supported by a song *(waiata)*, generally led by the women. When the mihi is finished the manuhiri reply. The tapu is deemed to have been lifted from the manuhiri when the replies are finished. The manuhiri then greet the tangata whenua with handshakes and the pressing of noses *(hongi)*. In some places the hongi is a single press, in others it is press, release, press.

attack from young, urban Maori who see the old leaders as too conservative and exclusive. With their adherence to traditional etiquette and Maori language, many urban Maori not brought up on the marae feel excluded and want a greater say in tribal affairs and negotiations with the government.

Many Pakeha also have a growing awareness of Maori culture. Certainly government and intellectuals have embraced the new Maori revival, and an understudying of Maori culture and at least a basic knowledge of Maori is seen as an advantage. However, there is an undercurrent of unease in the wider community, especially with radical Maori aspirations that call for Maori sovereignty – the establishment of a separate Maori government and judicial system.

The Maori occupation of the Moutoa gardens in Wanganui in 1995, which created great acrimony in the town and other parts of New Zealand, points to the difficulties of adjustment for the dominant Pakeha culture. Though New Zealand is not the utopia of racial harmony it is sometimes portrayed to be, there is no denying the genuine attempts by the Pakeha community to accommodate Maori aspirations. The overall good relations between the Maori and Pakeha communities continues, and New Zealand's record on race relations remains strong.

RELIGION

The most common religion in New Zealand is Christianity. The 'big three' denominations are Anglican (Church of England) with 25% of the population, Presbyterian with 18% and Roman Catholic with 16%. Many

Before the manuhiri leave the marae they make farewell speeches *(poroporoaki)* which take the form of thanks and prayer.

The important thing to remember, as a visitor, is that once invited you are extremely welcome on the marae, as a cornerstone of Maori culture is hospitality. Once protocol has been satisfied you have become part of an extended family and the concern of the tangata whenua is you – the manuhiri. They want to see you fed and looked after, almost spoiled, because you are a guest. Such hospitality is fantastic and lucky visitors to New Zealand are increasingly being given the opportunity to enjoy it, either as a guest or on one of the marae tours that are becoming popular. If you do receive hospitality such as food and lodging, it is customary to offer a *koha* or donation to help towards the upkeep of the marae. When the roles are reversed and you are the tangata whenua, remember that the care of *your* guests becomes your first concern. ■

other denominations also have followings, with Methodists, Baptists, Mormons, Brethren, Jehovah's Witnesses, Pentecostals, Assemblies of God and Seventh Day Adventists all well represented, along with various other faiths including Hindus, Jews, Muslims and Baha'is. The Ratana and Ringatu faiths, also with significant followings, are Maori adaptations of Christianity.

There is also a significant number of people (16.7%) who have no religion.

LANGUAGE

New Zealand has two official languages: English and Maori. English is the language that you usually hear spoken. The Maori language, long on the decline, is now making a comeback. You can use English to speak to anyone in New Zealand, as Maori people speak English. There are some occasions, though, when knowing a little Maori would be very useful, such as if you visit a marae, where often only Maori is spoken. It's also useful to know since many places in New Zealand have Maori names.

Kiwi English

As everywhere in the world where English is spoken, in New Zealand it is spoken in a unique way. The elision of vowels is the most distinctive feature of the Kiwi pronunciation of English. The NZ treatment of 'fish & chips', for example, is an endless source of delight for Australians when pronounced 'fush & chups'. In the North Island sentences often have 'eh!' attached to the end. In the far south a rolled 'r' is practised widely, a holdover from that region's Scottish heritage

– it is especially noticeable in Southland. There are some words in common usage which are peculiar to, or typical of, Kiwi English:

afghan – a popular home-made chocolate biscuit
All Black – a revered member of the national rugby team. The name comes from 'All Backs', which the NZ rugby team were called by the press on an early visit to England
baa – the most common greeting bleated by around 60 million Kiwis
bach – holiday home, usually a wooden cottage (pronounced 'batch')
Beehive – Parliament House in Wellington, so called because of its distinctive shape
box of birds – expression, usually a reply to 'How are you', meaning 'on top of the world'
bro – literally brother, usually meaning mate, as in 'just off to see the bros'.
choice – fantastic, great
ciggies – cigarettes
crib – Southland bach
cuzzies – cousins, relatives in general
chillie bin – cooler, esky; large insulated box for keeping beer etc cold
dairy – a small corner store which sells just about everything, especially milk, bread, the newspaper and ice cream; a convenience store. Cows are not milked here!
freezing works – slaughterhouse
Godzone – New Zealand (God's own)
good as – short for 'good as gold'
good as gold – very good
greenstone – jade; pounamu
handle – a beer glass with a handle
hard case – an unusual or strong character
hokey pokey – neither mischief nor magic but a delicious variety of ice cream
hooray – a rather 'bush' way of saying goodbye
huntaway – loud-barking sheepherding dog, usually a sturdy black-and-brown hound
Instant Kiwi – state-run lottery; a chance to become an instant millionaire
Is it what! – strong affirmation or agreement; Yes isn't it!
jandals – elsewhere in the world they may be referred to as sandals, flip flops or thongs; usually rubber footwear
judder bars – bumps in the road to make you drive slowly; speed bumps
kiwi – a flightless brown bird with a long beak; it is the national symbol and the name by which New Zealanders often refer to themselves; also an adjective to mean anything of or relating to NZ. Also a member of the national Rugby League team.
kiwi fruit – once called Chinese gooseberries; a small, succulent fruit with fuzzy brown skin and juicy green flesh
lounge bar – more upmarket and polite bar than a public bar; called a 'ladies' bar' in some countries
metal road or metalled road – gravel or gravelled road
motor camp – New Zealand caters well for its travelling population with a network of well-equipped camps. These have tent sites, caravan and campervan sites, on-site caravans, cabins and tourist flats
Nifty-fifty – 50 cc motorcycle
Pakeha – a fair-skinned person of European ancestry
Plunket – the Plunket Society is an organisation established to promote the health of babies. There are Plunket rooms (baby clinics), Plunket nurses (baby nurses) etc.
pushchair – baby stroller
Rheiny – affectionate term for Rheineck beer
scrap – a fight, not uncommon at the pub
section – a small block of land
Steinie – affectionate term for Steinlager beer
tarseal – the bitumen surface of a road
varsity – university or uni
wopwops – in the wopwops is out in the middle of nowhere; remote

A *Personal Kiwi-Yankee Dictionary* by Louis S Leland Jr, is a fine and often hilarious book of translations and explanations of quirks between the Kiwi and Yankee ways of speaking English. Yanks will love it.

Maori

The Maori have a vividly chronicled history, recorded in songs and chants which dramatically recall the Great Migration and other important events. It was the early missionaries who first recorded the language in a written form. They did this using only 15 letters of the English alphabet, with all syllables ending in a vowel.

The language is related to other Polynesian languages (including Hawaiian, Tahitian and Cook Islands Maori) and has some similarity to dialects found in Indonesia. It's a fluid, poetic language and surprisingly easy to pronounce if you just remember to say it phonetically and split each word (some can be amazingly long) into separate syllables.

Although the Maori language was never dead – it has always been used in Maori ceremonial events – in recent years there has been a revival of interest in the language, an important part of the renaissance of

Maoritanga. Many Maori people who had heard the language on maraes all their lives but had not spoken it in day-to-day living are now studying Maori and speaking it with fluency. Maori is now taught in schools throughout New Zealand, some TV programmes and news reports are broadcast in Maori, many of the English place names are being renamed in Maori, and even government departments have been rechristened with Maori names. The Inland Revenue Department is also known as Te Tari Taake (the last word is actually *take*, meaning levy, but the department has chosen to stress the long *a* by spelling it 'aa').

In many places, Maori people have got together to provide instruction in Maori language and culture for young children, so they will grow up speaking Maori in addition to English, and be familiar with Maori tradition. It is a matter of some pride to have fluency in the language and on some marae only Maori is allowed to be spoken, to encourage everyone to speak it and to emphasise the distinct Maori character of the marae.

Pronunciation Most consonants in Maori – h, k, m, n, p, t and w – are pronounced much the same as in English. The Maori *r* is a flapped sound with the tongue near the front of the mouth, but not rolled. It is closer to the English *l* in pronunciation.

Two combinations of consonants require special attention. *Ng*, pronounced as in the English suffix '-ing' (singing, running etc), can be used at the beginning of words as well as at the end; it's easy to practise this sound, just say the '-ing' over and over, isolate the *ng* part of it, and then practise using it to begin a word rather than end one.

The *wh* also has a unique pronunciation in Maori, generally being pronounced like a soft English *f*. This pronunciation is used in many place names in New Zealand, especially in the North Island, where there are place names such as Whangarei, Whangaroa and Whakapapa (all pronounced as if they began with a soft *f*). There is some regional variation, however; in the region around the Whanganui River, for example, the *wh* is pronounced the same as in English (as in when, why, etc).

When learning to speak Maori the correct pronunciation of the vowels is all important. We can only approximate the sounds here; to really get it right, you will have to hear someone pronounce it correctly, so take what is written here only as a rough guideline.

Each vowel has both a long and a short sound. The approximate sounds are:

ā	as in 'large' (long *a*)
a	as in 'but' (short *a*)
ē	a sort of combination sound, between 'get' and 'bait' (long *e*)
e	as in 'get' (short *e*)
ī	as in 'weed' (long *i*)
i	as in 'it' (short *i*)
ō	as in 'pork' (long *o*)
o	a shorter sound than *o*
ū	as in 'moon' (long *u*)
u	as in 'foot' (short *u*)

The diphthongs are pronounced approximately like this:

ae & ai	as in 'sky'
ao & au	as in 'how'
ea	as in 'lair'
ei	as in 'bay'
eo	eh-oh
eu	eh-oo
ia	as in 'beer'
ie	as the 'ye' in 'yet'
io	as the 'ye o' in 'ye old'
iu	as in 'cue'
oa	as in 'roar'
oe	as in 'towing'
oi	as in 'toy'
ou	as in 'sow'
ua	as in 'fewer'

Each syllable ends in a vowel and there is never more than one vowel in a syllable. There are no silent letters.

You can find a number of Maori phrasebooks, grammar books and Maori-English dictionaries if you want to study the language. Learning just a few basic greetings is an excellent thing to do, especially if you will be going onto a marae, where you will be greeted in Maori.

The *Collins Maori Phrase Book* by Patricia Tauroa is an excellent book for starting to speak the language, with sections on ordinary conversation and also on how the language is used in the context of the culture, ie on a marae. *Say It in Maori* compiled by Alan Armstrong is a smaller pocket-size book. *He Whakamarama: a New Course in Maori* by John Foster is a introductory language course with an accompanying cassette.

Other English-Maori dictionaries include the *English-Maori Maori-English Dictionary* by Bruce Biggs, and the *Reed Dictionary of Modern Maori* by PM Ryan, one of the most widely available and authoritative dictionaries.

The *Dictionary of the Maori Language* by HW Williams is a large volume which translates only from Maori to English; it's the standard classic dictionary used by serious students of the language.

Meanwhile, here are a few words you will probably hear:

atua – spirit or gods
haka – war dance
hakari – feast
hangi – oven made by digging a hole and steaming food in baskets over embers in the hole; a feast of traditional Maori foods
heitiki – carved, stylised human figure worn around the neck, usually shortened to 'tiki'
hoa – friend
hui – gather; meeting
iwi – people, tribe
kai – food; any word with kai in it will have some food connection
ka pai – good, excellent
karakia – prayer
kaumatua – elders
koe – you (singular)
koutou – you (plural)
kumara – sweet potatoes, a Maori staple food
mana – spiritual power or prestige
manuhiri – visitor; guest
Maoritanga – Maori culture
mere – flat, greenstone war club
moko – facial tattoo
ngati – people, tribe
o – of
pa – fortified village, usually on a hilltop
Pakeha – White person, European, non-Maori
tane – man
tangata – human beings
tangata whenua – people of the land; the local people
taniwha – fear-inspiring water spirit
tapu – holy; sacred; taboo; forbidden
te – the
tiki – an amulet or figurine, often a carved representation of an ancestor
tohunga – priest, wizard or general expert
Wahine – woman
wai – water; place names with 'wai' in them will often be on a river
whakapapa – genealogy
whare – house
whare runanga – meeting house
whare whakairo – carved house

Greetings & Small Talk Maori greetings are finding increased popularity; don't be surprised if you're greeted on the phone or on the street with 'Kia ora'.

Haere mai! – Welcome!
Haere ra. – Goodbye, farewell. (from the person staying to the one going)
E noho ra. – Goodbye, farewell. (from the person going to the person staying)
Kia ora. – Hello, good luck, good health.
Tena koe. – Hello. (to one person)
Tena korua. – Hello. (to two people)
Tena koutou. – Hello. (to three or more people)
Kei te pehea koe? – How are you? (to one person)
Kei te pehea korua? – How are you? (to two people)
Kei te pehea koutou? – How are you? (to three or more people)
Kei te pai. – Very well, thank you; that is satisfactory, OK.
Ka pai. – Thank you.

Place Names Many place names have a clear Maori influence. Maori words incorporated in New Zealand's place names include:

anatoki – axe or adze in a cave; cave or valley in the shape of an axe
awa – river or valley
ika – fish
iti – small
kahurangi – treasured possession, special greenstone
kai – food
kainga – village
kare – rippling
kotinga – boundary line
koura – crayfish
manga – branch, stream or tributary
mangarakau – plenty of sticks, a great many trees

manu – bird
maunga – mountain
moana – sea or lake
moko – tattoo
motu – island
nui – big
o – of
one – beach, sand or mud
onekaka – red-hot or burning sand
pa – fortified village
papa – flat, broad slab
parapara – the soft mud used for dyeing flax
patarua – killed by the thousands, site of early tribal massacres
pohatu – stone
puke – hill
rangi – sky, heavens
rangiheata – absence of clouds; a range seen in the early morning
repo – swamp
roa – long
roto – lake
rua – hole, two
takaka – killing stick for parrot, or bracken
tane – man
tata – close to, dash against, twin islands
te – the
totaranui – place of big totara trees
uruwhenua – enchanted objects
wahine – woman
wai – water
waikaremumu – bubbling waters
waingaro – lost, waters that disappear in certain seasons
wainui – big bay or many rivers, the ocean
waka – canoe
wero – challenge
whanau – extended family
whanga – bay or inlet
whare – house
whenua – land or country

Try a few – Whanga-roa is 'long bay', Roto-rua is 'two lakes', Roto-roa is 'long lake', Wai-kare-iti is 'little rippling water'. All those names with 'wai' in them – Waitomo, Waitara, Waioru, Wairoa, Waitoa, Waihi and so on – have something to do with water.

However, a little knowledge can be a dangerous thing, and words don't always mean the sum of their components. If you're interested, *A Dictionary of Maori Place Names* by AW Reed is an excellent reference for understanding Maori place names all over New Zealand, and it's small enough to be easy to carry around.

Flora & Fauna

R COLBORNE, DOC

Kea on southern rata

As is the case for most Pacific islands, New Zealand's native flora & fauna are, for the most part, not found anywhere else in the world. And, like other Pacific islands, NZ's native ecosystem has been dramatically affected and changed by plants and animals brought by settlers, mostly in the last 200 years. Wild pigs, goats, possums, wallabies, rabbits, dogs, cats and deer have all made their mark on the native wildlife, and blackberries, gorse, broom and agricultural weeds have infested huge areas of land.

New Zealand is believed to be a fragment of the ancient southern continent of Gondwanaland which became detached over 100 million years ago allowing many ancient plants and animals to survive and evolve in isolation. As a result, most of the NZ flora & fauna is indigenous/endemic. It has the worlds largest flightless parrot (kakapo), the only truly alpine parrot (kea), the oldest reptile (tuatara), some of the biggest earthworms, the smallest bats, some of the oldest trees, and many of the rarest birds, insects, and plants in the world. The first Maoris brought some rats and the now extinct Maori dog *(kuri)* with them but the only indigenous mammals at that time were bats.

Much of New Zealand's unique flora & fauna has survived, but today over 150 native plants – 10% of the total number of native species – and many native birds are threatened with extinction.

FAUNA

Birds

The endemic avifauna of NZ is not immense but it evolved in relative peace with very little threat, and certainly there were no large competitors. Thus ground dwelling parrots, kiwis and moas not only survived but thrived. The balance was altered by the coming of humans – first the Maori then the Pakeha and the predatory species which both groups introduced. Many species vanished in a 'blink of the eye' relative to New Zealand's evolutionary history.

So the NZ bird you *won't* see is the famous moa, a sort of oversized ostrich. Originally there were numerous types and sizes, but the largest of them – the giant moas – were as tall as four metres. They had been extinct for a few centuries by the time the Europeans arrived, but you can see moa skeletons and reconstructions in many NZ museums. Similarly, the huia, with its remarkable differentiation and function in male and female bills, is extinct.

R MORRIS, DOC

Great spotted kiwi

Kiwi

There are three species of kiwi: the brown kiwi *(Apteryx australis)*, of which there are several sub species; the little spotted kiwi *(A. owenii)*; and the great spotted kiwi *(A. haastii)*. The best known of NZ's birds, the kiwi has become the country's symbol.

It's a small, tubby, flightless bird and, because it's nocturnal, is not easy to observe. Kiwis have defunct vestigial wings, feathers that are more like hair than real feathers, short sight and a sleepy nature, but they have strong legs. Despite the fact that night-time is when they are most active, they are still fairly lazy, sleeping for up to 20 hours a day. The rest of the time they spend poking around for worms which they sniff out with the nostrils on the end of their bill.

R MORRIS, DOC

North Island brown kiwi

The female kiwi is larger than the male and much fiercer. She lays an egg weighing up to half a kg, huge in relation to her size (about 20% of her body weight), but having performed that mighty feat leaves the male to hatch it while she guards the burrow. When the kiwi hatches it associates with its father, completely ignoring its mother.

The kiwi is a threatened species but it is not endangered. Brown kiwis can be seen on Stewart Island, Waitangi State Forest, Little Barrier Island, Fiordland, Paparoa National Park and Mt Otanewainuku near Tauranga. Little spotteds are seen on Kapiti Island and the great spotted kiwi in the Paparoa National Park.

GR CHANCE, TRUST BANK, ROYAL ALBATROSS CENTRE

Royal albatross

Royal Albatross

These large birds *(Diomedea epomorphora;* Maori: toroa) range throughout the world and breed on a number of the island groups to the south and east of NZ. There is one mainland breeding colony, at Taiaroa Head on the Otago Peninsula. They breed from October to September. There is nothing quite like seeing these enormous birds swoop past at eye level. On land however, they are lumbering creatures.

In winter you may see a wandering albatross *(Diomedea exulans)* over NZ waters.

Westland Black Petrel

Near Punakaiki, Westland, are the world's only breeding grounds of the largest burrowing petrel *(Procellaria westlandica)*. Westland black petrels come to land only during the breeding season from March to December. Eggs are laid in May and chicks hatch in July/August. From August to November chicks are fed by one of the parents every three days. In December the fledgelings leave the colony, not to return for seven years.

Their daily flights to and from feeding grounds can best be observed near Punakaiki in the South Island. They fly out individually each morning but congregate offshore for the flight in at dusk. During the breeding season thousands can be seen at the colony en masse. (See the Paparoa National Park section in the West Coast chapter.)

R MORRIS, DOC

Westland black petrel

Fiordland Crested Penguin

This penguin *(Eudyptes pachyrhynchus;* Maori: pokotiwha) lives around the south-west coast of the South Island and around Stewart Island. You are most likely to see these birds when you're travelling down the West Coast in the World Heritage region, especially near the beach by Lake Moeraki, and in Milford Sound. It is now believed to be the rarest species of penguin in the world. It is very timid and is identifiable by its yellow crest, which distinguishes it from the yellow-eyed penguin.

A MUNN, DOC

Fiordland crested penguins

Little Blue Penguin

The little blue penguin *(Eudyptula minor;* Maori: korora) is common in coastal waters from the top of the North Island to Stewart Island. It is the smallest species of penguin and can often be seen coming ashore at night, most notably at Oamaru in Otago. Its upper parts are blue, underparts white and bill black. It is known as the fairy penguin in Australia.

R MORRIS, DOC

Little blue penguin

Yellow-Eyed Penguin

The yellow-eyed penguin *(Megadyptes antipodes;* Maori: hoiho) is the world's second rarest species of penguin, its numbers having diminished because of the loss of its coastal habitat. It can still be seen along the south-east coast of the South Island (see Oamaru, Otago Peninsula and the Catlins in the Otago Chapter). The streaked yellow head and eye are its most conspicuous characteristics.

NZ TOURISM BOARD, DUNEDIN

Yellow-eyed penguin

Australasian Gannet

This gannet *(Morus serrator;* Maori: takapu) is becoming increasingly common around NZ waters and there are three mainland breeding colonies (Farewell Spit in the South Island, Muriwai and Cape Kidnappers in the North Island). The juveniles migrate to Australia and return in four years to breed. These birds dive from

P BLOK, DOC

Australasian gannet

great heights, with wings folded back, to catch fish. Their yellow head against a white body is their most obvious feature. On land they are ungainly but in the air – poetry in motion.

Cormorants or Shags

Cormorants or shags are generally referred to as 'shags' in NZ, and seldom is the distinction made between species. There are seven species. The black shag *(Phalacrocorax carbo novahollandiae,* Maori: kawau), NZ's largest shag, is common on inland lakes and along sheltered parts of the coastline. It is seen in flocks near shellbanks and sandspits or perched on rocks.

Three other species of *Phalacrocorax* are found in NZ. The pied shag *(P. varius varius,* Maori: karuhiruhi), sometimes referred to as the pied cormorant; the little black shag *(P. sulcirostris)* and the little shag *(P. melanoleucos brevirostris;* Maori: kawaupaka). The little black is distinguished from the immature little shag by its long, narrow bill.

R MORRIS, DOC

Spotted shags

A separate genus of shags is *Leucocarbo*. The New Zealand king shag *(L. carunculatus)* is one of the rarest shags in the world and is only found in coastal waters on the southern side of Cook Strait. Its pink feet are its distinguishing feature. The Stewart Island shag *(L. chalconotus)* is found in coastal waters from the Otago Peninsula to Stewart Island. The last species of shag is the spotted *(Stictcarbo punctatus punctatus;* Maori parekareka). Recognised by the black spots on its back, it is found in coastal water around Auckland, in the Marlborough Sounds and on the Otago and Banks peninsulas.

White Heron

This heron *(Egretta alba modesta;* Maori: kotuku) is to NZ what the flamingos are to the Galapagos – it is widely spread throughout the world but seen in relatively few numbers in NZ.

MF SOPER, DOC

White heron

It is believed that there are only 200 birds in the country. The sole breeding colony is on the banks of the Waitangi-Taona River in South Westland (near Okarito) and the best time to see them is from September to November. After that they scatter to wetlands and tidal lagoons throughout NZ. Their scarcity led the Maori to believe that seeing them was a once-in-a-lifetime experience.

Blue Duck

This endemic and threatened species of duck (*Hymenolaimus malacorhynchos*; Maori: whio) is found in fast-flowing rivers of the high country of the North and South Islands; it doesn't occur further north than East Cape. You can almost be certain that it is a blue duck if it is seen surfing and feeding in fast-flowing, turbulent water.

M WILLIAMS, DOC

Male blue duck

Weka

The four subspecies of weka are found in a wide range of habitats, usually in scrub and on forest margins. The North Island weka *(Gallirallus australis greyi)* is found on Kapiti Island and in Northland and Poverty Bay. The western South Island weka *(G. australis australis)* is found in the north and western regions of the South Island, while the eastern South Island weka *(G. australis hectori)* is found in the drier east. The Stewart Island weka *(G. australis scotti)* has been introduced to Kapiti Island. The flightless weka is most active at dusk but can be seen scrounging during the day in areas where humans leave rubbish.

RICHARD TIMBURY

Weka

New Zealand Falcon

The falcon *(Falco novaeseelandiae;* Maori: karearea) is distinguished from the larger Australasian harrier by its rapid flight and longer tail. It inhabits high country in the Southern Alps and Fiordland and the forests of Westland and the North Island; it is rarely seen north of the central North Island. It has a rapid 'kek-kek-kek' call and feeds on smaller passerine birds.

R MORRIS, DOC

Immature New Zealand falcon

Pukeko

This bird *(Porphyrio porphyrio melanotus)* is common throughout the wetter areas in NZ, especially near swamps and lake edges where there are clumps of rushes; it is a good swimmer. Pukekos have very large feet and emit a high-pitched screech when disturbed.

Black Stilt

The Mackenzie country of south Canterbury is the home of the black stilt *(Himantopus novaezelandiae;* Maori: kaki), one of the world's rarest wading birds. It is found in swamps and beside riverbeds in the Waitaki River system, Otago. A single remnant population of 70 adults (11 breeding pairs) survives in the wild.

The DOC has established a captive breeding and release programme for this endangered species near Twizel. Approximately 30 juvenile birds have also been hand-reared (in isolation of humans) and will be released into the wild at nine months of age. Public

CR VEITCH, DOC

Black stilt

R MORRIS, DOC

Pukeko

R MORRISON, DOC

South Island takahe

M SOPER, DOC

New Zealand dotterel

CR VEITCH, DOC

Male wrybill on nest

CR VEITCH, DOC

Kakapo

viewing of these captive birds is welcome and guided tours leave daily from the DOC Information Centre in Twizel. A specially designed hide allows visitors to view the breeding birds without disturbance, and displays provide information on the programme.

South Island Takahe

The takahe *(Porphyrio mantelli hochstetteri)* disappeared and was believed extinct. It was then found again in the Murchison Mountains of Fiordland in 1948. It is a flightless bird that feeds on tussock shoots, alpine grasses and fern roots, whose habitat is tussock and small patches of beech forest. Numbers are estimated at about 160 (1991), including some in captivity, mostly at Te Anau Wildlife Park, Mt Bruce National Wildlife Centre and Maud Island in the Marlborough Sounds.

New Zealand Dotterel

The dotterel *(Charadrius obscurus;* Maori: tuturiwhatu) is a threatened species which is found north of the Bay of Plenty and Raglan and occasionally on Stewart Island. There are accessible breeding colonies on the sandy beaches of the eastern side of the Coromandel. Its nest is a simple sand scrape, sometimes lined with dry grass; nesting takes place from August to December. Listen for the 'pweep' when they are disturbed – then back off, as you are too close.

Wrybill

If you fail to recognise this bird with its unique bill with tip bent to the right then put your binoculars away and take up stamp collecting. Wrybills *(Anarhynchus frontalis;* Maori: ngutuparore) migrate within NZ, first nesting in the shingly riverbeds of Canterbury and Otago and then moving north to spend autumn and winter in the warmer climes of the estuaries and mudflats of the North Island. The wrybill swings its bill sideways through mud to trap marine organisms from the sludge.

Kakapo

The kakapo *(Strigops habroptilus)* is severely endangered and the remaining populations are on the predator-free Little Barrier and Codfish islands. The largest parrot in the world (males sometimes weigh up to three kg), it is nocturnal and flightless although it uses its wings for balance. There are probably only 50 or so birds left. You will only observe this bird with the assistance of the DOC.

Kaka

There are two distinct subspecies of kaka. The North Island kaka *(Nestor meridionalis septentrionalis)* inhabits lowland forest in the North Island and forested offshore islands. The South Island kaka *(N. meridionalis meridionalis)* inhabits forest in Nelson, the West Coast, Fiordland and Stewart Island. The South Island kaka is slightly larger and has a whitish crown (sometimes grey); both birds are generally bronze in colour with crimson tones on the underparts.

CR VEITCH, DOC

Kaka

Kea

The kea *(Nestor notabilis)* is a large parrot decked out in unparrot-like drab green except for bright red underwings It inhabits South Island high-country forests and mountains. They're amusing, fearless, cheeky and inquisitive birds. There are plenty of opportunities to observe them at the Fox and Franz Josef glaciers. At the car park at the terminal of the glaciers they hang around waiting for tourist hand-outs. Signs warn you of their destructive tendencies.

R MORRIS, DOC

Kea

Parakeets

There are two species of indigenous parakeet – the yellow-crowned *(Cyanoramphus auriceps auriceps)* and red-crowned parakeet *(C. novaezelandiae novaezelandiae)* – both are known to the Maori as kakariki. The yellow-crowned is seen high in the canopy of forests in the North, South and Stewart islands, and on many offshore islands (not pictured). The red-crowned is not likely to be seen on the mainland but rather in the lowland forests on many offshore islands. Both species lay their eggs from October to January and the males assist in the feeding of chicks.

Morepork

The endemic owl *(Ninox novaeseelandiae novaeseelandiae;* Maori: ruru) is found throughout NZ with the exception of the east of the South Island. It is the only endemic owl and differs from the introduced little owl *(Athene noctua)* in that it has a rounded head and larger tail. It gets its name from its cry of 'Quor-quo' which, with imagination, sounds like 'more pork'. It would probably eat this meat if offered but favours insects such as moths and wetas, with the occasional side dish of small birds and mice.

JL KENDRICK, DOC

Red-crowned parakeet

CR VEITCH, DOC

Morepork

JL KENDRICK, DOC

New Zealand pigeon

MF SOPER, DOC

Rifleman

New Zealand Pigeon

When you first encounter the New Zealand pigeon *(Hemiphaga novaeseelandiae novaeseelandiae*; Maori: kereru*)* in the forest it is likely that you will be startled by its thumping, whistling wingbeat as it flies from tree to tree.

It is widespread throughout NZ forests and is occasionally observed eating in open fields. A large bird, it is the only endemic species of pigeon. The West Coast, the Catlins, Fiordland and Stewart Island are good places to see them.

Rifleman

There are two subspecies of rifleman, NZ's smallest bird. The South Island rifleman *(Acanthisitta chloris chloris;* Maori: titipounamu) is found throughout the island, especially in mountainous beech forests. The North Island rifleman *(A. chloris granti)* is found on the Barrier Islands and in forests south of Te Aroha. The rifleman has a short tail and short, spiralling flight, flitting from tree to tree when feeding.

Rock Wren

This bird *(Xenicus gilviventris)* inhabits sub-alpine and alpine fields only in the South Island. Not much larger than the rifleman, it is recognisable because of its long legs and curious habit of bobbing up and down. It literally jumps from rock to rock looking for insects and spiders. During winter it lives in rock crevices under the snow.

Fantail

There are two subspecies of fantail, the North Island *(Rhipidura fuliginosa placabilis*; Maori: piwakawaka) and South Island *(R. fuliginosa fuliginosa*), both common throughout forest, scrub and in suburban gardens. The South Island fantail has more white on its outer tail feathers. Why do they follow you through the bush? They are attracted to the insects you disturb as you brush past the undergrowth.

R MORRIS, DOC

Rock wren

D CROUCHLEY, DOC

Fantail

Whitehead & Mohua (Yellowhead)

The whitehead *(Mohoua albicilla;* Maori: popokatea) inhabits forest and scrubland in the North Island only. Like the mohua, the most conspicuous feature is the single colour of the head. It doesn't occur north of Te Aroha except on Tiritiri and Little Barrier islands.

The mohua *(M. achrocephala)* or yellowhead, about the size of a house sparrow, is fairly hard to find and if observed in a forest it is unmistakable because of its bright yellow head. That is if you are in the ancient forests of Arthur's Pass National Park, Fiordland or the Catlins Forest Park (all in the South Island). If you see a similar bird in open grassland it is most likely that it is the introduced yellowhammer.

M F SOPER, DOC

Mohua (yellowhead)

Chatham Island Black Robin

In 1976 there were only seven black robins *(Petroica traversi)* left in the world, all on Little Mangere Island in the Chatham Islands. In the next few years attempts were made to transfer the birds to safer habitats on other islands. These relocations were largely unsuccessful and in 1980 there were only five black robins left. Such a small population would usually spell extinction of the species but as a last resort wildlife authorities began a cross-fostering programme using endemic warblers and, later, tom tits.

The robins must have sensed that the time for their emergence was right. By the end of summer 1984 there were 19 black robins, and at the end of the following summer 38. The tom tits were ideal foster parents. The future of the black robin is no longer bleak and one the most courageous attempts to save an endangered species has succeeded. In 1995, after a good breeding season there were 160 tough little birds.

D MERTON, DOC

Chatham Island black robin

North Island Kokako

The depletion of its habitat and the introduction of predators have severely endangered the populations of the North Island kokako *(Callaeas cinerea wilsoni).* It is a member of the wattle-bird family and is distinguished by its blue wattle (the skin hanging from its throat).

It is a weak flier and would most likely be observed bounding and gliding through the unmodified lowland forest of the Central North Island, Taranaki, Northland and the Coromandel. The South Island kokako, orange-wattled, may well be extinct by now.

R LALBOURNE, DOC

North Island kokako

Tui

The tui *(Prosthemadera novaeseelandiae novaeseelandiae)* is found throughout NZ's forests. It is conspicuous by its white throat feathers (hence a common name, 'parson bird'). It has an extremely large repertoire of sounds and can mimic many other birds.

You can see them around much of the country. Pelorus Sound, Ulva Island and Oban, Stewart Island are particularly fertile spotting grounds.

CR VEITCH, DOC

Tui

CR VEITCH, DOC

Bellbird

CR VEITCH, DOC

Saddleback

Bellbird

The bellbird *(Anthornis melanura melanura;* Maori: makomako) is common in both native and exotic forests and is easily identified by its beautiful bell-like call. It is found in all areas of NZ with the exception of Northland. Both sexes have curved honeyeater bills and short tail feathers.

Saddleback

There are two subspecies of saddleback, (you guessed it by now!) the North Island *(Philesturnus carunculatus rufusater;* Maori: tieke) and South Island *(P. carunculatus carunculatus).* The first is found on offshore islands off the East Coast region and Kapiti Island, and the second on small islands off the coast of Stewart Island. They differ in that the North Island saddleback has a narrow, buff-coloured band in front of the saddle. Both subspecies are weak fliers and tend to flit through the forest in short rapid movements. You will often be greeted into their territory with their distinctive chattering call.

Marine Mammals

Perhaps one of the greatest delights of a trip to New Zealand, especially the South Island, is a chance to observe the wealth of marine mammalia. There are 76 species of whales and dolphins on this globe and New Zealand, as small as it is, is blessed by the fact that 35 of these species have been observed in its waters. Kaikoura is particularly blessed as nearly half of that number of whales and dolphins have been seen in waters off its shores.

Of the 66 species of toothed whales and dolphins, the largest and the smallest are seen in New Zealand waters – the sperm whale and the Hector's dolphin. There are also baleen whales, seals and sea lions.

No longer does the blood of these species stain NZ waters as an indication of short-term reward. The

DOC ROSS

Bottlenose dolphin

whales, dolphins, seals and sea lions attract not the bludgeon and harpoon but the entranced eyes of foreign and local observers. The tourist dollars pouring into Kaikoura and elsewhere are worth many times the money made by the previous slaughter for oil and skins.

Humpback Whale

Sadly, sightings of the humpback *(Megaptera novaengliae)* are rare. There is a group which migrates from Tonga to Antarctic waters via the coast of NZ. Once there were an estimated 100,000 in the world's oceans, now the number is believed to be about 2000. These whales sieve their food through baleen (fine whalebones), hence their classification as mysticeti (baleen whales). The males are a little smaller than the females who usually reach 16 metres in length and about 50 tonnes in weight. Humpbacks have unique tail fluke patterns, long flippers (up to one third of their length) and throat grooves.

Sperm Whale

This whale *(Physeter macrocephalus)* is the largest of the toothed whales – the male often reaches up to 20 metres in length and the female is much smaller with a maximum length of 12 metres. This is the whale that 'watchers' come to Kaikoura to see or at least see 10% of the whale, as this is all that is seen from the boats until the whale dives and then exposes its tail flukes. Males weigh from 35-50 tonnes and females just over 20 tonnes, and both live up to 70 years. They dive for long periods, around 45 minutes.

They are hard to locate in the open ocean and the only real give away is the blow from their spout or their sonar clicks, detected with hydrophones. Because they require a huge feeding area for each individual they are normally seen singly. The sperm whales have a single blowhole, offset on the left side of their head.

JEFF WILLIAMS

Sperm whale diving

Orca ('Killer Whale')

Orca *(Orcinus orca)* are the largest of the dolphins and among the largest predators on earth, feeding on other dolphins and whales, as well as seals, sea birds, penguins and sharks. They are classified as members of the Odontoceti (toothed whales and dolphins). They grow up to 9.5 metres in length (females seven metres) and 8000 kg in weight (females 4000 kg).

They are distinguished by their huge dorsal fins, often reaching nearly two metres high. The NZ pods (groups) have not been extensively studied. Both sexes have up to 12 pairs of teeth in each jaw. The orca vocalises both for socialising and as a means of keeping contact when foraging for food. There is no record of an unprovoked attack by an orca, as powerful as it is, upon humans.

I JISSER, DOC
Stranded long-finned pilot whales

Long-Finned Pilot Whale

Of the two species of pilot whale, the long and short-finned, it is the long-finned *(Globicephala melas)* which is seen the most in NZ waters. This is the species which has become notorious for large-scale 'strandings'. Long-finned pilot whales grow to over six metres in length (females up to 5.5 metres) and 3000 kg (females 2500 kg).

Bottlenose Dolphin

This is the 'Flipper' dolphin and it is one of the larger species, often reaching four metres, although those seen in NZ waters are about 3.5 metres. The bottlenose *(Tursiops truncatus)* are very gregarious but occasionally they go 'solo', like Maui, whom you may see at Kaikoura.

It is the bottlenose that is most recorded in history, probably because of its commensal fishing activities with humans. They are also known to feed cooperatively among themselves, after encircling a shoal of fish.

DOLPHIN DISCOVERIES
Dusky dolphin

Dusky Dolphin

Dusky dolphins *(Lagenorhynchus obscurus)* can reach lengths of over two metres, but they usually average 1.6 to 1.8 metres. What they lack in size they make up for in spirit. These are the most playful dolphins and those which 'dolphin swimming' participants are most likely to encounter. While in the water, you will see them executing head-first re-entry leaps, noisy leaps and somersaults.

They feed on small schooling fish, and often round up hundreds of fish in a tight ball, from which the pod takes turns at feeding. They congregate near the shore from late October to May; the pods then break up as winter comes on and the dolphins move offshore.

Hector's Dolphin

This dolphin *(Cephalorhynchus hectori)* is confined to NZ waters. They have a rather dumpy shape, a distinctive rounded fin and reach a length of only 1.4 metres. Like the dusky they feed on small schooling fish, but they stay relatively close to shore all year round. Even though they are the world's rarest dolphin there is a good chance that you will see them when travelling in the South Island. Kaikoura, Banks Peninsula and Porpoise Bay (Southland) are all good locations.

Some years back Greenpeace reported that around Banks Peninsula 230 Hector's, about 30% of the population of the area, had been killed in gill nets over a four-year period. Fortunately, DOC has since declared Banks Peninsula a marine mammal sanctuary.

F BRUEMMER, DOC
Female Hooker's sea lion

Common Dolphin

This dolphin *(Delphinus delphis)* is the most widespread of dolphins, occurring throughout the world. They grow up to 2.5 metres, although are likely to average just over two metres. They dive to nearly 300 metres and can stay underwater for five or so minutes.

Near Kaikoura, they are often seen alongside pods of duskys, but are considered more an offshore (pelagic) species. Common dolphins are recognised by the golden coloration on their sides. Squid is their favoured food.

Hooker's Sea Lion

These sea lions *(Neophoca hookeri)* are visitors to the South Island, and you are most likely to see them on beaches in the Catlins and on the Otago Peninsula. They are much larger than the NZ fur seal. In 1995 a pup was born on the Otago Peninsula – an incredible event. It is believed that this has not occurred on the mainland for an estimated 700 years.

P MOORE, DOC
New Zealand fur seal

New Zealand Fur Seal

This seal *(Arctocephalus forsteri)* is most commonly seen in NZ waters. Mature male seals (bulls) are about two metres in length, and females (cows) are about 1.6 metres; average weight is about 140 kg. Once slaughtered for their dense, luxuriant two-layered skins, fur seals are now thriving as a protected species. You can see them basking on rocks, but they will probably enter the safety of the water if you get too close. Fur seals differ from sea lions in that they have a broader bear-shaped head, prominent ears and larger front flippers.

You can swim with them in a number of locations, especially near Kaikoura. They are a popular distraction for sea kayakers in the Abel Tasman region, and you will see them from boats in Milford and Doubtful sounds.

C ROBERTSON, DOC
Male southern elephant seal

Elephant Seal

This seal *(Mirounga leonina)*, with its distinctive trunk-like nose is not commonly seen in NZ. There is a small breeding colony at the Nuggets, Southland, in the fauna-rich Catlins. It is found in its thousands on NZ's Subantarctic islands. The male grows to over four metres long and can weigh more than 4000 kg, making it the largest seal.

Other Fauna

The tuatara *(Sphenodon punctatus)* is a lizard-like reptile dating back to the age of the dinosaurs and perhaps before (260 million years?). Active at night, it eats insects, small mammals and birds' eggs. It also has a rudimentary 'third eye', grows up to 60 cm in length and may live well over 100 years. The tuatara is found on protected offshore islands (eg The Brothers and Stephens Island in the Marlborough Sounds) for which you need special permission to visit. Some specimens are kept in captivity, such as at the Wellington Zoo and the Southland Museum in Invercargill, where they have been successfully bred .

New Zealand has no snakes and only one spider that is dangerous to humans, the rare katipo, a close relative of the North American black widow and the Australian redback.

If you hear something croaking during the night, you can be sure it's not one of the three species of NZ frogs – they lack a vocal sac, so can only produce a high-pitched squeak. They're also remarkable in not having a free-swimming tadpole stage, instead undergoing metamorphosis in a capsule. One frog is restricted to the high parts of the Coromandel Peninsula, another to the summit of Stephens Island, Marlborough Sounds and the other frog is only found in remnant rainforest in the Marlborough Sounds.

The sandfly *(Austrosimulium* spp, Maori: te namu) is the most ubiquitous of nuisances and leaves its impression on every traveller to New Zealand, especially those who venture to South Westland and Fiordland. Typically, it is only the females who bite, needing the blood they take from you to reproduce. The bite is extremely itchy so do all you can to avoid being bitten in the first place, or try not to scratch the bite.

There are a number of species of wetas, quite large invertebrates with a fearsome appearance. The cave weta has long legs and a small body, perfectly adapted for movement on cave walls. In contrast, the bush weta has a large body. In both cases the male looks fearsome with a large head and snapping mandibles. The wingless alpine weta, also known as the 'Mount Cook flea' lives in rock crevices above the snowline.

There are two species of native (indigenous) bat, New Zealand's only mammals prior to the arrival of humans. These are the long-tailed and the short-tailed bat. You may see both species flitting around forest margins at sunset seeking insects. Bats were the only mammals to reach NZ, which was isolated from other land masses prior to mammalian expansion.

All of the introduced species of mammals have done their fair share of damage since their introduction. Probably the most infamous is the brush-tailed possum *(Trichosurus vulpecula).* Also prevalent are the rabbit, chamois, thar, Virginia (white-tailed) deer, red deer, wild pigs and goats.

And fish. New Zealand is renowned as an angler's paradise, largely due to the introduction of rainbow and brown trout, perch, carp, Atlantic salmon and quinnat

P MORRISON, DOC

Tuatara

M AUSS, DOC

Giant weta

JL KENDRICK, DOC

Long-tailed bat

salmon to its rivers and estuaries. The native NZ grayling is believed to be extinct.

Sitting at a major confluence of warm and cold ocean currents, NZ's offshore waters have a great variety of tropical and cold-water species of fish; and its thousands of km of coastline are home to tasty crustaceans such as the crayfish (lobster; Maori koura).

FLORA

In the 1800s when the first Europeans arrived, about 70% of New Zealand was covered in native forest. Much of it was soon cleared for timber (as in the large kauri forests) or to make way for farming.

Despite there not being as much native forest around as there was before the arrival of Europeans, NZ still has some magnificent areas of native forest and bush. About 10% to 15% of the total land area of the country is native flora, much of it in protected parks and reserves.

The variety of vegetation types in NZ is enormous. Heading south from the giant kauri forests of Northland there are the luxuriant lowland kohekohe forests of the Bay of Plenty; the rainforests dominated by rimu, various beeches, tawa, matai and rata, and a great variety of tree ferns; the podocarp and hardwood forests of the lower parts of the North Island with its kahikatea, tawa, rimu, rata, and kohekohe; the summer-flowering alpine and subalpine herb fields; and the windswept scrub of the smaller islands.

In the South Island the vegetation changes dramatically as you climb into the mountains. The lowland supplejacks give way to rimu, miro, and then tree ferns at about 800 metres. Above 1000 metres the totara, wineberry, fuschias, rata and kaikomako are gradually left behind, to be replaced by subalpine scrub. At about 1200 metres the scrub gives way to the tussock grasses and alpine herb fields, and at the extreme heights only some hardy lichens hang on to the exposed rock.

Like the Australian species, most of the 72 NZ orchids are not large or brilliantly coloured; one exception is the beautiful *Earina autumnalis*, which has perfumed cream flowers.

Various introduced species have been planted in large tracts for the timber industry. The most obvious imports are the massive plantations of radiata or Monterey pine and Douglas fir (Oregon).

The Maori language has bestowed marvellous names on some of the native plants of NZ, names that are almost unpronounceable to Europeans – tawhairauriki, kowhai ngutukaka, whauwhaupaku, mingimingi, hangehange, kumarahou, and pua o te reinga, to name a handful. Some of the English names are nearly as colourful, and it's interesting to speculate about their derivations – gum digger's soap, wild Irishman, seven-finger, bog pine, flower of Hades and Dieffenbach's Spaniard.

L MOLLOY, DOC

Dracophyllum species

RICHARD TIMBURY

Mt Cook lily

T LILLEBY, DOC

Mangrove tree

L MOLLOY, DOC

Kahikatea forest

P de JAGER, DOC

Kauri

Trees

The progenitors of NZ's two major forest groups, the podocarps and the southern beeches, were to be found in the ancient supercontinent of Gondwanaland. When the continents drifted apart and the land bridges eventually lost, over 60 million years ago, NZ's flora evolved in isolation. Of the country's 2000 or so flowering plants about 75% are only found in New Zealand.

The podocarps are part of an ancient family, Podocarpaceae, which evolved before flowering plants. Fossil pollen indicates that trees very similar to kahikatea and rimu have been here for more than 60 million years. The *Nothofagus* (beech) species found in NZ are very similar to those found in the south of South America, adding weight to the Gondwanaland theory.

Plenty of books cover this topic: *Which Native Tree* and *Which Native Fern* by Andrew Crowe and *New Zealand Trees and Ferns*, by Murdoch Riley.

Kahikatea

The white pine *(Dacrycarpus dacrydioides)* is NZ's tallest tree, reaching 60 metres, and maturing to hundreds of years. An adult tree has green scaly leaves. The immature fruit is yellow, ripening into an orange-red berry that bears a seed at its tip – favoured by the native pigeon (kereru) and the Maori. It is not surprising that the Maori also snared many pigeons on this tree.

Kamahi

Pronounced 'car-my', the hardy black birch, *Weinmannia racemosa*, is found throughout NZ from Auckland down to Stewart Island. It grows to a height of 25 metres and attains a diameter of over one metre. It has grey bark with white blotches, glossy, dark green leaves, small lilac-coloured flowers and rusty red seeds.

Kauri

Kauris *(Agathis australis)* only grow in Northland and on the Coromandel Peninsula. These large native trees were once ruthlessly cut down for their excellent timber and Northland is covered with evidence of the kauri days (see the Northland chapter).

D CROUCHLEY, DOC

Kamahi in flower

Kauri gum was found to be an important ingredient for making varnish and at one time there were many 'gumdiggers' who roamed the forests, poking in the ground for hard lumps of kauri gum.

Kauris grow to 30 metres and are believed to attain an age of about 2000 years. They have distinctive blotchy mosaic on the bark which feels as good as it looks.

J GREENWOOD, DOC
Kowhai flowers

Kowhai

This tree *(Sophora microphylla)* grows to about 11 metres and has small green leaves and groups of bright yellow flowers. There are three species of this, NZ's national flower, and all are similar in appearance. It is found in open areas, near rivers and on the edge of forests. It is a good tree in which to spot birds, especially tuis, as they seek honey from the flowers.

J GREENWOOD, DOC
Pohutukawa

Matai

The black pine *(Prumnopitys taxifolia)* is one of the most majestic of NZ's trees and is found throughout the North and South Islands. It grows to 30 metres and often with a very wide girth (one easily seen at Lake Ianthe in Westland). Its thick, grey bark falls off to reveal blotchy red patches underneath. It has small, flat leaves, the male and female flowers are found on the same long yellow spikes and it produces purple edible berries.

Miro

The miro *(Prumnopitys ferrugineus)*, another member of the pine family, grows to 25 metres. It is found throughout lowland forests in NZ. Very slow growing it may take 500 years to reach maturity. It has pointed leaves which could be mistaken for matai.

J GREENWOOD, DOC
Pohutukawa flowers

Pohutukawa

This beautiful tree *(Metrosideros excelsa)* is predominantly found in the north of the North Island but has been successfully planted throughout the South Island. Its magnificent crimson flowers appear in December and the tree is popularly known as the 'Christmas tree'; thin brown seeds appear in May. It grows up to 20 metres in height and two metres across at its base. It is found close to the sea; good places to see it are East Cape and the Coromandel Peninsula.

CR VEITCH, DOC
Rata

Rata

The rata is another tree with beautiful crimson flowers like the pohutukawa, except that its leaves are shiny and pointed at both ends. The northern rata *(Metrosideros robusta)*, reaching a height of 25 metres, grows in the North Island and in Nelson in the South Island. Southern rata *(M. umbellata)* predominates in the South Island but is also found in Northland.

This tree starts as a climber (epiphyte) on a host tree which it eventually strangles. When this happens the aerial roots disappear and the tree takes on a gnarled appearance.

Rimu

The red pine *(Dacrydium cupressinum)*, the most easily recognised of the podocarps, is found throughout NZ in areas of mixed forest. It grows to a height of more than 50 metres with a girth of about 1.5 metres. The narrow, prickly leaves drape down and often have little red cones at the tips of the leafy clusters. The fruit appears as a black nut at the tip of the seed.

It was once the most common of the lowland podocarps but its popularity as a building timber has drastically led to its depletion.

L MOLLOY, DOC
Rimu

Cabbage Tree

The beautiful broad-leafed mountain cabbage tree *(Cordyline indivisa;* Maori: toii) is found in moist mountain areas where there is plenty of light. It grows to 20 metres and, when mature, its stems hang downwards. Captain Cook and his crew gave the cabbage tree its name – the shoots they ate reminded them of cabbage.

Beeches *(Nothofagus spp)*

The silver beech *(Nothofagus menziesii;* Maori: tawhai) is found in stands in mixed forest on both Islands and occurs in sub-alpine regions. It grows up to 30 metres and has a silver-grey trunk of up to two metres in diameter. The small rounded leaves have serrated edges, the flowers are small, green and brown, and the fruit is small and woody. It is closely related to the other beeches including the red beech *(N. fusca)* and black beech *(N. solandri var. solandri)*.

M WILLIAMS, DOC
Cabbage tree flowers

M WILLIAMS, DOC
Cabbage tree

The beautiful mountain beech *(Nothofagus solandri var. cliffortioides;* Maori: tawhairauriki) occurs in mountain and sub-alpine areas from the central North Island plateau to the far south of the South Island. It grows to 22 metres high in favoured sites (but usually to about 15 metres) and its trunk is about a metre in diameter. Its leaves are dark and pointy as opposed to the light leaves of the tawhai. It has small red flowers and woody fruit. It is seen in splendour in Arthur's Pass National Park and near the Lewis Pass. (not pictured)

L MOLLOY, DOC

Silver beech forest

Totara

This tree *(Podocarpus totara)* has special significance in NZ as it was the favoured tree for Maori war canoes because of its soft wood. It can grow to be extremely old, attaining an age of 1000 years or more. It has long pointy leaves, and the male and female cones occur on separate trees. Its red and pink stalks attract birds.

Nikau

The nikau *(Rhapalostylis sapida)* is found throughout lowland areas of the North Island and the north of the South Island as far south as Banks Peninsula. The best place to see nikau is on the north of the West Coast, from Punakaiki to Karamea, and their appearance here could fool you into thinking you are in the tropics. It can grow to 10 metres in height. Its fronds were interwoven and used for roofing material by the Maori.

L MOLLOY, DOC

Totora

CR VEITCH, DOC

Nikau grove

T LILLEBY, DOC

Ponga

T LILLEBY, DOC

Piupiu

Ferns

One of the prominent features of the NZ bush is the proliferation of tree ferns which are intertwined into the undergrowth. There are over 80 species of fern and five species of soft fern. Perhaps the most interesting are the mauku (hen & chickens fern; *Asplenium bulbiferum*) and the raurenga (Kidney fern; *Trichomanes reniforme*), and the rarest would be the para (horseshoe or king fern; *Marattia salicina*). A common sight on NZ hillsides is the bracken fern *(Pteridium aquilinum)*, growing to three metres or more.

The mamaku (black tree fern; *Cyathea medullaris)* is the largest of the NZ ferns and grows to a height of 20 metres, with the fronds extending up to seven metres. It grows throughout the country, common in damp forest gullies.

The ponga (silver tree fern; *Cyathea dealbata)* is the national symbol which adorns the jumpers of many of NZ's sports representatives. It grows up to 10 metres in height and the fronds, which extend up to four metres, are white on the underside and dull green on the upper side.

The piupiu (crown fern; *Blechnum discolor)* is found throughout the country and is very noticeable because its bright green fronds, up to 1.5 metres in length, often form a significant part of the ground cover. When the frond is turned over it reveals a silvery-grey side. Interestingly, it is the colour of the two types of fronds of *Blechnum* species, one brown and one green, which denotes whether they are fertile or sterile. The brown fronds look as though they are dead or dying, but they produce the reproductive spores. Other ferns produce spores seen as brown spots on the underside of green fronds.

Facts for the Visitor

VISAS & EMBASSIES

Everyone needs a passport to enter New Zealand. If you enter on an Australian or New Zealand passport, or any other passport containing an Australian or New Zealand residence visa, your passport must be valid on arrival. All other passports must be valid for at least three months beyond the time you intend to stay in New Zealand, or one month beyond the intended stay if the issuing government has an embassy or consulate in New Zealand that is able to issue and renew passports.

Australian citizens or holders of current Australian resident return visas do not need a visa or permit to enter New Zealand, and they can stay in New Zealand as long as they like provided that they do not have any criminal convictions. Australians do not require a work permit should they wish to work in New Zealand.

Citizens of the UK and other British passport holders who have evidence of the right to live permanently in the UK do not need a visa, and upon arrival in New Zealand they are issued with a permit to stay in the country for up to six months.

Citizens of the following countries do not need a visa, and upon arrival in New Zealand they are issued with a permit good for a three-month stay:

Austria, Belgium, Brunei, Canada, Denmark, Finland, France, Germany, Greece, Iceland, Indonesia, Ireland, Italy, Japan, Kiribati, South Korea, Liechtenstein, Luxembourg, Malaysia, Malta, Monaco, Nauru, the Netherlands, Norway, Portugal, Singapore, Spain, Sweden, Switzerland, Thailand, Tuvalu, USA

Citizens of all other countries require a visa to enter New Zealand, available from any NZ embassy or consular agency. Visas are normally valid for three months.

To qualify for a visitor's permit on arrival, or to qualify for a visa if you need one, you must be able to show:

- Your passport, valid for three months beyond the time of your intended stay in New Zealand.
- Evidence of sufficient funds to support yourself in New Zealand for the time of your intended stay, without working. This is calculated to be NZ$1000 per month (NZ$400 per month if your accommodation has been prepaid) and can be in the form of cash, travellers' cheques, bank drafts or the following credit cards: American Express, Bankcard, Diners Club, MasterCard or Visa.
- Onward tickets to a country to which you can show you have right of entry, with firm bookings if travelling on special rate air fares.

If you do not have sufficient funds, you can still come if you have a friend or relative in New Zealand who is willing to sponsor you, that is, who will guarantee your accommodation and maintenance.

Entry requirements can change, so always check the situation before departure.

Visitor's permits can be extended for stays of up to nine months, provided you apply for further permits and meet normal visitor requirements. 'Genuine tourists' and a few other categories of people can be granted stays of up to 12 months.

If you know in advance that you will want to stay longer than the permitted time, or if you intend to work or study in New Zealand, you must obtain a visa, work permit or student permit before coming to New Zealand, even if you are from a country that otherwise would not require a visa.

It is illegal for you to work in New Zealand on a visitor's permit. If you have an offer of employment, work permits valid for up to three years should be applied for overseas before arriving in New Zealand. You will be granted permission to work only if there are no suitable New Zealand job seekers who could do the job you have been offered. You can apply for a work permit in New Zealand after arrival, but if granted, it will only be valid for the remaining time you are entitled to stay as a visitor.

Citizens of Canada, Japan and the UK

aged 18 to 30 years can apply for a Working Holiday Work Visa valid for a 12-month stay. It allows you to engage in employment while travelling around the country. The visa must be applied for in the home country before entering New Zealand, and is only issued to those seeking a genuine working holiday, not for permanent work.

You can study for up to three months on a visitor's permit, provided it is one single course of not more than three months' duration. If you want to study longer, you will need to obtain a student permit.

You can apply for a work permit, a student permit or an extension of your visitor's permit at any office of the New Zealand Immigration Service. They have offices in Auckland, Manukau, Hamilton, Palmerston North, Wellington, Christchurch and Dunedin. Requirements for an extension are the same as those for your initial visa or visitor's permit.

Be careful not to overstay your time. Extensions are easy to get provided you meet the requirements. If you overstay your permit, however, you are subject to removal from the country.

New Zealand Embassies & Consulates

New Zealand embassies and consulates in other countries include:

Australia
- High Commission, Commonwealth Ave, Canberra, ACT 2600 (☎ (6) 270 4211; fax 273 3194)
- Consulate-General, Watkins Place Building, 288 Edward St (GPO Box 62), Brisbane, QLD 4001 (☎ (7) 3221 9933; fax 3221 9127)
- Consulate-General, 60 Albert Rd, South Melbourne (PO Box 7275, Melbourne, VIC 3004) (☎ (3) 9696 0501; fax 9690 0422)
- Consulate-General, 14th Floor, Gold Fields Building, 1 Alfred St, Circular Quay (GPO Box 365), Sydney, NSW 2000 (☎ (2) 9247 1999; fax 9231 6369)

Canada
- High Commission, Suite 701, Metropolitan House, 99 Bank St, Ottawa, Ont K1P 6G3 (☎ (613) 238 5991; fax 238 5707)
- Consulate-General, Suite 1200-888 Dunsmuir St (PO Box 10071, Pacific Centre), Vancouver, BC V6C 3K4 (☎ (604) 684 7388; fax 684 7333)

France
- Embassy, 7ter, rue Léonard de Vinci, 75116, Paris (☎ (1) 45 00 24 11; fax 45 01 26 39)

Germany
- Embassy, Bundeskanzlerplatz 2-10, 53113 Bonn (☎ (228) 22 80 70; fax 22 16 87)
- Consulate-General, Heimhuderstrasse 56, 2000 Hamburg 13 (☎ (40) 442 5550; fax 442 55549)

Ireland
- Consulate-General, 46 Upper Mount St, Dublin 2 (☎ (01) 762 464; fax 762 489)

Italy
- Embassy, Via Zara 28, Rome 00198 (☎ (6) 440 2928/30; fax 440 2984)

Japan
- Embassy, 20-4-Kamiyama-cho, Shibuya-ku, Tokyo 150 (☎ (3) 3467 2271/75; fax 3467 6843) (NZ also has consulates in Fukuoka, Hokkaido, Nagoya, Osaka and Sendai)

Netherlands
- Embassy, Carnegielaan 10, 2517 KH The Hague (☎ (70) 346 9324; fax 363 2983)

Switzerland
- Consulate-General, 28A Chemin du Petit-Saconnex, CH-1209 Geneva (PO Box 334, CH-1211, Geneva 19) (☎ (22) 734 9530; fax 734 3062)

UK
- High Commission, New Zealand House, The Haymarket, London SW1Y 4TQ (☎ (0171) 973 0366/63; fax 973 0370)

USA
- Embassy, 37 Observatory Circle NW, Washington, DC (☎ (202) 328 4848; fax 667 5227)
- Consulate-General, Suite 1150, 12400 Wilshire Blvd, Los Angeles, CA 90024 (☎ (310) 207 1605; fax 207 3605)
- Consulate, 6810 51st Ave NE, Seattle, WA 98115 (☎ (206) 525 9881; fax 525 0271) NZ also has consulates in Chicago, Houston, New York, Salt Lake City, San Diego and San Francisco

Foreign Embassies & Consulates in NZ

Foreign embassies in New Zealand are in Wellington, the capital city; see the Wellington chapter for details. A number of countries also have consulates in Auckland and Christchurch; see the Auckland chapter and the Christchurch section for details on these.

DOCUMENTS

No special documents other than your passport are required in New Zealand. Since no vaccinations are required to enter New Zealand, an international health certificate is not necessary.

If you are from a country whose driver's

licence is not recognised in New Zealand, you will need an International Driving Permit if you want to drive. It must be issued by your home country. See the Getting Around chapter for details.

If you'll be travelling by bus or aeroplane in New Zealand, get an International Youth Hostel card (called a YHA card in New Zealand) or a VIP Backpackers Card. They'll give you up to a 50% discount on domestic air travel and a 30% discount on major bus lines, plus dozens of other discounts. An ISIC card (International Student Identity Card) will also entitle you to certain discounts.

CUSTOMS

Customs allowances are 200 cigarettes (or 50 cigars or 250 grams of tobacco), 4.5 litres of wine or beer and one 1125 ml (40 oz) bottle of spirits or liqueur. There is an 'overallowance' provision of one carton of cigarettes and two 1125 ml bottles of spirits providing they are not worth more a combined value of $50; these must be declared.

As in most places the customs people are very fussy about drugs.

MONEY

The currencies of Australia, the UK, USA, Canada, Germany and Japan are all easily changed in New Zealand. Westpac banks, found throughout the country, will exchange these and about 30 other currencies.

American Express, Visa, MasterCard and Thomas Cook travellers' cheques are all widely recognised. Visa, MasterCard, Australian Bankcard, American Express and Diners Club credit cards are the most widely recognised. Banks will give cash advances on Visa and MasterCard, but for American Express card transactions you must go to an American Express office. American Express has offices or representatives in Auckland, Wellington, Christchurch, Queenstown, Dunedin, Nelson, Whangarei, Lower Hutt, Rotorua, Hamilton and Pukekohe.

As in most countries, if you need to have money sent to you it's probably easiest to do it by telegraphic transfer, bank to bank.

If you're intending a long stay it may be worth opening a bank account. Westpac and the Bank of New Zealand (BNZ) are probably the two banks with the most branches throughout the country and are easy to get to on your travels – you can also request a card for the 24-hour automatic teller machines (ATMs) which give you access to your money anytime.

PostBank, which was once a part of the post office but is now independent, is another bank with many branches but their services are a bit more limited.

Unless otherwise noted all prices quoted in this book are in NZ dollars.

Currency

New Zealand's currency is dollars and cents. There are five, 10, 20, 50 and 100 dollar notes and five, 10, 20 and 50 cent, $1 and $2 coins.

You can bring in as much of any currency as you like and unused foreign currency or travellers' cheques which you brought in with you may be exported without limitations. Unused NZ currency can be changed to foreign currency before you leave the country.

Exchange Rates

Australia	A$1	=	NZ$1.10
Canada	C$1	=	NZ$1.09
France	1FF	=	NZ$0.29
Germany	DM1	=	NZ$1.01
Japan	¥100	=	NZ$1.41
Singapore	S$1	=	NZ$1.05
United Kingdom	UK£1	=	NZ$2.26
United States	US$1	=	NZ$1.50

Banks are open from 9 am to 4.30 pm Monday to Friday. Exchange rates may vary a few cents from bank to bank; you'll get a slightly better rate for travellers' cheques than for cash. At most banks there's no service charge for changing travellers' cheques, only a five cent stamp fee per cheque.

Costs

It is possible to travel quite economically in New Zealand; alternatively, there's plenty of opportunity to spend up. If you stay in hostels, the cost will usually be around $14 to $18 per person, per night. In motor camps, costs are about $20 to $25 for one or two people in simple cabins, about half that for camping. Basic Department of Conservation (DOC) camp sites are even cheaper, ranging on average from $2 to $6 per person. Guesthouses, farmstays, homestays and B&Bs typically charge around $50 or $60 a night for two, but it *can* be that much per person. Cheaper hotels are about $35/50 for singles/doubles, while motels are usually around $60 to $70 for two.

Hostels, motor camps and motels all have kitchens for guests' use, so staying in these gives you the option of doing your own cooking. Eating out can cost anywhere from around $5 for a simple takeaway meal to around $50 or $60 for two for dinner at most medium-priced restaurants.

The average long-distance (three to five-hour) bus ride might cost around $30, or 30% less with an approved Backpacker/YHA card. If you have a few people together, hiring a car or buying one on the buy-back system may be just as economical as taking the bus. Hitchhiking and cycling are also popular ways to get around and they don't cost a thing.

Of course one of the main reasons people come to New Zealand is to participate in the host of activities the country is known for. Some cost nothing – tramping, swimming, birdwatching or whatever. There are so many enjoyable activities that do cost something, however, that activities can end up being a major part of the travel budget.

Tipping

Tipping is becoming more widespread in New Zealand, although many Kiwis still regard it as a rather odd foreign custom. Nevertheless, it is on the increase, principally in the major centres where there's been more foreign influence. You should tip in a restaurant (not in a simple cafe) if you feel you have received exceptional service. The tip would be about 5-10% of the bill.

Consumer Taxes

GST (Goods & Services Tax) adds 12.5% to the price of just about everything in New Zealand. Most prices are quoted inclusive of GST but when you're paying for something beware of any small print announcing that the price is GST exclusive.

WHEN TO GO

New Zealand's busiest tourist season is generally in the warmer months from around November to April, though of course there's some exceptions – ski resort towns, obviously, will be packed out in winter.

The most busy time to be travelling in New Zealand is during the summer school holidays from around 20 December to 30 January. To a lesser extent Easter weekend, Labour Weekend in late October, and the May and August school holidays are also busy periods. If you're travelling during the summer school holidays, when New Zealanders as well as visitors are out on the road, remember that every type of accommodation and transport is likely to fill up, especially the more economical places, so plan ahead. It may be more pleasant to visit New Zealand either before or after this hectic period, when the weather is still warm and there aren't as many other travellers around.

New Zealand is not like some countries, though, where the weather is so miserable at some times of year that there's no point in going. You'll need warmer clothes in winter but there are many things to see and do in New Zealand all year round.

WHAT TO BRING

The main thing to remember about New Zealand is that while it may be a small, compact country it has widely varying and very changeable weather. A T-shirt and shorts day at the Bay of Islands can also bring snow and sleet to a high pass in the Southern Alps. In fact, on any of New Zealand's mountains you can often meet T-shirt-and-snow-gear weather on the same day. So come prepared for widely varying climatic conditions and if you're planning on tramping come prepared for anything! Waterproof gear and a warm down sleeping bag will help to make your stay in New Zealand much more pleasant at any time of the year.

Come prepared for New Zealand's 'dress standards' too. An amazing number of restaurants, bars, clubs and pubs have signs proclaiming their equally amazingly varied dress rules. It sometimes seems that if you combined all the rules together (one place proclaims no denim, the next no leather, or no shirts without collars, no sandals, no gang insignia etc) the only thing you'd be permitted to wear would be your birthday suit! Seriously though, men should bring a tie if they're planning on eating in upmarket restaurants.

Otherwise there are no great preparations to be made. New Zealand is a modern, well-organised country and you should be able to find most visitor's requirements, from film to pharmaceuticals.

TOURIST OFFICES

Local Tourist Offices

There are local tourist information centres in nearly every city or town – almost any town big enough to have a pub and a corner shop seems to have a tourist information centre. Many are united by VIN, the Visitor Information Network, which in affiliation with the New Zealand Tourism Board (NZTB) strives to ensure that each of its members provides top quality information and service. Smaller tourist offices funded by local councils or business communities don't have the resources of the VIN network and are usually staffed by volunteers, but they are also very helpful and can answer most queries.

The centres have abundant information on local activities and attractions, they give out free brochures and maps, and many act as travel agents and will make bookings for accommodation, activities and transport. They are an excellent resource for travellers everywhere in New Zealand; make use of them.

Tourist Offices Abroad

The New Zealand Tourism Board has representatives in various countries around the world. Its purpose is to promote tourism in New Zealand. The NZTB Head Office can be contacted at PO Box 95, Wellington, New Zealand (☎ (04) 472 8860). NZTB offices include:

Australia
- Level 11, 145 Eagle St, Brisbane QLD 4000 (☎ (7) 3831 8315)
- Level 19, Como Tower, 644 Chapel St, South Yarra, Melbourne VIC 3141 (☎ (3) 9823 6283)
- Level 8, 35 Pitt St, Sydney NSW 2000 (☎ (2) 9247 5222)

Canada
- Suite 1200-888 Dunsmuir St, Vancouver BC, V6C 3K4 (☎ (604) 684 2117)

Germany
- Friedrichstrasse 10-12, 60323 Frankfurt am Main, Germany (☎ (69) 97 12 11 (0))

Hong Kong
- 1501 Universal Trade Centre, 3-5 Arbuthnot Rd, Central Hong Kong (☎ 2526 0141)

Japan
- Meiji Seimei Sakaisuji Honmachi Building, 2nd Floor, 1-7-15 Minami Honmachi, Chuo ku, Osaka-shi 541 (☎ (6) 268 8335)
- Shinjuku Monolity 21st Floor, 2-3-1 Nishi Shinjuku, Shunjuku-ku, Tokyo 163-09 (☎ (3) 5381 6331)

Singapore
- 391 Orchard Rd, Ngee Ann City, 15th Floor, Tower A, Singapore (☎ 738 5844)

UK
- New Zealand House, Haymarket, SW1Y 4TQ London (☎ (0171) 973 0363)

USA
- 501 Santa Monica Blvd, No 300, Santa Monica, CA 90401 (☎ (310) 395 7480)
- 780 3rd Avenue, Suite 1904, New York, NY 10017-2024 (☎ (212) 832 8482)

USEFUL ORGANISATIONS

A number of organisations provide useful services for travellers in New Zealand, especially the visitor information centres, the Department of Conservation (DOC) and the Automobile Association (AA). Most useful of all is the network of visitor information centres throughout the country. DOC also operates information and visitor centres in cities, towns and parks throughout New Zealand; these are great for maps and information about outdoor areas and outdoor activities, especially tramping.

The AA is a useful organisation to join if you are doing any driving; its benefits and services are described in the Car & Motorbike section of the Getting Around chapter. Like the visitor information centres and DOC offices, AA offices or agents are found in most cities and towns throughout New Zealand. In this book we've listed visitor information centres, DOC and AA offices wherever they exist. Among the three, you can find out almost anything you could want to know about New Zealand.

If you're a student of any age, or if you're under 26, the STA (Student Travel Agencies) is a good travel resource. They offer discounted air fares, sell International Student Identity (ISIC) Cards and provide other services for both international and domestic travel. STA has offices in Auckland, Hamilton, Palmerston North, Wellington, Christchurch and Dunedin.

BUSINESS HOURS

Office hours are generally Monday to Friday from 9 am to 5 pm. Most government offices are open Monday to Friday from around 8.30 am to 4.30 pm. Shops are usually open Monday to Friday from 9 am to 5 pm plus Saturday morning (9 am to 12.30 pm), with 'late-night shopping' to 9 pm one night of the week, usually Thursday or Friday. Many small convenience stores (called 'dairies' in NZ) stay open much longer hours and some of the larger supermarkets now also stay open seven days a week.

HOLIDAYS

People from the northern hemisphere never seem to become completely familiar with upside-down seasons. To them Christmas simply doesn't fall in the middle of summer and how is it possible to have mid-winter cold in August? But it's worth remembering, since Christmas is in the middle of summer and the school holidays, which means lots of Kiwis are on holiday, which in turn means crowds and higher prices. If you want to avoid the school-age hordes, they're out of captivity from mid-December until the end of January and then for a couple of weeks in May and again in August.

Public holidays include:

January
  New Year's Day and the next day (1st & 2nd)
February
  Waitangi Day or New Zealand Day (6th)
March or April
  Good Friday/Easter Monday
April
  Anzac Day (25th)
June
  Queen's Birthday (1st Monday)
October
  Labour Day (4th Monday)
December
  Christmas Day and Boxing Day (25th & 26th)

SPECIAL EVENTS

A number of cultural events and festivals are held annually around New Zealand. Some of the more noteworthy ones include:

January
  Annual Yachting Regatta – Auckland
  Summer City Programme – Wellington, beginning of January to end of February; two months of festivals and entertainment around the city
February
  Marlborough Food & Wine Festival – Blenheim, 2nd weekend in February
  International Festival of the Arts – Wellington; an entire month of national and international culture (even-numbered years only)
  Art Deco weekend (third weekend) – Napier; dinners, balls, fancy dress and Deco tours
March
  Fiesta Week – Auckland, mid-March; great fun with some terrific fireworks and the 'Round the Bays' run
  Golden Shears Sheep Shearing Contest – Masterton; a major event in this sheepish country!
  International Billfish Tournament – Bay of Islands
  Ngaruawahia Regatta for Maori Canoes – Hamilton
April
  Highland Games – Hastings
May
  National Woodcrafts Festival – Christchurch
June
  New Zealand Agricultural Field Days – a major agricultural show at Mystery Creek, Hamilton
September
  New Zealand Listener Women's Book Festival – week-long festival celebrating women's books, with events throughout the country
November
  Canterbury Show Week – Christchurch
  International Trout Fishing Contest – Rotorua

Each province also has its own anniversary-day holiday. Local holidays include Wellington, 22 January; Auckland, 29 January; Northland, 29 January; Nelson, 1 February; Otago, 23 March; Southland, 23 March; Taranaki, 31 March; Hawkes Bay, 1 November; Marlborough, 1 November; Westland, 1 December; and Canterbury, 16 December.

When these local holidays fall between Friday and Sunday, they are usually observed on the following Monday; if they fall between Tuesday and Thursday, they are held on the preceding Monday.

There are many smaller annual events held all over New Zealand; each little town seems to have its annual fair, often involving simple sports like racing horses on the beach, wheelbarrow and sugar bag races, woodchopping and sheep-shearing contests.

POST & COMMUNICATIONS

Post

NZ Post Shops are open from 9 am to 5 pm on weekdays. You can have mail addressed to you care of 'Poste Restante, CPO' in whichever town you require. CPO stands for Chief Post Office. Mail is usually held for 30 days.

For postage within New Zealand there are two options. Standard post costs 45c for medium letters and 80c for extra large letters; delivery time is two days between major centres, a bit longer for rural areas. Or there's Fast Post, promising next-day delivery between major centres (Auckland, Wellington, Christchurch), two-day delivery for rural areas. Fast Post costs 80c/$1.20 for medium/extra large letters. In both cases the maximum thickness is 20 mm.

For international mail, use Fast Post; just affix a Fast Post sticker or use a Fast Post envelope. This way it costs $1 to send postcards anywhere in the world. The cost for international letters with a maximum weight/thickness of 200 g/20 mm (prices given are for medium/large/extra large letters) include:

Zone A: Australia & South Pacific Islands; $1/$1.50/$3; three to eight days delivery

Zone B: North America & Asia; $1.50/$2.50/$6; six to 12 days delivery

Zone C: South America, Europe, Africa & Middle East; $1.80/$2.80/$6.80; six to 12 days delivery

Telephone

The phone system, formerly a government monopoly controlled by Telecom, has been deregulated and opened to competition from Clear, the new kid on the block. Telecom still operates the public phone and local call networks, and the changes only affect long-distance rates for New Zealand subscribers. From private phones, local calls cost 20c for unlimited time or are free for those subscribers who pay higher rent, while long-distance calls can be made through Telecom or Clear. Rates for long-distance calls are subject to change, but can be quite cheap depending on when you ring, which card you have, what club you belong to and various other promotional deals offered by the two companies.

The big losers are those forced to use pay phones. Local calls cost 20c per minute or part thereof, out-of-area calls start at around 50c per minute or part thereof, international calls have a minimum charge of $3 and tick over at an alarming rate. It can be cheaper to ring overseas from a private phone than to make a long-distance call within New Zealand from a pay phone.

Almost all pay phones in New Zealand are now of the card-operated type. Cardphones accept $5, $10, $20 or $50 cards, which you can buy from visitor information centres, news agencies, hostels and larger hotels or any shop displaying the lime-green 'phone cards available here' sign. Some credit-card phones are also found in the larger cities. Long-distance and international calls can be dialled directly from pay phones.

To avoid the high charges on long-distance calls from public phones, many places to stay have cardphones for guests and you can receive calls on these phones. You can make a short call to someone long distance or overseas and get them to ring you straight back. Another option for long-distance telephone calls is the call-back service. Dial 013 before you make the call and an operator will ring you back immediately after you hang up to tell you how much it cost. This service costs around $3 on top of the price for the call, but it means that many hostels, hotels and so on will allow you to place long-distance calls from their telephones, if you pay on the spot.

To reach the local and national operator dial 010; for directory assistance anywhere in New Zealand it's 018.

Toll-free numbers are preceded by the 800 code, but you'll still have to insert a card into a public phone to make the call even though it is not charged. Mobile phone numbers are preceded by the 025 code, and calls to these are charged at a higher rate.

For emergencies in the major centres dial 111 and say whether you want police, ambulance or fire brigade. Emergency calls are not charged.

Area Codes All cities and towns throughout the entire South Island and Stewart Island are on the (03) area code. The North Island has various regional area codes: (09) in Auckland and the Northland, (07) in the Coromandel Peninsula, Bay of Plenty, Waikato and Central Plateau, (06) in the East Coast, Whanganui, Manawatu and Taranaki regions, and (04) in and around Wellington. If dialling within a region you still have to use the area code between towns, often for a town just a few km down the road.

Area codes are listed in the introductory pages of the telephone directory.

In this book, we have not listed the area code for each telephone number. Unless indicated otherwise, the code for every telephone number in each chapter is given at the beginning of the chapter.

International Telephone Calls Direct dialling from private or cardphones is made by simply dialling '00' to get out of the country, then the country code, area code and number. The country code for New Zealand is 64.

You can make a price-required call to any another country by dialling 0160 rather than 00 to begin the call.

For the international operator dial 0170; international directory information is 0172.

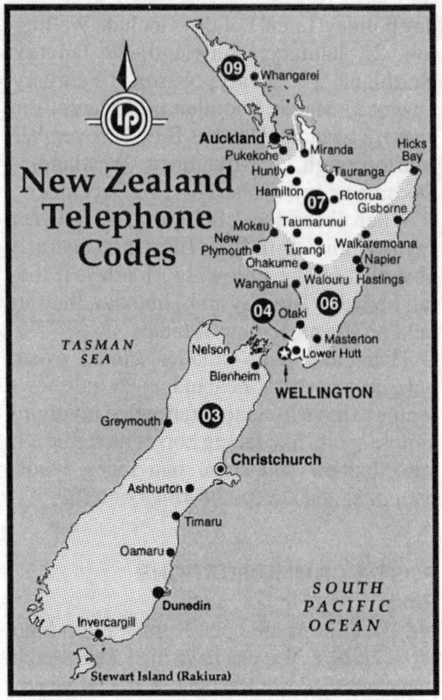

Country Direct Many countries have Country Direct services, enabling you to phone directly to the operator in that country, bypassing the operator in New Zealand. There are various times when using this service can be very convenient, such as when you want to charge a call to your telephone number in your home country. Details, including the Country Direct numbers for all the various countries that have the service, can be found in the introductory pages of the telephone directory or by asking the New Zealand international operator.

Fax

Fax machines are very common in New Zealand; many hotels, motels and even hostels have fax machines. Most centres of any size have some kind of business offering fax services. Typically the charge to send a fax is about $5 plus the telephone toll charges. Receiving a fax costs around $1 per page.

TIME

Being close to the international date line, New Zealand is one of the first places in the world to start a new day. New Zealand is 12 hours ahead of GMT (Greenwich Mean Time) and UTC (Universal Time Coordinated) and two hours ahead of Australian Eastern Standard Time.

In summer New Zealand observes Daylight Saving Time, an advance of one hour, which comes into effect on the last Sunday in October and lasts to the first Sunday of the following March. Of course some other countries also have Daylight Saving Time so it's not always the same, but usually the time differences are:

When it is:	*It is:*
noon in NZ	midnight in London
	8 pm in New York
	8 pm in Toronto
	5 pm in San Francisco
	10 am in Sydney
	9 am in Tokyo
	8 am in Hong Kong
	8 am in Singapore

ELECTRICITY

Electricity is 240 volts AC, 50 cycle, as in Europe and Australia, and Australian-type three-prong plugs are used. Appliances designed for DC supply or different voltages need a transformer.

WEIGHTS & MEASURES

New Zealand uses the metric system for all weights, measures, distances etc. In ordinary day-to-day usage the metric measures are used (kilometres of distance, kilograms of fruit and vegetables etc) but you will still encounter vestiges of the British Imperial system, in use until 1967. If you go skydiving they'll take you up to 9000 feet rather than 2743 metres, and if you ask someone how much they weigh, the answer may be in kilos, pounds or stone (a stone is 14 pounds).

LAUNDRY

You won't see many laundrettes in New Zealand, but virtually every accommodation place provides a coin-operated washing machine and dryer where you can clean a full load of clothes for about $2 to wash and $2 to dry (using coins or tokens).

BOOKS

For a description of New Zealand literature, including poetry, children's books and contemporary Maori & Pacific literature, see the Arts section in the Facts about the Country chapter. Most books are published in different editions by different publishers in different countries. As a result, a book might be a hardcover rarity in one country while it's readily available in paperback in another. Fortunately, bookshops and libraries search by title or author, so your local bookshop or library is best placed to advise you on the availability of the following/above recommendations.

History

A History of New Zealand by Keith Sinclair is a readable and entertaining general history of New Zealand, from the Maori account of the creation of the earth up to the present. *The People and the Land – Te Tangata me Te Whenua: An Illustrated History of New Zealand 1820-1920* by Judith Binney, Judith Bassett & Erik Olssen is another good illustrated history of New Zealand.

The award-winning *Two Worlds: First Meetings between Maori and Europeans 1642-1772* by Anne Salmond is an account of the first points of contact between the Maori and the European explorers, a fascinating anthropological history telling the story as it was experienced by both sides.

The 19th-century land wars between Pakeha and Maori are looked at in a new and interesting way in *The New Zealand Wars* by James Belich. Christopher Pugsley's *Anzac* is a pictorial account of NZ troops in the Gallipoli campaign in 1915, an important part of the modern national psyche.

Maori: A Photographic and Social History by Michael King is a comprehensive illustrated history of the Maori people.

The Old-Time Maori by Makereti is an important historical document. First published in London in 1938, the book was the first ethnographic account of the Maori people ever written by a Maori scholar. It's fascinating reading.

One of the continuously most controversial elements of New Zealand history is the Treaty of Waitangi. Many books have been written about the treaty and the debates surrounding it. One of the best is *The Treaty of Waitangi* by Claudia Orange. The same author has written several other books about the treaty, including *An Illustrated History of the Treaty of Waitangi*.

Another significant moment in New Zealand history, noted around the world, was when Greenpeace's ship *Rainbow Warrior* was sunk by the French government in Auckland Harbour in 1985. Several books have been written about the incident; *Making Waves: The Greenpeace New Zealand Story* by Michael Szabo tells the story of this and other Greenpeace activities in New Zealand and the Pacific, with lots of colour illustrations.

Historical Biography Some of the most fascinating history has been told in the form of biography. *The Dictionary of New Zealand Biography* is a multi-volume collection of hundreds of short New Zealand biographies. Volume One, published in 1990 with over 600 biographies from the years 1769 to 1869, and Volume Two, published in 1993 with biographies from the years 1870 to 1900, are already out and a third volume is said to be on the way.

A People's History: Illustrated Biographies from The Dictionary of New Zealand Biography, Volume One, 1769-1869 selected by WH Oliver contains over 100 biographies of early New Zealanders, illustrated with historic photos.

Of course there are many biographies written about historical NZ figures. Three about Maori elders are particularly interesting. *Eruera: The Teachings of a Maori Elder* by Eruera Stirling as told to Anne Salmond won the NZ Wattie Book of the Year Award, one of NZ's highest awards. *Te Puea* by Michael King tells the story of Te Puea Herangi, one of the most influential women in modern Maori history. *Whina*, also by Michael King, tells the story of Whina Cooper, another very important Maori figure, who organised her first public protest at age 18 and welcomed an international audience to the XIV Commonwealth Games in Auckland in 1990 at the age of 95.

NZ Women's Biography

The Book of New Zealand Women – Ko Kui Ma Te Kaupapa edited by Charlotte Macdonald, Merimeri Penfold & Bridget Williams is a large anthology of over 300 biographical essays of New Zealand women – a great resource.

Modern Autobiography

Check out *The Life and Times of a Good Keen Man* by Barry Crump. One of New Zealand's favourite characters, Barry Crump is an alcoholic, writer and rugged adventurer, very much the Bukowski rather than the bastard of the bush. He is the author of many popular books including *A Good Keen Man* (1960), *Hang On a Minute Mate* (1961) and a long list of books after that, which still sell even after all these years.

Being Pakeha by Michael King is the autobiography of one of New Zealand's foremost Maori historians, who is a Pakeha. *An Autobiography* by the poet Lauris Edmonds is a frank account of an emergent writer's life.

Mihi Edwards is a contemporary Maori elder who writes very readable books telling the story of her life – a lot about how some of the current generation of Maori elders were raised, how they were punished if they spoke their language in school, and many other things about what it has been like to grow up Maori in Pakeha culture. The two autobiographical books published so far include *Mihipeka: Early Years* and *Mihipeka: Time of Turmoil*.

Maori Culture

In recent years New Zealand has experienced a renaissance of interest in Maori culture, and many excellent books have been written about various aspects of it. Language books are mentioned in the Language section of the Facts about the Country chapter.

Some useful and insightful books have been written about the customs, protocol and meanings of things on the marae; it would be particularly useful to read one or more of these if you are going to visit a marae.

Te Marae: A Guide to Customs & Protocol by Hiwi & Pat Tauroa is a useful little 'how-to' book for non-Maori who may be visiting a marae for the first time. It gives a background and understanding of customs and procedures on the marae, and good, readable advice about how one is to behave.

Hui: A Study of Maori Ceremonial Gatherings by Anne Salmond is an excellent, more scholarly book about Maori gatherings on the marae. It's not written from a 'how-to' perspective, but as an insight into Maori culture.

Te Ao Hurihuri: Aspects of Maoritanga edited by Michael King is a collection of writings on many aspects of Maori culture, written by a number of respected Maori authors.

Tikanga Whakaaro: Key Concepts in Maori Culture by Cleve Barlow is a bilingual book in English and Maori, in which the author tells about Maori culture by taking 70 terms central to Maori culture and explaining their significance.

Maori Customs and Crafts compiled by Alan Armstrong is only a small book in the Pocket Guide series but it describes many different Maori customs and crafts, with illustrations.

Maori Myths, Legends & Stories

A number of good books have been written about the rich legends, myths and stories of the Maori people, from the creation myth forward. An excellent one is the illustrated *Maori Myths and Tribal Legends* retold by Antony Alpers. Another smaller volume is the illustrated *Maori Myth and Legend* by AW Reed.

Traditional Maori Stories introduced and translated by Margaret Orbell is a fine book of Maori stories told side by side in English and Maori.

Chatham Islands

Moriori: A People Rediscovered by Michael King tells about the Moriori people of the Chatham Islands and reveals that the truth about this people is very different from the common notions about them. The same author also wrote *A Land Apart: The Chatham Islands of New Zealand* with Robin Morrison (photographs), a good book of realistic photographs, history and stories of these remote islands.

Photography

There are innumerable coffee-table books of photographs of New Zealand. You'll find at least a dozen in almost any large bookstore in New Zealand, with titles like *New Zealand – the Glorious Islands*, *New Zealand – A Special Place*, *Beautiful New Zealand* and so on. Two of New Zealand's best photographers, Craig Potton and Robin Morrison, have published a number of books.

Art & Architecture

There are plenty of high-quality art books on NZ's well-known artists. Many books have also been written about Maori arts & crafts. A truly magnificent one is *Taonga Maori: A Spiritual Journey Expressed through Maori Art* by the Australian Museum. It's an impressive book with colour photographs and insightful text about some of the best Maori art in existence.

Architecture is not what people usually think of when contemplating New Zealand, but the book *The New Zealand House* by Michael Fowler (architect) & Robert van de Voort (photographer) is a fascinating presentation of an amazing variety of NZ home architecture, with a wealth of colour photos of everything from grand Victorian palaces to home-made rolling caravan inventions.

Travel Guides

Innumerable specialised travel guides have been written about all the kinds of things you can do in New Zealand. There are books about tramping, skiing, cycling, scuba diving, surfing, fishing, birdwatching and many more. They're mentioned in the

Outdoor Activities chapter in the appropriate sections.

The *Mobil New Zealand Travel Guides* by Diana & Jeremy Pope are excellent resources for historical background about hundreds of places you can visit if you're travelling around New Zealand. There's one book about the *North Island* and another about the *South Island*, both worth carrying if you like to know history, background and interesting stories about the places you visit.

The *Insight Guide – New Zealand*, with plenty of colour illustrations, is another guide for background about the country.

Cartoons

No overview of New Zealand publishing could be complete without mention of New Zealand's favourite comic strip, *Footrot Flats* by Murray Ball. Many books have been published of the adventures of the focal character, Dog, a mongrel black-and-white sheep dog, and his master Wal, the farmer. It's a delightful look into rural New Zealand farming life as told from the sheep dog's point of view.

Bookshops

Whitcoull's and London Bookshops are two large bookshop chains with a wide selection of books, including sections specialising in New Zealand books. Bennett's Government Bookshops, with many branches throughout the country, are also excellent bookshops with a wide variety of books and maps about New Zealand. For more information see Bookshops in the city sections of this book.

MAPS

Many excellent maps are widely available in New Zealand; you can easily find everything from street maps and road atlases to detailed topographical maps.

If you're a member of the Automobile Association you can go into any AA office, present your card, and get all the maps you want for free. The AA city, town, regional and highway maps are some of the best available. For car touring off the beaten track, pick up a set of their superb 1:350,000 District Maps covering the whole country. They also publish road atlases and large maps of the North and South Islands, which anyone can buy, member or not. The Shell road atlas, Wises maps and road atlases, and the Minimap series are also excellent; they are available at AA offices, Bennett's Government Bookshops, map shops and some other bookshops.

The Department of Land and Survey Information (DOSLI) publishes several series of excellent maps of all kinds – street, country and holiday maps, maps of national parks and forest parks, detailed topographical maps for trampers, and more. Their maps are available at DOSLI offices, at Bennett's Government Bookshops, at map shops and some other shops. Many DOC offices carry the DOSLI topographical and national park maps.

MEDIA

Newspapers & Magazines

There is no national paper although the *New Zealand Herald* (Auckland), the *Dominion* (Wellington) and the *Press* (Christchurch) all have wide circulations. Backing up the city newspapers are numerous local dailies, some OK, some not. The closest to a national weekly news magazine is the *Listener*, an excellent publication which provides a weekly TV & radio guide, plus in-depth articles on the arts, social issues and politics. The international publications such as *Time* and *Newsweek* are available almost anywhere.

Radio & TV

There are two national noncommercial radio stations and many regional or local commercial stations, broadcasting on the AM and FM bands.

There are three commercial TV stations (Channels One, Two & Three) plus Sky, a subscriber television service with news, sports, movie and documentary channels.

FILM & PHOTOGRAPHY

Photographic supplies, equipment and maintenance are all readily available in New

Zealand. You can probably find any kind of camera or equipment you're looking for, but it may cost more here than elsewhere.

Fuji and Kodak are the most popular films, with Agfa also available. Prices can vary quite a bit from shop to shop, so if you'll be buying much film or getting much processed it might pay to shop around. One-hour photo developing shops are found all over New Zealand, but they only do prints; slide processing takes considerably longer, usually about a week.

The only notable peculiarities of taking photos in New Zealand might be if you're taking photos in the bush. Native bush in New Zealand is quite dense, and it may be darker than you think, photographically speaking. If you'll be doing much tramping in heavy bush and want to record your journey, carry a couple of rolls of 400 ASA film.

HEALTH

There are no vaccination requirements to enter New Zealand. New Zealand is largely a clean, healthy, disease-free country. Medical attention is of high quality and reasonably priced but you should have medical insurance.

Travel health depends on your predeparture preparations, your day-to-day health care and how you handle any medical problem or emergency that does develop.

Travel Health Guides

There are a number of books on travel health:

Travellers' Health, Dr Richard Dawood, Oxford University Press, 1995. Comprehensive, easy to read, authoritative and highly recommended, although it's rather large to lug around.

Travel with Children, Maureen Wheeler, Lonely Planet Publications, 1995. Includes basic advice on travel health for younger children.

Predeparture Preparations

Health Insurance A travel insurance policy to cover theft, loss and medical problems is a good idea. There are a wide variety of policies and your travel agent will have recommendations. The international student travel policies handled by STA or other student travel organisations are usually good value. Some policies offer lower and higher medical expenses options but the higher one is chiefly for countries like the USA which have extremely high medical costs. Check the small print:

- Some policies specifically exclude 'dangerous activities' which can include scuba diving, motorcycling, even tramping. If such activities are on your agenda you don't want that sort of policy.
- You may prefer a policy which pays doctors or hospitals direct rather than you having to pay on the spot and claim later. If you have to claim later make sure you keep all documentation. Some policies ask you to call back (reverse charges) to a centre in your home country where an immediate assessment of your problem is made.
- Check if the policy covers ambulances or an emergency flight home. If you have to stretch out you will need two seats and somebody has to pay for them!

Medical Kit A small, straightforward medical kit is a wise thing to carry. A possible kit list includes:

- Aspirin or Panadol – for pain or fever.
- Antihistamine (such as Benadryl) – useful as a decongestant for colds, allergies, to ease the itch from insect bites or stings or to help prevent motion sickness.
- Antibiotics – useful if you're travelling well off the beaten track, but they must be prescribed and you should carry the prescription with you.
- Kaolin preparation (Pepto-Bismol), Imodium or Lomotil – for stomach upsets.
- Rehydration mixture – for treatment of severe diarrhoea, this is particularly important if travelling with children.
- Antiseptic, Mercurochrome and antibiotic powder or similar 'dry' spray – for cuts and grazes.
- Calamine lotion, antihistamine or anti-itch cream – to ease irritation from bites or stings.
- Bandages and Band-aids – for minor injuries.
- Scissors, tweezers and a thermometer (note that mercury thermometers are prohibited by airlines).
- Insect repellent (for those sandflies), sunscreen, suntan lotion, chap stick.
- Water purification tablets or other water purification system, if you'll be camping in the bush.

Health Preparations Make sure you're healthy before you start travelling. If you are embarking on a long trip make sure your teeth are OK.

If you wear glasses take a spare pair and your prescription. Losing your glasses can be a real problem, although in New Zealand you can get new spectacles made up quickly, cheaply and competently.

If you require a particular medication take an adequate supply, as it may not be available locally. Take the prescription, with the generic rather than the brand name (which may not be locally available), as it will make getting replacements easier. It's a wise idea to have the prescription with you to show you legally use the medication – it's surprising how often over-the-counter drugs from one country are illegal without a prescription or even banned in another.

Immunisations You don't need any vaccinations to visit New Zealand. It's always a good idea to keep your tetanus immunisation up to date no matter where you are – boosters are necessary every 10 years and protection is highly recommended – but even this is not strictly required.

Basic Rules

Care in what you eat and drink is the most important health rule; stomach upsets are the most likely travel health problem but the majority of these upsets will be relatively minor.

Water Tap water is clean, delicious and fine to drink in New Zealand. Water in lakes, rivers and streams will look clean and it could be OK, but since the parasitic protozoan *Giardia lamblia* has been found in lakes, rivers and streams. If in national parks and forest areas administered by DOC, you can ask DOC officers about the occurrence of giardia water in that area. If in doubt, water from these sources should be purified before drinking.

Water Purification The simplest way of purifying water is to boil it thoroughly, that is, for more than three minutes. Filtering is acceptable *only* if you use giardia rated filters, available from some outdoor equipment retailers.

If you cannot boil water it should be treated chemically. Iodine is very effective in purifying water and is available in tablet form (such as Potable Aqua), but follow the directions carefully and remember that too much iodine can be harmful. Before buying, check the manufacturer's specifications on the packet to ensure that the tablets will kill the giardia parasite.

If you can't find tablets, tincture of iodine (2%) or iodine crystals can be used. Four drops of tincture of iodine per litre or quart of clear water is the recommended dosage; the treated water should be left to stand for 20 to 30 minutes before drinking. Iodine crystals can also be used to purify water but this is a more complicated process, as you have to first prepare a saturated iodine solution. Iodine loses its effectiveness if exposed to air or damp so keep it in a tightly sealed container. Flavoured powder will disguise the taste of treated water and is a good idea if you are travelling with children.

Nutrition If your food is poor, if you're travelling hard and fast and therefore missing meals, or if you simply lose your appetite, you can soon start to lose weight and place your health at risk.

Make sure your diet is well balanced. Meat (lamb, beef, pork and poultry) is plentiful in New Zealand; eggs, tofu, beans, lentils and nuts are also good sources of protein. Fresh fruits and vegetables are a good source of vitamins. Also eat plenty of grains and bread. If your diet isn't well balanced or if your food intake is insufficient, it's a good idea to take vitamin and iron pills.

Everyday Health Normal body temperature is 98.6˚F or 37˚C; more than 2˚C (4˚F) higher indicates a 'high' fever. The normal adult pulse rate is 60 to 80 per minute (children 80 to 100, babies 100 to 140). You should know how to take a temperature and a pulse rate. As a general rule the pulse increases about 20 beats per minute for each 1˚C rise in fever.

Respiration (breathing) rate is also an

indicator of illness. Count the number of breaths per minute: between 12 and 20 is normal for adults and older children (up to 30 for younger children, 40 for babies). People with a high fever or serious respiratory illness (like pneumonia) breathe more quickly than normal. More than 40 shallow breaths a minute usually means pneumonia.

Many health problems can be avoided by taking care of yourself. Wash your hands frequently – it's quite easy to contaminate your own food. Avoid climatic extremes: keep out of the sun when it's hot, dress warmly when it's cold. Avoid potential diseases by dressing sensibly. You can avoid insect bites by covering bare skin when insects are around, by screening windows or beds or by using insect repellents. Seek local advice: if you're told the water is unsafe due to currents, riptides or for any other reason, don't go in. In situations where there is no information, discretion is the better part of valour.

Climatic & Geographical Considerations

Sunburn On the beach, in the snow or at high altitudes you can get sunburnt surprisingly quickly, even through cloud. The sun is particularly dangerous here in New Zealand, where the ozone layer is said to be considerably thinner than in other parts of the world. Use a sunscreen and take extra care to cover areas which don't normally see sun, eg your feet. A hat provides added protection, and you can also use zinc cream or some other barrier cream for your nose, lips and ears. Calamine lotion is good for mild sunburn.

Hypothermia Too much cold can be dangerous, particularly if it leads to hypothermia. Hypothermia is a real and present danger in New Zealand, due to the country's extremely changeable weather. A certain number of visitors die from hypothermia every year in New Zealand, mostly because they have gone out walking without adequate preparation, not realising that the weather can change abruptly and within the space of a few minutes a bright, warm day can change to freezing winds, rain and hail. You should always be prepared for cold, wet or windy conditions even if you're just out walking or hitching, and it's especially important if you're tramping out in the bush, away from civilisation.

Hypothermia occurs when the body loses heat faster than it can produce it and the core temperature of the body falls. It is surprisingly easy to progress from very cold to dangerously cold due to a combination of wind, wet clothing, fatigue and hunger, even if the air temperature is above freezing. It is best to dress in layers; silk, wool and some of the new artificial fibres are all good insulating materials. A hat is important, as a lot of heat is lost through the head. A strong, waterproof outer layer is essential, since keeping dry is vital. Carry basic supplies, including food containing simple sugars to generate heat quickly, and lots of fluid to drink.

Symptoms of hypothermia are exhaustion, numb skin (particularly fingers and toes), shivering, slurred speech, irrational or violent behaviour, lethargy, stumbling, dizzy spells, muscle cramps and violent bursts of energy. Irrationality may take the form of sufferers claiming they are warm and trying to take off their clothes.

To treat hypothermia, first get the patient out of the wind and/or rain, remove their clothing if it's wet and replace it with dry, warm clothing. Give them hot liquids – not alcohol – and some high-kilojoule, easily digestible food. This should be enough for the early stages of hypothermia, but if it has gone further it may be necessary to place the victim in a warm sleeping bag and get in with them. Do not rub the patient, don't place them near a fire or remove their wet clothes in the wind. If possible, place a sufferer in a warm (not hot) bath.

Motion Sickness Eating lightly before and during a trip will reduce the chances of motion sickness. If you are prone to motion sickness try to find a place that minimises disturbance – near the wing on aircraft, close to midships on boats, near the centre on buses. Fresh air usually helps; reading and cigarette smoke don't. Commercial motion-sickness preparations, which can cause drowsiness, have to be taken before the trip commences; when you're feeling sick it's too late. Ginger is a natural preventative and is available in capsule form.

Diseases of Insanitation

A change of water, food or climate can all cause diarrhoea, but given high standards of hygiene and food handling in New Zealand more serious infections from contaminated food is unlikely. About the only problem is giardia, which occurs in some areas.

Giardiasis This is caused by an intestinal parasite present in contaminated water; it has been found in many rivers, lakes and streams in New Zealand, so it's important to know about it if you will be out in the bush. It can be spread by any mammals such as possums, rats, mice or humans. Though drinking contaminated water is the most common way to catch giardia, it can also occur as a result of poor personal hygiene or unhygienic food handling.

The symptoms are stomach cramps, nausea, a bloated stomach, watery, foul-smelling diarrhoea and frequent gas. Giardiasis can appear several weeks after you have been exposed to the parasite. The symptoms may disappear for a few days and then return; this can go on for several weeks. Tinidazole, known as Fasigyn, or metronidazole (Flagyl) are the recommended drugs for treatment. Either can be used in a single treatment dose. Antibiotics are of no use.

Diseases Spread by People & Animals

Tetanus This potentially fatal disease is found around the world; it's not any particular problem in New Zealand but it's still a good idea to keep your tetanus booster up to date. Tetanus is difficult to treat but is preventable with immunisation. Tetanus occurs when a wound becomes infected by a germ which lives in the faeces of animals or people, so clean all cuts, punctures or animal bites. Tetanus is known as lockjaw, and the first symptom may be discomfort in swallowing, or stiffening of the jaw and neck; this is followed by painful convulsions of the jaw and whole body.

Amoebic meningitis This very serious disease can be a danger if you bathe in natural hot thermal pools. Fortunately, it's no danger at all if you know how to protect yourself from it.

The amoeba that causes the disease can enter your body through the orifices of your head, usually the nose but occasionally the ears as well. Once it gets inside the nose it bores through the tissues and lodges in the brain. It's very easy not to catch the disease – just keep your head out of the water!

Symptoms of amoebic meningitis may have a slow onset – it could be several days or even several weeks later that the first symptoms are noticed. Symptoms may be similar to the flu at first, later progressing to severe headaches, stiffness of the neck, hypersensitivity to light, and then even coma. It can be treated with intravenous anti-amoebic drugs.

Sexually Transmitted Diseases Sexual contact with an infected partner spreads these diseases. While abstinence is the only 100% preventative, using condoms is also effective. Gonorrhoea and syphilis are the most common of these diseases; sores, blisters or rashes around the genitals, discharges or pain when urinating are common symptoms. Symptoms may be less marked or not observed at all in women. Syphilis symptoms eventually disappear completely but the disease continues and can cause severe problems in later years. The treatment of gonorrhoea and syphilis is by antibiotics.

There are numerous other sexually transmitted diseases, for most of which effective treatment is available. However, there is no cure for herpes and there is also currently no cure for AIDS, which is present in New Zealand as in most other parts of the world.

HIV/AIDS HIV, the Human Immunodeficiency Virus, may develop into AIDS,

Acquired Immune Deficiency Syndrome. HIV is a major problem in many countries. Any exposure to blood, blood products or bodily fluids may put the individual at risk. In many developing countries transmission is predominantly through heterosexual sexual activity. This is quite different from industrialised countries where transmission is mostly through contact between homosexual or bisexual males, or via contaminated needles shared by IV drug users. Apart from abstinence, the most effective preventative is always to practise safe sex using condoms. It is impossible to detect the HIV-positive status of an otherwise healthy-looking person without a blood test.

HIV/AIDS can also be spread through infected blood transfusions, though blood and blood products are adequately screened in New Zealand. It can also be spread by dirty needles – vaccinations, acupuncture, tattooing and ear or nose piercing can potentially be as dangerous as intravenous drug use if the equipment is not clean.

Fear of HIV infection should never preclude treatment for serious medical conditions. Although there may be a risk of infection, it is very small indeed.

Toxic Shellfish It doesn't happen often but it has been known to occur: certain algae or other substances in sea water can cause shellfish that are normally safe to eat to become dangerous. Any instances are likely to be widely reported in the New Zealand media.

Cuts, Bites & Stings

Cuts & Scratches Skin punctures can easily become infected while travelling and may be difficult to heal. Treat any cut with an antiseptic solution and mercurochrome. Where possible avoid bandages and Band-aids, which can keep wounds wet; if you have to keep a bandage on during the day to protect the wound from dirt, take it off at night while you sleep to let it get air.

Bee & Wasp Stings Wasps are a problem in some places in New Zealand. They are attracted to food, especially at picnic sites; late summer is the worst time of year for them. There are especially many wasps in beech forests.

Bee and wasp stings are usually painful rather than dangerous. Calamine lotion will give relief; ammonia is also an effective remedy. Ice packs or antihistamine cream will reduce the pain and swelling. If you are allergic to bee or wasp stings, carry your medication with you.

Mosquitoes & Sandflies Mosquitoes appear after dusk. They are not a big problem in some parts of the country but in certain places – notably the west coast of the South Island, and especially in summer – they can come in clouds. Avoid bites by covering bare skin and using an insect repellent. Insect screens on windows and mosquito nets on beds offer good protection, as does burning a mosquito coil or using a pyrethrum-based insect spray. Mosquitoes may be attracted by perfume, aftershave or certain colours. They can bite you right through thin fabrics, or on any small part of your skin not covered by repellent.

Another New Zealand insect that can drive you wild is the sandfly, a tiny black creature that is found in inland areas as well as around the coasts, where it lives in bushes, trees or grasses. Sandfly bites can be even more irritating than mosquito bites; since the insects live on the ground, sandfly bites are mainly on the feet and ankles. Wearing shoes, thick socks and plenty of insect repellent is not only advisable but practically a necessity where sandflies are present.

The most effective insect repellent is called DEET (N,N-Diethylmetatoluamide); it is an ingredient in many commercially available insect repellents. Look for a repellent with at least a 28% concentration of DEET. DEET breaks down plastic, rubber, contact lenses and synthetic fabrics, though, so be careful what you touch after using it. It poses no danger to natural fibre fabrics.

New Zealand's DOC gave us a few other recommendations for keeping away the sandflies and mosquitoes. They say that eating plenty of vitamin B1 is an effective deterrent to sandflies, and we've heard the same thing about mosquitoes too. Externally, they recommend making up a half-and-half mixture of Dettol (the bathroom cleaner) and baby oil, and wiping it over your skin where sandflies may bite.

Other good insect repellents include Off! and Repel, which comes in a stick or a spray and will not eat through plastic the way DEET-containing repellents do.

Spiders Many types of spiders live in New Zealand but by far the most famous is the only poisonous one, the retiring little katipo spider, *Latrodectus katipo*. It has a poisonous bite that can be fatal, but though mention of its name strikes fear into the hearts of brave souls, in fact only a few deaths have ever been recorded and most of those were a long time ago. Nowadays antivenin is available from most hospitals, and it's effective even if administered as long as three days after the bite has occurred.

The katipo is found in coastal areas in all of New Zealand except for the far south. It lives in areas just back from the high tide zone, weaving a small, dense web in driftwood, grasses or any other suitable place close to the ground. The katipo is not aggressive; it's a shy animal which only bites if disturbed.

Only the mature female spider is dangerous; she is identified by a shiny black body, about six mm long, with a bright red patch on the rear of the abdomen. The harmless mature male is identified by the presence of white markings on both sides, in addition to the red patch; the white markings are also present on the immature spiders of both sexes.

Jellyfish Local advice is the best way of avoiding contact with these sea creatures with their stinging tentacles. Stings from most jellyfish are quite painful. The most effective folk remedy for jellyfish stings, used all over the world, is to apply fresh urine to the stings as soon as possible. This is also useful if you touch stinging coral. Ammonia is also effective. Dousing in vinegar will de-activate any stingers which have not 'fired'. Calamine lotion, antihistamines and analgesics may reduce the reaction and relieve the pain.

Women's Health

Gynaecological Problems Poor diet, lowered resistance due to the use of antibiotics and even contraceptive pills can lead to vaginal infections when travelling in hot climates. Maintaining good personal hygiene, and wearing skirts or loose-fitting trousers and cotton underwear will help to prevent infections.

Yeast infections, characterised by a rash, itch and discharge, can be treated with a vinegar or lemon-juice douche, or with yoghurt. Nystatin suppositories are the usual medical prescription. Trichomoniasis is a more serious infection; symptoms are a discharge and a burning sensation when urinating. Male sexual partners must also be treated, and if a vinegar-water douche is not effective medical attention should be sought. Metronidazole (Flagyl) is the prescribed drug.

Pregnancy Most miscarriages occur during the first three months of pregnancy, so this is the most risky time to travel. The last three months should also be spent within reasonable distance of good medical care, as quite serious problems can develop at this time. Pregnant women should avoid all unnecessary medication. Additional care should be taken to prevent illness and particular attention should be paid to diet and nutrition.

WOMEN TRAVELLERS

New Zealand is quite an easy country for women travellers, with very few hassles. Women should, however, exercise the same degree of caution as they would in most other countries. We recommend that you observe all the commonsense habits of safety, such as not walking through isolated urban areas alone when it's dark, not hitchhiking alone, and so on.

DANGERS & ANNOYANCES

Violent crime is not common in New Zealand. The newspapers report on murders and bashings in great detail, but this is a reflection of the lack of crime (or perhaps the lack of news). Whereas in many cities around the world violent crime no longer rates a mention, in New Zealand a murder will be splashed across the dailies from coast to coast.

Theft, primarily theft from cars, can be a problem and is on the rise as the rich get richer and the poor get poorer in New Zealand's restructured economy. Don't leave any valuables in a car, either outside accommodation or particularly at tourist parking areas, such as car parks at the start of walks. If you must leave your belongings in the car, make sure they are hidden from view.

The biggest dangers in New Zealand, though, may come not from your fellow humans but from nature. Remember to take all the recommended precautions when tramping, especially in the mountains; see the Tramping section in the Outdoor Activities chapter for advice on tramping safety, and follow the advice!

Sharks

Sharks exist in NZ waters but they are well fed by the abundance of marine life and rarely pose a threat to humans. However attacks do occasionally occur. Take notice of any local warnings when swimming, surfing or diving. Should you come face to face with a shark when diving, the best thing to do is move casually and quietly away. Don't panic, as they are attracted by things that thrash around in the water. Avoid swimming in places that would be obvious attractions to them as predators, such as areas where young seals or penguins are learning to swim. They are also attracted to blood, so don't swim where fish are being killed or cleaned in the sea.

LANGUAGE COURSES

People from around the world, especially Asia and the Pacific countries, come to New Zealand to study English. Some of the attractions are that the country is a native English-speaking country with a high standard of education that is accredited throughout the world and it's a country which is uncrowded, clean, green and friendly. Typically each language school arranges for its students to live in homes with New Zealand families, so that English is used outside as well as inside the classroom. They also arrange a variety of extracurricular evening and weekend activities for their students.

Auckland has the highest concentration of language schools, and there are a few in other parts of the country as well. The Auckland Visitor Information Centre keeps a complete, up-to-date list.

WORK

New Zealand has a moderately high unemployment rate, so it's fussy about foreigners coming in and taking jobs that its own citizens need. An ordinary visitor's permit or visa does not give you the right to work in New Zealand; if you work without a work permit, you are breaking the law. You can apply for a work permit before arriving in New Zealand or within the country at any office of the New Zealand Immigration Service. Generally you need to be sponsored by an employer with an offer of definite employment in an occupation that is in demand in New Zealand. Special working holiday visas are available to citizens of Canada, Japan and the UK aged 18 to 30. See the Visas & Embassies section at the beginning of this chapter for more about work permits.

One type of work that foreign visitors are often able to get in New Zealand is fruit picking. Apples, kiwi fruit and other types of fruit and vegetables need to be picked in summer and early autumn, and often there are not enough New Zealanders available to make up the picking crews. Picking season is from around January to April so that's when the most work is available, though there may be some agricultural work to be done all year round. Picking is hard work and the pay is by the amount picked. If you're slow you won't make much money; speedy pickers do well.

HIGHLIGHTS

New Zealand has so many superb physical features that you find yourself taking the beauty of the country for granted after a while. With hundreds of km of rugged coastline and sandy beaches, lush native forest, rugged mountains and volcanoes, abundant wildlife and many other beautiful natural features, New Zealand has 'highlights' practically everywhere you turn. But if we had to pick some 'not to be missed sights or things to do in New Zealand' here's what they'd be, from north to south:

- Northland. In particular the magnificent Waipoua Kauri Forest on the west side, home of some spectacular giant 1500-year-old kauri trees; isolated beaches; the Bay of Islands on the east side; and the trip to Cape Reinga on the top.
- Visit a museum, for an insight into New Zealand culture, both Maori and Pakeha. The museums at Auckland, Wellington, Christchurch, Hamilton and Wanganui are amongst the best, but there are also interesting museums in some smaller, out-of-the-way places such as the Otamatea Kauri & Pioneer Museum at Matakohe and the Wagener Museum at Houhora, both in the Northland. Fascinating whether you're interested in present history, pioneering times or prehistory.
- Waitomo Caves, south of Hamilton. The Waitomo area is riddled with limestone caves with stalactites and stalagmites; the Waitomo Cave has the added attraction of a magnificent glow-worm grotto. Waitomo also offers amazing and unusual activities including cave rafting, abseiling expeditions in the caves, horse trekking and more.
- Rotorua, Bay of Plenty. This is one of New Zealand's most interesting areas. Go there for the thermal activity (boiling mud pools, hissing geysers and eerie volcanic landscapes) and the Maori culture (don't miss the night-time Maori concerts or a *hangi)*.
- Tongariro National Park, Central Plateau. A World Heritage Area, this park has some of the best mountain/volcano scenery in the country, excellent tramping tracks, and skiing in winter.
- Kaikoura, east coast of the South Island. Whale-watching trips and swimming with dolphins have made this place famous, and there are many other activities.
- Fox and Franz Josef Glaciers, west coast of the South Island. Nowhere else do glaciers come so close to sea level so close to the equator. Steep mountains and heavy rainfall are the scientific answer but sitting in sub-tropical rainforest, looking at so much ice, drives the easy answers out of your head. To experience their full majesty, get above them in a plane or helicopter or walk on them.
- Mt Cook, west coast of the South Island. The highest mountain in New Zealand has fantastic scenery, good tramping and skiing, and the mighty Tasman Glacier.
- Queenstown, South Island. The adrenaline capital of New Zealand. This is a resort town which offers a host of activities in a fantastic setting.
- Fiordland, south-west coast of the South Island. Similar to the fiords of Norway. Milford Sound is one of the most spectacular, with towering Mitre Peak. You won't forget the dolphins frolicking in the boat's bow wave and the absolute silence of night in this unique wilderness.
- The Catlins, south coast of the South Island. This place is a living museum, with an amazing array of flora & fauna including species not found elsewhere, tracts of rainforest, waterfalls and magnificent kelp-strewn ancient beaches. A must!
- Stay on a farm. Farm life, especially sheep farming, is what rural New Zealand is all about.
- Activities. How can we choose a highlight here? New Zealand has some of the finest tramping in the world. It also has great skiing. Plus literally dozens of activities ranging from boat trips and visits to sheep stations to shooting rapids upstream in jet-boats or downstream in inflatables, white-water sledging/rafting/boogey boarding, tandem skydiving, rap jumping, mountain biking and bungy jumping from high bridges, pipelines and platforms. Is tandem skydiving more thrilling than white-water sledging? If you go swimming with hundreds of dolphins, will you ever forget it as long as you live? A visit to a marae may be the thing you'll treasure as your warmest memory.

ACCOMMODATION

New Zealand has a wide range of accommodation but there is one catch: the Kiwis are great travellers. A greater proportion of New Zealanders have passports than in any other country and when they are not jaunting around overseas they'll be jaunting around at home. So book ahead during the holiday season, particularly in the main tourist areas at peak times. The busiest times for domestic tourism are the summer holidays from Christmas to the end of January, and Easter. Prices rise in the beach resorts and other popular destinations, and finding a room can be difficult. International tourism also puts a strain on accommodation and is at its busiest from October to April.

Accommodation has been bracketed into several categories. Camping grounds are either motor camps or Department of Conservation (DOC) camping grounds. Another option is accommodation on farms or in private homes, known as 'farmstays' and 'homestays' in NZ parlance. There is considerable overlap between these various groups. Hostel accommodation is provided by the YHA, YWCA and YMCA, and the private, independent hostels called 'backpackers'. Then there are the guesthouses, B&Bs, hotels and motels.

The NZTB, in conjunction with the AA, is introducing the Qualmark classification system which will eventually classify all accommodation, from hostels to five-star hotels.

Information

Some good accommodation guides are available in New Zealand.

The AA produces two *Accommodation Guides*, one to the North Island and one to the South Island, revised every year. They list motor camps, hotels, motels and so on, but since they have changed to a glossy advertising format they contain fewer listings and are less useful. They are available from any AA office and are free to AA members or overseas visitors who belong to an automobile association enjoying reciprocal rights with the AA. Otherwise you can purchase them for a small fee.

Jason's accommodation directories are similar commercially produced guides, available free from motels and motor camps. They have the most complete listings in two guides, *Jason's Motels & Motor Lodges* and *Jason's Budget Accommodation*, which primarily list motor camps and camping grounds.

Other publications are useful for the latest rundown on hostels, DOC camping grounds, and B&Bs; see them in those sections.

One of the best resources for accommodation information is the local information centre, found in almost every town of any size. Most also act as booking agents for accommodation and you can fax them from overseas for information and accommodation bookings.

Camping

If you like to camp, New Zealand is a great place for it. For the tent camper, Kiwi campsites are some of the best in the world, and motor camps (or caravan parks) have excellent facilities for tent campers, caravans and campervans, plus cabins of varying degrees of luxury and often on-site caravans.

Camping grounds and motor camps are found just about everywhere, particularly in touristy places, and often in prime locations – right on the beach or next to a babbling brook in mountain areas. They are very well equipped. Most have kitchens and dining areas where the cooker, hot plates, kettles and toasters are provided, though you may have to supply your own pots and pans, utensils, plates etc. They're great places to meet people – you talk with other people while you fix your food and carry on when you share a table to eat it. They also have laundry facilities and often TV rooms. Though it's best to bring your own sleeping bag, most places also hire linen if you're staying in cabins.

Camping or caravan sites may be charged at fixed site rate for two, and then an additional charge for each extra person, or sometimes it's just a straight site charge, but often it's a per-person charge typically around $7 to $9 per adult, half-price for children. A powered site for a caravan or campervan as opposed to a tent site without power is usually a dollar or two more per person.

At most sites the kitchen and showers are free but a few have coin-in-the-slot operated hot plates and hot showers. At most sites laundry facilities are coin operated.

High-quality camping gear can readily be bought in New Zealand if you leave home without it, but prices are also high. Auckland, Wellington and Christchurch all have good second-hand camping and sports shops; many of the army and navy surplus shops around New Zealand also have inexpensive and/or second-hand gear.

Remember it gets cool in New Zealand in the winter, so camping becomes less practical then, especially in the south.

DOC Camping Grounds The Department of Conservation operates over 120 camping grounds all around New Zealand. There are DOC camping grounds in reserves and in national parks, maritime parks, forest parks and farm parks.

DOC camping grounds are of three types. Serviced camping grounds have flush toilets, hot showers, tap water, kitchen and laundry areas, outdoor lighting, picnic tables, rubbish collection, and usually have powered as well as non-powered sites. They may also have BBQ and fireplace facilities, a shop or a campervan waste disposal point. Fees are around $6 to $9 per adult, per night.

Standard camping grounds are more basic, with minimal facilities including cold running water, toilets, fireplaces and not much else – but they also have minimal charges, around $2 to $6 per adult.

Children aged five to 16 are charged half price at both types of sites; it's free for children under the age of five.

The third type of camping ground, informal camping grounds, are free. They have limited facilities, usually just a cold water tap and places to pitch tents. Sometimes the access to these sites is a bit more difficult – you may have to walk in, rather than drive in.

You can check with local DOC offices for details on facilities, what you need to take and whether you should book in advance. Bookings can be made for all serviced camping grounds; contact the DOC office nearest the camping ground. Standard and informal camping grounds operate on a first come, first served basis, and fees are paid by a self-registration system. Since all fees are used for the maintenance of the camping grounds, and are kept as low as possible, it's important to pay them (usually into an 'honesty box') even when there's no warden present.

Back Country Huts The DOC also operates numerous back country huts, most of which can only be reached on foot. See the Tramping section in the Outdoor Activities chapter for information on huts.

Cabins & Tourist Flats

Many camping grounds and motor camps have cabins. Standard cabins are simply free-standing rooms with bare mattresses where you have to provide your own sleeping gear (a sleeping bag is fine) and towels. Cabins can be very cheap, often around $20 or $25 for two which can make them even cheaper than hostels. They generally charge per two adults, plus so much for each additional person, but some charge per cabin and some per person. Linen can usually be hired.

Moving up from this basic standard, there is a variety of standards and prices of cabins. Often the cabins become 'tourist flats' and are equipped closer to motel standard with kitchens and/or bathrooms. They may also be serviced with linen provided. On-site caravans (trailer homes in US parlance) are another camping ground possibility. Many camping grounds also have regular motel rooms or an associated motel complex and hostel-style bunkrooms.

Farmstays (Farm Holidays)

New Zealand has been called the world's most efficient farm so a visit to a farm is an interesting way of getting to grips with the real New Zealand. Farmstays are a very popular activity as many farms take guests who can 'have a go' at all the typical farm activities and be treated as one of the household into the bargain. If you want to know more about it contact the new Zealand Tourism Board (NZTB; see the Tourist Offices section earlier in this chapter) or the visitor information centres. There are all sorts of farms you can choose from – dairy, sheep, high country, cattle or mixed farming farms. If you're staying in the homestead typical daily costs are in the $60 to $120 range including meals, but there are also many on a B&B only arrangement where costs may be more like $35 to $50 per day, with an extra $10 to $15 if you want dinner. Some farms have separate cottages where you fix your own food and have to supply your own bedding; these ones may charge by the week. Rates can get as cheap as $10 per night in basic sheep shearers' cottages, for example.

Other places offer accommodation and meals for nothing or at very cheap rates in exchange for work on the farm. Though some travellers have reported the occasional labour camp, many farms offering accommodation on this basis offer an excellent chance to work on a farm, learn about farm life and save money. FHINZ (☎ (06) 376 4582; fax (06) 358 1092), Kumeroa Lodge Stud, RD1 Woodville, produce a booklet for $15 that lists farms throughout New Zealand that provide lodging in exchange for four hours work per day.

WWOOF A very economical way to stay on a farm and do some work there is to join Willing Workers on Organic Farms (WWOOF). Membership in WWOOF provides you with a list of over 300 organic farms throughout the country where, in exchange for your 'conscientious work', the farm owner will provide food, accommodation and some hands-on experience in organic farming. Once you've made a decision about which farm you'd like to visit you have to contact the farm owner or manager directly by telephone or letter. They emphasise that you cannot simply turn up at a farm without warning.

To join WWOOF and receive the booklet, write to Janet & Andrew Strange, PO Box 1172, Nelson, New Zealand, or telephone mobile number (025) 345711. The cost is $15 if you join in New Zealand.

Homestays

In addition to farms there are also numerous possibilities for staying in private homes throughout New Zealand, whether in urban or rural areas. Most are B&B arrangements – see the B&Bs & Guesthouses section for additional details. Several of the agencies which handle farmstays are combination 'farm and homestay' services. Visitor information centres throughout New Zealand, especially in the smaller towns, keep lists of farmstays and homestays in their areas.

Possibilities for farmstays and homestays in New Zealand are limitless. Your best bet is to get hold of a copy of *The New Zealand Bed & Breakfast Book* mentioned earlier, make contact with one of the umbrella organisations specialising in farmstays and homestays, or ask at the visitor information centre for each area.

Home Exchange

If you want to spend some time in one area, an option is a holiday home exchange. It works the same way as in other parts of the world: you pay a fee to a matching agency, they facilitate connections between potential home-swappers, and once the connection is made, there are no more accommodation costs – it's an even swap, home for home. Home rentals can often also be arranged.

The Worldwide Home Exchange Club is a worldwide organisation with a representative in New Zealand. Write for information and a membership blank to Worldwide Home Exchange Club, CPO Box 4433, Auckland 1, New Zealand (☎ (09) 630-8732).

Hostels

Hostels offer cheap accommodation in locations all over New Zealand and are the real boom area in accommodation. At a hostel you basically rent a bed, usually for around $12 to $16 a night. Some hostels have bunkrooms for 10 or more people, sometimes segregated, sometimes not. Others have smaller bunkrooms or 'share rooms' with three or four beds, and almost all have at least a few twin or double rooms, and sometimes single rooms. All hostels have a fully equipped communal kitchen, a dining area, a lounge area and a laundry room.

Hostels are divided into two camps – YHA hostels and private hostels or backpackers. Due to intense competition, the YHA in New Zealand has gone to great lengths to change its image. Gone are the chores and curfews, as are many of the fuddy duddy managers traditionally associated with YHAs.

Hostels vary enormously from town to town, and hostel to hostel. The YHA hostels tend to be more consistent in standards as their hostels are purpose-built and run. Private hostels range from new, purpose-built hostels that offer excellent standards of accommodation to converted family homes that may lack good communal areas and adequate kitchens essential to a good hostel. On the other hand, YHA hostels may be in institutional buildings, while the home atmosphere of private hostels may be more attractive. Ultimately it boils down to the managers – some are just not in tune with backpackers, but many are right on the ball, promote a congenial atmosphere, offer excellent travel information, tours, activities etc. Many of the hostels, YHA and private, are just brilliant.

Many hotels, motor camps and even some motels are cashing in on the backpackers boom and also offer backpacker accommodation. They offer discounted rates in share or individual rooms, which can be good value but are often anonymous and lack the atmosphere of a hostel.

It's a good idea to travel with your own sleeping bag. At independent backpackers bedding usually costs extra. YHA hostels provide bedding for free; you just have to ask for it.

YHA Hostels The YHA in New Zealand produces a free annual *YHA Accommodation Guide* with details on all their hostels throughout New Zealand. You may be able to get a copy from your national YHA or you can request one from the YHA National Office, PO Box 436, Christchurch, New Zealand (☎ (03) 379 9970; fax 365 4476). It's also available at all YHA hostels and YHA travel centres throughout New Zealand. Like elsewhere in the world, the Youth Hostel Association also goes under the banner of Hostelling International, but the term 'YHA' is still more common in New Zealand.

YHA hostels are only open to members. You can either join the YHA in your home country or in New Zealand at any YHA hostel for $24. You can also pay in instalments of $4 per night at each hostel you stay at, and after six nights your card then becomes a full membership card. If you have a YHA card make sure you bring it, even if you don't want to stay in hostels. Backpackers discounts are offered by many bus companies (usually 30% discount), airlines, and for many activities and some attractions if you flash your YHA card.

New Zealand also has a number of Associate YHA Hostels – privately owned premises affiliated to the YHA. You don't need a membership card to stay at an Associate YHA Hostel, but they often charge $1 or more extra for non-members.

Particularly during school holidays and at popular hostels it pays to book ahead directly with the hostel in question, through the New Zealand YHA offices, or through another hostel. Reservations must be paid in advance at another hostel or you can reserve directly by phone or fax with a credit card (Visa, MasterCard or Bankcard). It is also possible to book from one country to another via YHA hostels.

Backpackers The numerous 'backpackers' (private or independent hostels) have basically the same facilities and prices as YHA hostels – fully equipped communal kitchens, common areas, laundry facilities and so on.

A couple of handy brochures are useful for the latest listings of the many backpackers, which are springing up all around the country with amazing rapidity. Hostels pay to be listed in these brochures, so they are not independent assessments or regulated organisations, but they are up-to-date and well prepared.

Budget Backpackers Hostels New Zealand is an excellent publication, commonly known as the 'Blue Book', put out by Budget Backpackers Hostels. Available through member hostels and some information centres, it has details, prices and a big selection of backpackers throughout New Zealand. Their BPP rating, based on guests' assessments, is an interesting and usually accurate guide to a hostel's atmosphere (not necessarily facilities). You can also get a copy through the Rainbow Lodge (☎ & fax (07) 377 1568), 99 Titiraupenga St, Taupo, or Foley Towers (☎ & fax (03) 379 3014), 208 Kilmore St, Christchurch.

The *VIP Backpackers Accommodation Guide* also has a wide range of hostels and most of the large, city hostels. All the backpackers listed are members of the VIP network; possession of a VIP Card gives you $1 off at every hostel, plus a host of other discounts (similar to those offered on a YHA card). The VIP accommodation guide is available at VIP hostels and information centres, or request one from VIP Backpackers Resorts, 9 Fort St, Auckland (☎ (09) 358 4852; fax (09) 358 4872) at Auckland Central Backpackers.

Another is the 'Red Guide'. This is a much less extensive selection of hostels and other budget, non-hostel accommodation put out by New Zealand Backpacker Lodges at the Kiwi Hilton (☎ (09) 358 3999), 430 Queen St, Auckland.

YMCA & YWCA Hostels There are YMCA and YWCA hostels in several larger towns which offer straightforward, no frills accommodation and are generally reasonably priced. A few are single-sex only but most take both men and women. Although the emphasis is on long-term accommodation – providing a place to stay for young people coming to study or work in the 'big city' – they do provide accommodation in the crowded summer season when their long-term residents go home or go off on holiday. Accommodation in these hostels is often in single or twin rooms.

B&Bs & Guesthouses

There's a wide variation in types and standards in this category. Guesthouses may be spartan, cheap, ultra-basic 'private' (unlicensed) hotels. Most are comfortable, relaxed but low-key places, patronised by people who don't enjoy the impersonal atmosphere of many motels. Others are very fancy indeed.

B&B accommodation in private homes is by far the biggest category. The best publication for B&B listings is the excellent *The New Zealand Bed & Breakfast Book* by J & J Thomas, available in New Zealand bookstores and updated annually, which has details on hundreds of B&Bs all over the country. Local visitor information centres also have a list of B&Bs.

Although breakfast is definitely on the agenda at the real B&B places it may or may not feature at guesthouses. Breakfast may be 'continental', ie not much, or a substantial meal of fruit, eggs, bacon, toast, tea and coffee. Many guesthouses pride themselves on the size, quality and 'traditional value' of their breakfasts. If you like to start the day heartily it's worth considering this when comparing prices.

Guesthouses can be particularly good value if you're travelling on your own. Most hotels and motels are priced on a 'per room' basis whereas guesthouses usually charge 'per person'. Typically B&Bs cost around $30 to $50 per person. Except at the most expensive B&B guesthouses, rooms generally do not have attached bathrooms.

Many B&Bs also offer the evening meal for an extra charge. A few B&Bs offer a kitchen where guests can do their own cooking, but most do not.

There are several cooperatively produced lists of B&B accommodation – usually available from guesthouses which appear on the list, and from visitor information centres.

Hotels

As in Australia a hotel has to be licensed to serve alcohol. So at one end of the scale the hotel category can include traditional older-style hotels where the emphasis is mainly on the bar and the rooms are pretty much a sideline. At the other end it includes all the five-star hotels in the big cities. At the cheapest old-style hotels, singles might cost as low as $20, while at the most luxurious new establishments a room could cost $200 or more.

Some of the older hotels now also have 'backpackers rooms' that usually cost about half the normal hotel rate. These are regular hotel rooms without the frills – no TV, radio etc – and towel and bedding are not provided or cost extra.

If you like staying in economical older hotels, a free *Pub Beds* brochure will give you a good discount when you present it at participating hotels. It's published by Pub Beds, PO Box 32-332, Auckland 9, New Zealand (☎ (09) 445 4400; fax 445 1010) and is available at many hotels and information centres around New Zealand.

Motels

Motels in New Zealand have all the facilities of motels everywhere, and more. Many motel units will have a kitchen with a stove, crockery and all the cooking utensils you need to prepare meals, though some studio units only have a fridge, and tea and coffee-making equipment. Most motels provide you with a small carton of fresh milk. Motels will often have a laundry for guests.

Many visitors find NZ motels a definite notch below international standards. Many motels date from the 1960s and look like it. Though comfortable enough, they are drab, pre-fabricated affairs. Newer motels are also often cheap constructions but usually brighter with better decor, and some are definitely luxurious. Motel rooms typically cost around $60 to $70 a double, and then $10 to $15 for every extra person. The more luxurious new motels cost around $70 to $100 a double. The difference in price between a single or double motel room, if there is one, is usually minimal. In tourist towns, motels can really hike prices in the main tourist season. At beach resorts popular with Kiwi holiday-makers, it may be difficult to find a motel room under $100 in summer.

A motor inn is a part motel/part hotel. It offers motel-style accommodation and usually has a bar and restaurant.

FOOD

In the last few years the dining scene has changed markedly. In the major cities, you can find Italian, Middle Eastern, Indian, Cambodian, Mexican and other cuisines represented. Curiously, however, despite the proliferation of international restaurants in the larger cities, there is little to be seen from the Pacific Islands, the source of New Zealand's largest number of immigrants. In the hinterlands, Chinese restaurants still predominate over any other sort of overseas cuisine.

There's not much of a NZ national cuisine – no moa & chips or Auckland fried kiwi. They're big meat eaters though and a NZ steak is every bit as good as an Aussie one. Lamb, of course, is top quality and available everywhere. New Zealand is also renowned for its dairy products and the milk, cheese and ice cream are excellent.

With all that coastline it's not surprising that seafood is pretty popular. There are some fine local varieties of oyster and the now rare and expensive shellfish toheroa or slightly less pricey tuatua. In some places, such as 90 Mile Beach in the North Island, and in the right season, a few minutes of digging in the sand at the beach can yield bucketfuls of shellfish, including tuatuas; pipis and periwinkles are other favourites.

The green-lipped mussels, available all over New Zealand, are easily the best in the world and though they're exported abroad they cost a fortune if you get them in other countries – compare $5 for *eight dozen* fresh ones in New Zealand (admittedly an excellent deal) to around $15 for a dozen in Australia. Likewise Bluff oysters are hard to beat – oyster fans shouldn't leave New Zealand without tasting them. Scallops are also good eating but ask local advice before you eat them; in 1993 there was a ban on them for several months, which was later lifted. Crayfish (lobster) is a speciality in some areas. Saltwater fish favourites include hoki, hapuka, groper, snapper, and kingfish.

New Zealand also has good freshwater fish, with incredibly large rainbow and brown trout. The areas around lakes Taupo and Rotorua in the North Island are particularly famous for giant-sized trout, but in fact they are found in many places in the country. You can't buy these trout in the shops but there are many opportunities to catch one yourself. There are a number of guidebooks

Kiwi Fruit

New Zealand's most famous fruit, the kiwi fruit, is a marvel of New Zealand agricultural know-how. Once known as the Chinese gooseberry, New Zealand took this obscure fruit, developed new strains suitable for local conditions and then marketed it internationally under the name kiwi fruit. In the 1980s, when no self-respecting nouvelle cuisine chef was without this colourful fruit on hand, the country was overtaken in the kiwi fruit rush that saw vines planted everywhere. The rich volcanic soils and temperate climate of the Bay of Plenty region were particularly suited to kiwi fruit, and overnight millionaires were made.

Since those heady days, other countries have started to grow the kiwi fruit and the price has dropped. However, New Zealand produces the largest and juiciest variety, and still accounts for two-thirds of all the kiwi fruit grown in the world. Kiwi fruit exports are in excess of $400 million a year.

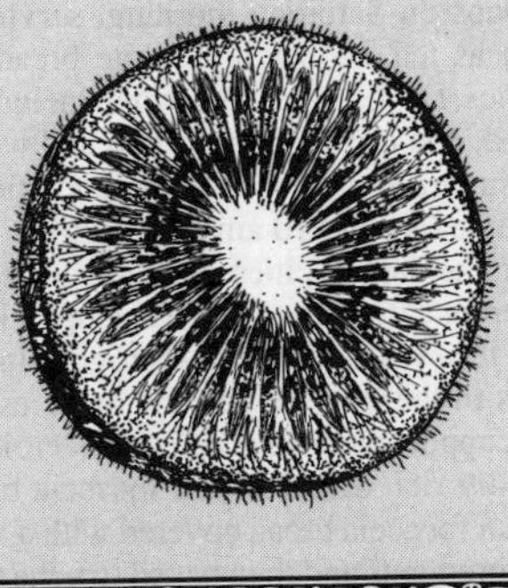

Imported from the Yangtze Valley in China, the first kiwi fruit climbers were grown as ornamental garden vines and it was only around 50 years ago that the first attempts were made to grow them commercially. The industry grew very slowly at first; only in the last couple of decades has it finally assumed the economic importance it enjoys today.

The New Zealand agricultural industry is always on the lookout to develop other exotic fruit, such as nashi pears and persimmons, which are also widely exported. Perhaps one of the most delightful fruits you'll find in New Zealand, grown in backyards all over the country for decades but never really developed as a commercial entity, is the sweet, highly perfumed feijoa, a South American import. ■

about fishing in New Zealand; see the Outdoor Activities chapter.

Eels, plentiful in New Zealand's rivers and creeks, are another local delicacy, especially smoked eels. Smoked fish is also quite popular.

Fast Food & Takeaways

Starting from the bottom (or the top for some itinerant diners) there are plenty of fast-food joints, along with those symbols of US culinary imperialism: McDonald's, Pizza Hut and KFC.

Of course there is fish & chips. Unlike in Australia where frying up good English fish & chips seems to be an Italian or Greek occupation, in New Zealand it's very often a Chinese one. (To the Americans in the crowd, note that 'chips' in New Zealand are the same thing as 'French fries' in the USA.)

New Zealanders are just about as tied to the meat pie as Australians but they probably do make a better job of them. To any Americans or Poms out there, the meat pie has as great a cultural significance to Australians as the hot dog does to a Noo Yorker – and is as frequently reviled for not being what it once was or currently should be. Georgie Pie, a chain of pie shops, has now fallen into this culinary void.

If you want to eat fast food and takeaways Kiwi style, fish & chips and hot meat pies are about as traditionally Kiwi as you can get. Try kumara chips sometime, for a variation.

Other snacks popular in New Zealand include nachos, potato skins, battered mussels and hamburgers like the great 'Kiwi burger' with a fried egg, beetroot and salad on it.

Tastebuds Mexican Cantina, found in several places around the North Island with more branches opening all the time, is a great local fast-food chain. You can get a good meal of a taco, burrito or enchilada, served with Mexican rice and either chile con carne or beans, plus a few crispy chips and whatever 'hotness' of sauce you like, all served on a paper plate for under $6 – such a deal.

Cafes & Tearooms

New Zealand's traditional cafes or coffee shops, called tearooms, are nothing to get very excited over. They're usually open on weekdays from around 9 am to 5 pm and perhaps on Saturday morning, serving fare such as tea, scones and white bread sandwiches. Devonshire teas, which include a pot of tea, one or two scones, jam and whipped cream, are served at morning and afternoon tea time (around 10 am and 3 pm).

In the larger cities, though, an entirely different cafe scene has sprung up in just the past few years. You can now go into many cafes in the larger cities and order espresso (or cappuccino, cafe latte etc), croissants, sinfully rich desserts, and focaccia bakes – Italian focaccia bread covered with a variety of ingredients and then baked (try the cheese and pesto one at Zoe's in Wellington). Some cafes, like the traditional tearooms, stay open only on weekdays until around 5 pm, but each city has some that are popular late-night hang-outs where you can sit and drink espresso, have a dessert, listen to music and generally hang out and be cool.

Pub Food

If you move into the pubs you'll probably find some of the best value for money. Counter meals (pie & chips, stews etc) have more or less died out, though some bars still sell pies from a pie warmer. A lot of pubs now have bistro meals – simple but good food like schnitzel, steak, fish or the like with chips and a good fresh salad or coleslaw. Average main courses range from $8 to $12 and they are usually excellent value. The Cobb & Co chain offer pub-style food in locations all over NZ. They're safe, sound and consistent and also open commendably generous hours, usually from 7 am to 10 pm seven days a week.

Restaurants

In New Zealand you will notice restaurants are either BYO or Licensed. BYOs (bring-your-own, or BYOG, bring-your-own-grog) mean that you can bring your own bottle of wine or whatever along with you and the food prices are generally a notch lower than in licensed restaurants. Check before you arrive if it is BYO or not. If you like reading about restaurants before you try them, Michael Guy's *Eating Out* is an interesting guide to restaurants all over New Zealand.

Vegetarian New Zealand has a number of great vegetarian restaurants, principally in the big cities. Auckland has several cheap and excellent vegetarian restaurants including Gopals, run by the Hare Krishnas. In Christchurch the Mainstreet Cafe is more expensive but the food, especially dessert, is superb.

Self-Catering

Buying food to cook yourself is generally far cheaper than eating out, of course, and with all camping grounds and hostels and most motels having cooking facilities it's a relatively easy alternative.

New Zealand has several large supermarket chains – Pak 'N Save, New World and Woolworth's for example – that have excellent prices and they're usually open seven days a week, with at least one or two 'late night' shopping nights when they're open until around 8 pm. The large supermarkets are not found only in large cities; sometimes there are unusually large supermarkets in towns which serve a large rural community.

When the supermarkets are shut, the good old corner dairy is the place to go. A dairy is a small shop found on many street corners throughout New Zealand, which sells milk, food, newspapers, chocolate, sweets – in fact a bit of everything, but mostly food lines. They're open longer hours than other shops and are far more widespread, but their selection is usually not as good as a larger shop, and their prices tend to be higher.

DRINKS

Beer & Pubs

New Zealanders are great drinkers, and both the beer and the pubs are pretty good. Almost all the beer is now brewed by only two companies, NZ Breweries and DB Breweries. Steinlager, the various types of DB (Bitter, Export etc) and Lion Red are probably the most popular beers. Down in the deep south you'll see some different labels like Speights and Southland Bitter. Monteith's, from the South Island's wild west coast, is as dark as the bituminous coal dug by the miners who drink it.

There are a smattering of small boutique breweries where the beer is made and consumed on the premises. Check out the Shakespeare Tavern & Brewery in Auckland or the popular Loaded Hog in Christchurch, Timaru and Wellington; the Loaded Hog makes four different types of grog and boasts that all are guaranteed 100% hangover-free! The Shakespeare Brewery makes six different varieties and if you manage to drink all of them in one evening you get a certificate of achievement. Probably the best of the boutique beers are from Marlborough and Nelson – Pink Elephant and Mac's. 'Dark' drinkers will appreciate the Black Mac. If your constitution is up to it seek out Hooker's Ale, a beer with a kick like an enraged moa.

New Zealand produces a variety of excellent beers

Cans aren't very popular and most beer is sold in bottles anyway as they're refundable and cheaper than cans. In a pub the cheapest beer is on tap. You can ask for a 'seven', which was originally seven fluid ounces but is now a 200 ml glass, the nearest metric equivalent (it's still called a 'seven' though – old ways die hard); a 'handle', which is a half-litre or litre mug with a handle; or a jug, which is just that.

Drinks at public bars are the cheapest, while lounge or other bars tend to mark their drinks up more, but prices vary widely.

In public bars you can pretty much wear anything, but lounge bars have a lot of 'neat dress required' signs around. You sometimes get the feeling they are determined that New Zealand should be the last home of the necktie. The bars with entertainment are normally lounge bars, which can sometimes make things a bit awkward for the traveller with jeans, sandals and T-shirt.

Wine & Wineries

New Zealand has a thriving wine-producing industry and many wineries have established international reputations, particularly for their whites. Air New Zealand has been a consistent winner of awards for the best wines served by an airline.

A few notable wine-producing areas are Henderson near Auckland, Martinborough in the Wairarapa, Hawkes Bay, Blenheim in the Marlborough region in the north part of the South Island, and now, Central Otago. Winery visits and tours are popular in all these places and of course there's free wine tasting. As New Zealand wine continues to achieve a better reputation, new wineries in these and other regions will probably continue to open. The two most well-known regions are Marlborough, noted for its Sauvignon Blanc, and Hawkes Bay, noted for its Chardonnay.

An unusual New Zealand speciality is kiwi fruit wine. There are lots of different varieties – still and bubbly, sweet and dry – and even a liqueur. You may not like it, but New Zealand's the best place to try it.

ENTERTAINMENT

As in many countries, there's plenty of nightlife in the major cities but not much in the small towns, where everything seems to shut with a bang after dark except the pub and the Chinese takeaway, and even they might be closed by around 9 or 10 pm. In the cities there's plenty of entertainment, with cinemas, theatre, discos, live-music venues, late-night cafes and plenty more.

In spectator sports, rugby union is practically a national mania, with cricket in a distant second place. It seems little boys in New Zealand learn to play rugby about as soon as they can walk, and continue to play it as late in life as they can manage. As you travel round New Zealand you'll see matches being played everywhere you go by teams of all ages. In rugby season when they're not out playing rugby, they're inside watching it on television. The All Blacks, New Zealand's national rugby team, are the national heroes. Rugby league, a variant of rugby, is also very popular.

THINGS TO BUY

You don't go to New Zealand intending to come back with a backpack full of souvenirs – a photograph of some flawless moment may be your best reminder – but there are some things worth checking out.

Woollen Goods

You can buy beautiful woollen gear in New Zealand, of course, particularly jumpers (sweaters) made from hand-spun, hand-dyed wool. Hand-knit jumpers are something of

Rugby Union

No book about New Zealand would be complete without mention of the national obsession – Rugby Union football. Try to escape the euphoria when the national team, the All Blacks, steamroll their international opponents into the mud of Eden Park – impossible. Look at the fear on the faces of the opposition as the All Blacks perform the fearsome haka at the start of a match for which they have become famous.

According to tradition, rugby had its beginnings in 1823 when William Webb Ellis picked up the ball during a game of soccer at Rugby School in England. The illegality of this move led to the popularity of such handling of the ball and the game was born. The Rugby Union was formed in 1871 and rugby was carried to the far outposts of the British Empire by British citizens travelling and living abroad.

The NZ Football Union was founded in 1892 and the country became a stronghold of the game. Interprovincial championships began in 1902 with play for the Ranfurly Shield which was donated by the then governor general, the earl of Ranfurly. New Zealand first played in Great Britain in 1888-89 and 1905-06.

The highest level of competition for rugby is now the World Cup, first held in 1987, when it was hosted jointly by Australia and New Zealand. New Zealand won that inaugural World Cup, went out in the semi-final stages of the 1991 tournament and lost 15-12 to South Africa in the 1995 final. During the 1995 event, New Zealand amassed the highest team score in World Cup history, by beating Japan 145-17.

The Bledisloe Cup competition (instigated by Lord Bledisloe, the former New Zealand governor general) has been contested by New Zealand and Australia since 1931 and by 1995 New Zealand had 57 wins and Australia 21; four matches were drawn.

The game is played on a quadrangular field. The maximum distance between the goal lines is 100 metres, the field is 69 metres wide, and goalposts are 5.6 metres apart with the crossbar three metres above the ground. The object is to get the ball across the opponents' goal line and

an art form in New Zealand and although they're not cheap – they sell in tourist shops for around $150 to $300 – they are of the highest quality and great if you can afford them. Other knitted goods include hats, gloves, scarves, mufflers and so on.

Woollen Swann-Dri jackets, shirts and pullovers are so practical and warm that they're just about the New Zealand national garment in the countryside, especially if you happen to be a farmer. Most common are the red-and-black or blue-and-black plaid ones, though they do also come in a few solid colours.

You can buy Swann-Dris (affectionately known as 'Swannies') in better outdoor-gear shops and again, though they're not cheap – a good pullover could cost you around $200 – they're top quality and if you buy one it will probably keep you from ever getting cold for at least the next decade or so. Great if you want a long-lasting souvenir!

Sheepskins

Sheepskins are also popular buys – the ones sold in the top tourist shops are beautiful and pure white, with long, thick, straight combed wool. Numerous other things are made of sheepskin, including toasty warm slippers.

Greenstone (Pounamu)

Jade, called greenstone or pounamu in New Zealand, is made into ornaments, brooches, earrings, cuff links and tikis. The latter are tiny, stylised Maori figures, usually depicted with their tongue stuck out in a warlike challenge, worn on a thong or chain around the neck. They've got great *mana* or power, but they also serve as fertility symbols so beware!

Bone Carvings

Maori bone carvings are another fine Maori art form which is undergoing something of a renaissance in NZ. Of course the Maori artisans have always made bone carvings, but

ground it (a try worth four points), or kick it over the goal posts (a conversion worth two points, a penalty worth three or a drop goal from the field worth three).

The oval ball is leather and weighs 440 grams. It is kicked off from the centre and then, by a combination of maul, ruck and scrum, is taken by one team. Without getting offside and without passing forward they attempt to get the ball to the opponents' line. Play stops only for a lineout, when the ball has gone out and is thrown back in to a line of players; for a scrum, when opposing forwards pack down against each other; for a penalty or conversion; or for a respite to remove an injured player. Get the full bottle from someone in the pub.

There are 15 players in each side – eight forwards and seven backs. The backs include a fullback, left wing, right wing, outside centre, inside centre, fly half and scrum half. They usually have slender builds and can move quickly with the ball. Looking at a number of forward packs you could be forgiven for thinking that brawn was a prerequisite. There are two burly props, a hooker to rake the ball in the scrum, two second rowers or locks, two flankers (or breakaways) and the last man down (No 8). The last three are referred to as loose forwards.

There are approximately 11,000 clubs in NZ. The All Blacks, over the years, have included many great players such as the famous lock forward Colin 'Pine Tree' Meads – 55 caps (representing New Zealand) and 133 appearances between 1957 and 1971; Brian Williams, the great winger; Don Clarke, fullback extraordinaire; Grant Fox, fly half; Ian Kirkpatrick, a scintillating loose forward; the great Waka Nathan; and the sensation of the 1995 World Cup, winger Jonah Lomu, nicknamed the 'human bulldozer'.

Seven-a-side competition is now popular with the advent of the Hong Kong sevens tournament. The All Blacks won this tournament in 1995.

If you're interested and are there at the right time, make sure you see a game at Eden Park. Tickets are available at the park itself and it's best to buy them well in advance.

Rugby league, with 13 instead of 15 players and slightly different rules, is also popular, especially in Auckland, but not as revered as rugby union. New Zealand reached the semi-final of the 1995 Rugby League World Cup. ■

nowadays it seems you see amazingly beautiful bone carvings a lot more often. Tikis can be carved of bone as well as greenstone, though the greenstone ones are more common, and there are some very interesting human and animal figures that are carved of bone. Fishhooks, carved in a variety of traditional Maori styles, are also commonly carved of bone; a certain type of fishhook represents the legend of how New Zealand was fished up from the sea by Maui. Dolphins, sea birds and other figures are also carved of bone. Bone figures are often worn on a thong or a chain around the neck.

Paua (Abalone)

Abalone shell, called paua in New Zealand, is another substance from which beautiful carvings and jewellery are made. It's illegal to take unadulterated paua shells out of New Zealand, but you can buy pendants, earrings and many other things made of paua and take them with you with no problems. You'll probably see whole shells used as ashtrays in places where paua is plentiful, but you can't take one of those out of the country.

Wood Carvings

Another distinctive Maori art form, Maori wood carvings are worth checking out, particularly in Rotorua. In a number of places, carvers are producing tremendous forms such as leaping dolphins, in addition to the sometimes highly intricate traditional Maori carvings. Of course, many poor examples are turned out for the tourist trade and they tend to dominate. In Auckland, try the China Oriental Markets where shops sell mostly souvenirs but also some good quality carvings, as well as interesting carvings from the entire Pacific region. For high-quality Maori art and high prices, check out the Taumata Art Gallery in the Finance Plaza on Queen St.

Other Arts & Crafts

New Zealanders have a reputation as great do-it-yourselfers and there are a lot of excellent shops selling arts & crafts where you'll find everything from hand-painted scarves to ceramics to home-made jams and preserves, in addition to all the handicrafts previously mentioned. The quality of the pottery and weaving is particularly fine: they make good presents to take back home and don't take up much room in your pack. Nelson, in particular, is noted for its excellent pottery. The quality of the local clay has attracted many potters there.

Fashion

City Kiwis have an independent flair when it comes to fashion, and consequently there are some great little clothes shops around. In Auckland, check out Ponsonby Rd, the markets and in the centre around High and O'Connell Sts. The more mainstream quality designers congregate around the central city and Parnell districts in Auckland. Thornton Hall is a successful women's label you'll find in all the major cities.

Outdoor clothing has also become very competitive and the durable yet stylish Canterbury sports clothing label is known internationally. New Zealand is making quite a name for itself with high-quality outdoor fashion, which is at home in the bush or the bar. In Auckland, Broadway in Newmarket has a number of outlets, including Action Downunder.

Camping Equipment & Souvenirs

If you're planning a camping trip around New Zealand you can buy quality sleeping bags, tents, clothes and other bush gear. You get what you pay for and if you don't mind paying the price you can get some of the world's best quality. The large cities have second-hand sports shops were you can sometimes pick up some good bargains.

You can find beautiful postcards everywhere you go in New Zealand and a postcard collection would make a great keepsake of the country. Books of New Zealand photography, in hardback or paperback, are sold in bookshops around New Zealand; the Whitcoull's chain has a large selection but you can find them in most bookshops. Or how about a book of *Footrot Flats* cartoons?

Of course there are also plenty of silly

souvenirs. How about a little tin can that goes 'baaaa' like a sheep when you turn it over? Or a miniature sheep? Then there are the snow-domes with a flock of sheep trapped in a perpetual snow shower. And how about everything you can think of, from T-shirts to key rings, emblazoned with little cartoon kiwis?

Outdoor Activities

New Zealand is a haven for visitors who seek to combine adventure with the wide open spaces. The land, air and water are not sacrosanct, and the Kiwis and their visitors move over or through these media in just about every way imaginable. They jet-boat, white-water sledge, raft, boogey board, canoe, kayak, surf, surf raft, scuba dive and ski through the water; bungy jump, parapente, skydive, abseil, fly, helicopter and barrel roll through the air; and tramp, mountain bike, ski, horse ride, rock climb and ice climb across and up terra firma. Not forgetting, beneath the surface – caving, cave rafting, *tomo* exploring and hydrosliding are all actively pursued.

To give you an indication of the lengths Kiwis will go to experience something different, read *Classic New Zealand Adventures* by Jonathan Kennett, Johnny Mulheron, Greg Carlyon & Malcolm O'Neill. It contains every adventure from a sedate paddle down a river to wharf jumping on a bicycle, pillocking across mud flats on a rubbish-tin lid, and bridge swinging on a climbing rope. Still bored? Then try a jump in the nude from the top of Maruia Falls!

The *New Zealand Adventure Annual & Directory* is another good resource, coming out annually with articles, colour photos and listings of all kinds of adventure and activity operators around New Zealand.

TRAMPING

Tramping, or bushwalking as it is often called, is the best way of coming to grips with New Zealand's natural beauty. It gives the traveller the satisfaction of being a participant rather than just a spectator.

The country has thousands of km of tracks, many well marked, some only a line on the maps. One thing that makes tramping especially attractive are the hundreds of huts available, enabling trampers to avoid the weight of tents and cooking gear. Many tracks are graded; some are easily covered by those with only moderate fitness and little or no experience, while others are more rewarding for experienced, fit walkers. Many travellers, once having tried a track, then gear the rest of their trip in New Zealand to travelling from one track to another, with side trips to see other sights. This section should open your eyes to the possibilities of tramping, but before attempting any track consult the appropriate authority for the latest information.

There are literally hundreds of tracks to be enjoyed all over New Zealand. Visitors tend to want to do the famous ones – the Milford, Routeburn, Abel Tasman, etc – and some of these tend to get so crowded with trampers that everyone gets annoyed, meanwhile an equally beautiful track may be just a few km away with nobody on it. Most of the time it's because they haven't heard about it.

The 'Great Walks' are the most famous tramping tracks in the country and they became famous because of their beauty. Their beauty does indeed make them worth experiencing but if you do walk these tracks, please don't do so and then be upset that they are crowded – especially the Abel Tasman Coastal Track, the most popular track in NZ. Of *course* these tracks are sometimes crowded, especially at the height of summer – people from all over the world come here to tramp.

The most walked tracks in New Zealand are the Abel Tasman Coastal Track, which 21,000 people walked in 1992/93; the Routeburn which had 10,200 visitors; the Milford with 10,100; the Tongariro Northern Circuit with 7400; the Kepler with 5000; and Lake Waikaremoana with 4500. If you like tramping but want to avoid the crowds, it's worth asking at Department of Conservation (DOC) offices and park headquarters for details on lesser known tracks – they will be happy to help you plan some enjoyable walks. There are DOC offices in every city and in dozens of towns, and they all give free information about tramping in their areas. Every national park, forest park and maritime park has its own DOC headquarters and they all have information on a number of long and short walks. There are also council parks, farm parks, regional parks and more, all of which have walking possibilities.

When to Go

The most crowded season for tramping is during the summer school holidays – from one to two weeks before Christmas to the end of January. The couple of weeks before school breaks up in December can also be bad as many school groups are on the trails. December-January on the main trails is a good period to avoid. The best weather is from January to March, though most tracks can be walked enjoyably anytime from about November to April. June and July are considered the middle of winter and not the time to be out on the tracks. Some are closed in winter because of avalanche danger. It's best to time your walks so that the most southerly are done in the middle of summer.

Surprisingly, most people on the tracks are from outside New Zealand. It's common to have a ratio of only one in 10 Kiwis in a hut, although on the Milford Track, of course, it can reach 50:50. Kiwis do tramp, but they tend to avoid the popular tracks, seeking the really wild and untouched regions.

What to Bring

For an enjoyable tramp the primary consideration is your feet and shoulders. Make sure your footwear is adequate and that your pack is not too heavy. Having adequate, waterproof rain gear is also important, especially on the South Island's West Coast, where you can get drenched to the skin in minutes if your rain gear is not up to the challenge.

Equipment This list is for someone who will be sticking to the main tracks, staying in huts and tramping during the summer months. It is inadequate for snow country or winter.

Boots – light to medium with good ankle support are recommended. The boots should be broken in or you'll get painful blisters. Cover your heels with moleskin before you start if you think there is any chance of blisters.

Alternative footwear – thongs (jandals/sandals) or

The Mt Cook region is inextricably linked to the history of mountaineering in New Zealand

running/tennis shoes for strolling around the huts or if the boots become just too painful to wear.

Socks – three heavy polypropylene or woollen pairs; two to be worn at once to reduce the chance of blisters. Frequent changes of socks during the day also reduces the chance of blisters but isn't too practical.

Shorts, light shirt – for everyday wear; swimsuits for the immodest.

Woollen sweater/jersey, woollen trousers – essential in case of cold weather. Some of the modern synthetics, such as polypropylene and polar fleece, are just as good as wool.

Waterproof raincoat and overtrousers – a combination of wet and cold can be fatal.

Dishes & cutlery – knife, fork, spoon, cup, plate, soup bowl. (You can cut this back to knife, spoon and bowl – a bowl is multipurpose: you can eat or drink out of it, and mix things in it.)

Pot/billy (one) – 1.5 to two litres capacity is sufficient.

Pans (two) – 15 cm across and five cm deep is plenty. The pot and pans are adequate for two to three-course meals for two people. Preferably the pots should fit into each other and be made of aluminium for lightness.

Camping stove – take one along, even if you'll be staying in huts. Many huts don't have cookers.

Matches/lighter – for cooking and lighting candles. Matches are difficult to keep dry.

Candle – half to one candle per day, depending on how many are sharing the hut. Some huts have lanterns supplied.

Torch (flashlight) – for nocturnal toilet visits and late arrival at the hut

Small first-aid kit, toilet paper and insect repellent – see the Health section in the Facts for the Visitor chapter for information on first-aid kits and insect repellents.

Small towel – should dry quickly

Sleeping bag – warm down or Hollofill, light to medium weight, including a light stuff bag for rapid and easy packing.

Pack of cards – brush up on crib, 500 and euchre.

Pen/pencil and paper.

Pot scrubber and tea towel – washing up is usually done in cold water, making pot cleaning difficult.

Map and compass

Water purifier (see the Health Section in the Facts for the Visitor chapter).

Sun protectors – hat, cream, glasses.

Books – for birdwatching, plant identification etc.

Camera, binoculars.

Food Take food which is nourishing, tasty and lightweight:

breakfast – the most important meal of the day:
- tea/coffee, sugar, instant milk
- muesli/porridge (quick cooking) – good with sultanas (raisins)
- bacon & eggs – bacon in vacuum pack will last days
- bread, butter/margarine, Vegemite/Marmite or honey

lunch – it's normally eaten between huts and therefore should not require too much preparation:
- bread/crackers, butter or margarine (there are some nice wholemeal crackers available, but 'Cabin Bread' is larger and stronger and so will stand up to being crammed in a pack better)
- cheese – tasty, not bland

dinner – must be hot and substantial:
- instant soups – help to whet the biggest appetites
- fresh meat – good for the first two days
- dehydrated meals – Alliance is excellent, Vesta is OK
- dehydrated vegetables, instant mashed potatoes – check preparation time: 20 minutes is the limit
- rice – goes with everything (couscous as a substitute)
- dessert – easy to cook, instant such as tapioca, custard or instant puddings

snacks – important source of energy while tramping:
- chocolate – 100 g per person per day
- raisins, sultanas, dried fruit
- scroggin – combination of all the above; make it yourself
- glucose – in the form of barley sugar, glucose tablets or powder from chemists; it gives almost instant energy
- biscuits – great before bed with tea or coffee. Get a recipe for 'Tararuas', an indestructible, calorie-packed life saver
- cordial concentrate – powder; a great thirst quencher, adds flavour to purified water
- instant noodles

This list of food is by no means complete for a long trek, but it should get you through the first tramp without suffering from withdrawal symptoms. For a three-day tramp, one loaf of bread, 200 to 300 grams of butter/margarine and 200 grams of instant dried milk are sufficient amounts to take for one person. Since so many dishes require milk it is important not to underestimate your requirements.

As all rubbish should be carried out, ensure that everything is in suitable containers. Extra lightweight metal and plastic containers are available from supermarkets and some chemists. Don't take glass bottles

Milford Sound (DW)

Top: Hangi, Te Kaha, Coromandel Peninsula (HL)
Bottom: Te Mata o Hoturoa war canoe, Whanganui Regional Museum, Wanganui (NK)

– transfer the ingredients, such as coffee or Vegemite, into light containers.

Everything should be kept in plastic bags, preferably two, for protection from the elements. Clothes must be kept dry under all circumstances. Plastic pack liners, 'survival bags', made by the NZ Mountain Safety Council, are sold in outdoors shops for about $4 and they are an excellent investment. Made of thick plastic that will not tear, a survival bag is large enough for you to climb into for survival if need be, or you could split it and make a shelter. If you can't find one, you could use large green plastic rubbish bags. Put the lot into a lightweight, waterproof backpack.

The total weight of your backpack should not exceed 14 kg for a three-day tramp.

Department of Conservation (DOC) – Te Papa Atawhai

The DOC looks after parks, tracks, walkways, huts and general tramping facilities. It also administers hundreds of scenic, historic, scientific and nature reserves, and wildlife refuges and sanctuaries. It also has responsibility for the Subantarctic Islands and the two World Heritage areas – Tongariro National Park and Te Wahipounamu (southwest New Zealand, which incorporates Fiordland, Mt Aspiring, Mt Cook and Westland national parks).

The local DOC office is usually the best place for information on nature and outdoor attractions in any area. They produce excellent pamphlets on almost any natural attraction. In some places the visitor information centres have the same information and a collection of DOC pamphlets.

Conservation Volunteer Programme The DOC has a programme in which you can volunteer to participate in all kinds of conservation projects. Work might include things like counting certain species of birds, guarding and protecting nesting areas at certain times of year, track and/or hut maintenance or any number of other activities. You don't get paid but you do get a chance to go to some wild out-of-the-way places and get hands-on experience in conservation. You can volunteer for any length of time. Check with DOC regional offices.

National Parks

New Zealand has many parks: 13 national, 19 forest, three maritime and two marine, plus a few other types of parks and reserves.

DOC information centres for the various national parks and maritime parks are found at:

Abel Tasman National Park – Totaranui, Nelson, Motueka, Takaka
Arthur's Pass National Park – Arthur's Pass township
Bay of Islands Maritime & Historic Park – Russell
Egmont National Park – Dawson Falls and North Egmont on Mt Egmont/Taranaki
Fiordland National Park – Te Anau
Hauraki Gulf Maritime Park – Auckland
Kahurangi National Park – Karamea, Motueka, Takaka, Nelson
Marlborough Sounds Maritime Park – Picton, Blenheim, Havelock
Mt Aspiring National Park – Wanaka, Makarora
Mt Cook National Park – Mt Cook villabge near the Hermitage
Nelson Lakes National Park – St Arnaud, Lake Rotoroa
Otago Goldfields Park – Dunedin, Alexandra
Paparoa National Park – Punakaiki
Stewart Island Stewardship Area – Oban
Te Urewera National Park – Aniwaniwa at Lake Waikaremoana
Tongariro National Park – Whakapapa on Mt Ruapehu
Westland National Park – Franz Josef and Fox glaciers
Whanganui National Park – Pipiriki

In addition to the national parks there are numerous forest areas. The excellent pamphlet *Exploring New Zealand's Parks* outlines the national, maritime and forest parks.

Books

The DOC produces very good books with detailed information on the flora & fauna, geology and history of New Zealand's national parks. The DOC has leaflets available on thousands of walking tracks throughout the country, and the local DOC office is usually the best source of information on specific tracks.

New Zealand
Parks
0
100
200 km
Bay of Islands Maritime & Historic Park
Kaitaia
Russell
Poor Knights Islands Marine Reserve
Northland Forest Park
Whangarei
Hauraki Gulf Maritime Park
Coromandel Forest Park
Auckland
Thames
Raukumara Forest Park
Kaimai-Mamaku Forest Park
Whakawerawera Forest Park
Hamilton
Tauranga
Pirongia Forest Park
Rotorua
WHANGANUI NATIONAL PARK
Pureora Forest Park
Whirinaki Forest Park
TE UREWERA NATIONAL PARK
Gisborne
Sugar Loaf Islands Marine Park
Taupo
Turangi
Kaimanawa Forest Park
New Plymouth
Kaweka Forest Park
TONGARIRO NATIONAL PARK
Napier
Hastings
EGMONT NATIONAL PARK
Wanganui
Ruahine Forest Park
ABEL TASMAN NATIONAL PARK
Marlborough Sounds Maritime Park
Palmerston North
Rimutaka Forest Park
Tararua Forest Park
Takaka
TASMAN SEA
KAHURANGI NATIONAL PARK
Nelson
Picton
Haurangi Forest Park
WELLINGTON
Mt Richmond Forest Park
Westport
Victoria Forest Park
St Arnaud
NELSON LAKES NATIONAL PARK
PAPAROA NATIONAL PARK
LEWIS PASS NATIONAL RESERVE
Greymouth
Lake Sumner Forest Park
Hanmer Forest Park
Hokitika
ARTHUR'S PASS NATIONAL PARK
SOUTH PACIFIC OCEAN
WESTLAND NATIONAL PARK
Craigeburn Forest Park
Christchurch
TE WAHIPOUNAMU WORLD HERITAGE AREA
MOUNT COOK NATIONAL PARK
Banks Peninsula
MT ASPIRING NATIONAL PARK
Timaru
Milford Sound
Milford
Wanaka
Otago Goldfields Park
Queenstown
Te Anau
Dunedin
FIORDLAND NATIONAL PARK
Catlins Forest Park
Invercargill
Oban
Stewart Island (Rakiura)
National & Forest Parks
World Heritage Areas

Tramping in New Zealand, by Jim DuFresne & Jeff Williams, is another Lonely Planet guide. It has descriptions of nearly 50 walks, of various lengths and degrees of difficulty, in all parts of the country. There are plenty of other books about tramping in New Zealand. *New Zealand's Top Ten Tracks* by Mark Pickering contains many of the obvious ones (Milford, Routeburn, etc). *101 Great Tramps* by Mark Pickering & Rodney Smith has 101 suggestions for two-day to six-day tramps around the country.

Tramping in North Island Forest Parks by Euan & Jennie Nicol and *Tramping in South Island Forest Parks* by Joanna Wright are good for shorter walking and tramping possibilities, with suggestions for everything from half-hour walks to tramps taking several days. The descriptions of flora, fauna and history in these books are outstanding.

The Forest and Bird Book of Nature Walks by David Collingwood & EV Sale, revised by Joanna Wright, has good suggestions for short walks half an hour to several hours in length.

BP (Penguin) publishes a series of pocket-size paperback guides to several of NZ's most popular walking tracks. There's also a series of Shell guides to the more popular tracks.

Moir's Trampers' Guide to the Southern Lakes & Fiordland by the New Zealand Alpine Club is the definitive work on tracks in the south of the South Island. It comes in two volumes: *Northern Section: Lake Wakatipu to the Ohau Watershed* and *Southern Section: Hollyford Valley South*.

Maps

The DOSLI (Department of Survey & Lands Information) topographical maps are the best, though stationery shops tend to have a very poor selection of them. DOSLI has map sales offices in the North Island in Auckland, Hamilton, Gisborne, Napier, Rotorua, New Plymouth, Palmerston North, Wellington and Whangarei; and in the South Island in Blenheim, Christchurch, Dunedin, Hokitika, Invercargill, Nelson and Timaru. The local DOC often sells a selection of DOSLI maps of the tracks in its immediate area.

DOSLI has various series of maps for specific uses. Parkmaps are produced for national, state and forest parks, and there are Trackmaps for some of the more popular walking tracks. There are also Holiday-maker maps, Touringmaps, Terrainmaps and Streetfinder maps and larger Aotearoa and Pacific maps covering all of New Zealand and many Pacific islands. The most detailed are the Topomaps series of topographical maps. They have the best details, but the problem is you may need two or three maps to cover one track. The maps cost about $12.50 each.

Track Classification

Tracks are classified according to their difficulty and many other features – how they are marked, degree of steepness etc. In this chapter we loosely refer to the level of difficulty, eg easy, medium, hard and difficult. The track classification system is relatively new but you will often hear the various classifications used. They are:

Path – easy and well formed; allows for wheelchair access or constructed to 'shoe' standard. Suitable for people of all ages and fitness levels.

Walking Track – easy and well formed; constructed to 'shoe' standard. Suitable for people of most ages and fitness levels.

Tramping Track – requires skill and experience. Constructed to 'boot' standard. Suitable for people of average physical fitness.

Route – requires a high degree of skill, experience and route-finding ability. Suitable for well-equipped trampers.

Track Safety

It's very important that you learn and follow some basic rules of safety if you'll be out tramping in New Zealand. Thousands of Kiwis and overseas visitors tramp in New Zealand every year without incident, but every year a few die in the mountains. Most fatalities could have been avoided if simple safety rules had been observed.

The main thing to be aware of when tramping in NZ is the extremely changeable weather. New Zealand has a maritime climate, which means that if you come from any of the large land masses with a continental climate (eg Australia, North America, Europe) you will be surprised by the degree and frequency of climate changes.

Always remember that the weather can change extremely quickly. Heavy rain, snow and high winds can hit mountain areas *even in summer*, and it can happen in a matter of minutes even on a warm sunny day. Always be mentally and physically prepared for all kinds of weather. Take along warm clothes, waterproof rain gear (raincoat and overtrousers) and a waterproof pack liner. If you should find your clothing and footwear are not adequate for the conditions, it's best to turn back.

Weather forecasts should be watched but taken with a grain of salt. New Zealand's prevailing weather comes from the southwest, an area which has no inhabited land and very little sea or air traffic, making accurate reporting difficult. In Fiordland it is considered that the forecast weather hits the area a day before it is forecast.

Hypothermia is the main health hazard to look out for when tramping in New Zealand. Be aware of what causes it so you can avoid it, and know what to do about it if it does occur. (Hypothermia is covered in the Health section of this book; see the Facts for the Visitor chapter.)

Drowning was once called the 'New Zealand disease'. Never attempt to cross a river when it is in flood. Many tracks have an emergency wire crossing upstream. If there is no emergency crossing, backtrack to shelter or wait until the creek or river subsides. You would be well advised to learn and practice river crossing techniques.

Getting lost is another very real danger, so stick to the tracks. It is another quirk of New Zealand that getting lost in the bush is more of a danger here than in many other places. The native bush is very dense. People have become hopelessly lost even when having set off to do something as simple as a 15-minute walk, and have only been found many days later or even not at all. It sounds so strange it's almost comical, but if you spend any length of time in New Zealand and keep up with the news you'll start to notice that people go missing in the bush quite frequently; and it's not always overseas visitors either, it's often experienced trampers who know the area they're tramping in.

Always make sure someone responsible knows where you're going, what route you intend to take, when you expect to come out, and that they must notify the police if you don't come out. Don't forget to let them know when you've come out safely!

Fill out an intentions and/or help form at the DOC office, national park headquarters, visitors centre or whatever at the start of the trip, and write in the logbooks of huts along the way, giving the names of the members of your party and details about when you were there and where you are going when you leave. Do this even if you don't stay in the huts – it will make it far easier to find you if you should go missing.

For safe tramping make sure you:

- Choose a track that suits your level of fitness and experience.
- Find out what to expect on the track. Always seek local advice about current track and weather conditions from the proper authority – the local DOC office, national park headquarters, etc – before you set out.
- Go with at least one other person, and stay on the track.
- Be sure to purify river or lake water before drinking it.
- Take along a first-aid kit and everything else you're supposed to – water purifier, warm clothes, etc.
- If you meet heavy rain, and rivers in your path have risen, stay where you are until the rivers go down, retrace your tracks, or take another route. Don't ever cross a flooding river unless you are absolutely certain you can get across safely.

The NZ Mountain Safety Council has published a number of pamphlets with good information on tramping, with titles like *Bushcraft, Mountaincraft, Outdoor First Aid, Hypothermia, Survival* etc. They are widely available at information centres and hostels. The DOC can also give you excellent safety advice. It's worth talking to them about it.

Going with tramping clubs can be a great way to tramp in New Zealand, as you'll be with like-minded people who know about the bush. Federated Mountain Clubs (PO Box 1604, Wellington) has information on local clubs all around New Zealand.

Accommodation & Wardens

The following notes on huts and wardens apply only to the popular 'tourist' tracks. Keep these factors in mind:

- When walking allow about four km per hour on easy ground.
- Huts are usually placed three to four hours apart.
- Huts usually cater for 24 or more, and beds are thick foam mattresses on bunks.
- Huts on the more popular tracks usually have wood stoves for heating and gas burners for cooking.
- There is a two-night limit on huts, if they are full.

If you venture off the popular tracks onto any other tracks, things will be quite different. For example, it may take you an hour to cover one km, huts may be eight hours or so apart, there won't be any wardens and you will have to be much better prepared.

Above all else, *toitu te whenua* – leave the earth undisturbed.

Camping on tracks is allowed on all except the Milford Track. On Great Walks tracks, where the huts can fill up, camping areas are provided beside all the huts for overflow. On the Milford and Routeburn tracks numbers are regulated so huts don't get overloaded.

The NZ Environmental Care Code provides guidelines for camping (it is reproduced in this chapter). Always leave firewood in huts for the next group, in case they arrive in heavy rain or the dark.

In the last decade or so, there has been an amazing improvement in the conditions of tracks and huts. Tracks are administered by

New Zealand's Environmental Care Code

1 **Protect plants and animals.** Treat New Zealand's forests and birds with care and respect. They are unique and often rare.

2 **Remove rubbish.** Litter is unattractive, harmful to wildlife and can increase vermin and disease. Plan your visits so as to reduce rubbish, and carry out what you carry in.

3 **Bury toilet waste.** In areas without toilet facilities, bury your toilet waste in a shallow hole well away from waterways, tracks, camp sites and huts.

4 **Keep streams and lakes clean.** When cleaning and washing, wash well away from the water source. Because soaps and detergents are harmful to water life, drain used water into the soil to allow it to be filtered. If you suspect the water may be contaminated, either boil it for at least three minutes, filter it, or chemically treat it.

5 **Take care with fires.** Portable fuel stoves are less harmful to the environment and are more efficient than fires. If you do use a fire, keep it small, use only dead wood and make sure it is out by dousing it with water and checking the ashes before leaving.

6 **Camp carefully.** When camping, *leave no trace of your visit.*

7 **Keep to the track.** By keeping to the track, you lessen the chance of damaging fragile plants.

8 **Consider others.** People visit the back country and rural areas for many reasons. Be considerate of other visitors who also have a right to enjoy the natural environment.

9 **Respect cultural heritage.** Many places in New Zealand have a spiritual and historical significance. Treat these places with consideration and respect.

10 **Enjoy your visit.** Enjoy your outdoor experience. Take a last look before leaving an area; will the next visitor know that you have been there?

Protect the environment for your own sake, for the sake of those who come after you, and for the environment itself.

Toitu te whenua – Leave the land undisturbed. ■

DOC officers and wardens; the former are permanent staff, well trained and very knowledgeable. The wardens are temporary; usually employed for the summer season to keep an eye on and maintain the huts, to provide track information and first aid, to collect hut fees and be helpful to trampers.

Wardens in the national parks collect hut fees when they're on duty, from November to April. Whether a warden is present or not, it's important that you always pay your hut fees, as all huts require maintenance and this is how it is paid for. Most DOC offices in the regional centres near the start of tracks sell back country hut tickets (see later in this section). Check with wardens or DOC staff in the regional offices for weather forecasts and track information.

Hut & Camping Fees The DOC has a network of back country huts in the national, maritime and forest parks. Hut fees range from $4 to a maximum of $30 per night for adults, paid with tickets purchased in advance at any DOC office or park visitors' centre. The tickets cost $4 each (you can buy them in booklets) and are valid for 15 months. Children under 11 years of age can use all huts free of charge. Children who are 11 years and older are charged half price and use a special 'youth ticket'.

Huts are classed into four categories and, depending on the category, a night's accommodation may require one or two tickets, except on Great Walks where special passes are required. On arrival at a hut, you simply date the tickets and deposit them in the box provided. Hut accommodation is on a first come, first served basis.

The best, category one, huts have cookers and fuel, bunks or sleeping platforms with mattresses, toilet and washing facilities, and a water supply. They may also have lighting, heating, radio communications, drying facilities, and a hut warden on duty. category one huts are found on the Great Walks, where Great Walks passes are required (see the following section). The cost in Great Walks huts ranges from $6 to $30 per night (youths are charged half price).

Category two huts have bunks or sleeping platforms with mattresses, toilet and washing facilities, and a water supply. They may also include cooking and heating facilities, but you may have to provide your own cooker and fuel. The cost is $8 (two tickets) per night.

Category three huts are more basic, with bunks or sleeping platforms (but no mattresses), toilet and water supply only. You provide your own cooker and fuel. These huts are $4 (one ticket) per night.

There is no fee for category four huts, which are usually just simple shelters – no bunks or other amenities.

Camping is permitted outside the huts (but not the ones on the Milford); the cost is $6.

If you plan to do much tramping, consider getting an Annual Hut Pass. The pass allows you to stay overnight at all category two and three huts on a first come, first served basis, and to camp outside all category one huts where this is allowed. The cost is $58 (children $29) and the pass is valid for one year from the date of purchase. It does not apply to the Great Walks.

A list of all huts and their categories is available at any DOC office. The Milford Track operates on a system all its own.

The Great Walks

All of the Great Walks are described in this book. The descriptions are designed to whet your appetite rather than deluge you with information. They are covered in detail in the pamphlets provided by DOC offices (and information centres) and in Lonely Planet's *Tramping in New Zealand* by Jim DuFresne & Jeff Williams. For information on a particular walk go to the relevant section, eg the Lake Waikaremoana Circuit is covered under Te Urewera National Park in the East Coast chapter. The Great Walks are:

- Lake Waikaremoana, Te Urewera National Park (North Island) – a three to four-day, easy to medium tramp with great views of the lake and surrounding bush-clad slopes.
- Tongariro Northern Circuit, Tongariro National Park (North Island) – a four-day, medium to hard

tramp through an active volcanic landscape. Part of this tramp can be done as the one-day Tongariro Crossing.

- Abel Tasman Coastal Track, Abel Tasman National Park (South Island) – an easy, two to three-day walk along the coast and close to beaches and bays. It is NZ's most popular walk so be prepared for lots of people!
- Heaphy Track, Kahurangi National Park (South Island) – a four to five-day, medium to hard tramp of 77 km through forest and limestone (karst) landscape. The last day is one of the great beach walks.
- Routeburn, Mt Aspiring and Fiordland national parks (South Island) – a medium, 40-km, three-day walk through stunning alpine scenery. It is now necessary to book a place on this walk.
- Milford, Fiordland National Park (South Island) – this 54-km, four-day/three-night walk is one of the best known in the world. It includes views of river valleys, glaciers, waterfalls and an alpine pass crossing. Bookings are essential.
- Kepler, Fiordland National Park (South Island) – this 67-km, four to five-day walk is a medium to hard tramp. It climbs to the top of a mountain and includes alpine, lake and river valley scenery.
- Rakiura Track (Stewart Island) – a three-day tramp, mostly on duckboards, for which medium fitness is required. The track goes along the coast and through forest.

The canoe trip down the Whanganui River in Whanganui National Park in the North Island is obviously not a walk – they call it the Whanganui Journey – but it, too, is one of the Great Walks (the Matemateonga Walkway is nearby).

Accommodation Ordinary tickets for back country huts and Annual Hut Passes are not valid on the Great Walks; all Great Walks require a special Great Walks Pass for that particular walk. These are sold at DOC offices, national park offices and other places in the vicinity of each walk; the local DOC office can advise you of all the places selling the passes.

The passes cost different amounts for different walks, but they are not expensive. They allow you either to use the huts or to camp in the designated camping grounds, whichever you prefer. Bring camping gear, since at peak times (summer, Easter weekend, etc) the huts can fill up.

On some tracks – the Tongariro Northern Circuit and the Whanganui Journey, for example – Great Walks passes are necessary only at certain times of year, when the tracks are busiest. During the times of year when Great Walks passes are not required on these tracks, ordinary back country hut tickets and Annual Hut Passes are accepted.

In addition to the back country huts, DOC also maintains over 100 camping grounds; these are outlined in the appropriate place in the various chapters.

Don't forget your walking pass if you're heading for the Great Walks

Other Tracks

In addition to the Great Walks there are numerous other tramping possibilities in all forest and national parks, especially Arthur's Pass, the Nelson Lakes, Coromandel and, of course, Mt Egmont/Taranaki. These are merely some of the possibilities:

North Island

- Ninety Mile Beach-Cape Reinga Walkway (Northland) – a 50-km, three-day, easy tramp. There are no huts but there are plenty of places to camp on this beach walk.
- Coromandel Track (Coromandel Peninsula) – an easy to medium, three-day walk near the Pinnacles at the top of Kauaeranga Valley in the Coromandel Forest Park.
- Great Barrier Forest Track (Great Barrier Island) – a four-day, easy to medium loop walk. There is the opportunity to see historic kauri dams, regenerating forest and hot springs.

- Tongariro Crossing (Tongariro National Park) – a long one-day, medium tramp designed to introduce the fit tramper to this active volcanic landscape.
- Round the Mountain, Mt Egmont/Taranaki, (Egmont National Park) – a 55-km walk of four days or more (depending on which of the many side trips you do). It is medium to hard tramping through forest and mountainous country.
- Mt Holdsworth Circuit & Totara Flats Track (Holdsworth, Tararua Forest Park) – two three-day tramps. The first tramp is a medium to hard walk through forest and over the top of alpine Mt Holdsworth. The second is a medium tramp mostly along the Totara River Valley, with three low saddles to cross.

South Island

- Queen Charlotte Walkway (Marlborough Sounds) – a three to four-day, medium walk from which you get great views of the Sounds and pass many historic places.
- Travers-Sabine Circuit & D'Urville Valley Track (Nelson Lakes National Park) – these are five to six-day circular tracks for experienced trampers only. The first is 80 km long and includes alpine passes and river valleys. The second is about 65 km and also includes a high-altitude pass.
- Wangapeka & Leslie-Karamea tracks (Kahurangi National Park) – the first is a four to five-day, medium tramp through river valleys and over passes (a good return walk after the Heaphy). The second is a 90-100 km, five to seven-day tramp for the experienced only. It includes river valleys, gorges and passes.
- Arthur's Pass tramps (Arthur's Pass National Park) – there are many walks to choose from in this park including Goat Pass, Three Passes, Harper Pass and Cass-Lagoon Saddle. Most tramps in this great park are difficult.
- St James Walkway (Lake Sumner Forest Park/Lewis Pass Reserve) – this 66-km, five-day, medium walk passes through subalpine scenery.
- Banks Peninsula Walk (private/public land near Akaroa) – a two-day (medium) or four-day (easy) walk over the hills and along the coast of Banks Peninsula. You have to book accommodation in advance.
- Mt Somers Subalpine Walkway (Canterbury Foothills) – a medium, three-day walk through river valleys, subalpine forest and pastures. There are harder variations for the fitter tramper.
- Inland Pack & Croesus tracks (Paparoa National Park) – the first of these walks, a medium tramp, follows river valleys through the karst landscape near Punakaiki on the West Coast. The second walk is a medium two-day crossing of the Paparoa Range from Blackball to Barrytown.
- Copland Valley & Pass (Mt Cook & Westland national parks) – the trip to Welcome Flat Hut and springs is a medium overnight tramp. The four-day alpine crossing of the Copland Pass from Mt Cook to Westland is extremely difficult and you are advised to engage the services of a guide.
- Matukituki Valley Walks (Mt Aspiring National Park) – there are a number of good walks in the Matukituki valley near Wanaka. The difficult Cascade Saddle Route joins this region with the Rees-Dart valleys.
- Greenstone/Caples tracks (Stewardship land just outside Fiordland National Park) – these two tracks are close to the Routeburn and a good way to finish this popular track.
- Rees-Dart Track (mostly Mt Aspiring National Park) – a 70-km, four to five-day, medium to hard walk through river valleys and over an alpine pass.
- Hollyford Track (Fiordland National Park) – there are several variants on this track but it will take eight days if you walk in and walk out, four days if you fly one way. It traverses through low level forest, often on muddy tracks, and includes lake, alpine, rainforest and coastal scenery.
- Dusky & George Sound tracks (Fiordland National Park) – just a couple more examples of the great wealth of tramping in this World Heritage region. The Dusky is a very challenging tramp, as is the George Sound route – you need lots of time if you plan to tramp in this region.
- North-West Circuit (Stewart Island – Rakiura) – this eight to 10-day route is just one of the many possibilities on Rakiura. The whole island offers the chance for wilderness walks.

Getting There & Away

Getting to and from tracks can be a real problem. Having a vehicle only simplifies the problem of getting there. Having two vehicles allows the positioning of one at each end of the track. If you have no vehicle then you have to take public transport or hitch in, and if the track starts or ends at the end of a dead-end road, hitching will be difficult. Fortunately, with the far greater number of trampers now walking NZ's tracks there is also more backpacker transport available.

Leave excess luggage behind or send it on to a point near the end of the track. Camping grounds and other accommodation places will often hold luggage for free. Bus companies will carry excess luggage at a very reasonable price and will hold it in their offices until it is picked up.

SKIING

New Zealand is one of the most popular places for skiing in the southern hemisphere. In addition to downhill (alpine) skiing, there are ample opportunities for cross-country downhill, ski touring, ski mountaineering and snowboarding. One ski area, the Waiorau Nordic Ski Area in the Pisa Range near Wanaka, specialises in Nordic skiing, but many of the downhill ski areas have areas with cross-country possibilities.

Heli-skiing is another attraction of skiing in New Zealand. New Zealand seems to have more helicopters than it knows what to do with and in winter many are used to lift skiers up to the top of long, isolated stretches of virgin snow, or even onto glaciers. The cost of these flights is surprisingly reasonable.

New Zealand's commercial ski areas are generally not very well endowed with on-field chalets, lodges or hotels. The places to stay are in surrounding towns, sometimes nearby and sometimes quite a long distance from the slopes. Either way, daily transport to and from the ski areas can be easily arranged. Often there's a good variety of accommodation in the nearby towns, ranging from cheap hostels to high-class hotels and ski lodges.

Club ski areas are open to the public and you are welcome to ski there; they are cheaper and much less crowded than the commercial ski areas. Although non-members pay a slightly higher rate, they can still work out to be cheaper than the commercial areas. There is usually accommodation at the areas, subject to availability; they may be fully booked during the busiest times, such as winter holidays or weekends, but mid-week you'll have no trouble finding a place to stay.

At the major ski areas, lifts cost from $35 to $55 a day and two-hour group lessons are around $35/$20 an hour for adults/children. These costs are much less at the smaller resorts. All the usual equipment can be bought or hired in NZ; for between $25 and $30/15 an adult/child can be fitted out.

The ski season is generally from June to October, although it varies considerably from one ski area to another. Snow-making machines assist nature at some areas.

There are plenty of ski-package tours both from Australia and within New Zealand. Information centres in New Zealand, and the NZTB internationally, have brochures on the various ski areas and packages available, and can make bookings.

The *New Zealand Ski & Snowboard Guide* by Brown Bear is an excellent free, annual reference filled with information on all the commercial and club ski areas in NZ. It has colour illustrations of the ski areas and ski runs, and information on heli-skiing, glacier skiing and so on.

North Island

Whakapapa Whakapapa ski area, the largest in New Zealand with a 161-hectare groomed area, is six km above Whakapapa Village on Mt Ruapehu in Tongariro National Park. It's the end of the road – known as the Top of the Bruce – and has the most popular ski slopes in NZ, including a downhill course dropping

On the piste? It's all downhill from here!

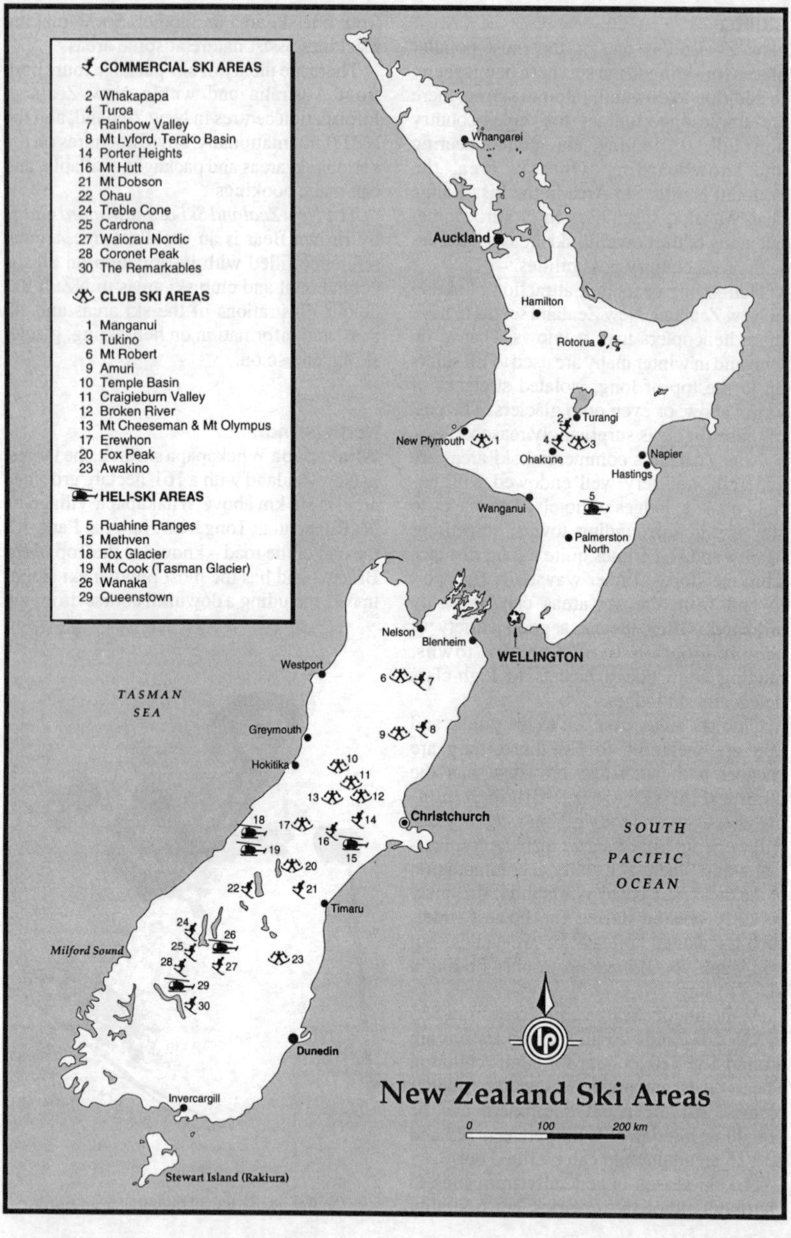
COMMERCIAL SKI AREAS
2 Whakapapa
4 Turoa
7 Rainbow Valley
8 Mt Lyford, Terako Basin
14 Porter Heights
16 Mt Hutt
21 Mt Dobson
22 Ohau
24 Treble Cone
25 Cardrona
27 Waiorau Nordic
28 Coronet Peak
30 The Remarkables
CLUB SKI AREAS
1 Manganui
3 Tukino
6 Mt Robert
9 Amuri
10 Temple Basin
11 Craigieburn Valley
12 Broken River
13 Mt Cheeseman & Mt Olympus
17 Erewhon
20 Fox Peak
23 Awakino
HELI-SKI AREAS
5 Ruahine Ranges
15 Methven
18 Fox Glacier
19 Mt Cook (Tasman Glacier)
26 Wanaka
29 Queenstown
Whangarei
Auckland
Hamilton
Rotorua
Turangi
New Plymouth
Ohakune
Napier
Hastings
Wanganui
Palmerston North
Nelson
Blenheim
WELLINGTON
Westport
TASMAN SEA
Greymouth
Hokitika
Christchurch
SOUTH PACIFIC OCEAN
Timaru
Milford Sound
Dunedin
Invercargill
Stewart Island (Rakiura)
New Zealand Ski Areas
0
100
200 km

nearly 675 metres over four km. There are chairlifts, T-bars, platters and rope tows, and plenty of possibilities for snowboarding including excellent pipes off the far western T-bar, cross-country, downhill, ski touring, and paragliding. The normal season is from June to mid-November.

Accommodation can be found at Whakapapa Village within the national park (see the Tongariro National Park section in the Central Plateau chapter), or in nearby towns including National Park (12 km away), Turangi and Ohakune (each about 50 km away). Accommodation bookings are very heavy during the ski season, especially on weekends, so make sure you plan ahead.

You can drive yourself up to the slopes or you can take a shuttle minibus from Whakapapa Village, National Park or Turangi; a taxi service is available from Ohakune.

Contact: Ruapehu Alpine Lifts Ltd, Private Bag, Mt Ruapehu (☎ (07) 892 3738, snowphone (07) 892 3833).

Turoa Around the other side of Mt Ruapehu from the Whakapapa ski area, the Turoa ski area on the south-western side of Mt Ruapehu is the country's second largest ski area. Quad and triple chairlifts, T-bars and platters take you up to the beginning of a four-km run. There's also a beginner's lift, snowboarding and cross-country downhill skiing. There is no road toll or parking fee and daily ski area transport is available from Ohakune, 17 km away, where there's plenty of accommodation – once again, accommodation bookings can be heavy during the ski season, especially for the more economical places, so plan ahead.

Ohakune has the liveliest après-ski scene in the North Island. There are three cafeterias and a snack shack on the ski area. Skis can be hired on the slopes or at many places around Ohakune. The season lasts from June to November.

Contact: Turoa Ski Resort Ltd, PO Box 46, Ohakune (☎ (06) 385 8456, snowphone (0900) 99 444).

Tukino This is a club-operated ski area, on the eastern side of Mt Ruapehu. The area is 50 km from Turangi, and it's quite remote – you have to traverse 14 km of gravel road once you leave the sealed Desert Rd (SH1), and you need a 4WD vehicle to get in (or make a prior arrangement to use the club transport). Because access is so limited, the area is uncrowded, however it is most suitable for the beginner or intermediate skier, since there are only a couple of advanced runs.

Accommodation is available at ski clubs here. It has a short season, July to October, because it is on the opposite side of the mountain from prevailing winds.

Contact: Tukino Mountain Clubs Association, 11 Grendon Rd, Titirangi (☎ (09) 817 8987, snowphone (06) 387 6294).

Manganui Ski Area, Mt Taranaki There's more volcano-slope skiing on the eastern slopes of Mt Taranaki in the Egmont National Park at the Manganui club ski area, 22 km from Stratford. You get to the ski area after a 20-minute walk along the scenic Manganui Gorge from the car park. It has a T-bar and three rope tows, and there is a day-visitor canteen. The season here is from mid-June to mid-September. There is limited accommodation on the ski area and at the Stratford Mountain House, with more accommodation available in Stratford and New Plymouth.

Early summer skiing is possible off the summit of Mt Taranaki; when conditions permit, it is an invigorating two-hour climb to the crater but an exhilarating 1300-metre descent.

Contact: Stratford Mountain Club, c/o 32 Mountain Rd, RD2 Stratford, (snowphone (06) 765 7669).

South Island

Coronet Peak New Zealand's southernmost slopes, near Queenstown, are rated the best in New Zealand and are comparable to any in the world. The season, mid-June to October, is reliable because of a multimillion dollar snow-making system. Access to the ski area is from Queenstown, 18 km away, and there's a shuttle bus service in the ski season. The rich often catch a helicopter.

Chairlifts, T-bars and beginners' lifts take you up the slopes. The treeless slopes and good snow provide excellent skiing – the chairlifts run to altitudes of 1585 and 1620 metres. Consistent gradient and the many undulations make this a snowboarder's paradise.

The ski area is operated by the Mt Cook Group and they have a licensed restaurant, overnight ski storage, a ski repair shop and ski lessons. The lift tickets are also valid at the Remarkables. For accommodation see the Queenstown section in the Otago chapter; there are a multiplicity of après-ski possibilities.

Contact: Mt Cook Group, PO Box 359, Queenstown (☎ (03) 442 4640, snowphone (0900) 34 444).

The Remarkables Like Coronet Peak, The Remarkables ski area is near Queenstown (23 km away), with shuttle buses running from Queenstown during the season (late June to late October). It, too, has beginner, intermediate and advanced level runs, with chairlifts and beginners' tows. Passes for Coronet Peak and The Remarkables, including weekend and multi-day passes, can be used interchangeably at either ski area. There is a $10 access road toll to The Remarkables.

Both Coronet Peak and The Remarkables have designated ski school areas, with group, private, and children's lessons. The Remarkables also offers a Nordic ski school with cross-country downhill skiing lessons. Snowboarding instruction is also available.

Contact: Mt Cook Group Ltd, PO Box 359, Queenstown (☎ (03) 442 4615, snowphone (0900) 34 444).

Treble Cone The season at Treble Cone, 29 km from Wanaka in the southern lake district, is from mid-June to mid-October. Reliability has been improved with the extension of snow-making to the top of the Deliverance chair. The highest of the areas in the southern lake area, Treble Cone is spectacularly situated overlooking Lake Wanaka. Slopes are steep and best for intermediate to advanced skiers. It has a chairlift, two T-bars and one learner tow, and a lift-serviced, natural half-pipe for snowboarding. Accommodation is available in Wanaka and shuttle buses run from there or from Queenstown, 1½ hours away; there is a $7 toll on the access road.

Contact: Treble Cone Ski Area, PO Box 206, Wanaka (☎ (03) 443 7443, snowphone (0900) 34 444).

Cardrona Cardrona is 33 km from Wanaka and is open from mid-June to mid-October. It has three chairlifts, a couple of beginners' tows and a radical half-pipe for snowboarders. It has numerous gentle runs to choose from over variable terrain suitable for beginning and intermediate level skiers. Buses run from Wanaka during the ski season, or from Queenstown, about 1½ hours away. There is a licensed cafeteria in the main facilities complex.

Cardrona has acquired a reputation for its services offered to disabled skiers and it is the first resort in the South Island to have an on-field crèche.

Contact: Cardrona Ski Resort, PO Box 117, Wanaka (☎ (03) 443 7411, snowphone (0900) 34 444).

Waiorau Nordic Area New Zealand's only commercial Nordic ski area is 26 km from Wanaka, on the Pisa Range high above Lake Wanaka. There are 25 km of groomed trails and thousands of hectares of open rolling country for the ski tourer. Huts with facilities are dotted along the top of the Pisa Range. So whichever Nordic or cross-country discipline you are into – skating, day or overnight touring, cross-country downhill – it is catered for here. The season is from late June to late September.

Contact: Waiorau Nordic Ski Area, Private Bag, Wanaka (☎ (03) 443 7542).

Awakino This is a club ski area on Mt St Mary in the Waitaki Valley, about 12 km from Kurow and 66 km from Omarama.

Awakino is known to get the odd powder blast during southerly storms but essentially it is for intermediate skiers. The season is from July to October. Although it has just three rope lifts, most of the runs are for intermediate and advanced skiers. There is good cross-country touring nearby. There's accommodation 500 metres below the main rope lift or at Kurow or Omarama. Access to the area is by 4WD.

Contact: Waitaki Ski Club, PO Box 191, Oamaru (☎ (03) 434 5110).

South Canterbury Region There are three ski areas in South Canterbury – Ohau, Mt Dobson and Fox Peak. The Mt Dobson and Fox Peak ski areas are between Fairlie and Tekapo, on the main Christchurch to Mt Cook road. Both towns are good bases for skiing in this region.

The most distant from Christchurch, the **Ohau** commercial ski area is 45 km from Twizel and has the longest T-bar in the southern hemisphere. It is situated on Mt Sutton and has a large percentage of intermediate and advanced runs, plus excellent terrain for snowboarding, cross-country downhill and ski touring to Lake Dumb Bell. Accommodation is available at the Lake Ohau Lodge, 15 minutes from the slopes, or in Twizel, 42 km away. The ski season is from July to October.

Contact: Ohau Ski Area Ltd, PO Box 51, Twizel (☎ & snowphone (03) 438 9885).

A three-km-wide basin provides **Mt Dobson**, a commercial ski area 26 km from Fairlie, with New Zealand's largest learners' area, as well as possibilities for intermediate and advanced skiers. From the summit of Mt Dobson, on a clear day, you can see Mt Cook and the Pacific Ocean. Accommodation is in Fairlie and Lake Tekapo. The season is from late June to mid-October.

Contact: Mt Dobson Ski Area Ltd, Alloway Rd, Fairlie (☎ (03) 685 8039, snowphone (0900) 39 888).

The **Fox Peak** club ski area, 23 km from Fairlie in the Two Thumb Range, has five rope tows; Skid Row, the learners' lift, is free. There is good ski touring from the summit of Fox Peak and parapenting is also popular here. There's accommodation at the ski area at Fox Lodge, or in Fairlie, 35 minutes away. The season is from early July to late September.

Contact: Fox Peak Ski Club, PO Box 368, Timaru (☎ (03) 688 1870, snowphone (03) 688 0044).

Mt Hutt Mt Hutt is one of the highest ski areas in the southern hemisphere and is rated as one of the best in New Zealand. It's 104 km west of Christchurch and you can get there by bus from Christchurch or from the local accommodation centres of Methven and Ashburton.

Mt Hutt has beginner, intermediate and advanced-level slopes, with a quad and a triple chairlift, three T-bars, various other lifts, and heli-skiing from the car park to slopes further afield. Instruction is offered at all levels, and there's also racing and racing instruction. The wide open faces are good for those learning to snowboard.

The ski season here is very long, usually from early May to mid-October, and is made reliable by extensive snow-making facilities. There's a variety of accommodation in Methven, 26 km away, or you can stay at Ashburton, 35 km from Methven on SH1.

Contact: Mt Hutt Ski & Alpine Tourist Co, PO Box 14, Methven (☎ (03) 302 8811, snowphone (0900) 34 444).

Erewhon The Erewhon club ski area must be one of the best gems in New Zealand. It is based on Mt Potts, above the headwaters of the Rangitata River, and is about 75 km from Methven. It has four rope lifts and one learners' lift. Accommodation and meals are available from a lodge at Mt Potts, eight km from the ski area. It has a good mix of beginner, intermediate and advanced slopes, with snowboarding and cross-country downhill also popular. Transport by 4WD is essential, and can be arranged through the club. The season is from June to September.

Contact: Erewhon Ski Club, c/o Mount Somers Station, Mt Somers (snowphone (03) 308 7091).

Porter Heights The closest commercial ski area to Christchurch, Porter Heights is about 90 km from Christchurch on the Arthur's Pass road. The 720-metre-long 'Big Mama' is the steepest run in New Zealand. There are three T-bars, one platter lift and a learners' tow. There's a half-pipe for snowboarders, plus good cross-country downhill areas, and ski touring out along the ridge. The season runs from mid-June to mid-October. Accommodation is available at the area or in neighbouring Springfield. The Snowman Shuttle & Tours (☎ (03) 364 7223) provides economical transport to and from the ski area ($4); there is a $6 toll on the access road.

Contact: Porter Heights Skifield, PO Box 536, Christchurch (☎ (03) 379 7087, snowphone (0900) 34 444).

Arthur's Pass & Craigieburn Regions There are five ski areas in the Arthur's Pass and Craigieburn regions.

The most distant from Christchurch, **Temple Basin**, is a club area just four km from the Arthur's Pass township. It is a 45-minute walk uphill from the car park to the lift area where there are four rope tows. From the summit of Mt Temple, on a clear day, you can see all the way from the Tasman Sea to the Pacific Ocean. At night there's flood-lit night skiing. Accommodation is available at two lodges on the area, or in Arthur's Pass. The season is from June to October. There are good back-country runs for snowboarders.

Contact: Temple Basin Ski Club, PO Box 1228, Christchurch (☎ (03) 355 9480, snowphone (03) 366 5865).

The **Craigieburn Valley** ski area, centred on Hamilton Peak, is 40 km from Arthur's Pass, 48 km from Springfield and 110 km from Christchurch. It is one of New Zealand's most challenging club areas, with mostly intermediate and advanced runs and a shredder's 'soggy dream'. It is a pleasant 10-minute walk through beech forest from the car park to the ski area. The season is from early July to mid-October.

Contact: Craigieburn Valley Ski Club, PO Box 2152, Christchurch (☎ (03) 348 2842, snowphone (03) 366 6644).

It is possible to ski from Craigieburn to the **Broken River** club ski area, 50 minutes away, where the ski passes are interchangeable; it will take twice that time to ski back, so plan accordingly. Otherwise access to Broken River is unsealed for the last six km, after which it's a 15-minute walk to the lodges and a further 10-minute walk to the ski area. Accommodation is available in three lodges, or you can stay in Springfield, 40 minutes away; it's 1½ hours to Christchurch. The season is from late June to late October.

Contact: Broken River Ski Club, PO Box 2718, Christchurch (☎ (03) 318 8713, snowphone (03) 366 6644).

Another good club area in the Craigieburn Range is **Mt Cheeseman**, 112 km from Christchurch. The ski area, based on Mt Cockayne, has a T-bar and a platter serving the wide, sheltered basin. Accommodation is available at two lodges at the area, or in Springfield. The season is from early July to late September. Transport to Cheeseman and Porter Heights is available with Mountain Adventures Shuttle & Tours (☎ (03) 355 3320).

Contact: Mt Cheeseman Ski Club, PO Box 22178, Christchurch (☎ (03) 379 5315, snowphone (03) 366 6644).

The fifth ski area is **Mt Olympus**. Hard to find, but worth the search, Mt Olympus, is 66 km from Methven and 12 km from Lake Ida. This club area has four tows which lead to a number of intermediate and advanced runs. It is on the south side of the Craigieburn Range, and the southerly aspect means that there is often good powder. Snowboarding is accepted, there are good cross-country downhill areas and ski-touring trails to other areas. Accommodation is available on the field and in a lower lodge, or there's accommodation in Methven. 4WD is advisable from the bottom hut. The season is from early July to October.

Contact: Windwhistle Winter Sports Club, PO Box 25055, Christchurch (☎ (03) 329 1823, snowphone (03) 366 5865).

Hanmer Springs Region There are three ski areas near Hanmer Springs. **Amuri**, a club area based on Mt St Patrick, is 27 km from Hanmer Springs and has a poma and two rope tows leading to runs suiting all types of skiers. There's accommodation at the area, or you can stay in Hanmer Springs, 45 minutes away. The season is from early July to mid-September.

Contact: Amuri Ski Area, PO Box 129, Hanmer Springs (☎ (03) 315 7125, snowphone (03) 366 5865).

New Zealand's newest commercial ski area is **Mt Lyford**, 60 km from Kaikoura, and 3.5 km from Mt Lyford Village, where accommodation is available. The Lake Stella field has skiing at all levels, basin and off-piste cross-country downhill skiing, 15 km of groomed trails for ski touring, and a natural pipe for snowboarding. Mt Lyford has been built in conjunction with a wilderness retreat where there is ice skating, fishing, golf and hot pools. It is open from early June to mid-October; there is a $5 toll on the access road.

The nearby **Terako Basin** ski field is being developed for advanced skiers and has separate access to Mt Lyford.

Contact: Mt Lyford Ski Area, Private Bag, Waiau, North Canterbury (☎ (03) 315 6178, snowphone (03) 366 5865).

Nelson Region In the north, near St Arnaud in Nelson Lakes National Park, there are two ski areas. The **Rainbow Valley** commercial ski area is just outside the park. There is a double chair and a T-bar which lift skiers to the top of a spacious bowl, two learners' tows, and it's good for cross-country ski touring. Accommodation is available in St Arnaud or in Nelson or Blenheim, each 1½ hours away. The season is from mid-June to mid-October; there is an $8 toll on the access road.

Contact: Rainbow Valley Ski Area, Private Bag, St Arnaud (☎ (03) 521 1861, snowphone (0900) 34 444).

Inside the park, 15 km from St Arnaud, **Mt Robert** is a club area with two lodges right at the ski area, but it's a 1½-hour walk from the car park, seven km from St Arnaud, to reach it. On weekends a helicopter lift is available from the car park (about $35 per person). This area is known for its powder and there are many cross-country opportunities for the suitably equipped. The season is from mid-June to late October.

Contact: Nelson Ski Club Inc, PO Box 344, Nelson (snowphone (03) 548 8336).

Heli-Skiing & Glacier Skiing

If you want to try heli-skiing New Zealand is a great place for it. Harris Mountains Heli-Skiing, based in Wanaka and Queenstown, has been suggested by many as the pick of the bunch. It operates from July to October over a wide area with over 100 peaks and 200 runs to choose from in The Remarkables, the Harris Mountains, the Buchanans Range, and the Branches, plus the Tyndall Glacier. They can be contacted at 99 Ardmore St, Wanaka (☎ (03) 443 7930). Three runs in a day, in the shoulder season, will cost $525, five runs $640 and eight runs $850.

Other heli-skiing companies in the South Island include:

Southern Lakes Heliski, based in Queenstown (☎ (03) 442 9792)
Alpine Guides Mt Cook, based in Mt Cook Village (☎ (03) 435 1834)
Methven Heli-ski, based in Methven (☎ (03) 302 8108, 302 8774)
Mt Hutt Heli-Ski, based in Rakaia (☎ (03) 302 8401)

In the North Island, Snowrange Heli-skiing does guided heli-ski trips to the Ruahine Ranges, south-east of Mt Ruapehu, operating from July to October. They are based in Taihape (☎ (06) 388 1696).

Although it is not strictly necessary to fly up to the **Tasman Glacier** (people have been known to walk!) this is really a ski resort for the jetsetter only – skiing down from the upper reaches of the Tasman Glacier usually requires a flight up from Mt Cook airfield in a ski-plane. You need to be a fairly competent skier as well as a rich one to savour this unique skiing experience. The lower reaches of the glacier are almost dead flat and are usually covered in surface moraine so you must either walk out – or fly once again. In exceptional circumstances the run down the glacier can be 20 km in length, although it's usually less than 10 km. Count on around $550 to $595 for a flight up, the guide fee, two runs down the glacier and the flight back. You must have a guide with you – contact Alpine Guides Mt Cook, based at Mt Cook Village (☎ (03) 435 1834). The season is from mid-July to late October.

Other glaciers that can be skied on Mt Cook include the **Murchison Glacier** and **Mannering Glacier**. On the other side of the divide, Fox Glacier Wilderness Skiing – Alpine Guides Westland (☎ (0800) 111 600) operate in the **Fox Glacier** and **Franz Josef Glacier** névés, in the Westland National Park. The season is from August to December. A day out costs about $440.

MOUNTAINEERING

New Zealand has a rich history of mountaineering, as it is an ideal training ground for greater adventures overseas. The Southern Alps offer a great number of challenging climbs, and are studded with a number of impressive peaks.

It is not a pursuit for the uninitiated as it is highly challenging, very physical and contains a number of dangers – fickle weather with storms, winds and extreme cold; avalanches; rotten, loose rock and the ever present danger of rockfalls; the possibility of falling; and equipment failure, all factors that can lead to accidents.

Don't be put off, though, as proper instruction and training will allow you to enjoy the mountains, and enable you to make commonsense decisions which enhance your safety and thus appreciation of the mountain environment. A list of recommended companies which provide expert instruction in mountaineering is included at the end of this section.

The Mt Cook region has always been the focus of climbing activity in New Zealand, and the history of climbing in this country is inextricably linked to it. On 2 March 1882, William Spotswood Green and two Swiss alpinists, after a 62-hour epic, failed to reach

Following in Sir Edmund Hillary's footsteps...

the summit of Cook (Aoraki). Two years later three local climbers, Tom Fyfe, George Graham and Jack Clarke, spurred into action by the news that two well-known European alpinists, Edward Fitzgerald and Matthias Zurbriggen, were coming to attempt Cook, set off to climb it before the visitors. On Christmas Day 1884 they ascended the Hooker Glacier and north ridge, a brilliant climb in those days, and stood on the summit.

In 1913 Freda du Faur, an Australian, was the first woman to reach the summit. In 1948 Edmund Hillary's party climbed the south ridge. (Hillary went on to become, with Tenzing Norgay, the first to the summit of Mt Everest in the Himalaya.) Since then most of the daunting face routes have been climbed. An extremely lucky Geoff Wayatt climbed the east face a week before a huge landslide (see Mt Cook in the Canterbury chapter). The Mt Cook region has many great peaks – Sefton, the beguiling Tasman, Silberhorn, Elie de Beaumont, Malte Brun, Aiguilles Rouges, Nazomi, La Perouse, Hicks, De la Beche, Douglas and the Minarets. Many of the peaks can be ascended from Westland National Park, and there is a system of climbers' huts on both sides of the divide.

Mt Cook is only one of a number of outstanding climbing areas. The others extend along the spine of the South Island from Tapuaenuku (in the Kaikouras) and the Nelson Lakes peaks, in the north, to the rugged mountains of Fiordland.

Arthur's Pass is an outstanding climbing area. There are a number of challenging routes on Mt Rolleston and 'away from it all' climbs on Mts Carrington and Murchison. To the south lie the remote Arrowsmiths, with true wilderness climbing possibilities.

Beyond the Cook region is Mt Aspiring National Park, centred on 'the Matterhorn of the South', Mt Aspiring, and the Volta, Therma and Bonar ice fields which cling to its sides. This is the second centre of mountaineering in New Zealand, and there are possibilities for all levels of climbs on Aspiring, Rob Roy, Avalanche, Liverpool, Barff, and peaks around the Olivine Ice Plateau. To the south, in the Forbes Mountains, is Mt Earnslaw, flanked by the Rees and Dart rivers.

Fiordland is not without its impressive peaks. The mightiest of these is Tutoko, the centrepiece of the Darrans Range, just to the north of Milford Sound. There are some walks in this area but, generally, if you wish to explore the Darrans you are forced to climb up sheer granite walls. This is the remotest and most daunting region of New Zealand, and the domain of the skilled, confident mountaineer.

For those seeking to learn the necessary skills, here's a list of climbing schools:

Mt Cook & Westland National Parks

Alpine Guides Mt Cook (☎ (03) 435 1834), PO Box 20, Mt Cook Village (mountaineering courses and guiding for Copland Pass)

Alpine Guides (Westland) (☎ (0800) 111 600), PO Box 38, Main Rd, Fox Glacier (ski mountaineering, mountaineering and Copland Pass)

Alpine Recreation Canterbury (☎ (03) 680 6736), PO Box 75, Lake Tekapo (ski touring, high altitude pass crossing – Ball Pass, mountaineering courses)

Southern Alps Guiding (☎ (03) 435 1890), PO Box 32, Mt Cook (private guiding)

Mt Aspiring National Park

Aspiring Guides (☎ (03) 443 7930) (heli-skiing, mountaineering courses, guiding)

Mountain Recreation (☎ (03) 443 7330), PO Box 204, Wanaka (also guiding for Cascade Saddle crossing – Matukituki to the Rees-Dart, mountaineering courses, high altitude walks in upper Matukituki)

Mountain Works (☎ (03) 442 7329), PO Box 647, Queenstown (for Mt Earnslaw and Copland Pass)

ROCK CLIMBING

This sport has increased in popularity in New Zealand. No longer is it just considered practice for mountaineering, it is now an activity in its own right. There are a number of companies set up to take beginners out for their first climbs, with all attention being paid to safety.

In the North Island, popular climbing areas include the Mt Eden Quarry in the heart of Auckland, Whanganui Bay and Motuoapa in the vicinity of Lake Taupo and, about 10 km south of Te Awamutu, the Wharepapa Rock Climbing Field.

The South Island has a great number of rock-climbing areas. Above Christchurch, in the Port Hills, there are a number of climbs, and 100 km away on the road to Arthur's Pass is Castle Hill and a number of great friction climbs. For the more adventurous there are the long, extreme routes of the Darrans, a range blessed with New Zealand's best rock.

Rap Jumping

A variation on abseiling or rappelling. Instead of the traditional face to the wall, feet first approach of descent, you go almost head first, face out. The Bay of Islands and Wanaka are good places where rap jumping operators are willing to teach you to come to grips with gravity.

CAVING

There are plenty of caving opportunities in New Zealand, as this is also a popular activity amongst local outdoor enthusiasts. Auckland, Westport and, of course, Waitomo are all areas where you'll find both active local clubs and organised tours. For more information contact the NZ Speleological Society (NZSS; ☎ (07) 878 7640), PO Box 18, Waitomo Caves.

MOUNTAIN BIKING & CYCLE TOURING

This mode of transport has taken off with phenomenal fury. Mountain bikes are seen everywhere, used either for recreation or as a form of daily transport.

New Zealand, with its great scenery as well as off-road possibilities, is great biking country. Many choose mountain bikes or touring cycles as the preferred mode of transport around New Zealand – the bike allows them to get off the beaten track, or to amble along at a leisurely pace.

Most towns have mountain bikes for hire – a good way to see the towns and their attractions as well as to take off into the countryside. Bikes can be hired by the hour, day, week or month; you can hire the bike alone, or hire a bike with a bike/bus option, or even go on an organised bicycle tour. The various options are discussed under Cycling in the Getting Around chapter.

If you'll be cycling through New Zealand, get a copy of *Cycle Touring in New Zealand – including both North & South Islands* by Bruce Ringer. With maps and suggestions for long-distance cycle tours as well as short side trips, it tells you all you need to know about cycling in this country, including where the steep hills are! *Classic New Zealand Mountain Bike Rides* by Paul, Simon & Jonathan Kennett is another good cycling book, suggesting a wide variety of short and long rides all over New Zealand.

For downhill fans, various companies will take you up to the top of mountains, hills and volcanoes (Mt Ruapehu, Christchurch's Port Hills, The Remarkables) so that you can hurtle down without the usual grunt of getting uphill beforehand.

Get on your bike to explore the country, but keep off the walking tracks in national parks

Many routes which were traditionally walked are now being cycled. One thing to remember, though, is *never* to bicycle on walking tracks in national parks unless it has been permitted. DOC will fine you if you're caught. Contact the NZ Mountain Bike Association (NZMBA; ☎ (07) 378 9552), PO Box 371, Taupo.

WATER ACTIVITIES

Travellers should be aware that adventure sports, particularly those on fast-flowing rivers such as rafting and kayaking, do entail risk. Make sure that the company you choose takes adequate safety precautions.

Jet-Boating

New Zealand is the home of the amazing jet-boats, invented by CWF Hamilton in 1957. An inboard engine sucks water into a tube in the bottom of the boat, and an impeller driven by the engine blows it out a nozzle at the stern in a high-speed stream. The boat is steered simply by directing the jet stream.

The boats are ideal for use in shallow water and white water because there are no propellers to damage, there is better clearance under the boat, and the jet can be reversed instantly for quick braking. The instant response of the jet enables the boats to execute 360° spins almost within the length of the boat. All that adds up to some hair-raising rides on NZ rivers.

The Shotover and Kawarau rivers near Queenstown and the Buller near Westport are renowned jet-boating rivers in the South Island, with the Dart River less travelled but also good. In the North Island, the Whanganui, Manganui-a-te-Ao, Motu and Rangitaiki rivers are excellent for jet-boating; and the Huka Jet, operating near Taupo, is also popular.

Just about every riverside and lakeside town throughout New Zealand has a jet-boat company that runs trips, sometimes in combination with other adventure activities such as bungy jumping, aerial sightseeing and rafting.

Rafting

There are almost as many white-water rafting possibilities as there are rivers in New Zealand. And there is no shortage of companies willing to take you on a heart-pounding, drenching, exhilarating and spine-tingling ride down some of the wildest and most magnificent rivers in the world. The Shotover and Kawarau rivers in the South Island, popular for jet-boating, are also popular for white-water rafting, as is the less accessible Landsborough River (often reached by helicopter or light plane). Canterbury has the Rangitata River, considered one of NZ's best.

The north of the South Island has great rafting possibilities, such as the Buller, Karamea, Mokihinui and Gowan rivers. Details about all the companies offering trips can be found in the respective sections. The West Coast has the Hokitika and Waiho rivers, plus many other rafting possibilities.

In the North Island there are plenty of rivers, like the Rangitaiki, Wairoa, Motu, Tongariro, Rangitikei and Ngaruroro, that are just as good. There is also the Kaituna Cascades near Rotorua, with a seven-metre waterfall, the Okere Falls, as its highlight. This is perhaps NZ's bumpiest raft ride, with 15 drops in 40 minutes. The drop over the six-metre Tawhai Falls in Tongariro National Park is another dramatic drop.

The rivers are graded from one to six, with six meaning 'unraftable'. The grading of the Shotover canyon varies from three to five plus depending on the time of year, the Kawarau River is rated four, and the Wairoa River is graded three to five. On the rougher stretches there's usually a minimum age limit of 12 or 13 years. The rafting companies supply wet suits and life jackets.

Rafting trips take anything from one hour to three days and cost between about \$75 and \$130 per person per day, depending on whether or not helicopter access is involved. Spring and summer are the most popular rafting times.

Be aware that people have been killed in rafting accidents – check at local tourist offices for the best and safest times for rafting. There are risks in all such adventure activities.

Cave Rafting Yet another variation on the rafting theme is not true rafting at all, but it is very unusual and exciting. It's known as 'black-water rafting' at Waitomo in the North Island, as 'underworld rafting' at Westport and as 'Taniwha adventure caving' at Greymouth in the South Island.

It involves donning a wet suit, a lighted hard hat and a black inner tube and floating on underground rivers through some spectacular caves. An added attraction is seeing glow-worms, those fascinating insects, glowing away like a Milky Way of stars in the bowels of the earth.

Canoeing & Kayaking

An open two-person canoe, called simply a canoe or sometimes an Indian canoe in other parts of the world, is called a 'Canadian canoe' in New Zealand. A kayak, a smaller, narrower one-person craft which is covered except for a hole for the paddler to sit in, is often called a 'kayak' in New Zealand but it can also be called a 'canoe'. It's a good idea to specify whether you mean a 'Canadian canoe' or a 'kayak' when talking about river trips in this country.

Many companies offer canoeing and kayaking trips on the same rivers where rafting is popular. You can go for a few hours of quiet paddling or white water excitement in hired canoes or kayaks without a guide, or take longer solo or guided camping trips with fishing and other activities thrown in.

Canoeing is especially popular on the Whanganui River in the North Island, where you can hire a canoe for days at a time; there are many other possibilities. Canoeing is also popular on lakes, notably Lake Taupo, and on lakes not far from Christchurch.

Kayaking is a very popular sport. Commercial trips (for those without their own equipment) are offered on a number of rivers and lakes in the North and South Island. One of the best is with Alpine River Guides on the Matukituki and Makarora rivers near Wanaka. Contact the NZ Canoeing Association (NZCA), PO Box 3768, Wellington.

Sea Kayaking Sea kayaking is very popular in New Zealand. Renowned sea kayaking areas are the Bay of Islands and Coromandel in the North Island, and in the South Island the Marlborough Sounds and along the coast of the Abel Tasman National Park, where sea kayaking has become a viable alternative to walking on the Abel Tasman Coastal Track (see those sections for further details).

Fiordland has become a popular destination for those wishing to hone their sea kayaking skills. There are tour operators in Te Anau, Milford and Manapouri who can arrange spectacular trips in the lakes and on the fiords.

River Sledging

This is a relatively new sport in 'find the new quick buzz' New Zealand. Discard the raft, kayak, canoe, Lilo or inflated inner tube if you think they lack manoeuvrability. Instead, grasp a responsive polystyrene sled or a modified boogey board, flippers, wet suit and helmet, a positive attitude, and go for it.

In the North Island, the Rangitaiki River near Rotorua seems to be the river to hurl yourself down and in the South Island, the Kawarau near Queenstown is both boogey boarded and sledged. The Chinese Dogleg, not far from the bungy bridge, provides all the fun (see the Wanaka and Queenstown sections in the Otago chapter).

Sailing

Auckland is appropriately the City of Sails, the insular nature of New Zealand throws up the world's best mariners and the Kiwis have swept the world before them in international yachting races. Most recently Kiwi sailors have dominated the Whitbread Around the World race and, in May 1995, *Kiwi Magic* captured the America's Cup from Dennis Connor's *Young America* team in a 5-0 finals 'sail'-over.

There are plenty of opportunities for travellers to experience sailing in New Zealand. The Bay of Islands, the southern lakes (Te Anau and Wakatipu) and the cities of Auckland and Dunedin are good venues to get out and experience the thrill of the wind in the sails.

Scuba Diving

Scuba diving also has its devotees. The Bay of Islands Maritime & Historic Park and the Hauraki Gulf Maritime Park in the North Island, and the Marlborough Sounds Maritime Park in the South Island, are obvious attractions but there are many more diving possibilities around both islands. Even Invercargill, with its notoriously cold water, has a club!

New Zealand has two marine parks, which are protected marine life reserves – interesting for diving. The Poor Knights Islands Marine Reserve is off the coast near Whangarei, north of Auckland. This reserve is reputed to have the best diving in New

Zealand, and French naturalist Jacques Cousteau rates it one of the 'top 10' diving spots in the world. The Sugar Loaf Islands Marine Park, another interesting reserve, is off Back Beach in New Plymouth, not far from the city centre.

Fiordland in the South Island is a surprisingly interesting place for diving. The diving here is most unusual because the extremely heavy rainfall leaves a layer of freshwater, often peaty brown, over the saltwater. You descend through this murky and cold freshwater into amazingly clear and warmer saltwater. The freshwater cuts out light which discourages the growth of seaweed and this provides ideal conditions for the growth of black coral *(Antipathes fiordensis)*, white when alive but black when dead, it is found much closer to the surface than is common elsewhere in the world. Leave it there, though. It's 100% protected in New Zealand.

Fiordland also has plenty of crayfish (lobster) and amazing pods of dolphins who display great interest in the relatively rare appearance of scuba divers. It also has snake stars which symbiotically live on the black coral; and brachiopods, true living fossils.

Coastal Fishes of New Zealand: A Diver's Identification Guide by Malcolm Francis is a field guide to all the fishes a diver in New Zealand is likely to encounter, with colour photos of the fishes in their natural environment. For more information contact the New Zealand Underwater Association (NZUA; ☎ (09) 849 5896), PO Box 875, Auckland.

Surfing

With its thousands of km of coastline, New Zealand has excellent surfing possibilities. Swells come in from every angle and while any specific beach will have better surfing at some times of the year than at others, there's good surfing to be found *somewhere* in NZ at any time of the year.

According to the surfing grapevine, Auckland is the best surfing area in the North Island, and Dunedin is the best in the South Island, especially in summer and autumn, but there are hundreds of possibilities. Among the guidebooks on surfing in New Zealand, look out for *The New Zealand Surfing Guide* by Mike Bhana. It has details about surfing at beaches all around NZ, including good surfing spots and what times of year to surf there, where to find right-hand and left-hand breaks, tidal advice and more.

A few spots recommended by surfies are:

North Island

Auckland area (within two hours drive of the city)
- West coast: Piha, Raglan, Muriwai
- East coast: Whangamata, Matakana Island

Gisborne
- city beaches, Mahia Peninsula

Taranaki
- Stent Rd, Puniho Rd, Greenmeadows Point

Wellington
- Titahi Bay, Palliser Bay, Castlepoint

South Island

Dunedin
- Sandfly Bay, Long Point, Lobsters near Akatore River

Kaikoura
- Meatworks, Mangawhau Point, Mangamanu Reef

Westport
- Westport beaches, Tauranga Bay

Greymouth
- Blaketown, Cobden breakwater

Fishing

New Zealand is renowned as one of the great sportfishing countries of the world, thanks largely to the introduction of exotic rainbow trout, brown trout, quinnat salmon, Atlantic salmon, perch, char and a few other fish. The lakes and rivers of central North Island are famous for trout fishing, especially Lake Taupo and the rivers that feed it. The rivers and lakes of the South Island are also good for trout, notably the Mataura River, Southland. The rivers of Otago and Southland also have some of the best salmon fishing in the world.

Saltwater fishing is also a big attraction for Kiwi anglers, especially in the warmer waters around the North Island where surfcasting or fishing from boats can produce big catches of grey mullet, trevally, mao mao, porae, John Dory, gurnard, flounder, mackerel, hapuku, tarakihi, moki and kahawai.

The Ninety Mile Beach and the beaches of the Hauraki Gulf are good for surfcasting.

The colder waters of the South Island, especially around Marlborough Sounds, are good for snapper, hake, trumpeter, butterfish, ling, barracouta and blue cod. The Kaikoura peninsula is great for surfcasting.

It is not easy to hire fishing gear in New Zealand, so bring your own if you can. Rods and tackle may have to be treated by NZ quarantine officials, especially if they are made with natural materials such as cane or feathers.

If you want to fish on inland waters you will need a fishing permit. They are available for particular regions and are available for a day, a week, a month or a season. If you plan to do a lot of fishing in different areas, you can get a special tourist licence that is valid throughout most of New Zealand for one month. Special tourist fishing licences are available only at Tourism Rotorua; see the Rotorua section for details. Local visitor information centres and DOC offices can give you more information about fishing licences and regulations.

Many books have been written about fishing in New Zealand. John Kent has written the *North Island Trout Fishing Guide* and the *South Island Trout Fishing Guide*. Tony Orman, a renowned NZ fisherman and author, has written *21 Great New Zealand Trout Waters* as well as *Fishing the Wild Places of New Zealand*, telling not only how to catch fish but also relating some of the author's adventures fishing in many of New Zealand's wilderness areas. For surfcasting, check out *Surfcasting: A New Zealand Guide* by Gil Henderson.

Marine-Mammal Watching

Kaikoura, on the north-eastern coast of the South Island, is the centre of marine-mammal watching in New Zealand. One company operates daily whale-watching tours, two offer swimming with dolphins, and another two offer seal swimming.

The main attraction is the sperm whale, which is the largest toothed whale, but there's also a lot of other beautiful wildlife to be seen on the tours: Hector's dolphin (the smallest and rarest of all dolphins), the dusky dolphin (found only in the southern hemisphere, often in huge groups), the NZ fur seal, the orca or killer whale (the largest of all dolphins), common dolphin and pilot whale. As well there are many sea birds, blue penguin, the royal albatross, cape pigeon and mollymawk.

Nature being what it is, there's no guarantee of seeing any specific animal on any one tour, but it's fairly certain that something of interest will be out there any time you go. In general, the sperm whales are most likely to be seen from October to August, and orcas from December to March. Most of the other animals are seen all year round.

There is also swimming with dolphins in the North Island at Whakatane, Paihia and Whitianga (it's mainly interaction with bottlenose dolphins), and in the Marlborough Sounds and Fiordland in the South Island.

Whales & Dolphins of New Zealand & Australia: An Identification Guide by Alan N Baker is a guide for identifying the species, with details on dorsal fins and so on, but it's sort of a ghoulish book since all the photos of animals show only dead ones!

AERIAL ACTIVITIES

Bungy Jumping

Bungy jumping was made famous by Kiwi AJ Hackett's bungy dive from the Eiffel Tower in 1986. He teamed up with New Zealand's champion speed skier, Henry van Asch, and looked for a way to make commercial jumping safe. Hackett and van Asch now operate bungy jumping companies in New Zealand, Australia and France, and they are continually on the lookout for spectacular eyries for clients to leap off. This company alone has sent many thousands of people hurtling earthward from bridges over the Shotover and Kawarau rivers near Queenstown, in Normandy, France, and even from a tower in Cairns, Australia, with nothing between them and kingdom come but a gigantic rubber bungy cord tied to their ankles.

The jump begins when you crawl into the

Five, four, three, two, one – bungy!

preparation area, get your ankles strapped up with a towel for padding, and have adjustments made to the cord depending on your weight. You then hobble out to the edge of the jumping platform, stand looking out over thin air, and get ready to jump. The crew shout out 'five, four, three, two, ONE!' and you dive off and are flying. Likely as not you will dunk head first into the river below before soaring upwards again on the bungy. The daring choose the 'escalator' and step off to watch the bridge above disappear rapidly, before the cord turns them 180° and they hurtle back up towards the bridge, upside down.

After bobbing up and down like a human yo-yo, you finally settle down, grab the pole held up to you by the crew down below, and are pulled into a rubber raft. There you're unstrapped and towed back to dry land. No doubt about it, it's a daredevil sport, and the adrenaline rush can last for days. But it's all very well organised, with every possible precaution and attention to safety. In fact, Hackett's rightly boast that their jump is fully approved to the NZ Safety Standards.

The historic Kawarau Suspension Bridge, near Queenstown, attracts the most jumpers; it's 43 metres above the Kawarau River. A more spectacular dive spot is Skippers Canyon Bridge, 71 metres above a narrow gorge on the Shotover River, also near Queenstown (see Queenstown in the Otago chapter). Recently another bunch of former Hackett crew members set up the massive 102-metre Pipeline where the first bounce brings you up to the height of the Skipper's Bridge!

You'll pay upwards of $89 for a bungy jump, which includes a bungy T-shirt that can only be obtained by actually doing the jump. It's even more expensive at the Shotover bridge, but there the price includes transport to the rather remote jump site ($145). You can also arrange for still photos or a video of your jump, to impress the folks back home.

Jumping is also done in the North Island at Taupo, where there's a bungy platform jutting out from a cliff 45 metres above the Waikato River, and from a 43-metre bridge (the same height as the Kawarau Bridge) over the Rangitikei River near Mangaweka (see Mangaweka in the Wanganui & Manawatu chapter). You can bungy off the Waiau River Bridge near Hanmer Springs, and off a platform on the way to the Heaphy Track, near Bainham. The highest jump in the country is now the 102-metre high Pipeline Bungy on the upper Shotover River, where brave (or slightly nutty) jumpers leap from a restored water pipeline towards the Shotover below (see the Queenstown section of the Otago chapter).

Parapenting & Paragliding

This is perhaps the easiest way for humans to fly, without the problems faced by Icarus. After half a day of instruction you should be able to do limited solo flights. Before you know it you could be doing flights from 300 metres.

The best place to learn the skills necessary to operate your parapente/paraglider is Wanaka. Initial instruction is conducted at Mt Iron, just outside the town, and the long jumps are from the road up to Treble Cone ski field (often up to six minutes air time). Communication between instructor and student is via a radio in your helmet. If you want a taste of flying without instruction consider taking a tandem flight from Treble Cone. Contact Air Action (☎ 443 9193) (see Wanaka and Queenstown in the Otago chapter).

Aerial Sightseeing

Planes and helicopters abound in all parts of New Zealand, and there are plenty of pilots willing to take you for sightseeing trips (called 'flightseeing' by the locals).

The incredible contrast in scenery and the spectacular mountain ranges make New Zealand one of the best places for aerial sightseeing. Some of the best trips are around the Bay of Islands, the Bay of Plenty, Tongariro National Park and Mt Taranaki in the North Island, and Mt Cook and the West Coast glaciers and fiords in the South Island. You can even arrange to be flown up to the top of the glacial ski fields, from where you have a clear run all the way down to the bottom.

If you get down to the south-western coast of the South Island, try to fit in a flight up the fiords; the scenery is sensational and you can often combine the flight with a trip on the water to see other places of interest.

Most aerial sightseeing companies operate from the local aerodrome. Ask at the local tourist office for information; in some places you can just turn up at the aerodrome during daylight hours and arrange a trip on the spot. We have included details of flight operators in the relevant sections in this book.

A far more sedate way to see the countryside is from a hot-air balloon. A company operating from near Methven takes you up to an altitude where you get spectacular views of the Southern Alps.

Skydiving

A lot of the aerial sightseeing companies also operate skydiving courses and trips. Many visitors are taking the 'ultimate' jump in tandem with a fully qualified instructor. It is not cheap, usually around $175, but the thrill is worth every dollar.

You can go tandem skydiving in the North Island at Taupo, Rotorua, at Parakai near Auckland, at Paraparaumu near Wellington and at Hastings near Napier. In the South Island there's tandem skydiving at Nelson, Christchurch and Queenstown. It's a popular activity in all these places and will probably become available at even more places.

An extra bonus is that by going up to skydiving height you also get in some great aerial sightseeing, so if you're only going to do it once, pick the place you would most like to get a bird's eye view of.

OTHER ACTIVITIES

Horse Riding

There are numerous places where you can see the countryside by horse in New Zealand, on anything from half-hour rides to 12-day treks. In the South Island, all-day adventure rides on horseback are a great way to see the surrounding country in Kaikoura, around Mt Cook, Queenstown and Dunedin. There are many treks offered in Westland, from all-day rides at Punakaiki, and excursions up to 12 days long at the Waitaha Valley, Ross.

In the North Island, Taupo has options for wilderness horse trekking and for rides in the hills overlooking the thermal regions. The Coromandel Peninsula and Waitomo are also good places for horse trekking.

There are many more options available, so check the index for individual mentions in this book, and ask at the local information centres for lists of operators.

Birdwatching

New Zealand is a birdwatcher's paradise in many ways. In such a small area there are many unique endemic species, a number of interesting residents and wave upon wave of visitors. It is as famous for extinct and point-of-extinction species as it is for common species.

The extinct species can't be 'watched' but a tour through museums, into caves where their bones are found and into former habitats is fascinating. These were the islands of the giant four-metre-tall moa and the Haast's eagle which was large enough to have preyed upon it; and the remarkable huia with its vastly different male and female beaks. The number of species on the point of extinction and the frenzied efforts to rebuild their populations is also a captivating story.

Any visiting birdwatcher will not be disappointed by the more accessible species. The kiwi is probably the species most sought after by birdwatchers and you are guaranteed to see the Stewart Island subspecies at all times of the year. Other birds sought after are the royal albatross, the white heron or kotuku, the cheeky kea which ranges throughout the Southern Alps, the yellowhead or mohua, Fiordland crested penguin, yellow-eyed penguin, Australasian gannet, wrybill, oystercatcher, and in the forests the kereru or New Zealand pigeon, rifleman, tui, kaka and the saddleback.

There is no shortage of places to see birds. Some of the best are Ulva Island (near Stewart Island); the Catlins Forest Park and south-east coast; Fiordland and the forests of Westland; Otago Peninsula; Cape Farewell; the Marlborough Sounds; Te Urewera National Park; the Firth of Thames (Miranda Naturalist's Trust); Opoutere and the Coromandel; and the forests and coasts of Northland. There are a number of islands established as wildlife refuges where threatened birds are being protected: you will need special permission to visit these.

There are a number of field guides for birdwatching in New Zealand. Jeff, an avid birder, reckons the two that a real twitcher should carry around are *A Field Guide to New Zealand Birds* by Geoff Moon and *Birds of New Zealand: Locality Guide* by Stuart Chambers. Both have excellent colour photos of the birds in their natural environments and lots of good information about them; the *Locality Guide* also gives valuable practical information on how and where to find each species.

See the Flora & Fauna section for descriptions of various birds.

Mazes

For some reason, Kiwis are mad on mazes, and there are some spectacular ones built as tourist attractions around the country. When they tired of ordinary mazes they made three-dimensional ones, most of which are incredibly convoluted – the original three-dimensional maze, at Wanaka in the South Island, can take hours to work through.

The Fairbank Maze, opposite the airport at Rotorua, is the largest hedge maze in New Zealand, with a 1.6-km pathway. Te Ngae Park, three km beyond the Rotorua airport, is a three-dimensional, 1.7-km wooden maze similar to the one at Wanaka.

There are usually other facilities that make them great fun for families. Recently New Zealand has even started to export its mazes – a maze craze has developed in Japan where Kiwi consultants advise on the designs.

Getting There & Away

The overwhelming majority of visitors to New Zealand arrive by air. Apart from cruise ships, no regular sea services are available to New Zealand.

However you're travelling, it's worth taking out travel insurance. Work out what you need. You may not want to insure that grotty old army surplus backpack – but everyone should be covered for the worst possible case: an accident, for example, that will require hospital treatment and a flight home. It's a good idea to make a copy of your policy, in case the original is lost. If you are planning to travel for a long time, the insurance may seem very expensive – but if you can't afford it, you certainly won't be able to afford to deal with a medical emergency overseas.

AIR

New Zealand has three airports that handle international flights – Auckland, Wellington and Christchurch. Most international flights go through Auckland. Wellington airport has limited runway capacity and international flights are all to and from Australia. Flights to and from Christchurch are also mainly with Australia although there are some connections to other countries.

There are some special ticket types and definitions which may be of interest to visitors to New Zealand.

Round-the-World & Circle Pacific Tickets

Round-the-World (RTW) tickets have become very popular in the last few years. The airline RTW tickets are often real bargains, and can work out to be no more expensive or even cheaper than an ordinary return ticket. Prices usually start at about £850, A$1800 or US$1300.

These tickets have become very popular in the last few years; basically, there are two types – airline tickets and agent tickets. An airline RTW ticket is issued by two or more airlines that have joined together to market a ticket which takes you around the world on their combined routes. It permits you to fly pretty well anywhere you choose using their combined routes as long as you don't backtrack, ie keep moving in approximately the same direction east or west.

Other restrictions are that you (usually) must book the first sector in advance and cancellation penalties then apply. There may be restrictions on how many stops you are permitted and usually the tickets are valid for 90 days up to a year.

The other type of RTW ticket, the agent ticket, is a combination of cheap fares strung together by an enterprising travel agent. These may be cheaper than airline RTW tickets, but the choice of routes will be limited.

Circle Pacific tickets use a combination of airlines to circle the Pacific – combining Australia, New Zealand, North America and Asia. As with RTW tickets there are advance purchase restrictions and limits to how many stopovers you can take. These fares are likely to be around 15% cheaper than RTW tickets. Air New Zealand sometimes offers good deals on tickets involving departure from Los Angeles that don't include Asia but do include New Zealand, Australia and many small Pacific islands.

Australia

The NZ cities with flights to or from Australia are Auckland, Christchurch and Wellington. Australian cities with flights to or from New Zealand are Adelaide, Brisbane, Cairns, Canberra, Hobart, Melbourne, Perth and Sydney. Air New Zealand, Qantas and United Airlines are the main carriers.

The fare depends on the day you fly out as well as where you fly to and from. The year is divided up into peak, shoulder and off-peak times, which can vary with the airline.

The main peak season is over the December-January summer school holidays. Typical low-season rock bottom fares from a travel agent specialising in discount tickets from Sydney would cost around A$400/450 one-way/return to Auckland, A$450/550 to Christchurch or Wellington. From Melbourne the equivalent fares would be A$420/450 to Auckland, A$450/550 to Wellington, or A$500/600 to Christchurch. Return fares in the high season cost around A$200 more, and tickets valid for two months or more are also more expensive.

If you're travelling from Australia to the US west coast via New Zealand, the high season varies but is generally during the US summer (June, July and August). Low-season fares start at around A$1000/1600 one-way/return, high season fares are more like A$2000 return.

RTW fares departing from Australia, which can include a stopover in New Zealand, vary with the season. The northern hemisphere summer (June, July and August) is usually the high season for RTW fares; they cost around A$2000 to A$2500 in high season but the price can be a few hundred dollars less in the low season.

In Australia, STA and Flight Centres are major dealers in cheap air fares. They have branches in all the major cities. Otherwise, check the travel agents' ads in the *Yellow Pages* and ring around.

The USA

Most flights between the USA and New Zealand are to/from the USA's west coast. Most go through Los Angeles but some also arrive and depart from San Francisco. If you're coming from some other part of the USA, your travel agent can arrange a discounted 'add-on' fare to get you to the city of departure.

Excursion (round-trip) fares are available with various airlines but are generally much higher than those obtained through travel agents. Cheaper 'short life' fares are frequently offered, for only limited periods. The easiest way to get a cheap air fare from the USA is through a travel agency selling discounted fares; these fares can be around US$900 return from Los Angeles or around US$1200 return from New York. For as little as $100 extra from Los Angeles you can fly to Australia with a stopover in New Zealand.

The Sunday travel sections of papers like the *New York Times*, the *Chicago Tribune*, the *Los Angeles Times* or the *San Francisco Examiner* always have plenty of ads for cheap airline tickets and there are often good deals on flights across the Pacific, especially in the west coast papers. Even if you don't live in these areas, you can have the tickets sent to you by mail.

Two of the most reputable discount travel agencies in the USA are STA and CIEE/Council Travel Services. Both of these are international travel agencies with a number of offices throughout the USA and in other countries. Both started out as student travel agencies. While they both still specialise in student travel, honouring and selling the International Student Identity Card (ISIC), they also offer discount tickets to non-students of all ages. You can contact their national head offices to ask about prices, find an office near you, purchase tickets by mail or buy an ISIC card.

The magazine *Travel Unlimited* (PO Box 1058, Allston, MA 02134) publishes details of the cheapest air fares and courier possibilities for destinations all over the world, departing from the USA.

If you want to visit other Pacific destinations on your way to or from New Zealand, compare carefully the stopover possibilities offered by each airline. Air New Zealand flights offer an excellent variety of stopover options on their route between Los Angeles and Auckland. You can tack on stopovers in Honolulu, Tahiti, Rarotonga, Western Samoa, Tonga and Fiji quite cheaply. Other airlines fly to New Zealand for the same price, or sometimes cheaper, but with more limited stopover options.

Canada

In Canada, the student and discount travel agent is Travel CUTS, which has about 35 offices around Canada. Once again, you don't

Air Travel Glossary

Apex Tickets Apex stands for Advance Purchase Excursion fare. These tickets are usually between 30 and 40% cheaper than the full economy fare, but there are restrictions. You must purchase the ticket at least 21 days in advance (sometimes more) and must be away for a minimum period and return within a maximum period. Stopovers are not allowed, and if you have to change your dates of travel or destination, there will be extra charges to pay. These tickets are not fully refundable – if you have to cancel your trip, the refund is often considerably less than what you paid for the ticket. Take out travel insurance to cover yourself in case you have to cancel your trip unexpectedly – for example, due to illness.

Baggage Allowance This will be written on your ticket; you are usually allowed one 20-kg item to go in the hold, plus one item of hand luggage. Some airlines which fly transpacific and transatlantic routes allow for two pieces of luggage (there are limits on their dimensions and weight).

Bucket Shops At certain times of the year and/or on certain routes, many airlines fly with empty seats. This isn't profitable and it's more cost-effective for them to fly full, even if that means having to sell a certain number of drastically discounted tickets. They do this by off-loading them onto bucket shops (UK) or consolidators (USA), travel agents who specialise in discounted fares. The agents, in turn, sell them to the public at reduced prices. These tickets are often the cheapest you'll find, but you can't purchase them directly from the airlines. Availability varies widely, so you'll not only have to be flexible in your travel plans, you'll also have to be quick off the mark as soon as an advertisement appears in the press.

Bucket-shop agents advertise in newspapers and magazines and there's a lot of competition so it's a good idea to telephone first.

Bumped Just because you have a confirmed seat doesn't mean you're going to get on the plane – see Overbooking.

Cancellation Penalties If you have to cancel or change an Apex or other discount ticket, there may be heavy penalties involved; insurance can sometimes be taken out against these penalties. Some airlines impose penalties on regular tickets as well, particularly against 'no show' passengers.

Check In Airlines ask you to check in a certain time ahead of the flight departure (usually two hours on international flights). If you fail to check in on time and the flight is overbooked, the airline can cancel your booking and give your seat to somebody else.

Confirmation Having a ticket written out with the flight and date on it doesn't mean you have a seat until the agent has confirmed with the airline that your status is 'OK'. Prior to this confirmation, your status is 'on request'.

Courier Fares Businesses often need to send their urgent documents or freight securely and quickly. They do it through courier companies. These companies hire people to accompany the package through customs and, in return, offer a discount ticket which is sometimes a phenomenal bargain. In effect, what the courier companies do is ship their freight as your luggage on the regular commercial flights. This is a legitimate operation – all freight is completely legal. There are two shortcomings, however: the short turnaround time of the ticket, usually not longer than a month; and the limitation on your luggage allowance.

Discounted Tickets There are two types of discounted fares – officially discounted (such as Apex – see Promotional Fares) and unofficially discounted (see Bucket Shops). The latter can save you more than money – you may be able to pay Apex prices without the associated Apex advance booking and other requirements. The lowest prices often impose drawbacks, such as flying with unpopular airlines, inconvenient schedules, or unpleasant routes and connections.

Economy Class Tickets Economy-class tickets are usually not the cheapest way to go, though they do give you maximum flexibility and they are valid for 12 months. If you don't use them, most are fully refundable, as are unused sectors of a multiple ticket.

Full Fares Airlines traditionally offer first class (coded F), business class (coded J) and economy class (coded Y) tickets. These days there are so many promotional and discounted fares available that few passengers pay full fare.

Lost Tickets If you lose your airline ticket, an airline will usually treat it like a travellers' cheque and, after inquiries, issue you with a replacement. Legally, however, an airline is entitled to treat it like cash, so if you lose a ticket, it could be forever. Take good care of your tickets.

MCO An MCO (Miscellaneous Charges Order) is a voucher for a value of a given amount, which resembles an airline ticket and can be used to pay for a specific flight with any IATA (International Air Transport Association) airline. MCOs, which are more flexible than a regular ticket, may satisfy the irritating onward ticket requirement, but some countries are now reluctant to accept them. MCOs are fully refundable if unused.

No Shows No shows are passengers who fail to show up for their flight for whatever reason. Full-fare no shows are sometimes entitled to travel on a later flight.

Open Jaw Tickets These are return tickets which allow you to fly to one place but return from another, and travel between the two 'jaws' by any means of transport at your own expense. If available, this can save you backtracking to your arrival point.

Overbooking Airlines hate to fly with empty seats, and since every flight has some passengers who fail to show up (see No Shows), they often book more passengers than they have seats available. Usually the excess passengers balance those who fail to show up, but occasionally somebody gets bumped. If this happens, guess who it is most likely to be? The passengers who check in late.

Promotional Fares These are officially discounted fares, such as Apex fares, which are available from travel agents or direct from the airline.

Reconfirmation You must contact the airline at least 72 hours prior to departure to 'reconfirm' that you intend to be on the flight. If you don't do this, the airline can delete your name from the passenger list and you could lose your seat.

Restrictions Discounted tickets often have various restrictions on them, such as necessity of advance purchase, limitations on the minimum and maximum period you must be away, restrictions on breaking the journey or changing the booking or route etc.

Standby This is a discounted ticket where you only fly if there is a seat free at the last moment. Standby fares are usually only available directly at the airport, but sometimes may also be handled by an airline's city office. To give yourself the best possible chance of getting on the flight you want, get there early and have your name placed on the waiting list. It's first come, first served.

Student Discounts Some airlines offer student-card holders 15% to 25% discounts on their tickets. The same often applies to anyone under the age of 26. These discounts are generally only available on ordinary economy-class fares.

Tickets Out An entry requirement for many countries is that you have an onward or return ticket, in other words, a ticket out of the country. If you're not sure what you intend to do next, the easiest solution is to buy the cheapest onward ticket to a neighbouring country or a ticket from a reliable airline which can later be refunded if you do not use it.

Transferred Tickets Airline tickets cannot be transferred from one person to another. Travellers sometimes try to sell the return half of their ticket, but officials can ask you to prove that you are the person named on the ticket. This may not be checked on domestic flights, but on international flights, tickets are usually compared with passports.

Travel Periods Some officially discounted fares, Apex fares in particular, vary with the time of year. There is often a low (off-peak) season and a high (peak) season. Sometimes there's an intermediate or shoulder season as well. At peak times, when everyone wants to fly, both officially and unofficially discounted fares will be higher, or there may simply be no discounted tickets available. Usually the fare depends on your outward flight – if you depart in the high season and return in the low season, you pay the high-season fare. ■

have to be a student to use their services. Their primary offices in Vancouver and Toronto will give you the address of their nearest office if it's not in your local phone book.

The *Vancouver Sun* and the *Toronto Globe & Mail* carry travel agents' ads. The magazine *Great Expectations* (PO Box 8000-411, Abbotsford BC V2S 6H1) is also useful.

Most flights coming from Canada will have at least one stopover. See the USA section; much of the same advice applies, especially as regards stopover options.

The UK

London-Auckland return tickets can be found in London bucket shops for around £700. Some stopovers are permitted on this sort of ticket. Depending on which airline you come with, you may fly across Asia or across the USA. If you're coming across Asia you can often make stopovers in places like India, Bangkok, Singapore and Australia; coming across in the other direction, stopover possibilities include places like New York, Los Angeles, Honolulu or a variety of Pacific islands. Stopover options will vary depending on which airlines you fly with.

Since New Zealand is about as far from Europe as you can get, it's not that much more to fly right on round the world rather than backtracking. Agents can organise an RTW route that goes through the South Pacific from around £650 to £900.

There has always been cut-throat competition between London's many 'bucket shops', and London is an important European centre for cheap fares. There are plenty of bucket shops in London and although there are always some untrustworthy operators most of them are fine. Look in the listings magazines *Time Out* and *TNT* plus the Sunday papers and *Exchange & Mart* for ads. Also look out for the free magazines widely available in London – start by looking outside the main railway stations. The Globetrotters Club (BCM Roving, London WC1N 3XX) publishes a newsletter called *Globe* which covers obscure destinations, and they can help in finding travelling companions.

Two good, reliable low-fare specialists are Trailfinders in west London, which produces a lavishly illustrated brochure including air fare details, and STA with a number of branches in London and around the UK. Most British travel agents are registered with the ABTA (Association of British Travel Agents). If you have paid for your flight to an ABTA-registered agent who then goes out of business, ABTA will guarantee a refund or an alternative. Unregistered bucket shops are riskier but also sometimes cheaper.

Continental Europe

Frankfurt is the major arrival and departure point for flights to New Zealand, with connections to other European centres.

There are many bucket shops where you can buy discounted air tickets in mainland Europe. In addition to the bucket shops, STA and Council Travel, the international student and discount travel agencies, also have a number of offices in various European countries. Any of their offices can give you the details on which office might be nearest you. In Amsterdam, NBBS is a popular travel agent.

Asia

There are far more flights to New Zealand from Asia than there were only a few years ago. There are direct flights to Auckland from Tokyo, Taipei, Hong Kong, Singapore and Denpasar/Bali, and connecting flights to most other places. Many of the connecting flights have stopovers in Australia. There are also a few direct flights to/from Christchurch including flights to/from Tokyo and Singapore.

Ticket discounting is widespread in Asia, particularly in Hong Kong, Singapore and Bangkok; Hong Kong is probably the discount air ticket capital of the region. There are a lot of fly-by-nights in the Asian ticketing scene so a little care is required. STA, which is reliable, has branches in Hong Kong, Tokyo, Singapore, Kuala Lumpur and Bangkok.

You can pick up some interesting tickets in Asia to include Australia and New Zealand on the way across the Pacific. See Circle Pacific Tickets.

SEA

Cruise ships apart, there are no longer any regular passenger ship services to New Zealand and these days arriving on some romantic tramp steamer (something you can still do in various Pacific Island nations) is pretty much a thing of the past. Ditto for the idea of working your passage.

Even working your way across the Pacific as crew on a yacht is much more difficult to arrange now than it used to be. There are many yachts sailing around the Pacific but nowadays they're usually only willing to take on experienced yachties as crew.

To try your luck finding a yacht, you have to go to the appropriate port at the appropriate time. There are lots of favourite islands, ports and harbours where you're likely to find yachts, such as Sydney and Cairns in Australia; Bali in Indonesia; various ports in Fiji or Tahiti; Hawaii, San Diego or San Francisco in the USA. In New Zealand, popular yachting harbours include the Bay of Islands and Whangarei (both in the Northland), Auckland and Wellington.

Yachts tend to move around the Pacific with the calendar – they sail with the prevailing winds and they stay out of the typhoon areas when it's cyclone season so there are certain times when you're more likely to find yachts. From Fiji, October to November is a peak departure season as cyclones are on their way. March-April is the main departure season for yachts heading to Australia. Be prepared for rough seas and storms crossing the Tasman Sea.

ORGANISED TOURS

As well as the host of tours you can arrange in New Zealand, many can be arranged from outside the country. The NZTB, which handles international promotion of tourism for New Zealand, can provide details of tour companies. NZTB offices around the world are listed in the Facts for the Visitor chapter. If you just want to add accommodation or car or campervan hire on to your air ticket, travel agents can often get better deals than that available on arrival.

LEAVING NEW ZEALAND

As in Australia, STA and Flight Centres International are popular travel agents specialising in discount fares. Flight Centres have some of the cheapest fares, and they have branches throughout New Zealand. STA has offices in Auckland, Hamilton (Waikato University), Palmerston North, Wellington, Christchurch and Dunedin.

Here are some sample discount fares offered from Auckland, quoted in NZ dollars:

Auckland to:	*one-way*	*return*
London	1250	2200
Frankfurt	1250	2200
New York	1450	2100
Los Angeles	1200	1600
San Francisco	1300	1800
Vancouver	1400	1800
Honolulu	1100	1400
Buenos Aires	1700	2300
Fiji	700	750
Singapore	650	1200
Bangkok	700	1250
Hong Kong	800	1400
Tokyo	1050	1350
Sydney	450	600
Melbourne	550	750
Brisbane	500	700
Cairns	700	1000

There's a $20 departure tax at the airport.

WARNING

The information in this chapter is particularly vulnerable to change: prices for international travel are volatile, routes are introduced and cancelled, schedules change, special deals come and go, and rules and visa requirements are amended. Airlines and governments seem to take a perverse pleasure in making price structures and regulations as complicated as possible. You should check directly with the airline or a travel agent to make sure you understand how a fare (and ticket you may buy) works. In addition, the travel industry is highly competitive and there are many lurks and perks.

The upshot of this is that you should get opinions, quotes and advice from as many airlines and travel agents as possible before you part with your hard-earned cash. The details given in this chapter should be regarded as pointers and are not a substitute for your own careful, up-to-date research.

Getting Around

AIR

Although New Zealand is a compact country and ground transport is generally quite good there are still places where flying can make a lot of sense, particularly if you've already done the same journey by land. There are also great views to be enjoyed, particularly if your flight takes you over the mountains or volcanoes. A variety of discounts makes flying in New Zealand quite economical.

New Zealand has two major domestic airlines: Air New Zealand and Ansett New Zealand. Several smaller airlines – Mt Cook Airline, Eagle Air and Air Nelson – are partly owned by Air New Zealand and have been grouped together as 'Air New Zealand Link' to complement the regular Air New Zealand services. With a host of connecting flights, the Air New Zealand National & Link network covers the country quite completely. Ansett's coverage is more limited but they, too, have many useful flights.

Discounts

Air New Zealand has regular listed economy fares, but it also has discounts which make it virtually unnecessary to ever have to pay the full fare. If you purchase your tickets before you arrive in New Zealand you can save 12.5% off the full fare, as the government's 12.5% GST tax is usually charged when you buy the tickets in New Zealand.

On the other hand, the various discount fares available can save you even more than that, some being up to 50% off the regular fare, while some fares, such as the Air New Zealand Visit New Zealand fare, are GST exempt for visitors. These all have certain requirements, which are spelled out in the airlines' timetables.

Both Air New Zealand and Ansett New Zealand offer very good deals if you have an International Student Identity Card (ISIC), giving you a 45% or 50% discount on stand-by flights. There's usually no problem getting a seat, except at the busiest times such as school holidays, Monday morning commuter flights and the like. It could be worth getting one of these cards just to save on air fares if you'll be doing much flying.

Air Passes

There are air passes available for all major flight destinations in New Zealand. The tickets are in the form of 'flight sector coupons'. Each flight uses between one and four coupons, depending on how many sectors there are to the flight (ie how many stops it makes). The passes can be open dated and even once you've set your dates, they can be changed again at little or no extra charge.

Ansett's routes are much more limited than Air New Zealand's, but you can change your itinerary anytime upon payment of a $25 surcharge. With Air New Zealand your route can be changed without penalty prior to starting the travel, but once you have taken your first flight, you cannot change your routing. Full refunds will be given prior to use of the coupons, but there is no refund after you've taken your first flight.

Air NZ Explore New Zealand Airpass – can only be bought outside NZ; minimum three coupons, maximum eight (also valid on Mount Cook Airline)

Ansett NZ New Zealand Airpass – can be bought outside or in NZ (subject to 12.5% GST tax if bought in NZ)

Prices vary between airlines, but should be within the following price brackets:

3 sectors/coupons	NZ$435–465
4 sectors/coupons	NZ$580–620
5 sectors/coupons	NZ$725–775
6 sectors/coupons	NZ$820–930
7 sectors/coupons	NZ$960–1085
8 sectors/coupons	NZ$1100–1240

Mt Cook Airline has a Kiwi Air Pass which gives you 30 days almost unlimited travel on Mt Cook Airline services for $963 (children $722, age four to 14). The only restriction is

Top: Australia vs New Zealand One-Day International, Nelson (JW)
Bottom: Sports Day, wood-chopping, Waitomo (NK)

Top: The Bath-House (Museum of Art and History), Rotorua (TW)
Bottom Left: Mt Tarawera, Rotorua (TW)
Bottom Right: Hell's Gate, Rotorua (CH)

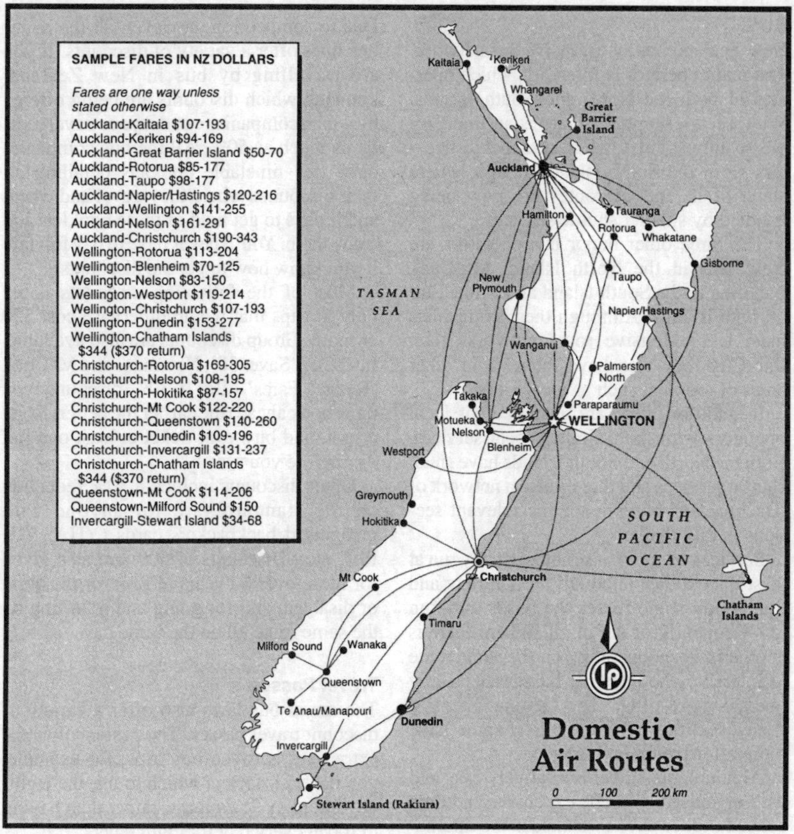

that you can only fly once in each direction on each of their scheduled flights. This pass is available only to overseas visitors, but you can buy it either outside the country or after you arrive in New Zealand.

Local Air Services & Aerial Sightseeing

Apart from the major operators there are also a host of local and feeder airlines. Services that may interest travellers include Southern Air's economic hop between Invercargill and Stewart Island, which is cheaper than the boat services and a favourite with trampers, flights to Great Barrier Island off Auckland, or flights to the Chatham Islands from Christchurch, Napier or Wellington. Flights between the North and South Islands are a popular alternative to the ferry services (see the Wellington section for details).

At some point in their travels many visitors also do a little aerial sightseeing. Popular trips include the flights in either helicopters or fixed-wing planes over the glaciers, mountains or fiords of the South Island or over the volcanoes of the central North Island. It is even possible to land on glaciers in either a skiplane or helicopter – for some the highlight of their trip to New Zealand.

BUS

New Zealand has an extensive bus network. The main operator is InterCity, which operates in both the North and South Islands. With a few exceptions there is an InterCity bus to almost any town of reasonable size – less so in the South Island, though, where some of its former routes are now being handled by smaller shuttle services.

The three other major bus operators are Newmans in the North Island, Mt Cook Landline in the South Island and White Star on both islands. Although these companies have less extensive route networks than InterCity they also have interests in other areas of tourism, such as local tours.

In addition there are a number of local operators with more limited local services. Both the North and South Islands have small shuttle services and there's also a network of 'Backpacker' buses – see the relevant sections in this chapter.

Services on main bus routes usually run at least once a day, although on Saturday and Sunday on some routes the buses may run less frequently or not at all. Where there is another service operating on the same route as InterCity, the InterCity buses will usually operate more often. The Getting There & Away sections within each chapter have more information on buses.

Although bus travel is relatively easy and well organised it can be expensive and time consuming. It pays to consider the alternatives carefully. Sometimes buying a car can actually work out cheaper than travelling by bus (see the Car & Motorcycle section later in this chapter). Slowness of travel seems particularly prevalent on the once-a-day InterCity services where the bus also operates as a means of local communication, picking up and dropping off mail at every little town along the way.

Discounts

Although fares do vary from company to company they are generally fairly close and seem to play leapfrog with one another. The sample fares given on the Bus Routes map are indicative of the normal, standard fares. Due to competition, however, all the major bus lines offer a variety of discounts. If you are travelling by bus in New Zealand, knowing which discounts are being offered by which companies can cut your travel costs by as much as 50%. All the bus companies have free timetable booklets detailing all their discounts, where they travel and when, and it pays to get hold of these booklets and study them. You'll never have to pay full fare if you know how to get the discounts.

Most of the following discounts apply only to trips that would otherwise cost $20 or more. Group discounts are also available. InterCity 'Saver 30', Newmans and Mt Cook 'Budget Fares' offer a 30% discount; you must book ahead (the earlier the better) to get a spot, and buy your ticket at least one full day before you travel.

Other discounts include a 30% reduction on the standard fare for anyone with recognised backpackers cards (YHA, VIP, ISIC etc). Discounts of 30% are also given for those over 60 years of age, for the blind or disabled, and for going and returning by the same route all on the same day.

Travel Passes

The major bus lines also offer a variety of discount travel passes. The passes allow for extra days between bus trips; for example, you have 21 days in which to use the eight-day InterCity Travelpass, rather than having to travel every day for eight days.

As with any unlimited travel pass of this type you have to do lots of travelling to make it pay off – they're best for people who want to see a lot within a short time. Book ahead on the buses to be sure of a seat.

InterCity New Zealand 3 in 1 Travelpass – unlimited travel on any InterCity bus, the train and on the Interislander ferry. Children under five travel free; those between five and 15 pay 67% of the adult fare. Costs are: eight-day pass, $453 for adults and $302 for children (travel to be completed in 21 days); 15-day pass, $569, $379 (35 days); and 22-day pass, $665, $443 (56 days).

Newmans Stopover Pass – 14 days travel in all parts of the North Island except Northland; you can travel only in one direction, ie no backtracking. It costs $99.

Newmans Flexi Pass – One Island Pass for either the North or South Island, or a Two Island Pass; valid for three months; travel can be at any time within the three-month period. The costs are: seven-day pass ($295 for One Island, $395 for Two Island); 10 days ($375, $495); 15 days ($495, $595); each additional day for the One Island Pass is $30, for the Two Island it is $40.

Mt Cook's Kiwi Coach Pass – covers both islands and includes a one-way air flight between Wellington and either Nelson or Blenheim; buy overseas or in NZ; children half-price. The costs are: seven-day pass, $418 (travel to be completed in 14 days); 10-day pass, $501 (21 days); and 15-day pass, $580 (35 days); 25-day pass, $692 (60 days); and 33-day pass, $735 (90 days).

Northliner Express – several discount passes for the Northland; valid 14 days from date of purchase; unlimited travel on various routes. Costs are Bay of Islands pass $49; Northland Freedom pass $109; Loop pass $79.

KiwiBus Network – a cover-all discount pass for most of New Zealand's smaller operators such as Kiwi Discovery, Kiwi Safaris, Northliner Express, Atomic Shuttles, Catlins Coastal Link, West Coast Express etc. The pass costs $45 and if you used it wisely you could make considerable savings. The advantage of this pass is that you are not committed to the same company for the length of the trip, which can vary from two weeks to six months.

Shuttle Buses

There are a number of small shuttle bus companies offering useful services throughout the country. Typically they are smaller, cheaper and friendlier than the regular large buses. Some of them are designed especially with foreign travellers and/or backpackers in mind, and have lots of little 'extras' that make them attractive.

Following are a few examples. In the North Island there are also shuttles around the East Cape, around Coromandel Peninsula, and up in Northland. In the South Island there are shuttles between Christchurch and Akaroa, Christchurch and Greymouth, Invercargill and Dunedin, Invercargill and Te Anau and between Westport and Karamea.

North Island

Alpine Scenic Tours (☎ (07) 378 6305) – between Turangi & National Park with stops at various spots in the Tongariro National Park that are especially useful for trampers, with extension services up to Taupo & Rotorua

C Tours (☎ (06) 758 1777) – shuttle from New Plymouth to Rotorua, with a one-hour stop at Waitomo; gets you there faster than if you took the major bus lines

Kiwi Safaris (☎ (0800) 800 616) – 'Mud & Worm Loop' circle trip Auckland, Waitomo, Rotorua, Te Aroha & Thames (or reverse – it makes the loop in both directions); free pick-up & drop-off; also Rotorua to Wellington via National Park (a full North Island Pass is $155)

Northliner Express (☎ (09) 307 5873) – Auckland to Paihia and a loop around Northland (see Travel Passes in this section)

South Island

Atomic Shuttles (☎ (03) 322 8883) – three services between Christchurch, Dunedin, Picton and Queenstown

Barry's Bus Services (☎ (03) 577 2100) – Hokitika to Nelson via Westport and return daily, Nelson to Picton via Queen Charlotte Drive and Blenheim, and Picton to Nelson via Blenheim

Catch-a-Bus (☎ (0800) 508 000) – between Queenstown and Dunedin

Catlins Coastal Link (☎ (03) 454 3179) – Dunedin to Invercargill via the scenic Catlins route

Coast to Coast Shuttle (☎ (0800) 800 847) – cross the South Island between Christchurch and Hokitika via Greymouth

Cunningham's (☎ (03) 789 7177) – Karamea to Westport for the southern end of the Heaphy Track

East West (☎ (0800) 500 251) – Christchurch to Westport via Reefton daily

Golden Bay Book-a-Bus (☎ (03) 525 9864) – Takaka to Collingwood (Tuesday and Friday only), Takaka to Nelson via Motueka, Nelson to Takaka with connections to Totaranui and Heaphy by arrangement

Kiwi Discovery (☎ (03) 442 7340) – Queenstown to Milford

Ko-op Shuttles (☎ (03) 366 6633) – Christchurch to Picton, Dunedin and Greymouth, all daily services

Nationwide Shuttles (☎ (03) 379 5531) – Christchurch to Queenstown via Tekapo, Christchurch to Dunedin via Oamaru and Timaru

Nelson Lakes Transport (☎ (03) 521 1887) – between Nelson & St Arnaud for the Nelson Lakes National Park

Sounds to Coast (Blenheim Taxis) (☎ (0800) 802 225) – Picton to Greymouth via St Arnaud (Monday, Wednesday and Friday)

Backpackers Buses

In addition to the regular bus services and the shuttle buses, there are several buses catering primarily to backpackers. A number of such bus companies operate tours lasting for several days in various parts of the country. In some places, notably the west coast of the South Island, these can be the best way of seeing the area if you don't have your own wheels, as hitchhiking is difficult and the more conventional bus services simply whiz past many of the most attractive spots. Some offer greater flexibility than others, allowing you to get off the bus for independent travel and then get on again when the bus next comes around. Mostly they are organised tours these days, and in summer, if you are allowed to get off it can be difficult to get a seat again on a crowded bus.

On all these trips the buses are comfortably fitted out, the atmosphere is casual and there are plenty of stops to see the sights along the way, plus stops for walks, picnics, boat cruises, recreational activities and so on. Usually all you need to bring is a sleeping bag, plus the usual travelling gear such as good walking shoes, warm clothes and rain gear, and your own food. Accommodation costs are extra; low-cost overnight accommodation is pre-booked, usually at hostels (the cost is about $13 to $16 a night), with an option to camp if you have your own tent ($8 a night). The exception is the Flying Kiwi bus, a 'rolling travellers home' which comes equipped with bunks and tents, included in the price.

Except for the Southern Explorer, which operates only in summer from October to May, all the buses operate all year round, with more frequent departures in summer. Often they have negotiated special deals so you can get discounts on activities, accommodation, etc as you travel with them.

All the buses have pamphlets detailing their itineraries, departure times and costs. Contact numbers are listed here for direct bookings. Many can also be booked through hostels and visitor information centres. All require advance booking, and usually a deposit. Be sure you understand the refund policy when you make your booking, in case you decide to cancel later on.

Kiwi Experience – Well known, and with a reputation for parties; North & South Islands; 12 routes; minimum of two to 18 days to complete one route, depending on the route; tickets valid for six months, so you can complete your travel any time within that period. For reservations: Auckland, 36 Customs St East, PO Box 1553, (☎ (09) 366 1665); Wellington (☎ (04) 385 2153); Christchurch (☎ (03) 311 0550); and in Sydney, Australia, (☎ (02) 977 2688).

Ice Bus – operates from Christchurch to Queenstown via the Glaciers, Queenstown to Christchurch via Dunedin. It is operated by Kiwi Experience

Magic Bus – North & South Islands, affiliated with InterCity buses. Bookings: at any hostel, or by telephoning Auckland (☎ (09) 358 5600); Wellington (☎ (04) 387 2018); Nelson (☎ (03) 548 3290); Queenstown (☎ (03) 442 8178); and Christchurch (☎ (03) 377 0951).

North Cape Green Beetle – North Island; departs from Auckland for the Northland region for a five-day ($179) or six-day trip ($199). Contact them in Auckland at the ACB Travel Centre (☎ (09) 358 4874).

Awesome Tours – North Island, affiliated with Kiwi Experience; Northland; tour lasts three days but passes are good for six months. Bookings: Auckland (☎ (09) 366 1665).

West Coast Express – South Island; six days Nelson to Queenstown via the West Coast route; cost $99; you can depart from either end of the line. For bookings in Nelson contact Tasman Towers (☎ (03) 548 7950) or the office (☎ (03) 546 6703); and in Queenstown contact the YHA Hostel (☎ (03) 442 8413) or Backpacking Specialists (☎ (03) 442 8178).

Southern Explorer – South Island; four-day trip from Queenstown to Dunedin via Te Anau, Milford Sound, the 'southern scenic route' to Invercargill, through the Catlins and on to Dunedin; cost $120; for $150 you can continue on from Dunedin to Queenstown or Te Anau. One-day sections available for individual day prices ($25 to $45). Book in Queenstown at the Backpacking Specialists (☎ (03) 442 8178) or in Te Anau at the Te Anau Motor Park (☎ (03) 249 7820).

Flying Kiwi – the 'rolling travellers home'; includes bunks, tents, hot shower and kitchen. They carry mountain bikes, a Canadian canoe, a windsurfer, fishing gear and more. South Island trips include 10-day ($550); 17-day ($890); and 24-day ($1190). In the North Island they operate a seven-day trip and a two-day Northern Express trip. Contact them at 2 Canterbury St, Picton (☎ (03) 573 8126).

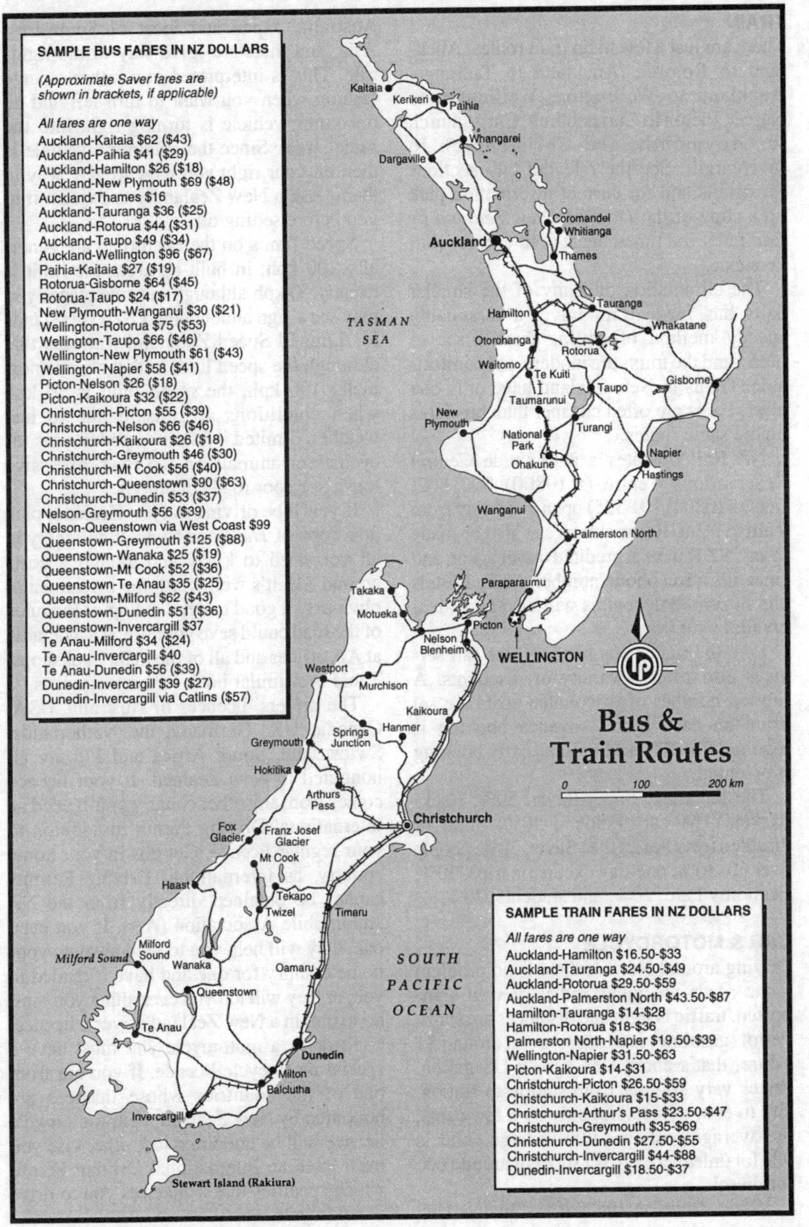

SAMPLE BUS FARES IN NZ DOLLARS

(Approximate Saver fares are shown in brackets, if applicable)

All fares are one way

Auckland-Kaitaia $62 ($43)
Auckland-Paihia $41 ($29)
Auckland-Hamilton $26 ($18)
Auckland-New Plymouth $69 ($48)
Auckland-Thames $16
Auckland-Tauranga $36 ($25)
Auckland-Rotorua $44 ($31)
Auckland-Taupo $49 ($34)
Auckland-Wellington $96 ($67)
Paihia-Kaitaia $27 ($19)
Rotorua-Gisborne $64 ($45)
Rotorua-Taupo $24 ($17)
New Plymouth-Wanganui $30 ($21)
Wellington-Rotorua $75 ($53)
Wellington-Taupo $66 ($46)
Wellington-New Plymouth $61 ($43)
Wellington-Napier $58 ($41)
Picton-Nelson $26 ($18)
Picton-Kaikoura $32 ($22)
Christchurch-Picton $55 ($39)
Christchurch-Nelson $66 ($46)
Christchurch-Kaikoura $26 ($18)
Christchurch-Greymouth $46 ($30)
Christchurch-Mt Cook $56 ($40)
Christchurch-Queenstown $90 ($63)
Christchurch-Dunedin $53 ($37)
Nelson-Greymouth $56 ($39)
Nelson-Queenstown via West Coast $99
Queenstown-Greymouth $125 ($88)
Queenstown-Wanaka $25 ($19)
Queenstown-Mt Cook $52 ($36)
Queenstown-Te Anau $35 ($25)
Queenstown-Milford $62 ($43)
Queenstown-Dunedin $51 ($36)
Queenstown-Invercargill $37
Te Anau-Milford $34 ($24)
Te Anau-Invercargill $40
Te Anau-Dunedin $56 ($39)
Dunedin-Invercargill $39 ($27)
Dunedin-Invercargill via Catlins ($57)

SAMPLE TRAIN FARES IN NZ DOLLARS

All fares are one way

Auckland-Hamilton $16.50-$33
Auckland-Tauranga $24.50-$49
Auckland-Rotorua $29.50-$59
Auckland-Palmerston North $43.50-$87
Hamilton-Tauranga $14-$28
Hamilton-Rotorua $18-$36
Palmerston North-Napier $19.50-$39
Wellington-Napier $31.50-$63
Picton-Kaikoura $14-$31
Christchurch-Picton $26.50-$59
Christchurch-Kaikoura $15-$33
Christchurch-Arthur's Pass $23.50-$47
Christchurch-Greymouth $35-$69
Christchurch-Dunedin $27.50-$55
Christchurch-Invercargill $44-$88
Dunedin-Invercargill $18.50-$37

TRAIN

There are just a few main train routes: Auckland to Rotorua, Auckland to Tauranga, Auckland to Wellington, Wellington to Napier, Picton to Christchurch, Christchurch to Greymouth, and Christchurch to Invercargill. See the relevant city sections for details and for current information pick up a copy of the *Discover New Zealand by Rail* fares and timetable at your earliest convenience.

The elimination of many of the smaller halts has made train travel a reasonably speedy method of getting from place to place, and the trains are modern and comfortable. Trains in New Zealand have only one class. Fares are often cheaper than bus fares on the same routes.

NZ Rail operates a nationwide Central Reservations Centre (☎ (0800) 802 802; freefax (0800) 101 525) open every day from 7 am to 9 pm. Reservations can also be made at any NZ Rail or accredited travel agent, and since it's a freephone number, many hostels and information centres will also make reservations for you.

Like the major bus services, the rail services also offer a variety of discounts. A limited number of discounted seats are set aside on each train. Advance booking is required for all these fares and early booking is essential.

The fares are: Super Saver, 50%; Backpacker/YHA card-holders, 30%; blind or disabled travellers, 50%; Saver, 30%; people over 60, 30%; one-day excursion trips, 30%; Economy Fare, 20%; and students, 20%.

CAR & MOTORCYCLE

Driving around New Zealand is no problem – the roads are good and very well signposted, traffic is light and distances are short. Petrol (gasoline) is expensive – at around $1 a litre, that's about US$3 for a US gallon. Prices vary slightly from station to station, city to countryside, but only by a few cents; the average costs per litre in large cities is 92c for unleaded, 97c for super or around 60c for diesel.

Kiwis drive on the left, as in the UK, Australia, Japan and most of South-East Asia, and there's a 'give way to the right' rule. This is interpreted in a rather strange fashion when you want to turn left and an oncoming vehicle is turning right into the same street. Since the oncoming vehicle is then on your right you have to give way to them. Ask a New Zealander to explain it to you before setting off.

Speed limits on the open road are generally 100 kph; in built-up areas the limit is usually 50 kph although in some places you may see a sign announcing LSZ. This stands for Limited Speed Zone and it means that although the speed limit in that zone is normally 100 kph, the speed limit is 50 kph when conditions are unsafe due to bad weather, limited visibility, pedestrians or cyclists or animals on the road, excessive traffic, or poor road conditions.

If you'll be driving in New Zealand, pick up a copy of *The Road Code*. It will tell you all you need to know and though it costs around $15 it's well worth the investment – obviously a good understanding of the rules of the road could save your life. It's available at AA offices and all of the main bookshops. There is a similar book for motorcyclists.

The drivers' licences of Australia, USA, Canada, UK, Germany, the Netherlands, Switzerland, South Africa and Fiji are all honoured in New Zealand. If your licence comes from any other country you'll need an International Driving Permit in addition to your regular licence. Get this in your home country, as International Driving Permits cannot be obtained directly from the NZ Automobile Association (AA). If you need one, they will help you to send away to your home country for one and have it mailed to you, or they will tell you everything you must do to obtain a New Zealand driver's licence.

To drive a motorcycle you must have a special motorcycle licence. If you are from one of the countries whose licences are honoured by New Zealand, your motorcycle licence will be honoured too, otherwise you must have an International Driving Permit which specifies that it licences you to drive a motorcycle.

Excellent road maps are readily available in New Zealand; see Books & Maps in the Facts for the Visitor chapter. If you're a member of the AA you can go into any AA office, present your card, and get all the maps you want for free. There are a number of other useful benefits of AA membership including emergency breakdown services, free technical advice about your car, free legal assistance if you should get a traffic ticket, help in understanding the NZ driving rules, and so on.

Membership in the AA costs $66 per year plus a joining fee of $20. The AA has reciprocal rights with the automobile associations of many countries, so members of an equivalent organisation may qualify for reciprocal benefits from the AA in New Zealand. Remember to bring your card. The AA also operates a mobile car inspection service, a very useful service if you're buying a used car.

Car Rental

The major operators – Avis, Budget, Hertz – have extensive fleets of cars in New Zealand with offices in almost every town. Unlimited km rental of a small car (Toyota Corolla, Mitsubishi Mirage) starts at around $70 per day, more for rental of only a few days. If you are just driving around town and don't choose an unlimited km option then expect to pay about 30c a km.

Medium-sized cars (Toyota Corona, Ford Telstar) are typically around $100 per day with unlimited km. In addition there's a daily insurance charge of around $15 a day, and a drop-off fee if you are not returning the car to the city of hire. For hire of a new car through a major operator, overseas travel agents can often get better deals than you can hunt out yourself in New Zealand.

Apart from the three major international operators there are also a number of others. Their rates often undercut the major operators but there may be more restrictions on use, and one-way rentals may not always be possible. All sorts of special deals are available. In peak season you may get a car for $55 (all inclusive) if you rent it for more than four days; in off-peak periods the cost may drop to $45.

Operators often want cars to be shifted from Wellington to Auckland and from Christchurch to Picton because most renters travel in the opposite directions. In these instances special rates may apply. Usually you must be at least 21 years old to rent a car in New Zealand and sometimes there will be an insurance excess if you're under 25.

Car rental is very competitive in the major cities, particularly Auckland. The surplus of operators means that you can often get special deals for longer rentals, especially outside the peak summer months. Shop around, and play one company off against the other – quoting a competitor's rates may bring a reduction, even from the major companies.

Many smaller operators have second-hand cars, advertised for as little as $20 per day, but you get what you pay for. Advertised rates (and even quotes over the phone) are often misleading, and business practices can leave a lot to be desired. Always check km rates to see if the price includes GST, minimum hire periods, bonds and insurance coverage. Always read the rental agreement before you sign. The rock-bottom rates usually apply to minimum one-month hire in the off season for a beat-up car over 10 years old with limited or even no insurance. Full payment in advance and a credit card bond may be required. Insurance from the cheaper rental agencies is usually subject to an excess of at least $500 (plus GST) for any accident or damage to the car (sometimes including tyre replacement and puncture repairs), even if it is not your fault.

If you are prepared to risk the insurance restrictions, second-hand car hire can be good value. For one month hire, you can get a late 1980s model Japanese import in the off season for as little as $25 a day or a recent model for $40 a day. Prices are up to 50% higher in the peak season, and prices are also higher outside Auckland. Insurance coverage for all hire cars is usually invalid on certain roads, typically beaches and unsealed roads in major tourist areas.

Campervan Rental

Renting a campervan (also known as mobile homes, motor homes or, in US parlance, Winnebago's or RVs) is an enormously popular way of getting around New Zealand. In some popular but out-of-the-way areas of the South Island almost every other vehicle seems to be a campervan. With a campervan you have your transport and accommodation all in one neat package, and you've also got your own kitchen on wheels.

There are numerous companies renting campervans and their costs vary with the type of vehicle and the time of year. For a small van, suitable for two people, the cost could be around $150 per day during the high season (usually from 1 October to 30 April), $90 per day in the low season (usually from 1 May to 30 September) through the main companies. Better deals can see prices drop to around $65 per day for longer rentals in off-peak periods, and overseas travel agents can also get good discounts.

Maui is one of the main operators and the main car hire operators also rent campervans. For details on companies renting campervans in Auckland, see that chapter in the Getting There & Away section. Smaller operators rates start at around $40 per day, though these may be kitted out minivans rather than true campervans.

House Trucks

When travelling around New Zealand, watch out for colourful and exotic house trucks. These individually built constructions often look like a collision between an elderly truck and a timber cottage, sometimes complete with shingle roof and bay windows! Many of these uniquely Kiwi contraptions look far too fragile for road use but they seem to travel all over the country and are often parked for days or even months in the most idyllic settings.

Motorcycle Rental

It's also possible to hire a motorcycle for touring in New Zealand. Most of the motorcycle hire shops are in Auckland, and Christchurch has a few too; see those sections for details. You can hire anything from a little 50 cc moped or 'Nifty-fifty', for zipping around town, to a big 750 cc touring motorcycle.

Remember you will need a motorcycle licence; a car licence might get you by if you want to do something like toodle around on a moped, but if you want to drive a regular motorcycle (rental bikes are usually from 250 cc to 750 cc in size) then you'll have to have a motorcycle licence. As with cars, you can find motorcycles to buy on the buy-back system.

Buying a Car

If you're planning a longer stay and/or you're travelling in a group, buying a car and then selling it again at the end of your travels can be one of the cheapest ways of seeing New Zealand. You're not tied to the bus schedules, nor do you find yourself waiting by the roadside with your thumb out looking for a ride.

Since most travellers arrive in New Zealand at Auckland, that's where most look to buy a car. Fortunately this is easy to do; it seems the city is inundated with cars for sale.

There are many ways to buy cars in Auckland. One convenient option is the 'buy-back system', where the dealer guarantees to buy the car back from you at the end of your travels. The buy-back amount varies, but may be 50% less than the purchase price if you've had the car for a long time and taken it all around the country. It is often cheaper to hire a car or buy and sell elsewhere if you have the time. Some dealers give you the right to sell the car to anyone else – a very convenient option since you can try to get the best price you can, but have the guaranteed offer of a sale if time is running short.

A company that combines buy-back and long-term rental is Car Link NZ Ltd in Auckland. You post a bond to the value of the vehicle and at the end of your 'purchase' period the bond is refunded, minus a fixed 'usage fee' regardless of how long you've had the vehicle (up to a maximum of six months) – it's basically a cheap long-term rental with increased responsibility for you to look after the vehicle. Enquiries and bookings should be made through Travel Action (☎ +49-2764-78 24; fax +49-2764-79 38), Einsiedeleiweg 16, D-57399 Kirchhundem, Germany, a few months in advance to ensure the vehicle of your choice.

Other dealers who sell cars on the buy-back system are listed in the Auckland section. There is at least one similar dealer operating in Christchurch – Wheels (☎ (03) 366 4855) at 20 Manchester St. The Christchurch/Canterbury tourist information centre can probably tell you of others.

There are many other ways of buying and selling cars in Auckland. You can find cars in the newspaper small ads just like anywhere else in the world. Auckland has a number of auctions and car fairs, where private individuals bring their cars to sell. For details, see the Auckland chapter. The car fairs and auctions have lots of cars available from around $1000 to $4500. These are the real cheapies; a good, late-model used car from a dealer could cost around $8500 (with warranty).

In general, the cheapest prices are found at the auctions. Next cheapest prices will be found at car fairs, where you have more time to browse around. You might try buying at an auction and selling at a fair to get the best overall deal.

Another way to find cheap cars for sale is to look on the notice boards of hostels, where you'll often see ads from other travellers keen to sell their cars and move on. Though less so than Auckland, Christchurch is another popular arrival and departure point; it has lots of cars.

Make sure any car you buy has a WOF (Warrant of Fitness) and that the registration lasts for a reasonable period. You have to have the WOF certificate proving that the car is roadworthy in order to register it, and the WOF must be current (not more than 28 days old). To register a car, both you and the seller fill out a form which is filed at any post office. Registration can be purchased for either six months or a year.

Auckland has a very useful mobile inspection service, Car Inspection Services Ltd (☎ (09) 309 8084), who come to wherever you are and perform a thorough inspection on any car you are considering buying. The cost is $75 but it's worth it. The AA also does car inspections; the cost is the same for their mobile inspection service, or about $10 cheaper if you bring the car to an AA-approved mechanic. The car fairs and auctions have inspection services standing by to provide on-the-spot inspections. Car inspections are highly recommended and the cost may well save you in repair bills later. Another wise precaution before you buy a car is to ring the freephone Credit Check telephone number (☎ (0800) 658 934). With the licence plate and chassis numbers, they can confirm the ownership of the car and tell you if any outstanding debts are owed on it.

Car prices in New Zealand, which a few years ago were amazingly expensive due to high duties, have come down remarkably due to large numbers of used cars from Japan having been shipped to NZ. There are now so many Japanese second-hand imports in the country that getting spares for them is no longer a problem.

BICYCLE

In recent years there has been a marked increase in the number of cyclists touring New Zealand. You seem to see touring bicycles almost everywhere, especially in summer. There are lots of hills, so it's hard going at times, but it's a compact country and there's always plenty of variety. Many cyclists call New Zealand a cyclists' paradise – it's clean, green, uncrowded, unspoiled, friendly, there are plenty of places where you can camp out or get cheap accommodation in hostels, plenty of fresh water, the climate is not too hot or too cold, the roads are good, bikes (whether to rent or buy) and cycling gear are readily available, as are bicycle repair services – you get the idea. Pick up a copy of *Cycle Touring in New Zealand* by Bruce Ringer – it's full of useful information for cyclists, like where the steep hills are!

Occasionally a cyclist may resort to public transport. The best way to carry a bike on public transport is often on one of the shuttle buses or backpackers buses; you can bus it on the major bus lines or on the train, but they'll only take it on a 'space available' basis (meaning it may not get on) and you'll have to pay extra for it (around $10). Some of the shuttle or backpackers buses, on the other hand, make sure they always have enough storage space to accommodate bikes and they usually will take them along as baggage for free.

Many international airlines will carry your bicycle at no additional cost as 'sporting equipment'. Remember to bring your helmet, as NZ regulations require that you wear one.

Many bicycle rental operators in New Zealand offer daily and weekly bicycle hire, with negotiable monthly rates. Bicycle rental is listed in the Getting Around sections of cities and towns throughout this book. Costs vary widely – daily rates can be anywhere from around $10 to $25, weekly rates anywhere from around $50 to $125, and monthly rates anywhere from around $120 to $360; it all depends what kind of bike you get and where you get it from. A bit of time spent comparing prices will probably be time well spent. Practically all rental companies also have bicycle touring gear and repair kits available.

The Kiwi Experience bus people offer a bus-bike combination called Wild Cycles; for more details ring ☎ (09) 366 1665. Adventure South (☎ (09) 486 5327; (03) 332 1222) have four choices of back-road cycle tours: Clarence, Queenstown, West Coast and Milford – all in the South Island.

Bicycle Tours of New Zealand (☎ (09) 276 5218) at 22 Walmsley Rd, Otahuhu, opposite the train station, has cheap rentals and Pedaltours (☎ (09) 302 0968) in Parnell, Auckland, offers a variety of guided cycle tours but they're not cheap.

Of course you can also buy bicycles in New Zealand but prices are high for new bikes. If you want to 'own your own' you're better off bringing one in, or buying a used one. Hostel notice boards frequently have signs offering mountain bikes for sale, or check the newspaper ads.

HITCHING

Overall, New Zealand is a great place for hitching and, although almost anybody who does a fair amount of hitching will get stuck somewhere uncomfortable for an uncomfortably long period of time, most travellers rate it highly. It's pretty safe, the roads are not crowded but there are just enough cars to make things fairly easy, and the locals are well disposed towards hitchhikers.

The usual hitching rules apply. If you're standing in one spot, pick your location so drivers can see you easily and stop safely. Some hitchhikers report they have better luck hitching while walking alongside the road than when standing planted in one spot. You may find you have better luck getting picked up if you stand in a 50 kph speed zone rather than a 100 kph zone, as it's easier for the cars to stop. Often you'll have better luck the earlier it is in the day.

In larger towns it usually pays to get out of town before starting to hitch, either by local bus or walking. You may pick up a lift on the way out, but don't count on it; it's much harder to get a ride in town with a pack. On the other hand, on the open road it's a lot easier to get a lift if you're wearing a pack. Learn which rides not to take – not just crazy drivers but also rides that leave you at inconvenient locations; wait for the right one.

Dress for the occasion – not in your fancy clothes ('they can afford to take the bus') or too shabbily ('don't want them in my car'). If someone else is already hitching on the same stretch of road remember to walk ahead of them so they get the first ride, or leave the road until they get a ride. Most importantly, be cautious and careful – there are some unpleasant people on the road in New Zealand just as there are anywhere else in the world.

Generally hitching on the main routes in the North Island is good. In the South Island hitching down the east coast from Picton through Christchurch to Invercargill is mostly good. Elsewhere in the South Island there are hundreds of km of main roads with very little traffic. Expect long waits – even days – in some places. It's a good idea to have the InterCity, Newmans and Mt Cook timetables with you so you can flag a bus down if you're tired of hitching. Make sure you show the driver the colour of your money. Quite a few drivers have been stopped by hitchhikers who have then decided they can't afford the fare, so some bus drivers are wary about stopping unless they know you're prepared to pay.

It's easier hitching alone if you are male. Unfortunately, even though New Zealand is basically a safe country for women, a woman on her own may experience some tricky – if not dangerous – situations. It is better to travel with someone else if possible. Many hostels have local hints for hitching (such as what bus to get out of town, where to hitch from) on their notice boards.

Please note that hitching is not always a safe way of getting around. The well-publicised murder of two Swedish hitchhikers a few years ago highlights the fact that even in relatively safe New Zealand hitchhiking can be a risky undertaking. Just because we explain how it works doesn't mean we recommend it.

BOAT

Inter-Island Ferries

The *Interislander* ferry and the *Lynx* services, operating between Wellington in the North Island and Picton in the South Island, are covered in detail in the Wellington chapter.

Other regularly scheduled inter-island ferry services in New Zealand include those to the various islands off Auckland; see the Auckland chapter. A ferry also connects Stewart Island (Rakiura) with the South Island at Bluff, near Invercargill.

Other Water Transport

There are various places where transport is more convenient by water than by land, especially in the Marlborough Sounds area where a number of places to stay can only be reached by water. Regular launch and water-taxi services operate along the coast of the Abel Tasman National Park.

Other convenient ferry services include the ferries to Russell on the east side of the Northland, including the passenger ferry from Paihia and the car ferry crossing over from Opua. On the west side of the Northland is the convenient car ferry from Rawene to Kohukohu.

In other places transport over lakes is a significant way to get around and see things, such as at Wakatipu, Taupo and Waikaremoana. Sometimes the most interesting things to see are reached by water rather than by land; cruises on Milford and Doubtful Sounds in Fiordland in the South Island and on the Bay of Islands in the Northland are especially popular.

LOCAL TRANSPORT

To/From the Airport

In all the large cities and even many smaller ones, shuttles operate to and from the airports. A taxi shared between three or four people may work out cheaper.

Suburban Buses & Trains

There are bus services in most larger cities but with a few honourable exceptions they are mainly daytime, weekday operations. On weekends and particularly on Sunday, buses can be hard to find.

The only city with a good suburban train service is Wellington.

Taxi

Although there are plenty of taxis in the major towns they rarely 'cruise'. If you want a taxi you usually either have to phone for one or go to a taxi rank.

Bicycle

Bicycles can be rented by the hour, day or week in most major cities and in many smaller locales. Rentals by the week for longer trips are becoming more common. See the Bicycle section earlier in this chapter.

ORGANISED TOURS

Tours can sometimes be a useful way of getting around, especially if you're travelling in an area that is otherwise hard to reach, or when you have limited time, or when you want the benefit of commentary. Backpackers often use the 'alternative' buses as a sort of informal tour; see these in the Bus section.

Otherwise there are a variety of more conventional tours. Thrifty Tours, operated by InterCity, are indeed thrifty, using a combination of tour buses and public transport to create a variety of short and long tours all over New Zealand. Mt Cook Line, operators of the Mt Cook Landline bus network and Mt Cook Airline, also offers a variety of tours around New Zealand. Gray Line (☎ (0800) 800 904) is another major tour operator, offering a variety of one-day tours in various cities and towns, plus inter-city tours. All of these are major companies which can be contacted through virtually any travel agent or visitor information centre in New Zealand, or through travel agents or the NZTB before you arrive in New Zealand.

Where there are specific, worthy and interesting tours (some of several days) they have been listed under the towns where they depart from.

Bushwise Women (☎ & fax (03) 332 4952) specialises in trips for women only with an emphasis on women's ambience. They range from working on conservation projects to tramping but all are a good opportunity to meet other women travellers.

NORTH ISLAND

Auckland

On the shores of Waitemata and Manukau harbours, Auckland is surrounded by water and covered in volcanic hills. It has a population of around one million – over a quarter of all New Zealanders – and is also the 'big city' for the Polynesian islands of the South Pacific. So many islanders from New Zealand's Pacific neighbours have moved to Auckland that it now has the largest concentration of Polynesians in the world, and more recently it has been attracting immigrants from Asia as well. All these foreign influences help to give Auckland a much more cosmopolitan atmosphere than other cities in New Zealand.

Sprawling between the two large harbours, Auckland has a lot of enthusiastic yachties who sail back, forth and around on weekends and make it look very picturesque – the city is nicknamed 'the City of Sails'.

Like Sydney it has a harbour bridge, which was opened in 1959 with due pomp and ceremony and four traffic lanes. Probably to no-one's surprise it was discovered that the reason not many people lived on the North Shore was because there hadn't been a bridge – and as soon as there was one, so many people moved there to live that the bridge wasn't big enough. Fortunately, the Japanese came to the rescue and 'clipped' two more lanes on each side (known locally as the 'Nippon Clippons') to convert it to eight streams of cars.

Auckland is the main arrival point for international visitors. It has a large variety of attractions, accommodation, restaurants and night-time entertainment.

HIGHLIGHTS

- A harbour cruise
- A ferry ride and visit to Devonport
- Auckland Museum and its Maori collection
- A stroll and a meal in one of Auckland's genteel inner suburbs such as Parnell
- The Islands of the Hauraki Gulf, ranging from Rangitoto (an extinct volcano) and Waiheke (a village extension of Auckland), to the much wilder and remote Great Barrier Island
- A walk through the rugged forest of the Waitakeres or a pleasant tour of the wineries in West Auckland

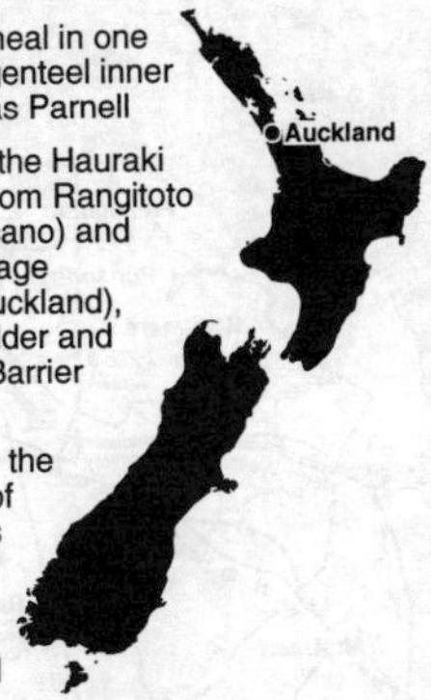

History

Maori settlement in the Auckland area dates from as early as 1350 AD. Other Maori peoples wanted the fertile land in succeeding years, and eventually the volcanic cones around the area were topped by *pas* (fortified Maori settlements). However, tribal wars and epidemics ravaged the settlements and by 1840, when Europeans came to settle here, the area was almost deserted.

From early colonial times the administrative centre of New Zealand had been at Russell in the Northland, but after the signing of the Treaty of Waitangi in 1840, Captain William Hobson, New Zealand's first governor, decided to move the capital south to a more central position. The site of Auckland was chosen principally for its fine harbour and good soil, and in September 1840 officials came down from Russell to formally proclaim Auckland capital of New Zealand. Governor Hobson named the new settlement after his former commander, Lord Auckland, who was at that time the viceroy of India and a British hero.

The new settlement did not get off to a good start, and 25 years later, in 1865, the capital was moved once again, this time south to Wellington.

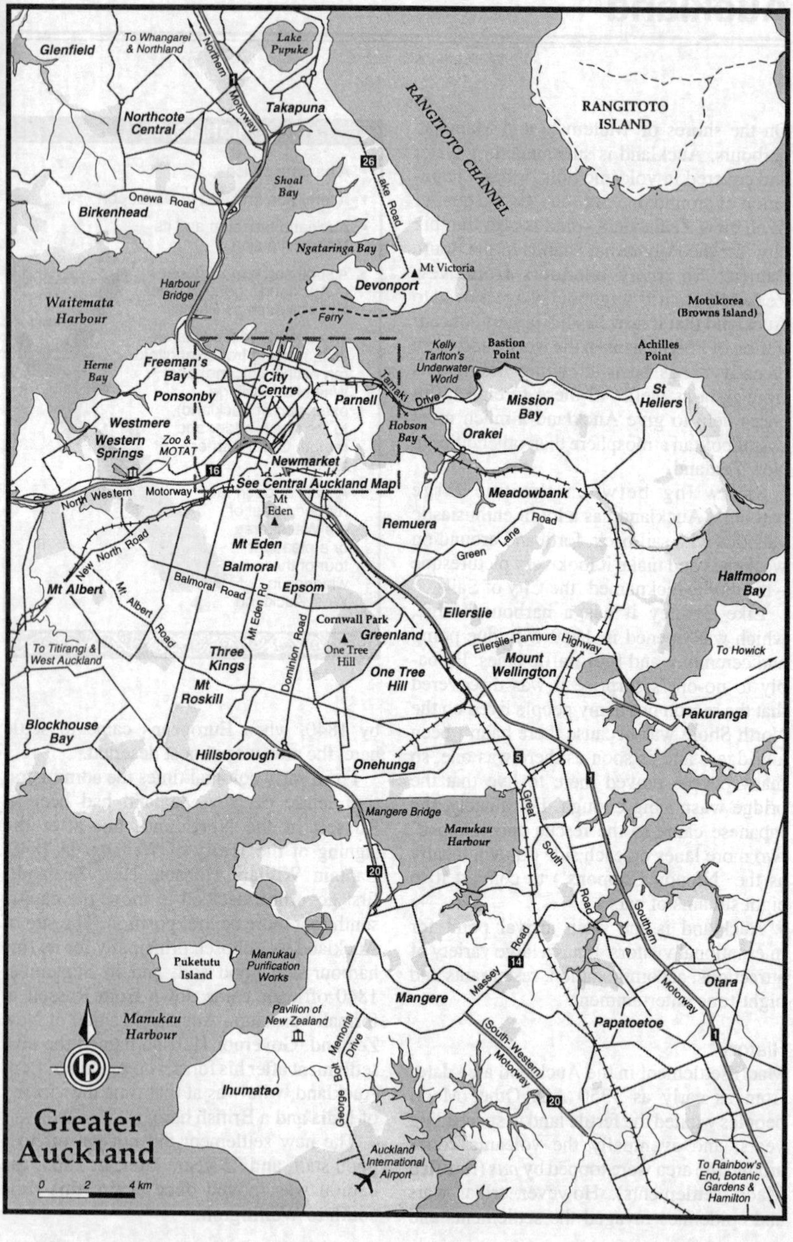
Greater Auckland
0 2 4 km
To Whangarei & Northland
Glenfield
Northern Motorway
Lake Pupuke
Takapuna
Northcote Central
RANGITOTO CHANNEL
RANGITOTO ISLAND
Shoal Bay
Lake Road
Onewa Road
Birkenhead
Ngataringa Bay
Mt Victoria
Devonport
Harbour Bridge
Waitemata Harbour
Ferry
Motukorea (Browns Island)
Kelly Tarlton's Underwater World
Bastion Point
Achilles Point
Herne Bay
Freeman's Bay
City Centre
Tamaki Drive
Parnell
Mission Bay
St Heliers
Ponsonby
Westmere
Western Springs
Zoo & MOTAT
Hobson Bay
Orakei
Newmarket
See Central Auckland Map
North Western Motorway
Meadowbank
Mt Eden
Remuera
Green Lane Road
New North Road
Mt Eden
Balmoral
Halfmoon Bay
Balmoral Road
Mt Eden Rd
Epsom
Mt Albert
Mt Albert Road
Ellerslie
Cornwall Park
Greenland
One Tree Hill
Dominion Road
Ellerslie-Panmure Highway
To Titirangi & West Auckland
Three Kings
One Tree Hill
Mount Wellington
To Howick
Mt Roskill
Pakuranga
Blockhouse Bay
Hillsborough
Onehunga
Mangere Bridge
Manukau Harbour
Great South Road
Southern Motorway
Massey Road
Puketutu Island
Manukau Purification Works
Otara
Mangere
Pavilion of New Zealand
Papatoetoe
Manukau Harbour
George Bolt Memorial Drive
(South-Western) Motorway
Ihumatao
Auckland International Airport
To Rainbow's End, Botanic Gardens & Hamilton

Later in the century, a gold rush in Thames and a great increase in the area's agricultural production did much to revive Auckland. Since the turn of the century Auckland has been New Zealand's fastest-growing city and its main industrial centre. While political deals may be done in Wellington, Auckland is the commercial centre dominating the country.

Orientation

The commercial heart of Auckland is Queen St, which runs from Queen Elizabeth II Square – usually called 'QE II Square' by the locals – near the Ferry Building by the waterfront, uphill to Karangahape Rd (called simply 'K Rd'), passing Aotea Square with the visitor centre and large Aotea Centre.

The Downtown Airline Terminal is near the waterfront, the railway station is about one km to the east, and the airport is about 21 km south-west of the centre.

To the east of Queen St is Albert Park, a popular lunch-time haven for city workers and students. Beyond the park is Auckland University; it's New Zealand's largest university and visitors are welcome at most activities.

Quay St runs along the waterfront, and Customs St is parallel, one block inland; it's called Customs St East on one side of Queen St, Customs St West on the other.

While the commercial district has much of the accommodation, many restaurants and most of Auckland's nightlife, it suffers from the 'dead heart' syndrome of many cities. Suburban shopping areas outside the city are often more appealing and lively. Parnell, just east of the city centre, is a fashionable area of renovated wooden villas, and Parnell Rd is lined with boutiques and restaurants. Just west of the city centre is Ponsonby, another old area packed with restaurants.

Administratively, Auckland comprises a number of cities, all blending into one vast urban sprawl. Auckland City proper lies between Waitemata and Manukau harbours. North Shore City, centred around Takapuna, lies to the north over the harbour bridge. Manukau City is to the south of Auckland, around the airport, and Waitakere City is west of Auckland.

Maps The mini-map series is very handy for finding your way around Auckland – small to carry, yet detailed enough to show everything. You can get good maps of Auckland and other places in New Zealand from the Auckland Visitor Centre, the AA, DOSLI (see Tourist Information) and bookshops. The free tourist information booklets *Auckland A to Z Visitors Guide* and the *Auckland Great Time Guide* contain good maps of the city centre.

Information

The free annual *Auckland A to Z Visitors Guide* booklet and the monthly *Auckland Great Time Guide* booklet are useful publications. See Newspapers in this section for more information.

Tourist Offices The Auckland Visitor Centre (☎ 366 6888; fax 366 6893), 299 Queen St on Aotea Square, can answer most queries and makes bookings for transport, tours, activities and accommodation in Auckland and further afield. A travellers' notice board has personal ads for cars, bicycles, camping gear, etc. The office is open Monday to Friday from 8.30 am to 5.30 pm and from 9 am to 5 pm on weekends and holidays. It also operates an information kiosk (☎ 366 0691), open from 9 am to 5 pm every day, on QE II Square at the foot of Queen St.

The Airport Visitor Centre (☎ 275 6467) in the International Terminal is well stocked with brochures and can answer queries and make bookings. There is also a small information booth in the Domestic Terminal. Near the airport on George Bolt Memorial Drive, heading towards the city, is the drive-in Automobile Association (AA) Host Information Centre.

Other information centres include the North Shore Visitor Information Centre (☎ 486 8670) on Hurstmere Rd in Takapuna, on the North Shore.

The Department of Conservation (DOC) and Auckland Regional Parks have a combined information centre (☎ 366 2166) at the Ferry Building, open every day from 8.30 am to 6 pm in summer, and 8.30 am to 5 pm Monday to Friday the rest of the year. They have brochures on the parks and natural attractions for Auckland and the whole country, and can help you plan an itinerary to New Zealand's natural attractions. The main DOC office (☎ 307 1465; fax 377 2919) is in the Sheraton complex on the corner of Karangahape Rd and Liverpool St.

Money The Bank of New Zealand branch at the airport is open for all international arrivals and departures.

Queen St has plenty of moneychangers and banks, open Monday to Friday from around 9 am to 4.30 pm. Rates are similar but it pays to shop around. Thomas Cook has bureaux de change on the corner of Queen and Customs Sts and at 96 Queen St. Travelex changes money in the Ansett Travel Shop at 75 Queen St. The American Express Travel Services Office (☎ 379 8243) is at 101 Queen St.

For after-hours transactions, an automatic 24-hour change machine is outside the Downtown Airline Terminal on Quay St – stick in notes of most major currencies and out will pop the equivalent amount in New Zealand money. Nearby at the Ferry Building on Quay St, Interforex changes money every day from 8 am to 8 pm, but rates are lower than at banks.

Post & Communications A number of post offices are scattered around the city centre. Poste restante is held at the Chief Post Office (CPO) in the Bledisloe Building in Wellesley St West, near the corner of Queen St. Post offices are open Monday to Friday from 9 am to 5 pm.

The telephone area code for Auckland is 09.

Useful Organisations The Automobile Association (AA) (☎ 377 4660) is at 99 Albert St, on the corner of Albert and Victoria Sts. Members of an equivalent overseas auto club can use its services; it has accommodation directories and excellent maps. It's open Monday to Friday from 8.30 am to 5 pm. In the same building, the Department of Survey and Land Information (DOSLI; ☎ 377 1899) sells a complete selection of DOSLI maps, including topographical maps, national park maps, street maps, road atlases and so on. It's open Monday to Friday from 8 am to 4.30 pm.

Foreign Consulates Consulates in Auckland include:

Australia
Union House, 32-38 Quay St, City (☎ 303 2429)
Canada
9th floor, Jetset Centre, 48 Emily Place, City (☎ 309 3690)
Cook Islands
127 Symonds St, City (☎ 309 1875)
Fiji
4th floor Federal House, 86 Federal St, City (☎ 377 3955)
Finland
10 Heather St, Parnell (☎ 309 2969)
Germany
5th floor, 52 Symonds St, City (☎ 377 3460)
Japan
6th floor, National Mutual Building, 37-45 Shortland St, City (☎ 303 4106)
Netherlands
7th floor, 90 Symonds St, City (☎ 379 5399)
Sweden
Targetti House, 60 Parnell Rd, Parnell (☎ 373 5332)
UK
Fay Richwhite Building, 151 Queen St, corner Queen & Wyndham Sts, City (☎ 303 2973)
USA
General Building, corner Shortland & O'Connell Sts, City (☎ 303 2724)

Travel Agencies For international air tickets, good places to try include: Student Travel Agency (STA; ☎ 309 0458), 10 High St; Flight Centres (☎ 309 6171, 377 4655) with several offices around Auckland; and Skytrain (☎ 309 6896) at 37 High St.

Auckland has a number of backpackers travel centres which book tours, buses and activities throughout New Zealand. They can offer good deals and discounts on activities, but remember many are weather dependent (dolphin watching, tandem skydiving, etc) and if cancelled you'll usually have to return to Auckland to collect your refund.

Agents to try include the YHA Holiday Shoppe (☎ 379 4224) at 36 Customs St East, on the corner of Gore St, and in the lobby of the Auckland City YHA Hostel (☎ 309 2802); Auckland Central Backpackers Travel Centre (☎ 358 4874), 9 Fort St; and Independent Travel Services (☎ 303 3442) on the ground floor of the Central City Backpackers at 26 Lorne St. Anyone can use the services of these travel agencies.

The NZ Adventure Centre (☎ 358 5868; fax 358 5878) in the Downtown Shopping Centre on QE II Square also specialises in NZ travel.

Bookshops Whitcoull's, on the corner of Queen and Victoria Sts, is a huge bookshop with good sections on New Zealand, travel, fiction, etc as well as audiovisual products, and it also has a cafe. Whitcoull's has plenty of other shops around Auckland, including one in the Downtown Shopping Centre at the bottom of Queen St.

Books Pacifica, 283 Karangahape Rd, has an excellent selection of books on Maori culture and the South Pacific islands.

Auckland has a large selection of secondhand bookshops. Look in the *Yellow Pages* phone directory, or try Bloomsbury Books upstairs at 10 O'Connell St off Shortland St, Jason Secondhand Books at 50 High St beside the Simple Cottage vegetarian restaurant, or Anah Dunsheath Rare Books at 6 High St.

Newspapers The *Auckland Tourist Times* is a useful free weekly newspaper for visitors, containing information on events and activities in the city. The *New Zealand Herald* is the Auckland morning daily.

Things to See

Most of Auckland's main attractions are close to the city centre. Those further out, such as Kelly Tarlton's, the zoo and Motat, can be reached by public transport or the tourist loop buses such as Bus-A-Bout and Explorer Bus.

If you intend doing a lot of sightseeing, various promotional cards cover a number of attractions and include transport – the Auckland Visitor Centre has full details. Some offer good savings, especially those that include ferry tours, while others offer no savings at all.

Auckland Museum If you're only going to see one thing in Auckland, see Auckland's magnificent museum. Situated in the Domain, it has a tremendous display of Maori artefacts and culture: pride of place goes to a magnificent 25-metre-long war canoe. The museum also houses a fine collection of South Pacific items and NZ wildlife, including a giant moa model, and exhibits from around the world. The Volcanoes & Giants exhibition retells New Zealand's natural history from volcanoes to the moa.

The museum is open daily from 10 am to 5 pm; admission is free but entry to Volcanoes & Giants is $7 (children $4). It's about a 25-minute walk from Queen St up through the Domain, or you can catch bus No 63, 64 or 65 from the Downtown Bus Terminal to Parnell Rd; or the Bus-A-Bout and Explorer Bus stop at the front.

Pounamu Ventures run an excellent 1½-hour programme that includes a guided tour of the Maori exhibits, followed by a half-hour performance of traditional Maori music and dance. This excellent introduction to Maori culture begins at 10.30 am and 12.45 pm daily and costs $6.50 (children $1.50 to $2).

Hobson Wharf Maritime Museum Auckland isn't called the City of Sails for nothing, and this museum on the downtown waterfront is dedicated to one of New Zealand's national obsessions – sailing. This extensive museum is a must for lovers of the sea and explores 1000 years of the seafaring history of this Pacific island nation. Dozens of sailing craft and displays are exhibited, including the giant 76-foot (25-metre) outrigger canoe *Taratai* that modern navigator Jim Siers constructed using 1000-year-old methods and sailed across the Pacific.

There are other vessels inside the museum and on the water, some taking visitors out

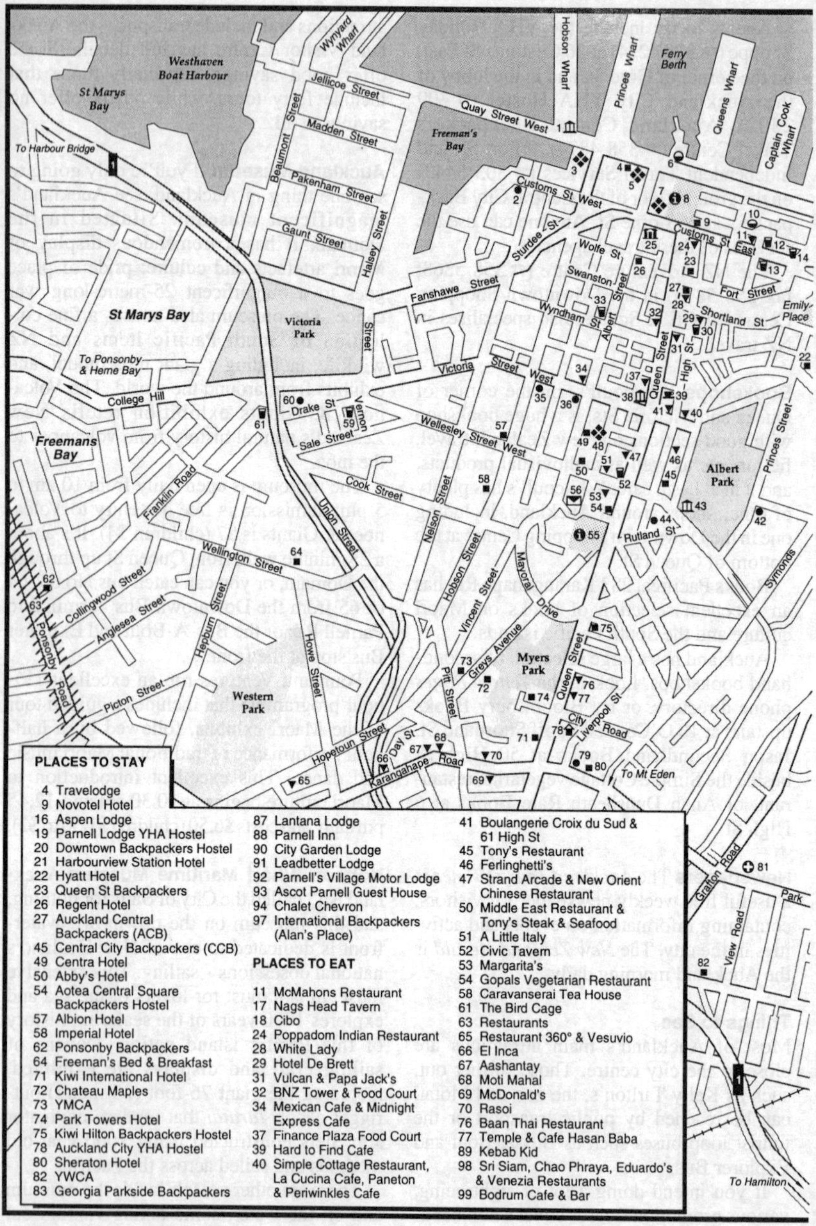
Westhaven Boat Harbour
St Marys Bay
Wynyard Wharf
Jellicoe Street
Madden Street
Beaumont Street
Pakenham Street
Gaunt Street
Halsey Street
To Harbour Bridge
Hobson Wharf
Princes Wharf
Ferry Berth
Queens Wharf
Captain Cook Wharf
Quay Street West
Freeman's Bay
Customs St West
Customs St East
Sturdee St
Wolfe St
Swanston
Fanshawe Street
Wyndham St
Albert Street
Fort Street
Shortland St
Emily Place
Queen Street
High St
St Marys Bay
Victoria Park
To Ponsonby & Herne Bay
College Hill
Victoria Street West
Drake St
Vernon Street
Wellesley Street West
Sale Street
Freemans Bay
Franklin Road
Cook Street
Union Street
Nelson Street
Hobson Street
Princes Street
Albert Park
Rutland St
Symonds
Wellington Street
Collingwood Street
Anglesea Street
Ponsonby Road
Hepburn Street
Howe Street
Vincent Street
Mayoral Drive
Greys Avenue
Pitt Street
Myers Park
Liverpool St
City Road
Picton Street
Western Park
Hopetoun Street
Day St
Karangahape Road
To Mt Eden
Grafton Road
Park
View Road
To Hamilton
PLACES TO STAY
4 Travelodge
9 Novotel Hotel
16 Aspen Lodge
19 Parnell Lodge YHA Hostel
20 Downtown Backpackers Hostel
21 Harbourview Station Hotel
22 Hyatt Hotel
23 Queen St Backpackers
26 Regent Hotel
27 Auckland Central Backpackers (ACB)
45 Central City Backpackers (CCB)
49 Centra Hotel
50 Abby's Hotel
54 Aotea Central Square Backpackers Hostel
57 Albion Hotel
58 Imperial Hotel
62 Ponsonby Backpackers
64 Freeman's Bed & Breakfast
71 Kiwi International Hotel
72 Chateau Maples
73 YMCA
74 Park Towers Hotel
75 Kiwi Hilton Backpackers Hostel
78 Auckland City YHA Hostel
80 Sheraton Hotel
82 YWCA
83 Georgia Parkside Backpackers
87 Lantana Lodge
88 Parnell Inn
90 City Garden Lodge
91 Leadbetter Lodge
92 Parnell's Village Motor Lodge
93 Ascot Parnell Guest House
94 Chalet Chevron
97 International Backpackers (Alan's Place)
PLACES TO EAT
11 McMahons Restaurant
17 Nags Head Tavern
18 Cibo
24 Poppadom Indian Restaurant
28 White Lady
29 Hotel De Brett
31 Vulcan & Papa Jack's
32 BNZ Tower & Food Court
34 Mexican Cafe & Midnight Express Cafe
37 Finance Plaza Food Court
39 Hard to Find Cafe
40 Simple Cottage Restaurant, La Cucina Cafe, Paneton & Periwinkles Cafe
41 Boulangerie Croix du Sud & 61 High St
45 Tony's Restaurant
46 Ferlinghetti's
47 Strand Arcade & New Orient Chinese Restaurant
50 Middle East Restaurant & Tony's Steak & Seafood
51 A Little Italy
52 Civic Tavern
53 Margarita's
54 Gopals Vegetarian Restaurant
58 Caravanserai Tea House
61 The Bird Cage
63 Restaurants
65 Restaurant 360° & Vesuvio
66 El Inca
67 Aashantay
68 Moti Mahal
69 McDonald's
70 Rasoi
76 Baan Thai Restaurant
77 Temple & Cafe Hasan Baba
89 Kebab Kid
98 Sri Siam, Chao Phraya, Eduardo's & Venezia Restaurants
99 Bodrum Cafe & Bar

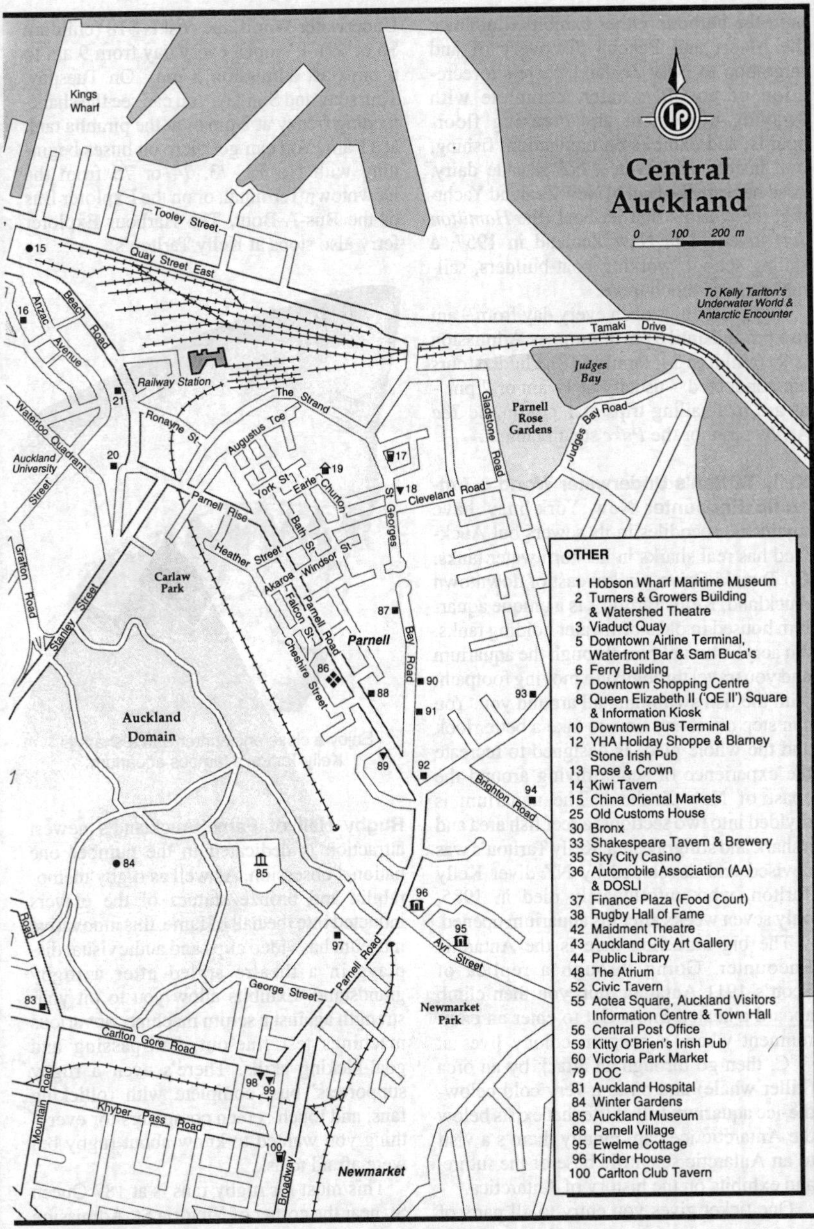
Central Auckland
0 100 200 m
Kings Wharf
Tooley Street
Quay Street East
Beach Road
Anzac Avenue
Railway Station
Waterloo Quadrant
Auckland University
Ronayne St
The Strand
Augustus Tce
York St
Earle
Churton
Cleveland Road
St Georges
Parnell Rise
Bath St
Windsor St
Heather Street
Akaroa
Falcon St
Parnell Road
Cheshire Street
Carlaw Park
Grafton Road
Stanley Street
Parnell
Bay Road
Gladstone Road
Parnell Rose Gardens
Judges Bay Road
Judges Bay
Tamaki Drive
To Kelly Tarlton's Underwater World & Antarctic Encounter
Brighton Road
Auckland Domain
Ayr Street
George Street
Carlton Gore Road
Newmarket Park
Khyber Pass Road
Mountain Road
Broadway
Newmarket
OTHER
1 Hobson Wharf Maritime Museum
2 Turners & Growers Building & Watershed Theatre
3 Viaduct Quay
5 Downtown Airline Terminal, Waterfront Bar & Sam Buca's
6 Ferry Building
7 Downtown Shopping Centre
8 Queen Elizabeth II ('QE II') Square & Information Kiosk
10 Downtown Bus Terminal
12 YHA Holiday Shoppe & Blarney Stone Irish Pub
13 Rose & Crown
14 Kiwi Tavern
15 China Oriental Markets
25 Old Customs House
30 Bronx
33 Shakespeare Tavern & Brewery
35 Sky City Casino
36 Automobile Association (AA) & DOSLI
37 Finance Plaza (Food Court)
38 Rugby Hall of Fame
42 Maidment Theatre
43 Auckland City Art Gallery
44 Public Library
48 The Atrium
52 Civic Tavern
55 Aotea Square, Auckland Visitors Information Centre & Town Hall
56 Central Post Office
59 Kitty O'Brien's Irish Pub
60 Victoria Park Market
79 DOC
81 Auckland Hospital
84 Winter Gardens
85 Auckland Museum
86 Parnell Village
95 Ewelme Cottage
96 Kinder House
100 Carlton Club Tavern

onto the harbour. Other exhibits illuminate the Maori and Pakeha discovery of and migration to New Zealand; there's a recreation of an old whaler, complete with swaying movement and creaking floorboards; and exhibits on navigation, fishing, oral history and even a NZ seaside dairy. Also here are the Hall of New Zealand Yachting, the world's first jet-boat (the *Hamilton Jet)* invented in New Zealand in 1957, a sailing school, working boat-builders, sailmakers, and much more.

The museum is open every day from 9 am to 5 pm and until 6 pm in summer. Admission is $9 (children $4, family $18). Guided tours are conducted – usually at 11 am or 2 pm – as are free sailing trips at 1 pm on the *Ted Ashby* scow or the *Puke* steam launch.

Kelly Tarlton's Underwater World & Antarctic Encounter New York may have mythical crocodiles in its sewers but Auckland has real sharks in its stormwater tanks. On Tamaki Drive, six km east of downtown Auckland, Kelly Tarlton's is a unique aquarium housed in old stormwater holding tanks. An acrylic tunnel runs through the aquarium and you travel through on a moving footpath, with the fish swimming all around you. You can step off at any time to take a better look and the whole place is designed to recreate the experience of scuba diving around the coast of New Zealand. The aquarium is divided into two sections: a reef fish area and a shark and stingray area. Kelly Tarlton's was devised and developed by NZ diver Kelly Tarlton, who unfortunately died in 1985, only seven weeks after his aquarium opened.

The big attraction here is the Antarctic Encounter. Going through a replica of Scott's 1911 Antarctic hut, you then climb aboard a heated Snow Cat to enter an environment where a penguin colony lives at -7°C, then go through an attack by an orca (killer whale) and on to a very cold below-the-ice aquarium full of life that exists below the Antarctic ice cap. Finally there's a visit to an Antarctic scientific base of the future, and exhibits on the history of Antarctica.

One ticket gives you entry to all parts of Underwater World; the cost is $18 (children $6 or $9). It's open every day from 9 am to 6 pm (last admission 5 pm). On Tuesday, Thursday and Sunday, you can see the shark-feeding frenzy at 2 pm or at the piranha tank at 11 am. You can get there on buses beginning with No 72, 73, 74 or 75 from the Downtown Terminal, or on the Explorer Bus or the Bus-A-Bout. The Harbour Explorer ferry also stops at Kelly Tarlton's.

Enjoy a close enclounter with a shark at Kelly Tarlton's famous aquarium

Rugby Hall of Fame Auckland's newest attraction is dedicated to the number one national obsession. As well as rugby memorabilia and bronze statues of the players inducted into the hall of fame, this innovative museum has video clips and audiovisual displays in a theatre styled after a rugby grandstand. Exhibits allow you to pit your strength against a scrum machine, or various machines test line-out, ball-passing and goal-kicking skills. There's even a rugby supporters' bus, complete with rollicking fans, and touch-screen computers for everything you wanted to know about rugby but were afraid to ask.

This must for rugby fans is at 187 Queen St, near the corner of Victoria St. Admission is $10 (children $5). Opening hours are 9.30 am to 5 pm daily. The Rugby Hall of Fame also has a shop and the Front Row rugby bar and restaurant.

Auckland City Art Gallery The Auckland City Art Gallery is two blocks off Queen St, on the corner of Wellesley St East and Kitchener St, beside Albert Park. The gallery has an extensive collection of NZ art including many works by Colin McCahon and Frances Hodgkins, along with international works and rotating special exhibits. It's open every day from 10 am to 4.30 pm; admission is free.

Museum of Transport & Technology The Museum of Transport & Technology (Motat) is out at Western Springs near the zoo, just off the Great North Rd. Motat comprises two sections, lying on either side of the zoo.

Motat I has transport, communications, energy and other exhibits including one about pioneer aviator Richard Pearce. It's quite possible that this eccentric South Island farmer flew before the Wright brothers, but to Pearce a mere hop off the ground wasn't flying and he made no personal claims. During his life he produced a steady stream of inventions and devices, though not surprisingly he was a lousy farmer! Also at Motat I is the infotainment Science Centre, with hands-on exhibits.

Motat II at the Sir Keith Park Memorial Airfield features displays of rare and historic aircraft. Exhibits include a V1 flying bomb and Lancaster bomber from WWII, but pride of place goes to the huge Solent flying boat that ran a Pacific islands loop in the luxury days of flying.

Motat is open from 10 am to 5 pm. Admission to Motat I & II is $8 (children $4), or $4 (children $2) for Motat II only. Electric trams run regularly from Motat I around to the zoo entrance and Motat II.

Motat is signposted just off the North Western Motorway and can be reached by a Pt Chevalier bus No 045 departing from Customs St West in the city, or take the Bus-A-Bout or Explorer Bus.

Auckland Zoo The Auckland Zoo is on Motions Rd off Great North Rd in the same area as Motat. Though not a large zoo by world standards, it is beautifully landscaped and a continuing renovation program has replaced many of the old animal houses with more spacious, naturalistic compounds.

It has a nocturnal house where you can see kiwis foraging for worms. Kiwis are not in fact rare, it's just that they are rarely seen in their natural setting because of their nocturnal habits. There's also a large walk-through aviary where you can observe native birds. Among the real rarities in the zoo are the tuataras, the prehistoric NZ reptiles. The usual lions, hippos, rhinos, etc can also be seen. Tui Farm is a farm animal compound and a favourite with children. The zoo also stages animal shows on Sundays and holidays.

The zoo is open every day from 9.30 am to 5.30 pm (last admission 4.15 pm); entry is $9 (children $4.50). The Pt Chevalier bus No 045 from Customs St West will get you to both Motat and the zoo (a tram connects the two), as will the Bus-A-Bout and Explorer Bus.

Historic Buildings There are a number of restored and preserved colonial-era historic buildings around the city. The oldest building in the city is **Acacia Cottage** in Cornwall Park at the foot of One Tree Hill. Built in 1841 by Sir John Logan Campbell and his partner William Brown, the cottage originally stood near where Shortland St is today.

Highwic, at 40 Gillies Ave, Epsom, and **Alberton**, at 1 Kerr-Taylor Ave, Mt Albert, on the corner of Kerr-Taylor Ave and Mt Albert Rd, are both large houses of wealthy mid-Victorian New Zealanders. They were originally built in the 1860s, added on to with time, and ultimately bequeathed to the Historic Places Trust. **Ewelme Cottage**, at 14 Ayr St, Parnell, off Parnell Rd, was built of fine native kauri wood by an 1860s clergyman. All are open daily from 10.30 am to noon and from 1 to 4.30 pm. It costs $5 to visit Ewelme Cottage, $3.50 (children $1) to visit each of the others.

Just five doors from Ewelme Cottage, **Kinder House** at 2 Ayr St on the corner of Parnell Rd is a fine example of early (1857) architecture and contains two galleries of artwork and memorabilia of the Rev Dr John Kinder. The restored home is open from 11 am to 3 pm; admission is $1 (children 50c).

Renall St, coming off Ponsonby Rd, has been declared a conservation area by the Auckland City Council, and is a registered place of historic interest for its 19th-century atmosphere. The houses along this block are still used as private homes and are not open to the public, but you can stroll along and see the 20 or so early artisans' houses and the larger Foresters' Hall at No 5.

Mt Wellington Stone Cottage is at the shopping centre in Panmure. To get there take Bus Nos 51 and 52 from the Downtown Bus Terminal. There are several of the early **Fencible Cottages**, including one from the 1840s, at Jellicoe Park, Quadrant Rd, Onehunga. It's open from 1.30 to 4.30 pm on weekends. To get there, take Bus Nos 301 and 302 from Victoria St East.

In south-east Auckland, **Howick Historical Village** in Lloyd Elsmore Park, Bells Rd, Pakuranga, is a restored village of the 1840 to 1880 period, on the old military settlement of Howick. It has over 20 restored colonial buildings including a thatched sod cottage, forge, schoolhouse, village store, church and settlers' houses. It's open daily from 10 am to 4 pm (until 5 pm in summer); entry is $8 (children $3). Take the Howick bus from the Downtown Bus Terminal.

Parnell Parnell is an old inner suburb, only a couple of km from the centre, where there was a concerted effort to stave off the office developers and restore the old houses and shops, many of them with a decidedly eccentric touch. Parnell Rd is one of the most appealing streets in New Zealand with lots of arts & crafts shops, good (and expensive) restaurants, galleries and trendy Kiwis. It's a great place to people-watch.

Parnell Village is the most interesting area. This is a unified cluster of restored shops and houses, linked by paved alleyways, courtyards and boardwalks. Browse in the exclusive shops even if you can't afford to buy. The Elephant House at No 237 Parnell Rd has one of the largest and most innovative arrays of crafts, while The Cupboard boutique at No 333 gets the Most Pretentious Award for its sign proclaiming: 'Clothes for those that understand the difference'.

Further east on Gladstone Rd, the Parnell Rose Gardens has harbour views and is in bloom from November to March.

Parnell is a pleasant 20-minute walk via the Domain from Queen St, or you can take bus No 63, 64 or 65 from the Downtown Bus Terminal. The Explorer Bus and the Bus-A-Bout make regulaı stops at Parnell Village and the rose gardens.

Mt Eden & One Tree Hill Auckland is built across more than 50 extinct volcanoes, and many of the volcanic cones that dot the city provide parkland retreats and fine views. Mt Eden and One Tree Hill are the most interesting.

The view from Mt Eden, the highest volcanic cone in the area at 196 metres, is the best in Auckland. From Mt Eden you can see the entire Auckland area – all the bays and both sides of the isthmus – or look 50 metres down into the volcano's crater. Like the other extinct volcanic cones in the Auckland area, it was used by the Maori as a pa and you can also see the old Maori pa terracing and storage pits. It's worth the trouble to get up there. You can drive to the top or take bus No 274 or 275 from Customs St East and then walk.

One Tree Hill (183 metres) is a distinctive bald hill, topped only by a lone pine tree and a huge obelisk dedicated to the Maori by Sir John Campbell. It was the largest and most populous of the Maori pa settlements, and the terracing and dugout storage pits are visible. One Tree Hill was named after a sacred totara tree which stood on the hilltop until 1876. It has since been replaced by a (now huge) pine tree, which is looking decidedly sick after a chainsaw attack by a Maori protester. Get there on any bus beginning with the No 30 or 31 from the corner of Queen and Victoria Sts.

Auckland Observatory The Auckland Observatory, in the One Tree Hill Domain, off Manukau Rd, is open to the public every Tuesday and Thursday from 7.30 to 10 pm. There is an illustrated talk on some aspect of astronomy and, on clear nights, there is viewing by telescope and help in finding the southern hemisphere constellations. Admission is $6 (children $3).

Markets On Victoria St West, opposite Victoria Park, is the large **Victoria Park Market** open from 9 am to 6 pm (until 7 pm on weekends). It's an alternative, renovated market concentrating mostly on crafts, souvenirs and clothes. It also has outdoor cafes, occasional entertainment and a big concentration of New Age eclectics (have your fortune told or buy some crystals). It's about a 20-minute walk west from the centre, or take Bus No 005 from Customs St West (this bus does not run on weekends), the Explorer Bus or the Bus-A-Bout.

China Oriental Markets on Quay St, a few blocks east of the centre, is another interesting market, housed in a huge, brightly coloured warehouse with lots of imported goods, craft shops, herbal healers, an international food court, the usual merchandise and some good deals. It's open every day from around 10 am to 6 pm, and on Sunday there's a flea market in the car park.

Auckland also has traditional markets selling fruit, vegetables and everyday goods. The biggest and most interesting is the **Otara Markets**, held every Saturday from around 6 am to noon in the car park between the Manukau Polytec and the Otara town centre on Newbury St in Otara. Otara Markets has a definite Polynesian market feel, being situated in one of Auckland's main Polynesian residential areas. There are also a number of regular and one-off markets selling food, arts & crafts, antiques, clothing etc in the city and surrounding suburbs; the Auckland Visitor Centre keeps an up-to-date list.

Auckland Suburbs Though Auckland's population is only one million, it covers a vast area with a suburban sprawl stretching almost 60 km north-south and 30 km east-west. Like many cities, much of it is suburban conformity, but some areas are interesting for their history, vistas or unique character.

Auckland's most prestigious and historic real estate is found around the city's many delightful bays and beaches. For architecture buffs, the older suburbs have fine, 19th-century wooden villas, built mostly of durable kauri, which was once plentiful and cheap.

Just south of the central city area, straight up the hill from Queen St, is **Karangahape Rd**, known universally as K Rd. After WWII, the area around K Rd was a popular inner suburb for Maori and then Polynesian residents. With its South Pacific clubs, it maintains its Polynesian feel but now K Rd also has a strong Indian presence. It has always been a disreputable area, but the strip clubs and sex shops are giving way to restaurants and renovation. It still has plenty of character as a mixed shopping area.

K Rd runs south-west to Ponsonby Rd, the main street of fashionable **Ponsonby**. Housed in historic shopfronts, Ponsonby Rd's many restaurants are abuzz with the chat of diners, the hiss of cappuccino machines and the bleep of mobile phones. Ponsonby has many fine old houses, though the adjoining **Herne Bay**, right on the harbour, has some of Auckland's best Victorian houses, some found on small, private bays.

To the east of the city centre, the already mentioned Parnell is one of Auckland's most interesting suburbs. Just south of Parnell, is **Newmarket**, a lively and increasingly trendy shopping area along Broadway. Newmarket is well known for its furniture and clothes shops, particularly those selling designer outdoor fashion.

Tamaki Drive, which starts at the railway station, runs east past sheltered bays to the wealthy suburbs facing Rangitoto Island. From the city centre, Tamaki Drive crosses

Hobson Bay and the first suburb you reach is **Orakei**, which contains Auckland's most expensive real estate. Parakai Drive in Orakei is millionaires' row, with great views across the city. Tamaki Drive continues on past Kelly Tarlton's and the Tamaki Yacht Club to **Bastion Point**. A 19th-century fort was built here to protect the entrance to the harbour, but Bastion Point is best known for the Maori land occupation of 1977-78. The squatters were eventually evicted in a huge police operation, but the historic protest halted the subdivision of the claimed Maori land.

Tamaki Drive leads further around to chic **Mission Bay**, Auckland's smaller answer to California's Santa Monica. Mission Bay is most popular in summer, with a park area, sidewalk cafes and a pleasant, calm beach. Further on, **St Heliers Bay** is similar but smaller. Further east along Cliff Rd, the **Achilles Point Lookout** has dramatic views of the city, harbour and Hauraki Gulf islands. Bus Nos 719 and 769 run along Tamaki Drive from the Downtown Bus Terminal.

Rainbow's End Adventure Park This large amusement park on the Great South Rd (corner of Wiri Station Rd) at Manukau is open every day from 10 am to 5 pm (until 8 pm in January). Super passes for $29 (children $19) are good for unlimited rides, all day long; otherwise, a $15 admission includes three rides. Take bus No 327, 347, 447, 457, 467, 487 or 497 from the Downtown Bus Terminal or take the Manukau exit off the Southern Motorway and drive 400 metres to the park.

Pavilion of New Zealand On Montgomerie Rd, off George Bolt Memorial Drive near the airport, this exhibition centre has a variety of displays and shows about New Zealand, plus family-oriented activities and rides. From Christmas to the end of January it is open daily from 10 am to 8 pm . The rest of the year it tends to be more geared towards conference facilities and opens from 10 am to 4 pm on weekends only. Admission is $10 (children $5).

Lion Breweries Lion Breweries (☎ 377 8840) is New Zealand's largest multinational brewery and gives free tours of the plant at 368 Khyber Pass Rd in Newmarket. See the process, guzzle a Steinie and try other popular commercial beers. Free tours are held Tuesday, Wednesday and Thursday at 10.30 am and 2 pm; bookings are essential.

Monterey Park North-west of Auckland, on the north shore of Waitemata Harbour near Hobsonville, Monterey Park is a large motor museum featuring 40 vintage cars. The site also has gardens and tearooms. Entry is $6 (children $3) and it is open Wednesday to Sunday from 11 am to 4 pm.

Parks & Gardens Covering about 80 hectares, the **Auckland Domain**, right near the centre of the city, is a lovely public park that contains the Auckland Museum and the Winter Gardens with its hot-house fernery. It's a pleasant walk down through the Domain and back through the university grounds and Albert Park to Queen St.

Popular for jogging, picnics and walks, **Cornwall Park**, adjoining One Tree Hill on Greenlane Rd, is an extensive pastoral retreat only six km south of the city centre. It has sports grounds, fields of grazing sheep, a good visitors centre, historic Acacia Cottage, and a kiosk/restaurant.

Keen gardeners will appreciate **Eden Garden**, on the slopes of Mt Eden, noted for its camellias, rhododendrons and azaleas. Entry is via Omana Ave and costs $3. The extensive and relatively new **Auckland Regional Botanic Gardens** are 27 km south of the city. Take the Southern Motorway to the Manurewa turn-off (the one past Rainbow End).

Pick up a copy of the Auckland Regional Council pamphlet guide to the Auckland Regional Parks from the Auckland Visitor Centre or the Regional Parks/DOC office at the Ferry Building. The colour pamphlet contains photos, details of facilities and activities, and maps for over 20 parks (mostly former grazing land and coastal parks) in the Auckland area. Some allow camping, others are interesting day parks.

Activities

Walks The Auckland Visitor Centre and the Regional Parks/DOC office at the Ferry Building have pamphlets on walks in and around Auckland. *Inner City Strolling* outlines self-guided walks along the city waterfront, Tamaki Drive and Parnell. DOC's *Auckland Walkways* pamphlet has a good selection of forest and coastal day walks outside the metropolitan area. The *Coast to Coast Walkway* pamphlet covers the walk marked out between the Waitemata Harbour on the east coast and the Manukau Harbour on the west. The four-hour walk encompasses Albert Park, Auckland University, the Auckland Domain, Mt Eden, One Tree Hill and other points of interest, keeping as much as possible to reserves rather than city streets.

Beaches & Swimming Auckland is known for its fine and varied beaches, which are dotted all around the harbours and up and down the coast. You can run around them with 80,000 fit New Zealanders in the Round the Bays run which is held in March or April every year – one of the largest fun runs in the world.

The east coast beaches along Tamaki Drive, including Mission Bay and St Heliers Bay, are very popular. With most east coast and harbour beaches, swimming is better at high tide. Popular North Shore beaches include Takapuna and Milford. To get to them, take Bus No 83 or 85, departing from Victoria St West.

For good surf less than 50 km from the city, try Bethells on the west coast where the water is often very rough. You should also check out Karekare, Muriwai and Whatipu. Most of the surfing beachers have surf clubs and lifeguards. Further afield, but possible as day trips, Piha and Raglan on the west coast and Tawharanui, east of Warkworth on the east coast, have some of New Zealand's best waves.

Swimming pools in the city include the Olympic Pool in Newmarket, the Parnell Baths on Judges Bay Rd in Parnell with a saltwater pool right on the waterfront (closed in winter), the heated Point Erin pool on Shelly Beach Rd in Herne Bay, and the Takapuna Pools on Killarney St in Takapuna on the North Shore.

Outside the city, hot pool and swimming complexes are popular with Auckland residents. These include the Aquatic Park at Parakai, 45 km north-west of Auckland, and Waiwera Thermal Pools, 48 km to the north; see the Around Auckland section for details.

Scenic Flights There are scenic flights over Auckland, the Hauraki Gulf Islands and the Coromandel Peninsula. Try Auckland Scenic Air Safaris (☎ 298 5210) or Christian Aviation (☎ 298 9846) based at Ardmore Airfield. Alternatively, you can go sightseeing by helicopter. The Helicopter Line (☎ 377 4406), Auckland Helicopters (☎ 256 0648) and North Shore Helicopters (☎ 426 8287) all do sightseeing trips over the city. The Auckland Visitor Centre has all the details and can make bookings.

Adventure Activities Auckland is not to be outdone in adventure activities, and though you can't swim with the dolphins or go whale-watching in the Hauraki Gulf, you can do just about anything else that is offered around the country. The *Auckland Adventure* booklet from the Auckland Visitor Centre has extensive listings of activities and operators.

Auckland's latest adrenaline-pumping activity is rap jumping (face-down abseiling) off the Novotel Hotel building in QE II Square. The cost is $40; ring Absolute Adrenalin Adventures (☎ 483 8553) for details.

The Parakai Parachute Centre (☎ 838 6963) at Parakai, near Helensville, does tandem skydiving every day, weather permitting. The cost is $185; for an extra $10 they'll provide transport to/from Auckland. Wings & Waves (☎ 483 2619) has one-day or longer paragliding courses. Balloon

Safaris (☎ 415 8289) does hot-air balloon trips for $195.

Auckland has a host of sea kayaking operators with trips on the harbour and out to the islands. They include Ian Ferguson (☎ 529 2230), the Olympic gold medallist, who does evening trips to Rangitoto, and Ross Adventures (☎ 357 0550), which has moonlight trips from Waiheke Island. Mainly Kayaking (☎ 817 4560) runs seven-day kayaking trips to Northland with a German-speaking guide, and other adventure tours.

Scuba diving trips are organised by the Dive Centre (☎ 444 7698) in Takapuna, Kiwi Diver (☎ 298 1941) in Papakura and other operators. Sailboards, mountain bikes and camping gear can be hired from Windsurf Kiwi (☎ 629 0952). Windscene Windsurf (☎ 528 5277) has windsurfing courses and gear for rent. Jet Ski Safaris (☎ 376 0532) has jet ski tours around the Hauraki Gulf from Wenderholm Park, near Orewa.

Horse riding can be enjoyed around Auckland at Muriwai (☎ 411 8480) and Helensville (☎ 420 7629) to the west, or Pakiri (☎ 420 7269) near Wellsford up north. Mountain bike rentals and tours abound, and trails range from the very easy at Cornwall Park in the city, to the very strenuous at Dome Valley, north of Auckland near Warkworth.

The Auckland Climbing School (ACS) Adventures (☎ 837 3620) conducts courses in rock climbing, abseiling, kayaking, caving, mountaincraft and more. There are also many possibilities for fishing, tennis, golf and other sports in and near Auckland. The Auckland Visitor Centre and the various agencies specialising in NZ adventures can tell you about these and many other activities, and they will make bookings.

The Hauraki Gulf Maritime Park is one of the best scuba diving locations in New Zealand

Language Courses

People from around the world, especially Asia and the Pacific countries, come to New Zealand to study English. Auckland has the highest concentration of language schools, and the Auckland Visitor Information Centre keeps a complete, up-to-date list.

Tours

You can do your own tour of the major attractions around Auckland by getting a Bus-A-Bout All Day Bus Pass for $10 (children $5). It departs from the Downtown Airline Terminal on Quay St hourly from 9.30 am to 3.30 pm, making a circular route with stops at the China Oriental Markets, Kelly Tarlton's Underwater World, the Parnell Rose Gardens, Parnell Village, Auckland Museum, Auckland Zoo, Motat, Victoria Park Market, Hobson Wharf Maritime Museum, and back to the Downtown Airline Terminal. You can get off wherever you wish and get on the bus when it comes around the next hour. You can join the tour at any point along the way, getting your ticket from the bus driver.

The United Airlines Explorer Bus does a similar but more extensive route for $15 ($7 children. It departs from the Ferry Building on the hour and goes to Mission Bay, Kelly Tarlton's, the Parnell Rose Gardens, Auckland Museum, Parnell Village, Victoria Park

Market and back to the Ferry Building. At the museum you can pick up their Satellite Link (operating from October to April only) to Mt Eden, St Lukes shopping mall, Auckland Zoo, Motat and the Aotea Visitors Centre.

Auckland has dozens of tour operators doing very similar tours in and around the city. Three-hour tours will typically drive around the central city, over the harbour bridge and out along Tamaki Drive and include stops at Mt Eden, the Auckland Museum and Parnell. The going rate is $34 (children $17). Other tours do the above and include Kelly Tarlton's for around $50, a harbour cruise for $75 or both for $95. Gray Line (☎ 377 0904), Great Sights (☎ 303 1170) and Scenic Tours (☎ 634 0189) are the largest operators, but plenty of smaller tour companies also offer good trips. Hotel pick-up and drop-off is usually included in the price.

Trips to West Auckland take in the gannet colony at Muriwai and/or the Waitakere Ranges for around $50 (half day) to $80 (full day). Bush & Beach Nature Tours (☎ 478 2882) offers small-group nature tours to West Auckland and the Antipodean Explorer (☎ 302 2400) has tours to West Auckland and further afield; both tours have an excellent reputation.

There are many other specialised tours around Auckland including golf, fishing and garden tours. Maori Heritage Tours (☎ 486 3296) does tours that take in a marae, Mt Eden and the Auckland Museum. New Zealand Country Tours (☎ 377 9067) takes in sheep, cattle and horse stud properties around Auckland. In winter there are ski tours to the North Island ski areas, principally Whakapapa. The Auckland Visitor Centre can tell you about various specialised tours.

Many other tours depart from Auckland to places all over New Zealand, including tours to Waitomo, Rotorua and the Bay of Islands; the Auckland Visitor Centre has details.

Harbour Cruises One of the best ways to appreciate the City of Sails is to take to the water. A great variety of cruises and ferries depart from the Ferry Building on the downtown waterfront. Fullers Cruises (☎ 367 9102) is the main operator; it has the largest selection of cruises and operates almost all the ferries.

The cheapest way to get out on the harbour is to take the short ferry ride to picturesque Devonport ($7 return). Ferries also go to many of the nearby islands in the Hauraki Gulf, including Rangitoto, Waiheke, Great Barrier, Rakino, Motutapu and Motuihe. Rangitoto ($17 return) and Waiheke ($22 return) are easy to reach and make good day or half-day trips from Auckland. Children travel half price on all ferries. Fullers also puts together a large selection of combined ferry and onshore tours. Details on tours and attractions for Devonport and all the main islands are covered later in this chapter.

Fullers also has popular tours around the inner harbour, including a 1½-hour coffee cruise ($22), and a 1½-hour luncheon cruise ($38). The *Harbour Explorer* loops from Devonport to Kelly Tarlton's Underwater World, Rangitoto Island and back to Devonport, with connecting ferries to the downtown Ferry Building. An all-day Harbour Explorer boat pass allowing you to get on and off at will costs $22, or for $59 ($35 children) you can buy the Harbour Explore Super Ticket, a two-day boat pass that includes entry to Hobson Wharf, Kelly Tarlton's, the summit shuttle on Rangitoto Island, and other complimentary offers.

Plenty of other companies offer cruises and sailing trips – the Auckland Visitor Centre has full details. The Pride of Auckland Company (☎ 373 4557) has large blue and white sailing yachts doing two-hour luncheon cruises ($39) and three-hour dinner cruises ($75) around the harbour. It also offers Experience Sailing trips for $30, depending on demand.

The *Kestrel* ferry from Devonport does dinner and jazz trips. The Hobson Wharf Maritime Museum also does sailing trips from the museum at 1 pm on the *Ted Ashby*.

Among the most interesting cruises are those offered by the 1909 wooden auxiliary schooner *Te Aroha*, sailing from the Marsden Wharf in central Auckland every few days from October to April. Their nature-oriented tours go around the islands of the Hauraki Gulf and further afield to the Coromandel Peninsula, Bay of Islands and Bay of Plenty. Popular day trips to Tiritiri Matangi run at least once a week in January and February and cost $27. Other trips last for several days and visit a number of islands, eg the three-day Rare & Endangered Species tour, led by noted naturalist Geoff Moon, lands on Tiritiri Matangi, Kawau and Little Barrier islands and costs $400 per person. Ring Adventure Cruising (☎ 444 9342) for bookings and schedules.

In summer, a host of other boats ply the harbour. Auckland makes particularly good use of its fine harbour on the annual Auckland Anniversary Day Regatta in late January.

Special Events

Of the large number of annual events held in Auckland, some of the more important ones follow. The Auckland Visitor Centre keeps a complete list of annual and current events, and can supply exact dates.

January
Open Tennis Tournament; Opera in the Park; Auckland Anniversary Day Regatta

February
Symphony under the Stars; Devonport Food & Wine Festival

March/April
Around the Bays Fun Run; Ironman Competition; Pasifika Polynesian Festival; Royal Easter Show

June
New Zealand Boat Show

July
Rally of New Zealand

December
Great New Zealand Crafts Show

Places to Stay

Camping & Cabins There are camping grounds and motor parks both north and south of the city centre, many very conveniently situated.

North of the city, the four-star *Auckland North Shore Caravan Park, Cabins & Motel* (☎ 418 2578) is at 52 Northcote Rd in Takapuna, four km north of the Harbour Bridge; take the Northcote Rd exit and it's 700 metres west of the motorway, beside Pizza Hut. Accommodation includes tent and caravan sites at $16/23 for one/two people, cabins ranging from $27/37 to $45/55, tourist flats and leisure lodges for $68 and motel units for $80 a double.

Also in Takapuna, the *Takapuna Beach Caravan Park* (☎ 489 7909), 22 The Promenade, Takapuna, is eight km from the city and right on the beach on the north shore, with a view of Rangitoto Island. It's an easy walk to the shops and centre of Takapuna, and a 10-minute drive or bus ride into downtown Auckland. Tent sites are $17 for two people, powered sites are $22.50 to $27, cabins are $31.50 for two and on-site caravans cost $40 for two.

Further north of Auckland, the *Tui Glen Camping Park* (☎ 838 8978) is beside the swimming pool complex at Henderson, 13 km north-west of Auckland in the wine country. Sites are $6 per person, $9 with power. Cabins are $35 for two, and it also has tourist flats at $48.

South of the city centre, the closest camping ground to the city is the quiet and secure *Remuera Motor Lodge* (☎ 524 5126) at 16 Minto Rd, off Remuera Rd. It's eight km from downtown Auckland; take bus No 64 or 65 from the Downtown Bus Terminal. It has plenty of trees, a large swimming pool, and is just 100 metres from the shops and bus stop. Tent and powered sites start at $12 per person, a self-contained bunkroom with beds costs $20 per person, and tourist flats cost $60 for two.

The *Avondale Motor Park* (☎ 828 7228) at 46 Bollard Ave, off New North Rd, is nine km south of central Auckland and fairly close to Motat and the zoo. Sites are $9 per person, $10 with power, and it also has on-site caravans at $35 a double, cabins at $45 and tourist flats at $55.

South Auckland has plenty of other caravan parks, such as the *Manukau Central Caravan Park* (☎ 266 8016) at 902 Great South Rd, Manukau, a quiet place away from the motorway. The *Meadow Court Motor Camp* (☎ 278 5612) is also in Manukau at 630 Great South Rd, close to Manukau city centre and handy to the airport and Rainbow's End amusement park. Sites here cost $7 per person, $8 with power.

The *South Auckland Caravan & Camping Park* (☎ 294 8903) is on Ararimu Rd, 300 metres off the Great South Rd at Ramarama, 35 km south of Auckland city centre. It's a large park on a dairy farm with a private lake. Tent sites are $16 for two people, powered sites are $18 and cabins are $28.

The Auckland Regional Council has camping grounds in the regional parks around Auckland, many of which are in coastal areas. Some are accessible by vehicle, others are reached by tramping. Contact the Auckland Regional Parks/DOC information centre (☎ 366 2166) at the Ferry Building for information and bookings.

Hostels Auckland has plenty of good hostels in the city centre and inner suburbs. The suburban hostels are smaller, homier and quieter, but the city hostels are conveniently located and some offer excellent facilities and services. The international YHA has two hostels in Auckland and the rest are independent hostels, known as 'backpackers'.

Prices given here are summer prices. Despite the large number of hostels, they may still all be full in summer and it pays to book, especially if you want a single or double room. In winter it's not so hectic, and most hostels give up to a 25% discount off normal prices. The hostels may have touts waiting at the airport to meet incoming flights; they offer a free ride into town and sometimes discounts. Some hostels use the free phone service in the international terminal to arrange a free shuttle into town.

All the hostels have kitchens where you can do your own cooking; some have cafes and even bars.

Hostels – city centre Just off Queen St and right behind the Sheraton Hotel, the *Auckland City YHA Hostel* (☎ 309 2802) on the corner of City Rd and Liverpool St is one of Auckland's biggest hostels, with mostly twin, double and family rooms, many with great views of the city and harbour. Comfortable, student-style rooms cost $19 per person in double and twin rooms and $28 in the few single rooms available. This hotel-style YHA is open 24 hours a day, has a shop, luggage safes and a YHA travel agency.

Heading down the hill, both literally and in quality, the *Kiwi Hilton* (☎ 358 3999), nearby at 430 Queen St, is a more basic, mid-sized backpackers costing $13 for a dorm bed and $24/35 in singles/doubles, including breakfast. Slightly better is the nearby *Aotea Central Square Backpackers Hostel* (☎ 303 3350), on the 2nd floor of 295 Queen St. This is another central hostel, sleeping 50 or 60 people in rooms that are simple but OK. The cost is $14 in the dorms or $36 for a double room.

At 9 Fort St, near the corner of Queen St, the *Auckland Central Backpackers* (☎ 358 4877) is Auckland's largest hostel, with room for 300 people. Amenities include made-up beds, a good cafe, a lively rooftop bar, a video theatre and a backpackers travel agency. A bed in a three or four-bed dorm costs $16; singles/doubles are $25/40, including linen and duvet.

Right opposite at 4 Fort St, the *Queen St Backpackers* (☎ 373 3471) is a reasonable place that sleeps around 90. The main drawback is the Park in the Bar disco downstairs, which makes a lot of noise until the early hours of the morning, especially on weekends. Dorms start at $15, singles/doubles are $24/37.

Another good, large hostel is the *Central City Backpackers* (CCB) (☎ 358 5685) at 26 Lorne St. Though large it manages to maintain a homey feel, and the rooms are spotless, if a little dark. It sleeps 120 and has all the usual amenities, including a backpackers travel agency. The cost per person is $15 in 10-bed dorms, $17 in four-bed dorms, $25 in twins. Double rooms are $40.

The much smaller *Downtown Backpackers Hostel* (☎ 366 1444) is conveniently located at 6 Constitution Hill, near Auckland University. It has a good atmosphere, parking is available and the house has a small garden. The cost per person is $12 in the dark downstairs dorm or $15 in the much better upstairs dorm. A double is also available downstairs for $36.

The *Georgia Parkside Backpackers* (☎ & fax 309 8999) is at 189 Park Rd on the corner of Carlton Gore Rd, Grafton, overlooking the Auckland Domain. This rambling old place is slowly being upgraded and has a variety of rooms. Dorm beds cost $12, and doubles range from $30 to $34 for more private rooms.

Though the hostels are a better option, the YWCA and YMCA also have accommodation. The Ys are usually full with students and long-term residents in winter, but often have rooms in summer when everything else is full.

The *YWCA* (☎ 379 4912), 10 Carlton Gore Rd, Grafton, costs $20 per person (women only) in single or twin rooms inside the main house, linen included. Out the back a small backpackers cottage costs $13 or $17 if you want to use inside facilities.

The *YMCA* (☎ 303 2068) is in a tall, modern building on the corner of Pitt St and Grays Ave. It takes men and women, in single/twin rooms costing $27/49, linen included.

Hostels – Parnell One of Auckland's more stylish districts, Parnell also has a good selection of hostels. From the city centre, it's a 20-minute walk or you can take bus No 635, 645 or 655.

The *Parnell Lodge YHA Hostel* (☎ 379 0258/3731) is at 2 Churton St on the corner of Earle St, three short blocks east of Parnell Rd. It sleeps 81; the cost is $16 in dorms ($13 in winter), $19 per person in doubles and twins.

Three backpackers hostels can be found on St Georges Bay Rd, which branches off from Parnell Rd at the top of the hill by the library. The first one you come to as you head down the hill is the *Leadbetter Lodge* (☎ 358 0665) at 17 St Georges Bay Rd. It's a basic place costing $10 to $13 in the dorm, $17.50 per person in double and twin rooms.

The next place along, the *City Garden Lodge* (☎ 302 0880) at No 25 is a fine hostel in a large, elegant old home originally built for the queen of Tonga. It has undergone a facelift and is one of the best in Parnell. The cost is $13 to $15 in dorms, $17.50 per person in double or twin rooms.

Further down the hill at 60 St Georges Bay Rd, *Lantana Lodge* (☎ 373 4546) is quite basic but a friendly, well-run place; the cost is $15 in dorms, $17.50 per person in doubles and twins.

International Backpackers (Alan's Place) (☎ 358 4584), 8 Maunsell Rd, is in a quiet residential location, right near the Auckland Museum. The large brick building was once student housing, so it has plenty of individual rooms, a well-equipped, commercial-style kitchen, a lounge, TV room, dining area and a reading room, plus plenty of off-street parking. A dorm bed costs $14, though most of the accommodation is in doubles and twins for $36 or singles for $22.

Hostels – Mt Eden A couple of good hostels are found at Mt Eden, a pleasant residential area about four km south of the city centre. These hostels tend to be the last to fill up in summer, so if you have a car, it's a good area to head for. Bus Nos 274 and 275 run from the Downtown Bus Terminal to Mt Eden Rd.

The *Eden Lodge Tourist Hostel* (☎ 630 0174), 22 View Rd, Mt Eden, is fairly upmarket, set in a huge colonial-era home and surrounded by gardens. The rooms are very comfortable and the house has large, pleasant communal areas. Dorm beds cost $12 in the outside prefab bunkhouse, but the $14 dorms inside are much better. Twin or double rooms cost $34. Buses stop on the corner of Mt Eden and View Rds.

Further up the hill, *Berlin Lodge* (☎ 638 6545) is at 5A Oaklands Rd, Mt Eden, just off Mt Eden Rd, in a quiet tree-lined residential street at the foot of Mt Eden; the bus stops at the Mt Eden shops on the corner, 100 metres away. English, French and German are spoken here. The cost is $13 and $14 in dorm rooms, $38 for twin and double rooms, and $25 in single rooms. Ring for free pick-up.

Hostels – other areas Ponsonby, like Parnell, is another happening area close to the city. *Ponsonby Backpackers* (☎ & fax 360 1311), 2 Franklin Rd, is in a historic house only one street from lively Ponsonby Rd and within easy reach of the centre. Dorm beds cost $12 or $15, singles are $20 and doubles or twins $17. The rooms vary in quality and the bathroom facilities are light on, but all in all this is a good place.

At Epsom, just past Mt Eden, *Rocklands* (☎ & fax 630 0836), 187 Gillies Ave, is a residential college for students. It always has a few rooms for backpackers, but the main backpacker trade is in summer when the students are on holiday. The main building is a magnificent mansion, and there's a large kitchen, TV lounge, pool room, etc. The scores of student-style rooms are in newer blocks out the back. Single rooms cost $15 and $20, doubles and twins are $40 and there are some dorm beds for $14. Bus Nos 30 to 35 run to Gillies Ave from the corner of Victoria and Queen Sts.

The *Ivanhoe Lodge* (☎ 846 2800) is at 14 Shirley Rd in Grey Lynn, out towards Motat and the zoo. It's a large 80-bed hostel with a bar, pool table, games room and sauna. It costs $12 to $14 in dorms, $20/34 in singles/doubles. Take bus No 045 to Grey Lynn shops, then walk down Turangi Rd and follow the signs.

Near the airport are a couple of places with backpackers rooms as well as motel units. Both offer courtesy airport transport. The *Airport Skylodge International* (☎ 275 1005) at 144 McKenzie Rd, Mangere, has hostel facilities at $20 per person. The *Skyway Lodge* (☎ 275 4443) at 30 Kirkbride Rd, Mangere, has bunkroom accommodation at $15 per person.

B&Bs & Guesthouses Guesthouses and bed & breakfasts (B&Bs) are popular in Auckland. All those mentioned here are attractive, clean, comfortable and friendly, with a 'home away from home' feeling, and the room rate includes a substantial breakfast. Most have off-street parking. Unless mentioned otherwise, the rooms usually have shared bathroom facilities.

In the city centre, *Chateau Maples* (☎ & fax 358 2737) at 100 Greys Ave is only about 300 metres from Queen St, but is quiet and cosy. The cost is $48/72 for singles/doubles.

Also in the city centre, the *Aspen Lodge* (☎ 379 6698) looks out on a delightful little park at 62 Emily Place, about a five-minute walk from Queen St. This is more of a hotel-style B&B with a convivial dining/common area. Singes/doubles cost $45/65.

Still quite central, about a 10-minute walk from Queen St, the *Freeman's Bed & Breakfast* (☎ 376 5046) at 65 Wellington St, Freeman's Bay, has a private garden area behind the house and 12 rooms at $43/65, plus self-contained apartments at $85 a double.

The fashionable Parnell district has two good guesthouses, both with private bath in every guest room. The *Ascot Parnell* (☎ 309 9012) at 36 St Stephens Ave, off Parnell Rd, is a long-running favourite in Auckland, with 11 guest rooms in a restored historic home. The cost is $75/103. Nearby, *Chalet Chevron* (☎ 309 0291) at 14 Brighton Rd has beautiful views over the harbour; the cost is $55 in single rooms, $95 in doubles or twins.

The *Heathmaur Lodge* (☎ 376 3527) at 75 Argyle St, Herne Bay, is in a large three-storey mansion, a two-minute walk to a sandy beach, an easy walk to restaurants and a 10-minute ride to the city centre. With the water nearby, an open view, quiet neighbourhood and homey atmosphere, it seems far removed from the big city even though it's so close. Basic room rates are $40/60, $65 and $75 with private bathroom; weekly rates are lower.

Mt Eden is another residential district with two attractive guesthouses. The *Bavaria Guest House* (☎ 638 9641) at 83 Valley Rd is a lovely place with a private sun deck and garden; both English and German are spoken. Rooms, all with private bath, are $49 to $62 for singles, $79 to $92 for doubles, with discounts for longer stays and in the off-season. Also in Mt Eden, the *Pentlands Tourist Hotel* (☎ 638 7031) at 22 Pentland

Ave, off Valley Rd, has large outdoor grounds with a tennis court, a BBQ area and picnic tables, and a lounge with a pool table and open fire; the cost is $39/59 to $45/65 for singles/doubles.

Aachen House (☎ 520 2329) at 39 Market Rd, Remuera, about four km south-east of the centre, is a bit further out but it's worth the trip. A fine old Victorian home with just seven guest rooms and a lot of style, it's set in half an acre of private garden at the foot of Mt Hobson. Inside it has spacious rooms and many fine touches, including original NZ art works. Singles/doubles are $58/82.

Also in Remuera is the *Remuera House* (☎ 524 7794) at 500 Remuera Rd, an attractive English-style guesthouse with B&B at $39/58.

Hotels Several hotels are conveniently situated in the heart of the city. The *Albion Hotel* (☎ 379 4900), on the corner of Wellesley St West and Hobson Sts, has 20 rooms in an old building which has been restored with a bit of style. Singles and doubles, all with private bath, are $75/80, less on weekends.

In the same price range, *Abby's Hotel* (☎ 303 4799) on the corner of Wellesley St West and Albert St has rooms with private bath at $89. This is a reasonably priced business hotel with a good selection of bars and restaurants – though some of the rooms are very small.

More expensive, but an excellent place to stay, the *Imperial Hotel* (☎ 357 6770) at 131-139 Hobson St has 61 rooms, all with private bath and other amenities, priced at $150.

The *Park Towers Hotel* (☎ 309 2800) at 3 Scotia Place, just off Queen St, has rooms with simple, student-like decor and private bath for $130.

Nearby, the *Kiwi International Hotel* (☎ 379 6487) at 411 Queen St is a large, fairly old hotel that has had a facelift. Older economy singles/doubles with shared facilities cost $30/49, renovated rooms with private facilities are $69, and business rooms with more amenities are $79.

Directly opposite the railway station, the *Harbourview Station Hotel* (☎ 303 2463) at 131 Beach Rd looks a bit decrepit on the outside but the interior has been renovated. Rooms with private bath and telephone cost $50/70.

Auckland's best business hotels start at around $200 per room, but substantial discounts are usually available, especially if you book through a travel agent before arriving in Auckland. The *Travelodge* (☎ 377 0349), 96-100 Quay St, and the *Novotel* (☎ 377 8920), 8 Customs St, are older luxury hotels and hence are cheaper. Next up the rung are the *Hyatt* (☎ 366 1234), on the corner of Princes St and Waterloo Quadrant, and the *Centra* (☎ 302 1111), 128 Albert St.

Auckland's best hotels are the *Sheraton* (☎ 379 5132) at 83 Symonds St, the *Carlton* (☎ 366 3000) in Mayoral Drive, or the top of the heap, the *Regent* (☎ 309 8888) on the corner of Albert and Swanson Sts, where double rooms are around $400 a night.

Motels Auckland has over 100 motels scattered around the city. Costs start around $55/65 for singles/doubles. Some of the camping grounds have tourist flats or motel units (see Camping & Cabins).

Several areas reasonably close to the city have a good selection of motels. *Parnell's Village Motor Lodge* (☎ 377 1463) at 2 St Stephens Ave, on the corner of Parnell Rd, has studio units from $70 to $85, one-bedroom units from $95 and a range of units including a family one sleeping nine for $115. All are self-contained and well equipped, and reasonably priced for the good location.

Going down Parnell Rd towards the city, the *Parnell Inn* (☎ & fax 358 0642) at No 320 is another reasonably priced motel with studio units from $65/70, and prices are negotiable, especially for longer stays.

Another alternative is Jervois Rd in Herne Bay, after its junction with Ponsonby Rd. A number of motels are on, or just off, Jervois and Shelly Beach Rds. This is close to the southern end of the Harbour Bridge. At 6 Tweed St, off Shelly Beach Rd, the *Harbour Bridge Motel* (☎ 376 3489) has units from

$58/68, with larger family units for $75 a double. It's an 1886 building full of character, with a more recent extension. It has an outdoor BBQ and an attractive garden, and is in a convenient location.

Also in Herne Bay, the *Sea Breeze Motel* (☎ 376 2139) at 213 Jervois Rd is near beaches, fishing, tennis courts, restaurants and shops – and a bus stops outside the door! It has studio units for $79 and one-bedroom units for $86. The *Abaco Spa Motel* (☎ 376 0119) at 59 Jervois Rd has units for $89 and $99.

Five km south-east of the city centre, Remuera just past Newmarket has a motel row along Great South Rd. Motels include the *Siesta Motel* (☎ 520 2107) at No 70, *Aaberdeen Motel* (☎ 524 5381) at No 76, *Double Tree* (☎ 522 2011) at No 80 and the *Ascot* (☎ 523 3794) at No 92. *Hansen's* (☎ 520 2804) at No 96 and the *Tudor Court* (☎ 523 1069) at No 108 are two of the cheapest, with units from $60.

Across the Harbour Bridge, Takapuna and Birkenhead have plenty of motels. Out near the airport, Mangere has dozens of motels, particularly along Kirkbride Rd and McKenzie Rd. Almost all manage to get the words 'airport' or 'sky' into their names and most are from around $70 a night. The *Skyway Lodge* (☎ 275 4443) at 30 Kirkbride Rd has single/double rooms at $40/50, a bunkroom with beds at $15 per person, and two-bedroom family units starting at $65 a double. There's a swimming pool, sauna and TV lounge, and the motel offers pick-up from the airport, which is five minutes away.

Also near the airport, the *Kiwi Motel* (☎ 275 1005) at 144 McKenzie Rd has standard units at $69, family units at $102 and hostel facilities at $20 per person. It also offers courtesy airport transport.

Places to Eat

Auckland, because of its size and greater ethnic diversity, has the best range of dining possibilities in the country. Unlike some cities, there are no distinct ethnic areas – you can find almost anything almost anywhere.

A wide variety of cafes and restaurants are scattered around the city centre. High St/Lorne St is the haunt for lunch-time cafe society, while those up on Queen St towards Karangahape Rd (K Rd) are full of character.

The most densely packed concentrations of cafes and restaurants are found in Ponsonby and Parnell. Other suburban areas, such as Newmarket, Mt Eden and Herne Bay, have smaller restaurant enclaves. The restaurants in Devonport (see Around Auckland) are only a short ferry ride from central Auckland – a pleasant trip for lunch or dinner.

Food Courts & Fast Food Food courts are popular for quick eating in central Auckland, but most are open during shopping hours only. The Downtown Shopping Centre on QE II Square, on the corner of Queen St and Customs St West, has the *Downtown Food Court*. The Baron Supreme stall here has good all-day bacon & egg breakfasts for $6. Other food courts can be found on the lower ground floor of the *BNZ Tower* on the corner of Queen and Shortland/Swanson Sts; on the 4th floor of the *Finance Plaza* on the corner of Queen and Durham Sts; and on the 4th floor of *Countrywide Bank Centre* in Queen St down from Wellesley St.

The large markets also have good food courts for inexpensive meals. The *Victoria Park Market* has several eating places and a food court area. The *China Oriental Markets* on Quay St has the best general food court in Auckland with plenty of choice, ranging from vegetarian to Chinese or American-style fast food.

For an Asian food court, you can't beat *Food Alley* at 9 Albert St. Excellent, authentic Thai, Chinese, Malay, Korean etc meals cost $5 to $7. Juices, beer and wine are available from the drink stall. It's open every day from 10 am to 10 pm.

The *Kebab Kid* opposite the library near the top of the hill at 363 Parnell Rd is one of the cheapest in Parnell with tasty Middle Eastern food to take away or eat there.

If *McDonald's* is your favourite food, you won't starve in Auckland. You'll find one in the Downtown Food Court, two on Queen St and another on Karangahape Rd. There's a *Wendy's* upstairs in Queen St, just down from Wellesley St. In the same block but a bit further down the hill, opposite McDonald's, there's a *Pizza Hut* downstairs in the Strand Arcade.

Cafes & Cheap Eats In the city, High St and Lorne St have the best collection of cafes. They are very busy at lunch time, and many stay open in the evening.

On the corner of High St and Victoria St East, *Boulangerie Croix du Sud* is a French bakery with a good selection of croissants, breads, baguette sandwiches and lunch-time snacks. Next door, *61 High St* at, yes, 61 High St, is good for sandwiches at lunch time, as is the *Periwinkles Cafe* opposite.

Also near the corner of High St and Victoria St East, are *Paneton* at 60 High St and *La Cucina* at 58 High St. These are popular sidewalk cafes with espresso, sandwiches, focaccia bakes and so on. Paneton is also a bakery. Still on High St/Lorne St, the *Simple Cottage* is a vegetarian restaurant.

Vulcan Lane is a paved alleyway running between High and Queen Sts. The *Vulcan* is a fashionable lunch-time cafe, and above it *Papa Jack's* is popular in the evenings when the music is turned up. Just over High St, the *Rupin Cafe* is good for coffee, pasta and moderately priced light meals. It's one of the few places open until the early hours of the morning (24 hours a day on weekends).

Several other good places are up the hill on Queen St, between Aotea Square and K Rd. The *Caravanserai Tea House* at 430 Queen St – next to the Kiwi Hilton – is a casual, relaxing Middle Eastern caravanserai (way-station) for relaxation and revitalisation of weary travellers where you can get cheap lunch specials – eg a chicken kebab for $10 – or just hang out over coffee.

Keep going up Queen St for more good cafes and restaurants. The *Baan Thai* restaurant on the corner of Queen and Turner Sts is open for dinner every night. A little further up the hill, the *Cafe Hasan Baba* has Turkish food and pleasant decor. The lunch special is $7, evening meals are around $10. Up the block a bit more, the *Temple* at 486 Queen St is a hip little cafe featuring 'cool coffee, kai and music', and it also doubles as a comedy venue.

In K Rd, the *Verona Cafe* at No. 169 is a popular cafe open long hours. Though not dirt cheap, you can get some excellent, innovative NZ fare for around $16 a main course. *Rasoi*, at No 211 opposite McDonald's, is a straightforward, vegetarian Indian place with laminex tables. Their thali meals, starting at $3 and going up to $12.95 for all you can eat, are very tasty and great value for lunch or dinner.

The cheap eats and late nights quandary can be solved by *The White Lady* mobile hamburger stand, an Auckland institution. It's on Shortland St just off Queen St and is open in the evenings only until around 3 am during the week, and 24 hours a day on weekends and holidays. It's a good place for burgers, toasted sandwiches or a steak.

Auckland, as the main gateway to the country, always has plenty of backpackers, and some places cater primarily for backpackers. The *Cafe at the World's End*, on the 7th floor of the Auckland Central Backpackers at 9 Fort St, is a good, cheap cafe next to the bar. *Margarita's*, on Elliot St opposite the post office, is a Mexican restaurant with cheap $5 meal specials and a sometimes lively bar. It is hard to find – go around the back of the buildings on Elliot St and then downstairs.

Pub Food The various city pubs are another economical eating possibility, particularly for lunch. The three pubs at the *Shakespeare Brewery*, on the corner of Albert and Wyndham Sts, all serve food, as does the bistro of the *London Bar* on the 1st floor at Wellesley St West near the corner of Queen St.

The *Blarney Stone Irish Pub* at 50-52 Customs St East has good lunch and dinner menus. The *Kiwi Tavern*, around the corner in Britomart Place, serves good, inexpensive meals. Both are popular with backpackers and offer backpacker specials.

The *Bird Cage* on the corner of Victoria St West and Franklin Rd, opposite Victoria St

Market, is a fancier pub that serves meals but it is mainly noted for its good-value $5 breakfasts.

The English-style *Nags Head Tavern* at 117 St Georges Bay Rd near The Strand, at the bottom of the hill in Parnell, serves lunch, dinner and snacks in its restaurant section, and is especially popular at lunch time.

Several places provide drinks and meals with a stylish air. Try the Wine Bar in the *Hotel De Brett* on the corner of High and Shortland Sts. The *Loaded Hog*, at Viaduct Quay on Quay St, is the most popular brewery pub in town and serves moderately priced meals. Upstairs in the Downtown Airline Terminal on Quay St, the *Waterfront Bar & Restaurant* is more upmarket and serves lunch and dinner both inside and out on the patio.

Restaurants – city centre There are many good restaurants around the centre, many of them reasonably priced.

Tony's at 32 Lorne St must be doing something right because it's been carrying on unchanged while plenty of other places have come and gone. It has a basic steakhouse menu which also features NZ lamb dishes and pastas. Steaks cost around $24 for dinner, less for lunch.

For cheap Italian food, *A Little Italy* at 43 Victoria St West has good pizzas or pasta. *Papa Luigis*, on Wellesley St right near the corner of Queen St, has takeaway pizzas and a small dining area. Great pizzas, with crusty bases and not too much oil, cost around $10 and you can wash it down with a glass of the cheap house wine.

For Mexican food, the *Mexican Cafe* upstairs at 67 Victoria St West has a fun, casual atmosphere. It has equally popular bar and restaurant sections, it's not too expensive and offers vegetarian and meat dishes. Another fine Mexican restaurant, the tiny *Hard to Find Cafe* at 47 High St has a bright Mexican decor and healthy food. It is indeed hard to find, tucked away in an off-street arcade. Main courses are around $15 at either place.

Chinese restaurants range from cheap takeaways to flash eateries that attract wads of $HK. For value, the *New Orient Chinese Restaurant* in the Strand Arcade on Queen St does a great yum cha every day, and buffet dinners on Wednesday ($18) and Sunday ($19). For something fancier, try the bright, cavernous *Dragon Boat*, a modern Cantonese banquet house in The Atrium on Elliot St.

Auckland has a significant Indian community – mostly from Fiji – and plenty of good, cheap Indian restaurants. *Poppadom*, downstairs at 55 Customs St, is a long-running favourite with curries for around $16, cheaper vegetarian dishes, and banquets. Across the road at No 34, *McMahons* is an old-fashioned, dowdy Indian restaurant that scores low on ambience but high on value. The lunch buffets ($9) and Friday and Saturday night dinner buffets ($12.50) are great for the price.

K Rd is also good for Indian restaurants. The *Moti Mahal* at No 271 is good value with curries for $10 to $12, though for only a little extra, *Aashantay* at No 309 has excellent North Indian food, and a bar.

Middle Eastern fare – usually Turkish – is also cheap and popular. The *Middle East* at 23A Wellesley St West is tiny and often crowded – deservedly so since the food is excellent and reasonably priced. Check out their great collection of camel art. For authentic Turkish food, try the similarly priced *Midnight Express Cafe* at 59 Victoria St West, near the Mexican Cafe. Despite the reference to the film, you won't find any prison chains – just good food and atmosphere. It's open until 11 pm.

For vegetarian food, *Gopals*, run by the Hare Krishnas, is on the 1st floor at 291 Queen St near Aotea Square. This relaxed, comfortable place has Indian vegetarian snacks, à la carte meals and unbeatable value buffets. It's open for dinner from 5 to 8.30 pm every night, for lunch from noon to 2.30 pm Monday to Saturday. The *Simple Cottage* at 50 High St is another popular vegetarian place with good, economical vegetarian food and some fine desserts. It's open until 9 pm. *Ferlinghetti's*, 12-14 Lorne St, is a small cafe with organic vegetarian and vegan food.

For great views of the city, try the revolving *Restaurant 360°* on the top floor of the Telecom Building in Hereford St, just behind the Karangahape Plaza on K Rd. Buffets cost $22 for lunch, dinner is $30 to $35. In the same building, the *Vesuvio* Italian restaurant doesn't revolve, but the views are still great and you'll get some of the best Italian food in town for about $20.

For fine views of the ferries and harbour, *Cin Cin on Quay*, in the Ferry Building at 99 Quay St, is an innovative and stylish restaurant that attracts the glitterati and visiting VIPs. It's not cheap but isn't outrageously expensive for the quality.

In a similar vein, *Kermadec* in the Viaduct Quay complex on Quay St, serves top-quality food, with an emphasis on seafood.

Restaurants – Parnell The Parnell Village conglomeration of shops has some good medium-priced restaurants hidden away, several with tables in open courtyards so you can enjoy the fresh air. There's *Valerio's* for Italian food or *Thai Friends* for good Thai food at reasonable prices. The bright and pleasant *Konditorei Boss* German pastry shop/cafe is highly enjoyable for European pastries, espresso concoctions and light meals; it's also great for people-watching on a sunny day. Tucked away in the rear of Parnell Village is the arty little *Boardwalk* cafe.

Parnell is good for Italian food. *La Trattoria Cafe* at 259 Parnell Rd is a fancy Italian/Continental restaurant with dining inside or on a torch-lit patio. Less-expensive Italian places along Parnell Rd include the ever-busy *Italian Cafe & Bar* at No 207, and the *Milano Pizzeria* at No 111.

Cafe Birak at 161 Parnell Rd is another trendy place with an eclectic menu, though moderately priced. The large *Maruhachi Restaurant* on the corner of Parnell Rd and Akaroa St is a Japanese restaurant with a sushi bar, tempura, teppanyaki and big, reasonably-priced salmon rolls.

Cibo at 91 St Georges Bay Rd is one of Parnell's finest restaurants – take your credit card and cellular phone! Most of the main meals are marinated, smoked, sautéed or provençal, doused in booze and accompanied by a variety of colourful things you're not really meant to eat – but they are surprisingly good and the desserts are even better.

Restaurants – Ponsonby Ponsonby is Auckland's busiest restaurant district, with numerous restaurants and cafes strung out over many blocks along Ponsonby Rd. You can walk along here in the daytime or evening and see what captures your fancy. On Saturday nights, get there early or book.

Heading down Ponsonby Rd from the corner with Jervois Rd, a couple of fine eateries are one block down on the corner with Pompallier Terrace. *Freiya's* is a Parsee restaurant, the Parsees (or Zoroastrians) being ancient Persians who migrated to India. It has fine atmosphere, music and good food, but is really just a more expensive Indian restaurant.

Opposite Freiya's, *Java Jive* has a reasonably priced menu with a selection of meat and vegetarian dishes, plus strong coffees and good desserts. Live jazz and blues music start every night around 9.30 or 10.30 pm (see Entertainment); the restaurant/cafe opens every night at 6 pm.

Cafe Cézanne at 296 Ponsonby Rd is a small, casual place with a great atmosphere and good food at good prices. Breakfasts, light meals, gourmet burgers and unusual pies are served all day, all at around $7, and there's a good dinner menu, late-night desserts and espresso. Someone will come around to your table and serve you bottomless coffee. Next door at No 294, the *Turkish Cafe* is one of the cheapest restaurants in Ponsonby, with main courses for around $10 to $12 or a mixed platter for two at $20. The food is good and the service excellent. Across the road, *Hasan Baba* at No 263 is another cheap Turkish cafe with a good lunch special.

Further down Ponsonby Rd, the ever-popular *Prego* at No 226 has a varied Italian menu with a good range of pastas for around $15, and a large selection of wine to wash it down with.

Two of the trendiest eating spots in Auckland are the *Tuatara* at 198 Ponsonby Rd and *SPQR* at No 150. The *Tuatara* has straightforward, well-prepared food and good coffee. The tables outside are popular during the day, but it also packs them in until late at night. The smaller *SPQR* is similar with stylish decor and a good range of moderately priced snacks and light meals. The food is a prelude or complement to the wine quaffing, which goes on to the early hours. Opposite SPQR, the *Atomic Cafe* at No 121 is a breakfast and day-time hang-out, with arguably the best coffee in Auckland (their roasters supply many of the other cafes). It's cosy, and there's a sandpit for the kids.

Ponsonby Rd also has a couple of good Thai restaurants, and Thai food is always moderately priced in Auckland. Try the *Thai House* at No 25 or the *Sawadee* at 42A.

Restaurants – other areas Just west of Ponsonby, along Jervois Rd, the Herne Bay shopping centre has a small selection of good cafes and restaurants. *Sierra Coffee* at 50 Jervois Rd is good for a coffee and a cheap light meal during the day. *Andiamo* at No 194 is licensed, very trendy and open until midnight. The food is always good, from breakfast through to supper. Of the other Herne Bay eateries, *Borobudur Satay House* at No 234A is one of Auckland's few Indonesian restaurants; it serves satay on rice for $13 and other similarly priced meal.

The busy Newmarket shopping district also has a small enclave of good, cheap restaurants on Khyber Pass Rd, near Broadway. For Thai food, there's *Chao Phraya* at No 477 and, right next door, *Sri Siam* at No 473. Just along, *Eduardo's* at No 483 or the slightly fancier *Venezia* at No 479, have Italian food, pizzas and pasta. Around the corner at 2 Osborne St, the very popular *Bodrum Cafe & Bar* has large meals for $12 to $15, and a belly dancer often performs.

Entertainment

Auckland has a good variety of places to go to after the sun sets. The entertainment section in the Saturday *Herald* has a limited run-down on events for the week, mostly movies. Gig guides tend to come and go – the Auckland Visitor Centre will have any available copies. *Auckland Alive & Happening* is a monthly pamphlet from the Auckland Visitor Centre that lists the latest events, music, concerts, theatre, opera, dance, sports and anything else you can think of.

Whatever you're doing late at night in Auckland, keep your eye on the time if you're dependent on buses, which finish at about 10.30 pm, Sunday at 7 pm.

Pubs, Bars & Music Venues Auckland has plenty of convivial pubs and bars, many with music, though live bands are disappearing in favour of cheaper DJs and taped music. Most bands play Irish or folk music and revival oldies, though a few venues specialise in alternative music. Big-name rock concerts are held at *The Power Station* at 33 Mt Eden Rd in Mt Eden.

Nightlife tends to be quiet during the week, with everyone saving up their energies for Friday and Saturday nights. On weekends the popular spots are full to overflowing and dress standards apply at many of the fancier bars, where a beer costs around $4. The central city area is by far the liveliest for nightlife, though a few spots are found in the inner suburbs.

The *Loaded Hog*, at Viaduct Quay down by the waterfront on Quay St, is currently one of the most popular pubs in town. This pub brewery is favoured by the cellular phone brigade and enforces dress codes, but it has a good atmosphere and is always lively.

The *Civic Tavern* at 1 Wellesley St West near the corner of Queen St has three bars on three floors, each specialising in a different part of the British Isles. *Murphy's Irish Bar* is on the ground floor, *Younger's Tartan Bar* is downstairs, and upstairs is the *London Bar*, an English-style pub. On weekends, the London Bar has jazz combos while Murphy's has higher-energy bands.

Kitty O'Brien's Irish Pub at 2 Drake St, Freemans Bay, is on the corner of Drake and Wellesley Sts near the Victoria Park Market. Kitty's always packs them in and is

Auckland's most popular Irish pub with the best reputation for pouring a good Guinness. Live music, Irish and other, is featured every night of the week.

The *Blarney Stone Irish Pub* at 50-52 Customs St East is another convivial Irish pub revolving around the Guinness tap. Irish bands play on the weekends, though this pub doesn't have to put on anything to attract custom.

Over the road, the *Rose & Crown* is another renovated pub on the corner of Custom St East and Commerce St with occasional bands, especially on a Saturday night.

The *Kiwi Tavern*, in Britomart Place, just off Customs St East opposite the China Oriental Markets, is popular with backpackers. It has three separate floors with the Moa Bar on the ground floor, the Haka Bar on the 1st floor with occasional live music and the Loft Bar upstairs where you can hang out, relax, play pool or darts, have a coffee or beer, read international newspapers, check out the notice board and generally take it easy. The Kiwi Tavern is open every day until late.

The *Bar at the World's End* in the Auckland Central Backpackers on Fort St is the liveliest and most popular backpackers hang-out. It has low prices and is always active, even during the week, when most of Auckland is sleeping. It has an outdoor 7th-floor rooftop deck, plus an indoor cafe and a bar with weekly pool competitions. It's a bar especially for backpackers, guests and non-guests alike.

Across the road on Fort St, underneath the Queen St Backpackers, the *Park in the Bar* is an incredibly popular pick-up spot with young suburbanites. On weekends the music is loud, but the place is too crowded for dancing.

High St is good for a music/pub crawl. The *Hotel de Brett* has a variety of bars for wining, dining and playing pool, and the upmarket *DOS Bar* ('Department of Sound') upstairs has a DJ disco on Friday and Saturday nights. Downstairs is *Bob*, a more interesting student hang-out with experimental bands that are sometimes good, sometimes Dunedin dropouts.

A few doors south at 35 High St, the *Bronx* is a lively rap-oriented bar with a DJ, pulsating strobes and the liveliest dance floor in town. Further along, the *CCB Bar*, underneath the Central City Backpackers, gets a few backpackers and an interesting regular clientele with a gay/straight/Polynesian mix.

Small Vulcan Lane, between Queen and High Sts, is also lively on weekends. *Papa Jack's*, the upstairs bar at the Vulcan, turns up the volume and attracts a mixed crowd with a bent for alternative music. Or lace up your Doc Martens and do a bit of head banging at the *Occidental Pub* opposite.

Albert St is another area to cruise for music and bars. In the Downtown Airline Terminal, the *Waterfront Bar*, upstairs on the corner of Albert and Customs Sts, attracts a younger, moneyed crowd at weekends. A few doors further along Albert St, *Sam Buca's* is a place to be seen and also enforces dress codes.

The more down-to-earth *Shakespeare Tavern & Brewery* on the corner of Wyndham and Albert Sts has a number of bars and a variety of brews on the premises. It's a popular spot, featuring live music on weekends and some nights during the week. *Abby's Hotel* on the corner of Wellesley St East and Albert St has several bars featuring DJs.

In the 'other' category, the *Temple* at 486 Queen St is a hip little cafe with live music, usually folk, several nights a week and a Saturday comedy night. The *Empire Tavern*, on the corner of Nelson and Victoria Sts, has poetry nights every Monday from 7.30 pm. *El Inca* at 373 K Rd is a lively place with salsa music for dancing from Thursday to Sunday nights, with no cover charge. A restaurant area is in the rear.

In Parnell, the *Nags Head Tavern* at the bottom of St George's Bay Rd near The Strand is a popular English-style pub with meals served in a restaurant section off to one side. *Iguacu* at 269 Parnell Rd is a very trendy bar/restaurant where it's a challenge to squeeze through the door on Friday nights.

The *Carlton Club* on the corner of Broadway and Khyber Pass in Newmarket is a renovated pub with a popular rugby/sports bar. It's a good spot to watch an Auckland Warriors game on a weekend afternoon; it also has bands on Saturday nights.

Java Jive at 12 Pompallier Terrace, just off Ponsonby Rd in Ponsonby, is one of those rarities that has live music every night, mostly jazz and blues. Sunday is country music night, Monday is blues jam night, and there's always good music playing.

Gay & Lesbian Venues Auckland is undoubtedly New Zealand's gay capital with dozens of gay organisations and venues, ranging from spa houses to haka groups. *MtM* is New Zealand's leading gay newspaper, offering a complete guide to the gay community in Auckland. The Centre (☎ 378 4987) is a good contact point for the gay and lesbian community.

Auckland's gay nightlife is concentred around Karangahape Rd and Albert St. *The Staircase* at 340 K Rd is a very popular nightclub, disco and bar, while a few doors west, *Footsteps* is a popular women's club. *Legend* on the other side of K Rd opposite the Staircase is another gay bar.

The Bar in the large, glossy building on the corner of Albert and Wolfe Sts, opposite the Regent Hotel, is a more low-key gathering place. Opposite the Regent at 17 Albert St, *The Oven* is another nightclub open Wednesday to Sunday from 10 pm.

Ponsonby Rd is another 'gay way' with meeting places like the *Summer Street Cafe* on the corner of Summer St and Ponsonby Rd or the *Atlas Power Cafe* further north on Ponsonby Rd.

Theatre There are a number of live theatre venues around the city centre. They include the *Galaxy Theatre* (☎ 302 0095) in the Old Customs House on the corner of Customs St West and Albert St, and the *Maidment Theatre* (☎ 379 3685) on the corner of Princes and Alfred Sts. The *Watershed Theatre* (☎ 357 0888) in the Turners & Growers Building on the corner of Customs St West and Market Place specialises in alternative theatre.

Other Entertainment One of Auckland's biggest entertainment venues is the new Sky City Casino complex on the corner of Victoria and Hobson Sts. The biggest attraction here is, of course, the gambling, but when completed it will contain a 700-seat theatre as well as restaurants, bars, a hotel and observation tower.

The Aotea Centre in Aotea Square on Queen St is a venue for all kinds of performances and concerts; stop by or phone for their current schedule (☎ 309 2678). Also check out the Auckland Philharmonia Orchestra (☎ 638 7073), the New Zealand Symphony Orchestra (☎ 358 0952) and the New Zealand Ballet Co (☎ 358 3580).

Auckland University has a restaurant, pub, live music, plays, film series, lectures and more. Art films can be seen at the University or at the *Vogue, Academy, Capitol* or *Bridgeway* theatres, the last being in Northcote. Many good cinemas around the city show first-run films; check the newspaper for listings.

For a well-rounded look at New Zealand, Auckland is a good place to see a rugby match. Eden Park is the home of rugby union in Auckland. The Mt Smart Stadium is the home of the Auckland Warriors rugby league team, and their matches against visiting Australian teams are guaranteed to attract an enthusiastic crowd.

Getting There & Away

Air Auckland is the major arrival and departure point for international flights to/from New Zealand. See Air in the Getting There & Away chapter for information on international flights.

Air New Zealand, Ansett New Zealand and Mt Cook Airline connect Auckland with the other major centres in New Zealand. See the Getting Around chapter for fare details. A number of local operators also have flights in and out of Auckland.

The Auckland airport is 21 km south-west of the centre. It has two terminals – an International Terminal and a Domestic Terminal, each with a tourist information centre. A free shuttle service operates between the two, and there's also a signposted footpath.

At the International Terminal there's a free telephone for making accommodation bookings, and many places to stay also provide a free shuttle. A bank is open to change money for all arriving and departing flights, but they charge a transaction fee of $3. The domestic and international terminals have left-luggage facilities and there are also a few car rental desks, though you'll get better rates from car rental companies in town.

Airlines International airlines with representatives in Auckland include:

Aerolíneas Argentinas
ASB Centre, 135 Albert St (☎ 379 3675)
Air New Zealand
QE II Square, Quay St; 139 Queen St (☎ 357 3000)
Air Pacific
404 Queen St (☎ 379 2404)
British Airways
corner Queen & Customs Sts (☎ 367 7500)
Cathay Pacific
191 Queen St (☎ 379 0861)
Continental Airlines
99 Albert St (☎ 379 5680)
Delta Airlines
87 Queen St (☎ 379 3370)
Garuda Indonesia
120 Albert St (☎ 366 1862)
Japan Airlines
120 Albert St (☎ 379 9906)
Polynesian Airlines
283 Karangahape Rd (☎ 309 5396)
Qantas
154 Queen St
(☎ 357 8900, freephone (0800) 808 767)
Singapore Airlines
West Plaza Building, corner Albert & Fanshawe Sts (☎ 379 3209)
Thai Airways International
22 Fanshawe St (☎ 377 3886)
United Airlines
7 City Rd (☎ 379 3800)

Domestic airlines operating from Auckland include:

Air New Zealand
QE II Square, Quay St; 139 Queen St (☎ 357 3000)
Ansett New Zealand
75 Queen St (☎ 302 2146)
Great Barrier Airlines
Auckland Domestic Terminal (☎ 275 9120)
Gulf Island Air
Waiheke Island (☎ 372 7428)
Mt Cook Airline
34 Queen St (☎ 377 8389); Downtown Airline Terminal

Bus InterCity buses have services from Auckland to just about everywhere in New Zealand. See individual destinations for details. InterCity buses operate from the Auckland InterCity Travel Centre (☎ 358 4085) beside the railway station. The ticket office is open Monday to Thursday from 7.25 am to 6 pm, Friday 7.45 am to 6 pm, and weekends from 7 am to 2.30 pm.

Newmans buses (☎ 309 9738) operate from the Downtown Airline Terminal, Quay St, and their buses go just about everywhere in the North Island. Northliner Express buses (☎ 307 5873) also operate from the Downtown Airline Terminal, with services heading north from Auckland to Whangarei, the Bay of Islands and Kaitaia.

A number of backpackers buses operate in and from Auckland; all offer door-to-door service, picking you up and letting you off at any hostel in Auckland. See Bus in the Getting Around chapter for details.

Train Trains arrive and depart from the railway station (☎ freephone (0800) 802 802) on Beach Rd, about one km east of the city centre. You can telephone for reservations and information every day from 7 am to 9 pm.

Two trains operate between Auckland and Wellington (10 hours). The *Overlander* train runs every day, departing from both venues in the morning and arriving around dinnertime. The *Northerner* is an overnight train operating every night except Saturday, departing from both venues in the evening and arriving early in the morning.

The *Geyserland* operates twice daily between Auckland and Rotorua (four hours). The *Kaimai Express* operates daily between Auckland and Tauranga (3½ hours) with a stop in Hamilton on the way.

Hitching As usual, it's easier to get a lift from out of town, but if you want to hitch from central Auckland, use the Beaumont St motorway ramp near Victoria Park to go north and the Grafton Bridge ramp behind the hospital to go south.

Otherwise, to start hitching northwards, take a bus from the Downtown Bus Terminal to Waiwera (bus No 895), Hatfields Beach (bus No 894), Orewa (bus No 893) or Silverdale (bus No 899). All leave about six times a day and cost about $6. Alternatively, you can take an hourly bus to Albany and start hitching from there.

To get an early start hitching north, you can take a bus to Orewa, stay overnight there (the Marco Polo hostel is very convenient) and be on the highway first thing in the morning.

Going south, take any southbound long-distance bus and get off at the Bombay Hills crossroads. Buses leave many times daily; the cost is around $10.

Getting Around

To/From the Airport The Auckland airport is 21 km south-west of the centre. The Airbus shuttle runs every 20 minutes between the airport and the Downtown Airline Terminal (☎ 275 9396), Quay St, starting at 6.10 am and finishing at 8.50 pm, with scheduled stops along the way. The cost is $10 one way, $15 return, and the trip takes about 45 minutes (allow an hour during rush hour).

Door-to-door shuttle services also run to and from the airport, and competition is cut-throat. The two main operators are Super Shuttle (☎ 307 5210) and Johnston's Shuttle Link (☎ 256 0333). The cost between the airport and the city centre is around $15 for one person, but all sorts of deals are available. Super Shuttle's rates are as low as $8 or $9 for backpackers if you're going to or from a hostel.

Bus Local bus routes operate every day from around 6.30 am to 10.30 pm, finishing earlier (around 7 pm) on Sunday.

The Downtown Bus Terminal is on Commerce St, between Quay St and Customs St East, but not all buses leave from here. Local bus route timetables are available from the bus terminal, newsagents, the Auckland Visitor Centre, or you can phone Buz-a-Bus (☎ 366 6400) for information and schedules. It operates from 7 am to 7 pm on weekdays, until 9 pm on Friday, from 8 am to 7 pm on Saturday and 8 am to 6 pm on Sunday, although on weekends you may have trouble getting an answer as there aren't enough people to answer the phone. There's a bus information kiosk at the Downtown Bus Terminal; it's open from 7.15 am to 6.30 pm Monday to Friday, 9.15 am to 4.45 pm on weekends. The Bus Place at 67 Victoria St West is another source of information, open from 8.15 am to 4.30 pm Monday to Friday. The *Auckland Busabout Guide* shows bus routes and departure points for the city's major attractions.

Inner city fares cost 40 cents, further distances cost $1, then $2 and so on. Busabout passes are available for unlimited daily bus use from 9 am onwards (anytime on weekends) for $8 (children $4, families $12). The passes can be bought on board the bus. Weekly passes are also available.

Train Auckland has a limited Cityrail (☎ 0800 103 080) train service with just two main lines running west to Waitakere and south to Papakura. The first stop out from the main railway station is at Newmarket. Trains run roughly every hour from 6 am to 7 pm.

Taxi Deregulation is the name of the game in New Zealand, and when the taxi industry was deregulated, small companies cropped up all over the place offering cut-price fares. Now the companies have got together to 'self-regulate' (fix) prices, though driver training still seems to be non-existent. Flagfall is $2 and then around $1.50 per km. A taxi to the airport from the city will cost around $35.

There are plenty of taxis in Auckland that usually work from ranks but they also cruise the popular areas. You often have to phone for a taxi – Auckland Taxi Co-op (☎ 300 3000) is one of the biggest companies.

Car & Campervan Auckland is crawling with car and campervan hire operators and is the best city in which to hire a vehicle for touring around New Zealand. Some good deals can be had for long-term hire, but be warned that cheapest is not necessarily the best. Renting a bomb is one thing, renting a bomb with limited or no insurance and being liable for repairs is another.

The major companies – Avis, Budget, Hertz and Thrifty – are the most reliable, offer full insurance, and have offices at the airport and all over the country. They are expensive, but rates are often negotiable for longer rentals.

If you are prepared to take limited insurance and risk losing an excess of around $700, then the cheaper operators offer some pretty good deals. Prices vary with the season, the age of the car and length of rental. In the off-season, for rental of a month or more, a good 1990 model car costs as little as $25 per day. For shorter rentals in the high season, expect to pay $40 or more a day. A campervan or kitted-out minibus starts at around $40 per day.

Ignore prices quoted on brochures and shop around by phone. Check km rates, whether the price includes GST, minimum hire periods, bonds, responsibility for repairs and insurance coverage. Always read the rental agreement thoroughly before you sign. See the Getting Around chapter for a full discussion of car hire and the pitfalls.

Auckland had over 60 rental operators at last count. The following are either the larger operators or they can offer drop-off in the South Island, usually Christchurch.

Ace	☎ 378 8002
Adventure*	☎ 275 8994
Avis	☎ 379 2650
Avon*	☎ 275 3034
Big Save	☎ 303 3928
Breakaway*	☎ 874 8833
Budget*	☎ 379 6768
Cheapa	☎ 827 4577
Country Wide Rentals	☎ 376 4000
Garden City*	☎ 377 1813
Gypsy Hire*	☎ 480 5098
Hertz	☎ 303 4924
Holiday Rentals*	☎ 357 6593
Leisureport Campervans* (Maui, Mt Cook, Budget, Newmans & Horizon)	☎ 275 3013
Matthew*	☎ 256 0555
Maui*	☎ 275 3013
McDonalds	☎ 276 8574
Nationwide	☎ (0800) 803 003
National	☎ 309 3336
NZ Rent a Car	☎ 275 2422
Pegasus*	☎ 358 5757
Percy	☎ 303 1122
Realistic*	☎ 302 2985
Rent-a-Wreck	☎ 357 0019
Southern Cross	☎ 275 3099
Suntrek*	☎ 520 1404
Take It Easy*	☎ 817 4387
Thrifty	☎ 358 4488
Value	☎ 360 0099
Wenderkreisen*	☎ 810 9582

* Those with an asterisk have campervans as well as rental cars.

Buying a Car For stays of two months or more, many people look at buying a car. You can buy through dealers, on the buy-back scheme, at car fairs or though ads in the newspapers. The hostels in Auckland also have notice boards where travellers leaving the country advertise their cars, and the Auckland Visitor Centre on Aotea Square has a similar board.

For newspaper listings, cars are advertised in the *NZ Herald* on Wednesday, the *Trade & Exchange* on Thursday, and the *Auto Trader* magazine.

Buy-backs, where the dealer agrees to buy back your car for an agreed price, are not usually a great deal but are an easier option. Dealers who work on this system include:

Budget Car Sales	☎ 379 4120
Downtown Rentals	☎ 303 1847
Gerarty McGregor Motors	☎ 307 6700
Rex Swinburne Motors	☎ 620 6587
Rock Bottom Rentals	☎ 622 1592

The most popular way to buy a car is through the car auctions, where private individuals bring their cars to sell. Manakau is the biggest and best, but the Ellerslie Racecourse car fair is also good. In the city centre, there is a car fair next to the China Oriental Markets, but it is relatively small. Arrive early, between 8.30 and 9.30 am, for the best choice of cars – the car fairs are all over by about midday. Mechanical inspection services, credit agencies and Auto Check details are all on hand at the fairs, which are listed below:

Manukau car fair, South Auckland – in the parking lot of the giant shopping mall near the Manukau motorway offramp (☎ (09) 358 5000); Sunday
Ellerslie Racecourse car fair – near the Greenlane roundabout (☎ (09) 810 9212); Sunday
China Oriental Markets – on Beach Rd in the city centre (☎ (09) 524 9183); Saturday

Alternatively, you could try the car auctions. Two of the best known are:

Turner's Car Auction (☎ (09) 525 1920), McNab St, Penrose – several times a week, with a special day set aside for budget vehicles
Hanmer Auctions (☎ (09) 579 2344), 830 Great South Rd, Penrose – also holds auctions several times a week

Motorcycle If it's just a small scooter you're looking for, Pegasus (☎ 358 5757) at China Oriental Markets will hire you a scooter for $25 for 24 hours. Only a car licence is needed.

For larger motorcycles, some will rent and others will sell it on a buy-back system. They usually hire anything from 250 cc to 750 cc.

Bill Russell Motorcycles (☎ 377 8739) at 22 Mt Eden Rd, Mt Eden sells 250 cc to 750 cc motorcycles on the buy-back system. When they buy it back from you they deduct about $800 for one month, $1000 for two months or $1200 for three months.

Other places that hire motorcycles include Colemans Suzuki (☎ 303 1786) at 538 Karangahape Rd and Graeme Crosby (☎ 376 3320) at 299 Great North Rd.

Bicycle Several companies around Auckland hire bicycles, usually mountain bikes, by the day, week, month or longer. They also hire all the gear you need for longer journeys – helmets, panniers, tents and so on. Most will help you work out a cycle touring route.

Some operate on a buy-back system, which can work out cheaper than long-term hire.

A handy place in the city centre is *Adventure Cycles* (☎ 309 5566), in Fort Lane, just off Fort St opposite the Queen St Backpackers. Mountain bike rentals with panniers and a bike kit start at $25 per day, $100 per week or $245 per month.

The Penny Farthing Cycle Shop (☎ 379 2524, 379 2002; fax 309 1559) on the corner of Symonds St and Khyber Pass Rd hires mountain and hybrid bikes. The Mountain Bike Hire Co (☎ 358 4885) hires 21-speed mountain bikes in five sizes and they offer free delivery to wherever you're staying.

For a bike around town, Cycle Xpress (☎ 379 0779) at 11 Beach Rd rents good 15-speed bikes at $17 per day plus deposit (bring your credit card), or arranges longer-term rental and sells bikes. Pack 'n Pedal (☎ 522 2161) at 436 Broadway in Newmarket hires mountain bikes at $25 per day and sells bikes on the buy-back system (buy-backs at half price) and also sells cycling gear and camping equipment.

Pedaltours (☎ 302 0968; fax 302 0967) at 28 Birdwood Crescent, Parnell, offers interesting guided group cycling tours of both the North and South Islands, and you can hire a bike from them even if you don't join one of their tours. Quality bikes with touring equipment are $110 per week or $305 for four weeks.

Boat Fullers (☎ 367 9102 for schedules) are the main ferry operators to Devonport and the islands of the Hauraki Gulf. Ferries to Devonport ($7 return) leave roughly every 30 minutes, about a dozen ferries a day go to Waiheke ($22 return), and three or four ferries a day go to Rangitoto ($17 return). Less frequent ferries go to Great Barrier, Rakino, Motutapu and Motuihe. All Fullers ferries depart from the Auckland Ferry Building.

Apart from Fullers, Sinclairs Ferry (☎ 372 6892) also operates to Rakino, and car ferry services operate to Waiheke and Great Barrier.

Around Auckland

REGIONAL PARKS

The Auckland Regional Council administers 21 regional parks around the Auckland region, all within 15 to 90 km of the city (20 minutes to 1½ hours driving time). There are several coastal and beach parks with swimming and surfing beaches, plus bush parks, a kauri park, the Waitakere Ranges west of Auckland, and a gannet colony at Muriwai on the coast north-west of the city. All the parks have good walks and tramping tracks, ranging from 20 minutes to several hours in length; several allow camping.

An Auckland Regional Parks pamphlet with photos, descriptions and a list of facilities in each regional park is available from the Auckland Visitor Centre, or the DOC/Auckland Regional Parks information centre (☎ 366 2166) at the Ferry Building.

DEVONPORT

Devonport is an attractive suburb on the tip of Auckland's North Shore peninsula. One of the earliest areas of European settlement,

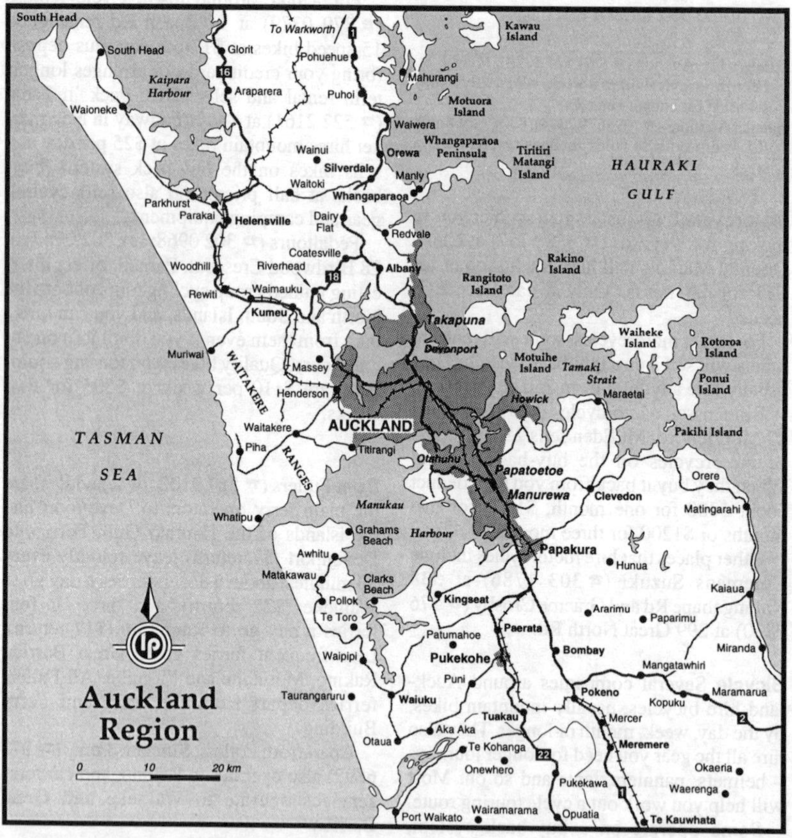

it still retains a 19th-century atmosphere with its many well-preserved Victorian buildings. It also has a tourist atmosphere – it's the most popular excursion from downtown Auckland, only 15 minutes away by ferry – and has lots of small shops, arts & crafts galleries, cafes and takeaways in the area surrounding the ferry dock.

Things to See

Devonport also has several points of interest. Two volcanic cones, **Mt Victoria** and **North Head**, were once Maori pa settlements – you can see the terracing they made on the sides of the cones. Mt Victoria is the higher of the two, with a great 360° view and a map at the top pointing out all the landmarks and giving the names of the many islands you can see. You can walk or drive to the summit of Mt Victoria; the road is open all the time except from 6 pm to 7 am Thursday, Friday and Saturday.

North Head, on the other cone, is a historic reserve riddled with old tunnels built at the end of the last century in response to fears of a Russian invasion. The fortifications were extended and enlarged during WWI and WWII but dismantled after WWII. Some of the old guns are still up here and a ranger is on hand with historical information. The reserve is open to vehicles every day from 6 am to 6 pm and to pedestrians until 10 pm.

The **waterfront promenade** of Devonport, with a view back towards the city, makes a good stroll. Near the ferry wharf is a children's playground and a large lawn area where families picnic on sunny days.

Walk west from the wharf along the promenade (left as you come out of the wharf building) for about five blocks until you reach the navy base, then turn right into Spring St. At the end of the street is the small **Naval Museum**, open from 10 am to 4.30 pm daily; admission is free. The **Devonport Museum**, in Mt Cambria Reserve just east of Mt Victoria, chronicles Devonport and is open on weekends from 2 to 4 pm. Another museum, **Jackson's Museum** at 10 Victoria Rd – the main drag – is filled with automobiles and old bric-a-brac, but the doors remain closed while the owner's battles with the local council continue.

Just past the foot of North Head, **Cheltenham Beach** is a lovely little beach with a superb view of Rangitoto Island.

Tours

The Old Devonport Ferry & Coach tour (☎ 357 6366) meets the ferry every hour from 10 am to 3 pm, and an enjoyable minibus tour takes you around Devonport's many sights, including the summits of North Head and Mt Victoria, which are quite a climb otherwise. The tour takes about an hour and costs $22 (children $11).

On Friday and Saturday evenings the *Kestrel*, a historic ferry sometimes affectionately called the 'jazz ferry', goes back and forth across the harbour from Auckland to Devonport, departing hourly from each side (Auckland on the hour, Devonport on the half-hour) from 7 pm to 11 pm. There's a jazz band for dancing, a restaurant for dining, and all in all it's a very pleasant evening. Reservations are recommended if you intend to dine on the ferry (☎ 377 1771), but not needed otherwise.

Places to Stay

Devonport is an enjoyable and convenient place to stay, and it has several good, small B&B guesthouses to choose from.

Pride of place goes to the *Peace & Plenty Inn* (☎ 445 2925) at 6 Flagstaff Terrace, just a one-minute walk from the ferry wharf, facing the little triangular grassy park on Victoria Rd. In a restored historic kauri house, it's one of the most artistically and unusually decorated places we've seen. The cost for B&B is $85 to $110 for a single, $110 to $140 for a double.

Near Cheltenham Beach and North Head, the *Garden Room* (☎ 445 2472) at 23 Cheltenham Rd is a self-contained bungalow in the grounds of an Edwardian villa. The cost is $75/95 a single/double including breakfast. Down the other end of Cheltenham Beach, *Cheltenham by the Sea* (☎ 445 9437) at 2 Grove Rd just off Wairoa Rd, is a guesthouse in a family home; the cost is $45/70 B&B in one of three guest rooms, each with private entrance but all sharing bathroom facilities.

The historic, renovated *Esplanade Hotel* (☎ 455 1291) is directly opposite the ferry dock at 1 Victoria Rd. The rooms are simple but stylish with TV and phone, and the bathrooms range from big to huge. Singles cost $55 with shared facilities, doubles with private bathroom are $75 to $85, and suites are $195 to $225.

Places to Eat

Most of Devonport's restaurants and cafes are strung out along Victoria Rd, the main street leading from the ferry wharf.

The ferry building itself has a small food court with fast-food counters and dining facilities. Upstairs are two popular bar/restaurants, *Port-O-Call* and *Torpedo Bay*, where you can dine inside or out, day or night, overlooking the harbour.

Heading up Victoria St, the Esplanade Hotel has a couple of flash dining rooms, including the *Grapevine Wine Bar*, which has varied NZ fare; dinner costs around $15 to $20.

Victoria Rd has plenty of fashionable cafes and bars such as the *Devonport Bar & Brasserie* at No 5-7, the *Left Bank* at No 14, or the most popular *Carpe Diem* at No 49 with a good blackboard menu.

Good restaurants on Victoria Rd are the *Portofino Bar & Restaurant* at No 26 with good pasta dishes, *Monsoon* at No 71 with reasonably priced Thai and Malaysian curries or *Low Flying Duck* at No 99, with nouvelle-NZ dishes for around $20.

For great views over lunch, *McHugh's of Cheltenham*, 46 Cheltenham Rd, is right on Cheltenham beach directly opposite Rangitoto Island. Buffet lunches cost $18 on weekdays, $20 on weekends. Bookings are recommended (☎ 445 0305).

For takeaway fish & chips to eat down at the waterfront, the *Catch 22* fish shop at No 19 Victoria Rd has a good selection of fish, but *Gloria's* further up at No 26 is cheaper and has great fish & chips. For a cheap counter meal, the *Masonic Tavern*, on the corner of Church St and the waterfront parade, is a local boozer with good views of the harbour.

Getting There & Away

Bus Buses to Devonport run regularly from the Downtown Bus Terminal in Auckland, but the ferry crossing is quicker and more enjoyable.

Boat The Devonport ferry departs from the Auckland Ferry Building every 30 minutes from 6.15 am to 7 pm, then every hour until 11 pm. The return fare is $7 (children $3.50) and the crossing takes 10 to 15 minutes.

The Fullers' *Harbour Explorer* stops at Devonport, Kelly Tarlton's Underwater World and Rangitoto Island; an all-day pass entitles you to jump on and off the boat wherever you like. Fullers (☎ 377 1771) has information on all the Devonport ferries.

WEST AUCKLAND

No more than an hour's drive from the city, West Auckland has excellent surf beaches, nature reserves and the Waitakere Ranges, which offer good walking tracks and temperate rainforest. West Auckland is also the place to go for vineyards and craft outlets.

Vineyards

New Zealand's wines have earned themselves a worldwide reputation and there are numerous vineyards in the West Auckland area. The *Winemakers of West Auckland* pamphlet – available from the Auckland Visitor Centre – details the vineyards, their addresses and opening hours. Some, such as Corbans, are within walking distance of Henderson, which can be reached by bus or Cityrail from Auckland. Other large and well-known vineyards, such as Matua Valley, Nobilo and Coopers Creek, are further out near Kumeu.

Some of the wineries have excellent restaurants. For fine dining in a beautiful setting, the *Hunting Lodge* (☎ 411 8259) at the Matua Valley wineries is open Fridays and weekends for lunch and dinner. A set meal costs $42.50.

Waitakere Ranges

These scenic ranges once supported important kauri forests, but these were logged almost to extinction in the 19th century, though a few stands of kauri and other mature trees such as rimu survive. The **Centennial Memorial Park** now protects many native plants in the regenerating forest. Bordered to the west by the beaches on the Tasman Sea, the park's sometimes rugged terrain with steep-sided valleys is the most significant forest area close to Auckland and is popular for picnics and walks.

The **Arataki Visitor Centre** (☎ 817 7134) on SH24, six km past Titirangi on Scenic Drive, is a good starting point for exploring the ranges. As well as providing a host of information on the area, this impressive centre with its Maori carvings and spectacular views is an attraction in its own right. The nature trail at the centre points out native species and contains a few mature kauris.

The visitor centre has pamphlets and maps for walking over 200 km of trails in the ranges, or you can also get information from the Auckland Regional Parks office in Auckland. Noted walks are the Karamatura Loop Walk near Huia, leading to waterfalls and northern rata forest, and the Cascade Falls walk at the north of the park, which passes mature kauri.

Piha & Whatipu

Piha, about 40 km west of Auckland at the edge of Centennial Memorial Park, is a small seaside village inhabited by many artists, craftspeople and alternative types that comes alive in summer with hundreds of beachgoers, holidaymakers and surfers. In summer, in addition to the beach life, there's tennis, lawn bowling, live bands playing at the surf club on weekends, and lots of partying going on. Surfing competitions are held in Piha, and there are many good bushwalks through the surrounding Waitakere Ranges and along the rocky coastline. All in all it's a very enjoyable, picturesque spot – a refreshing change from Auckland. Karekare, south of Piha, has a surf-pounded beach and nearby rain-drenched forest. It was the location for the award-winning film *The Piano*.

The *Piha Domain Campground* (☎ 812 8815) right on the beach is open all year round and has tent sites at $14 for two, powered sites at $15 for two, and on-site caravans at $30 for two. Non-campers will find private homestays, baches and caravans available in Piha.

Another attractive spot is Whatipu, on the northern side of Manukau Harbour at Manukau Heads, 40 km from Auckland via Titirangi and Huia, about a 50-minute drive from the city. The *Whatipu Lodge* (☎ 811 8860), set in a quiet and isolated area good for tramping and fishing, has basic non-powered camp sites at $8 per vehicle (up to four people), plus hostel-style accommodation with single, twin and double rooms at $18 per person. Take the bus to Huia and they'll come to pick you up.

Muriwai Beach & Gannet Colony

The road to Muriwai Beach is well sign-posted at Waimauku on SH16. Apart from the renowned surf beach, the main attraction here is the colony of Australasian gannets *(Sulidae sula bassana)*. The colony was once confined to a nearby rock stack but now it has overflowed to the shore cliffs, even past the barriers erected to keep observers out. If you haven't seen these beautiful birds at close range before, take the opportunity to see them here.

A good way to explore the beach and forest around Muriwai is on a horse trek which can be organised the Muriwai Riding Centre (☎ 411 8480).

Places to Stay At the small settlement of Muriwai, the *Muriwai Waterfront Camp* (☎ 411 7426) is adjacent to the beach and an 18-hole golf course. Tent and powered sites are $8 per person, on-site caravans $10 per person. A small shop and cafe, the only one in Muriwai, is at the entrance to the camp. Away from the beach, the *Muriwai Country Motel* (☎ 837 3363) has units for around $70.

Helensville

This town is less than an hour's drive from Auckland, four km inland from the southern end of Kaipara, New Zealand's biggest harbour.

Helensville itself is no great attraction, but you can take interesting **harbour cruises** on the MV *Kewpie Too* (☎ 420 8466) – advance bookings are essential. Tours range from a four-hour, $12 cruise to an all-day cruise costing $35 (children $15) that lands at Pouto Point on the northern head of the harbour and joins a 4WD sand dune tour from Dargaville.

Four km from Helensville, at Parakai, **Aquatic Park** is a huge hot pool/swimming complex with indoor and outdoor hot mineral pools and various waterslides. The centre is open from 10 am to 10 pm daily; admission is $9 (children $6) and the waterslides cost extra. The Helensville bus from Auckland continues on to Parakai and stops at the front of Aquatic Park.

Tandem skydiving at the Parakai Parachute Centre (☎ 838 6963) is a popular activity and good value at $185.

Places to Stay & Eat The *Point of View Backpackers* (☎ 420 7331) is a small, no-frills place a long way from town. It costs $15 per person. The *Grand Hotel* (☎ 420 8427), Railway St, has singles/doubles for $25/50 and a restaurant. The best options are the various homestays and farmstays in the area. The small Helensville Information Centre (☎ 420 7468) on the main street has listings.

Out at Parakai, the *Aquatic Park Holiday Camp* (☎ 420 8884) is adjacent to the thermal complex. Here a tent site is $8.50 per person, with the added incentive of free admission to the hot pools. Parakai also has three motels, one of which offers basic backpacker accommodation.

Hauraki Gulf Islands

The Hauraki Gulf off Auckland is dotted with islands. Some are within minutes of the city and are popular for day trips. Waiheke Island in particular is a favourite weekend escape and has become almost a dormitory suburb of the city. Waiheke also has some fine beaches and hostels so it's a popular backpackers' destination. Great Barrier Island, once a remote and little visited island, is also becoming a popular destination and it can be used as a stepping stone to the Coromandel Peninsula. The islands are generally accessible by ferry services or light aircraft. There are also some 'getting there is half the fun' possibilities, like the elderly wooden auxiliary schooner *Te Aroha*.

There are 47 islands in the Hauraki Gulf Maritime Park, administered by DOC. Some are good-sized islands, others are simply rocks jutting out of the sea. The islands in the park are roughly classified into two categories: recreation islands and conservation islands. The recreation islands can be visited, transport is available to them, and their harbours are dotted with yachts in summer. The conservation islands, on the other hand, have severely restricted access. Special permits are required to visit some of them, and others cannot be visited at all, since these islands are refuges for the preservation of plants and animals, especially birds, some of which are extremely rare or even endangered species.

Information

The Hauraki Gulf Islands are administered by the DOC, so their information centre at the Downtown Ferry Building in Auckland is the best place for information. It produces leaflets on several of the islands and can tell you about natural features, walkways, camping and so on. The Auckland Visitor Centre is the place to go for information on the more commercial aspects of the islands – hotels, ferry services, etc. If you're planning to spend some time exploring, look for the DOSLI maps on Waiheke and Great Barrier islands.

RANGITOTO & MOTUTAPU ISLANDS

These two islands, joined by a causeway, are part of the Hauraki Gulf Maritime Park. Rangitoto is just 10 km north-east of the city. The youngest of the 50 or so volcanic cones in the Auckland region, Rangitoto rose from the sea only about 600 years ago, in a series of volcanic explosions. The last eruption was 250 years ago. Rangitoto is the short version

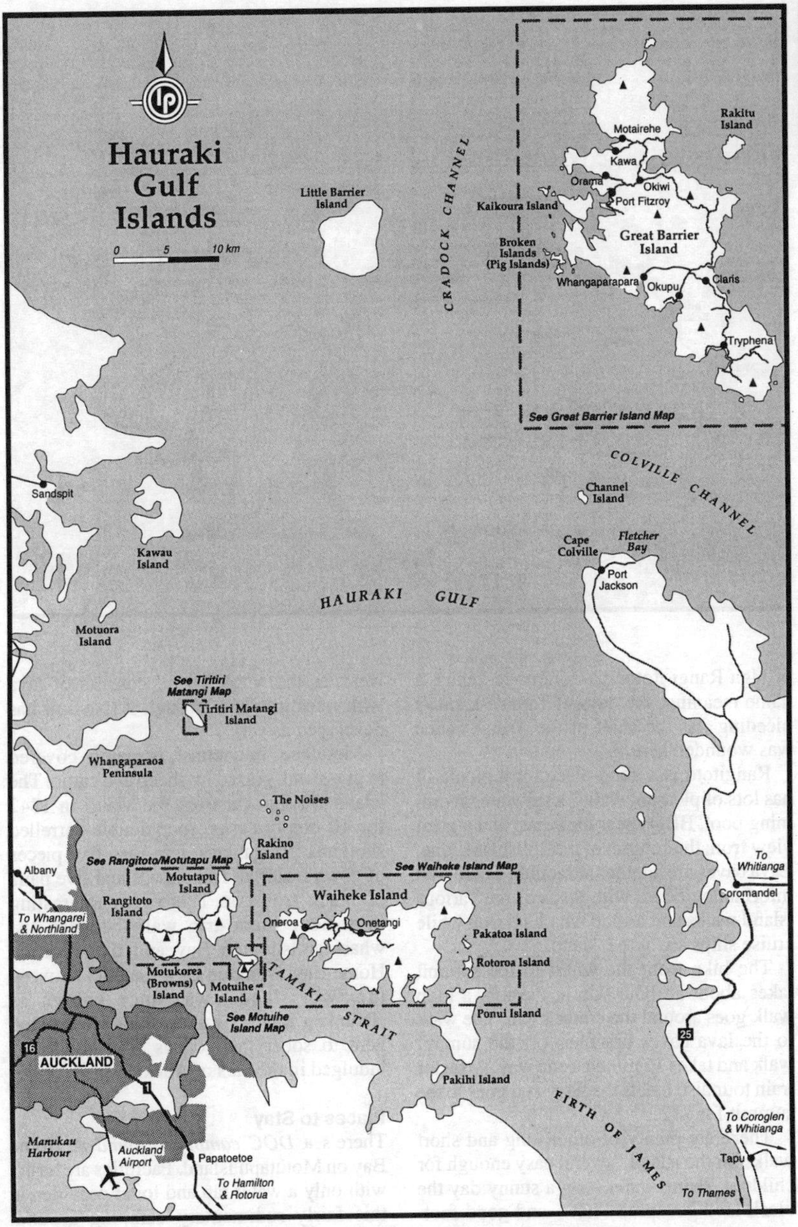
Hauraki Gulf Islands
0 5 10 km
Little Barrier Island
CRADOCK CHANNEL
Kaikoura Island
Broken Islands (Pig Islands)
Whangaparapara
Motairehe
Kawa
Orama
Okiwi
Port Fitzroy
Great Barrier Island
Okupu
Claris
Tryphena
Rakitu Island
See Great Barrier Island Map
COLVILLE CHANNEL
Channel Island
Cape Colville
Fletcher Bay
Port Jackson
Sandspit
Kawau Island
HAURAKI GULF
Motuora Island
See Tiritiri Matangi Map
Tiritiri Matangi Island
Whangaparaoa Peninsula
The Noises
Rakino Island
See Rangitoto/Motutapu Map
Motutapu Island
Rangitoto Island
See Waiheke Island Map
Waiheke Island
Oneroa
Onetangi
Pakatoa Island
Rotoroa Island
Ponui Island
Pakihi Island
Motukorea (Browns) Island
Motuihe Island
See Motuihe Island Map
TAMAKI STRAIT
FIRTH OF JAMES
Albany
To Whangarei & Northland
AUCKLAND
Manukau Harbour
Auckland Airport
Papatoetoe
To Hamilton & Rotorua
To Whitianga
Coromandel
To Coroglen & Whitianga
Tapu
To Thames
1
16
25

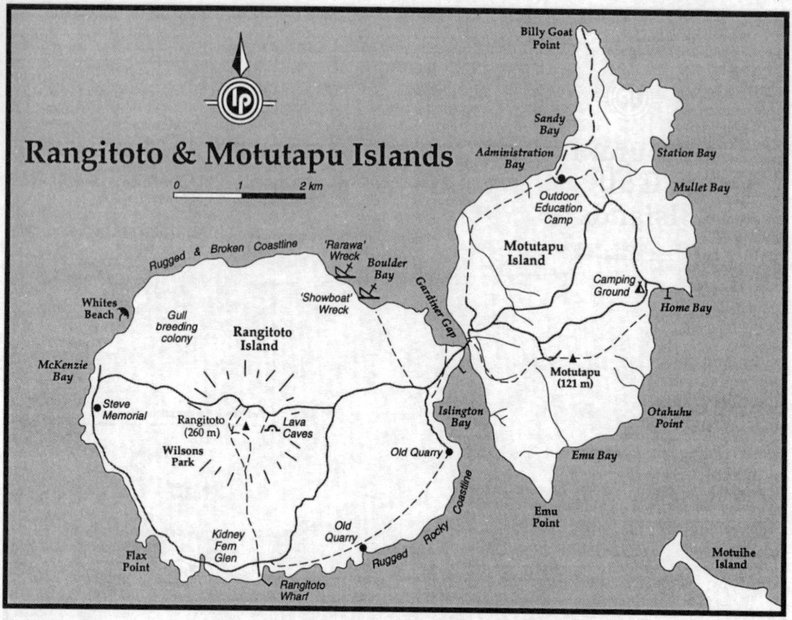

of Nga Rangi-itotongia-a-Tama-te-kapua, a name meaning 'the days of Tamate-kapua's bleeding', as the chief of the *Arawa* canoe was wounded here.

Rangitoto is a good place for a picnic. It has lots of pleasant walks, a saltwater swimming pool, BBQs near the wharf and a great view from the summit of the 260 metre cone. Lava caves are another attraction. There's an information board with maps of the various island walks and a shop which is open while cruise ships are at the island.

The hike from the wharf to the summit takes about an hour. Up at the top, a loop walk goes around the crater's rim. The walk to the lava caves branches off the summit walk and takes 15 minutes one way. A tractor train tour also meets the ferry and goes to the summit for $12.

There are plenty of other long and short walks on the island, several easy enough for children. Bring water – on a sunny day the black lava gets pretty hot – and good footwear, as the whole island consists of lava with trees growing through it (No soil has developed as yet).

Motutapu, in contrast, is mainly covered in grassland, grazed by sheep and cattle. The island was bought from the Maori in 1842 for 10 empty casks, four double-barrelled shotguns, 50 blankets, five hats, five pieces of gown material, five shawls and five pairs of black trousers. There's an interesting three-hour round-trip walk between the wharf at Islington Bay and the wharf at Home Bay. Islington Bay, the inlet between the two islands, was once known as 'Drunken Bay' as sailing ships would stop here to sober their crews who had over-indulged in the bars of Auckland.

Places to Stay

There's a *DOC camping ground* at Home Bay on Motutapu Island. Facilities are basic, with only a water tap and toilet provided at this fairly rudimentary camping ground.

Bring your own cooking equipment as open fires are not permitted. Camping fees are $3 per night. For more information contact the island's Senior Ranger (☎ 372 7348) or the DOC in Auckland.

Getting There & Away

The ferry trip to Rangitoto from the Ferry Building in Auckland takes about an hour. Fullers (☎ 377 1771) has ferries departing every day at 9.30 and 11.30 am and 2 pm. They depart from Rangitoto for the return trip at 10.30 am and 12.30 and 3 pm, with an extra departure leaving the island at 5 pm on Sunday. The return fare is $17 (children $8.50).

Fullers' *Harbour Explorer* ferry stops at Rangitoto Island and other places; see Harbour Cruises under Tours in the Auckland section.

WAIHEKE ISLAND

Waiheke is the most visited of the gulf islands and at 93 sq km is one of the largest. It's reputed to be sunnier and warmer than Auckland and there are plenty of picturesque bays and beaches. A popular day trip from the city, it also has plenty of accommodation for those staying longer.

The island attracts all kinds of artistic and 'alternative lifestyle' folk, who exhibit their work in galleries and craft shops on the island. There is also an increasing number of retirees and commuters. While it is slowly becoming an Auckland suburb, it is still a relaxed, rural retreat.

Waiheke was originally discovered and settled by the Maori. Legends relate that one of the pioneering canoes came to the island, and traces of an old fortified pa can still be seen on the headland overlooking Putiki Bay. The Europeans arrived with the missionary Samuel Marsden in the early 1800s and the island was soon stripped of its kauri forests.

Orientation

The island's main settlement is Oneroa, at the western end of the island. From there it's fairly built up through Palm Beach to Onetangi in the middle. Beyond this the eastern end of the island is lightly inhabited. The coastline is a picturesque mixture of coves, inlets and private little beaches. The island can explored by bus or hired bicycle, scooter or car.

Information

The Waiheke Island Visitor Information Office (☎ 372 9999; fax 372 9919) is at the Artworks complex, on the main road in Oneroa, one km from the ferry dock. It has maps and information about the island, and makes bookings for tours and accommodation. It is open daily from 9 am to 5 pm (until 4 pm in winter).

The *Gulf News* is a weekly newsmagazine of island events. *Waiheke Island – A Tour*, an interesting little booklet produced by the Waiheke Historical Society, is available at the information office and at the museum. *Island Time – a visitor's guide to Waiheke* is another useful book.

Oneroa has a post office, banks and 24-hour ATMs.

Things to See

The **Artworks Living Art Centre** is home to a variety of art and crafts galleries, other businesses and community groups. Artworks is on Ocean View Rd on the corner of Kororoa Rd, between Oneroa and Matiatia Wharf; it's open every day from 10 am to 4 pm.

On the road to Onetangi, between the airstrip and the golf club, is the small **Historic Village** and **Waiheke Island Museum**. The Historic Village is just an old cottage, an old woolshed and a couple of baches, but the little museum is interesting enough, with photos and relics of the old days on the island. It is open from 11 am to 2 pm on weekends most of the year and every day during school holidays.

Waiheke also has some **vineyards** you can visit on a tour or by arrangement. Some charge for tours and tastings. The information office has brochures on the vineyards.

The **Piritahi Marae** in Blackpool, just down the hill from Oneroa, welcomes visitors.

There's a produce and general **market** at Ostend Hall on the main road in Ostend from 7 am to noon on Saturday mornings.

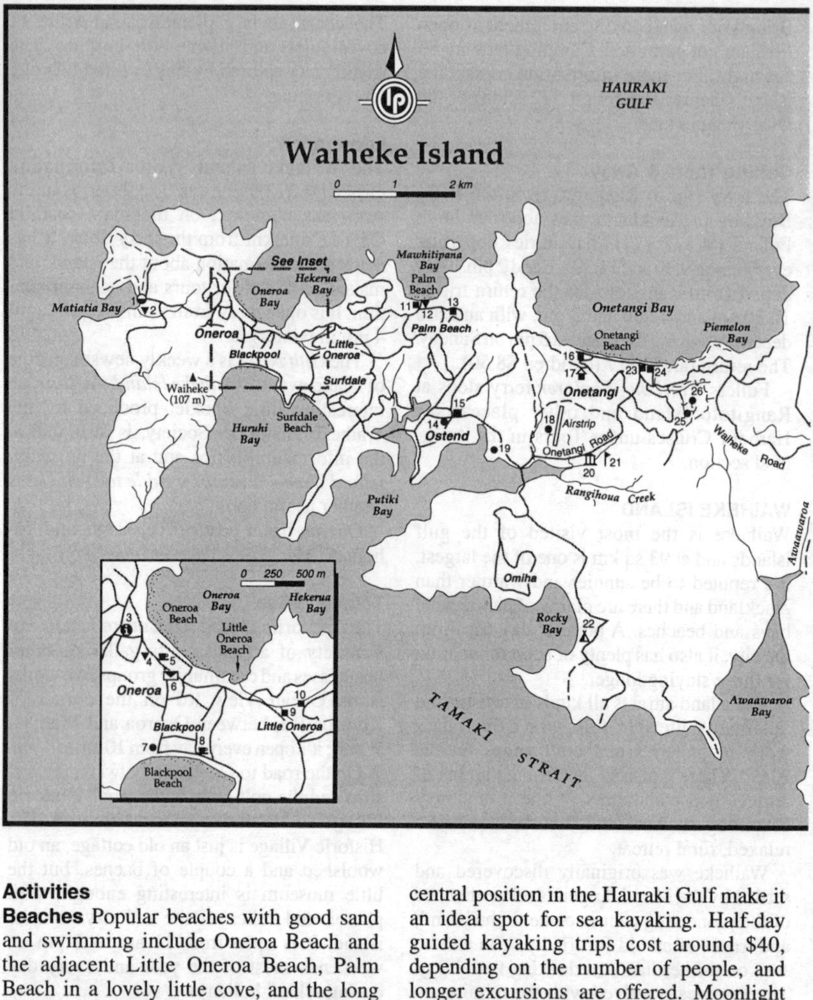

Activities

Beaches Popular beaches with good sand and swimming include Oneroa Beach and the adjacent Little Oneroa Beach, Palm Beach in a lovely little cove, and the long stretch of sand at Onetangi Bay. A number of the beaches have shady pohutukawa trees. You can find nudist beaches at Palm Beach and on the western end of Onetangi Beach. Surf skis and boogie boards can be hired on Onetangi Beach and there's snorkelling at Hekerua Bay.

Sea Kayaking Waheke's many bays and central position in the Hauraki Gulf make it an ideal spot for sea kayaking. Half-day guided kayaking trips cost around $40, depending on the number of people, and longer excursions are offered. Moonlight kayaking is also becoming popular. Operators include Gulf Adventures (☎ 372 7262), Wilderness Expeditions (☎ 372 9020), and Ross Adventures (☎ 357 0550), based at Matiatia.

Walks Waiheke has a system of walkways, outlined in the *Waiheke Islands Walkways* pamphlet, readily available on the island or

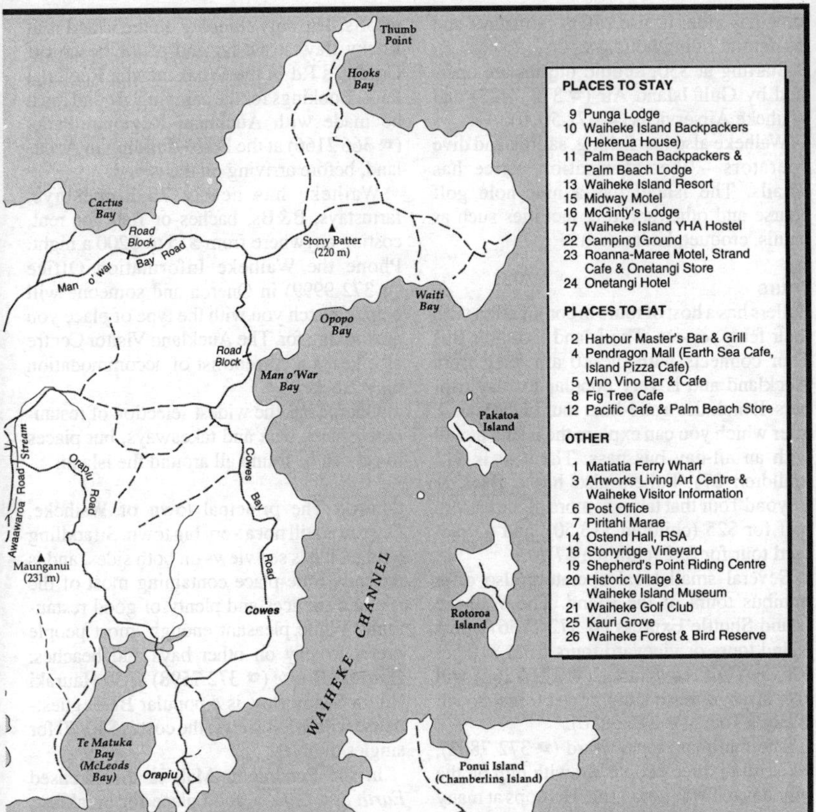

from the DOC/Auckland Regional Parks office in Auckland.

In Onetangi there's a forest and bird reserve with several good walks, one of them a walk up to three large kauri trees. For coastal walks, a good, well-marked track leads right around the coast from Oneroa Bay to Palm Beach. It's about a two to 2½-hour walk; at the Palm Beach end you can jump on a bus to come back to town. Another good coastal walk begins at the Matiatia ferry landing.

The best walks are in the less developed eastern part of the island. The Stony Batter walk, leading through private farmland, derives its name from the boulder-strewn fields. From Man o' War Bay Rd, the track leads to the old WWII gun emplacements with their connecting underground tunnels and sweeping views, then you can continue walking north to Hooks Bay or south to Opopo Bay.

Other Activities The Shepherd's Point Riding Centre (☎ 372 8104) at 6 Ostend Rd, between Ostend and the airstrip, has guided **horse rides** from $20 for one hour and $70 for a day ride; it also offers farmstays and residential riding holidays.

Starting at $30, **scenic flights** are operated by Gulf Island Air (☎ 372 7428) and Waiheke Airservices (☎ 372 5000).

Waiheke also has fishing, sailing and dive operators – the information office has details. The island has a nine-hole golf course and other sporting facilities such as tennis, croquet, badminton.

Tours

Fullers has a host of tours in conjunction with their ferry service. The Island Explorer Bus Tour connects with the 10 am ferry from Auckland and is very popular for day trippers. It includes a one-hour tour of the island, after which you can explore the island at will with an all-day bus pass. The cost is $12 (children $7). Fullers also has a Back & Beyond Tour that takes in more of the eastern half for $25 (children $13.50), and a vineyard tour for $22 (children $7).

Several small local operators also offer minibus tours of the island. The Waiheke Island Shuttle Express (☎ 372 7756) offers island tours or vineyard tours from $10 per person. Gulf Adventures (☎ 372 7262) will also arrange reasonably priced tours as will Wally's Tours (☎ 372 5010).

The mailman, Peter Ward (☎ 372 7802), takes up to three people out with him on the Monday to Friday mail run. He stops at many scenic spots for a look, stops to chat with the locals, and tells stories about the island. The trip lasts from about 8.30 am to noon and costs $10.

Special Events

Summer events include the Onetangi Beach Races in February, which feature horse racing on Onetangi Beach. The Waiheke Jazz Festival is held at Easter each year, and the Waiheke Arts & Crafts Fair is held on Labour Weekend in late October.

Places to Stay & Eat

Waiheke has three good hostels (in Little Oneroa, Palm Beach and Onetangi), a few hotels and motels, a lodge and two posh resorts. The only *camping* on the island is at Rocky Bay, at the far end of the beach off Gordon's Rd in the Whakanewha Regional Park. Bookings for the camping ground must be made with Auckland Regional Parks (☎ 366 2166) at the Ferry Building in Auckland, before arriving on the island.

Waiheke has nearly 70 homestays, farmstays, B&Bs, baches or flats for rent, costing anywhere from $15 to $200 a night. Phone the Waiheke Information Office (☎ 372 9999) in Oneroa and someone will help to match you with the type of place you are looking for. The Auckland Visitor Centre also keeps a current list of accommodation on Waiheke.

Oneroa has the widest selection of restaurants, snack bars and takeaways, but places to eat can be found all around the island.

Oneroa The principal town of Waiheke, Oneroa is still not a very big town. Straddling a ridge, it has sea views on both sides, and is a trendy little place containing most of the island's services and plenty of good restaurants. While pleasant enough, most people prefer to stay on other bays and beaches. *Hauraki House* (☎ 372 7598) at 50 Hauraki Rd, in Sandy Bay, is a popular B&B guesthouse with good views; the cost is $40/70 for singles/doubles.

In the Pendragon Mall is the licensed *Earth Sea Cafe*, a good place for breakfast, a light meal or snack. For pizza, *Island Pizza Cafe* is also in the mall. Across the street in the Oceanview Mall, the *Vino Vino Bar & Cafe* is a very popular bar and gathering place with good food and an outdoor deck offering great views over Oneroa Bay. Oneroa has plenty of other good restaurants, cafes and takeaways.

The *Fig Tree Cafe* is near the waterfront on the corner of the Esplanade and Moa Ave in Blackpool, between Surfdale and Oneroa. This small, attractive place has meat, seafood and vegetarian dishes for around $20 and is one of the island's favourite restaurants, so reservations are recommended (☎ 372 6363).

Near Matiatia Wharf, the large *Harbour*

Master's Bar & Grill is noted for its fine food and has several dining areas, plus a garden bar and swimming pool under shady trees with a view of the bay – beautiful in summer.

Little Oneroa Just beyond Oneroa, Little Oneroa has a reasonable beach and one of the island's few areas of native bush.

Waiheke Island Backpackers (Hekerua House; ☎ 372 8371) is a delightful backpackers nestled in native bush at 11 Hekerua Rd. It is comfortably furnished, has a swimming pool and deck, and is not far from the shop and the beach. The cost per person is $16 in dorms and $40 in a double (both prices include linen). Barbecues and meals are offered in summer. From the ferry landing, the WISE shuttle bus will bring you to the door for $2, otherwise you have to take the bus and then walk up the steep hill. Phone ahead from Auckland to make sure there's room. It is closed in winter.

Also in Little Oneroa, *Punga Lodge* (☎ 372 6675) at 223 Ocean View Rd is in a tranquil bush setting. The summer rate is $55/70 for B&B singles/doubles.

Palm Beach Palm Beach is in a beautiful little cove with a pleasant beach. *Palm Beach Backpackers* (☎ 372 8662) at 54 Palm Rd is a sprawling place with a school camp feel to it, but it's right on the beach and rents windsurfers, kayaks, mountain bikes and so on. The cost is $16 per person in dorms, $40 for double rooms, and camping is $10 per person.

Next door, the *Palm Beach Lodge* (☎ 372 7763) is a much more upmarket place with double rooms at $160. The cost includes an assortment of activities.

On the hill overlooking Palm Beach, the *Waiheke Island Resort* (☎ 372 7897) at 4 Bay Rd is very posh. Chalets with their own private decks and beautiful sea views cost from $100. Facilities include a restaurant, dance floor and entertainment in summer.

Right by the beach, the *Pacific Cafe* at 39 Palm Rd, has a cheap cafe menu with a salad bar. Next door, the general store offers takeaways and groceries.

Ostend Ostend village has shops and a couple of places to eat but it is a fair way from the beach. On the main road, the *Midway Motel* (☎ 372 8023), 1 Whakarite Rd, has motel units for $55 to $78 a double.

In the centre of Ostend village, the *RSA* serves good, cheap pub food and the cheapest beer on the island. Opposite this is a *Chinese takeaway*.

Onetangi Onetangi's long, sandy beach is one of the best on the island – it's popular in summer for swimming, surfing, windsurfing and other activities. Surf skis, surfboards and boogie boards can be hired at the store or on the beach in summer.

The popular *Waiheke Island YHA Hostel* (☎ 372 8971) is on Seaview Rd in Onetangi, up on the hill overlooking the bay. The cost is $14 a night (only $1 extra for non-members) and most of the rooms are twins. Doubles cost $30 and $33, and a self-contained flat is available for $60. Bicycles, kayaks, surfboards etc can be rented and tours are offered. The last stop on the Onetangi bus route is at the bottom of the hill, or the WISE shuttle from the ferry to the door costs $2.50.

Right on the beach, the *Roanna-Maree Motel* (☎ 372 7051) has a swimming pool, spa pool and well-equipped units for $85 to $100 in the high season. The *Onetangi Hotel* (☎ 372 8028) is a modern hotel directly opposite the beach with singles/doubles for $40/65. The hotel also has good-value meals in the *Rumourz Bistro*.

At the Onetangi Store right by the beach, the *Strand Cafe* does takeaways and sit-down meals, with seating inside or out. It's open all day every day, all year round.

Entertainment

The *Baracuda Bar* at the Harbour Masters Restaurant in Matiatia has bands or a DJ on weekend nights, and other events such as comedy nights. The *Vino Vino Bar & Cafe* in Oneroa also has live entertainment on weekends, as does the *RSA* in Ostend and the *Onetangi Hotel*.

Getting There & Away

Air Gulf Island Air (☎ 372 7428) flies to Auckland airport for $50/90 one way/return, Coromandel for $50/90, Thames for $65/120, Great Barrier Island for $65/120 or Ardmore Aerodrome in Papakura for $45/80. They also do charter and scenic flights.

Waiheke Air Services (☎ 372 5000) and Great Barrier Airlines also have flights to/from Waiheke.

Boat Fullers' (367 9102) high-speed ferry service takes about half an hour from Auckland's Ferry Building to Matiatia Wharf at a return cost of $22 (children $11). Ferries depart Auckland at 8 and 10 am, noon, 2, 4, 5.30 and 7 pm, returning 45 minutes later, and extra services are provided at differing times of the year. Fullers buses connect with all arriving and departing ferries.

Subritzsky Shipping Company (☎ 534 5663) operates a vehicle ferry between Kennedy Point on Waiheke and Half Moon Bay in Auckland. Ferries leave two to four times every day, and the voyage takes about 1½ hours. The cost is $55 or $60 each way ($100 or $110 return) for a car and driver, $30 for motorcycles cost each way and $10 for passengers ($5 children). Bookings must be made in advance.

Getting Around

Bus Two bus routes operate on the island, both connecting with the arriving and departing ferries. The Onetangi bus goes from Matiatia Wharf, through Oneroa, Surfdale and Ostend, ending at Onetangi. The Palm Beach bus goes from Matiatia through Oneroa, Blackpool, Little Oneroa, Palm Beach and Ostend, ending at Rocky Bay. Return bus fares (children half price) from Matiatia Wharf are: Oneroa $2, Palm Beach $5, Rocky Bay $5 and Onetangi $5. You can buy bus tickets from Fullers when you buy your ferry ticket. For $12, the Island Explorer bus tour includes a one-hour tour and an all-day bus pass.

Door-to-ferry, ferry-to-door shuttle bus services also operate. Waiheke Island Shuttle Express (WISE) (☎ 372 7756) and Waiheke Coach (☎ 372 7151) both charge about the same prices – $3 to Little Oneroa, $5 to Palm Beach or Onetangi – with discounts depending on the number of people and your choice of accommodation. Both companies also do island tours.

Taxi Two taxi services operate on Waiheke: Waiheke Taxis (☎ 372 8038) and Dial-a-Cab (☎ 627 9666). If you have a group of four together, taking a taxi may cost about the same as the bus.

Car, Scooter & Bicycle The best way to explore Waiheke is with your own transport. Cycling is a good way to explore the island, though the hills make it tough-going in places. Most fun are the little nifty-fifty scooters, favoured by Auckland daytrippers who buzz around and scare the island's residents witless.

Waiheke Rental Cars (☎ 372 8635) has an office by the ferry wharf at Matiatia Bay. It hires out cars, Jeeps and utes (pick-up trucks) for $40 per day plus 35c/km. Automatic 50 cc scooters are $20 for four hours or $30 for a full day. The scooters are easy to ride and only a car licence is required, but be careful, especially on gravel. Motorcycles and minibuses can also be rented. Drivers must be 21 and a driver's licence is required (foreign licences are accepted).

Bicycles can be rented at various places around the island, including at the ferry wharf. The going rate is $20 per day. Pick up a copy of the *Bike Waiheke* pamphlet, available from Fullers or the information centre. Attitude (☎ 372 9914) in the Artworks complex rents motorised mountain bikes, a quieter alternative to the scooters, for $25 a half day or $35 a full day.

PAKATOA ISLAND

Pakatoa Island is a small tourist resort 36 km from Auckland and just off the east coast of Waiheke. The resort has a restaurant, bar, coffee shop, swimming pool and various sporting facilities. There are great views of the gulf and across to the Coromandel Peninsula from the island's high point.

The *Pakatoa Island Resort Hotel* (☎ 372 9002) is the only place to stay on the island. The resort mainly offers packages, such as two-night package for $230 per person, including meals and ferry transport.

GREAT BARRIER ISLAND

Great Barrier Island, 88 km from the mainland, is the largest island in Hauraki Gulf. It is a rugged scenic island, resembling the Coromandel Peninsula to which it was once joined.

With a population of around 1000 living on the 110-sq-km island, there's plenty of open space. Great Barrier has hot springs, historic kauri dams, a forest sanctuary, and a network of tramping tracks. Because there are no possums on the island to eat it, the native bush is lush.

The island's main attractions are its beautiful beaches and its fine tramping. The west coast has safe sandy beaches; the east coast beaches are good for surfing. The best tramping trails are in the Great Barrier Forest between Whangaparapara and Port Fitzroy, where there has been much reforestation. Cycling, swimming, fishing, scuba diving, boating, sea kayaking and just relaxing are other popular activities on the island.

Named by Captain Cook, the island later became a whaling centre. It has also been the site of some spectacular shipwrecks, including the *SS Wairarapa* in 1894 and the *Wiltshire* in 1922. There's a cemetery at Katherine Bay where many of the victims of the *Wairarapa* wreck were buried.

Great Barrier Island is decidedly isolated. Only two hours by ferry from Auckland, the Barrier (as it is called locally) is 20 years away. The island has no electricity supply, only private generators, most of the roads are unpaved and it has only a handful of shops.

Tryphena is the main settlement and arrival point for the ferries. It consists of a few dozen houses, two shops, a school, a ferry wharf and a handful of accommodation places dotted around the harbour. From the wharf it is a couple of km to the Mulberry Grove Store, and then another km over the headland to Pa Beach and the Stonewall Store.

The airport is at **Claris**, a small settlement with a shop, motel and petrol pump. **Whangaparapara** is an old timber town and the site of the island's 19th-century whaling activities. **Port Fitzroy** is the other main town; it is also very small, but is the home of the DOC office.

From around mid-November to Easter the island is a very busy holiday destination, especially during the Christmas holidays until the end of January, Easter, and Labour Weekend. At these times transport, accommodation and activities should be booked in advance.

Information

In Tryphena, the Fullers Office (☎ 429 0004), next to the Stonewall Store, is a mine of information on the island. Talk to Tamara, who can provide information and make accommodation bookings. The office maintains an extensive list of homestays and lodges. In summer it is open from 8.30 am to 5 pm every day and in winter from 9 am to 3 pm.

On the island, the main DOC office (☎ 429 0044; fax 429 0071) is in Port Fitzroy, a 15-minute walk from the ferry landing. It has information and maps on the island, collects camping fees and sells hut tickets, and has a good camping ground. It's open Monday to Friday from 8 am to 4 pm – if there's enough tourist interest, it also opens on weekends during the height of summer. Whangaparapara also has a small DOC post, which opens at irregular hours.

The Auckland Visitor Centre and the DOC information centre in Auckland also have plenty of information about Great Barrier Island.

There's no power on the island, so bring a torch (flashlight). Most people on the island generate their own power by using solar, wind or diesel energy, but there are no street lights anywhere. Great Barrier does have an automatic telephone service and card-operated phones are dotted around the island –

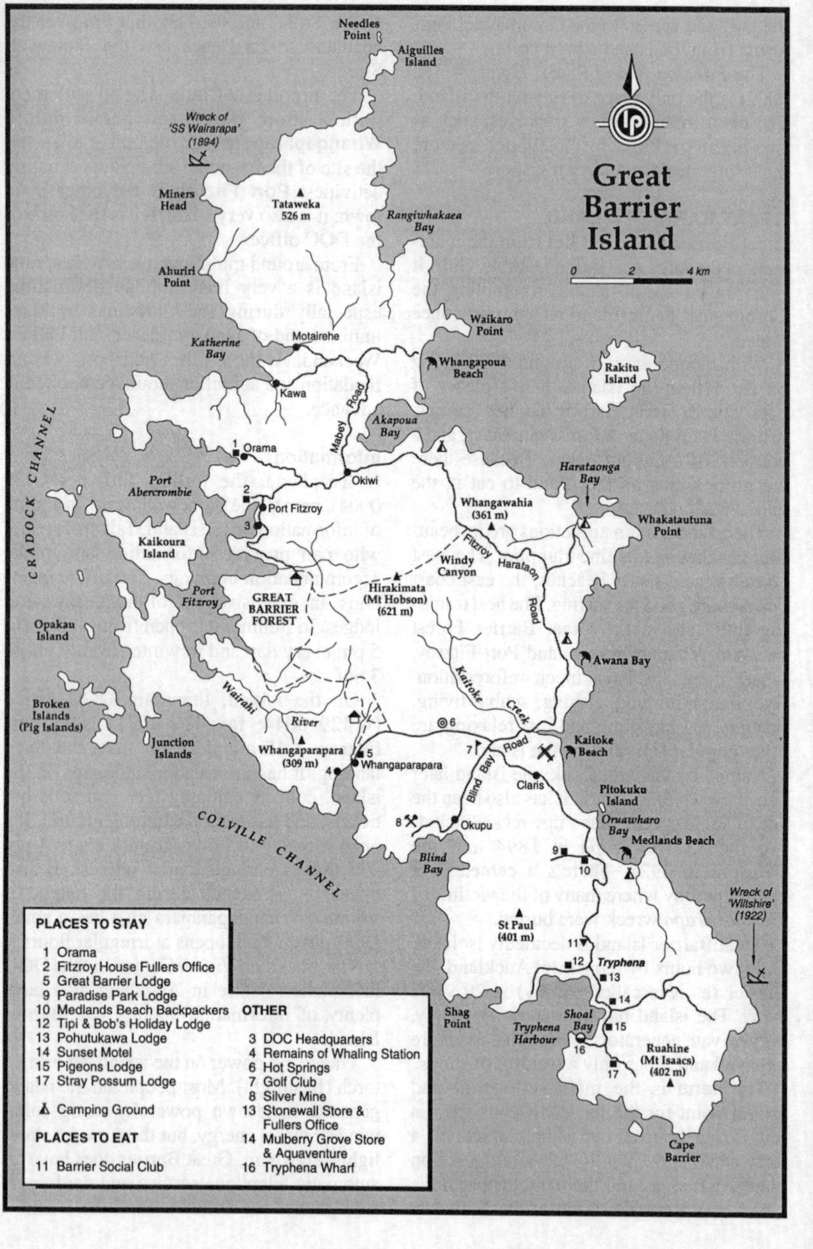
Great Barrier Island
0 2 4 km
Needles Point
Aiguilles Island
Wreck of 'SS Wairarapa' (1894)
Miners Head
Tataweka 526 m
Rangiwhakaea Bay
Ahuriri Point
Waikaro Point
Katherine Bay
Motairehe
Whangapoua Beach
Kawa
Mabey Road
Rakitu Island
Akapoua Bay
CRADOCK CHANNEL
Orama
Okiwi
Harataonga Bay
Port Abercrombie
Port Fitzroy
Whangawahia (361 m)
Whakatautuna Point
Kaikoura Island
Fitzroy
Harataonga Road
Windy Canyon
Hirakimata (Mt Hobson) (621 m)
Port Fitzroy
GREAT BARRIER FOREST
Opakau Island
Awana Bay
Kaitoke Creek Road
Wairahi River
Broken Islands (Pig Islands)
Junction Islands
Whangaparapara (309 m)
Whangaparapara
Blind Bay Road
Kaitoke Beach
Claris
Pitokuku Island
Oruawharo Bay
Medlands Beach
Okupu
COLVILLE CHANNEL
Blind Bay
Wreck of 'Wiltshire' (1922)
St Paul (401 m)
Tryphena
Shag Point
Tryphena Harbour
Shoal Bay
Ruahine (Mt Isaacs) (402 m)
Cape Barrier
PLACES TO STAY
1 Orama
2 Fitzroy House Fullers Office
5 Great Barrier Lodge
9 Paradise Park Lodge
10 Medlands Beach Backpackers
12 Tipi & Bob's Holiday Lodge
13 Pohutukawa Lodge
14 Sunset Motel
15 Pigeons Lodge
17 Stray Possum Lodge
Camping Ground
PLACES TO EAT
11 Barrier Social Club
OTHER
3 DOC Headquarters
4 Remains of Whaling Station
6 Hot Springs
7 Golf Club
8 Silver Mine
13 Stonewall Store & Fullers Office
14 Mulberry Grove Store & Aquaventure
16 Tryphena Wharf

you'll find them in the most unlikely places. Food is available but more expensive than on the mainland.

Things to See & Do

Of the **beaches**, Medlands Beach, with its wide sweep of white sand, is one of the best on the island and easily accessible from Tryphena. Whangapoua is a fine surfing beach, while Kaitoke, Awana Bay and Harataonga are also good. Whangapoua has an excellent right-hand break, while Awana has both left and right-hand breaks. Tryphena's bay, lined with pohutukawa trees, has good sheltered beaches.

Many people come just for the **walks**. The Great Barrier Forest walks are most easily accessed from Port Fitzroy or Whangaparapara. You can take the ferry to either of these destinations and walk 45 minutes to one of the two huts that can be used as bases for exploring the forest. The most spectacular short walk is from Windy Canyon to Mt Hobson. **Windy Canyon**, only a 15-minute walk from the main road, has spectacular rock outcrops and great views of the island. From Windy Canyon, an excellent trail continues for another 1½ hours through scrubby forest to **Mt Hobson** (621 metres), the highest point on the island with views right across to the Coromandel Peninsula and Auckland on a fine day. Near the top of the mountain are lush forests and a few mature kauri that survived the logging days. From Mt Hobson it is two hours though forest to the hut closest to Port Fitzroy, and then 45 minutes to Port Fitzroy itself.

Many other trails traverse the forest. From the road outside Whangaparapara you can also walk to the **hot spring**, though the trail is usually very muddy and not well maintained. There is also a good, four-hour walk west from Tryphena to Okupu Bay that eventually joins the Blind Bay Rd.

Mountain biking is popular on the island. There is diverse scenery, and biking is not too difficult here, even though the roads are unsealed. Here is one popular ride: you can cycle from Tryphena to Medlands Beach in about an hour, stop for a swim, then cycle another hour to the hot springs; from there it's another half-hour to accommodation in Whangaparapara. You could catch the ferry out from Whangaparapara, or spend another day cycling through the forest up to Port Fitzroy, stopping on the way for a hike up to the kauri dams on a good, well-marked 4WD track. It's about a three to 3½-hour ride, not counting stops, but allow all day if you're going to the kauri dams.

Great Barrier Island provides some of the most varied **scuba diving** in New Zealand. There's pinnacle diving, shipwreck diving, lots of fish, and over 33-metre (100-foot) visibility at some times of year; February to April is probably the best time of all. Aquaventure (☎ 429 0033) in Tryphena conducts diving trips and also offers diving instruction. Aquaventure also rent kayaks for **sea kayaking**, as do many of the places to stay. Fitzroy House (☎ 429 0091) in Port Fitzroy will guide kayaking groups for $70 per day and rent kayaks at $35 per day.

Horse treks can be arranged through Fitzroy House (☎ 429 0091) and Nagle Cove Horse Treks (☎ 429 0212).

A number of operators offer boat and fishing trips. Safari Tours (☎ 429 0448), and Bob from Tipi & Bob's (☎ 429 0550) have informative tours around the island for $40 per person.

Places to Stay

Most of the accommodation is found in Tryphena, but places are scattered all over the island. Prices are steep in summer, when bookings are essential, but rates drop dramatically outside the peak summer period. Summer prices are quoted here.

DOC Camping Grounds & Huts DOC operates camping grounds at Harataonga Bay, Medlands Beach, Akapoua Bay and Awana Bay, all with basic facilities including water and pit toilets. Fires are permitted on the island only in the designated fireplaces in the camping grounds, using only the firewood provided by DOC. It's a good idea to bring your own cooker. Camping is not allowed outside the designated camping grounds without a permit from DOC. Camping costs are $4 per adult, or $2 if you bring your own cooker.

As well as the camping grounds, DOC has two huts in the Great Barrier forest near Port Fitzroy and Whangaparapara, each 45-minutes walk from the nearest wharf. Each hut sleeps up to 24 people in two bunkrooms; facilities include cold water, pit toilets and a kitchen with a wood stove but no pots or pans. Bring your own sleeping bag and cooking equipment. The cost is $8 (two tickets). From November to January the huts are very busy; accommodation is first come, first served, so the early birds get the bunks!

Hostels *Pohutukawa Lodge* (☎ 429 0211) next to the Stonewall Store in Tryphena is about as centrally located as you can get on the Barrier. It is an associate YHA hostel, meaning you can stay with or without a YHA card. Bunks are $14 per night ($15 for non-YHA members), and linen is available for an extra $5. You can fix your own food or have meals provided. A separate lodge has self-contained doubles costing $85 B&B. Kayaks and bicycles are rented, and trips can be arranged from the hostel.

The *Stray Possum Lodge* (☎ 429 0109) in Tryphena is the best backpackers on the island, providing quality accommodation in a lovely bush setting. The only drawback is that it is a long walk to the shops. Dorms cost $14 and $16, twins and doubles are $36. Two self-contained chalets are also available for $75 and $85 a double. The Stray Possum has its own bus for transport around the island, and has snorkelling gear, boogie boards, mountain bikes, etc for hire.

The backpackers accommodation at the *Sunset Motel* in Tryphena (see Lodges & Motels) is also good.

Medlands Beach Backpackers (☎ 429 0320) is on Mason Rd, just inland from the main road at Medlands Beach. The hostel is fairly basic and is expensive at $20 per person in shared rooms, but it's only a five-minute walk to the superb beach. The price drops to a more reasonable $12 outside the summer season. There is no shop at Medlands Beach.

Cabins & Baches Great Barrier Island has a big array of holiday baches, all privately owned and maintained. The going rate is around $60 to $80 a double, and many sleep four or more. Some are listed below but this list is by no means exhaustive. Fullers (☎ 429 0004) keeps a list, so check with them.

Bubbles Wheeler's	☎ 429 0530
Crosswinds Homestead	☎ 429 0557
The Granny Flat	☎ 429 0451
Hi Look Cottage	☎ 429 0537
Kowhai Cottage	☎ 429 0473
Lovell's Holiday Bach	☎ 429 0468
Macadamia Heights	☎ 429 0497
Nancy's Nest	☎ 429 0433
Sherwood Orchids	☎ 429 0445
Tom & Rose Bone	☎ 429 0479
Whale Cottage	☎ 429 0211

Lodges & Motels *Pigeons Lodge* (☎ 429 0437) at Shoal Bay on the beachfront is in a bush setting. The cost is $85 for two, but caters mostly for pre-sold packages.

The *Sunset Motel* (☎ 429 0568) in Tryphena has motel units, which sleep up to six, for $90 a double. It also has a well-equipped hostel section with good lounge and kitchen facilities for $15 per person in two, four and six-bed rooms.

The very central *Tipi & Bob's Holiday Lodge* (☎ 429 0550) has motel-style accommodation 50 metres from the sea, with a garden bar, restaurant and takeaways. Good self-contained units, most with great sea views, cost $85 to $120 a double. An older cottage sleeping up to eight costs $85 a double and $15 per extra person.

The *Paradise Park Lodge* (☎ 429 0352) on Mason Rd, Medlands Beach, is set in 10 acres of park-like grounds at the foot of the hills inland from the beach. Excellent self-contained units sleeping four cost $90 for two, and there's also a five-bed bunkroom. You can cook, or meals can be ordered.

At Whangaparapara Harbour, the *Great Barrier Lodge* (☎ 429 0488) at the water's edge is a big place overlooking the inlet. It has a restaurant and bar and rooms range in cost from $40 to self-contained cabins for $80 for two.

Fitzroy House (☎ 429 0091) is on the other side of the bay from the ferry wharf at Port Fitzroy. This old homestead offers fine views of the bay, and two self-contained cottages starting at $90 a double. This is a particularly good place for organising activities such as horse riding, sea kayaking, sailing and tramping, with transport arranged to the trails.

At Karaka Bay, the next bay north of Port Fitzroy, *Orama* (☎ 429 0063) is a Christian fellowship hostel that provides B&B accommodation in self-contained flats for $25 per person and will pick up from the Port Fitzroy ferry wharf. It has good facilities, including a swimming pool.

Places to Eat

There aren't many restaurants on the island, so all the places to stay make provisions for their guests to eat by providing meals or a place for their guests to cook, or both. *Tipi & Bob's* in Tryphena is the only fully fledged restaurant and has a garden bar, restaurant and takeaways. They serve main meals for around $18 or cheaper burgers and snacks. The *Barrier Social Club* in Tryphena has good-value meals and cheaper bar prices. Claris also has a social club and you can get a meal at the golf club in Claris.

Tryphena has two grocery stores, the Mulberry Grove Store and the Stonewall Store, though food is more expensive than on the mainland. The Stonewall Store has the *Driftwood Cafe* next door for breakfast and lunch. Claris, Whangaparapara and Port Fitzroy have general stores.

Getting There & Away

Air Great Barrier Airlines (☎ 275 9120), the main airline servicing the island, flies twice daily from the Air New Zealand Domestic Terminal at Auckland airport to Claris. The flight from Auckland takes half an hour and costs $70. Special deals are often available in the off-season or there's a fly-boat combination whereby you fly one way and go by boat the other way for $110. The airline operates a transfer bus ($7) from Claris to Tryphena and from Okiwi to Port Fitzroy. Great Barrier Airlines also flies to Tauranga on Wednesday and Sunday and Whangarei on Friday and Saturday.

Tipaka Air (☎ 429 0088) flies to Auckland for $65/120 one way/return or $50 one way standby and to Ardmore airport in Papakura. New Zealand Air Services (☎ 426 3930) flies to Auckland's North Shore airport.

Boat Fullers Cruises has high-speed ferries departing from the Auckland Ferry Building on Tuesday, Thursday and Sunday at 9 am, stopping first at Tryphena, then Whangaparapara and Port Fitzroy. The ferry returns to Tryphena in the afternoon, departing for Auckland at 4 pm. In addition, a 5.45 pm Friday ferry goes from Auckland to Tryphena only, returning at 8 pm, and extra services run in summer. The voyage takes two hours and costs $99 return (children $49.50). Fullers also has a day-trip package for $50 (children $25) with an optional $17 bus tour. Ferries sail subject to weather conditions. Cancellations are rare but do happen.

The cheapest way to get to Great Barrier is with Gulf Trans (☎ 373 4036), which operates a car and passenger service from Auckland's Wynyard Wharf to Tryphena every Tuesday at 7 am, returning from Fitzroy every Wednesday at 8 am. The crossing takes six hours, costs $20 ($10 for children) and the ferry has a lounge bar. A small car costs $270/400 one way/return – this price includes the driver's fare, but any passengers must pay the usual fee. The beat-up *Nivanga* (☎ 307 1405) is another freighter that also takes passengers.

An increasingly popular way to visit the island is to travel from Auckland to Great Barrier and from there to the Coromandel Peninsula. Aquaventure (☎ 429 0033) has a boat service from Tryphena to Fletcher Bay on the northern tip of the Coromandel Peninsula, costing $25/45 one way/return for the 40-minute journey. It operates all through the summer, but not in winter. From Fletcher

Bay a bus goes to Coromandel township, from where other buses connect to the rest of the peninsula and back to Auckland. The loop is made easy by the Barrier Island Pass, which for $99 ($50 children) includes the Fullers ferry from Auckland to Great Barrier, the boat connection to Fletcher Bay, and then bus connections back to Auckland. The pass is available from Fullers and allows stopovers.

Getting Around

From Tryphena in the south to Port Fitzroy in the north is about 47 km by gravel road, or 40 km via Whangaparapara using the walking tracks. The roads are graded but rough.

Great Barrier Travel (☎ 429 0469) has a bus that meets the ferry and takes passengers into Tryphena for $5. In theory it continues on through Medlands Beach and Claris to Port Fitzroy, but unless enough passengers want to go you will have to charter. Many of the places to stay will come to pick you up if notified in advance.

Taxi and shuttle services are available but they aren't cheap. The Stray Possum Lodge has a bus that goes from Tryphena most days in summer for $8/10 one way/return to Medlands Beach or Claris, $15/20 to the hot springs or Windy Canyon.

For rental cars, Budget (☎ 429 0094) has excellent 4WD vehicles for $95 per day; Wheels (☎ 429 0110) has smaller Suzuki Samurai's for $85. Sedans can also be hired at various places on the island but are no cheaper.

Mountain bikes are readily available for hire for $20 to $25 per day. Most of the places to stay rent bikes and often give guests a discount.

MOTUIHE ISLAND

Halfway between Auckland and Waiheke, small **Motuihe Island** was once a quarantine station, and the cemetery at the north-western tip has graves of victims of the 1918 influenza epidemic. In WWI it was used as a prisoner-of-war camp and it was from here that the German captain Count Felix von Luckner made a daring but ultimately unsuccessful escape.

The peninsula pointing out north-west has fine sandy beaches on both sides so one side is always sheltered from the wind. The beaches make it popular with day trippers, and on a sunny weekend there may be over 500 boats anchored in the bay! There are several walking tracks on the island – it takes about three hours to walk all the way around.

Places to Stay

If you want to stay overnight on the island, ask DOC about their basic camping ground and farmhouse. You can reach them at the kiosk on the island (☎ 534 8095), or check with the Auckland DOC office.

Getting There & Away

Fullers stops at Motuihe on its Wednesday, Saturday and Sunday mail run leaving Auckland at 9.30 am and also stopping at Rangitoto, Motutapu and Rakino. There are extra sailings in summer. The fare is $20 return ($10 children).

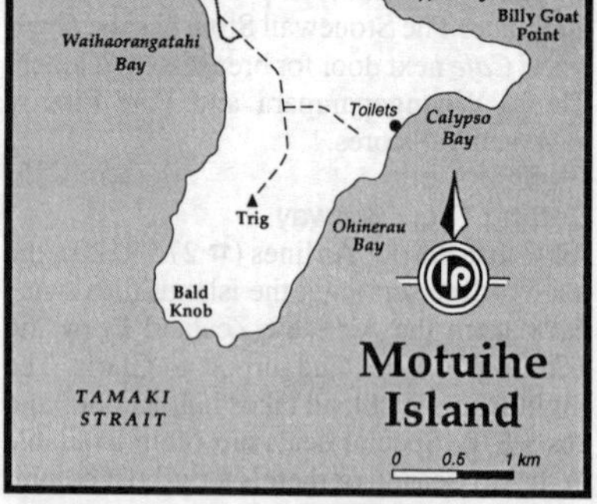

RAKINO ISLAND

This small island, just to the north of Motutapu Island, was originally known as Hurakia and was purchased from its Maori owners in 1840. At one point the island was used for prisoners taken in the Maori Wars. The island has sandy beaches, rugged coastlines and deep-water coves. Beyond Rakino there is a cluster of tiny islands collectively known as The Noises.

Fullers stops at Rakino on its Wednesday, Saturday and Sunday mail run.

TIRITIRI MATANGI ISLAND

Part of the Hauraki Gulf Maritime Park, this island – about four km off the coast of the Whangaparaoa Peninsula – is further north, about halfway between the islands close to Auckland and Kawau Island.

The 220-hectare island is an 'open sanctuary' where native wildlife is protected but visitors are permitted. The island has some original coastal broadleaf forest with large pohutukawa trees and some re-vegetated forest. Native birds, including many rare species, thrive on the island and are practically tame, since there is nothing to threaten them. They include the rare takahe, black robins, bellbirds, brown teal ducks, parakeets (Maori: kakariki), whiteheads, saddlebacks, tuis, wood pigeons, little spotted kiwis and many other species. Ornithologists from all over the world come to the island.

There are a number of good walks on the island. Starting from the wharf there are one, two and three-hour walks, and in a day you could explore most of the coastal and ridge walks.

Places to Stay

Camping is absolutely prohibited on the island, in the interest of protecting the wildlife, but it may be possible to stay overnight in the lighthouse keeper's house. Contact the DOC officer (☎ 479 4490).

Getting There & Away

A ferry from Whangaparaoa Peninsula (☎ 424 5561 for details) leaves at 9.30 am on Sunday and Thursday from the Gulf Harbour Marina, returning at 3.30 pm, and costs $22 (children $12). The *Te Aroha* schooner also comes here (see Tours in the Auckland section).

OTHER ISLANDS

Dotted around Rangitoto-Motutapu and Waiheke or further north are many smaller islands.

South of Rangitoto, the small island of **Motukorea**, or 'Island of the Oystercatcher', is also known as Browns Island. The island had three fortified Maori pa settlements on the volcanic cones by 1820, and it was purchased from the Maori by John Logan Campbell and William Brown in 1839, before the founding of Auckland, and used as a pig farm. It's now part of the Hauraki Gulf Maritime Park.

Another small island, just off the east coast of Waiheke Island between Pakatoa

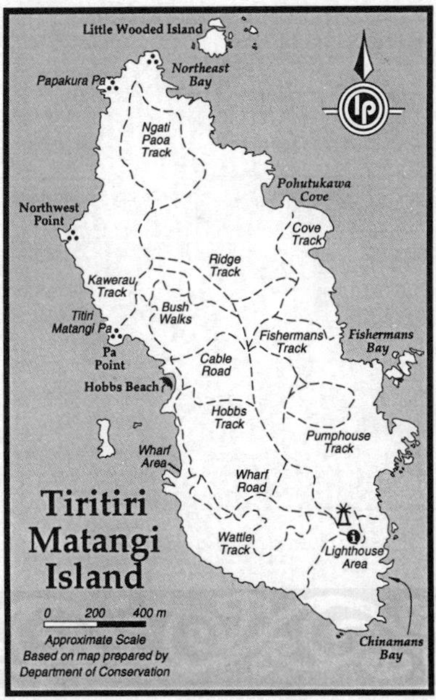

and Ponui islands, is **Rotoroa**, a private island which the Salvation Army uses for a residential treatment programme for recovering alcoholics.

Ponui Island, also known as Chamberlins Island, is a larger island just south of Rotoroa and has been farmed by the Chamberlin family ever since they purchased it from the Maori in 1854. South again from Ponui is Pakihi, or Sandspit Island, and the tiny Karamuramu Island.

Little Barrier Island, 25 km from Kawau Island, is one of New Zealand's prime nature reserves, being the last area of NZ rainforest that remains unaffected by humans, deer or possums. Several rare species of birds, reptiles and plants live in the varied habitats on the volcanic island. Access to the island is strictly restricted and a DOC permit, which is very difficult to obtain, is required before any landing is made on this closely-guarded sanctuary. The easiest way to gain access to this island is to come on a *Te Aroha* cruise, (see Tours in the Auckland section).

Motuora Island is halfway from Tiritiri Matangi to Kawau. A wharf and a camping ground are on the west coast of the island but there is no regular ferry service to Motuora. A camping permit can be obtained from the ranger (☎ 422 8882) on Kawau Island, or from the caretaker on Motuora.

The most remote islands of the Hauraki Gulf Maritime Park are the **Mokohinau Islands**, 23 km north-west of Great Barrier Island. They are small, low-lying islands that receive little rain. They are all protected nature reserves, requiring a permit for landing.

The other main island in the Hauraki Gulf is **Kawau Island**, which is connected by regular ferry from Sandspit (not Pakihi Island), east of Warkworth, and therefore covered in the Northland chapter.

Northland

Geographically, the region is shaped like a finger pointing north from Auckland. Often referred to as the 'winterless north', its climate tends to be mild compared to the rest of New Zealand. Northland is also the cradle of modern New Zealand – it was here that Europeans first made permanent contact with the Maori, where the first squalid sealers' and whalers' settlements were formed, and where the Treaty of Waitangi was signed between the settlers and the Maori. To this day there is a greater proportion of Maori in the Northland population than elsewhere in New Zealand.

The big attraction of Northland is the beautiful Bay of Islands, though scenic, sheltered bays and superb, but far less touristy, beaches can be found all along the east coast.

The west coast is a long stretch of sand pounded by the surf of the Tasman Sea. It also has scenic harbours, such as Hokianga, but the main attraction is the 'Kauri Coast', where the best remaining stands of New Zealand's once mighty kauri forests can be seen

Kaitaia and the Far North feature some great beaches, and are home to Maori communities, offering travellers the chance to learn about Maori culture.

The telephone area code throughout Northland is 09.

HIGHLIGHTS

- The Bay of Islands, the most beautiful of Northland's wonderful coastal scenery
- The ancient kauri forests of the Kauri Coast
- The desolate landscapes of Ninety Mile Beach and Cape Reinga
- Any number of good beaches, complemented by the best climate in New Zealand – try Mangawhai, Omaha or Ocean Beach near Whangarei or Coopers Beach
- Fishing – anywhere around the coast, but especially Tutukaka, Bay of Islands or Whangaroa

Getting Around

There are two main routes – east and west – through Northland to the top of New Zealand. To reach Northland, go through Helensville or Warkworth to Wellsford and then on to Brynderwyn, 112 km north of Auckland. From here, the simplest and fastest route is to head straight up through Whangarei on the eastern side of the peninsula, through the Bay of Islands to Kaitaia.

The west coast route is longer and slower, though the road is now sealed virtually all the way. It goes along the Kauri Coast through Matakohe, Dargaville, the Waipoua Kauri Forest and the remote and scenic Hokianga Harbour.

The two main bus lines serving Northland are Northliner Express (☎ Auckland 309 5873), leaving from the Downtown Airline Terminal in Auckland, and InterCity (☎ 357 8400), leaving from their depot near the railway station. These services follow the east coast from Auckland to Whangarei, Bay of Islands and Kaitaia, but both connect with the West Coaster service for the west coast. Northliner has bus passes ranging from $49 for travel between Auckland and the Bay of Islands to $109 for travel throughout Northland. InterCity bus passes can be used in Northland.

The West Coaster (☎ Auckland 358 4085) links Paihia with Dargaville via Kaikohe, Rawene, Opononi and the Waipoua forests, allowing time for photo stops at the big trees. It leaves Paihia for Dargaville every day

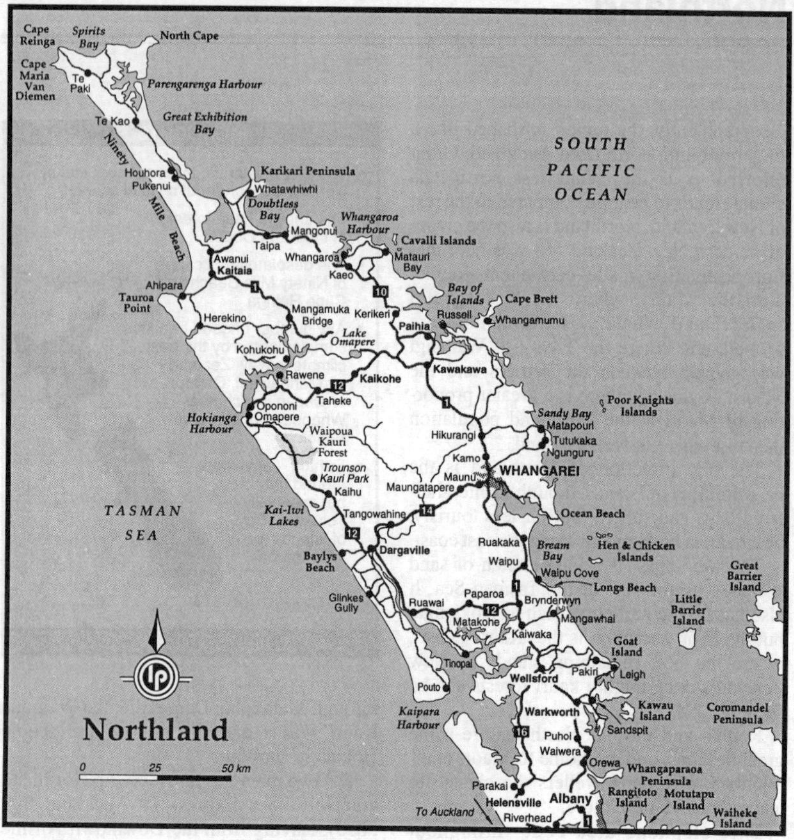

Monday to Friday, in the reverse direction on Tuesday and Thursday only. On Monday, Wednesday and Friday it also runs from Dargaville to Whangarei, and Dargaville to Matakohe and Brynderwyn and return.

Dargaville is connected to Auckland by Mains Coachlines and Pioneer (see under Dargaville).

Backpacker tours and connections running through Northland are: the Green Beetle, New Sea-Land Adventures, and Kiwi Experience's Awesome Adventures. See the Auckland and Getting Around chapters for more details on tour possibilities.

Auckland to Whangarei

While many visitors do this trip along SH1 in just a few hours in their haste to get to the Bay of Islands, the east coast between Auckland and Whangarei has many delightful bays and beaches.

Just north of Auckland, the Hibiscus Coast between Whangaparaoa and Warkworth is a favourite with Auckland holidaymakers, especially in summer. It is also becoming an extension of Auckland as more people move out to enjoy the beaches and semi-rural lifestyle within commuting distance of Auckland. Heading further north, the coast is less developed and less accessible but no less beautiful.

WHANGAPARAOA PENINSULA

Now virtually a suburb of Auckland, the Whangaparaoa Peninsula – just north of Auckland off SH1 – is good for water-based activities: windsurfers flock to Manly Beach, boaties leave from the Weiti River and Gulf Harbour, and swimmers find great beaches around the tip of the peninsula, at Shakespeare Regional Park. Many native bush birds and waders can be seen, and the native forests of the park contain karaka, kowhai, taraire and old puriri. A number of walking tracks traverse the park. The park is just beyond the huge Gulf Harbour Marina development, an upmarket real estate blot on the landscape.

Whangaparaoa has a small **narrow gauge railway** with steam trains offering rides ($3, children $1.50) on the weekends. Whangaparaoa is also the place for boats to Tiritiri Matangi Island (see under Hauraki Gulf Islands in the Auckland chapter).

OREWA

Orewa is another Auckland satellite suburb with a large mall-style shopping centre. Its main attraction is the great beach that runs next to the highway. The town also has a statue of Sir Edmund Hillary, one of the first two people to stand on top of Mt Everest. City buses from Auckland run to Orewa, so it is an easy first stop out of Auckland to the north.

The Hibiscus Coast Information Centre (☎ 426 0076; fax 426 0086) is on the highway south of town, next to KFC. Pick up a copy of *Walks of the Hibiscus Coast*, outlining many good walks in the area.

Places to Stay

A good reason to stop in Orewa is the *Marco Polo Backpackers Inn* (☎ 426 8455) at 2a Hammond Ave, Hatfields Beach, just off the highway on the northern outskirts of Orewa. Take Auckland city bus Nos 894, 895 or 899. At this purpose-built hostel, nestled into hillside greenery, dorm beds are $13, and singles/doubles are $24/32. The owners arrange a variety of trips, including snorkelling trips to Goat Island ($25), and they run popular bone-carving courses.

Run by the same owners, *Pillows Travellers Lodge* (☎ 426 6338), 412 Hibiscus Coast Highway, is a sparkling new hostel providing excellent standards of accommodation for $14 or $16 for a dorm bed, $28/34 for singles/doubles. It is conveniently located near the centre of Orewa – opposite the beach, but right on the highway.

In addition, Orewa has a dozen motels and three motor camps/camping grounds. *Puriri Park* (☎ 426 4648) on Puriri Ave is a well-equipped motor camp with a swimming pool in a quiet, park setting. Camp sites are $9 per person, cabins and caravans $35 for two and tourist flats $50 for two.

WAIWERA

The coastal village of Waiwera, 48 km north of Auckland (bus No 895 from the Downtown Bus Terminal), is noted for its thermal pools . This huge complex of hot pools, spa pools, waterslides etc is open daily from 9 am to 10 pm, apart from Friday and Saturday when it closes at 11 pm; admission is $12 (children $7). A private spa costs $10. Horse riding is offered by Ti Tree Hills (☎ 426 7003).

Just north of Waiwera is the **Wenderholm Regional Park**, a coastal farmland park with a good beach, estuary and walks. Within the park is a kiosk and the historic **Couldrey House**, open at weekends from 1 to 4 pm.

Places to Stay & Eat

Near the hot pools are a range of accommodation choices. At the *Waiwera Thermal Caravan Park* (☎ 426 5270) has camp sites for $10 per person and on-site vans for $40 a double and backpackers vans at $12 per person. The grand hotel that was a popular escape from Auckland earlier this century has gone, but the present *Waiwera Resort Hotel* (☎ 426 4089) has motel-style units for

$65 a double or large, self-contained family units for $120.

PUHOI

North of Waiwera, a few hundred metres from SH1, Puhoi is a picturesque, historic village that claims to be New Zealand's first Bohemian (Yugoslav migrant) settlement. The small **Puhoi Bohemian Museum** is open irregular hours, but the main point of interest here is the historic pub, crammed with old artefacts, including some relics of rustic Kiwi machismo behind the bar. At Puhoi you can hire canoes (☎ 422 0891) at $12 per hour for a paddle down the river to Wenderholm Regional Park on the coast.

WARKWORTH

Just off the main highway, nestled by the Mahurangi River, this pretty town was once connected to Auckland by steamships that docked at the town's old wharf. Warkworth is mainly just a lunch stop on the drive north, but the surrounding area is a popular summer holiday destination.

On the outskirts of town, the **Parry Kauri Park** has short forest walks and a couple of monstrous mature kauri, including the 800-year-old McKinney kauri. Also at the park, the small **Warkworth Museum**, open from 10.30 am to 3.30 pm, has well-presented pioneering exhibits.

The Warkworth Visitor Information Centre (☎ 425 9081; fax 425 7584), 1 Baxter Street, near the river and bus station, has a complete rundown on the area.

Places to Stay & Eat

Warkworth has a backpackers hostel, lodges, motels and an old kauri hotel.

Boss Lodge (☎ 425 8185), 26 View Rd, is an excellent hostel about one km west of the highway on a hill overlooking the town and surrounding farmland. The two-storey hostel has good communal areas and dorm beds for $15, double rooms for $36.

Warkworth's historic pub, the *Warkworth Inn* (☎ 425 8569) on Queen St, has typical old pub rooms with shared facilities for $30/47 including a continental breakfast. Next to the river on Elizabeth St, the *Bridge House Lodge* (☎ 425 8351) is a part old, part new establishment with some style. Rooms with attached bathroom start at $60.

Warkworth has a good selection of places to eat. *Ducks Crossing* is one of the best cafes with a fine outlook over the river and the old wharf.

Getting There & Away

Gubbs Motors (☎ 425 8337) has buses to the Auckland Downtown Bus Terminal ($15, 1½ hours) from Monday to Friday at 8.15 am and 1.30 pm, returning at 10 am and 3.30 pm. Connection on to Sandspit for Kawau Island can be arranged for $5 per person.

AROUND WARKWORTH

The biggest unabashedly touristic attraction is four km north of Warkworth on SH1. **Sheepworld** demonstrates many aspects of NZ sheep farming, including sheepdog manoeuvres, shearing, and things you can try for yourself such as carding, spinning, weaving and feeding tame sheep and lambs. You can also buy woollen products, such as expensive pullovers, and eat lamb. It's open daily from 9 am to 5 pm, with shows at 11 am and 1 pm, with an extra show in January at 3 pm; admission is $8 (children $4).

The **Dome State Forest**, 10 km north of Warkworth on SH1, is a regenerating forest that was logged about 90 years ago. A walking track to the Dome summit (336 metres) and its great views leads from the car park and takes about an hour return. A three-hour walk leads beyond the summit to the Waiwhiu Kauri Grove, an unlogged stand of 20 mature kauri trees.

Six km south of Warkworth, the **Earth Satellite Station** has an information centre with hands-on exhibits explaining satellite communications. It is open to the public from 9 am to 4 pm. Opposite the satellite station entrance, the **Mahurangi Honey Centre** has interesting displays on bees and bee-keeping. Entry is free to both.

To the east of Warkworth on the scenic Mahurangi Peninsula is **Sandspit**, where the ferry departs for Kawau Island. To the south of Sandspit are the new beach suburbs of **Snells Beach**, which has a trendy ye olde English pub, shopping centre, motel and B&Bs, and **Algies Bay** further on. These shallow bays are pleasant enough, but three km further, **Martins Bay** is the pick of the beaches and has a motor camp.

KAWAU ISLAND

Directly east of Warkworth, Kawau Island's main point of interest is **Mansion House**, an impressive historic house built in 1846 by Sir George Grey, an early governor of New Zealand. It was a hotel for many years before being restored and turned into a museum.

Kawau has many beautiful walks, starting from Mansion House and leading to beaches, an old copper mine, and a lookout. An unusual sight in this part of the world are the numerous wallabies, introduced from Australia.

Vivian Bay is the only sandy bay with accommodation on the island; attractions include a white sandy beach, swimming, fishing, snorkelling and bush walks.

Places to Stay

There are several places to stay at Vivian Bay, on the north side of Kawau Island, and a couple of others on Bon Accord Harbour.

Kawau Island Cottages for Couples (☎ 422 8835) has three chalets on the beach; the cost is $160 a double, with all meals included. Also right on the beach, *St Clair Lodge* (☎ 422 8850) is another upmarket B&B, costing from $200 a double, including all meals.

Bon Accord Harbour's accommodation is mostly in homestays, such as the *Katy Clark Homestay* (☎ 422 8835) and the *Cedar Lodge* (☎ 422 8700) on the waterfront at Smelting Cove. *Pah Farm* (☎ 422 8765) has camping at the top of harbour.

Getting There & Away

Two ferryboat companies operate trips to Kawau from Sandspit. Travelling time is about one hour.

The Kawau Island Mansion House Ferryboat Company (☎ 425 8006) has ferries to Mansion House at 7.45 am and 2 pm, and other sailings in summer for $18 return (children $9). Their mail-run cruise, departing from Sandspit at 10.30 am on the fast Kawau Kat, delivers the mail, stopping at Mansion House and many coves, bays and inlets. A full commentary on the island is given as you go. The cost is $25 (children $10).

Matata Cruises (☎ 425 6169) has a coffee cruise to Kawau for $18 return (children $8) at 10 am every day, with an additional sailing at 2 pm in summer. It also offers a combined three-hour lunch and Mansion House cruise for $35.

WARKWORTH TO BREAM BAY

Less frequented than the main road north to Whangarei is the scenic route from Warkworth out to Leigh on the east coast, and then north via Mangawhai and Waipu to Bream Bay. This route has a number of places where you can relax, off the not-so-beaten path. Additionally there are walks and great birdwatching opportunities.

The first good beach, **Omaha**, is a short detour from the Leigh Rd and has a sweeping stretch of white sand, good surf and a life-saving club. For a pleasant, sheltered beach, try **Mathesons Bay** just before you enter the small town of Leigh. **Leigh** sits above a picturesque harbour dotted with fishing boats. Leigh has a motel, a sometimes lively pub popular with fishermen, and a great fish & chip shop that cooks up the fresh, local catch.

Further north, around the cape from Leigh, **Goat Island** is the site of the Cape Rodney-Okakari Point Marine Reserve, where Auckland University has a marine laboratory. The reserve is teeming with fish that can be hand fed in the water or viewed from a glass-bottomed boat (☎ 422 6334) that operates in summer for $16 ($8 for children). Snorkelling and diving gear can be hired at Seafriends (☎ 422 6212), one km before the beach. The beach has a good, inexpensive restaurant and a small aquarium. *Goat Island Camping* (☎ 422 6185) has a few powered and non-powered sites.

Continuing along the coast, a gravel road

leads to **Pakiri**, a tiny rural settlement with a white-sand surf beach. A good way to see the unspoilt beach and the forests behind is on horseback. *Pakiri Beach Horse Rides* (☎ 422 6275), on Rahuikiri Rd, has very popular horse rides along the beach; rides cost from $25 for a one-hour ride to $85 for all-day treks and they also organise three-week riding tours of the whole country. They also arrange farmstays for $70 per person including meals or basic cabins on the beach costing $67 for two.

From Pakiri, the gravel road via Tomatara eventually meets the sealed road to Mangawhai. You rejoin the coast at **Mangawhai Heads**, a growing summer resort town with a great surf beach and a lifesaving club. The Mangawhai Cliffs Walkway (1½ to two hours one way) starts at the beach and affords extensive views inland and out to the Hauraki Gulf islands. For those who want to stay overnight, Mangawhai has motels and caravan parks.

A particularly scenic part of the road goes over the headland to Langs Beach and then on to Waipu.

WAIPU & BREAM BAY

Near the mouth of the Waipu River is an estuary which provides home to many species of wader birds, including the rare New Zealand dotterel, variable oyster-catchers and fairy terns. The *Ebb & Flow Backpackers* (☎ 432 0217) is well situated overlooking the Waipu River estuary on Johnsons Point Rd. A bunk bed in this place costs $10 to $13, and twins and doubles are $30. The Ebb & Flow overlooks the estuary, and views from the verandah include the Hen & Chicken Islands, Sail Rock and Bream Head. For $35 you can tour the Waipu Caves, 16 km west of Waipu. George, your blind guide, ensures part of the tour fee goes to the Royal Guide Dog Society. At nearby Waipu Cove are a motel and motor camp.

At Uretiti, DOC have a camping ground. Book with them on ☎ 438 0299. You can buy camping supplies from the Four Square store.

In Waipu is an unusual, small museum, the House of Memories, which has displays relating to early Nova Scotian settlers of Waipu and the surrounding district.

Kauri Coast

Heading towards Whangarei, you can turn off SH1 past Wellsford and travel along SH12 to the area known as the Kauri Coast. At the northern end of the Kaipara Harbour and extending along the west coast to Hokianga, the Kauri Coast is so-called because of the Kauri timber and gum industry that flourished here in the 19th century, generating much of New Zealand's wealth. The massive kauri forests are all but gone; however, the Waipoua Kauri Forest has untouched kauri forest and is the best place in New Zealand to see these magnificent trees. A prior visit to Matakohe is worthwhile for an understanding of kauri and the kauri industry.

MATAKOHE

Turning off at Brynderwyn for Dargaville you pass through Matakohe, where the **Matakohe Kauri Museum** has a strange and wonderful collection of kauri gum. It also has lifelike displays of various aspects of the life of the kauri bushpeople and an extensive photographic collection. It's a superb museum, well worth the short detour to see it.

The museum shop has some excellent bowls and other items crafted from kauri wood. They're expensive but very well made. Look for the items made of 'swamp kauri', ancient kauris which lay in swamps for thousands of years, their gum-saturated wood still remaining in good condition. The museum is open daily from 9 am to 5 pm; admission is $5 (children $1.50).

Facing the museum is the **Matakohe Pioneer Church**, built between 1866 and 1867 of local kauri. The tiny church served both Methodists and Anglicans, and doubled as the town hall and schoolhouse for the pioneer community.

Places to Stay

Near Matakohe are two excellent backpackers. The *Old Post Office Guesthouse* (☎ 431 7453) is at Paparoa, seven km from Matakohe. It is a very pleasant hostel with all the facilities; a share room is $13.50 and singles/doubles are $18/33. The pleasant outdoor area overlooks a sylvan valley, and they arrange transport to the museum. At Ruawai, west of Matakohe on the main road to Dargaville, is the small *Ruawai Travellers Hostel* (☎ 439 2283). All beds cost $15 in this clean place which has the only drawback of being on the main road. Pluses are free linen and laundry facilities.

DARGAVILLE

Founded in 1872 by Joseph McMullen Dargaville, this once-important river port thrived on the export of kauri timber and gum. As the kauri forests were decimated, Dargaville declined, and today it is a quiet backwater servicing the agricultural Northern Wairoa area.

Dargaville is the main town on the Kauri Coast, and access point for the Waipoua kauri forests to the north. Dargaville's only other claim to fame is its title as the 'kumara capital of New Zealand'.

Information

The helpful information centre (☎ & fax 439 8360), on Normanby St, is open in winter from 8.30 am to 5 pm Monday to Friday, and in summer from 8 am to 5.30 pm and 9 am to 3 pm on weekends. It can help with tours, bus tickets, and accommodation in Dargaville and has a list of homestays and farmstays in the area. This office also houses the AA office.

Harding Park & Maritime Museum

On a hill overlooking the town and the sweeping Wairoa River, Harding Park is the site of an old Maori pa, Po-tu-Oterangi, and tucked into the bottom of the hill is an early European cemetery.

On top of the hill, the small Maritime Museum has an eccentric collection of anything over 50 years old, including settlers' items, kauri gum samples and a huge slab of kauri. The maritime section has models of ships built or repaired in the Kaipara Harbour, notorious for its shipwrecks, and a massive Maori war canoe. Nearly 18 metres long, the 18th-century canoe is the only surviving example from pre-European times. In front of the museum are the masts from the *Rainbow Warrior*, the Greenpeace flagship bombed by the French secret service in 1985. The museum is open daily from 9 am to 4 pm; admission is $3 (children 50c).

Tours

The information centre has details on tours to the Waipoua Kauri Forest, the Trounson Kauri Park, Kai-Iwi Lakes, and 4WD tours along the beach to the Kaipara Lighthouse, returning to Dargaville or connecting with a boat ride south to Shelley Beach. Maxi's Tours (☎ 439 6695) is one of the main operators.

Places to Stay

Camping & Cabins *Selwyn Park* (☎ 439 8296) in Onslow St has camp sites for $14 ($18 with power), simple cabins at $28 and fully equipped tourist cabins at $39 for two.

Hostels The pleasant YHA associate *Greenhouse Hostel* (☎ 439 6342), 13 Portland St, costs $13 in dorms; singles/doubles are $25/32. It has a pool table, surfboards and bicycles, and arranges Baylys Beach horse rides and walks in the Waipoua Forest.

Hotels & Motels The two most convenient hotels are the *Northern Wairoa Hotel* (☎ 439 8923) on Hokianga Rd, which has single/doubles from $27/54, and the *Central Hotel* (☎ 439 8034) at 18-22 Victoria St with rooms from $30/50.

Motels range from the straightforward *Dargaville Motel* (☎ 439 7734) at 217 Victoria St with singles/doubles from $50/60, to the well-appointed *Hobson's Choice Motel* (☎ 439 8551), 212 Victoria St, with a swimming pool and a variety of studio, one and two-bedroom units starting at $75 a double.

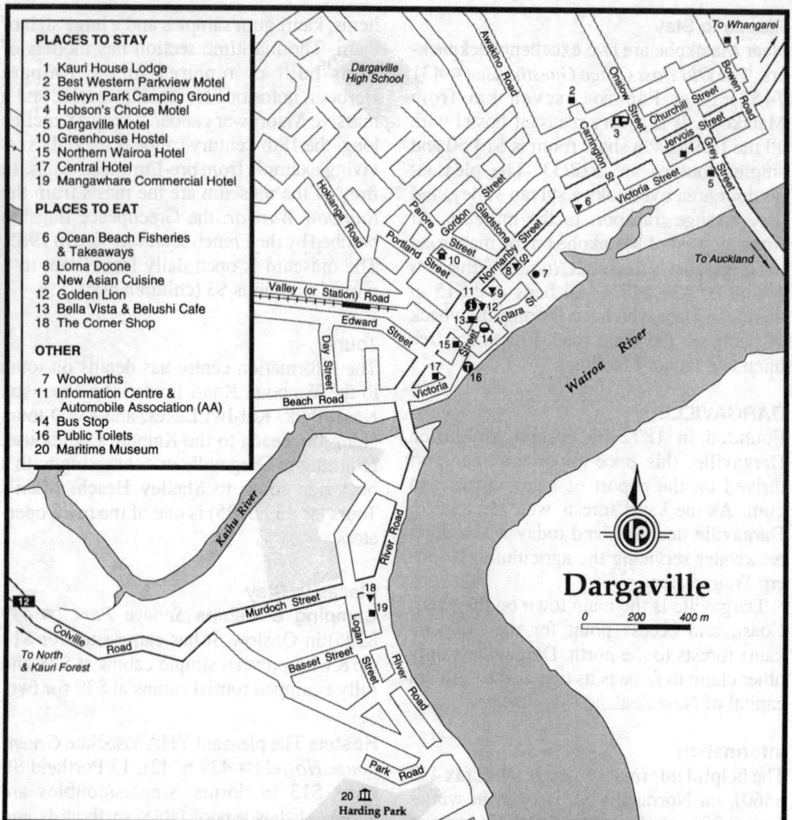

The delightful *Kauri House Lodge* (☎ 439 8082) on Bowen Rd is a rambling old colonial homestead furnished with antiques. This fine B&B, set on 100 acres, has only two double rooms (bookings essential) for $125, and there's a swimming pool.

Places to Eat

The main street, Victoria St, has plenty of eating options. *Ocean Beach Fisheries & Takeaways* at No 164 is the place for fish & chips. For moderately priced Chinese food, try the *Golden Lion* or the brighter *New Asian Cuisine* at No 114. The *Bella Vista* at No 100 is a standard coffee shop, or next door the *Belushi Cafe* is Dargaville's answer to cafe society, with such bohemian offerings as cappuccino. The *Northern Wairoa Hotel* has pub food, a Friday night smorgasbord and huge Sunday roasts. The *Lorna Doone* on the corner of Victoria and Gladstone Sts is one of Dargaville's fanciest restaurants but moderately priced.

Getting There & Away

The bus stop is on Kapia St. Main Coachlines has a bus to/from Auckland ($20, 3¼ hours) via Matakohe every day except Saturday. Pioneer Coachlines, which comes under the InterCity umbrella, also does this run.

The West Coaster bus service runs from Paihia to Dargaville (four hours) via Kaikohe, Rawene, Opononi and Waipoua every day Monday to Friday; and from Dargaville to Paihia on Tuesday and Thursday only. On Monday, Wednesday and Friday it goes from Dargaville to Whangarei (one hour) and Paihia, looping back to Dargaville and then on to Matakohe, Brynderwyn and return.

AROUND DARGAVILLE

Kaipara Lighthouse

A worthwhile trip from Dargaville, if you can find a way to get there, is the 71-km run south-east to Kaipara Lighthouse; the last 6.5 km is on foot along the foreshore. If you don't have wheels check with the information centre about tours that go there. Built in 1884, the lighthouse has been restored to its original condition.

Baylys Beach & Ripiro Ocean Beach

Only a 15-minute drive from Dargaville is Baylys Beach, lying on the 100-km-long Ripiro Ocean Beach which is backed by high, yellow sand dunes. This stretch of surf-pounded coast is the site of many shipwrecks, including a French man o' war and an ancient Portuguese ship.

Ripiro Ocean Beach is a gazetted highway and you can drive along its hard sands at low tide, although it is primarily for 4WD vehicles. Ask locals about conditions before venturing on to the sands. There is also access at Glinks Gully, Mahuta Gorge and Omamari.

Horse rides on Baylys Beach are a popular activity from Dargaville. Baylys Beach Horse Treks (☎ 439 6342) offer regular half-day beach rides for $27.

Places to Stay The *Baylys Beach Motor Camp* (☎ 439 6349) at Baylys Beach, 14 km from Dargaville, has sites for $15 to $17 and cabins from $26 for two. *Ocean View Home Stay* (☎ 439 6356) is a small, simple bach turned B&B for $60 a double.

DARGAVILLE TO HOKIANGA

En route to the big trees from Dargaville you can make a number of excursions. There are many walks you can undertake in Waipoua Kauri Forest and in the smaller reserves. Any visit to this area should be preceded by a visit to the Kauri Museum in Matakohe. An excellent set of brochures – *Walks of the Kauri Coast Northland 1, 2 & 3* – is available from the information centre in Dargaville. The brochures cover more than 28 walks, including all the main ones in Waipoua Kauri Forest.

Kai-Iwi Lakes

Only 34 km north of Dargaville are three freshwater lakes called the Kai-Iwi Lakes (Taharoa Domain), which are popular for swimming, trout fishing and boating. The lakes are Kai-Iwi, Taharoa and Waikere. The largest of the lakes, Taharoa, has deep blue water fringed with gleaming white sand beaches and pine groves. Activities are outlined in the *Taharoa Domain: Kai-Iwi Lakes* pamphlet available from the small office-cum-information centre at the lakes or from visitor information centres throughout Northland.

A three to four-hour return walk from the lakes leads to the coast, then north along the beach to the base of Maunganui Bluff. You can also climb the summit (three hours return) or continue north for the three-day walk to Omapere (see Walks under Opononi).

Places to Stay There are two rustic *camping grounds* at the Kai-Iwi Lakes, one at Pine Beach right on the main lake, and another at Promenade Point (book these at the information centre at Kai-Iwi Lakes or at Dargaville's information centre). They have toilets, cold showers, fireplaces, and no power, and cost $5 per person.

Waterlea (☎ 439 0727) is a farm with self-contained accommodation right at the entrance to the lakes. The owners organise trout fishing tours ($37 for two) and other activities.

Trounson Kauri Park

Heading north from Dargaville you can take a route passing by the 573-hectare Trounson Kauri Park, 40 km north of Dargaville. There's an easy half-hour walk leading from the parking and picnic area by the road, passing through beautiful forest with streams and some fine kauri stands, a couple of fallen kauri trees and the 'four sisters' – two trees each with two trunks. There's a ranger station and camping in the park.

Guided night-time nature walks are organised through the Kauri Coast Motor Camp. These excellent, informative walks cost $9 and explain the flora and nightlife. You might see a kiwi if you're lucky; you will certainly see possums.

Places to Stay The turn-off for the Trounson Kauri Park is 32 km north of Dargaville. Just after the turn-off, the *Kauri Coast Motor Camp* (☎ 439 0621) is in a lovely riverside spot central to the lakes and the kauri forest. Bushwalks, pony rides, river, lake and sea fishing can be organised here. Tent or powered sites cost $18, basic cabins cost from $30, or $40 in self-contained cabins.

There's also a *DOC camping ground* at the Trounson Kauri Park (☎ 439 0615). It's a beautiful place, ringed by superb kauris. Sites are $6 per person, with or without power. There are cabins that cost $8 per person ($4 for children), or the whole place is $60 a week.

On SH12, two km north of the Trounson turn-off, the *Kaihu Farm Hostel* (☎ 439 4004), has twins and doubles for $14 per person. It has a small shop where you can stock up before going on one of the many bushwalks in the area. Waipoua Kauri Forest and Kai-Iwi lakes are both close by.

Waipoua Kauri Forest

The highlight of a west coast visit, this superb forest sanctuary – proclaimed in 1952 after much public pressure and antagonism at continued milling – is the largest remnant of the once extensive kauri forests of northern New Zealand. There is no milling of mature kauri trees nowadays, except under extraordinary circumstances such as for the carving of a Maori canoe.

The road through the forest passes by some splendid huge kauris. Turn off to the forest lookout just after you enter the park – it was once a fire lookout and offers a spectacular view. A little further north, the park visitor centre (☎ 439 0605) has plenty of information and excellent exhibits on kauri trees, native birds and wildlife. Here you can pick up a brochure on the park which tells the full story of the trees. A fully grown kauri can reach 60 metres and have a trunk five metres or more in diameter. They are slow growing and some kauris are 2000 years old.

Several huge trees are easily reached from the road. Te Matua Ngahere, the 'father of the forest', has a trunk over five metres in diameter, believed to be the widest girth of any kauri tree in New Zealand. This massive tree is a short drive then a 10-minute walk from the main road. Close by are the Four Sisters, a graceful collection of four tall trees

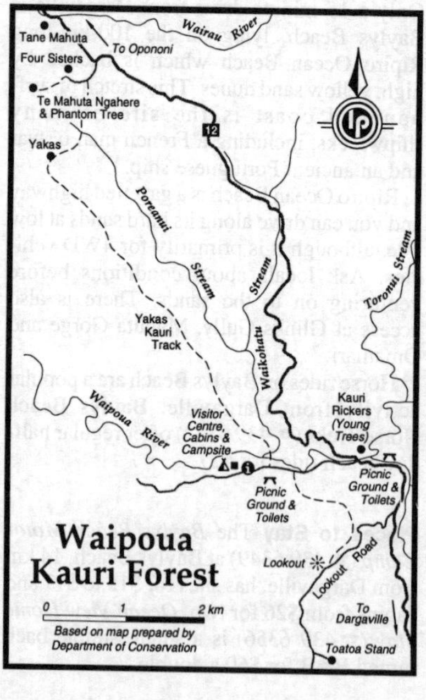

in close proximity. Also near Te Matua Ngahere is the Phantom Tree, believed to be the second largest in the forest. Unfortunately, theft from cars has been a problem – take your valuables with you.

From the same access road you can follow a half-hour walking track to the Yakas Tree, the eighth largest kauri in New Zealand, and continue if you like for the whole two to three-hour trek to the park information centre.

Further up the road is Tane Mahuta, 'lord of the forest', the largest kauri tree in New Zealand, which stands close to the road and is estimated to be 1200 years old. At 52 metres, it's much higher than Te Matua Ngahere but doesn't have the same impressive bulk – although its cubic volume is said to be even greater.

On the south-eastern boundary of the Waipoua Kauri forest is the 250-hectare McGregor Memorial Reserve. It contains regenerating kauri and podocarp forest and is the habitat of the kiwi and kauri snail. As manuka (tea-tree) is an ideal cover under which native trees grow, it is being planted over former grassland in the reserve. To reach the reserve turn off SH12 onto Marlborough Rd, about one km south of Katui Homestead. The entrance to the reserve is four km down Marlborough Rd.

Places to Stay Right in the heart of the forest, next to the Waipoua River and just past the information centre, camp sites (with shared showers and toilets) cost $6. Cabins with showers and kitchen facilities cost $10 per person (four-bed cabins) and $14 (two-bed). Children are half-price. A furnished three-bedroom lodge is also available; bookings through DOC (☎ 439 0605).

On SH12 at the southern edge of the forest, 48 km north of Dargaville, *Waipoua Lodge* (☎ 439 0422) is a fine old homestead with B&B accommodation for $70 a double. In Waimamaku, just north of the forest, the pleasant *Solitaire Guesthouse* (☎ 405 4891) is a B&B in a well-restored old kauri house and costs $35/56 a single/double.

Hokianga

Further north from the Kauri Coast, the road winds down to the Hokianga Harbour and the tiny twin townships of Omapere and Opononi. Hokianga is a depressed rural area with no industry and little development, but the harbour is beautiful and the area unspoilt – much less commercial than the Bay of Islands. It is a good place to take time out and drift for a while, as plenty of alternative lifestylers have found out.

As you come up over the hill from the south, the rest stop on Pakia Hill has a great view of the harbour and is worth a stop.

Further down the hill, two km west of Omapere, Signal Station Rd leads out to the **Arai-Te-Uru Recreation Reserve & lookout**, on the South Head of the Hokianga Harbour. It's about a 30-minute walk from Omapere, or if you're driving, a five-minute walk from the car park to Signal Station Point. This overlooks the harbour entrance, the massive sand dunes of North Head, and the turbulent confluence of the harbour and the open sea. There's a swimming beach here, people fish off the rocks, and it's also the northern beginning/ending point of the Hokianga-Waipoua Coastal Track.

OMAPERE

Omapere has a tiny museum, on the main road through town, which also houses the Hokianga Visitors Information Centre (☎ 405 8869) It's open in summer from 9 am to 5 pm Monday to Saturday and 10 am to 2 pm on Sunday. Winter hours are shorter.

Places to Stay & Eat

Globetrekkers (☎ 405 8183) is a good new hostel on the main road in Omapere overlooking the harbour. Dorm beds cost $14 or doubles are $35. It offers a variety of activities and the Northland hostel special – bone carving courses.

The *Motel Hokianga* (☎ 405 8847) has units for $78 a double and the *Omapere Tourist Hotel/Motel* (☎ 405 8737) has a variety of accommodation, ranging from camp sites for $9 per person to motels units at $80 a double. *Whaley B&B* (☎ 405 8641) is on the way to the heads on Signal Station Rd, overlooking the harbour. It is reasonably priced at $25 per person.

For a dining splurge there is the fancy *Harbourmaster's Restaurant* at the Omapere Tourist Hotel & Motel, where you can eat outside, watching the boats and all activity in the bay. The *Green Cafe* is good for vegetarian food, and it also rents windsurfing equipment. About two km outside Omapere, heading south, the *Panorama Tea Rooms* has, yes, a panoramic view of the harbour, whether from inside or out on the deck. It serves light meals and takeaways plus home-baked goods and has a separate dinner menu.

OPONONI

Only 3.5 km past Omapere the road passes through the tiny settlement of Opononi. The stone walls along Opononi's seafront were constructed from rock ballast used in timber ships which were sailed out from Sydney by convicts.

Back in 1955 a dolphin paid so many regular, friendly visits to the town that it became a national attraction. Opo, as the dolphin was named, played with children and learned to perform numerous tricks with beach balls. Unfortunately, Opo was killed, some say accidentally, by illegal dynamite fishers. A sculpture of Opo marks the dolphin's grave outside Opononi's pub. You can see a video of Opo at the Hokianga Visitors Information Centre & Museum in Omapere.

Walks

The **Hokianga-Waipoua Coastal Track** leads south from South Head at the entrance of Hokianga Harbour along the coast: it's four hours to the Waimamaku Beach exit; six hours to the Kawerua exit which also has a camping ground and hut; 12 hours to the Kerr Rd exit where there's a camping ground at Waikara Beach; or you could continue the entire 16 hours (allow about three days) to the Kai-Iwi Lakes. Pick up a brochure from any information centre or DOC office in Northland for details.

From Cemetery Rd on the eastern outskirts of Opononi, a half-hour climb leads up **Mt Whiria**, one of the oldest unexcavated pa sites, with a splendid view of the harbour.

Two km east of Opononi the Waiotemarama Gorge road turns south for six km to the **Waiotemarama bush track**, the best short walk from Opononi. This track climbs to Mt Hauturu, 680 metres high. It's a four-hour walk to the summit (eight hours return), but there's a shorter loop walk starting from the same place which takes only about two hours and passes kauri trees and a picturesque waterfall. The highest point in Northland, Te Raupua (781 metres), is nearby but there is no regular track.

Between Waima and Taheke is the **old Waoku coach road**, once the sole route to Dargaville and, because of the rainfall, only open during summer. This is a more adventurous walk, muddy and not well marked, so proper gear and preparation are required. Get information from DOC before starting out.

Other Activities

The MV *Sierra* is a 12-metre (40-foot) boat built of local Hokianga kauri wood in 1912, at the end of the logging boom. The boat recreates the historic 'mail run' around the harbour in summer, and this cruise costs $32 (children free). You can hire the *Sierra* (☎ 405 8702) for $75 per hour.

Fishing and shellfishing are excellent around the Hokianga Harbour. Fishing trips are easily arranged; even fishing off the wharf or the rocks near the harbour entrance is not bad. Okopako Pony Trekking (☎ 405 8815), at the Okopako Lodge, has two-hour horse treks and longer rides through the bush.

The Hokianga Visitors Information Centre has a full rundown on all activities.

Places to Stay

The *Opononi Beach Motor Camp* (☎ 405 8791) has camp sites at $9 per person, a handful of on-site caravans and a couple of chalets for $40 per unit. This camp is closed from May until the Labour weekend (late October).

The *Opononi YHA Hostel* (☎ 405 8792) is two km east of Opononi at Pakanae, on Waiotemarama Gorge Rd. It's a good, rustic hostel in the former old Pakanae schoolhouse, but a little far from the town. It costs $10 per night ($14 for non-members), $25 in total for three nights or you can camp for $6 ($10 for non-members). The dorms are simple but it has a large airy kitchen and a quiet location.

The House of Harmony (Te Rangimarie) (☎ 405 8778) is more conveniently located and costs $15 a night per person in dorm or double rooms. It's up the steep driveway beside the South Hokianga War Memorial Hall in the centre of Opononi.

Five km east of Opononi, off the highway just before Whirinaki on Mountain Rd, *Okopako* (☎ 405 8815) is a peaceful farm and backpackers lodge with good views. Dorm beds cost $14, doubles are $36 and family rooms are available. Horse rides in the nearby hills and harbour activities can be arranged.

In central Opononi, the *Opononi Resort Hotel* (☎ 405 8858) has one-bedroom motel units for $74.25 and two-bedroom units for $85.50, less in winter. Most of the hotel rooms have shared facilities and cost $25/35, or $45 a double with private bath. There is also a backpackers section, where beds are just $12 a night.

Also in Opononi the *Taha Moana Motel* (☎ 405 8824) has one-bedroom units at $60 a double and two-bedroom units at $80 for two.

Places to Eat

Opononi has cafes and takeaways, and the restaurant at the *Opononi Resort Hotel* provides basic food at moderate prices. Seafood is the local speciality, and it's excellent. The South Hokianga RSA (☎ 405 8723) accepts non-members and the attraction is really cheap beer and a kitbag of reminiscences.

Getting There & Away

InterCity buses stop at Omapere and Opononi on their Monday-to-Friday run from Paihia to Dargaville, each about two hours distant. From Dargaville to Paihia, buses only go on Tuesday and Thursday.

RAWENE

Rawene is a tiny settlement on a point on Hokianga Harbour, from where ferries cross to Kohukohu for the pleasant back route to Kaitaia. The shallow waters around Rawene become mud flats at low tide, but though it lacks beaches, Rawene is full of history.

While you wait for the ferry you can visit historic **Clendon House**, built in the late 1860s by James Clendon, the Resident Magistrate. It is open from 10 am to 4 pm daily in summer, weekends only in winter. Admission is $2 (children $1). In addition to Clendon House, the Wharf House – now housing a restaurant – is the oldest building in town and Rawene's hotel dates from the 1870s.

Further up Hokianga Harbour, three km west of Horeke, **Mangungu Mission** is another historic building dating from 1839. The Hokianga chiefs signed the Treaty of Waitangi in this Wesleyan mission house in 1840.

Places to Stay

Rawene has a *motor camp* (☎ 405 7720) in Marmon St just off Manning St, with tent sites at $8 per person ($9 with power), cabins at $15 per person, and two self-contained units at $20 per person. The *Masonic Hotel* (☎ 405 7822), just a few steps up from the ferry landing, has rooms from $25/35. Rawene also has two B&Bs: *Hokingamai* (☎ 405 7782) on Bundry St has singles/doubles for $35/55 and *Searell Homestay* (☎ 405 7835) on Nimmo St costs $35/60.

Getting There & Away

The ferry departs from Rawene roughly every hour on the half-hour between 7.30 am and 5.45, and from the Narrows on the Kohukohu side at 7.45 am until 6 pm. The crossing takes 15 minutes, and fares are $8 for cars ($12 return), $1 for people.

KOHUKOHU

This pleasant town is in a very quiet backwater on the north side of Hokianga Harbour. It is a good example of a completely preserved town with a number of historic kauri buildings. There are a number of kauri villas over 100 years old and other fine buildings including the Masonic Lodge, the Anglican Church and an old school.

Places to Stay & Eat

Backpackers are spoilt at the *Kohukohu Tree House* (☎ 405 5855), one of the finest backpacker retreats in the country. Constructed of wood and stained glass, it is nestled in the hills not far from the waters of Hokianga Harbour and two km from the northern ferry terminus. Dorms cost $15 per person and doubles, including two private sleep-outs, are $36. The main room is impressive. This is a good place to relax, go mountain biking, walking or take a bone-carving course.

B&Bs in Kohukohu are the *Kohukohu Farmstay* (☎ 405 5534) in Hawkins Rd, with singles/doubles for $25/50; *Harbour Views* (☎ 405 5815) on Rakautapu Rd, costing $30/60; and *Yarborough House* (☎ 405 5896), a wonderful old homestead on Yarborough St, which costs $35/65.

KAIKOHE

Kaikohe is the main town of central Northland, with strong Maori traditions. A centre for the Ngapuhi tribe, it was the scene of bloody battles during the Maori land wars. Hone Heke eventually settled in Kaikohe and died here in 1850. His monument lies on **Kaihoke Hill**, on the western outskirts of town, from where there are fine views across Hokianga Harbour.

Kaikohe's only real tourist attraction is the **Pioneer Village** on the back road through town. The village houses a historic court house, cottage, school, jail, general store, fire station and saw mill, and features various memorabilia, farm machinery and steam engines. Opening hours are 10 am to 4 pm weekdays in summer; weekends only in winter. Admission of $5 ($1 for children) includes a guided tour.

The Kaikohe information centre (☎ 401 1693) is on the main road to the east of the town centre. Accommodation includes the historic but basic *Kaikohe Hotel*, the *Kaikohe RSA* and the *Motel New Haven*.

AROUND KAIKOHE

Ngawha Springs

Eight km from Kaikohe, Ngawha Springs has a series of hot springs of varying temperatures, but the bathing facilities are run down. Admission is $2 at the Wairiki Pools, $2.50 at the better Ngawha Spa.

Puketi & Omahuta Kauri Forests

North of Kaikohe, the Puketi Forest and the Omahuta Forest comprise one large forest area with kauri sanctuaries and other native trees, camping and picnic areas, streams and pools, and viewpoints. Kauri milling in the Puketi Forest was stopped some years back not only to protect the kauri but also because this area was the home of the rare native bird, the kokako.

The two forests are reached by several entrances and contain a network of walking tracks varying in length from 10 minutes to two days. A pamphlet detailing the tracks and features of the forests is available from any DOC office. Camping is permitted in Puketi Forest and there are basic trampers huts and a camping ground at the Puketi headquarters on the Waiare Rd, 28 km north of Kaikohe. Book at the DOC office in Kaikohe (☎ 401 0109).

The Far North

KAITAIA

Kaitaia, the second-largest commercial centre in the north, is the jumping-off point for trips up Ninety Mile Beach to Cape Reinga.

Entering Kaitaia you'll see a welcome sign in three languages – Welcome, Haere Mai (Maori) and Dobro Dosli (Dalmatian) – as many Maoris and Dalmatians live in the area. Both groups are culturally active, with a Maori marae and a Yugoslav Cultural Club being the focus of activities.

Information

The Northland Information Centre (☎ 408 0879), in Jaycee Park on South Rd, has information on Kaitaia and all the Far North, and books accommodation, tours and activities. The office is open from 8.30 am to 5 pm on weekdays and 8.30 am to noon on Saturday and Sunday.

Far North Regional Museum

The Far North Regional Museum, near the information centre, houses an interesting collection including a giant moa skeleton, various bits and pieces from shipwrecks, and the Northwood Collection – photographs taken around 1900 by a professional photographer. The giant 1769 de Surville anchor, one of three the explorer lost in Doubtless Bay, is one of the museum's prize pieces. It's open Monday to Friday from 10 am to 5 pm and 1 to 5 pm on weekends, with extended summer hours. Admission is $2.50 (children 50c).

Activities

The Aero Club (☎ 406 7320) has scenic flights to Cape Reinga. Various sailing and fishing trips can be arranged from Kaitaia. Northland Information Centre has details on all activities.

Every year a special marathon is conducted along the length of Ninety Mile Beach. It celebrates the legend of Te Houtaewa. This great runner ran the length of the beach from near Te Kao to Ahipara to steal kumara from the Rarawa people, returning with two full baskets after being angrily pursued.

Tours

Kaitaia is a small town but it's quite a centre for tours to surrounding areas, notably Cape Reinga and the gumfields of Ahipara. See the sections on Ahipara and Ninety Mile Beach for information on those tours.

Kaitaia is a good place to gain an understanding of Maori culture. The Main Street Backpackers Hostel (☎ 408 1275) has fascinating and informative marae tours for $20 per person. Fishing, sand tobogganing, Cape Reinga tours and other activities can be arranged.

Places to Stay

Camping & Cabins *Dyer's Motor Camp* (☎ 408 0333) at 67 South Rd on the southern end of town, and the basic *Pine Tree Lodge Motor Camp* (☎ 409 4864), 18 km west on the coast at Ahipara, have tent and powered sites at $8.50 per person.

The *Park Ninety Mile Beach* (☎ 406 7298) is 18 km north on the Cape Reinga road at Waipapakauri Ramp and has tent and powered sites at $9 per person, basic cabins at $28 for two and fully equipped tourist cabins at $40 for two. There's a licensed restaurant on the premises.

Hostels The *Kaitaia YHA Hostel* (☎ 408 1840) is very central at 160 Commerce St (the main drag). It sleeps 39 and since there are plenty of twin rooms and family rooms you have a pretty good chance of getting a room to yourself. The cost is $13 for a dorm bed, $18/30 for singles/doubles.

In the next block north, at 235 Commerce St, *Main Street Backpackers* (☎ 408 1275) is a good hostel that organises many activities. The live-in owner, Peter, is active in the Maori community and takes visitors to see the local marae (see Tours earlier in this section). It's a good place to stay and rates are $10 or $13 for shared rooms, and singles/doubles are $20/30.

Hotels & Motels The *Kaitaia Hotel* (☎ 408 0360) on Commerce St is a venerable hotel with 30 rooms at $35/40, all with bathroom. Right at the centre of town, the hotel is a Kaitaia institution and has a good licensed restaurant plus a house bar, a lounge bar and a popular pub.

Kaitaia has a surprising number of motels, all along the stretch from South Rd to North

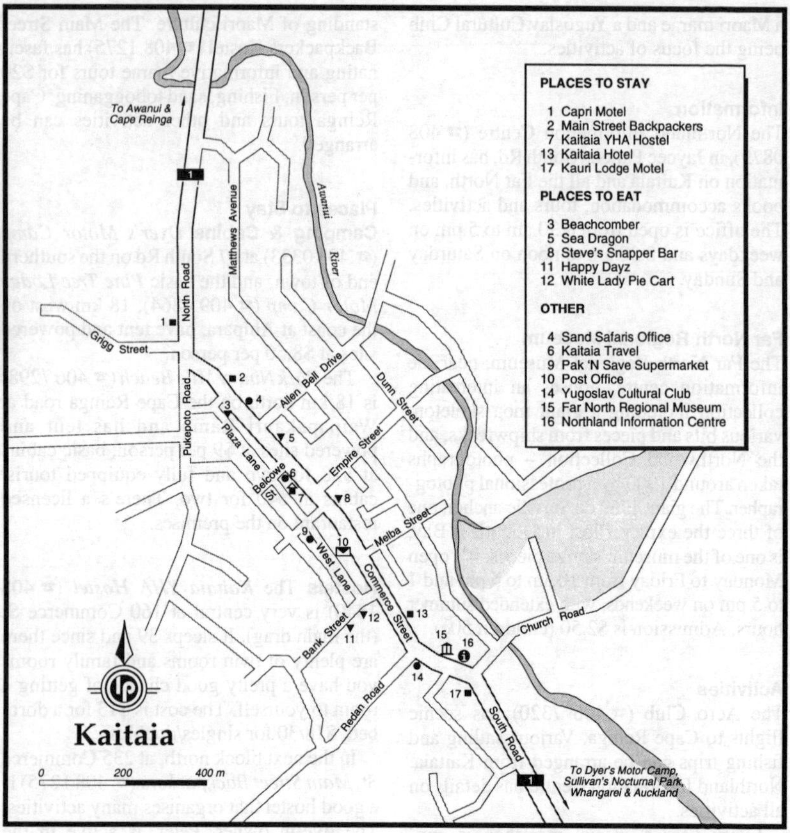

Rd. Motels, with prices for singles/doubles, include:

Kaitaia Motor Lodge	☎ 408 1910	$60/70
Kauri Lodge Motel	☎ 408 1190	$45/65
Capri Motel	☎ 408 0224	$55/75
Orana Motor Inn	☎ 408 1510	$60/70
Sierra Court Motor Lodge	☎ 408 1461	$60/80

Places to Eat

Kaitaia is not a culinary paradise, but has enough variety for a short stay. Just don't bother trying to find a place open for Sunday breakfast.

Steve's Snapper Bar at 123 Commerce St is a good and economical takeaway but you can also eat there. It has fish & chips, chicken, pizzas, etc. The *Kauri Arms Tavern*, *Collard's Tavern* and the *Kaitaia Hotel Pub* all serve pub food.

For a late-night bite the *White Lady Pie Cart*, just off Commerce St, is open some nights until 3 am. Next door, *Happy Dayz* is a spic-and-span cafe recreating the 1950s with sundaes and standard coffee-shop fare.

The *Sea Dragon*, on Commerce St is a reasonable BYO Chinese restaurant. Large mains for around $12 to $14 are enough for two. Kaitaia's top restaurant by far is the award-winning, licensed *Beachcomber* on Commerce St, featuring good seafood and other dishes.

The gigantic Pak 'N Save on the main drag is the cheapest supermarket for self-catering.

Entertainment

Kaitaia's three pubs, the *Kaitaia Hotel*, *Kauri Arms Tavern* and *Collard's Tavern* all have to try hard to attract customers and have live bands at weekends. The bar at Collard's has a huge screen which draws in rugby devotees in winter.

Getting There & Away

Air Eagle Air (☎ 407 7411) has daily flights between Kaitaia and Auckland, and Kaitaia and the Bay of Islands.

Bus InterCity (☎ 408 0540) leaves from the Kaitaia Travel on Blencowe St. Northliner also leaves from the same place. Buses go every day between Kaitaia and Auckland via Doubtless Bay and Whangarei. InterCity buses go via the Bay of Islands. Travel time is 30 minutes to Doubtless Bay, 2½ hours to Paihia, 3½ hours to Whangarei or seven hours all the way to Auckland.

Getting Around

The major rental car companies have agents in Kaitaia: Budget is at Star Garage (☎ 408 2510), Avis is at Kaitaia Travel and Hertz is at Kaitaia Toyota (☎ 408 0440).

AROUND KAITAIA

Ahipara

It's easy hitching a ride out to the beach at Ahipara, 14 km west of Kaitaia. Ahipara is the southernmost section of Ninety Mile Beach and is popular with locals and visitors. It offers fishing, surfing, horse riding, a motor camp and picnic grounds.

Ahipara is best known for the massive Gumfields sand dunes. Sand tobogganing, beach safaris and quad-bike rides are popular activities on the dunes above Ahipara and further around the Tauroa Peninsula. Tu-Tu Tours (☎ 408 0200) in Kaitaia have five-hour adventure bus tours over the sand hills, including sand tobogganing, for $40 ($20 children). Sand toboggans can also be hired at Ahipara, or from the information centre in Kaitaia for $10 per day. The Adriaan Motel (☎ 409 4888) in Ahipara rents quad-bikes at $40 for one hour, $70 for two hours.

Kaitaia Walkway

The Kaitaia Walkway, also known as the Kiwanis Bush Walk, on the edge of the Herekino Forest makes a good day trip and has excellent views. Originally planned as a road, the track has a gentle gradient along its nine km, and you should allow five hours to walk it. To get to there head south from Kaitaia on SH1 for three km, then turn right into Larmer Rd and follow it to the end. Here you'll find the Kiwanis Club Bush Camp Hut, where you can stay overnight if you've made prior arrangements.

The track finishes at Veza Rd, off Diggers Valley Rd, which can be an awkward place to get out of as there is no transport and it's quite a long way from the main road. There is a good short walk from the Larmer Rd end to the lookout or Kauri grove. Get information from the local DOC office, which also has information on the beautiful Raetea Forest, 20 km east of Kaitaia.

Sullivan's Nocturnal Park

In Fairburn, about a 30-minute drive from Kaitaia or Doubtless Bay, Sullivan's Nocturnal Park (☎ 408 4100) is open from 9 am to 5 pm in June and July and from 9 am to 10 pm the rest of the year. The main attraction is a glow-worm grotto beside a waterfall; in the dark of night you're taken on a guided nature walk for a close-up view of the glow-worms in their natural habitat. There's also a nocturnal kiwi house and areas for picnics in the daytime. Entry is $8 for adults, $3 for children.

To reach the park from Kaitaia, go eight km south-east on SH1, turn left at the Fairburn signpost and continue for another nine km along the gravel road. From Doubtless Bay, take the road from Taipa inland to Oruru and Peria.

NORTHLAND

CAPE REINGA & NINETY MILE BEACH

At the tip of the long Aupouri Peninsula, Cape Reinga is at the northern tip of New Zealand. As such it is a pilgrimage site for those who want to travel from one end of the country to the other. Contrary to popular belief, Cape Reinga is not the northernmost point of New Zealand – that honour belongs to Surville Cliffs on North Cape, 30 km to the east. Nor is it the most western part of the North Island – Cape Maria van Diemen, just one bay around, claims that title. But standing at the windswept **Cape Reinga lighthouse** and looking out over the endless sea certainly has an end-of-the-world feel to it. Directly below the lighthouse is the Columbia Bank maelstrom, where the waters of the Tasman Sea and Pacific Ocean meet, generating waves of up to 10 metres high in stormy weather.

The Aupouri Peninsula is known to the Maori as *Te Hika o te Ika (tail of the fish)* from the creation legend that tells of how Maui hauled a great fish from the sea, which became the North Island. The peninsula is a rugged, desolate landscape dominated by high sand dunes and flanked by Ninety Mile Beach. When they metricate it to Ninety Kilometre Beach the name will be a lot more accurate as it's a good bit short of 90 miles! Bus tours along Ninety Mile Beach to Cape Reinga are very popular.

The **Aupouri Forest**, about 75 km long and five km wide, covers two-thirds of the western side of the peninsula. It's an exotic forest, mostly pine, planted for timber. Kauri forest used to cover the area; in fact traces have been found of three separate growths of kauri which were buried and then grew up again. This was a fruitful area for gumdiggers. On the northern edge of the Aupouri Forest, a volcanic rock formation called The Bluff is part of a 36-hectare private reserve used for fishing by the Maori tribe living in nearby Te Kao. A colony of white-fronted terns can be seen just past **The Bluff** on a prominent sandspit.

North of The Bluff, the Te Paki Reserves are public land with free access; just leave the gates as you found them and don't disturb the animals. There are about seven sq km of giant sand dunes on either side of where the Te Paki Stream meets the sea; a stop to take flying leaps off the dunes is one of the highlights of the locally operated tours.

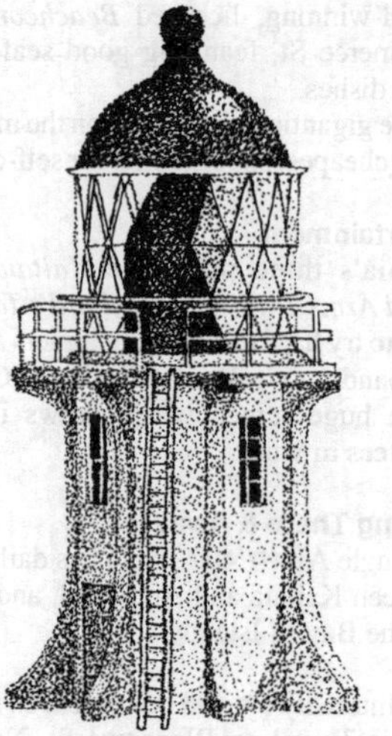

The Cape Reinga lighthouse overlooks the often stormy meeting of the Tasman Sea and Pacific Ocean

Bus tours travel along the hard sands of Ninety Mile Beach to Cape Reinga, or vice versa, depending on the tides. Private vehicles can also do the beach trip but all hire-car agreements prohibit use on the beach. The usual access point for vehicles is Waipapakauri, just north of Kaitaia. Tours go as far as Te Paki Stream, though most cars only go as far as The Bluff. The beach 'road' is only for the well-prepared, with rugged vehicles. Cars have hit soft sand and been swallowed by the tides – you may see the roof of an unfortunate vehicle poking through the sands. Motorcycling on the beach is OK but take it slow and be extra careful, a few bikers have been killed when they suddenly rode into washouts or soft sand.

DOC have a shop right at Cape Reinga serving drinks and snacks, and this tiny outpost even has a post office.

Wagener Museum & Subritzky Homestead

The Wagener Museum at Houhora houses an unrelated collection of oddities but the sheer number of items makes this museum astonishing. Exhibits include stuffed animals and birds, Maori artefacts, antique gramophones and washing machines, a huge commode collection, pianolas and other musical instruments that the guide will play for you.

The museum has a cafe and is open daily from 8 am to 5.30 pm; entry costs $6 (children $2). All the Cape Reinga tours stop here.

For an extra $3 (children $1.50) you can also visit the Subritzky homestead next door. Dating from 1862, the homestead is constructed of local kauri.

Walks

The coastline is scattered with beautiful beaches, connected by a network of tracks. You can walk the **Ninety Mile Beach** but you'll need to be well prepared as there are no huts, and although it may not be as long as 90 miles, it certainly feels like it when walking!

From Cape Reinga you can walk along Te Werahi Beach to **Cape Maria van Diemen** in about five hours return. Beautiful **Tapotupotu Bay** is a two-hour walk east of Cape Reinga, via Sandy Bay and the cliffs. From Tapotupotu Bay it is about an eight-hour walk to **Kapowairua** at the eastern end of Spirits Bay. Both Tapotupotu Bay and Kapowairua have camping grounds and road access. For details of walking tracks in the area inquire at the DOC shop and information centre at Cape Reinga.

Tours

Bus tours go from Kaitaia, Doubtless Bay and the Bay of Islands. Tours from Kaitaia or Doubtless Bay are preferable since they're much closer to Cape Reinga. Tours from the Bay of Islands are larger, more commercial tours, and involve a couple of hours extra travel at each end of the day.

From Kaitaia, Sand Safaris (☎ 408 1778), 221 Commerce St, has small buses for day trips taking in the Aupouri Forest, the beach, Te Paki Stream, sand hills, Cape Reinga, Tapotupotu Bay, Rarawa Beach and the Wagener Museum. The cost is $50 (children $25), including a light lunch. Other smaller operators in Kaitaia offer good tours, but Sand Safaris goes every day.

Nor-East Coachlines (☎ 406 0244) is another good local company, operating from Mangonui. Nor-East costs the same and goes to the same places as Sand Safaris.

Both Sand Safaris and Nor-East give backpacker discounts and allow you to get off the tour and be picked up on another day.

Fullers and King's tours come from the Bay of Islands only. In addition to being a bit more costly these tours are also more formal, done in big buses with tighter time schedules.

Places to Stay & Eat

DOC has several camping grounds in the Cape Reinga area costing $5 per person. There's a site at *Kapowairua* on Spirits Bay, with cold water and limited toilet facilities, and another at *Tapotupotu Bay*, with toilets and showers; neither has electricity. Bring a cooker as fires are not allowed. Both bays have mosquitoes and biting sandflies, so come prepared with coils and insect repellent. The *Rarawa Beach* camping ground, three km north of Ngataki, has water and toilet facilities only. No prior bookings can be made and no open fires are permitted.

At Waitiki Landing, the last settlement before Cape Reinga, *Waitiki Landing Cabins* (☎ 409 7508) is the northernmost accommodation in New Zealand. Singles/doubles with private facilities cost a very reasonable $17.50/38. Waitiki Landing has a shop and restaurant.

Northwind Backpackers (☎ 409 8515) is six km down an unmade road at Henderson Bay on the east side of the peninsula. It is small (10 people maximum), quiet, very friendly and near a great stretch of beach. A dorm bed costs $13, and there is one twin for $26.

The *Pukenui Lodge Motel & Hostel* (☎ 409 8837) is in a lovely setting overlooking Pukenui Harbour. The motel has singles, twins or doubles for $77. It has a comfortable and homey hostel section with dorm rooms at $13 and twins/doubles at $30.

Follow Lamb Rd west about 500 metres to the *Pukenui Motor Camp* (☎ 409 8803) with tent and powered sites at $7.50 per person, on-site caravans at $35 for two and a cabin at $40 for two.

The *Houhora Camping Ground* (☎ 409 8564) is next to the Wagener Museum. It has limited facilities but is cheap at $5 per person or $7.50 with power. The museum has a good cafe. At the turn-off to the museum, on the highway, the *Houhora Chalets Motel* (☎ 409 8860) has six A-frame units for $65 a double.

KARIKARI PENINSULA

Remote Karikari Peninsula forms the western end of Doubtless Bay. Roads are mostly unsealed and facilities are limited, but the peninsula's beaches are among Northland's finest.

Rangiputa has beautiful white-sand beaches that are easy to reach. A turn-off on the road to Rangiputa takes you to remote **Puheke Beach** with it white sand dunes and long, lonely walks on windswept beaches.

On the east coast of the peninsula, **Tokerau Beach** is a depressed place, while further north **Whatuwhiwhi** is more attractive, but loveliest of all is **Matai Bay** with its tiny 'twin coves'.

Places to Stay

Rangiputa is a small settlement with a dozen or so houses, and the *White Sands Motor Lodge* (☎ 408 7080), which has an attached shop. Pleasant, modern units cost $115 for four people in summer, or only $50 a double in the off-season.

DOC has a camping ground at *Matai Bay* (☎ 402 2100). During the Christmas holidays it is very popular, but is usually not full at other times of the year. There is a good walking track from the end of the beach which takes you up onto the southern peninsula. The cost at this place is $6 for adults and $3 for children.

The *Karikari Motor Camp* (☎ 408 7051) is off Matai Bay Rd at Karikari Bay. A camp site is $9.50 per day for two adults and three children, and cabins and caravans are $26.

DOUBTLESS BAY

The bay gets its unusual name from an entry in Captain Cook's logbook, where he wrote down that the body of water was 'doubtless a bay'. Lying between the Bay of Islands and Kaitaia, Doubtless Bay has picturesque bays, coves and beaches. The whole area is great for fishing and shellfishing, boating, swimming and all other water sports.

The principal town, Mangonui, is a charming historic village. Stretching west around the bay are the modern, popular beach resorts of Coopers Beach, Cable Bay and Taipa, forming suburban extensions of Mangonui. With its glorious climate and beautiful beaches, Doubtless Bay is a go-ahead area, attracting moneyed retirees and other rat race escapees.

Doubtless Bay competes with Kaitaia as a good base for exploring the Far North. On the northern and western sides the bay is bounded by the Karikari Peninsula. Nor-East Coachlines (☎ 406 0244) in Mangonui have good tours for exploring Cape Reinga and Ninety Mile Beach (see under that section).

Mangonui

Mangonui is a small, picturesque fishing village – the name means 'Big Shark' – with numerous old kauri buildings lining the shallow Mangonui harbour. It has all the basic services and a few interesting spots to visit.

The **Mangonui wharf** has a small saltwater aquarium and is a spot to cast a line.

The **Mangonui Courthouse** is a historic reserve and the nearby Wharf Store has a variety of arts & crafts. The area attracts many craftspeople, and Doubtless Bay has plenty of craft outlets.

Also at Mangonui is attractive **Mill Bay**, dotted with tiny boats; you can take Silver Egg Rd out to Mill Bay's Mangonui Cruising Club and an assortment of historical markers. This was the spot where Mangonui's first European settler made his base, and the whaling boats replenished their water from the stream.

Rangikapiti Pa
Between Mangonui and Coopers Beach is the Rangikapiti Pa Historic Reserve, with ancient Maori terracing and a spectacular sweeping view of Doubtless Bay. There is a walkway from Mill Bay, just west of Mangonui, to the top of the pa.

Beaches
The first beach west of Mangonui is **Coopers Beach**, a fine sweep of sand lined with pohutukawa trees. Coopers Beach is quite developed and has a small shopping centre. The next bay along, less developed **Cable Bay**, was once the home of the longest cable in the world: from 1902 to 1912 a cable stretched 3500 nautical miles from here to Queensland, Australia. The cable station was closed down in 1912 when another cable was laid between Sydney and Auckland.

Across the river from Cable Bay, **Taipa** is another popular summer destination. According to Maori legend, Taipa is the place where Kupe, the original Polynesian discoverer of New Zealand, first set foot on the new land. Today it has a fine beach, a harbour where the Taipa River meets the sea, and several motels and motor camps. You can get a good view overlooking Taipa by turning off the main road onto Bush Point Rd.

Places to Stay
Camping & Cabins The closest motor camp to Mangonui is on Hihi Beach, 11.5 km from Mangonui across the bay. The *Hihi Motor Camp* (☎ 406 0307) has camp sites for $8.50 per person and cabins from $50, less in winter. Taipa is a more attractive destination than Hihi. The *Taipa Caravan Park* (☎ 406 0995), on the river close to the beach, has camp sites from $8.50 per person.

Hostels The *Old Oak Inn* (☎ 406 0665), 19 Waterfront Drive, in Mangonui is a pleasant 1861 kauri house with hostel accommodation from $13.50 in dorms, $22 for a single and a variety of doubles and twins from $28 to $38. It's a small lodge with a good restaurant and an arts & crafts shop. Many inexpensive activities are organised from the hostel and you can hire canoes and mountain bikes for $15 a day. It takes just a couple of hours to bike to the Karikari Peninsula and the area has many other good spots to visit.

Further along the waterfront, just behind Cafe Nina, *Waterfront Backpackers* (☎ 406 0347) is also a historic house, but it's plainer and has less character than the Old Oak Inn. Shared rooms are $11 per bed, doubles are $30.

Hotels & Motels In Mangonui the historic *Mangonui Hotel* (☎ 406 0003) is comfortable and refurbished, with regular rooms at $35 for a single and doubles with bathroom for $75 (breakfast included).

There are many motels in the area costing around $60 to $70 a double, but most charge $100 or more from Christmas to the end of January. Motels include the *Mangonui Motel* (☎ 406 0346) in Mangonui, the *Blue Pacific Motel* (☎ 406 0010) and the *Taipa Sands Motel* (☎ 406 0446) in Taipa. The *Driftwood Lodge* (☎ 406 0418) in Cable Bay is a standard motel but right on the beach. The *Coopers Beach Motel* (☎ 406 0271) is also very popular.

Not your average motel, the *Beach Lodge* (☎ 406 0068) at Coopers Beach has very classy, beautifully appointed two-storey units with balconies overlooking the sea. Definitely for those seeking a bit of luxury, which can be hard to find. Rates are $130 a double or $165 in summer, and $20 to $30 for each extra adult.

Guesthouses Doubtless Bay is not over-endowed with B&Bs, but *Mac 'n' Mo's* (☎ 406 0538), on the highway in Coopers Beach, is a reasonably-priced guest house at $30/50, and they can arrange activities.

Just off the road to Hihi, two km from the highway, *Abraham Lincoln's B&B* (☎ 406 0090) is a pleasant farmstay high on a hill with expansive views across Mangonui Bay. Doubles cost $60.

NORTHLAND

Places to Eat

In Mangonui *Cafe Nina* is a cosy little cafe with good food and music – an ideal place to drink cappuccino and have a game of chess or backgammon. The pizzas are described as 'southern Italian', which apparently means insubstantial.

Similar in style, but a touch classier, the *Cafe du Port* is opposite the Four Square supermarket. Snacks during the day will set you back around $5, and the dinner menu – which features seafood – runs to around $20 for main courses. The *Old Oak Inn* has a good à la carte restaurant, and hostel guests get discount meals at the back.

The award-winning *Mangonui Fish Shop*, near the wharf, is on stilts over the water. You can eat your fish & chips on tables overlooking the bay. Shellfish, smoked fish and seafood salads are also sold at this excellent fish shop.

The *Mangonui Hotel* has a restaurant with a pleasant outdoor garden area to one side. The beaches have a few takeaways, and at Coopers Beach the Coopers Beach Motel has the *Pamir Restaurant* with steak and seafood.

Entertainment

This is not exactly Auckland for entertainment but the *Mangonui Hotel* often has bands on the weekend.

Getting There & Away

InterCity buses pass through Mangonui once a day on the Bay of Islands-Kaitaia route. Northliner buses do the same run, stopping at Mangonui, Coopers Beach and Taipa every day but Saturday. The travel time is 30 minutes to Kaitaia, 1½ hours to Paihia.

WHANGAROA

Whangaroa Harbour is a picturesque inlet of small bays and bright green water, surrounded by high, rugged cliffs and curious hills. The area was once well known for its kauri forests. The timber was milled at Whangaroa and across the harbour at Totara North, often ending up as sailing vessels.

The small town of Whangaroa, six km off the main road, is now a popular gamefishing centre. This is a very quiet town but good tours and activities are available. Totara North, on the other side of the bay, is an even sleepier town with an old timber mill.

The Boyd Gallery (☎ 405 0230), the general store in Whangaroa, is also a souvenir gallery and the town's informal tourist information office.

Cruises & Other Activities

Many travellers rave about the yacht *Snow Cloud* (☎ 405 0523), which operates out of Whangaroa Harbour (Te Ngaere) to the Cavalli Islands where there are excellent beaches, diving spots (including the *Rainbow Warrior*), snorkelling and walks. The cost is a mere $45 per person (minimum two) for this excellent full-day trip.

Sea Fever Cruises operate harbour cruises and several other boats are available for deep sea fishing, water-skiing and diving. Book boats through the Boyd Gallery, Marlin Hotel or other places to stay.

The area around Whangaroa Harbour is ideal for **sea kayaking**. Northland Sea Kayaking (☎ 405 0381) is located east on the coast, past Tauranga Bay (pick-up from Kaeo can be arranged for $5 return). This coast is magical, with bays, beaches, sea caves, tunnels and islands to explore. The kayak tours 'comb' the coast, visiting different areas each day for a very reasonable $55 per day, including accommodation.

For **walks**, the domed, bald summit of St Paul's offers fine views. It is a half-hour walk above Whangaroa town to the south. The Wairakau track north to Pekapeka Bay (1½-hours) begins near the church hall on Campbell Rd in Totara North and passes through farmland, hills, flats, shoreline, the Wairakau Stream, and Bride's Veil Falls before arriving at DOC's Lane Cove Cottage.

Guided horse treks also go through native and pine forest, and up to scenic lookouts.

Places to Stay

Camping & Cabins The *Whangaroa Motor Camp* (☎ 405 0306) costs $8 per person for tent sites, $10 for caravan sites, and cabins cost from $26. The camp is about 2.5 km before the wharf.

DOC's *Lane Cove Cottage*, reached by the Wairakau track or by boat, costs $8 per night. It is has showers and flush toilets but you have to bring your own cooker. Book through DOC Kerikeri (☎ 407 8474).

Hostels The *Sunseeker Lodge* (☎ 405 0496), is up on a hill about 500 metres beyond the wharf, with a great view of the harbour. The cost is $14 in nine or six-bed dorms. Motel units are $70 a double, and one is set aside for backpackers at $20 per person. They provide free pick-up and drop-off from Kaeo, and can give you information on tours.

At Totara North the *Historic Gumstore Hostel* (☎ 405 1703) dates from 1890 and has dorms for $12.50 and doubles/twins are $25 to $30. Totara North is a backwater (literally – the mangrove-fringed creek is right beside the old store) but you can rent dinghies and go fishing.

Just west of the Totara North turn-off, 24 km south of Mangonui, the *Kahoe Farm Hostel* (☎ 405 1804) has dorm beds for $14 and doubles or twins for $34. Numerous activities include nearby walks, organised horse treks, sailing and kayaking. Camping is possible and meals of the day include excellent pizza.

Hotels & Motels Right by the wharf the *Marlin Hotel* (☎ 405 0347) has share-facility rooms at $30/40 for singles/doubles, one twin room with private facilities at $45 and a one-room self-contained flat for $50. The hotel is the centre of life in town. The *Motel Whangaroa* (☎ 405 0022) and the *Truant Lodge Motel* (☎ 405 0133) have motel rooms from $56 and $73 respectively.

At the exclusive *Kingfish Lodge* (☎ 405 0164), reached by boat, the cost is $140 per person, including transfers.

Places to Eat

The *Marlin Hotel* does dinner, breakfast and lunch, or visitors can gain temporary membership at the *Whangaroa Big Gamefish Club*, opposite the pub, where fish, of course, features heavily on the menu. Come during the day in summer and see them weigh in the marlin.

AROUND WHANGAROA

For a scenic drive, you can visit the beautiful bays and fine beaches east of Whangaroa. From the SH10, just south-east of Kaeo, the road via Otoroa is sealed almost all the way to Matauri Bay, except for the final descent to the beach. From Matauri Bay through to Whangaroa the road is unsealed almost all the way, but the great scenery makes the strain on the nerves worthwhile!

The trip out to **Matauri Bay** is one of *the* surprises of Northland. Matauri Bay is Maori land, home to the Ngati Kura people, and this superb stretch of beach sees few tourists. The view from the ridge above the bay is spectacular with the beach, Cavalli Islands and headland way down below. At the top of the headland in Matauri Bay is a monument to the *Rainbow Warrior*. The boat itself lies offshore in the waters of the Cavalli Islands, and *Rainbow Warrior* dives can be arranged at the Matauri Bay Holiday Park, or in Paihia.

Heading west from Matauri Bay, the road leads to **Te Ngaire**, a small settlement with a lovely quiet beach, then to nearby **Wainui Bay** for cast fishing. You can then detour to **Mahinepua Bay** or continue on to **Tauranga Bay**, another fine sweeping beach with good surf and accommodation.

Places to Stay

The *Matauri Bay Holiday Park* (☎ 405 0525) has sites for $18 and cabins from $30. The *Oceans Beachfront Holiday Village* (☎ 405 0417) at the end of the road has five comfortable units from $75 a double and two larger lodges. It also has a licensed restaurant. DOC has a very basic hut at Papatara Bay on Motukawanui Island, one of the Cavallis. Bookings are through DOC in Kerikeri.

The *Tauranga Bay Holiday Park* (☎ 405 0436), right on the beach at Tauranga Bay, has sites for $8 per person ($9 with power)

NORTHLAND

The *Rainbow Warrior* Trail

New Zealand is seldom mentioned on the world stage. With a population of three and half million and its relative isolation, New Zealand is in many eyes a small, almost inconsequential Pacific nation. In 1985 an explosion in Auckland Harbour made world headlines and put New Zealand on the map.

The Greenpeace flagship *Rainbow Warrior* lay anchored in Auckland Harbour, preparing to sail north of Tahiti to protest against French nuclear testing.

The *Rainbow Warrior* never left Auckland. French saboteurs, with the backing of the French government, attached explosives to the side of the ship and sank her. In the explosions one green campaigner, Fernando Pereira, was killed.

It took some time to find out exactly what had happened, but in inquisitive, rural New Zealand the comings and goings of foreigners are not easily forgotten. Two of the saboteurs were captured, tried and found guilty, while the others have never been brought to justice.

The incident caused an uproar in France – not because the French government had conducted a wilful and lethal act of terrorism on the soil of a friendly nation, but because the French secret service had bungled the operation and been caught. The French used all their political and economic might to force New Zealand to release the two saboteurs, and in a farcical turn of events the agents were imprisoned on a French Pacific island as if they had just won a trip to Club Med. Within two years, and well before the end of their sentence, they returned to France to receive a hero's welcome.

Northland was the stage for this deadly mission involving several secret service agents. Explosives for the sabotage were delivered by a yacht (which had picked them up from a submarine) from Parengarenga Harbour in the far north. They were driven to Auckland in a Kombi van, by French agents posing as tourists. Bang – an innocent man dead, and international outrage – Auckland Harbour was in the news.

The skeletal remains of the *Rainbow Warrior* were taken to the waters of the beautiful Cavalli Islands. The masts of this oceanic crusader were sent to the Maritime Museum in Dargaville. The memory of the Portuguese photographer who died, Fernando Pereira, endures in a peaceful bird sanctuary in Thames. A haunting memorial to the once-proud boat sits in peace atop a Maori pa site at Matauri Bay.

The world recently focused on the *Rainbow Warrior* again in 1995. Ten years after the sinking the French announced that they were going to resume nuclear testing in the Pacific, and Greenpeace's new flagship bearing the name of its ill-fated ancestor set sail for the Mururoa test site. ■

and cabins for $30 for two people ($10 each extra adult). Four-person minimum rates apply in summer. The *Tauranga Bay Motel* (☎ 405 0222) is a plain but comfortable motel for $75 a double (from $90 in summer).

Bay of Islands

Long famed for its stunning coastal scenery, the Bay of Islands is one of the country's major tourist attractions. The bay is punctuated by dozens of coves, and its clear waters range in hue from turquoise to deep blue. Dotted with nearly 150 islands, the Bay of Islands is aptly named. The islands have escaped development and the Bay of Islands townships are all on the mainland.

The Bay of Islands is also of enormous historical significance. As the site of New Zealand's first permanent English settlement, it is the cradle of European colonisation. It was here that the Treaty of Waitangi was drawn up and first signed by 46 Maori chiefs in 1840, and the treaty remains the lynch pin of race relations in modern New Zealand.

Paihia is the centre of the Bay of Islands. Though only a small town, its population swells dramatically in summer. It's a neat, modern town with dozens of motels, restaurants, shops and a host of tour operators

NORTHLAND

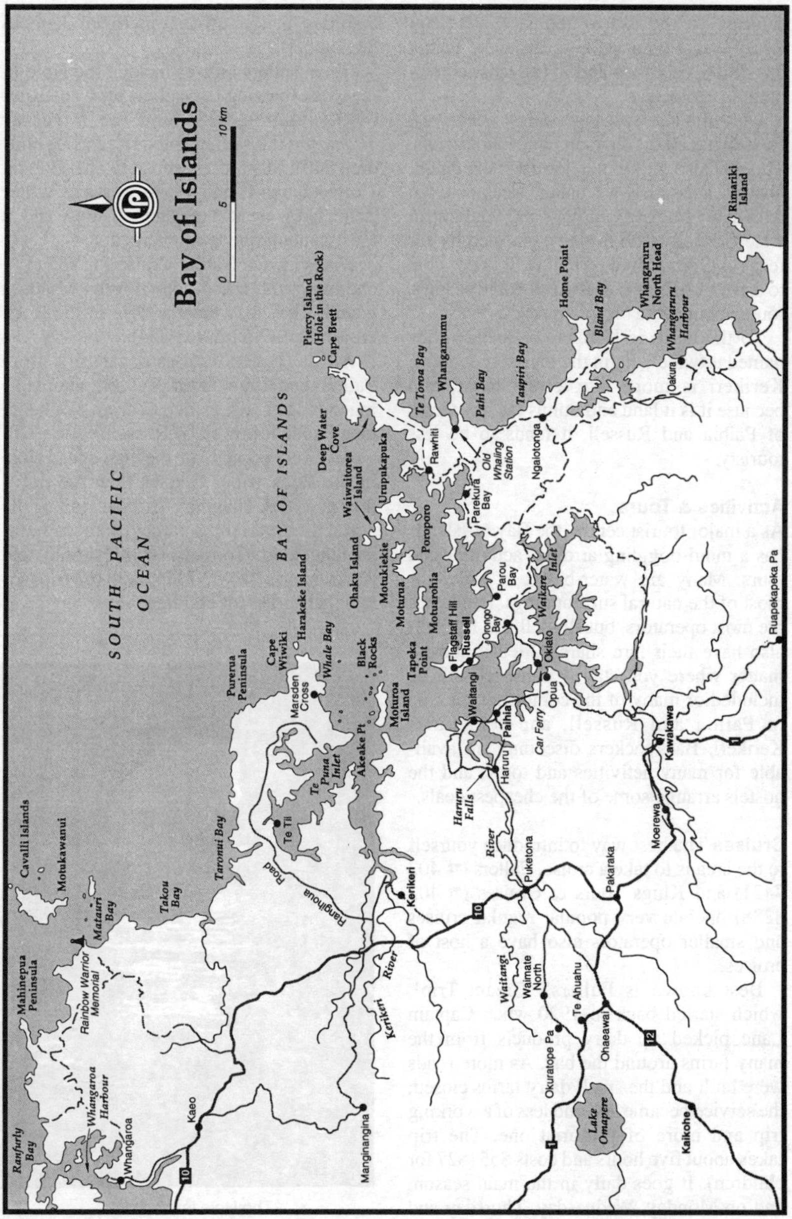
Bay of Islands
0
5
10 km
SOUTH PACIFIC
OCEAN
BAY OF ISLANDS
Cavalli Islands
Motukawanui
Mahinepua Peninsula
Rainbow Warrior Memorial
Matauri Bay
Takou Bay
Taronui Bay
Ranfurly Bay
Whangaroa Harbour
Whangaroa
Kaeo
Purerua Peninsula
Te Tii
Te Puna Inlet
Rangitoua Road
Kerikeri
Kerikeri River
Manginangina
Cape Wiwiki
Marsden Cross
Whale Bay
Harakeke Island
Akeake Pt
Black Rocks
Moturoa Island
Ohaku Island
Motukiekie
Moturua
Motuarohia
Waiwaitorea Island
Urupukapuka
Poroporo
Tapeka Point
Flagstaff Hill
Russell
Orongo Bay
Parou Bay
Parekura Bay
Waitangi
Paihia
Haruru
Haruru Falls
Waitangi River
Car Ferry
Opua
Okiato
Waikare Inlet
Kawakawa
Moerewa
Pakaraka
Puketona
Waimate North
Te Ahuahu
Okuratope Pa
Ohaeawai
Lake Omapere
Kaikohe
Ruapekapeka Pa
Deep Water Cove
Piercy Island (Hole in the Rock)
Cape Brett
Rawhiti
Te Toroa Bay
Whangamumu
Pahi Bay
Old Whaling Station
Ngaiotonga
Taupiri Bay
Home Point
Bland Bay
Whangaruru North Head
Whangaruru Harbour
Oakura
Rimariki Island
10
12
1

catering to the tourist industry. Waitangi Reserve is within walking distance. Paihia has all the facilities and is the most convenient place to stay.

Only a short passenger ferry ride away, Russell has all the character that Paihia lacks. Though also a popular tourist destination, historic Russell is a smaller, sleepier town with many fine old buildings and a delightful waterfront. Russell is also connected by car ferry to Opua, south of Paihia. It is possible to drive from Paihia to Russell but it's a long, roundabout route on rough roads.

To the north is Kerikeri – 'so nice they named it twice', claim the tourist brochures. Kerikeri is more like a real town, and because it is inland and minus the bay views of Paihia and Russell, it tends to be less touristy.

Activities & Tours

As a major tourist centre, the Bay of Islands has a mind-boggling array of activities and tours. Many are water-based to make the most of the natural surroundings. Paihia has the most operators, but Russell and Kerikeri also have their fare share. Often it doesn't matter where you stay – transport will be included or many of the companies pick up in Paihia and Russell, and sometimes Kerikeri. Backpackers discounts are available for many activities and tours, and the hostels arrange some of the cheapest deals.

Cruises The best way to introduce yourself to the area is to take a cruise. Fullers (☎ 402 7421) and Kings Tours & Cruises (☎ 402 8288) operate very popular regular cruises and smaller operators also have a host of cruises.

Best known is Fullers' 'Cream Trip', which started back in 1920 when Captain Lane picked up dairy products from the many farms around the bay. As more roads were built and the small dairy farms closed, the service became less and less of a working trip and more of a tourist one. The trip takes about five hours and costs $55 ($27 for children). It goes daily in the main season, and on Monday, Wednesday, Thursday and Saturday in the off-season (from June to September).

Other Fullers cruises include the Hole in the Rock (passing through it) off Cape Brett ($49, children $25), and the *R Tucker Thompson* tall sailing ship cruise ($75, children $40). Most tours stop at Otehei Bay on Urupukapuka Island where westerns writer Zane Grey went big game fishing and a tourist submarine is submerged.

Kings have a Nature Cruise for $65 ($35 children) with a 2½-hour stop on Moturua Island. They also have a Hole in the Rock cruise for $47 (children $24).

All the Fullers cruises depart first from Paihia and then from Russell about 15 minutes later. Kings depart from Waitangi, then Paihia followed by Russell.

Also very popular are the high-speed Hole in the Rock trips. Cruises they are not – this is a neck-snapping jet-boat ride of the adrenaline-pumping rather than camera-priming kind. Tornado (☎ 402 8668) and Reefrunner's (☎ 402 7355) both run trips for $45, half-price for children.

The Hole in the Rock

Sailing A very pleasant way to explore the Bay of Islands is on a sailing trip. Fullers has been mentioned, but there are also a number of other operators.

Carino (☎ 403 7230) has a 40-foot (12-metre) keel yacht and 42-foot catamaran offering full-day sailings for $48.

Great Escape Charters (☎ 407 8920) in Kerikeri has bareboat yacht charters; five-metre two berth/six-metre three berth/6.3 metre four berth yachts cost $70/90/130 per 24 hours.

Gungha New Zealand (☎ 407 7930) is a 14-metre ocean-going sloop departing Kerikeri and picking up in Russell. Full-day cruises are $60 or evening cruises are $30.

A Place in the Sun (☎ 403 7615) organises cruises for $40 for a half day, and longer sailings can also be arranged.

Straycat (☎ 407 7342) has day trips in a catamaran departing from Russell, Kerikeri and Paihia for $60, including lunch.

Vigilant (☎ 403 7596) has full-day cruises, during which you can help sail, for $55 or evening Wine & Cheese cruises for $40.

Dolphin Swimming This is a popular and fast growing activity in a country blessed with many types of marine mammals. Though Kaikoura in the South Island is still the premier destination for swimming with the dolphins, trips from the Bay of Islands are becoming increasingly popular. The big plus for Bay of Islands trips is that they operate all year, even in winter when Kaikoura trips stop.

The Bay of Islands trips have a high success rate, so high that operators have been offering another free trip if dolphins are not sighted. The dolphins most often observed are the common and bottlenose dolphins, although it is likely that you will see other marine mammals. Whale sightings are less common, but minke, brydes and killer whales frequently visit these waters. Dolphin swims are, of course, subject to weather and sea conditions.

Dolphin Discoveries (☎ 403 7350) got this activity under way in this region in 1991, have small groups and provide all equipment for $65. Their tours have a very good name.

Fullers, the big tour conglomerate, are not to be outdone and also run Dolphin Adventures for the same price. Fullers have larger groups, but regulations restrict the number of people that can go into the water at any one time.

Sea Kayaking Sea kayaking trips in the bay have become very popular, with a number of operators offering trips that are highly recommended by travellers. Coastal Kayakers (☎ 402 8105) does a trip from Waitangi around the mangrove forests up to Haruru Falls, passing right underneath the falls, and

The frolicsome dusky dolphin.
Swimming with the dolphins is an increasingly popular activity in the Bay of Islands, even in winter

out to Motumaire Island all in one day. The full-day trip costs $60 or shorter four-hour trips cost $40. Kayaks and gear can be rented for $10 per hour, $25 per half day or $35 for a full day. Kayaks can also be hired at Down 'N' Under (☎ 402 8428), 12 Marsden Rd near Paihia's hostels, or at the kiosk on the beach opposite.

Over in Russell, Kaptain Kayak (☎ 403 7584), near the corner of Matauwhi Rd and Florence Ave, hire out kayaks and canoes in addition to mountain bikes and windsurfers. Ring them for details of extended guided tours. The Bay of Islands Kayak Co (☎ 403 7672) in Russell has a good reputation and offers guided sea kayak trips from $80 per day. It also arranges independent rentals.

Scuba Diving Moving from above the water to under it, there is a handful of companies available to get you below the surface. Paihia Dive Hire (☎ 402 7551) on Williams Rd hires full sets of scuba gear to qualified divers. It also offers scuba and snorkelling courses, tank filling and scuba gear servicing, a dive shop, and diving trips, including expeditions to the sunken *Rainbow Warrior* for $145 all up.

Bay Guides (☎ 402 7906), in addition to abseiling and hiking trips, offer guided diving trips. All levels of divers are catered for. Their trips depart from Paihia wharf daily all year round.

Target Dive Charters (☎ 404 7971), Okitao Point Rd, Russell, also have diving and snorkelling trips.

Other Activities The Bay of Islands is noted for its **fishing**, particularly snapper and kingfish. Fishing charter boats abound and can be booked at the Maritime Building in Paihia or at the Russell wharf.

Surprisingly inexpensive are the **scenic flights** over the Bay of Islands: you can take a short aerial tour (about 15 minutes) for around $30, or longer flights at varying prices. Bay of Islands Aero Club (☎ 407 8400) at Kerikeri has scenic flights, or you can take seaplane flights from the Paihia wharf (☎ 402 7811).

Bay Guides organises **abseiling trips**, and can be contacted at Down 'N' Under, 12 Marsden Rd, which makes bookings for many activities and rents a wide range of equipment. The abseiling trips go down cliffs ranging in height from 10 metres to the spectacular 30-metre Rainbow Falls; you get wet on the last abseil, but no previous experience is necessary.

Lanes Rd Farm (☎ 403 7673) in Russell has **horse riding** through a particularly beautiful part of the peninsula.

Cape Reinga Trips If you're heading to the Far North, it's easier to make trips to Cape Reinga and Ninety Mile Beach from Kaitaia or Doubtless Bay. However, there are a number of popular trips leaving from the Bay of Islands.

King's Tours & Cruises (☎ 402 8288) has trips departing from Paihia with pick-ups in Kerikeri daily at 7.30 am, returning at 6.30 pm. The tour also stops at Puketi Kauri Forest and Wagener Museum. The cost is $67 (children $34), less if you also have taken their Cape Brett tour. Fullers (☎ 402 7421) charges $79 (children $45) for a similar trip with lunch thrown in. Their deluxe version at $89 (children $51) includes entry to the Wagener Museum, and Sullivan's Glow Worm Grotto & Kiwi House.

Other Tours Fullers have a shorter trip which includes Kerikeri and the Puketi Forest. It's about four hours in duration and costs $35 (children $17). They also have a Kerikeri & Crafts tour for $30 (children $15).

Getting There & Away

Air Eagle Airways (☎ 402 7421) has daily flights to Kerikeri from Auckland, with Air New Zealand connections to other destinations. Eagle Airways also has one flight every day except Sunday to Kaitaia.

Bus All the buses serving Paihia arrive and depart from the Maritime Building by the wharf, where there are booking agents.

InterCity has buses daily from Auckland to the Bay of Islands, via Whangarei and Opua.

The trip takes about four hours to Paihia and proceeds to Kerikeri before continuing north to Kaitaia, two hours farther on.

Northliner has an Auckland-Whangarei-Bay of Islands-Kaitaia bus service. It departs from the Downtown Airline Terminal in Auckland and stops at the Paihia Maritime Building, Haruru Falls, Puketone Junction and Kerikeri. There's a connecting service to Russell and also a direct Whangarei-Russell service.

The West Coaster has a four-hour trip going from Paihia to Dargaville via the Waipoua Kauri Forest from Monday to Friday (see the introductory Getting Around section for Northland).

Getting Around

Passenger ferries connect Paihia with Russell, running from around 7 am to 7 pm (to 10 pm from October to June). Three ferries, the large Fullers ferry and two smaller, local services operate on average every 20 minutes from Russell to Paihia in summer. The fare is $3 one way; return tickets are no saving and are less flexible.

To get to Russell with your car you cross from Opua to Okiato Point using the car ferry (see Getting There & Away for Russell for more details).

There's also a water taxi (☎ 403 7123, 403 7378) for getting around the bay.

BAY OF ISLANDS MARITIME & HISTORIC PARK

The Bay of Islands Maritime & Historic Park is comprised of about 40 different sites extending all the way from Mimiwhangata Bay in the south to Whangaroa Harbour in the north. Marked walks of varying levels of difficulty (many very easy) take anywhere from 10 minutes to 10 hours and include tramps around islands, Maori pas and other historical sites, scenic, historic and recreational reserves and the Mimiwhangata Marine Park.

The Bay of Islands Maritime & Historic Park Visitor Centre is at Russell (☎ 403 7685). DOC Kerikeri (☎ 407 8474) can also supply you with information. There are a number of good books which will guide you in the right direction. *The Story of the Bay of Islands Maritime & Historic Park*, produced by DOC, is indispensable. Its frontispiece is haunting: 'Whatungarongaro te tangata toitu te whenua' (People are perishable but the land endures). You can also get the two useful pamphlets *Huts & Camping* and *Walking* from the DOC visitor information centre.

Development of the islands in the Bay of Islands is limited, though **Urupukapuka Island** has some facilities. Fullers tours stop at Otehei Bay, where they have a submarine-styled vessel for underwater viewing and a restaurant/bar. As well as camping, the island also has a hostel (see Places to Stay).

Places to Stay

The DOC office in Russell (☎ 403 7685) has details of accommodation in the park. The *Cape Brett Hut* is a very popular destination. You can arrange to walk there and stay in the hut by ringing ☎ 403 7923. A 'koha' or donation should be made to the Maori landowners.

Camping is permitted at most of the bays on *Urupukapuka Island* but you need food, stove and fuel and a shovel for digging a toilet. At Oteihei Bay, *Otehei Bay Hostel* (☎ 403 7803) is a YHA associate hostel with dorm beds for $16 and twin rooms for $36. Accommodation is in simple cabins, but the position in the middle of the Bay of Islands is hard to beat. To reach Urupukapuka Island, take one of the Fullers tours, get off at Otehei Bay and arrange to catch the tour on another day.

Also popular are the *Mimiwhangata Cottage & Lodge* in the coastal Mimiwhangata park, equidistant from Russell or Whangarei on the east coast (see the Russell to Whangarei section).

PAIHIA & WAITANGI

The main town in the area, Paihia, was settled by Europeans as a mission station in 1823 when the first raupo (bullrush) hut was built for the Reverend Henry Williams. Paihia still has a very pretty setting but the missionary zeal has been replaced with an equally fervent tourist industry. It's basically an accommodation, eating and tours centre and a good starting point to see the rest of the Bay of Islands.

Adjoining Paihia to the north is Waitangi, the site of the historic signing of the 6 February 1840 treaty between the Maori people and the representatives of Queen Victoria's government.

The Treaty of Waitangi is a momentous document that on the one hand saw the Maori tribes accept British governorship, but on the other granted the Maori citizenship and land rights. The treaty lies at the heart of Maori grievances and land claims today.

Information

Most of the information places are conveniently grouped together in the Maritime Building right by the wharf in Paihia. Here you'll find the Bay of Islands Visitor Information Centre (☎ 402 7426; fax 402 7301), Marsden Rd, which can give information, advice, and make bookings for every single thing you might want to do while you're in the region.

Also in the Maritime Building are the Fullers and King's offices for cruises and tours, a centre for fishing boat bookings, the bus station, and the terminal for the ferry to Russell. The offices are open every day from 8 am to 5 pm.

Maori Land Rights

At the heart of Maori grievances and race relations in New Zealand today, the Treaty of Waitangi signalled the annexation of the country by Britain and laid the foundation of modern New Zealand. Though the treaty was soon ignored as land-grabbing settlers colonised the country, its most remarkable feature is that it was ever drawn up at all. In a colonial era when land was just taken with the force of guns, the treaty represents a unusual spirit of equality and accommodation with an indigenous people.

Since its signing in 1840, Maori leaders have continued to petition the government to uphold the treaty. Come self-government, the treaty was never ratified by a New Zealand parliament, but in 1975 the government sought, at least in part, to honour the terms of the treaty by establishing the Waitangi Tribunal to investigate Maori land claims. In 1994 the government announced a billion dollar 'settlement envelope' to settle all outstanding claims on Crown land once and for all.

The treaty remains hotly debated. The Maori chiefs signed a shortened Maori version, which differs from the English, as did Maori and Pakeha concepts of sovereignty and land ownership. Here is the full English text of this short but contentious document:

Treaty Of Waitangi 1840

Her Majesty Victoria Queen of the United Kingdom of Great Britain and Ireland regarding with Her Royal Favour the Native Chiefs and Tribes of New Zealand and anxious to protect their just Rights and Property and to secure to them the enjoyment of Peace and Good Order has deemed it necessary in consequence of the great number of Her Majesty's Subjects who have already settled in New Zealand and the rapid extension of Emigration both from Europe and Australia which is still in progress to constitute and appoint a functionary properly authorized to treat with the Aborigines of New Zealand for the recognition of Her Majesty's Sovereign authority over the whole or any part of those islands.

Her Majesty therefore being desirous to establish a settled form of Civil Government with a view to avert the evil consequences which must result from the absense of the necessary Laws and Institutions alike to the native population and to Her subjects has been graciously pleased to empower and to authorize 'me William Hobson a Captain' in Her Majesty's Royal Navy Consul and Lieutenant Governor of such parts of New Zealand as may be or hereafter shall be ceded to Her Majesty to invite the confederated and independent Chiefs of New Zealand to concur in the following Articles and Conditions.

Waitangi National Reserve
The Treaty House in Waitangi has special significance as the start of the European history of New Zealand. Built in 1832 as the home of British Resident James Busby, eight years later it was the setting for the signing of the historic Treaty of Waitangi. The house, with its beautiful sweep of lawn running down to the bay, is preserved as a memorial and museum.

A few metres across the lawn, the magnificently detailed Maori Whare Runanga (Meeting House) was completed in 1940 to mark the centenary of the treaty. The carvings represent the major Maori tribes.

Down by the cove is the largest war canoe in the world – the Maori war canoe *Ngatokimatawhaorua*, named after the canoe in which the Maori ancestor Kupe discovered New Zealand. It too was built for the centenary, and a photographic exhibit details how the canoe was made from two gigantic kauri trees. Traditionally the canoe was launched every year on 6 February (New Zealand Day) for the annual treaty-signing commemoration ceremonies, when dignitaries gathered and Maori activists protested. For the Maori, the Treaty of Waitangi remains a symbol of the expropriation of their land, and highlights the failure of the government to honour its responsibilities under the treaty. After a protest in 1995 when the

Article the First The Chiefs of the Confederation of the United Tribes of New Zealand and the separate and independent Chiefs who have not become members of the Confederation cede to Her Majesty the Queen of England absolutely and without reservation all the rights and powers of Sovereignty which the said Confederation or Individual Chiefs respectively exercise or possess, or may be supposed to exercise or to possess, over their respective Territories as the sole Sovereigns thereof.

Article the Second Her Majesty the Queen of England confirms and guarantees to the Chiefs and Tribes of New Zealand and to the respective families and individuals thereof the full exclusive and undisturbed possession of their Lands and Estates Forests Fisheries and other properties which they may collectively or individually possess so long as it is their wish and desire to retain the same in their possession; but the Chiefs of the United Tribes and the individual Chiefs yield to Her Majesty the exclusive right of Preemption over such lands as the proprietors thereof may be disposed to alienate at such prices as may be agreed upon between the respective Proprietors and persons appointed by Her Majesty to treat with them in that behalf.

Article the Third In consideration thereof Her Majesty the Queen of England extends to the Natives of New Zealand Her royal protection and imparts to them all the Rights and Privileges of British Subjects.

Signed **W Hobson Lieutenant Govenor**

Now therefore We the Chiefs of the Confederation of the United Tribes of New Zealand being assembled in Congress at Victoria in Waitangi and We the Separate and Independent Chiefs of New Zealand claiming authority over the Tribes and Territories which are specified after our respective names, having been made fully to understand the Provisions of the foregoing Treaty, accept and enter into the same in the full spirit and meaning thereof in witness of which we have attached our signatures or marks at the places and the dates respectively specified

Done at Waitangi this Sixth day of February in the year of Our Lord one thousand eight hundred and forty. ■

governor-general was spat at, the prime minister announced that the ceremony would no longer be held.

Beyond the Treaty House a road climbs Mt Bledisloe, from where there are commanding views of the area. Beginning from the visitors centre, a walking track takes off through the reserve, passing through the mangrove forest around Hutia Creek and on to Haruru Falls. The walkway has a boardwalk among the mangroves so you can explore them without getting your feet wet. The walk to the falls takes about 1½ hours each way.

Admission to Waitangi Reserve is $5 (children free) and it's open from 9 am to 5 pm daily. At the visitors centre an audiovisual presentation relating the story of the developments surrounding the signing of the treaty begins every half-hour.

Kelly Tarlton's Shipwreck Museum

Beached beside the bridge over the Waitangi River is the barque *Tui*, an old sailing ship, imaginatively fitted out as a museum of shipwrecks. It's open from 9 am to 5.30 pm daily (the cafe is open later), longer during holiday periods; admission is $5 (children $2.50). Recorded sea chants, creaking timbers and swaying lights accompany the collection of over 1000 bits and pieces Kelly Tarlton dragged up from wrecks around the coast.

Haruru Falls

A few km upstream from the *Tui* are the very attractive Haruru Falls, also accessible via the walkway through the Waitangi National Reserve. At the foot of the falls there's good swimming, several motor camps, a licensed restaurant and a tavern. If you wish to kayak to the base of the falls see Sea Kayaking earlier in this section.

Walks

Just behind Paihia is the **Opua Forest**, a regenerating forest with a small stand of kauris, and a number of walking tracks ranging from 10 minutes to three hours in length. If you walk up from School Rd for about 20 minutes, you'll find a couple of good lookout points. DOC publishes pamphlets with details on all the Opua Forest walks. You can also drive into the forest by taking the Oromahoe Rd west from Opua.

There is a variety of good short and long walks around the Bay of Islands and on the islands themselves. The park information centre in Russell and DOC Kerikeri have lots of information on walks. You could start with the two-minute stroll to the top of the headland on the southern end of Paihia, or take the mangrove walk near the *Tui* barque, or the coastal walk from Paihia to Opua.

Other Activities

Small boats, kayaks and windsurfers can be hired on the beach and mountain bikes are readily available for hire. Paihia is the main centre for the many activities in the Bay of Islands (see Activities & Tours at the start of this section); the hostels book many activities at good prices and the Visitor Information Centre can also help.

Places to Stay

The Bay of Islands Visitor Information Centre (Paihia Wharf) will tell you what is available and will make bookings. They're particularly good for B&B bookings which can be a worthwhile deal in Paihia, where accommodation is often quite expensive.

Camping & Cabins There are many camping grounds around Paihia and Waitangi, most of them a few km back from the coast near the Haruru Falls. The *Panorama Motor Lodge & Caravan Park* (☎ 402 7525), beside the river and facing the falls, has sites at $9 per person in peak summer season, and motel units at $85 to $95 at peak season but $55 to $65 at other times. The camp is well equipped with a large swimming pool, bar and restaurant.

The *Twin Pines Tourist Park* (☎ 402 7322) on Puketona Rd at the Falls has tent and powered sites at $8.50 per person, cabins and on-site caravans at $38 a double, and tourist flats for $49. Next door the *Falls Caravan Park* (☎ 402 7816) has tent and powered sites at similar rates. At Puketona Junction

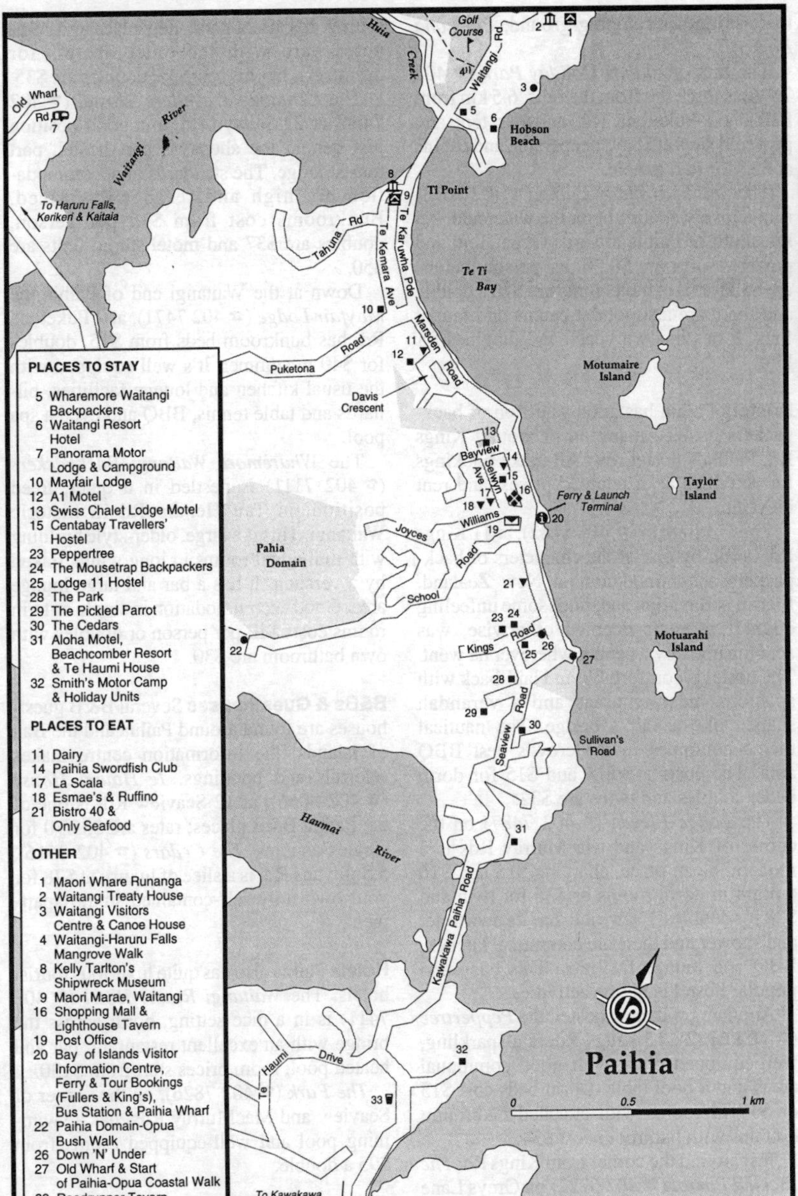
Golf Course
Waitangi Rd
Huia Creek
Old Wharf Rd
Waitangi River
To Haruru Falls, Kerikeri & Kaitaia
Hobson Beach
Ti Point
Tahuna Rd
Te Kemara Ave
Te Karuwha Pde
Te Ti Bay
Marsden Road
Puketona Road
Davis Crescent
Motumaire Island
Bayview
Selwyn Ave
Ferry & Launch Terminal
Williams
Joyces
Road
Taylor Island
Pahia Domain
School
Kings
Road
Motuarahi Island
Seaview Road
Sullivan's Road
Haumai River
Kawakawa Paihia Road
Te Haumi Drive
To Kawakawa, Opua & Whangarei
Paihia
0
0.5
1 km
PLACES TO STAY
5 Wharemore Waitangi Backpackers
6 Waitangi Resort Hotel
7 Panorama Motor Lodge & Campground
10 Mayfair Lodge
12 A1 Motel
13 Swiss Chalet Lodge Motel
15 Centabay Travellers' Hostel
23 Peppertree
24 The Mousetrap Backpackers
25 Lodge 11 Hostel
28 The Park
29 The Pickled Parrot
30 The Cedars
31 Aloha Motel, Beachcomber Resort & Te Haumi House
32 Smith's Motor Camp & Holiday Units
PLACES TO EAT
11 Dairy
14 Paihia Swordfish Club
17 La Scala
18 Esmae's & Ruffino
21 Bistro 40 & Only Seafood
OTHER
1 Maori Whare Runanga
2 Waitangi Treaty House
3 Waitangi Visitors Centre & Canoe House
4 Waitangi-Haruru Falls Mangrove Walk
8 Kelly Tarlton's Shipwreck Museum
9 Maori Marae, Waitangi
16 Shopping Mall & Lighthouse Tavern
19 Post Office
20 Bay of Islands Visitor Information Centre, Ferry & Tour Bookings (Fullers & King's), Bus Station & Paihia Wharf
22 Paihia Domain-Opua Bush Walk
26 Down 'N' Under
27 Old Wharf & Start of Paihia-Opua Coastal Walk
33 Roadrunner Tavern

there's another camping ground, *Puketona Park.*

The *Bay of Islands Holiday Park* (☎ 402 7646) is three km from the falls, 6.5 km from Paihia on Puketona Rd, and has tent and powered sites at $8.50 per person, and cabins at $35 for two people.

The *Smiths Holiday Camp* (☎ 402 7678) is at a lovely spot right on the waterside, 2.5 km south of Paihia towards Opua. Tent and powered sites are $9.50 per person, cabins are $38 for two, motel units are $70 a double and there are also tourist cabins and tourist flats. It has its own beach and dinghies for hire.

Hostels Paihia has good selection of backpackers hostels, many on or around Kings Rd, Paihia's hostel row. All make bookings for activities at discounted prices, and rent bicycles.

The Mousetrap (☎ 402 8182), at 11 Kings Rd, is run by one of the characters of backpackers accommodation in New Zealand. Martin is Bavarian and, until some unfeeling council officials deemed otherwise, was accompanied by a pet pig wherever he went. The hostel is comfortable and laid-back with spacious meeting areas and a verandah shaped like a ship's bridge. The nautical theme continues in the crow's nest BBQ area. The costs are $14 and $15 for dorm beds; doubles and twins are $32.

The *Lodge Eleven* (☎ 402 7487) on the corner of Kings and MacMurray Rds is a modern, clean place, charging $15 and $16 a night in dorm rooms or $36 for twin and $38 for doubles. Each room has its own toilet and shower and there are communal kitchen, BBQ and lounge facilities. This busy and popular hostel is big on activities.

Another good, new hostel, the *Peppertree* (☎ 402 6122), 15 Kings Rd, is a sparkling, well-equipped place with good communal areas and a pool table. Dorm beds cost $15 or $17 in rooms with attached bathroom; doubles with bathroom cost $34.

Just around the corner from Kings Rd, *The Pickled Parrot* (☎ 402 6222) on Greys Lane is another spic-and-span place in a nice setting. It's also a good, new place and competes hard with the other hostels for customers. Dorms cost $15; doubles are $35.

The *Centabay Travellers' Hostel* (☎ 402 7466) at 27 Selwyn Rd, in a good position just behind the shops, is part hostel, part tourist lodge. The standards of accommodation are high and reasonably priced. Bunkrooms cost from $15 per person, doubles are $37 and motel studio units are $50.

Down at the Waitangi end of Paihia the *Mayfair Lodge* (☎ 402 7471), at 7 Puketona Rd, has bunkroom beds from $15, doubles for $40 in summer. It's well equipped with the usual kitchen and lounge facilities, billiards and table tennis, BBQ and even a spa pool.

The *Wharemore Waitangi Backpackers* (☎ 402 7111) is nestled in a quiet, treed position on Tau Henare Rd in historic Waitangi. This is a large, older-style building with individual rooms in long wings linked by a veranda. It has a bar and large lounge area. Good accommodation in single or twin rooms costs $12 per person or doubles with own bathroom are $30.

B&Bs & Guesthouses Several B&B guesthouses are found around Paihia and the Bay of Islands; the information centre makes referrals and bookings. *Te Haumi House* (☎ 402 8066), at 12 Seaview Rd, is one of the Paihia B&B places; rates are $35/70 for singles/doubles. *The Cedars* (☎ 402 8516), 5 Sullivans Rd, is a slice of luxury at $78 for your own fully self-contained studio apartment.

Hotels Paihia also has quite luxurious tourist hotels. The *Waitangi Resort Hotel* (☎ 402 7411) is in a nice setting, north across the bridge with an excellent restaurant, bar and heated pool; room prices start from $130.

The Park (☎ 402 7826), on the corner of Seaview and MacMurray Rds, has a swimming pool and well-equipped rooms from $95 a double.

Motels Paihia is motel city, with dozens to

choose from. Motels stand shoulder to shoulder along the waterfront and double rates are around $100 during the peak summer season, dropping to $60 or $80 during the low season. Rates tend to vary with the room, the season, current demand and probably a few other secret factors as well.

Paihia motels offer good standards and most have good kitchen facilities. A few likely places to try, listed with their high season rates (winter rates will be considerably lower) are:

A1 Motel, 46 Davis Crescent (☎ 402 7684); $120 for doubles
Ala-Moana Motel, Marsden Rd on the waterfront (☎ 402 7745); $120 for doubles or twins
Aloha Motel, Seaview Rd (☎ 402 7540); doubles from $125
Ash Grove Motel, Blackbridge Rd, Haruru Falls (☎ 402 7934); $120 for doubles
Blue Pacific Motel, corner of Marsden and Puketona Rds (☎ 402 7394); $115 for doubles
Dolphin Motel, 69 Williams Rd (☎ 402 8170); singles/twins are $77/89
Swiss Chalet Lodge Motel, 3 Bayview Rd (☎ 402 7615); $150 for doubles

Places to Eat

Paihia has a big selection of restaurants and takeaway places scattered around, particularly in the shopping mall opposite the Maritime Centre and the post office.

The *Blue Marlin Cafe* in the shopping mall overlooking the bay, is a no-frills greasy spoon but has cheap, filling breakfasts and other snacks and grills.

The *Cafe Over the Bay*, upstairs in the shopping mall, has a good view of the bay and good, reasonably priced food too, with lots of European snacks and dishes (mostly French and Italian).

In the lane that runs though the shopping mall, *King Wah* is a licensed Chinese restaurant with dark decor and reasonably priced banquets. Also here is the *Fishpot Cafe*, a small cafe with moderately priced seafood and fish & chips, and the *Sidewalk Bar & Grill*, a good place for a drink or meal at the tables out on the pavement.

On the Williams Rd side of the mall, the *Odeon Pub* is another, fancy bar/restaurant with good, cheap meals but expensive drinks.

The *La Scala* licensed restaurant on Selwyn Ave is about the priceyest place in town, with a mixed seafood platter, including lobster, for two at about $75.

At 41 Williams Rd, *Esmae's* is a fancy, licensed restaurant with interesting nouvelle Kiwi cuisine at around $20 to $22 a main. Meat dishes predominate but fresh fish is also featured. Upstairs at 39 Williams Rd, *Ruffino* is a little pizza cafe with cheap meals. Pastas and small pizzas are around $9.

Bistro 40 and *Only Seafood* are in a converted old home on Marsden Rd with attractive decor and areas indoors and out overlooking the sea. Both have good food, with Only Seafood getting the best marks for moderately priced, excellent seafood.

Entertainment

The *Lighthouse Tavern* upstairs on Marsden Rd has various sections including a restaurant, bars and a pub, and it features live bands. At Haruru Falls the *Twin Pines* has a tavern with house brews on tap and entertainment on weekends. The *Roadrunner* is a pub about a five-minute drive south of Paihia en route to Opua. The *Odeon Pub* on Williams Rd is a lively drinking hole in evenings and also has entertainment.

Getting There & Away

For information on travel to/from Paihia, see Getting There & Away in the Bay of Islands section.

RUSSELL

A short ferry ride across the bay is Russell, originally a fortified Maori settlement which spread over the entire valley, then known as Kororareka.

Russell's early European history was turbulent. In 1830 it was the scene of the 'war of the girls', which occurred when two Maori girls from different tribes each thought they were the favourite of a whaling captain. This resulted in conflict between the tribes, which the Maori leader, Titore, who was recognised as the chief of chiefs in the area, attempted to resolve by separating the two tribes and making the border at the base of the Tapeka Peninsula. A European settlement quickly sprang up in place of the abandoned Maori village.

In 1845 the government sent in soldiers and marines to garrison the town when the Maori leader, Hone Heke, threatened to chop down the flagstaff – symbol of Pakeha authority – for the fourth time. On 11 March 1845 the Maoris staged a diversionary siege on Russell. It was a great tactical success, with Chief Kawiti attacking from the south and another Maori war party attacking from Long Beach. While the troops rushed off to protect the township, Hone Heke felled the hated symbol of European authority on Maiki Hill for the final time. The Pakehas were forced to evacuate to ships lying at anchor off the settlement. The captain of HMS *Hazard* was wounded severely in the battle and the first lieutenant ordered the ships' cannons to be fired on the town, during the course of which most of the buildings were razed.

Traditional Maori dress and Moko (tattoo)

Russell today is a relaxed, peaceful and pretty little place. It's a marked contrast to the neon hustle of Paihia across the bay.

Information

The Bradley's Information Office (☎ 403 7596), out at the end of the pier, books tours and fishing boats and can answer questions on Russell. There's a Fullers office (☎ 403 7866) at the land end of the pier.

The excellent Bay of Islands Maritime Park Visitor Information Centre (☎ 403 7685) has displays about the area and lots of information on walks, camping, snorkelling, diving and many other activities. The centre is open every day from 9 am to 5 pm (May to August until 4.30 pm) and has an audiovisual show beginning every half-hour. The free *Russell Heritage Trails* pamphlet outlines one walking tour of town and three driving tours on the peninsula.

Russell Museum

The Russell Museum was built for the bicentenary of Cook's Bay of Islands visit in 1769. It's small but it houses maritime exhibits, displays relating to Cook and his voyages, and a fine 1:5 scale model of his barque *Endeavour* – a real working model – in addition to a collection of early settlers' relics. The museum is open from 10 am to 4 pm every day; admission is $2.50 (children 50c).

Pompallier House

Close by, and on a lovely waterfront site, is Pompallier House, built to house the printing works for the Roman Catholic mission founded by the French missionary Bishop Pompallier in 1841. It also served as a tannery and only in the 1870s was converted to a private home. It is one of the oldest houses in New Zealand and has a small museum. It is open 10 am to 5 pm daily (closed on weekends from June to September) and entry is $5.

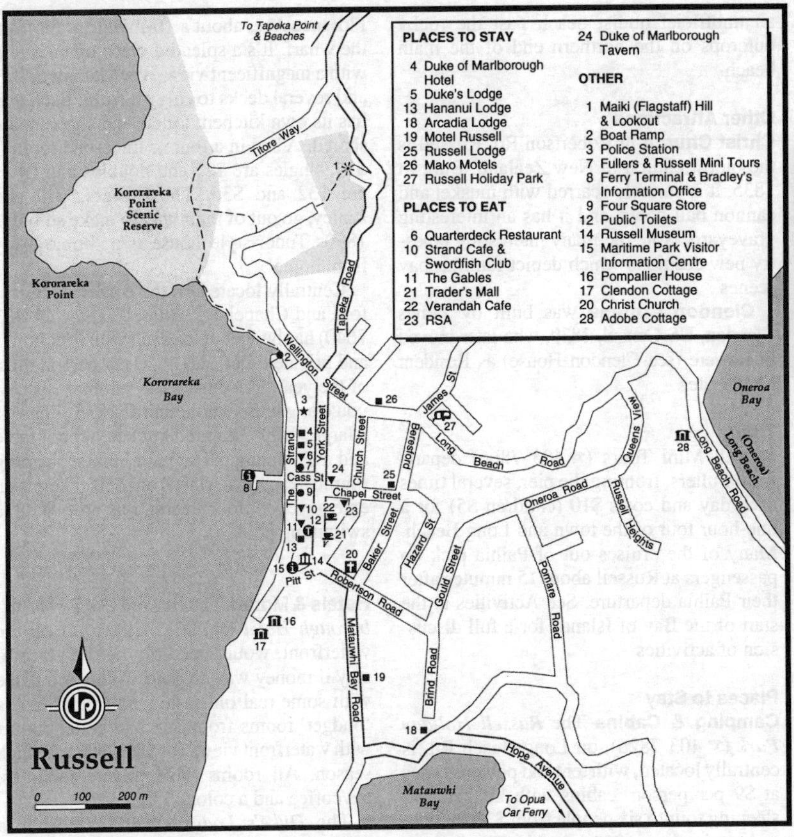

NORTHLAND

Flagstaff Hill

Overlooking Russell is Maiki (Flagstaff Hill), where Hone Heke made his attacks – this, the fifth flagpole, has stood for a lot longer than the first four. The view is well worth the trouble to get up there, and there are several routes to the top. If you go by car, take Tapeka Rd, or on foot take the track west from the boat ramp along the beach at low tide, or up Wellington St at high tide. The track passes through the Kororareka Point Scenic Reserve. Alternatively, simply walk to the end of Wellington St and take the short track up the hill, about a 30-minute climb.

Oneroa Bay

About one km behind Russell to the east is Oneroa Bay, with a beautiful beach known variously as Oneroa Bay Beach, Donkey Beach or Long Beach. It's about a 15-minute walk from the Russell wharf, heading over the hill on Long Beach Rd. When you reach the summit of the hill, at the intersection with Queen's View Rd, there's a tiny old grave-yard with benches and a good view of Oneroa Bay. Take a turn here and go about one block up Queen's View Rd to where it meets Oneroa Rd and the view is even better – a sweeping vista of the peninsula. There's an unofficial nudist beach past the rocky outcrops on the northern end of the main beach.

Other Attractions

Christ Church in Robertson Rd, Russell is the oldest church in New Zealand. Built in 1835, it is suitably scarred with musket and cannon ball holes, and it has an interesting graveyard. Note the many interesting tapestry pew cushions which depict familiar bay scenes.

Clendon Cottage was built by James Clendon, US Consul, 1839, who later moved to Rawere (see Clendon House) as Resident Magistrate.

Tours

Russell Mini Tours (☎ 403 7866) departs from Fullers, fronting the pier, several times each day and costs $10 (children $5) for a one-hour tour of the town and Long Beach. Many of the cruises out of Paihia pick up passengers at Russell about 15 minutes after their Paihia departure. See Activities at the start of the Bay of Islands for a full discussion of activities.

Places to Stay

Camping & Cabins The *Russell Holiday Park* (☎ 403 7826), on Long Beach Rd, is centrally located, with tent and powered sites at $9 per person, cabins with kitchen and sleeping four to six people from $38 for two, and tourist flats at $59 a double. The Orongo Bay Holiday Park (see Hostels) also has camp sites.

Hostels Three places around Russell offer hostel-style accommodation. *Orongo Bay Holiday Park* (☎ 403 7704) is three km south of Russell on the road to the Opua car ferry, and provides a free pick-up service if you arrive in Russell by ferry. Orongo Bay is a YHA associate Hostel and costs $12.50 per night in one to four-bed rooms, whether you're a YHA member or not. It also provides camp sites at $7 per person. There's a swimming pool and a TV/games room.

The *Arcadia Lodge* (☎ 403 7756) is on Florance Ave, about a 10-minute walk from the wharf. It's a splendid place up on a hill, with a magnificent view over Matauwhi Bay and several decks to enjoy it from. Each unit has its own kitchen; toilets and showers are shared. A bed in a four or three-bed room is $14, singles are $25 and doubles and twins are $32 and $36. The owners, Bill and Linley, go out of their way to make sure this 1890s Tudor-style house is a 'home away from home'.

Centrally located on the corner of Beresford and Chapel Sts, *Russell Lodge* (☎ 403 7640) has budget units, each with four bunks and private toilet, at $12.50 per person most of the year, $15 during the summer rush, or you can get the whole unit for $35. There is a large, fully-equipped kitchen, a pool table and a TV lounge. The motel units, sleeping four to six people, start from $60. There's an extensive outdoor recreation area with a swimming pool.

Hotels & Motels The fine old *Duke of Marlborough Hotel* (☎ 403 7829), right on the waterfront, would certainly be the place to stay if money was no object. This is a place with some real old-fashioned charm. It has 'budget' rooms from $68 and better rooms with waterfront views for $80/120 in the high season. All rooms have private facilities, tea/coffee and a colour TV.

The *Duke's Lodge* (☎ 403 7899) is a stylish, old building right on the waterfront. Well-equipped units with kitchens sleeping up to six people cost $135 in summer or smaller units without kitchen are $110. There is a swimming pool in the central courtyard and rates are halved in the off season.

Similar, though more modern, is the *Hananui Lodge* (☎ 403 7875), which backs on to the waterfront. Self-contained motel units cost from $70 up to $150 in the peak season. Russell also a range of other motels. Two of the more moderately priced are *Motel Russell* (☎ 403 7854) with doubles for $100 ($80 in the off-season) and *Mako Motel* (☎ 403 7770), which charges $120 a double ($65 in the off-season).

Places to Eat
There are several cafes and takeaways in Russell, including the waterfront *Strand* with sandwiches, snacks, a courtyard at the back and a verandah in front. They serve great lunches and a good-value soup of the day. In the Traders Mall, *Penny's Place* is a licensed cafe and takeaway with everything ranging from Chinese food and pizzas to haute cuisine.

The *Duke of Marlborough Tavern* has typical pub food in its family section, with main dishes around $10. More refined dining can be had in the restaurant at the Duke of Marlborough Hotel on the waterfront, or the lounge bar and tables out front are a great place for a meal or drink on a sunny day. Also on the waterfront are the more upmarket *Quarter Deck Restaurant* and the licensed *The Gables*, with main courses for around $20. Both of these places are well recommended, and The Gables has a particularly interesting menu and excellent food.

Entertainment
The *Duke of Marlborough Tavern* was the first pub in New Zealand to get a licence, back on 14 July 1840. Its three predecessors all burnt down. The tavern, in the block behind the hotel, has both a family room and a more serious, perhaps 'rougher', bar. If you want cheaper beer then get one of the RSA members to sign you in to their very friendly club.

Getting There & Away
Basically your choices are to come on the passenger ferry from Paihia (see that section for details), to drive or hitch in via the Opua car ferry, or take the Northliner bus.

Fullers run a continuous shuttle service during the day from Opua to Okiato Point, still some distance from Russell. This ferry operates from 6.50 am to 9 pm (10 pm on Friday). The one-way fare is $7 for a car and driver, $12 for a campervan and driver, $3.50 for a motorcycle and rider, plus $1 for each additional adult passenger. InterCity go to Paihia, from where you catch the ferry. There's a much longer dirt road which avoids the Opua ferry, but it's a long haul to Russell via this route.

OPUA
As well as being the car ferry terminus, Opua is a deep-sea port from which primary produce (meat, wool and butter) is exported. The town was established as a coaling port in the 1870s when the railway line was constructed. Before the wharf was built, after WWI, the coal was transported out to ships on lighters (flat-bottomed barges). Today, the occasional cruise ship may be seen alongside the wharf, as well as many local and foreign yachts during the summer.

The Opua Forest, for the most part a regenerating forest, is open to the public. There are lookouts up graded tracks from the access roads and a few large trees have escaped axe and fire, including some fairly big kauris. You can enter the forest by walking in from Paihia on School Rd (see Paihia), driving in from Opua on the Oromahoe Rd, or a couple of other access roads. Get a leaflet from the visitor information centres in Paihia, Russell or Kerikeri.

Vintage Railway
There's a historic steam train service that operates from Opua to Kawakawa, running from Saturday to Tuesday in winter and every day except Friday in summer. The trip takes 45 minutes each way and a one-way/return costs $10/16 (children $6/10).

Places to Eat
At Opua there's the *Ferryman's Restaurant & Bistro* by the car ferry dock. The restaurant section is expensive but the bistro is a great place to sit out by the waterside and enjoy a light meal, sandwich or burger.

KERIKERI
At the northern end of the bay, Kerikeri is a laid-back provincial town. It has plenty of accommodation and can be used as a base for exploring the Bay of Islands, but is primarily a service town for the surrounding agricultural district.

The word *kerikeri* means 'to dig' and it

was right here, in 1820, that the first agricultural plough was introduced to New Zealand, and here that the Maori grew large crops of kumaras (sweet potatoes) before the Pakeha arrived. Today it is still primarily an agricultural region, with kiwi fruit, citrus and other orchards. Large numbers of itinerant farmworkers congregate in Kerikeri for the six-week kiwi fruit harvest beginning the first week in May, but orchard work of one kind or another is usually available all year round except perhaps during February. It is also a centre for a wide variety of arts & crafts.

Kerikeri is significant in NZ history. It became the site of the country's second mission station when the Reverend Samuel Marsden chose the site at the head of the Kerikeri inlet under the protection of the Maori chief, Hongi Hika. In November 1819 the Reverend John Butler arrived at the site and set up the mission headquarters. New Zealand's oldest wooden building, Kemp House, and its oldest stone building, the Stone Store, were part of the mission station and are still in superb condition.

PLACES TO STAY

- 8 Kerikeri YHA Hostel
- 9 Abiline Motel
- 12 Homestead Lodge & Restaurant
- 14 Aranga Holiday Park
- 17 Cottle Court Motel
- 18 Pagoda Lodge Caravan Park
- 19 Hone Heke Lodge
- 21 Hideaway Lodge, Adventure Park
- 22 Puriri Park

PLACES TO EAT

- 1 Adam & Eve's Restaurant
- 7 Stone Store Tearooms & Restaurant

OTHER

- 2 Rainbow Falls
- 3 Scenic Reserve & Carpark
- 4 Kemp House
- 5 Rewa's Maori Village & Visitors' Centre
- 6 Kororipo Pa
- 10 Price Choppers
- 11 New World Supermarket
- 13 Information Centre
- 15 Post Office, Bus Station
- 16 Public Toilets
- 20 The Orange Centre

Information

There is a small information centre on the main street, or the visitors centre at Rewa's Maori Village has pamphlets. Information on walking tracks and huts is available from DOC Kerikeri (☎ 407 8474).

Stone Store

The Stone Store is the oldest stone building in New Zealand; construction began in 1833 and was completed in 1836. The river in front of the Stone Store is subject to flooding, and floods and time have taken their toll on the building. Long-standing renovations are still in progress, and the building is closed until they are completed.

Kemp House

Near the Stone Store is Kemp House – New Zealand's oldest surviving building, a remarkable fact given that it is constructed of wood. It was erected in 1821 by John Butler, who was the first head of the Church Missionary Society's new station. It is still complete with original fittings and chattels. It's open daily from 10 am to 4.30 pm; admission is $5 (students and children $2). Get a copy of the informative pamphlet *Kemp House*.

Rewa's Maori Village & Visitors Centre

Just across the river from the Stone Store, Rewa's Maori Village is built on a site thought to have been occupied at one time by Chief Rewa. The various buildings are an authentic reproduction of a *kainga*, a pre-European unfortified Maori village, with various habitations, kitchen buildings, storerooms and so on, and exhibits of the many plants the Maoris used. It's open every day, admission is $2 (children 50c) and there are fine views across the inlet.

Waimate Mission House

This is New Zealand's second oldest surviving house. Built of kauri between 1831 and 1832, it was the Anglican Waimate Mission

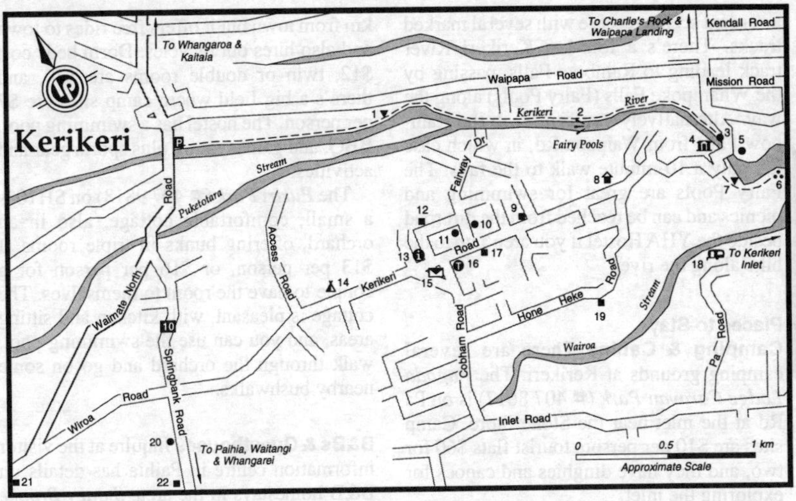

from 1832 to 1841 and the home of New Zealand's first Anglican bishop, Bishop Selwyn, from 1842 to 1844. It can be reached from SH1 between Ohaeawai and Okaihau by turning off at Te Ahuahu. It can also be reached from SH10 by turning off at Puketona. It is open daily, except Thursday and Friday, from 10 am to 4.30 pm. Adjacent to the building are the Church of St John the Baptist (1871) and a Sunday school building dating from the 1880s. An admission fee is charged.

Arts & Crafts Shops

The Kerikeri area is home to many artists and artisans. Several shops display their work, and in most you can see work in progress, especially pottery. On Kerikeri Rd at the northern end of town is Red Barn Pottery; at the south side, also on Kerikeri Rd is The Studio and the Kauri Workshop. North of Kerikeri, Earthlight Pottery on Waipapa Rd, Lilly's Pots near the junction of SH10 and Waipapa Rd, and Northland Woodcraft Workshop at Waipapa Landing have crafts on display. On SH10 there are several good shops including the Origin Art & Craft Cooperative with many kinds of crafts, Blue Gum Pottery and the Potting Shed with pottery and weaving.

Other Attractions

The Orange Centre (☎ 407 9397) by the Kerikeri crossroads on SH10 has guided tours of the orange, kiwi fruit and other orchards in the 'orange-mobile' for $8. It also sells expensive orange juice.

For children the Adventure Park on Wiroa Rd has 2½ hectares of amusements for the kids, including mini golf, a flying fox and pony rides. It's open daily from 10 am to 5 pm (summer only).

The Aero Club at Kerikeri Airport has scenic flights and charters.

Walks

Just up the hill behind the Stone Store Tearooms is a marked Historical Walk which takes about 10 minutes and leads to **Kororipo Pa**, the fortress of Maori chief Hongi Hika, from which huge warfaring parties of Maoris once departed on raids, terrorising most of the North Island. The walk emerges near the St James Anglican church, built in 1878.

Across the bridge from the Stone Store is

a verdant scenic reserve with several marked tracks. There's a four-km Kerikeri River track leading to Rainbow Falls, passing by the Wharepoke Falls (Fairy Pools) along the way. Alternatively you can reach the Rainbow Falls from Waipapa Rd, in which case it's only a 10-minute walk to the falls. The Fairy Pools are great for swimming and picnics and can be reached from the dirt road beside the YHA Hostel if you aren't up to the hike along the river.

Places to Stay

Camping & Cabins There are several camping grounds at Kerikeri. The *Pagoda Lodge Caravan Park* (☎ 407 8617) is on Pa Rd at the inlet near the Stone Store. Camp sites are $10 per person, tourist flats $60 for two, and they have dinghies and canoes for exploring the inlet.

The *Aranga Holiday Park* (☎ 407 9326) is on Kerikeri Rd in a lovely setting beside the Puketotara River, only five minutes walk from town. Tent sites are $8 per person, powered sites $9, and cabins are $30 for two people. A tourist flat with private facilities is $52 for two. The *Hideaway Lodge* (☎ 407 9773) on Wiroa Rd has camp sites (see also Hostels).

Hostels Kerikeri's hostels attract both tourists and itinerant agricultural workers, catered for in large dormitories. Some of the lodges can help travellers to find orchard work.

The *Kerikeri YHA Hostel* (☎ 407 9391) is on the main road (Kerikeri Rd). The nightly cost is $13 or $32 a double and various trips are organised from the hostel, including full-day Bay of Islands sailing trips, kayaking and horse riding. The lounge room is spacious and decorated with murals.

The *Hone Heke Lodge* (☎ 407 8170) is on Hone Heke Rd in a quiet residential area about 10 minutes walk from the town centre. The cost per person is $13 in bunkrooms, $32 for twin or double rooms.

The *Hideaway Lodge* (☎ 407 9773) is on a 3½-hectare orchard on Wiroa Rd, west of and out beyond the SH10 junction. It's four km from town but it offers free rides to town and also hires out bicycles. Dorm beds cost $12, twin or double rooms are $30, and there's a big field where camp sites are $7 per person. The hostel has a swimming pool, BBQ, and games room, plus sports gear and activities.

The *Puriri Park* (☎ 407 9818) on SH10 is a small, comfortable cottage, also in an orchard, offering bunks in triple rooms at $13 per person, or $16 per person for a couple to have the room to themselves. The cottage is pleasant, with kitchen and sitting areas, and you can use the swimming pool, walk through the orchard and go on some nearby bushwalks.

B&Bs & Guesthouses Inquire at the visitor information centre in Paihia has details on B&B homestays in the area. *Stoney Brooke* (☎ 407 7371 on Edmonds Rd, 12 km east of Kerikeri, is near the Kerikeri inlet and has singles/doubles for $35/60. In town, *The Pines* (☎ 407 6150), next to the Abilene Motel at 132 Kerikeri Rd, costs $40/67.50 and it arranges fishing and sailing trips.

Motels Several motels are found along Kerikeri Rd. Near the youth hostel, *Kemp Lodge* (☎ 407 8295) is small, with a swimming pool and three chalets costing $80/90 for singles/doubles; off-season rates will be lower. Next door the *Abilene Motel* (☎ 407 9203) has a swimming pool and 10 units, two with private spa pools, from $72/75.

The *Central Motel* (☎ 407 8921) has 14 units with features like a waterbed suite, swimming and spa pools, colour TVs and so on. Summer rates start at $70, dropping to $65/70 in winter. There are plenty of other motels. The *Cottle Court Motel* (☎ 407 8867) is also priced from $65/70.

Places to Eat

Kerikeri has several fast food places and cafes. On the main road the *Calypso* has good fish & chips and other takeaways. Cafes include *Scandals Cafe*, with sandwiches, light meals and cakes, and *Food Affair*.

Across from the Stone Store the *Stone Store Tearooms & Restaurant* is open daily from 9 am to 9 pm. It's a lovely spot to eat indoors or out on the verandah overlooking the lawn and the boats moored in the inlet. It has a great selection of mains and desserts in the evening.

More expensive places include *Adam & Eve's Restaurant* (licensed) five minutes out of town on Waipapa Rd and the *Homestead Lodge & Restaurant* behind the main shopping area on Homestead Rd.

Getting There & Away

InterCity and Northliner buses come and go from Travel Lee's (☎ 407 8013) on Cobham Rd, just off Kerikeri Rd in the town centre. See the Getting There & Away section in the Bay of Islands chapter for more details on long-distance buses.

Both companies have buses departing from Kerikeri in the morning for the half-hour trip to Paihia, returning in the afternoon or evening.

Bay of Islands to Whangarei

This description assumes that you are heading back in the direction of Auckland from the Bay of Islands to complete the loop around Northland.

In particular, there are two very scenic drives out on the east coast: the back road from Russell to SH1, and the drive out to Tutukaka from Hikurangi on SH1, which loops around to Whangarei. Out to sea are the Poor Knights islands.

Heading straight back via SH1, the limestone **Kawiti Caves**, one km from the highway at Waiomio just south of Kawakawa, are privately owned glow worm caves. You'll see plenty of the illuminating wrigglers, but at $10 entry (including a corny, half-hour guided tour), skip it and wait until you get to Waitomo.

Russell Rd

The back road from Russell skirts around the coast before joining SH1 at Whakapara. The road is long, unsealed and rough for the most of the way but very scenic. It is only for those with their own transport, plenty of time and a desire to get off the beaten track.

From Russell, the road starts near Orongo Bay and skirts along the Waikare Inlet before reaching the Waikare Rd to Waihaha. This turn-off eventually leads back to the highway and Paihia, about a 1½-hour drive all up from Russell.

Continuing along the Russell Rd past the Waihaha turn-off, there's access to the **Ngaiotonga Scenic Reserve** which preserves the mixed forest that once predominated throughout Northland. There are two short walks, suitable for families. The 20-minute **Kauri Grove Nature Walk** and the 10-minute **Twin Bole Kauri Walk** both provide good opportunities to see fine specimens of these majestic trees. There's a longer walk passing through the Ngaiotonga reserve before heading into the Russell Forest.

Another side trip from the Russell Rd is to take the northern Manawaora Rd, which passes many small bays, including **Parekura Bay** where the *Carpe Diem B&B* has accommodation and boat rental.

Further on is the turn-off to isolated **Rawhiti**, a small Maori settlement where life still revolves around the marae. Past the marae on the headland is the *Rawhiti Motor Camp*, which has a small shop, camp sites, some on-site vans and stunning views of the Bay of Islands. Boat hire and dive refills are available.

Rawhiti is also the starting point for the trek to **Cape Brett**, a hard 7½-hour walk to the top of the peninsula where overnight stays are possible in the Cape Brett Hut. Book the hut, and obtain information on the walk before heading off, through the Bay of Islands Maritime Park Visitor Centre (☎ 403 7685) in Russell.

Closer to the Rawhiti turn-off, a shorter one-hour walk leads through Maori land and over the headland to Whangamumu

NORTHLAND

Harbour. At the main beach on the harbour, the **Whangamumu Scenic Reserve** has a 'back to nature' camping ground. There are over 40 prehistoric sites on the peninsula and the remains of an unusual whaling station. A net, fastened between the mainland and Net Rock, was used to ensnare or slow down whales so the harpooners could get an easy shot in. The whales taken were mainly humpbacks and in 1927 over 70 whales were trapped in this fashion.

Further south, another side road leads to the **Whangaruru North Head Scenic Reserve**, which has beaches, camping grounds, walks and fine coastal scenery in a farmland park setting. Pohutukawa, puriri and kowhai abound and many bird species can be seen in the area. The small settlement of Whangaruru North, just before the reserve, also has a motor camp, as does Oakura on the other side of the harbour.

At Helena Bay, Russell Rd returns to tarseal and leads back to SH1. About eight km from Helena Bay along a rough, winding side road is the **Mimiwhangata Coastal Park**. This is a truly scenic part of the coastline, with coastal dunes, pohutukawa, jutting headlands and picturesque beaches. Birdwatchers might glimpse the rare brown teal here. DOC has a luxurious lodge sleeping 10 that costs $550 per week ($450 in winter) and a simpler but comfortable cottage for eight people at $350 per week ($250 in winter). Camping is also possible. Book at the DOC offices in Whangarei or Russell.

Tutukaka Coast

At Hikurangi on SH1 you can turn off and take a very scenic route to Whangarei. When driving from Hikurangi the first place you come to on the coast is Sandy Bay surf beach, where you can go horse riding on a little-frequented piece of the east coast. There is a succession of idyllic bays from here on – Woolley's, Whale (with some excellent walks), Matapouri, Church, Kowharewa, Pacific, Dolphin and Whangaumu (Wellingtons). All have scope for walking, boating, swimming and, perhaps most popularly, fishing.

Small, exclusive **Tutukaka** is the home of the Whangarei Deep Sea Anglers Club and the beautiful harbour is cluttered with yachts and fishing boats. The tiny yacht club here launched its own multi-million dollar challenge for the 1995 America's Cup, eventually won by Auckland-based *Black Magic*. Tutukaka is best known as a premier gamefishing destination, and late in the day marlin and other catch are weighed in. The well-organised Tutukaka Charter Boat Association (☎ 434 3818) at the marina handles fishing, diving and cruise charters.

The large town of the area is Ngunguru, a few km south of Tutukaka. Here you'll find all the facilities you need, such as food outlets, accommodation, petrol and laundrette, plus a sports complex.

Places to Stay & Eat At Sandy Bay, *Whananaki Trail Rides* (☎ 433 8299), has backpackers farmhouse accommodation for $15 and camping is free. The bonus is that you can horse trek ($30 for two hours, a two-day trek is $90), or they have surfboards and can arrange kayak trips ($65) through Ocean Kayak Adventures (☎ 025 775 117).

Tutukaka has accommodation at the *Tutukaka Hotel* (☎ 434 3854) for $60 a double. *Pacific Rendezvous* (☎ 434 3847) is an exclusive resort on its own headland just south of Tutukaka. One to three-bedroom, self-contained chalets are $110 to $150 in summer ($85 to $125 in winter). If you love seafood, Tutukaka is paradise. The places to go for a meal are the *Tutukaka Hotel*, *Snapper Rock Cafe* and the *Whangarei Deep Sea Anglers Club*.

At Ngunguru, *Coastal Backpackers* (☎ 434 3419), Waitoti Rd, is about one km from the beach in a quiet farm setting. All accommodation is $12 per person. Motels include the *Chalet Court Motel* (☎ 434 3786) at $60 a double. The best dining is at *Shelley's Licensed Restaurant*.

Poor Knights Islands Marine Reserve

The Poor Knights Islands Marine Reserve, 24 km off Northland's east coast near Tutukaka, was established in 1981. The reserve is reputed to have the best scuba diving in all New Zealand and has been rated by many as one of the top diving spots in the world.

The two large islands, Tawhiti Rangi and Aorangi, were once home to members of the Ngati-wai tribe, but since a massacre in the early 1800s by a raiding party, the islands have been tapu. You are *not* allowed to land on the islands – but you can swim around them.

Since the northern islands are bathed in a subtropical current, varieties of tropical and subtropical fish not seen in other coastal waters are observed by divers. The waters are clear and there are none of the problems with sediment that there are on the mainland. The underwater cliffs drop steeply, about 70 metres, to a sandy bottom, where there is a labyrinth of archways, caves and tunnels, packed with a bewildering variety of fish.

As the islands are relatively isolated from the mainland they have acted as a sanctuary for flora & fauna, the most famous example of which is the prehistoric reptile, the tuatara.

Diving trips depart from Tutukaka, Whangarei and elsewhere. Boat hire costs around $65 a day, and count on another $65 for full diving equipment for two dives. Operators in Tutukaka are Tutukaka Charter Boat Association (☎ 434 3818), Pacific Hideaway (☎ 434 3675) and Aqua Action Adventures (☎ 434 3867). In Whangarei contact The Dive Shop (☎ 438 3521) on Water St, The Dive Connection (☎ 430 0818) at 140 Lower Cameron St and Sub Aqua Dive (☎ 438 1075) on Clyde St.

Whangarei

Whangarei (population 40,000) is the major city of Northland and a haven for yachts. Whangarei is a pleasant, thriving city with an equable climate, though its main attractions are in the surrounding area. The beaches at Whangarei Heads about 35 km east of town are incredibly scenic, with many tiny bays and inlets, and the Tutukaka and Bream Bay Coasts can be done as day trips from Whangarei.

The climate and soil combine to make this city a gardener's paradise, reflected in the many parks and gardens which thrive in this city.

Information

The Whangarei Visitor Information Centre (☎ 438 1079) is at Tarewa Park, Otaika Rd, on SH1 at the southern entrance to town. It's open every day from 8.30 am to 5 pm and the staff are very helpful and friendly, providing good maps and suggestions on things to do in the area. There is a cafe which overlooks a very 'kid-friendly' park, with toy train rides on the weekend. The AA office, on the corner of Robert and John Sts, has good maps of town and of the surrounding region.

The DOC office (☎ 438 0299) at 149-151 Bank St has information on camping, recreational activities, maps and hut tickets, as well as an environmental shop with posters, publications, T-shirts and souvenirs.

Things to See

Boats from around the world are moored in **Town Basin**, an attractive area right on the edge of the town centre along Quay St. The waterfront along the river has been renovated and the redevelopment includes the **Clapham Clock Museum**, which has an awesome 1300 timepieces, all ticking away furiously. Don't worry, clepsydra, skeleton, speaker's, 'nark', chess, gravity, tower, coconut, balloon, grandfather, 400-day and hickery dickery dock are all types of clock. The museum is open from 10 am to 4 pm every day; admission is $3.50 (children $1.20) including a guided tour.

Also at the Town Basin is the **Museum of Fisheries**, open 10 am to 4 pm, entry $3.50 (children $1.50). Fishing enthusiasts will appreciate the stuffed game fish; otherwise forget it. At the end of Quay St, 100 metres away, **Reyburn House** is a historic homestead dating from 1845 and now houses an art gallery.

Spanning a stream in the centre of town, **Cafler Park** has well-tended flowerbeds, a conservatory and fernery. The Margie Maddren Fernery & Snow Conservatory is New Zealand's only all-native fernery with over 80 varieties on display. Both are open daily from 10 am to 4 pm; admission is free.

The Northland Craft Trust, known simply as **The Quarry**, is about 500 metres west of the town centre in an old converted quarry. This artists' cooperative has studios where you can observe work in progress or buy crafts at the showroom. It is open daily from 10 am to 4 pm.

Six km west of Whangarei, on the Dargaville road at Maunu, is the **Whangarei Museum**, open from 10 am to 4 pm daily. The museum is set in a large park which includes a kiwi house, the 1885 Clarke Homestead and the Exhibition Centre museum, which houses European relics and an impressive collection of Maori artefacts (the feather cloaks in particular are superb). The park also includes an old locomotive which runs in summer, an abandoned mercury mine and more. Admission is $7 (children $3.50), less for only one or two attractions. The museum has popular 'live days', when children's rides operate, bands play and the park has a carnival atmosphere.

Scenic Reserves & Walks The **Whangarei Falls** are very photogenic, with water cascading over the edge of an old basalt lava flow. Next to the Ngunguru Rd, in the suburb of Tikipunga, five km north of the town centre, the falls can be reached by Tikipunga bus (weekdays only). The surrounding domain has three natural swimming pools in the river, and numerous picnic spots.

The **AH Reed Memorial Kauri Park** spans a pretty stream and has a waterfall, several easy walkways and over 50 kinds of native trees including punga, totara and a few large kauris (some up to three metres in diameter). It's about five km from the town centre, going out Whareora Rd.

There are two scenic reserves handy to the centre of town, on the hills on either side of the valley. **Coronation Scenic Reserve**, on the west, has a lookout, an old pa site, Maori pits and an old gold mine, as well as lots of bush. It is accessible from Kauika Rd.

On the eastern side is the **Parahaki Scenic Reserve**. There is a road to the summit of Parahaki, turning off Riverside Drive (the road towards Onerahi and the airport). Three tracks lead down from the summit, two finishing at Mair Park and one at Dundas Rd.

The Onerahi Mangrove Walk in Onerahi is an easy, level walk along an old (1880) railway embankment, lasting two hours and passing through mangrove swamps and over a harbour bridge. There's a shorter, 10-minute mangrove walk over boardwalks in the centre of town, just behind the Olympic swimming pool.

Ten minutes up from Dundas Rd are some falls, with lots of glow-worms on the cliffs nearby, making a good 20-minute evening walk. *Whangarei Walks* is a useful pamphlet for these and other walks.

Activities

The Whangarei Visitor Centre produces an excellent leaflet on dozens of activities and operators in the region.

Whangarei is a popular centre for diving and fishing, mostly organised out of Tutukaka. The Whangarei Tramping Club (☎ 436 1441) welcomes visitors. Northland Districts Aero Club (☎ 436 0890) has scenic flights or Whangarei City Riding Centre (☎ 437 5710) has horse treks.

You can go caving right in Whangarei city at Abbey Caves. Hatea House Hostel (☎ 437 6174) runs 1½-hour tours for only $10, longer three-hour adventure tours for $18.

In addition to the Ted Eliott Memorial Pool Complex with its Olympic-size indoor and outdoor pools, saunas and spas, Whangarei has an impressive array of sporting facilities.

Places to Stay

Camping & Cabins The *Alpha Caravan Park* (☎ 438 9867) at 34 Tarewa Rd is the most centrally located camping ground, less than a km from the town centre. Camping is $7 per person, $9 with power, cabins are $35 to $38 for two, and self-contained units are $50 for two. The *William Jones Park* (☎ 437 6856) on Mair St, 2.5 km from the town

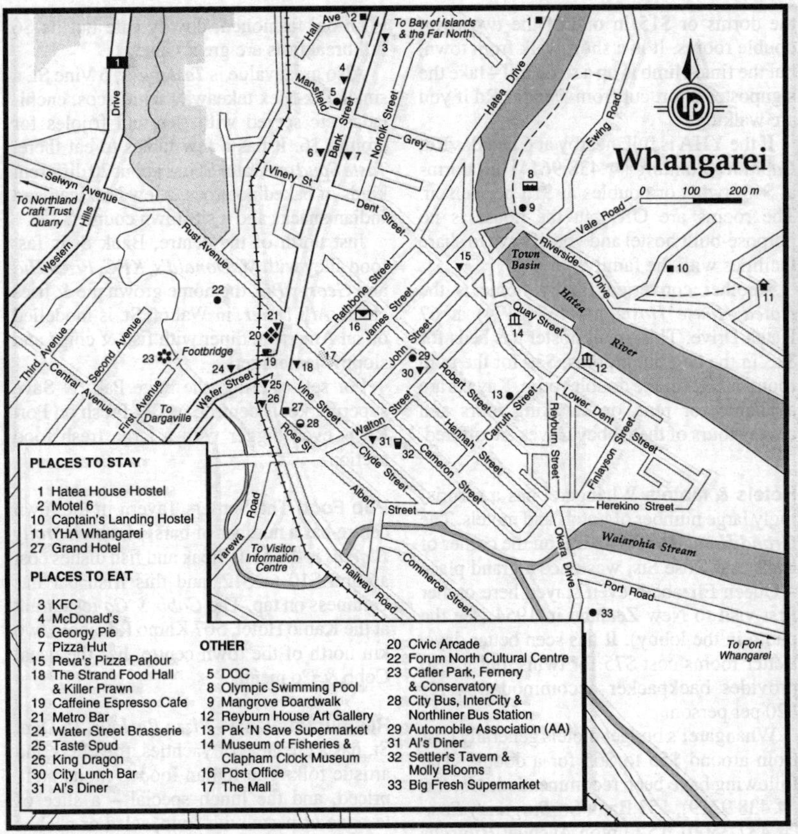

centre by Mair Park, has tent or powered sites at $6.50 per person, cabins at $15/25.

The *Otaika Motel Caravan Park* (☎ 438 1459), 136 Otaika Rd, is situated at the southern entrance to Whangarei, with tent and powered sites at $7.50 per person, well-equipped tourist flats at $33/40 for one/two people and motel units at $48/60.

The *Whangarei Falls Motor Camp* (☎ 437 0609) near the falls, five km from the town centre, is a good place with swimming and spa pools and cheap backpacker accommodation. There are tent and caravan sites at $7.50 per person, a hostel-style bunkroom at $13, doubles/twins for $32, and cabins at $48 a double.

Other camping and caravan sites include *Kamo Springs Caravan Park* (☎ 435 1208) at 55 Great North Rd, Kamo; the *Blue Heron Holiday Park* (☎ 436 2293), on Tamaterau Beach; and *Tropicana Holiday Park* (☎ 436 0687) on Whangarei Heads Rd by the beach, 10 km from Whangarei.

Hostels The *YHA Whangarei* (☎ 438 8954), 52 Punga Grove Ave, is a small, easy-going hostel with fine views across the city and good travel information. A bed costs $13 in the dorms or $15 in one of the two twin/double rooms. It is a short walk from town, but the final climb is up a steep hill – take the signposted short cut from Dundas Rd if you are walking.

If the YHA is full, nearby at 6 Dundas Rd, *Captain's Landing* (☎ 438 9614) has dorms at $13, twins or doubles at $15 per person. The rooms are OK, but the house is no purpose-built hostel and you'll have to share facilities with the family.

Another converted family home is the *Hatea House Hostel* (☎ 437 6174) at 67 Hatea Drive. This small hostel has beds for $13 in the two bunkrooms, $30 for the twin room or $32 for the double room. Kayaks are available for rent, or kayaking tours and caving tours of the Abbey Caves are offered.

Hotels & Motels Whangarei has a surprisingly large number of hotels and motels. The *Grand Hotel* (☎ 438 4279), on the corner of Bank and Rose Sts, was once a grand place – Queen Elizabeth even stayed here on her first visit to New Zealand in 1954 (see the photo in the lobby). It has seen better days. Better rooms cost $75 for twins, but it also provides backpacker accommodation for $20 per person.

Whangarei's budget motels generally cost from around $55 to $65 for a double. The following have been recommended: *Motel 6* (☎ 438 9219), 153 Bank St; *Burgundy Rose* (☎ 437 3500), 15 Lupton Avenue; *Hibiscus Motel* (☎ 437 6312), 2 Deveron St; *Redwood Lodge Motel* (☎ 437 6861), Hatea Drive & Drummond St; *San Jose* (☎ 438 5669), 10 Cross St; *Regency* (☎ 438 3005), 11 Cross St; and the *Continental Motel* (☎ 437 6359), 67 Kamo Rd.

Places to Eat

Cafes & Fast Food During the day, *The Strand Food Hall* has fish & chips, *McDonald's* and, upstairs, the classier *Robert Harris* coffee house has balcony tables. Another trendy coffee house is the very popular *Caffeine Espresso Cafe*, 4 Water St. The *City Lunch Bar*, 67 Walton St, is an old-fashioned, dowdy cafe but its $6 full breakfasts are great value.

Also great value is *Tastebuds*, 6 Vine St, a small Tex-Mex takeaway with tacos, enchiladas etc served with rice and frijoles for around $6. It has a few tables to eat there. *Taste Spud* on Water St has about 20 different kinds of baked potatoes, a few Mexican and Indian snacks and a sit-down counter.

Just north of the centre, Bank St is fast food alley with *McDonald's*, *KFC*, *Pizza Hut* and *Georgy Pie*, the home grown pie & fries chain. *Al's Diner*, in Walton St, is modelled on an American diner with fish & chips and sloppy hamburgers.

For self-catering, the huge Pak 'N Save supermarket is central, or Big Fresh on Port Rd is even bigger with a large fresh food section.

Pub Food The Settlers Tavern in the town centre has a number of bars, of which *Molly Blooms* is the best. Steak and fish dishes cost around $10 to $12, and this Irish bar has Guinness on tap. The *Cobb & Co* restaurant at the Kamo Hotel, 567 Kamo Rd, about two km north of the town centre, has the usual Cobb & Co menu.

Restaurants *Reva's Pizza Parlour*, 15 Dent St, has a clientele of yachties, travellers and artistic folk. The Italian food is moderately priced, and the lunch special – a slice of lasagne or pizza with soup, salad or nachos – is hard to beat at $4.95.

The *King Dragon Chinese*, 11-13 Bank St, is good for Cantonese banquets and does lunchtime buffets on weekdays.

The *Metro Bar*, on Bank St opposite The Stand, is a trendy bar/restaurant. *Killer Prawn!*, 26-28 Bank St next to The Strand, is currently the place to be seen. This bar/restaurant serves up mostly seafood at around $20 for a main course. In a similar price range, *Water Street Brasserie*, 24 Water St, has a typical lamb/fish/venison/steak menu and a long-running reputation as one of Whangarei's best restaurants. *Le Grand Monet* in the Grand Hotel on Bank St is another of Whangarei's top restaurants.

An *Eating Out* guide is available from the visitor information centre for a comprehensive rundown on Whangarei's many restaurants.

Entertainment

Molly Blooms is always popular and features Irish bands. The *Grand Hotel* also has bands on the weekends. The *Metro Bar* has jazz, blues and acoustic performers on Friday and Saturday nights, and *Reva's* is another restaurant with live music from Wednesday to Friday.

Some of the best venues are out of town. The *Tutukaka Hotel* on the north-east coast and the *Parua Bay Hotel*, south-east at Whangarei Heads, are popular on weekends. Closer in, the suburban *Tikipunga Tavern* on Denby Crescent has entertainment.

Getting There & Away

Air Eagle Air, flying under the Air New Zealand umbrella, and Ansett have flights daily between Auckland and Whangarei, with connections to other centres. Great Barrier Airlines, the small provincial airline servicing Great Barrier Island, flies twice a week to/from the island.

The Whangarei Airport Shuttle (☎ 437 0666) has a door-to-door airport bus service for $6.

Bus The InterCity bus depot (☎ 438 2653) is on Rose St. InterCity has frequent buses between Auckland and Whangarei (three hours), continuing north to Paihia (1½ hours) in the Bay of Islands, Hokianga Harbour and Kaitaia, with another route to Dargaville (one hour).

Northliner has a daily bus service Auckland-Whangarei-Bay of Islands, with a route to Kerikeri via Paihia or directly to Russell on the Opua ferry. The bus operates from the Northliner Terminal (☎ 438 3206) in Rose St.

Hitching Being the only big town between Auckland and the Bay of Islands, and the principal town of the region, Whangarei is a very busy spot for hitchhikers going north and south.

Heading north, the best hitching spot is on SH1 just after the Three Mile Bush Rd intersection, in the Kamo suburb about five km north of the town centre. Any Kamo bus from the town centre will drop you there. Heading south, the best hitching spot is on SH1 opposite Tarewa Park or, second best, about 500 metres further south, by the New World supermarket.

Getting Around

Whangarei Bus Services (☎ 438 3104) operates a limited local bus service. On Saturday the problem is particularly acute and there are no buses at all on Sunday. The Onerahi bus route serves the airport on this same schedule. Rental cars are available from Avis (☎ 438 2929), Budget (☎ 438 7292) and Renta-Cheapy (☎ 438 7373).

AROUND WHANGAREI

Whangarei Heads

From Whangarei, Heads Rd winds its way around the northern shore of Whangarei Harbour, passing picturesque coves and bays on its way to the heads at the harbour entrance. This drive (there is no bus) has magnificent scenery and passes small settlements such as Parua Bay, McLeod Bay and McKenzie Bay. There are great views from the top of 419-metre Mt Manaia, a sheer rock outcrop above McLeod Bay, but it is a hard, steep climb and requires a fair degree of agility and a reasonable head for heights.

Urquarts Bay near the heads has good views (blighted by the oil refinery on the other side) and from adjoining Woolshed Bay it is a 30-minute walk over the headland to the delightful beach at Smugglers Cove.

Keep going past the heads to Ocean Beach, a great surf beach, probably the Whangarei area's best beach.

You can also make a detour from Parua Bay to beautiful Pataua, a sleepy fishing settlement that lies on a shallow inlet. A long footbridge leads to the small offshore island, which has a good surf beach on the other side.

An alternative return route is to go via the

Waikaraka Scenic Reserve on Mt Tiger, with excellent views (turn-off at Parua Bay).

Marsden Point

New Zealand's oil refinery is at Marsden Point, across the harbour from Whangarei Heads. It has an information centre (☎ 432 8194) you can visit to learn about oil refining; there is a 130-sq-metre scale model of the refinery, accurate down to the last valve and pump. The centre is open daily from 10 am to 4 pm; admission is free.

New Zealand Fudge Farm

At Tangiteroria, between Whangarei and Dargaville on SH14, is the home of 'creamy farm-fresh fudge'. Fudgeaholics can satisfy their addiction from 10.30 am to 4 pm, Monday, Wednesday, Thursday and Sunday.

Waikato & the King Country

The Waikato and King Country regions lie south of Auckland. The Waikato, one of the world's richest dairy and agricultural areas, is about one hour's drive from downtown Auckland. It includes four fertile plains and Hamilton, New Zealand's fifth-largest city, is its major centre. The region also encompasses the central and lower reaches of the Waikato River, New Zealand's longest river, which starts in the central North Island, flows out from Lake Taupo and meets the sea on the west coast.

Further south is a historic region known as the King Country, extending roughly from the towns of Otorohanga in the north to Taumarunui in the south, and from western Lake Taupo to the coast.

The telephone area code throughout Waikato and the King Country is 07.

HIGHLIGHTS

- The glow-worms and caves of Waitomo
- The surf beaches of Raglan
- Exploring the coastal backwaters
- The rich agricultural lands of the Waikato, and the older, English-style settlements of Cambridge and Te Aroha

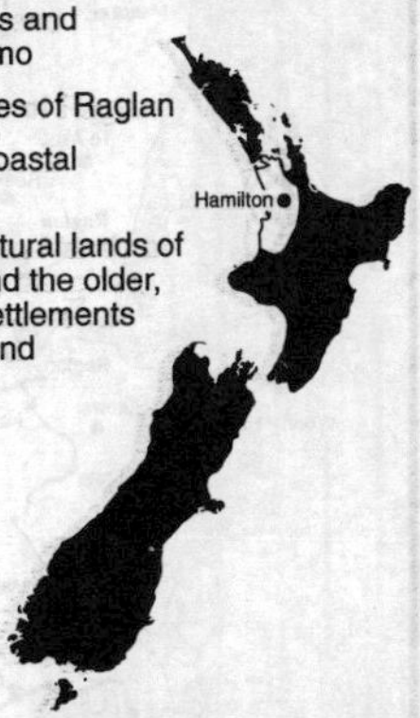

Waikato

The Waikato region was cultivated by the Maori in pre-European times, with archaeological evidence showing that thousands of hectares were under cultivation with kumaras (sweet potatoes) and other crops.

When the Europeans settled in Auckland in 1840, relations with the local Maori were peaceful at first; missionaries in the 1830s introduced European crops and farming methods to the Waikato region, and by the 1840s the Maori were trading their agricultural produce with the European settlers in Auckland.

Relations between the two cultures soured during the 1850s, largely due to the Europeans' eyeing of the Maori's land for settlement. By the early 1860s the Waikato Maori had formed a 'King Movement' and united to elect a king. The movement probably stemmed both from a need for greater organisation of the Maori tribes against the Pakeha invaders and from a desire to have a Maori leader equivalent to the British Queen when dealing with the Pakeha.

The first Maori king, Potatau Te Wherowhero, was a paramount high chief of the Waikato tribes when he was made king in 1859. He died one year later at the age of about 85 and was succeeded by his son, the second and most widely-known Maori king, Matutaera Te Wherowhero – commonly known as King Tawhiao – who ruled for the next 34 years until his death in 1894.

The King Movement was a nationalistic step on the part of the Maori, who were unwilling to sell or otherwise lose their homeland to the Europeans. The Europeans, however, were equally unwilling to take no for an answer, and in July 1863 they sent a fleet of gunboats and small craft up the Waikato River to put down what they regarded as the 'open rebellion' of the Maori King Movement. After almost a year of warfare known as the Waikato Wars, involving many historic battles, the Europeans finally won in April 1864 and the Maori retreated south to the area now known as the

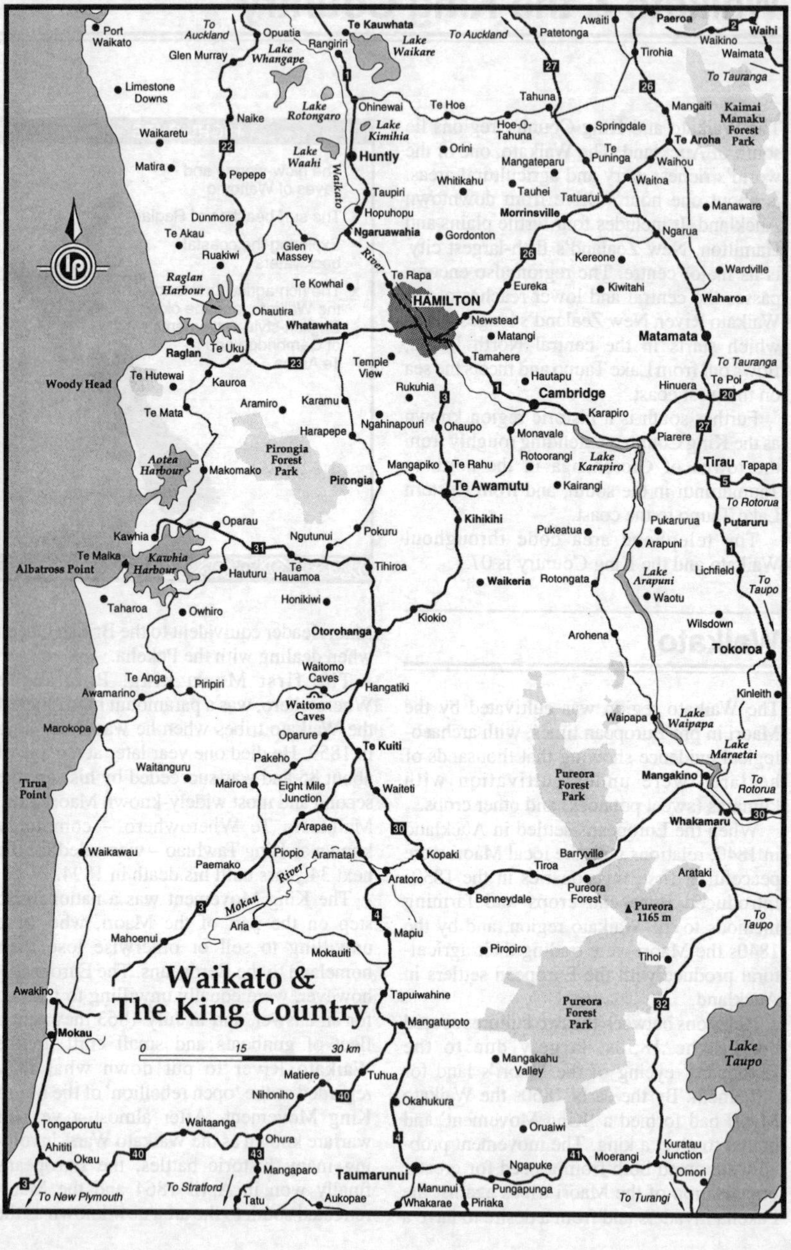
Waikato &
The King Country
0
15
30 km
Port Waikato
To Auckland
Opuatia
Te Kauwhata
Rangiriri
Lake Waikare
To Auckland
Patetonga
Awaiti
Paeroa
Waihi
Waikino
Waimata
To Tauranga
Glen Murray
Lake Whangape
Tirohia
Limestone Downs
Lake Rotongaro
Ohinewai
Te Hoe
Tahuna
Mangaiti
Kaimai Mamaku Forest Park
Naike
Lake Kimihia
Hoe-O-Tahuna
Springdale
Te Aroha
Waikaretu
Lake Waahi
Huntly
Orini
Te Puninga
Mangateparu
Waihou
Matira
Pepepe
Waikato
Taupiri
Whitikahu
Tauhei
Waitoa
Tatuarui
Manaware
Hopuhopu
Dunmore
Morrinsville
Te Akau
Ngaruawahia
Gordonton
Ngarua
Glen Massey
River
Ruakiwi
Kereone
Wardville
Raglan Harbour
Te Kowhai
Te Rapa
Eureka
Kiwitahi
HAMILTON
Waharoa
Ohautira
Newstead
Whatawhata
Matangi
Matamata
Raglan
Te Uku
Temple View
Tamahere
To Tauranga
Woody Head
Te Hutewai
Kauroa
Hautapu
Hinuera
Te Poi
Rukuhia
Cambridge
Aramiro
Karamu
Te Mata
Karapiro
Ngahinapouri
Ohaupo
Monavale
Piarere
Harapepe
Pirongia Forest Park
Rotoorangi
Lake Karapiro
Aotea Harbour
Makomako
Mangapiko
Te Rahu
Tirau
Tapapa
Pirongia
Te Awamutu
Kairangi
To Rotorua
Kihikihi
Oparau
Pukeatua
Pukarurua
Putaruru
Kawhia
Ngutunui
Pokuru
Arapuni
Te Maika
Kawhia Harbour
Albatross Point
Hauturu
Te Hauamoa
Tihiroa
Lichfield
To Taupo
Waikeria
Rotongata
Lake Arapuni
Honikiwi
Waotu
Taharoa
Owhiro
Kiokio
Wilsdown
Otorohanga
Arohena
Tokoroa
Waitomo Caves
Te Anga
Piripiri
Awamarino
Hangatiki
Kinleith
Waitomo Caves
Marokopa
Oparure
Lake Waipapa
Waipapa
Te Kuiti
Lake Maraetai
Pakeho
Waitanguru
Pureora Forest Park
Mairoa
Tirua Point
Eight Mile Junction
Waiteti
Mangakino
To Rotorua
Whakamaru
Arapae
Waikawau
Kopaki
Barryville
Piopio
Aramatai
Tiroa
Paemako
Arataki
Aratoro
Mokau River
Benneydale
Pureora Forest
Pureora 1165 m
Aria
To Taupo
Mahoenui
Mapiu
Mokauiti
Piropiro
Tihoi
Awakino
Tapuiwahine
Pureora Forest Park
Mokau
Mangatupoto
Lake Taupo
Mangakahu Valley
Matiere
Tuhua
Nihoniho
Okahukura
Tongaporutu
Waitaanga
Ohura
Oruaiwi
Ahititi
Okau
Mangaparo
Kuratau Junction
Moerangi
Ngapuke
Omori
To New Plymouth
To Stratford
Taumarunui
Manunui
Pungapunga
To Turangi
Tatu
Aukopae
Whakarae
Piriaka
1
2
3
4
5
20
22
23
26
27
30
31
32
40
41
43

King Country, where the Europeans dared not venture for several more decades.

AUCKLAND TO HAMILTON

The trip to Hamilton by road from Auckland takes about 1½ hours and there are a few points of interest along the way. If you're a steam train enthusiast you can pause at the **Glenbrook Vintage Railway** (☎ (09) 236 3546), where on Sunday and public holidays you can take a 12-km steam train ride for $8 (children $3). To get there follow the yellow signs after leaving the Southern Motorway at Drury, 31 km south of Auckland, and head for Waiuku. There is also an **animal farm and deer park** at Glenbrook.

Te Kauwhata, 67 km south of Auckland and just off SH1, is a good place for a bit of wine tasting. From here the road follows the Waikato River all the way to Hamilton. Along the way is **Huntly**, a coal-mining town with the large Huntly Power Station (☎ 828 9590) which can be visited by appointment – free 1½ to two-hour guided tours are offered for groups of one to 60 people. You will need to arrange it a couple of days in advance.

At the lookout on SH1, a couple of km north of the town, there are a restaurant, a crafts shop and the **Pukeroa Native Timber Museum**, open every day from 9.30 am to 5 pm, with samples of woodturning and all kinds of New Zealand and exotic timbers. Also at Huntly is the **Huntly Mining & Cultural Museum** at 26 Harlock Place, open from 10 am to 3 pm every day except Monday.

South of Huntly the road enters Taupiri Gorge, a gap through the ranges. On your left as you emerge from the gorge is a Maori cemetery on the hillside.

Ngaruawahia, 19 km north of Hamilton on SH1, is an important centre for the Waikato Maori people and the home of the Maori queen, Te Arikinui Dame Te Atairangikaahu. A few hundred metres off SH1, beside the river on River Rd, is the impressive Turangawaewae Marae.

If you're fit, there's an excellent view from the top of Taupiri Mountain, and on the opposite side of the river there are also good views from the Hakarimata Track. The northern end leads off Parker Rd, which can be reached by crossing the river at Huntly and following the Ngaruawahia-Huntly West Rd. The southern end meets the Ngaruawahia-Waingaro Rd just out of Ngaruawahia. To walk the length of the track takes seven hours.

A shorter walk, and easier to get to if you have no transport, is the three-hour return trek from Brownlee Ave, Ngaruawahia, to Hakarimata Trig (371 metres). The top part of this is fairly steep but the view is rewarding. Tracks from each access point meet at the trig.

About 25 km west of Ngaruawahia are the popular Waingaro Hot Springs.

HAMILTON

New Zealand's largest inland city and fifth-largest overall, Hamilton (population 105,000) is 129 km south of Auckland. Built on the banks of the Waikato River, it is the Waikato region's major centre, and in the past few decades the city has undergone spectacular growth.

Archaeological evidence shows that the Maori had long been settled around the Hamilton area, but when the Europeans arrived, the site was deserted. European settlement was initiated by the 4th Regiment of the Waikato Militia, who were persuaded to enlist with promises of an acre (less than half a hectare) in town and another 50 acres in the country. The advance party, led by Captain William Steele, travelled up the Waikato River on a barge drawn by a gunboat and on 24 August 1864 went ashore at the deserted Maori village of Kirikirioa. The township built on that site was named after Captain John Fane Charles Hamilton, the popular commander of HMS *Esk* who had been killed in Tauranga at the battle of Gate Pa four months earlier on 30 April.

The Waikato River was once Hamilton's only transport and communication link with other towns including Auckland, but it was superseded by the railway in 1878, and later by roads.

Orientation & Information

Running north to south a block from the Waikato River, Victoria St is the main drag of the commercial centre; you'll find most things you'll need on or near this busy thoroughfare.

The Hamilton Visitor Centre (☎ 839 3580) is in the city council building in Garden Place, between Victoria and Anglesea Sts right in the centre of town. It's open weekdays from 9 am to 4.45 pm and from 10 am to 2 pm on Saturday, Sunday and public holidays. It has information on Hamilton, Waitomo and the Waikato region and also sells bus and train tickets.

The DOC office (☎ 838 3363) is on the ground floor of the BDO House at 18 London St, near the river.

The Map Shop (☎ 834 6725), 820 Victoria St on the corner of Rostrevor St, operated by DOSLI, has maps of every description on New Zealand and most other parts of the world.

The AA (☎ 839 1397) is on the corner of Victoria and Bryce Sts.

Waikato Museum of Art & History

The Waikato Museum of Art & History is in a modernistic building on the corner of Victoria and Grantham Sts near the river. It has a good Maori collection, with carvings and the impressively large and intricately carved *Te Winika* war canoe, dating from 1836. The canoe has been beautifully restored, a project detailed in photos along the wall. It's open every day from 10 am to 4.30 pm; admission is $2 (children 50c). The attractive Museum Cafe is good for a snack.

Also at the museum is Exscite, the Science & Technology Exhibition Centre with science exhibits and hand-on activities. Entry costs $5 (children $3).

Gardens, Parks & Walks

The huge **Hamilton Gardens** complex contains about 100 different theme gardens – rose gardens, a riverside magnolia garden, a scented garden, cacti and succulents, vegetable and glasshouse gardens, carnivorous plants, and many more, with new ones still under construction. The complex is on Cobham Drive on the east side of the Cobham Bridge, and can be reached by walking south from the city centre along the river walkway. The gardens are always open; admission is free.

Other relaxing spots are **Hamilton Lake (Rotoroa)** and the green domains along the **Waikato River**. Walkways pass through verdant parks and bushy areas on both sides of the river through the city centre all the way south to Cobham Bridge. The area below the traffic bridge (Bridge St) is particularly attractive. Embedded in the riverbank walkway are the remains of the gunboat SS *Rangiriri*, which played a part in the Maori Wars in 1864.

The visitor centre has a free map showing the walkways around the lake, along the river and down to Hamilton Gardens. The DOC office has info on many other walks in and around Hamilton.

Hamilton Zoo

New, more natural pens, walkways and a programme to house endangered species from around the world has made Hamilton Zoo one of New Zealand's better zoos. Though still relatively small, it is well laid with spacious grounds. The zoo is eight km from the city centre – take SH23 west towards Raglan, turn right at Newcastle Rd and then right again onto Brymer Rd. The zoo is open from 9 am to 5 pm every day; admission is $6 (children $3).

National Agricultural Heritage Complex

The interesting National Agricultural Heritage Complex incorporates the Clydesdale Agricultural Museum, the National Dairy Museum, a Heritage Village with historical buildings, and farm animals the kids can touch and feed. It's open every day from 9 am to 4.30 pm; admission is $5 (children $2.50). Animal shows are daily at 11.30 am and 2 pm.

The complex is on Mystery Creek Rd at Mystery Creek, 16 km south of Hamilton and 1.5 km south-east of Hamilton airport. Buses

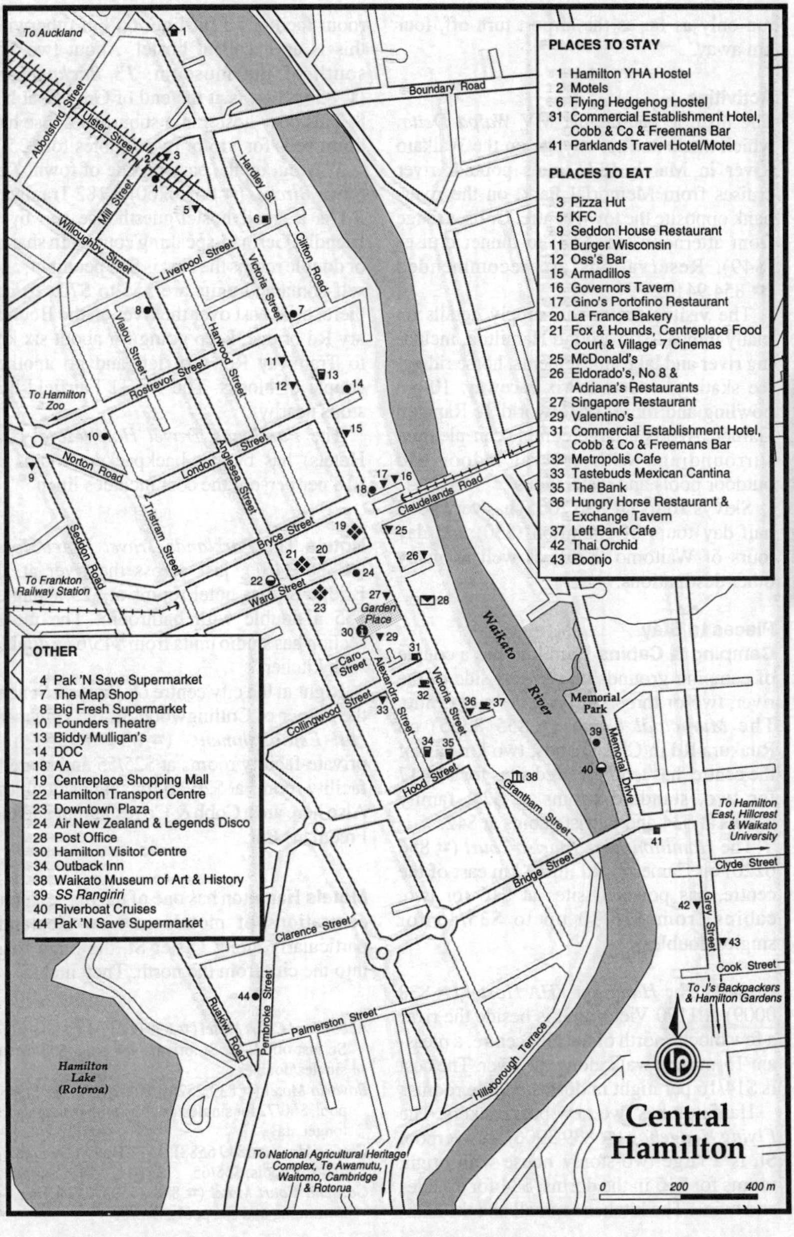
Central Hamilton
PLACES TO STAY
1 Hamilton YHA Hostel
2 Motels
6 Flying Hedgehog Hostel
31 Commercial Establishment Hotel, Cobb & Co & Freemans Bar
41 Parklands Travel Hotel/Motel
PLACES TO EAT
3 Pizza Hut
5 KFC
9 Seddon House Restaurant
11 Burger Wisconsin
12 Oss's Bar
15 Armadillos
16 Governors Tavern
17 Gino's Portofino Restaurant
20 La France Bakery
21 Fox & Hounds, Centreplace Food Court & Village 7 Cinemas
25 McDonald's
26 Eldorado's, No 8 & Adriana's Restaurants
27 Singapore Restaurant
29 Valentino's
31 Commercial Establishment Hotel, Cobb & Co & Freemans Bar
32 Metropolis Cafe
33 Tastebuds Mexican Cantina
35 The Bank
36 Hungry Horse Restaurant & Exchange Tavern
37 Left Bank Cafe
42 Thai Orchid
43 Boonjo
OTHER
4 Pak 'N Save Supermarket
7 The Map Shop
8 Big Fresh Supermarket
10 Founders Theatre
13 Biddy Mulligan's
14 DOC
18 AA
19 Centreplace Shopping Mall
22 Hamilton Transport Centre
23 Downtown Plaza
24 Air New Zealand & Legends Disco
28 Post Office
30 Hamilton Visitor Centre
34 Outback Inn
38 Waikato Museum of Art & History
39 SS Rangiriri
40 Riverboat Cruises
44 Pak 'N Save Supermarket
To Auckland
Abbotsford Street
Ulster Street
Mill Street
Willoughby Street
Boundary Road
Hardley St
Clifton Road
Liverpool Street
Victoria Street
Vialou Street
Harwood Street
Rostrevor Street
To Hamilton Zoo
Norton Road
London Street
Anglesea Street
Tristram Street
Seddon Road
Claudelands Road
Bryce Street
Ward Street
To Frankton Railway Station
Garden Place
Caro Street
Alexandra Street
Collingwood Street
Victoria Street
Hood Street
Grantham Street
Memorial Park
Memorial Drive
Waikato River
Bridge Street
To Hamilton East, Hillcrest & Waikato University
Clyde Street
Grey Street
Cook Street
To J's Backpackers & Hamilton Gardens
Clarence Street
Pembroke Street
Ruakiwi Road
Palmerston Street
Hillsborough Terrace
Hamilton Lake (Rotoroa)
To National Agricultural Heritage Complex, Te Awamutu, Waitomo, Cambridge & Rotorua
0 200 400 m

run only as far as the airport turn-off, four km away.

Activities

The historic paddleboat MV *Waipa Delta*, which made its first voyage on the Waikato River in March 1877, runs popular river cruises from Memorial Park, on the river-bank opposite the town centre. Cruises range from afternoon tea ($18) to dinner cruises ($49). Reservations are recommended (☎ 854 9415).

The visitor centre can supply details on many things to do around Hamilton, including river and lake amusements, horse riding, ice skating, a Grand Prix raceway, 10-pin bowling and more. Waterworld Te Rapa on Garnett Ave is a large complex in pleasant surroundings with several indoor and outdoor pools and waterslides.

Skivys Tours (☎ 856 2005) has very good half-day tours of Hamilton ($30) and day tours of Waitomo ($75), as well as many other destinations.

Places to Stay

Camping & Cabins Hamilton has a couple of camping grounds on the east side of the river, two or three km from the city centre. The *Municipal Camp* (☎ 855 8255) on Ruakura Rd in Claudelands, two km east of the centre, has tent/powered sites for $14/17 for two, standard cabins at $24, family cabins at $34 and tourist cabins at $42.

The *Hamilton East Tourist Court* (☎ 856 6220) on Cameron Rd, three km east of the centre, has powered sites at $16 for two, cabins from $16/30 up to $35/45 for singles/doubles.

Hostels The *Hamilton YHA Hostel* (☎ 838 0009) at 1190 Victoria St is beside the river a few blocks north of the city centre, a pleasant 15-minute walk along the river. The cost is $14/16 per night in dorms/double rooms.

Hamilton has two new backpackers. The *Flying Hedgehog* (☎ 839 3906), 8 Liverpool St, is a large two-storey house with bright rooms for $15 in the dorms, $34 for doubles and twins. The kitchen is small and the bathroom facilities a bit light on but otherwise this is an excellent hostel. About two km south of the museum, *J's Backpackers* (☎ 856 8394) is at the end of Grey St at No 8. This cosy hostel in a suburban house has dorm beds for $15 or two doubles for $35.

Way out on the eastern side of town, *The Silver Birches* (☎ 855 6260) at 182 Tramway Rd is a small hostel/guesthouse run by a friendly, German-speaking couple. In shared or double rooms the cost is $15 per night, and self-contained units are $55 to $70. To get there, head east over the river on the Boundary Rd bridge, keep going for about six km to Tramway Rd, turn left and go another couple of blocks. The No 11 Fairfield bus stops nearby.

The *Parklands Travel Hotel/Motel* (see Hotels) has budget backpackers rooms at $18 per person; the cost includes linen.

Hotels The *Parklands Travel Hotel/Motel* (☎ 838 2461), just across the river at 24 Bridge St, has hotel rooms at $25 a single, $55 a double with bathroom. The motel section has studio units from $45/67 a double with kitchen.

Right in the city centre on Victoria St near the corner of Collingwood St, the *Commercial Establishment* (☎ 839 1226) has private-facility rooms at $25/55 and shared-facility rooms at $20/40 for singles/doubles. Also here are a Cobb & Co restaurant and the Freemans Bar.

Motels Hamilton has one of the biggest concentrations of motels in New Zealand, particularly along Ulster St, the main road into the city from the north. They include:

Abbotsford Court Motel (☎ 839 0661), 18 Abbotsford St, just off Ulster St, private spa pool, $58/69 for singles/doubles
Bavaria Motel (☎ 839 2520), 203-207 Ulster St, spa pool, $60/72 for singles/doubles with discounts for longer stays
Classic Motel (☎ 849 6588), 451 Ulster St, swimming and spa pools, $55/65
Gardena Court Motel (☎ 838 1769), 257 Ulster St, swimming and spa pools, $75/89

Farmstays & Homestays The visitor centre has listings for farmstays and homestays in the Waikato region.

Places to Eat

Snacks & Fast Food The modern *Centreplace* shopping centre is good for a quick and cheap meal. On the ground floor is an international food court with a variety of counters offering Italian, Chinese, Singaporean and other fast food. Just outside the centre at 68 Ward St is *La France Bakery* for cakes and pastries.

The *Downtown Plaza* mall across Ward St also has a small food court with McDonald's and Asian food featured.

Tastebuds Mexican Cantina in the Farmers Building on Collingwood St on the corner of Alexandra St serves its usual mix of Mexican snacks at cheap prices, but this one has an identity crisis and also serves Korean food. Nearby, the *Metropolis Cafe* at 241 Victoria St near Collingwood St is a hip cafe with lunches, dinners, snacks, rich desserts and espresso.

In the Garden Place on Victoria St the *Valentino's* has pizza, coffee and Italian gelato, while *Burger Wisconsin* at 789 Victoria St boasts gourmet char-grilled burgers.

And yes, the big three American fast food chains are all in Hamilton: *McDonald's* on the corner of Victoria St and Claudelands Rd, and on Ulster St, *Pizza Hut* and *KFC*.

Pub Food Moving on to pub food, there's a popular *Cobb & Co* in the Commercial Establishment on the corner of Victoria and Collingwood Sts, and a block away, the similar *Hungry Horse*.

The friendly, olde English-style *Fox & Hounds* in Ward St does pub lunches and ploughman's platters. Nearby, the *Governor's Tavern* on Bryce St by the river has indoor areas plus a riverside garden bar, which is pleasant in summer; lunch and dinner are served on Thursday, Friday and Saturday. *Oss's Bar* at 711 Victoria St has a good selection of inexpensive bar meals with tasty food, huge portions and interesting dishes you don't usually see in pubs, as well as all the old favourites.

Restaurants Hamilton has plenty of good restaurants. *Eldorado's Mexican Restaurant* at 10 Alma St has great atmosphere and serves large portions of tasty Mexican and Tex-Mex food. Next door at 8 Alma St, the *No 8 Restaurant* has innovative Italian-style cuisine, while next door again, *Adriana's Cafe & Restaurant* at 6 Alma St is an authentic Italian BYO with a relaxed atmosphere and interesting art on the walls.

Gino's Portofino at 8 Bryce St is a bit more expensive but it's popular with the yuppie crowd for Italian and continental cuisine.

The *Singapore Restaurant* on Garden Place, is a good, licensed Chinese restaurant, but has little in the way of Singaporean cuisine on the menu. For some South-East Asian flavour, *Boonjo* across the river at 316 Grey St has good Malaysian food. Nearby, the *Thai Orchid* at 435 Grey St is cheap and the pick of Hamilton's multiplying Thai restaurants.

The Bank on Hood St is a very popular bar/restaurant with cheap snacks and music in the evenings. At 592 Victoria St, *Armadillos* has Mexican food and American ribs in a trendy setting.

There are plenty of places you can spend more money in Hamilton if you want to go upmarket. Top of the top include the *Left Bank Cafe* beside the river on Marlborough Place just off Victoria St and *Seddon House* at 67 Seddon Rd.

Entertainment

Pubs, Bars & Nightclubs Hamilton has plenty of lively nightspots on Friday and Saturday night. Most venues have DJs, though a few have bands.

Down on Hood St, *The Bank* is a trendy bar in a renovated historic building and is always a popular place for a drink. The dance floor gets active. Next door, the *Outback Inn* is popular with students and also has a lounge dance floor.

Biddy Mulligan's at 742 Victoria St is an Irish pub, and one of the most popular places in town. Live bands play regularly. *Freemans Bar* in the Commercial Establishment on the corner of Victoria and Collingwood Sts has live bands for dancing on Thursday, Friday and Saturday nights. The *Exchange Tavern* at 188 Victoria St has head-banging bands on the weekend. *Oss's Bar* at 711 Victoria St is a popular sports bar with good bar meals and occasional entertainment.

The *Fox & Hounds*, in Ward St just off Victoria St, is a popular English-style pub with 27 varieties of imported beer, plus Newcastle Brown, Guinness and cider on tap, pub lunches, and live entertainment on Thursday and Saturday nights.

Legends upstairs over the Air New Zealand office in Ward St is a good, lively disco.

Cinema & Theatre The *Village 7 Cinemas*, upstairs in Ward St, has seven movie theatres showing the latest films. Live theatre venues include the *Founders Memorial Theatre* (☎ 838 6600) in Tristram St and the *Riverlea Theatre & Arts Centre* (☎ 856 5450) in Riverlea Rd off Cambridge Rd.

Getting There & Away

Air The Air New Zealand office (☎ 839 9835) is at 33-35 Ward St near Victoria St. It has direct flights to Auckland, Christchurch, Dunedin, Gisborne, Napier, Palmerston North and Wellington, with connections to several other centres.

Kiwi Travel Air Charters (☎ 834 1121) is a charter company offering good deals on return flights to Brisbane ($649) and Cairns ($849) as well as other destinations in Australia. Discounts for full-time students and seniors over 50 are offered.

Bus All local and long-distance buses arrive and depart from the Hamilton Transport Centre on the corner of Anglesea and Ward Sts. Newmans (☎ 838 3114), InterCity (☎ 834 3457) and Mt Cook Landline (☎ 839 3360) are all represented.

Frequent buses make the connection between Hamilton and Auckland (two to 2½ hours). Buses also depart for Thames (1½ to two hours), Tauranga (two hours), Whakatane (3½ hours), Opotiki (4½ hours), Rotorua (1½ hours), Taupo (two to 2½ hours), New Plymouth (four hours) and Wellington (8½ to nine hours). For Waitomo, Newman's drop off in Otorohanga where a connecting service goes to the caves and InterCity has a daily Auckland-Hamilton-Waitomo-Rotorua tour bus.

A number of local bus operators run regular services to nearby towns including Raglan, Huntly, Te Awamutu, Morrinsville, Te Aroha and Thames.

Of the backpackers services, Magic Bus stops at Hamilton on its way from Auckland to Waitomo.

Train Hamilton is on the main rail line and all trains between Auckland and Wellington, Rotorua and Tauranga stop at Hamilton's Frankton railway station on Queens Ave, about a 20-minute walk west of the city centre. Tickets can be bought at the Frankton station, or more conveniently at the Hamilton Travel Centre or the Visitor Centre.

Hitching Hamilton is a bit spread out, and from the centre it's a distance to good hitching spots on the outskirts. It may be best to take a local bus to the edge of town and hitch from there.

Heading south to Waitomo or New Plymouth, catch a Glenview bus to the outskirts. For hitching to Rotorua, Taupo, Tauranga or Wellington, catch a Hillcrest bus and get off by the Hillcrest School. Hitching north to Auckland is easiest if you take a Huntly bus to the outskirts or to Huntly.

Getting Around

To/From the Airport Hamilton Airport is 12 km south of the city. The Airport Shuttle (☎ 847 5618) offers a door-to-door service between the city and the airport for $7 per person. Roadcat Transport (☎ 856 7192) has a shuttle service to Auckland airport for $36 ($70 for two).

Bus Hamilton's city bus system operates on weekdays only, with services from around

7 am to 5.45 pm, Friday until 8.45 pm. All local and long-distance buses arrive and depart from the Hamilton Transport Centre on the corner of Ward and Anglesea Sts.

A complete timetable of local city bus routes plus local buses travelling further afield (to Raglan, Huntly, Te Aroha, Thames, etc) is available at the Hamilton Transport Centre or from the visitor centre. Both places can answer any questions you may have about buses; for bus information, ring the visitor centre (☎ 839 3360) or Busline (☎ 856 4579).

Car There are many car rental agencies, including Waikato Car Rentals (☎ 856 9908) and Rent-a-Dent (☎ 839 1049) which are more economical than most.

AROUND HAMILTON

Waingaro

Waingaro Hot Springs is a popular day trip from Hamilton, with three thermal mineral pools, private spa pools, giant waterslides, children's play areas, BBQs and a deer park. The complex is open every day from 9 am to 10 pm; admission is $5 (children $2.50).

You can stay near the hot springs in the *Waingaro Hot Springs Motel & Caravan Park* (☎ & fax 825 4761). Camp sites with power cost from $24 for two, on-site caravans are $40 for two people and motel units are $70. To get there, turn west at Ngaruawahia, 19 km north of Hamilton, and go 23 km; it is clearly signposted.

Candyland

East of Ngaruawahia at Komakorau, Candyland on Henry Rd is a candy and chocolate factory turning out a huge array of sweets. Candyland has tours to see the candy-making process at 1 pm for $5 (children $3), including sampling of the wares and entry to the candy museum.

RAGLAN

On the coast 48 km west of Hamilton, Raglan is Hamilton's closest and most popular beach. Raglan is world famous for its surfing, attracting top surfers from around the world to Te Manu Bay and Whale Bay, especially in summer when international ProAm surfing competitions are held here.

The relaxed little town of Raglan lies on a beautiful sheltered harbour, good for windsurfing, boating and swimming. The famous black-sand surfing beaches are west of town.

Information

The Raglan Information Centre (☎ 825 0556) is on Bow St, right in the centre of town. Here you can pick up free maps of the town and region and find out everything you want to know about the area. The office is open Monday to Friday from 9 am to 4 pm, and weekends from 10 am to 2 pm, closing daily for an hour at lunch time.

Beaches

The beach at the **Kopua Recreational Reserve** near the camping ground, a five-minute walk over the footbridge from town, is a safe, calm estuary beach popular with families. On the other side of the tiny peninsula is a popular windsurfing beach, reached via the camping ground (a day use fee is charged). Other sheltered inner-harbour beaches close to town include **Cox's Bay**, reached by a walkway from Government Rd or from Bayview Rd, and **Puriri Park**, towards the end of Wallis St, a safe swimming spot at high tide.

About five km west of town, **Ngarunui Beach (Ocean Beach)**, is a popular surf beach for swimming. Swim on the left side of the beach, away from the riptides, where lifeguards are posted in summer.

Manu Bay, eight km west of Raglan, is a world-famous surfing beach, said to have the longest left-hand break in the world. Featured in the 1966 cult surfing film *Endless Summer*, this was the beach where a surfer caught a wave which he was still riding about 10 minutes later. The very long, uniform waves at Manu Bay are created by the angle at which the ocean swell, coming in from the Tasman Sea, meets the coastline here. **Whale Bay**, a couple of km further west of Manu Bay, is another excellent surfing spot.

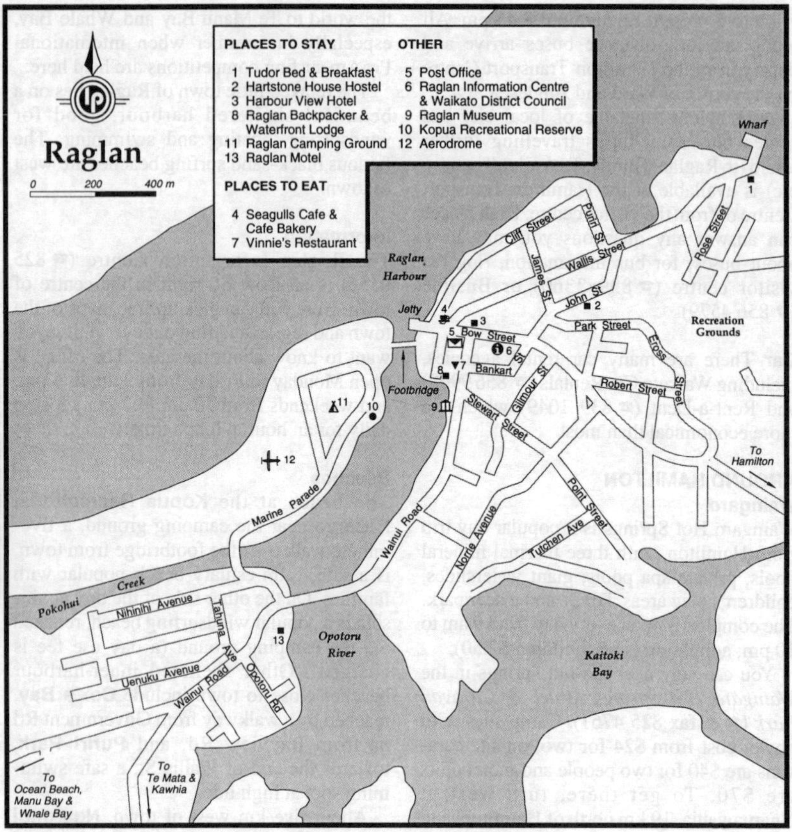

Ruapuke Beach, a rugged stretch of coastline still further past Whale Bay, is good for surfcasting but not so good for swimming due to treacherous cross-currents; it can be reached from Ruapuke Rd.

Other Attractions

The small **Raglan Museum** on Wainui St has exhibits on the history of the Raglan area. It's open every day during the summer school holidays, less frequently the rest of the year.

It is always pleasant and relaxing to walk down to the **wharf** around sunset and meet the trawlers returning from the day's fishing. A few locals are often hanging around to inspect the day's catch. The wharf is four blocks east of the centre of town.

Some good **walks** can be done in the area. About midway between Hamilton and Raglan, the Karamu Walkway goes through the Four Brothers Scenic Reserve. The Bryant Memorial Scenic Reserve is nine km south-west of Raglan on Whaanga Rd, past Ocean Beach. From there a track leads down to the beach. Other walking possibilities are in the Pirongia Forest Park, south of Raglan.

Raglan Harbour Cruises (☎ 825 0300) has

1½-hour **cruises** in summer for $15. The information office also has information on canoeing and mountain biking in the area.

Places to Stay

Camping & Cabins The beachside *Raglan Camping Ground* (☎ 825 8283) is on a sheltered, sandy inner-harbour beach across the estuary from town, popular for swimming and windsurfing. It has tent/caravan sites at $14/16 for two, cabins at $40 and tourist flats at $50 a double.

Raglan Wagon Cabins (☎ 825 8268) on Wainui Rd is six km west of Raglan, on a hill with magnificent views of the coast, two km before Manu Bay surfing beach. Comfortable cabins, imaginatively constructed from restored railway carriages, cost $12.50 per person. Self-contained houses cost $50 a double and tent sites are $7 per person. There's a kitchen and TV lounge and the friendly owner has a copy of the *Endless Summer* surfing film on video.

Hostels & Guesthouses *Raglan Backpacker & Waterfront Lodge* (☎ 825 0515) is on the edge of the water and has fine views. This new, purpose-built hostel provides excellent standards of accommodation for $12 in shared rooms, or doubles and twins are $32.

The *Hartstone House* (☎ 825 8670) at 15 John St is a hostel with a bunkroom at $12 per person, but was up for sale at the time of writing, so it pays to phone first.

The *Tudor Bed & Breakfast* (☎ 825 8771), on Wallis St facing the wharf, is a well-equipped little place with kitchen and sitting areas, and just one double room, one twin room and one single room. Bed & breakfast is $36/47 for singles/doubles.

Hotels & Motels The *Harbour View Hotel* (☎ 825 8010) on Bow St in the centre of town has single/double rooms at $38/48. Across the bridge on the west side of town, the peaceful *Raglan Motel* (☎ 825 8153) at 14 Wainui Rd is right on the shore of the estuary, with singles/doubles at $50/60.

Places to Eat

Vinnie's on Wainui Rd is the best restaurant in town. *Seagulls* and the *Cafe Bakery* near the corner of Bow St and Cliff St are also good.

Entertainment

The *Harbour View Hotel* on Bow St has bands, often Midge Marsden and his band.

Getting There & Away

The Hamilton-Raglan Shuttle (☎ 825 8966) departs for Raglan from the Hamilton Transport Centre at 9 am returning at 2.15 pm, Monday to Friday. On Saturday, buses depart at 9.30 am and 4 pm, returning at 8.30 am and 3 pm. The cost is $5 one way.

RAGLAN TO KAWHIA

The back roads between Raglan and Kawhia, on the coast 55 km to the south, are slow and winding, but scenic and enjoyable for travelling off the beaten track. The gravel roads take a while to traverse – allow at least 1½ hours' driving time between Raglan and Kawhia, not counting stops. Traffic is light.

There are two routes between Raglan and Kawhia. From Raglan you can head west along the coast, out past Ocean Beach, Manu Bay and Whale Bay, and keep following the coast road until it turns inland and meets the interior road at Te Mata, 20 km south of Raglan. Along the way is the *Ruapuke Motor Camp* near the beach at Ruapuke. Alternatively, from Raglan you can head towards Hamilton and take the signposted Te Mata-Kawhia turn-off.

About 12 km south-west of Raglan is **Mt Karioi**. You can take a good round-the-mountain drive, over mostly gravel roads, in a couple of hours from Raglan.

Along this route the **Te Toto Track**, starting from the Te Toto car park on Whaanga Rd (the coast road) on the western side of Mt Karioi, is strenuous but scenic, ascending steeply from the car park to a lookout point (two hours) followed by an easier stretch up to the summit of Mt Karioi (one hour). From the east side of the mountain, the **Wairake Track** is a steeper two-hour climb to the summit and meets the Te Toto Track.

The *Tainui* Canoe

Though it's only a small town, Kawhia has an illustrious history. It was here that the *Tainui* canoe, one of the canoes of the Great Migration of around 1350 AD, made its final landing.

Before the *Tainui* canoe departed from the Maori homeland island of Hawaiki, the priests there prophesied that the departing canoe would eventually come to a favourable place where its people would make a new home, have a good life and prosper. Their prophecy went something like this:

Te Tauranga mou e Tainui	Your resting place Tainui
Ko te Taihauauru	Is the west coast
Ka whia te mataitai	(There is) an abundance of shellfish
Ka whia te ika	An abundance of fish
Ka whia te kai.	An abundance of food.

The priests told the leaders of the *Tainui* canoe which landmarks to look for so they would know they had arrived at the new home they were destined to find.

The *Tainui* canoe left Hawaiki, stopping at Easter Island, Raiatea (an island in French Polynesia) and Rarotonga (the principal island of the Cook Islands) as it crossed the Pacific. It landed in New Zealand at Maketu on the Bay of Plenty, accompanied by the *Arawa* canoe. The *Arawa* canoe stopped there, its people becoming the Arawa people, a large Maori tribe that still lives in the Bay of Plenty and Rotorua areas today.

The leaders of the *Tainui* canoe – Hoturoa, the captain, and Rakataura, the expert tohunga or high priest – knew that the *Tainui's* home was destined to be on the west coast. So the *Tainui* canoe continued on. The story of how it found its final resting place is a long and heroic one.

WAIKATO

Mt Karioi is in one part of the Pirongia Forest Park; a larger part lies within the triangle formed by the towns of Raglan, Kawhia and Te Awamutu, with the 959-metre summit of **Mt Pirongia** clearly visible throughout the district. Tracks going through the forest park lead to the summit of Mt Pirongia – the mountain is usually climbed from Corcoran Rd on the Hamilton side. There's a hut near the summit if you want to spend the night. Maps and information about the Pirongia Forest Park are available at the DOC office in Hamilton. The township of Pirongia is 32 km south-west of Hamilton.

Near Te Mata, 20 km south of Raglan, are the **Bridal Veil Falls**. From the car park it's an easy 10-minute walk through native bush to the top of the falls, with a further bush walk leading down to the pool at the bottom, where you could swim to cool off.

Places to Stay

Near Te Mata, *Marcus Vernon's Farmstays* (☎ 825 6892) is a friendly, easy-going place to learn about life on a sheep and cattle farm, high on a hill with stunning views. For $15 a day, and four hours help on the farm, you get a bed in a shared room in the farmhouse with all meals, and activities such as horse riding are thrown in. Marcus is flexible – B&B with no work costs $20, or rooms with private facilities in a separate house can be rented. The farm is on Houchen Rd, off the main road just north of Te Mata. Follow the Houchen Rd all the way to the end.

KAWHIA

Kawhia is a sleepy, crumbling, little port on the Kawhia Harbour. The harbour is large, with many extensions, but its entrance is narrow – the people of the *Tainui* canoe missed it on their first trip down the coast around 1350 AD, and Captain Cook also missed it when he sailed past in 1770, naming Albatross Point on the south side of the harbour but failing to note the harbour itself.

Today Kawhia is still easy to miss, though

Seeking, first one way and then another, to get to the west coast, the Tainui people finally dragged their canoe overland at Manukau Harbour, near Auckland. Setting off south in search of the prophesied landmarks, they journeyed all the way to the South Island, still without finding their place. They turned around and came north again, still searching, and finally recognised their prophesied new home at Kawhia Harbour.

When they landed the canoe, they tied it to a pohutukawa tree on the shore, naming the tree Tangi te Korowhiti. Though the tree is not marked, it still grows with a few other pohutukawa trees on the shoreline between Kawhia town and the Maketu Marae; you can easily see it. At the end of its long voyage, the *Tainui* canoe was dragged up onto a hill and buried. After burying the canoe, Hoturoa and Rakataura placed sacred stones at either end to mark its resting place. Hani, on higher ground, is the stone marking the bow of the canoe, and Puna, the lower stone, marks the stern. These sacred stones are still there, a powerful remembrance to the Tainui people. You can walk up behind the marae and see the stones behind a wooden fence.

The prophecy that this place would be a good home for the long-journeying Tainui people did come true for them. Kawhia Harbour indeed turned out to be abundant with shellfish, fish and food. Today the Tainui tribe extends over the entire Waikato region, over the Coromandel Peninsula, north to Auckland and south to Lake Taupo and south past Mokau on the coast. Kawhia, the Maketu Marae and the burial place of the *Tainui* canoe are supremely sacred to all the Tainui people.

Another point of historical significance for Kawhia is that it was once the home of Te Rauparaha, the great Maori warrior. When pushed out of Kawhia by warring Waikato tribes in 1821, Te Rauparaha moved southwards, making his base on Kapiti Island off the west coast of the southern end of North Island, from there making raids all the way down to the South Island. See the Kapiti Coast section in the Wellington chapter for more on Te Rauparaha. ■

it gets a few fishing enthusiasts and beachgoers during summer. Kawhia's main event of the year is the whaleboat rowing regatta on New Year's Day, which has been held since early this century and draws thousands of visitors.

Things to See

The **Kawhia Museum** is in the historic former Kawhia County Building right near the wharf in the centre of town. It has some interesting exhibits and also has pamphlets and information on the town. The museum is open irregular hours but if you ask around, someone might open it for you. Marae visits can be arranged through the museum.

From the museum and the wharf, a pleasant walk extends seaward along the coast, to the **Maketu Marae** with its impressively carved meeting house, Auaukiterangi. Through the marae grounds and behind the wooden fence, two stones, Hani and Puna, mark the burial place of the *Tainui* canoe.

Three km behind the town, through the Tainui Kawhia Pine Forest, is windswept **Ocean Beach** and its black dunes, but swimming can be dangerous. Two hours either side of low tide you can find the **Puia Hot Springs** in the sands – just dig a hole for your own little natural spa. There's a drivable track over the dunes.

Places to Stay & Eat

Kawhia's three camping grounds fill up at busy periods in summer, so plan ahead. The *Forest View Motor Camp* (☎ 871 0858) on Waiwera St has tent sites, caravan sites and cabins, as does the *Beach View Motor Camp* (☎ 871 0727) on the beachfront. The *Kawhia Motor Camp* (☎ 871 0774) on Karewa St is smaller and simpler, with just tent and caravan sites.

The *Kawhia Motel* (☎ 871 0865) is a friendly place in the centre of town on the corner of Jervois and Tainui Sts; units cost $55/65 for singles/doubles.

Kawhia has a general store, a hotel, a fish shop and *Wozzies Cafe & Crafts*.

Getting There & Away

Kawhia Bus & Freight (☎ 871 0701) takes passengers on the freight run to Te Awamutu every day except Sunday.

The 50-minute drive to Kawhia from Te Awamutu or Otorohanga is a scenic route offering fine views of the harbour. Along the way is the Te Kauri Park Nature Reserve, with a one-hour walk from the road to a kauri grove – they say that Kawhia Harbour marks the southernmost limit that kauri trees grow naturally.

You can drive or cycle down the mostly unsealed coastal back roads all the way from Raglan in the north to Awakino and Mokau in the south, finally coming to New Plymouth (or vice versa, south to north). It's slow going but scenic.

TE AWAMUTU

Te Awamutu is a service town for the local dairy-farming community. It is noted for its rose gardens, hence its title 'the Rose Town of New Zealand'.

Te Awamutu was an important site in the Waikato wars – you can still see the flat-topped hill where there was a fort. After the wars, it became a frontier town. The name Te Awamutu means 'river cut short', since the river above this point was unsuitable for canoes.

Information

The Te Awamutu Information Centre (☎ 871 3259), on the corner of Gorst Ave and SH3, opposite the Rose Garden, is open from 9 am to 4.30 pm, on weekends from 9 am to 3 pm.

Things to See

The **Te Awamutu Rose Garden** has over 2000 rosebushes. The garden is on the main road in town, opposite the information centre. The roses are at their best from November to April; a Rose Festival is held in November each year.

Beginning behind the Rose Garden, the Pioneer Walk goes beside the river for about 1.5 km to Memorial Park and the **Aotearoa Centre**, where there's a Maori carving and weaving institute.

The **Te Awamutu Museum** in the Civic Centre on Roche St houses a fine collection of Maori *taonga* (treasures), the centrepiece of which is the Uenuku, a Maori totara carving, said to have been brought to New Zealand on the *Tainui* canoe. The museum is open Tuesday to Friday from 10 am to 4 pm; weekends from 2 to 4 pm.

On the third Sunday of each month, the **Waikato Railway Museum** on Racecourse Rd has the biggest static display of large steam locomotives in New Zealand.

Every Thursday from around 10 am to 3 pm, farm animals are auctioned off at the **Te Awamutu Sale**, held at the sale yard on Gorst Ave, near the information centre. It's a rural event which visitors often find fascinating.

The **Wharepapa Rock Climbing Field**, with 42 rock climbs ranging from beginner's to advanced levels, is 22 km south-west of Te Awamutu in the Pirongia Forest Park.

Places to Stay & Eat

The *Selwyn Park Motor Camp* (☎ 871 7478) on Gorst Ave behind the information centre has tent sites, powered sites and cabins. *Rosetown Lodge* (☎ 871 7650) at 494 Kihikihi Rd, on SH3 one km south of the centre of town, is a small hostel sleeping eight in a self-contained bunkroom out behind the house. The cost is $15 per person, or $7.50 per person for tent sites on the lawn.

Motels in Te Awamutu include the *Rosetown Motel* (☎ 871 5779) at 844 Kihikihi Rd, the *Road Runner* (☎ 871 7420) at 141 Bond Rd and the *Park Lodge Motel* (☎ 871 5179) on the Main Ohaupo Rd.

Te Awamutu has a selection of eateries on Alexandra St, the town's main commercial street, including *KFC* and the *Gold Star Restaurant & Takeaways* for Chinese food. The most popular establishment in the *Rose & Thorn* for good, cheap grills.

Getting There & Away

Buses and trains between Auckland and Wellington stop at Te Awamutu, as do local buses between Te Awamutu and Hamilton.

MORRINSVILLE

About 33 km north-east of Hamilton, Morrinsville is a small centre for the Waikato dairy industry. In fact its tourist literature boasts that 'there are more cows within a 25 km radius of Morrinsville than in any other part of the world'! The **Morrinsville Museum & Pioneer Cottage** on the corner of Lorne and Anderson Sts is open on Sunday afternoons from 1.30 to 4 pm. A couple of scenic reserves are nearby, or you could climb **Mt Misery** for a view over the town.

The Morrinsville Information Centre (☎ 889 5575) in Thames St, the main street through town, is open every day from 10 am to 4 pm. They can arrange accommodation in farmstays and homestays, or Morrinsville has a camping ground, hotel and motel.

TE AROHA

Te Aroha, 55 km north-east of Hamilton on SH26, is at the foot of the mountain of the same name. Te Aroha means 'love', since this is where Kahu-mata-momoe sat on the summit of Mt Te Aroha and was filled with love for the land and people of Te Paeroa-o-Toi. From the summit on a clear day you can see as far as Tongariro and Mt Egmont/Taranaki so it's well worth the climb.

In European times, Te Aroha became a favourite spa resort, and the hot mineral and soda pools in the historic domain are still a favourite place to relax after walking in the area.

Orientation & Information

The clock tower at the intersection of Whitaker and Kenrick Sts marks the centre of town. Whitaker St is the town's 'main drag', with most businesses found along it. The Domain, a large park on Whitaker St a block or two south of the clock tower, contains most of the town's attractions including the Te Aroha Museum, the hot spa baths, a geyser, and walking tracks to Mt Te Aroha, a restaurant and the information centre and DOC offices.

The Te Aroha Information Centre (☎ 884 8052), on Whitaker St in the Domain, is open Monday to Friday from 10 am to 4.30 pm, weekends from 10 am to 3 pm. It also serves as the town's AA agent.

DOC (☎ 884 9303), in the Domain near the spa baths, has maps and information on Mt Te Aroha and the Kaimai-Mamaku Forest Park.

Museums

The **Te Aroha Museum** in the Cadman Building in the Domain, occupying the town's original bathhouse building, has exhibits on the mining and agricultural development of the town. It's open 1 to 3 pm on weekends, daily during the school summer holidays.

Cobbers Museum at 60 Kenrick St is a private agricultural and colonial museum, which an avid collector put together at home until it got so extensive he decided to open it to the public. It's open on weekends from 10 am to 5 pm, or by arrangement (☎ 884 8769). History fans might also like to see New Zealand's oldest **organ**, the 1712 Renatus Harris pipe organ in St Mark's church.

Hot Pools & Geyser

The Hot Soda Water Baths in the Domain at the foot of Mt Te Aroha have two types of thermal water: hot soda water and hot mineral water. All the baths are in private hot-tub pools; the cost is $4 (children $2.50) for half an hour's soak, less with a YHA card. The baths are open every day from noon to 9 pm; it's a popular place so if you want to go on the weekend it might be good to book yourself a spot in advance.

Behind the hot pools is the Mokena geyser, said to be the only hot soda water geyser in the world. It's quite active, going off about every half hour or so.

Activities

The **walking tracks** going up Mt Te Aroha start at the rear of the Domain, from behind the hot pools and geyser. It takes about an hour on a relatively easy track to ascend to the Bald Spur Lookout, also called the Whakapipi Lookout (350 metres); after that it's another two hours' steep climb to reach the summit of Mt Te Aroha (950 metres). The climb is worth it for the magnificent view.

Other tramping possibilities and things to see around Te Aroha include Wairongamai, five km south of town off Loop Rd, with many old relics of the gold mining era; the Killarney Lakes, 11 km south of town; and the Wairere Falls, two waterfalls, 73 and 80 metres high, which are 26 km south of Te Aroha.

There's **trout fishing** all year round in the Waihou River; get a fishing licence from Cockerton's Variety Store.

Places to Stay

The *Te Aroha Holiday Park* (☎ 884 9567), about two km west of Te Aroha on Stanley Rd after the racecourse, has a swimming pool and tennis courts. Tent/powered sites are $13/15 for two, cabins start at $22 and tourist flats cost $42 a double.

The *Te Aroha YHA Hostel* (☎ 884 8739) on Miro St, a few blocks from the centre of town, is a pleasant small hostel and costs $10 a night. Double rooms and free bicycles are available. It has heaps of information about Te Aroha.

The Palace Hotel (☎ 884 9995) on Whitaker St by the clock tower has rooms at $35/60 for singles/doubles. The *Te Aroha Motel* (☎ 884 9417) at 108 Whitaker St has units at $55/66.

The information centre can provide referrals for farmstays in the area.

Getting There & Away

Murphy and Tavs City Connections (both part of the InterCity umbrella) have buses between Hamilton and Thames, stopping in Te Aroha, every day except Saturday.

CAMBRIDGE

On the Waikato River 20 km south-east of Hamilton, Cambridge is a small, peaceful town with a charming rural English atmosphere. Cricket is played on the village green in the centre of town, and the avenues are lined with broad, shady European trees, at their best in autumn. The Cambridge region is famous for the breeding and training of thoroughbred horses. One well-known Cambridge-bred horse is Charisma, winner of the Olympic three-day event in both 1984 and 1988, ridden by New Zealander Mark Todd.

Information

The Cambridge Information Centre (☎ 827 6033) on the corner of Victoria and Queen Sts is open Monday to Friday from 8 am to 4.30 pm.

Things to See

Cambridge has a number of arts & crafts and antiques shops, adding to the town's twee atmosphere. Best known is the award-winning **Cambridge Country Store**, in an old church on SH1 near the centre of town. Another old church worth seeing, also on SH1, is the 100-year-old **St Andrew's Anglican Church**, a white church with a beautiful wooden interior, fine stained-glass windows and a high steeple sheathed in copper. The outside is beautiful but it's still a surprise to see the beauty of the interior.

The **Cambridge Museum**, occupying the historic 1909 former Cambridge Courthouse building on Victoria St, is open Tuesday to Saturday from 10 am to 4 pm, Sunday and public holidays from 2 to 4 pm. **Te Koutu Lake** at the Te Koutu Park in the centre of Cambridge is a peaceful bird sanctuary.

The **Cambridge Thoroughbred Lodge**, ideal for horse lovers, is three km south of town on SH1, is a magnificent horse stud that has tours at 10.30 am and 2.30 pm daily for $9 (children $4). The thoroughbreds are brought out on show with commentaries, and there are show jumping and dressage exhibitions.

Activities

Other attractions in Cambridge include jet-boat rides and canoeing on the Waikato River, and walking on tracks along both sides of the Waikato River and around Te Koutu Lake. The information centre has free pamphlets showing all the town's walking tracks.

There are also walks further afield. From SH1 take the turn-off at Cambridge and in about a five-minute drive you'll reach the Maungakawa Scenic Reserve, a regenerating forest with some exotic timber species and a fairly easy short bush walk. From the eastern side of Mt Maungakawa, a track suitable for experienced trampers ascends from Tapui Rd; it takes half a day to walk there and back. Also about a five-minute drive from town, Mt Mungatautri is another good walking spot; it takes about 1½ hours to climb to the summit.

Places to Stay

The *Cambridge Domain Motor Camp* (☎ 827 5649) in Scott St, Leamington, about 1.5 km from the centre of town, has tent sites at $6.50 per person, powered sites at $7.50 per person and cabins at $10 per person.

The *Cambridge Country Lodge Backpackers* (☎ 827 8373) is a pleasant hostel in a rural setting on a two-hectare farmlet 100 metres down Peake Rd, turning off from SH1, a km north of Cambridge. They provide courtesy transport and bicycles. You can do your own cooking, or home-prepared meals are available. The cost is $15 per person double and dorm rooms.

Hotels include the *Masonic Hotel* (☎ 827 5500) in Duke St East with singles/doubles at $45/60 and the *National Hotel* (☎ 827 6731) in Lake St with rooms at $32/55.

Motels in Cambridge include the *Cambrian Lodge Motel* (☎ 827 7766) at 63 Hamilton Rd and the *Captains Quarters Motor Inn* (☎ 827 8989) at 57A Hamilton Rd, both costing $70/80 for singles/doubles. The *Colonial Court Motel* (☎ 827 5244), 37 Vogel St, has units from $65/70 and the *Leamington Motel* (☎ 827 4057), 90 Shakespeare St, costs $58/70.

Cambridge also has a good selection of B&Bs, ranging in price from the *River Close B&B* (☎ 827 8333) on Duke St, which costs $40/60, to the *Park House B&B* (☎ 827 6368) overlooking the town square at 70 Queen St and costing $80/100. The information centre has a full list of B&Bs and farmstays in the area.

Getting There & Away

Lying on SH1, Cambridge is well connected by bus. Most of the long-distance buses from Hamilton to Rotorua or the Bay of Plenty stop in Cambridge. Cambridge Travel Lines (☎ 827 7363) and Cesswell Motors (☎ 827 7789) both have buses during the week between Cambridge and the Hamilton Transport Centre.

KARAPIRO & ARAPUNI

Karapiro, furthest downstream of a chain of hydroelectric power stations and dams on the Waikato River, is 28 km south-east of Hamilton, eight km past Cambridge, just off SH1. The road passes over the dam and the lake is popular for aquatic sports. For camping at the lake, the Karapiro Lake Domain (☎ 827 4178) beside the lake has tent sites, powered sites and bunkrooms.

Arapuni, the first government-built hydroelectric station on the river, is 66 km from Hamilton via Te Awamutu. Take SH3 to just south of Te Awamutu, and turn left (east) at Kihikihi. It is also accessible from Karapiro or Tirau on SH1. The dam was built across the Arapuni Gorge and is worth a look. Visitors are allowed access to most of the works.

The King Country

The King Country is named after the Maori King Movement, which developed in the Waikato in the late 1850s and early 1860s. When King Tawhiao and his people were forced to move from their Waikato land after the Waikato Wars of 1863 to 1864 against British troops, they came south to this region which was as yet unaffected by Pakeha invasion. Legend has it that King Tawhiao placed his white top hat, symbol of the kingship, on a large map of New Zealand and declared that all the land it covered would be under his mana or authority. The area coincided roughly with the present-day districts of Otorohanga, Waitomo and Taumarunui,

Te Arikinui Dame Te Atairangikaahu

The Maori 'King Movement', in which local chief Te Wherowhero was elected as the first Maori king in 1859, is still very much alive among the Waikato Maori tribes. Te Arikinui Dame Te Atairangikaahu, who currently holds the title of Maori queen, is sixth in the line of succession.

Her father, Koroki Mahuta, was the fifth Maori king. When he died in 1966, there was widespread concern over who his successor should be, since he had no sons but two daughters, Tura and Piki, and there had never been a Maori queen.

According to ancient tradition, if an *ariki* (the first-born of a noble family) died and had no sons, office would be passed on to a close male relation. Therefore the inheritance of royal office posed a major question: should it be passed on to one of Koroki Mahuta's female descendants, or should it be bestowed upon someone else?

After much discussion and debate, the Maori chiefs and elders decided that the office should pass to Piki, Mahuta's daughter. Princess Piki became the first Maori queen on 23 May 1966. In 1970 Queen Elizabeth II conferred upon her the title of Dame Commander of the British Empire, and her official title became Te Arikinui Dame Te Atairangikaahu.

Many Westerners misunderstand her position, believing her to be queen of all the New Zealand Maori just as Queen Elizabeth II is queen of all of the UK; in fact Te Arikinui Dame Te Atairangikaahu is queen only of the tribes who united to form the Maori King Movement in the 1850s. She is head of the Tainui tribal confederation, which consists of four major tribes: the Waikato, Maniapoto, Hauraki and Raukawa. This is one of New Zealand's largest Maori confederations, estimated to contain around 70,000 to 75,000 people (out of the entire Maori population of around 330,000).

Te Arikinui Dame Te Atairangikaahu's marae is the magnificent Turangawaewae Marae, beside the Waikato River in Ngaruawahia. If you are travelling through Ngaruawahia on SH1, you can see the marae as you cross the bridge over the river. The queen has houses in various places significant to her people – for example, there is a house for the Maori queen beside the Maketu Marae in Kawhia, where the *Tainui* canoe is buried.

Te Arikinui Dame Te Atairangikaahu is an eloquent speaker and a gracious leader who is much loved by her people. She uses her influence to try to promote equality between Maori and Pakeha, and mutual understanding and respect for each culture. ■

extending westwards to the coast and eastwards as far as Lake Taupo.

For several decades the King Country remained the stronghold of King Tawhiao and other Maori chiefs, who held out against the Pakeha longer than the Maori did anywhere else in New Zealand. This area was forbidden to the Pakeha by Maori law until the 1880s, and was even then not much penetrated by Pakeha until, with the consent of the Maori chiefs, the Auckland-Wellington Main Trunk Railway Line entered the region in 1891. The earliest Europeans to settle in Otorohanga were timber millers, the first of them arriving in 1890. The laying of the railway to form a continuous line from Auckland to Wellington in 1908 marked the end of the region's isolation, though even today a powerful Maori influence is still present.

From 1884, when Pakeha were allowed into the district, until 1955, the King Country was 'dry' (alcohol was prohibited). This condition was apparently imposed by Maori chiefs when they agreed to the Europeans building the railway through their country, opening it up even more to the outside world. Needless to say there are now numerous hotels everywhere, so you won't go thirsty.

OTOROHANGA

Otorohanga, in the upper Waipa basin, is on SH3, 59 km south of Hamilton and 16 km from Waitomo Caves. A dairy and sheep farming community, it is the northernmost township of the King Country. Otorohanga's only real tourist attraction is its impressive kiwi house and most people pass through Otorohanga on the way to Waitomo Caves.

The name Otorohanga means 'food for a long journey'. Legend says that a Maori chief who was on his way to Taupo passed through Otorohanga carrying little food, but that through magic incantations he was able to make the food last for the journey.

Information

The Otorohanga Visitor Information Centre (☎ 873 8951) on the corner of Maniapoto and Tuhoro Sts is open Monday to Friday from 9 am to 5 pm, Saturday and public holidays from 10 am to 3 pm and Sunday from 11 am to 2 pm. It is also the AA agent and sells bus and train tickets.

Otorohanga Kiwi House

'Not another kiwi house', you may groan – but this one is worth a visit. In a kiwi house night and day are reversed, so you can watch the kiwis in daytime under artificial moonlight. There are also various other native birds including some keas, which more than live up to their reputation for being inquisitive. The walk-in aviary is the largest in New Zealand. Other birds you can see include

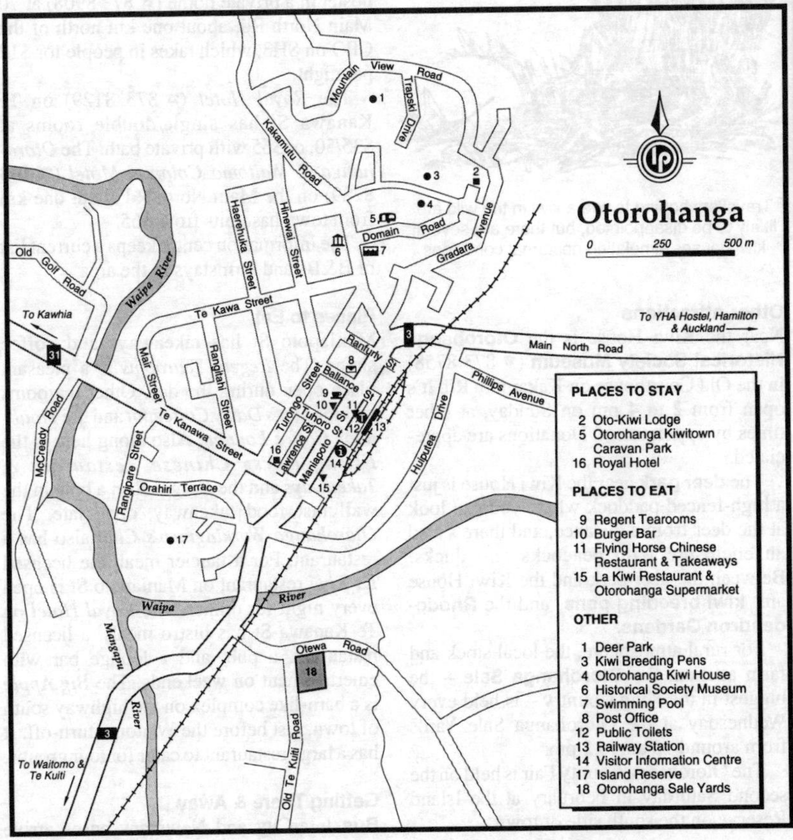

morepork owls, hawks and wekas. There are tuataras also on display.

The Kiwi House is open from 9.30 am to 5 pm every day. The last admission is half an hour before closing time. Admission is $7 (children $2).

Travellers hoping to see a kiwi in the wild are likely to be disappointed, but there are several kiwi houses simulating nocturnal conditions

Other Attractions

Near the Kiwi House is the **Otorohanga Historical Society Museum** (☎ 873 8758) in the Old Courthouse on Kakamutu Rd. It's open from 2 to 4 pm on Sunday, at other times by appointment. Donations are appreciated.

The **deer park** near the Kiwi House is just a high-fenced paddock where you can look at the deer from a distance, and there's also an enclosure with peacocks and ducks. Between the deer park and the Kiwi House are **kiwi breeding pens** and the **Rhododendron Gardens**.

For rural atmosphere, the local stock and farm auction, the **Otorohanga Sale** – the biggest in the King Country – is held every Wednesday at the Otorohanga Sale Yards from around 10 am to 2 pm.

The Otorohanga County Fair is held on the second Saturday in February at the Island Reserve on the south side of town.

Places to Stay

The *Otorohanga Kiwitown Caravan Park* (☎ 873 8214) is on Domain Rd, adjacent to the Kiwi House – you can hear the kiwis calling at night. There's a BBQ area, with free wood for BBQs; tent sites are $13 for two, powered sites are $15, and on-site caravans are $27.

Also near the kiwi house, *Oto-Kiwi Lodge* (☎ 873 6022), 1 Sangro Crescent, is a new backpackers opened by the Rt Hon Jim Bolger no less. It's a well-equipped hostel with small, four-bed dorms at $13 per person, and two doubles/triples costing $18.50 per person. There is also a friendly hostel in a private home (☎ 873 8908) at 70 Main North Rd, about one km north of the CPO on SH3, which takes in people for $12 per night.

The *Royal Hotel* (☎ 873 8129) on Te Kanawa St has single/double rooms at $35/50, or $65 with private bath. The *Otorohanga & Waitomo Colonial Motel* (☎ 873 8289) on the Main North Rd about one km from town has units from $65.

The information centre keeps a current list of B&Bs and farmstays in the area.

Places to Eat

Maniapoto St has takeaways and coffee shops. The *Regent Tearooms* is a pleasant place open during the day. Other tearooms include *Dot's Dairy Coffeepot* and the *Troubador Coffee Lounge*. Also along here is the *Flying Horse Chinese Restaurant & Takeaways* and the *Burger Bar*, a hole in the wall fast food takeaway, open late. The *Otorohanga Workingmen's Club* also has a restaurant. For a fancier meal, the licensed *La Kiwi* restaurant on Maniapoto St is open every night for dinner. The *Royal Hotel* on Te Kanawa St has bistro meals, a licensed restaurant, a pub, and a lounge bar with entertainment on weekends. The *Big Apple* is a barn-like complex on the highway south of town, just before the Waitomo turn-off. It has a large restaurant to cater for tour groups.

Getting There & Away

Bus InterCity and Newmans buses arrive

and depart from the information centre, which sells the bus tickets. There are several buses a day in each direction. It's about 30 minutes to Waitomo Caves, one hour to Hamilton, 3½ hours to Auckland and three hours to New Plymouth. Via Hamilton there are connecting services to Rotorua and Tauranga. C Tours also have a daily Auckland-New Plymouth service that stops at Otorohanga.

To get to Waitomo, change buses in Otorohanga. The Waitomo Shuttle (☎ 873 8279) runs between Otorohanga and Waitomo for $6, dropping off wherever you wish. The shuttle usually meets the main buses, but goes on request at other times; bookings through the information centre.

Train The day and evening Auckland-Wellington trains stop at Otorohanga. The railway station is in the centre of town.

AROUND OTOROHANGA

Otorohanga Carnation Growers

Ten km out from Otorohanga on the highway to Kawhia (SH31), the Otorohanga Carnation Growers (☎ 873 7400) have about 10,000 sq metres of glasshouses. They're open every day and visitors are welcome; they request that you telephone before you arrive.

WAITOMO

Waitomo is famous for its limestone caves, and the whole region is riddled with caves and strange limestone formations. Tours through the Waitomo Cave (now more commonly called the Glow-worm Cave), the Ruakuri Cave and the Aranui Cave have been feature attractions for decades and are still one of the North Island's main tourist attractions.

Visitors used to stop for an hour or a day, just to see the caves; now there's plenty to do during a longer stay. Waitomo has a host of activities – organised caving expeditions, rafting through caves, abseiling, horse trekking, canoeing and more.

The name Waitomo comes from *wai* (water) and *tomo* (hole or shaft). It's aptly named: dotted throughout the countryside are a number of tomos, shafts dropping abruptly through the surface of the ground into underground cave systems.

> Rivers going underground, great springs emerging from the ground, independent hollows and basins instead of connecting valleys, deep potholes and vast caves, isolated tower-like hills ... these are some of the distinctive features of karst, the name given to the kinds of country that owe their special characteristics to the unusual degree of solubility of their component rocks in natural waters.
>
> **JN Jennings in *Karst*, Australian National University Press, Canberra, 1971**

Information

Waitomo is eight km west of the main highway, SH3. The information centre is at the Museum of Caves (☎ 878 7640), which also serves as the post office and as the booking agent for most of the activities. It's open every day from 8.30 am to 5.30 pm; until 5 pm in winter from Easter to the end of October; and later, until around 8 pm, in January.

Serious cavers can get more caving information from the Tomo Group Hut (see Hostels).

Groceries are available at the store next to the New Zealand Trade Centre, but the choice is wider at nearby towns like Otorohanga or Te Kuiti.

Museum of Caves

This museum has excellent exhibits about how caves are formed, the flora and fauna that live in caves, the history of caves and cave exploration. Exhibits include a cave model, fossils of extinct birds and animals that have been discovered in caves, and a cave crawl for the adventurous. There are also audiovisual presentations about caving, glow-worms and the many other natural attractions found in the Waitomo area.

The museum is open every day from 8.30 am to 5.30 pm; until 5 pm in winter from Easter to the end of October; and later, until around 8 pm, in January. Admission is $3.50 (children free); free admission is sometimes included with various activities, or you can

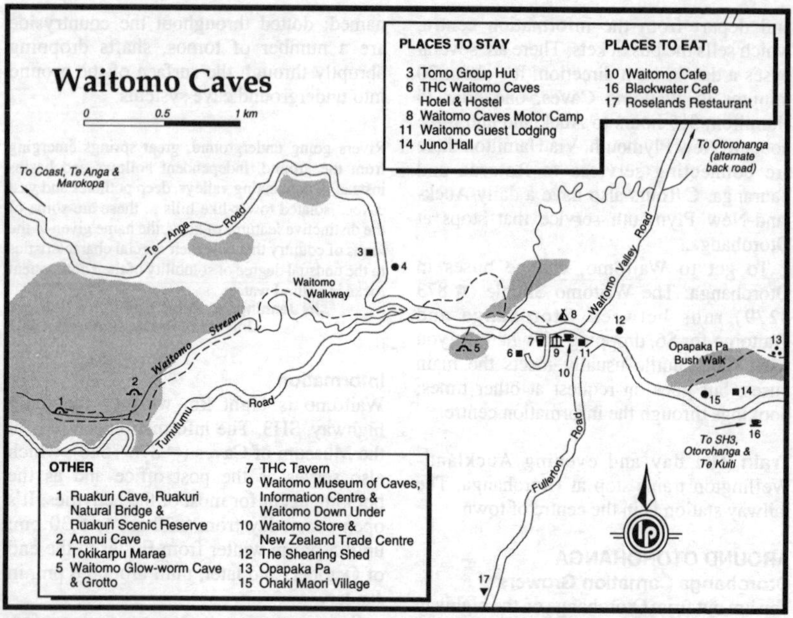

get a 'museum-cave special' for $18 if you visit the Glow-worm Cave.

Between the museum and the general store is a carved Maori canoe and some limestone formations with interesting plaques telling about karst and the area's limestone geology.

The Caves

Glow-Worm Cave This cave had been known to the local Maori for a long time, but the first European to explore it was English surveyor Fred Mace, who was shown the cave on 28 December 1887 by the Maori chief Tane Tinorau. Mace prepared an account of the expedition, a map was made and photographs given to the government, and before long Tane Tinorau was operating tours of the cave, over a century ago.

The Glow-worm Cave is just a big cave with the usual assortment of stalactites and stalagmites – until you board a boat and swing off onto the river. As your eyes grow accustomed to the dark you'll see a Milky Way of little lights surrounding you – these are the glow-worms. You can see them in other caves and in other places around Waitomo, and in other parts of New Zealand, but the ones in this cave are still something special to see; conditions for their growth here are just about perfect, so there is a remarkable number of them. The tour takes about 45 minutes.

The Glow-worm Cave is the most popular cave, crammed with tourists being shuttled through, one tour after the other. Many feel disappointed with the tourist rush-through, especially given the price, but this is the most spectacular cave and the main attraction of Waitomo. The big tour buses peak around lunch time. Try to go on the first tour of the day.

Aranui & Ruakuri Caves These caves are three km further up the road from the Glow-worm Cave.

The Aranui Cave has no river running through it and hence no glow-worms. It is a large cave with thousands of tiny, hollow 'straw' stalactites hanging from the ceiling. It takes about 45 minutes to tour this cave. Various scenes in the formations are pointed out and photography is permitted. Transport to the Aranui Cave is not included with the tour ticket. You may be able to catch a ride with the tour guide or other visitors, or else walk.

From the Aranui Cave car park it is a beautiful bush walk through the Ruakuri Scenic Reserve to the Ruakuri Cave. The Ruakuri Cave is an active cave, with large, dripping caverns where stalactites and stalagmites are still being formed. The cave is open only for Black Water Rafting (see the Cave Activities section), which the most exciting way to see any caves, but you can see into the cave from the walkway. The Ruakari Cave has glow-worms (though not as many as in the Waitomo cave) and fossils of scallops as big as your hand, as well as interesting limestone formations.

Tours & Tickets The Waitomo and Aranui caves can be visited individually or with a combined ticket. Tickets are sold at the entrance to the Glow-worm Cave. Entry to the Glow-worm Cave is $16.50 (children $8.25), the Aranui Cave costs $16.50 (children $8.75) or a combined two-cave ticket is $25 (children $13, family $55). The 'museum-cave special' includes the Glow-worm Cave tour and a visit to the Museum of Caves for $18.

The 45-minute tours of the Glow-worm Cave depart every day on the hour from 9 am to 4 pm, with a final tour at 4.30 pm. From late October to Easter there's also a 5.30 pm tour, with more at the height of the summer season. Aranui Cave tours go at 10 and 11 am, 1, 2 and 3 pm, and also take about 45 minutes.

KING COUNTRY

Glow-Worms

Glow-worms are the larvae of a type of gnat called a fungus gnat, which looks much like a large mosquito without mouth parts. The larvae glow-worms have luminescent organs which produce a soft, greenish light. Living in a sort of 'hammock' hanging down from an overhang, they weave sticky threads which hang down and catch unwary insects attracted by their lights. When an insect flies towards the light, it gets stuck in the hanging threads and becomes paralysed, after which the glow-worm reels the thread up and then eats the insect.

The larval stage lasts for six to nine months, depending on how much food the glow-worm gets – the more food, the quicker it can mature. When the glow-worm has grown to about the size of a matchstick it goes into a pupa stage, much like a cocoon. The adult fungus gnat emerges about two weeks later.

The adult of the species may be caught and eaten by the larval glow-worm. Even if it avoids that fate, the adult insect does not live very long because it does not have a mouth; it emerges, mates, lays eggs and dies, all within about two or three days. The sticky eggs, laid in groups of 40 or 50, hatch in about three weeks to become larval glow-worms.

Glow-worms thrive in moist, dark caves, but they can survive anywhere if they have the requisites of moisture, an overhang to hang from, and insects to eat. Waitomo is famous for its glow-worms but you can see them in many other places around New Zealand, both in caves and outdoors. Similar glow-worms exist in south-east Australia but the New Zealand variety is a distinct species, *Arachnocampa luminosa*.

When you come upon glow-worms, don't touch their hammocks or their hanging threads, try not to make loud noises, and don't shine a light right on them. In daylight their lights fade out, and if you shine a torch right on them they will dim their lights. It takes the lights a few hours to become bright again, during which time the glow-worm will catch no food. The glow-worms that shine most brightly are the ones that are the hungriest. ■

Check out the large Tane Mahuta carving outside the Glow-worm Cave ticket office. It was commissioned in 1987 for the centennial of the first recorded exploration of the Glow-worm Cave and has many interesting figures relating to the area and the caves. A pamphlet explains the various details of the carving.

Cave Activities

Black Water Rafting I & II Black-water rafting started in Waitomo in 1987 and quickly became one of New Zealand's most popular adventures.

Black Water Rafting I is a three-hour trip down a subterranean river through the Ruakuri Cave. First you get into a wetsuit and caver's helmet with a light on the front, grab a black inner tube, and you're off on a trek through the cave which involves leaping over a small waterfall, floating through a long glow-worm covered passageway, and plenty of Kiwi-style joking and laughs. At the end of the journey there's a hot shower and soup to warm up your innards, but in the wetsuit you probably won't get too cold.

The $55 fee includes admission to the Museum of Caves for more education on glow-worms and caves, and if you want something more than just a tour of the Glow-worm Cave, it is worth the extra. Trips leave from the Blackwater Cafe several times daily, and a shuttle runs between the museum and the cafe. During the busy summer holiday period, book as far in advance as possible through the Museum of Caves. This tour is raved about by just about everyone who goes on it.

Black Water Rafting II is a more adventurous caving experience. It goes through a different part of the Ruakuri Cave and this all-day caving expedition includes all the features of BWR I but also involves a 30-metre abseil, and a caving expedition out of the cave. The trip takes six hours; the cost is $110.

Waitomo Down Under Waitomo Down Under operates a variety of adventures. Its three-hour Adventure I cave tubing trip is similar to Black Water Rafting I & II; wearing a wetsuit and caving helmet, you go through the Te Ana Roa cave (long cave) in inner tubes, going over *two* waterfalls (one on a slide) and getting a good close-up view of some glow-worms along the way. It, too, ends with a hot shower, hot soup and tea, and includes a visit to the local marae along with some Maori culture; the cost is $50.

Waitomo Down Under's Adventure II combines the above with a 50-metre abseil down into the 'Baby Grand' tomo. Thrill seekers can also try this one rapseiling, ie upside down. The cost is $100. Their six-hour Adventure III combines the first two with exploration of a different cave which includes glow-worms and a crystalline white section known as 'The Pretties'. The cost is $130.

The Waitomo Down Under office (☎ 878 6577) is next door to the Museum of Caves. It is operated by descendants of Tane Tinorau, the Maori chief who introduced Fred Mace to the Waitomo Cave and who led tours there a century ago.

Lost World And now... to try to describe the indescribable. This is what the first explorers had to say:

'... We had fallen upon a 'wonderland'. The sight that met our view was enchanting. Fairyland was before us. Away down, near what appeared to be its very depths was a large plateau of moss and ferns, but so far down that they appeared only small topped matter showing all the tints of green. As we looked we more than half expected to see the pixies come dancing out. This is no imagination. It was fairyland without fairies.'

***The King Country Chronicle*, 16 December 1906.**

We found it the same when we went through. With 100 metres (300 feet) of free-hanging abseiling to get into the Lost World cave, it's right up there as one of the most amazing things you can do in this country. And you don't even need prior abseiling or caving experience.

The principal trip to Lost World is a 1½-day affair, including a half-day abseiling instruction on the first day, and then a full day at Lost World. This is when you abseil down into the cave, then by a combination of walking, rock climbing, spider-walking, inching along narrow rock ledges, wading and swimming through a subterranean river, you take a three-hour journey through a 30-metre-high cave to get back out, passing glow-worms, amazing rock and cave formations, waterfalls and more. The cost is $395.

The other option is a tandem abseil into the cave, with a guide right beside you on another rope, so you don't need the first day's detailed instruction. At the bottom, you walk half an hour into the cave, and exit via another vertical cavern back to the surface, without doing the underground river trip. The tandem trip takes only four hours and costs $195.

The Lost World can also be visited as a 'Gruesome Twosome' combo with the Haggas Honking Hole trip. Bookings are made through the Museum of Caves.

Haggas Honking Hole Yet another amazing trip presented by the Lost World people, this four-hour caving trip includes professional abseiling instruction followed by a caving trip with four abseils, rock climbing, and going along a subterranean river with waterfalls. Along the way you see glow-worms and a variety of cave formations – stalactites, stalagmites, columns, flowstone, cave coral and all the rest. It's a good experience for seeing real caving in action, using caving equipment and going through caverns of various sizes, squeezing through some tight spots and narrow passageways as well as traversing huge caverns.

The cost is $100; or the 'Gruesome Twosome' combines this with the Lost World tandem abseil for $270. Both four-hour trips, they can be done together on one day, or on different days.

Canoeing Yes, you can even canoe the caves. Waitomo Wilderness Tours (☎ 025 83574), in addition to regular canoeing trips, will lower you 22 metres into a cave stream from where you canoe with the glow-worms. These 3½ hour trips cost $75. There are also four-hour gorge canoeing trips to a glow-worm cave for $60, three-hour river trips through native bush for $50 or six to eight-hour trips for $120. A minimum of two people is required and a maximum of only four go on each trip.

Other Attractions

The **Ohaki Maori Village** is a replica of a pre-European Maori pa, with traditional Maori arts & crafts on sale. Demonstrations and displays of Maori weavings are put on for groups. The centre is open every day from 10 am to 4.30 pm. Admission to the Maori village is $2.50 (children $1.50), a weaving demonstration is $5 (children $1.50).

The **Shearing Shed** is a centre for products made with the fur of Angora rabbits. The craft shop here sells a variety of crafts and souvenirs as well as Angora products. You can pat the furry bunnies out the back, and see them being shorn at 1 pm. It's open every day from 9 am to 5 pm. Admission is free.

Next to the museum, the **New Zealand Trade Centre** sells deer products catering to the Asian market. It's worth a look for the bizarre array of deer velvet and other medicinal oddities such as deer penis on sale at astronomical prices.

Horse Treks

Waitomo Horse-Trekking operates from the Juno Hall hostel (see Hostels), with a variety of rides through Waitomo wilderness areas. The cost is $20 for a one-hour ride, $30 for two hours, $50 for a half day, $70 for a full-day ride and $150 for overnight treks. Waitomo Down Under, next to the Museum of Caves, also does horse treks.

Walks

The Museum of Caves has free pamphlets on various walks in the area. The walk from the Aranui Cave to the Ruakuri Cave is an excellent short work (see under Caves). From the Glow-worm Cave ticket office, it's a 15-minute forest walk to a grove of California redwood trees. Also from here, the five-km, three-hour Waitomo Walkway takes off through farmland and follows the Waitomo Stream to the Ruakuri Scenic Reserve, where a half-hour return walk passes by the river and caves and a natural limestone bridge.

A one-hour return walk, the Opapaka Pa Bush Walk takes off from the car park of the Otaki Maori Village & Crafts Centre, leading up to a pre-European Maori pa site on a hill. Plaques along the way describe traditional Maori medicinals found in the forest, traditional forest lore and the pa site itself.

Many other good walks are found west of Waitomo on the Marokopa Rd; see Around Waitomo for more on these.

Places to Stay

Camping & Cabins The *Waitomo Caves Motor Camp* (☎ 878 7639) is opposite the museum. Camp sites cost $6 per person, or $7 with power. It also has cabins at $24 a double.

Both hostels will also allow you to pitch a tent.

Hostels The *Waitomo Caves Associate YHA Hostel* (☎ 878 8227) is at the THC Waitomo Caves Hotel right in the centre of Waitomo, in a separate building that once served as the staff housing. The cost is $16 per night, $17 for non-YHA members. It also has twin rooms in the hotel at hostel rates.

Juno Hall (☎ 878 7649) is on the main road in from the highway to the caves, roughly one km before the Museum of Caves. Its communal area has the feel of a ski lodge and it offers good standards of accommodation. The cost is $14 in dorm rooms, $35 in twins and $45 in double rooms with own facilities. You can camp for $7 per person. Activities include horse trekking, hunting and fishing trips.

Two km further on past the Glow-worm Cave, the *Tomo Group Hut* (☎ 878 7442) is the clubroom of the Hamilton Tomo Group, the largest caving club in New Zealand. They welcome visitors, and the cost of $10 for the first night and $8 for each successive night helps to support the club. The hut is quite 'rustic' but has good lounge and kitchen areas, even if the beds in the share rooms are hard. Bring your own sleeping bag. The helpful caretaker can tell you about walks and free activities in the area, or if you're lucky you may be invited on a caving trip, particularly on weekends when cavers come to the hostel.

The Waitomo region has over 100 km of caves, many still unexplored, so there's ample field for caving adventure. The hut has detailed maps on many caves but it's not advisable to go off caving alone in the area. In 1995 one of the world's most experienced cavers tragically lost his life in a record cave-diving attempt.

Guesthouses & Farmstays *Waitomo Guest Lodging* (☎ 878 7641) is conveniently situated just 100 metres from the Museum of Caves in the centre of the village. It's a pleasant, friendly B&B. Rooms, each with private bath, cost $50/60 for singles/doubles, including breakfast.

Several homes and farms in the area offer lodging and B&B arrangements for around $35/60. Check with the Museum of Caves, where many are listed.

Hotels The *THC Waitomo Caves Hotel* (☎ 878 8227), high on the hill in the centre of the village, is a historic hotel built in 1908, and was *the* place to stay. This grand, old hotel is not quite as sophisticated or as expensive as it looks. Though one wing has refurbished rooms for $112 a night, many of the rooms are economy class with one set of bunk beds. It provides good accommodation with some old-fashioned style for $35, or $40 with attached bathroom. Economy rooms are popular, so book ahead. The hotel – and the caves – have been sold to new owners, so the hotel may be destined for upgrading.

Motels There are a couple of motels on SH3 at the junction of the Waitomo turn-off, eight km from Waitomo. The *Glow Worm Motel* (☎ 873 8882) on the corner of the two roads has units for $69 and $79. About 100 metres south on SH3, the *Caves Motor Inn* (☎ 873 8109) has a variety of accommodation including a lodge at $20 per person on a share basis, standard units at $55/65 and premium units at $65/75. There is also a bar and restaurant.

Places to Eat

The store beside the Museum of Caves is open every day, with a cafe off to one side where you can get inexpensive meals to take away or eat in. *Blackwater Cafe*, two km from the caves out towards the main highway, has both indoor and patio seating and is open every day from 9 am to 5 pm for breakfast, lunch and Devonshire teas.

The *THC Tavern* near the Museum of Caves is excellent value for light meals and snacks – and some of the snacks for around $5 are bigger meals than many restaurants serve. Drinks are also reasonably priced.

For more elegant and expensive dining the *THC Waitomo Caves Hotel* has the *Fred Mace Restaurant*, which in addition to its regular menu also does lunch and Sunday night buffets for around $20.

The upmarket *Roselands Restaurant* is open for lunch, with an ample BBQ of steak or fish, a salad buffet, dessert and coffee in an attractive setting with garden, veranda or indoor seating. From Waitomo village, go 400 metres east towards the highway, then follow the signs for three km.

Entertainment

The *THC Tavern* is the popular local watering hole, with cheap food and regular activities. Bands also play sometimes on weekends.

Getting There & Away

Bus The Waitomo Shuttle operates a pick-up and drop-off service between Waitomo and Otorohanga. The cost is $6 between Otorohanga and Waitomo, $4.50 from Waitomo to the SH3 turn-off. Scheduled departures from Waitomo go at 9.30 am, noon and 4 pm. At other times ring for pick-up but you'll have to charter if numbers are small. Bookings are essential and can be made through the Waitomo Museum of Caves or directly through Otorohanga Taxis (☎ 873 8279).

On weekdays Perry's Bus makes a round trip from the coast to Te Kuiti on the Marokopa Road – see the Marokopa Road section for information.

InterCity has round-trip excursion bus services to the Glow-worm Cave from Auckland and Rotorua. You only get to spend an hour at the caves so it's a very rushed trip. If you are already in Otorohanga you can catch the InterCity bus to the caves as it passes through at about noon. Since the Auckland and Rotorua excursion buses arrive and depart from the caves at the same times, you could arrive on the bus from Auckland and leave an hour later on the bus to Rotorua, or vice versa. You can also take these buses just one way to or from Waitomo. Leaving Waitomo, both buses depart from the Glow-worm Cave at 1.30 pm every day. Regular full fare is $43 to Auckland or Rotorua. Otherwise, frequent bus services along SH3 will drop you at the Waitomo turn-off, eight km from Waitomo.

Magic Bus, Kiwi Safaris and the Kiwi Experience also come to Waitomo.

Hitching Hitching to Waitomo from the turn-off on SH3 is usually pretty easy, as is hitching around Waitomo once you're out there. Hitching out towards Te Anga and Marokopa can be more difficult because there's so little traffic.

AROUND WAITOMO

There are many scenic reserves around the Waitomo area; the Waitomo Museum of Caves has plenty of printed information about them.

Marokopa Rd

Heading west from Waitomo, the Marokopa Rd follows a rewarding and scenic route with a couple of natural beauties worth visiting. DOC produces a useful *West to Marokopa* pamphlet, or *A Trip Through Time* by Peter Chandler, available from the museum, outlines a geological driving tour of the 53-km road from Waitomo to Kiritehere on the coast, with suggestions for walks.

On weekdays Perry's Bus runs from Taharoa on the coast along the Marokopa Rd to Te Kuiti via Te Anga and Waitomo. It departs from the Te Kuiti railway station at 1 pm for the return trip.

The **Tawarau Forest**, about 20 km west of Waitomo village, has various walks outlined in a DOC pamphlet, including a one-hour walk to the Tawarau Falls from the end of Appletree Rd. The Alpiger Hut shown in the DOC pamphlet is now closed.

The **Mangapohue Natural Bridge Scenic Reserve**, 26 km west of Waitomo, is a 5½-hectare reserve with a giant natural limestone bridge formation; this is a 20-minute walk from the road on a wheelchair-accessible pathway. At times you may see cavers practising their manoeuvres by dangling from the summit on ropes. You can easily walk to the summit. On the far side, big rocks full of oyster fossils jut up from the grass. At night you'll see glow-worms.

Not far from the Natural Bridge, the **Marokopa Tunnel** is another massive limestone formation – a natural tunnel 270 metres long and 50 metres high at its highest point, going right through a limestone hill. Limestone formations, fossils and glow-worms can be seen in the tunnel.

The tunnel is on private land, owned by a friendly farming couple who run Marokopa Tunnel Treks (☎ 876 7865). They conduct guided walks through the tunnel, departing from their farmhouse near the Mangapohue Natural Bridge car park and leading on a bush walk beside the Marokopa River, then up a small tributary to the tunnel. A picnic lunch and afternoon tea are provided; plan to spend about 3½ to four hours. The cost is $18 ($10 for students). Torches are provided.

About four km further west is the **Piripiri Caves Scenic Reserve**, where a 30-minute track leads to a large cave containing fossils of giant oysters. Bring a torch if you want to explore the cave.

The impressive 36-metre **Marokopa Falls** are 32 km west of Waitomo. You can view them from the road above, or walk to the bottom on a track starting just downhill from the roadside vantage point.

The falls are near **Te Anga** where you can stop for a drink at the pleasant Te Anga Tavern. From Te Anga you can turn north to Taharoa or Kawhia, 53 km away (see the Around Hamilton section) or south-west to **Marokopa**, a small village on the coast, 48 km from Waitomo. The whole Te Anga-Marokopa area is riddled with caves. The bitumen road ends just out of Marokopa at Kiritehere, but it is possible to continue, on a difficult but scenic road, 60 km further south until you meet SH3 at Awakino (see Te Kuiti to Mokau below). About 20 km south of Marokopa is the **Whareorino Forest**, which has forest walks and overnighting at Leitches Hut (enquiries through DOC in Te Kuiti).

Places to Stay In Te Anga, the *Bike 'n' Hike* (☎ 876 7362) is a small backpackers operated by an outdoorsy fellow knowledgeable about caving, geology and fossils; he organises a host of activities and rents mountain bikes.

About 10 km south of Te Anga on the road to Marokopa, *Hepipi Farm* (☎ 876 7861) offers B&B and also has three self-contained units at the beach in Marokopa for $40 per unit, each sleeping four or five people. Also at the beach in Marokopa is the *Marokopa Motor Camp* (☎ 876 7546).

TE KUITI

This small provincial town, south of Otorohanga and 19 km from Waitomo, has few attractions, but it does have basic services and makes another base for visiting Waitomo.

The name Te Kuiti probably comes from Te Kuititanga, 'the narrowing in', referring not only to the narrowing of the Mangaokewa Valley here but also to the confiscation of Maori property after the Waikato wars. Locals will proudly tell you, however, that the town is named for Te Kooti, a prominent Maori rebellion leader who settled here in 1872, seeking refuge from the Pakeha, and remained for a number of years.

The magnificently carved Te Tokanganui a Noho Marae, overlooking the south end of Rora St, was a gift from Te Kooti to his hosts, the Ngati Maniapoto people.

Te Kuiti, home to many champion sheep shearers, is known as 'the Shearing Capital of the World'. A 'big shearer' statue is the most prominent feature of the town.

Information

The Te Kuiti Information Centre (☎ 878 8077) on the main drag, Rora St, is open Monday to Friday from 9 am to 5 pm, weekends from 10 am to 4 pm. It has information on Waitomo and the surrounding area as well as Te Kuiti, homestays and farmstays, and it's also the AA agent for the town.

The DOC office (☎ 878 7297) is at 78 Taupiri St.

Things to See & Do

Apart from the big shearer, Te Kuiti's main attraction is the **Te Kuiti Muster**, held on the first weekend in April (or the following weekend, if Easter falls then). This popular event has all kinds of entertainment including sheep and goat shearing championships, a country parade, arts & crafts, live music, sheep races, Maori culture groups, BBQs and hangis, a duathlon, a town-wide bargain day, and more. Sometimes a steam locomotive comes from Auckland for the day.

Many NZ sheep stations welcome visitors and put on sheep-shearing and sheepdog displays

Tours can be arranged to **Te Tokanganui a Noho** meeting house at the Te Kuiti marae. Wharenui Tours (☎ 025 757415) explain marae protocol and Maori teachings as well as the carvings at the house. The cost is $15 per person (children $6); tours by appointment only.

Te Kuiti has some fine gardens and parks. If you're a garden fan, ask the information centre for their King Country Gardens brochure, giving details on 20 private gardens you can visit in the region.

The **Mangaokewa River** winds through the town, with a pleasant riverside walkway. Beside the river, the Mangaokewa Scenic Reserve, three km south of town on SH30, has picnic and BBQ areas, a waterhole for safe swimming, and overnight camping.

On the north-western boundary of Te Kuiti, the attractive **Brook Park Recreation Reserve** has walking tracks leading to the summit of the Ben Lomond hill. Besides affording a fine view, the hill is the site of the historic Matakiora Pa, constructed in the 17th century by Rora, son of Maniapoto. Camping is permitted in the park.

The **Te Kuiti Lookout**, on Awakino Rd (SH3) as it climbs out of town heading south, provides a great view over the town, especially at night with the sparkling lights stretching out below.

Places to Stay & Eat

The *Domain Motor Camp* (☎ 878 6223) on the north side of town beside the Mangaokewa River, about 800 metres north of the information centre, is a peaceful camping ground with tent sites at $5.50 per person, powered sites at $6.50 per person, on-site caravans at $20 and cabins at $25 for two.

Camping is also permitted at the Brook

KING COUNTRY

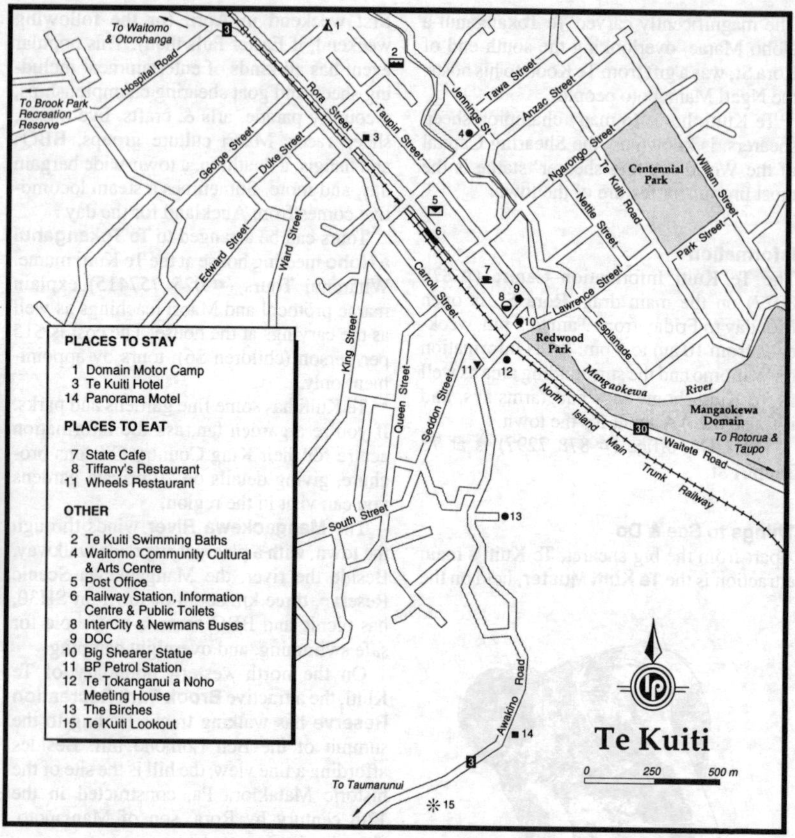

Park Recreation Reserve on the north-western boundary of Te Kuiti, and at the Mangaokewa Scenic Reserve beside the Mangaokewa River (see Things to See & Do); both have BBQs, picnic areas and toilets, but no other facilities. Payment is by donation.

On Rora St in the centre of town, the *Te Kuiti Hotel* (☎ 878 8172) has rooms with private facilities costing $45/55 for singles/doubles. The *Panorama Motel* (☎ 878 8051) at 59 Awakino Rd (SH3), about 1.5 km south of town, has a swimming pool and units from $57/70.

Te Kuiti has day-time cafes on Rora St, or the *State Cafe* is open until 8 pm for standard takeaways, or you can eat there. Also on Rora St, *Tiffany's Restaurant* is open late or *Wheels Restaurant*, beside the BP Petrol Station, is a friendly, casual restaurant popular with Te Kuitians and travellers passing through. It has both European and Chinese food, with a restaurant and a takeaways section.

Getting There & Away

Bus InterCity and Newmans buses arrive and depart from Tiffany's Restaurant on the south end of Rora St; the ticket office (☎ 878 8872) is open daily from 8.30 am to 5 pm.

Long-distance bus services include those to New Plymouth (two hours), Taumarunui (one hour) or north to Hamilton (1½ hours) and on to Auckland (3¾ hours).

Buses also operate in the local region. On weekdays the Perry's bus runs between Taharoa on the coast and Te Kuiti passing through Waitomo Caves, Te Anga and the other scenic attractions along the Waitomo-Marokopa Road. It departs Te Kuiti railway station at 1 pm.

Train The railway station is on Rora St in the centre of town. Tickets are sold at Tiffany's Restaurant on the south end of Rora St. The Auckland-Wellington trains stop at Te Kuiti.

AROUND TE KUITI

Mason's Limestone Valley

This private farm has limestone caves that can be visited on a three-hour tour for $35 (children $15). The cave tour includes a boat trip along the underground river where you will see glow-worms, and the you also get a tour of the farm on a tractor trolley. Bookings are by appointment (☎ 878 7622) and tours go at 9.30 am and 1.30 pm. To get there, take SH3 north of Te Kuiti for three km, then take the turn-off to Oparure, four km away. The farm is on the Boddie Rd, three km past Oparure.

Pureora Forest Park

The large Pureora Forest Park, about 50 km east of Te Kuiti, has camping, lodge and hut facilities, swimming, fishing, and long and short forest treks, including tracks to the summits of Mt Pureora (1165 metres) and Mt Titiraupenga (1042 metres). Logging was eventually stopped in the park in the '80s after long campaigns by conservationists. Hunting is permitted in the northern section of the park, designated as a recreational hunting area, but you must obtain a permit from the park headquarters. The DOC office in Te Kuiti has pamphlets, maps and information on the park.

TE KUITI TO MOKAU

From Te Kuiti SH3 runs south-west to Mokau on the rugged west coast before continuing on to New Plymouth in Taranaki. The road runs through a lightly populated farming area, and is very scenic in parts. InterCity, Newmans and C Tour buses between Hamilton and New Plymouth all take this route.

The road passes through the small towns of **Piopio**, which has a small museum, and then tiny Mahoenui, from where the road follows the Awakino River. The road along the river is the most spectacular part of the route. Through a short road tunnel you enter the steep **Awakino Gorge**, lined with dense bush and giant pongas.

The road follows the river all the way to **Awakino**, a small settlement on the coast where boats shelter on the river estuary away from the windswept coast. Awakino can also reached via the Marokopa Rd from Waitomo. Just south of Awakino is the **Manioroa marae**, which contains the anchor stone of the *Tainui* canoe, whose descendants populated the King Country. Ask at the organic farm opposite the marae on SH3 for permission to enter. Marae protocol should be observed.

Five km further south, the little town of **Mokau** is at the edge of the King Country before you enter Taranaki. The town's Tainui Museum, open 10 am to 4 pm, has a fascinating collection of old photographs from the time when this once isolated outpost was a coal and lumber shipping port for pioneer settlements along the Mokau River. Mokau River Cruises (☎ 752 9775) has good three-hour trips up the river in summer for $30. Mokau is otherwise just a speck on the map, but it does have a good stretch of wild beach and good fishing. The river mouth contains some of the best white bait to be found in the North Island.

Places to Stay

The *Awakino Hotel* (☎ (06) 752 9815) has singles/doubles for $40/70 and offers backpackers accommodation at $12 per person. The *Palm House* (☎ (06) 752 9081) in

Mokau is a good little hostel on the highway near the museum and close to the beach. Dorms are $14, twins or triples $16 per person or a double room costs $38. Enquire at the fish & chip shop next door if no one is around. Mokau also has two motor camps and a motel, the *Mokau Inn* (☎ (06) 759 9725).

TAUMARUNUI

Taumarunui is a quiet little town on SH4, 82 km south of Te Kuiti and 43 km north of the town of National Park. Its name, meaning 'big screen', comes from an episode in the town's history when a Maori chief, Pehi Taroa, was dying and asked for a screen to shade him from the sun. They say that he died before the screen was in place, still asking for it with his final words – *taumaru nui.*

In winter Taumarunui operates as a ski town, but is really too far from the snow to be convenient. In summer it is one of the main access points for canoeing the Whanganui River (see the Whanganui National Park section for details).

History

At the confluence of the Whanganui and Ongarue Rivers, both major transport waterways, Taumarunui was already an important settlement in pre-European days. It was also significant as the historical meeting place of three important Maori tribes: the Whanganui tribes, the Tuwharetoa and the Maniapoto.

Pakeha did not settle in the area until the 1880s, but even then European influence was minimal until the Main Trunk Railway Line came south from Te Kuiti in 1903. In the same year, the riverboat service coming from the coast at Wanganui was extended up the Whanganui River to Taumarunui. Te Kuiti flourished, as the rail link, running all the way to Auckland, became a much-travelled route and timber from the area's sawmills was freighted out.

Information

The Taumarunui Information Centre (☎ 895 7494) is at the railway station on Hakiaha St in the centre of town. It's open Monday to Friday from 9 am to 4.30 pm, Saturday and Sunday from 10 am to 4 pm. It's also the agent for AA and for InterCity bus and train tickets. It is worth a stop just for a look at the operating model of the Raurimu Spiral.

The DOC office (☎ 895 8201) at Cherry Grove, beside the river, is the place to go for information on the Whanganui National Park and canoeing the river.

Raurimu Spiral

The Raurimu Spiral is a feat of rail engineering that was declared a 'wonder of the world' when it was completed in 1908. The spiral's three horseshoe curves, one complete circle and two short tunnels, allowed the Main Trunk Railway coming south from Auckland and north from Wellington to finally be joined at Horopito. The information centre has an excellent working model of the spiral and pamphlets explaining its construction. At Raurimu, 37 km south of Taumarunui and six km north of National Park, you can see the real thing from a lookout just off the highway.

Rail buffs can experience the spiral on any train between Wellington and Auckland. For a day trip, you can take the train from Taumarunui to National Park and bus back to Taumarunui the same day – the information office has all the relevant schedules.

Museums

There are a couple of interesting museums just outside Taumarunui.

The **Nukunuku Museum** (☎ 896 6365) is a private museum devoted to the Whanganui River and the area around it, with Maori and pioneer artefacts, and pioneer buildings. The museum is at Nukunuku, 17 km down the Whanganui River from Taumarunui. It can visited by river, or via Saddlers Rd, off the Whanganui River Rd.

Shoebridge's Gun Collection (☎ 896 6749) on Mahoe Rd off SH4, about eight km east of Taumarunui, is a large collection of antique guns. Ring before arrival.

Walks

The information centre has suggestions for several enjoyable walks around Taumarunui.

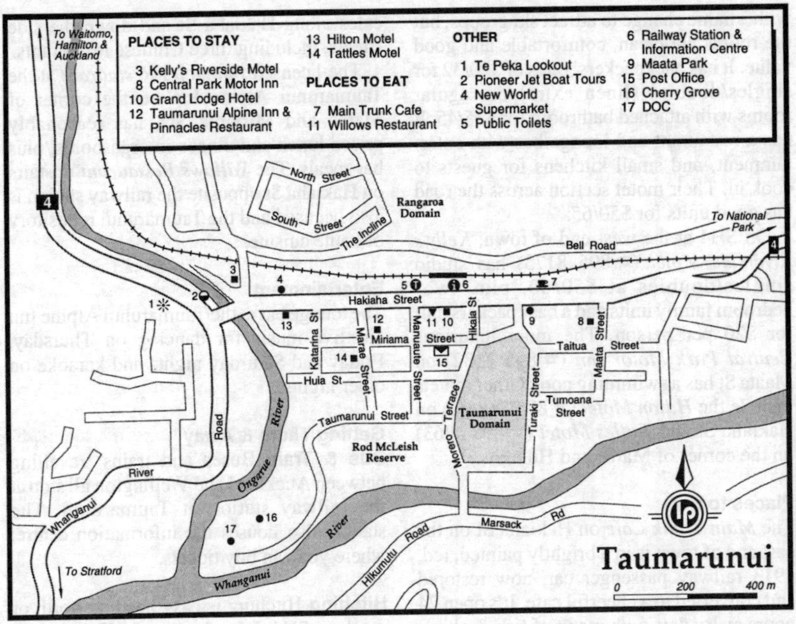

A pleasant walkway extends east along the Whanganui River from Cherry Grove to the Taumarunui Camping Ground, about three km away. Another track leads to the Rangaroa Domain with a good view over the town, its rivers and mountains; go over the railway line, up The Incline and through the native bush behind the scout den to reach it. The Te Peka Lookout across the Ongarue River on the west side of town is another good vantage point.

For even better views extending all the way to Tongariro National Park in the south, climb to the summit of the flat-topped Mt Hikurangi (770 metres) north-east of the town. The curious hill can be seen from far and wide. Before climbing, you must first ask permission from the owner, Mr Skelton (☎ 895 3031).

The Ohinetonga Scenic Reserve on the banks of the Whakapapa River, 26 km south of town at Owhango, has bush walks lasting from one to three hours.

Stratford-Taumarunui Heritage Trail

See the Taranaki chapter for details on this interesting route between Taumarunui and Stratford, in the Taranaki region.

Places to Stay

The *Taumarunui Camping Ground* (☎ 895 8514) is on the banks of the Whanganui River near SH4, three km east of town. Tent sites cost $7 per person, powered sites $8, cabins are $25 a double, and a family unit costs $45. Features of the camp include kayaks and bicycles for hire, bush walks, overnight tramping and guided tours.

Taumarunui has no hostels, but the *Grand Lodge Hotel* (☎ 895 7876) on the main drag, Hakiaha St, is a private hotel with basic singles/doubles for $25/37, and backpacker rates of $15/36 without linen. It has kitchen facilities.

A better bet is the *Taumarunui Alpine Inn* (☎ 895 7033) on the corner of Marae and Miriama Sts. This is basically a large pub with a name change to attract ski groups, but the rooms are clean, comfortable and good value. It has backpackers' rates of $20/32 for singles/doubles (linen extra) or regular rooms with attached bathroom for $35/45. It has a restaurant and lounge bar with entertainment, and small kitchens for guests to cook in. Their motel section across the road has good units for $50/65.

On SH4 at the west end of town, *Kelly's Riverside Motel* (☎ 895 8175) has studio singles/doubles at $50/60, plus two-bedroom family units and a backpackers unit for $20 per person. The more luxurious *Central Park Motor Inn* (☎ 895 7132) on Maata St has a swimming pool. Other motels include the *Hilton Motel* (☎ 895 7181/2) on Hakiaha St and *Tattles Motel* (☎ 895 8063) on the corner of Marae and Huia Sts.

Places to Eat

The *Main Trunk Cafe* on Hakiaha St on the east end of town is in a brightly painted, red, 1913 railway passenger car, now restored and converted to a cheerful cafe. It's open 24 hours every day, with menu of fish & chips, burgers, sandwiches and the like. There are also plenty of other tearooms, takeaways and cafes along Hakiaha St and down the side streets, including three Chinese restaurants.

The licensed *Pinnacles Restaurant* at the Taumarunui Alpine Inn on the corner of Marae and Miriama Sts, has reasonably priced lunch and dinner smorgasbords, plus bar meals. The *Willows Restaurant* upstairs on Hakiaha St opposite the railway station is also licensed and the Taumarunui repository of haute cuisine.

Entertainment

The lounge bar at the Taumarunui Alpine Inn has live music for dancing on Thursday, Friday and Saturday nights and karaoke on other nights.

Getting There & Away

Bus & Train Buses and trains travelling between Auckland and Wellington all stop at the railway station at Taumarunui. The station also houses the information centre, where you can buy tickets.

Hitching Hitching is easy heading north or south on SH4. It is a lot more difficult to get a ride on the lightly-trafficked Stratford-Taumarunui Road.

Taranaki

The Taranaki region juts out into the Tasman Sea on the west coast of the North Island, about halfway between Auckland and Wellington. The region is named after the large Mt Taranaki volcano, also called Mt Egmont, whose massive cone dominates the landscape. Conditions are excellent for agriculture and dairy farming, with rich volcanic soil and a climatic pattern of abundant rainfall.

The names Taranaki and Egmont are both widely used around the region, with Taranaki being the traditional Maori name for the volcano (there are several theories as to its meaning) and Egmont being the name Captain James Cook gave it in 1770, after the earl of Egmont, who had encouraged his expedition. Today the region is called Taranaki, the cape is called Cape Egmont, and the waters on either side of the cape are called the North and South Taranaki bights. Egmont National Park remains the name of the national park, but in 1986 the New Zealand government ruled that Mt Taranaki and Mt Egmont are *both* official names for the volcano.

In addition to the obvious attraction of Egmont National Park – Mt Taranaki is the 'most climbed' mountain in New Zealand – the region is also popular for its world-class surfing and windsurfing beaches.

The telephone area code throughout Taranaki is 06.

HIGHLIGHTS

- Mt Taranaki, Taranaki's awe-inspiring volcano, for walking, mountain climbing or skiing
- Maori and Pakeha historical sites
- Windsurfing and surfing the beaches of Oakura and New Plymouth

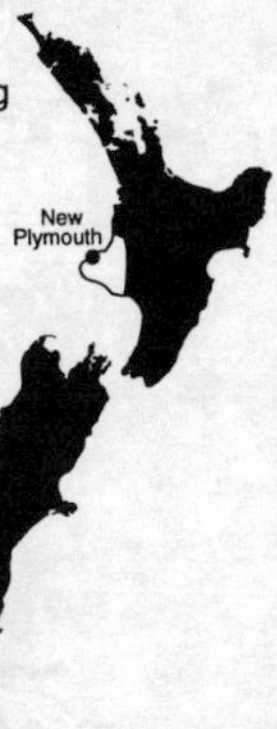

NEW PLYMOUTH

Principal centre of the Taranaki region, New Plymouth is about equal distance from Auckland (373 km) and Wellington (357 km) and has a population of around 50,000. A coastal city, with Mt Taranaki towering it behind it and surrounded by rich agricultural and dairy lands, New Plymouth is a good base for visiting Egmont National Park. In parts it is attractive, featuring fine parks and the spectacular backdrop of Mt Taranaki, but looking towards the sea the city's port and petrochemical installations blight the landscape.

History

Archaeological evidence shows that the Taranaki region was settled by Maori from early times. In the 1820s the Taranaki Maori took off to the Cook Strait region in droves to avoid a threatened attack by the Waikato tribes, but it was not until 1832 that the Waikato tribes attacked and subdued the remaining Te Ati-awa tribe, except at Okoki Pa (New Plymouth) where whalers had joined in the battle. So when the first European settlers arrived in the district in 1841, the coastlands of Taranaki were almost deserted. Initially it seemed there would be no opposition to land claims, so the New Zealand Company was able to buy extensive tracts from the Te Ati-awa who had stayed.

When the other members of the Te Atiawa and other tribes returned after years of exile and slavery they objected strongly to the sale of their land. Their claims were substantially upheld when Governor Fitzroy ruled that the New Zealand Company was only allowed to retain just over 10 sq km around New Plymouth – of the 250 it had

Taranaki
0
7.5
15 km
TASMAN SEA
To Auckland & Waitomo
Awakino
3
Mokau
Mohakatino
Tongaporutu
White Cliffs
Ahititi
Okau
40
Kotare
Pukearuhe
Uruti
To Taumarunui
Waitoetoe
Onaero
Urenui
Motonui
Okoki
Waitara
Bell Block
Brixton
Huirangi
3A
Tahora
43
Kohuratahi
NEW PLYMOUTH
Pukarangiora Pa
Lake Mangamahoe
Waitara River
Oakura
Hurworth
Huatoki Stream
Carrington Road
Egmont Village
Whangamomona
Lucy's Gully
Tataraimaka
Waitui
Tarata
Kaimata
Inglewood
Okato
Pukeiti Rhododendron Trust
Kaimiro
Mangaonui River
Matau
45
Stony River
Waiwhakaiho River
Cape Egmont Lighthouse
Egmont National Park
Tariki
Huiroa
Te Wera
Tamahu
Tuna
Te Popo
Huiakama
Pungarehu
North Egmont
Strathmore
Midhurst
Parihaka Pa
Mt Egmont/Taranaki (2518 m)
East Egmont
Wharehuia
Douglas
Makahu
Pembroke
Tututawa
Puniwhakau
Rahotu
Pembroke Road
Dawson Falls
Stratford
43
Waiaua River
Mahoe
Cardiff
Pukengahu
Omoana
Rowan
Lowgarth
Ngaere
Oaonui
Kapuni Stream
Mangamingi
Eltham
Rawhitiroa
Te Kiri
Awatuna
Kaponga
Mangatoki
Rukumoana
Moeroa
Riverlea
Opunake
Maata
Lake Rotokare
Kapuni
Whenuakura River
Auroa
Pihama
Ararata
3
Oeo
Otakeho
Normanby
Manaia
Tawhiti
45
Meremere
Hawera
Ohangai
Ngamatapouri
Ohawe Beach
Mokoia
Hurleyville
Manutahi
Alton
Kakaramea
Kohi
Omahina
Whenuakura
Patea
Waverley
Ngutuwera
3
Waitotara
To Wanganui
TASMAN SEA

TARANAKI

claimed. The Crown slowly acquired more land from the Maori, but the Maori became increasingly reluctant to sell and the European settlers increasingly greedy for the fertile land around Waitara, just north of New Plymouth.

The settlers' determination finally forced the government to abandon its policy of negotiation, and in 1860 war broke out. For 10 years the Maori kept the military engaged in guerrilla warfare. During this time, settlers moved in on Waitara and took control there, but the Maori came and went as they pleased throughout the rest of the province. The Taranaki chiefs had not signed the Treaty of Waitangi and did not recognise the sovereignty of the British queen, so they were treated as rebels. By 1870 over 500 hectares of their land had been confiscated and much of the rest acquired through extremely dubious transactions.

The Taranaki province experienced an economic boom with the discovery of natural gas and oil at Kapuni in 1959 and more recently at the Maui natural gas field off the coast of South Taranaki.

Orientation & Information

Devon St (East and West) is New Plymouth's main street; its central section is a mall.

The New Plymouth Information Centre (☎ 759 6080; fax 759 6073) on the corner of Liardet and Leach Sts is open Monday to Friday from 8.30 am to 5 pm, weekends and public holidays 10 am to 3 pm, with a computerised information line operating 24 hours a day. The office staff are very helpful and they have lots of free printed information, including a good city map and up-to-date details on restaurants and places to stay.

You'll find a DOC office (☎ 758 0433; fax 758 0430) at 220 Devon St West, opening hours are Monday to Friday from 8 am to 4.30 pm. The AA office (☎ 757 5646) is at 49-55 Powderham St.

Museums & Galleries

The **Taranaki Museum** on Ariki St, between Brougham and Egmont Sts, has a collection of Maori artefacts, wildlife exhibits including moa and whale skeletons, and an early colonists' exhibition. The museum is open Tuesday to Friday from 10.30 am to 4.30 pm, weekends and public holidays from 1 to 5 pm; admission is free, but donations are always welcome.

The **Govett-Brewster Art Gallery**, on the corner of Queen and King Sts, is a renowned contemporary art gallery with a good reputation for its adventurous shows. Fans of abstract animation on film should seek out the films of Len Lye, pioneer animator of the 1930s, whose works are held here and shown from time to time. It's open daily from 10.30 am to 5 pm; admission is free except during some special exhibitions.

Historic Places

If you like historic sites, pick up a free New Plymouth Heritage Walkway leaflet from the information centre, which outlines a self-guided tour of 30 historic sites around the city centre. Some are mentioned here but there are plenty of others.

Richmond Cottage, on Ariki St on the corner of Brougham St, was built in 1853. Unlike most early cottages, which were made of timber, Richmond Cottage was sturdily built of stone. From June to October it's open on Friday from 2 to 4 pm, and on weekends from 1 to 4 pm. The rest of the year it's also open on Monday, Wednesday and Friday from 2 to 4 pm. Admission is $1 (children 20c).

St Mary's Church, on Vivian St between Brougham and Robe Sts, built in 1846, is the oldest stone church in New Zealand. Its graveyard has numerous interesting gravestones of early settlers and of soldiers who died during the Taranaki wars. Impressed by their bravery, the British also buried several of the Maori chiefs here.

Beside Brooklands Park, **The Gables** is an early hospital built in the late 1840s. In 1854 a notable Maori chief died here from wounds received in a tribal feud. The hospital consequently became tapu, which saved it during the Taranaki wars as its forbidden status prevented the Maori from burning it down! It's now a medical museum and the home of the local arts society, with regular exhibitions.

On Devon St at the eastern end of the city is the **Fitzroy Pole**, erected by Maori in 1844 to mark the point beyond which Governor Fitzroy had forbidden settlers to acquire land. The carving on the bottom of the pole depicts a sorrowful Pakeha topped by a cheerfully triumphant Maori.

If you're wandering around the city, have a look at the curious transparent **clock tower** on the corner of Devon St West and Queen St. It was erected in 1985 to replace the old post office tower which was demolished 16 years earlier.

Marsland Hill & Observatory

The New Plymouth Observatory is on Marsland Hill off Robe St. Public nights are held every Tuesday, and include a planetarium programme and viewing through a six-inch refractor telescope if the weather is clear; times are 7.30 to 9.30 pm from March to October, 8 to 10 pm during daylight savings from November to March. The cost is $2 (children $1).

Also on Marsland Hill is a carillon, and St Mary's Church is directly below. From the hill you'll get fine views over the central city.

Power Station

At the western end of the city is the New Plymouth Power Station, designed to run on oil or gas. The original intention was to burn coal, but the discovery of natural gas in Taranaki changed this. The station is dominated by its towering 200-metre chimney. Free one-hour tours are conducted at 10 am on Wednesday and at 2 pm on Sunday.

Paritutu & Other Viewpoints

Above the power station is Paritutu, a steep hill with a magnificent view from the top. The name means 'rising precipice' and it's worth the tiring but quick scramble to the summit. Not only do you look down on the station but out over the city and the rocky Sugar Loaf Islands rising just offshore.

Yet another good viewpoint is Churchill Heights, with a trig marker on top showing directions and distances to places near and far. You can walk up from Morley St or drive up from the entrance on Cutfield St.

Arts & Crafts Centre

Just below the Paritutu car park and within easy walking distance, is the Rangimarie Arts & Crafts Centre on Centennial Drive. It features a display of traditional Maori arts & crafts and you can watch the members working on their carving, weaving and other skills. It's open Monday to Thursday from 8.30 am to 4 pm and Friday from 8 am to noon.

Parks

New Plymouth is renowned for its superb parks. **Pukekura Park**, a 10-minute walk from the city centre, is worth a visit, with 49 hectares of gardens, bush walks, streams and ponds and a kiosk cafe. Display houses with orchids and other exotic plants are open every day from 10 am to noon and 1 to 4 pm. Rowing boats on the lake can be hired on weekends, holidays and summer evenings. The lights and decorations in Pukekura Park from mid-December to early February are worth making a special trip to see, as hundreds of people stroll through the park in the evening to enjoy them. The park also has a delightful cricket oval in the English tradition, and visiting international teams sometimes play one-day games. If the West Indies are in town, go and see them smash a swag of sixes on this small oval.

Adjoining Pukekura is **Brooklands Park,** another lovely park, and between the two, the Bowl of Brooklands, an outdoor soundshell in a bush and lake setting. Brooklands Park was once the land around an important early settler's home; the fireplace and chimney are all that remain of the house after the Maori burnt it down. Highlights include a 2000-year-old puriri tree, a rhododendron dell with over 300 varieties of rhododendrons, The Gables historic hospital (see Historic Places) and, beside it, a children's zoo open daily from 9 am to 6 pm.

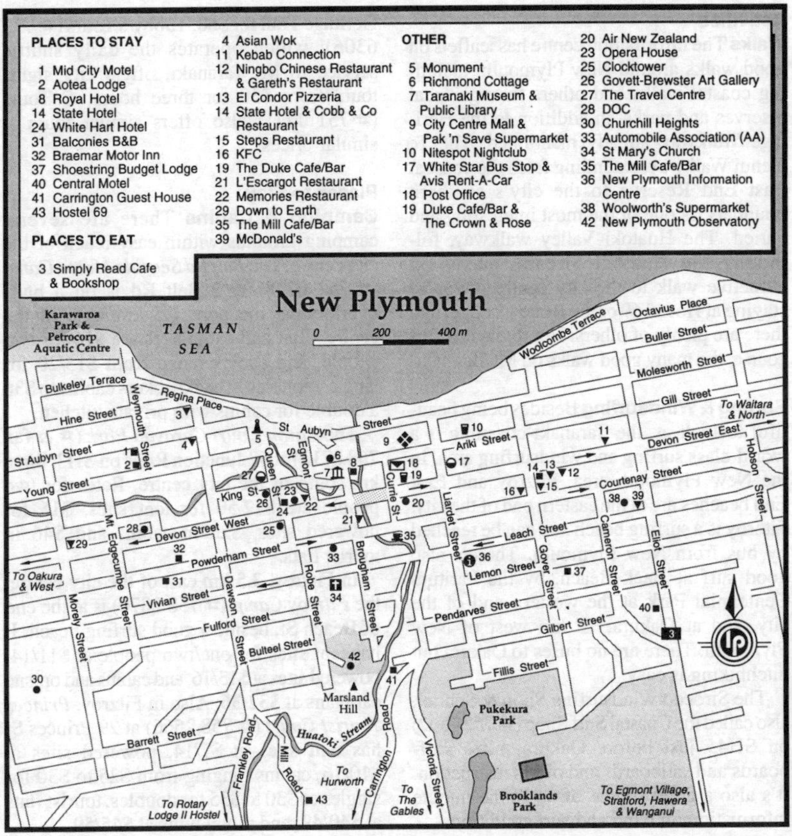

On the waterfront is **Kawaroa Park**, with green areas, squash courts and the Petrocorp Aquatic Centre which has a waterslide, an outdoor swimming pool, and an indoor pool open all year. Also on the waterfront in the central city area is Pukeariki Landing, a historic area with a number of sculptures on display.

Sugar Loaf Islands Marine Park

New Plymouth has parks not only on land but also offshore. The Sugar Loaf Islands Marine Park, established in 1986, includes the rocky islets offshore from the power station, Back Beach on the west side of Paritutu, and the waters up to about one km offshore. The islands are a refuge for birds, seals and marine life; the greatest number of seals present is from August to October but some are there all year round.

Activities in the park include boating and sailing, diving, birdwatching, pole fishing, surfing and beach walks. Boat trips to the islands are popular in summer. Happy Chaddy's Charters (☎ 758 0228) depart from Lee Breakwater hourly, 8.30 am to 5.30 pm; the cost is $15 (children $7).

Activities

Walks The information centre has leaflets on good walks around New Plymouth, including coastal walks and others through local reserves and parks, in addition to the Heritage Walkway already mentioned. The Te Henui Walkway, extending from the coast at East End Reserve to the city's southern boundary, is one of the most interesting and varied. The Huatoki Valley walkway, following the Huatoki Stream, makes an attractive walk to the city centre if you're staying at Hostel 69 or the Rotary Lodge, and there are plenty of others. Not to mention, of course, the many good walks on Mt Taranaki.

Surfing & Windsurfing Besides being beautiful to look at, the Taranaki coastline is a world-class surfing and windsurfing area. In the New Plymouth area, Fitzroy and East End beaches are at the eastern end of the city. Fitzroy is a surfing beach and can be reached by bus from New Plymouth. There's also good surf at Back Beach, by the Paritutu Centennial Park at the western end of the city, and at Oakura, 15 km west of New Plymouth. There are no buses to Oakura but hitchhiking is easy.

The Sirocco Windsurfing Shop & School, also called the Coastal Surf Shop (☎ 752 7562) on SH45 just before Oakura, hires surfboards and sailboards and offers instruction. It's also a good source of up-to-the-minute information on wind and surf conditions.

Aerial Sightseeing Several operators offer scenic flights around the area including flights over the snow-capped summit of Mt Taranaki – superb if the weather's clear. They include Air Taranaki (☎ 745 4375), the New Plymouth Aero Club (☎ 755 0500) and the Stratford Aero Club (☎ 756 6628/756 7771).

Organised Tours

Neuman's Sightseeing Tours (☎ 758 4622) at 78-80 Gill St – not the national Newmans bus line – offers a variety of 16 local sightseeing tours, ranging from a $30 half-day scenic city tour to a full-day tour around Mt Taranaki or down the Stratford-Taumarunui Heritage Trail for $60. Tubby's Tours (☎ 753 6306), which operates the daily shuttle service to Mt Taranaki, offers city sights tours from $30 for three hours; C Tours (☎ 751 1711) also offers similar tours at similar prices.

Places to Stay

Camping & Cabins There are several camping grounds within easy reach of the city centre. The *Belt Rd Seaside Motor Camp* (☎ 758 0228) at 2 Belt Rd is on a bluff overlooking the port, 1.5 km west of the centre. Tent and camp sites are $16 for two people, and cabins range from $15/20 for singles/doubles in backpackers cabins to $36 a double for cabins with private kitchen.

The *Aaron Court Caravan Park* (☎ & fax 758 8712) at 57 Junction Rd is on SH3, three km south of the city centre. Rates for two people are $12.50 for tent sites, $15 for powered sites, $28 in cabins and $46 in tourist flats.

In Fitzroy, 3.5 km east of the city centre, the *Fitzroy Camp* (☎ 758 2870) is at the end of Beach St, beside a good surfing beach. It has tent sites for one/two people at $11/14, powered sites at $13/16, and cabins and on-site caravans at $32/36. Also in Fitzroy, *Princes Tourist Court* (☎ 758 2566) at 29 Princes St has tent sites at $7/14, powered sites at $10/16, cabins ranging from $25 to $30 for singles or $30 to $35 for doubles, tourist flats at $40/49, and motel units at $45/59.

Heading around the coast in the other direction, the *Oakura Beach Camp* (☎ 752 7861) is an attractive camping ground right on Oakura Beach, a beautiful beach for surfing and windsurfing. The turn-off to the beach is one km west of Oakura, which is 15 km west of New Plymouth. The cost for two people is $13 in tent sites, $14.50 in powered sites.

Hookner Park (☎ 753 9506, 753 9168) at 551 Carrington Rd is a quiet, peaceful camp on a commercial dairy farm 10 km south of the city centre. Campers are welcome to join in the farm life. The cost for two people is $16 in tent and powered sites, $26 in cabins or $30 in on-site caravans.

Hostels The *Rotary Lodge* (☎ 753 5720) at 12 Clawton St is a tranquil hostel in large, park-like grounds with a stream running through. It's a fair way (1.5 km) from town – a 15-minute walk on a pleasant streamside walkway or phone for free pick-up from the bus station. The hostel is well set up for information on walks and other activities. The cost is $14 in dorms, and $30 in double and twin rooms or you can pitch a tent. It's a YHA associate hostel, so you can stay with or without a YHA card.

About the same distance from the centre, *Hostel 69* (☎ 758 7153) at 69 Mill Rd is a small, pleasant hostel with convenient services including mountain bike hire, free pick-up when you arrive and free rides to good hitching spots when you leave. It's a friendly place with a large, well-kept garden, and when it's clear the views of Mt Taranaki are stunning. The cost is $13 in dorms, $28 for double rooms.

More central, the *Shoestring Budget Lodge* (☎ 758 0404) at 48 Lemon St is in a large, stately old home; the cost is $13 in dorm rooms, $25/40 in singles/doubles. It's a well-equipped, friendly place and the rooms are excellent, but it can't make up its mind whether it's a hostel or a boarding house.

B&Bs & Guesthouses *Balconies Bed & Breakfast* (☎ 757 8866) at 161 Powderham St is a fine B&B with singles/doubles at $40/60. Also central, the *Aotea Lodge* (☎ 758 2438) on the corner of Young and Weymouth Sts has singles/doubles for $30/50 with breakfast included.

Carrington Guest House (☎ 758 2375), 32 Carrington St, near Pukekura Park, is also quite central. It's a good guesthouse – even if the backyard looks like a landslide – with B&B rooms for $40/60.

Other B&Bs include the *Brooklands B&B* (☎ 753 2265) at 39 Plympton St near Brooklands Park off Brooklands Rd, the extension of Victoria Rd, with singles/doubles for $35/55.

The information centre can make recommendations for other B&Bs, homestays and farmstays in the area.

Hotels & Motels There are several old-style hotels around central New Plymouth. The *White Hart Hotel* (☎ 757 5442) on the corner of Devon St West and Queen St has singles/doubles for $30/45. Or there's the *State Hotel* (☎ 758 5373) on the corner of Devon St East and Gover St, with rooms for $42/55 and a Cobb & Co restaurant.

More modern, the *Braemar Motor Inn* (☎ 758 0859) at 157 Powderham St has hotel rooms for $29/50 and motel rooms for $68/77.

New Plymouth has plenty of motels, starting from around $55/60 and up. The *Mid City Motel* (☎ 758 6109) on the corner of St Aubyn and Weymouth Sts is reasonably central, with singles/doubles for $60/70. The *Central Motel* (☎ & fax 758 6444) at 86 Eliot St, a few blocks east of the centre, is small but convenient, with units at $60 for singles, $65 or $75 for doubles. The *Timandra Unity Motel* (☎ 758 6006) at 31B Timandra St off Coronation Ave, the extension of Eliot St, has singles/doubles for $58/68.

The *Aaron Court Motel* (☎ & fax 758 8712) at 57 Junction Rd is at the Aaron Court Caravan Park, on SH3 three km south of the centre; motel units are $55/65 or there are tourist flats at $46. At Oakura, a pleasant beachside community 15 km west of New Plymouth, the *Oakura Beach Motel* (☎ 752 7680) on Wairau Rd has singles/doubles for $52/65.

Places to Eat

Snacks & Fast Food New Zealand is a small country and New Plymouth is a small city but the *McDonald's* on the corner of Leach and Eliot Sts is absolutely huge. There's an equally large *KFC* on the corner of Courtenay and Gover Sts. There are plenty of Chinese takeaways around the centre, especially on Devon St.

Opposite KFC, the *Steps Restaurant* at 37 Gover St is a popular wholefood restaurant offering good lunches and a pleasant atmosphere. The blackboard menu has plenty of inexpensive selections and you can eat there or take away.

El Condor Pizzeria on Devon St East near the corner of Gover St is a trendy little pizza and pasta place with a difference. It's Argentinian, and open Tuesday to Sunday for dinner. In the same block, the *Kebab Connection* at 211A Devon St East features doner kebab and other Middle Eastern takeaways.

In the City Centre shopping mall on Gill St there's a food court with Chinese and Italian food, seafood, wholefood, sandwich and dessert counters. Also in the City Centre shopping mall is the large Pak 'n Save supermarket for grocery shopping. Woolworth's is on Leach St between Eliot and Cameron Sts, beside McDonald's. For wholefood, *Down to Earth* is a bulk wholefood grocery on the corner of Devon St West and Morley St with 'healthy takeaways'.

Simply Read Cafe & Bookshop on the corner of Dawson and Hine Sts is a bookstore cafe and an ideal place for a coffee and snack during the day with views across the sea.

TARANAKI

Pub Food *The Mill* cafe/bar on Courtenay/Powderham St on the corner of Currie St, popular for its evening entertainment, has a dining area with bar meals always available; it's open every day except Sunday, from 11 am until late.

There's a *Cobb & Co* restaurant in the State Hotel on the corner of Devon St East and Gover St.

Restaurants *Memories Restaurant* on Egmont St near the corner of Devon St West has a curious menu – half of it consists of straightforward, pub-style dishes like steak, mixed grill and fisherman's basket, and the other half is cosmopolitan and changes every month. Main courses cost $16 to $20 and it's licensed.

The *Asian Wok*, on the corner of St Aubyn and Dawson Sts, has great value smorgasbords of Chinese, Thai and Indonesian food for $8.50. It's a pleasant little cafe, open evenings only. The *Ningbo Chinese Restaurant* on Devon St East is a cavernous, licensed restaurant offering smorgasbords for Friday, Saturday and Sunday dinner at $15.80, and children pay the imaginatively priced $1 per year of age.

Quality licensed restaurants include *Gareth's* at 182 Devon St East, or the 'genuinely French' *L'Escargot* in a historic building at 37-39 Brougham St.

Entertainment

The *Bowl of Brooklands* at the entrance to Brooklands Park is a large, fine outdoor theatre where concerts are held; the information centre will have current schedules and ticket prices. The *Opera House* on Devon St West stages operas and other performances.

The Mill cafe/bar on the corner of Courtenay/Powderham and Currie Sts is a popular place for a night out, with a section for bands from Wednesday to Saturday nights and a separate disco. Bar meals are available and it's known for having something enjoyable for all ages.

Other popular dancing spots include *The Crown & Rose* cafe/bar upstairs on Devon St East near the corner of Currie St, and the more alternative *Nitespot* nightclub at 51 Gill St near Liardet St; both have bands Thursday to Saturday.

The *White Hart Hotel* on the corner of Devon St West and Queen St has live bands in the bar on Friday nights.

Getting There & Away

Air Air New Zealand (☎ 757 9057) at 12-14 Devon St East, has direct flights to Auckland, Hamilton, Nelson, Wanganui and Wellington, with connections to other centres.

Bus InterCity (☎ 759 9039) and Newmans (☎ 757 5482) both stop at the Travel Centre on the corner of Queen and King Sts. Both companies have several buses daily heading north to Hamilton (four hours) and Auckland (5¾ hours), and south-east to Wanganui (2½ hours) and Palmerston North (five hours), from where buses proceed south to Wellington or east to Napier and Gisborne.

White Star (☎ 758 3338) buses depart

from the Avis Rent-A-Car office at 25 Liardet St. They operate every day except Saturday, with two buses a day heading to Wellington via Wanganui and Palmerston North.

C Tours (☎ 758 1777) has daily buses to Auckland via Otorohanga and Hamilton.

Hitching For hitching north towards Auckland, a good spot is on Courtenay St about 1.5 km east of the centre; anywhere from about Hobson St eastwards is good, the further out the better.

South towards Wanganui, a good hitching spot is on the corner of Coronation Ave and Cumberland St, about 1.5 km south of the centre; Coronation Ave is the southern extension of Eliot St.

To hitch west around the Taranaki coast towards Oakura, head west out of town on Devon St West, which becomes South Rd.

Getting Around

To/From The Airport The New Plymouth airport is 11 km east of the centre. Withatruck (☎ 751 1777) operates a shuttle service to and from the airport; the cost is $10.

Bus City buses operate every day except Sunday. The information centre has local bus timetables.

Tubby's Tours (☎ 753 6306) operates a daily shuttle service from New Plymouth to Mt Taranaki; see the Mt Egmont/Taranaki section for details.

AROUND NEW PLYMOUTH

Egmont National Park, of course, is the primary attraction of the New Plymouth area, but there are several other places of interest. Those mentioned here are all within about 20 km of New Plymouth. Hurworth, the Pouakai Zoo Park and the Pukeiti Rhododendron Trust can all be reached by heading south from the centre on Carrington Rd. Other attractions, further afield, are mentioned in the Around Taranaki section later in this chapter.

Tupare

Tupare, seven km south of New Plymouth, is a fine three-storey Tudor-style house surrounded by 3.6 hectares of lush English garden. It's part of the Queen Elizabeth II National Trust; look for it at 487 Mangorei Rd on the Waiwhakaiho River. The garden is open every day from 9 am to 4 pm; admission is $5 (children free).

Hurworth

This early homestead, at 552 Carrington Rd about eight km south of New Plymouth, dates from 1856. Its pioneer builder and first occupant, Harry Atkinson, was later to become premier of New Zealand four times. The house was the only one at this site to survive the Taranaki wars and is today owned by the New Zealand Historic Places Trust. It's open Wednesday to Sunday from 10 am to 4 pm; admission is $3.50.

Pouakai Zoo Park

Further on towards Pukeiti is the Pouakai Zoo Park at 590 Carrington Rd, about 10 km south of New Plymouth. Formerly a wildlife reserve, this small zoo has deer, donkeys, goats, possums, zebras, wallabies and other animals. It's open every day; admission is $3.50 (children 80c).

Pukeiti Rhododendron Trust

The Pukeiti Rhododendron Trust is a 400-hectare garden surrounded by native bush, and internationally renowned for its large collection of rhododendrons and azaleas. Peak flowering of rhododendrons generally takes place in September, October and November, though the garden is worth seeing at any time of year.

Pukeiti is 20 km south of New Plymouth; to get there, just keep following Carrington Rd all the way from town. The road passes between the Pouakai and Kaitake ranges, both part of Egmont National Park, but separated by the trust. Pukeiti is open every day from 9 am to 4.30 pm; admission is $6 (children free).

Lake Mangamahoe & TATATM

If you're heading out towards Stratford or North Egmont on SH3, stop off at Lake Mangamahoe, about 9.5 km south of New Plymouth. The lake is the setting for many famous photographs of Mt Taranaki, reflected in its waters.

Opposite the lake, on the corner of SH3 and Kent Rd, is the Taranaki Aviation, Transport & Technology Museum (TATATM), with vehicles, railway and aviation exhibits, farm equipment, and household and other items. It's open Sunday and most public holidays from 10.30 am to 4.30 pm; admission is $3 (children 50c).

Waitara

Waitara is 13 km east of New Plymouth on SH3. If you turn off SH3 at Brixton, just before Waitara, and head seven km south, you'll reach the site of the Pukerangiora Pa. It's beautifully situated on a high cliff by the Waitara River, but historically it was a particularly bloody battle site.

Rafting and canoeing on the Waiwhakaiho and the Waitara rivers are popular local activities. For details, phone Waiawaka Rafting/Canoeing (☎ 755 2068).

Just beyond Waitara on SH3 heading east from New Plymouth is the Methanex New Zealand's Motunui Plant. Opened in 1986, it was the world's first plant to convert natural gas to petrol (gasoline) and it remains the world's largest methanol production facility. Natural gas is piped here from the Maui natural gas field, 34 km offshore from Cape Egmont; the synthetic fuel produced here meets 30% of New Zealand's petrol needs. You can stop by the visitors centre near the plant's main entrance to see exhibits on the plant; it's open every day from 8 am to 5 pm and admission is free.

North via SH3

Heading north towards Waikato from New Plymouth, SH3 is a scenic route. This is the route to take for Waitomo, and buses heading north go this way to Otorohanga and Hamilton.

Heading past Waitara the highway follows the west coast with its high sand dunes and surf beaches. **Urenui**, 16 km past Waitara, is a popular beach destination in summer for Kiwis. *Urenui Beach Motor Camp* (☎ 752 3838) has a variety of accommodation right next to the beach and the sand dunes. About five km past Urenui, you can sample natural beers at the **White Cliffs Brewing Company**, a boutique brewery open during the week and on Saturday from 10 am to 5 pm, except Wednesday when it is open from 3 to 5 pm.

The brewery is near the turn-off to Pukearuhe and the **White Cliffs**, huge cliffs resembling their namesake in Dover. The cliffs dominate the coastal landscape along this stretch of coast and contain two-million-year-old marine sediments. A walkway along the cliffs leads from Pukearuhe to Tongaporutu via a tunnel from the beach, accessible only at low tide. On a fine day the full-day walk has spectacular views of the coastline and of Mt Taranaki and Mt Ruapehu.

SH3 continues further north from Tongaporutu to Mokau, on the border of Taranaki and the Waikato. Mokau has a backpackers and other accommodation (see the Waikato chapter).

Mt Egmont/Taranaki

The Taranaki region is dominated by the massive cone of 2518-metre Taranaki – a dormant volcano that looks remarkably like Japan's Mt Fuji or the Philippines' Mayon. After a long-standing dispute about whether the volcano should be called Taranaki, its Maori name, or Mt Egmont, the name it was given in 1770 by Captain James Cook, the New Zealand government ruled in 1986 that both names would be official.

Geologically, Mt Taranaki is the youngest of a series of three large volcanoes on one fault line, the others being Kaitake and Pouakai. Mt Taranaki last erupted 350 years ago, but it is regarded as being dormant

TARANAKI

Top: Cape Reinga, Northland (JW)
Middle: Mt Ruapehu, Tongariro National Park (RS)
Bottom: Wainui Inlet, Golden Bay, Marlborough (VB)

Top: Rangitoto Island from Cheltenham Beach, Auckland (PT)
Middle: View of Auckland from Mt Victoria (PT)
Bottom: West Coast beach, Coromandel (PT)

rather than extinct. The top 1400 metres is covered in lava flows and a few descend to 800 metres above sea level. An interesting feature is the small subsidiary cone on the flank of the main cone and two km south of the main crater, called Fantham's Peak (1962 metres).

There's a saying in Taranaki that if you can see the mountain it's going to rain, and if you can't see the mountain it's already raining! The mountain is one of the wettest spots in New Zealand with about 7000 mm of rain recorded annually at North Egmont (compared with 1584 mm in nearby New Plymouth), as it catches the moisture-laden winds coming in from the Tasman Sea and sweeps them up to freezing heights. Naturally it tends to be quite windy up there too!

Still, it doesn't *always* rain there, and the volcano is a spectacular sight on a clear day.

History

Mt Taranaki was supremely sacred to the Maori, both as a burial site for chiefs and as a hide-out in times of danger.

According to legend, Taranaki was once a part of the group of volcanoes at Tongariro. He was forced to leave rather hurriedly when Tongariro caught him with the beautiful Pihanga, the volcano near Lake Taupo – who was Tongariro's lover.

So angry was Tongariro at this betrayal that he blew his top (as only volcanoes can when upset) and Taranaki took off for the coast. Fleeing south in anger, pain and shame, the defeated Taranaki gouged a wide scar in the earth as he fled, meeting the sea at Wanganui and then moving still further west to his current position, where he's remained in majestic isolation ever since.

The Maori did not settle the area between Taranaki and Pihanga very heavily, perhaps because they feared the lovers might be reunited, with dire consequences. Most of the Maori settlements in this district were clustered along the coast between Mokau and Patea, concentrated particularly around Urenui and Waitara.

The Egmont National Park was created in 1900 and is the second-oldest national park in New Zealand.

Information

If you plan to tramp in Egmont National Park, get hold of local information about current track and weather conditions before you set off. DOC operates two visitor information centres on the mountain, offering maps and advice on weather and track conditions. The North Egmont Visitor Centre (☎ 756 8710) is the closest to New Plymouth and so the most visited. It is open from 9 am

TARANAKI

Mt Egmont/Taranaki dominates the skyline and attracts mountaineers, skiers & trampers

to 5 pm every day in summer (1 December to 30 April). The rest of the year it is open from 9 am to 4 pm during the week except Tuesday, when it is closed, and 9 am to 5 pm on weekends. On the other side of the mountain, the Dawson Falls Visitor Centre (☎ (025) 430 248) is open from 9 am to 5.30 pm Thursday to Monday.

Other places for maps and information on the mountain include DOC's Stratford Field Centre on Pembroke Rd coming up the mountain from Stratford (☎ 765 5144) and the DOC office in New Plymouth (☎ 759 6080). There are also general information centres around the mountain in New Plymouth (☎ 758 6086), Stratford (☎ 765 6708) and Hawera (☎ 278 8599).

Tramping & Skiing

In winter, the mountain is popular with skiers, while in summer it can be climbed in one day. There are a number of excellent tramping possibilities including hikes to the summit or right round the mountain. Shorter tracks ranging from easy to difficult and in length from 30 minutes to several hours start off from the three roads heading up the mountain.

Due to its easy accessibility, Mt Taranaki ranks as the 'most climbed' mountain in New Zealand. Nevertheless, tramping on this mountain holds definite dangers and should not be undertaken lightly. The principal hazard is the erratic weather, which can change from warm and sunny to raging gales and white-out conditions amazingly quickly and unexpectedly; snow can come at any time of year on the mountain, even in summer. There are also precipitous bluffs and steep icy slopes. In good conditions tramping around the mountain, or even to the summit, can be reasonably easy, but the mountain has claimed over 50 lives. Don't be put off, but don't be deceived.

If you intend to go tramping, get a map and consult a conservation officer for current weather and track conditions before you set off. Some tracks marked on maps have been closed and other planned ones may have opened; the North Egmont Chalet, marked on many maps, no longer exists. Be sure to register your tramping intentions and some emergency contact numbers with a DOC office.

A trip to the North Egmont Visitor Centre at the end of Egmont Rd is worthwhile for the view, and there are numerous long and short tracks and bush walks as well. The centre has interesting displays on the park and the mountain, an audiovisual feature, and a cafe.

The roads to the Stratford Mountain House, East Egmont, and Dawson Falls also have many worthwhile tracks and bush walks. From the Mountain House, Pembroke Rd continues three km to the Stratford Plateau and from there a 1.5 km walk takes you to the Manganui ski area. Skiing equipment can be hired at the Stratford Mountain House (see Places to Stay).

There are two main routes to the summit. The safest and most direct route takes off from the North Egmont Visitor Centre; allow about six to eight hours for the return trip. This route on the north side of the mountain loses its snow and ice soonest in the year. Another route to the summit, taking off from the Dawson Falls Visitor Centre, requires more technical skill and keeps its ice longer; if you go up this way, allow seven to 10 hours for the return trip.

The round-the-mountain track, accessible from all three mountain roads, goes 55 km around the mountain and takes four days or more to complete. You can start or finish this track at any park entrance. There are a number of huts on the mountain.

If you are an inexperienced climber or want other people to climb or tramp with, DOC can put you in contact with tramping clubs and guides in the area. Mountain Guides Mt Egmont (☎ 758 8261) offers guided trips to the summit all year round. Camp 'n Canoe (☎ 764 6737) also offers trips.

Places to Stay

Most visitors stay in New Plymouth, the nearest large town to the park, from where there's a convenient daily, door-to-door shuttle service to the mountain. Other options are to stay in the park itself or in other nearby towns.

Camping, Huts & Bunkhouses There are a number of tramping huts scattered about the mountain, administered by DOC and reached only by trails. Most cost $8 a night (for two tickets, which can be purchased from any DOC office), but some cost only $4 (one ticket). You provide your own cooking, eating and sleeping gear, they provide bunks and mattresses, and no bookings are necessary – it's on a first-come, first-served basis.

The Camphouse, a bunkhouse beside the North Egmont Visitor Centre (☎ 756 8710), has bunks at $8, with hotplates for cooking and hot showers; bring your own sleeping bag and kitchen utensils. There were plans to close this facility in mid 1996.

By the Dawson Falls Visitor Centre (☎ (025) 430 248), *Konini Lodge* has bunkhouse accommodation at $12 per person. Bring your own sleeping bag, food supplies and kitchen utensils.

There are motor camps at New Plymouth, Stratford, Eltham, Hawera, Opunake, Oakura and Waitara, but camping is not encouraged within the park itself – you're supposed to use the tramping huts.

Guesthouses The *Dawson Falls Tourist Lodge* (☎ 765 5457) beside the Dawson Falls Visitor Centre is an attractive alpine-style lodge with lots of carved wood and painted decorations, good views, comfortable rooms and sitting rooms and a dining room where guests dine together. They have a few rooms from $35 but most are around $100 for doubles; meals are extra. A courtesy car will meet public transport in Stratford.

On the eastern side of the mountain, the *Mountain Lodge* (☎ 765 6100) on Pembroke Rd, about 15 km up the mountain from Stratford, has rooms from $90, chalet cabins with kitchens at $80. They hire skis in winter for use at the nearby ski area.

Getting There & Away

There are several points of access to the park, but three roads lead almost right up to where the heavy bush ends. Closest to New Plymouth is Egmont Rd, turning off SH3 at Egmont Village, 12 km south of New Plymouth, and heading another 16 km up the mountain to the North Egmont Visitor Centre. Pembroke Rd enters the park from the east at Stratford and ascends 18 km to East Egmont, Stratford Mountain House, the Plateau car park and the Manganui ski area. From the south-east, Manaia Rd leads up to Dawson Falls, 23 km from Stratford.

Public buses don't go to Egmont National Park but Tubby's Tours in New Plymouth (☎ 753 6306) operates a daily door-to-door shuttle bus from New Plymouth to the mountain. The cost is $10 one way or $15 return ($20 if less than three are travelling), whether you return on the same or a different day. Tubby's also offers guided tours of the mountain, as do the other New Plymouth tour companies.

AROUND MT EGMONT/TARANAKI

Mt Taranaki is the principal attraction but there are also other places of interest around the Taranaki region.

There are two principal highways around the mountain. SH3, on the inland side of the mountain, is the most travelled route, heading south from New Plymouth for 70 km until it meets the coast again at Hawera. The coast road, SH45, heads 105 km around the coast from New Plymouth to Hawera, where it meets up again with SH3. A round-the-mountain trip on both highways is 175 km, although short cuts can be taken. A Taranaki Heritage Trails booklet, available free from information centres and DOC offices, points out many places of interest.

Stratford

Stratford, 40 km south of New Plymouth on SH3, is named after Stratford-upon-Avon in England, Shakespeare's birthplace, and almost all of its streets are named after a Shakespearean character. Stratford has a good Visitor Information Centre (☎ 765 6708; fax 765 7500) on Broadway, the main street; a DOC Field Centre (☎ 765 5144) on

Pembroke Rd, heading up to Mt Taranaki; and an AA office (☎ 765 7331) at 298 Broadway North.

On SH3 one km south of the centre, the **Taranaki Pioneer Village** is a four-hectare outdoor museum featuring 50 historic buildings and other items pertaining to the heritage of the Taranaki region. It's open every day from 10 am to 4 pm; admission is $5 (children $2).

At Stratford is the turn-off for Pembroke Rd, heading up the mountain for 18 km to East Egmont, the Stratford Mountain House and the Manganui ski area. Stratford is also the southern end of the Stratford-Taumarunui Heritage Trail.

Places to Stay Accommodation in Stratford includes hotels, motels, B&Bs and the *Stratford Holiday Park* (☎ 765 6440) in Page St beside the King Edward Park. It has tent sites, powered sites, cabins, tourist flats and a backpackers bunkhouse with two dorms costing $15 person, a kitchen/lounge area and an indoor heated swimming pool.

Stratford-Taumarunui Heritage Trail

From Stratford, the Whangamomona-Tangarakau Gorge route (SH43) heads off towards Taumarunui in the central North Island. The route has been designated a Heritage Trail, passing by many historic sites, including the historic town of Whangamomona, Maori pa sites, small villages, waterfalls, abandoned coal mines and small museums. You can pick up a free Heritage Trails booklet from information centres or DOC offices in Stratford, Taumarunui or New Plymouth giving details of 32 places of interest along the route; keep an eye out for the blue-and-yellow Heritage Trail signs along the way, with explanatory plaques.

It takes a minimum of 2½ to three hours to drive the 150 km from Stratford to Taumarunui (or vice versa), as the road winds through hilly bush country and 30 km of it is unsealed. Nevertheless it's a good trip if you can put up with the road. It's best to start early in the day; allow at least five hours for the trip if you plan to make stops to see the historic sites. Fill up with petrol from the Stratford or Taumarunui ends, as petrol stations are limited once you're on the road. This is definitely a way to get right off the beaten track in New Zealand.

Eltham & the Lakes

About 10 km south of Stratford is Eltham, well known for its cheeses. Eleven km south-east down the Rawhitiroa Rd is Lake Rotokare, the largest stretch of inland water in Taranaki, where there's a 1½ to two hour walk around the lake through native bush. The artificial Lake Rotorangi, 46 km long and popular for boating and fishing, is also nearby, with cruises operating on the lake.

Hollard Gardens

On Manaia Rd three km north of Kaponga, which is about 13 km west of Eltham on the road to Opunake, are the large Hollard Gardens, administered by the Queen Elizabeth II National Trust. It's most colourful from September to November when the rhododendrons are in bloom but many other plants provide colour all year round. The vast array of rare plants makes it a horticulturist's delight, with posted half and one-hour walks through various gardens. It's open every day from 9 am until dusk; admission is $5 (children free).

Manaia Rd continues north right into the Egmont National Park, leading up to Dawson Falls.

Kapuni

About seven km south of Kaponga is Kapuni. Natural gas discovered at Kapuni was the first such find of any size in New Zealand. It is now piped to Auckland and Wellington. Oil condensate is also piped from Kapuni to New Plymouth, from where it is shipped to New Zealand's oil refinery at Marsden Point near Whangarei, north of Auckland.

Hawera

Hawera is on the coast 70 km south of New Plymouth and 90 km from Wanganui. It has an Information Centre (☎ 278 8599) at 55 High St, beside the historic water tower that dominates the town. The AA office (☎ 278 5095) at 121-123 Princes St.

Elvis fans might be interested in visiting the **Kevin Wasley Elvis Presley Memorial Room** (☎ 278 7624) at 51 Argyle St, which has a collection of Elvis records and souvenirs. Please telephone before you arrive.

Peter Pan fans might be interested in the Wendy statue surrounded by fairies and gnomes in **King Edward Park** on the corner of High and Vogel Sts. The large park has rose and scented gardens and an ornamental lake.

Hawera also has the excellent **Tawhiti Museum**, a private collection of remarkable exhibits, models and dioramas covering many aspects of Taranaki heritage. The life-like human figures were cast from real people around the region; it's quite a unique museum. A bush railway operates the first Sunday of each month and every Sunday during school holidays. The museum is on Ohangai Rd near the corner of Tawhiti Rd, four km from town. It's open Friday to Monday from 10 am to 4 pm, but on Sunday only in winter (June, July and August).

Two km north of Hawera on the Turuturu Rd are the remains of the pre-European Turuturu Mokai Pa. The reserve is open to the public every day. The Tawhiti Museum has a model of the pa.

Places to Stay Accommodation in Hawera includes hotels, motels and the *King Edward Park* camping ground (☎ 278 8544) on Waihi Rd, adjacent to the park, gardens and municipal swimming pool it has tent sites, powered sites, cabins and on-site caravans.

Hawera has two farm backpackers beyond the Tawhiti Museum. *Ohangai Backpacker Farm* (☎ 272 2878) on the Urupa Rd in Ohangai is a dairy farm with a well-equipped backpackers in the paddocks. The cost is $15 per person in good four-bed rooms; twin rooms are $30. German and French are spoken. Free pick-up from Hawera is offered, or take the Tawhiti Rd from Hawera, turn right in front of the museum and keep following the signs for another five km.

Wheatly Downs (☎ 278 6523) is another good farmstay backpackers also past the Tawhiti Museum – don't turn right but keep going straight on the Ararata Rd (the extension of Tawhiti Rd) for four km beyond the museum. Dorm beds cost $14, doubles and twins are $28.

Oakura

If you're starting round the mountain from New Plymouth on the coast road, SH45, the first settlement you'll come to is the small town of Oakura, 15 km west of New Plymouth, known for its beautiful beach, which is great for swimming, surfing and windsurfing.

Oakura has a town pub with an attractive beer garden, a craft shop called the Crafty Fox that is open every day, a surfing and windsurfing shop, and accommodation including a motor camp and motel.

Lucy's Gully

Lucy's Gully, 23 km from New Plymouth on SH45, is one of the few places where exotic trees are being maintained in a national park. A pleasant picnic area, it is also the start of a couple of tracks into the Kaitake Ranges. Further along SH45, turn west at Pungarehu onto Cape Rd to reach the Cape Egmont Lighthouse – it's an interesting sight, but is closed to visitors.

Parihaka

Inland one km or two from Pungarehu is the Maori village of Parihaka (population 100), formerly the stronghold of the Maori prophet and chief Te Whiti and once one of the largest Maori villages in New Zealand. Te Whiti led a passive resistance campaign against the ruthless land confiscation that was taking place with the expansion of European settlement. In the last military campaign in Taranaki, Te Whiti was defeated and jailed, and in 1881 Parihaka was razed. The heavily-armed troops found themselves opposed only by dancing children.

The spirit of Te Whiti still lives on, and his descendants and followers meet at Parihaka annually; it is not open to the public. Many other places in Taranaki are steeped in their Maori past.

Oaonui
Further south along the coast is Oaonui, the landfall of the gas pipeline from the Maui platform and site of the onshore processing plant. A model room is open to visitors daily from 8.30 am to 4.30 pm.

Opunake
Opunake (population 1600) is the largest town on the west side of the mountain. There's a fine beach in the small Opunake Bay, a peaceful place good for swimming and surfing. Right on the beach, the *Opunake Beach Motor Camp Resort* (☎ 761 8235) has tent sites for $7 per person, powered sites for $8, on-site caravans, and backpackers accommodation for $10 per night. In town, the *Opunake Motel & Opunake Backpackers* (☎ 761 8330), 36 Heaphy Rd, has motel units for $55/70, a cottage and a large house for backpackers out the back where dorms cost $15.

Coromandel Peninsula & Hauraki Plains

The Coromandel Peninsula is a rugged, densely forested region, where rivers force their way through gorges and pour down steep cliffs to the sea. The peninsula, with its beautiful coastal scenery and fine beaches, is a haven for Auckland holiday-makers and gets very busy in summer. There are a number of small towns and holiday resorts scattered up and down the coast on both sides of the peninsula. The Coromandel Forest Park stretches almost the entire length of the peninsula, and the landscape gets more rugged and more isolated the further north you head.

South of the peninsula are the pancake-flat Hauraki Plains and to the west the bird-watchers' heaven, the Firth of Thames. Hauraki also has a few places of historical interest but it is mostly by travellers on their way to the delights of the Coromandel Peninsula.

The telephone area code throughout the Coromandel Peninsula and Hauraki Plains is 07.

HIGHLIGHTS

- Coromandel beaches are among New Zealand's best, especially those on the eastern side such as Hahei, Hot Water, Pauanui, Matarangi and Whangamata
- The drive right around the peninsula taking in the west and east coasts offers some of the finest coastal scenery in New Zealand
- Exploring the isolated and rugged north Coromandel for walks, mountain biking or swimming at undisturbed coves
- Walking in the Coromandel Forest Park – the most popular walk is to the Pinnacles
- The historic town of Thames or the craft and alternative lifestyle scene of Coromandel

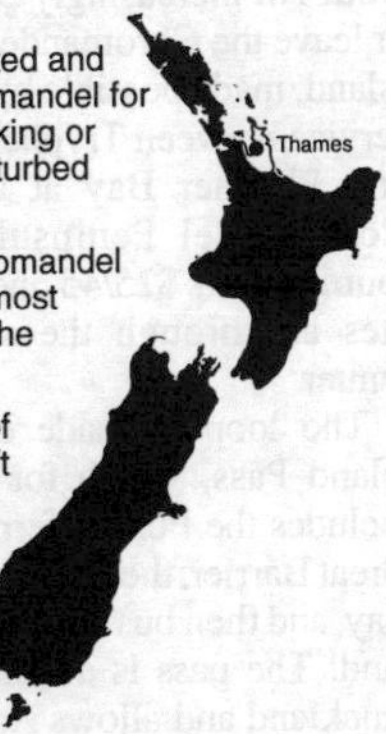

Getting There & Away

Bus The Coromandel has a good bus network, run by a variety of operators. Thames is the main access point for the Coromandel Peninsula.

InterCity has daily buses from Auckland railway station to Thames ($16, 1 hour 40 minutes), continuing on to Paeroa, Waihi, Tauranga and Rotorua. Murphy buses for Thames leave from the downtown bus terminal in Auckland, Monday to Friday at 1 pm. Tavs City Connection buses run from Hamilton to Thames ($20, two hours) via Morrinsville, Te Aroha and Paeroa, with connections to Coromandel.

Of the backpackers buses, Kiwi Safaris runs from Rotorua to Thames to Auckland, and Kiwi Experience stops at Thames on their run between Auckland and Rotorua.

Once in Thames there is a good network established so you can reach the far-flung parts of the peninsula. Murphy travels daily from Thames to Coromandel, Whitianga, Tairua and back to Thames. There are also small shuttle buses to other destinations. Sunkist Lodge in Thames can arrange transport to the Kauaeranga Valley and has a shuttle between Coromandel and Fletcher Bay. On the east coast, a shuttle goes to/from the ferry landing at Whitianga to Hahei and then on to the highway; and from Whangamata buses go to Hikuai via Opoutere and to Waihi.

The $75 Coromandel Busplan is valid for three months and can be used on all the various buses around the Coromandel. It also includes the fare to and from Auckland; alternatively, you can start or finish in Rotorua or Tauranga. For travel on the peninsula only, a

$45 pass is available. It can be booked through the bus companies or on ☎ 0800 800 838.

Hitching Hitching is OK between Thames and Coromandel but can sometimes be difficult beyond there. Be prepared for long waits if you're heading up to Colville or across to Whitianga. Traffic on the east coast is busy during holiday periods, but otherwise light.

Boat An increasingly popular way to reach or leave the Coromandel is via Great Barrier Island, made possible by the connecting boat service between Tryphena, on Great Barrier, and Fletcher Bay at the northern tip of Coromandel Peninsula. The 40-minute journey costs $25/45 one way/return. It operates all through the summer, but not in winter.

The loop is made easy by the Barrier Island Pass, which for $99 ($50 children) includes the Fullers ferry from Auckland to Great Barrier, the boat connection to Fletcher Bay, and then bus connections back to Auckland. The pass is available from Fullers in Auckland and allows stopovers.

Hauraki Plains

The Hauraki Plains cover the triangular area which stretches from Miranda on the south-west side of the Firth of Thames, across to Waihi on the east coast, and down to Paeroa and Te Aroha, which are inland at the southern apex of the triangle. For more information about the area, get a free copy of *Hauraki: Part of the Coromandel Experience*.

COROMANDEL

MIRANDA

Avid birdwatchers will love this area as it is one of the most accessible places to study birds. It's off the Thames/Pokeno Rd, only an hour's drive from Auckland. The vast 8500-hectare mudflat on the western side of the Firth of Thames is teeming with aquatic worms and crustaceans which attract many thousands of Arctic-nesting shore-birds over the Arctic winter.

The two main species are the bar-tailed godwit and the lesser knot, but it isn't surprising to see turnstones, curlew sandpipers, sharp-tailed sandpipers, and the odd vagrant red-necked stint and terek sandpiper.

Miranda also attracts internal migrants after the godwits and knots have departed, including the pied oystercatcher and the wrybill from the South Island, and banded dotterels and pied stilts from both main islands. The wrybill, as its name suggests, is distinguishable by its blackish-brown bill which curves to the right at its tip.

For information on this avifauna extravaganza, visit the modern Miranda Naturalists' Trust Education Centre, just north of Miranda, and pick up a copy of the pamphlet *Shore Bird Migration to and from Miranda*.

The other attraction here is the **Miranda Hot Springs** complex. It has open and covered hot pools, private spas, children's play areas, and camp sites with power. It's open from 10 am to 9 pm daily; admission is $5 (children $2.50).

Places to Stay & Eat

The *Miranda Naturalists' Trust* (☎ Auckland 232 2781) has clean and modern accommodation with all facilities at their Education Centre. A bed here costs a very reasonable $12.50 for non-members ($7.50 for members), and an apartment costs $20 (members $35). Membership of the trust is $20 per year.

Not far south of the centre, next to the hot springs, is the *Miranda Holiday Park* (☎ 867 3205) where tent and caravan sites are $15 for two people.

NGATEA

Originally known as 'Orchard', Ngatea is the hub of the Hauraki Plains and lies 24 km north-west of Paeroa. Before the draining of the plains, access to Ngatea was by small steamer.

The main attraction in town is **Wilderness Gems**, at 13 River Rd, which is a large factory outlet selling jade, semi-precious stones, and marble and rocks from around the world in natural, polished and carved forms. Rockhounds and crystal worshippers will drool, but even the uninitiated will find it a fascinating place to browse and prices are very reasonable.

Ngatea has accommodation and a few cafes. The *Ngatea Hotel* (☎ 867 7189) has singles/doubles for $25/40 and the *Thames Valley Motel* (☎ 867 7189) has units for $55/65.

PAEROA

The Maori name for the Coromandel range was Te Paeroa-o-Toi or 'The Long Range of Toi' and local Maori are believed to be descendants of the *Arawa* and *Tainui* canoes of the Great Migration fleet. In the days before the plains were drained Paeroa was a thriving port, and evidence of this can be seen in the Paeroa Historical Maritime Park. The main display here is the double paddle steamer *Kopu* which once operated between Paeroa and Auckland but there are other interesting displays for boat-lovers, including the 'cream boat' *Scotty* and the navy diving tender HMNZS *Manawanui*.

Lemon & Paeroa, NZ's own soft drink 'internationally famous in NZ', had its beginnings in this town but all that is left now is one discarded giant empty bottle – left here after Gulliver's travels.

The Paeroa Information Centre (☎ 862 8636) is on Belmont Rd (SH2) and is open daily. The town has a small museum, open Monday to Friday from 10.30 am to 3 pm. The Melody Park Radio & Clock Museum is at 4 Prospect Terrace.

Karangahake Gorge

The Karangahake Gorge Historic Walkway, along the Ohinemuri River, commenced when the Paeroa to Waihi railway line was closed in 1979. Waikino is at the eastern end of the gorge and after floods in 1981 the only building left standing was the Waikino Hotel.

The visitor centre in Waikino, now the terminus of the six-km Waihi to Waikino vintage railway, has information on the history and walks of the area. The booklet *Karangahake Gorge Historic Walkway* by Derek Beisly, and the DOC pamphlet of the same name, outline several easy walks in the area and suggest other harder ones.

Three of the highlights of the walkway are the **Owharoa Falls** and the Talisman and Victoria **gold battery sites**. There is a small museum and craft shop in Waikino; admission is $5 for adults and $1 for children.

Places to Stay & Eat

The *Paeroa Backpackers* (☎ 862 6609), at 3 Seymour St (behind the Caltex service station), has beds for $12 ($10 for each subsequent night); sheets and blankets are provided free. A camp site is $8.

Other accommodation includes the *Paeroa Hotel* (☎ 862 7099), the *Casa Mexicana Motel* (☎ 862 8216), *Paeroa Motel* (☎ 862 8475) and *Racecourse Motel* (☎ 862 7145).

Belmont Rd is a good place to hunt out eats. Here you'll find the *Tui Coffee Lounge* at No 18 and the *Four Seasons Chinese Restaurant & Takeaways* at No 70, as well as other cafes. On Normanby Rd (SH2) is the *Cosy Kitchen Tearooms*, and *Talisman Tearooms & Crafts* at Waikino serves light lunches and afternoon teas.

Entwined kiwis are a symbol of good luck – these are an example from the Ngati Maru tribe, Hauraki

WAIHI

Waihi, once a booming gold-mining town, has a number of architectural reminders of its heyday. Gold was first discovered in 1878, and the Martha mine became the richest gold mine in New Zealand and was worked up until 1952. It has since been reopened.

The Waihi Information Centre (☎ 863 6715) is on Seddon St next to the towering old brickworks.

Things to See

The **Waihi Arts Centre & Museum** on Kenny St has superb models and displays about the local Martha Hill mine and is open from 10 am to 4 pm, Monday to Friday, and from 1.30 to 4 pm on weekends. Admission is $2 (children $1).

Along with the Martha mine, the **Golden Cross mine** is now operating again after a long hiatus; weekday tours are by prior arrangement (☎ 863 8192).

Railway buffs, gathered together as the **Goldfields Steam Train Society** (☎ 863 8251), have acquired eight km of track between here and Waikino and run trains between the two townships. To get to the train station turn off SH2 at Wrigley St and proceed to the end.

From 10 am to 4 pm, November to April, you can visit the **Waihi Waterlily Gardens** out on Pukekauri Rd.

Waihi Beach, 11 km east of Waihi, is a small, expanding town with a fine surf beach which is popular in summer.

Places to Stay

Waihi has plenty of accommodation in town and at Waihi Beach. The *Waihi Motor Camp* (☎ 863 7654) is at 6 Waitete Rd in Waihi. At Waihi Beach you'll find *Athenree Motor Camp* (☎ 863 5600), Waihone Ave; *Beachhaven Camp & Caravan Park* (☎ 863 5505), Leo St; and *Bowentown Motor Camp* (☎ 863 5381), Waihi Beach South.

The *Golden Cross Hotel* (☎ 863 6306) on the Corner of Rosemount and Kenny Sts is an old pub offering backpackers accommodation at $15 per person in shared rooms, doubles and twins. There are also two motels in town.

At Waihi Beach, the *Waihi Beach Hotel* (☎ 863 5402) is a modern beer-barn-style pub with rooms for $50 and $60 with private facilities. The *Shalmar Motel* (☎ 863 5439), 40 Seaforth Rd, has units for $82 a double.

The information centre has an up-to-date list of B&Bs and homestays in the area, such as the *Russek's*, 3 Dillon St in Waihi Beach, which has an excellent self-contained, two-bedroom apartment opposite the beach for $55.

Coromandel Peninsula

The Coromandel Peninsula has some of the North Island's finest coastal scenery and beaches. It is very much a bastion for those seeking an alternative lifestyle away from the bustle of Auckland, a serenity only briefly punctuated by the hordes of Christmas holiday-makers. Despite its popularity as a retreat for Aucklanders, it is still a relaxing place for lying around on beaches, fishing, lazing and walking.

The west coast of the peninsula, bounded by the shallow Firth of Thames, is very scenic and contains the picturesque historic towns of Thames and Coromandel, though the most spectacular coastal scenery is on the east coast. The east coast, with its superb beaches, quiet bays and small islands scattered off the coast, is the main resort area.

As a backdrop to this beautiful coastline, a rugged, forest-clad mountain range runs along the spine of peninsula, with many good opportunities for hiking. The mountains extend up to the undeveloped north, which is more rugged and very beautiful but less accessible.

History

Maori have lived on the peninsula since the first settlers arrived, and the sheltered areas of the east coast supported a large population. This was one of the major moa-hunting areas of the North Island, although people also drew on the many other food sources

Coromandel Peninsula
0 10 20 km
Fletcher Bay
To Great Barrier Island
Cape Colville
Port Jackson
Poley Bay
Stony Bay
Fantail Bay
Paritu
Mt Moehau 982 m
Port Charles
Te Anaputa Point
Cuvier Island
Te Hope
Waiaro
Otautu
Waikawau Bay
Colville Bay
Colville
Waitete Bay
Great Mercury Island
MERCURY ISLANDS
Red Mercury Island
Amodeo Bay
Kennedy Bay
Papa Aroha
New Chums Beach
Otama Beach
Oamaru Bay
Shelly Beach
Whangapoua
Matarangi Beach
Waimate Island
Coromandel
Kuaotunu
Opito Bay
Ohinau Island
Long Bay
Te Rerenga
Motutapere Island
Whanganui Island
Coromandel Harbour
Waitaia Bay
309
Te Kouma
Manaia Harbour
Whitianga
Ferry Landing
Cathedral Cove
Manaia
Road
Hahei
Cooks Beach
Kereta
Hot Water Beach
FIRTH OF THAMES
Waikawau
Coroglen
Whenuakite
Te Mata
Tapu
Ruamahanga Bay
Ocean Beach
Shoe Island
Waiomu
COROMANDEL FOREST PARK
Tairua
Te Puru
Pauanui
Thorntons Bay
Ngarimu Bay
Slipper Island
Whakatete Bay
DOC Park HQ
Puketu
Hikuai
Ohui
Tararu
Thames
Opoutere
Kauaeranga
Miranda
Wharekawa
Kopu
Onemana
Tairua Block
Orongo
To Auckland
Matatoki
Waitakaruru
Whangamata
Puriri
Whangamata Harbour
Turua
Ngatea
Mangatarata
Hikutaia
Waiharakeke
Whiritoa
Hauraki Plains
Paeroa
Homunga Bay
Waihi
Golden Valley
Waikino
Tirohia
Karangahake Gorge
Waihi Beach
Athenree
KAIMAI-MAMAKU FOREST PARK
To Te Aroha & Morrinsville
25
25A
26
2

COROMANDEL

available through fishing, sealing, bird-hunting and horticulture.

The history of European colonisation on the peninsula and the plains to the south is steeped in gold-mining, logging and gum-digging. Gold was first discovered in New Zealand at Coromandel in 1852 by Charles Ring, but the rush was short-lived once the miners found it was not alluvial gold but gold to be wrested from the ground by pick and shovel. More gold was discovered around Thames in 1867 and over the next few years other fields were proclaimed at Coromandel, Kuaotunu and Karangahake. In 1892 the Martha mine at Waihi began production and by the time it was closed in 1952 around $60 million of gold had been extracted. Interest in minerals is still strong today because the area is rich in semi-precious gemstones like quartz, agate, amethyst, jasper, chalcedony and carnelian. In fact, if you walk along Te Mata beach you will probably stumble over some agate.

Kauri logging was a big business on the peninsula for around 100 years. Allied to the timber trade was ship-building which took off after 1832 when a mill was established at Mercury Bay. By the 1880s Kauaeranga, Coroglen (Gumtown) and Tairua were the main suppliers of kauri to the Auckland mills. Things got tougher once the kauri around the coast became scarce due to indiscriminate felling, and the loggers had to penetrate deeper into the bush for the timber. Getting the logs out became more and more difficult. Some logs were pulled out by bullock teams, others had to be hauled to rivers and floated out after dams had been

Cycling in the Coromandel

The compact nature of the peninsula makes it an ideal place for a cycling tour. Some people choose to get their bikes dropped off in Thames and then do a peninsula circuit. It is becoming much easier to do a full loop – Auckland-Coromandel-Great Barrier Island-Auckland – now that there are transport possibilities from Fletcher Bay and then on the QuickCat from Great Barrier.

The most preferred route is Thames to Coromandel along the coast; Coromandel to Whitianga via 309 Rd; followed by either Whitianga to Tairua via SH25 or the ferry to Ferry Landing, then Cook's Beach, Hahei, Cathedral Cove and Hot Water Beach, rejoining the road at Whenuakite.

Here are notes on each of the road sections:

Hauraki Plains: straight, sealed, with no steep hills

Thames to Coromandel: Thames has a busy residential area; the coast road is flat, narrow and has blind bends; last section to Coromandel is steep but sealed

North of Coromandel: to Colville the road is steep and narrow in places; north of Colville roads are unsealed and more suited to mountain bikes; there's a new mountain-bike track from Stony Bay to Fletcher Bay, well away from Coromandel Walkway

Coromandel to Whitianga: the two roads across the peninsula are unsealed; SH25 is the longer and has two steep hills; 309 Rd is potholed and has corrugations but there are a number of accessible, scenic features

Whitianga to Tairua: this road is sealed and has one steep hill; the reverse direction is harder

Kopu to Hikuai: not suitable for the beginner as it is steep and slippery in places; more suited to the fit cyclist

Maratoto/The Wires: the walking tracks are off-limits to cyclists

Whangamata: there are large hills on both sides of Whangamata; the forests around Whangamata contain some great mountain-bike tracks; the bush around Opoutere and Ohui have dirt and clay single-tracks with occasional water crossings

Karangahake Gorge: this road is sealed all the way but it is dangerous in conditions of low visibility as there are a number of blind bends; the plus is that it is flat, scenic and there are plenty of interesting rest stops. ■

built, and tramways were built on the west coast. But by the 1930s the logging of kauri on the peninsula had all but finished.

A useful brochure entitled the *Coromandel Peninsula: Heritage Trails* outlines urban heritage trails in Thames, Coromandel and Whitianga, and 15 spots which are worth stopping at on the peninsula.

THAMES

Thames is the gateway and main town of the Coromandel Peninsula, lying on the shallow Firth of Thames. Its streets are lined with old wooden houses and pubs dating from the 19th century, when the gold rush and kauri trade made Thames one of the biggest towns in New Zealand.

Thames is now a quiet town of historic interest, though most visitors merely pass through on their way to the scenic bays and beaches to the north and east.

Information

The Thames Information Centre (☎ 868 7284), 405 Queen St, is in front of the large Goldfields shopping mall. This well-run centre is a mine of information about the whole peninsula. It is open from 9 am to 5 pm every day in summer, with shorter weekend hours in winter. Pick up a copy of the very useful *Coromandel Directory*. Another excellent publication is *The Coromandel Travellers Guide*, available from the information centre or the Sunkist Lodge hostel.

The DOC office (☎ 868 6381) in the Kauaeranga Valley is open from 8 am to 4 pm, Monday to Friday. There's an AA office at 424 Pollen St, and the CPO is on Pollen St.

Things to See

At the northern end of town, the **gold mine & stamper battery** can be visited for a look at the town's gold-mining history. The Hauraki Prospectors' Association has set up a working stamper battery, displays and photographs, and tours of the mine are conducted twice daily. It is open from 9 am to 4 pm, but usually closed in winter; the cost is $4 (children $1).

The **Mineralogical Museum**, on the corner of Brown and Cochrane Sts, has a comprehensive collection of NZ rocks, minerals and fossils. It's open from 11 am to 4 pm daily.

The local **historical museum**, on the corner of Cochrane and Pollen Sts, has pioneer relics, rocks and old photographs of the town. It is open from 1 to 4 pm in summer; admission is $2 (children 50 cents).

The large concrete phallus overlooking town on Monument Hill is in fact the **WWI Peace Memorial**, from where there are good views of Thames and the surrounding countryside. Another good vantage point is the **Totara Pa**, once occupied by the Ngati Maru tribe until their defeat by Hongi Hika in 1821. It is now a cemetery, but if you look carefully you will see the remains of fortifications and deep trenches.

Activities

The visitor information centre can provide details on self-guided **walks** around town, taking in the buildings and sites of historic interest. About three km from town at the Dickson Holiday Park, a walking trail takes you 2½ to three hours through the forest to the Rocky's Goldmine.

The **Kakara Hide** is an excellent birdwatching hide at the edge of the mangroves just off Brown St.

One of Thames' more innovative attractions is its **Mystery, Murder & Intrigue Weekends**, held twice a month at the Brian Boru Hotel. Each of the 30 to 45 guests dons fancy-dress costume and is a suspect in the Agatha Christie-style murder mystery that takes place. These popular weekends attract visitors from many countries. The fun begins on Friday night, includes a Saturday tour of the Coromandel, and ends with a Sunday 'postmortem' over breakfast. The cost is $355, all inclusive.

For **crafts**, the Thames Society of Arts & Crafts shows local work at the Old North School on Tararu Rd, north of Thames.

Bicycles and kayaks can be rented for exploring further afield. The aeroclub at the airport offers scenic flights for spectacular

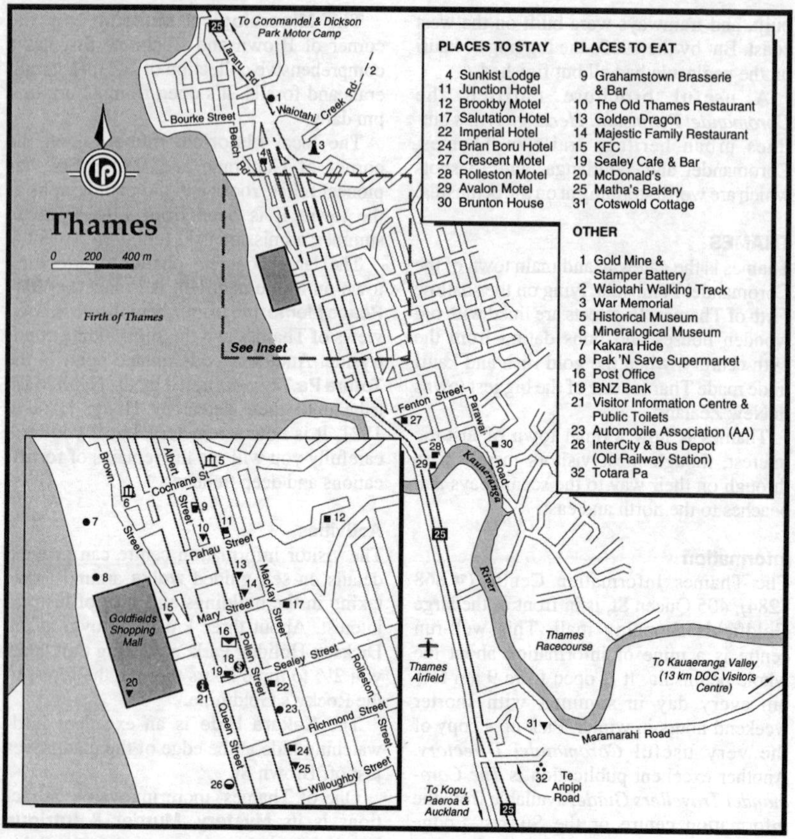

views of the peninsula on a fine day, and jet-boat tours run along the Waihou River – the visitor information centre has details.

Places to Stay

Camping & Cabins The *Dickson Holiday Park* (☎ 868 7308) is three km north of Thames in an attractive quiet valley beside a stream and four minutes from the beach. Tent sites cost $7 per person, power sites cost $18 for two people. The backpackers bunkroom costs $10 per person, cabins start from $37 a double, and a tourist flat with bathroom and colour TV costs $54 for two people. It's a pleasant camping ground with a swimming pool.

See the North of Thames section for other camp sites on the coast north of Thames.

Hostels *Sunkist Lodge* (☎ 868 8808), 506 Brown St, is a relaxed hostel in a historic building that was the Lady Bowen Hotel from 1868 to 1952; it's reputed to have a resident ghost. Dorm beds cost $14 and $16, and twins and doubles are $35. The upstairs verandah is a fine place to laze and watch the sunset over the placid Firth of Thames; there is a pool table in the lounge downstairs. The manager, Geoff, is a mine of information on the Coromandel, and you can arrange all your transport around the peninsula here.

Hotels & Motels The *Brian Boru Hotel* (☎ 868 6523), 200 Richmond St, on the corner of Pollen St, has double rooms with their own bathroom for $66 to $88, some imaginatively decked out as theme rooms complete with indoor waterfalls. The pub also has run-down budget rooms for $25, or $15 for 'genuine' backpackers. The motel section next to the hotel has the best accommodation at $68/88 for singles/doubles.

The town's other hotels also have standard pub rooms. The *Imperial Hotel* (☎ 868 6200), on the corner of Sealey and Pollen Sts, has singles/doubles at $38/48, or $50/60 with bathroom. If you are desperate, the *Junction Hotel* (☎ 868 6008), on the corner of Pollen and Pahau Sts, and the *Salutation* (☎ 868 6488), 400 Mary St, also have rooms.

There are plenty of motels in Thames and north along the coast towards Coromandel. The plain *Brookby Motel* (☎ 868 6663) at 102 Redwood Lane is one of the cheapest at $50/65 for singles/doubles. The *Coastal Motor Lodge* (☎ 868 6843), three km north of Thames on SH25, is considerably more expensive with singles/doubles for $76/89 or chalets for $97/110, but it's very attractive and pleasantly situated.

B&Bs & Guesthouses The information centre keeps a list of B&Bs and homestays for the area. Of note for its historic charm is *Brunton House* (☎ 868 5160), 210 Parawai Rd, a large, verandahed house with a swimming pool. Singles/doubles with breakfast cost $40/75.

Places to Eat

Pollen St, reputed to be one of the longest straight shopping streets in New Zealand, has plenty of takeaways and coffee lounges such as *Martha's Bakery* for baked goodies. *KFC* and *McDonald's* are both close to the Goldfields Mall. In the mall itself is a *Robert Harris Coffee Shop* and a number of other lunch-time outlets.

Thames also has a good range of restaurants. For value, the licensed *Old Thames Restaurant* on Pollen St is very popular for moderately priced steak, seafood and pizzas. It also has Bluff oysters – not to be missed. It's open every day from 5 pm. The *Majestic Family Restaurant*, 640 Pollen St, has a fish & chip takeaway at the front and good seafood meals in the restaurant around the back for $12 to $16, with slightly cheaper steaks. The *Golden Dragon* is the place for a cheap Chinese meal or takeaways.

The fancy restaurant at the *Brian Boru Hotel* serves three-course dinners, or you can dine à la carte. The restaurant features flounder, a Thames' speciality, and the bar serves flounder & chips for $13.50. The *Imperial Hotel* also has pub fare and a fancier bistro.

Bars and cafes are proliferating. Most fashionable is the *Grahamstown Brasserie & Bar* at 719 Pollen St in a beautifully restored building. The food is expensive but good.

The *Sealey Cafe & Bar*, 109 Sealey St, is another fine establishment for a meal or just a drink. It has a pleasant courtyard out front where you can take it easy on a sunny afternoon or warm evening. Just out of town on Maramarahi Rd, *Cotswold Cottage* is fully licensed and the menu combines seafood and game caught locally.

Getting There & Away

Thames is the main transport hub for the Coromandel Peninsula with bus connections to Auckland, Hamilton, Tauranga and Rotorua (see Getting There & Away at the start of this chapter for more information). Buses depart from the old railway station (☎ 868 7251), where you can buy tickets. Sunkist Lodge (☎ 868 8808) also sells bus tickets and the Coromandel Busplan for travel around the peninsula. The lodge also runs buses to the Kauaeranga Valley and from Coromandel to Fletchers Bay, linking up with the boat crossing to Great Barrier Island.

From Thames, the Murphy bus departs for Coromandel at 10 am from the old railway station. It will pick up passengers at Sunkist Lodge, and costs $12. From Coromandel, the bus continues on to Whitianga and then loops back to Thames. Tavs City Connection also has buses to Coromandel from Monday to Friday at 11 am and 3 pm for $10 ($16 return).

COROMANDEL FOREST PARK

There are over 30 walks and tramps through Coromandel Forest Park, covering the area from the Maratoto Forest, near Paeroa, to Cape Colville. The most popular region is the Kauaeranga Valley which cuts into the Colville Range behind Thames. There are many old kauri dams in the valley, including the Tarawaere, Waterfalls, Dancing Camp, Kauaeranga Main, Moss Creek and Waterfalls Creek dams. You are requested not to climb on them.

Walks in the **Kauaeranga Valley**, especially on weekends, have become so popular that DOC has built a new 80-bed hut to accommodate trampers. One of the best, most accessible walks on the peninsula is through the valley to the Pinnacles. The three to four-hour hike through regenerating forest to the jagged limestone outcrop of the Pinnacles is rewarded with great views of the peninsula. A number of other walks can be done in the area, though some trails are hazardous and have been closed – check with DOC before heading off.

Information

All of the walks are outlined in the excellent DOC pamphlet *Coromandel Recreation: A Forest and Coastal Experience*, free from DOC offices and visitor information centres.

Sunkist Lodge Hostel in Thames also has lots of information about walks in the area.

The DOC Visitor Centre (☎ 868 6381), is in the Kauaeranga Valley about 15 km from Thames. It is open on weekdays from 8 am to 4 pm, as well as on weekends in the summer.

Places to Stay

There are DOC camping grounds at various places throughout the Coromandel Forest Park. You'll find them on the west coast and northern tip of the peninsula at Fantail Bay, Port Jackson and Fletcher Bay, and at Stony Bay and Waikawau Bay on the east coast. All charge only a nominal fee, and you don't have to book.

There are camping grounds ($4 for adults and $2 for children) all along the Kauaeranga Valley Rd past the visitors centre. From the end of the road it is a three-hour walk to the Moss Creek Hut or the Pinnacles Hut, which have bunks, toilets, cooking and washing facilities. Bring your own cooking gear. The nightly cost for these is $8, and you can buy your tickets from DOC or the Thames Information Centre.

Getting There & Away

The headquarters and main entrance to the park are reached from the southern edge of Thames along Kauaeranga Valley Rd. Sunkist Lodge in Thames has a bus going on demand to the end of the Kauaeranga Valley Rd for $15/30 one way/return, $20 return if you have bought the Coromandel Busplan. The bus leaves at 1.15 pm; phone ☎ 868 8808 for bookings.

NORTH OF THAMES

Travelling north from Thames, SH25 snakes along the coast for 32 km past lots of pretty little bays and calm beaches. Fishing and shellfishing are excellent all the way up the coast, and the landscape turns crimson when pohutukawa trees bloom in the summer.

Along the way, you pass through Whakatete, Ngarimu Bay, Te Puru, Tapu and other small settlements. The **Rapaura Watergardens**, six km inland from Tapu on the Tapu-Coroglen Rd, are open daily from 10 am to 5 pm in summer; admission is $5 (children $1) and there are tearooms. Also on the Tapu-Coroglen Rd is the 'square' kauri tree, a huge kauri estimated to be 1200 years old.

Places to Stay

The *Boomerang Motor Camp* (☎ 867 8879) in Te Puru, 11 km north of Thames, has camping facilities, cabins and on-site caravans. Nearby is the *Puru Park Motel* (☎ 868 2686) and the luxurious *Te Puru Coast View*

COROMANDEL

Lodge (☎ 868 2326), a Mediterranean-style villa with singles/doubles for $85/99.

Another couple of km north is the *Waiomu Bay Holiday Park* (☎ 868 2777) which has camping, on-site caravans, cabins, tourist flats and motel units. The *Seaspray Motel* (☎ 868 2863) is also in Waiomu.

At Tapu, 22 km north of Thames, the *Tapu Motor Camp* (☎ 868 4837) has camp sites, on-site caravans and cabins. The backpackers rate is $10 per person in bunkrooms or caravans. Also in Tapu, the *Te Mata Lodge* (☎ 868 4834) has rustic, hostel-style accommodation set in the bush, at $12/20 for singles/doubles. There are plenty of bush walks, including one to the beach, and the rivers are good for swimming. To reach Te Mata Lodge go 1½ km north past Tapu on the coast road, turn inland past the concrete bridge down Te Mata Creek Rd, and follow the road to the end.

COROMANDEL

When you get to Wilsons Bay the road leaves the coast and cuts through hills and valleys until you arrive at the next major town, Coromandel. This town, 55 km north of Thames, was named after HMS *Coromandel* which visited the harbour in 1820 to pick up a load of kauri spars for the navy. It was here, on Driving Creek, three km north of the township, that kauri mill owner Charles Ring discovered gold in 1852. At the height of the gold rush the town's population rose to over 10,000, but today it's a soporific little township of fewer than 1000 souls, and is noted for its crafts and alternative lifestylers.

Information

The Coromandel Information Centre (☎ 866 8598) is in the Thames-Coromandel District Council building on Kapanga Rd. In summer it's open from 9 am to 5 pm, Monday to Friday, and 10 am to 1 pm on weekends. The centre has many useful leaflets on the surrounding area, and takes bookings for all the accommodation in town. There's also a DOC field centre here with information on parks and walking.

Things to See

The small **Coromandel Mining & Historic Museum** has gold-mining and colonial era exhibits. It's open daily from 10 am to 4 pm in summer; admission is $2 (children free). In winter, hours are variable but it is usually open on the weekend.

The **Coromandel Stamper Battery** (☎ 866 8765), also on Ring's Rd, demonstrates the process of crushing ore, the first step in extracting gold, and shows various amalgamation processes. Tours are arranged by appointment.

Driving Creek, three km north of Coromandel, is where Charles Ring discovered gold. It is now the site of various fascinating enterprises masterminded by one of Coromandel's leading artists, Barry Brickell. A potter who discovered excellent clay on his land, Brickell had to work out a way of moving it down the hill to his kiln. So he built his own railway to do it! The **Driving Creek Railway** runs up steep grades, across three high trestle bridges, along a spiral and a double switchback, and through two tunnels! It's a 50-minute round trip and Brickell takes visitors up to the top at 2 and 4 pm every day, with an extra 10.30 am run from October to Easter. The cost is $6 (children $3). Also at Driving Creek are Brickell's pottery stall and his commendable native forest restoration project.

For **crafts**, Coromandel has interesting craft shops along Kapanga Rd, or pick up a copy of the *Coromandel Craft Trail* pamphlet for exploring further afield.

Walks

Coromandel is in the middle of a region abounding in natural beauty, scenic reserves, and attractive bush walks. The visitor information centre has a big map on the wall showing all the scenic reserves and the two farm park recreation reserves with camping (at Cape Colville and Waikawau Bay).

A few of the more notable walks in the area include a three-km one from Coromandel to Long Bay through a grove of large kauris, and a climb through Whangapoua State Forest to the 521-metre Castle Rock on

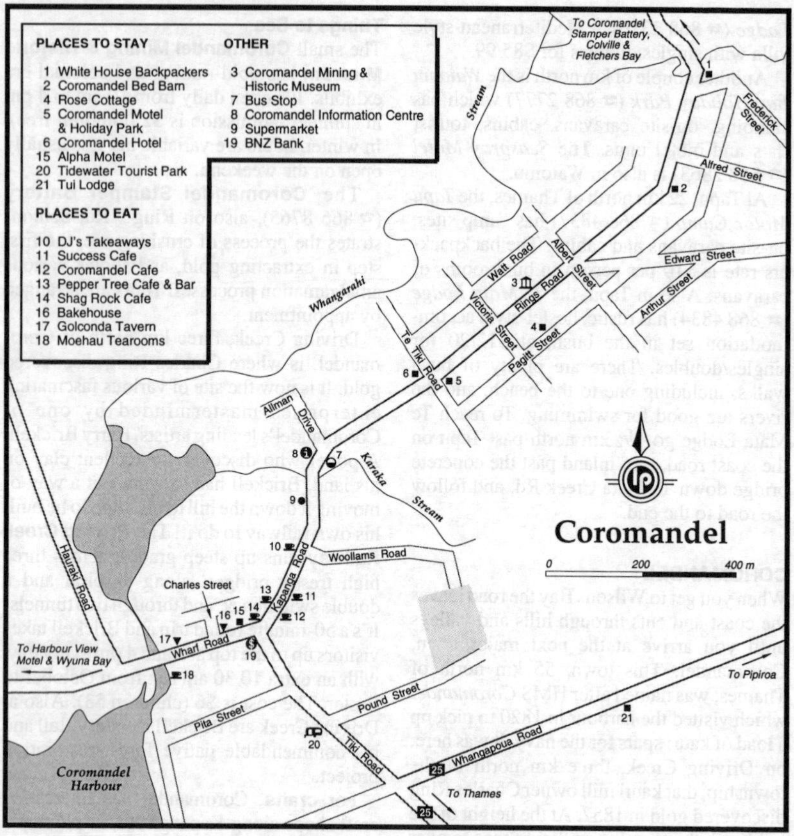

309 Rd. There are many old abandoned gold mines in the area and these, too, make for good exploration.

Places to Stay

Camping & Cabins There are several motor camps in and around Coromandel. The *Coromandel Motel & Holiday Park* (☎ 866 8830), 400 metres from the post office, has tent/power sites at $8/9 per person. Cabins cost $36 for two people, and motel units cost $80. Off-season and family tariffs are available.

On the beachfront, three km west of Coromandel, *Long Bay Motor Camp* (☎ 866 8720) has sites from $8.50 per person and on-site caravans. At *Shelly Beach Motor Camp* (☎ 866 8988), five km north of Coromandel, tent sites are $7.50 and powered sites $10.50.

There are more motor camps north of Coromandel: the *Oamaru Bay Tourist Flats & Caravan Park* (☎ 866 8735), on Oamaru Bay seven km north of Coromandel; *Papa Aroha Motor Camp* (☎ 866 8818) at Papa Aroha, 12 km north; and *Angler's Lodge & Motor Park* (☎ 866 8584) at Amodeo Bay, 18 km north of Coromandel.

Hostels The *Tidewater Tourist Park* (☎ 866 8888), 270 Tiki Rd near the harbour, is a YHA associate hostel. This friendly, spotless place has new hostel cabins and tourist flats. It costs $14 per person ($13 for YHA members) in dorms, twins or doubles. Self-contained two-person tourist flats cost $55.

Tui Lodge (☎ 866 8237), 600 Whangapoua Rd, is a quiet hostel 10 minutes walk from town. The Whitianga bus will stop at the gate or there's free pick-up on request. The backpackers house has a variety of accommodation; it's $13 in the dorms or $28 for twins and doubles. Tours are arranged, free bikes are available, and all-in-all this is a well-run, good-value place.

The *White House Backpackers* (☎ 866 8468), on the corner of Frederick St and Rings Rd, has three houses, which are a little run-down but spacious enough. Dorm rooms are $13 and twins and doubles $34. They offer free transport one way from Auckland if you stay a minimum of two nights (subject to bookings), and they offer a number of peninsula trips.

The *Coromandel Bed Barn* (☎ 866 8327), 327 Rings Rd, is a small new hostel with dorm beds for $13 and a double room for $30.

B&Bs & Guesthouses There are a number of B&Bs and guesthouses including the *Rose Cottage* (☎ 866 7047) on Pagitt St opposite the mining museum. This simple guesthouse, in a private home, offers backpackers discounted rates of $18/25 for singles/doubles. The *Jackaranda B&B* (☎ 866 8002) is a new house set back off the highway three km south of town and has singles/doubles for $35/60. The four-bed bunkroom caters to backpackers and costs $15 per person. The information centre has other B&Bs on file.

Hotels & Motels The *Coromandel Hotel* (☎ 866 8760) is on the main street and has rooms for $25 per person. Coromandel has many motels costing around $75 a double. Possibilities include the *Wyuna Bay Motel* (☎ 866 8507), the *Harbour View Motel* (☎ 866 8690), the *Alpha Motel* (☎ 866 8709) and the *Colonial Cottages* (☎ 866 8856).

Places to Eat

Try the *Bakehouse* on Wharf Rd, with its lasagne with smoked snapper and oysters for $8, or the bistro bar at the *Coromandel Hotel*. The *Coromandel Cafe* has sandwiches and hot meals. It's open for breakfast and lunch and, during summer, for evening meals as well. The *Success Cafe* on Kapanga Rd has light lunches during the day and a full menu at night, and the *Shag Rock Cafe*, also on Kapanga Rd, has inexpensive snacks, sandwiches, cappuccinos and a garden area out the back. Opposite the Golconda Tavern is the *Moehau Tearooms & Takeaways*.

The *Pepper Tree Cafe & Bar* on Kapanga Rd has excellent seafood and other meals in the dining room or the more casual bar. Out on Tiki Rd about one km south of town is the *Old Loft Cafe & Gallery* (☎ 866 8427), a seafood place and one of the town's finest restaurants.

If you're heading north from Coromandel you can't buy stores or food beyond Colville, so stock up before you go. There's an excellent market in Main St from 9 am to 3 pm every Saturday. Buy some fish from the local fishing fraternity and cook it yourself.

Getting There & Away

Air Coromandel (☎ 866 4016) will put down or pick up passengers from Coromandel on demand during their scheduled Auckland-Whitianga service.

Murphy buses serve Coromandel on their Thames-Coromandel-Whitianga-Thames route daily (except Saturday in winter). Buses to Coromandel ($10, 1½ hours) leave at 11.30 am from the information centre. Tavs City Connection buses leave Coromandel for Thames at 7.30 am and 2 pm.

The shuttle to Fletcher Bay meets the Murphy bus on Monday, Wednesday, Friday and Saturday, leaving for Fletcher Bay at 11.30 am. It costs $16/30 one way/return.

Paradise Shuttle Tours (☎ 866 6856) arranges tours around the peninsula.

AROUND COROMANDEL

North of Coromandel

The road heading north is sealed to the tiny town of **Colville**, 85 km north of Thames. Colville was formerly known as Cabbage Bay, so named by Cook who insisted that his crew eat the leaves of native cabbage trees, to guard against scurvy. Now it is home to alternative-lifestylers; there is a small wholefood cafe and a cooperative store.

North of Colville the roads are rough and hitching may not be so easy. From Colville you can head north along the west coast to Fletchers Bay or head over the ranges to Port Charles.

Port Charles is just a small collection of holiday baches on a scenic bay with a pleasant beach. The road leads to another small bay with more holiday houses and then over a headland with fine views to **Sandy Bay**, with its pebble beach and DOC camping ground. From Sandy Bay, tracks lead to Fletcher Bay and Mt Moehau.

Following the west coast road, 12 km north of Colville is Te Hope and the start of the walk to **Mt Moehau**, the peninsula's highest peak (892 metres). This is a demanding three to four-hour walk but is rewarded with fine views of Coromandel and the Hauraki Gulf. The trail continues on to the Sandy Bay – it's a full day's walk to cross the peninsula.

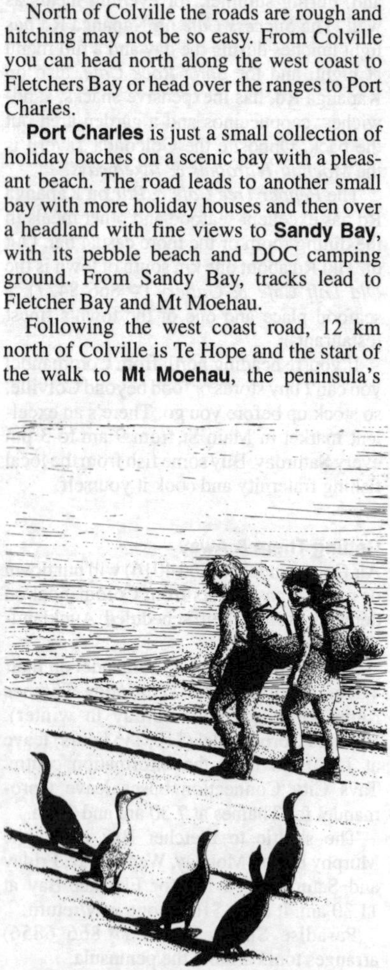

The west coast road leads eventually to **Fletcher Bay** – a real land's end. This is a magic place with deserted beaches, forest and coastal walks, sea kayaking, fishing trips, boat rides to Great Barrier, mountain biking, endless native birds and splendid views across to Great Barrier, Little Barrier and Cuvier islands. Fletcher Bay is reached by the shuttle from the Fletcher Bay hostel to Coromandel town (see under Coromandel) and is also the departure point for the boat to Great Barrier Island.

From Fletcher Bay, it's about a three-hour walk to Stony Bay on the east coast. Sometimes groups who have access to transport drive as far as possible and walk the rest of the way, with a driver meeting them on the other side. The Fletcher Bay hostel can also arrange boat or bus transport to Stoney Bay. A lot of people elect to walk both ways. It is an easy, pleasant walk with great coastal views and then an ambling section across open farmland. Mountain bikers must use the longer marked stock route that runs between the two bays along the flank of Mt Moehau.

Places to Stay DOC has camping grounds at Fletcher Bay, Waikawau Bay and Stony Bay on the eastern side of the peninsula, and at Port Jackson and Fantail Bay on the western side.

Colville Backpackers & Farmstay (☎ 866 6820) is on a 1260-hectare farm. A bed in the backpackers cottage is $13 to $15 per person, the bush lodge is $12 per person or $50 for the whole place. Camping costs $9.

Isolated Port Charles has two backpackers. *Beach Cottage* (☎ 866 8191) on Carey Rd has a simple backpackers at the back of the house. It's a friendly place right opposite the beach and it organises activities and transport to walks. The cost is $13 in dorm beds and $36 for a double room. *Paradise*

Backpackers (☎ 866 6856) is on Little Sandy Bay a couple of km further north. The hostel is small and nestled in greenery; it's back from the beach up Adlor Hill Rd. The cost is $15 in four-bed dorms and there is also a double cabin for $34. The owners also run Paradise Shuttle Tours, which offers a host of tours around north Coromandel.

Sunkist Lodge in Thames operates the *Fletcher Bay Backpackers* (☎ 866 8989), a small, comfortable 16-bed place perched up on a hill overlooking the farm and beach. It has all facilities and organises transport for hiking and the boat to Great Barrier Island. The cost per night is $15 per person.

SH25 to Whitianga

From Coromandel south-east to Whitianga there are two possible routes. SH25 is longer (46 km, 1¼ hours) and much of it is still gravel, but it's the more scenic route, following the coast and offering exquisite beach views. The other road is the unsealed Highway 309.

If you continue on SH25 east of Coromandel you come to Te Rerenga, almost on the shore of Whangapoua Harbour. The road forks here; if you head north you come to the end of the road at Whangapoua. From Whangapoua you can walk along the rocky foreshore to the isolated and pristine **New Chum's Bay**. The walk takes about 30 minutes and starts by the picnic area at the end of the road. At Whangapoua, the *Woodfish Farm* (☎ 866 5566/5377) is on SH25, 19 km from Coromandel and 27 km from Whitianga. It's on a beautiful promontory jutting out into Whangapoua Harbour and guests are welcome to stay in the flat behind the farmhouse for $15 per person.

Continuing east you can visit the beachside towns of Matarangi, Kuaotunu, Otama and Opito before heading south to Whitianga. This whole stretch has beautiful beaches. **Matarangi** has a good beach but it is a dull real estate development that seems to be the eventual fate for other parts of the Coromandel. **Kuaotunu** is a small settlement with a delightful beach and a camping ground. Off Opito Bay is the spectacular **Needle Rock**, so named because the hole through the rock is tapered in the shape of the eye of a needle.

Highway 309

Highway 309 (known locally as 309 Rd) is the shorter way to Whitianga (32 km, 45 minutes) but it's rather rough going as the road is unsealed. It's a bush road and is generally not as scenic as SH25, unless you want to get out and do some walking. It does have some excellent spots including the **Chiltern Scenic Reserve**, **Waiau Falls**, a grove of large kauri trees, and a two-hour return walking track to the summit of **Castle Rock**. Two private gardens that can be visited are the **Marmony Gardens** and **Waiau Water Works**, a herbal garden with various water-driven gadgets.

The **kauri grove** is particularly interesting as there is a Siamese kauri, which forks just above the ground. The roots of the kauri are protected by a system of boardwalks.

The 309 Honey Cottage (☎ 866 5151) is about 12 km from Whitianga on 309 Rd. It's a lovely place, relaxing and scenic, with 40 hectares of farm and bush. The cost is $15 a night in an old kauri cottage beside a river, or you can camp for $5 a night. There are plenty of farm animals about and there's a glass beehive where you can see bees at work (in spring). Activities include rafting, horse riding and bushwalking. There's no bus but they will pick you up in Whitianga if you phone.

WHITIANGA

The pleasant Whitianga area of Mercury Bay has a long history by NZ standards. The Polynesian explorer Kupe landed near here around 950 AD and the area was called Te Whitianga-a-Kupe (the Crossing Place of Kupe). Prior to that the land was abundant with moas and there is evidence that there were moa hunters here 2000 years ago.

Mercury Bay was given its modern name by Captain Cook when he observed the transit of Mercury while anchored in the bay in November 1769.

Whitianga is the main town on Mercury

Bay. Buffalo Beach, Whitianga's principal frontage onto the attractive bay, takes its name from HMS *Buffalo*, wrecked there in 1840. The beach itself is reasonable, and there are seven good beaches all within easy reach of the town.

The town is a big game-fishing base for tuna, marlin, mako (blue pointer shark), thresher shark and kingfish. It is very much a tourist town, whose small population swells to mammoth proportions during the January holidays.

Information

The Whitianga Information Centre (☎ 866 5555; fax 866 2222), 66 Albert St, is open 9 am to 5 pm, Monday to Friday, and 10 am to 3 pm on weekends.

Museum

The little Mercury Bay Historic Society Museum opposite the ferry wharf has many historic photos of Mercury Bay and the kauri logging era, and exhibits on mining, blacksmithing, the colonial era, Maori carvings, the HMS *Buffalo* and other shipwrecks. The jaws of a 1350-kg white pointer shark caught in the Hauraki Gulf in 1959 hang on the wall overlooking all.

The museum is open daily in summer from 10 am to 3 pm. Winter hours are shorter: 11 am to 2 pm, four days a week. Admission is $2 (children 50 cents).

Ferry Landing

From the Narrows on the southern side of town, a passenger ferry crosses over to Ferry Landing, site of the original township on the southern side of Mercury Bay. The stone wharf at Ferry Landing was built in 1837 by Gordon Browne, who had a trading post, warehouse and boat-building business. Stone for the wharf came from Whitianga Rock, a pa site of which Captain Cook said 'the best engineers in Europe could not have chosen a better site for a small band of men to defend against a greater number'. The view from Shakespeare's Lookout, on top of the white cliffs above Ferry Landing, is particularly lovely, a great spot to see all of Mercury Bay with its many beaches and coves.

The five-minute ferry crossing costs 75 cents (children 40 cents); 40 cents for bicycles. The ferry does not take cars, which have to take a circuitous route around the bay to the south, via Coroglen. In summer the ferry runs continuously from 7.30 am to 10.30 pm; in winter from 7.30 am to noon and from 1 to 6.30 pm.

Bicycles can be hired from beside the store in Ferry Landing. You can walk, cycle or drive to a number of excellent spots on this side including the town of Cook's Beach, Lonely Bay, Front Beach and Flaxmill Bay (where Cook is believed to have careened the *Endeavour)*, and further on to Hahei. A bus also runs from Ferry Landing (see Getting There & Away below). Purangi Winery (☎ 866 3724), six km south of Ferry Landing, has kiwi fruit and other wines for tasting, and a restaurant. It also operates cruises on the Purangi River.

Activities

Whitianga has many activities for visitors and the information centre can supply details on all of them. On the water there are scenic yacht trips, cruises, kayak trips, fishing excursions, windsurfing, sailing, jet-boating and safe swimming. In summer you can fish from the wharf. River rafting is popular on the nearby Waiwawa River. Back on land there are horse treks, bus tours, and numerous scenic drives and walks.

Dolphin Quest (☎ 866 5555) has a **swim with the dolphins** experience. The bottlenose dolphins were once regular visitors close inshore but now are not so common and the tours are dependent on definite sightings. Wet suits, snorkels and flippers are supplied; the cost is $75 for a three-hour trip.

Mercury Bay is rich in interesting **walks**. Watch your step, though – some of the mine shafts are quite deep. One of the more popular gold mines is reached by an enjoyable two-hour walk along a stream. The track starts on Waitaia Rd, 10 km north-east of Whitianga. Many other good walks are across the river, five minutes away by ferry.

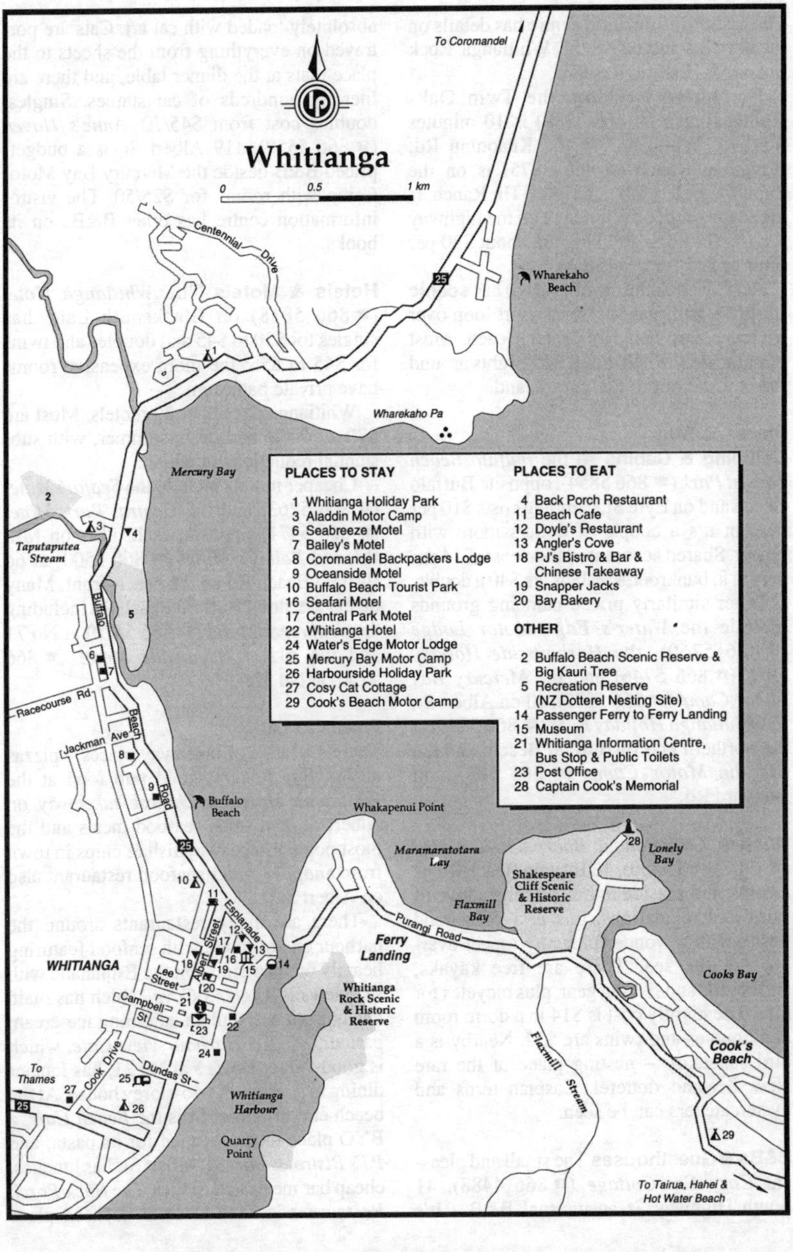

Whitianga
0
0.5
1 km
To Coromandel
Centennial Drive
Wharekaho Beach
Wharekaho Pa
Mercury Bay
Taputaputea Stream
Buffalo Beach Road
Racecourse Rd
Jackman Ave
Buffalo Beach
Esplanade
Albert Street
Lee Street
Campbell St
Cook Drive
Dundas St
WHITIANGA
To Thames
Whitianga Harbour
Quarry Point
Ferry Landing
Whitianga Rock Scenic & Historic Reserve
Whakapenui Point
Maramaratotara Bay
Purangi Road
Flaxmill Bay
Shakespeare Cliff Scenic & Historic Reserve
Lonely Bay
Cooks Bay
Cook's Beach
Flaxmill Stream
To Tairua, Hahei & Hot Water Beach
PLACES TO STAY
1 Whitianga Holiday Park
3 Aladdin Motor Camp
6 Seabreeze Motel
7 Bailey's Motel
8 Coromandel Backpackers Lodge
9 Oceanside Motel
10 Buffalo Beach Tourist Park
16 Seafari Motel
17 Central Park Motel
22 Whitianga Hotel
24 Water's Edge Motor Lodge
25 Mercury Bay Motor Camp
26 Harbourside Holiday Park
27 Cosy Cat Cottage
29 Cook's Beach Motor Camp
PLACES TO EAT
4 Back Porch Restaurant
11 Beach Cafe
12 Doyle's Restaurant
13 Angler's Cove
18 PJ's Bistro & Bar & Chinese Takeaway
19 Snapper Jacks
20 Bay Bakery
OTHER
2 Buffalo Beach Scenic Reserve & Big Kauri Tree
5 Recreation Reserve (NZ Dotterel Nesting Site)
14 Passenger Ferry to Ferry Landing
15 Museum
21 Whitianga Information Centre, Bus Stop & Public Toilets
23 Post Office
28 Captain Cook's Memorial

The visitor information centre has details on local walks including the Whitianga Rock Scenic & Historic Reserve.

For **horse trekking**, the Twin Oaks Riding Ranch (☎ 866 5388) is 10 minutes north of Whitianga on the Kuaotunu Rd; Rangihau Ranch (☎ 866 3875) is on the Tapu-Coroglen Rd; and Ace Hi Ranch is eight km south of Whitianga on the highway – costs for horse trekking are about $20 per hour or $35 for a half-day.

Air Coromandel (☎ 866 4016) has **scenic flights** starting at $25 for a short loop over Mercury Bay and Hot Water Beach. Most popular are the half-hour, $45 flights around the bay and out to Mercury Island.

Places to Stay

Camping & Cabins At the *Buffalo Beach Tourist Park* (☎ 866 5854), opposite Buffalo Beach and on Eyre St, camping costs $10 per person; it's a couple of dollars more with power. Shared accommodation costs $14 per person in bunkrooms; cabins are $40 a double.

Other similarly priced camping grounds include the *Water's Edge Motor Lodge* (☎ 866 5760), the *Harbourside Holiday Park* (☎ 866 5746) and the *Mercury Bay Motor Camp* (☎ 866 5579), all on Albert St; the *Whitianga Holiday Park* (☎ 866 5896) at the northern end of Buffalo Beach; and the *Aladdin Motor Camp* (☎ 866 5834) on Bongard Rd.

Hostels *Coromandel Backpackers Lodge* (☎ (907) 866 5380), 46 Buffalo Beach Rd, is a converted seaside motel. Despite a love of rules and regulations, this is a very good hostel with a wonderful sunny aspect overlooking the sea. There are free kayaks, surfboards and fishing gear, plus bicycles for hire. The nightly cost is $14 in a dorm room and doubles and twins are $32. Nearby is a bird sanctuary – nesting place of the rare New Zealand dotterel. Caspian terns and oystercatchers can be seen.

B&Bs & Guesthouses The small and pleasant *Cosy Cat Cottage* (☎ 866 4488), 41 South Highway, is an unusual B&B – it's absolutely loaded with cat art. Cats are portrayed on everything from the sheets to the place mats at the dinner table, and there are literally hundreds of cat statues. Singles/doubles cost from $45/70. *Anne's Haven* (☎ 866 5550), 119 Albert St, is a budget-priced B&B beside the Mercury Bay Motor Camp with rooms for $25/50. The visitor information centre has other B&Bs on its books.

Hotels & Motels The *Whitianga Hotel* (☎ 866 5818) on Blacksmith Lane has singles for $30 to $45 and doubles and twins for $45 to $55; the more expensive rooms have private bathroom.

Whitianga has about 20 motels. Most are $70 a double and up in summer; with substantial reductions in winter.

Cheaper motels include the *Seafari Motel* (☎ 866 5263) and the *Central Park Motel* (☎ 866 5471) opposite each other on Mill Rd, and *Bailey's Motel* (☎ 866 5500) at 66 Buffalo Beach Rd on the beach-front. Many others are along Buffalo Beach Rd including the *Seabreeze Motel* (☎ 866 5570) at No 71 and the ritzier *Oceanside Motel* (☎ 866 5766) at No 32.

Places to Eat

There's a range of takeaway places – pizzas at *The Bay Bakery*, good pub food at the *Whitianga Hotel*, a *Chinese takeaway* on Albert St, and fresh seafood meals and the most popular takeaway fish & chips in town from *Snapper Jacks* seafood restaurant also on Albert St.

There are many restaurants around the harbour end of town, with seafood featuring heavily on the menu. On the Esplanade with sea views is *Angler's Cove*, which has main meals from $15 and an adjoining ice-cream parlour, and the *Harbour View Cafe*, which is good value. *Doyle's* at No 21, has fancier dining in a restored, two-storey house. At the beach end of Albert St is the *Beach Cafe*, a BYO place recommended for its pasta, and *PJ's Bistro & Bar*, 31 Albert St, has lunches, cheap bar meals and dinner. *The Back Porch Restaurant* is an à la carte licensed place attached to the Mercury Bay Beachfront Resort, on Buffalo Beach Rd; diners get great views out over the bay and main meals cost around $20.

Getting There & Away

Air Coromandel (☎ 866 4016) has two flights daily between Whitianga and Auckland, costing $90, or $50 on standby (ring before departure to check availability).

Murphy buses call into Whitianga twice a day, departing at 8 am and 12.50 pm for Thames via Tairua. These buses connect with services to Auckland, Tauranga and Rotorua.

Three days a week there is a service from Opoutere to Whitianga. Bookings are essential and schedules vary; inquire at the visitor information centre for departure times.

Hot Water Beach Conxtions runs a bus from Ferry Landing at 7.30, 10 am, 12.30, 3 pm and 4.30 pm to Cook's Beach, Hahei and Hot Water Beach, with some services continuing to Dalmeny Corner on the highway for connection with Murphy buses to Auckland and Whitianga. It offers a $15 explorer pass, allowing you to get on and off along the way.

HAHEI & HOT WATER BEACH

This section of the coast is a popular area, accessible from the Stone Steps Wharf at Ferry Landing and from the highway. The offshore islands provide protection for the beaches around Hahei, arguably the best of the Coromandel's many fine beaches. The waters offshore and the islands have been incorporated as a **marine park** and offer some excellent diving.

At the eastern end of Hahei beach is a former Maori pa, which still has much evidence of the elaborate terracing used as fortifications. The tiny town of Hahei revolves around the general store where you can get information on the area. Just north of Hahei is **Cathedral Cove**, accessible only at low tide through a gigantic arched cavern which separates it from Mares Leg Cove. This headland was also the site of a Maori pa.

To the south of Hahei is the Hot Water Beach, where thermal waters are brewing just below the sand. You can go down to the beach two hours before and after low tide, dig a hole in the sand and sit in your own little natural spa pool; allow about 15 minutes to prepare your pool.

The *Hahei Explorer* (☎ 866 3532), a rigid inflatable boat operates scenic trips to Cathedral Cove and Hot Water Beach daily from Hahei – landings are made whenever the sea allows.

Places to Stay

Sites at the *Hot Water Beach Motor Camp & Thermal Pools* (☎ 866 3735) cost $8 per person, more with power. The *Hahei Holiday Resort/Cathedral Cove Backpackers* (☎ 866 3889) is right on the beach and has camp sites from $8.50 per person, cabins from $32 and tourist flats from $54. Their backpackers hostel has beds from $14.

Hahei also has a couple of good backpackers not far from the beach. *Tatahi Lodge* (☎ 866 3992), on Grange Rd behind the Hahei Store, is a new motel with a sparkling, purpose-built backpackers building. The excellent facilities cost $15 in the bunkrooms, or $36 for twin rooms. Classy self-contained, two-bedroom motel units cost $92 a double (less in winter). Nearby, closer to the beach, the *Summer House* (☎ 866 3886), 17 Beach Rd, is much more basic but it's a friendly, laid-back place that organises sailing trips, kayaks and excursions. The cost is $10 for a camp site, or $14 per person in the dorms or twin room.

The luxury end of the market is looked after by the *Hay-Lyn Park Lodge* (☎ 866 3888) at Hahei Beach; it also has a coffee shop.

TAIRUA & PAUANUI

This twin-town with a split personality is separated by Tairua Harbour. A passenger ferry links the two, otherwise it is a long drive around the harbour.

Tairua is small, older and lies on the highway; its tourist highlight is the climb to the top of Paku (an old pa site), which provides great views.

Pauanui is a sprawling, real estate agent's

dream with canal-side homes for the rich and famous. Pauanui has the pretty harbour on one side, a great surf beach on the other and pine-clad mountains behind. The only problem is that it's a boring, suburban development. Bylaws prohibit after-hours drinking in an attempt to discourage the riff-raff from flocking here in summer.

The area has a number of walks, including some good ones in the Broken Hills, and activities include game fishing, canoeing and horse trekking.

Places to Stay & Eat

You have the choice of five motor camps in this area; a camp site is about $9 to $10 per person and each camping ground usually has on-site caravans and cabins available. On SH25 in Tairua you'll find *The Flying Dutchman* (☎ 864 8448), a good hostel with a balcony area leading off the recreation room. The cost is $13 and $14 per person in shared rooms and $32 for twin and double rooms.

The *Sir George Grey Hotel* (☎ 864 8451), on Main Rd in Tairua, has singles for $25. There are at least eight motels or lodges in Tairua and Pauanui; inquire at the visitor information centre (Pauanui Activity Booking Centre; ☎ 864 7101) in the Pauanui shopping centre about their location and current rates. For five-star luxury, *Puka Park Lodge* (☎ 864 8088) in Pauanui is favoured by visiting dignitaries and hotel-trashing rock stars.

In the Pauanui shopping centre on Pauanui Boulevard is *Keith's Licensed Restaurant*. The place serves a wide range of New Zealand foods, has a great wine selection and has won a stack of awards.

COROMANDEL

OPOUTERE

Opoutere has a fine beach and one of the best situated youth hostels in New Zealand. Additionally, about a 15-minute walk from the road, the Wharekawa Wildlife Refuge is the breeding ground of the endangered New Zealand dotterel and variable oystercatcher. Keep dogs out of here and don't cross into the roped-off area during the breeding season. There is a Monday to Friday Waihi to Opoutere shuttle – it departs at noon.

The *Opoutere YHA Hostel* (☎ 865 9072) is a fine place to get right away from it all. It's in a country setting, almost encircled by native bush and overlooking Wharekawa Harbour. You can take one of the hostel's kayaks and paddle around, and there are plenty of bushwalks. The cost is $14 per night in dorms, $16 per person in doubles, or you can camp on the expansive lawn. The management are friendly and informative.

Just down the road from the Opoutere YHA Hostel is the *Opoutere Park* (☎ 865 9152) with camp sites from $7.50 per person.

WHANGAMATA

Whangamata is a sprawling hotch-potch of single-storey buildings, but its saving grace is the great, four-km surf beach with an excellent break by the bar for surfers. This well-equipped resort town has a population of 4000 but gets 10 times that number of visitors in summer.

The Whangamata Information Centre (☎ 865 8340) on Port Rd, the main street, is open daily from 9 am to 5 pm in summer, with shorter weekend hours in winter. It provides information on all activities, accommodation and walks in the area.

Activities

Whangamata has a number of **craft** outlets outlined in a pamphlet available from the information centre. Craft trail tours leave from the Memorial Hall at 9.30 am on the last Sunday of every month and cost $25, including lunch.

The area has some excellent **walks**. The most popular is the Wentworth Falls walk, which takes one hour one way through beautiful bush. To get to the track, take the highway south for three km to the turn-off, and then four km to the camping ground. From the falls a harder trail (get advice at the camping ground) leads to the top of the ranges and on to the Marakopa Rd.

Horse riding, game fishing, kayaking, windsurfing and mountain biking can be arranged. The information centre has details.

Places to Stay

The *Pinefield Holiday Park* (☎ 865 8791), Port Rd, has powered and tent sites for $20, and cabins and tourist flats from $40 a double. Similarly, the *Whangamata Motor Camp* (☎ 865 9128), Barbara Ave, has sites for $8 per person and cabins for $33 for two. The DOC owned *Wentworth Valley Campground* (☎ 865 7032) is in a beautiful valley setting at the start of the trek to Wentworth Falls, seven km from Whangamata. It has gas BBQs and cold showers; camping costs $5 per person in summer.

Whangamata has two backpackers hostels. *Whangamata Backpackers Hostel* (☎ 865 8323) at 227 Beverley Terrace is one street back from the beach. It's basic and charges $15 per person. The *Bedshed* (☎ 865 9580), on the corner of Port Rd and Mayfair Ave, is a combined backpackers and motel on the main road about one km from the shopping centre heading south. It has excellent accommodation for $15 in shared rooms and $36 for doubles and twins. Motel units cost $90, or $105 with kitchen, in summer. This new, pristine hostel has everything, including a small video theatre.

Whangamata also has a selection of motels and B&Bs. *Tukere House* (☎ 865 8009) on Tukere Drive is an attractive B&B in an A-frame lodge costing $35/65 or families can rent the whole unit. It's two km north of town, over the bridge. Right near the start of the Wentworth Valley walk, *Wentworth Valley Lodge* (☎ 8657632) has excellent homestay accommodation in a beautiful setting for $80/100.

Places to Eat

Whangamata has plenty of takeaways and coffee lounges but is not overly endowed with good restaurants. The *Port City Chinese Restaurant*, 606 Port Rd, also has a takeaway section. The *Whangamata Hotel*, on the main highway three km north of town, serves bistro meals and has a beer garden. *Pinky's*, 703 Port Rd, is an unpretentious bar/restaurant with moderately priced meals.

Getting There & Away

A daily bus shuttle service operates between Whangamata, Opoutere and Hikua, south of Tairua. There is also a connection from Whangamata to Waihi.

Bay of Plenty

The sweeping Bay of Plenty is blessed with a good climate, some fine beaches and is a thriving agricultural district most noted for its kiwifruit. The bay stretches from the main city of Tauranga-Mt Maunganui on the western half to Whakatane and Opotiki, the main focal points of the eastern Bay of Plenty.

Just inland in this region is one of New Zealand's premier tourist attractions, Rotorua. The Rotorua region is famous throughout the world for its geysers, hot springs, mud pools, shimmering lakes, trout fishing, tramping and a host of other activities. The region is also of great significance to the Maori population, whose presence dates back to its discovery and exploration by Maori in the 14th century.

The telephone area code throughout the Bay of Plenty is 07.

HIGHLIGHTS

- A visit to Whakarewarewa at Rotorua to see the geysers and boiling mud pools, as well as the Maori Arts & Crafts Institute
- Cruising on one of the lakes around Rotorua – Lake Rotorua, Lake Rotomahana or Lake Tarawera
- A Maori hangi and concert at Rotorua for a taste of Maori culture
- An excursion to White Island to see one of New Zealand's most active volcanos
- The eastern Bay of Plenty and Whakatane

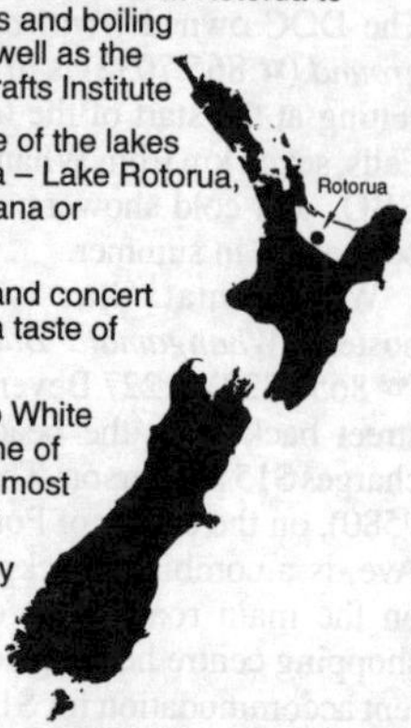

Rotorua

Rotorua (regional population 66,000) is the most popular tourist area of the North Island, if not of New Zealand. Nicknamed 'Sulphur City', it has the most energetic thermal activity in the country with bubbling mud pools, gurgling hot springs, gushing geysers and evil smells. All around the city, steam drifts up from behind bushes, out of road drains and around rocks. A strong smell of rotten eggs still pervades the town, despite efforts by the city to curb this natural product of thermal activity.

Rotorua also has a large Maori population whose cultural activities are among the most interesting and accessible in New Zealand.

The city itself is thriving, buoyed by the huge influx of tourism; it's also scenically located 280 metres above sea level on the shores of Lake Rotorua, teeming with trout. The whole area has the world's best trout fishing and some interesting trout springs and wildlife parks.

Despite all these attractions and the consequent hordes of tourists it's not too much of a rip-off. In fact Rotorua has many attractions that don't cost a cent – magnificent walks, lakes and forests to visit, waterfalls, steamy areas and just spending time along the Rotorua waterfront.

HISTORY

The district of Rotorua was probably first settled during the middle of the 14th century by descendants of the navigators who arrived at Maketu in the central Bay of Plenty in the *Arawa* canoe from Hawaiki. Originally they were of the Ohomairangi tribe, but soon after they reached Maketu they changed their tribal name to Te Arawa to commemorate the vessel that brought them so far in safety.

Much of the inland forest was explored by Ihenga in the late 14th century and it was he who discovered and named the lakes of Rotorua and many other geographical features of the area. The name Rotorua means 'the second lake' (*roto* means lake; *rua*, two) as it was the second lake that Ihenga discovered.

In the next few hundred years various sub-tribes spread into the area and as they grew in numbers, they split into more sub-tribes and began to fight over territory. In 1823 the Arawa lands were invaded by the Ngapuhi chief, Hongi Hika, of Northland. Although their primitive stone weapons were no match for the newly acquired muskets of the Ngapuhi, the Arawa managed to rout the Northlanders and forced them to withdraw.

The first Pakeha to visit Rotorua was a Dane, Philip Tapsell, who set up a trading station on the coast at Maketu and gave the Maori guns in exchange for flax, which he exported to Sydney where it was used to make rope. In 1831 Thomas Chapman, a missionary, visited Rotorua, returning to settle permanently in 1838, a date signifying the beginning of European occupation.

During the 1850s, wars erupted between the Arawa and the Waikato tribes. In 1867 the Waikato tribes attacked in retaliation for the part the Arawa had played in preventing

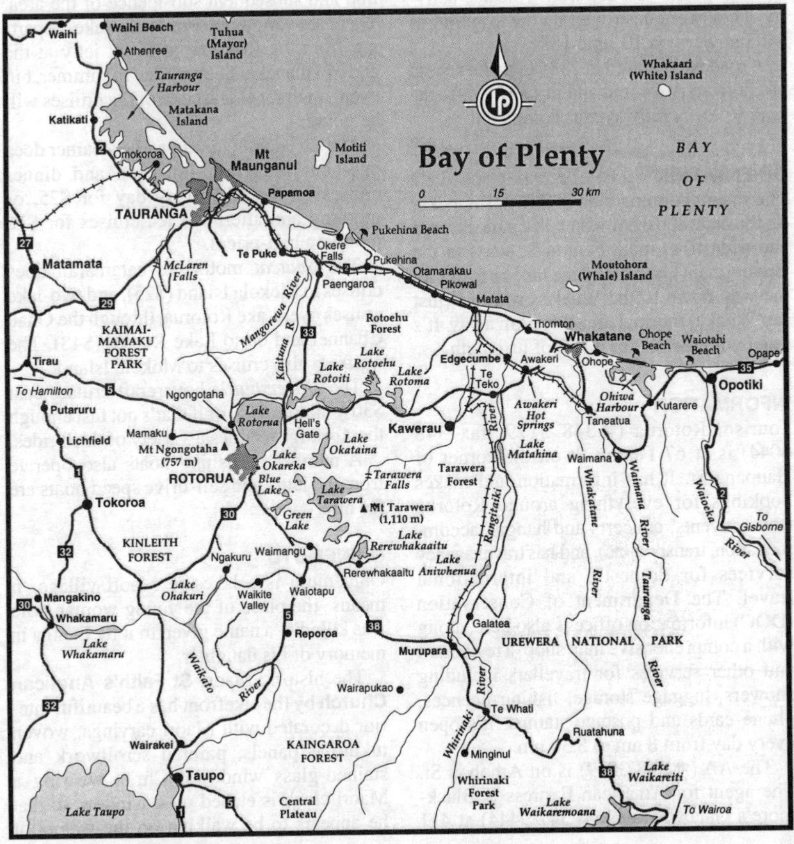

the east coast reinforcements getting through for the Maori King movement. In the course of these wars the Arawa threw in their lot with the government and thus gained the backing of government troops.

With the wars virtually over in the early 1870s European settlement around Rotorua took off with a rush, particularly as the army and government personnel involved in the struggle had broadcast the scenic wonders of the place. People came to take the waters in the hope of cures for all sorts of diseases, and so Rotorua's tourist industry was founded. Rotorua's greatest attraction was the fabulous Pink and White Terraces, formed by the sinter deposits of silica from volcanic activity. They were destroyed by the eruption of Mt Tarawera on 10 June 1886.

A road was cleared in 1884 to make access easier from Auckland and in 1894 the Auckland-Rotorua railway was completed.

ORIENTATION

The main shopping area is down Tutanekai St, the central part of which is a parking area and pedestrian mall. Fenton St starts in the Government Gardens by the lake and runs all the way down to the Whakarewarewa (just say Whaka) thermal area three km away. It's lined with motels for much of its length.

INFORMATION

Tourism Rotorua (☎ 348 5179; fax 348 6044) is at 67 Fenton St on the corner of Haupapa St. It has information and makes bookings for everything around Rotorua (tours, events, concerts and hangis, accommodation, transport etc), and has travel agency services for domestic and international travel. The Department of Conservation (DOC) information office is also here, along with a comprehensive map shop, a restaurant and other services for travellers including showers, luggage storage, fishing licences, phone cards and postage stamps. It's open every day from 8 am to 5.30 pm.

The AA (☎ 348 3069) is on Amohau St. The agent for American Express is Blackmore's Galaxy Travel (☎ 347 9444) at 411 Tutanekai St. Thomas Cook has a foreign-exchange desk in the Air New Zealand office, or there are plenty of banks that will change foreign currency. The post office is on Hinemoa St between the Tutanekai Mall and Amohia St.

Thermal Air is a useful free weekly tourist publication. The excellent *Gateway to Geyserland* map, available for $1 at Tourism Rotorua, includes a good map of the city and surrounding area.

LAKE ROTORUA

Lake Rotorua is the largest of 12 lakes in the Rotorua district. It was formed by an eruption and subsequent subsidence of the area. There are various cruises on the lake, departing from the Rotorua lakefront jetty at the end of Tutanekai St every day in summer, but even in winter at least one of the cruises will be going.

The *Lakeland Queen* paddle steamer does one-hour breakfast, luncheon and dinner cruises on the lake every day for $25, or morning and afternoon tea cruises for $16 (children half-price).

The *Scatcat* motorised catamaran does cruises to Mokoia Island ($25), and two-lake cruises over Lake Rotorua, through the Ohau Channel and on to Lake Rotoiti ($48). The *Ngaroto* also cruises to Mokoia Island.

The *Hovershuttle* hovercraft cruises cost $30 (children $15) or if that's not fast enough the *Aorangi Jet* does a variety of thrill rides.

A number of fishing boats also operate from the jetty, and self-drive speed boats are for hire.

OHINEMUTU

Ohinemutu is a lakeside Maori village. It means 'the place of the young woman who was killed' – a name given to it by Ihenga in memory of his daughter.

The historic Maori **St Faith's Anglican Church** by the lakefront has a beautiful interior decorated with Maori carvings, woven tukutuku panels, painted scrollwork and stained-glass windows. Christ wearing a Maori cloak is etched on a window so that he appears to be walking on the waters of

Hinemoa & Tutanekai

The story of Hinemoa and Tutanekai is one of the most well-known lovers' tales in New Zealand. It is not a legend but a true story, though you may hear one or two variations. The descendants of Hinemoa and Tutanekai still live in the Rotorua area today.

Hinemoa was a young woman of a sub-tribe that lived on the western shore of Lake Rotorua. Tutanekai was a young man of the sub-tribe that lived on Mokoia Island, on the lake.

The two sub-tribes sometimes visited one another, and that was how Hinemoa and Tutanekai met. But though both were of high birth in their respective tribes, Tutanekai was illegitimate and so, while the family of Hinemoa thought he was a fine young man and could see that the two young people loved one another, they were not in favour of them marrying.

At night, Tutanekai would play his flute on the island, and sometimes the wind would carry his melody across the water to Hinemoa. In his music she could hear his declaration of love for her. Her people, meanwhile, took to tying up the canoes at night to make sure she could not take off and go to him.

Finally one night as she heard Tutanekai's music wafting over the waters, Hinemoa was so overcome with longing that she could stand it no longer. She peeled off her clothes to get rid of the weight, and set off to swim the long distance from the shore to the island. In some versions of the story she also buoyed herself up with calabash gourds.

When she arrived on Mokoia, Hinemoa was in a quandary. She had had to shed her clothing in order to swim to the island, but now there, she could scarcely walk into the settlement naked! She sought refuge in a hot pool and tried to figure out what to do next.

Time passed and eventually a man came to fetch water from a cold spring beside the hot pool. In a deep man's voice, Hinemoa called out, 'Who is it?' The man replied that he was the slave of Tutanekai, come to fetch water. Hinemoa reached out of the darkness, seized the calabash and broke it. This happened a few more times, until finally Tutanekai himself came to the pool and demanded that the interloper identify himself. He was amazed when it turned out to be Hinemoa.

Tutanekai stole Hinemoa into his hut. In the morning, when Tutanekai was sleeping very late, a slave was sent to wake him and came back reporting that someone else was also sleeping in Tutanekai's bed! The two lovers emerged, it was discovered what Hinemoa had done in order to come to Tutanekai, and their union was celebrated. ■

The gateway of the model village of Whakarewarewa depicts the two lovers entwined

Lake Rotorua. Seen from this window, it's surprising how much Lake Rotorua does resemble the Sea of Galilee.

Opposite the church is the impressive **Tamatekapua Meeting House**, built in 1887. Named for the captain of the *Arawa* canoe, this is an important meeting house to all Arawa people. Maori concerts are held here every evening at 8 pm. Also in this complex are the Ohinemutu Craft Centre and the Te Huia Souvenir Shop.

MUSEUMS

The impressive **Rotorua Museum of Art & History**, better known as the Bath House, is housed in a Tudor-style building in the

Government Gardens. The building was an elegant spa retreat, built in 1908. The museum has small but fascinating exhibits on the local Te Arawa Maori people; the 1886 Mt Tarawera eruption, with videos about how it happened; the Pink and White Terraces; the history of this magnificent neo-Tudor building, and changing displays. It's open every day from 10 am to 4.30 pm; admission is $4 (children $1).

In the gardens around the Bath House are typical English touches like croquet lawns and rose gardens – not to mention atypical steaming pools.

Te Amorangi Museum has Maori and colonial artefacts, working demonstrations of agricultural machinery, and a miniature steam railway which is operated on the second Sunday of each month. The museum is in Robinsons Ave near the airport at Holdens Bay, six km from central Rotorua, and is open from 10 am to 4 pm on Sunday and holidays; admission is free.

WHAKAREWAREWA

Whakarewarewa is Rotorua's largest and best-known thermal zone and a major Maori cultural area. It's OK if you can't get your tongue around Whakarewarewa (Faka-raywa-raywa) – many people call it simply 'Whaka'. On the other hand, even the name Whakarewarewa is actually short for the place's real name, Te Whakarewarewa-tangaoteopetauaawahiao, meaning 'the gathering together of the war forces of Wahiao'. See if you can get your tongue around that!

Whakarewarewa's most spectacular geyser is **Pohutu** (Maori for 'big splash' or 'explosion'), an active geyser which usually erupts at least once an hour. Pohutu spurts hot water about 20 metres in the air but sometimes shoots up over 30 metres in brief 'shots'. The average eruption lasts about five to 10 minutes, though the longest one is reputed to have lasted for 15 hours! You get an advance warning because the Prince of Wales' Feathers geyser always starts off shortly before Pohutu.

Other Whaka attractions include the **Maori Arts & Crafts Institute** with working craftspeople, an art gallery, a replica Maori village, kiwi house and a Maori concert held every day at 12.15 pm, rated one of the best of the many Maori concerts around Rotorua.

Whaka is three km south of the city centre, straight down Fenton St. City buses drop you near a rear entrance, or the Sightseeing Shuttle bus will drop you at the main gate. Whaka is open daily from 8 am to 5 pm (last entry 4.30 pm); admission is $10.50 (children $4). The Maori concert is another $10.50.

THERMAL POOLS

Of course you won't want to visit Rotorua without taking a dip in some thermal pools. The **Polynesian Spa**, off Hinemoa St in the Government Gardens, is open daily from 6.30 am to 10 pm. The first building in Rotorua, a bath house, was opened at these springs in 1886 and people have been swearing by the health-giving properties of the waters ever since. The modern complex has several pools at the lake's edge. Admission to the main pools is $7 (children $2), private pools are $8 per half-hour (children $2). Towels and swimsuits can be hired, as can the sauna, or an Aix massage is available by appointment.

The **Waikite Thermal Mineral Baths** is an open-air natural mineral pool (39°C) with medicinal mineral waters, out in Waikite, a rural area. To get there, go 30 km south on SH5 (the highway to Taupo), to a signposted turn-off which is opposite the turn-off to Waiotapu. The pool is another six km down this road. It is open every day from 10 am to 9.30 pm; admission is $4 (children $2).

ORCHID GARDENS

The Orchid Gardens in Hinemaru St house not only an extensive orchid hothouse blooming all year round but also a Micro-world display, where you can get a microscopic view of living reptiles and insects, and a big water organ.

Water organs are very unusual. The sound is not produced by the water. The organ is really a huge fountain with over 800 jets

Art Deco architecture, Napier, East Coast
Top photograph (TW)
Other photographs (JW)

Top: Wellington (RS)
Bottom: Jerusalem, Whanganui River Road, Central North Island (NK)

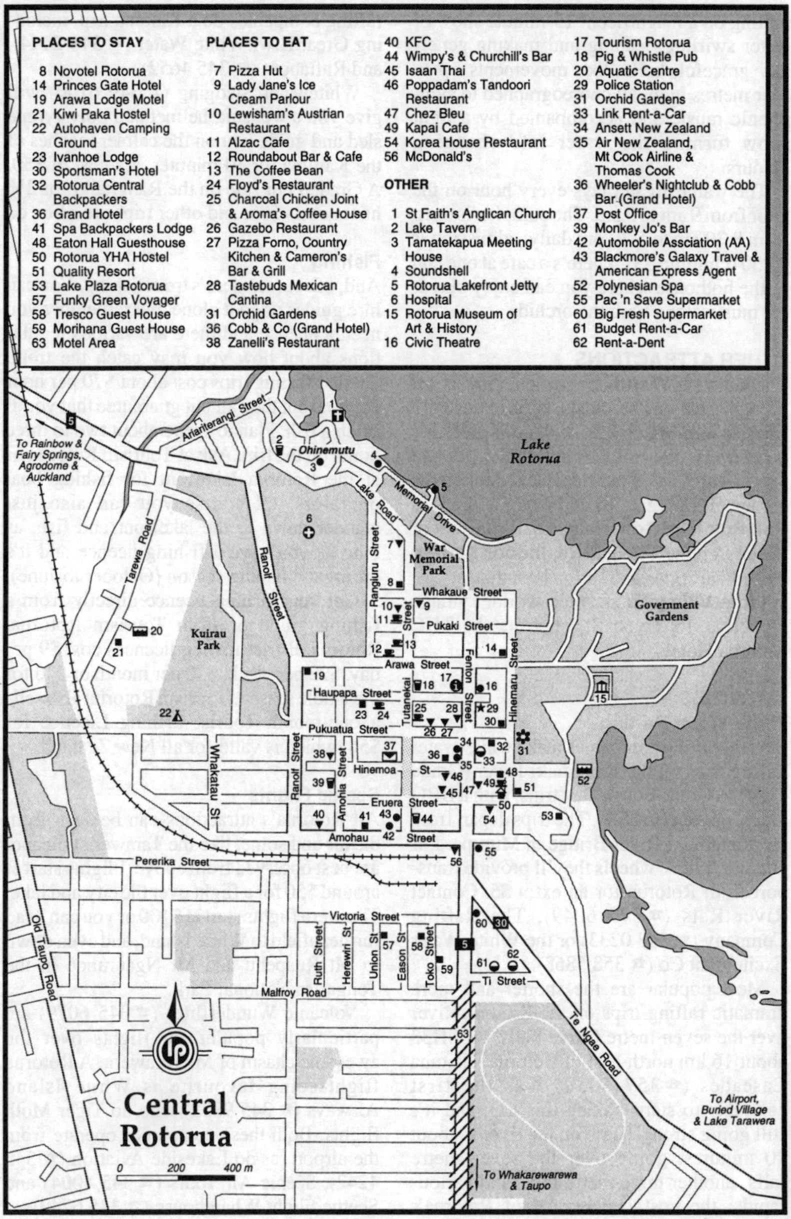

BAY OF PLENTY

putting on a magnificent 15-minute show of water swirling, leaping and making generally graceful, ballet-like movements up to four metres high, all choreographed to symphonic music and accompanied by a light show turning the water into changing colours.

The water organ plays every hour on the hour from 9 am to 5 pm. The complex is open from 8.30 am to 5.30 pm daily; admission is $7.50 (children $3). There's a cafe at one end of the hothouse where you can enjoy classical music along with the orchids.

OTHER ATTRACTIONS

The **Leisure World** amusement park is off Te Ngae Rd on the outskirts of town, with rides, a big waterslide and mini-golf. It's open every day from 10 am until 5 pm and you pay around $5 per ride. Next door on the corner of Te Ngae Rd and Marguerita St is **Putt Putt Mini Golf**. Half a km further out of the city on the Te Ngae Rd, **Indoor Karting** has go-cart rides at $10 for 10 minutes.

Little Village is an 'olde worlde' village replica at 15 Tryon St, opposite the THC Rotorua Hotel.

ACTIVITIES

White-Water Rafting

Several rafting companies make white-water rafting trips on the Rangitaiki River (Grade Three to Grade Four). Day trips, with a BBQ lunch, cost around $85. The trips depart from the Rangitaiki River Bridge in Murupara; if you don't have wheels they'll provide transport from Rotorua for an extra $5. Contact River Rats (☎ 347 6049), The Rafting Company (☎ 348 0233) or the White-Water Excitement Co (☎ 358 5868).

Most popular are the shorter and more dramatic rafting trips on the Kaituna River over the seven-metre Okere Falls, off SH33 about 16 km north-east of Rotorua. Kaituna Cascades (☎ 357 5032) was the first company to start making this trip, and it's still going strong. Time on the river is about 40 minutes, going over the seven-metre falls, another three-metre falls, and various rapids; the cost is $49. All of Rotorua's rafting companies do a Kaituna trip, including Great Kiwi White Water (☎ 348 2144), and Raftabout (☎ 345 4652).

Whitewater Sledging (☎ 349 6100) will give you a wet suit, helmet and polystyrene sled and guide you on the calmer reaches of the Kaituna for 30 minutes at a cost of $50. A Grade Four ride on the Rangitaiki for 2½ hours costs $95, and other trips are offered.

Fishing

And, of course, there's trout fishing. You can hire guides or go it alone, but remember you need a licence and there are various regulations about how you may catch the trout. Guided fishing trips cost about $70 per hour per boat but they all but guarantee that you'll catch a fish. Plan to spend about two to three hours on the trip. Ask at Tourism Rotorua or at the Rotorua lakefront for fishing boat operators. Of course you can also just wander down to the lakefront and fish, as long as you have a fishing licence and it's during the fishing season (October to June).

Get your fishing licence directly from a fishing guide or from Tourism Rotorua. Rotorua district fishing licences cost $9 per day, $22 per week, $30 per month or $46 for the whole season. Tourism Rotorua also sells a one-month Tourist Fishing Licence for $56, which is valid for all New Zealand.

Scenic Flights

All Rotorua's attractions can be seen from the air and some, like the Tarawera volcano, are best observed from above. Flights start at around $50 for a flight over the city and lake. Tarawera flights start at $100 or you can head further afield to White Island, and even down to Mt Ruapehu and Mt Ngauruhoe in the Tongariro National Park.

Volcanic Wunderflites (☎ 345 6079) are particularly popular for flights over the awesome chasm of Mt Tarawera. A Rotorua flightseeing favourite is White Island Airways (☎ 345 9832) who do Tiger Moth flights. Both these companies operate from the airport, as do Lakeside Aviation (☎ 345 4242), Scenic Air Tours (☎ 345 4004) and Scenic Flight Wharehouse (☎ 345 6749).

Volcanic Air Safaris (☎ 348 9984/4069) do helicopter and floatplane flights departing from the Rotorua lakefront. Other helicopter flightseeing operators include Marine Helicopters (☎ 357 2512), based at the Agrodome, and Tarawera Helicopters (☎ 348 1223) at Whakarewarewa.

Other Activities

You can go **tandem skydiving** from the Rotorua Airport (☎ 345 7520) for $195. In addition to the obvious thrill of the skydiving itself, the flight includes some amazing views over all the lakes and volcanoes of the region.

Waka Hikoi (☎ 362 7878) operates half-day guided **kayaking** trips on Lake Rotoiti and other lakes for $49 per person. Adventure Kayaking (☎ 348 9451) has full-day trips on Lake Okataina for $75 and rents kayaks for $75 per day.

Operators that do **horse treks** for around $20 per hour include Trakar Horse Riding (☎ 357 4350), The Farmhouse (☎ 332 3771) and Foxwood Park (☎ 345 7003).

The Blue Lake has lots of summertime activities including water-skiing, jet-skis, parasailing etc. The Green Lake, though, is sacred to the Maori people and you're not allowed to go on it.

A good craft market is held every second weekend at the Soundshell. The Lakeside Cafe here has a large collection of crafts and souvenirs at other times.

TOURS

Rotorua offers a mind-boggling array of tours. You can go to volcanic and thermal sites, out into the mountains and forests, up Mt Tarawera, across lakes and down rivers. There are tours in vans, 4WD vehicles and on bicycles – there's something for every taste. Tourism Rotorua can give you the low-down and book any tours, as can hostels and hotels.

Mud 'n Mountain (☎ 345 3264) does some of the most adventurous tours, visiting places way out in the bush by 4WD including Mt Tarawera, forests, sink holes, a disappearing river, waterfalls and thermal areas, including a dip in some secluded hot springs. The Longest Day tour from 8 am to 8 pm costs $120 and shorter budget tours are available.

Carey's Sightseeing Tours (☎ 347 1197) is one of the biggest local operators with a large range of tours. They originally started out with backpackers tours, still running as Carey's Capers, which visit most of Rotorua's favourite volcanic and thermal attractions, with a dip in an isolated hot water stream along the way. The cost ranges from $50 for a half-day to $95 for a full-day tour.

Other Carey's tours take in all the main attractions of Rotorua in a variety of combinations, including the thermal reserves, trout springs, lake cruises, Kaituna River rafting and 4WD trips to Mt Tarawera.

Carey's also runs the World Famous Waimangu Round Trip, which has been well known in these parts since 1902 at least, and is one of the best for appreciating this beautiful area of volcanoes and lakes. Focusing on the 1886 Mt Tarawera eruption, it includes the Waimangu Volcanic Valley, a cruise on Lake Rotomahana past the site of the Pink and White Terraces, another cruise on Lake Tarawera, a visit to the Buried Village, and a dip in the Polynesian Spa. The cost is $125 (children $65) for the full day.

4WD tours are very popular for bush bashing or visits to Mt Tarawera. Three-hour tours cost around $60. Mt Tarawera 4WD Tours (☎ 357 4026), Tarawera Mountain Sightseeing Tours (☎ 348 9333) and Mountain Magic (☎ 348 6399) all go to Mt Tarawera. 4WD Bush Safaris (☎ 332 5748) has wheel-spinning, mud-throwing and rut-gouging tours over some very rugged tracks through native bush. You can drive it yourself or they drive. Mountain Adventures Farm Bike Tours (☎ 348 6399) does similar tours on quad bikes.

There are plenty of other tours around Rotorua's more sedate attractions such as the Agrodome, thermal areas, and so on; InterCity, Gray Line and Taylor's are three established companies and there are plenty more. Tourism Rotorua can give you all the details. Some of the most popular and worthwhile tours are the Maori concert and hangi trips (see the Entertainment section). Another option is to take the Sightseeing Shuttle bus and visit them on your own (see the Getting Around section).

PLACES TO STAY

With all the Rotorua region's tourist attractions, it's not surprising that it is well endowed with places to stay. Hot mineral pools are a bonus in many establishments, no matter how humble, and almost every place is thermally heated.

Camping & Cabins

Rotorua has a big selection of camping grounds, although some are simply 'caravan only' places. Almost all have cabins.

Closest to the centre is the *Autohaven Camping Ground* (☎ 348 1886) at 129-137 Pukuatua St, beside Kuirau Park. It has tent/powered sites at $7.50/8.50 per person, and tourist flats from $45 for two, with higher rates from Christmas to the end of January.

Two km from the centre, Whittaker Rd off Lake Rd has two good camping grounds near Lake Rotorua. The *Cosy Cottage International Holiday Park* (☎ 348 3793) at 67 Whittaker Rd may be the only place in the world with heated tent sites – the warmth from under the ground gradually warms your tent at night. They also have a mineral pool, a heated swimming pool, canoes for loan and bicycles and fishing tackle for hire. Tent sites are $8.50 per person and powered sites $19. Tourist cabins cost $35 a double, tourist flats $46 to $55.

The *Lakeside Thermal Holiday Park* (☎ 348 1693) at 54 Whittaker Rd, beside the lake, has hot mineral pools and spas. Tent sites are $8 per person, powered sites $18, on-site caravans $30, cabins $35, tourist flats $45 and chalets are $55 (all prices for two people).

The *Rotorua Thermal Holiday Park* (☎ 346 3140), on the southern end of the Old Taupo Rd opposite the golf course, is a large camping ground with hot mineral pools and a heated swimming pool. Tent and caravan sites are $8.50 per person and campervan sites $10 per person – cabins cost from $30 a double and tourist flats are $50 a double. There is also a hostel with beds at $12 and a lodge with B&B at $26 per person, linen included. There's a bus service which stops at the gate.

A little further out, the *Holdens Bay Holiday Park* (☎ 345 9925) at 21 Robinson Ave is about 500 metres from Lake Rotorua, 6.5 km from central Rotorua on SH30. The *Blue Lake Holiday Park* (☎ 362 8120) is on Tarawera Rd on the shores of the Blue Lake, 10 km from the centre of Rotorua. Kayaks, canoes, fishing boats, fishing tackle and bicycles are all available for hire.

There are a few places to camp at Ngongotaha, eight km from Rotorua on the western shore of Lake Rotorua, and plenty more places out from the city. The following is a list of possibilities:

Redwood Holiday Park (☎ 345 9380), three km from the Rotorua city centre at 5 Tarawera Rd, Ngapuna, at the intersection of Te Ngae Rd.

All Seasons Holiday Park (☎ 345 6240), 7.5 km from the city centre on Lee Rd, Hannahs Bay, off SH30, opposite the lakefront.

Rainbow Resort (☎ 357 4289), eight km from the city centre at 24 Beaumonts Rd, Ngongotaha, close to the lake.

Waiteti Trout Stream Holiday Park (☎ 357 5255), beside Waiteti Stream at 14 Okana Crescent, Ngongotaha.

Greengrove Holiday Park (☎ 357 4429), corner Hall & School Rds, Ngongotaha.

Lake Rotoiti Lakeside Holiday Park (☎ 362 4860), 21 km from Rotorua on Okere Rd, Okere Falls, on the shore of Lake Rotoiti.

Ohau Channel Lodge and Tourist Cabins (☎ 362 4761), 17.5 km from Rotorua on Hamurana Rd, at the northern end of Lake Rotorua between Lake Rotorua and Lake Rotoiti.

Fisherman's Lodge (☎ 362 8754), on old mission site at Lake Tarawera, surrounded by native bush, a two-minute drive or 20-minute walk from the lake.

Hostels

The *Rotorua YHA Hostel* (☎ 347 6810) is on the corner of Eruera and Hinemaru Sts, close to the city centre. Formerly known as the Colonial Inn, it has plenty of twin and family rooms, a thermal spa pool, and it's open all day. The nightly cost is $16 in dorm rooms, $36 for a double room.

Rotorua Central Backpackers (☎ 349 3285) at 10 Pukuatua St has spacious rooms and a spa pool in a classic older building with plenty of character. The cost is $14 and $15 per person in dorm rooms, twins are $32 and doubles $36. It's very centrally situated and quiet.

The *Kiwi Paka* (☎ 347 0931) is at 60 Tarewa Rd, near Kuirau Park one km or so from the city centre. It is a huge place with a variety of accommodation, and recent extensions and renovations provide good-quality accommodation. It has a thermal pool, bicycles and a courtesy van. The cost per person is $13 in four-bed shared rooms; twins and doubles are $28, and new en-suite chalets are also available. You can also pitch a tent on the large lawn for $6.

The smallest of Rotorua's hostels is the funky little *Funky Green Voyager* (☎ 346 1754) at 4 Union St. In a quiet residential neighbourhood close to the centre, the hostel is comfortable and casual, with a spacious backyard, and plenty of travel information. The cost is $14 in dorms, or $32 for double and twin rooms.

The *Spa Backpackers Lodge* (☎ 348 3486) at 69 Amohau St, is older and a little cramped, but in a convenient location. There are plenty of single and double rooms: the cost is $13 and $14 in dorms and singles/doubles are $18/32.

The *Ivanhoe Lodge* (☎ 348 6985) at 54 Haupapa St is also central. Accommodation is in rooms or cabins: the cost is $13 per person in dorms and singles/doubles are $18/30.

B&Bs & Guesthouses

There are a number of guesthouses and B&Bs around Rotorua, including a couple on Toko St. Although it's reasonably central, Toko St is a quiet street and well away from the tourist hustle of central Rotorua. At 3 Toko St there's the *Tresco Guest House* (☎ 348 9611), where B&B costs $45/68 for singles/doubles. There are sinks in the rooms and it's a neat, tidy and comfortable place.

The same can be said for the *Morihana Guest House* (☎ 348 8511) a bit further down at 20 Toko St. Singles/doubles cost $45/80, including breakfast. Both places have hot mineral pools.

Eaton Hall (☎ 347 0366) at 39 Hinemaru St, centrally located opposite the Quality Resort, is a comfortable, homely guesthouse with B&B at $45/68 for singles/doubles (lower in the off season). Book ahead in summer, as this is a popular place.

Hotels

Right in the centre on the corner of Hinemoa and Fenton Sts, the *Grand Hotel* (☎ 348 2089) has singles/doubles with private facilities for $45/60. Rooms have tea and coffee-making facilities and there's a sauna, a Cobb & Co Restaurant and the Wheelers Bar nightclub.

Conveniently situated on the corner of Hinemaru and Pukuatua Sts, the *Sportsman's Hotel* (☎ 348 1550) has typical pub rooms for $43/51. It has a large thermal pool and the Dobbo's Sports Bar.

The *Princes Gate Hotel* (☎ 348 1179) at 1 Arawa St on the corner of Hinemaru St is a beautiful, luxurious hotel with crystal chandeliers, canopies over the beds, an elegant restaurant and bar, a health facility and much more. It costs $101/135.

Rotorua has some big hotels, to cater for those big tour groups. In an approximate progression of price and quality are the *Regal Geyserland* (☎ 348 2039), *THC Rotorua* (☎ 348 1189), *Quality Resort* (☎ 348 0199), *Lake Plaza Rotorua* (☎ 348 1174), *Quality Inn* (☎ 348 0199) and then a definite jump to the *Sheraton Rotorua* (☎ 349 5200). Prices start at $120 a double and go up to around $250 a double at the Sheraton. The new *Novotel Rotorua* is due to become one of Rotorua's best when construction is finished. If expense is no obstacle, Rotorua has a few exclusive and secluded lodges such as the *Solitaire Lodge* (☎ 362 8208) at Lake Tarawera, and the *Woodlands Country Lodge* (☎ 332 2242) on Hamurana Rd, Ngongotaha, where doubles cost $560 including meals.

Motels

Rotorua has over 80 motels and Fenton St, as it heads south from town past the Big Fresh supermarket, is a 'motel row' with wall-to-wall motels for as far as the eye can see. In the off season they are all competing with discounts displayed out front, offering some of the best motel deals in New Zealand. Prices may not be drastically cheaper than you'll pay elsewhere, but the standards of Rotorua motels are higher on average. Just a few of the cheaper places to try in Rotorua include:

Aywon Motel (☎ 347 7659), 18 Trigg Ave; studio and one-bedroom units $70/79 for singles/doubles, spa units $86/102.

Bel Aire Motel (☎ 348 6076), 257 Fenton St; $55 and $61 a double.

Forest Court Motel (☎ 346 3543), 275 Fenton St; from $48/56.

Havana Motor Lodge (☎ 348 8134), 12 Whakaue St; $60/70.

Heywoods Motor Lodge (☎ 349 5586), 249 Fenton St; $65 to $90 a double.

Lake Lodge Motel (☎ 348 5189), 16 Lake Rd; $65 a double.

Monterey Motel (☎ 348 1044), 50 Whakaue St; $55 to $65 a double.

Tom's Motel (☎ 347 8062), 6 Union St; $65 to $85 a double.

Waiteti Lakefront Motel (☎ 357 4294), Arnold St, Ngongotaha, on the lakefront; from $60/66.

Farmstays & Homestays

The Tourism Rotorua office has listings for nearly 50 homestays and farmstays, and can make bookings. Try to ask a couple of days in advance.

PLACES TO EAT

Snacks & Fast Food

Rotorua has plenty of snack and fast-food places. *Tastebuds Mexican Cantina* at 93 Fenton St, near the corner of Pukuatua St, serves up the usual cheap and tasty Tex-Mex fare to take away or eat there.

The *Charcoal Chicken Joint* at 286 Tutanekai St has charcoal-grilled chicken and hot carvery sandwiches. Next door *Aroma's Coffee House* has good coffee, pastries and cakes, as does the *Robert Harris Coffee House* directly opposite at No 227.

Pizza Forno at 31 Pukuatua St makes pretty good pizzas, to eat there or take away; phone for free delivery (☎ 347 9854). Two doors away, *Country Kitchen* does good sandwiches. The *Coffee Bean* at 189 Tutanekai St near the corner of Arawa St also makes good sandwiches, and good breakfasts too; it's open during the day, every day but Sunday.

The *Roundabout Bar & Cafe* upstairs at 83 Arawa St is a cafe, bar, resource centre and general hang-out for backpackers and travellers. It has a good menu with plenty of inexpensive meals and snacks; also here are a travellers' notice board, games, fax and phone services and discounted tour tickets. It's open every day from 11.30 am until late.

Most of the tourist attractions have cafes but the one at the *Orchid Gardens* on Hinemaru St is especially enjoyable, and it's not expensive. It's at one end of the large indoor orchid garden.

Chez Bleu on Fenton St near the corner of Hinemoa St is said to make the best burgers in town. It's open until the wee hours on weekends. *Wimpy's*, on Tutanekai St near Amohau St, is not so much hamburgers as good, old-fashioned filling lunches and dinners at cheap prices. The roasts are very good value.

The American 'big three' are all represented in Rotorua. *McDonald's* is on the corner of Fenton and Amohau Sts, *KFC* is further west on Amohau St and *Pizza Hut* is on Tutanekai St, up near the lake.

Pub Food

Cobb & Co in the Grand Hotel on Hinemoa St between Tutanekai and Fenton Sts has its usual dinner menu.

Churchill's Bar at 426 Tutanekai St is another good place for a meal. A comfortable English-style bar, it serves up a lot of lunches and finger food in big, satisfying portions; food is always available. *Cameron's Bar & Grill* upstairs on the corner of Fenton and Pukuatua Sts serves snacks and light meals for lunch and dinner at under $10.

Restaurants

The *Alzac Cafe* on Tutunekai St is a European-style cafe where you can come for a meal or just to hang out over coffee. The menu is 'California-style', emphasising fresh ingredients and eclectic international dishes.

Lewisham's Austrian Restaurant at 115 Tutanekai St specialises in traditional Austrian-Hungarian food. *Zanelli's* at 23 Amohia St is a very popular Italian dinner house, with good Italian gelati to round off your meal. The *Gazebo Restaurant* at 45 Pukuatua St is a popular restaurant with a menu featuring French, Asian and European food. There are good lunch specials or more expensive evening meals. *Floyd's Restaurant* at 44 Haupapa St is also good, with an eclectic menu.

Rotorua also has a Thai restaurant, *Isaan Thai* at 30 Eruera St. The dishes have been blandified a little for Kiwi tastes, but the servings are huge, prices moderate and it also has a bar. For Indian food, the licensed or BYO *Poppodam's Tandoori Restaurant* at 44 Hinemoa St is also moderately priced.

Rotorua was turning Japanese but now seems to be turning Korean, with plenty of large souvenir shops and restaurants catering to Korean tour groups. *Korea House Restaurant* at 16 Eruera St is a pleasant, large and fancy restaurant serving Korean food. The smaller *Kapai Cafe* around the corner on Hinemaru St is much plainer but has cheaper Korean fare.

ENTERTAINMENT

Maori Concerts & Hangis

Maori culture is a major attraction in Rotorua, and although it's commercialised

Pokarekare ana

The song *Pokarekare ana* is New Zealand's most cherished traditional song. Though most people probably think its origin is more ancient, the song was actually adapted from a poem by Paraire Henare Tomoana (1868-1946) of the Ngati Kahungunu tribe. His original lyrics were not about Rotorua, but rather Waiapu. Nevertheless the song seemed to fit the story of Hinemoa and Tutanekai so perfectly that in popular song the lake's name was changed to Rotorua, and the song is thought to be about the two lovers.

Almost anyone from New Zealand can sing this song for you. Often you will hear only the first verse and the chorus sung, but there are several verses. If you want to sing along, it goes like this:

Pokarekare ana nga wai o Rotorua. *Whiti atu koe, e hine, marino ana e.*	Troubled are the waters of Rotorua. If you cross them, oh maiden, they will be calm.
CHORUS: *E hine e, hoki mai ra,* *Ka mate ahau i te aroha e.* *E kore te aroha e maroke i te ra,* *Makuku tonu i aku roimata e.*	 Come back to me, maiden, I love you so much. My love will never dry in the sun. It will always be wet with my tears.
Tuhi atu taku reta, tuku atu taku ringi, *Kei kite to iwi, raruraru ana e.*	I have written my letter, I have sent my ring. If your people see them, there will be trouble.
CHORUS	
Kua whati taku pene, kua pau aku pepa, *Engari te aroha, mau tonu ana e.*	My pen is broken, my paper is all used up. But my love for you will always remain. ■

it's a worthwhile investment to get out and enjoy it. The two big activities are concerts, and hangis or feasts. In many cases the two are combined.

A hangi is a Maori earth oven – a large pit is dug and a fire is lit to heat stones placed in the pit. Food in baskets, covered with wet cloths, is then put in the pit, covered with soil and steamed to perfection.

The concerts are put on by local people and they seem to get as much of a kick out of them as you will. Chances are by the time the evening is over you'll have been dragged up on stage, experienced a Maori *hongi* (nose-to-nose contact), joined hands for a group sing-in, and thought about freaking out your next-door neighbour with a haka war dance when you get home. Other features of a Maori concert are poi dances, action songs and hand games.

Poi dances are performed by women only and consist of whirling round the flax poi balls on lengths of string. Action songs are a recent addition to the Maori activities – story-songs illustrated by fluid hand and arm movements. There are also hand games – a reaction-sharpening pastime. The best game is where the two players make rapid gestures and try to catch their opponent making the same one!

Basically, your choice is between attending a concert only, or a concert and hangi combined. For concert only, one of the best performances is presented every evening at 8 pm at the impressive **Tamatekapua Meeting House** in Ohinemutu, opposite St Faith's Church down by the lake. The cost is $13; you can show up at the door or book directly (☎ 348 4894).

Another option for concert only is the daily concert commencing at 12.15 pm at Whakarewarewa, which costs $10.50 (not including entry – see the Whakarewarewa section).

For a combined concert and hangi, Tamaki Tours (☎ 346 2823) do an excellent Twilight Cultural Tour to a marae and Maori village complex. They pick you up at your accommodation and along the way explain the traditional customs involved in visiting a marae – the *wero* (challenge), the welcome, the protocol for speaking on the marae – and a 'chief' is chosen among the group to represent the visitors. The concert is followed by a hangi. The cost is $52.

Other marae-based tours follow the same format. Rotoiti Tours (☎ 348 8969) is another excellent tour with an authentic flavour that takes you on to the Rakeiao Marae on the shore of Lake Rotoiti. The cost is $45. The Paruahanui Marae (☎ 332 3446) on Lake Rotorua also has hangi and cultural performance tours for $48, and Tumuni Station (☎ 348 2727) visit the same marae for $42.

Big hotels in Rotorua also offer Maori concerts and hangis that attract thousands of tourists each year. They present professional tourist performances and the traditional hangi foods, even if they don't dig holes out the back to cook it all. When they're not fully booked, you can opt for the performance only and skip the hangi. Big hotels with concerts and hangis include:

	Concert only	*Concert & Hangi*
Quality Resort, Eruera St (☎ 348 1234)	$20	$47
Lake Plaza, Eruera St (☎ 348 1174)	$17.50	$40
Quality Hotel, Fenton St (☎ 348 0199)	$17	$41
Sheraton Rotorua, Fenton St (☎ 348 7139)	$20	$47
THC Rotorua Hotel, Froude St (☎ 348 1189)	$16	$45

Pubs & Nightclubs

Rotorua has a selection of places for going out for a good time in the evening. The popular *Pig & Whistle*, on the corner of Haupapa and Tutanekai Sts, is a renovated police station with a number of brews on tap including their own Swine Lager. You guzzle a Swiney and listen to bands on Thursday, Friday and Saturday nights.

Monkey Jo's on Amohia St is a trendy bar and popular pick-up spot that packs them in most nights of the week.

Churchill's Bar at 426 Tutanekai St is a safe, relaxed, English-style bar with plenty of different beers on tap, New Zealand wines and meals. *Cameron's Bar & Grill* upstairs on the corner of Fenton and Pukuatua Sts sometimes has live music. They, too, serve food, and boast Guinness on tap and a huge range of whiskies.

The *Cobb Bar* in the Cobb & Co at the Grand Hotel on Hinemoa St between Tutanekai and Fenton Sts has middle-of-the road entertainment from Thursday to Saturday nights. Also at the Grand Establishment, *Wheeler's Nightclub* is a disco popular with a young crowd.

Dobbo's Bar at the Sportsman's Hotel on the corner of Hinemaru and Pukuatua Sts is a sports bar with live bands on weekends.

For just hanging out, the *Roundabout Bar & Cafe* upstairs at 83 Arawa St has games and an ambience catering to travellers.

GETTING THERE & AWAY

The Tourism Rotorua office books and sells tickets for every form of transport serving Rotorua – air, bus, shuttle, train, or anything else you can think of, and most buses stop out front.

Air

The Air New Zealand and Mt Cook Airline office (☎ 347 9564) on the corner of Fenton and Hinemoa Sts is open Monday to Friday from 8.30 am to 5 pm; they also have a counter at the airport (☎ 345 6175) open seven days a week. They offer daily direct flights to Auckland, Christchurch, Mt Cook, Queenstown, Taupo and Wellington, with connections to other centres.

Ansett New Zealand (☎ 347 0596) has a city office at 113 Fenton St, and an airport ticket counter (☎ 345 5348). Ansett offers daily direct flights to Christchurch, Queenstown, Invercargill and Wellington, with connections to other centres.

Bus

All the major bus companies stop at the Tourism Rotorua centre (☎ 348 5179) on Fenton St, which handles bookings.

InterCity has daily buses to and from Auckland (four hours), Wellington (5½ hours), Taupo, Tauranga, Whakatane and Hamilton (all 1½ hours), and Opotiki (2½ hours). On the east coast routes, InterCity goes daily to Gisborne (five hours) via Opotiki and to Napier (3½ hours) via Taupo. A Monday, Wednesday and Friday service operates between Rotorua and Wairoa on the east coast, stopping at Lake Waikaremoana.

Newmans buses go from Rotorua to Hamilton, Auckland, Taupo, Wellington, Palmerston North (5½ hours), Tauranga and Napier (3½ hours).

Mt Cook Landline stops at Rotorua on its run between Auckland and Wellington. It also stops at Hamilton, Taupo and Palmerston North. Alpine Scenic Tours has a Monday to Friday service between Rotorua and Turangi via Taupo.

Most of the backpackers buses stop in Rotorua, including the Magic Bus, Kiwi Safaris and Kiwi Experience.

East Bay Connections (☎ 347 9200), 85 Fenton St, is a door-to-door service that does day trips out to Hick's Bay on the East Cape for $99 and can drop off in Whakatane and Opotiki.

Train

The railway station is on Dingsdale Rd off Lake Rd, about one km north-west of the centre. The station opens only when trains are departing. Buy train tickets at Tourism Rotorua, not the railway station.

The Geyserland Express train operates twice daily between Auckland and Rotorua, stopping at Hamilton on the way. Travel time from Rotorua is two hours to Hamilton, four hours to Auckland.

Hitching

Hitching to Rotorua is generally not bad except on SH38 from Waikaremoana – once past Murupara the road is unsealed and traffic is very light.

The hitching problem out of Rotorua is often just the sheer number of backpackers leaving town. You may have to simply join the queue and wait.

GETTING AROUND

To/From the Airport

The airport is about 10 km out, on the eastern side of the lake. Airport Shuttle (☎ 346 2386) and Super Shuttle (☎ 349 3444) offer a door-to-door shuttle service to/from the airport for $8 for the first person, and $2 for each additional passenger in the group. A taxi from the centre to the airport costs about $15.

Bus

Rotorua Sightseeing Shuttle (☎ (025) 957399) makes a constant loop every day from 8.15 am to 5.10 pm. The route begins at the Tourism Rotorua office and goes to the Whakarewarewa thermal reserve, back to Tourism Rotorua again, then on to the Orchid Gardens, the Polynesian Spa, the Bath House museum, Rotorua lakefront, Skyline Skyrides, Rainbow Springs, Agrodome and back to Tourism Rotorua. Half-day passes for up to five hours cost $15, full-day passes $22 (children half-price), and you can jump on and off wherever you like. Ring for hotel pick-up.

The Pink Bus (☎ 348 2302) has a service at approximately 8.15 am and 12.30 pm, picking up at Tourism Rotorua and some accommodations, to Skyline Skyrides and Rainbow Springs for $5. Buses return at 12.30 pm and 5.30 pm. They also have tour buses to Waiotapu ($25 including admission) and Waimangu ($20 bus only) at 9 am, and also to other destinations.

Reesby Coachlines (☎ 347 0098) operates several suburban bus routes Monday to Friday, with limited Saturday service. Route 3 runs to Whakarewarewa, Route 2 along the lakeside to Rainbow Springs.

Car

Rotorua has a host of rental car companies. The competition is fierce and they all seem to offer 'specials' to try to undercut the others. Rent-a-Dent (☎ 349 1919) on Ti St and Link Rent-a-Car (☎ 347 8063) at 108 Fenton St are two economical companies. Ask about relocating cars to Auckland, whereby you drive the car to Auckland for them and pay only for insurance and fuel.

Bicycle

Rotorua is fairly spread out and public transport is not that good, so a bicycle is worthwhile. Lady Jane's Ice Cream Parlour (☎ 347 9340) on the corner of Tutanekai and Whakaue Sts hires bikes from $15 per day. A deposit is required.

AROUND ROTORUA

Hell's Gate

Hell's Gate (Tikitere), another highly active thermal area, is 16 km east of Rotorua on the road to Whakatane (SH30). The reserve covers 10 hectares, with a 2.5-km walking track to the various attractions, which include the largest hot thermal waterfall in the southern hemisphere. It's open daily from 8.30 am to 5 pm; admission is $10 (children $4).

George Bernard Shaw visited Hell's Gate in 1934. 'I wish I had never seen the place,' he said. 'It reminds me too vividly of the fate theologians have promised me.'

Waimangu Volcanic Valley

The Waimangu Volcanic Valley is another interesting thermal area, created during the eruption of Mt Tarawera in 1886. A walk through the valley – an easy downhill stroll – first passes the Waimangu Cauldron (a pale-blue lake steaming quietly at 53°C) then many other interesting thermal and volcanic features. Waimangu means 'black water', as much of the water here was a dark muddy colour. In this valley the Waimangu Geyser used to perform actively enough to be rated the 'largest geyser in the world'. Between 1900 and its extinction in 1904 it would occasionally spout jets nearly 500 metres high!

The walk continues down to Lake Rotomahana (warm lake), from where you can either get a lift back up to where you started or take a half-hour boat trip on Lake Rotomahana, taking you past steaming cliffs and the former site of the Pink and White Terraces.

The Waimangu Volcanic Valley is open every day from 8.30 am to 5 pm. The cost is $10 (children $4) for the valley walk only;

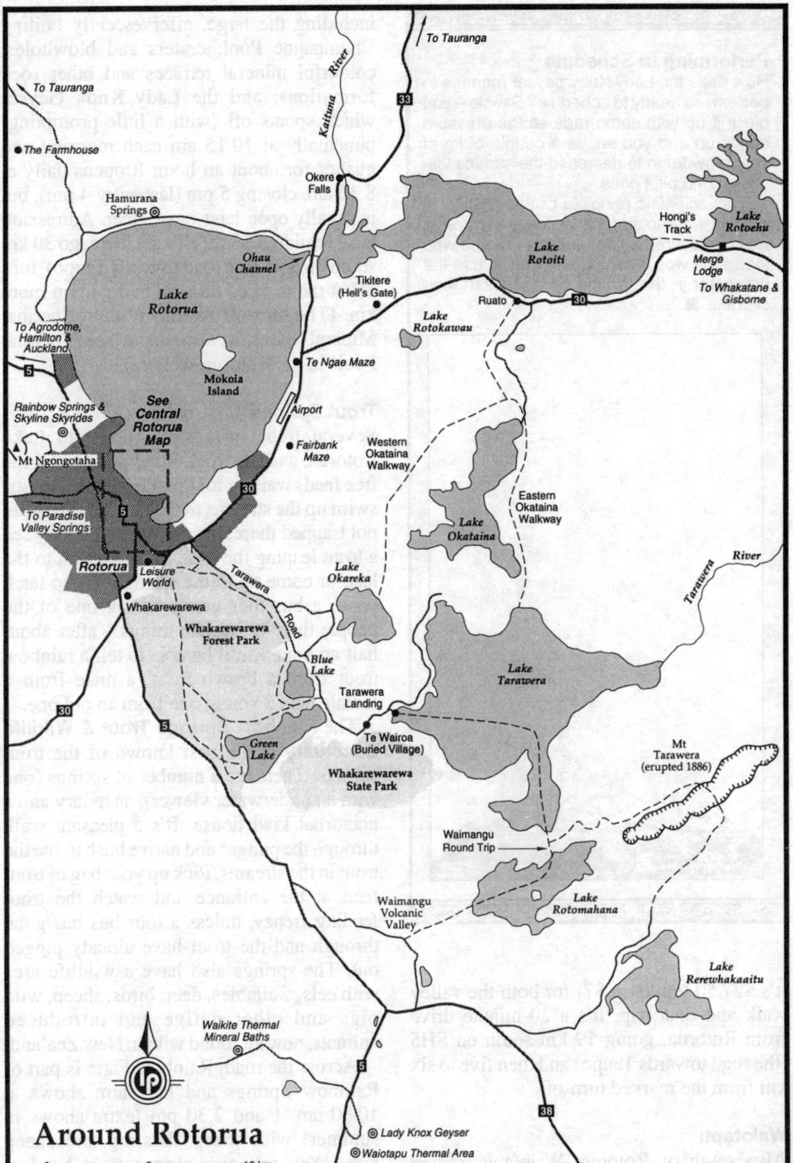
Around Rotorua
0
5
10 km
To Tauranga
To Tauranga
Kaituna River
33
The Farmhouse
Okere Falls
Hamurana Springs
Hongi's Track
Lake Rotoehu
Lake Rotoiti
Merge Lodge
To Whakatane & Gisborne
Ohau Channel
Tikitere (Hell's Gate)
Ruato
30
Lake Rotorua
Lake Rotokawau
To Agrodome, Hamilton & Auckland
5
Mokoia Island
Te Ngae Maze
See Central Rotorua Map
Rainbow Springs & Skyline Skyrides
Airport
Mt Ngongotaha
Fairbank Maze
Western Okataina Walkway
Eastern Okataina Walkway
30
To Paradise Valley Springs
5
Lake Okataina
Rotorua
Leisure World
Tarawera Road
Lake Okareka
Tarawera River
Whakarewarewa
Whakarewarewa Forest Park
Blue Lake
Lake Tarawera
Tarawera Landing
30
5
Green Lake
Te Wairoa (Buried Village)
Whakarewarewa State Park
Mt Tarawera (erupted 1886)
Waimangu Round Trip
Waimangu Volcanic Valley
Lake Rotomahana
Lake Rerewhakaaitu
Waikite Thermal Mineral Baths
5
38
Lady Knox Geyser
Waiotapu Thermal Area
To Lake Waikaremoana
To Taupo

Performing to Schedule

How does the Lady Knox geyser manage to perform so neatly to schedule? Simple – you block it up with some rags so the pressure builds up and you shove a couple of kg of soap powder in to decrease the surface viscosity. And off it goes.

This scientific principle of the relation of soap powder to surface viscosity of geysers was discovered by some early Pakeha who thought it would be a great idea to use the hot water in the ground here to wash their clothes. ■

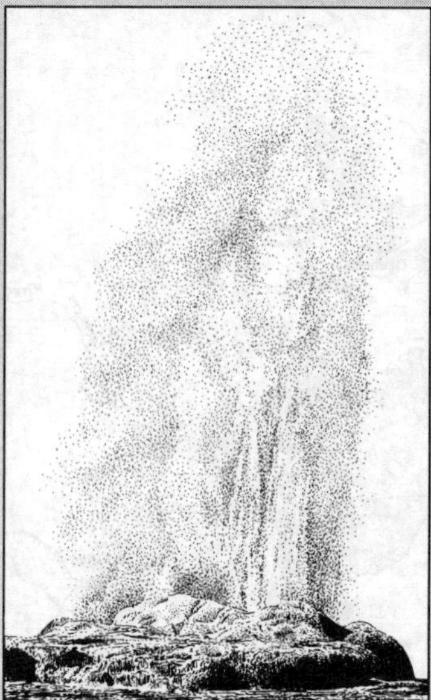

it's $27.50 (children $7) for both the valley walk and boat trip. It's a 20-minute drive from Rotorua, going 19 km south on SH5 (the road towards Taupo) and then five to six km from the marked turn-off.

Waiotapu

Also south of Rotorua, Waiotapu (sacred waters) is yet another thermal area worth visiting. It has many interesting features, including the large, effervescently boiling Champagne Pool; craters and blowholes; colourful mineral terraces and other rock formations; and the Lady Knox Geyser which spouts off (with a little prompting) punctually at 10.15 am each morning and gushes for about an hour. It opens daily at 8.30 am, closing 5 pm (last entry 4 pm), but is usually open later in summer. Admission is $9 (children $3.50). To get there, go 30 km south on SH5 (the road towards Taupo), turn off at the marked turn-off and go two more km. (The turn-off for the Waikite Thermal Mineral Baths is also there; see Thermal Pools in the Rotorua section.)

Trout Springs

Several trout springs run down to Lake Rotorua, and the trout, lured perhaps by the free feeds waiting for them from the tourists, swim up the streams to the springs. They are not trapped there; if you watch you may see a trout leaping the little falls to return to the lake or come up to the springs. Try to latch on to a bus tour group or ask one of the people there to explain things – after about half an hour you'll be able to tell a rainbow trout from a brown trout, a male from a female, and a young one from an old one.

The **Rainbow Springs Trout & Wildlife Sanctuary** is the best known of the trout springs. There are a number of springs (one with an underwater viewer), an aviary and a nocturnal kiwi house. It's a pleasant walk through the pungas and native bush to see the trout in the streams. Pick up your bag of trout feed at the entrance and watch the trout feeding frenzy, unless a tour bus has gone through and the trout have already pigged out. The springs also have a wildlife area with eels, wallabies, deer, birds, sheep, wild pigs and other native and introduced animals, now all found wild in New Zealand.

Across the road, Rainbow Farm is part of Rainbow Springs and has farm shows at 10.30 am, 1 and 2.30 pm (extra shows in summer) with sheep shearing and sheep dogs. You can also chance your hand at milking a cow or go champion bull riding.

Rainbow Springs is four km north of

central Rotorua, on the west side of Lake Rotorua – take SH5 towards Auckland or Hamilton, or catch the Sightseeing Shuttle Bus. It is open from 8 am to 5 pm daily; admission is $9.70 (children $3.50), the farm shows cost $7.80 (children $3.50) or a combined ticket is $13.50 (children $6).

Paradise Valley Springs are similar trout springs, set in an attractive six-hectare park with various animals, including a pride of lions. If you've never been in a lion's cage this is your chance – the cubs, from a few weeks to a few months old, are kept in an enclosed area and you can go in and play with them. The springs, 13 km from Rotorua on Paradise Valley Rd, at the foot of Mt Ngongotaha, are open daily from 9 am to 5 pm; admission is $9.50 (children $3).

Skyline Skyrides

Skyline Skyrides is on the west side of Lake Rotorua, near the Rainbow and Fairy Springs. Here you can take a gondola ride up Mt Ngongotaha for a panoramic view of the lake area, and once up there go flying 900 metres back down the mountain on a luge (a sort of sled without snow) or a flying fox, coming back up again on a chairlift. Also up there are a cafe and a restaurant for twilight dining. The gondola costs $10 (children $3.50) for the return trip and the luge is $4 for one ride, less per ride for multiple trips. It's open from 10 am daily.

Also at the top is a flight simulator, shooting range, mini-golf course and other attractions to spend your money on, or there are walking tracks around the mountain.

Agrodome

If seeing the millions of sheep in the NZ countryside has stimulated your interest in these animals, visit Agrodome. Going to see a bunch of sheep seems a rather strange thing to do in New Zealand, but for $9 (children $4) you get an interesting, educational and entertaining one-hour show at 9.15 am, 11 am and 2.30 pm daily. There are sheep-shearing and sheep dog displays; by the time you're through you may even be able to tell the difference between some of the 19 breeds of sheep on show. A dairy display, farmyard nursery and cow milking are also included.

You can hire horses for a guided tour or take a farm buggy tour of the 120-hectare farm. Farm Buggy Tours are $10 (children $5). Trakar Horse Riding has half-hour horse treks for $15, one-hour treks for $25. Agrodome is seven km north of Rotorua on SH1, and again, the Sightseeing Shuttle bus can drop you off here.

Mazes

Near the airport are a couple of large mazes. The **Fairbank Maze**, opposite the airport, is the largest hedge maze in New Zealand, with a 1.6-km pathway. There are also gardens, ponds, an orchard, picnic areas, birds and animals. The maze is open from 9 am to 5 pm daily; admission is $3 (children $1.50).

Te Ngae Park, three km beyond the airport, is a three-dimensional, 1.7-km wooden maze similar to the original Wanaka maze on the South Island. It's open every day from 9 am to 5 pm; admission is $4 (kids $2).

Buried Village

The Buried Village is reached by a 15-km scenic drive along Tarawera Rd, passing the Blue and Green Lakes. On display are many artefacts unearthed from the village, displays on the Mt Tarawera eruption which buried the village in ash, and excavated buildings. Of particular interest is the story of Tuhoto Ariki, who foretold the destruction of the village; his house has been excavated and is here on display. There's a good bush walk through the valley to Te Wairoa Falls, dropping about 80 metres over a series of falls.

The village is open from 8.30 am to 5 pm daily (until 6 pm in summer); admission is $8 (children $2).

Lake Tarawera

About two km further on past the Buried Village is Tarawera Landing on the shore of Lake Tarawera. Tarawera means 'burnt spear', named by a visiting hunter who left his birdspears in a hut and, on returning the following season, found both the spears and the hut had been burnt.

Tarawera Launch Cruises (☎ 362 8595) has a cruise at 11 am crossing over Lake Tarawera towards Lake Rotomahana. It stays on the other side for about 45 minutes, long enough for people to walk across to Lake Rotomahana, then returns to Tarawera Landing. Altogether the trip takes two hours and costs $20. A shorter 45-minute, $15 cruise on Lake Tarawera departs at 1.30, 2.30 and 3.30 pm. Boats from Tarawera Landing can also provide transport to Mt Tarawera and to Hot Water Beach on Te Rata Bay. The beach has hot thermal waters and a basic DOC camping ground.

Parks & Walks

Check in at the DOC office at the Tourism Rotorua centre for pamphlets and excellent maps outlining the many fine walks in the area.

On the south-east edge of town, **Whakarewarewa Forest Park** was planted earlier this century as an experiment to find the most suitable species to replace New Zealand's rapidly dwindling and slow-growing native trees. The Forestry Corporation Visitor Information Centre (☎ 346 2082) in the park is open daily and has a woodcraft shop, displays and an audiovisual on the history and development of the forest. Check in here if you want to go walking. Walks range from half an hour to four hours, including some great routes to the Blue and Green Lakes. Several walks start at the Visitor Centre, including a half-hour walk through the

The Eruption of Mt Tarawera

In the 19th century, Lake Tarawera near Rotorua was a major tourist attraction. It attracted visitors from around the world to see the Pink and White Terraces: large and beautiful terraces of multi-levelled pools, formed by silica deposits from thermal waters which had trickled over them for centuries. The Maori village of Te Wairoa, on the shores of the lake, was New Zealand's principal tourist resort, being the base from where Sophia, a Maori guide, took visitors on boat trips over the lake to view the terraces, which were regarded as one of the seven wonders of the world. Mt Tarawera towered silently over the lake, although the Maori believed that a powerful fire spirit lived inside it.

One day in June 1886, Sophia took a party out on the lake as usual, to go to see the terraces. As they were on the lake, they suddenly saw a phantom Maori war canoe gliding across the water, the Maori botamen inside it paddling rapidly. It was an ancient war canoe of a kind which had never existed on this lake. It was seen by all the people in the tourist boat, both Maori and Pakeha.

To Maori people, the appearance of a phantom Maori war canoe is an omen of impending disaster. Back at Te Wairoa, an old tohunga, Tuhoto Ariki, said the sighting of the canoe foretold disaster. He predicted that the village would be 'overwhelmed'.

Four days later, on 10 June 1886, in the middle of the night, there were earthquakes and loud sounds and the eruption of Mt Tarawera suddenly lit up the sky, with fire exploding from many places along the top of the mountain. By the time it was finished, six hours later, over 8000 sq km had been buried in ash, lava and mud, the Maori village of Te Wairoa was obliterated, the Pink and White Terraces were destroyed, 153 people were killed, Mt Tarawera was sliced and opened along its length as if with a huge cleaver, and Lake Rotomahana was formed.

Excavations were carried out at Te Wairoa to rescue the survivors. The guide Sophia became a heroine because she saved many people's lives, giving them shelter in her house.

The old tohunga, however, was not so fortunate. His house was buried in volcanic ash, with him trapped inside. The Maori people working to rescue the survivors refused to dig him out. They feared he had used his magic powers to cause the eruption – he had been saying for some time that the new orientation of the villagers towards tourists and a money economy were not traditional, and that neglect of the old traditions would anger the fire spirit inside the mountain. Finally, after four days had passed, he was dug out alive by Europeans, who took him to be cared for in Rotorua. He died a week later, aged around 104. ■

Redwood Grove, a grove of large Californian redwood trees.

Other walks in the Rotorua area include the 22.5-km **Western Okataina Walkway** through native bush from Lake Okareka to Ruato, on the shores of Lake Rotoiti. There's public transport past the Ruato end only; the whole walk takes about six hours, and you need good boots or stout shoes.

The **Eastern Okataina Walkway** goes along the eastern shoreline of Lake Okataina to Lake Tarawera – about a 2½-hour, eight-km walk. A connecting track makes it possible to do a two-day walk from either Lake Okataina or Ruato to Lake Tarawera and camp overnight at a DOC camp site ($5 per site), from where you can walk another hour to the Tarawera Falls.

To go tramping on **Mt Tarawera**, the easiest access is from Ash Pit Road at the northern end of Lake Rerewhakaaitu, but there is no public transport. Mt Tarawera is Maori Reserve land and permission should be obtained. DOC can tell you how to arrange it in Rotorua, but in summer there is usually someone on the track to collect the $2 fee. From the parking area it is a two-hour walk along a 4WD track to the crater chasm and Ruawhaia Dome. From here, most walkers return along the same route but it is possible to follow another track leading down to Lake Rotomahana and Lake Tarawera. You can complete a loop if you can arrange to be dropped off on the Ash Pit Rd and time your return to meet the Tarawera Launch at the Tarawera outlet for transport back to the Tarawera Landing.

It is essential to take water and wear good tramping shoes – it's easy to slip on the volcanic scoria. The weather on Mt Tarawera can be very changeable, so bring warm and waterproof clothing to protect you against wind and rain.

The **Okere Falls** is about 16 km north-east of Rotorua, on SH33 – the turn-off is well signposted. It's about a 30-minute walk through native podocarp forest to the falls. This is the seven-metre falls that the rafting companies are taking people over. Several other walks are also here, including walks up the Kaituna River to Hinemoa's Steps and some caves.

Just north of Waiotapu on SH5, a good trail leads to **Rainbow Mountain** with its small crater lakes and fine views. It is a good, short, but fairly strenuous 1½-hour walk to the Maungakakakatamea Lookout.

Other short walks can be made around Lake Okataina, Mt Ngongotaha (just north of Rotorua) and Lake Rotorua.

WHIRINAKI FOREST PARK

About 50 km east of Rotorua, signposted off the main road, is the 60,900-hectare Whirinaki Forest Park. Access is off SH38 on the way to Te Urewera National Park; take the turn-off at Te Whaiti to Minginui. The park is noted for the sheer majesty and density of its native podocarp forests; it has walking tracks, scenic drives, camping and huts, lookouts, waterfalls, the Whirinaki River, and some special areas including the Oriuwaka Ecological Reserve and the Arahaki Lagoon. For more information about this excellent forest park get a copy of the booklet *Tramping & Walking in Whirinaki Forest Park*.

The DOC has a field centre in the sawmill village of Minginui, but the park headquarters' office is the Ikawhenua Visitor Centre (☎ 366 5641) in Murupara.

Ask for details on the fine Whirinaki Track walk, an easy two-day walk that can be combined with Te Hoe Loop Walk, for a four-day walk with seven huts that starts in some of New Zealand's finest podocarp forest and proceeds along a series of river valleys.

Places to Stay

Just before Minginui is the *Whirinaki Recreation Camp* (☎ 366 3601) and in Minginui is the *Ohu Forest Users' Camp*; both cost $5 per night for adults and $2.50 for children. Down by the Whirinaki River, at the Mangamate Waterfall, there is an informal camping area; a tent site is $5. The forest has nine back country huts costing $4 per person. There are all types of accommodation in Murupara as well as food outlets.

Western Bay of Plenty

The western region of the Bay of Plenty extends from Katikati and Waihi Beach to Papamoa and Te Puke on the coast, and south to the Kaimai Ranges.

Captain Cook sailed into the Bay of Plenty on the *Endeavour* in October 1769, giving it its name because of the numbers of thriving settlements of friendly Maori he encountered (and the amount of supplies they gave him). It was a sharp contrast to the 'welcome' he received from the Maori of Poverty Bay several weeks earlier, when lives were lost and no food was available.

The area is not as popular with tourists as the far more commercial Bay of Islands, but in summer it hums along rather nicely. It enjoys one of the highest proportions of sunny days in New Zealand, the climate is consistently mild all year round, and in summer the coastal towns and beaches are popular with Kiwi holiday-makers.

The region is rapidly becoming the horticultural centre of New Zealand, with its main exports being kiwi fruit and timber products, including logs and woodchips. There is a growing mineral water industry, with springs being 'tapped' all over the place. Naturally there are several hot mineral spas around.

TAURANGA

Tauranga is the principal city of the Bay of Plenty, and its port – one of the largest export ports in New Zealand – ships out the produce from the rich, surrounding region. The days of the overnight kiwi-fruit millionaires have gone, but the area is still thriving economically and draws increasing numbers of retirees attracted by the temperate climate and a city well supplied with facilities. Tauranga is indeed a pleasant place to live, but its tourist attractions are limited mostly to the beaches and headland scenery of Mt Maunganui across Tauranga Harbour.

Tauranga is a Maori name meaning the 'resting place for canoes', for this was where some of the first Maori to arrive in New Zealand landed.

As the centre of New Zealand's principal kiwi fruit region, work is available when kiwi fruit is being picked (May and June) but you may be able to find orchard work of some kind at almost any time of year. Check with the hostels for orchard work contacts.

Information

The Tauranga Information & Visitors Centre (☎ 578 8103) is on the Strand by Coronation Pier. It's open in summer on weekdays from 7.30 am to 5 pm, and in winter on weekdays from 9 am to 3 pm.

The DOC office (☎ 578 7677) on the corner of McLean and Anson Sts is open from 8 am to 4.35 pm, Monday to Friday. The AA office is on the corner of Second Avenue and Cameron Rd.

Historic Attractions

The **Historic Village** (☎ 578 1302) on Seventeenth Ave features restored period buildings, vintage vehicles, farming equipment, an 1877 steam locomotive, an old tugboat, a Maori culture section and relics from the gold-mining era. It's open from 9 am to 5 pm every day; admission is $6 (children $2).

Te Awanui, a fine replica Maori canoe, is on display in an open-sided building at the top end of the Strand, close to the centre of town. Continue uphill beyond the canoe to **Monmouth Redoubt**, a fortified site during the Maori Wars. A little further along is **Robbins Park**, with a rose garden and hothouse.

The **Elms Mission Station House** on Mission St, was founded on the site in 1835, and the present house was completed in 1847 by a pioneer missionary. It is furnished in period style. The grounds contain gardens and several historic buildings. It is open 11 am to 2 pm on Sunday.

There's also the historic **Brian Watkins House**, built in 1887, near the corner of Elizabeth St and Cameron Rd. It's open on Sunday; a donation is requested.

Activities

Walks There are many walking possibilities in the region. A good number of these are outlined in the free pamphlet *Walkways of Tauranga & the Western Bay of Plenty*, available from visitor information centres. Over 20 walks, in Tauranga and Mt Maunganui (including the fascinating **Waikareao estuary**) and further afield, are described. Each is accompanied by a handy map. The backdrop to the Western Bay of Plenty is the rugged 70-km-long **Kaimai-Mamaku Forest Park**, with tramps for the more adventurous; DOC should be able to provide more detailed information on walks in this area. **McLaren Falls**, in the Wairoa River valley, 11 km from Tauranga just off SH29, is worth a visit. There's good bushwalking, rock pools and, of course, the falls. It's picturesque, but not exactly awe-inspiring.

Sea Activities Tauranga is surrounded by water, so if you like the sea you'll find plenty to do. Charter and fishing trips operate from Tauranga all year round. During the summer the place comes alive with sea activities of all kinds including jet-skiing, swim with the dolphins, water-skiing, windsurfing, parasailing, sea kayaking, diving, surfing, swimming, line fishing, deep sea fishing and sailing. Ask at the visitor information centre for details on these and other activities, and see the Around Tauranga section for details of trips to Mayor Island.

Recommended activities include sailing on Tauranga Harbour on the *Slipstream* yacht (☎ 576 1841), from $25 for 1½ hours to $80 for a full day. Gemini Galaxsea (☎ 578 3197) have swim-with-the-dolphin experiences on a motorised yacht for $60 per day. Even if you don't meet the dolphins (they claim a high success rate) it is good value for a day cruise and you get to snorkel on the reefs. Aquanauts Adventures (☎ 575 0060) also have swim with the dolphin expeditions and other activities such as surf rafting.

White-Water Rafting White-water rafting is popular around Tauranga, particularly on the Wairoa River, which has some of the best falls and rafting in New Zealand. It's definitely a rafting trip for thrill-seekers – one highlight of the trip is a plunge over a four-metre waterfall! The water level is controlled from a dam, so the Wairoa can only be rafted on a few days of the year. Operators include Wet 'N Wild Rafting (☎ 578 4093) and Woodrow Rafting Expeditions (☎ 576 2628). They do trips on other rivers too.

Flying & Skydiving Tauranga is home to lots of air enthusiasts. The Tauranga Airport, just across the harbour in Mt Maunganui, is the base for a number of air clubs. Scenic flights can be arranged at the airport. The Tauranga Glider Club (☎ 575 6768) flies every weekend, weather permitting, and an instructor will take you gliding and give you a flying lesson as you go. You can also do a flight in a microlight (a sort of powered hang-glider) with the Microlight Association (☎ 575 2321). Tandem skydiving is extremely popular and costs $190 with Tandem Skydiving (☎ 576 7990).

Places to Stay

Camping & Cabins The *Mayfair Caravan Park* (☎ 578 3323) is on Mayfair St, off Fifteenth Ave, beside the harbour. Tent facilities are limited. Powered sites cost $8.50 per person and cabins cost $30 a double.

The *Silver Birch Motor Park & Thermal Pools* (☎ 578 4603) is at 101 Turret Rd (the extension of Fifteenth Ave) by the Hairini Bridge to Maungatapu. Sites here cost $9, cabins cost from $40 for two, and there are also tourist flats and motel flats. It has thermal mineral pools, a boat ramp, dinghies for hire, and lots of recreational facilities.

The small waterside *Sixth Avenue Tourist Court* (☎ 578 5709) is close to the centre on Sixth Ave. Camp sites cost $16 for two and cabins cost from $34.

At the *Palms Caravan Park* (☎ 578 9337), 162 Waihi Rd, about four km south of the town centre, sites cost from $9 per person and on-site caravans cost $33 for two. The *Bayshore Leisure Park* (☎ 544 0700), on SH29, has sites from $8 per person and

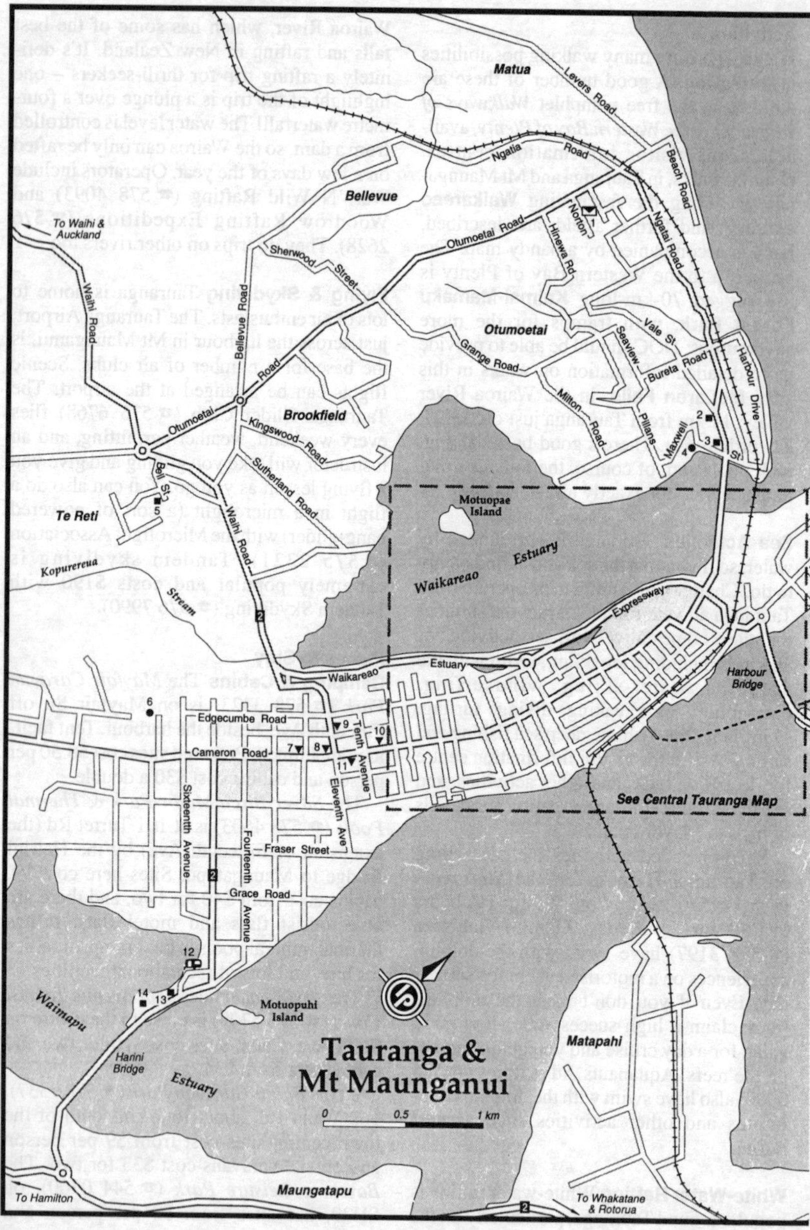
Tauranga &
Mt Maunganui
Matua
Levers Road
Beach Road
Ngatia Road
Bellevue
Norton
Hinewa Rd
Ngatai Road
Otumoetai Road
Sherwood Street
Bellevue Road
To Waihi & Auckland
Waihi Road
Otumoetai
Vale St
Seaview
Grange Road
Bureta Road
Harbour Drive
Milton Road
Pillans
Maxwell St
Otumoetai Road
Brookfield
Kingswood Road
Sutherland Road
Bell St
Te Reti
Motuopae Island
Waikareao Estuary
Kopurereua Stream
Expressway
Waikareao Estuary
Harbour Bridge
Edgecumbe Road
Cameron Road
Tenth Avenue
Eleventh Ave
Sixteenth Avenue
Fourteenth Avenue
Fraser Street
Grace Road
See Central Tauranga Map
Motuopuhi Island
Waimapu Estuary
Hairini Bridge
Matapahi
Maungatapu
To Hamilton
To Whakatane & Rotorua
0 0.5 1 km

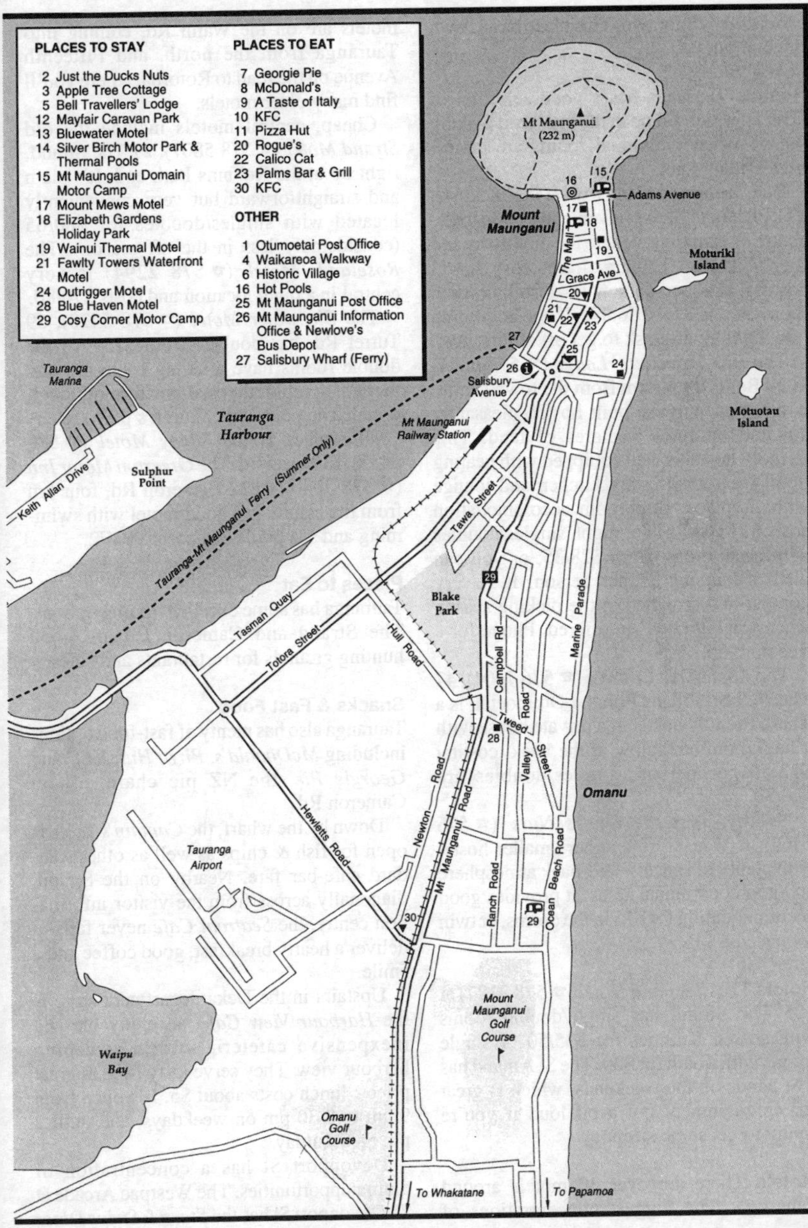

BAY OF PLENTY

cabins for $28 for two. This place has its own mineral pools.

Hostels Tauranga has a good selection of hostels, which fill up in the kiwi fruit picking season when individual rooms are almost impossible to get.

The *Waireinga YHA Hostel* (☎ 578 5064), 171 Elizabeth St, is conveniently close to the centre of Tauranga, next to the motorway and the Waikareao Estuary. It's a cosy hostel costing $14 per person in dorms or twin rooms and $32 for a double. If you're coming into town by bus, ask to get off at First Ave.

The *Bell Travellers' Lodge* (☎ 578 6344) at 39 Bell St, four km from the town centre, is a newer, purpose-built hostel, pleasantly situated on three hectares of land. This friendly hostel is well equipped with heating in all the rooms, a big kitchen and lounge with fireplace. Bunkroom accommodation costs $14 and $15 per night, singles/doubles with ensuite cost from $28/35, or you can pitch a tent for $7 per person. It is very popular and crowded in the picking season when weekly rates are offered. Phone for a free pick-up.

The *Apple Tree Cottage* (☎ 576 7404), 47 Maxwell St, Pillans Point at Otumoetai, is a small, friendly hostel in a private house with a bunkroom bungalow at the back, costing $12.50 per person; singles/doubles are $20/30.

Nearby, *Just the Ducks Nuts* (☎ 576 1366), 6 Vale St, is another smaller hostel with plenty of space, a laid-back atmosphere and good communal areas. It provides good accommodation for $15 in the dorms, or twin rooms cost $36.

Hotels The *St Amand Hotel* (☎ 578 8127) at 105 The Strand has single/double rooms with shared facilities for $35/50 or single rooms with a bath for $20. The St Amand has live bands on the weekends, which is great for entertainment but a bit loud if you're trying to get some sleep.

Motels There are over 30 motels around Tauranga. The biggest concentrations of motels are on the Waihi Rd, coming into Tauranga from the north, and Fifteenth Avenue on the road to Rotorua, where you'll find many older motels.

Cheap, central motels include the old *Strand Motel* (☎ 578 5807), 27 The Strand, right up at the Robbins Park end. It's plain and straightforward but very conveniently located with singles/doubles for $60/65 (considerably less in the off season). The *Roselands Motel* (☎ 578 2294) is very central in a quiet location and costs $70/80.

The *Bluewater Motel* (☎ 578 5420), 59 Turret Rd, has doubles from $75. All the double rooms have a sitting room too and there's a tepid thermal swimming pool, private spa pool and children's play area. A similar place is the *Savoy Motel* (☎ 578 6435), 53 Turret Rd. The *Greerton Motor Inn* (☎ 578 7040), 1222 Cameron Rd, four km from the centre, is a good motel with swimming and spa pools and costs $60/72.

Places to Eat

Tauranga has some excellent dining options. The Strand and Cameron Rd are good hunting grounds for restaurants and cafes.

Snacks & Fast Food

Tauranga also has plenty of fast-food options including *McDonald's*, *Pizza Hut*, *KFC* and *Georgie Pie*, the NZ pie chain, all on Cameron Rd.

Down by the wharf, the *Captain's Table* is open for fish & chips as well as other standard cafe-bar fare. Nearby on the Strand, diagonally across from the visitor information centre, the *Seafront Cafe* never fails to deliver a hearty breakfast, good coffee and a smile.

Upstairs in the Deka department store is the *Harbour View Cafe*, an enjoyable and inexpensive cafeteria with a sweeping harbour view. They serve tasty food at great prices; lunch costs about $5. It's open from 9 am to 3.30 pm on weekdays, and until 2 pm on Saturday.

Devonport St has a concentration of dining opportunities. The Westpac Arcade at 75 Devonport St has the *Stars & Strips Diner*

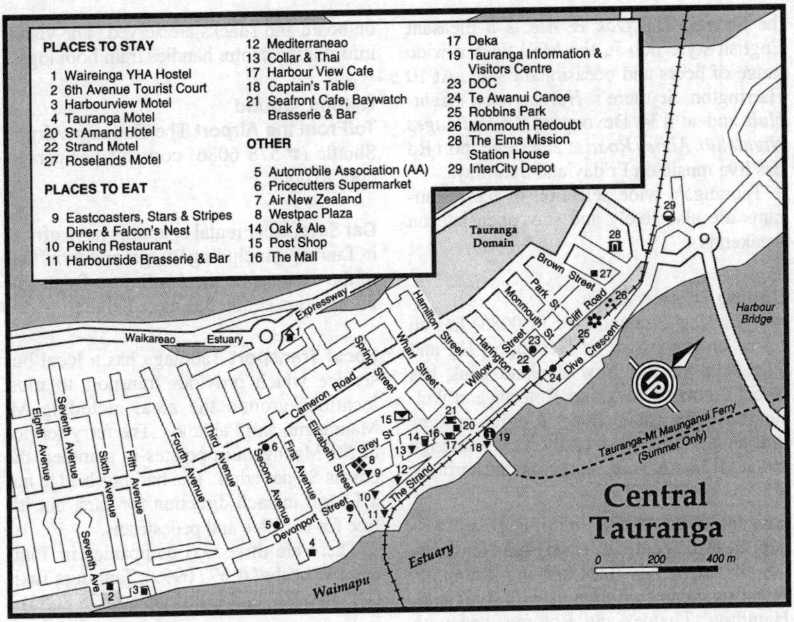

for burgers, nachos and other Kiwi Americana. *Falcon's Nest* is a good little cafe bar with meals in the $12 range and it sometimes has jazz and folk music. Above Falcon's Nest, *Eastcoasters* is a spacious place specialising in Mexican and Tex-Mex food, light meals, burgers and huge sandwiches, with something to please both vegetarians and meat-eaters.

Across the street, the *Peking Restaurant* is a better-than-usual Chinese restaurant with a takeaway section, à la carte meals in the restaurant or a set menu costing $22.

Restaurants

One of the most popular 'ethnic' restaurants is the reasonably priced *Collar & Thai* upstairs in the Goddards Centre, 21 Devonport Rd. The food is Thai – dress is casual. At 62 Devonport Rd is the gourmet *Mediterraneao*, a European-style cafe with a changing menu, great cakes and coffee.

The *Baywatch Brasserie & Bar*, on the corner of the Strand and Wharf St, is one of Tauranga's most popular restaurants. The menu is certainly innovative, combining a number of international treatments of local produce, and the desserts are great.

For Italian food, *A Taste of Italy* is a very popular licensed and BYO restaurant, on the corner of Eleventh Ave and St John St, with entree pastas for $9; mains such as veal marsala are around $20.

You can dine inside or outside, overlooking the water, at the *Harbourside Brasserie & Bar* in the Old Yacht Club Building, the Strand Extension, from 11.30 am until late. A three-course meal costs from $35 to $40 here but the choice of dishes is good and combines a variety of local produce; there's a supper menu as well.

Entertainment

Several hotel bars have live entertainment nightly from Thursday to Saturday, such as *Scotty's* which is in the St Amand Hotel on the Strand. The *Oak & Ale* is a pleasant English-style pub in the Mall with a wide range of beers and occasional bands. At 10 Harrington St there's *Harrington's Nightclub* and at 134 Devonport Rd is *Images Nightclub*. *Abbey Road* at 22a Devonport Rd has live music on Friday and Saturday.

Tauranga's wide selection of bar/restaurants are also lively and stay open late on weekends.

Getting There & Away

Air Air New Zealand (☎ 578 0083) has an office on the corner of Devonport Rd and Elizabeth St. Air New Zealand Link has direct flights to Auckland, Rotorua and Wellington, with connections to other centres. Tauranga's airport is actually not at Tauranga but at Mt Maunganui, just across the harbour.

Bus InterCity (☎ 578 2825), in Dive Crescent near the centre of town, and Newmans are the main bus lines serving Tauranga. InterCity connects Tauranga with Auckland, Hamilton, Thames and Rotorua, and with Gisborne via Whakatane and Opotiki. Newmans run to Hamilton, Auckland, New Plymouth, Rotorua, Taupo and Napier. Supa Travel (☎ 577 6595) is a local company with buses to Auckland ($29) every day but Saturday. Newmans and Super Travel stop at the visitor information centre, which also handles bookings for these buses. All bus lines continue to Mt Maunganui after stopping in Tauranga.

It's 2½ hours by bus from Tauranga to Thames, 4½ hours to Auckland (via Thames), two hours to Hamilton and 1½ hours to Rotorua.

Call-a-Bus (☎ 576 2089) has a door-to-door service to Auckland for $45 and a service to Rotorua.

Train The Kaimai Express to Auckland departs from Tauranga at 8.05 am; transfers and other connections can be made in Hamilton before it goes on to Auckland. It departs from Auckland for Tauranga at 5.45 pm, arriving in Tauranga at 9.05 pm; there is a bar on board and snacks are served. The visitor information centre handles train bookings.

Getting Around

To/From the Airport The Tauranga Airport Shuttle (☎ 578 6086) costs $7 per person, door to door.

Car Several car rental operators have offices in Tauranga, including Budget and Avis. One of the most economical is Rent-a-Dent. The information centre has more details.

Local Transport Tauranga has a local bus service which provides transport to most locations around the area, including Mt Maunganui and Papamoa. The ferry service to Mt Maunganui operates in summer; the cost is $5 per adult. The harbour bridge has a $1 toll in each direction for cars, but it's free for bicycles and pedestrians.

There are three taxi companies in Tauranga: Citicabs (☎ 577 0999), Tauranga Taxis (☎ 578 6086) and Coastline (☎ 578 8095).

AROUND TAURANGA

Matakana Island

Sheltering Tauranga Harbour, this elongated island is a quiet rural retreat just across the harbour from Tauranga. Two-thirds of the island is pine forest, providing the island's main industry, and the rest is farmland on the western side of the island. Matakana Island has 24 km of pristine white-sand surf beach on its eastern side and is also good for windsurfing, kayaking and fishing. An ideal way to explore the island is by bicycle, which you can take on the ferry. The island has a general store and social club, but not much else – bring your own supplies.

Places to Stay *Matakana Island Retreat* (☎ 578 0375) at the southern end of the island on the harbour side is a large house with single or double rooms for $25 per person. They have free bicycles, surfboards and windsurfers, and will pick up from the ferry landing. There is a kitchen for guests to cook, or meals are provided by arrangement.

It is also possible to stay in one of the island's three maraes, by prior arrangement. Check with the visitors centre in Tauranga.

Getting There & Away The main ferry (☎ 025 927251) departs from Omokoroa at 7.45 am and 4 pm for the western side of the island. It costs $2 for the 15-minute crossing. You can also take the *Forest Lady* (☎ 025 937426), a barge for the logging trucks that runs from the docks at Sulphur Point in central Tauranga to the southern end of the island. It shuttles across daily from Monday to Friday, but there is no fixed schedule. The island has no public transport.

Omokoroa

This town is 22 km west of Tauranga, and is situated on a promontory which protrudes well into the sheltered harbour and has fine views of the harbour and Matakana Island. It is a popular summer destination and has two caravan parks. From Omokoroa you can visit Matakana Island by the regular ferry service.

Katikati

In the past few years Katikati (to locals, Catty-Cat) on the Uretara River has become an open-air art gallery and many of its buildings are adorned with **murals**. Two good ones are Athenree Homestead and Waitekohe School – the latter one dates from around 1914. There's an excellent small brochure called *Mural Town: Katikati* available from the visitors centre (☎ 549 1658), Cherry Court.

Off SH2 not far from Katikati, the **Katikati Bird Gardens** are a bird sanctuary and botanic gardens, open daily (except during July). **Morton Estate** is one of New Zealand's bigger wineries on SH2, eight km south of Katikati. Wine tastings and tours are very popular and the vineyard also has a good restaurant.

Places to Stay The *Sapphire Springs Holiday Park* (☎ 549 0768) is set in 78 hectares of bush which backs on to the Kaimai Ranges. Sites cost from $8 per person, cabins $30 for two, tourist flats $50 for two, and motels $65 for two. A bunk bed in the lodge is $12.50; the springs are free to visitors but there are private spas available. In town is the *Katikati Motel* (☎ 549 0385) where singles/doubles are $60/74.

The visitors centre has information on numerous *homestays/farmstays* in the area, many providing budget accommodation from $12.

Kiwi Fruit Wineries

Prestons Kiwi Fruit Winery, on Belk Rd off SH29, is just one place where you can sample this uniquely NZ wine. It's open Monday to Saturday from 10 am to 4.30 pm. There are a number of other wineries in the district; inquire at the visitor information centre.

Tuhua Island

Tuhua (Mayor) Island is a dormant volcano about 40 km north of Tauranga in the Bay of Plenty. There are walking tracks through the now overgrown crater valley and an interesting walk around the island. The north-west corner is a marine reserve but specialist groups can seek permission to land there. (Permission needs to be obtained from the Maori Trust Board – inquire at the Tauranga visitor information centre.) Visitors pay a $5 landing fee (children $2).

Getting There & Away Ferries to the island operate three or four days a week from Christmas Day until the end of January. They depart from Coronation Pier in Tauranga, going out via Mt Maunganui at 7 am and returning at 4 pm. The trip takes about three hours in each direction. The cost is $35 (children $25) for a day trip, or $50 (children $30) if you go out on one day and return on another.

Minden Lookout

From Minden Lookout, about 10 km from Tauranga, there's a superb view back over the Bay of Plenty. To get there, take SH2 to Te Puna and turn off south on Minden Rd; the lookout is about four km up the road.

Papamoa

Papamoa, 13 km south of Mt Maunganui, is blessed with miles of beaches; digging for tuatua is popular when the tide is right. There are a couple of motor camps at Papamoa, all of them along Papamoa Beach Rd. They are the *Papamoa Beach Holiday Park* (☎ 542 0816) and *Beach Grove Holiday Park* (☎ 542 1337); camp sites are about $9 at each place and both have cabins as well. You can get takeaway food from a number of places on Beach Rd, and the *Papamoa Family Tavern* has bistro meals.

Te Puke

Hailed as the 'Kiwi Fruit Capital of the World', Te Puke is not as bad as its civic plaudits have made it sound. There is much native bush nearby and the town is not far from several good beaches and exciting rivers. Te Puke is certainly busy in the kiwi fruit picking season when there is plenty of work in the area.

The Te Puke Visitor Information Centre (☎ 573 9172) is at 72 Jellicoe St and has lots of information on activities and sights in the surrounding area.

Things to See The Bay of Plenty is kiwi fruit country and you can learn a little more about this fruit that is so important to New Zealand's economy. Gardening enthusiasts can visit many private gardens in the area.

Kiwi Fruit Country (you won't miss the garish 'big kiwi fruit' sign, which looks like a green-dyed sectioned human kidney) is on SH33, six km east of Te Puke and 36 km from Tauranga. You can visit the orchards and shop, see a video about kiwi fruit and sample some kiwi fruit or kiwi fruit wine. The complex is also a theme park with a Dragon Maze, 'magic taps', miniature hydro dam – all quite tacky but the kids might enjoy it. Including a kiwi-kart ride through the orchards and an exhibition on how the fruit is grown and packed, it costs $8 (children $4). Kiwi Fruit Country is open daily from 9 am to 5 pm.

Next to Kiwi Fruit Country is the **Te Puke Vintage Auto Barn**, with over 60 vintage cars on display. It is open 8.30 am to 5 pm daily. Admission is $5 (children $2).

Activities Longridge Jets (☎ 533 1515) does jet-boating on the Kaituna River near Te Puke, east of Tauranga. This river is renowned as having the most exciting white-water in New Zealand.

Faraway Farm (☎ 573 5400) has guided walks and horse rides through native bush, and is also a farmstay.

Places to Stay The *Te Puke Holiday Park* (☎ 573 9866) has sites from $8 per person, hostel-style accommodation for $12 per person, and on-site caravans and cabins for $32 for two. At 173 Jellicoe St is the *Beacon Motel* (☎ 573 7825) which has singles/doubles for $58/69 to $79.

Just south of town is *Lodore Lodge* (☎ 573 8258), 51 Atahua Way off No 3 Rd, a home-stay offering backpackers accommodation for $18 per person, including breakfast. The lodge is a homestead in a kiwi fruit orchard and has a swimming pool. Activities are organised. *De Haven* (☎ 533 1025) is a new backpackers at Paengoroa, about eight km east of Te Puke past Kiwi Fruit County. This small hostel has beds for $15 per person.

The visitors centre produces a glossy brochure listing many farm and homestays in the area.

Maketu

There's a Maori pa site at Town Point, near the township of Maketu, north-east of Te Puke. Maketu was the landing site of the *Arawa* canoe, more than 600 years ago, and there is a stone monument on the foreshore which commemorates this. The name Maketu comes from a place in Hawaiki. The small Maketu visitor information centre (☎ 533 2343) can't be missed, if for nothing else than the beautiful mural which decorates its front.

To get to Maketu from Tauranga, take SH2 through Te Puke and turn left into Maketu Rd just past Rangiuru.

Eastern Bay of Plenty

The eastern Bay of Plenty extends from Maketu and Pukehina to Opotiki, in the far east of the bay, and takes in Whakatane and Ohope.

MT MAUNGANUI

The town of Mt Maunganui stands at the foot of the 232-metre hill of the same name (also called the Mount, and the name Maunganui means 'large mountain'). It's just across the inlet from Tauranga and its fine beaches make it a popular holiday resort for Kiwis. Like Tauranga, Mt Maunganui is built on a narrow peninsula.

The downside of the drive to the Mount is the unsightly industrial area that they have routed the road through, reminiscent of the factory-pocked towns of the eastern US seaboard.

Information

The Mt Maunganui Information Office (☎ 575 5099), on Salisbury Avenue is open the same hours as its Tauranga counterpart.

Things to See & Do

Walking trails go around and up Mt Maunganui for magnificent views. You can climb around on the rocks on Moturiki Island, which is actually joined to the peninsula. The beach between Moturiki and Mt Maunganui is good for surfing, bodysurfing and swimming.

There are excellent hot saltwater pools at the foot of the Mount, on Adams Ave – the hot pools are open daily from 8 am to 10 pm and admission is $2.50 (children $1.50). Private pools are $3.50 (children $2.50).

Places to Stay

Camping & Cabins Mt Maunganui is a popular summer resort so there are plenty of camping grounds. At the foot of the Mount, the *Mt Maunganui Domain Motor Camp* (☎ 575 4471) has waterfront sites at $16 for two people, cabins and on-site vans from $40.

At the *Cosy Corner Motor Camp* (☎ 575 5899), 40 Ocean Beach Rd, camp sites cost $10 per person and on-site caravans are $36 for two. At 75 Girven Rd, the *Golden Grove Motor Park* (☎ 575 5821) has sites for $10 per person, and on-site vans and cabins at $40 for two.

The *Ocean Pines Motor Camp* (☎ 575 4265) on Maranui St has camp sites for $9.50 per person. On-site caravans cost $40 for two, and tourist flats cost $55 for two.

On the Mall, overlooking Pilot Bay on the Tauranga side of the peninsula, the *Elizabeth Gardens Holiday Park* (☎ 575 5787) has caravan sites for $10 per person. Cabins cost $35 to $45 for two and tourist flats cost $45 to $70 for two adults; there's also a five-bed backpackers bunkhouse, costing $20 per person ($15 in the off season).

Hotels & Motels The only hotel accommodation is at the rather expensive *Hotel Mt Maunganui* (☎ 575 5089), Girven Rd, where the Monday to Friday tariff for a double room is $96; on weekends it is $10 less.

Mt Maunganui has fewer motels than Tauranga, and their prices spiral outrageously in summer to over $100. At other times of the year prices are around the usual $60/70. Motels include *Fawlty Towers Waterfront Motel* (☎ 575 5883) at 28 The Mall, *Blue Haven Motel* (☎ 575 6508) at 10 Tweed St, *Wainui Thermal Motel* (☎ 575 3526) at 35 Maunganui Rd, and the *Outrigger Motel* (☎ 575 3250), 48 Marine Parade.

The *Mount Mews Motel* (☎ 575 7006), 8 Maunganui Rd, is an excellent new motel and a definite cut above the rest. Well-appointed units cost $90 a double or spa bath units are $110, and these rates apply all year round.

Places to Eat

The shopping centre along Maunganui Rd has plenty of takeaways and restaurants.

Fast-food addicts can go to *KFC* on the corner of Newton St and Hewletts Rd or *McDonald's* in the Bayfair Centre. At 114

Maunganui Rd, the *Calico Cat* has standard cafe fare, but the menu is spiced up with satay and good curries for around $6. For fancier dining, the *Palm Bar & Grill* and *Rogue's*, both on Maunganui Rd, are bistro-style, licensed restaurants with mixed menus.

Getting There & Away

Air The Tauranga airport is actually at Mt Maunganui; see the Tauranga section for flight details and how to get to/from the airport.

Bus Newmans and Super Travel buses serving Tauranga also stop at Mt Maunganui, in front of the visitor information centre. InterCity stops outside their agent, Davies Drycleaners (☎ 575 4669), 409 Maunganui Rd. Newlove's buses run from Wharf St in Tauranga to Mt Maunganui, stopping outside the visitor information centre and the hot pools. The fare is $3.

Car You can reach Mt Maunganui across the harbour bridge from Tauranga, or from the south via Te Maunga on SH2. If you're driving across the harbour bridge there's a $1 toll in each direction.

Ferry This only operates in the summer from Salisbury Wharf in Mt Maunganui to Tauranga; the fare is $5.

WHAKATANE

Whakatane (population 13,000) lies on a natural harbour at the mouth of the Whakatane River. The *Mataatua* canoe landed at the mouth of the river in about 1350, during the Great Migration, and Whakatane became an important Maori centre. Only around the turn of the century did Europeans discover the richness of the land and settle in any numbers. Whakatane today is the principal town for the eastern Bay of Plenty, and a service centre for the Rangitaiki agricultural and milling district.

Whakatane is a pleasant town in one of the sunniest parts of the North Island. Many visitors are attracted to the nearby beaches, especially in summer, and two major attractions are offshore – White Island, New Zealand's most active volcano, and swim-with-the-dolphin tours.

Information

The well-organised visitor information centre (☎ 308 6058) is on Boon St and half a block off the Strand, the town's main street. The centre is open from 9 am to 5 pm on weekdays, 9 am to 1 pm on Saturday. The staff can provide brochures on just about everything; they also make tour bookings. The AA office is opposite the visitor information centre on Boon St. The DOC office (☎ 308 7213) is being relocated to the new Regional Council Building.

Things to See

The **Whakatane Museum** on Boon St is one of the more interesting regional museums with photographic and artefact exhibits on early Maori and European settlers, and the natural environment, including the smoking White (Whakaari) Island volcano just offshore. It's also a centre of historical research, with an archive of historical publications. It's open from 10 am to 4.30 pm during the week, 11 am to 1.30 on Saturday, 2 to 4.30 pm on Sunday. Admission is $1.

Just to one side of the traffic circle on the corner of the Strand and Commerce St is **Pohaturoa**, a large rock outcrop and important Maori sacred site. The coastline used to come right up to here and there's a tunnel in the rock where baptisms and other rites were performed. Today the rock is set apart in a little park, with a plaque explaining its historical and religious significance. Also in the park are a Maori canoe, carved benches and a monument to a chief of the Mataatua tribes.

The **Whakatane Astronomical Observatory** (☎ 312 4618) in Hurunui Ave, Hillcrest, opens to the public every Tuesday evening.

The small **botanical gardens** are at the river end of McGarvey Rd, beside a children's playground. **Lake Sullivan** is on King St.

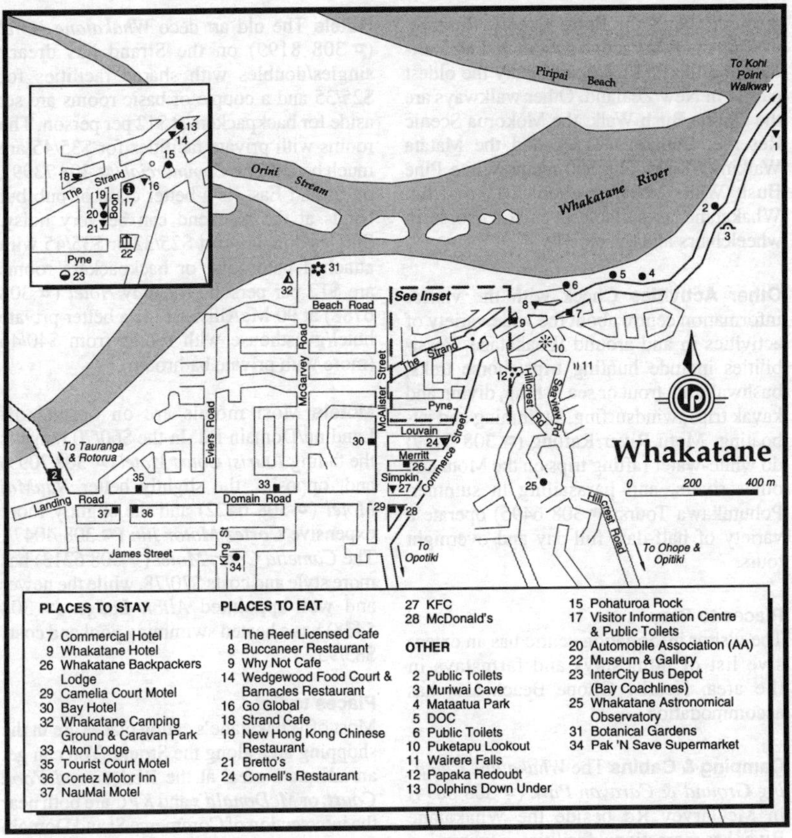

Activities

Swim with the Dolphins Dolphins Down Under (☎ 308 4636), 92 The Strand, run popular trips year round, subject to weather, to swim with the dolphins. They have a very high success rate for dolphin spotting in summer, when up to three trips per day operate for $75 per person. All the necessary equipment, including a wet suit, is supplied. You will see many pelagic bird species and, if you are lucky, whales. In winter the dolphins move further offshore and trips are subject to demand, but there is still a reasonable chance of finding dolphins at this time. Ring for details of their bus service from Rotorua.

Walks The information centre and DOC have lots of information on walks. An interesting 2½-hour town centre walk encompasses a number of scenic and historic spots including Muriwai Cave, Wairere Falls, Puketapu Lookout, Hapaka Redoubt, the Pohaturoa rock and a big game fishing facility.

Other notable walks include the 3½-hour Kohi Point Walkway, Nga Tapuwae-o-Toi (Sacred Footsteps of Toi), which extends through the Kohi Point Scenic Reserve, passing many attractive sites including lookouts and the Pa of Toi, reputedly the oldest pa site in New Zealand. Other walkways are the Ohope Bush Walk, the Mokorua Scenic Reserve, Latham's Track and the Matata Walking Track. The 300-metre White Pine Bush Walk, starting about 10 km from Whakatane, is suitable even for people in wheelchairs and the elderly.

Other Activities Check with the visitor information centre about the wide variety of activities in and around Whakatane. Possibilities include hunting trips, horse treks, bushwalking, trout or sea fishing, diving and kayak trips, windsurfing, swimming and jet-boating. Motu River Rafting (☎ 308 5449) do white-water rafting trips on the Motu and other rivers, and parasailing in summer. Pohutukawa Tours (☎ 308 6495) operate a variety of half-day, full-day and overnight tours.

Places to Stay

The visitor information centre has an extensive list of homestays and farmstays in the area. Nearby Ohope Beach also has accommodation.

Camping & Cabins The *Whakatane Camping Ground & Caravan Park* (☎ 308 8694) in McGarvey Rd beside the Whakatane River has recreational facilities, a swimming pool and a spa pool. Tent or powered sites are $8 per person, cabins are $30, or tourist flats cost $39. The *Whakatane Motor Lodge Park* (☎ 308 5189), three km south of town off Valley Rd, has camp sites at $10 per person, and a motel-style lodge section with units from $50.

Hostels *Whakatane Backpackers Lodge* (☎ 308 0406), 11 Merritt St near the centre of town, is a friendly backpackers in a large old house. A dorm bed costs $14 or there are two doubles at $30. The Whakatane and Commercial hotels (see the next section) also have backpackers rooms.

Hotels The old art deco *Whakatane Hotel* (☎ 308 8199) on the Strand has dreary singles/doubles with shared facilities for $25/35 and a couple of basic rooms are set aside for backpackers at $12 per person. The rooms with private facilities for $35/45 are much better. The *Commercial* (☎ 308 7399), on Strand East, is a better class of pub but bands at the weekend can be very noisy. Singles/doubles cost $25/32 or $35/45 with attached bathroom, or backpackers rooms are $12 per person. The *Bay Hotel* (☎ 308 6788) at 90 McAllister St is a better private hotel/guesthouse with rooms from $40/46 (more with private bathroom).

Motels Most motels are on or just off Landing/Domain Rd. In the $60/70 range is the fading *Tourist Court Motel* (☎ 308 7099) and, opposite, the slightly better *NauMai Motel* (☎ 308 6422) and the slightly more expensive *Cortez Motor Inn* (☎ 308 4047). The *Camelia Court Motel* (☎ 308 6213) has more style and costs $70/78, while the newer and well-appointed *Alton Lodge* (☎ 308 5438) has a heated swimming pool and costs $85/95.

Places to Eat

Most of Whakatane's eating places are in the shopping area along the Strand. You can get an adequate meal at the *Wedgewood Food Court*, or *McDonald's* and *KFC* are both near the intersection of Commerce St and Domain Rd. Try *Bretto's*, in Boon St, for fish & chips or burgers with the lot, or the unfortunately named *Dago's Famous Pizzeria* for crusty pizza base adorned with the Super Special mix.

The *New Hong Kong Restaurant*, on Richardson St, has Chinese food, with a separate counter for takeaways straight back through the block in Boon St. You can get a hearty steak meal at the *Buccaneer Restaurant*, between the Quay and the Strand, and continental food at *Go Global*, on the corner of Commerce St and Shapley Place. The popular *Why Not Cafe*, in the Whakatane Hotel, has a better class of pub fare, while the licensed *Barnacles* has upmarket fish &

chips. *Cornell's Restaurant* in Commerce St has a well-priced, comprehensive menu, and the *Strand Cafe* has an innovative blackboard menu and some of the best fare in town.

Getting There & Away

Air Air New Zealand (☎ 0800 737 000) has daily flights linking Whakatane to Auckland and Wellington, with connections to other centres.

A taxi (☎ 0800 807 038) to and from the airport costs $20. There is no bus service.

Bus The InterCity bus depot (☎ 308 6169) is in Pyne St (Bay Coachlines). InterCity has buses connecting Whakatane with Rotorua and Gisborne, with connections to other places; all buses to Gisborne go via Opotiki. It's two hours to Tauranga or Rotorua, about an hour to Opotiki, and another 2½ hours from Opotiki to Gisborne via the Waioeka Gorge route (SH2). Buses around the East Cape originate from Opotiki and Gisborne (see Getting There & Away for the East Cape).

East Bay Connections (☎ 347 9200) run tours to the East Cape from Rotorua, with pick-up and drop-off in Whakatane. Rotorua to Whakatane return costs $45.

OHOPE BEACH

The town of Ohope and its fine beach is seven km 'over the hill' from Whakatane. It is a pleasant area in which to spend a few days, with all types of accommodation available, and there are a number of walks in the area. Halfway between Whakatane and Ohope **Itchykoo Park** offers grass skiing and tobogganing.

Places to Stay & Eat

The *Ohope Backpackers* (☎ 312 5173), 1A West End, has bunks for $14 or double rooms for $30. This place is a grand three-storey building near the beach and has fine sea views from the verandah.

There are two motor camps: *Ohope Beach Holiday Park* (☎ 312 4460), Harbour Rd, has sites for $10 per person, cabins for $32 and $36 for two and tourist flats for $50 for two. *Surf 'n Sand Holiday Park* (☎ 312 5884), on the beachfront in central Ohope, has sites for $9 per person, cabins from $30 for two and tourist flats for $52 for two. There are about eight motels, most of them along West End, costing about $65/75 for singles/doubles, and a number of homestays.

If you are after takeaway food, there is the *Pink Caddyshack*, and the *Ohope Beach Resort* is a hotel/motel with a restaurant.

WHITE ISLAND

White Island, or Whakaari, is New Zealand's most active volcano, smoking and steaming away just 50 km off the coast from Whakatane. It's a small island of 324 hectares formed by three separate volcanic cones, all of different ages. Erosion has worn away most of the surface of the two older cones and the youngest cone, which rose up between the two older ones, now occupies most of the centre of the island. Hot water and steam continually escape from vents over most of the crater floor, and temperatures of 600°C to 800°C have been recorded. The highest point on the island is Mt Gisborne at 321 metres. Geologically, White Island is related to Whale Island and Mt Putauaki (Edgecumbe), as they all lie along the same volcanic trench.

The island is privately owned and the only way you can land on it is with helicopter or boat tours which have arranged permission. The island has no jetty so boats have to land on the beach, which means that boat landings are not possible in rough seas. A visit to White Island is an unforgettable, if disconcerting, experience, but the constant rumblings and large plume of steam do not necessarily mean that the island is about to explode.

History

Before the arrival of Europeans the Maori caught sea birds on the island for food. In 1769 Captain Cook named it White Island because of the dense clouds of white steam hanging above it.

The first European to land on the island

was a missionary, the Reverend Henry Williams, in 1826. The island was acquired by Europeans in the late 1830s and changed ownership a number of times after that. Sulphur production began but was interrupted in 1885 by a minor eruption, and the following year the island was hurriedly abandoned in the wake of the Tarawera eruption. The island's sulphur industry was resumed in 1898 but only continued until 1901, when production ceased altogether.

In the 1910s further mining operations were attempted and abandoned due to mud flows and other volcanic activity, and ownership of the island continued to change. In 1953 White Island was declared a Private Scenic Reserve.

The island was at its most active between 1976 and 1981 when two new craters were formed and 100,000 cubic metres of rock was ejected.

Getting There & Away

Several operators take trips to White Island, and include a one or two-hour tour on foot around the island. A landing by boat is definitely weather dependent. Operators include the following:

Pee Jay (☎ 312 9075) has good tours on a 40-foot (12-metre) sportscruiser for $75 per person, including lunch.

Kahurangi (☎ 323 7829) offers a good five-hour trip in a 20-foot (six-metre) foil cat – $65 per person, minimum of four people.

Island Princess (☎ 312 4236) is a bigger boat catering to groups with tours for $60 (children $30). It also runs from Tauranga.

White Island Volcano Adventure (☎ 307 0663) offers 2½-hour helicopter flights for $280 per person, minimum of four people. This is the only sure way to be able to land on the island.

All trips incur a $10 landing fee, often not included in the quoted price.

MOUTOHORA

Moutohora, or Whale Island, so-called because of its shape, is nine km north of Whakatane and has an area of 414 hectares. It's another volcanic island, on the same volcanic trench as White Island, though much less active, and along its shore are hot springs which can reach 93°C. The summit is 350 metres high and the island has several historic sites including an ancient pa site, an old quarry and a camp.

Whale Island was settled by Maori before the 1769 landing by Captain Cook. In 1829 there was a Maori massacre of sailors from the trading vessel *Haweis* while it was anchored at Sulphur Bay, followed by an unsuccessful whaling venture in the 1830s. In the 1840s the island passed into European ownership and is still privately owned, although since 1965 it has been an officially protected wildlife refuge administered by DOC.

Whale Island is principally a haven for sea and shore birds, some of which are quite rare. Some of the birds use the island only for nesting at certain times of the year, while others are present all year round. The island has a large colony of grey-faced petrels, estimated to number 10,000.

The island's protected status means landing is restricted. Contact the Whakatane DOC office, and enquire about tours to the island operated at Christmas time.

WHAKATANE TO ROTORUA

Travelling along SH30 from Whakatane to Rotorua, the **Awakeri Hot Springs**, 16 km from Whakatane, has a hot springs, spa pools, picnic areas and a motor camp (☎ 304 9117).

Lying just off SH30, **Kawerau** is a timber town surrounded by pine forest and dependent on the huge Tasman Pulp & Paper Mill. Kawerau has an information centre (☎ 323 7550) on Plunket Street in the centre of town, and a selection of accommodation, but the only real reason to come here is to visit the waterfalls outside town.

Tawerau Falls are a half-hour drive from Kawerau along a well-graded road through the pine forests (watch out for the logging trucks). From the end of the road it is a 15-minute walk through native forest to the falls, which emerge from a hole in the canyon wall. The track continues another two hours up to the top of the falls and on to

Lake Tarawera – a good walk with views of the lake and Mt Tarawera.

Also near Kawerau, **Mt Putauaki (Edgecumbe)** is a commanding volcanic cone with panoramic views of the entire Bay of Plenty from the top. You need a permit to climb it; contact Tasman Forestry (☎ 323 4599).

OPOTIKI

Opotiki, the easternmost town of the Bay of Plenty, is the gateway to the East Cape and the rugged forests and river valleys of the Raukumara and nearby ranges. The town itself is nothing special, but many visitors stop over on the way to East Coast and there are some reasonable surf beaches, such as Ohiwa and Waiotahi, nearby.

The Opotiki area was settled from at least 1150, 200 years before the Great Migration. In the mid-1800s Opotiki was the centre of Hauhauism, a Maori doctrine advocating, amongst other things, the extermination of Europeans. In 1865 the Reverend Karl Volkner was murdered in his church, St Stephen the Martyr, which culminated in the church being transformed into a fortress by government troops.

Information

The Opotiki Visitor Information Centre (☎ 315 8484), on the corner of St John and Elliot Sts, is open Monday to Friday from 8.30 am to 4.30 pm. DOC (☎ 315 8484) has an office in the same building. The centre does bookings for a range of activities, and can organise visits to a local marae.

Hukutaia Domain

Just over seven km from Opotiki is the fascinating Hukutaia Domain, which has one of the finest collections of native plants in New Zealand, many of the species rare and endangered. One example, a puriri tree – named Taketakerau – is estimated to be over 2000 years old. The remains of the distinguished dead of the Upokorere sub-tribe of the Whakatohea were ritually buried beneath it. The tree is no longer tapu (sacred) as the bones of the dead have been reburied elsewhere.

Historical & Agricultural Society Museum

This small museum contains historic local items. Hours are extremely variable.

Activities

Dreamers and East-Capers (☎ 315 5577), opposite the visitor information centre in St John St, organise a variety of mountain-bike trips in the bush around Opotiki. Their single-track trip follows a scenic river valley and passes through patches of virgin bush – watch the slippery bridges or you will end up in the creek! They have a fully escorted trip on the Old Motu coach road which takes in awesome drops, native bush and breathtaking views. The six-day, five-night 'Search for the Source of the Sun' trip sees Tim and Paula fill their van up with mountain bikes, snorkelling gear, kayaks and fishing rods for your use – you stop where you like along the coastal road and do whatever takes your fancy. Discounts are given on all trips if you bring your own bike.

Places to Stay

Camping & Cabins The *Opotiki Holiday Park* (☎ 315 6050) on the corner of Grey St and Potts Ave has powered sites and tent sites for $8 per person, cabins cost $26 for two and tourist flats cost $38.

There are several beachfront camping grounds near Opotiki. The *Island View Family Holiday Park* (☎ 315 7519), on Appleton Rd, four km from town, has camp sites and cabins. The *Tirohanga Beach Motor Camp* (☎ 315 7942) on the East Coast Rd, six km from town, has camp sites, cabins and tourist flats. Also on the East Coast Rd, 12 km from Opotiki, the *Opape Motor Camp* (☎ 907) 315 8175) has camp sites and an on-site caravan.

Hostels *Central Oasis Backpackers* (☎ 315 5165), 30 King St, is in the centre of town in an old cottage. It's a friendly, small hostel with dorm beds for $12 and $14, doubles for $30. Out at Waiotahi Beach, about five minutes west of Opotiki, is the *Opotiki Backpackers Beach House* (☎ 315 5117). It is a

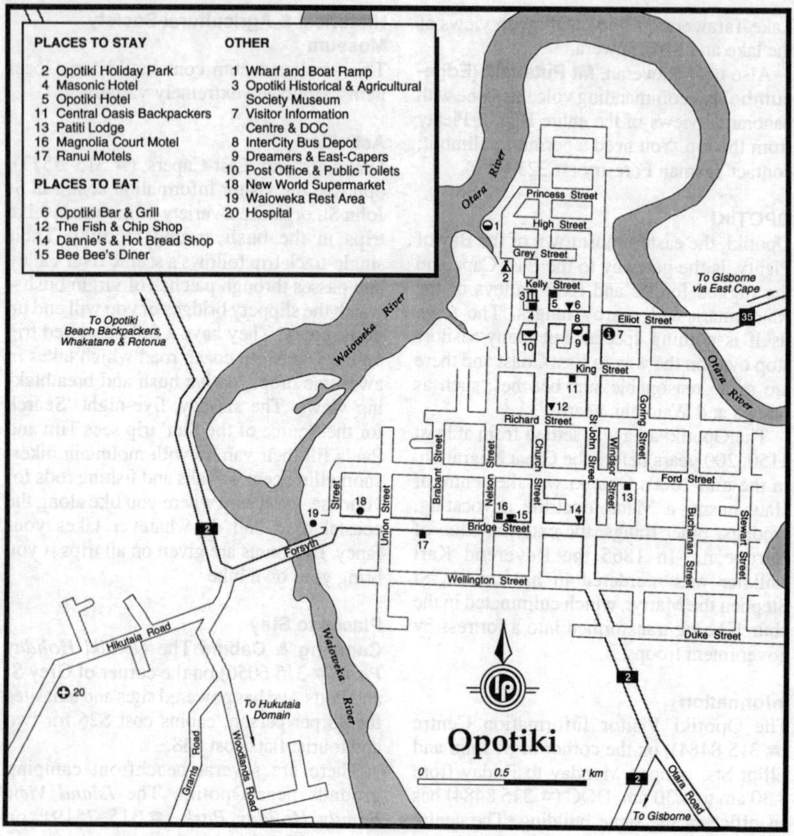

nice small place with adjoining kitchen and recreation room; the $12 beds are in the loft. It's right on the beach.

Hotels & Motels Opotiki has a couple of nondescript hotels with budget accommodation: the *Opotiki Hotel* (☎ 315 6078) in Church St and the *Masonic Hotel* (☎ 315 6115), also in Church St. The *Patiti Lodge Travel Hotel* (☎ 315 6834) at 112 Ford St has single/double rooms for $35/50; you can order meals here for extra.

The *Ranui Motel* (☎ 315 6669), at 36 Bridge St, has singles/doubles for $58/70, and the *Magnolia Court Motel* (☎ 315 8490), on the corner of Bridge and Nelson Sts, costs $64/72.

Places to Eat

Although not exactly gourmet capital of the Bay, Opotiki does have a small range of places to eat. *Dannie's & Hot Bread Shop*, near the corner of St John and Bridge Sts is a fast-food place; another is *The Fish & Chip Shop* on Church St for battered mussels & chips. For a hearty breakfast go to *Bee Bee's Diner* on Bridge St – they also serve full meals at other times of the day. The pubs have bistro meals and for Kiwi fare there is the *Opotiki Bar & Grill* on Elliott St. On Looney's Rd (I'm serious), out at Waiotahe, is the *Cottage Garden Cafe*, a place for afternoon and Devonshire teas.

Getting There & Away

Travelling east from Opotiki there are two routes to choose from. SH2 crosses the spectacular Waioeka Gorge. There are some fine walks of one day and longer in the Waioeka Gorge Scenic Reserve. The gorge gets progressively steeper and narrower as you travel inland, before the route crosses typically green, rolling hills, dotted with sheep, on the descent to Gisborne.

The other route east from Opotiki is SH35, around the East Cape, described fully in its own section.

The InterCity bus depot (☎ 315 6450) is on Elliott St. InterCity has daily buses connecting Opotiki with Whakatane (one hour), Rotorua (three hours), and Auckland (7½ hours via Rotorua). Heading south they connect Opotiki with Gisborne (two hours), Wairoa and Napier on Wednesday, Friday and Sunday.

The longer route to Gisborne (about eight hours), along the coast around the East Cape, is not serviced by regular bus but can be done by courier services (see the East Cape section in the East Coast chapter).

Central Plateau

The Central Plateau is at the heart of the North Island and is the centre of New Zealand's volcanic activity. New Zealand's main volcanic area, the Taupo Volcanic Zone, stretches in a line from White Island, north of the Bay of Plenty, through Rotorua and down to the Tongariro National Park.

The Central Plateau was at its most active some 2000 years ago. The remaining volcanoes do not match the destructive fury of some of the world's other hot spots, but still put on spectacular shows from time to time. Most recently, in 1995, Mt Ruapehu in Tongariro National Park exploded in a series of eruptions, spewing forth rock and billowing clouds of ash and steam.

Taupo is the main resort town of this volcanic plateau and lies on large Lake Taupo, itself a remnant of a massive volcanic explosion. Taupo caters for a whole range of tastes, from trout fishing to bungy jumping. The plateau extends south to the majestic, snow-capped volcanoes in the Tongariro National Park, one of New Zealand's premier parks with many fine walks.

The telephone area code for all places listed in this chapter is 07, except for those on the southern edge of Tongariro National Park – Ohakune and Waiouru – where telephone numbers are preceded by 06.

HIGHLIGHTS

- Tongariro National Park, dominated by smoking Mt Ruapehu. The park's many fine walks include the famous Tongariro Crossing and the Northern Circuit
- Lake Taupo for trout fishing or boating
- Wairekei Park and its thermal regions
- Skiing at Whakapapa and Turoa
- Tandem skydiving or bungy jumping at Taupo

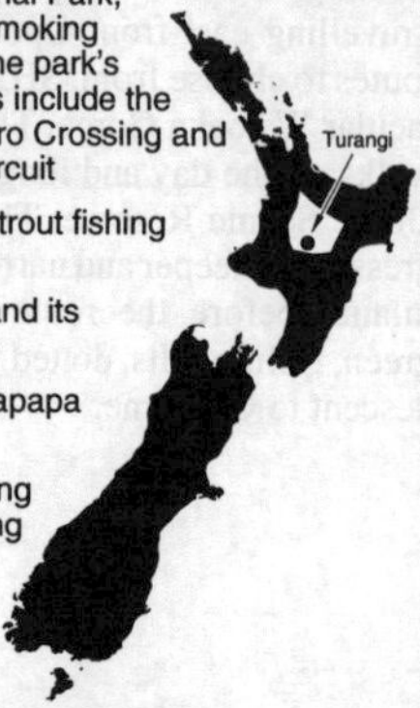

Lake Taupo

New Zealand's largest lake, Lake Taupo, is in the very heart of the North Island.

Lake Taupo, 606 sq km in area and 357 metres above sea level, was formed by one of the greatest volcanic explosions the world has experienced. Historical chronicles of darkened skies in the daytime and blood-red sunsets were recorded in around 186 AD in places as faraway as China and Rome, and are believed to refer to the effects of the Taupo explosion in the atmosphere. Pumice from this explosion is found as far away as Napier and Gisborne and forms a layer – in some places just one cm thick, in others metres – over a vast area of the central North Island. The area is still volcanically active and, as in Rotorua, thermal areas can be visited.

Today serene Lake Taupo is claimed to be the world's trout fishing capital. If you

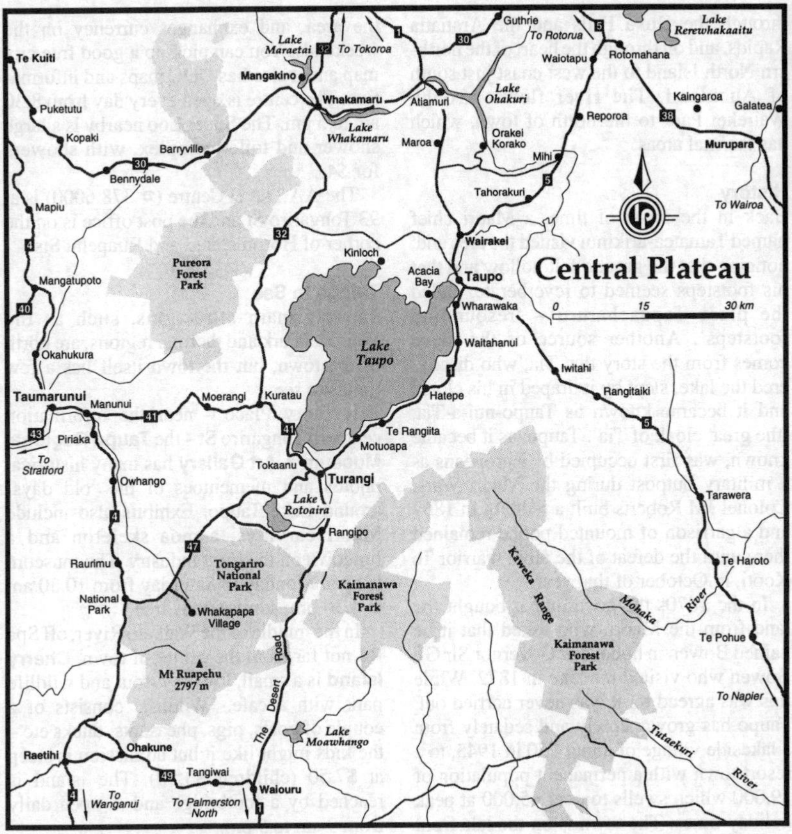

thought those trout in the Rotorua springs looked large and tasty, they're nothing compared to the monsters found in Lake Taupo. All of New Zealand's rainbow trout are descended from a single batch of eggs brought from California's Russian River nearly a century ago. International trout-fishing tournaments are held in Lake Taupo each year on Anzac weekend, on or around 25 April.

Taupo is the tourist centre of the region and Turangi, further south, is noted for its excellent fishing and is a stopover point on the way to Tongariro National Park.

TAUPO

Taupo (population 19,000) lies on the north-east corner of Lake Taupo with scenic views stretching across the lake to the volcanic peaks of the Tongariro National Park. This relaxed resort is the main town of the area and makes a good base to explore its attractions. Many activities can be done in Taupo, ranging from fishing and boating on the lake, to adrenaline-pumping bungy jumping and skydiving.

Lake Taupo is also the source of the longest river in New Zealand, the Waikato, which leaves the lake at the township, flows through the Huka Falls and the Aratiatia Rapids, and on through the heart of the northern North Island to the west coast just south of Auckland. The river flows through Wairekei Park to the north of town, which has thermal areas.

History

Back in the mists of time, a Maori chief named Tamatea-arikinui visited the area and, noticing that the ground felt hollow and that his footsteps seemed to reverberate, called the place Tapuaeharuru – 'resounding footsteps'. Another source of the name comes from the story that Tia, who discovered the lake, slept by it draped in his cloak, and it became known as Taupo-nui-a-Tia, 'the great cloak of Tia'. Taupo, as it became known, was first occupied by Europeans as a military outpost during the Maori Wars. Colonel JM Roberts built a redoubt in 1869 and a garrison of mounted police remained there until the defeat of the rebel warrior Te Kooti, in October of that year.

In the 1870s the government bought the land from the Maori, who asked that it be named Bowen in honour of Governor Sir GF Bowen who visited the lake in 1872. While this was agreed to, it was never carried out. Taupo has grown slowly and sedately from a lakeside village of about 750 in 1945, to a resort town with a permanent population of 19,000 which swells to over 45,000 at peak holiday times. The town is on the lakefront where SH1, the main road from the north, first meets the lake.

A fascinating book about Taupo's history is *The Remotest Interior – A History of Taupo* by Barbara Cooper, tracing the area's history from the violent volcanic formation of the lake and volcanoes, to when Taupo was considered 'the remotest interior' of the North Island, and up to modern times.

Information

The Taupo Information Centre (☎ 378 9000; fax 378 9003), on Tongariro St near the corner of Heu Heu St, has full information and handles bookings for all accommodation, transport, activities and attractions in the area, and exchanges currency on the weekends. You can pick up a good free city map and it also has DOC maps and information. The centre is open every day from 8.30 am to 5 pm. The Super Loo nearby is a large shower and toilet complex, with showers for $4.

The AA Travel Centre (☎ 378 6000) is at 93 Tongariro St and the post office is on the corner of Horomatangi and Ruapehu Sts.

Things to See

Taupo's main attractions, such as the Wairekei Park and thermal regions, are north of the town, but the town itself has a few things to see.

In Story Place – near the information centre in Tongariro St – the **Taupo Regional Museum & Art Gallery** has many historical photos and mementoes of the 'old days' around Lake Taupo. Exhibits also include Maori carvings, a moa skeleton and a rundown on the trout industry. The museum is open Monday to Saturday from 10.30 am to 4.30 pm; admission is free.

In the middle of the Waikato River, off Spa Rd not far from the centre of town, **Cherry Island** is a small, low-key trout and wildlife park with a cafe. 'Wildlife' consists of a couple of goats, pigs, pheasants, ducks etc – the kids might like it but admission is steep at $7.50 (children $3.50). The island is reached by a footbridge and is open daily from 9 am to 5 pm.

Right near Cherry Island is the **Taupo Bungy** site where jumpers leap off a platform jutting 20 metres out over a cliff and hurtle down towards the Waikato River, 45 metres below. If you don't want to jump, it is a scenic spot with plenty of vantage points for a good view of the jumpers.

On Spa Rd, next to the Spa Hotel, **Spa Dinosaur Valley** is Taupo's answer to Jurassic Park with giant concrete dinosaurs to impress the kids. It is open 10 am to 4 pm; entry is $5 (children $3). **Trainsville**, upstairs at 35A Heu Heu St, is a model railway exhibition in a shop for model trains and aeroplanes; the cost is $3 (children $1.50).

Under the SH1 bridge over the Waikato River in Taupo are control gates regulating the level of Lake Taupo and the amount of flow down the Waikato River through its string of hydroelectric power stations. Just up the hill from here is the turn-off to **Acacia Bay**, a pleasant, peaceful beach a little over five km west of Taupo. There's a short walk from here to Little Acacia Bay.

Activities

Taupo doesn't have any swim-with-the-trout experiences yet, but it has just about every other activity.

Thermal Pools The AC Thermal Baths (☎ 378 7321), at the top of Spa Rd, about two km east of the town centre, has a big, heated swimming pool with a waterslide, private mineral pools and a sauna. It's open from 8 am to 9.30 pm every day. Admission is $4 (children $2), saunas are $4 and the waterslide $3.

The De Brett Thermal Pools (☎ 378 8559) are on the Taupo-Napier Highway (SH5), one km from the lake. There are also large outdoor pools, a big hot waterslide, and private pools. The pools are open from 8 am to 9.30 pm daily and admission is $5 (children $3). Private pools are $6 per person.

Lake Cruises Three boats specialise in cruises on the lake: the *Barbary*, the *Spirit of Musick* and the *Ernest Kemp*. The *Barbary*, built in 1926, is a 15-metre ocean-going racing yacht once owned by Errol Flynn. 'Barbary Bill', the skipper, is much loved by tourists and locals alike and his trip is probably the most popular. The *Spirit of Musick* is an elegant 44-foot (13-metre) ketch. The *Ernest Kemp* is a different kind of boat, a replica 1920s steam ferry.

All three boats offer similar cruises, visiting a modern Maori rock carving beside the lake. The carving is on private land so it cannot be reached by foot; the only way to see it is by boat. All three boats offer morning, afternoon and evening cruises in summer. The cruises last about 2½ to three hours; the cost is $20 (children $10) on all boats. All the boats leave from the wharves at the Taupo Boat Harbour, off Redoubt Rd. Bookings for all the cruises can be made at the Taupo Information Centre or at the launch office by the wharves (☎ 378 3444). You may receive a discount if you book through a hostel.

Fishing A number of fishing guides and charter boats operate in Taupo; check with the information centre. A trip costs about $60 per person. Boats can also be hired from the launch office (☎ 378 3444), starting at $65 per hour for a whole boat taking up to six people, up to around $120 per hour for the larger boats. The hostels also book fishing boat trips. Count on a fishing trip lasting around two or three hours. If you go on a boat trip they'll supply all the gear, and you can get your fishing licence through them.

Taupo is world-famous for its trout fly fishing. Fly fishing is the only kind you can do on all rivers flowing into the lake, and in a 300-metre radius of the river mouths. Spin fishing is allowed on the Waikato River (flowing *out* of the lake) and on the Tokaanu tail race, flowing into the lake from the Tokaanu Power Station. On the lake, both spin fishing and fly fishing are allowed. Several fly fishing guides operate around Taupo, some of them very good, but the price is not cheap – around $200 a day, everything included.

If you're going it on your own, Bob Sullivan's Taupo Sports Depot (☎ 378 5337) on Tongariro St by the waterfront and the Fly & Gun Shop (☎ 378 4449) on Heu Heu St have fishing tackle for hire.

Fishing licences are available from the information centre, or from the launch office at the harbour. Fishing licences for fishing on Lake Taupo and the nearby rivers cost $9 per day, $22.50 per week, $30.50 per month or $46.50 for the entire year (1 July to 30 June). A special tourist fishing licence, valid for one month anywhere in New Zealand, costs $56, but you can only get it from the Tourism Rotorua office in Rotorua.

Any time you go fishing, be certain you have your fishing licence and that you obey

Trout

The Department of Conservation (DOC) operates three trout hatcheries in New Zealand – one in Wanaka in the South Island, one near Rotorua and one in Turangi. The Wanaka hatchery is more for salmon than trout, while the two North Island hatcheries are almost exclusively for rainbow trout. There are other private hatcheries, some of which obtain their eggs from the DOC operations.

The first brown trout eggs arrived in New Zealand from Tasmania in 1867. They had originally come to Australia from England. Rainbow trout eggs first arrived from California in 1883. Hatcheries were established at that time to rear the first young fish, and although many fish are hatched naturally nowadays, there is still a need for artificial hatcheries. This is because New Zealand's lakes and rivers may be ideal for trout but some of them have insufficient good spawning grounds. Plus there's a lot of fishing going on (although there are tight limitations on the number of fish that can be caught).

In the wild, fully grown trout migrate each winter to suitable spawning beds. This usually means gravel beds in the upper reaches of rivers and streams. Here a female fish makes a shallow depression and deposits eggs which are quickly fertilised by an attendant male fish. The female fish then sweeps gravel over the eggs. Over two or three days this process is repeated to create a redd with several pockets of eggs. All through this process the fish do not feed and a female fish may lose one-third of her body weight by the time she returns to the lake. Male fish are in even worse shape because they arrive at the spawning grounds before the females and leave afterwards.

Less than one per cent of the eggs survive to become mature fish. The eggs may be damaged or destroyed by gravel movement and even when hatched they may be eaten by other fish, birds or rats. Even other trout will happily make a meal of them.

Because there were only a few shipments of eggs, from which all of today's trout are descended, New Zealand's rainbow trout are considered to be a very pure strain. The hatchery eggs are collected by capturing fish during their spawning run. Eggs are gently squeezed from a female fish and milt from males added and stirred together in a container. Incubator trays containing about 10,000 eggs are placed in racks and washed over by a continuous flow of water.

After 15 days the embryos' eyes start to appear and by the 18th day the embryos, previously very sensitive and frail, have become quite hardy. They need to be because on that day the eggs are poured from a metre height into a wire basket. Any weak eggs are killed off by this rough treatment, ensuring that only healthy fish are hatched out. The survivors are now placed 5000 to a basket and about 10 days later the fish hatch out, wriggle through the mesh and drop to the bottom of the trough. They stay there for about 20 days, living off the yolk sac.

When they have totally absorbed their yolk sac they are known as fry and although they can be released at this stage they are normally kept until they are 10 to 15 cm long. At this time they are nine to 12 months old and are known as fingerlings. They are moved outside when they are about four cm long and reared in ponds. Fingerlings are transported to the place where they will be released in what looks rather like a small petrol tanker, and simply pumped out the back down a large diameter pipe! ■

all the rules listed on it. Fishing is taken very seriously around these parts, and there are fines of thousands of dollars for violation of fishing regulations.

Kayaks, Canoes & Boats The Acacia Bay Lodge (☎ 378 6830) at 868 Acacia Bay Rd in Acacia Bay hires motorboats at $24 per hour, rowing boats and Canadian canoes at $12 per hour, and kayaks at $10 per hour. It takes about one hour to go from there to the Maori rock carvings in a motorboat.

The Sail Centre (☎ 378 3299) at Two Mile Bay, south of Taupo, hires Canadian canoes, windsurfers, catamarans and sailboats in the summer. Bruce Webber Adventures (☎ 378 4715) has a very good name for his kayak school and kayaking trips. A guided two-hour trip on the Waikato River costs $25.

During summer there are lots of activities

on Lake Taupo including swimming, water skiing, windsurfing, paragliding and sailing. The information centre has details on all of them. Gear can be hired at the lakefront.

Several white-water rafting companies operate from Taupo with one-day trips on the Tongariro and Rangitaiki rivers, longer trips on other rivers. Book these trips through the hostels or the information centre.

Bungy Jumping The bungy jump in Taupo is the most popular in the North Island, largely because of its scenic setting on the cliffs of the Waikato River right in the town. The cost for a jump is $85 but there is a bewildering array of discounts for groups, certain hostels, certain buses that you arrived on, or whatever. The Taupo Bungy office (☎ 377 1135) is open every day from 9 am to 5 pm.

Tandem Skydiving This is another of Taupo's popular adrenaline-rush activities. In addition to the skydiving itself, offered at the cheapest rate in NZ, you get a brilliant view over Lake Taupo and the entire region. Vaughan Brady's Taupo Tandems (☎ (025) 428 688) does tandem skydiving trips for $165.

Aerial Sightseeing & Gliding You can go for a scenic flight on the floatplane (☎ 378 7500) next to Taupo Boat Harbour; a number of operators also go from the airport. They all offer similar flights for similar prices, ranging upwards from about $30 for a short flight around the Taupo area to about $120 for flights across Lake Taupo and Tongariro National Park.

Helistar Helicopters (☎ 374 8405), with an office and helipad on the Huka Falls Rd north of town, offers a variety of scenic helicopter flights including a 10-minute flight over Taupo for $75 per person.

The Taupo Gliding Club (☎ 378 5627) goes gliding all day Sunday and every Wednesday afternoon (when the weather is suitable) at Centennial Park on Centennial Drive, about five km up Spa Rd from the centre, out past the AC Baths. A gliding trip starts at about $40.

Horse Trekking Taupo Horse Treks (☎ 378 0356) based on Karapiti Rd (the road leading to Craters of the Moon) has a good reputation for their treks – they're off-road, through some fine forest with good views over the Craters of the Moon area. One hour costs $20, two hours is $35.

Huka Village Riding Centre at Huka Village also do horse riding along the road.

Mini-Golf Taupo Mini-Golf on the lakefront is open every day from 9 am until late; the cost is $5.50 (children $3).

Walks You can walk all the way from Taupo to Aratiatia. From the centre of town head up Spa Rd by Woolworth's, passing by the Taupo Bungy site. Turn left at County Ave and continue through Spa Thermal Park at the end of the street, past the skateboard bowl and over the hill, following the rough roadway to the left until you hit the track.

The track follows the river to Huka Falls crossing a hot stream and riverside marshes en route. It's about a one to 1½-hour walk from the centre of Taupo to Huka Falls, depending on your walking speed. From Huka Falls you can cross the footbridge along the seven-km Taupo Walkway to Aratiatia (another two to 2½ hours). There are good views of the river, Huka Falls, and the power station across the river. It's easy walking.

If you're going to Craters of the Moon as well, you can make it a round trip, using the walkway in one direction between Taupo and Aratiatia, and the road in the other.

Another walk worth mentioning is Mt Tauhara, with magnificent views from the top. Take the Taupo-Napier Highway (SH5) turn-off, two km south of the Taupo town centre. About six km along SH5, turn left into Mountain Rd. The start of the track is sign-posted on the right-hand side. It will take about two hours to get to the top, walking slowly.

A pleasant walkway goes along the lake-front to the south of town all the way from the Taupo lakefront to Four Mile Bay. It's a flat, easy walk along public-access beaches. Heading south from Taupo, there's a hot water beach on the way to Two Mile Bay. At Two Mile Bay the walkway connects with the Lions Walk, going from Two Mile Bay (3.2 km south of Taupo) to Four Mile Bay (6.4 km). Anywhere along here you can easily get back to SH1, the lakeside road.

There are plenty of other good walks and tramps in the area, including river, lake, forest and mountain walks. Pick up a copy of the *Walking Trails* booklet for $2 from the Taupo Information Centre.

Tours

Walter's Backpackers Tours are run by a delightful, spry old fellow who is also Taupo's radio weatherman and foremost cyclist. He does three-hour tours of the local sights (Huka Falls, Aratiatia, Craters of the Moon, Mt Tauhara and so on) for $20, plus full-day trips further afield to Tongariro National Park for $40 and Waitomo Caves for $50. Book directly with him (☎ 378 5924), through the hostels, or through the information centre.

Paradise Tours (☎ 378 9955) does 2½ hour tours to the Aratiatia Rapids, Geothermal Information Centre, Craters of the Moon and Huka Falls for $24 (children $10). Rapid Sensations (☎ 378 7902) does guided three-hour mountain-bike tours through the geothermal areas for $45. The Double Decker Bus (☎ 377 0774) does 2½-hour tours from the information centre to Wairakei Park for $15 (children $7) but departures are irregular.

Places to Stay

Camping & Cabins Camping is free beside the river at Reid's Farm about 1.5 km south of the Huka Falls towards Taupo.

The *Taupo Motor Camp* (☎ 377 3080) is on Redoubt St by the river, right near the centre of town. It has tent and powered sites at $9 per person, cabins at $25/35 for one/two people, and on-site caravans at $40 for two. Rates are lower outside the January holidays.

Taupo Cabins (☎ 378 4346) at 50 Tonga St doesn't have camping but has a variety of cabins. The cheapest and most basic are $12 per person, tourist cabins with cooking facilities are $35 and self-contained tourist flats are $45. Bedding and towels can be hired.

The *All Seasons Holiday Park* (☎ 378 4272) is at 16 Rangatira St, on the corner of Matipo St. It, too, is about 1.5 km from the centre. It has a hot thermal pool and a variety of accommodation including tent and powered sites at $9 per person, standard cabins and rooms in a 40-bed lodge at $12 per person, tourist cabins at $35 for two, and tourist flats at $45 for two.

The *De Brett Thermal Resort* (☎ 378 8559) is beside the De Brett Thermal Pools, one km from the lake on SH5, the Taupo-Napier Rd. Camp sites are $9 per person, leisure lodges are $60 for two, and motel-style units are $48 for two.

The *Hilltop Motor Caravan Park* (☎ 378 5247) at 39 Puriri St, off Taharepa Rd, has hot mineral spas and a cold swimming pool. Tent sites are $7 to $8 per person, caravan sites $1 extra, and cabins and on-site caravans are $37 for two.

The *Lake Taupo Holiday Park* (☎ 378 6860) is on Centennial Drive off Spa Rd, opposite the AC Thermal Baths and the Taupo Golf Club. It's a seven-hectare park with tent and caravan sites at $8 per person, family cabins at $35 for two and tourist flats at $45 for two.

Great Lake Holiday Park (☎ 378 5159) on Acacia Bay Rd, three km west of the town centre, has tent and powered sites at $9 per person, cabins at $26 for two, on-site caravans at $33 for two and tourist flats at $49 for two.

The *Windsor Lodge & Caravan Park* (☎ 378 6271) at Waitahanui, 12 km south of Taupo on SH1, has camp sites at $15 for two, cabins at $20/25 for one/two people, and two-bedroom motel units at $55 for two.

Hostels Taupo has a good range of hostels, offering extras including breakfast, free coffee, bicycles etc. Price wars have seen dorm beds drop to as low as $10. Several of Taupo's hostels, particularly the Rainbow and Sunset Lodges, arrange a host of activities at significantly discounted prices.

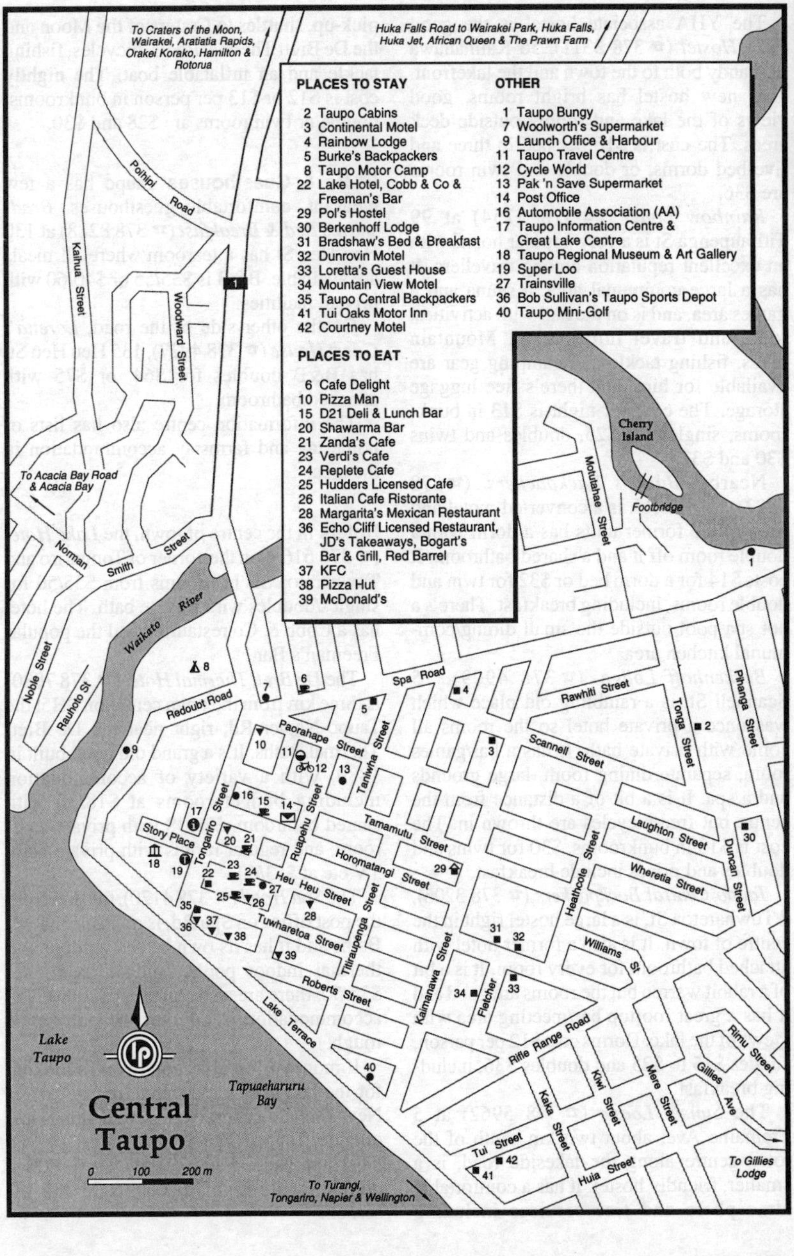
Central Taupo
PLACES TO STAY
2 Taupo Cabins
3 Continental Motel
4 Rainbow Lodge
5 Burke's Backpackers
8 Taupo Motor Camp
22 Lake Hotel, Cobb & Co & Freeman's Bar
29 Pol's Hostel
30 Berkenhoff Lodge
31 Bradshaw's Bed & Breakfast
32 Dunrovin Motel
33 Loretta's Guest House
34 Mountain View Motel
35 Taupo Central Backpackers
41 Tui Oaks Motor Inn
42 Courtney Motel
PLACES TO EAT
6 Cafe Delight
10 Pizza Man
15 D21 Deli & Lunch Bar
20 Shawarma Bar
21 Zanda's Cafe
23 Verdi's Cafe
24 Replete Cafe
25 Hudders Licensed Cafe
26 Italian Cafe Ristorante
28 Margarita's Mexican Restaurant
36 Echo Cliff Licensed Restaurant, JD's Takeaways, Bogart's Bar & Grill, Red Barrel
37 KFC
38 Pizza Hut
39 McDonald's
OTHER
1 Taupo Bungy
7 Woolworth's Supermarket
9 Launch Office & Harbour
11 Taupo Travel Centre
12 Cycle World
13 Pak 'n Save Supermarket
14 Post Office
16 Automobile Association (AA)
17 Taupo Information Centre & Great Lake Centre
18 Taupo Regional Museum & Art Gallery
19 Super Loo
27 Trainsville
36 Bob Sullivan's Taupo Sports Depot
40 Taupo Mini-Golf
To Craters of the Moon, Wairakei, Aratiatia Rapids, Orakei Korako, Hamilton & Rotorua
Huka Falls Road to Wairakei Park, Huka Falls, Huka Jet, African Queen & The Prawn Farm
To Acacia Bay Road & Acacia Bay
To Turangi, Tongariro, Napier & Wellington
To Gillies Lodge
Poihipi Road
Kaihua Street
Woodward Street
Norman Smith Street
Waikato River
Noble Street
Rauhoto St
Redoubt Road
Spa Road
Paorahape Street
Taniwha Street
Story Place
Tongariro Street
Ruapehu Street
Tamamutu Street
Horomatangi Street
Heu Heu Street
Tuwharetoa Street
Titiraupenga Street
Roberts Street
Lake Terrace
Rawhiti Street
Tonga Street
Pihanga Street
Scannell Street
Heathcote Street
Laughton Street
Duncan Street
Wheretia Street
Williams St
Kaimanawa Street
Fletcher
Rifle Range Road
Kiwi Street
Kaka Street
Mere Street
Rimu Street
Gillies Ave
Tui Street
Huia Street
Mututahae Street
Cherry Island
Footbridge
Lake Taupo
Tapuaeharuru Bay
0 100 200 m

The YHA associate hostel is the good *Pol's Hostel* (☎ 378 3311), 56 Kaimanawa St, handy both to the town and the lakefront. This new hostel has bright rooms, good views of the lake and roomy outside deck areas. The cost is $16 per bed in three and five-bed dorms, or double and twin rooms are $36.

Rainbow Lodge (☎ 378 5754) at 99 Titiraupenga St is a very popular hostel with an excellent reputation among travellers. It has a large communal area, a sauna and a games area, and is on the ball with activities, tours and travel information. Mountain bikes, fishing tackle and camping gear are available for hire, and there's free luggage storage. The cost per night is $13 in bunkrooms, singles are $25, doubles and twins $30 and $32.

Nearby, *Burke's Backpackers* (☎ 378 9292), 69 Spa Rd, is a converted motel and each of the former units has a dorm with a double room off it and a shared bathroom. It costs $14 for a dorm bed or $32 for twin and double rooms, including breakfast. There's a hot spa pool outside the small dining/communal kitchen area.

Berkenhoff Lodge (☎ 378 4909), 75 Scannell St, is a rambling old place which was once a private hotel so the rooms all come with private bath. It has a bar/games room, separate dining room, large grounds and a spa. It is a bit of a distance from the centre but free bicycles are thrown in. The cost is $13 in bunkrooms, $30 for twins and doubles and prices include breakfast.

Taupo Central Backpackers (☎ 378 3206), 7 Tuwharetoa St, is a large hostel right in the centre of town. It is also a former hotel with attached bathroom for every room. It is a bit of a rabbit warren but the rooms are good and it has a great rooftop bar/meeting area with views of the lake. Dorms cost $12 per person, singles $15 to $25 and doubles $36, including breakfast.

The *Sunset Lodge* (☎ 378 5962) at 5 Tremaine Ave, about two km south of the town centre along the lakeside road, is a smaller, friendly hostel. It has a comfortable atmosphere and free services including pick-up, shuttles to Craters of the Moon and the De Brett Thermal Pools, bicycles, fishing tackle and an inflatable boat. The nightly cost is $12 or $13 per person in bunkrooms; double or twin rooms are $28 and $30.

B&Bs & Guesthouses Taupo has a few pleasant, comfortable guesthouses. *Bradshaw's Bed & Breakfast* (☎ 378 8288) at 130 Heu Heu St has a tearoom where all meals are available. B&B is $35/55 or $40/60 with private facilities.

On the other side of the road, *Loretta's Guest House* (☎ 378 4927), 135 Heu Heu St, has B&B doubles for $64, or $75 with attached bathroom.

The information centre also has lists of homestay and farmstay accommodation in the area.

Hotels In the centre of town, the *Lake Hotel* (☎ 378 6165) on the corner of Tongariro and Tuwharetoa Sts has rooms from $35/50 for singles/doubles with private bath. The hotel has a Cobb & Co restaurant and the popular Freeman's Bar.

The *De Brett Thermal Hotel* (☎ 378 7080) is three km from the town centre on SH5, the Taupo-Napier Rd, right near the De Brett Thermal Baths. It's a grand old hotel built in 1889, with a variety of accommodation including budget rooms at $18/30 with shared bathroom, $28/38 with private bathroom, and regular rooms with private bath, TV etc at $53/60.

The *Spa Hotel* (☎ 378 4120), two km from the post office on Spa Rd, is opposite the AC Baths and it has its own heated outdoor and thermal indoor pools. Budget rooms are $35/50; there are also chalets at $60/80. The accommodation is OK but the pub bar is rough.

If money is no object and you're looking for the height of understated luxury, one of New Zealand's most expensive hotels is just outside Taupo. The *Huka Lodge* (☎ 378 5791) at Huka Falls costs over $1000 a double, with slight discounts in the off season.

Motels Taupo is packed with motels and, as in Rotorua, the competition tends to keep prices down, though many of them have minimum rates during holiday periods. Economical, good-value motels include the *Dunrovin Motel* (☎ 378 7384) at 140 Heu Heu St, a '50s-style motel with a classic '50s name. It's basic but smart and singles/doubles cost $49/65. The *Continental Motel* (☎ 378 5836) at 9 Scannell St on the corner of Motutaiko St and the *Golf Course Motel* (☎ 378 9415) at 123 Tauhara Rd are similarly priced.

The *Courtney Motel* (☎ 378 8398) at 15 Tui St has a variety of units including studios from $60, and one, two and three-bedroom units at $78 for two and $12 for each extra person. The *Mountain View Motel* (☎ 378 9366) at 12-14 Fletcher St has singles at $45, doubles from $56 to $81.

The better motels line the lakefront along Lake Terrace. Typical of these is the *Tui Oaks Motor Inn* (☎ 378 8305) on the corner with Tui St. It a more modern, well-appointed motel with doubles from $85 to $120.

Places to Eat

Self-Catering The huge *Pak 'n Save* and *Woolworth's* supermarkets are open seven days a week.

Snacks & Fast Food Taupo has the usual collection of sandwich places and takeaway bars. Down by the lakefront are a *Pizza Hut*, *KFC* and a *McDonald's*. Also along here is *Maxi's Diner*, a 24-hour greasy spoon place with inexpensive burgers, grills and breakfasts. On Tongariro St near the lakefront, *JD's Takeaways* does good fish & chips. The *Shawarma Bar* at 3 Horomatangi St has a selection of inexpensive middle eastern food, with vegetarian and meat selections – it's primarily a takeaway, but you can eat there.

The city centre has plenty of day-time cafes for a coffee and snack or a light meal. *Zanda's Cafe* has inexpensive food with both vegetarian and meat selections. It's in the Marama walking arcade between Heu Heu and Horomatangi Sts. On Horomatangi St, the *D21 Deli & Lunch Bar* has a wide selection of sandwiches and snacks to eat there or take away. On Heu Heu St, *Verdi's Cafe* is slightly expensive but has excellent coffee, as does the very popular, in-vogue *Replete Cafe* a few doors along.

Over on Spa Rd, *Cafe Delight* behind Woolworth's is good for breakfast and lunch. Opposite, the *Pizza Man* is popular for pizzas and has a selection of $5 meals (pasta, nachos and squid rings) to take away or eat there – phone for free delivery (☎ 378 3400) on orders of $15 or more.

Pub Food There's a *Cobb & Co* in the Lake Hotel on the corner of Tongariro and Tuwharetoa Sts, open from 7.30 am to 10 pm daily with the usual steaks, salad bar etc.

The *Red Barrel*, the popular restaurant/pub on the lakefront, serves bar meals. Nearby on the lake end of Tongariro St, *Bogart's Bar & Grill* has a menu featuring steak and other dishes.

Restaurants *Margarita's* at 63 Heu Heu St is a popular restaurant/bar with good Mexican food and decor. Regular dinner main courses are $12 to $19 but you can order from the special $5 backpackers menu. There are a few not-so-Mexican selections on the menu too. Margarita's is open every day from 4 pm to 2 am, and can be a lively drinking hole.

Hudders Licensed Cafe at 22 Tuwharetoa St is a small licensed and BYO restaurant featuring an eclectic menu, giant portions and various specials. It's a very popular place to drink as much as to eat.

A few doors from Hudders, the *Italian Cafe Ristorante* has a good selection of pizzas and pastas for around $16. The blackboard specials offer excellent, authentic Italian dishes such as scaloppine. It's not cheap but very good.

Just around the corner on the Tongariro St side, the *Echo Cliff Licensed Restaurant* is a more upmarket restaurant with a good view over the lake; count on spending around $25 for a three-course meal.

If you're going upmarket, the *Edgewater Restaurant* on the lakefront is an elegant and expensive but top-notch restaurant specialising in New Zealand food. Also situated there is *Peppers Brasserie*, a more reasonably priced family restaurant. Both restaurants have a fine view of the lake, which is especially beautiful around sunset.

Entertainment

The *Great Lake Centre* (☎ 377 1200) on Tongariro St has a theatre and hall for performances, exhibitions, conventions and events of all kinds. The information centre will have the current schedule.

The *Red Barrel* on the lakefront near Tongariro St is a lively pub, good for socialising and dancing. It has live bands for dancing on Wednesday, Friday and Saturday nights.

Around the corner on the lake end of Tongariro St, *Bogart's Bar & Grill* is another pleasant hang-out. Further along on Tongariro St at the corner of Tuwharetoa St, *Freeman's Bar* has live bands for dancing on Thursday, Friday and Saturday nights.

De Brett's Thermal Hotel, three km from the centre and one km back from the lake on SH5, has a homestyle country & western band in the lounge bar on Thursday nights; the atmosphere is casual and friendly and anyone can come and sit in for a song. On weekends there is other live music.

The *Spa Hotel*, two km east of the town centre along Spa Rd, has live bands every Friday and Saturday night. The Spa is the place to go if you've been kicked out of every other hotel in town and want to drink beer by the jug.

Getting There & Away

Air Air New Zealand and Mt Cook Airline (☎ (0800) 800 737) have direct flights to Auckland, Christchurch, Rotorua and Wellington, with connections to other centres.

Neither of these airlines has an office in town; their offices are at the airport. In town, their ticketing is handled through travel agencies, including the AA Travel Centre (see Information), Budget Travel (☎ 378 9799) at 37 Horomatangi St, and the James Holiday Shoppe (☎ 378 7065) in the same block of Horomatangi St.

Bus Taupo is about halfway between Auckland and Wellington. Being at the geographical centre of the island, it's a hub for bus transport.

InterCity, Newmans and Alpine Scenic Tours arrive and depart from the Taupo Travel Centre (☎ 378 9032) at 16 Gascoigne St. The travel centre also sells tickets for trains and the Interislander ferry.

InterCity and Newmans have several daily buses to Turangi (45 minutes), Auckland (four hours), Hamilton (two hours), Rotorua (one to 1½ hours), Tauranga (2½ hours), Napier (two hours), Wanganui (five hours), Palmerston North (3½ hours) and Wellington (6½ hours).

Alpine Scenic Tours (☎ 378 6305) operates a daily shuttle service between Taupo and Turangi. Take the 9 am bus from Taupo to connect with their other shuttle service going from Turangi to National Park at 11 am. This includes several stops in the Tongariro National Park, including the walking tracks. There's also a Monday to Friday shuttle service between Turangi and Rotorua, stopping in Taupo on the way.

Mount Cook Landline stop in Taupo on their daily run between Auckland and Wellington. Their buses stop at the information centre, which handles bookings.

In winter, ski shuttle services operate between Taupo and the Whakapapa Ski Area, a 1¼-hour trip. They go every day and may include package deals for transport and ski hire. Bookings can be made from the information centre or from the hostels.

Getting Around

Taupo has no regular bus service around town. Taupo Taxis (☎ 378 5100) and Stop Taxis (☎ 378 9250) both have door-to-door airport shuttle services for $8.

Mountain bikes can be hired from Cycle World (☎ 378 6117) at 126 Ruapehu St, opposite the large Pak 'n Save supermarket, Ski Yer Heart Out (☎ 378 7400) on Roberts St near Lake Terrace and other outlets in town. Most hostels have bikes and the Rainbow Lodge will also rent to non-guests for $15 per day or $3 per hour. Bikes are forbidden on the track from Spa Park to the Huka Falls due to track damage.

AROUND TAUPO

Wairakei Park

Crossing the river at Tongariro St and heading north from town on SH1, you'll arrive at the Wairakei Park area, also known as the Huka Falls Tourist Loop, where there are a number of interesting places to visit. Take the first right turn after you cross the river and you'll be on Huka Falls Rd, which passes along the river. At the end, turn left, back onto the highway, and you'll pass other interesting spots on your way back to town. The following points of interest follow this route, though of course you can do the loop in the other direction, going up the highway first and back down Huka Falls Rd.

There's no public transport serving this route, despite the obvious need. Tours will take you to a few places along here, otherwise you can walk (see Walks) or hire a bicycle for the day.

Beyond the Wairakei Park area, on the way to Rotorua, Orakei Korako is one of New Zealand's most interesting thermal areas.

Huka Falls A little further along Huka Falls Rd are the Huka Falls, *hukanui* in Maori meaning 'great body of spray'. A footbridge crosses the Waikato River above the falls – a great torrent of water, more like a giant rapid – that plunges through a narrow cleft in the rock. The water here is incredibly clear and turquoise, particularly on a sunny day.

Honey Hive New Zealand This is the place for budding apiarists – there are displays on everything you wanted to know about bee-keeping. It has viewing hives (a glass hive, a commercial hive and a bush hive), educational videos about bees, and a number of honeys and bee products for sale. It is past the Helistar Helicopters helipad, five km north of Taupo, and is open daily from 9 am to 5 pm. Admission is free.

Taupo Observatory This is the place for budding vulcanologists. The observatory monitors volcanic activity in the volatile Taupo Volcanic Zone, and the visitor centre has excellent displays on New Zealand's geothermal and volcanic activity.

Exhibits include a large relief map with push-button highlighters to show you the volcanic regions, and old documentaries about the eruptions of Ngauruhoe and Ruapehu in 1945, the largest this century. Pick up a monitoring report to tell you about this week's earthquakes or to see if Mt Ruapehu is about to blow.

The visitor centre, which also has a good bookshop, is open daily from 10 am to 4 pm. Admission is free.

New Zealand Woodcraft Further along is New Zealand Woodcraft, a showroom and workshop where you can see wood turning in action, and buy wood-turned items made from native New Zealand timbers. It's open every day from 8 am to 5 pm. Admission is free.

African Queen & Huka Jet Next along, nine km north of Taupo, Huka Jet and the African Queen share a dock on the river. Together they make a bit of a strange pair, exemplifying 'the old and the new' of New Zealand river boating.

The African Queen (☎ 374 8338) is actually the historic MV *Waireka*, a 62-foot (18.6-metre), 46-passenger riverboat built by Yarrow & Co in Scotland in 1908. It once operated on the Whanganui River and is still going after nearly 90 years of continuous service. It makes cruises daily at 11 am and 3 pm, and the Moonlight Glow-worm Cruise goes at 9 pm in summer, 6 pm in winter. The cruises all cost $18 (children $8).

Partly inspired by the engineering of river boats like the *Waireka*, which has a draught of only 12 inches (30.5 cm) laden, New Zealander CWF Hamilton was inspired to invent the jet-boat in 1958. The *Huka Jet* (☎ 374 8572) departs from the same dock for a 30-minute ride down to the Aratiatia Dam and up to the Huka Falls. Half-hourly trips

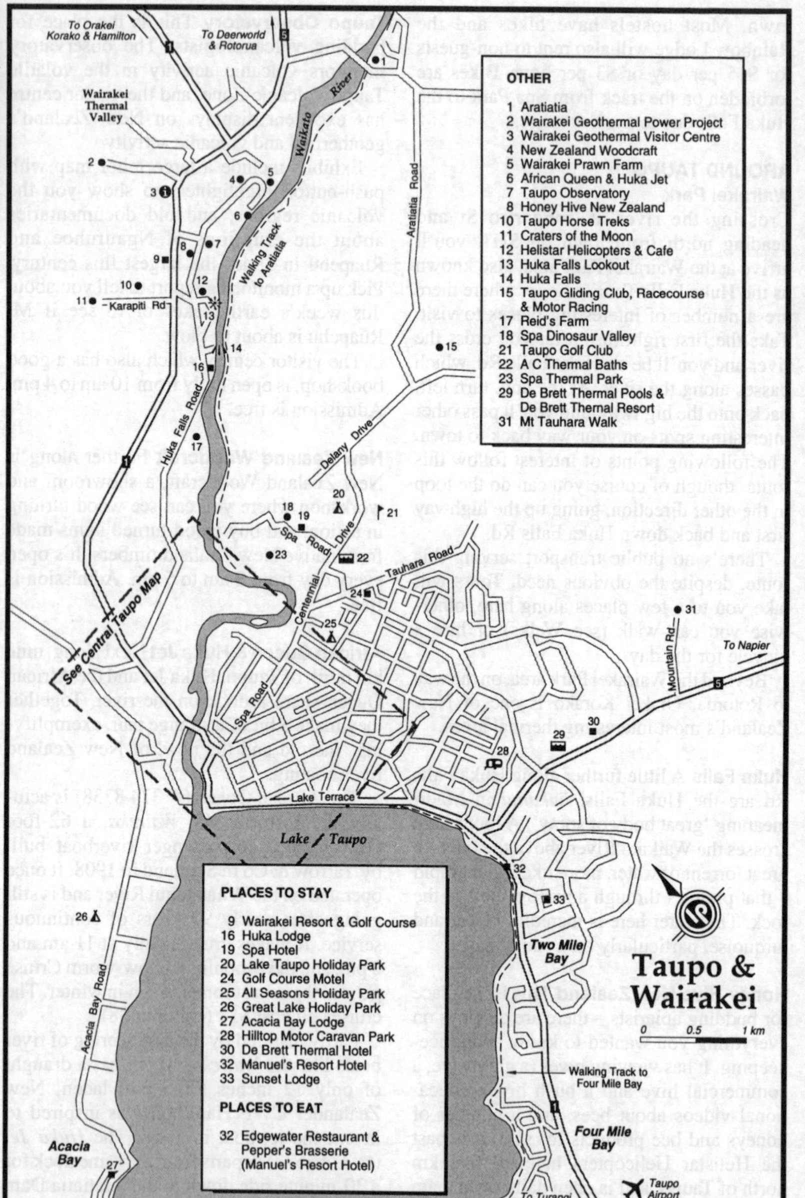
Taupo &
Wairakei
OTHER
1 Aratiatia
2 Wairakei Geothermal Power Project
3 Wairakei Geothermal Visitor Centre
4 New Zealand Woodcraft
5 Wairakei Prawn Farm
6 African Queen & Huka Jet
7 Taupo Observatory
8 Honey Hive New Zealand
10 Taupo Horse Treks
11 Craters of the Moon
12 Helistar Helicopters & Cafe
13 Huka Falls Lookout
14 Huka Falls
15 Taupo Gliding Club, Racecourse & Motor Racing
17 Reid's Farm
18 Spa Dinosaur Valley
21 Taupo Golf Club
22 A C Thermal Baths
23 Spa Thermal Park
29 De Brett Thermal Pools & De Brett Thermal Resort
31 Mt Tauhara Walk
PLACES TO STAY
9 Wairakei Resort & Golf Course
16 Huka Lodge
19 Spa Hotel
20 Lake Taupo Holiday Park
24 Golf Course Motel
25 All Seasons Holiday Park
26 Great Lake Holiday Park
27 Acacia Bay Lodge
28 Hilltop Motor Caravan Park
30 De Brett Thermal Hotel
32 Manuel's Resort Hotel
33 Sunset Lodge
PLACES TO EAT
32 Edgewater Restaurant & Pepper's Brasserie (Manuel's Resort Hotel)
To Orakei Korako & Hamilton
To Deerworld & Rotorua
Wairakei Thermal Valley
Waikato River
Walking Track to Aratiatia
Aratiatia Road
Karapiti Rd
Huka Falls Road
Delany Drive
Spa Road
Centennial Drive
Tauhara Road
See Central Taupo Map
Lake Terrace
Lake Taupo
Acacia Bay Road
Acacia Bay
Two Mile Bay
Four Mile Bay
Mountain Rd
To Napier
Walking Track to Four Mile Bay
To Turangi
Taupo Airport
0
0.5
1 km

run all day long; the cost is $45 (children $20), including transport from town.

Wairakei Prawn Farm Almost next door to the Huka Jet and the African Queen, the Wairakei Prawn Farm (☎ 374 8474) is the world's only geothermally heated freshwater prawn farm. Interesting guided tours of the prawn farm explain how the prawns are grown, and tell you about their life cycle. The tours last 20 to 25 minutes and depart every hour on the hour from 11 am to 4 pm in summer, less frequently in winter; the cost is $4.

If all the talk about prawns makes you hungry, prawn BBQ lunches and dinners are put on daily (phone for bookings).

Aratiatia Two km off SH5 are the Aratiatia Rapids, a spectacular part of the Waikato River until the government, in its wisdom, plonked a power house and dam down here, shutting off the water to the rapids. To keep the tourists happy they open the control gates at noon and 2 pm daily, and in summer also at 4 pm. You can see the water flow through from three good lookout points. It's all open land, with no admission charge.

From Aratiatia, if you're doing the loop, head back down the highway towards Taupo and you'll pass some amazing thermal areas.

Wairakei Thermal Valley If you are not too distracted by all the steam from the Geothermal Power Project, you'll see a 1.5-km road on your right leading to the Wairakei Thermal Valley. Wairakei, like Orakei Korako, gets its name from being the place where the waters were used as mirrors. This is the remains of what was once known as Geyser Valley. Before the geothermal power project started in 1959 this was one of the most active thermal areas in the world, with 22 geysers and 240 mud pools and springs. Now the neighbouring geothermal power project has sucked off the steam, and only eight or nine mud pools remain active. There's a bush walk to the Huiata pools but they're only active after a heavy rain. Entry is $5 (children 75c) and it's open from 9 am to 5 pm every day. Also here is the Barn Tearooms.

Wairakei Geothermal Power Project New Zealand was the second country in the world to produce power from natural steam. If you dive into all that steam you will find yourself at the Wairakei Geothermal Power Project which generates about 150,000 kW, providing about 5% of New Zealand's total electrical power.

The Wairakei Geothermal Visitor Centre is close to the road, where you can make an educational stop between 9 am and 4 pm daily. Information on the bore field and power house is available and an audiovisual is shown. You can drive up the road through the project and from a lookout see the long stretches of pipe, wreathed in steam.

Just south of here is the big Wairakei Resort and its golf course.

Craters of the Moon Craters of the Moon is an interesting and unexploited thermal area. It's run by the DOC, so is free of the more touristy aspects you'll find at some other, commercially exploited thermal areas.

This thermal area sprang up in the 1950s because the power station lowered underground water levels, which reduced the pressure of the heated water, causing more vigorous boiling and steam. New mud pools and steam vents appeared here, and you can wander through them on a plank-walk.

It is open from dawn to dusk. There is a small kiosk staffed by volunteers at the car park. Admission is free but donations are appreciated.

Craters of the Moon is signposted on SH1 about five km north of Taupo.

Orakei Korako

Between Taupo and Rotorua, Orakei Korako is one of the finest thermal areas of New Zealand but receives far fewer visitors than the other thermal areas because of its remote location.

After the destruction of the Pink and White Terraces by the Tarawera eruption, Orakei Korako was possibly the best thermal area left in New Zealand and one of the finest in the world. Although three-quarters of it now lies beneath the waters of artificial Lake Ohakuri, which was formed by a hydroelectric dam, the quarter that remains is the best part, and still very much worth seeing.

A well laid-out walking track takes you around the large, colourful silica terraces for which Orakei Korako is famous, as well as geysers and Ruatapu Cave – a magnificent natural cave with a pool of jade-green water. The pool is said to have been used by Maori as a mirror during hairdressing ceremonies; the name Orakei Korako means 'the place of adorning'.

Entry is $12.50 (children $5), including a boat ride across Lake Ohakuri. It's open daily from 8.30 am to 4.30 pm. Canoes and dinghies are available for hire, and there are two hot tubs. Accommodation (☎ 378 3131) is available in a lodge with a fully equipped kitchen. The cost is $16 per person in rooms with two to six beds. Tourist flats sleeping six cost $40 for two. Tent and caravan sites are free.

Orakei Korako is a 25-minute drive north from Taupo or a 45-minute drive south from Rotorua. From Taupo take SH1 to Hamilton for 23 km, and then it is 14 km from the turn-off. From Rotorua the turn-off is on SH5, via Mihi.

Deerworld

Deerworld is a deer farm with a deer museum, a cafe serving venison, and a shop selling deer products. Helicopter rides and 4WD tours are also offered. Deerworld is on SH5, 30 km north of Taupo heading towards Rotorua. It is open 8.30 am to 5.30 pm. Admission is free.

TURANGI

Developed for the construction of the nearby hydroelectric power station built in 1973, Turangi is Taupo's smaller, poorer cousin at the southern end of Lake Taupo. The town itself is four km inland from the lake, and access to the lake is from nearby Tokaanu.

Turangi's main attraction is excellent trout fishing (the Tongariro River is world-

Introduced red deer are the focus of a thriving farming industry in Taupo

renowned). Turangi can also be used as an access point to the northern trails of nearby Tongariro National Park, though Whakapapa is the main base for treks in the park.

Information

The Turangi Information Centre (☎ 386 8999; fax 386 0074), just off SH1, has a detailed relief model of the Tongariro National Park and is the place to stop for information on the park, Kaimanawa Forest Park, trout fishing, walks around town, and snow and road conditions during the ski season. The office also makes bookings for activities, accommodation and transport, and issues fishing licences. The centre is open every day from 9 am to 5 pm.

The DOC office (☎ 386 8607) is near the junction of SH1 and Ohuanga Rd.

The information centre is the AA agent for the town. The post office and banks are in the Turangi Shopping Mall, opposite the information centre.

Tongariro National Trout Centre

Five km south of Turangi on SH1 is the DOC-managed Tongariro National Trout Centre, an important trout hatchery. It's open every day from 9 am to 4 pm and entry is free. This landscaped centre has a self-guided walk to an underwater viewing area, keeping ponds and a pleasant picnic area, and you can also try your hand at trout fishing in the Tongariro River which runs close by.

Tokaanu

About five km west of Turangi on the lake, this little settlement has a collection of motels and fishing lodges. The **Tokaanu Thermal Park** is an interesting thermal area with hot baths. A 15-minute boardwalk leads around the bubbling mud pools and thermal springs. In the park, Tokaanu Thermal Pools has hot pools, a sauna and interesting exhibits. The walk is free, while the public pool costs $3.50 (children $1); slightly more for private pools and sauna. The pools are open every day from 10 am to 9 pm.

The **Tokaanu Power Station Visitor Centre**, just off SH41, has exhibits, a video documentary on hydroelectricity and free tours through the power station. It is open Monday to Saturday from 10 am to 4 pm.

Just past Tokaanu around the lake is Waihi with its fine old church, but the secessionist-minded Ngati Turumakina people have closed their village to visitors.

Activities

Walks The DOC *Turangi Walks* and the *Central Volcanic Plateau Trail Map* leaflets outline walks in the area. Notable walks include the Tongariro River Walkway (three hours return), Tongariro River Loop Track (one hour), Hinemihi's Track near the top of Te Ponanga Saddle (15 minutes return), a walk on Mt Maunganamu (40 minutes return) and a walk around Lake Rotopounamu, which abounds in birdlife (20 minutes to the lake, then 1½ hours around the lake).

Trout Fishing February and March are the best months for brown trout, June to September are best for rainbow trout, but fishing is good most of the year. Don't forget your fishing licence.

Turangi has a variety of fishing guides starting at around $40 per hour, including all gear, or you can hire your own gear from Greig Sports (☎ 386 7713) in the shopping mall. Boats can be hired for lake fishing – aluminium dinghies cost $13 per hour from Braxmere Lodge just before Waihi Village, and they rent fishing gear.

Other Activites River rafting is popular, and the Tongariro River has grade 3 river rafting, or for families, grade 1 on the lower reaches in summer. All rafting trips and other activities can be booked through the information centre.

The Turangi information centre also arranges horse treks, hunting and fishing trips, cruises and charter boats, mountain biking, kayaking, scenic flights and just about any other outdoor activity you can think of.

Places to Stay

Camping & Cabins *Turangi Holiday Park* (☎ 386 8754) is on Ohuanga Rd, off SH41. Tent sites are $8 per person, powered sites $8.50 per person, pokey cabins $15.50 per person, other cabins $34 for two, and on-site caravans $38 for two people. There's also a backpackers rate of $7/13 per person in tent sites/cabins. At one time this was the power station construction workers' quarters, which accounts for the large number of cabins.

At Tokaanu the *Oasis Motel & Caravan Park* (☎ 386 8569) on SH41 has camp sites at $6.50 per person, $8 with power, cabins at $15 per person, and motel units at $50 for two. It also has hot pools and spa pools.

Other motor camps north of Turangi on the lakeside road to Taupo are: the *Motuoapa Domain Camp* (☎ 386 7162), eight km out at Motuoapa, *Tauranga-Taupo Lodge & Caravan Park* (☎ 386 8385), 11 km north, and the *Motutere Bay Caravan Park* (☎ 386 8963), 17 km north at Motutere Bay.

Hostels The *Bellbird Lodge* (☎ 386 8281) at 3 Rangipoia Place is a small, friendly hostel with a spacious lounge area and kitchen. The cost is $16 per person in twin, double and dorm rooms. This popular, well-run hostel is about the best reason to stay in Turangi – one bonus is the cheap fishing trips on offer.

Club Habitat (☎ 386 7492) on Ohuanga

Rd is a huge place with blockhouse rooms scattered all around the grounds. The fancy name is to attract the cheap ski tours that stay here, and River Rats rafting tours also use this place. Backpackers rooms are rather bare and anonymous but OK for $14 in dorm rooms, $32 for twin rooms. The better-furnished cabins with kitchens and shared bathrooms are comfortable but no bargain at $50, or en-suite motel units cost $70 for two. The best thing about this place is the fancy restaurant/bar/games complex and there is a sauna and spa.

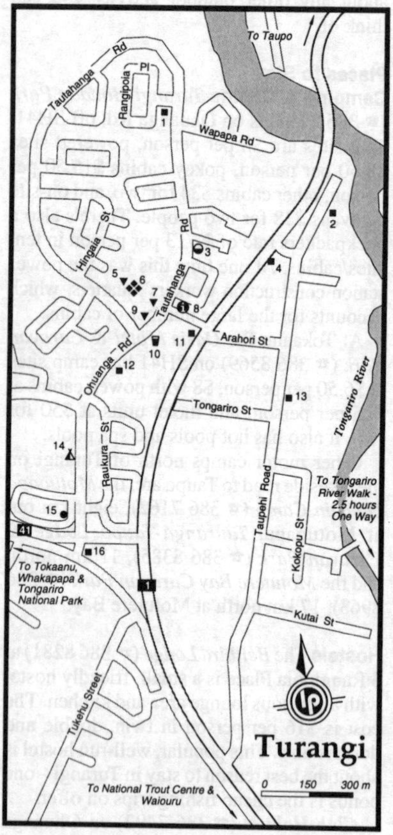

Lodges The *Sportsman's Lodge* (☎ 386 8150) at 15 Taupehi Rd has rooms with shared kitchen and TV lounge at $35/45 for singles/doubles. Along SH1, the *Turangi Motor Lodge* (☎ 386 0115) has studio units from $67.50; there's a spa pool, house bar and licensed restaurant. The *Creel Lodge* (☎ 386 8081) at 165 Taupehi Rd has units from $50/67.

There's some interesting accommodation in nearby Tokaanu including the *Tokaanu Lodge* (☎ 386 8572) with three private mineral pools, a covered outdoor pool, a fish cleaning area and a fish freezer/smoker. The cost is $72 for one-bedroom units, $105 for two-bedroom family units.

Places to Eat

The Turangi Shopping Mall has two large *supermarkets*, open seven days a week, and a variety of places to eat. *Vaughan's Takeout* is good, and you can take away or eat in at the *Hong Kong Chinese Takeaways*. *Valentino's* is a good Italian restaurant, a solid reminder of the many Italian construction workers here at the time the power station was built. *Club Habitat* has a cafeteria-style restaurant with good, cheap meals.

PLACES TO STAY

1 Bellbird Lodge
2 Sportsmans Lodge
4 Tongariro River Motel
10 Huckleberry's Pub
11 Turangi Motor Lodge
12 Club Habitat
13 Creel Lodge
14 Turangi Holiday Park
16 Anglers Paradise Motel

PLACES TO EAT

5 Vaughan's Takeout
7 Hong Kong Chines Takeaways
9 Valentino's

OTHER

3 Turangi Bus & Travel Centre
6 Turangi Shopping Mall & CPO
8 Turangi Information Centre & AA
15 DOC

Getting There & Away

InterCity and Newmans buses stop at the Turangi Bus & Travel Centre. Auckland-Wellington and Rotorua-Wellington buses running along the eastern side of the lake to/from Taupo, 45 minutes to the north, all stop at Turangi.

Alpine Scenic Tours (☎ 386 8918) runs a shuttle service several times daily between Turangi and National Park, stopping in the Tongariro National Park – at the Ketetahi trail head, the Mangatepopo trail head, Whakapapa Village (the Chateau), and in winter the Whakapapa Ski Area (Top of the Bruce) – an excellent service for skiers and trampers. It also has services to/from Taupo and a weekday service to/from Rotorua.

Tongariro National Park

Tongariro, established in 1887, was New Zealand's first national park. It was given to the country in September 1887 by Horonuku Te Heuheu Tukino, a far-sighted paramount chief of the Ngati Tuwharetoa people who realised that this was the only way to preserve an area of such spiritual significance in its entirety. The name Tongariro originally covered the three mountains of the park (Tongariro, Ngauruhoe and Ruapehu) and means *tonga*, south wind; *riro*, carried away. The story goes that Ngatoro-i-rangi was stuck on the summit and had almost perished from the cold. He called to his sisters in Hawaiki for fire and his words were carried to them on the south wind.

With its collection of mighty (and still active) volcanoes, Tongariro is one of the most interesting and spectacular parks in New Zealand. In summer it has excellent walks and tramps, most notably the Great Walks of the Tongariro Northern Circuit and the Tongariro Crossing. In the winter it's an important ski area.

Information

In Whakapapa Village, on the north side of the park, the Whakapapa Visitor Centre (☎ 892 3729; fax 892 3814) is open every day from 8 am to 5 pm. It has maps and lots of information on the park, including walks, huts and current skiing, track and weather conditions. Two interesting audiovisual presentations, one on the park and one on volcanoes, cost a small fee to see but they're worth it; these and the many displays on the geological and human history of the park, plus a small shop, make this an interesting place to visit whatever the weather. The excellent *Tongariro National Park* map costs $11 and is well worth having a look at or purchasing before you go off trekking.

Other DOC visitor centres serving the park are in Ohakune and Turangi.

In December and January, ask the park visitor centres about their summer activities programme of special walks, heli-bikes, heli-hikes and more.

Volcanoes

The long, multi-peaked summit of Mt Ruapehu is the highest of the volcanoes at 2797 metres and the most active. The upper slopes were showered with hot mud and water in the volcanic activity of 1969 and 1975, and in December 1988 the volcano threw out some very hot rocks. However, these were just tame precursors to the spectacular eruptions of September 1995, when Ruapehu sprayed volcanic rock and emitted massive clouds of ash and steam. No lava overflows occurred, but potentially destructive lahars (slurries of rock, ash, soil and water) swept down the mountain. Fortunately these missed the ski runs, which are all found on the mountain's slopes, and no lives were lost.

At the time of writing, Mt Ruapehu was still rumbling, but volcanic activity had substantially declined. Crater Lake near the summit was still off limits, though all the main trails were open. The Tongariro Northern Circuit was not affected, while the Round-the-Mountains Track was open but alternative trails had to be used to complete parts of the walk on the southern slopes of Ruapehu. Check with the DOC office in Whakapapa for the latest track conditions.

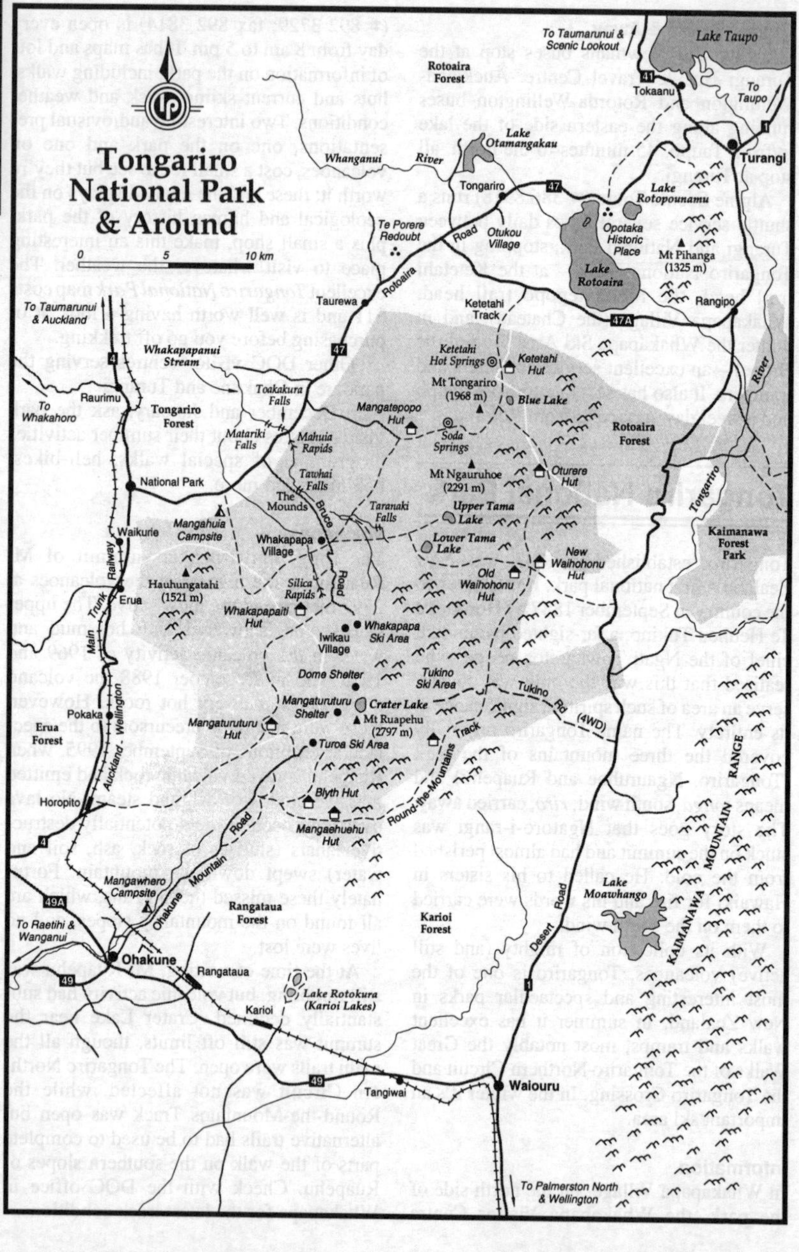
Tongariro National Park & Around
0
5
10 km
To Taumarunui & Scenic Lookout
Lake Taupo
Rotoaira Forest
41
Tokaanu
To Taupo
1
Lake Otamangakau
Whanganui
River
Turangi
Tongariro
47
Lake Rotopounamu
Te Porere Redoubt
Road
Otukou Village
Opotaka Historic Place
Lake Rotoaira
Mt Pihanga (1325 m)
Rotoaira
Taurewa
Ketetahi Track
Rangipo
47A
To Taumarunui & Auckland
Whakapapanui Stream
47
Ketetahi Hot Springs
Ketetahi Hut
Mt Tongariro (1968 m)
Blue Lake
4
Raurimu
To Whakahoro
Tongariro Forest
Toakakura Falls
Mangatepopo Hut
Soda Springs
Rotoaira Forest
River
Matariki Falls
Mahuia Rapids
Tawhai Falls
Mt Ngauruhoe (2291 m)
Oturere Hut
National Park
The Mounds
Bruce
Taranaki Falls
Tongariro
Mangahuia Campsite
Upper Tama Lake
Waikune
Railway
Whakapapa Village
Lower Tama Lake
Kaimanawa Forest Park
New Waihohonu Hut
Hauhungatahi (1521 m)
Silica Rapids
Road
Old Waihohonu Hut
Erua
Trunk
Main
Whakapapaiti Hut
Whakapapa Ski Area
Iwikau Village
Dome Shelter
Tukino Ski Area
Tukino Rd (4WD)
Mangaturuturu Shelter
Crater Lake
Mt Ruapehu (2797 m)
Pokaka
Wellington
Mangaturuturu Hut
Erua Forest
Auckland
Turoa Ski Area
Round-the-Mountains Track
Horopito
Blyth Hut
Mangaehuehu Hut
Road
4
Mountain
MOUNTAIN
RANGE
KAIMANAWA
Mangawhero Campsite
Ohakune
Desert Road
49A
Rangataua Forest
Karioi Forest
Lake Moawhango
To Raetihi & Wanganui
Ohakune
Rangataua
49
Lake Rotokura (Karioi Lakes)
1
Karioi
49
Tangiwai
Waiouru
To Palmerston North & Wellington

Though the eruption of 1995 was the most explosive in recent memory, it was not the most destructive. Between 1945 and 1947 the level of Crater Lake rose dramatically when eruptions blocked the overflow. On Christmas Eve 1953 the overflow burst and the flood that resulted led to one of New Zealand's worst disasters. The torrent swept away a railway bridge moments before a crowded express train arrived and in the resulting crash 153 people lost their lives.

Mt Tongariro, at 1968 metres, is another old volcano but it is still considered active – it last erupted in 1926. It has a number of coloured lakes dotting its uneven summit as well as hot springs gushing out of its side at Ketetahi. The Tongariro Crossing, a magnificent walk, passes beside the lakes, right through several craters, on to the hot springs, and down the other side through lush native forest.

Mt Ngauruhoe is much younger than the other volcanoes in the park – it's estimated to have formed in the last 2500 years and the slopes to the 2291-metre summit are still perfectly symmetrical. In contrast to Ruapehu and Tongariro which have multiple vents, Mt Ngauruhoe is a conical, single-vent volcano. It can be climbed in summer, but in winter and under snow conditions it is definitely suitable only for experienced mountaineers. It's a very steep but rewarding climb. Between Ngauruhoe and Ruapehu are the Tama Lakes, explosion craters which have filled with water.

Tongariro Northern Circuit

The long, circular Round-the-Mountains Track embracing Mt Ruapehu, Mt Ngauruhoe and Mt Tongariro requires five to six days to complete, but more popular is the shorter northern circuit, normally done in four days. One of New Zealand's Great Walks, it has several possibilities for shorter walks taking from a few hours to overnight, and includes the famous Tongariro Crossing.

Highlights of the Northern Circuit include tramping through several volcanic craters including the South Crater, Central Crater and Red Crater; brilliantly colourful volcanic lakes including the Emerald Lakes, Blue Lake and the Upper and Lower Tama Lakes; the steaming Ketetahi Hot Springs and the cold Soda Springs and Ohinepango Springs; various other volcanic formations including cones, lava flows and glacial valleys; and spectacular views extending right over Lake Taupo and as far as Mt Taranaki on a fine day.

The most popular side trip from the main track is to Mt Ngauruhoe summit, but it is also possible to climb Mt Tongariro from Red Crater (1½ hours), or walk to the Ohinepango Springs from the New Waihohonu Hut (30 minutes).

Walking the Track The track is served by four huts: the Mangatepopo, Ketetahi, Oturere and New Waihohonu huts. The huts have mattresses, gas heating, gas cookers, toilets and a water supply. Camping is permitted beside all the huts.

During the full summer season – from late October to 31 May – a Great Walks pass is required and must be bought in advance, whether you stay in the huts or camp beside them; the cost is $14 per night in huts or $6 for camping (children half-price). Ordinary back country hut tickets and annual passes cannot be used during these months. The Tongariro National Park Visitor Centres sell Great Walks passes.

The rest of the year, ordinary back country hut passes or annual passes may be used; the cost is $8 per night (two tickets) for huts, $4 (one ticket) for camping. However, this track is quite different in winter, when it is covered in snow and becomes a challenging alpine trek.

Estimated walking times are:

Whakapapa Village to Mangatepopo Hut	2½ to three hours
Mangatepopo Hut to Emerald Lakes	three to four hours
Emerald Lakes to Ketetahi Hut & Hot Springs	two to three hours
Emerald Lakes to Oturere Hut	one to two hours
Oturere Hut to New Waihohonu Hut	two to three hours
New Waihohonu Hut to Whakapapa Village	five to six hours

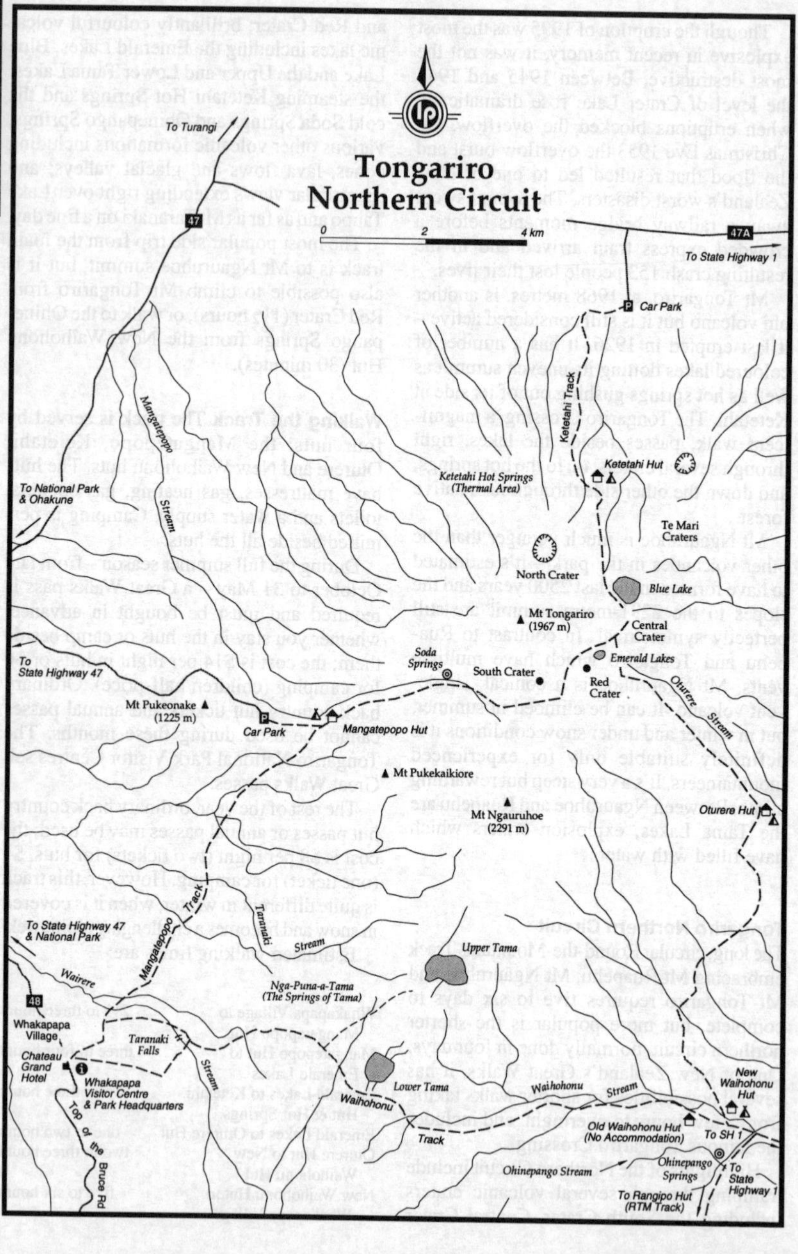
Tongariro
Northern Circuit
0
2
4 km
To Turangi
47
47A
To State Highway 1
Car Park
Ketetahi Track
Ketetahi Hot Springs
(Thermal Area)
Ketetahi Hut
Te Mari
Craters
North Crater
Blue Lake
Mt Tongariro
(1967 m)
Central
Crater
Emerald Lakes
Soda
Springs
South Crater
Red
Crater
Oturere
Stream
To National Park
& Ohakune
Mangatepopo
Stream
To
State Highway 47
Mt Pukeonake
(1225 m)
Car Park
Mangatepopo Hut
Mt Pukekaikiore
Mt Ngauruhoe
(2291 m)
Oturere Hut
Mangatepopo
Track
Taranaki
Stream
To State Highway 47
& National Park
Wairere
Upper Tama
Nga-Puna-a-Tama
(The Springs of Tama)
48
Whakapapa
Village
Chateau
Grand
Hotel
Whakapapa
Visitor Centre
& Park Headquarters
Taranaki
Falls
Stream
Top of the Bruce Rd
Lower Tama
Waihohonu
Track
Waihohonu
Stream
New
Waihohonu
Hut
Old Waihohonu Hut
(No Accommodation)
To SH 1
Ohinepango Stream
Ohinepango
Springs
To
State
Highway 1
To Rangipo Hut
(RTM Track)

Track Safety Check with one of the DOC offices for current track and weather conditions before you set out. The weather on the mountains is extremely changeable – warm brilliant sunshine, snow, hail, wind etc can all alternate within a few minutes of one another, at any time of year. Bring a rain coat and warm woollen clothing.

A lot of accidents occur on this track when people misjudge loose rocks, or go sliding down the volcanic slopes – watch your step!

On Mt Ngauruhoe, watch out for the loose scoria, and be careful not to dislodge rocks onto those coming up behind you.

Around the Ketetahi Hot Springs, be careful of unstable ground caused by the thermal activity.

In winter, alpine or mountaineering experience is essential, especially to climb the peaks. If you don't know how to use ice axes, crampons and avalanche gear, come with an experienced guide.

Tongariro Crossing

Often called 'the finest one-day walk in New Zealand', the Tongariro Crossing covers many of the most spectacular features of the Tongariro Northern Circuit between the Mangatepopo Hut and the Ketetahi Hut. On a clear day the views are magnificent. This is basically what many trampers do as day two of the Northern Circuit, with the extra walk along the Ketetahi track. Because of its popularity, shuttle transport is available to both ends of the track.

There are a couple of steep spots, but most of the track is not terribly difficult. However, it is a long, exhausting day's walk – you'll feel you have accomplished something after you've done it. It's billed as a seven to eight-hour walk, but expect it to take longer if you're not in top condition. Some prefer to do it as a two-day walk, especially if side trips are included.

The track passes through a variety of vegetation zones ranging from alpine scrub and tussock, to places where there is no vegetation at all on the higher altitudes, down into lush podocarp forest as you descend from Ketetahi Springs to the end of the track.

Worthwhile side trips from the main track include ascents to the summits of Mt Ngauruhoe and Mt Tongariro. Mt Ngauruhoe can be ascended most easily from the Mangatepopo Saddle, reached near the beginning of the track after the first steep climb. The summit of Mt Tongariro is reached by a poled route taking off from Red Crater.

Walking the Track Near the start of the track is the Mangatepopo Hut, accessed by Mangatepopo Rd, or there's the Ketetahi Hut near the Ketetahi Hot Springs, a couple of hours before the end of the track. To stay at or camp beside either hut, you must have a Great Walks pass, purchased in advance, from the end of October until 31 May.

The Ketetahi Hut, beside the steaming Ketetahi Hot Springs, is the most popular hut in the park. It has bunks to sleep 24 people, but regularly has 50 to 60 people trying to stay there on Saturday nights and at the busiest times of year (summer and school holidays). Bunks are claimed on a first come, first served basis, so you have the best chance of getting a bunk if you arrive early. It's obviously not a bad idea to bring camping gear with you, just in case. Campers can use all the hut facilities – except for the bunks – which can make the kitchen a bit crowded, especially at busy times of year.

Estimated walking times are as follows:

Mangatepopo Rd end to Mangatepopo Hut	30 minutes
Mangatepopo Hut to Mangatepopo Saddle	1½ hours
(Side trip) Mangatepopo Saddle to summit of Mt Ngauruhoe	three hours return
(Side trip) Red Crater to Mt Tongariro Summit	1½ hours return
Mangatepopo Saddle to Emerald Lakes	1½ to two hours
Emerald Lakes to Ketetahi Hut	two to three hours
Ketetahi Hut to Ketetahi Hot Springs	15 minutes
Ketetahi Hot Springs to Ketetahi Rd end	two hours

Crater Lake

At the time of writing, the area within 1.5 to two km around Crater Lake remains off limits due to Mt Ruapehu's eruption. If and when it is again possible to walk to the lake, new scoria will make this difficult walk even more demanding. Given the likelihood that the walk to Crater Lake will open again, pre-eruption details are given, but check with any DOC office at the park for the latest information.

The walk to Crater Lake in the crater of Mt Ruapehu begins at Iwikau Village, at the top of Mt Bruce Rd above Whakapapa village, and takes about seven hours return (about four hours up, three hours down). It's definitely not an easy stroll and the track is not marked. Even in summer, there may be ice and snow to get through; in winter, forget it unless you are an experienced mountaineer. Check with the Whakapapa Visitor Centre for current weather conditions before you set off. Boots, sunglasses and windproof clothing are always essential; ice axes and crampons may be needed.

From December to April you can use the chair lift at the Whakapapa Ski Area to get you up the mountain, cutting about three hours off the walk. Guided walks to Crater Lake go from the chair lift (☎ 892 3738 for reservations) for $30 (children $20).

It is also possible to reach Crater Lake starting from the Ohakune side, but the track is steeper and ice axes and crampons are necessary all year round since you must climb up a steep glacier. If you do start from the Ohakune side, allow at least five hours up and three hours to get back down.

Other Walks

The park visitor centres at Whakapapa, Ohakune and Turangi have maps, brochures and current information on a number of interesting short and long walks in the park. Be sure to ask them about current track and weather conditions before you set off.

Keen trampers can do the entire Round-the-Mountains Track, circling around both Mt Ruapehu and Mt Ngauruhoe. It can be accessed at various points around the national park and it requires about five to six days to complete. The 1995 eruption saw the destruction of some trail bridges on the southern slopes of Mt Ruapehu and access to some huts was impossible. Using alternative trails the walk was still possible and, barring the possibility of melting snow unleashing further lahars, the southern section of the Round-the-Mountains Track is expected to return much to normal. Consult with one of the park visitor centres about current track and weather conditions and get a map before embarking on this track.

A number of fine walks begin at or near the Whakapapa Visitor Centre and from the road leading up to it; these are covered here. Several other good walks take off from the Ohakune Mountain Rd, leading from Ohakune up to the Turoa Ski Area; they are covered in the Ohakune section.

DOC's *Whakapapa Walks* pamphlet outlines a number of walks starting near the visitor centre. Some of the more popular walks are:

Whakapapa Nature Walk – A 15-minute loop track suitable for wheelchairs, beginning about 200 metres above the Visitor Centre. The track passes through beech forest and a number of gardens demonstrating the various vegetation zones of the park.

Ridge Track – A 30-minute return walk, climbs through beech forest to alpine shrublands for panoramic views of Mt Ruapehu, Mt Ngauruhoe and the surrounding area.

Silica Rapids – A 2½-hour, eight-km loop track to the Silica Rapids, named for the silica mineral deposits formed here by the rapids on the Waikare Stream. A waterfall and other interesting alpine features are passed along the way; the final two km is back down the Bruce Rd above Whakapapa Village.

Taranaki Falls – A two-hour, six-km loop track to the 20-metre Taranaki Falls on the Wairere Stream.

Tama Lakes – This 16-km track to the Tama Lakes takes about five to six hours return. On the Tama Saddle between Mt Ruapehu and Mt Ngauruhoe, the Tama Lakes are great for a refreshing swim in summer. The upper lake affords fine views of Mt Ngauruhoe and Mt Tongariro. Beware of windy conditions on this walk, as the Tama Saddle acts as a wind funnel for the prevailing westerly winds.

Both the Tongariro Northern Circuit and Tongariro Crossing can be accessed from Mangatepopo Road off SH47, and as well as the full walks you can do just parts of them and some other shorter trips. DOC has a full rundown.

Still more tracks take off from SH47, on the north side of the park, and include:

Mahuia Rapids – About two km north of the SH48 turn-off leading to Whakapapa Village, SH47 crosses the Whakapapanui Stream just below these rapids, which can be seen from the car park on the south side of the road.

Matariki Falls – A 20-minute return track through private farmland to see the Matariki Falls takes off from SH47 about 200 metres from the Mahuia Rapids car park.

Lake Rotoaira – On the shores of Lake Rotoaira, on the north side of the park, are some interesting excavations of a pre-European Maori village site.

Lake Rotopounamu – A beautiful, secluded lake set in podocarp forest on the saddle between Lake Rotoaira and Lake Taupo, Lake Rotopounamu can be reached by a 20-minute walk from SH47. The lake is on the west side of Mt Pihanga. You can walk around the lake in 1½ hours – there's no camping, though.

Skiing

The two main ski areas are the Whakapapa Ski Area, above Whakapapa Village on the north side of the park, and the Turoa Ski Area, on the south side of the park near Ohakune. The Tukino Ski Area on the east side of Mt Ruapehu is a private club ski area and much less popular, requiring a 4WD vehicle to get to it and it has limited tows. The only accommodation at the ski fields are private lodges, so most skiers stay at Whakapapa Village, National Park and Ohakune. See the Skiing section in the Outdoor Activities chapter for more details on skiing in the park.

Other Activities

The most popular activities in the park are tramping in summer and skiing in winter; opportunities for both are magnificent. But there are several other interesting things you can see and do in the park.

The Grand Chateau Hotel in Whakapapa has a nine-hole golf course and tennis courts open to the public, with hire of golf clubs, tennis racquets etc. Even if you can't afford to stay at the hotel, you can stop in for a drink in the lobby just to savour the elegant atmosphere.

The ski lifts at the Whakapapa Ski Area (☎ 892 3738) also operate for sightseeing and for trampers' transport up the mountain from December to April – subject to weather conditions. A return ride costs $12 (children $7).

Mountain Air (☎ 892 2812), with an office on SH47 near the SH48 turn-off to Whakapapa Village, has flights over the national park for amazing views of the volcanoes. Flights cost from $45; cheaper specials are offered when it's quiet.

Plateau Outdoor Adventure Guides (☎ 892 2740), based at Raurimu six km north of National Park township, offers a wide variety of activities around Tongariro National Park, Whanganui National Park and the surrounding region. Some of their specialities include canoeing, white-water rafting, mountaineering, tramping and ski touring.

Places to Stay

You can stay in the national park or outside the park in one of the nearby small towns. Within the park itself, Whakapapa Village has an expensive hotel, a motel and a motor camp. Also in the park are two DOC camping grounds – one near National Park and one near Ohakune – and the huts, accessible only by walking tracks. Small towns near the park include National Park, Ohakune and Turangi; see the separate sections on each of these towns for their accommodation possibilities.

Camping, Cabins & Huts There are two basic DOC camping grounds in the park with cold water and pit toilets; the cost is low and you place your money (about $2) into an honesty box. The *Mangahuia camping ground* is on SH47, between National Park and the SH48 turn-off heading to Whakapapa. The *Mangawhero camping ground* is near Ohakune, on the Ohakune Mountain Rd heading up to Mt Ruapehu.

The popular *Whakapapa Holiday Park* (☎ 892 3897) is up the road from the Grand Chateau Hotel, opposite the Whakapapa Visitor Centre. It's in a pretty spot and couldn't be more conveniently located. Tent sites cost $8 per person, powered sites $1 extra, cabins are $33 for two and tourist flats are $50 for two, with prices the same all year round. From December to June there's also a special backpackers share rate of $12.50 per person in cabins.

Scattered around the park's tramping tracks are nine huts, with access by foot only. The cost is $8 (two tickets) in huts, $4 for camping beside the huts, with back country hut tickets and annual hut passes both acceptable. However, in the summer season from the end of October to the end of May a Great Walks hut or camp site pass is required for the four Tongariro Northern Circuit huts: the Ketetahi, Mangatepopo, New Waihohonu and Oturere huts. The cost is $14 per night in huts, $6 per night for camping. Back country hut tickets and annual hut passes are not valid in these huts during this period.

All the park visitor centres have information on huts and can sell hut tickets or Great Walks passes, or provide information on several other places in the area where Great Walks passes can be bought.

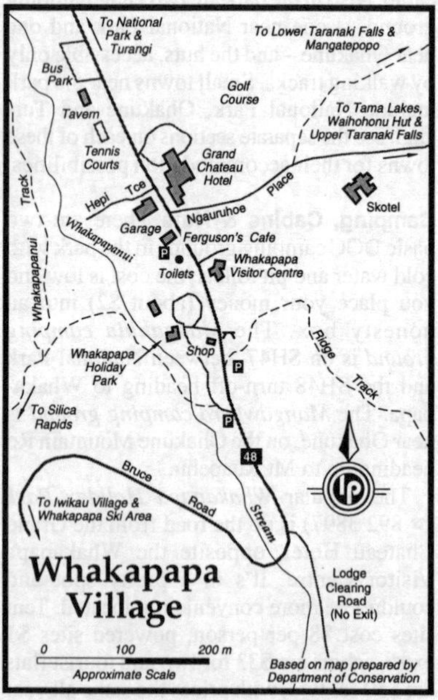

Hotels & Motels At Whakapapa Village, the *Grand Chateau Hotel* (☎ 892 3809) is indeed a grand hotel; apart from the Hermitage at Mt Cook it is the best-known hotel in New Zealand. Built in 1929 in an opulent style, it has been well preserved and is priced accordingly. For most of the year, economy rooms are $107, standard rooms are $126, premium rooms are $158. There are also more expensive suites and villas. In the ski season, standard rooms cost $259 on Friday and Saturday, $180 during the week, and various packages are offered. Discount packages are sometimes available.

Behind the Chateau is the *Skotel* (☎ 892 3719) with both deluxe and budget accommodation. From the end of October to early July, hostel-style twin rooms are $36, standard rooms are $82 and deluxe rooms are $110. In the ski season, hostel rooms are $81 and other rooms are around 50% more. There are also self-contained chalets sleeping six people for $110 a double in summer, $225 in winter. There's a communal kitchen for the regular rooms (you provide crockery and cutlery, they provide pots and pans), as well as a sauna, spa pool, gym, games room, restaurant and house bar.

Places to Eat

The *Whakapapa Store* sells takeaway snacks and food for self-catering – as usual it's more expensive than elsewhere.

Ferguson's Cafe is reasonably priced for snacks, light meals and coffee. Their cakes are superb.

The *Skotel* has a licensed family restaurant and house bar, serving all meals. The restaurant at the *Whakapapa Tavern*, opposite the Chateau, may be open only in winter.

Of course the fancy place to eat is at the *Grand Chateau Hotel*. Its Ruapehu Room is an elegant restaurant serving expensive à la carte meals, or you can try the $35 Saturday night buffet or the $25 Sunday lunch buffet – they're both good value. Also at the Chateau, the *Carvery* is a less-expensive family restaurant, open seasonally.

During the ski season there is a takeaway food van at Whakapapa Village. The *restau-*

rant at the Top of the Bruce, where the lifts and tows start, is there for hungry skiers and sightseers over summer.

Getting There & Away

Trains and InterCity buses stop at National Park village, the main gateway to Whakapapa and the park.

Bus Alpine Scenic Tours (☎ 386 8918) has an inexpensive shuttle bus departing Turangi at 7.30 am and 3.30 pm – with an extra service at 11 am in summer – to Whakapapa Village, the Mangatepopo car park (for the start of the Tongariro Crossing track), National Park and Ketetahi car park (at the end of the Tongariro Crossing) along the way. They will go up to the ski area at the Top of the Bruce above Whakapapa by request; their services also continue north from Turangi to Taupo and Rotorua. Since seats are limited, book in advance to guarantee yourself a spot.

From National Park township other shuttles run to Whakapapa, Mangatepopo and Ketetahi for the Tongariro Crossing and other walks; see the National Park section for details. Transport is also available from Ohakune; see the Ohakune section for details.

Car The park is encircled by roads. SH1 (at this point it's called the Desert Rd) passes down the eastern side of the park; SH4 passes down the western side; SH47 crosses the northern side and SH49 the southern side. The main road up into the park is SH48 which leads to Whakapapa Village, continuing further up the mountain as Bruce Rd to the Top of the Bruce and the Whakapapa Ski Area. The Ohakune Mountain Rd leads up to the Turoa Ski Area from Ohakune in the south-west.

For the Tongariro Crossing, access is from the end of Mangatepopo Road off SH47, and SH47A from the end of Ketetahi Rd off National Park Rd, which runs between SH1 and SH47. Theft from parked vehicles has become a problem at both ends of the track. Don't leave any valuables in your car.

NATIONAL PARK

Situated at the gateway to Tongariro National Park, the small settlement of National Park is at the junction of SH4 and SH47, 15 km from Whakapapa Village. It's just a small village catering to the ski season crowds, with plenty of accommodation but little else apart from great views of Mt Ruapehu. In the quiet summer season it makes a convenient base for the walks and attractions of the park. Several daily shuttle buses leaving from here serve both ends of the Tongariro Crossing walking track and Whakapapa Village in summer, and the Whakapapa Ski Area in winter.

National Park is also a base to organise other activities, notably canoe trips on the Whanganui River.

Activities

Chalet on the Rocks (see Places to Stay) organises a variety of guided mountain bike tours which you can do either with your bike or theirs. Both Howard's Lodge and the Ski Haus also hire tramping boots and other gear for going on the Tongariro Crossing or other treks. The spa pool at the Ski Haus can be hired by guests and non-guests.

Go For It Tours (☎ 892 2705) at the Petticoat Junction building, which is also the railway station, does guided off-road motorcycle tours and rents mountain bikes for $10 per hour.

National Park has no organisation doing canoe trips on the Whanganui River, but operators just up the road further north can arrange transport from National Park. Plateau Outdoor Adventure Guides (☎ 892 2740) and Whanganui River Jet (☎ 895 5995), at Raurimu six km north, are the closest. See the Whanganui National Park section for details on canoe hire and other operators.

Places to Stay

National Park has three good hostels/ski lodges, and a wide range of other accommodation. Prices increase dramatically in the ski season, when accommodation is tight and bookings essential, especially on weekends.

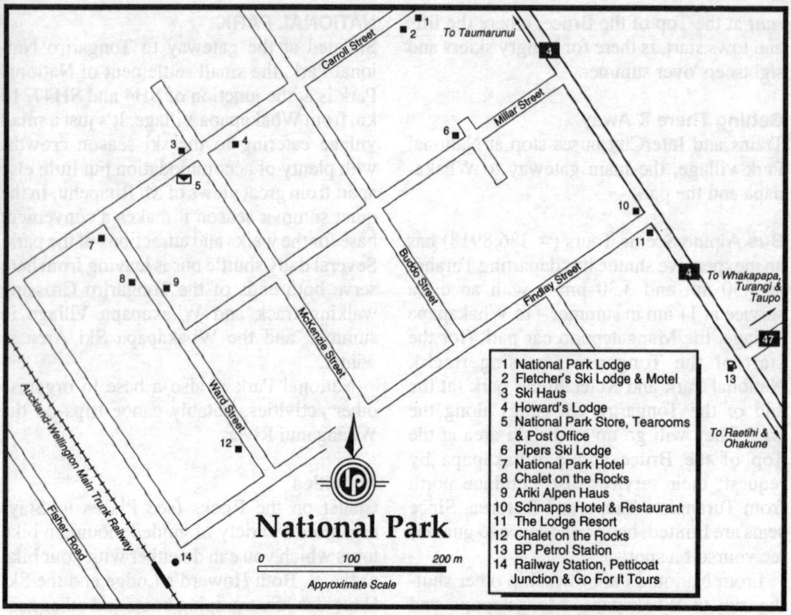

Hostels The *Ski Haus* (☎ 892 2854) on Carroll St has good amenities such as a spa pool, billiards table and a sunken fireplace area in the large lounge. It has a house bar, an inexpensive restaurant and a kitchen to do your own cooking. The hostel organises a variety of activities and transport to Whakapapa and the Tongariro Crossing trail heads. Rooms are simple but comfortable. In summer a dorm bed costs $15, doubles and twins are $40. You can camp on the lawn for $8 per person. From June to the end of October, doubles start at $58 during the week and at $78 on weekends; B&B is also offered.

Also on Carroll St, *Howard's Lodge* (☎ 892 2827) is a good hostel with amenities including a spa pool, BBQ, ski hire, bicycle hire and comfortable lounge and kitchen areas. You can do your own cooking all year round, and inexpensive meals are also available. They provide the same transport for the same prices as the Ski Haus, plus free transport coming from Taupo each Monday. In summer, a bed in the simple bunkhouse out the back costs $15, or a bed in the inside four-bed rooms costs $17, while singles/doubles are $25/40. Winter rates are at least 50% higher, and new chalets are being built.

Further down Carroll St, the *National Park Lodge* (☎ 892 2846) is part of the Fletcher's Motel next door. This older-style ski lodge has a large lounge area and comfortable rooms for $15 in share rooms, or $40 for doubles. It also has a motel block with units from $60. In winter, shared rooms are $20 per person, and other rooms are around 50% higher.

Hotels, Chalets & Motels The *National Park Hotel* (☎ 892 2805) on Carroll St near the railway tracks has bunkroom accommodation at $15 per person with linen included. Regular hotel rooms are $20/45 for singles/doubles. Prices remain the same all year round. There's a kitchen where guests can cook.

Near the hotel, on Ward St, *Chalet on the Rocks* (☎ 892 2938) has two self-contained three-bedroom houses with single and double rooms. Meals are available on request and it also organises bicycle tours. The cost is $20 per person.

Also on Ward St, the *Ariki Alpen Haus* (☎ 892 2801) is open only in ski season. It sleeps 14 to 19 people and offers accommodation in the European tradition – similar to a homestay – with beds from $25 to $55 per person, more in peak seasons. Attractions include a sauna, spa pool and ski hire shop.

Fletcher's Ski Lodge and Motel (☎ 892 2846) on Carroll St offers accommodation, plus spa pools, billiards, volleyball, BBQ, fireplace lounge etc. In summer, motel units are $50 or $60. In winter the prices rise to $80 for studio units and $100 for motel units (more on weekends). In summer, guests can cook in the kitchen; in winter, you have to eat in the restaurant.

The *Mountain Heights Lodge* (☎ 892 2833) on SH4, two km south of National Park township, has motel units at $48 in summer, $110 in winter. It also has lodge accommodation open only during ski season, with a variety of twin rooms and bunkrooms; the cost is $45 per person for dinner, bed & breakfast.

Discovery Motel & Caravan Park (☎ 892 2744) on SH47, halfway between National Park and Whakapapa Village, has chalets and motel units in addition to camp sites for $8. In summer, motel units and chalets are $66 and cabins sleeping two are $12.50 per person. In winter, cabins are $42, and motel units and chalets range from $82 a double to $183 for six people. It has a spa pool, a licensed restaurant and bar.

Other ski lodges include the *Erua Ski Lodge* (☎ 892 2894), six km south of National Park on SH4, open only during the ski season, and the *Slalom Ski Lodge* (☎ 892 2855) at Raurimu, six km north of National Park on SH4.

Places to Eat

All the accommodation places in National Park make provisions for their guests' meals, with meals provided, kitchens where you can do your own cooking, or both.

The bar and restaurant at the *Ski Haus* are open to guests and non-guests alike. Its restaurant is open all year round; several other places to stay have restaurants, such as *Schnapps* on the highway, but are usually open only in winter.

Getting There & Away

Bus Daily InterCity buses arrive and depart from the National Park Store on Carroll St. Tickets are sold at the Ski Haus and Howard's Lodge. The trip either north to Auckland via Hamilton or south to Wellington via Palmerston North takes about five hours.

Alpine Scenic Tours (☎ 386 8918) operates several daily shuttle buses making a round trip between Turangi and National Park, with stops at Whakapapa Village, the Whakapapa Ski Area by request, the Mangatepopo and Ketetahi car parks for transport to the Tongariro Crossing track, and on from Turangi to Taupo and Rotorua. For the track ends, make sure you arrange transport beforehand, as there are no phones at the trail heads.

Tongariro Track Transport (☎ 892 2610) operates a daily shuttle bus from behind the National Park BP petrol station on the highway to either end of the Tongariro Crossing track, stopping at Whakapapa Village on the way. The Ski Haus and Howard's Lodge provide similar services for $16 and $15 respectively.

During the ski season most of the accommodation places make some provision for transport to the Whakapapa Ski Area.

Train Some trains running north and south between Auckland and Wellington stop at National Park. *Interislander* ferry tickets and train tickets are sold not from the railway station, but from the Ski Haus or Howard's Lodge, both on Carroll St.

HOROPITO

A few km south of National Park on SH4 at Horopito is a monument to the Last Spike – the spike that marked the completion of the

Main Trunk Railway Line connection between Auckland and Wellington in November 1908, a most significant event which opened up transport to, communication with, and settlement of the central North Island. A plaque at the monument relates how they had struggled to complete the line ever since the 1860s.

OHAKUNE

The pretty town of Ohakune is the closest town to the Turoa Ski Area on the south side of Mt Ruapehu. It's very much a skiing town with lots of motels and even more restaurants – a lot of effort goes into catering for those snow-season big-spenders from mid-June to late October, and many places don't even bother opening up outside this season. Ohakune tries to attract tourists year-round, and many outdoor activities can be organised in summer, including canoeing trips on the Whanganui River.

Ohakune's main commercial district is to the south of the town on the highway. The north end of town by the railway station comes alive during the ski season but is quiet the rest of the year.

While you're in town check out the Big Carrot on SH49, paying homage to the town's primary agricultural product. Kids will like the old tank in the children's play park on Clyde St.

Information

The Ruapehu Visitor Centre (☎ 385 8427; fax 385 8527), 54 Clyde St, has an excellent three-dimensional model of the Tongariro National Park – great for tracing where you're going to walk. The staff make bookings for all the area's activities and accommodation, for InterCity buses and for the train. From June to October it's open Monday to Friday from 8.30 am to 5.30 pm, weekends from 9 am to 2 pm. The rest of the year it's open weekdays from 9 am to 4.30 pm, weekends from 10 am to 2 pm. The centre is also the AA office.

The Ohakune Ranger Station (☎ 385 8578; fax 385 8128) is on Ohakune Mountain Rd, which leads to the ski fields. It's open Monday to Friday from 8 am to 4.30 pm, and daily in the ski season from 8 am to 2.30 pm. It offers maps, current weather reports and other advice about this side of the Tongariro National Park.

The Turoa Ski Area operates an information line (☎ 385 8456) with up-to-the-minute information on ski and road conditions.

Walks

The Ohakune Mountain Rd goes 17 km from the north end of Ohakune to the Turoa Ski Area on Mt Ruapehu. Several walking tracks lead off from this road into the Tongariro National Park. Stop by the Ohakune Ranger Station at the bottom of this road for maps and information about the tracks before you set off. Weather on the mountains is highly changeable, so come prepared for all weather, and let someone know where you're going and when you'll be back.

Two of the most delightful walks are the short 15-minute **Rimu Track** and the longer 1½-hour **Mangawhero Forest Walk**, both departing from opposite the Ohakune Ranger Station. They both pass through a lovely section of native forest; the Rimu Track is marked with plaques pointing out various features of the forest.

Other popular tracks leading from Ohakune Mountain Rd include a 1¼-hour return walk to the **Waitonga Falls**, beginning 11 km past the Ranger Station, and the five-hour return walk to **Lake Surprise**, beginning 15 km past the Ranger Station. If you continue past the falls on the Waitonga Falls track, you'll be on the Round-the-Mountains Track (see the Tongariro National Park section). Other tracks taking off from the Mountain Rd include a 10-minute return walk to the **Mangawhero Falls** and a four to five-hour walk on the **Old Blyth Track**.

There's no regularly scheduled transport up the mountain, and traffic is light for hitching. The Snowliner Shuttle (☎ 385 8573) can be chartered to the tracks, but tends to be expensive. Or you could go to the top with a bicycle (see Cycling) and do some tramping on your way back down.

Cycling
The Powderhorn Ski Shop (☎ 385 8888) hires mountain bikes at $10 per hour, $25 for half a day or $35 per day. A cheaper and highly enjoyable way to do some cycling in Ohakune is to go with Ride the Mountain (☎ 385 8257), who for $20 will take you in a van to the Turoa Ski Area at the top of the Ohakune Mountain Rd and set you loose with a bicycle, helmet and all the other gear you need.

Bicycles are not allowed on any of the trails in the national park.

Other Activities
Ask at the information centre about activities around Ohakune. There's horse trekking, white-water rafting, fishing, canoe, kayak and jet-boat trips on the nearby Whanganui River, golf and more. Or you could go for a hot swim at the Powder Keg restaurant/bar's pool.

Ohakune can be used as a base to organise canoeing trips on the Whanganui River. Two operators in town are Canoe Safaris (☎ 385 9237), which has an office on Miro St, and Yeti Tours (☎ 385 8197). Raetihi Motor Camp (☎ 385 4176) in Raetihi, 11 km west of Ohakune, also has canoeing equipment and arranges transport. See the Whanganui National Park section for more details.

Places to Stay
Finding a place to stay is no problem in summer, but during the ski season you should definitely book ahead, especially for economical accommodation. More places can found in Raetihi, 11 km west. The information centre can make bookings for all of them.

Camping & Cabins The *Ohakune Motor Camp* (☎ 385 8561) at 5 Moore St near the centre is a pleasant camp beside a gurgling

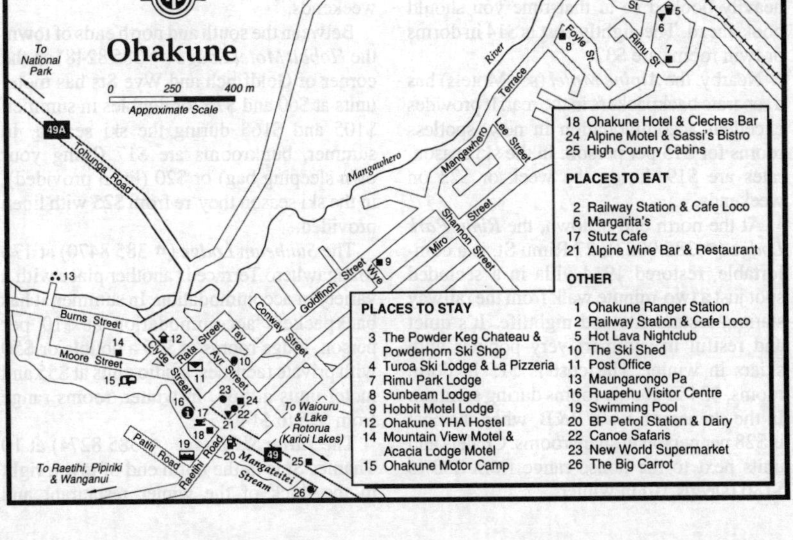

stream, with plenty of trees and green areas and a comfortable TV lounge-dining room. Tent sites are $7 per person, powered sites $9, and backpackers cabins or on-site caravans are $16 per person ($32 in the ski season).

The *Raetihi Motor Camp* (☎ 385 4176) in Raetihi, 11 km west of Ohakune, is a friendly camping ground with tent sites at $7 per person, powered sites at $12 or on-site caravans and cabins at $20 to $25 for two people. They offer free glow-worm tours and feeding of wild possums in the evening, and there are squash and tennis courts, swimming pools, a roller-skating rink and a children's playground nearby. This is also a popular and inexpensive place to hire canoes or kayaks for trips on the Whanganui River.

The *Mangawhero Campsite* is a simple DOC camping ground on Ohakune Mountain Rd. Facilities include cold water and pit toilets; the cost is $2 per night.

Hostels The *Ohakune YHA Hostel* (☎ 385 8724) is on Clyde St, near the post office and information centre. It's a good hostel with twin, triple and bunkrooms; you have your own room key so you can come and go as you wish. During the ski season it is very heavily booked so at that time you should book ahead. The nightly cost is $14 in dorms or twin rooms are $32.

Nearby, the *Alpine Motel* (see Motels) has a separate backpackers in the rear. It provides excellent accommodation in new, spotless rooms for $15 per person. In the ski season, rates are $19 during the week or $23 on weekends.

At the north end of town, the *Rimu Park Lodge* (☎ 385 9023), 27 Rimu St, is a comfortable, restored 1914 villa in a secluded spot just a two-minute walk from the railway station, restaurants and nightlife. It's quiet and restful in summer; very popular with skiers in winter. The cost is $15 in dorm rooms, $34 in double rooms during summer. In the ski season it's a B&B, when the cost is $28 per person in share rooms. Chalets and units next to the house range from $80 to $180 (sleeps 10) in winter.

A number of cabins, motels and lodges in town offer backpackers accommodation; see the other sections for details.

Hotels, Motels & Lodges At the south end of town, the *Ohakune Hotel* (☎ 85 8268) on the corner of Clyde St and Raetihi Rd has singles/doubles for $30/40 or doubles with private facilities are $60.

Nearby, the *Alpine Motel* (☎ 385 8758) at 7 Miro St is a popular place, with studio units, family units, chalets and a separate backpackers in the rear, plus a spa pool and a popular restaurant/bar. Double units are $65, or $110 in winter. Chalets sleeping up to four are $70 a double and $10 for each extra person in summer, or $165 for four in winter.

Also at the southern end of town, the *Mountain View Motel* (☎ 385 8675) at 2 Moore St – opposite the motor camp – has motel units at $65 in summer and $115 in the ski season. There is also a 14-bed bunkhouse for $12 per person ($16 in winter), plus six-bed cabins for $14 per person; bring your own sleeping bag and kitchen utensils.

Next door, at 6 Moore St, the *Acacia Lodge Motel* (☎ 385 8729) has kitchen units at $65 and serviced units at $55 in summer; add another $20 mid-week in winter, $40 on weekends.

Between the south and north ends of town, the *Hobbit Motel Lodge* (☎ 385 8248) on the corner of Goldfinch and Wye Sts has motel units at $60 and $75 for doubles in summer, $105 and $165 during the ski season. In summer, bunkrooms are $17 (bring your own sleeping bag) or $20 (linen provided); in the ski season they're from $25 with linen provided.

The *Sunbeam Lodge* (☎ 385 8470) at 178 Mangawhero Terrace is another place with a variety of accommodation. In summer, it has backpackers accommodation at $10 per person, lodge rooms at $35 a double or $50 with private facilities, studio units at $55 and motel units at $65. In winter, rooms range from $75 to $140.

The *Turoa Ski Lodge* (☎ 385 8274) at 10 Thames St is in the north end of town, right in the thick of the winter restaurant and nightlife scene. It's open only during the ski season with doubles for $90 and there's a bunkroom. It has a popular licensed restaurant.

Ohakune has a number of other lodges that come to life in the ski season. Top of the heap is the *Powderkeg Chateau* (☎ 385 8888), the place to be for après ski, with brand new chalet rooms for $150 a double.

Four km east of town on SH49, the *Ruapehu Homestead* (☎ 385 8799) has a variety of fancy accommodation and a licensed restaurant; it also organises plenty of activities through its Ruapehu Outback Adventures. It has lodge rooms at $30/45 per person in summer/winter, motel units at $80/125 a double in summer/winter, and the bunkroom is $20 per person all year round.

Places to Eat

The restaurant district on the north side is active during the winter with the après ski crowd, but little is open in summer. Those on the south side of town are open all year round.

On the south side, the pleasant *Stutz Cafe* on Clyde St is open every day from breakfast until dinner, with European food, Chinese food, pizza and a takeaways section. Nearby, *Cleches* at the Ohakune Hotel on the corner of Clyde St and Raetihi Rd is also open long hours and has a better class of pub food. On the opposite corner, the *Alpine Wine Bar & Restaurant* is open for wining and dining every evening. Half a block away, *Sassi's Bistro* at the Alpine Motel on Miro St is also open for dinner every evening, all year round; it's a pleasant little place with a varied, changing blackboard menu with something to suit all budgets.

At the northern end of town are many popular restaurants along Thames St, including *La Pizzeria*, which does pretty good pizzas. Or in winter there's the licensed restaurant at the *Turoa Ski Lodge* and, just around the corner, *Margarita's* have their usual brand of Tex-Mex food and lots of drinking.

The most popular place on Thames St is the *Powderkeg* on the corner of Thames St and Mangawhero Terrace. Especially popular for its bar, the yuppie après-ski hang-out, it's also popular for its restaurant with good food and for its indoor heated swimming pool. It's hard to squeeze in the door here at times.

Entertainment

Ohakune is known as the good-fun place in the nightlife department during the ski season; the rest of the year it's pretty quiet. The *Hot Lava* nightclub on Thames St is a popular spot, open every night during the ski season with live music on weekends and disco music on other nights. Other places with live music in the ski season include the always popular *Powderkeg* and the *Turoa Ski Lodge* on Thames St, and the *Ohakune Hotel* on Clyde St in the south part of town.

Getting There & Away

InterCity buses serve Ohakune every day except Saturday, arriving and departing from the Ruapehu Visitor Centre, which sells the tickets. The Kiwi Experience bus also comes here.

The Auckland-Wellington trains stop at Ohakune. Buy tickets at the Ruapehu Visitor Centre, not at the railway station.

Getting Around

In winter several companies have transport between Ohakune and the Turoa Ski Area, all charging $14 for round-trip door-to-door transport from wherever you're staying. A bus also operates from the corner of Clyde and Goldfinch Sts for $10 return.

The Snowliner Shuttle (☎ 385 8573) offers a variety of transport around the area. In winter, the cost is $15 return to the Turoa Ski Area, and $25 to the Whakapapa Ski Area. In summer they can be chartered to the trail heads in the Tongariro National Park, but the price is expensive for only a few people.

LAKE ROTOKURA

Lake Rotokura is about 11 km south of Ohakune on SH49, at Karioi in the Karioi Forest, about a km from the Karioi turn-off. It's called Lake Rotokura on the map and the sign but it's actually two lakes not one, and the locals call them the Karioi Lakes. Karioi means 'places to linger', and they couldn't be more aptly named. They are two little jewels, one above the other, great for picnicking, fishing and relaxing.

WAIOURU

At the junction of SH1 and SH49, km east of Ohakune, Waiouru is primarily an army base. In a large grey concrete building with tanks out front, the **Queen Elizabeth II Army Memorial Museum** tells the history of the New Zealand Army in times of war and peace, with an extensive collection of artefacts from early colonial times to the present and a 23-minute audiovisual presentation. It's open every day from 9 am to 4.30 pm; admission is $7 (children $4).

SH1 from Waiouru to Turangi is known as the Desert Rd and is often closed in winter because of snow, but can also close at other times of the year. It runs through the Rangipo Desert east of Mt Ruapehu. It's not a desert in the true sense of the word, but was so named because of its desert-like appearance caused by its cold, exposed, windswept situation.

Wanganui & Manawatu

The Wanganui region is dominated by the Whanganui River, historically one of the most important rivers in New Zealand. Once the only access to the region, it is still the only way to reach the isolated interior of the Whanganui National Park. Apart from the national park, the main places of interest are Wanganui city, and Palmerston North in neighbouring Manawatu district.

The difference in spelling between 'Whanganui' and 'Wanganui' is mostly a political issue. It was originally spelt Wanganui, because the Maori tribes of the river region do not pronounce 'Wh' as an 'F', contrary to most Maori dialects. However, the sound is aspirated and strictly speaking should be 'Wh'. The 'h' has been officially restored to the name of the river and national park, but not to the city or the region as a whole. The split in spellings is in many way a reflection of the split in attitudes over Maori issues, which came to a head at Moutoa gardens in Wanganui (see that section). Interestingly, the Pakeha dominated town and region retain the old spelling, while the river area, very much Maori territory, takes the new spelling.

You may be startled by the screeching alarm call of the pukeko, a bird commonly found in the rushes of the Whanganui River

HIGHLIGHTS

- Canoeing and jet-boating on the Whanganui River in the Whanganui National Park
- Driving along the Whanganui River Road to Pipiriki
- The historic riverport city of Wanganui

Wanganui

The main artery of the Wanganui district is the Whanganui River, which flows from Mt Tongariro down to the sea at Wanganui, the main city and service centre for the surrounding region. The main highlight of the district is the Whanganui National Park, based around the river. The park has dense forest and good walks but it is noted mainly for canoeing trips and jet boating on the Whanganui River.

WHANGANUI NATIONAL PARK

Whanganui National Park's main attraction is the Whanganui River, which winds its way 329 km from its source on the flanks of Mt Tongariro in the central North Island to the Tasman Sea at the city of Wanganui. The river is not the longest in the country – that honour goes to the Waikato River – but the fact that it is the longest *navigable* river in the country has been shaping its destiny for

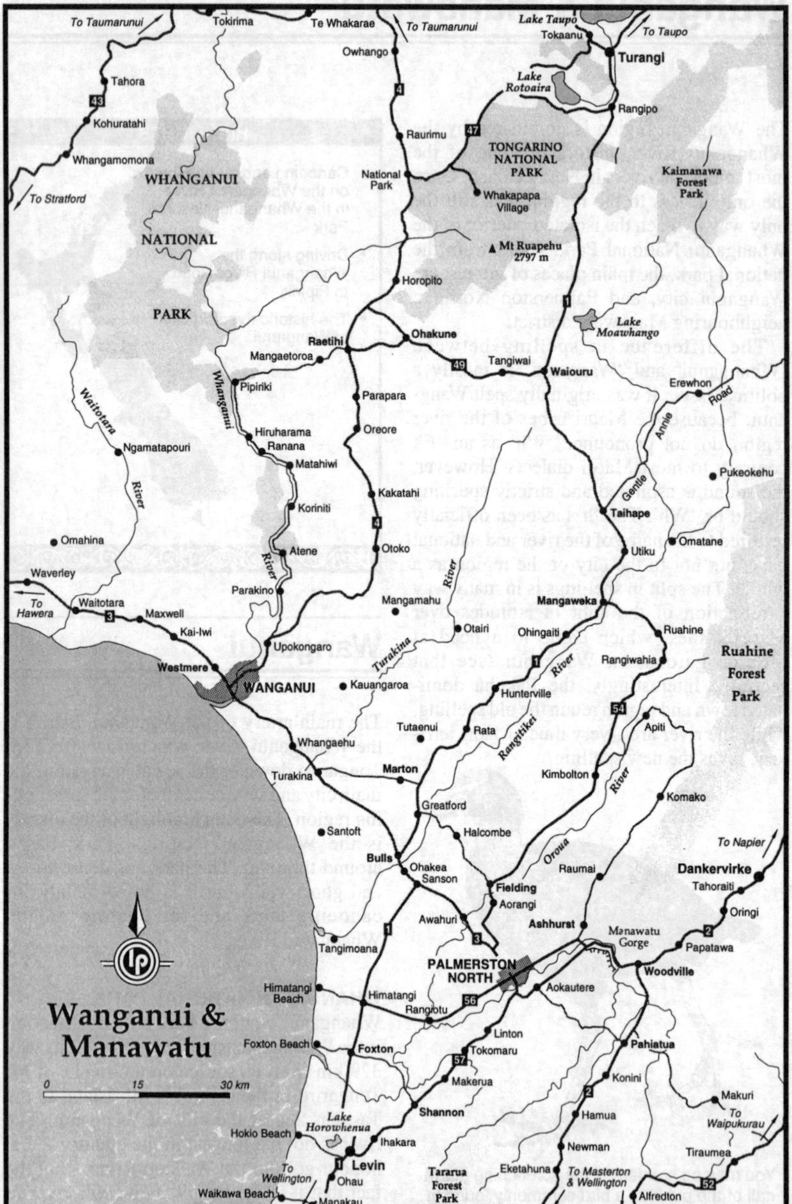
Wanganui &
Manawatu
To Taumarunui
Tokirima
Te Whakarae
To Taumarunui
Lake Taupo
Tokaanu
To Taupo
Turangi
Owhango
Tahora
Lake Rotoaira
Rangipo
Kohuratahi
Raurimu
TONGARINO NATIONAL PARK
Whangamomona
Kaimanawa Forest Park
National Park
Whakapapa Village
WHANGANUI
To Stratford
NATIONAL
Mt Ruapehu 2797 m
Horopito
PARK
Lake Moawhango
Ohakune
Raetihi
Mangaetoroa
Tangiwai
Waiouru
Pipiriki
Whanganui
Erewhon
Parapara
Waitotara
Annie
Road
Oreore
Hiruharama
Ranana
Ngamatapouri
Matahiwi
Gentle
Pukeokehu
River
Kakatahi
Koriniti
Taihape
Omahina
Utiku
Omatane
Atene
Otoko
River
Waverley
Parakino
River
To Hawera
Waitotara
Maxwell
Mangamahu
Mangaweka
Kai-Iwi
Otairi
Ohingaiti
Ruahine
Upokongaro
Turakina
Rangiwahia
Ruahine Forest Park
Westmere
River
WANGANUI
Kauangaroa
Hunterville
Apiti
Tutaenui
Rata
Rangitikei
Whangaehu
River
Kimbolton
Turakina
Marton
Komako
Greatford
Santoft
Halcombe
To Napier
Bulls
Oroua
Dankervirke
Ohakea
Sanson
Raumai
Tahoraiti
Fielding
Aorangi
Oringi
Awahuri
Ashhurst
Manawatu Gorge
Papatawa
Tangimoana
PALMERSTON NORTH
Woodville
Himatangi Beach
Himatangi
Aokautere
Rangiotu
Linton
Foxton Beach
Foxton
Tokomaru
Pahiatua
Konini
Makerua
Makuri
0
15
30 km
Shannon
Hamua
To Waipukurau
Lake Horowhenua
Hokio Beach
Ihakara
Newman
Tiraumea
Levin
To Wellington
Ohau
Tararua Forest Park
Eketahuna
To Masterton & Wellington
Waikawa Beach
Manakau
Alfredton
43
4
47
1
49
4
3
1
54
1
3
2
56
57
2
52
1

centuries. Historically a major route for travel between the sea and the interior of the North Island, first by the Maori and then by the Pakeha, the route was eventually superseded by rail and road. In recent years, however, recreational canoe, kayak and jetboat enthusiasts have once again made the river a popular thoroughfare.

The stretch of the river from Taumarunui south to Pipiriki has been added to the New Zealand Great Walks system and called the 'Whanganui Journey'. A Grade Two river, the Whanganui is easy enough to be enjoyed by people of any age, with or without previous canoeing experience, yet there is enough movement and small-size rapids to keep it interesting. A canoe trip down the river is a great way to relax in one of New Zealand's last great wilderness areas.

Though the river ends at Wanganui, most canoe hire and trip operators are based upstream and canoeing trips are usually arranged in Taumarunui, National Park, Ohakune or Raetihi.

Other attractions of the park include two very good walking tracks, the Matemateaonga Walkway and the Mangapurua Track. Fishing and hunting are also popular sports in the park.

History

In Maori legend, the Whanganui River was formed when Mt Taranaki, after his fight with Mt Tongariro over the lovely Mt Pihanga, fled the central North Island and headed for the sea, leaving a long gouge in the earth in his wake. When he reached the sea he turned westwards, finally coming to rest in the place where he stands today. Mt Tongariro sent forth cool water from his side, to flow down and heal the wound in the earth – and so the Whanganui River was born.

The river was settled from very early in New Zealand's history. The great Polynesian explorer Kupe explored some distance upriver from the river's mouth in around 900 AD. Maori genealogy traces a group of people living on the river from about 1100. Major Maori settlement began along the river in around 1350, and flourished along this major route from the sea to the interior.

The first European to travel the river was Andrew Powers in 1831, but he didn't do it of his own free will – he was brought up the river as a captive by some Maori of the Ngati Tuwharetoa tribe.

European influence did not begin on the river until missionaries arrived in the 1840s. The missionary settlements of Hiruharama (Jerusalem), Ranana (London), Koriniti (Corinth) and Atene (Athens) still survive today, though the population along the river has dwindled from its former numbers. A French Catholic missionary established the Daughters of Our Lady of Compassion in Hiruharama in 1892. St Joseph's church is still the most prominent feature of the town and the large, white wooden convent still stands in a beautiful garden beside it.

Steamers first voyaged up the river in the mid-1860s when, encouraged by Maori from the Taranaki region, some of the river tribes joined in the Hauhau Rebellion – a Maori movement seeking to oust Europeans from New Zealand.

In 1886 the first commercial steamer transport service was established by a Wanganui company, and others soon followed, connecting parts of the river all the way from Wanganui to Taumarunui. They serviced the river communities and grew in importance as a transport link from the sea to the interior of the island, especially after 1903 when the Main Trunk Railway reached Taumarunui from the north.

Tourism was another major development on the river. Internationally advertised tourist trips on the 'the Rhine of Maoriland' became so popular that, by 1905, 12,000 tourists a year were making the trip upriver from Wanganui or downriver from Taumarunui to Pipiriki House, a magnificent 65-room hotel in Pipiriki that burnt down in 1959.

The engineering feats and skippering ability required to operate the steamboats and paddle steamers on the Whanganui River became legendary, spawning something like the lore that Mark Twain made famous on the Mississippi River. It required some imaginative engineering in some places, such as cables and channelling of the river's currents.

Around 1918, land along the river above Pipiriki was given as grants to returning WWI soldiers. This rugged area was a major challenge to clear, and eventually the combined factors of isolation, economic difficulty (especially in the 1930s Depression), declining soil fertility, floods, road washouts and erosion all became too much for the settlers. Some families struggled for as long as 30 years to make a go of their farms, but by the early 1940s only a few farms remained.

One of the most famous features of the river, the Bridge to Nowhere, was built in 1936 as part of a road from Raetihi to the river. It stands as mute testimony to the failed efforts to settle the region. The track from the Mangapurua Landing to the bridge, though now only walking track, used to be a 4½-metre-wide roadway leading down to the river-boat landing. The Matemateaonga Walkway and the Mangapurua Track also follow former roads and are now being reclaimed by the forest.

Improved roads and the Auckland-Wellington Main Trunk railway line gradually superseded the riverboats, the last of which made its final voyage in 1959. Today only one vessel of the old fleet still operates on the river: the *Otunui* makes river cruises on the lower reaches of the river from Wanganui. Another of the old fleet, the MV *Ongarue*, has been restored and is on display at Pipiriki, and the *Waimarie*, which had sunk at its mooring in Wanganui in 1952, has been raised and is undergoing restoration in Wanganui. The MV *Waireka* has been moved from the Whanganui River and now operates tourist cruises at Huka Falls near Taupo.

Information

Maps, brochures and information about the park are available at the DOC offices in Wanganui (☎ 345 2402; fax 345 8712), Taumarunui (☎ (07) 895 8201; fax 895 9036) and Pipiriki (☎ 385 4631; fax 385 3162). Tourist Information Centres in the area – at Taumarunui, Ohakune, Raetihi and Wanganui – also have some information on the park.

Good books about the river, available locally, include the *Guide to the Whanganui River* by the New Zealand Canoeing Association, and *The Wanganui River – a scenic, historic and wilderness experience* published by the Department of Lands and Survey. The Canoeing Association's *Guide* is an excellent companion on canoe trips. *In and Around Whanganui National Park*, a paperback booklet published by the DOC, is good if you want to do some walking or tramping.

Whanganui River

The native bush is thick podocarp-broadleaf forest, with many types of trees and ferns. Occasionally you will see poplar and other introduced trees along the river, evidence of where people planted them in settlements that have long since vanished.

There are also traces of former Maori settlement along the river in various places, with pa sites, old *kainga* (village) sites, and the unusual Hauhau niu poles of war and peace at Maraekowhai, at the confluence of the Whanganui and Ohura rivers. The Ratakura, Reinga Kokiri and Te Rerehapa Falls, all near Maraekowhai on the Ohura River, were popular places for Maori to come to catch small 'tuna riki' eels. Several of the landings marked along the Whanganui River's banks were once riverboat landings. The small but fascinating Nukunuku Museum beside the river at Nukunuku, just downriver from Ohinepa, is a popular feature of river trips beginning at Ohinepa or Taumarunui.

Canoe & Kayak Trips The most popular part of the river for canoeing and kayaking is the section from Taumarunui to Pipiriki. Entry to the river is made from the boat ramps at Taumarunui (Cherry Grove), Ohinepa and Whakahoro (Wades Landing).

Taumarunui to Pipiriki is a five-day/four-night trip. Ohinepa to Pipiriki is a four-day/three-night trip and Whakahoro to Pipiriki is a three-day/two-night trip. Taumarunui to Whakahoro is a popular overnight trip, especially for weekenders, or you can do a one-day trip from Taumarunui to Ohinepa or Ohinepa to Whakahoro. From Whakahoro to Pipiriki, 87 km downstream, there's no road access so you're committed to being on the river for a few days.

Most canoeists stop in Pipiriki. Below Pipiriki the river widens out, the current is more sluggish and about 30 km from the sea the river becomes tidal and paddling is more difficult.

The season for canoe trips is usually from around September to Easter. Up to 5000 people do this trip each year, the majority of them over the summer holidays from Christmas to the end of January. Weekends and Easter are also popular. During winter the river is almost deserted, with good reason. The cold weather and shorter days deter most people, and the winter currents are swifter. Macho types who want to do it in winter should probably wear a wetsuit.

Canoe and kayak operators will provide you with everything you need for the journey, including life jackets and waterproof drums – essential if you should capsize in rapids. Most operators also have tents, sleeping bags and other camping gear for hire at very reasonable rates.

Prices range from about $15 to $30 per day for single-person kayaks, $30 to $35 per day for two-person Canadian canoes (transport not included). Transport in and out can be just as costly as the canoes themselves; the cost may be around $25 to $40 per person, depending where you're starting out from, sometimes much higher. Some operators include the transport cost in the bargain when they hire the canoes. When comparing prices among different companies, ask about transport in and out and figure this amount into the overall cost of the trip. Two of the cheapest we found were Raetihi Motor Camp in Raetihi and Wades Landing Outdoors, based at Whakahoro in summer.

Another option is a guided canoe or kayak trip that provides all equipment, transport, food, cooking, setting up and taking down of tents, etc. Typical prices are around $200 to $250 per person for a two-day guided trip and around $550 per person for a five-day guided trip.

Canoe and kayak operators that offer independent hiring and/or guided trips include:

Pioneer Jet-Boat Tours, Taumarunui (☎ 895 8074). Hire only.
Kellys Motel, Taumarunui (☎ 895 8175). Hire only.
Wades Landing Outdoors, Raurimu (☎ 894 5995). Hire only.
Plateau Outdoor Adventure Guides, Raurimu (☎ 892 2740). Guided trips and hire.
Raetihi Motor Camp, Raetihi (☎ 385 4176). Hire only.
Yeti Tours, Ohakune (☎ 385 8197). Guided trips and hire.
Canoe Safaris, Ohakune (☎ 385 9237). Guided trips only.
Whanganui River Experiences, Wanganui (☎ 345 7933). Guided trips and hire.
Rivercity Tours, Wanganui (☎ 344 2554). Guide trips and hire.

Jet-Boat Trips Jet-boats are another alternative for getting around on the river. Quite different from canoe trips, jet-boat trips are loud and fast – and they give you a chance to see parts of the river in just a few hours that would take you days to cover in a canoe or kayak. Jet-boat trips depart from Pipiriki, Taumarunui and Whakahoro. All the jet-boat operators will provide transport to the river ends of the Matemateaonga Walkway and the Mangapurua Track.

Departing from Pipiriki, you can take a number of trips including a four-hour return trip to the Bridge to Nowhere for $60 per person (children half price) with Bridge to Nowhere Jet Boat Tours (☎ 385 4128). Trips to and from Wanganui can also be arranged.

From Taumarunui you can do anything from a short 15-minute jet-boat tour for $12 per person (minimum three people) to a two-day trip to Wanganui with Pioneer Jet-Boat Tours (☎ 895 8074).

Whakahoro is a bit off the beaten track – it's a long drive down an unsealed road to get there, whichever way you come – but Wades Landing Outdoors (☎ 894 5995) has one-hour trips for $30 per person, and a host of other options.

Other River Trips In the summer you can have a five-day trip on the MV *Wakapai*, which holds 15 people, for about $550 (children $350), everything included. Phone ☎ 385 4443 for schedules and bookings.

Baldwin Adventure Tours (☎ 343 6346) in Wanganui also has two, three and five-day trips on a motorised flat-bottom boat vessel holding 10 people).

River Safety & Etiquette At the height of summer, numerous canoes, kayaks and jet-boats ply the river. A few simple 'rules of the road' on the river make travel safer and more pleasant for everyone. When an oncoming craft is approaching, keep to the right, unless you are already so far to the left that you'd have to cross in the path of the oncoming craft. The craft heading downriver towards the sea has the right-of-way.

If you're in a canoe or kayak and a jet-boat is approaching from either direction, you should move to the true right of the river if possible – 'true right' is the right side of the river as you face downstream. You can minimise the effect of jet-boat wake by turning at right angles to it.

When beaching a canoe or kayak, especially at the end of the day, pull it well clear of the water and secure it tightly. Water levels on the river are extremely changeable and can rise quickly.

Don't drink the river water unless it's boiled. Clean drinking water is available at huts and at the posted camping grounds where rain water is collected in tanks. Water from the tributary streams may be safe to drink, but use your own judgement.

Tramping

There are various tramping possibilities in the park. Probably the most famous and most travelled is the 40-minute bush walk from the river's Mangapurua Landing to the Bridge to Nowhere, 30 km upstream from Pipiriki.

The Matemateaonga Walkway and the Mangapurua Track are excellent for longer tramps. Both are one-way tracks beginning (or ending) at remote spots on the river, so you must arrange for jet-boat transport to or from these ends of the tracks. Any jet-boat operator on the river will do this, but if they have to make a special trip from Pipiriki or Whakahoro to pick you up expect to pay around $200 for four people. If you arrive at the Ramanui Lodge, and jet-boats are already there, the price is substantially cheaper for the transfer to the Mangapurua trail head.

Several good walks are found along the section of river between Pipiriki and Wanganui; see the Whanganui River Road & Pipiriki section for details on these. The DOC offices in Wanganui, Pipiriki and Taumarunui have information, maps and brochures on all the walking tracks in the area.

Matemateaonga Walkway Taking four days to complete, the 42-km Matemateaonga Walkway has been described as one of New Zealand's best walks. Nevertheless it is not widely known and does not attract the crowds that can form on some of New Zealand's more famous tracks, probably due to its remoteness.

Penetrating deep into bush, wilderness and hill country, the track follows an old Maori track and a disused settlers' dray road between the Wanganui and Taranaki regions. It traverses the Matemateaonga Range along the route of the Whakaihuwaka Rd, started in 1911 to create a more direct link from Stratford to Raetihi and the Main Trunk Railway. The track was cut and was to be widened to a road, but the outbreak of WW I interrupted the plans and the road was never completed.

The track passes through thick bush and regenerating bush. Much of it follows the crest of the Matemateaonga Range. On a clear day, a 1½-hour side trip to the summit of Mt Humphries affords a panoramic view of the Wanganui region all the way to

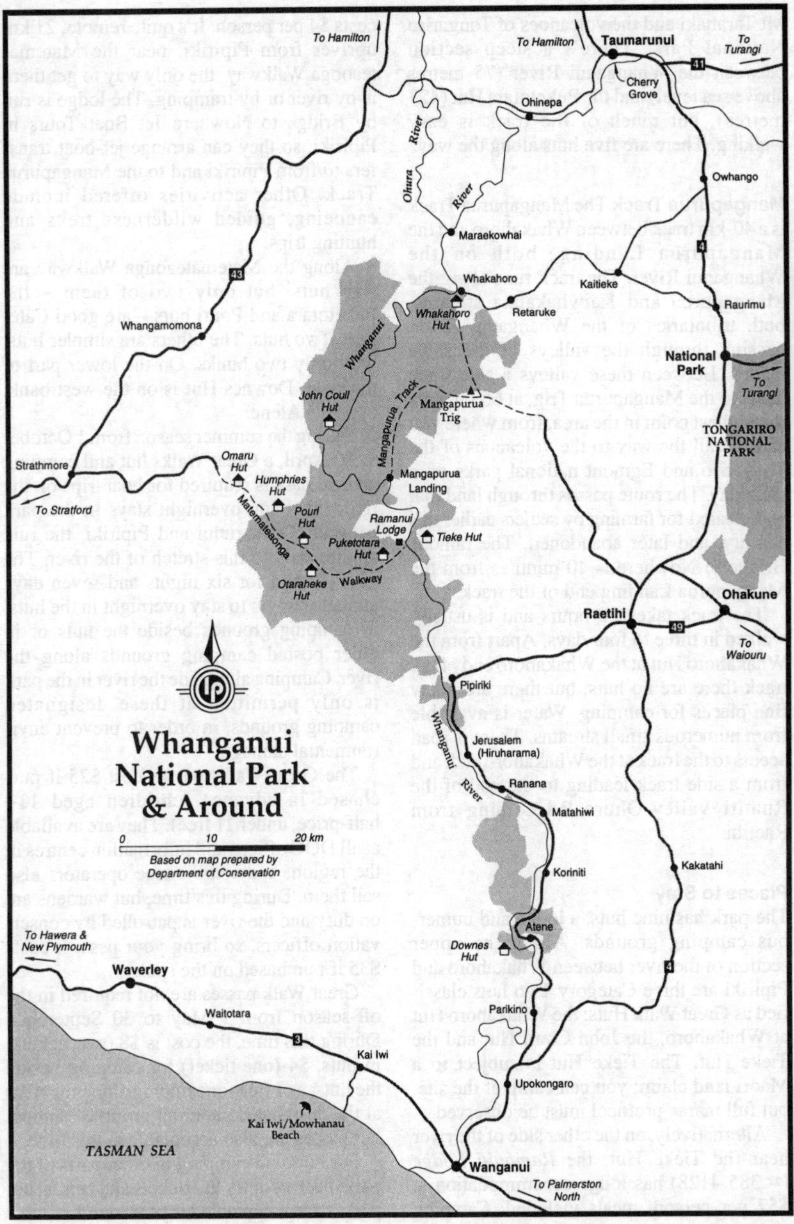
Whanganui
National Park
& Around
0
10
20 km
Based on map prepared by
Department of Conservation
To Hamilton
To Hamilton
Taumarunui
To Turangi
41
Cherry Grove
Ohinepa
Ohura River
River
Owhango
Maraekowhai
4
Kaitieke
Whakahoro
Whakahoro Hut
Retaruke
Raurimu
43
Whangamomona
Whanganui
National Park
To Turangi
Mangapurua Track
John Coull Hut
Mangapurua Trig
TONGARIRO NATIONAL PARK
Strathmore
Omaru Hut
Humphries Hut
Mangapurua Landing
To Stratford
Matemateaonga
Pouri Hut
Ramanui Lodge
Tieke Hut
Puketotara Hut
Walkway
Otaraheke Hut
Ohakune
Raetihi
49
To Waiouru
Pipiriki
Whanganui
Jerusalem (Hiruharama)
Ranana
River
Matahiwi
Koriniti
Kakatahi
To Hawera & New Plymouth
Atene
Downes Hut
4
Waverley
Waitotara
Parikino
3
Kai Iwi
Upokongaro
Kai Iwi/Mowhanau Beach
TASMAN SEA
Wanganui
To Palmerston North

WANGANUI

Mt Taranaki and the volcanoes of Tongariro National Park. There's a steep section between the Whanganui River (75 metres above sea level) and the Puketotara Hut (427 metres), but much of the track is easy walking. There are five huts along the way.

Mangapurua Track The Mangapurua Track is a 40-km track between Whakahoro and the Mangapurua Landing, both on the Whanganui River. The track runs along the Mangapurua and Kaiwhakauka streams, both tributaries of the Whanganui River, passing through the valleys of the same names. Between these valleys a side track leads to the Mangapurua Trig, at 663 metres the highest point in the area, from where you can see all the way to the volcanoes of the Tongariro and Egmont national parks on a clear day. The route passes through land that was cleared for farming by settlers earlier this century, and later abandoned. The famous Bridge to Nowhere is 40 minutes from the Mangapurua Landing end of the track.

The track takes 20 hours and is usually walked in three to four days. Apart from the Whakahoro Hut at the Whakahoro end of the track there are no huts, but there are many fine places for camping. Water is available from numerous small streams. There is road access to the track at the Whakahoro end, and from a side track leading to the end of the Ruatiti Valley-Ohura Rd coming from Raetihi.

Places to Stay

The park has nine huts, a lodge and numerous camping grounds. Along the upper section of the river between Whakahoro and Pipiriki are three Category Two huts classified as Great Walk Huts: the Whakahoro Hut at Whakahoro, the John Coull Hut and the Tieke Hut. The Tieke Hut is subject to a Maori land claim; you can camp at the site, but full marae protocol must be observed.

Alternatively, on the other side of the river near the Tieke Hut, the *Ramanui Lodge* (☎ 385 4128) has lodge accommodation at $57 per person, meals included. Camping costs $4 per person. It's quite remote, 21 km upriver from Pipiriki, near the Matemateaonga Walkway; the only way to get there is by river or by tramping. The lodge is run by Bridge to Nowhere Jet Boat Tours in Pipiriki, so they can arrange jet-boat transfers to/from Pipiriki and to the Mangapurua Track. Other activities offered include canoeing, guided wilderness treks and hunting trips.

Along the Matemateaonga Walkway are five huts, but only two of them – the Puketotara and Pouri huts – are good Category Two huts. The others are simpler huts, with only two bunks. On the lower part of the river, Downes Hut is on the west bank, opposite Atene.

During the summer season from 1 October to 30 April, a Great Walks hut and camping ground pass is required for boat trips on the river involving overnight stays in the park between Taumarunui and Pipiriki; the rule applies only to this stretch of the river. The pass is valid for six nights and seven days and allows you to stay overnight in the huts, in camping grounds beside the huts or in other posted camping grounds along the river. Camping alongside the river in the park is only permitted at these designated camping grounds, in order to prevent environmental damage.

The Great Walks passes cost $25 if purchased in advance (children aged 11+ half-price, under 11 free). They are available at all DOC offices and information centres in the region, and some canoe operators also sell them. During this time, hut wardens are on duty and the river is patrolled by conservation officers, so bring your pass. It costs $35 if purchased on the spot.

Great Walk passes are not required in the off-season from 1 May to 30 September. During this time, the cost is $8 (two tickets) in huts, $4 (one ticket) for camping beside the huts, and free for camping along the river at the designated camping grounds. Annual hut passes are also acceptable at this time.

For huts and camping in other parts of the park, back country hut tickets and annual hut passes are acceptable all year round.

Getting There & Away

If you're going on a canoe or kayak trip, the canoe company will make some arrangement for transport to get you and the canoe to and from the river.

Camp 'n Canoe (☎ 764 6737) in Kaponga, Taranaki, has guided trips and transport in and out to both ends of the Matemateaonga Walkway. You can check with the DOC and information centres at Stratford in Taranaki, as well as the usual ones for the park, to see if anyone else is also offering this service.

There's road access to the river at Taumarunui, Ohinepa and Whakahoro. Whakahoro is a long drive in through a remote area, along a road that is unsealed for much of its distance; roads leading to Whakahoro take off from Owhango or Raurimu, both on SH4. There isn't any further road access to the river until you reach Pipiriki, 87 km downstream from Whakahoro. From Pipiriki, the Whanganui River Rd heads south 79 km to Wanganui and east 28 km to Raetihi.

The only way to reach any part of the river by public transport is at Taumarunui, served by buses and trains, and at Pipiriki, where the mail-run bus makes a round trip coming up from Wanganui on weekdays. See the Taumarunui and Wanganui sections for details.

WANGANUI

Midway between Wellington and New Plymouth, Wanganui is an attractive coastal city on the banks of the Whanganui River. The town has many fine old buildings and the central city has been rejuvenated by the restoration of historic buildings on the main street, Victoria St, down by the river. The block from Taupo Key and Ridgway St has many restored reminders of Wanganui's days as a prominent port.

The Whanganui River, which enters the sea at Wanganui, is the longest navigable river in New Zealand. It starts off on Mt Tongariro and travels 329 km, passing through the Whanganui National Park named for the river, to its mouth in the Whanganui basin. The estuary, over 30 km long, is the area known to the early Maori as Whanganui, meaning 'great estuary' or 'great wait'.

History

Kupe, the great Polynesian explorer and navigator, is believed to have travelled up the Whanganui River for about 20 km around 900 AD. There were Maori living in the area around 1100, and they fully established themselves soon after the great Polynesian migration from Hawaiki around 1350. By the time the first European settlers came to the coast around the late 1830s there were numerous Maori settlements scattered up and down the river.

European settlement at Wanganui was hastened along when the New Zealand Company was unable to keep up with the supply and demand for land around Wellington. In 1840 many Wellington settlers moved to Wanganui and founded a permanent settlement there, the signing of the deed being conducted on the site now known as Moutoa Gardens.

The settlement was initially called Petre after one of the directors of the New Zealand Company, but his name wasn't destined to last on the maps for long. In 1844 it was changed to Wanganui, the name Kupe had given the river.

When the Maori understood that the gifts the Pakeha had presented them were in exchange for the permanent acquisition of their land, seven years of bitter opposition followed. The Pakeha brought in thousands of troops to occupy Queen's Park, and the Rutland Stockade dominated the hill. Ultimately, the struggle was settled by arbitration and when the Maori Wars were waged with the Taranaki tribes, the Wanganui Maori actively assisted the Pakeha.

Information

The Wanganui Information Centre (☎ & fax 345 3286) is on Guyton St between St Hill and Wilson Sts, 1½ blocks from Victoria Ave. It's open Monday to Friday from 8.30 am to 5 pm, Saturday and Sunday from 10 am to 2 pm, with extended hours during the

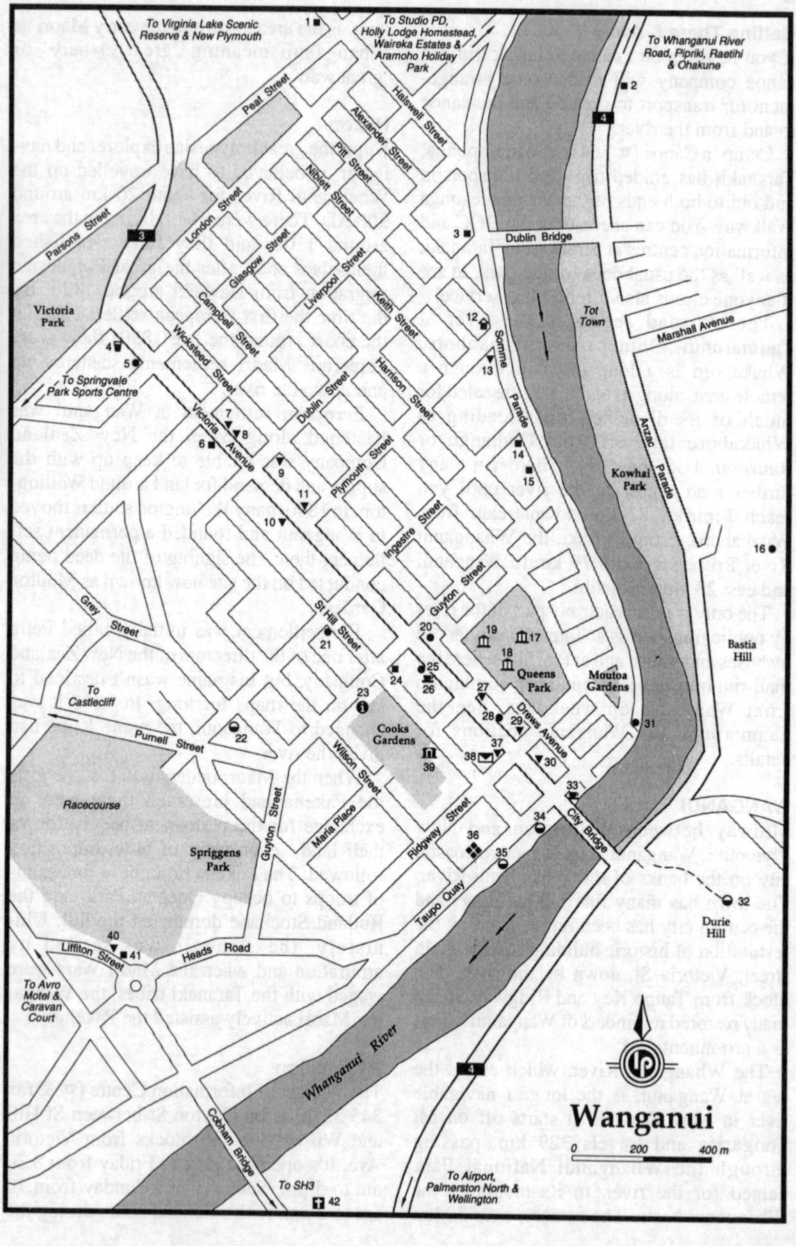

To Virginia Lake Scenic Reserve & New Plymouth
To Studio PD, Holly Lodge Homestead, Waireka Estates & Aramoho Holiday Park
To Whanganui River Road, Pipiriki, Raetihi & Ohakune
Peat Street
Halswell Street
Alexander Street
Pitt Street
Niblett Street
London Street
Parsons Street
Glasgow Street
Liverpool Street
Campbell Street
Keith Street
Dublin Bridge
Tot Town
Marshall Avenue
Victoria Park
Wicksteed Street
Harrison Street
Somme Parade
To Springvale Park Sports Centre
Victoria Avenue
Dublin Street
Plymouth Street
Anzac Parade
Kowhai Park
Ingestre Street
Guyton Street
Grey Street
St Hill Street
Queens Park
Basti Hill
Moutoa Gardens
Drews Avenue
To Castlecliff
Cooks Gardens
Pumell Street
Wilson Street
Racecourse
Maria Place
Guyton Street
Ridgway Street
City Bridge
Spriggens Park
Taupo Quay
Durie Hill
Liffiton Street
Heads Road
To Avro Motel & Caravan Court
Whanganui River
Cobham Bridge
To SH3
To Airport, Palmerston North & Wellington
Wanganui
0
200
400 m

PLACES TO STAY

1 River City Motel
2 Acacia Park Motel
3 Astral Motel
6 Mid Town Motor Inn
12 Riverside Inn & YHA Hostel
14 Riverside Motel
15 Tamara Backpackers
24 Grand Hotel & Cobb & Co Restaurant
41 Coachman's Lodge

PLACES TO EAT

7 Wing-Wah Chinese Restaurant
8 McDonald's
9 Michaels Restaurant
10 KFC
11 Pizza Hut
13 Riverside Restaurant
26 Dr Johnson's Coffee House
27 Oriental Thai Restaurant
29 Rutland Arms Inn
30 George's Fish & Chips
33 Quay Cafe & Bar
37 Chamomile Cafe & Cables Restaurant & Bar
40 Liffiton Castle

OTHER

4 Celtic Arms Pub
5 Woolworth's Supermarket
16 Water Tower
17 Sarjeant Gallery
18 War Memorial Hall
19 Whanganui Regional Museum
20 Barristers Disco
21 DOC
22 White Star Bus Stop
23 Information Centre
25 Air New Zealand
28 Automobile Association (AA)
31 Whanganui Riverboat Centre
32 Durie Hill Elevator
33 Quay Cafe & Bar
34 *Otunui* Dock
35 Wanganui Travel Centre
36 Trafalgar Square Shopping Mall & Foodtown Supermarket
38 Post Office
39 Opera House
42 Pukiti Maori Church (St Paul's)

summer. The staff are very helpful and there's a great model of the area from Wanganui right up to the Tongariro National Park.

The DOC office (☎ 345 2402; fax 345 8712), on the corner of Ingestre and St Hill Sts, is a good resource for maps, pamphlets and information on the Whanganui National Park, Whanganui River Rd, and natural attractions around Wanganui.

The AA office (☎ 345 4578) is at 78 Victoria Ave.

Wanganui Regional Museum

The Wanganui Regional Museum, opposite the War Memorial Hall on Wicksteed St near Maria Place, is one of the largest and best regional museums in New Zealand with excellent Maori exhibits. The Maori collection includes the magnificently carved Te Mata-o-Houroa war canoe, other fine carvings and some nasty-looking *meres*, those elegant but lethal greenstone clubs. The museum also has good colonial and wildlife collections – the display of moa skeletons is particularly worth seeing. The museum is open Monday to Saturday from 10 am to 4.30 pm, Sunday from 1 to 4.30 pm; admission is $2 (children 60c).

Sarjeant Gallery

On the hill beside the museum is Wanganui's art gallery, with an extensive permanent exhibition, as well as frequent special exhibits. It's open Monday to Friday from 10.30 am to 4.30 pm and weekends and public holidays from 1 to 4.30 pm; admission is free, donations gratefully accepted.

Parks & Gardens

Wanganui has several parks right in the city centre including the pleasant **Queens Park** in which the museum, gallery and war memorial hall are situated.

Wanganui's most famous town gardens is undoubtedly **Moutoa Gardens**, claimed as Maori land and subject to a four-month Maori occupation in 1995. The occupation signalled a new chapter in Maori-Pakeha relations in New Zealand and caused great acrimony in the town. The city council, abandoned by Wellington, fought the claim in the High Court, angry Pakeha counter-demonstrated under the banner of 'One New Zealand', and police raids flamed Maori anger. When the claim was eventually rejected by the High Court, the country looked on expecting violence, but the occupation was peacefully abandoned after a moving night-long meeting addressed by Maori leaders. The gardens remained fenced off and have acquired a sacred status in the eyes of many Maori visitors.

Across the river from the town centre, **Kowhai Park** is a pleasant riverside park with an arboretum, plantings of exotic trees, a rose garden and a children's section with a Tot Town Railway, bumper boats, mini-golf and an imaginative playground. The **Glenlogie Rose Gardens** are on the corner of Anzac Pde and Marshall Ave, opposite Kowhai Park.

The **Virginia Lake Scenic Reserve (Rotokawau)**, about one km north from the top end of Victoria Ave, is a beautiful reserve with a lake, theme gardens, a walk-in aviary, numerous statues, and the Higginbottom Fountain, colourfully lit up at night. The winter gardens and aviary are open from 10 am to 4 pm daily, and the rest of the reserve is always open.

Whanganui Riverboat Centre

On the riverbank beside Taupo Quay, the Whanganui Riverboat Centre houses the old *Waimarie* side-paddle steamer, currently being restored. The 260-passenger vessel was launched on the Whanganui River in 1900, and plied the river for over 50 years until 1952, when it sank at its original berth. It remained submerged for another 40 years until it was raised for restoration with the goal of getting the *Waimarie* on the river again. Entry is free.

Durie & Bastia Hills

Across the river from the town centre is the carved gateway to the Durie Hill elevator. You can follow a tunnel into the hillside and then, for $1, ride up through the hill to the summit 65 metres above.

There are two viewpoints at the top: a lower one on the top of the lift machinery room, and the higher War Memorial Tower from where there's a fine view over the town all the way to Mt Taranaki, Mt Ruapehu or the South Island if the weather is clear.

In summer the elevator operates Monday to Friday from 7.30 am to 6 pm, Saturday 10 am to 6 pm and Sunday from 11 am to 5 pm.

Bastia Hill, with a large water tower, is another good viewpoint. You can climb up the water tower on a spiral staircase, but only to the first couple of levels.

Putiki Church

If you turn right after the Victoria Ave bridge and continue for one km or so you come to Putiki Church, also called St Paul's Memorial Church. It's a plain little place from the outside but the interior is magnificent, completely covered in Maori carvings and *tukutuku* wall panels. The church is usually open during the day but if it's locked you can ask for the key at the caretaker's house on the corner of Anaua St and SH3, a couple of doors away.

Holly Lodge & Waireka Estates

Six km upstream from the Dublin St Bridge, the Holly Lodge Homestead is a historic homestead by the river. The homestead is open every day from 8 am to 8 pm; you can reach it by road, or come on the *Otunui* paddle steamer. Out on the grounds are a swimming pool and a playground for the kids. Admission is free.

Two km further upstream, the Waireka Estate (☎ 342 5729) is a 19th-century homestead with a fascinating private museum collection. Interesting tours of the homestead are given to groups. Phone for bookings.

The *Otonui* paddle steamer comes to Holly Lodge and may continue on to Waireka Estate.

Activities

The best way to get a feel for the Whanganui and its history is to take a **river cruise** on the 16-metre (55 ft), *Otunui* paddle steamer. It has a long history on the river, beginning in 1907 when it was shipped in pieces from England and reassembled at Hatrick's Foundry in Wanganui. After plying the Whanganui River for 40 years, the vessel had a varied history which included being sunken for 20 years, relocated to other parts of the North Island around Taupo and Rotorua, and finally returned to Wanganui in 1984, where it was restored and is once again in service and capable of carrying 85 passengers. Cruises depart from the City Marina beneath the City Bridge. The paddle steamer usually sails twice a day at 10 am and 2 pm during summer and once a day at 11 am the rest of the year. To go up the river as far as Holly Lodge costs $14 (children $8).

A variety of other river trips are possible – by canoe, kayak, jet-boat or motorised vessel, starting further up the river in the Whanganui National Park. Rivercity Tours (☎ 344 2554) is one company offering additional tours up the Whanganui River Rd and on to the Drop Scene or the Bridge to Nowhere by jet-boat, returning to Wanganui via SH4. See the Whanganui National Park section for more details on river activities.

If you prefer sightseeing from the air, the Wanganui Aero Club (☎ 345 0914) offers a variety of **scenic flights** and Wanganui Aero Work (☎ 345 3994) offers Tiger Moth flights.

Tours

A very interesting trip up the Whanganui River Rd can be made with the weekday mail run, going up the river from Wanganui to Pipiriki Monday to Friday. The mailman, Don Adams, will pick you up at around 7.30 am for an all-day trip up the river, stopping at many interesting and historic sites including the Kawana Flour Mill, the Jerusalem church and the Koriniti Marae; he'll tell you about the river's past and present roles along the way. Coffee and tea is provided, but bring your own lunch – you'll get back to town around 3 or 4 pm. The cost is $22 per person, with an optional half-hour jet-boat trip from Pipiriki to Drop Scene for another $30. Contact Don (☎ 344 2554) for bookings.

Places to Stay

Camping & Cabins Closest in is the *Avro Motel & Caravan Court* (☎ 345 5279) at 36 Alma Rd, 1.5 km from the city centre. It has 10 powered sites at $12/18 for one/two people plus motel units at $60/72; there's an indoor spa pool and swimming pool but no kitchen facilities.

The *Aramoho Holiday Park* (☎ 343 8402) at 460 Somme Parade, six km north of the Dublin St Bridge, is a peaceful, parklike camp on the town-side bank of the Whanganui River. It has tent and caravan sites at $16 for two people, cabins from $23 to $32, tourist flats at $47 and chalets at $50. Local Aramoho buses run there from Monday to Friday.

Other camps and cabins are at Castlecliff, a seaside suburb eight km from the centre. The local Castlecliff bus runs there every day except Sunday. The *Castlecliff Camp* (☎ 344 2227) by the beach on the corner of Karaka and Rangiora Sts has tent sites at $7.50 per person, powered sites at $16 for two, backpackers cabins at $15/26 for one/two people, larger cabins at $32 for two and on-site caravans at $16/30.

Also in Castlecliff, the *Alwyn Motel & Cabins* (☎ 344 4500) opposite the beach at 65 Karaka St doesn't have camping but it does have cabins at $32, tourist flats at $45 and motel units at $58. All the cabins have private kitchens, and there's a swimming pool.

Hostels The friendly *Riverside Inn* (☎ 347 2529), at 2 Plymouth St opposite the river, is part-YHA hostel and part-guesthouse. The cost is $15 for the dormitories, or $40 for double and twin rooms.

Also overlooking the river is *Tamara Backpackers* (☎ 347 6300), 24 Somme Parade, a rambling old guesthouse turned hostel. It's a well-run, friendly place that also serves as student accommodation in the winter months. Dorm beds cost $12 and $13, singles are $20, doubles and twins are $26 and $30.

B&Bs & Guesthouses The guesthouse half of the *Riverside Inn* (☎ 347 2529) costs $40/55 for singles/doubles including a continental breakfast. There's a hostel in the rear part of the building. Don't confuse it with the *Riverside Motel* nearby on Somme Parade.

Hotels & Motels The *Grand Hotel* (☎ 345 0955) at 99 Guyton St on the corner of St Hill St is about the only hotel of the old school still surviving in Wanganui. Singles/doubles are $50/60; all rooms have private facilities and there's a Cobb & Co restaurant downstairs.

The *River City Motel* (☎ 343 9107) at 59 Halswell St is attractively situated on a quiet tree-lined street at the foot of St John's Hill; the cost is $60 a double. The *Mid Town Motor Inn* (☎ 345 8408) at 321 Victoria Ave has units from $59 to $80. *Coachman's Lodge* (☎ 345 2227) at 30 Liffiton St beside the racecourse has singles/doubles at $50/55.

The *Astral Motel* (☎ 347 9063) at 45 Somme Parade on the corner of Dublin St, by the Dublin St Bridge, has units at $60. Across the river, the *Acacia Park Motel* (☎ 343 9093) at 140 Anzac Parade has studio units at $60/65, $70 with kitchen.

Places to Eat

The *Chamomile Cafe* on the corner of Victoria Ave and Ridgway St is a pleasant cafe with a good selection of light meals and snacks. *Dr Johnson's Coffee House* in the Tudor Court on Victoria Ave between Guyton St and Maria Place is a courtyard cafe.

George's Fish & Chips on Victoria Ave between Ridgway St and Taupo Quay sometimes turns out good fish & chips; it has both restaurant and takeaway sections.

The big three American fast-food chains are all represented in Wanganui, within a couple of blocks on Victoria Ave. *Pizza Hut* is on the corner of Victoria Ave and Plymouth St, *KFC* is almost opposite, and *McDonald's* is in the next block, between Dublin and Liverpool Sts.

For pub food, *Cobb & Co* tucked away in the recesses of the Grand Hotel on the corner of Guyton St and St Hill St, a block from Victoria Ave, has the usual Cobb & Co menu and hours. The *Rutland Arms Inn*, 48 Ridgway St, is one of Wanganui's most pleasant pubs for a meal or drink in a magnificently restored historic building. The *Quay Cafe & Bar* is also popular for meals; see Entertainment.

Wanganui has several good restaurants. *Cables* on the corner of Victoria Ave and Ridgway St has plenty of atmosphere. So does the *Riverside Restaurant* on the corner of Somme Parade and Plymouth St by the river; it offers smorgasbord lunches every day except Saturday, and there's also a bistro and beer garden section.

For Chinese food, the *Wing-Wah* on Victoria Ave is very popular for a cheap meal. The *Oriental Thai Restaurant* at 5 Maria Place, near the museum, has added a bit of spice to Wanganui's dining with good Thai food and it has a bar. *Liffiton Castle*, 26 Liffiton St, is interesting for the kitsch castle-style architecture complete with drawbridge, but it also serves decent Indian and English-style fare for around $17 a main.

If you want to pull out all the stops and splurge, head for *Michaels* at 281 Wicksteed St on the corner of Dublin St. It's a consistently award-winning restaurant with an elegant atmosphere in a classic converted home.

Entertainment

The *Quay Cafe & Bar* on the corner of Victoria Ave and Taupo Quay is a popular place with a variety of entertainment including live music, classical music nights, jazz jam nights, chess and backgammon nights, a soap box night, guest chefs once a month, and so on. It's open Monday to Saturday from 11 am to 3 am, Sunday from 11 am to midnight.

Barristers in Victoria Ave is a popular disco that occasionally has bands.

Getting There & Away

Air Air New Zealand (☎ 345 4089) at 133 Victoria Ave has daily direct flights to Auckland and Wellington, with connections to other centres.

Bus InterCity and Newmans buses operate from the Wanganui Travel Centre (☎ 345 4433) on Taupo Quay between St Hill and Wilson Sts, beside the river. Both companies operate buses to Auckland (eight hours) via Hamilton (four hours), and to New Plymouth (2½ hours). Heading south, buses go to Palmerston North (1½ hours) and on to Wellington (four hours) or Napier (4½ hours). For services north to Tongariro, Taupo and Rotorua, you have to transfer at Bulls, on the way to Palmerston North.

White Star buses (☎ 345 7612) operate from a bus stop in front of the Avis Rent-A-Car office at 161 Ingestre St, with buses to New Plymouth, Palmerston North and Wellington.

The mail-run bus (☎ 344 2554) heads up the Whanganui River Rd to Pipiriki and back on weekdays; see Tours.

Car Between Wanganui and the centre of the North Island the highway (SH4) passes through the Paraparas, an area of interesting papa hills with some beautiful views, and also passes close by the impressive Raukawa Falls and along the Mangawhero River Gorge.

Alternatively you can take the Whanganui River Road – see the Whanganui River Road & Pipiriki section. This is a popular scenic drive, with points of interest marked along the way.

Getting Around

To/From the Airport The Wanganui Airport is about four km from the town centre, across the river and out towards the sea. Ash's Transport Services (☎ 343 8319, mobile (025) 958 693) operates a shuttle service to the airport, the bus station and other points around town. It also operates a shuttle service to the airport at Palmerston North.

Bus Wanganui Taxi-Bus (☎ 343 5555) operates a limited local bus service from Monday to Friday, including routes to Castlecliff, to Aramoho and others, all departing from the taxi-bus stop on Maria Place near Victoria Ave.

WHANGANUI RIVER RD & PIPIRIKI

The Whanganui River Rd, running along the Whanganui River most of the way from Wanganui to Pipiriki, is a scenic and historic area worth making the detour to see. The DOC has dubbed it 'The River Road Scenic and Historic Drive', with plaques along the river pointing out sites of scenic and historic interest. The River Rd meets SH4, the highway from Wanganui to the centre of the North Island, 14 km north of Wanganui and again at Raetihi, 91 km north of Wanganui.

It takes about 1½ to two hours to drive the 79 km between Wanganui and Pipiriki – that's not counting stops. If you come on the mail-run bus from Wanganui to Pipiriki the trip will take most of the day, but you'll have the benefit of lots of social and historical commentary. The full circle from Wanganui to Pipiriki to Raetihi and back down SH4 through the scenic Paraparas and the Mangawhero River Gorge to Wanganui takes about four hours. The River Rd is also becoming increasingly popular with cyclists as an alternative route to SH4.

Information

Pick up a copy of the *The River Road Scenic and Historic Drive* pamphlet, available at the DOC offices and information centres in Wanganui and Pipiriki. It gives a map and commentary about various interesting spots along the road. The Pipiriki DOC office (☎ 385 4631) is open Monday to Friday from 8 am to 5 pm, but is not always staffed.

A Motorist's Guide to the Wanganui River Road by Judith Crawley is a 40-page booklet for $4.95 with much more detail.

Things to See

The main attraction of the drive is the scenery and wonderful views of the Whanganui River. A few notable sights include the Maori villages of Atene (Athens), Koriniti (Corinth), Ranana (London) and Hiruharama (Jerusalem) where you can visit the historic Catholic church; the historic flour mill at Ranana; the Operiki Pa and other pa sites; the Aramoana hill from where there's a panoramic view; and Pipiriki.

Pipiriki Pipiriki is beside the river at the north end of the River Rd, 79 km from Wanganui and 28 km from Raetihi. This is the ending point for canoe trips coming down the Whanganui River and jet-boat rides (see the Whanganui National Park).

The **Colonial House** in Pipiriki is a historic house now converted to a museum with

WANGANUI

many interesting exhibits on the history of Pipiriki and the river. If it's locked, ask at the DOC office about entry.

Beside the Colonial House, some old steps and foundations are all that remain to mark the site of the old **Pipiriki House** hotel, a glamorous 65-room wooden hotel popular with tourists around the turn of the century. Pipiriki was a bustling place served by several river steamers and paddleboats back then, with 12,000 tourists a year recorded in 1905.

Another interesting historic relic at Pipiriki is the **MV *Ongarue***, a 20-metre (60-foot), 65-passenger riverboat that was once one of the A Hatrick & Co riverboat fleet. Built by Yarrow & Co in London in 1903 and shipped in sections to Wanganui where it was assembled, the riverboat plied the river from 1903 to 1959, when the Pipiriki House burned down and the Hatrick riverboat fleet ceased operating. The vessel was restored in 1983 and is now on display on land, about 50 metres from the turn-off to the DOC office.

Walks

The Wanganui Information Centre and DOC office have brochures on a couple of good walks starting from the Whanganui River Rd. Or ask them for the DOC booklet *Walks In and Around Whanganui National Park*, with details on these and other walks along the river.

The **Aramoana Walkway** begins across the road a few metres south of the Aramoana Lookout, near the southern end of the Whanganui River Rd three km north of its junction with SH4. A seven-km, 2½-hour loop track, the walkway passes through farmland and forest to higher ground from where there's a panoramic view of the river area and all the way to Mt Ruapehu to the north, Mt Taranaki to the west and Kapiti Island to the south. Other features include fossilised cockle shell beds, evidence that this land – now 160 metres high – was once at the bottom of the sea. Take drinking water, warm clothing and be prepared for mud after wet weather.

The **Atene Skyline Track** begins at Atene (Athens), on the River Rd about 22 km north of the SH4-River Rd junction. The 18-km track takes six to eight hours and features native forest, sandstone bluffs, and the 523-metre Taumata Trig, commanding broad views. The track ends back on the River Rd, two km downstream from where it began.

Places to Stay

There are various places to stay along the River Rd. The nuns at the Catholic *church* in Hiruharama (Jerusalem) take in travellers. Accommodation is in a large room, divided by curtains into individual cubicles; the cost is around $10 a night.

Beside the river at Ranana, the *Kauika Campsite* (☎ 342 8133) has hot showers, kitchen and laundry facilities. Tent sites are $6 for two people, powered sites $10 for two.

The *Ahu Ahu Ohu* (☎ 345 5711) is a remote farming community four km up the Ahu Ahu Stream from where it meets the Whanganui River at the Te Tuhi Landing, between Atene and Koriniti on the other side of the river. This small alternative community farm welcomes visitors – WWOOFers, backpackers, campers and farmstayers. Contact them before you arrive to be picked up at the Te Tuhi Landing.

At Pipiriki there's a DOC camping ground with toilets and cold water. Another basic DOC camping ground is the *Otumaire Camping Site* between Atene and Koriniti.

Getting There & Away

One of the most convenient and congenial ways to travel the Whanganui River Rd is with the mail-run bus, which goes from Wanganui to Pipiriki on weekdays and takes passengers along with the mail for an interesting tour. See Tours in the Wanganui section.

If travelling by car, petrol is available at Raetihi on the north end of the journey and at Upokongaro and Wanganui on the south end, but nowhere in between.

This route is also becoming a favourite of cyclists, despite the steep hills in parts. SH4 is also fine, but the River Rd has less traffic and is generally considered more interesting.

WESTMERE TO LAKE WIRITOA

Heading north-west from Wanganui on SH3 as if you were going to New Plymouth, after about 5.5 km you reach Rapanui Rd. Turn towards the sea on this road and you come to some pleasant spots.

First is the **Westmere Reserve & Wildlife Refuge**, where there's lots of birdlife and a 40-minute walk around Lake Westmere.

Next along, **Bason Botanical Reserve** is a 25-hectare botanical reserve with a lake, conservatory, gardens of many kinds, a deer park, a lookout tower and an old homestead. The reserve is open every day from 9.30 am until dusk; the conservatory is open from 10 am to 4 pm on weekdays and from 2 to 4 pm on weekends.

At the end of Rapanui Rd, nine km from the SH3 turn-off, **Mowhanau Beach**, also called Kai Iwi Beach, is a beautiful beach. The Mowhanau Creek meets the sea here and provides a safe place for children to swim, and there's also a motor camp and scenic papa cliffs.

Bushy Park

Bushy Park is 24 km north-west of Wanganui. Following the signs as if you were going to New Plymouth, take SH3 to Kai Iwi, turn off where you see the signs and go eight km further on a sealed side road. Owned by the Royal Forest & Bird Protection Society, the park is a 96-hectare scenic reserve with spacious grounds, picnic and BBQ areas, bush walks and a historic 1906 homestead. It's open every day from 10 am to 5 pm; admission is $3 (children $1).

Accommodation is available (☎ 342 9879) in the homestead; it's like staying in a well-preserved museum. Singles/doubles are $45/60 for B&B. It also has an 11-bed bunkroom at $12 per person, and caravan and tent sites at $6 per site.

Ashley Park

Ashley Park (☎ 346 5917), 34 km north-west of Wanganui on SH3, is another attractive park, with gardens and trees surrounding a picturesque lake. Activities include fishing, eeling, birdwatching, and kayaking on the lake. There's also an antiques and crafts shop and Devonshire teas. The park is open every day from 9 am to 5 pm; admission is free.

Here, too, accommodation is available and you can join in the farm activities, go boating on the lake or hunting. B&B in the house is $30 per person, with dinner by arrangement. It also has basic cabins at $11 per person and for camping powered sites cost $10/14.50 for one/two people and tent sites are $6 per person.

Lake Wiritoa

About 12.5 km south-east of the city, off SH3, Lake Wiritoa is popular for swimming and water-skiing. To get there, turn left at Lake Kaitoke and keep going past it to Lake Wiritoa.

Manawatu

The rich sheep and dairy farming district of Manawatu is centred around the provincial city of Palmerston North, dominated by Massey University, and includes the surrounding districts of Rangitikei to the north and Horowhenua to the south.

PALMERSTON NORTH

On the banks of the Manawatu River, Palmerston North is the principal centre of the Manawatu region and a major crossroads. With Massey University, the second-largest university in New Zealand, and several other colleges based here, Palmerston North has the relaxed feel of a rural university town. Though not really a tourist destination, it is a well-ordered, pleasant town.

Orientation & Information

The wide open expanse of The Square with its gardens and fountains is very much the centre of Palmerston North. You can get your bearings from a lookout on top of the Civic

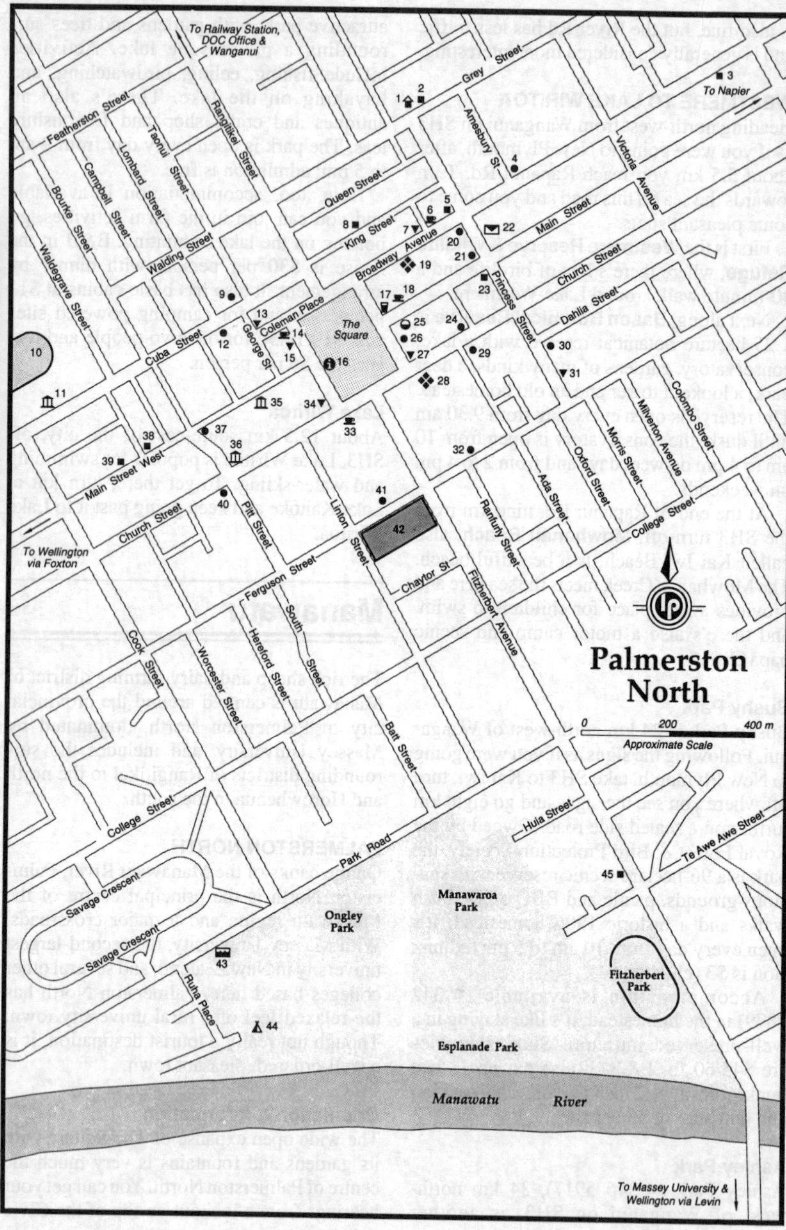
To Railway Station, DOC Office & Wanganui
Grey Street
To Napier
Featherston Street
Taonui Street
Rangitikei Street
Amesbury St.
Victoria Avenue
Lombard Street
Campbell Street
Bourke Street
Queen Street
Main Street
King Street
Broadway Avenue
Walding Street
Waldegrave Street
Church Street
Dahlia Street
Princess Street
Coleman Place
The Square
George St
Cuba Street
Colombo Street
Milverton Avenue
Morris Street
Oxford Street
Main Street West
Ada Street
Ranfurly Street
College Street
Pitt Street
Linton Street
Church Street
To Wellington via Foxton
Ferguson Street
Chaytor St
Fitzherbert Avenue
South Street
Hereford Street
Cook Street
Worcester Street
Batt Street
Palmerston North
200
400 m
Approximate Scale
College Street
Hula Street
Te Awe Awe Street
Park Road
Savage Crescent
Savage Crescent
Manawaroa Park
Ongley Park
Ruha Place
Fitzherbert Park
Esplanade Park
Manawatu River
To Massey University & Wellington via Levin

PLACES TO STAY

1 Peppertree Hostel
2 Grey's Inn
3 Broadway Motel
5 Consolidated Mid City Motel
8 King St Backpackers
23 Empire Hotel & Cobb & Co Restaurant
38 Shamrock Inn
39 Masonic Hotel
42 Quality Hotel
44 Palmerston North Holiday Park
45 Emma's Place

PLACES TO EAT

6 Dr Jerkyll's Cafe Bar
7 Celtic Inn & Sun Sing Chinese Restaurant
13 Deano's Bar & Grill
14 Bella's Cafe, Deano's Bar & Grill & Oscar's Wine Bar
15 Pizza Piazza
18 Orleans Cafe & Bar
27 McDonald's
31 KFC
33 Sage Cafe & Square Edge Community Arts Centre
34 Puddleducks, Cafe Ojakbashe & Truelife Bakery

OTHER

4 Automobile Association (AA)
9 Gotham City Nightclub
10 Palmerston North Showgrounds
11 New Zealand Rugby Museum
12 Three Guys Supermarket
16 Information Centre & Civic Centre
17 Eagle Rock Bar
19 Downtown Arcade, Food Court & Downtown Cinema 7
20 Ansett New Zealand
21 Air New Zealand
22 Post Office
24 Abbey Theatre
25 White Star & Local Bus Stop
26 Bassline Nightclub
28 Plaza Shopping Centre
29 Municipal Opera House
30 Palmerston North Travel Centre
32 Foodtown Supermarket
35 Manawatu Art Gallery
36 Manawatu Museum & Science Centre
37 Globe Theatre
40 Centrepoint Theatre
41 Pak 'N Save Supermarket
43 Lido Swimming & Recreation Centre

Centre building in The Square, open on weekdays.

The Palmerston North Information Centre (☎ 358 5003; fax 356 9481) in the Civic Centre building on The Square has plenty of information on the area. It's open Monday to Friday from 8.30 am to 5 pm, Saturday and Sunday from 10 am to 3 pm.

The DOC office (☎ 358 9004) is at 717 Tremaine Ave, on the north side of town. The AA office (☎ 357 7039) is at 185 Broadway Ave, near the corner of Amesbury St.

Things to See

The **Science Centre & Manawatu Museum**, on the corner of Church and Pitt Sts, has a museum specialising in the history of the Manawatu region, including its Maori history, culture and art. The Science Centre has rotating science exhibits and the hands-on displays are fun for kids and adults alike. It's open every day from 10 am to 5 pm. Admission is free to the museum, while the Science Centre costs $6 (children $4).

Around the corner is the modern and spacious **Manawatu Art Gallery** at 398 Main St West. It's open Monday to Friday from 10 am to 4.30 pm, weekends from 11.30 am to 4.30 pm; admission is free, donations are welcome.

Rugby fans shouldn't miss the **New Zealand Rugby Museum** at 87 Cuba St, a few blocks from The Square. This interesting museum contains exhibits and memorabilia relating to the history of rugby in New Zealand from the first game played in the country, in Nelson in 1870, up to the present. It also has mementos from every country where rugby is played, and videos of the most famous international games. The museum is open Monday to Saturday from 10 am to noon and 1.30 to 4 pm and on Sunday from 1.30 to 4 pm; admission is $3 (children $1).

The **Esplanade** is a beautiful park stretching along the shores of the Manawatu River, a few blocks south of The Square. At the park are gardens, bush walks, a nature trail, an aviary, a conservatory and lathe house, rose gardens, a playground, a miniature railway and a miniature golf course. The Manawatu Riverside Walkway & Bridle Track, extending 10 km along the Manawatu River, passes through the park.

Palmerston North is well supplied with sporting venues. The Palmerston North

Showgrounds include the Manawatu Sports Stadium, other stadiums, rugby pitches, sports fields, a speedway stockcar track, concert halls and more. Other sports venues include the Awapuni Racecourse for thoroughbred horse racing, and the Manawatu Raceway on Pioneer Highway for trotting and greyhound racing.

Places to Stay

Camping & Cabins The *Palmerston North Holiday Park* (☎ 358 0349) at 133 Dittmer Drive, off Ruha Place, is pleasantly situated beside the Esplanade, about two km from The Square. It has tent sites at $7.50 per person, powered sites at $17 for two, cabins at $32 to $39 for two and tourist flats at $52 for two.

Hostels The *Peppertree Hostel* (☎ 355 4054) at 121 Grey St, at the junction with Princess St, has a well-appointed kitchen, off-street parking and a homely atmosphere. The cost is $14 per night for a dorm bed, or $20/32 for singles/doubles; they offer free pick-up from the bus/train station and since it's an associate YHA hostel, you can stay with or without a YHA card.

King St Backpackers (☎ 358 9595) at 95 King St is a large hostel upstairs in a converted former hotel, 1½ blocks from The Square. The cost is $14 per person in dorm and shared rooms, with reduced weekly rates.

B&Bs & Guesthouses *Grey's Inn* (☎ 358 6928) at 123 Grey St, at the junction with Princess St, is an attractive, homey guesthouse with B&B at $54/80. Or there's *Emma's Place* (☎ 357 5143) at 250 Fitzherbert Ave with B&B at $35/45.

Hotels The *Empire Hotel* (☎ 357 8002) on the corner of Princess and Main Sts has nine rooms with private bath, off-street parking and a Cobb & Co restaurant downstairs; singles/doubles are $60/65. The *Masonic Hotel* (☎ 358 3480) at 249 Main St West near the corner of Domain St costs $39/50 with private facilities.

The *Shamrock Inn* (☎ 355 2130) at 267 Main St West on the corner of Domain St is a refurbished hotel with good budget rooms for $25/36, double rooms with ensuite for $45 and it has a bunk room with beds for $15. The bar downstairs often has bands on weekends.

Top of the range by far is the *Quality Hotel* (☎ 356 8059), 110 Fitzherbert Ave, with doubles for $140. The entrance is on Ferguson St.

Motels Palmerston North has a wide selection of motels. The *Consolidated Mid City Motel* (☎ 357 2184) at 129 Broadway Ave is a fancy, central motel with doubles from $80. Further along at 258 Broadway Ave, the *Broadway Motel* (☎ 358 5051) is more budget with singles/doubles for $55/65.

There's a 'motel row' on Fitzherbert Ave, south of The Square; motels along here are a bit more expensive. They include the *Hibiscus Motel* (☎ 356 1411) at No 248, the *Avenue Motel* (☎ 356 3330) at No 116, the *Rose City Motel* (☎ 356 5388) at No 120, the *Coachman Motel* (☎ 357 3059) at No 134 and the *Tokyo Motel* (☎ 356 7074) at No 167.

Places to Eat

Palmerston North has more than its fair share of good cafes and bar/restaurants serving inexpensive fare to cater for the town's student population.

On Broadway Ave, the *Downtown Arcade* has a good food court with counters serving Italian, Chinese, fish & chips, coffee, ice cream etc. It is open late to cater for moviegoers. Opposite at 69 Broadway, *Sun Sing* is a cheap Chinese buffet restaurant, serving grills for around $10. The *Celtic Inn* in the Regent Arcade between Broadway and King Sts is a small, Irish-style pub serving lunches and dinners plus a variety of snacks. Popular student bar/restaurants with reasonably priced meals and snacks are *Dr Jerkyll's* at 113 Broadway Ave, and the slightly fancier *Orleans Cafe & Bar* on Main St.

The *Sage Cafe* in the Square Edge Arts Centre at the south-western corner of The Square is a pleasant wholefood cafe. Nearby at 49 The Square, the tiny *Truelife Bakery* also specialises in wholefoods.

Also along the south-west side of The Square, *Puddleducks* at 42 The Square is a popular cafe for lunches and teas. Beside it, the *Cafe Ojakbashe* serves moderately priced Turkish dishes, or for pizza there's *Pizza Piazza* at 16-17 The Square. *Oscar's Wine Bar*, on the corner of Coleman Place and The Square, is a fancy bar but the blackboard menu features inexpensive light meals. Next to it, *Bella's Cafe* is a popular lunch spot. *Deano's Bar & Grill* on the corner of Coleman Place and George St is a popular older style bar & grill with good steaks from $14.

The chains are well represented in Palmerston, including *McDonald's*, *KFC*, *Pizza Hut*, and *Cobb & Co* in the Empire Hotel. For self-catering, *Pak 'N Save* and *Foodtown* supermarkets are on Ferguson St at the rear of the Plaza Shopping Centre.

Entertainment

Palmerston North's nightlife fluctuates according to the student year and is quiet during the holidays.

The *Celtic Inn* in the Regent Arcade between Broadway and King Sts is a small, pleasant, low-key Irish pub with live music on Friday and Saturday nights. *Orleans Cafe & Bar* on Main St and *Dr Jerkyll's* on Broadway Ave are popular student watering holes. The *Eagle Rock Bar* on the corner of The Square and Main St has alternating entertainment, ranging from keg racing and 'Joe's Bucking Bull' to karaoke and bands.

For nightclubs, there's *Gotham City Nightclub* on Cuba St, or the *Bassline Nightclub*, upstairs on The Square near McDonald's, has a big dance floor.

Palmerston North has a lot of culture for its size, with theatre and music performances staged at the *Centrepoint Theatre*, *Globe Theatre*, *Abbey Theatre* and the *Municipal Opera House*. Palmerston North's population are avid movie-goers – the large *Downtown Cinema 7* complex, upstairs in the Downtown Arcade on Broadway Ave, shows the latest films and art house selections.

Getting There & Away

Air Milson Airport on the northern outskirts of town is a new, modern airport bigger than you'd expect from the size of the town; planes often get diverted here when the weather at Wellington Airport is bad.

Air New Zealand (☎ 351 8800) on the corner of Princess and Main Sts has daily direct flights to Auckland, Christchurch, Hamilton and Wellington, with connections to other centres.

Ansett New Zealand (☎ 355 2146) is at 50-52 Princess St, near the Air New Zealand office. It has daily direct flights to Auckland, Christchurch, Invercargill, Nelson, Queenstown and Wellington, with connections to other centres.

Bus InterCity, Newmans and Tranzit Coachlines buses operate from the Palmerston North Travel Centre (☎ 351 5633) at 95 Princes St. InterCity and Newmans buses go from Palmerston North to most places in the North Island; Tranzit Coachlines operates one route only, from Palmerston North through Masterton to Wellington.

White Star buses (☎ 358 8777) operate from a bus stop in front of the Courthouse, on Main St near The Square, with buses to Wellington, Wanganui and New Plymouth.

Many direct Auckland-Wellington services bypass Palmerston North, stopping instead at nearby Bulls. The Wellington-Napier buses do stop at Palmerston North. Travel times from Palmerston North are 1½ hours to Wellington or Wanganui, 3½ hours to New Plymouth, three hours to Napier, and eight hours to Auckland via Taupo and Hamilton.

Train The railway station is off Tremaine Ave, about a dozen blocks north of The Square.

Trains between Auckland and Wellington stop at Palmerston North, as do trains between Wellington and Napier. The Auckland-Wellington trains run twice daily in each direction (morning and evening); from Palmerston North it's about two hours to Wellington and 8½ hours to Auckland. The Wellington-Napier train runs once daily in each direction, taking two hours to Wellington and three hours to Napier.

Getting Around

Local minibuses operate from the bus stop in the middle of Main St, on the east side of The Square. They operate Monday to Friday from 7 am to 6 pm, Saturday until 1 pm, and not at all on Sunday. All rides cost $1.50; No 12 goes to Massey University but none go to the airport. Palmerston North Shuttle (☎ 358 4499) to/from the airport costs $6 to the centre, $10 to Massey University.

AROUND PALMERSTON NORTH

Manawatu is not noted as a prime tourist destination but the area does have scenic nature reserves, walkways, lakes and so forth, many with camping and huts. The information centre and DOC office in Palmerston North have leaflets detailing attractions.

Manawatu Gorge

North of Palmerston North, SH2 heading to Napier runs through the spectacular Manawatu Gorge. Manawatu Jet Tours (☎ 326 8190, 358 4188) operate jet-boat trips on the river, and will arrange transport for small groups from Palmerston North for no extra cost. The information centre also has information on horse trekking in the area.

Tokomaru Steam Engine Museum

The Tokomaru Steam Engine Museum, in Tokomaru on SH57 about 20 km south of Palmerston North, exhibits a large collection of working steam engines and locomotives. It's open every day from 9 am to noon and from 1 to 3.30 pm; admission is $5 (children $2).

Gardens

The **Cross Hills Gardens**, with one of New Zealand's largest and most varied collections of rhododendrons and azaleas, is five km north of Kimbolton, on SH54 about a 45-minute drive north of Palmerston North. It's open from 10.30 am to 5 pm every day during the blooming season from September to April.

There are also a number of other gardens in the area; ask the Palmerston North information centre for their Garden Tour pamphlet.

Ohakea

Ohakea is a whistle stop town, west of Palmerston North on SH1 near Bulls. It is dominated by a large air force base, where you'll find the **Ohakea Museum** dedicated to the exploits of the Royal New Zealand Air Force. This small museum with mostly air force memorabilia is open Monday to Saturday from 7.30 am to 4.30 pm, on Sunday from 10 am to 4.30 pm. Admission is $4.50 (children $2).

Beaches

Himatangi Beach (29 km west of town) and Foxton Beach (40 km) are popular beaches near Palmerston North.

Mangaweka

Located north on SH1, 52 km south of Waiouru, Mangaweka's most noticeable attraction is the **Aeroplane Cafe**, a cafe in an old DC-3 plane right beside the highway, open every day.

Beside the plane, Rangitikei River Adventures (☎ 382 5747) offers various activities including a 43-metre bungy jump over the Rangitikei River. This is the same height as the famous Kawerau Bridge jump at Queenstown. The cost is $70 for the Rangitikei River jump.

They also do a number of Rangitikei River trips, including jet-boating and rafting, and they can arrange accommodation. Bookings are essential for all their activities.

East Coast

The East Coast is an area full of interest, with the sea on one side and towering forested hills in the hinterland. It is also a place of contrasts, from the Art Deco and Spanish Mission-style architecture of bustling Hastings and Napier to the serene, primeval forests that girt Lake Waikaremoana in Te Urewera National Park.

The area includes three of the larger cities of the North Island and their adjoining bays – Gisborne on Poverty Bay and Napier and Hastings on Hawke Bay. In the latter case, the actual bay is known as Hawke Bay and the area as Hawkes Bay.

From Opotiki on the eastern Bay of Plenty, circling around to Gisborne, the East Cape is a rugged landscape with stunning scenery along the coast and dense forest inland. This long-isolated region has retained its strong Maori influence, and even though now accessed by good roads, it remains largely undeveloped and is well off the main tourist routes.

The telephone area code throughout most of the East Coast is 06, except for the north-western half of the East Cape. Just west of Hicks Bay the area code changes to 07.

HIGHLIGHTS

- Napier with its Art Deco architecture and seaside ambience
- Te Urewera National Park and its Lake Waikaremoana Great Walk
- The rugged East Cape
- The wild, windswept Mahia Peninsula

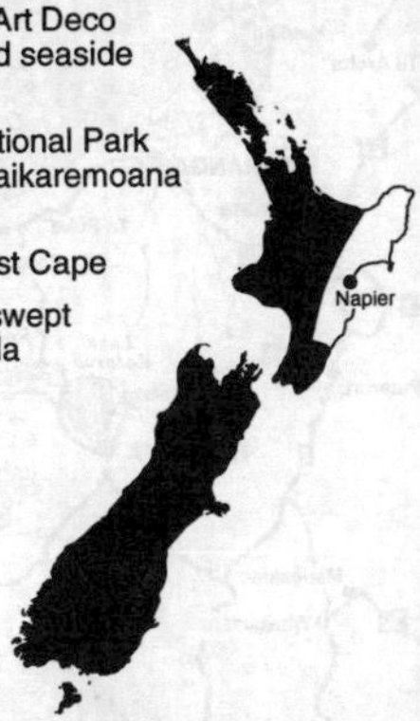

East Cape

The East Cape is a scenic, isolated and little-known region of the North Island. The small communities scattered along the coast are predominantly Maori and the pace of life is peaceful and slow. Geographically, the area has few natural harbours and, until the road network was completed, goods had to be loaded off the beaches onto waiting barges. The interior is still wild bush, with the Raukumara Range extending down the centre of the cape. The western side of the range is divided into several state forest parks: Ruatoria, Raukumara, Urutawa, Waioeka and Mangatu.

The coast is now circled by 330 km of highway, SH35, which took decades to build. It is an excellent road (open all year round), and has made the coast more accessible than ever before. The drive is worthwhile if only for the magnificent views of this wild coast, which is dotted with picturesque little bays, inlets and coves that change aspect with the weather – on a sunny day the water is an inviting turquoise colour, at other times a layer of clouds hangs on the craggy mountains rising straight up from the beaches and everything turns a misty green. Dozens of fresh clear streams flow through wild gorges to meet the sea. During the summer the coastline turns crimson with the blooming of the pohutukawa trees lining the seashore.

Getting There & Away

Getting around the East Cape by bus is not easy. The only options are the various courier services, which do sections of the cape and take passengers. This situation

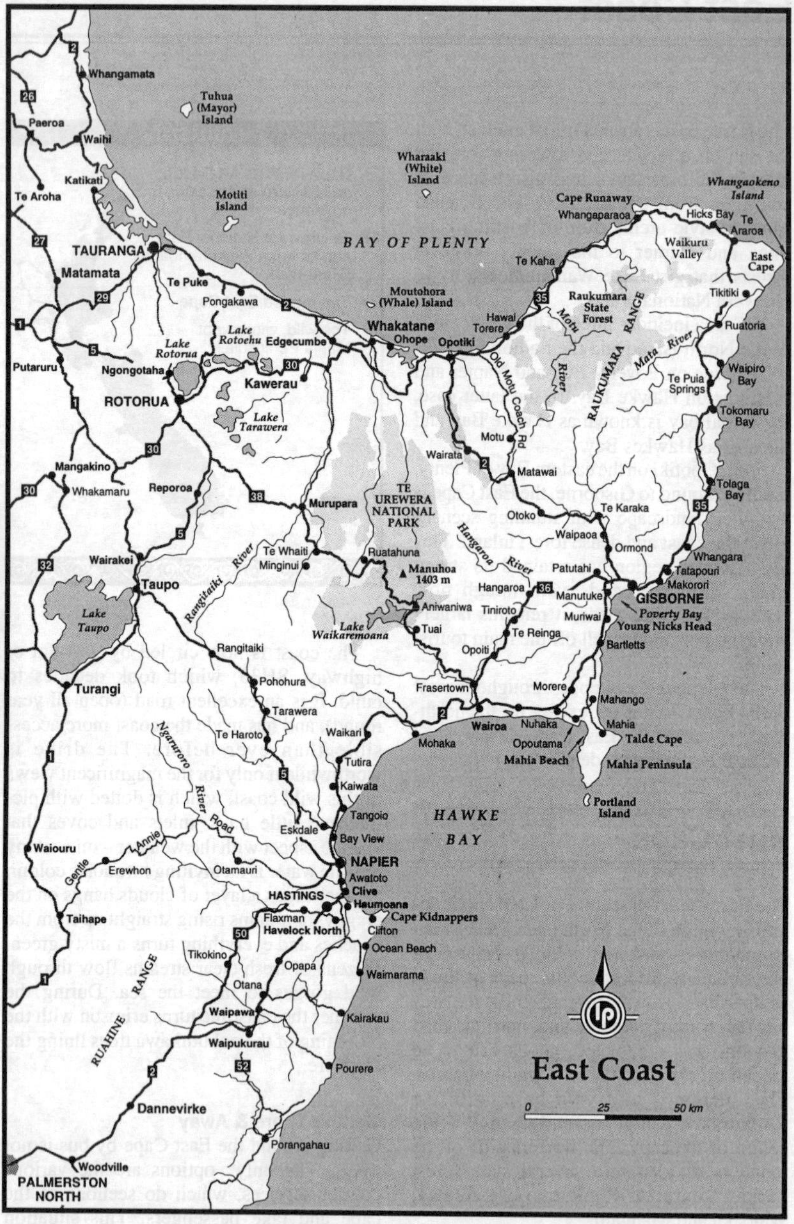
East Coast
0 25 50 km
BAY OF PLENTY
HAWKE BAY
Whangamata
Tuhua (Mayor) Island
Paeroa
Waihi
Katikati
Te Aroha
Wharaaki (White) Island
Motiti Island
Whangaokeno Island
Cape Runaway
Whangaparaoa
Hicks Bay
Te Araroa
Waikuru Valley
East Cape
TAURANGA
Matamata
Te Puke
Pongakawa
Moutohora (Whale) Island
Te Kaha
Raukumara State Forest
Tikitiki
Ruatoria
Whakatane
Ohope
Opotiki
Hawai
Torere
Edgecumbe
Lake Rotoehu
Lake Rotorua
Putaruru
Ngongotaha
Kawerau
ROTORUA
Lake Tarawera
Motu River
Old Motu Coach Rd
RAUKUMARA RANGE
Mata River
Te Puia Springs
Waipiro Bay
Tokomaru Bay
Motu
Wairata
Matawai
Mangakino
Whakamaru
Reporoa
Murupara
TE UREWERA NATIONAL PARK
Tolaga Bay
Te Karaka
Otoko
Waipaoa
Ormond
Whangara
Wairakei
Te Whaiti
Minginui
Ruatahuna
Manuhoa 1403 m
Rangitaiki River
Hangaroa River
Patutahi
Tatapouri
Makorori
Taupo
Lake Taupo
Hangaroa
Manutuke
GISBORNE
Aniwaniwa
Tiniroto
Muriwai
Poverty Bay
Young Nicks Head
Tuai
Lake Waikaremoana
Te Reinga
Opoiti
Bartletts
Rangitaiki
Turangi
Pohohura
Frasertown
Morere
Mahango
Tarawera
Wairoa
Nuhaka
Mahia
Te Haroto
Waikari
Ngaruroro River
Mohaka
Opoutama
Mahia Beach
Talde Cape
Mahia Peninsula
Tutira
Kaiwata
Portland Island
Tangoio
Eskdale
Bay View
Waiouru
Annie
Gentle
Erewhon
Otamauri
Road
NAPIER
Awatoto
HASTINGS
Clive
Haumoana
Taihape
Flaxman
Havelock North
Cape Kidnappers
Clifton
Ocean Beach
Tikokino
Opapa
RUAHINE RANGE
Otana
Waimarama
Waipawa
Kairakau
Waipukurau
Pourere
Dannevirke
Porangahau
Woodville
PALMERSTON NORTH
2
26
27
29
1
5
30
38
32
35
36
50
52

might change, so contact the Opotiki or Gisborne information centres.

From Opotiki, Eastland Courier Services (☎ 315 6350) leaves at 10.30 am for Hicks Bay and Te Araroa and return. The cost is $26 to Te Araroa.

From Gisborne, Fastways (☎ 868 9080), on the corner of Grey St and Awapuni Rd, has a service at 9 am every day except Saturday to Hicks Bay ($25), returning from Hicks Bay at 1 pm. Departing from Gisborne's bus terminal on Bright St, Matakaoa Transport also goes to Hicks Bay, Cooks Couriers goes as far as Te Araroa, and Coastline Couriers (part of the InterCity umbrella) goes to Ruatoria.

Hitching around the cape was once notoriously slow, with not much traffic passing by. Many locals say the hitching situation really isn't that bad. Of course there would be more traffic in summer than in winter.

OPOTIKI TO EAST CAPE

This trip is well described in *Opotiki & East Cape*, a comprehensive booklet available free from the Opotiki Visitor Information Centre. Along the first stretch of road from Opotiki there are fine views across to the steaming White Island volcano. At the Waiaua River is the turn-off for the road to Gisborne via Toa Toa and the **Old Motu Coach road**, probably more suited to mountain bikes.

The beaches at **Torere** and **Hawai** are steeply shelved and covered with driftwood – good spots for seascape photography. About 45 km from Opotiki the road crosses the **Motu River**, famed for its jet-boating, white-water rafting and kayaking possibilities.

Some 25 km further on is **Te Kaha**, once a whaling centre, now a small town popular for boating and fishing. It has a rocky beach, a pub, a store and accommodation. At the large marae, the Tukaki meeting house is magnificently carved. A succession of picturesque bays, including the beautiful Whanarua Bay, are passed before **Whangaparaoa (Cape Runaway)** is reached. You cannot miss the Raukorore Anglican Church, nestled under Norfolk pines on a lone promontory, about 100 km north of Opotiki. Cape Runaway can only be reached on foot; seek permission before going onto private land.

Hicks Bay (once named Te Wharekahika) gets its name from a crew member of Cook's *Endeavour*. It is a magnificent place, complemented by nearby Horseshoe Bay. Nearly 10 km 'round the corner' as you turn south-east is the sizeable community of **Te Araroa**, which has an information centre. At Te Araroa there is a distinct change in geography from the volcanic rock outcrops to the sandstone cliffs standing above the town on the bay. At Te Araroa you turn off for **East Cape lighthouse**, the most easterly tip of New Zealand. Because it lies right next to the dateline, sunrise at the lighthouse is the start of new day for the world. Hicks Bay Backpackers Lodge conducts trips to the lighthouse.

Places to Stay & Eat

There is no shortage of budget and other accommodation along the cape's western side. In addition to *Tirohanga Motor Camp* and its soulmate at Opape, there is *Coral's B&B* (☎ (07) 315 8052), also in Opape. Famished? – the fish & chips at *Torere Seafoods* are legendary! At Maraenui there is the *Oariki Homestay* (☎ (07) 325 2678) where they make their own cheeses and wine; you can stay in a room in the house or in the fully equipped cottage outside.

Te Kaha is the central point on the west side of East Cape. The *Te Kaha Holiday Park* (☎ (07) 325 2894) has camp sites, cabins and tourist flats, and 'luxury' backpackers accommodation from $12 per person. The *Te Kaha Hotel* (☎ (07) 325 2837) has budget accommodation and the usual hotel bedrooms. At pretty Whanarua Bay, *Rendezvous on the Coast Holiday Park* (☎ (07) 325 2899) has sites from $14 for two, and cabins from $30.

At Waihau Bay, the *Waihau Bay Holiday Park* (☎ (07) 325 3844), Oruati Beach, has camp sites, cabins and on-site caravans. Also in this area is the *Waihau Bay Lodge* (☎ (07) 325 3804), an old pub that has had a bit of a facelift. Doubles start at $70 and it also offers backpackers accommodation and camping. *Waihu Bay B&B* (☎ (07) 325 3674) is opposite the beach and has doubles for $50.

On the northern tip of the cape are Hicks Bay and Te Araroa, both beautiful areas convenient for an overnight stopover. Hicks Bay has a takeaway and a general store. If you take the dirt road around the peninsula from the Hicks Bay township, you'll come to the spic-and-span *Hicks Bay Backpackers Lodge* (☎ 864 4731), on Onepoto Beach Rd. It's a small place with a backpackers bunkroom off to one side of the home, and it fronts a beautiful beach, only 50 metres away. The nightly cost is $14 and $15 in dorms or $35 for a double room. They organise trips to the East Cape lighthouse, and various other activities. Also at Hicks Bay, on the hill overlooking the bay, is the *Hicks Bay Motel Lodge* (☎ 864 4880) with double rooms starting at $70.

Te Araroa Holiday Park (☎ 864 4873), midway between Te Araroa and Hicks Bay, is another lovely spot, in a sheltered 15-hectare parklike setting near the beach. The park has lots of amenities, including its own cinema. Tent/powered sites cost $7/8 per person, bunkroom accommodation is $10 per person, cabins are $30 for two people and tourist flats cost $45. Two km from town, *Te Aroha Holiday Motor Park* (☎ 884 9567) is also well equipped and similarly priced. Te Araroa also has the *Kawakawa Hotel* (☎ 864 4809) for pub rooms.

EAST COAST

EAST CAPE TO GISBORNE

Going south from Te Araroa the first place of interest you come to is **Tikitiki**. The Anglican Church is well worth visiting for its Maori architectural design.

A few km off the road is **Ruatoria**, which has powerful Mt Hikurangi as a backdrop. Ruatoria is a very important Maori town. It is the centre of the Ngati Porou tribe and has been home to many eminent Maori. Sir Apirana Ngata, a politician from the early 1900s to 1930, lived here, and the Maori war hero Lieutenant Ngarimu VC was born here. The town had a short sojourn into Rastafarianism, which produced the popular reggae band Herbs.

About 25 km south is **Te Puia**, a pretty little town with hot springs nearby, and the pleasant **Waipiro Bay**. Another 10 km further on is **Tokomaru Bay**, a crumbling but picturesque town with a good beach and sweeping cliffs at the southern end of the bay.

Tolaga Bay is the next main concentration of population and, although popular with surfers, is not particularly exciting when contrasted with Tokomaru or bays to the north. The aspect gets better the further you get from town towards the beach. South of Tolaga Bay is a small settlement called Whangara, the setting for Witi Ihimaera's wonderful fictional work *The Whale Rider*. This is a great little book to read for a feel of the Maori culture and mythology of the area. After passing Tatapouri and Wainui beaches you reach Gisborne.

Places to Stay

Heading south along the east coast from Te Araroa you come to the Waiapu River and the town of Tikitiki, which has a *hotel* and *caravan park*. Ruatoria has the old *Manutahi Hotel* (☎ 864 8437) with standard pub rooms. At Te Puia is the *Hot Springs Hotel* (☎ 864 6861), a Historic Trust building, with singles/doubles for $35/55. Te Puia also has a motel and the information centre here can tell you about homestays in the area.

At Waipiro Bay on the coast, *Waikawa Lodge* (☎ 864 6719) is a small backpackers cottage for getting away from it all. It has just four twins/doubles at $15 per person.

Tokomaru Bay is another exceptionally scenic spot. The *House of the Rising Sun* (☎ 864 5858) is a small, comfortable and homely hostel about a block from the beach. Hiking, swimming, surfing, tennis, fishing, cycling, horse riding on the beach and visits to the new beachside pub are all popular activities from the hostel; the nightly cost is $13 for a dorm bed and $30 for twins and doubles. Out at Anaura Bay, *Anaura Bay Motor Camp* (☎ 862 6380) has sites at $14 for two. Further south, the well-equipped *Tolaga Bay Motor Camp* (☎ 862 6716) is on the beach at Tolaga Bay, with sites from $15 for two, and a variety of cabins from $40 for two. Their backpacker bunkroom costs $13 per person. The historic *Tolaga Inn* (☎ 862 6856) has singles/doubles for $30/55 and the *Tolaga Bay Motel* (☎ 862 6888) has units from $55/60.

INLAND: THE RAUKUMARA & WAIOEKA

Inland the Raukumara Range offers tramping (the highest mountain in the range is Hikurangi at 1752 metres), hunting and white-water rafting on the Waioeka and Motu rivers – contact Motu River Expeditions (☎ 308 7760) for more information on rafting the rivers in the region. The most popular access to this rugged, untamed region is via SH2 (the Waioeka Gorge Rd), the 144-km road which connects Opotiki to Gisborne at the base of the East Cape triangle.

There are many great walks in this region and the Department of Conservation (DOC) have quite a deal of information on possibilities. See their *Raukumara Forest Park* and *Waioeka Gorge Scenic Reserve* pamphlets. The rare blue duck may be seen in the Raukumara, and Hochstetter's frog *(Leiopelma hochstetteri)* is quite common in the park. Some parts of the region are penetrable by mountain bike, others are certainly not. Consider this region one of New Zealand's last frontiers, as wild as sections of South Westland and Fiordland – a must for those with a sense of adventure.

There are a couple of interesting accommodation possibilities along this road: the *Wairata Station Farmstays* (☎ 315 7761) and the *Matawai Hotel* (☎ 862 4874), 43 km and 76 km from Opotiki respectively.

Poverty Bay

GISBORNE

Gisborne (population 30,000) is New Zealand's most easterly city and one of the closest to the International Date Line. Therefore, dawn in Gisborne marks the new day for most of the world. It was here that Captain Cook made his first landfall in New Zealand on 9 October 1769. He named it 'Poverty Bay', after deciding it had nothing to offer. It was an inauspicious first meeting. Cook's landing party was attacked and several Maori were killed in the altercation.

The fertile alluvial plains around Gisborne support intensive farming of subtropical fruits, maize, market-garden produce and vineyards. Recently, kiwi fruit and avocados have been important crops. The city itself is right on the coast at the confluence of three rivers, the Turanganui, Waimata and Taruheru. Often described as the city of bridges, it is also noted for its fine parks.

History

European settlement of the region did not occur until the late 19th century. A man of considerable drive, John Williams Harris, was first to purchase a small area on the west bank of the Turanganui River. He set up the region's first whaling venture, and in 1839 began farming up the Waipaoa River near Matunuke.

As whaling became increasingly popular the missionaries also began to move into the area. Two of them, Father Baty and Reverend William Colenso, were the first Europeans to tramp into the heart of Te Urewera and see Lake Waikaremoana.

Gradually more Pakeha arrived but organised settlement was limited due to Maori resistance. When the Treaty of Waitangi was signed in 1840 many chiefs from the east coast did not acknowledge the treaty, let alone sign it. In the 1860s, numerous battles with the Maori broke out.

The Hauhau insurrection that began in the Bay of Plenty reached its height at the battle of Waerenga-a-hika in November 1865. By the following year the government had crushed opposition and transported a number of the survivors, including the charismatic Maori leader Te Kooti, to the remote Chatham Islands. This paved the way for an influx of Europeans who brought with them their flocks of sheep, but in 1868 Te Kooti escaped and with an army of 200 exacted revenge on the settlement at Matawhero, killing 33 Europeans and 37 Maori.

Even today, however, much of the pasture land is leased from the Maori and a large part of it is under their direct control. Unfortunately, the pioneer farmers were so anxious to profit from the land they ripped out far too much forest cover, with disastrous results. Massive erosion occurred as the steeply sloping land was unable to hold the soil after heavy rains.

Information

The Gisborne Visitor Information Centre (☎ 868 6139; fax 868 6138) is at 209 Grey St. Look for the fine Canadian totem pole beside it. It's open daily from 8 am to 5 pm, with longer hours in summer. The office has useful brochures and good city maps, and children (and a fair number of adults) love the mini-golf course behind the centre.

The DOC office (☎ 867 8531) at 63 Carnarvon St is open from 8 am to 4.30 pm on weekdays; they request that you first seek information on parks and walks from the visitor information centre which stocks all the pamphlets. The AA is near the corner of Disraeli St and Palmerston Rd. There's a laundrette on the corner of Gladstone Rd and Carnarvon St.

Gisborne Museum & Arts Centre

The fact that Gisborne and the surrounding district are strongly influenced by Maori culture is clearly exhibited at this interesting regional museum at 18 Stout St. The gallery has changing exhibitions of local, national and international art, and the museum has numerous displays relating to the east coast Maori and colonial history, as well as geology and natural history exhibits. Outside there are more exhibits – a sled house, stable, Wyllie Cottage (first house on the site, 1870), and Lysnar House with working artists' studios (not open to the public).

The ***Star of Canada* Maritime Museum** behind the main museum is part of the museum complex. One wild night in 1912 the 12,000-ton ship *Star of Canada* was blown ashore on the reef at Gisborne. The ship's bridge and captain's cabin were salvaged and eventually installed in a house that became the best known home in Gisborne. The unique home was bequeathed to the city and moved to its present site, restored and made into a museum. There are displays on Maori canoes, early whaling and shipping and Captain Cook's Gisborne visit but the most interesting items relate, of course, to the *Star of Canada*.

The museum complex is open from 10 am to 4 pm Monday to Friday, 1.30 to 4 pm on weekends and public holidays; admission is $3.50 (children $1.50). The price admits you to both museums.

Statues & Views

There's a **statue** of 'Young Nick' (Nicholas Young), Cook's cabin boy, in a little park on the river mouth. He was the first member of Cook's crew to sight New Zealand. Across the bay are the white cliffs which Cook named 'Young Nick's Head'.

Across the river at the foot of Kaiti Hill is a **monument** to Captain Cook, near the spot where he first set foot on New Zealand (9 October 1769 in 'ship time' in Cook's journal, but actually it was the 8th). Nearby Waikahua Cottage once served as a refuge during the Hauhau unrest.

Titirangi (Kaiti Hill) has fine views of the area. There's a walking track up from the Captain Cook monument which starts near Waikahua Cottage. Near the top is another monument to Captain Cook, this one with a fine statue of the captain. At the 135-metre summit is the **James Cook Observatory**, with a sign proclaiming it the 'World's Easternmost Observatory'. The Gisborne Astronomical Society (☎ 868 8653) meets here at 7.30 pm on Tuesday; all are welcome.

Down on **Kaiti Beach**, low tide attracts a wealth of birdlife including stilts, oystercatchers and pelagic visitors.

Another good view of Gisborne is from **Gaddum's Hill**. To get there, head out to the suburb of Kaiti on Wainui Rd (SH35 heading to East Cape), turn inland onto De Lautour Rd and follow it up the hill. It's a short walk from here to the trig station, a nine-km return trip from Gisborne.

Poho-o-Rawiri

Also at the foot of Titirangi is the Poho-o-Rawiri Maori meeting house, one of the largest meeting houses in New Zealand. It has a richly decorated interior and its stage is framed by carved *maihi* (ornamental carved gable boards). The human figure kneeling on the right knee with right hand held upwards is the *tekoteko* (carved figure) representing the ancestor who challenges those who enter the marae. It is open daily at any time except when a function is in progress; seek permission before entering. A little Maori church, **Toko Toru Tapu**, stands on the side of Titirangi, not far from the meeting house.

The leaflet *Tairawhiti – Heritage Trails: Gisborne District* contains a wealth of information on historic sites in this ancestral land of the Maori. It covers the area from the tip of East Cape to the south of Poverty Bay.

Other Attractions

The Gisborne area has a number of attractive gardens that can be visited, including the huge **Eastwoodhill Arboretum** (☎ 863 9800), 35 km from town, which is open daily from 10 am to 4 pm. It contains the largest collection of northern hemisphere temperate trees, shrubs and climbers in New Zealand. To get there follow the Ngatapa-Rere road; there is a 45-minute marked track through the trees. The visitor information centre has details on many other private gardens in the area. The **Botanic Gardens** are in town beside the river off Aberdeen Rd.

Gisborne is a major wine-producing area, noted for its Chardonnay. The **wineries** that can be visited include: Parker Methode Champenoise, 24 Bank St; Matawhero Wines, Riverpoint Rd; and Harvest Wines, Bell Rd, in Matawhero. Tours are available to the larger wineries such as Montana and Corbans. There is also a brewer of natural beers, the Sunshine Brewing Company, 109 Disraeli St.

Near the A&P Showgrounds in Makaraka there's the **East Coast Museum of Transport & Technology** (ECMOT). It is open daily from 9.30 am to 4.30 pm; admission is $2 (children 50c).

At Matawhero, a few km south along SH2, the historic Presbyterian Church is the only building in the immediate vicinity to have survived the conflicts of 1868, and is one of a handful still standing from this period.

Activities

You can swim right in the city at Waikanae Beach – in fact there's good swimming, fishing and surfing all along the coast. Midway Beach has an Olympic swimming complex with a big waterslide and children's playground.

The Motu and Waioeka rivers are both in the Gisborne district; ask at the visitor information centre about white-water rafting trips. The centre also has information on walks, horse trekking, fishing, hunting and tours.

A new walk of interest is the **Te Kuri Walkway**, a three-hour walk through farmland and some forest to a commanding viewpoint. The walk traverses the farm of Murray Ball, the famous cartoonist and creator of *Footrot Flats*, whose beloved hero is 'The Dog' (*Te Kuri* in Maori). The walk starts four km north of town at the end of Shelley Rd.

Places to Stay

Camping & Cabins The *Waikanae Beach Holiday Park* (☎ 867 5634) is on Grey St at Waikanae Beach, very near the centre. Sites cost $14 for two, cabins range upwards from $20 for two, and tourist flats are $46.

The *Showgrounds Park Motor Camp* (☎ 867 4101), at Makaraka near the showgrounds, is cheaper – only $10.50 for two; $12.50 with power – but it's not so conveniently central. The cabins here are also cheap at $15 to $20 for two people but they're pretty spartan.

Hostels The *Gisborne YHA Hostel* (☎ 867 3269) is at 32 Harris St, 1.5 km from the town

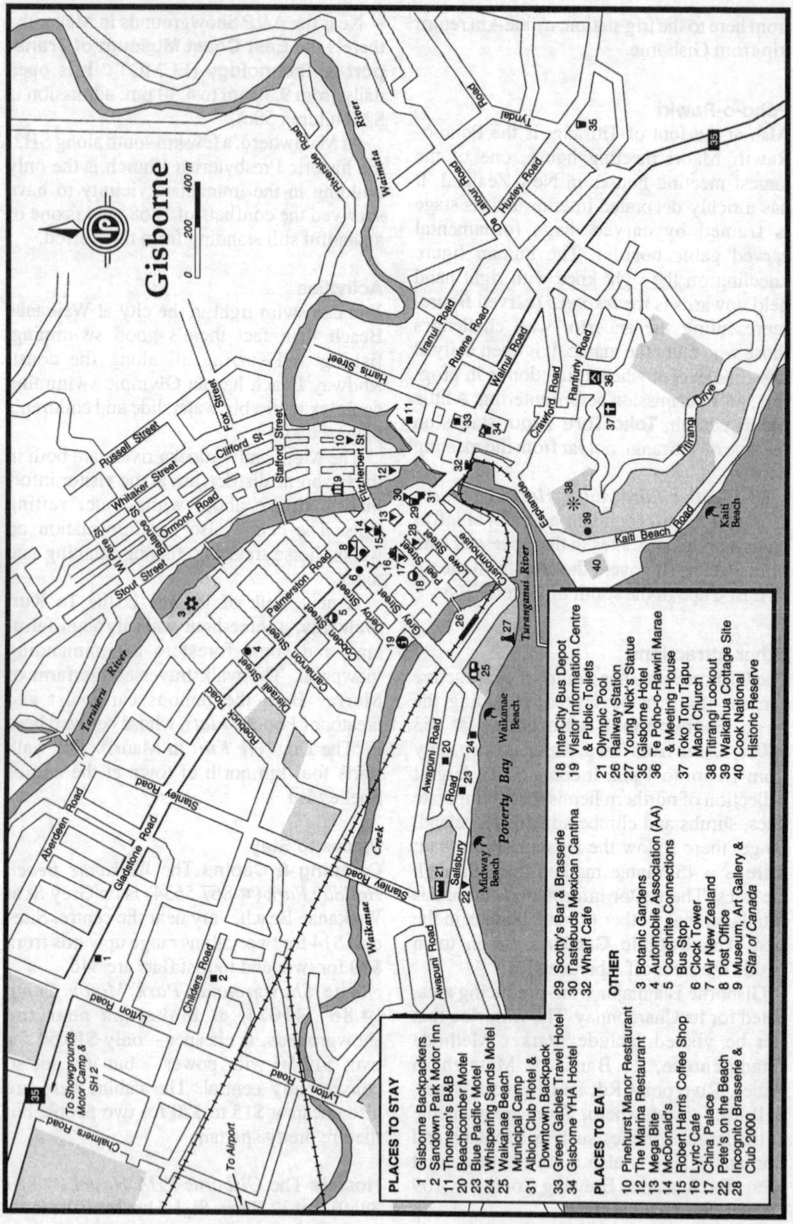
Gisborne
0 200 400 m
PLACES TO STAY
1 Gisborne Backpackers
2 Sandown Park Motor Inn
11 Thomson's B&B
20 Beachcomber Motel
23 Blue Pacific Motel
24 Whispering Sands Motel
25 Waikanae Beach Municipal Camp
31 Albion Club Hotel & Downtown Backpack
33 Green Gables Travel Hotel
34 Gisborne YHA Hostel
PLACES TO EAT
10 Pinehurst Manor Restaurant
12 The Marina Restaurant
13 Mega Bite
14 McDonald's
15 Robert Harris Coffee Shop
16 Lyric Cafe
17 China Palace
22 Pete's on the Beach
28 Incognito Brasserie & Club 2000
29 Scotty's Bar & Brasserie
30 Tastebuds Mexican Cantina
32 Wharf Cafe
OTHER
3 Botanic Gardens
4 Automobile Association (AA)
5 Coachrite Connections Bus Stop
6 Clock Tower
7 Air New Zealand
8 Post Office
9 Museum, Art Gallery & Star of Canada
18 InterCity Bus Depot
19 Visitor Information Centre & Public Toilets
21 Olympic Pool
26 Railway Station
27 Young Nick's Statue
35 Gisborne Hotel
36 Te Poho-o-Rawiri Marae & Meeting House
37 Toko Toru Tapu Maori Church
38 Titirangi Lookout
39 Waikahua Cottage Site
40 Cook National Historic Reserve
To Showgrounds Motor Camp & SH 2
To Airport
Poverty Bay
Waikanae Beach
Midway Beach
Kaiti Beach
Turanganui River
Taruheru River
Waimata River
Waikanae Creek
Gladstone Road
Stanley Road
Lytton Road
Childers Road
Aberdeen Road
Chalmers Road
Awapuni Road
Salisbury Road
Roebuck Road
Disraeli Street
Carnarvon Street
Cobden Street
Derby Street
Grey Street
Palmerston Road
Peel Street
Lowe Street
Customhouse
Esplanade
Stout Street
Ormond Road
Whitaker Street
Russell Street
Fox Street
Clifford St
Stafford Street
Fitzherbert St
Harris Street
Riverside Road
Rutene Road
Iranui Road
Wainui Road
Crawford Road
Ranfurly Road
Latour Road
De Huxley Road
Tyndal Road
Titirangi Drive
Kaiti Beach Road
Balance St
W Pere St

centre across the river, in a big rambling old home with spacious grounds. The nightly cost is $13 in dorms or $30 for doubles or twins. Doonas are available but make sure you return them!

Gisborne Backpackers (☎ 868 1000) is at 690 Gladstone Rd, about two km from the town centre. This large, former orphanage retains some of its old atmosphere but provides good standards of accommodation in dorm rooms for $13 and $14, or singles/doubles cost $20/28. Most of the buses stop outside.

The *Downtown Backpack* (☎ 867 9997) is part of the Albion Club Hotel at 13 Gladstone Rd. It costs $10 per person, plus a key deposit, in basic pub rooms above a noisy bar.

B&Bs & Guesthouses The visitor information centre has full details on B&Bs and guesthouses in and around Gisborne. They include the *Green Gables Travel Hotel* (☎ 867 9872) at 31 Rawiri St, Kaiti, across the river from the city centre, where singles/doubles are $35/58, or $48/80 including breakfast. *Thomson's B&B* (☎ 868 9675), 195 The Esplanade, is pleasantly situated in the historic riverfront district and costs $40/55.

Repongaere (☎ 862 7717), near Patutahi, is a more upmarket B&B in a large historic homestead. This fine retreat costs $120 to $150 a double, and dinner can be arranged.

Motels Most Gisborne motels start from around $65 for singles and $75 for doubles. Marginally cheaper ones include the *Coastland Motel* (☎ 868 6464) at 114 Main Rd, the *Endeavour Lodge* (☎ 868 6075) at 525 Gladstone Rd, and the *Highway Motel* (☎ 868 4059) at 60 Main Rd.

Salisbury Rd is close to the city centre and right near the beach is a good (if more expensive) motel hunting ground. Motels here include the *Blue Pacific* (☎ 868 6099) and *Whispering Sands* (☎ 867 1319), right on the beach, or the *Beachcomber* (☎ 868 9349) on the other side of street is cheaper.

Places to Eat

Gisborne has the usual selection of sandwich places, particularly along Gladstone Rd – or you could try Peel St, where there are two excellent sandwich places. *Mega Bite* has good hot lunches (quiche, samosas and the like), sandwiches, rolls, and drinks, and it's a relaxed and pleasant place to eat them. Opposite this, in the pedestrian mall leading to McDonald's, is the *Robert Harris Coffee Shop* with an equally good selection of sandwiches.

For Chinese food, the most popular place is *China Palace* in Peel St, which has a takeaway counter at front and a no-frills dining section where you can eat at takeaway prices. Next door is a flash but usually empty bar and upstairs is a more expensive licensed restaurant.

At 124 Gladstone Rd the *Lyric Cafe* is a fine, old-fashioned seafood restaurant with fish & chips and a variety of meals at around $12. There is a separate counter for takeaways. Down at the Gisborne wharf, the *Wharf Cafe* serves meals, decadent desserts, coffee and local wine by the glass.

Tastebuds Mexican Cantina on the corner of Lowe St and Reads Quay is part of a chain of popular Tex-Mex places, serving nachos, burritos, tacos and enchiladas. *The Marina*, wonderfully situated beside the river, is expensive in the evening, but the à la carte lunches are reasonably priced.

Pete's on the Beach, on Midway Beach, is a seafood and steak restaurant, open for lunch and dinner. The *Incognito Brasserie*, 90 Peel St, is a very flash bar/restaurant with a range of continental dishes at about $20 for a main course. The top of the town's dining pile is the *Pinehurst Manor*, at 4 Clifford St, which is a winner of several Taste NZ and lamb cuisine awards and justifiably so.

Entertainment

Longjohn's in the Sandown Park Motor Inn on Childers Rd has bands. For a *Once Were Warriors* experience, the *Albion Club*, Gladstone Rd, and the *Gisborne Hotel* on Huxley Rd are rough pubs with live music most weekends. The *Tatapouri Hotel* on the main

EAST COAST

road in Tatapouri, about 12 km north of Gisborne, is one of the region's most popular and enjoyable nightspots, right on the beach with both indoor and outdoor bars.

You find the young trendy set at *Club 2000*, part of the Incognito complex on Peel St. During the summer holidays local bands, musicians and poets perform in the parks.

Getting There & Away

Air The Air New Zealand office (☎ 867 9490) is at 37 Bright St. They have daily direct flights to Wellington, Napier, Hamilton and Auckland, with connections to other centres.

Bus The InterCity depot (☎ 868 6196) is on the corner of Bright St and Childers Rd. InterCity has at least one bus every day to Napier (3½ hours) via Wairoa (1½ hours). From Napier there are connections to Palmerston North and Wellington. InterCity also runs buses between Gisborne and Auckland (nine hours) via Opotiki (two hours), Whakatane (three hours) and Rotorua (five hours).

Coachrite Connections (☎ 868 9969) has a 7.45 am bus every day except Saturday to Wairoa ($18), Napier ($32) and Hastings ($35), with student/backpacker discounts of around 20% available. It departs from opposite Georgy Pie on Gladstone Rd.

Newmans also share some of these services and their passes can be used on the InterCity buses to Napier and the Coachrite Connections buses.

The much longer, but very scenic, East Cape route to Opotiki can be done by a combination of courier services. See the beginning of the East Cape section for details.

Another route from Rotorua to Gisborne runs through the Te Urewera National Park, passing by Lake Waikaremoana and joining the Napier route at Wairoa, 97 km south of Gisborne. For the national park you must change buses in Wairoa.

Hitching Hitching is OK from the south, and not too bad through Waioeka Gorge to Opotiki – it's still best to leave early. To hitch a ride out head along Gladstone Rd to Makaraka, six km west, for Wairoa and Napier, or the turn-off to Opotiki and Rotorua. Hopefully you may get a ride before Makaraka but most of Gladstone Rd is a built-up area.

Hitching from Wairoa to Waikaremoana is hard going. For hitching around the East Cape head out along the Wainui road.

Getting Around

Gisborne City Buses (☎ 868 6761) run only on weekdays until about 5.30 pm. Ring Gisborne Taxis (☎ 867 2222) for a taxi. Link Shuttles (☎ 867 4765) run to Gisborne airport. The various rental car companies include Budget, Avis and Hertz. Check out Scotties (☎ 867 7947) for the lowest prices.

GISBORNE TO WAIROA

Heading south towards Napier you have two choices. The bus follows the SH2 coastal route, passing close to the Wharerata Forest Reserve, Morere Hot Springs and the Mahia Peninsula before meeting SH36 in Wairoa. SH36 is the inland route and is equally scenic.

Coastal Route

The coastal route runs just inland most of the way south from Gisborne, before entering the Wharerata State Forest. At the southern edge of the state forest, 56 km from Gisborne, Morere is a pretty little town noted for its hot springs. The **Morere Hot Springs**, with various pools and bush walks, are a popular day trip from Gisborne. The well-presented hot spring pools are complemented by short walks of up to two hours through the beautiful native forest of the surrounding reserve. The hot springs, managed by DOC, are open from 10 am to 5 pm daily, until 8 pm on weekends in summer. The cost is $3 (children $1.50) in the public pool, $4 (children $2) in private pools.

You can stay in Morere at the delightful *Peacock Lodge* (☎ 837 8824), about two minutes walk from SH2. Follow the road next to the tearooms across the stream. This

EAST COAST

old colonial farmhouse has a spacious lounge, fully equipped kitchen and a large, wide verandah – it costs $13 per person in shared rooms, or doubles and twins are $30. The *Morere Springs Tavern* has a small restaurant.

SH2 continues south to Nuhaka on the northern end of the sweep of Hawke Bay, where you can head west to Wairoa or east to the superb, windswept and wild **Mahia Peninsula** – *mahia* translates as 'indistinct sounds', although the peninsula is said to be named after a place in Tahiti. There are long, curving beaches popular with surfers, clear water for diving and fishing, birdwatching at Mangawhio Lagoon and walks to a number of reserves. The isthmus was once an island, but sand accumulation has formed New Zealand's largest tombolo landform (where a sand or shingle bar ties an island to another island or the mainland). The Mahia is a magical, atmospheric place, majestic in either sun or storm.

Facilities are limited and you'll need your own transport to get around. Accommodation can be found at the *Mahia Beach Motor Camp* (☎ 837 5830) at Opoutama where sites cost from $8 per person, cabins are $38.50 for two and motel-style units for $65 a double. The similarly priced *Blue Bay Motor Camp* (☎ 837 5867) at Mahia Beach is right on the beach. Some six km from Opoutama is the *Tunanui Farmstay* (☎ 837 5790) which has a fully self-contained cottage sleeping six – there is a lot to do in the area and the view out over the Mahia Peninsula is stupendous.

Inland Route

Along SH36, the inland route to Wairoa and Napier, there are also several things to see and do. You can climb up **Gentle Annie Hill** for a good view over the Poverty Bay area. **Doneraille Park** (53 km from Gisborne), a native bush reserve, is a popular picnic spot with good swimming when the water is clear. There's fine trout fishing at **Tiniroto Lakes**, 61 km from Gisborne, and about 10 km further on, the **Te Reinga Falls** are worth a detour off the main road.

Hawkes Bay

WAIROA

The two highways, SH2 and SH36, merge in Wairoa, 98 km south of Gisborne and 118 km north of Napier. Wairoa has a reasonable beach but the main reason to stop in this provincial town is to get transport connections to Te Urewera National Park. The reconstructed lighthouse by the river, built in 1877 of solid kauri, used to shine from Portland Island at the tip of the Mahia Peninsula. Not far east of Wairoa is the Whakaki Lagoon, an important wetlands area renowned for its bird populations.

The Wairoa Information Centre (☎ & fax 838 7440) is on the corner of SH2 and Queen St in the centre of town.

Places to Stay

If you have to wait in Wairoa to get a bus up to Te Urewera, the *Riverside Motor Camp* (☎ 838 6301) is a pleasant place on the banks of the Wairoa River with sites from $8 per person and cabins for $31 a double. Wairoa also has pub rooms at the *Clyde Hotel* (☎ 838 7139), Marine Parade, and motels include the *Three Oaks* (☎ 838 8204), on the corner of Campbell St and Clyde Rd, where singles/doubles start at $57/68.

At Frasertown, eight km north of Wairoa, *Tipi Backpacker* (☎ 838 7960) makes an excellent base for visiting Te Urewera National Park. This quiet, rural retreat is on SH38 on the way to the park – look for the big tipi in the garden. A dorm bed in the well-equipped farmhouse costs $14, doubles are $34 or in summer you can stay in the tipi for $11. They organise various trips, such as to the Te Reinga Falls and local glow-worm caves. Best of all they arrange transport to the national park, and rent camping and cooking gear at reasonable rates. They can pick up from Napier or Gisborne for $15 – ring for details.

Getting There & Away

All InterCity (☎ 838 6049) and Coachrite

Connections buses between Gisborne and Napier pass through Wairoa. InterCity also has a service between Rotorua and Wairoa ($55, $33 with discount) on Monday, Wednesday and Friday, passing right through Te Urewera National Park.

WAIROA TO NAPIER

There are some good reserves along this stretch of road, all accessible from SH2, to break the twisting drive.

Lake Tutira has a farmland setting; there are walkways around the lake and a bird sanctuary. The **Hawkes Bay Coastal Walkway** is 12 km from SH2, down Waikari Rd. The walkway is 16 km long, goes from the Waikari River to the Aropaoanui River, and involves equal portions of boulder hopping, track walking and beach walking.

Off Waipati Rd and 34 km from Napier is the **Waipatiki Scenic Reserve**; the **White Pine Bush Scenic Reserve**, 29 km from Napier, is notable for the dominant kahikatea (white pine); and the **Tangoio Falls Scenic Reserve**, two km south of White Pine, has the Te Ana Falls, stands of ponga and whekiponga and podocarps. The White Pine and Tangoio Falls reserves are linked by the **Tangoio Walkway**, which follows Kareaara Stream.

EAST COAST

TE UREWERA NATIONAL PARK

Te Urewera National Park is one New Zealand's most attractive parks. This is a marvellous area of lush forests, lakes and rivers, with lots of tramps ranging from half an hour to several days, and plenty of birds, trout, deer and other wildlife. The main focus of the park is the superbly scenic Lake Waikaremoana (sea of rippling waters). Most visitors to the park come by boat on the lake or walk the Lake Waikaremoana Track, one of New Zealand's Great Walks, but many other walks are possible.

The park protects part of the largest untouched native forest area in the North Island. Diverse forest in the park ranges from podocarp and tawa forest in the river valleys to rimu and beech at higher altitudes. The rivers and lakes of the park offer good fishing for rainbow and brown trout. The further reaches of the park are popular with pig and deer hunters (licences required from DOC).

Information

The Aniwaniwa Visitor Centre (☎ 837 3803; fax 837 3722) is within the park on Lake Waikaremoana. It has interesting displays on the park's natural history and supplies detailed information on the many walking tracks, camping grounds and huts around the park.

The Ikawhenua Visitor Centre (☎ (07) 366 5641) is the park's other main information centre near Murupara on the western edge of the park. Hut and camping ground passes for the Lake Waikaremoana Track can also be bought at DOC offices in Gisborne, Opotiki, Whakatane, Napier etc, and at the Gisborne Visitor Information Centre.

Lake Waikaremoana Track

This three to four-day walk is one of the most popular walks in the North Island. The 46-km walk has spectacular views from the Panekiri Bluff, but all along the walk through fern groves, beech and podocarp forest there are vast panoramas and beautiful views of the lake. The walk is rated as easy, and the only difficult section is the climb to Panekiri Bluff. Because of its popularity it is very busy from mid-December to the end of January and at Easter. The walk can be done all year round, but the cold and rain in winter deter most people and make conditions much more challenging. Because of the altitude, temperatures can drop quickly even in summer.

Five huts are spaced out along the track, but at peak time it may be wise to carry a tent. Huts and camp sites cost $6.

Walking the Track The track can be done from either end. The bus between Rotorua and Wairoa can drop you at either Onepoto or Hopuruahine Landing. Starting from Onepoto all the climbing is done in the first few hours – water on this section of the track is limited so make sure you fill your water bottle before heading off. For those with

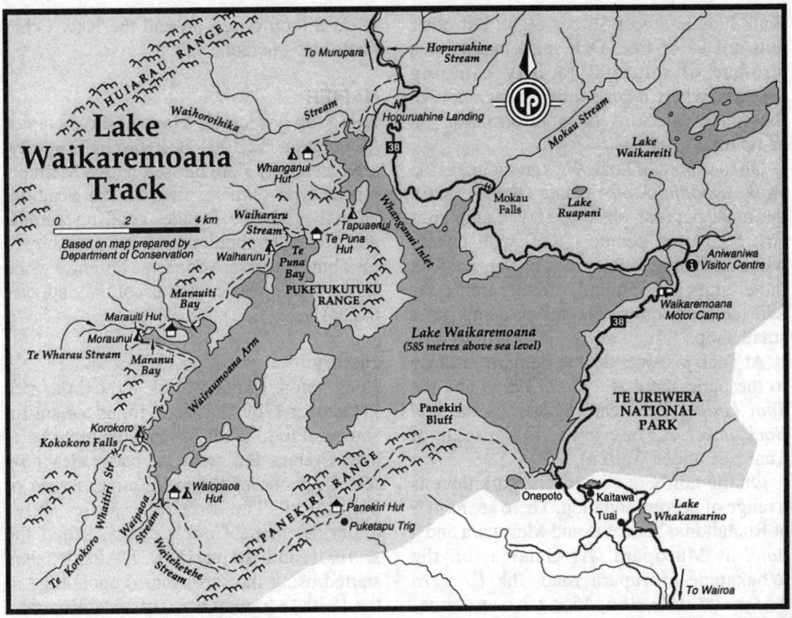

their own car, it is safest to leave the car at Waikaremoana and then take either a boat or bus to the trail heads.

Estimated walking times are:

Onepoto to Panekiri Hut	five hours
Panekiri to Waiopaoa Hut	four hours
Waiopaoa to Marauiti Hut	4½ hours
Marauiti to Te Puna Hut	2¾ hours
Te Puna to Whanganui Hut	two hours
Whanganui to Hopuruahine Landing	three hours

Other Walks

The other major walk in the park is the **Whakatane River Round Trip**. The four to five-day walk starts at Ruatahuna on SH38, 45 km from the Aniwaniwa Visitor Centre towards Rotorua. The track follows the Whakatane River then loops back via the Waikare River, Motomuka Stream and the Whakatane Valley. The track has six huts. The Aniwaniwa Visitor Centre has track notes for this walk and sells topographical maps.

Another good walk is the **Lake Waikareiti Track**, which begins near the Aniwaniwa Visitor Centre and leads to the Sandy Bay Hut. There are at least 20 other walks along the park's 600 km of tracks.

Kayaking

Bay Kayaks (☎ 837 3818) at the Waikaremoana Motor Camp has guided kayaking trips on the lake starting at $80 for one day up to $320 for a four-day trip. There is a tramp-paddle option allowing you to, say, walk three sections of the track and kayak one for variety. Kayaks can also be rented for $25 a half-day or $45 per day.

Places to Stay

There are various camps and cabins spaced along SH38, including a camp, cabins and motel 67 km inland from the Wairoa turn-off.

DOC has over 50 huts along the walkways throughout the national park. The Lake Waikaremoana Track huts are rated as Great

Walk huts and cost $6 per night, but other huts are $4 or free. DOC also maintains a number of minimal facility camping grounds, where it costs only $2 to camp. All the ranger stations have information on camping.

On the shore of Lake Waikaremoana is the *Waikaremoana Motor Camp* (☎ 837 3826), the most popular place to stay. Camp sites cost $7.50 per person, $8.50 with power, while cabins are $30 for two, chalets are $50, motel units are $56 and a family unit costs $85 for four adults. The motor camp has a small shop.

At Tuai, just outside the southern entrance to the park, there is a *motor camp* and the *Tuai Lodge*. The nearest hostel is the *Tipi Backpacker* at Frasertown, 42 km south of Tuai (see under Wairoa).

On the northern edge of the park there is a range of accommodation. There are *motels* at Ruatahuna, Taneatua and Murupara and a *hotel* at Murupara. At Galatea, on the Whakatane-Murupara road, the *Urewera Lodge* (☎ (07) 366 4556) has a three-bedroom cottage with bunkrooms for $22 per person.

Getting There & Away

Most of the 120-km road through the park between Frasertown and the town of Murupara is unsealed, winding and time-consuming. Traffic is light on this road, making it a slow go for hitching.

InterCity buses run the five-hour trip between Rotorua and Wairoa on Monday, Wednesday and Friday and can drop off and pick up at the trail heads and the Waikaremoana Motor Camp. The Waikaremoana Shuttle service (☎ 837 3836) operates on demand from Tuai to Onepoto, the motor camp, visitor information centre, Mokau landing, and Hopuruahine. Depending on the number of people, the cost from Tuai is around $10 to Onepoto, $20 to Hopuruahine.

From the Waikaremoana Motor Camp, a ferry service (☎ 837 3729) across the lakes does a loop trip twice a day in summer, on demand in winter. It costs $10 to Onepoto, $15 to Hopuruahine, or $20 if you just want to do a loop cruise around the lake. Other boats also operate.

NAPIER

Lying on sweeping Hawke Bay, Napier (population 52,100) is a fascinating city, architecturally rich, blessed with a Mediterranean-type climate, fine coastal position, attractive Marine Parade, good restaurants and a friendly population. It is a great city to visit but try to avoid domestic holidays when it becomes crowded and accommodation is expensive.

History

Long before Captain Cook sighted the area in October 1769, the Maori found a plentiful source of food in the bay and the hinterland. The Otatara Pa, with its barricades now rebuilt, is one of the pre-European sites of habitation. The French explorer Jules d'Urville, using Cook's charts, sailed the *Astrolabe* into the bay in 1827. After whalers started using the safe Ahuriri anchorage in the 1830s, a trading base was established by one Captain Barney Rhodes in 1839. The town was planned in 1854, named after the British general and colonial administrator, Sir Charles Napier, and soon flourished as a commercial centre for the region.

In 1931 Napier was dramatically changed when a disastrous earthquake, measuring 7.9 on the Richter scale, virtually destroyed the city. In Napier and nearby Hastings over 250 people died, and waterlocked Napier suddenly found itself 40 sq km larger. The quake heaved that amount of water-covered land above sea level, and in places the land level rose by over two metres. The Napier airport is built on that previously submerged area. The rebuilding programme that followed has left us with one of the world's best examples of an Art Deco city.

Orientation

At the northern end of town Bluff Hill looms, acting as a natural boundary between the centre and the Ahuriri and port areas. The many fine wooden villas on the hill that survived the quake give this district a genteel

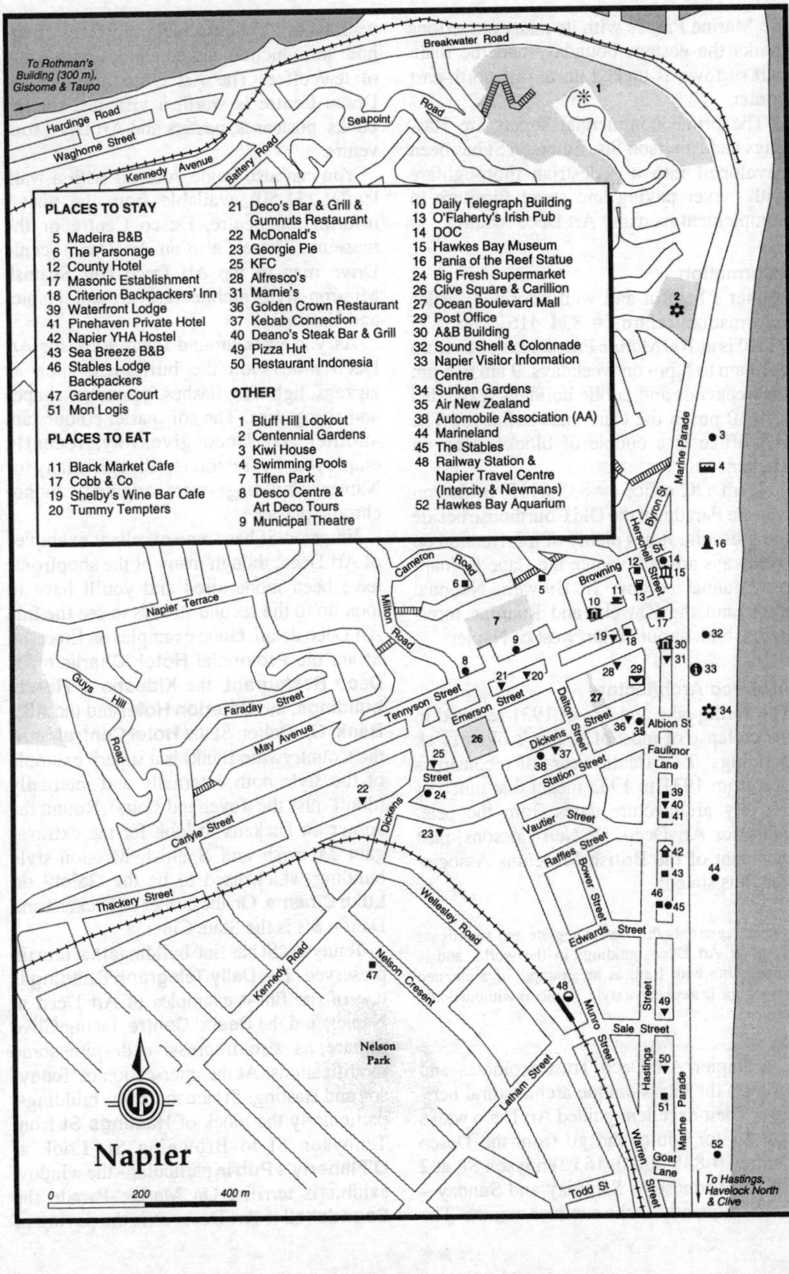
Napier
To Rothman's Building (300 m), Gisborne & Taupo
PLACES TO STAY
5 Madeira B&B
6 The Parsonage
12 County Hotel
17 Masonic Establishment
18 Criterion Backpackers' Inn
39 Waterfront Lodge
41 Pinehaven Private Hotel
42 Napier YHA Hostel
43 Sea Breeze B&B
46 Stables Lodge Backpackers
47 Gardener Court
51 Mon Logis
PLACES TO EAT
11 Black Market Cafe
17 Cobb & Co
19 Shelby's Wine Bar Cafe
20 Tummy Tempters
21 Deco's Bar & Grill & Gumnuts Restaurant
22 McDonald's
23 Georgie Pie
25 KFC
28 Alfresco's
31 Mamie's
36 Golden Crown Restaurant
37 Kebab Connection
40 Deano's Steak Bar & Grill
49 Pizza Hut
50 Restaurant Indonesia
OTHER
1 Bluff Hill Lookout
2 Centennial Gardens
3 Kiwi House
4 Swimming Pools
7 Tiffen Park
8 Desco Centre & Art Deco Tours
9 Municipal Theatre
10 Daily Telegraph Building
13 O'Flaherty's Irish Pub
14 DOC
15 Hawkes Bay Museum
16 Pania of the Reef Statue
24 Big Fresh Supermarket
26 Clive Square & Carillion
27 Ocean Boulevard Mall
29 Post Office
30 A&B Building
32 Sound Shell & Colonnade
33 Napier Visitor Information Centre
34 Sunken Gardens
35 Air New Zealand
38 Automobile Association (AA)
44 Marineland
45 The Stables
48 Railway Station & Napier Travel Centre (Intercity & Newmans)
52 Hawkes Bay Aquarium
Breakwater Road
Hardinge Road
Waghorne Street
Kennedy Avenue
Battery Road
Seapoint Road
Marine Parade
Byron St
Herschell Street
Browning St
Cameron Road
Milton Road
Napier Terrace
Guys Hill Road
Faraday Street
Tennyson Street
May Avenue
Emerson Street
Dalton Street
Dickens Street
Station Street
Albion St
Faulknor Lane
Vautier Street
Raffles Street
Bower Street
Edwards Street
Carlyle Street
Dickens Street
Thackery Street
Wellesley Road
Kennedy Road
Nelson Cresent
Nelson Park
Munro Street
Latham Street
Warren Street
Hastings Street
Sale Street
Goat Lane
Todd St
To Hastings, Havelock North & Clive
0 200 400 m

EAST COAST

air. Marine Parade with its many attractions marks the eastern boundary and the main part of town is tucked up in this north-east corner.

The prime commercial streets are Hastings and Emerson Sts. Emerson St has been developed into a pedestrian thoroughfare with clever paving and street furniture to complement its many Art Deco features.

Information

Napier's helpful and well-informed visitor information centre (☎ 834 4161; fax 835 7129) is at 100 Marine Parade. It's open from 8.30 am to 5 pm on weekdays, 9 am to 5 pm on weekends and public holidays (extended to 8.30 pm in the Christmas holidays). The AA office is a couple of blocks away on Dickens St.

The DOC office (☎ 835 0415) is also on Marine Parade, in the Old Courthouse beside the museum. It has plenty of information on walkways around Napier, the Cape Kidnappers gannet colony, Te Urewera National Park, and the Kaweka and Ruahine forest parks, both about 50 km west of Napier.

Art Deco Architecture

The earthquake and fire of 1931 resulted in the collapse of most of Napier's older brick buildings. Two frantic years of reconstruction from 1931 to 1933 meant that much of the city architecture dates from the peak years for Art Deco. Dr Neil Cossons, past president of the British Museums Association, has stated:

> Napier represents the most complete and significant group of Art Deco buildings in the world, and is comparable with Bath as an example of a planned townscape in a cohesive style. Napier is without doubt unique.

The Napier Art Deco Trust promotes and protects the city's unique architectural heritage. Their excellent guided Art Deco walks cost $7 for adults and go from the Desco Centre (☎ 835 0022), 163 Tennyson St, at 2 pm on Wednesday, Saturday and Sunday – more frequently in the summer months. The walk takes 1½ hours, is preceded by a half-hour introduction and concludes with a cup of tea/coffee. The Art Deco Shop in the Desco Centre is worth a visit just for the books, postcards, posters and Art Deco souvenirs.

You can also guide yourself with a walk leaflet ($1.50) available from the visitor information centre, Desco Centre or the museum. There's also an Art Deco Scenic Drive map to the Art Deco and Spanish Mission-style architecture around Napier and Hastings.

As you walk around town, look for Art Deco motifs on the buildings, such as zigzags, lightning flashes, geometric shapes and rising suns. The soft pastel colours are another Art Deco giveaway, recently employed by restorers, though many of Napier's buildings were originally monochrome plaster.

Emerson St has some excellent examples of Art Deco, though many of the shopfronts have been modernised and you'll have to look up to the second storeys to see the fine Art Deco detail. Good examples on Emerson St are the **Provincial Hotel**, **Charlie's Art Deco Restaurant**, the **Kidsons & Hursts buildings**, the **Criterion Hotel** and the **ASB Bank**. On Dalton St the **Hotel Central** (now the Countrywide Bank) is a superb example of the style both externally and internally (don't miss the foyer and stairs). Round the corner on Dickens St look for the extravagant Moorish and Spanish Mission-style building which used to be the **Gaiety de Luxe Cinema**. On the corner of Dickens and Dalton Sts is the State Cinema.

Tennyson St has fine buildings that remain preserved. The **Daily Telegraph Building** is one of the finest examples of Art Deco in Napier, and the **Desco Centre**, facing Clive Square, is also impressive despite some modifications. At the intersection of Tennyson and Hastings Sts are more fine buildings, particularly the block of **Hastings St** from Tennyson St to Browning St. Look at **O'Flaherty's Pub** in particular – the window exhibit is terrific. On Marine Parade the **Soundshell** is Art Deco, as is the paving of the plaza which used to be a skating rink. From here you can admire the Art Deco **clocktower** (neon lit at night) of the A&B building and also the **Masonic Hotel**.

In the third week of February, Napier holds an Art Deco weekend where there are dinners, balls and much fancy dress.

Marine Parade

Lined with Norfolk pines, some fine old wooden buildings that survived the quake and many attractions, Marine Parade is one of New Zealand's premier seaside boulevards. Marine Parade has retained its air of an old-fashioned English seaside resort complete with pebble beach, but the strong riptide makes for hazardous swimming.

Marine Parade has parks, sunken and scented gardens, and amusements including mini-golf, swimming pools and a rollerblading rink. The statue of **Pania of the Reef**, a sort of Maori equivalent of Copenhagen's Little Mermaid, is at the parade's northern end.

Marineland has a collection of performing seals and dolphins; displays take place at 10.30 am and 2 pm, with an additional 4 pm show in summer. Admission is $7.50 (children $4). The kids enjoy the show but in these days of eco-tourism it is a little outdated, so they also have swim-with-the-dolphin experiences in the pool ($30 by appointment), as well as dolphin and shark feeding and other close-encounter tours.

Not far away on the parade, the **Hawkes Bay Aquarium** has sharks, crocodiles, piranha, turtles and other animals including New Zealand's unique tuataras. It's open daily from 9 am to 5 pm. Feeding time is 3.15 pm, admission is $6.50 (children $3.25).

Marine Parade also has a **Kiwi House**, where every day at 1 pm there's a half-hour show with an educational talk on kiwis. After that, at 2 pm, it's feeding time and sometimes the children can come in to feed the birds. The centre has other animals and birds, including moreporks, sugar gliders, night herons, bush geckoes and whistling frogs. It's open daily from 11 am to 3 pm; admission is $3 (children $1.50).

At No 321, **The Stables** is a small complex with a waxworks pioneer museum, a small Shantytown and Earthquake '31, a good video documentary of the quake, which you can view in 'quake-a-rama'. The complex is open from 8 am to 6 pm daily and entry costs $6 (children $2.50) or $4.50 ($2) for the museum or video only.

Hawkes Bay Museum & Cultural Trust

Also on Marine Parade is the well-run art gallery and museum. Quality Maori artefacts of the east coast's Ngati Kahungunu tribe are displayed, as well as European antiques and Art Deco items; there's also a dry but informative audiovisual of the 1931 earthquake. The museum also has regular exhibitions. It is open from 10 am to 4.30 pm daily; admission is $2 (children free). The museum's shop has good-quality souvenirs.

Bluff Hill Lookout

There's an excellent view over all of Hawkes Bay from Bluff Hill, 102 metres above the Port of Napier. It's a sheer cliff-face down to the port, however, and rather a circuitous route to the top. It's open every day from 7 am until one hour after sunset.

Activities

At Napier there are many water activities including fishing, windsurfing, kayaking, canoeing, parasailing, jet-boating, waterskiing, tandem skydiving and so on – ask at the visitor information centre to find the current operators.

Although the beach along Marine Parade is not good for swimming, there's great swimming and surfing on the beach up past the port. The swimming pool on Marine Parade costs just $1, but is closed in winter. The Onekawa Pool Complex is larger and fancier, with waterslides and other attractions.

More activities can be found at Riverland (☎ 834 9756), 50 km north of Napier on SH5, where there's horse trekking, white-water rafting and backpackers accommodation. Hawkes Bay Jet Tours (☎ 874 9703) organises trips on the scenic Ngaruroro River, which range from 30 minutes to one day.

Places to Stay

Camping & Cabins Napier has a number of camping grounds, but none of them is conveniently central. Closest to the centre is *Kennedy Park* (☎ 843 9126) off Kennedy Rd at Marewa, 2.5 km from the central post office. Powered sites cost $18 for two. There are also some basic huts at $25 for two, cabins at $38 and tourist flats at $56.

The *Westshore Holiday Camp* (☎ 835 9456) is on Main Rd near Westshore Beach, six km north of town. Camp sites here are $7 per person, $8 with power, cabins are $25 to $30 for two and there are also tourist flats from $40.

At Taradale, 9.5 km out, *Taradale Holiday Park* (☎ 844 2732) at 470 Gloucester St has sites from $7.50 per person, plus on-site caravans and cabins from $40.

Hostels Napier has a good selection of hostels.

The *Napier YHA Hostel* (☎ 835 7039), 277 Marine Parade, is a former guesthouse in an excellent location opposite the beach. It's more luxurious than most hostels and costs $14 a night in a dorm or twin room. The kitchen, dining room and recreation area are all separate, making it more spacious.

Right in the centre the *Criterion Backpackers Inn* (☎ 835 2059), at 48 Emerson St, is upstairs in what was formerly the Criterion Hotel, a classy Art Deco building. It has the usual kitchen and dining facilities plus a large recreation area; downstairs are a bistro and bar, The Cri. The nightly cost is $12 and $14 in the dorms and $30 for twin or double rooms.

The *Stables Lodge Backpackers* (☎ 835 1937), 321 Marine Parade, is part of The Stables museum complex. The hostel is behind the museum – enter from Hastings St after hours. It's a brand new hostel with spotless rooms and a good kitchen/dining area. A dorm bed costs $14, doubles and twins are $30.

The *Glenview Farm Hostel* (☎ 836 6232) is a hill-country sheep and cattle station, where horse riding and walking are popular activities. You can join in the farm activities, and go hunting for geese or eels. The cost is $12 a night. The hostel is 31 km north of Napier off SH2, two km along the Arapaoanui Rd towards the sea.

B&Bs & Guesthouses Since it is a summer resort of the old-fashioned variety, Napier has some good guesthouses along Marine Parade beside the beach. However, as this is a large and busy thoroughfare, it can be quite noisy. The *Pinehaven Private Hotel* (☎ 835 5575) at No 259 has singles/doubles for $38/60; it's a strictly non-smoking place. The front rooms have fine views of the seafront. The *Waterfront Lodge* (☎ 835 3429) at No 217 is another old, wooden guesthouse offering B&B for $30/50, but it also has budget rooms for $15/30. It's good value. At No 415 is the charming French-style *Mon Logis* (☎ 835 2125), built in 1915 as a private hotel, but it is very expensive at $150 a double. Opposite Marineland on the parade, the *Sea Breeze B&B* (☎ 835 8067) has a lounge room with a great view and costs $40/50.

Another good hunting ground for B&Bs is on Bluff Hill, just a short walk down to the city centre (but a long walk back up). A number of fine wooden villas offer accommodation – the visitor information centre has listings. They include *Madeira B&B* (☎ 845 5185), 6 Madeira Rd, at the end of a very steep street. It costs $65 a double and the upstairs balcony is *the* spot to take breakfast; the view is terrific. Nearby, *The Parsonage* (☎ 835 1527), 29 Cameron Rd, is a fine old villa, with a new, self-contained flat at the back of the house costing $45/65.

Hotels Cheaper hotels include the *Taradale Hotel* (☎ 844 2338), in Gloucester St, Taradale, which has singles/doubles for $35/45, and the *Victoria Hotel* (☎ 835 3149) at 367 Marine Parade, where singles are $40 to $55, doubles $65.

The fine old *Masonic Establishment* (☎ 835 8689) on the corner of Marine Parade and Tennyson St is very central. The rooms with a bathroom are $51/54 or singles without bath cost $31. They also do a B&B

special at $59 a double and have some backpacker rooms at $25 per person. Freeman's Bar is underneath so the rooms can be noisy.

For something special, the *County Hotel* (☎ 835 7800), 12 Browning St, is a boutique hotel in a newly refurbished and converted city council building. Rooms offering real luxury start at $125, though most are $175 or suites are $375.

Motels Napier has plenty of motels, particularly around Westshore, coming into town on the road from Gisborne and Taupo. The *Albatross Motel* (☎ 835 5991), on this stretch at 59 Meeanee Quay, has singles/doubles from $45/50. It regularly offers discounts, and motels nearby follow suit.

The *City Close Motel* (☎ 835 3568) at 50 Munroe St is conveniently located and costs $57/68. The *Snowgoose Lodge Motel* (☎ 843 6083), at 376 Kennedy Rd, costs $66/77, and at 335 Kennedy Rd, the *Tropicana Motel* (☎ 843 9153) has units for $56/68. The *Gardener Court Motel* (☎ 835 5913), 16 Nelson Crescent, costs $60/70.

Places to Eat

Snacks & Takeaways Emerson St has some good sandwich bars. Places to try include *Tummy Tempters* at 204 Emerson St for healthy sandwiches and snacks.

Kebab Connection on Dickens St has huge kebabs to take away or eat in for $7. Of course there are plenty of Chinese restaurants and takeaways in Napier. Try the *Golden Crown* on Dickens St, which does both. The Wednesday to Friday lunch-time smorgasbord is unbeatable value at $7.50.

McDonald's, *KFC*, *Pizza Hut* and *Georgie Pie* are all represented in Napier.

On the small pedestrian street of Market St, opposite the Cri on Emerson St, *Shelby's Wine Bar Cafe* specialises in pizzas and is reasonably priced.

Pub Food There's a *Cobb & Co* in the fine old Masonic Establishment looking out onto Marine Parade. The *Victoria Hotel* at 76 Marine Parade does pub food. *Deco's Bar & Grill*, in the Provincial Hotel, is licensed and has a standard, reasonably priced dinner menu.

Deano's Steak Bar & Grill on Marine Parade serves good, old-fashioned pub food. Their excellent, large steaks and grills are very good value.

Restaurants & Cafes Napier has an excellent selection of restaurants, cafes and bars, and many places act as all three.

Alfresco's, upstairs at 65 Emerson St, has a good range of food and great liqueur coffees. The *Black Market Cafe*, 53 Hastings St, is as much a place to drink as to eat, and the menu could feature Cajun, Mexican or Italian fare.

Anatoles at the County Hotel on Browning St is a cafe/bar open for breakfast, lunch and dinner. This is the place to be seen, and is upmarket but not outrageously expensive for the good and varied food.

Indonesian cuisine is hard to find in New Zealand, so if you are hankering for satay or rendang head to *Restaurant Indonesia* at 409 Marine Parade. This is a licensed and BYO restaurant with attractive decor and interesting food. Their rijsttafels, that Dutch-Indonesian-smorgasbord blend, range from $23 to $30 per person.

You can get more vegetarian food from *Gumnuts* in the Art Deco Provincial Hotel – this is the only exclusively vegetarian and seafood place in town and it is open Wednesday to Saturday from 6 pm.

For more traditional fare try *Marnie's*, in Hastings St, which specialises in seafood. Three of the upmarket places are *Bayswater on the Beach* and *East Pier* on Hardinge Rd and *Pierre sur le Quai* at 63 West Quay.

Entertainment

Popular rock pubs include the *Shakespeare Hotel* on Shakespeare Rd and the *Onekawa* in, you guessed it, Onekawa. The *Cri* in Emerson St, underneath the Criterion Backpackers, is always a good bar for a drink and often has bands on Friday and Saturday, and out by the port the *Iron Pot Cafe* also has live music. The *Freeman's Bar* in the Masonic Hotel has a DJ Wednesday to Saturday and

O'Flaherty's Irish Pub on Hastings St is yet another Irish pub that packs them in with bands on weekends.

Many of Napier's cafes and restaurants are also lively drinking and meeting places on the weekends. Marine Parade is a good place to cruise on weekends.

Getting There & Away

Air Air New Zealand (☎ 835 3288) is on the corner of Hastings and Station Sts. They have direct flights to Auckland, Gisborne, Hamilton and Wellington several times daily, with connections to other centres.

Bus InterCity and Newmans both operate from the Napier Travel Centre (☎ 834 2720) at the railway station in Munro St. InterCity has services to Auckland (seven hours), Hamilton (4¾ hours), Rotorua (3¼ hours), Taupo (two hours), Tauranga (five hours), Gisborne (3¾ hours), Palmerston North (3½ hours) and Wellington (six hours).

Newman's routes head north to Taupo, Rotorua and Tauranga; through Palmerston North and Wanganui to New Plymouth; and to Wellington via Palmerston North.

As well as InterCity, Coachrite Connections travel every day except Saturday between Gisborne, Wairoa and Napier. From Wairoa, you can catch an InterCity bus to Rotorua via Waikaremoana on Monday, Wednesday and Friday.

All the long-distance buses coming to Napier continue for the extra half-hour ride to Hastings.

Train The railway station (☎ 834 2720) is in Munro St. The Bay Express train operates daily between Napier and Wellington, with several stops including Hastings and Palmerston North on the 5½-hour run.

Hitching Hitching is OK around here. If you're heading north catch a long-distance bus and get off at Westshore, or try thumbing closer in. If you're heading south stick to SH2. The alternative inland route, SH36, is much harder going with very little traffic.

EAST COAST

Getting Around

To/From the Airport There's an airport shuttle bus (☎ 879 9766) which costs $7. A taxi to the airport costs about $12. The Napier Taxi Service (☎ 835 7777) goes to and from the airport and operates local tours.

Bus Nimbus (☎ 877 8133) operates the suburban bus services on weekdays, with regular buses between Napier and Hastings via Taradale, plus other local services. There's no service at all on weekends. All the local buses depart from the corner of Dickens and Dalton Sts.

Bicycle Napier Cycle World (☎ 835 9528) at 104 Carlyle St hires 10-speeds and tandems at $12 for a half-day and $17 a day, and Bike Torque (☎ 835 0709), also in Carlyle St, has similar rates.

AROUND NAPIER

Cape Kidnappers Gannet Colony

From late October until late April one of Hawkes Bay's most dramatic sights is at the Cape Kidnappers Gannet Colony. These large birds usually make their nests on remote and inaccessible islands but here they nest on the mainland and are curiously unworried by human spectators.

The gannets (takapu) usually turn up in late July after the last heavy storm of the month. Supposedly, the storm casts driftwood and other handy nest-building material high up the beach so very little effort has to be expended collecting it. In October and November eggs are laid, which take about six weeks to hatch. By March the gannets start to migrate and by April only the odd straggler will be left.

You don't need a permit to visit the gannet sanctuary and the best time to see them is between early November and late February (the sanctuary is closed from June to October).

Three tour operators run to Cape Kidnappers (so named because Maori tried to kidnap a Tahitian servant boy from Cook's expedition here). Gannet Beach Adventures (☎ 875 0898) at Te Awanga, 21 km from

Napier, has rides on a tractor-pulled trailer along the beach for $18 (children $12). From where they drop you, it is a 20-minute walk to the main saddle colony. The guided return trip takes about four hours altogether. Unimog (☎ 835 4446) departs from Napier and goes along the beach in a Mercedes Benz for $30 (children $20). Both trips are dependent on the tides. Gannet Safaris (☎ 875 0511) from Summerlee Station beyond Te Awanga has 4WD tours through a farm right to the main saddle colony for $36 (children $17). A minimum of six people is required.

Alternatively, the eight-km walk along the beach from Clifton, just along from Te Awanga, takes about two hours. You must leave no earlier than three hours after high tide and start back no later than 1½ hours after low tide. It's another eight km back and there are no refreshment stops so go prepared! The tide schedule is available in Napier from the visitor information centre or DOC, or ask at Clifton. No regular buses go to Te Awanga or Clifton from Napier, but Kiwi Shuttle (☎ (025) 475578) goes on demand for $15 per person.

There is a rest hut, with refreshments, at the colony. The katipo, New Zealand's only poisonous spider, is known to inhabit the driftwood above the high tide mark, so leave it alone!

DOC, which administers the reserve, has a handy leaflet and booklets on the gannet colony. Accommodation is available in Te Awanga at *Sullivan's Motor Camp* (☎ 875 0334), which is good for information on the gannet colony. At Clifton, the *Clifton No 2 Reserve* has camp sites and cabins.

Arts, Crafts & Antiques

Many craftspeople reside in the Hawkes Bay region. A number open their studios to the public. Their locations range from Wairoa in the north to Waimarama and Waipukurau in the south. Get a copy of the informative *Hawkes Bay Arts & Crafts Guide* from the visitor information centres. A number of antique dealers are listed in the *Napier Antique Trail* leaflet.

Wineries

The Hawkes Bay area is one of New Zealand's premier wine-producing regions and a number of vineyards can be visited for tastings. Hawkes Bay is very much the Chardonnay capital of New Zealand, but Cabernet Sauvignon grapes from the area are highly regarded and many other varieties are produced.

Vineyards to visit include Brookfields Vineyards at Meeanee, Mission Vineyards at Taradale (the oldest vineyard in the country), Esk Valley Estate Winery, Vidal of Hawkes Bay and Ngatarawa Wines in Hastings, Te Mata Estate Winery and Lombardi Wines in Havelock North, and Church Road Winery in Taradale. A number of the wineries are open for lunch and offer excellent dining.

The Hawkes Bay Vintners produce a handy *Guide to the Wineries of Hawkes Bay*, which lists opening hours. Every year around February, the Harvest Hawkes Bay weekend has activities focusing on food and wine. Around the same time an international concert is held at the Mission Bay winery and a special label is produced for each entertainer.

A fine way of visiting the wineries is on a bicycle (hire one in Napier), since most of them are within easy cycling distance and it's all flat land. From Napier, Bay Tours (☎ 843 6953) does four-hour winery tours for $25, and Eastland Tours (☎ 836 6705) has a similar vineyard and sightseeing tour.

Te Mata Peak

Te Mata Peak is about 31 km south of Napier, 11 km from Hastings. It rises up in some dramatically sheer cliffs to the Te Mata trig, 399 metres above sea level, commanding a spectacular view over the Heretaunga Plains to Hawke Bay. On a clear day you can see all of Hawkes Bay up to the Mahia Peninsula, and to Mt Ruapehu in the Tongariro National Park. You can also see oyster shells in the rocks at your feet!

Te Mata Peak is part of the 98-hectare Te Mata Park, with several walkways. You can drive right up to the trig at the summit.

The peak is a favourite spot for hang-gliding. In addition to the thrill of leaping straight out over a vertical cliff with nothing but fresh air under them for 399 metres or so, gliders get remarkable possibilities from the updraughts breezing in from the Pacific Ocean, just a few hundred metres away.

Peak Paragliding (☎ (025) 441 572) offer tandem paraglider flights off the spectacular cliffs of Te Mata Peak. You can 'Summit Plummet' for $45 ($60 with transport) down to the plains below, or climb to the clouds and return to the summit for $90 (conditions permitting). There are also 10-km cross-country flights for $200.

HASTINGS

Hastings (population 27,400), only 20 km south of Napier, shared the same fate as Napier in the 1931 earthquake, and is also noted for its Art Deco and Spanish Mission-style architecture. The paved Civic Square is particularly attractive, with the Art Deco clocktower as its centrepiece (but watch out for the trains that hurtle through the middle of the square).

Hastings is just a flat country town in comparison to Napier, but drinkers can appreciate the wineries and the local brewery, and the surrounding area also has a few attractions. Hastings is an agricultural centre, popular in the apple harvest season from February to April with those looking for work.

Information

The Hastings Visitor Information Centre (☎ 878 0510; fax 878 0512) in Russell St is open from 8.30 am to 5 pm on weekdays, and from 10 am until 3 pm on Saturday and Sunday. They have a good city map outlining a scenic drive around Hastings, Havelock North and Flaxmere with many examples of Art Deco and Spanish Mission-style architecture and other points of interest, including Te Mata Peak. Garden lovers should obtain the free pamphlet *Hastings: Parks and Amenities*. The AA office is at 124 Market St North.

Things to See

The legacy of the 1931 earthquake is an impressive collection of **Art Deco & Spanish Mission buildings** in and around Hastings. A pamphlet is available from the information centre to explore Hastings' architecture in depth, but the highlights are undoubtedly the **Westerman's Building**, with its impressive bronze and leadlight shopfronts that have largely survived modernisation, and the magnificent **Municipal Theatre** on Hastings St, the most imposing example of Spanish Mission style in the Hawkes Bay area.

Travelling with children? In Windsor Park, two km from the town centre on Grove Rd, **Fantasyland** is a leisure park. It has a miniature of the Disneyland castle, a Mother Hubbard's shoe, merry-go-round, pirate ship, Noddy Town, go-karts, bumper boats, other boats you can take out on the lake fronting the castle, a flying fox, narrow gauge train rides, and much more. It's open every day from 9 am to 4.30 pm and admission is $3 (children free). Also in Windsor Park is a swimming pool, skating rink, motor camp and more.

The **Hawkes Bay Exhibition Centre** in the Civic Square, Eastbourne St, is associated with the Hawkes Bay Museum in Napier and hosts a wide variety of changing exhibitions. It's open from 10 am to 4.30 pm on weekdays and from noon to 4.30 pm on weekends and holidays.

For something less highbrow, the **Hawkes Bay Brewery** has tours on Monday, Wednesday and Friday at 10.30 am for $2.

Havelock North is only a few km east of Hastings but is well worth a visit for its gardens, wineries and, if you have children, the **Keirunga Park Railway**, a miniature railway.

Places to Stay

In Windsor Park, adjacent to Fantasyland, *Hastings Holiday Park* (☎ 878 6692) has camp sites at $9 per person. Cabins start at $25 for two, and tourist flats are $50 to $65. The camp is in Windsor Ave, 2.5 km from the post office. The *Raceview Holiday Park*

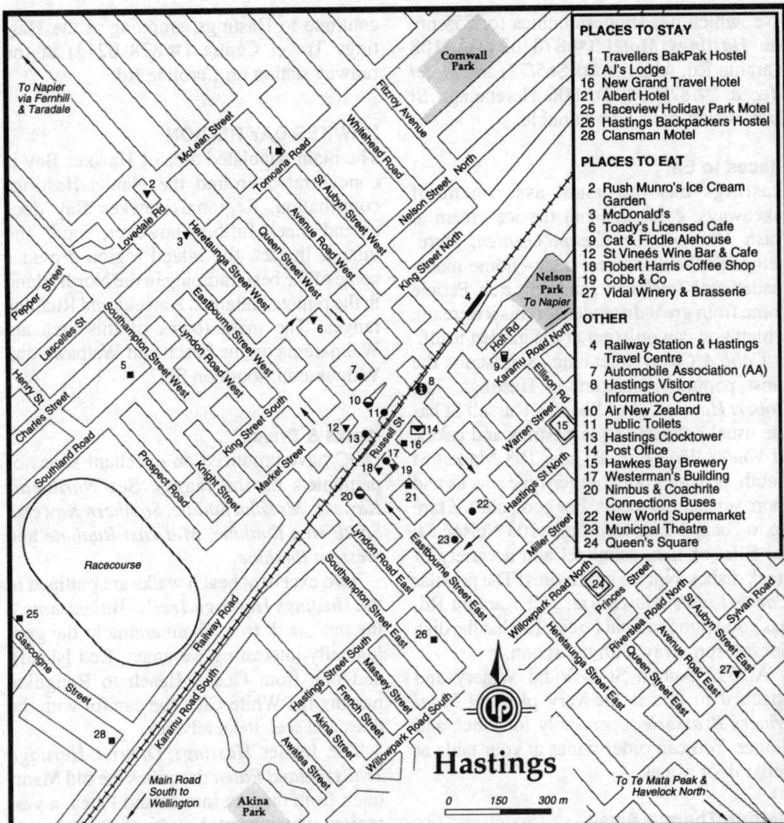

Motel (☎ 878 8837) at 307 Gascoigne St, adjacent to the racecourse, has camping at $13, on-site caravans at $25, and tourist flats at $47 – all prices are for two people.

Hastings' backpackers are at their busiest in the harvest season. The *Hastings Backpackers Hostel* (☎ 876 5888), 505 Lyndon Rd East, has dorm beds for $10 and $12, doubles and twins for $24. It is in a suburban area, not far from the city centre. *AJ's Lodge* (☎ 878 2302), a spacious Edwardian house at 405 Southland Rd, is a tidy, well-run place costing $13 for a dorm bed, $32 for a twin room. *Travellers BakPak Hostel* (☎ 878 7108), 606 St Aubyrn St West, is yet another hostel in a suburban house; it's crammed with pickers during the season but is quiet the rest of the year. Dorm beds cost $13 per person, twins and doubles in rooms and caravans at the back are $32.

There are several hotels and motels, plus many home and farmstays available around Hastings. At 114 Heretaunga St, the *New Grand Travel Hotel* (☎ 878 4363) is a sad hotel full of elderly long-termers, and has backpackers beds for $12 or $15 with linen. Hastings' many motels include: *Aladdin Lodge Motel* (☎ 876 6322), 120 Maddison

Ave, which has singles/doubles for $55/66; the *Hastings Motel* (☎ 878 6243), 1108 Karamu Rd, which costs $65/72; and *Motel Mecca* (☎ 878 3192), 806 Heretaunga St East, which costs $74 a double.

Places to Eat

Hastings has the usual assortment of takeaways, cafes etc, but the ice cream at *Rush Munro's Ice Cream Garden*, Heretaunga St West, is a real treat – home-made, loaded with fresh fruit, and very rich. People come from great distances for this ice cream, which you can only get at the garden itself.

Cobb & Co on Heretaunga St is, sadly, the most popular restaurant in Hastings. The *Robert Harris Coffee Shop* on Russell St has the usual cafeteria-style pastries and cakes. *St Vineés Wine Bar & Cafe*, 108 Market St South, provides both burger-type snacks and more substantial meals. For good old NZ fare go to *Toady's Licensed Cafe*, 103 Nelson St, for fillet of fish, schnitzel and a variety of steak dishes. Not for herbivores! The popular *Cat & Fiddle Ale House*, 502 Karamu Rd, has good pub food but be careful that the dish doesn't run away with the spoon.

At 913 Aubyn St is Vidal Winery and attached to this is the very pleasant *Vidal Winery Brasserie*, open daily for lunch and dinner. You can order wines at your table at cellar door prices.

Getting There & Away

It's easy to get to Hastings by bus from Napier, a half-hour away. Nimbus (☎ 877 8133) operates a frequent local bus service from Napier ($4) on weekdays. Coachrite Connections buses to Gisborne stop at the Nimbus bus stop on Eastbourne St. All InterCity and Newmans buses going to Napier continue to Hastings, stopping at the Hastings Travel Centre (☎ 878 0213) at the railway station on Caroline Rd.

HAWKES BAY REGION

The main populated area of Hawkes Bay is concentrated around the Napier-Hastings conurbation. Regional Hawkes Bay does extend much further, however, south and inland. In fact, the inland region provides some of the best tramping in the North Island in the remote, untamed Kaweka and Ruahine ranges. The main towns of this area are Waimarama on the beach and Waipawa and Waipukurau, south on SH2.

Walks & Drives

DOC have produced an excellent series of pamphlets on the ranges. See *North-east Kaweka*, *Makahu Saddle*, *Southern Kaweka*, *South-east Ruahine*, *Mid-east Ruahine* and *Western Ruahine*.

Two excellent beach walks are outlined in the *Hastings Heritage Trails: Waimarama* – the one south from Waimarama to the geologically interesting Karamea (Red Island), and one from Ocean Beach to Rangiika, passing the White Cliff (be careful with the tides and seek local advice).

The leaflet *Hastings District Heritage Trails: Inland Patea* describes the old Maori track from the bay into Inland Patea, a vast region which stretches from Ruapehu to Taihape and across to the gorges of the Wanganui River. The route is now a road which heads from Fernhill near Hastings via Omahu, Okawa, Otamauri, Blowhard Bush and the Gentle Annie towards Taihape. It is a three-hour return car journey from Fernhill to the top of the Kawekas.

Wellington Region

Wellington, the capital of New Zealand, is situated on a beautiful harbour at the southern tip of the North Island. Approaching it from the north you will pass through one of two regions – the Kapiti Coast on the west side (SH1) or the Wairarapa on the east side of the North Island (SH2) – before you enter the heavily populated Hutt Valley or the city itself. All of these areas have interesting activities and places to visit.

Information

Most telephone numbers in this region have an 04 prefix if you are calling them long distance (even within the region). The prefix for the Kapiti Coast changes between Waikanae (04) and Otaki (06). In the Wairarapa, use an 06 prefix.

HIGHLIGHTS

- Wellington Harbour – the view over the harbour from Mt Victoria, a cruise across the harbour to Eastbourne or a walk along the city foreshore
- The Cable Car to the Botanic Gardens – an exhilarating ride followed by trails through stands of native trees
- The Maori collection in the National Museum (Te Papa Tongarewa)
- Mystical Kapiti Island and the scenic Kapiti Coast
- The vineyards of the Wairarapa and the rugged Wairarapa coastline
- Walking in and exploring the Tararua Ranges

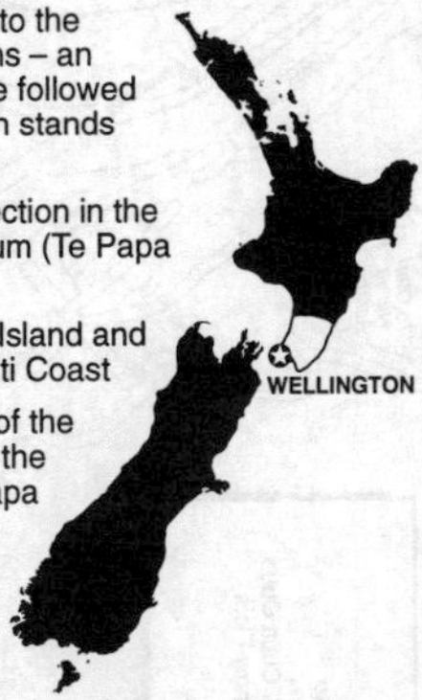

Wellington

Wellington takes part in friendly rivalry with larger Auckland. The town, with a regional population of 400,000 and 150,000 in the city itself, is hemmed in by its magnificent harbour, with buildings marching picturesquely up the steep hills. It's a lively city with plenty to see and do – it's a centre for culture and the arts, there's a plethora of restaurants, cafes, nightlife and activities – and it's home to the country's government and national treasures. Many travellers pass through Wellington as, apart from its importance as the capital, it's also a major travel crossroads between the North and South islands.

The city is built around a fine harbour formed by the flooding of a long-extinct, and very large, volcano crater. The city runs up the hills on one side of the harbour, and so cramped is it for space that many Wellington workers live in two narrow urban valleys leading northwards between the steep, rugged hills – one is the Hutt Valley, and the other follows SH1 northwards through Tawa and Porirua. The city's nickname is 'Windy Wellington'. You'll discover why!

History

Traditionally, the Maori maintain that the explorer, Kupe, was the first person to discover Wellington harbour. The original Maori name for the place was Te Whanga-Nui-a-Tara, Tara being the son of a Maori chief named Whatonga who had settled on the Hawkes Bay coast. Whatonga sent Tara and his half-brother off to explore the southern part of the North Island but it was over a year before they returned. When they did, their reports were so favourable that Whatonga's followers moved to the harbour, founding the Ngati Tara tribe.

The first European settlers arrived on 22 January 1840 in the New Zealand Company's ship *Aurora*, not long after

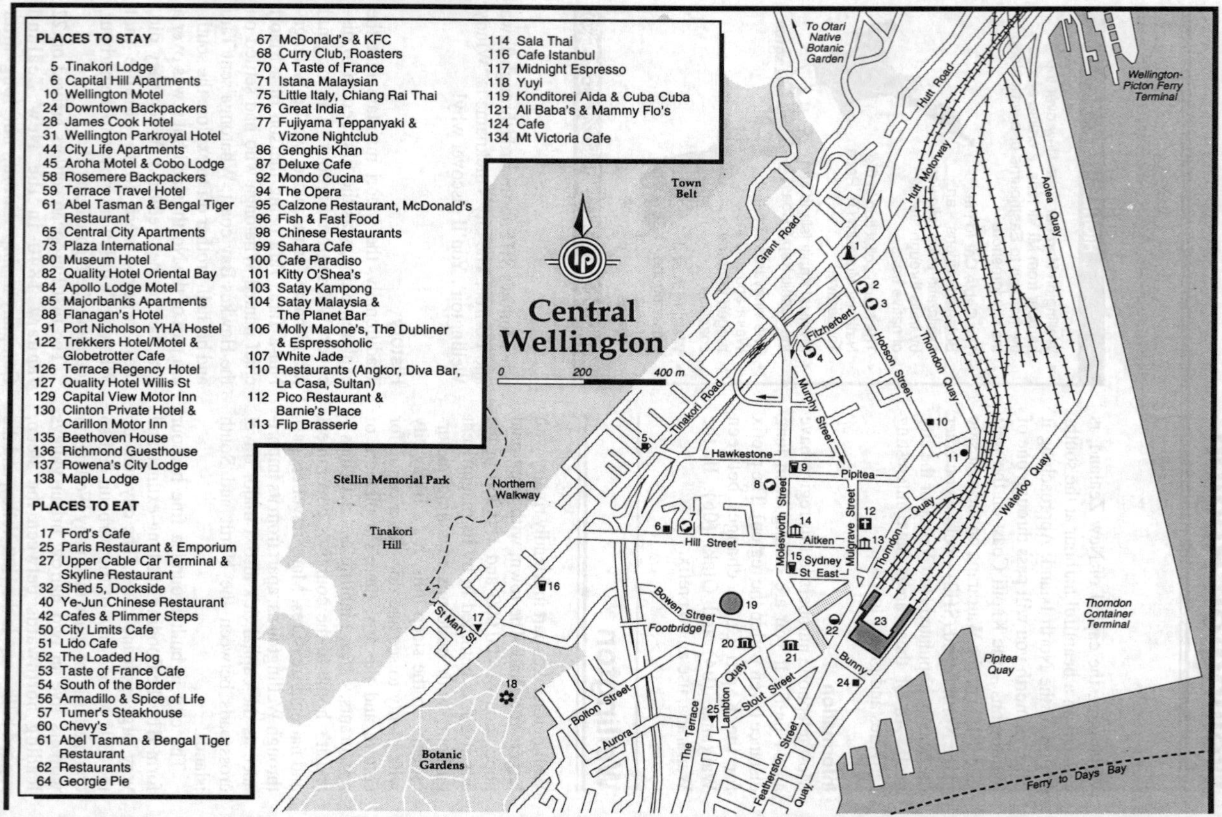
PLACES TO STAY
5 Tinakori Lodge
6 Capital Hill Apartments
10 Wellington Motel
24 Downtown Backpackers
28 James Cook Hotel
31 Wellington Parkroyal Hotel
44 City Life Apartments
45 Aroha Motel & Cobo Lodge
58 Rosemere Backpackers
59 Terrace Travel Hotel
61 Abel Tasman & Bengal Tiger Restaurant
65 Central City Apartments
73 Plaza International
80 Museum Hotel
82 Quality Hotel Oriental Bay
84 Apollo Lodge Motel
85 Majoribanks Apartments
88 Flanagan's Hotel
91 Port Nicholson YHA Hostel
122 Trekkers Hotel/Motel & Globetrotter Cafe
126 Terrace Regency Hotel
127 Quality Hotel Willis St
129 Capital View Motor Inn
130 Clinton Private Hotel & Carillon Motor Inn
135 Beethoven House
136 Richmond Guesthouse
137 Rowena's City Lodge
138 Maple Lodge
PLACES TO EAT
17 Ford's Cafe
25 Paris Restaurant & Emporium
27 Upper Cable Car Terminal & Skyline Restaurant
32 Shed 5, Dockside
40 Ye-Jun Chinese Restaurant
42 Cafes & Plimmer Steps
50 City Limits Cafe
51 Lido Cafe
52 The Loaded Hog
53 Taste of France Cafe
54 South of the Border
56 Armadillo & Spice of Life
57 Turner's Steakhouse
60 Chevy's
61 Abel Tasman & Bengal Tiger Restaurant
62 Restaurants
64 Georgie Pie
67 McDonald's & KFC
68 Curry Club, Roasters
70 A Taste of France
71 Istana Malaysian
75 Little Italy, Chiang Rai Thai
76 Great India
77 Fujiyama Teppanyaki & Vizone Nightclub
86 Genghis Khan
87 Deluxe Cafe
92 Mondo Cucina
94 The Opera
95 Calzone Restaurant, McDonald's
96 Fish & Fast Food
98 Chinese Restaurants
99 Sahara Cafe
100 Cafe Paradiso
101 Kitty O'Shea's
103 Satay Kampong
104 Satay Malaysia & The Planet Bar
106 Molly Malone's, The Dubliner & Espressoholic
107 White Jade
110 Restaurants (Angkor, Diva Bar, La Casa, Sultan)
112 Pico Restaurant & Barnie's Place
113 Flip Brasserie
114 Sala Thai
116 Cafe Istanbul
117 Midnight Espresso
118 Yuyi
119 Konditorei Aida & Cuba Cuba
121 Ali Baba's & Mammy Flo's
124 Cafe
134 Mt Victoria Cafe
Central Wellington
0
200
400 m
Town Belt
To Otari Native Botanic Garden
Wellington-Picton Ferry Terminal
Hutt Road
Hutt Motorway
Aotea Quay
Grant Road
Fitzherbert
Hobson Street
Thorndon Quay
Murphy Street
Tinakori Road
Hawkestone
Pipitea
Waterloo Quay
Stellin Memorial Park
Northern Walkway
Tinakori Hill
Molesworth Street
Mulgrave Street
Aitken
Hill Street
Sydney St East
Thorndon Quay
Thorndon Container Terminal
Bowen Street
Footbridge
Bunny
St Mary St
Pipitea Quay
Bolton Street
Lambton Quay
Stout Street
Aurora
The Terrace
Featherston Street
Quay
Botanic Gardens
Ferry to Days Bay

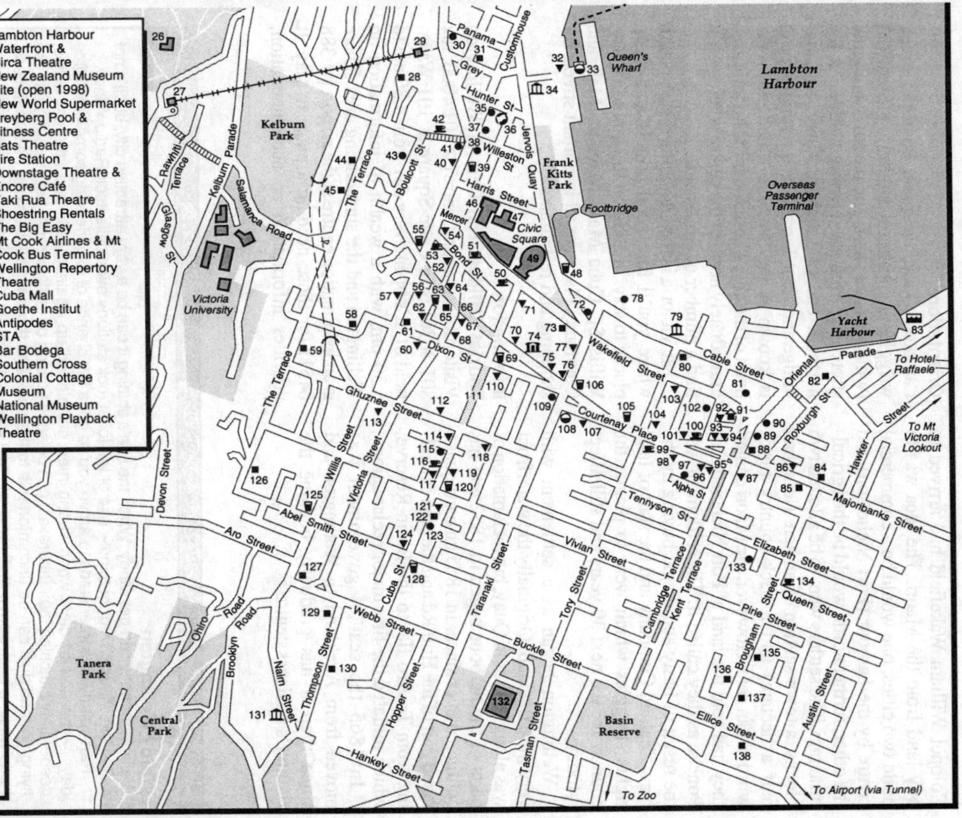

OTHER

1 Katherine Mansfield Birthplace
2 German Embassy
3 Australian High Commission
4 US Embassy
7 UK High Commission
8 Canadian High Commission
9 Thorndon Tavern
11 The Map Shop (DOSLI)
12 Old St Paul's Cathedral
13 National Archives & Portrait Gallery
14 National Library & Gallery
15 The Backbencher Pub
16 Western Park Tavern
17 Art & Craft Shops
18 Lady Norwood Rose Garden
19 The Beehive & Parliament
20 Bowen House
21 Old Government Building
22 City Bus Terminal
23 Railway Station, Newmans, Bus Depot & GPO
26 New Zealand Astronomy Centre
27 Upper Cable Car Terminal & Skyline Restaurant
29 Lower Cable Car Terminal
30 Air New Zealand
33 Trust Bank Ferry, Cruises
34 Maritime Museum
35 Ansett NZ
36 Japanese Embassy
37 Japan Information & Cultural Centre
38 BNZ Building
39 The Malthouse
41 Automobile Association (AA)
43 DOC & Antrim House
46 Wellington Art Gallery & Continuum Cinema
47 Wellington Library & Tourist Information
48 St John's Bar
49 Michael Fowler Centre
55 Aqua Vitae Wine Bar
63 Mid City Tavern & Metro Disco
66 Manners Mall
69 La Luna Bar
72 Wakefield Market
74 State Opera House
78 Lambton Harbour Waterfront & Circa Theatre
79 New Zealand Museum Site (open 1998)
81 New World Supermarket
83 Freyberg Pool & Fitness Centre
89 Bats Theatre
90 Fire Station
93 Downstage Theatre & Encore Café
97 Taki Rua Theatre
102 Shoestring Rentals
105 The Big Easy
108 Mt Cook Airlines & Mt Cook Bus Terminal
109 Wellington Repertory Theatre
111 Cuba Mall
115 Goethe Institut
120 Antipodes
123 STA
125 Bar Bodega
128 Southern Cross
131 Colonial Cottage Museum
132 National Museum
133 Wellington Playback Theatre

Colonel William Wakefield had arrived to buy land from the Maori. The idea was to build two cities: one would be a commercial centre by the harbour (Port Nicholson) and the other, further north, would be the agricultural hub. The settlers were to be allotted two blocks, a town section of an acre (less than half a hectare) and a back-country block worth £1 an acre. However, the Maori denied they had sold the land at Port Nicholson, or Poneke as they called it. The settlement was the result of hasty and illegal buying by the New Zealand Company and the start of land rights struggles which were to plague the country for the next 30 years and still affect it today.

Wellington began as a settlement with very little flat land. Originally the waterfront was along Lambton Quay, but reclamation of parts of the harbour began in 1852 and has continued ever since. In 1855 an earthquake razed part of the Hutt Rd and the area extending from Te Aro flat to the Basin Reserve, which initiated the first major reclamation.

In 1865 the seat of government was moved from Auckland to Wellington and since then it has gradually become the country's business centre.

Orientation

Lambton Quay, the main business street, wriggles along almost parallel to the seafront (which it once was). The part of Wellington stretching from the railway station, at the northern end of Lambton Quay, to Cambridge and Kent Terraces at the southern end is known as the 'Miracle Mile' and is the heart of the city. Thorndon is the historic area immediately north of the centre where you'll find a number of embassies.

Mt Victoria is the area immediately south where you'll find good hostels and cheap places to stay. In addition to Lambton Quay, Willis St, Cuba Mall, Manners Mall and Courtenay Place are all important streets for shopping and restaurants.

Information

Tourist Offices The Central Wellington Visitor Information Centre (☎ 801 4000; fax 801 3030) is in Civic Square at 101 Wakefield St. It's open every day from 8.30 am to 5.30 pm, with a wealth of information on Wellington and the surrounding area. There is an information centre at the airport (☎ 388 6451) for those needing a place to stay. It provides information on accommodation,

Windy Wellington

Wellington really can get windy. When the sun's shining it can be a very attractive city, but it's not called the windy city for nothing – one of the local rock stations even calls itself Radio Windy.

Particularly as winter starts to arrive you've got a fair chance of experiencing some gale-force days – the sort of days when strong men get pinned up against walls and little old ladies, desperately clutching their umbrellas, can be seen floating by at skyscraper height. Seriously, the flying grit and dust can be uncomfortable to the eyes and the flying rubbish can be a real mess. I was walking back from a restaurant late one windy night when a sudden gust blew several bags of garbage out of a doorway, a passing car hit one and a veritable snowstorm of soft-drink cans, pizza boxes and assorted debris rushed down the street like tumbleweeds from an old western movie. The wind was blowing so hard that this blizzard of rubbish actually overtook the offending car!

One blustery day back in 1968 the wind blew so hard it pushed the almost-new Wellington-to-Christchurch car ferry *Wahine* on to Barrett's Reef just outside the harbour entrance. The disabled ship later broke loose from the reef, drifted into the harbour and then sank causing the loss of 51 lives. The Wellington Maritime Museum has a dramatic model and photographic display of the disaster.

Nancy Keller

events, transport etc and also sell tickets for the *Interislander* ferry, trains, buses, South Island shuttle and backpacker bus services.

The DOC Information Centre (☎ 471 0726) at 59 Boulcott St has information on walks, parks, outdoor activities and camping in the region. *Let's Do It! Your Guide to the Outdoors*, a valuable publication with information on outdoor attractions in the Wellington-Wairarapa area, is available for $6. The office is open Monday to Friday from 8.30 am to 4.30 pm.

The AA (☎ 473 8738) is upstairs on the 1st floor at 342 Lambton Quay. In addition to the usual AA maps and services it also offers an array of travel books on NZ and the world, DOSLI and Wises maps and road atlases. AA members receive a 10% discount. It's open from 9 am to 5.30 pm, Monday to Thursday; 9 am to 8.30 pm Friday; and 9.30 am to 12.30 pm Saturday.

A number of useful free publications will inform you about attractions and events around Wellington. Look for the weekly *Capital Times*. Also check out the *Wellington: Great Time Guide*, *Kia Ora: Wellington*, *City Map* and *Wellington's Great Events*. All are freely available at the visitor information centre.

Money The American Express office (☎ 473 7766) in the Sun Alliance Centre on Lambton Quay at Grey St, near the lower cable-car terminal, is open Monday to Friday from 8.30 am to 5 pm. Thomas Cook has a travel services office in Greenock House at 108 Lambton Quay (☎ 473 5167). There are also many banks where you can change money.

Post The main post office is in the railway station lobby. Poste restante mail can be collected here Monday to Friday, between 8.30 am and 5 pm. There are plenty of other post offices spread around the centre.

Foreign Embassies & Consulates As the capital city of NZ, Wellington is the base for consulates and embassies of many countries, including the following:

Australian High Commission
  72-78 Hobson St (☎ 473 6411)
Canadian High Commission
  61 Molesworth St (☎ 473 9577)
French Embassy
  Willis Corroon House, 1-3 Willeston St (☎ 472 0200)
German Embassy
  90-92 Hobson St (☎ 473 6063)
Japanese Embassy
  7th Floor, Norwich Insurance House, 3-11 Hunter St (☎ 473 1540)
Netherlands Embassy
  10th Floor, Investment Centre, cnr Featherston & Ballance Sts (☎ 473 8652)
Swiss Embassy
  Panama House, 22 Panama St (☎ 472 1593)
UK High Commission
  44 Hill St, Thorndon (☎ 472 6049)
US Embassy
  29 Fitzherbert Terrace, Thorndon (☎ 472 2068)

Cultural Centres A German cultural centre, the Goethe Institut (☎ 499 2469), is at 150 Cuba St on the corner of Garret St, just south of Ghuznee St; the entrance to the building is on Garret St. It's open Monday to Thursday from 9 am to 5 pm, and Friday from 9 am to 3 pm. The Alliance Française (☎ 472 1272), 24 Johnson St, is open 9 am to 5 pm weekdays.

The Japan Information & Cultural Centre (☎ 472 7807) at 113 Customhouse Quay, near the corner of Lambton Quay, is open Monday to Friday from 9 am to 5 pm.

Travel Agencies There are plenty of travel agencies in Wellington. The Hub (☎ 385 3580), in the Trekkers Hotel at 213 Cuba St, caters for backpackers' needs, can book all travel and accommodation and arrange cheap rental cars on both islands.

The YHA travel agency (☎ 801 7238) is in the lobby of the YHA hostel, on the corner of Wakefield St and Cambridge Terrace. It's open every day from 8 am to 8 pm and you don't have to be a YHA member to get their discounted rates. STA, specialising in student and youth travel, is at 207 Cuba St (☎ 385 0561) and in the Student Union building at Victoria University (☎ 499 1017). They're open Monday to Friday from 9 am to 5 pm, and Saturday from 10 am to 12.30 pm.

Books & Maps Wellington has some fine bookshops including Unity Books on the corner of Willis and Manners Sts; Ahradsen's in the BNZ underground shopping centre (near the junction of Lambton Quay and Willis St), with a good travel section; Whitcoulls at 312 Lambton Quay and 91 Cuba St; and London Bookshops at 326 Lambton Quay and 89 Cuba Mall.

Bennett's Government Bookshop in Bowen House, corner of Lambton Quay and Bowen St, has a great selection of books on NZ and a good travel section. It's open Monday to Friday from 8 am to 5.30 pm.

Bellamy's at 106 Cuba St is a good second-hand bookshop. There are a few others along Courtenay Place. Metro Mags at 226 Lambton Quay has a mind-boggling selection of magazines and newspapers from around the world – about 4000 different titles. The Nature Shop in Cuba Mall also has a selection of German magazines.

The Map Shop at 103-115 Thorndon Quay is operated by the Department of Survey and Land Information (DOSLI) and carries their complete line of maps, plus a range of aerial photographs. It's open Monday to Friday from 8.30 am to 5 pm.

The Beehive & Parliament

Three buildings form New Zealand's parliamentary complex. By far the most distinctive and well known is the modernist building known as the Beehive – because that is just what it looks like. Designed by British architect Sir Basil Spence, it was begun in 1969 and completed in 1980. This building houses the executive offices.

Next door, the Old Parliament Building, completed in 1922, was closed in 1990 for renovation due to more stringent earthquake safety standards but should reopen in 1996. Beside this, the neo-Gothic Parliamentary Library building is the oldest building in the parliamentary complex.

Free public tours of the Beehive and the House of Representatives are offered most days, but the schedule depends on what functions or meetings are being held. Phone ☎ 471 9999 to ask about tour times.

The public is also welcome to attend meetings of the House of Representatives. It usually meets three out of four weeks every month, with sessions Tuesday to Thursday from 2 to 5.30 pm and again from 7.30 to 10.30 pm, during which you are free to come and go as you please from the public gallery.

The statue of Richard Seddon, also known as 'King Dick', stands proudly before the Beehive

Old Wooden Buildings

Opposite the Beehive, at the northern end of Lambton Quay, stands the **Old Government Building**, one of the largest all-wooden buildings in the world – there's a wooden temple in Japan (the Daibutsu-den in Nara) which beats it for 'the biggest' honours. The building was closed in 1992 due to a fire and is now being restored.

Wood was used widely in the construction of buildings in Wellington's early days. There are some fine old **wooden houses** still to be seen, especially along Tinakori Rd in the historic Thorndon area which was Wellington's first suburb, just uphill from the Parliament buildings. The best examples of genuine 19th-century architecture are in Ascot St, just off Sydney Rd West. One of the oldest pubs in NZ still on its original site is the **Thistle Inn** (1840), on the corner of Mulgrave St and Sydney St East.

National Library & Archives

Opposite the Beehive on the corner of Molesworth and Aitken Sts, the National Library (Te Puna Matauranga o Aotearoa) houses by far the most comprehensive book collection in NZ. Also at the National Library is the Alexander Turnbull Library, an early colonial collection complete with many historical photographs, often used for genealogical and other research on NZ.

The library hosts lectures and cultural events which are free and open to the public and there are interesting art exhibits in the National Library Gallery. Free tours are conducted weekly. The library is open Monday to Friday from 9 am to 5 pm, Saturday from 9 am to 4.30 pm and Sunday from 1 to 4.30 pm.

A block away, at 10 Mulgrave St at the junction of Aitken St, the National Archives (Te Whare Tohu Tuhituhinga o Aotearoa) display several interesting national treasures including the original Treaty of Waitangi and other historical treaties and documents. Also here are the New Zealand Portrait Gallery (Te Pukenga Whakaata) and other galleries with changing art exhibits. All can be visited free of charge. Opening hours are Monday to Friday from 9 am to 5 pm and Saturday from 9 am to 1 pm.

Old St Paul's Cathedral

Just a few doors up the hill on Mulgrave St is Old St Paul's Cathedral. It was built from 1863 to 1864 and looks quaint from the outside, but the interior is a good example of Early English Gothic design in timber. Old St Paul's is open Monday to Saturday from 10 am to 4.30 pm, Sunday 1 to 4.30 pm (with shorter opening hours in winter). Admission is free.

Museums & Art Galleries

National Museum & Art Gallery The National Museum (Te Papa Tongarewa) – just look for the carillon on Buckle St – is a museum of art, history, Maori culture and the natural environment. It has an excellent Maori and Pacific Islands collection plus many other interesting exhibits. The National Art Gallery and New Zealand Academy of Fine Arts are also housed here. Admission is free (donations accepted) and it's open every day from 9 am to 5 pm. The art gallery is open on weekdays from 9 am to 5 pm, Saturday from 9 am to 1 pm and is closed on Sunday. You can get here on bus No 11.

Maritime Museum This museum is near the corner of Queens Wharf and Jervois Quay. It has many maritime relics associated with the city and a fine three-dimensional model of the harbour. The collection of ship models includes a great one of the inter-island ferry *Wahine*, in the process of sinking, with a photo exhibit documenting the tragedy. The museum is open Monday to Friday from 9.30 am to 4 pm, and weekends from 1 to 4.30 pm. Admission is $2 (children 50 cents).

Wellington City Art Gallery Also on Civic Square, in the Old Library building, the Wellington City Art Gallery is a contemporary art gallery open every day from 11 am to 5 pm and on Thursday until 8 pm; admission is $2 (children 50 cents). The information centre has details on other art galleries around town.

The Capital Discovery Place This museum of sorts is in Civic Square behind the town hall. It is a hands-on science centre designed for children. It's open from 10 am to 5 pm, Tuesday to Sunday; admission is $6 (children $4).

Other Museums The **Colonial Cottage Museum** at 68 Nairn St is one of the oldest colonial cottages in Wellington, built in 1858 by carpenter William Wallis and lived in by his family until 1977. It's open from 10 am

Katherine Mansfield

Katherine Mansfield is New Zealand's most distinguished author, known throughout the world for her short stories and often compared to Chekhov and Maupassant. Born Katherine Mansfield Beauchamp in 1888, she left Wellington when she was 19 for Europe, where she spent the rest of her short adult life. She mixed with Europe's most famous writers, such as DH Lawrence, TS Eliot and Virginia Woolf, and married the literary critic and author John Middleton Murry in 1918. In 1923, aged 34, she died of tuberculosis at Fontainebleau in France. It was not until 1945 that her five books of short stories (*In a German Pension*, *Bliss*, *The Garden-Party*, *The Dove's Nest* and *Something Childish*) were combined into a single volume, *Collected Stories of Katherine Mansfield*.

She spent five years of her childhood at 25 Tinakori Rd in Wellington; it is mentioned in her stories *The Aloe* (which in its final form became *Prelude*) and *A Birthday* (a fictionalised account of her own birth). ■

to 4.30 pm Monday to Friday, and from 1 to 4.30 pm on weekends and public holidays; admission is $3 (children $1). To get there take bus No 8 to Aro St or No 7 to Brooklyn; get off at Webb St and walk up to Nairn St.

If you are familiar with the expressions 'silly mid on', 'leg spin' and 'maiden over' you will gravitate to the **National Cricket Museum**, in the old grandstand of the Basin Reserve. Aficionados will be bowled over by the 1743 Addington bat (one of the oldest) and Dennis Lillee's controversial aluminium bat banned in 1979. It's open daily from 10.30 am to 3.30 pm, October to April; otherwise it's open on weekends, again from 10.30 am to 3.30 pm. Admission is $3 (children $1, free if accompanied by an adult).

The **Alexander McKay Geological Museum** is in the Cotton Building at Victoria University. It's open from 9 am to 5 pm on weekdays; admission is free.

Katherine Mansfield's house is open from 10 am to 4 pm every day except Monday; admission is $4 (children $1). They screen an excellent video *A Portrait of Katherine Mansfield*, and the 'Sense of Living' exhibition displays photographs of the period alongside excerpts from her writing. A doll's house has been constructed from details mentioned in the short story of the same name. The house is at 25 Tinakori Rd.

Cable Car

From a narrow alley off Lambton Quay a cable car runs up to Kelburn which overlooks the city. It's one of Wellington's historic attractions – the cable-car service began in 1902, carried nearly half a million passengers in its first year and by 1912 was transporting a million passengers a year. In the late 70s the track was reconstructed and the two old wooden cable cars were replaced with shiny red Swiss-made ones.

A ride to the top costs $1.50 (children 70 cents) or $2.50 return (children $1.40). It operates at 10-minute intervals from 7 am to 10 pm, Monday to Friday; 9 am to 6 pm on Saturday; and 10.30 am to 6 pm on Sunday. The Skyline restaurant at the top offers great views over the city and harbour; it's open every day from 11 am to 4 pm. From the top you can stroll back down through the Botanic Gardens or return to town by a series of steps which interconnect with roads.

The **NZ Astronomy Centre** is in the Botanic Gardens near the top cable-car terminal. It has displays, videos and computers relating to astronomy, and is open Monday to Friday from 10 am to 5 pm; admission is $3 (children $1.50). It has good displays of the night sky.

Botanic Gardens

The tranquil Botanic Gardens are worth a visit, with 26 hectares of native bush and a wide variety of gardens including the Lady Norwood Rose Garden which has over 100 kinds of roses blooming from November to the end of April. Other gardens include succulents, ferns, threatened species, Australian plants, rhododendrons, fuchsias, camellias, begonias and herbs. The large gardens are always open.

The main entrance to the **Otari Native Botanic Garden** is at the junction of Wilton Rd and Gloucester St. It can be reached by the No 14 bus (Wilton). This is a sanctuary devoted to the cultivation and preservation of indigenous New Zealand plants, and incorporates a number of walks through densely forested areas and flax clearings. There is also a fernery and an information centre.

Wellington Zoo

This zoo has a wide variety of native and other wildlife, including outdoor lion and chimpanzee parks plus a nocturnal kiwi house also housing tuataras and giant wetas. The kiwis are on view from 10 am to 4 pm daily but the best time to see them is from 10 am to noon. The zoo is four km from the city centre, at the end of the Newtown Park bus route No 10. It is open daily from 8.30 am to 5 pm; admission is $7.50 (children $3.50).

Views

The best view of the entire city, harbour and surrounding region can be seen from the lookout at the top of **Mt Victoria**. It's a good walk up there and it's well worth the effort; otherwise you can take bus No 20 departing from the railway station or Courtenay Place and walk or ride back down. To drive, head up the hill on Majoribanks St and follow the signs saying 'Lookout', turning left onto Hawker St. Other good views are from the top cable-car terminal and from the Northern, Southern and Eastern walkways.

There is also a good view from the **wind turbine** on Brooklyn Hill. To get there head up Victoria St to Brooklyn Rd, turn left into Ohiro Rd and then right into Todman St; it is signposted from there. Bus No 7 will take you within walking distance of the turbine.

Walks

Wellington has numerous possibilities for enjoyable walks. Ask at the visitor information centre for their brochures on walks in the city and surrounds. Get the free leaflets on the Eastern, Northern and Southern walkways, and Red Rocks Coastal Walk.

The DOC office on Boulcott St is another good source of information on walks. Their free brochure *Walking Around Wellington*, available at the DOC office and the visitor information centre, gives details of over 50 walks in the Wellington area including the city itself, the Kapiti Coast, Hutt Valley and Wainuiomata on the eastern side of the harbour.

Activities

Mountain Biking In the city there are several places to bike including Mt Victoria, most of the Southern Walkway, along the ridgetop at Tinakori Hill, in firebreaks around Karori Reservoir, and a track to Mt Kau Kau. Longer rides can be enjoyed (or endured) in Belmont, East Harbour and Kaitoke regional parks; up the Rimutaka Incline and along Tunnel Gully; in Queen Elizabeth II Park on the Kapiti Coast; and in Battle Hill Forest Park. For more information on these mountain-bike trails (and others) contact the visitor centre for free maps. Take careful note of the mountain-biking code and avoid 'recto-cranial inversion'.

Surfing & Windsurfing With all the wind, water and bays around, Wellington is a great place for windsurfing – choose from sheltered inlets, rough harbours and wave-beaten coastal areas, all within half an hour's drive of the city and of one another. There are some good surfing breaks around too, including one near the airport and the many fine breaks on Palliser Bay.

Wild Winds Extreme (☎ 384 1010), Chaffers Marina, Oriental Bay, have a six-hour beginners' windsurfing course for $90. Phone them for a free recorded wind/surf report, updated daily.

Rollerblading You can't beat rollerblading along the waterfront on a sunny day. Cheapskates (☎ 499 0455), at 60 Cuba St, hires rollerblades from their shop and from their roving van which is normally stationed at the foot of Taranaki St by the waterfront on weekends during the day and at Frank Kitts Park on Monday and Wednesday evenings. The cost is $7/15 for hourly/overnight hire.

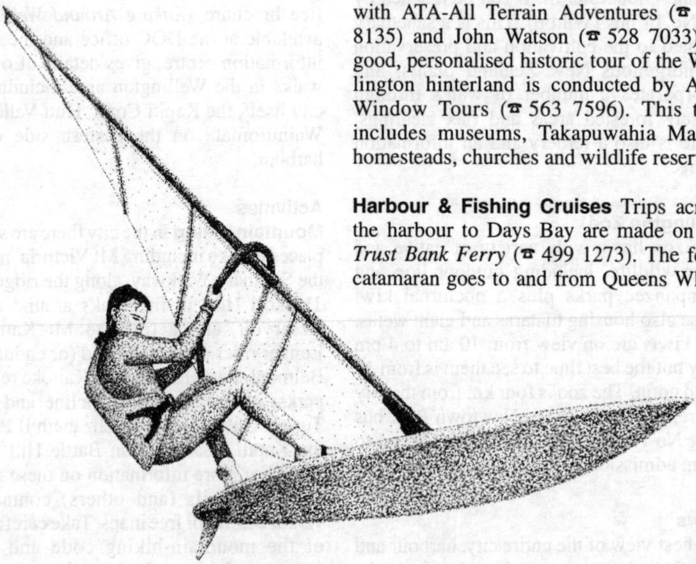

Tours

Bus A number of interesting and worthwhile tours are offered in Wellington; the information centre has more details.

Harbour Capital Tours (☎ 499 1282) offers one-hour tours of the faultline, which is basically the city ($15); two-hour tours of the city skyline ($18); and three-hour afternoon tours of the coastline ($21).

Wally Hammond (☎ 472 0869) takes a 2½-hour city-highlight tour, departing at 10 am and 2 pm. The cost is $20 (children $10), with discounts for backpackers. Their three-hour Kapiti Coast Tour ($55, children $26) departs daily at 9.30 am and 1.30 pm.

Also emphasising the city's heritage, Newlands (☎ 478 8315) operates a three-hour Wellington Heritage Highlights Tour with departures at 9.30 am and 2 pm, with an optional harbour cruise and lunch. The cost is $24 (children $10) for the tour only, $53 (children $33) with the cruise and lunch.

Unique Tours (☎ 389 2057) have tours of Wellington that highlight the Maori and colonial history of the region.

Tours further afield include 4WD safaris with ATA-All Terrain Adventures (☎ 388 8135) and John Watson (☎ 528 7033). A good, personalised historic tour of the Wellington hinterland is conducted by Attic Window Tours (☎ 563 7596). This tour includes museums, Takapuwahia Marae, homesteads, churches and wildlife reserves.

Harbour & Fishing Cruises Trips across the harbour to Days Bay are made on the *Trust Bank Ferry* (☎ 499 1273). The ferry catamaran goes to and from Queens Wharf on a regular daily schedule. The one-way fare is $6.50 (children $3.50). It's a 30-minute trip to Days Bay, where there are beaches, a fine park and a couple of houses that Katherine Mansfield's family kept for summer homes; her story *At the Bay* recalls summer holidays at Days Bay.

Bluefin Harbour Cruises (☎ 569 8203) does 1½-hour 'coffee cruises' for $14, a 90-minute lunch cruise for $17, and two-hour dinner cruises for $25 (children half-price on all tours). They depart from the wharf at the end of Whitmore St, between Queens Wharf and the railway station.

Also departing from the wharf at the end of Whitmore St, Lady Fisher Ltd (☎ 380 8888) does reasonably priced fishing trips around the harbour and out into Cook Strait. Fishing rods and tackle are available for hire on the boat.

Festivals & Annual Events

It seems like Wellington is always celebrating one event or another; check the *What's On* from the information centre for current events. Some notable annual events include:

January
: *Wellington Anniversary Weekend* – the Wellington marathon and half-marathon races, plus horse racing

February
: *City Dragon Boat Festival* – towards the end of February, with an international flavour; held between Queens and Taranaki St wharves

February/March
: *International Festival of the Arts* – a month of culture including theatre, music, opera and fringe activities (held only in even-numbered years)

March
: *Irish Festival* – first three weeks, leading up to St Patrick's Day on the 17th
: *Benson & Hedges Fashion Design Awards* – mid to late-March, top fashion show of the year

July
: *International Film Festival* – two-week extravaganza

September
: *Listener Women's Book Festival* – week-long women's writing festival, mid-September

October
: *Wine & Food Festival* – held on Daylight Saving Day, either in October or November

November/December
: *Wellington Waterfront St Race & Streets Ahead Festival* – this race roars through the streets of Wellington on the last weekend of November or the first weekend in December.

Places to Stay

Wellington has a good selection of places to stay in all categories.

Camping & Cabins Areas of green grass (or even no grass) where you can pitch a tent in Wellington are rarities. If you find a place, write and let us know so that other campers can pitch their tents. Closest is the *Hutt Park Holiday Village* (☎ 568 5913) at 95 Hutt Park Rd in Lower Hutt, 13 km from the centre of Wellington. It has tent/powered sites at $16/18, standard cabins at $28, tourist cabins at $39, tourist flats at $52 and motel units at $65 (all prices are for two people). The camping ground is a 15-minute drive from the ferry terminal, a five-minute walk from the bus stop (take the Eastbourne bus) or a 20-minute walk from Woburn railway station.

The *Harcourt Holiday Park* (☎ 526 7400), at 45 Akatarawa Rd in Upper Hutt, about 30 minutes drive from Wellington, is in a lovely native-bush setting. Tent/powered sites are $16/17 for two, and tourist flats $44/56 for two/three people.

A bit further out, 45 minutes drive from Wellington, the *Rimutaka Forest Park* (☎ 564 3066) has basic cold-water camping facilities at Catchpool Valley near the DOC's Catchpool Visitor Centre. The cost is $4/2 for adults/children and the bush cabins, only reached by walking, are $9 per person.

Hostels The *Port Nicholson YHA Hostel* (☎ 801 7280) on the corner of Cambridge Terrace and Wakefield St, is conveniently situated, queer-friendly (in that it was the first in Wellington to 'come out') and quite a luxurious hostel. Most rooms in this hostel have views right over the harbour, and all have private bath. The cost is $17 in dorm rooms ($15 from May to November), or

$25/38/40 for singles/twins/doubles. There's a well-organised travel agency in the lobby.

Also convenient is *Downtown Backpackers* (☎ 473 8482) on the corner of Waterloo Quay and Bunny St, opposite the railway station. It's a large, impersonal hostel with a big-city feel but is quite a distance from the attractions of Courtenay Place and Cuba St; among its amenities are an in-house restaurant, a bar with billiards and other games, a pub next door, a huge kitchen, and lounge facilities. All rooms have private bathroom; the cost is $16 for a dorm bed or $25/39 for singles/doubles.

Trekkers Hotel/Motel (☎ 385 2153) is another central place, stretching through from Cuba St to Dunlop Terrace, just a few doors from the Cuba and Vivian Sts corner. While it also has hotel and motel rooms, it's a popular spot for backpackers; the cost is $15 per person in double and triple rooms if you bring your own sleeping bag, $5 extra with linen provided; singles are $40 or $60 with bathroom. Facilities include spa, sauna, laundry, guests' kitchen, restaurant, bar and off-street parking. The Hub travel agency is in this building.

The dilapidated *Rosemere Backpackers* (☎ 384 3041) at 6 MacDonald Crescent is a short walk uphill from the centre, with good city views especially from the tiny 3rd-storey balcony. The friendly management more than compensates for its basic feel – they even provide juggling lessons. The cost is $14 in dorm rooms and $20/34 for singles/doubles.

Several other hostels are found on and near Brougham St in the pleasant Mt Victoria area. To get there from the railway station end of town catch bus No 2 or 5 to Brougham St, or bus No 1 or 3 to the KFC on Kent Terrace. From the Courtenay Place end of town it's only a five-minute walk.

Beethoven House (☎ 384 2226) at 89 Brougham St, Mt Victoria, is known for its eccentric atmosphere, largely due to the personality of its owner. The guests are woken up by classical music each morning in time for a big communal breakfast at 8 am – the $13 for a dorm bed and $30 double-room rate includes this now infamous breakfast. All birthdays, including Ludwig's, the house's, yours and Christmas are celebrated. Note however that this place inspires either love or hate and as many people positively hate it as love it! There's no prominent sign outside, just a small 'BH'. The No 2 bus stops near the Brougham and Pirie Sts corner.

Nearby, *Rowena's City Lodge* (☎ 385 7872) at 115 Brougham St is a larger hostel, up a driveway above the street. There are three separate lounges and various things to play with such as billiards, a trampoline, a grand piano and more. The staff here could do with some hospitality training. Rates are $14 in dorm rooms, $17/34 for singles/doubles.

Around the corner at 52 Ellice St is *Maple Lodge* (☎ 385 3771), a small, friendly hostel with rates of $14 in dorms and $18/32 for singles/doubles. It has safe off-street parking, a confined kitchen, dining room, TV lounge and laundry facilities.

A new place, *Wide World Backpackers* (☎ 473 2255), has opened at 2/28 Hinau Rd in Hataitai, at the eastern side of the Mt Victoria Tunnel. The hostel, a little way out of the city, is a good retreat from the hustle and bustle as it is surrounded by trees and gardens. A dorm bed is $15 per person, and doubles are $24. The owners will pick you up from the city or you can get off at the Hinau Rd stop on bus No 2 or 6.

Guesthouses & Apartment Hotels There is an excellent selection of guesthouses in Wellington. At 116 Brougham St in the Mt Victoria area, the *Richmond Guest House* (☎ 385 8529) is a clean, comfortable 'home away from home' with a guests' kitchen, laundry and TV lounge. B&B is $35/50 for share singles/doubles, or $60 for doubles with private bath.

Also on the south side of town, the *Clinton Private Hotel* (☎ 385 9515) at 35 Thompson St has singles/doubles for $30/45, with breakfast an extra $6.50, plus a backpackers rate of $15 in a five-bed dorm with linen provided. There's no guests' kitchen but you can request meals.

Nearby, the *Terrace Travel Hotel* (☎ 382 9506) at 291 The Terrace is a comfortable home-style guesthouse with singles/doubles for $45/65, all with private bath. Breakfast is $6 extra but there's also a guests' kitchen where you can do your own cooking. Out behind the house are backpackers cabins where a bed is $15 with your own sleeping bag, $5 extra with linen provided.

A bit more luxurious, the *Tinakori Lodge* (☎ 473 3478) at 182 Tinakori Rd in the historic Thorndon district offers attractive rooms, each with TV, with a lavish buffet breakfast at $66/80 for singles/doubles.

Wellington also has some apartment hotels, a cross between an apartment and a hotel. You can rent them nightly and they often give discounts for long-term stays. *Capital Hill Apartments* (☎ 472 3716) at 54 Hill St, just behind the Beehive, has bedsit (studio) apartments for $110. *Majoribanks Apartments* (☎ 385 7305) at 38 Majoribanks St has double apartments for $100 nightly, providing you book for a week or more; extra adults are charged $15 each. *City Life Apartments* (☎ 472 3413) at 202 The Terrace is at the top of the line, luxury-wise, with one, two and three-bedroom apartments starting at $180 per night; there are reductions for longer-term stays and on weekends. The *Central City Apartments* (☎ 385 4166) on the corner of Victoria and Edward Sts have singles and doubles for about $130.

Hotels There are cheap old hotels and plenty that head up towards the sky pricewise. A cheaper central one is *Flanagan's Hotel* (☎ 385 0216) on the corner of Kent Terrace and Majoribanks St, which has rooms for $40, $45 with private bath, and family rooms for $60.

The popular, centrally situated *Trekkers Hotel* (see Hostels) has 100 hotel rooms, with singles/doubles for $40/50 and rooms with private bath, TV, telephone, clock radio and desk for $60/70. Also central, the *Abel Tasman* (☎ 385 1304) on the corner of Willis and Dixon Sts has singles or doubles at $60 on weekends, rising to $110/118 on weekdays.

Much more expensive hotels include the *Terrace Regency Hotel* (☎ 385 9829) at 345 The Terrace, with doubles/suites at $151/192 from Monday to Thursday, considerably less on weekends; the *Museum Hotel* (☎ 385 2809) at 51-61 Cable St with a range of rooms from $105 to $160, also much less on weekends; the *Quality Hotel Willis St* (☎ 385 9819) at 355 Willis St with standard rooms/suites for $156/169; the *James Cook Hotel* (☎ 499 9500) at 147 The Terrace with singles and doubles at $253 during the week, considerably less on weekends; the *Bay Plaza* (☎ 385 7799) at 40-44 Oriental Parade with twins for $112/90 during the week/weekends; the *Quality Hotel Oriental Bay* (☎ 385 0279) at 73 Roxburgh St with rooms/suites from $162/225; and the *Wellington Parkroyal* (☎ 472 2722) on the corner of Grey and Featherston Sts with rooms starting at around $315. The *Hotel Raffaele* (☎ 384 3450) at 360 Oriental Parade is recommended; its doubles and triples are $190 during the week, weekend specials are $107.

The *Plaza International* (☎ 473 3900) at 148-176 Wakefield St is centrally located. But as any real-estate agent will tell you, 'position' doesn't come cheap; doubles are about $250 and suites are from $450 to $850.

Motels The *Aroha Motel & Cobo Lodge* (☎ 472 6206) at 222 The Terrace has single/double self-contained motel units at $90, plus family units at $145. The *Wellington Motel* (☎ 472 0334) at 14 Hobson St is clean and comfortable with single/double studios at $87, or two-bedroom family units at $97.

Motels close to the centre include *Apollo Lodge Motel* (☎ 385 1849), 49 Majoribanks St, the *Capital View Motor Inn* (☎ 385 0515), 12 Thompson St, and *Academy Motor Lodge* (☎ 389 6166) at 327 Adelaide Rd.

Places to Eat

Wellington probably has the widest variety of international cuisines to be found in NZ and there are many restaurants to choose from. Courtenay Place and Cuba St in particular are packed with restaurants.

Snacks & Takeaways The US fast-food giants are well represented in Wellington. *McDonald's, KFC* and *Pizza Hut* can all be found in Manners Mall in the centre. There's also a *KFC* on Kent Terrace on the corner of Pirie St, another *McDonald's* on Courtenay Place near the Cambridge Terrace junction and yet another on Lambton Quay near the lower cable-car terminal. At the corner of Victoria and Lombard Sts is *Georgie Pie*, a NZ chain that churns out various fillings in pastry casings – the end product is said by some to be not too bad.

Wellington is a great place for a sandwich or snack at lunch time. You'll find lots of places along Courtenay Place and Manners Mall, up Plimmer Steps and along Lambton Quay right in the centre, or along Cuba St and Cuba Mall. Also try the basement level under the BNZ building at the Willis St/Lambton Quay junction – Wellingtonians go underground to escape the wind. Places here sell sandwiches, pizzas, Chinese food, doners, fish & chips and other light meals.

Climb Plimmer Steps off Lambton Quay and you'll come to the *Cafe Mamba* and *Zoe's Cafe* (see Cafes). At 101 Manners St, close to the Cuba St junction, *A Taste of France* French bakery has a variety of interesting sandwiches and baked goods. They have a sit-down cafe branch on the corner of Willis and Bond Sts.

Ali Baba, 203 Cuba St, sells doner kebabs with salad and bread for around $8. Other doner places are the *Sultan* at 39 Dixon St and the *Sahara Cafe* at 39 Courtenay Place.

An important port like Wellington naturally has plenty of fish & chips specialists. The *Wellington Fish Supply* at 40 Molesworth St, opposite the Beehive, has good fish & chips. On Courtenay Place near the corner of Cambridge Terrace are the *Capital Fish Shop* and *Courtenay Fish & Chips*, open daily from 11 am to 9.30 pm. *Shed 5* on the waterfront also serves very fresh fish.

Cafes Wellington has a number of enjoyable cafes where you can go for a cappuccino or a relaxed meal, snack or dessert. Typical cafe menus include sandwiches, pizza, quiche, focaccia, muffins and cakes. There are cafes on Courtenay Place, on Cuba St and up the Plimmer Steps.

Konditorei Aida at 181 Cuba St is a traditional Viennese-style cafe with rich pastries, chocolates, fruit cakes and coffees. There's another branch in Lambton Square.

Up on Plimmer Steps in the centre, *Zoe's Cafe* is a most enjoyable cafe-restaurant with a great menu of focaccia, pasta, omelettes, espresso, wine and beer, and rich desserts.

Other cafes in the centre include the licensed (but oh so trendy) *Lido Cafe* on the corner of Victoria and Wakefield Sts, *City Limits Cafe* at 122 Wakefield St opposite the Old Town Hall, and the excellent *Clark's Cafe* upstairs on the mezzanine floor of the public library on Wakefield St. It's open daily and is worth a visit even if you weren't planning to go to the library.

For Internet junkies there is *Roasters* at the corner of Victoria and Dixon Sts next to the Curry Club. You can surf the information superhighway as you get high on caffeine. Choices on offer are latte, World Wide Web, cappuccino, InterRelayChat etc.

There are a number of hip cafes where the decor is graffiti, the music is underground, and the customers may include hipsters with spiky purple hair or dreadlocks down to their waists, international hitchhikers, visiting intergalactic guidebook researchers, or librarians from Taupo. *Espressoholic* at 128 Courtenay Place near the corner of Taranaki St is trendy indeed and it's open long hours, beginning at 8 am every day and staying open well past 1 am most nights. Over on Cuba St are a couple of similar places. Check out the *Midnight Espresso* at 178 Cuba St near the corner of Vivian St, or *Cuba Cuba* opposite it at No 179, which is not only a cafe but also a bar with live music some nights.

The *Deluxe Cafe* at 10 Kent Terrace, beside the Embassy Theatre and facing Courtenay Place, is a smaller and quieter but still hip little cafe, open from 7.30 am to midnight most days. The small and pleasant *Cafe Roti* at 103 Willis St, near Manners St, is open on weekdays from 11 am to 6 pm, and until midnight on Friday night.

Vegetarians are also well catered for in Wellington. The *Mt Victoria Cafe* on the corner of Brougham and Queen Sts in the Mt Victoria area at the south end of town, is a pleasant vegetarian wholefood cafe with delicious food and live jazz and board games on Sunday evening. The *Spice of Life* at 149 Willis St is often crammed with locals.

Judging by the number of cabbies there, the most popular cheap eatery in town (especially for breakfast) is the nameless *cafe* near the corner of Abel Smith and Cuba St. A huge breakfast (eggs, toast, chips, sausages and bacon) is about $6 and includes a bottomless cup of coffee.

Pub Food The *Loaded Hog, Backbencher, Thorndon Tavern, Paris, Flanagan's, Malthouse, Bull & Bear*, and *Molly Malone's* are all good pubs serving food; read more about pubs in the Entertainment section.

Restaurants Wellington has a great number of restaurants from which to choose, including many popular ethnic ones. Typically they are open for lunch Monday to Friday and seven nights a week for dinner.

Asian One of the best Asian restaurants in Wellington is the *Satay Malaysia*, upstairs at 46 Courtenay Place, serving traditional Malaysian food. A giant feast will cost around $15 to $22 per person, or you can order from the à la carte menu. It's open for dinner every night from 5.30 pm, and for lunch Wednesday to Friday. A good Malaysian place, passed on to us by readers, is the *Istana* in lower Cuba St (between Manners Mall and Wakefield St). A cheaper restaurant serving traditional Malaysian food is *Satay Kampong* at 262 Wakefield St, with nothing over $8 on the menu. The atmosphere is basic and functional, but the tiny restaurant is enormously popular.

For great Thai food head for Cuba St, and *Sala Thai* at No 134. It is open for dinner every night from 5.30 pm for those craving tom yam goong ($9.50). The *Oriental Thai* at 58 Cambridge Terrace (run by the renowned Suzie, ex of Suzie's) may well be the city's best but is expensive. The *Chiang Rai Thai* on Courtney Place near the corner of Taranaki St is also worth consideration.

Cambodian restaurants are rare, but the *Angkor* at 43 Dixon Street fills this void. Here you can sample such delights as mahope kari, a curry selection of chicken, lamb or prawn; amok trei, spicy steamed fish; and yao horn, a charcoal broiler steam boat. It is open for dinner daily.

Wellington has many of Chinese restaurants – every block on Courtenay Place seems to have several. With all the possibilities, one place stands out as a particularly good deal, but it's not on Courtenay Place. It is the *Ye-Jun* Cantonese restaurant upstairs at 40 Willis St, where an all-you-can-eat 10-course buffet is served every evening. Dinner cost $12 and weekday lunches are $10. It's not gourmet food but the price and the all-you-can-eat aspect of it makes it especially popular with travellers. A good place for yum cha is the *White Jade*, on the 1st floor of the Olympic Building at 97-99 Courtenay Place; their banquet meals are $25 per head.

The *Genghis Khan* at 25 Majoribanks St on the south end of town is a Mongolian BBQ place and the one price includes 'bottomless portions' – keep going back as many times as you like. Dinner is served daily from 6 to 10.30 pm (to 9.30 pm on Sunday).

The sub-continent is also well represented with a number of popular Indian places. The *Great India* at 141 Manners St gets rave reviews from Wellingtonians and serves delicious tandoori specialities. The chicken tikka is $16, seekh kebab is $13.50 and tandoori prawns are $21.50.

Japanese The *Donbeh Cafe* on Plimmer Steps is a Japanese snack and lunch bar open from 8 am to 3 pm, Monday to Thursday; 8 am to 8 pm Friday; and 10 am to 2 pm Saturday. Or there's the more expensive *Sakura* restaurant up on the 3rd floor of the Japan Seamans' Insurance Hall at 181-195 Wakefield St, open for lunch and dinner, Tuesday to Saturday. For teppanyaki, try the pricey *Fujiyama* on lower Taranaki St.

Middle Eastern *Ali Baba* at 203 Cuba St has expanded its restaurant section into a very pleasant place to dine – with seating on Turkish pillows, of course, or chairs if you prefer. It's casual and great for an inexpensive meal, snack, or just a baklava and coffee, and is open every day from 10.30 am to 9 pm, until 10 pm on Friday. Also on Cuba St at No 156 is *Cafe Istanbul*, another Turkish restaurant/cafe with a pleasant Turkish decor.

The *Sultan* at 39 Dixon St is a fancier Turkish restaurant, with a more complete menu, open Monday to Saturday from 11.30 am until late. The *Sahara Cafe* at 39 Courtenay Place is a similar place with Turkish, Lebanese and Syrian food.

European Italian food is represented at several restaurants including *La Casa Pasta* upstairs at 37 Dixon St, with home-style Italian cuisine. Other Italian restaurants include *Little Italy* at 125 Manners St and *Calzone* on the corner of Courtenay Place and Cambridge Terrace, a yuppie sort of place serving gourmet pizzas, pastas, salads and desserts, open every day from 10 am to 1 am.

If your wallet allows then head to *Mondo Cucina* in Blair St north of Courtney Place. It is open daily from 6 pm for dinner, and Wednesday to Sunday for brunch. Just around the corner at 14-16 Courtney Place is the very swish *Opera* where 'overtures' are about $11, various 'acts' (pastas and mains) are between $18 and $23, and 'finales' (desserts) are $9.50. *Il Casino* restaurant and piano bar is a very upmarket place on the corner of Vivian and Tory Sts. It has won lots of awards and the elevated snob factor is reflected in the price; a three-course meal with coffee would be about $50.

The *Cafe Paradiso* on the corner of Courtenay Place and Blair St is an intimate, pleasant cafe with a mostly French menu. With main courses at over $20 it's not cheap, but it's an enjoyable place with good music playing and candles on the tables, quite popular with the well-heeled set.

The *Paris* in Massey House at 132 Lambton Quay is there if you need it. How is this for a review: 'Drawing it's (sic) Clientele from the corporate sector, parliament and the nearby judiciary, Paris celebrates the new mood of business confidence with a menu of unabashed luxury'.

Tex/Mex The *Mexican Cantina* at 19 Edward St, just off Manners Mall, is a pleasant restaurant and good value for an enjoyable lunch or dinner out. They have all the usual Mexican dishes – enchiladas, tacos etc – from around $4 to $6, main meals and combination plates for $13, and some options for vegetarians. It's open for lunch on weekdays, and for dinner every night except Sunday.

In the same area, *Armadillo* at 129 Willis St is another Wellington institution – a loud, Texas cowboy-style restaurant/bar specialising in American food like steaks, ribs, southern chicken and burgers in Texas-size portions. It's not cheap at $18 plus for mains, but you get big portions and the place, complete with John Wayne decor, is lots of fun.

Around the corner at 97 Dixon St, *Chevy's* is a colourful pseudo-US restaurant with fancy burgers, hot Texan chilli, and appetisers like chicken wings, nachos and potato skins, all from around $11 to $15. Beware, if you want fries with your expensive burger then it will cost an extra $4.50. *South of the Border* (actually the corner of Willis and Bond Sts) is another place where you can be guaranteed a good margarita.

Mammy Flo at 201 Cuba St is popular as locals are fast learning the delights of Cajun cuisine. In season you can get Dixieland crab for $19, blackened fish for $16.50 and jambalaya for $14.

Other Restaurants The attractive, upmarket *Shed 5* and *Dockside* restaurants/bars on Queens Wharf are both fine places for seafood. They were opened as part of the city's waterfront revamp. *Shed 5* also has a cafe section, outdoor dining, and dance music on weekends.

Pico is an elegant little restaurant that's a favourite with travellers, set back from the street at 60 Ghuznee St, near Cuba Mall. It serves an eclectic menu of delicious and

Top: Abel Tasman National Park, Nelson (VB)
Bottom: Picton Harbour, Nelson (TW)

Top: Knights Point, West Coast (NK)
Bottom: Punakaiki Pancake Rocks, West Coast (JW)

interesting international foods, with plenty of dishes for vegetarians. It's open for lunch and dinner every day except Sunday.

We haven't forgotten those who enjoy a steak. The licensed *Turners* in the Willis St Village has an open BBQ. Their motto is 'If you leave us hungry ... you've only got yourself to blame'. A huge steak, bottomless salad bowl and fries or baked potato is $18.50. It is open seven days from 5.30 pm.

Entertainment

Pubs The *Loaded Hog* at 12-14 Bond St, just off Willis St, is one of the city's most popular pubs, with a lively atmosphere, live music Wednesday to Sunday nights (no cover charge) and a good menu. They brew their own beers on the premises, including Hog's Head dark ale, Port Nick lager, and Weiss German-style lager. All are 100% natural and guaranteed to be hangover-free. It's open every day from 11 am till late, and until 10 pm on Sunday.

Molly Malone's, an Irish pub at the Glass House on the corner of Courtenay Place and Taranaki St, is another rousing, popular pub. Live music is mostly Irish, playing Tuesday to Saturday nights with no cover charge; on Sunday nights there's an Irish jam session where you're welcome to sit in. It's open daily from 11 am till late Monday to Saturday, and until 9 pm on Sunday. You can get traditional Irish fare upstairs in the *Dubliner*.

Another popular pub is *The Backbencher* on the corner of Molesworth St and Sydney St East, opposite the Beehive. It does a thriving business at lunch time, serving large portions of food, and dinners are becoming popular too. The atmosphere is casual, friendly and fun. It's open every day from 11 am until late.

Also on Molesworth St, a couple of blocks up the hill at No 110, the *Thorndon Tavern* is a sports bar with a big-screen sports TV, billiards, darts and TAB racing downstairs. It also has pub food. On Thursday, Friday and Saturday nights there's live music, mostly laid-back country style. A pub with a bit more of a suburban feel is the *Western Park Tavern* on Tinakori Rd, not far from the main entrance to the Botanic Gardens.

On Plimmer Steps in the centre off Lambton Quay, the *Bull & Bear* is a bar & grill pub with an emphasis on sports – they run buses

Gay & Lesbian Wellington

The most popular gay venue is *Caspars Bar* at 120 Victoria St on the ground floor of MRL House (opposite McDonald's). There are gay, lesbian (last Saturday night of every month) and friends' nights at the *Escape Niteclub*, 9 Edward St, and special evenings on long weekends. Downstairs at 9 Edward St is *ESC*, a cool cafe and bar. Their motto is: 'It doesn't matter if you are black or white, straight or gay, leave your attitude on the outside and come on in and meet some really warm people'. The *Toledo Bar* on the ground floor of the Oaks Complex, Manners St, has a quiet, friendly atmosphere.

Madison at 106 Oriental Parade, *Goudy's* at 105 Vivian St, *Paris* at 132 Lambton Quay, the *Lido Café* on the corner of Victoria and Wakefield Sts and *Flip Brasserie* in the RSA Building at 103 Ghuznee St (a great, but not cheap, place for good Mediterranean food and company) are all gay-friendly restaurants.

There is a good gay and lesbian book section at Unity Bookshop on the corner of Willis and Manners Sts. A good fortnightly national gay newspaper is *MtM (Man to Man)*. Get a copy of the *Lesbian & Gay in Wellington Guide to Groups and Venues*. If you are hoping to meet a friendly bunch of people when you arrive in Wellington try the Gay Switchboard (☎ 385 0674) or the Lesbian Line (☎ 389 8082), Tuesday, Thursday and Saturday 7.30 to 10 pm. AIDS services include the NZ Aids Foundation Awhina Centre (☎ 389 3169) at 35 Mein St, Newtown, and the hotline number (☎ (0800) 802 437). ■

to rugby games and you're welcome to go along. There's live music on Thursday, Friday and Saturday nights. Further along Lambton Quay at No 134-136 is the trendy *Paris*. Not far from the corner of Lambton Quay and Willis St (No 47) is the *Malthouse*, a good place for a meal but an absolute shrine for the lover of naturally brewed beer. All of NZ's best beer (with the exception of Hooker's Ale) are on offer – Mac's Gold, Black Mac, Pink Elephant Mammoth and the antithetical Sunshine Sundowner, some of which are brewed following the Bavarian 'Reinheitsgebot'.

La Luna upstairs on Manners St near the corner of Cuba St has live music Wednesday to Saturday nights, mainly blues bands for dancing. It's open every day except Sunday from 11 am until late.

Wine buffs should check out the *Aqua Vitae Wine Bar* on the corner of Willis and Boulcott Sts, featuring over 100 wines.

Discos & Nightclubs There's dancing at several of the pubs mentioned above, and at other places around town. Popular discos include the *Metro* on Manners St, on the underground floor below Pizza Hut. The *MidCity Tavern* above the metro on ground level is divided into a couple of areas. You can get a meal or a beer, dance if you have a partner or dodge the punches as the evening wears on. The *Big Easy* (often referred to locally as the 'big sleazy') is a 'singles' venue on Courtney Place.

The *Antipodes* on the corner of Cuba and Vivian Sts is popular with travellers and it has live music on Thursday, Friday and Saturday nights. *Cuba Cuba* at 179 Cuba St is a hip cafe/bar with live dance music Thursday, Friday and Saturday nights.

Shed 5 at Queens Wharf and *Flanagan's* on the corner of Kent Terrace and Majoribanks St are both popular with the yuppie set for more upmarket dancing (and dining if you like) on weekends. The *St Johns Bar*, at 5-9 Cable St, in the old St John's Ambulance building, not far from the wharf, is a good after-dark venue popular with locals.

The *Planet Bar* on the corner of Courtenay Place and Tory St is one place people come to after the pubs shut down. Large and pleasant with interesting decor and a long twisted bar, it has live dance music on Wednesday night, and DJs on Thursday, Friday and Saturday. It's open from 11 am to 3 am, Sunday to Tuesday, and until 5 am on other days.

The *Bar Bodega* on the corner of Abel Smith and Willis Sts is popular with alternative types, lovers of good brews and those who like their music a little different. It is open from morning until late at night. There is live music from Wednesday to Saturday in the evening and a DJ on Tuesday and Sunday (on these nights it is usually the last bar in town to shut).

Theatre Wellington is the most active place in New Zealand for live theatre, supporting a number of professional theatre companies and quality amateur companies.

Downstage Theatre (☎ 384 9639) presents plays in the Hannah Playhouse on the corner of Cambridge Terrace and Courtenay Place; the pleasant Encore cafe is here. *Circa Theatre* (☎ 801 7992), near the corner of Cable and Taranaki Sts on the Lambton Harbour waterfront, presents a variety of drama. The *Bats Theatre* (☎ 384 9507), 1 Kent Terrace, is a more avant-garde, alternative theatre.

The *Taki Rua Theatre* (☎ 384 4531) at 12a Alpha St specialises in New Zealand drama, with new and Maori plays and local themes. The *Repertory Theatre* (☎ 385 4939) at 13 Dixon St is a community theatre company.

Half-price theatre tickets for the Bats, Circa and Downstage theatres are available at the information centre Monday to Friday from noon to 4 pm, subject to availability.

The Wellington City Opera (☎ 384 4434) and the Royal New Zealand Ballet (☎ 238 5383) both perform in town, usually at the State Opera House; ring for current events.

Shows & Films The *State Opera House* (☎ 385 0832) in Manners St, the *Michael Fowler Centre* (☎ 801 4263) in Wakefield St, the *Wellington Town Hall* (☎ 471 1573) on Wakefield St and the *Victoria University Theatre* (☎ 473 3120) are all popular performance venues. The ritzy Michael Fowler Centre, part of the Civic Square complex, has its main entrance on Wakefield St. It is host to all sorts of performances from bands to the NZSO. Check the newspapers or the information centre for current shows. The *amphitheatre* at Frank Kitts Park on the waterfront and the *Dell* in the Botanic Garden are popular venues for outdoor concerts and shows.

The *Wellington Film Society* (☎ 384 6817) presents interesting international and art films at the Paramount and Continuum theatres, the National Library, and the Memorial Theatre at Victoria University's Student Union, phone for a current schedule.

There are plenty of cinemas: *Midcity* in Manners St, the *Regent* in Manners Mall and the *Embassy* in Kent St screen commercial films; the *Paramount* in Courtney Place has 'hard-edged' art-house movies; the *Penthouse* in Brooklyn is 'middle of the road' art house; the *Rialto* in Cable St boasts 'quality independent productions'; and the *Continuum* in Civic Square has 'alternative' movies.

Things to Buy

The market is in the Old St James building near the corner of the Cuba Mall and Manners St. It has dozens of tiny shops selling everything from international arts & crafts to homemade jams, with several little restaurants for a snack. It's open daily from 10 am to 6 pm, Friday night until late.

New Zealand's answer to Bloomingdale's or Harrod's is Kirkcaldie & Stains in Lambton Quay. Let the kids off the rope in Lost Forests in Lambton Square, where trees talk and pigs fly!

There is a well-stocked New World supermarket is on the corner of Cambridge Terrace and Wakefield St.

Camping & Sports Gear If you need gear for camping, tramping or other sports, Wellington is a good place to buy it. The Kathmandu store, on the ground floor of the Rural Bank Building at 34 Manners St, is a great place to purchase good-quality tramping clothing. Second Wind Sports at 120 Wakefield St sells both new and used sports and outdoor equipment of all kinds. They have good prices on used stuff, or you can trade-in your old gear. Ski 'n' Camp, 181 Wakefield St, is a good place to find a tent.

Getting There & Away

Air Wellington airport has two terminals, each with restaurants, gift shops and its own information centre. The information centre at the Air New Zealand/domestic terminal (☎ 388 6451) is open Monday to Friday from 7 am to 8.30 pm, and from 7 am to 8 pm on the weekend. The one at the international terminal (☎ 388 2953) is open at similar times. Left-luggage lockers are in the domestic terminal and are always available.

Wellington is served by two major international airlines (Qantas and Air New Zealand), two major domestic airlines, and two small-craft airlines specialising in short flights across Cook Strait.

Air New Zealand and Ansett offer direct domestic flights to many places in NZ, with connections to other centres. Air New Zealand has direct flights to Auckland, Blenheim, Christchurch, Dunedin, Gisborne, Hamilton, Motueka, Napier, Nelson, New Plymouth, Palmerston North, Rotorua, Taupo, Tauranga, Timaru, Wanganui and Westport. Ansett has direct flights to Auckland, Blenheim, Rotorua, Palmerston North, Nelson, Christchurch, Dunedin, Invercargill and Queenstown.

To get to the South Island you have to either take the ferry or fly. Some travellers take the ferry in one direction and fly in the other, to experience both. The flight between Wellington and Picton takes 25 minutes in a small plane. Note that the strait can be just as bumpy up above as it often is at sea level.

Soundsair (☎ 388 2594) Wellington-Picton/Wellington-Blenheim flights cost $52/65 one way. They have return flights to the Heaphy Track ($349, minimum of two passengers).

Float Air Picton (☎ 236 6870) operates from Porirua Harbour, north of Wellington. Its floatplanes take off and land on the sea. It costs $70 from Wellington to Picton.

Each of these small airlines also fly to any destination around the Marlborough Sounds; Float Air Picton in its floatplanes, Soundsair in small amphibious aircraft. The cost is around $85 to $90 for most flights, more if you're going to a very remote sound.

International flights serving Wellington are limited to Air New Zealand and Qantas flights to/from Sydney, Brisbane and Melbourne. International airlines with offices in Wellington (though not all of these fly to/from Wellington) include:

Air New Zealand
  179 Featherston St, 79 Willis St (☎ 388 9737)
Ansett New Zealand
  corner Customhouse Quay & Hunter St (☎ 471 1146)
British Airways
  Royal Insurance Bldg, corner Featherston & Panama Sts (☎ 472 7327)
Mt Cook Airline
  Saachi & Saachi Bldg, corner Taranaki St & Courtenay Place (☎ 388 9900; (0800) 800 737)
Qantas Airways
  DFC Harbour Tower, corner Jervois Quay & Hunter St (☎ 472 1100; (0800) 808 767)
Singapore Airlines
  3-11 Hunter St (☎ 473 9749)
United Airlines
  26 Brandon St (☎ 472 0470)

Bus Wellington is an important junction for bus travel, with buses coming into and heading out of town on several major routes.

InterCity (☎ 472 5111) and Newmans buses (☎ 499 3261) depart from Platform 9 at the railway station, as well as from the *Interislander* ferry terminal. Tickets for these buses are sold at the travel reservations & tickets centre in the railway station. Mount Cook Landline (☎ (0800) 800 287) buses depart from the Mt Cook depot at the corner of Taranaki St and Courtney Place. City to City: White Star (☎ 478 4734) buses depart from Bunny St near Downtown Backpackers.

The Kiwi Experience (☎ 385 2153) and Magic Bus (☎ 387 2018) also come in and out of Wellington. Bookings for all buses can be made at most Wellington hostels.

Train Wellington railway station (☎ 498 3413; (0800) 802 802) is a large station with a travel centre offering reservations and tickets for trains, buses, the *Interislander* ferry, airlines, tours and more. Also here are Wellington's main post office, and luggage lockers open every day from 6 am to 10 pm.

A free shuttle bus operates between the railway station and the ferry terminal, departing from the station 35 minutes before each sailing and meeting each arriving ferry.

Two trains operate between Wellington and Auckland, running through the central North Island. The daytime *Overlander* runs every day, departing from each end in the morning. The overnight *Northerner* runs every night except Saturday, departing from each city in the evening, and arriving early the next morning. The *Bay Express* operates daily between Wellington and Napier, departing from Wellington in the morning, arriving in Napier in the early afternoon, and departing from Napier an hour later to arrive back in Wellington in the evening.

Hitching It's not easy to hitch out of Wellington because the highways heading out of the city, whether SH1 heading up the Kapiti Coast or SH2 heading up the Hutt Valley, are motorways for a long distance and it's illegal to hitch right on the motorway. It's best to catch a bus or train out to the Kapiti Coast or to Masterton and hitch from there.

Vehicle Storage If you need to store your vehicle while you go across on the ferry or for any other reason, Wellington has a few reputable vehicle-storage services. There is an overnight lock-up service at the ferry terminal. Securaport (☎ 387 3700) at 57-61 Kingsford Smith St, Lyall Bay charges $10 per day. They offer under-cover and fully insured storage, and will arrange for your transport between the car park and the airport or ferry terminal. Another option is Car Storage (☎ 472 3215), 138 Old Hutt Rd,

Kaiwharawhara; they pick up and drop off at the ferry terminal.

Ferry The *Interislander* ferry shuttles back and forth between Wellington and Picton. There are usually four services daily in each direction and the crossing takes about three hours. It's best to do the trip in daylight, if the weather's good, to see Wellington Harbour and the Marlborough Sounds.

The fares vary with the seasons; normal fares are $30 during off-peak times, $38 during standard times. Off-peak means most of the time; standard means the usual holiday periods. Children aged four to 14 travel at half-price and infants under four travel free. Return fares are double the one-way fares.

Day-excursion return fares cost the same as one-way fares and there is a variety of fares such as 'weekend savers', and family, group and senior fares, which provide a substantial discount. Cars or motorhomes cost $92 to $114 off-peak fare, $114 to $150 standard fare. Bicycles cost $12, motorbikes $30, and it's $16 each for canoes, sailboards, hang-gliders and dogs.

At peak periods you must book well ahead – the ferries can be booked solid at certain popular holiday times, especially for the limited vehicle space, which can get booked up months in advance. All the discount fares except the day excursions *must* be booked in advance, they are not available at the ferry terminal. You can book up to six months in advance, either directly (☎ (0800) 658 999) or at most travel agents and information centres throughout New Zealand.

There are faster services across Cook Strait. The *Lynx* (☎ (0800) 658 999) operates in summer only from December to April, doing the trip to Picton in less than two hours; it operates from both ends three times daily. The off-peak rate for adults/children is $35/20 and the peak rate $35/15; cars are from $125 to $165 in peak season and $105 to $125 in off-peak times; motorcycles $45/$35 for peak/off peak; bicycles are $12; and other articles such as windsurfers and dogs are $16. There are also 'one-dayer' and 'combo' return discounted fares.

A free shuttle bus service is provided for ferry sailings on both sides of the strait. In Wellington it operates between the ferry and railway station, departing from the railway station 35 minutes before each sailing. This is convenient for both train and bus connections, since the long-distance buses depart from either the ferry terminal or the railway station, as well as for just getting between town and the ferry. The shuttle meets all arriving ferries except the one late-night ferry on Monday. On the Picton side, a free shuttle is provided between the ferry and the Picton-Christchurch *Coastal Pacific Express* train.

If you're planning to hitch out of Picton note that the cars drive off the ferry almost as soon as the ferry docks. Foot passengers are likely to find every vehicle has gone by the time their feet hit terra firma!

Getting Around

To/From the Airport There are two types of shuttle service to the airport in Wellington, and two companies providing it: Johnston's Shuttle Express (☎ 384 7654) and Super Shuttle (☎ 387 8787), both with the same prices.

Door-to-door service to or from the airport costs $8 for one person, $10 for two people, $12 for three with either company, and they'll also go to the ferry and the bus or railway station. Less expensive at $4 per person, both companies also operate a shuttle directly from the railway station to the airport, departing from the railway station every half-hour from 7.15 am to 5.45 pm, but note that this service operates only from Monday to Friday.

A taxi between the city centre and airport costs around $12 to $14.

Bus Wellington has a good local bus system with frequent buses operating every day from around 7 am to 11 pm on most routes. Most routes depart from beside the railway station and from the major bus stop on Courtenay Place at the intersection of Cambridge Terrace. Useful colour-coded bus route maps and timetables are available at the information centre.

Phone Busline (☎ 801 7000) for all questions about public transport around the Wellington area; the service operates Monday to Saturday from 7.30 am to 8.30 pm, Sunday from 9 am to 3 pm. They offer information on all bus and train schedules, fares, connections etc.

Bus fares are determined by zones. The 'Miracle Mile', between the railway station and the Courtenay Place/Cambridge Terrace bus stops, costs $1; otherwise it's $1.10 to ride in one section, $1.70 for two sections etc.

There's also a Daytripper Pass, good for riding all day and evening on any Big Red bus (most local buses); these passes can be used on weekdays from 9 am (after the rush hour), and weekends at any time of day. The cost is $5, and two children can ride free with each adult.

Train Four suburban electric train routes, with frequent trains daily from around 6 am to midnight, depart from Wellington railway station. These routes are: Johnsonville, via Khandallah and Ngaio; Paraparaumu, via Porirua and Paekakariki; Melling, via Petone and Lower Hutt; and Upper Hutt, going on to Masterton. Phone Ridewell (☎ 801 7000) for questions on their services, or pick up a timetable from the railway station or visitor information centre.

In addition to the regular fares there is also a day pass available which, for $15, allows two adults and two children (or one adult and three children) to ride these suburban trains anywhere, all day long.

Bicycle The Penny Farthing Cycle Shop (☎ 385 2279) at 89 Courtenay Place hires mountain bikes at $25/140/450 per day/week/month, plus a full range of panniers and other gear.

Bicycles Unlimited (☎ 385 1233) at 65 Courtenay Place hires mountain bikes at $25/100 per day/week, road bikes at $15/60 per day/week, with special weekend rates of $25/40 for road/mountain bikes hired from Friday afternoon to Monday morning. Both shops offer a full range of bicycle gear, clothing, bicycle repairs, and bicycles for sale.

Around Wellington

To the north of Wellington is the Hutt Valley, and to the north-west the Kapiti Coast. The Hutt Valley is an urban extension of Wellington, the Kapiti Coast a beach escape and the summer playground of the windy city.

Getting There & Away

Getting from Wellington to the west coast is a breeze – this is the major route from Wellington to the rest of the North Island whether you're coming by bus, train or car.

InterCity, Newmans, Mount Cook Landline, Kiwi Experience and Magic Bus all stop at Paraparaumu and Otaki on their north-south routes to/from Wellington. From Wellington it's about an hour to Otaki and 45 minutes to Paraparaumu.

Trains between Wellington and the coast operate even more frequently than the buses. Coming from Wellington, the Paraparaumu electric train runs hourly in both directions every day from around 6 am to midnight, with stops at Paekakariki and Paraparaumu.

All the long-distance trains serving Wellington stop at Paraparaumu and Otaki, making three trains a day in each direction. Travel time on these is 50 minutes to Paraparaumu and 1¼ hours to Otaki

Running along the coast, SH1 is the principal route connecting Wellington to the rest of the North Island, so there's plenty of traffic. Hitching is good along here.

HUTT VALLEY

The Hutt River acts as the western boundary for land-starved Wellington's dormitory cities, Lower Hutt and Upper Hutt. There are a number of sights and activities in these sizeable cities. Lower Hutt has the **Petone Settlers Museum** on the Esplanade, Petone, which is open from noon to 4 pm, Tuesday to Friday and from 1 to 5 pm on the weekend. For more information contact the Lower Hutt Visitor Information Centre in the Pavilion, 25 Laings Rd (☎ 570 6699); it is open from 9 am to 5 pm daily.

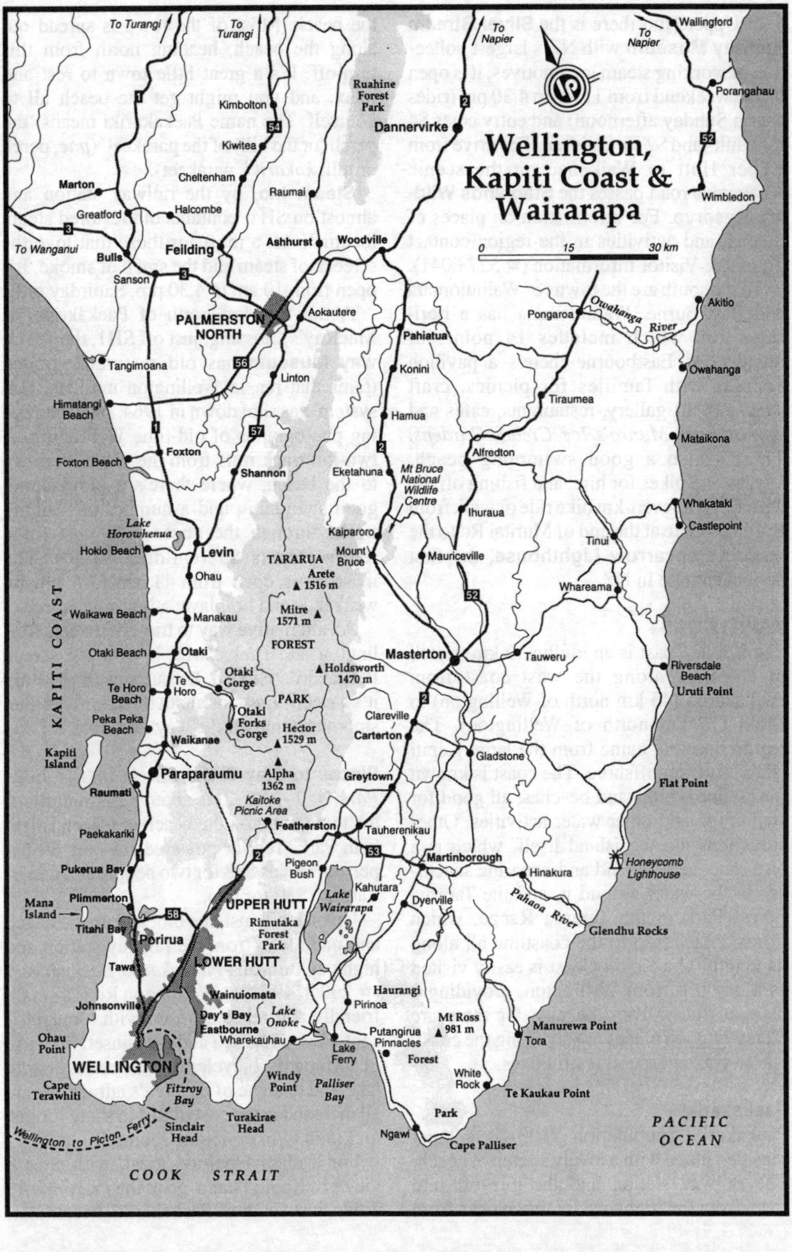

Wellington, Kapiti Coast & Wairarapa
0
15
30 km
To Turangi
To Turangi
To Napier
To Napier
To Wanganui
Wallingford
Porangahau
Wimbledon
Ruahine Forest Park
Kimbolton
Kiwitea
Cheltenham
Dannervirke
Marton
Greatford
Halcombe
Raumai
Bulls
Feilding
Ashhurst
Woodville
Sanson
Aokautere
PALMERSTON NORTH
Pahiatua
Pongaroa
Owahanga River
Akitio
Owahanga
Tangimoana
Linton
Konini
Himatangi Beach
Hamua
Tiraumea
Mataikona
Foxton
Foxton Beach
Shannon
Eketahuna
Mt Bruce National Wildlife Centre
Alfredton
Whakataki
Castlepoint
Lake Horowhenua
Ihuraua
Tinui
Hokio Beach
Levin
Kaiparoro
Mount Bruce
Mauriceville
TARARUA
Arete 1516 m
Ohau
Whareama
Waikawa Beach
Manakau
Mitre 1571 m
FOREST
KAPITI COAST
Otaki Beach
Otaki
Holdsworth 1470 m
Masterton
Tauweru
Riversdale Beach
Uruti Point
Te Horo Beach
Te Horo
Otaki Gorge
PARK
Peka Peka Beach
Otaki Forks Gorge
Hector 1529 m
Clareville
Carterton
Kapiti Island
Waikanae
Gladstone
Paraparaumu
Alpha 1362 m
Greytown
Flat Point
Raumati
Kaitoke Picnic Area
Paekakariki
Featherston
Tauherenikau
Martinborough
Pukerua Bay
Pigeon Bush
Hinakura
Honeycomb Lighthouse
Mana Island
Plimmerton
UPPER HUTT
Lake Wairarapa
Kahutara
Dyerville
Pahaoa River
Titahi Bay
Porirua
Rimutaka Forest Park
Glendhu Rocks
Tawa
LOWER HUTT
Johnsonville
Wainuiomata
Haurangi
Pirinoa
Day's Bay
Eastbourne
Lake Onoke
Mt Ross 981 m
Manurewa Point
Ohau Point
Wharekauhau
Lake Ferry
Putangirua Pinnacles
Tora
Forest
WELLINGTON
White Rock
Te Kaukau Point
Cape Terawhiti
Fitzroy Bay
Windy Point
Palliser Bay
Wellington to Picton Ferry
Sinclair Head
Turakirae Head
Park
Ngawi
Cape Palliser
PACIFIC OCEAN
COOK STRAIT
1
1
1
2
2
2
3
3
52
52
53
54
56
57
58

In Upper Hutt there is the **Silver Stream Railway Museum** with NZ's largest collection of working steam locomotives; it is open on the weekend from 11 am to 4.30 pm (rides are on Sunday afternoon) and entry costs $4 for adults and $2 for children. The drive from Upper Hutt to Waikanae on the scenic Akatarawa road passes the **Staglands Wildlife Reserve**. For information on places of interest and activities in the region contact Tourist & Visitor Information (☎ 527 6041).

To the south are the towns of Wainuiomata and Eastbourne. Wainuiomata has a **heritage trail** which includes 14 points of interest. At Eastbourne there's a pavilion popular with families for picnics, craft shops, an art gallery, restaurants, cafes and one of *Rush-Munro's Ice Cream Gardens*. There's also a good swimming beach, kayaks and bikes for hire, and fishing off the wharf. It is a seven-km bike ride or walk from Burdan's Gate at the end of Muritai Rd to the historic **Pencarrow Lighthouse**, the first permanent one in NZ.

KAPITI COAST

The Kapiti Coast is an idyllic 30-km stretch of coastline along the west coast from Paekakariki (45 km north of Wellington) to Otaki (75 km north of Wellington). The region takes its name from the large Kapiti Island five km offshore. The coast is known for its fine white-sand beaches, all good for swimming and other water activities. Other attractions are the island itself, which is a bird sanctuary on land and a marine sanctuary in the water around it, and the Tararua Forest Park in the Tararua Range, which forms a backdrop to the coastline all along its length. The Kapiti Coast is easily visited as a day trip from Wellington, providing a pleasant relief from the city. Or there are plenty of good places to stay along the coast, where you can spend restful days.

Paekakariki

Paekakariki (population 2100) is a quiet seaside village with a lovely stretch of beach. The railway station and the turn-off into town from the highway are two blocks from the beach. Most of the town is spread out along the beach, heading north from this turn-off. It's a great little town to rest and relax, and you might get the beach all to yourself. The name Paekakariki means 'the perch (or the hill) of the parakeet' (*pae*, perch or hill; *kakariki*, parakeet).

Steam Inc, by the railway station and almost on SH1, contains old restored steam locomotives, a must for those that love the screech of steam and the smell of smoke. It's open from 10 am to 4.30 pm, Saturday only.

About five km north of Paekakariki at MacKay's Crossing, just off SH1, the **Tramway Museum** has old restored wooden trams that ran in Wellington until its tram system was shut down in 1964, plus interesting photographs of old-time Wellington. A two-km track runs from the museum down to the beach, where there's a playground, good swimming and a number of walking tracks through the dunes. The cost for a return ride is $3 (children $1.50). The museum is open from 11 am to 5 pm on weekends and holidays; admission is free.

An alternative way to travel between Wellington and Paekakariki is over the scenic Paekakariki Hill Rd. If you're cycling south, it's a steep climb for about three km and then smooth sailing all the way after that.

Places to Stay & Eat *Batchelor's Holiday Park* (☎ 292 8292) is about 1.5 km north of the town, right on the beach in Queen Elizabeth Park. Tent or powered sites are $9 per person, cabins $38 for two people and tourist flats are $50 for two.

Up on a hill just one block from the beach and one block from the railway station and highway turn-off, *Paekakariki Backpackers* (☎ 292 8749) at 11 Wellington Rd is a small, friendly and relaxed hostel with a magnificent view of the sea and the sunset. Free use of surfboards, bicycles, and a courtesy car to take you to some of the area's attractions are all included in the cost of $14 in share rooms, or $35 in twin or double rooms.

For a classy seafood meal, with superb views of Kapiti Island, go to the *Fisherman's Table*, just south of Paekakariki. Meals start

WELLINGTON

at $12 and include one of those divine all-you-can-eat salads.

Paraparaumu

Paraparaumu (population 3000) is the principal tourist town of the Kapiti Coast. It's actually two towns, not one: Paraparaumu on the main highway, and Paraparaumu Beach, a pleasant community on the beach three km to the west. The beach here is the most developed along the coast, with a beachside park, a big waterslide, playgrounds and plenty of water activities. Boat trips to Kapiti Island depart from here.

The name Paraparaumu is rather a mouthful, but not really difficult to pronounce ('para-para-umu'). Some of the locals affectionately call the town 'para-par-AM' for short, but this is a corruption of the original. The name means 'scraps from an oven' (*parapara*, scraps or waste fragments; *umu*, underground oven) and is said to have originated in the old days when a Maori war party attacked the settlement and found only scraps of food in the oven.

Most things you'll need in Paraparaumu town (the part by the highway) are right on the highway within a block or two of the one set of traffic lights. The Kapiti information centre (☎ 298 5139), in the shopping centre, is open on weekdays.

Things to See The main attraction is **Paraparaumu Beach**, with its beachside park with good swimming, a big waterslide and other water activities (jet-skiing, windsurfing etc).

On SH1 about two km north of Paraparaumu, the **Lindale Agricultural Centre** is where the famous Kapiti cheese and Kapiti ice cream are made – drop in for a taste. It's open every day from 9 am to 5 pm.

About another km north, just off SH1, the **Southward Car Museum** is one of the coast's main attractions. It holds one of the largest collections of antique and unusual cars in Australasia, with over 130 cars including the three oldest cars in New Zealand – the 1895 Benz 'horseless carriage' is the oldest of the lot – and an array of motorbikes, three-wheeled cars, inventive homemade vehicles, some antique airplanes, and bicycles. See also Marlene Dietrich's Rolls Royce and a gull-winged Mercedes Benz. It's open daily from 9 am to 4.30 pm; admission is $4 (children $1).

Nyco Chocolates, on SH1 about one km south of town, is open every day from 8 am to 5.30 pm with all kinds of chocolates and other confections for sale; there are tours at 10.30 am and 2.30 pm daily.

Places to Stay & Eat The *Lindale Motor Park* (☎ 298 8046) is about two km north of the town near SH1, just south of the Lindale Agricultural Centre. Rates are $14/16 for two in tent/powered sites, and $26/37 for a single/double in cabins and $25/33 in on-site caravans.

Just opposite the beachside park at Paraparaumu Beach, the *Barnacles Seaside Inn* (☎ 298 4856), 3 Marine Parade, has views of the sea and is convenient to everything. The cost is $20/30 for a single/double.

There are plenty of motels both in the town and at the beach; most cost around $65 to $75 for a double. In Paraparaumu Beach there's the *Ocean Motel* (☎ 298 6458) at 42-44 Ocean Rd, *Wright's by the Sea* (☎ 298 7646) at 387-389 Kapiti Rd, the *Kapiti Court* (☎ 298 7982) at 341 Kapiti Rd, and the *Golf View* (☎ 298 6089) at 16 Golf Rd. Motels along SH1 include the *Beechwood* (☎ 298 8091), the *Belvedere* (☎ 292 8478) and the *Paraparaumu* (☎ 298 4476).

Restaurants, cafes and takeaways are plentiful near Paraparaumu Beach. Out on the highway, just south of the town's one traffic light, *Pizza Hut*, *McDonald's* and *KFC* are all strategically located to ensnare the passing motorists.

Kapiti Island

About 10 km long and two km wide, Kapiti Island is the coastline's dominant feature. Its name is short for Te-Waewae-Kapiti-o-Tara-raua-ko-Rangitane, meaning 'the place where the boundaries of Tara and Rangitane divide'; historically it formed the boundary between the Ngati Tara and Rangitane tribal lands. In the early 1800s the island was the base for Te Rauparaha, a mighty warrior who came down from Kawhia with his forces and took over the entire region. Later in the 19th century, the main island and the three small islands between it and the mainland became bases for seven whaling stations.

Since 1897 the island has been a protected wildlife reserve. Many species of birds that are now rare or extinct on the mainland still thrive on Kapiti Island.

The island is maintained by DOC and access is extremely limited. To visit you must obtain a permit from the DOC office in Wellington. Permits are often booked solid for six months in advance; with luck, you might be able to grab a space at the last minute if a permit-holder hasn't shown up, but of course you can't count on it. To arrange a permit, contact the Department of Conservation, Wellington Conservancy, 2nd floor, Bowen State Bldg, Bowen St, Wellington (☎ 472 5821; fax 499 0077). Permits cost $30 (for a group of up to 15 people) and only 50 people are able to visit on any one day. The reserve is closed to visitors on Monday and Tuesday, or Tuesday and Wednesday if Monday is a public holiday. The DOC office will advise you how to get out to the island; the boats depart from Paraparaumu Beach.

Although access to the island itself is restricted, there's no limitation on boat trips going *around* the island, or on diving in the marine reserve; these can be done anytime. A variety of tours around the island, lasting from 1½ hours to a full day, are offered by Kapiti Alive Tours (☎ 298 6044) in Paraparaumu; they also run fishing and diving trips. Kapiti Marine Transport (☎ (04) 298 6085) offers scenic boat trips around the island and fishing trips, as do Kapiti Marine Charter (☎ 297 2585).

WELLINGTON

Waikanae

About five km north of Paraparaumu, Waikanae is another town with two sections, one on SH1 and another by the beach. The Waikanae Field Centre (☎ 293 2191) at 10 Parata St is the main DOC office for the Kapiti Coast.

Waikanae's main attraction is the **Nga Manu Sanctuary**, a 15-hectare bird sanctuary with habitats including ponds, swamp, scrubland, coastal and swamp forest, and birds including mute swans, keas, pied stilts, parakeets (kakariki), ducks and wood pigeons. Other features include picnic areas, bush walks and a nocturnal house with kiwis, owls and tuataras.

To reach the sanctuary, turn seaward from SH1 onto Te Moana Rd and then follow the signs; the sanctuary is several km from the turn-off. It's open every day from 10 am to 5 pm; admission is $3 (children $1.50).

Places to Stay Waikanae has several motels including the *Safari Park Motel* (☎ 293 6053) on SH1; the *Sand Castle Motel* (☎ 293 6072) on the beach at Paetawa Rd; the *Toledo Park Motel* (☎ 293 6199) at 95 Te Moana Rd and the *Ariki Lodge Motel* (☎ 293 6592) at 4 Omahi St. One B&B about which we have received letters of commendation is *Waimoana* (☎ 293 7158) at 63 Kakarirki Grove; here singles/doubles are $60/100 and dinner is $30 per person. This place has a swimming pool, garden and waterfall which are all under the one roof.

Otaki

Otaki is only a small town but it has three distinct sections. The section on SH1 serves the passing traffic, with shops, takeaways, petrol stations and a railway station which doubles as the bus station. The main centre of Otaki, with the post office and more shops, is two km seawards. Three km further on the same road brings you to Otaki's beachside community.

Otaki is quiet and friendly, with a strong Maori history and influence: the little town has nine maraes, a Maori university and a historic Maori church. Its name means 'the place of sticking in' – relating to a story that this is the place where Hau stuck his staff in the ground when he was pursuing his wife.

Rangiatea Maori Church In late 1995 one of the country's most historic buildings, the Rangiatea Church (also known as the Maori

Cathedral) burnt down. The church was of great spiritual significance to the Maori. All that is left now are the totara pillars and ridgepole brought here at the command of Ngati Toa chief Te Rauparaha nearly 150 years ago.

This was the original burial site of Te Rauparaha and it is also the burial place of the internationally recognised opera singer, Inia Te Wiata.

Other Attractions Two km south of the town, Otaki Gorge Rd takes off inland from SH1 and leads 19 km to **Otaki Forks**, the main western entrance to the Tararua Forest Park. The scenic half-hour drive up through the Otaki Gorge to the Forks has a number of posted walking tracks along the way. The road is sealed most of the way, but the last five km is a gravel road.

Also along here is the **Tararua Outdoor Recreation Centre** (☎ (06) 364 3110) with canoe, kayak and rafting trips on the grade-2 Otaki River. You can hire the gear for a morning, afternoon or whole day, and they also offer guided river trips, abseiling, rock climbing, mountain biking, horse treks and other outdoor activities. It's open on weekends and school and public holidays, from October to April only.

At Otaki Forks there are picnic and swimming areas, camping areas and a hut, and a resident conservation officer (☎ (06) 364 3111) who has maps and information on the Tararua Forest Park. There are bush walks from 30 minutes to 3½ hours in length around the immediate area, and longer tracks leading to huts. Ask for advice on longer tracks in the park – you could do some good tramps lasting several days. Bring adequate clothing if you're planning to do a lot of tramping as the weather can be changeable, and sign the intentions book.

Places to Stay Otaki has two motor camp sites just a block from the beach. The *Capitol Seaside Resort* (☎ (06) 364 8121) at 20 Tasman Rd has single/double tent sites at $8/14, powered sites at $13/17, and tourist flats at $40/45. Facilities include a licensed restaurant, swimming pool, spa, sauna, tennis and other games courts, a trampoline and playgrounds.

The *Otaki Beach Holiday Camp* (☎ (06) 364 7107) on Moana St is a simpler place with tent sites at $7/11, powered sites at $9.50/13.50, and cabins and on-site caravans at $25 to $30.

The *Otaki Oasis* (☎ (06) 364 6860) at 33 Rahui Rd is a small, pleasant and well-tended hobby farm. Nonetheless it's not too remote; it's on the inland side of the railway tracks, about a block south of the railway station. If you're driving, turn inland at the BP petrol station on SH1 and then right (south) just over the tracks. The cost is $15 per person in the dorm or $35 for a double room.

A bit farther from town, *Bridge Lodge* (☎ (06) 364 5405) is on Otaki Gorge Rd just inland from SH1, about two km south of the town. The cost is $15.50/19.50 per person in four-bed/twin rooms.

The *Family Hotel* (☎ (06) 364 7180) at 30 Main St in the centre of town, two km towards the sea from SH1, charges $25/45 for singles/doubles. The *Capitol Seaside Resort* has units for $62/70; the *Otaki Motel* (☎ (06) 364 8469) on SH1 is about $10 cheaper.

The Wairarapa

The large region east and north-east of Wellington is known as the Wairarapa, taking its name from Lake Wairarapa ('shimmering waters'), a shallow but vast 8000-hectare lake. This region, very much the apotheosis of rural New Zealand, is principally a sheep-raising district – it boasts that it has three million sheep within a 16-km radius of Masterton, the region's principal town. It also has a few interesting attractions for visitors including the National Wildlife Centre at Mt Bruce, wineries at Martinborough, and very good tramping and camping in several regional and forest parks. Obtain a copy of the free, excellent *Wairarapa: Capital Country Escape*.

MASTERTON

The main town of the Wairarapa, Masterton (district population 23,000), is not a particularly exciting place, although it's a fair-sized town. Probably its main claim to fame is the international Golden Shears competition held annually the first week in March, in which sheep shearing is raised to the level of sport and art, with the world's top shearers competing for finesse as well as speed.

You will pass through Masterton if you're travelling north-south on SH2. The major bus and train routes serving Wellington go along the Kapiti Coast on the SH1.

The information centre, Tourism Wairarapa (☎ (06) 378 7373; fax 378 7042) at 5 Dixon St is open weekdays from 8.30 am to 5.30 pm and weekends from 9 am to 4 pm, except in winter when the weekend hours are shortened from 10 am to 4 pm. It has information on the entire Wairarapa region.

The DOC field office (☎ (06) 378 2061) on South Rd, two km on the outskirts of town, is open Monday to Friday from 8.30 am to 5 pm. The AA (☎ (06) 378 2222) is on the corner of Chapel and Jackson Sts.

Things to See

The large 32-hectare **Queen Elizabeth Park** in Park St off Queen St has sports grounds, an aviary, aquarium, deer park, small lake where boats are hired, children's playgrounds and a miniature railway where trains are run on weekends and holidays. Entry to the park is free.

The **Wairarapa Arts Centre** in Bruce St off Queen St has several galleries and the Stidolph Museum of Early Childhood, with a fascinating collection of antique items pertaining to childhood including dolls, toys, games, clothing and an array of teddy bears.

The centre is open Monday to Friday from 9 am to 4.30 pm and weekends from 1 to 4.30 pm; admission is free and donations are welcome.

Places to Stay

The *Mawley Park Motor Camp* (☎ (06) 378 6454) is in Oxford St on the bank of the Waipoua River. Tent/powered sites are $12/15, and cabins are $24 to $31 for two.

Masterton Backpackers (☎ (06) 377 2228) at 22 Victoria St in the centre of town is a homely, colonial-style hostel with four clean dorm rooms (it is now an Associate YHA). The cost of a bed in this friendly place is $14 per night. The *Victoria House Guesthouse* (☎ (06) 377 0186) offers B&B at $35/56 for singles/doubles.

Inexpensive hotels and motels include the *Station Hotel* (☎ (06) 378 9319) at 145 Perry St with singles/doubles at $30/45, the *Colonial Cottage Motel* (☎ (06) 377 0063) at 122 Chapel St with singles/doubles at $58/67 and the *Cornwall Park Motel* (☎ (06) 378 2939) at 119 Cornwall St with the same prices.

The *Masterton Motor Lodge* (☎ (06) 378 2585) is on SH2 in South Masterton. Singles, twins and doubles are $90 and it is $15 for each extra adult. The upmarket *Solway Park Travelodge* (☎ (06) 377 5129) on High St is $130 for a double or twin. Just about every sporting whim is satisfied here – there's even a jogging track.

The information centre has referrals for farmstays and homestays in the Wairarapa; singles/doubles are generally from $30/60.

Places to Eat

There are a number of good dining places in Masterton. *Cobb & Co* on High St South is open seven days, *Burridges* in Queen St North has its own in-house brewery and the *Slug & Lettuce* at 94 Queen St doesn't (fortunately!) serve the first item of its name.

If you have kids you will probably be dragged to *McDonald's* on the corner of Lincoln Rd and Chapel St. The cafe to laze in is *Bloomfields*, also on the corner of Lincoln Rd and Chapel St.

Getting There & Away

Tranzit Coachlines (☎ (06) 377 1227) operates two buses daily between Wellington and Masterton, but only on weekdays – on weekends take the train. The train service between the two cities is faster, cheaper and more frequent, with four trains daily on weekdays and two daily on weekends. An adult day excursion ticket is $15.

Tranzit Coachlines also operates buses between Masterton and Palmerston North, passing through Mt Bruce on the way.

CARTERTON, GREYTOWN & FEATHERSTON

There are a number of rural communities in the Wairarapa living up to the title of 'Capital Country Escapes'. Carterton has the Paua Shell Factory at 54 Kent St which is open daily. Here you can see shellfish in a live paua aquarium. Later, when the paua meat has been removed, the shells are turned into alternately tacky or tasteful souvenirs.

For cyclists who find themselves in this part of the world there is a backpackers in historic *Daleton Farm* (☎ (06) 379 8944) on the Main Rd in South Carterton. Beds in this atmospheric farmhouse are from $12 and 'sleepers' are invited to participate in farm activities. The *Buck Horn Bar & Grill* is the place to head for a meal.

Greytown is New Zealand's oldest inland Pakeha town and there are good examples of Victorian architecture along the main street. Historic walking tours (☎ (06) 304 9465) of the town are $5. The quaint Cobblestones Museum at 169 Main St is open daily from 9 am to 4.30 pm. To the east of Greytown is the scenic **Waiohine Gorge** where there is a vast choice of outdoor activities, conducted in an amphitheatre of native forests of rimu, kahikatea, beech and rata.

In Featherston, the Fell Engine Museum on the corner of Lyon and Fitzherbert Sts is well worth a look. It houses the only remaining Fell locomotive in the world and once ran on three rails to climb 265 metres up the Rimutaka Incline. The museum is open on weekends from 10 am to 4 pm, and on Sunday in winter from 1 to 4 pm. The information centre (☎ (06) 308 8051) is in the court house on Fitzherbert St.

MARTINBOROUGH

This town, south of Greytown, has become the vineyard centre of the Wairarapa. There are some 17 wineries close to the town and on any day a few are guaranteed to be open. Get a free copy of the *Winemakers of Martinborough*.

The information centre (☎ (06) 306 9043) in Kitchener St provides instructions on how to get to the spectacular **Ruakokopatuna Chasm** and glow-worm caves. The centre is open from 11 am to 2 pm, Monday to Thursday, and from 10 am to 4 pm, Friday to Sunday. A number of local tour operators include the wineries on their itineraries: Laura's Tours (☎ (06) 377 3534); South Wairarapa Tours (☎ (06) 308 9352); and McGill's Safaris (☎ (06) 378 6327).

There is plenty of homestay and farmstay accommodation in and around the town; enquire at the visitor centre; $70 for a double seems to be the norm, and this includes breakfast at a number of places. One really nice place is the *Oak House Homestay* (☎ (06) 306 9198) at 45 Kitchener St, housed in a 70-year-old Californian bungalow.

For those who wish to sample local wines with their meals there is the brasserie-style *Cafe Célèbre* in the square. The mains, from $16, are Asian influenced but there is a fair smattering of NZ cuisine and a selection of boutique beers for the 'vino-phobes'. If you need a picnic basket to take on your wine tour go to *Woodlands Cafe* at 48 Oxford St.

WAIRARAPA COAST

The Wairarapa coast from Palliser Bay to Castlepoint is one of the most remote and intriguing in the North Island and well worth exploring. The road to Cape Palliser is really scenic, hemmed in as it is by the sea and the Aorangi Mountains. It also offers grand views across to the South Island, a spectacular sight in winter when the far-off hills are cloaked in snow. On the way, the Wairarapa Wetlands and The Spit at Onoke are passed – both are good birdwatching sites.

The **Putangirua Pinnacles**, a 'badlands' formed by rain washing silt and sand away and exposing the underlying bedrock, stand like giant organ pipes. Well worth a visit, they're accessible by a track near the car park on the Cape Palliser road. It's a one-hour return walk to the pinnacles.

Not far to the south is the archetypal fishing village of **Ngawi**. The first thing that will impress you is the collection of bulldozers used to pull the fishing boats ashore. Continue on to the Cape Palliser **seal colony**, the North Island's largest breeding area. Whatever you do in your quest for that *National Geographic* shot, don't get between the seals and the sea.

There are 250 steps up to the Cape Palliser **lighthouse**, from where there are even more breathtaking views of the South Island. Occasionally you will see surfers relishing in the southerly and south-easterly swells. This place is replete in Maori mythology.

Castlepoint, with its reef and the lofty 162-metre-high Castle Rock, is an awesome place, with good protected swimming and plenty of walking tracks. There is a 45-minute return walk across the reef to the lighthouse, with over 70 species of fossil shells in the rock you pass over. Two other walks are the 1½-hour trip to a huge limestone cave and another two-hour track from Deliverance Cove to Castle Rock. Keep well away from the lower reef when heavy seas are running; many lives have been lost here.

MT BRUCE

Thirty km north of Masterton on SH2, the **Mt Bruce National Wildlife Centre** is a sanctuary for native NZ wildlife, mostly birds. Large aviaries and outdoor reserves feature some of the country's most rare and endangered species, which you probably won't get to see anywhere else, in addition to more common species and a nocturnal house with kiwis (you may not see one), tuataras and other endangered reptiles. There are breeding programmes of endangered species here. Each species is given as natural a habitat as possible, so you have to look closely to find the birds.

The centre is open every day from 9 am to 4.30 pm; admission is $6 (children $1.50). The visitor facilities have been upgraded so there is better food in the cafe and a good audiovisual is screened. The last admissions to the centre are at 4 pm; get there much earlier as there's a lot to see.

The **Mt Bruce Pioneer Museum** on SH2, 10 km south of the National Wildlife Centre, is the largest private museum in the Wairarapa region, with over 3000 items including working displays of gramophones, milking machines, stationary engines and waterwheels, plus farming equipment and other interesting relics of NZ's pioneering days. It is open every day from 9 am to 4.30 pm; admission is $2.50 (children 50 cents).

Both the Mt Bruce Pioneer Museum and the National Wildlife Centre are right on SH2. Any bus going between Masterton and Palmerston North can drop you at the gates. It's also easy to hitchhike.

FOREST PARKS

There are plenty of good opportunities for tramping in the Wairarapa, especially in the Tararua, Rimutaka and Haurangi (Aorangi) forest parks. There are some fine coastal walks too. Maps and information are available from the DOC offices in Wellington and Masterton.

A favourite spot for tramping in the Wairarapa is at **Holdsworth**, the principal eastern entrance to the Tararua Forest Park, where there is some beautiful virgin forest with pleasant streams running through. The park entrance has swimming, picnic and camping areas, a good hut and a number of fine walks including short, easy family walks, excellent one or two-day walks, and longer, more challenging treks for experienced trampers.

A resident conservation officer (☎ (06) 377 0022) has maps and information on tramping in the area, and an intentions book where you can sign in. Ask there about current weather and track conditions before you set off, and come prepared for all types of weather – the Tararuas Forest Park has a notoriously changeable climate. The turn-off to Holdsworth is on SH2, 35 km south of Masterton; from there it's 15 km to the park entrance.

Closer to Wellington, the Rimutaka Incline walk is a five to seven-hour walk each way along a historic old railway line which operated trains between Wellington and the Wairarapa between 1878 and 1955. The walk begins from SH2 (look for the signpost) nine km north of Upper Hutt. A little further north, 16 km north of Upper Hutt on SH2, the Kaitoke Regional Park is good for swimming, rafting, camping, picnicking and a number of good walks ranging from 20 minutes to six hours.

The *Black Stump YHA Hostel* (☎ 526 4626) is at Kaitoke, 42 km north of Wellington at the top of the Hutt Valley, in Marchant Rd just off SH2. The hostel, in hill country at the edge of the Tararua Forest Park, is 1.5 km from bushwalking tracks, swimming holes, horse and kayak hire, and 45 minutes drive from Wellington – or take the Tranzit bus to Masterton. The nightly cost is $9 in this rather basic hostel.

SOUTH ISLAND

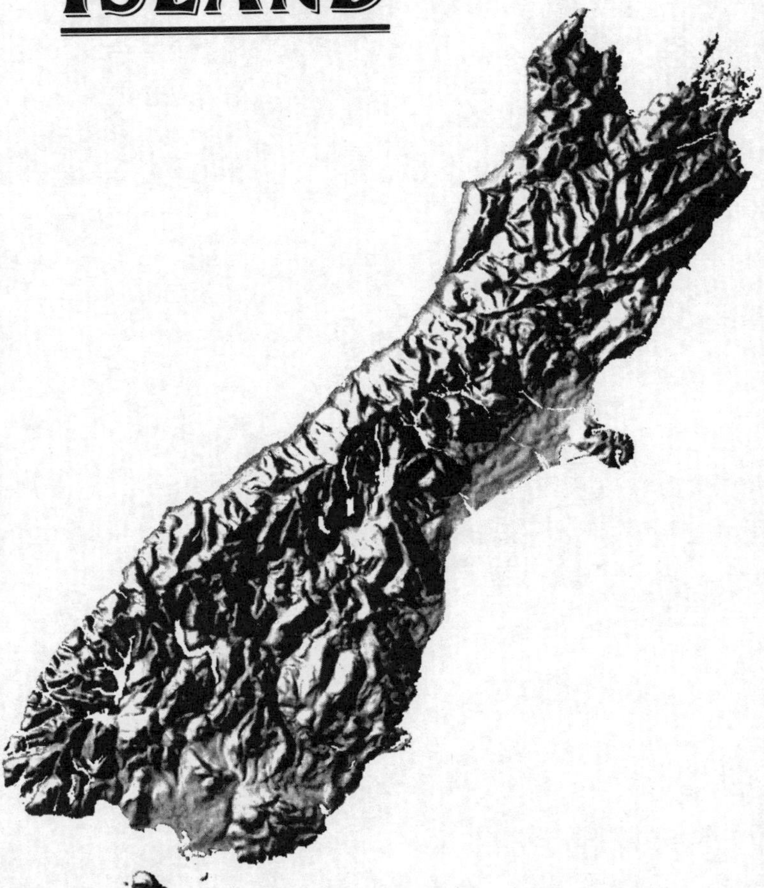

Marlborough & Nelson

To some people, crossing Cook Strait from Wellington to Picton in the South Island is like entering a new country. Many visitors strike out further afield immediately after crossing, but there is much that is of interest in this area, in particular the inlets and bays of Marlborough Sounds.

To the west is the Nelson region with great tramping possibilities in national parks. Nelson is a great city to relax in, as are the towns of Motueka and Takaka. If you are lucky and make it over to the far west then you can tour up to Farewell Spit.

HIGHLIGHTS

- The waterways of the Marlborough Sounds – a haven for boating, walking and relaxing
- The remote walks and rugged scenery of Kahurangi National Park – the Heaphy, Wangapeka and Leslie-Karamea tracks
- Kaikoura – one of the best ecotourism destinations anywhere – for whale-watching, dolphin and seal swimming
- The ferry journey from Wellington to Picton – across Cook Strait and through the Tory Channel
- Nelson – a town ideally suited to relaxing and holidaying
- The Abel Tasman Coastal Track – undoubtedly the most popular in the country and deservedly so
- The trip to the gannet colony and the lighthouse at the end of Farewell Spit
- Walking, boating or fishing in the Nelson Lakes National Park

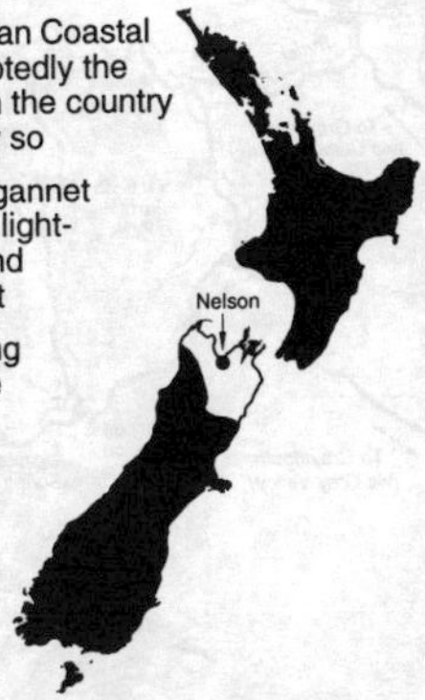

Marlborough Province

The first sight of the South Island for many visitors, especially those on the ferry, are the convoluted waterways of the Marlborough Sounds. There is plenty of opportunity to head back out from Picton to the many hideaways in the Sounds, where you can set up a base and go walking, fishing, sailing and kayaking. To the south of Picton is the sedate city of Blenheim and many nearby vineyards. Further south is the marine wildlife centre of Kaikoura, and inland there are mountainous regions with good walking possibilities.

History

The first European to come across the Marlborough district was Abel Tasman, who spent five days sheltering on the eastern coast of D'Urville Island, in 1642. It was to be over 100 years before the next Pakeha, James Cook, turned up in January 1770, remaining there for 23 days. Between 1770 and 1777 Cook made four visits to the stretch of water he named Queen Charlotte's (now Charlotte) Sound. Near the entrance of Ship Cove there's a monument that commemorates the explorer's visits. Because Cook spent so much time there he was able to make detailed reports of the area, so that it became the best known haven in the southern hemisphere. In 1827 the French navigator Jules Dumont d'Urville discovered the narrow strait now known as French Pass, and his officers named the island just north of there in his honour.

In the same year a whaling station was set up at Te Awaiti in Tory Channel, which brought about the first permanent European settlement in the district. In June 1840 Governor Hobson's envoy, Major Bunbury, arrived on

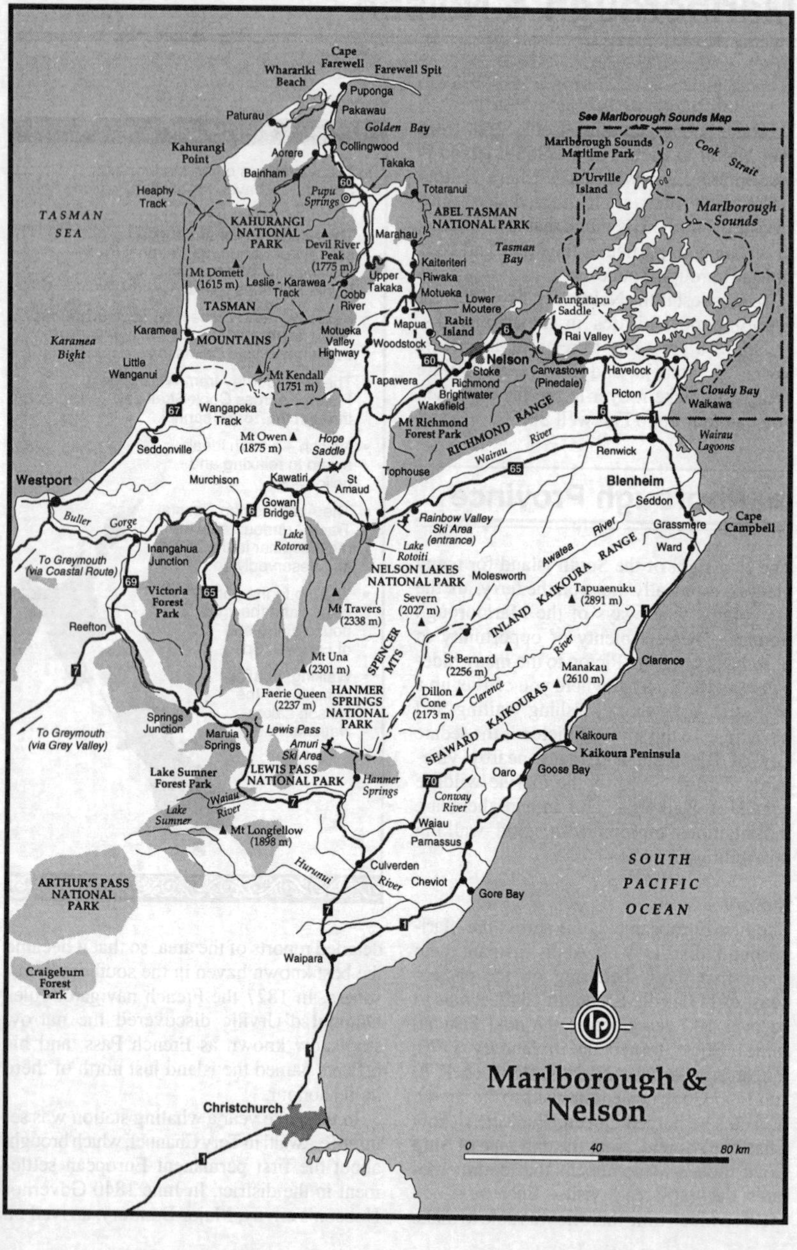

Marlborough & Nelson
Cape Farewell
Farewell Spit
Wharariki Beach
Puponga
Pakawau
Paturau
Golden Bay
Collingwood
Aorere
Kahurangi Point
Bainham
Takaka
Pupu Springs
Totaranui
Heaphy Track
TASMAN SEA
KAHURANGI NATIONAL PARK
Devil River Peak (1775 m)
ABEL TASMAN NATIONAL PARK
Marahau
Tasman Bay
Kaiteriteri
Mt Domett (1615 m)
Upper Takaka
Riwaka
Leslie - Karawea Track
Cobb River
Motueka
Lower Moutere
TASMAN MOUNTAINS
Mapua
Rabit Island
Karamea
Motueka Valley Highway
Woodstock
Karamea Bight
Little Wanganui
Mt Kendall (1751 m)
Tapawera
Nelson
Stoke
Richmond
Brightwater
Wakefield
Wangapeka Track
Mt Owen (1875 m)
Hope Saddle
Mt Richmond Forest Park
Seddonville
Westport
Murchison
Kawatiri
St Arnaud
Tophouse
Gowan Bridge
Buller Gorge
Rainbow Valley Ski Area (entrance)
Lake Rotoroa
Lake Rotoiti
Inangahua Junction
To Greymouth (via Coastal Route)
Victoria Forest Park
NELSON LAKES NATIONAL PARK
Mt Travers (2338 m)
Reefton
SPENCER MTS
Mt Una (2301 m)
Faerie Queen (2237 m)
HANMER SPRINGS NATIONAL PARK
Springs Junction
To Greymouth (via Grey Valley)
Maruia Springs
Lewis Pass
Amuri Ski Area
LEWIS PASS NATIONAL PARK
Hanmer Springs
Lake Sumner Forest Park
Waiau River
Lake Sumner
Mt Longfellow (1898 m)
ARTHUR'S PASS NATIONAL PARK
Culverden
Hurunui River
Craigeburn Forest Park
Waipara
Christchurch
See Marlborough Sounds Map
Marlborough Sounds Maritime Park
Cook Strait
D'Urville Island
Marlborough Sounds
Maungatapu Saddle
Rai Valley
Canvastown (Pinedale)
Havelock
Picton
Cloudy Bay
Waikawa
RICHMOND RANGE
Wairau River
Renwick
Wairau Lagoons
Blenheim
Seddon
Cape Campbell
Grassmere
Awatea River
Ward
Molesworth
INLAND KAIKOURA RANGE
Severn (2027 m)
Tapuaenuku (2891 m)
St Bernard (2256 m)
Clarence River
Clarence
Manakau (2610 m)
Dillon Cone (2173 m)
SEAWARD KAIKOURAS
Kaikoura
Kaikoura Peninsula
Goose Bay
Oaro
Conway River
Waiau
Parnassus
Cheviot
Gore Bay
SOUTH PACIFIC OCEAN
0
40
80 km

the HMS *Herald* on the hunt for Maori signatures to the Treaty of Waitangi. On 17 June Bunbury proclaimed the British Queen's sovereignty over the South Island at Horahora Kakahu Island. Towards the end of that year a Wesleyan mission was set up at Ngakuta Bay in the north-western corner of the port.

In spite of this, the Marlborough area was not the site of an organised company settlement; it was more an overflow of the Nelson colony. Around 1840 the opportunistic and unscrupulous New Zealand Company tried to settle part of the Wairau Plain after buying the alleged rights from the widow of a trader, John Blenkinsopp. He had claimed to have bought the land from the Maoris for one 16-pound cannon, and had obtained a dubious deed signed by Maori chiefs who couldn't read English. The cannon is now on display in Blenheim.

By 1843 the pressure for land from the Nelson settlers was so great that it led to conflict with the Maoris, who denied all knowledge that any part of Wairau was sold. Two Maori chiefs, Te Rauparaha and Te Rangihaeata, arrived from Kapiti to resist survey operations. The Pakehas sent out a hurriedly co-opted armed party led by Arthur Wakefield and Police Magistrate Thompson to arrest the chiefs. The party was met peacefully by the Maoris at Tuamarina, but the Pakehas precipitated a brief skirmish during which Te Rangihaeata's wife was shot. The Pakehas were then forced to surrender and Rangihaeata, mad with rage, demanded vengeance. Twenty-two of the party, including Wakefield and Thompson, were clubbed to death or shot; the rest escaped through the scrub and over the hills. The whole event came to be known as the Wairau Massacre.

Te Rauparaha was a formidable Ngati Toa chief who was, indirectly, a major reason for the British government taking control of New Zealand. He cultivated the captains and crews of visiting whaling ships (they nicknamed him the 'old sarpint') and, with muskets and other weapons he acquired, set out on the wholesale and horrific slaughter of other South Island tribes. In his most gruesome raid he was aided by a Pakeha trader, who transported his warriors and decoyed the opposing chiefs on board, where they were set upon by Te Rauparaha's men. The ensuing slaughter virtually wiped out the local tribe. When news of this event and the captain's part in it reached Sydney, the British Government finally decided to bring some law and order to New Zealand and to their unruly citizens operating there. (For a detailed account of Te Rauparaha's life see the biography, *Te Rauparaha: A New Perspective*, by Patricia Burns.)

In March 1847 Wairau was finally bought and added to the Nelson territory. It was not long before the place was deluged by people from Nelson and elsewhere. However, when the Wairau settlers realised that revenue from land sales in their area was being used to develop the Nelson district they petitioned for independence. The appeal was successful and the colonial government called the new region Marlborough and approved one of the two settlements, Waitohi (now Picton) as the capital. At the same time, the other settlement known as 'The Beaver' was renamed Blenheim. After a period of intense rivalry between the two towns, including legal action, the capital was transferred peacefully to Blenheim in 1865.

MARLBOROUGH SOUNDS

The convoluted waters of the Marlborough Sounds have many bays, islands, coves and waterways, formed by the sea invading its deep valleys after the ice ages. Parts of the sounds are now included in the Marlborough Sounds Maritime Park. The park is actually many small reserves separated by private land. There is a small paperback, *Marlborough Sounds Maritime Park*, which is a good introduction to the area ($10.65). To get an idea of how convoluted the sounds are, Pelorus Sound is 42 km long but has 379 km of shoreline!

Information

The best way to get around the sounds is still by boat, although the road system has been extended. Permits are required for hunting or

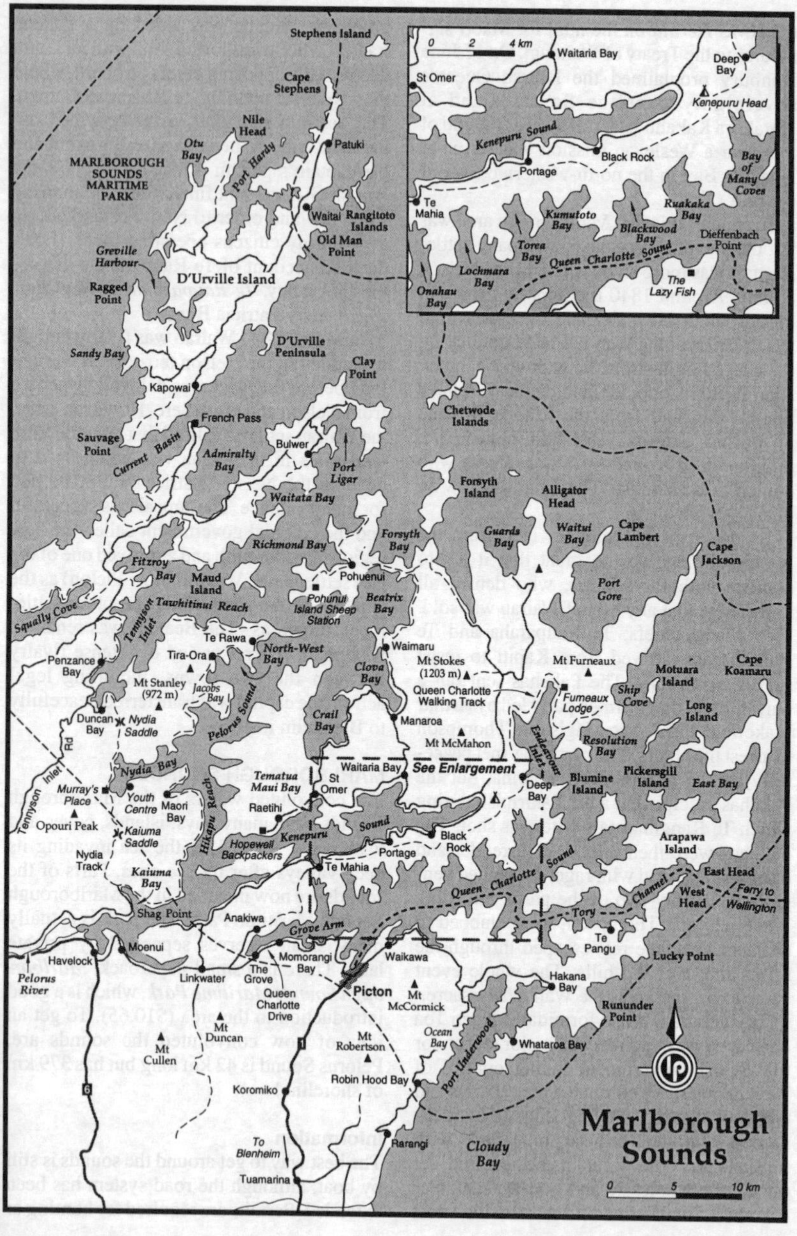
Marlborough Sounds
0 5 10 km
0 2 4 km
Waitaria Bay
Deep Bay
St Omer
Kenepuru Head
Kenepuru Sound
Black Rock
Portage
Bay of Many Coves
Te Mahia
Kumutoto Bay
Blackwood Bay
Ruakaka Bay
Dieffenbach Point
Torea Bay
Queen Charlotte Sound
Lochmara Bay
The Lazy Fish
Onahau Bay
Stephens Island
Cape Stephens
Nile Head
Otu Bay
Port Hardy
Patuki
MARLBOROUGH SOUNDS MARITIME PARK
Waitai
Rangitoto Islands
Old Man Point
Greville Harbour
Ragged Point
D'Urville Island
D'Urville Peninsula
Sandy Bay
Kapowai
Clay Point
French Pass
Chetwode Islands
Sauvage Point
Current Basin
Admiralty Bay
Bulwer
Port Ligar
Waitata Bay
Forsyth Island
Alligator Head
Guards Bay
Waitui Bay
Cape Lambert
Richmond Bay
Forsyth Bay
Cape Jackson
Fitzroy Bay
Maud Island
Pohuenui
Tawhitinui Reach
Pohuenui Island Sheep Station
Beatrix Bay
Port Gore
Squally Cove
Tennyson Inlet
Te Rawa
North-West Bay
Waimaru
Penzance Bay
Tira-Ora
Clova Bay
Mt Stokes (1203 m)
Mt Furneaux
Motuara Island
Cape Koamaru
Mt Stanley (972 m)
Jacobs Bay
Queen Charlotte Walking Track
Ship Cove
Furneaux Lodge
Long Island
Duncan Bay
Nydia Saddle
Pelorus Sound
Crail Bay
Manaroa
Mt McMahon
Endeavour Inlet
Resolution Bay
Rd
Nydia Bay
See Enlargement
Waitaria Bay
Deep Bay
Blumine Island
Pickersgill Island
East Bay
Tennyson Inlet
Murray's Place
Youth Centre
Maori Bay
Hikapu Reach
Tematua Maui Bay
St Omer
Opouri Peak
Kaiuma Saddle
Raetihi
Kenepuru
Sound
Black Rock
Arapawa Island
Nydia Track
Hopewell Backpackers
Portage
Te Mahia
Kaiuma Bay
Queen Charlotte Sound
East Head
Shag Point
Anakiwa
West Head
Ferry to Wellington
Tory Channel
Grove Arm
Havelock
Moenui
Te Pangu
Lucky Point
Pelorus River
Linkwater
The Grove
Momorangi Bay
Waikawa
Picton
Hakana Bay
Queen Charlotte Drive
Mt McCormick
Runnder Point
Mt Cullen
Mt Duncan
Ocean Bay
Mt Robertson
Port Underwood
Whataroa Bay
6
1
Robin Hood Bay
Koromiko
To Blenheim
Rarangi
Cloudy Bay
Tuamarina

camping and there's plenty of good swimming, tramping and fishing. Information on the park is available in Picton from the visitor centre and DOC.

Activities

Queen Charlotte Walkway Those put off by the hordes doing the Abel Tasman Track may wish to try this alternative. It is a 58-km-long track that connects historic Ship Cove with Anakiwa. You pass through privately owned land and DOC reserves. The coastal forest is lush, and from the ridges you can look down on either side to Queen Charlotte and Kenepuru sounds.

You can arrange to complete the walk in sections (using local boat services – see Getting There & Away) or do the whole three to four-day journey. There are many camp sites for those tenting it, as well as a number of hostels and hotels. Remember that you are here only through the cooperation of local landowners, so respect their property and carry out what you carry in.

The track is well defined and suitable for people of all ages and average fitness. Between Kenepuru Saddle and Portage Saddle you'll find the going toughest. Carry water between Kenepuru and Te Mahia saddles; this is available at the Bay of Many Coves Saddle camping ground. For more information, get a copy of the pamphlet *The Queen Charlotte Track* from DOC in Picton. It is possible to do a leg of the trip by sea kayak; contact Marlborough Sounds Adventure Company (☎ 573 6078) for advice. Estimated distances and walking times are:

	Distance	*Time*
Anakiwa-Te Mahia	9 km	4 hr
Te Mahia-Portage	8 km	4 hr
Portage-Bay of Many Coves Saddle	10 km	6 hr
Bay of Many Coves-Kenepuru Saddle	5 km	3 hr
Kenepuru Saddle-Endeavour Inlet	8 km	4 hr
Endeavour Inlet-Resolution Bay	6 km	3 hr
Resolution Bay-Ship Cove	3 km	2 hr

Getting There & Away If you are planning to walk the whole track, Cougar Line (☎ 573 7925), 10 London Quay, Picton, operate a drop-off service at Ship Cove, the preferred starting end for the walk. The approximate cost is $34 each. It leaves at 8.45 am and arrives at the drop-off point at about 10 am. At the Anakiwa end Barry's Buses (☎ 577 2100) can pick you up from Monday to Friday, at approximately 4.30 pm, for the return trip to Picton; subject to confirmation.

Sea Kayaking The Marlborough Sounds Adventure Company (☎ 573 6078), Picton, organises sea-kayak trips and bush walks around the sounds. The kayak trips range from one ($60) to four days ($450). Longer expeditions can be arranged but the complexity depends on paddlers' experience. Prices include the kayak, guide, camping equipment and all meals. They also hire kayaks for solo trips at a daily cost of $35 for a single kayak (minimum of two days) or $65 for a double kayak. For $70 they will drive you and your kayaks to Tennyson Inlet.

Two other operators provide sea kayaking trips out of Picton. They are Sea Kayaking & Adventure Tours (☎ 574 2765) and Waikawa Sea Kayaks (☎ 573 6800).

Places to Stay

There are plenty of places to stay on the sounds, although some are accessible only by boat or floatplane. Prices are usually fairly reasonable, and practically all offer free use of dinghies and other facilities. The fact they are only accessible by boat means they're often in some beautiful settings.

Camping Following is a list of DOC camping grounds in the area:

- Bay of Many Coves Saddle, Queen Charlotte Walkway
- Camp Bay, Endeavour Inlet, Queen Charlotte Sound
- Cowshed Bay, Portage, Kenepuru Sound
- Elaine Bay, Tennyson Inlet
- French Pass, Roadend of Croiselles/French Pass Rd, Marlborough Sounds
- Harvey Bay, Tennyson Inlet
- Jacobs Bay, Dillon Bell Point, Pelorus Sound

- Kenepuru Head, head of Kenepuru Sound
- Kumutoto Bay, Queen Charlotte Sound
- Momorangi, Momorangi Bay, Queen Charlotte Drive (FS)
- Nikau Cove, Picnic Bay, Kenepuru Sound
- Pelorus Bridge, adjacent SH6, NW of Havelock (FS)
- Picnic Bay, Kenepuru Sound
- Ratamira Bay, near Ruakaka Bay, Queen Charlotte Sound
- Titirangi Farm Park, outer Marlborough Sounds
- Waimaru, Waimaru Bay, Pelorus Sound
- Whatamonga Bay, Port Underwood Rd, Queen Charlotte Sound

FS = Fully serviced

Hostels Various places around the sounds offer cheap backpacker accommodation and do their bookings through The Villa in Picton. They include *Resolution Bay Camp & Cabins* (☎ 579 9411) in Resolution Bay and *Furneaux Lodge* (☎ 579 8259) on the Endeavour Inlet section of the Queen Charlotte Sound Track, both charging just $12.50 a night. On Kenepuru Sound there is *Mary's Holiday Cottage* (☎ 573 4376) at Waitaria Bay, 95 km from Picton via Linkwater, where it costs $14 per person. Check with the YHA in Havelock before going out there.

The *Lazy Fish Hostel* (☎ 579 9049) on Queen Charlotte Sound, 12 km from Picton, is accessible only by boat. The cost in this renovated homestead-turned-hostel is $16 per person in dorms, and doubles or twins are $36. This includes free use of windsurfer, dinghy, canoe, fishing gear, snorkels, volleyball, BBQ and so on. The front deck is just seven metres from the secluded beach. In summer lots of boats will take you out there. Enjoy the spa pool – it's out on the beach underneath the palm trees. It is popular so book ahead before you catch a boat out there.

Hopewell (☎ 573 4341) is the place to choose if you really want to stay in a remote part of Kenepuru Sound. Doubles and twins are $32, and the price lets you have use of a full range of equipment such as rowing boats, fishing lines and table tennis. Access by road is possible but time consuming as the road is often under repair and extremely winding. The best way to get there is by water taxi from Portage or by floatplane from Picton; with a group of four the plane should work out reasonable and it would be an interesting way of arriving.

Hotels & Lodges The well-known *Portage Hotel* (☎ 573 4309) is on Kenepuru Sound. Double rooms cost $89 per night but there is also bunkroom accommodation for $22 per person, which still allows you to use all the resort's facilities. The hotel has sail boats, windsurfers, fishing, spa, gym and tennis courts. It can easily be reached by road, boat or floatplane from Picton.

The *Bulwer Guesthouse* (☎ 576 5285) on Waihinau Bay in Pelorus Sound has one self-contained flat for $18 per person, or guesthouse beds including all meals for $60. Road access (70 km) is via the Rai Valley.

Other accommodation options at Kenepuru Sound include the *Raetihi Lodge* (☎ 573 4300), costing $75 per night including all meals; they have reduced rates for backpackers. *St Omer House* (☎ 573 4086) has cottage accommodation from $18 to $22 per person, or chalets for $70 per person including all meals. There's road access to these places.

The *Furneaux Lodge* (☎ 579 8259) is a century-old place set amidst lovely gardens in Endeavour Inlet; chalets for two are $60 in winter ($70 in summer). There is some backpacker accommodation available. The *Te Mahia Resort* (☎ 573 4089) is on the Queen Charlotte Walkway. Self-contained units cost $30 to $35, caravan and camp sites are $15 for two and there are backpackers' beds available. It is accessible by road, water taxi, or floatplane (30 minutes from Porirua in the North Island). *Craglee Lodge* (☎ 579 9223) in the Bay of Many Coves is recommended; a floatplane to Craglee is $90.

At the *Te Pangu Bay Lodge* (☎ 579 9755) on Te Pangu Bay, Tory Channel, self-contained units for two to seven people cost $25 per person (minimum unit charge $40). The *Tira-Ora Lodge* (☎ 579 8253) on Northwest Bay, Pelorus Sound, is more expensive;

rooms there cost $112.50 per night for one or two people. Both lodges can only be reached by boat or floatplane.

One place recommended by readers is the *Pohuenui Island Sheep Station* (☎ 597 8161), Pohuenui, via Havelock. Accommodation is budget priced at $12.50, with the added bonus that you are staying on a working sheep station.

Resorts & Cabins There are cabins at *Gem Resort* (☎ 579 9771) at the Bay of Many Coves. Cabins for two cost between $60 and $65; there's no road access. The *Te Rawa Boatel* (☎ 579 8285), 27 km by launch from Havelock, is a bit cheaper, with rooms at $45 for two people. *Punga Cove Tourist Resort* (☎ 579 8561) on Endeavour Inlet, Queen Charlotte Sound, is more expensive; double rooms cost between $68 and $115 per night; there is a licensed restaurant here. The *Endeavour Resort* (☎ 579 8381), also set in historic Endeavour Inlet, has chalets and units from $70 to $150 for two per night. You can get to it with the Cougar Line.

Getting There & Away

The 'mail run' boat and Cougar Line runs to the Lazy Fish Hostel on Queen Charlotte Sound all year round on Tuesday and Friday, and costs about $13. A water taxi costs about the same if you have a group of four or five to split the fare; prices to accommodation in the area vary. There are two floatplane choices – Float Air Picton (☎ 573 6433) and Soundsair (☎ (04) 388 2594) – which service the many hotels, lodges and guesthouses.

See the Picton and Havelock sections for transport information around the Sounds.

PICTON

The ferry from the North Island comes into Picton, a pretty little port at the head of Queen Charlotte Sound. Picton, originally called Waitohi, is a small borough. It's a hive of activity when the ferry is in and during the peak of summer, but rather slow and sleepy any other time.

Information

The Picton Visitor Information Centre (☎ 573 7477; fax 573 8362) is located with the DOC, about 200 metres from the ferry terminal. They have good maps, information on boats and walking in the sounds area, and do transport and accommodation bookings. It is open daily from 8.30 am to 6.30 pm in winter and until 8 pm in summer. The Railway Station (☎ 573 8857) in the Picton railway station between the ferry terminal and the town centre also has lots of information. The DOC office (☎ 573 7582) is open from 8.30 am to 4.30 pm Monday to Friday. You can get information here on the Sounds Maritime Park, Mt Richmond Forest Park with its many walking tracks and huts, and the greater district.

The ferry terminal in Picton has a convenience that you will not come across often in NZ – a laundrette – so if you've got a pile of dirty clothes in your backpack, take them along. The Marlin Motel (☎ 573 6784) at 33 Devon St is the AA agent.

The Edwin Fox

Between the museum and the ferry wharf is the battered, but still floating, hull of the old East Indiaman *Edwin Fox*, believed to be the ninth oldest ship in the world. Built of teak in the Bengal region of India, the 157-foot (48-metre), 760-ton vessel was launched in 1853 and in its long and varied career carried convicts to Perth, troops to the Crimean War and immigrants to NZ.

The *Edwin Fox* is slowly being restored. The project will take at least 10 years to complete, and may cost several million dollars – but that should keep the boat in the water for another 200 years! The metal-sheathed hull is open to visitors from 8.45 am to 5 pm every day (closing at 4.30 pm in winter) and admission is $4 (children $1).

Other Attractions

The excellent little **museum** is on the foreshore, right below London Quay. The old building is being rebuilt with fancier quarters. There are a number of interesting

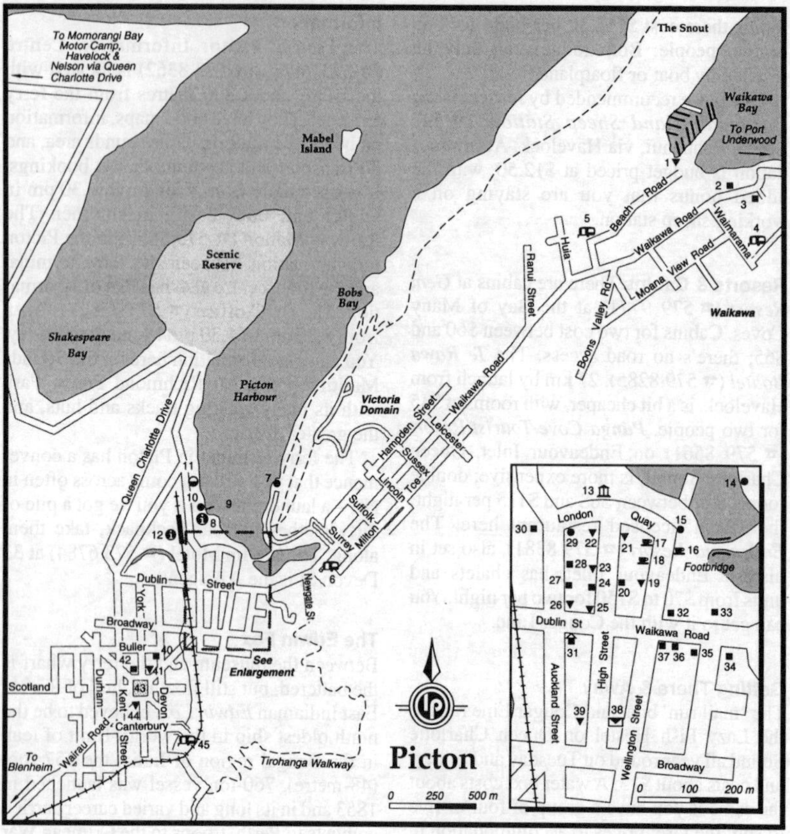

whaling exhibits, including a harpoon gun, and numerous other unusual items such as an old Dursley Pederson bicycle built around 1890. The museum is open from 10 am to 4 pm daily; admission is $3 (children 50c).

On the eastern side of Shakespeare Bay, across the inlet from the town centre via the footbridge, is the scow ***Echo***, now used as the clubrooms of the Marlborough Cruising Club. Built on the Wairau River in 1905, the *Echo* traded between Blenheim and Wellington, shipping around 14,000 tons of freight a year, and was only retired in 1965 after the railway ferries were introduced.

Near Koromiko, six km south of Picton, is an alpaca park – complete with picnic area and children's playground. Tuamarina, 13 km further on, is historically interesting as the site of the **Wairau Massacre**. The tree near where the skirmish started still stands on the riverbank. In the cemetery, just above the road, is a Pakeha monument designed by Felix Wakefield, youngest brother of Arthur Wakefield, who was killed in the affray.

Walks

There are many scenic walks around Picton, as well as longer tramps. The information

PLACES TO STAY

2 Bay Vista Motel
3 Bayview Backpackers
4 Waikawa Bay Holiday Park
5 Parklands Caravan Park
6 Blue Anchor Holiday Park
20 Americano Motor Inn & Restaurant
21 London Quay Dairy & Tearooms, Carousel & Federal Hotel
22 Terminus Hotel
24 Tourist Court Motel
27 Deluxe Backpackers
28 The Villa
30 Baden's Picton Lodge
31 Wedgewood House Youth Hostel
33 Picton Beachcomber Inn
34 Harbour View Motel
35 Marineland Private Hotel
36 Admiral's Lodge
37 The Gables
40 Marlin Motel
42 Picton Backpackers
45 Alexander's Motor Park

PLACES TO EAT

1 Neptune's
16 Kiwi Takeaways & Book Exchange
17 Seaspray Cafe & Oxleys Hotel
18 Village Cafe
19 5th Bank, Carousel & Federal Hotel
23 Ship Cove, Le Cafe, Marlborough Terranean
25 Holty's
26 Picton Bakery
32 Ancient Mariner
39 Lord Thompson
41 Wiseway Super 7
44 Crow's Nest Restaurant

OTHER

7 Marlborough Cruising Club
8 Visitor Information Centre, DOC
9 *Edwin Fox* & Boat Ramp
10 Vehicle Hire Places
11 Cook Strait Ferry Terminal & Laundrette
12 Railway Station, Booking Office, Stoker's Bar & Restaurant & Toot 'n' Whistle
13 Museum
14 *Echo*
15 Marlborough Sounds Adventure Company, Cougar Line & Marlborough Sounds Yacht Charter
29 Diver's World
38 Mariners Mall & Post Office
43 Nelson Square

centre has a map showing several good walks in and near town, as well as others further afield in the sounds and the Maritime Park. The DOC also has plenty of maps and leaflets on walks in the area.

An easy one-km track runs along the eastern side of Picton Harbour to Bob's Bay, where there's a BBQ area in a sheltered cove. Now added on to this is the **Snout Walkway**: carry on along the Bob's Bay path and follow it along the ridge. Allow three hours for the walk. There are great views of the length of Queen Charlotte Sound.

There's also the **Tirohanga Walkway**, beginning in Newgate St behind the hospital, which takes about 45 minutes each way and features panoramic views of Picton and the sounds.

Tours

The main access around Queen Charlotte Sound is by water, which means there are innumerable cruises and fishing trips.

There are a number of round-the-bay cruises. Beachcomber Fun Cruises (☎ 573 6175) has popular cruises on the MV *Beachcomber*, including an all-day 'mail run' cruise around the sounds on Monday, Tuesday, Thursday and Friday for $45, and two-hour scenic cruises for $27. A full-day trip to the Portage Hotel on Kenepuru Sound is another possibility ($30). Children travel for half price on all the *Beachcomber* tours.

On land, Sounds Connection (☎ 573 8843), the Corgi Bus Company (☎ 573 7125) and Fuller's (☎ 573 8159) are three local (Picton) tour operators; winery visits are a speciality. Deluxe Coach-lines (☎ 578 5467) operate all-day wine-trail tours from Blenheim but they also pick-up in Picton.

Alternatively, you can get up above it all on a floatplane. Float Air Picton (☎ 573 6433), between the *Edwin Fox* and the ferry terminal, does scenic flights and normal transport trips to any point around the sounds and also to Lake Rotoiti and Wellington.

The Picton Underwater Centre at 41 Wellington St hires diving equipment for underwater explorations. Diver's World (☎ 573 7323), corner of London Quay and Auckland St, also hires equipment and organises charters.

Places to Stay

Camping & Cabins The *Blue Anchor Holiday Park* (☎ 573 7212), on Waikawa Rd about 500 metres from the town centre, has powered sites at $18, various cabins for around $28 to $38, and tourist flats at $45; prices are for two. The ageing *Alexander's Motor Park* (☎ 573 6378) is a km out on Canterbury St and has sites at $15 for two, plus a variety of cabins and on-site caravans at $24 to $32 for two.

The *Parklands Caravan Park* (☎ 573 6343) is on Beach Rd at Waikawa Bay, three km from town. Other possibilities include *Waikawa Bay Holiday Park* (☎ 573 7434) and *Momorangi Bay Motor Camp* (☎ 573 7865), on Queen Charlotte Drive, 13 km from Picton. At Momorangi Bay there are dinghies for hire.

Hostels *The Villa* (☎ 573 6598) at 34 Auckland St has dorm beds for $15 per person, or doubles or twins for $36. It's a well-equipped hostel which also serves as a centre for information and bookings for backpackers activities around Marlborough Sounds. They provide a cheap and hearty soup for their guests, and often cook up local seafood.

Around the corner is *Wedgwood House* (☎ 573 7797), an Associate YHA Hostel at 10 Dublin St. It's a converted guesthouse with two, four or six beds to a room; the cost is $14 per person, or $32 for twin rooms. One drawback is its cramped kitchen. It is open until 11 pm at night for passengers from the late ferry.

The closest accommodation to the ferry terminal is *Baden's Picton Lodge* (☎ 573 7788) at 3 Auckland St. Dorms/share rooms are $14.50/15.50 per person, and twins and doubles are $34. The facilities in this large place are good and they even have a smokers' terrace with harbour views. It is 200 metres from the ferry (important if you are lugging a pack) and next to the railway station.

Another backpackers is the *Flying Kiwi Hostel* (☎ 573 8126), at 2 Canterbury St, about five minutes walk south of town; beds here are $13.50 per person. They rent equipment for the Queen Charlotte Walkway.

On Waikawa Bay there is *Bayview Backpackers*, at 318 Waikawa Rd (☎ 573 7668). As it is four km from Picton town centre it offers free pick-up and drop-off services. Doubles and twins are $32, triples are $45 for three and the share rooms are from $13.50 per person. There are heaters in all the rooms, two kitchens, and two lounges. There is a range of water sports equipment and bicycles free for guests.

There is a little place on 42 Auckland St next to The Villa which is good for overflow. The *Deluxe Backpackers* (☎ 573 6536) lacks a backpacker atmosphere; the cost of a dorm bed is $15 per person. *Picton Backpackers* (☎ 573 8399) on Nelson Square has ramshackle dorm beds for $13.50 per person, a free breakfast included (and a cluster of ramshackle semi-permanent guests).

Guesthouses, B&Bs & Hotels Picton has a number of guesthouses and private hotels, including the *Marineland Guesthouse* (☎ 573 6429) at 28 Waikawa Rd which has a 'shark-free swimming pool'. Singles/doubles are $38/55 with breakfast or there are self-contained units at $66 for two – the staff here are friendly and helpful. There are minimum rates in the peak season. Centrally located is the *Terminus Hotel* (☎ 573 6452) at 1 High St, with singles/ doubles for $36/57.

The *Admiral's Lodge* (☎ 573 6590) at 22 Waikawa Rd has single/double B&B rooms for $45/72, and low-season discounts. Next door at 20 Waikawa Rd is *The Gables* (☎ 573 6772), a very comfortable B&B where they serve excellent breakfasts (eg salmon and fresh fruits); a single is $50, doubles or twins are from $75 to $85.

Motels Picton also has plenty of motels, most priced from $65 for two. The *Tourist Court Motel* (☎ 573 6331), in the centre of town at 45 High St, is a simple place with studio units from around $52 for two, or two-bedroom units for $65; low-season discounts might be available. The *Bay Vista Motel* (☎ 573 6733), four km out at Waikawa Bay, is also good value at $69 to $72 for two. Highly recommended is the *Harbour View*

Motel (☎ 573 6259) at 30 Waikawa Rd; the cost for two varies from $67 to $72 but there are also off-season reductions. As the name suggests, you get great views from here.

The *Americano Motor Inn* (☎ 573 6398) at 32 High St has singles/doubles at $67/77.50; it is a classy place with spa, automatic laundry, a restaurant and bar.

Places to Eat

Snacks & Fast Food Most of the food in Picton would be better than the indigestible cardboard you get tossed at you on the ferry. There are plenty of takeaways and fast-food places around the town centre. The *Village Cafe* is on Wellington St; the sign announces 'A Good Eating Place' but a number of diners have suggested otherwise. There are several cafes along the waterfront including the attractive little *Seaspray Cafe*, the *London Quay Dairy & Tea Rooms* on the corner of London Quay and High St, the *Carousel* takeaway next door, and the ever popular (with locals) *Kiwi Takeaways* near the corner of the Quay and Wellington St.

Further down High St, *Lord Thompson's* has good fish & chips and pizzas, and it's one of the few places open until late.

The *Picton Bakery*, on the corner of Dublin and Auckland Sts, has been recommended by an enthusiastic German traveller for its 'dark long-baked rye bread ... real German style'. You'll also find that the doughnuts sold here have real cream in them.

Restaurants The *Americano Restaurant* at 32 High St has main courses from $14.50: the great Ship 'n' Shore (ribeye steak with scallops and mussels) is $22. A block away at 33 High St, the licensed *Ship Cove* and the BYO *Le Cafe* in the Strand Arcade are both rather fancy.

Some locals favour the *Marlborough Terranean*, at 31 High St, a sophisticated place which has a good wine selection. In this artistic interior an entrée costs about $9 and a main course $25 (it closes in the winter). *Holty's* on the corner of High and Dublin Sts provides kids meals; those travelling with children will appreciate this place.

Neptune's at Waikawa Bay is an excellent seafood restaurant with 'million dollar' views; and the *Ancient Mariner* on the corner of Wellington St and Waikawa Rd has a carvery buffet from $20 to $25.

There are four pubs along or near London Quay and all four – the *Terminus*, the *Federal* the *Oxley* and the *Toot 'n' Whistle* – have pub food, with bistro meals from about $6 to $8. On the south side of Nelson Square you will find the *Crow's Nest* in the Crow Tavern – the seafood is really fresh.

Getting There & Away

Air Soundsair (☎ 573 6184) has a regular service across the strait to and from Wellington. The short flight costs $54 and operates about six times a day. The Picton airstrip is at Koromiko, eight km out of town, and a Corgi shuttle bus connects to the flights for $5 (children $2).

The floatplane operated by Float Air Picton (☎ 573 6433) also flies to and from Wellington, where it lands at Porirua Harbour. The one-way fare is $70 (to or from lodges in the Sounds costs $90).

Bus There are many choices out of Picton. You can choose to go south to Christchurch and beyond, west to Nelson or through the island's centre to the West Coast. There are plenty of services from Picton to Christchurch. Mt Cook Landline buses (☎ 573 6687), also at the ferry terminal, continue all the way to Dunedin and Invercargill. There are connecting services through Blenheim around the northern coast to Havelock, Nelson, Motueka and Takaka, with connections to Collingwood. They also have buses heading south-west through Nelson to Westport and Greymouth, and south through Kaikoura to Christchurch and Dunedin.

InterCity (☎ 573 6855), also at the ferry terminal, has a service to Christchurch with connections to Dunedin and Invercargill, and another route east to Nelson via Blenheim and Havelock with connections to Greymouth and the glaciers. At least one bus daily on each of these routes connects with a ferry sailing to and from Wellington.

A new operator between Nelson and Picton is Barry's Buses (☎ (0800) 802 300). It has services at 7 am leaving from the Station information centre via Blenheim to Nelson, arriving at 9.15 am, and from the ferry terminal at 1 pm arriving in Nelson at 3.15 pm. Another of Barry's services leaves from the ferry terminal at 9 am, arriving in Nelson at 3.15 pm; it returns via scenic Queen Charlotte Drive.

There is a 'confusion' of small operators heading south to Christchurch and beyond. You can choose from Atomic Shuttles (☎ 573 6855), Nationwide Shuttles (☎ 379 5531), South Island Connections (☎ 578 9904), Compass Coachlines (☎ 578 7102), Ko-op Shuttles (☎ 366 6633) and the Midnight Express (☎ (0800) 508 400). Check details with the information centres; they will advise you on the best service and the current cheapest rate. Blenheim Taxis (☎ (0800) 802 225) travel from Picton to Blenheim to Greymouth via St Arnaud (Nelson Lakes) on Monday, Wednesday and Friday. Catch-a-Bus (☎ 577 9994) runs an on-demand bus in summer, Blenheim-Picton-Nelson with connections to Christchurch.

All buses serving Picton operate from the ferry terminal or the information centre.

Train The *Coastal Pacific* train between Picton and Christchurch, via Blenheim and Kaikoura, operates daily in each direction. The train connects with the ferry and a free shuttle service is provided between the railway station and ferry terminal on both sides of the strait. This trip is highly recommended for its coastal scenery.

Car There are basically two directions you can take to the rest of the South Island from Picton: the west coast route and the east coast route. If you opt for the east coast route it's a straight run south from Picton through Blenheim and on down SH1. If you're heading west, you can either take the scenic Queen Charlotte Drive westwards from Picton, or go south to Blenheim and head west from there.

Hitching Hitching out on SH1 towards Blenheim is possible if you've got patience. It can take a few hours to get a ride or at other times you may not get one at all. Most traffic is on the road just after a ferry arrives – there is not much between sailings. The trouble with being on the road just after the ferry docks is that other hitchhikers are also there.

If you're heading west, the best bet is to go to Blenheim and head west from there. Queen Charlotte Drive between Picton and Havelock is the shortest way to Nelson but has little traffic, so it's easier to hitch via Blenheim on the Spring Creek bypass: follow the Blenheim road (SH1) 22 km to Spring Creek, where you turn right towards Renwick. On average it will take a day to reach Christchurch or Nelson.

Ferry The *Interislander* ferry service (☎ (0800) 658 999) shuttles back and forth between Wellington and Picton. There are usually four services daily in each direction and the crossing takes about three hours. The faster *Lynx* operates in summer three times daily. (See Getting There & Away in the Wellington chapter for fares and details.)

Getting Around

A shuttle bus connects Picton with flights to and from the Picton airstrip at Koromiko for $5 (children $2). Avis, Hertz, Thrifty, Budget and Avon Cars (Shoestring Rentals) all have rental offices at the ferry terminal. Pegasus has an office at the railway station.

Kiwi Roadrunner and Buzzy Boats & Bikes hire nifty-fifty (50 cc) motorbikes (for which you need a current car licence). These can be hired from the kiosk beside the MV *Beachcomber* office. The cost is $15 for the first hour and $10 per hour thereafter.

Picton has several water taxis that can take you anywhere you want to go around the sounds, including the various out-of-the-way hotels and walking tracks that can be reached only by water. Check at the wharf in Picton, at the Station information office or at the visitor information centre.

BLENHEIM

The largest town in the Marlborough Sounds region, Blenheim is 29 km south of Picton, on the Wairau Plains – a contrasting landscape to the Sounds – at the junction of the Taylor and Opawa rivers. The town of over 23,000 is particularly well laid out, but more by accident than design as early development was confined to the high ground to avoid the swamp in the centre. The swamp has been reclaimed and is now Seymour Square with its attractive lawns and gardens.

During the second weekend in February Blenheim hosts the now famous Marlborough Food & Wine Festival at Montana's Brancott Estate. Get a copy of the comprehensive *A Taste of Marlborough: Gourmet Paradise* which tells of the festival and outlines restaurant, wineries and has profiles of the winemakers.

Information

The Blenheim Information Centre (☎ 578 9904; fax 578 6084) is in the Forum Building on Queen St. It has a number of DOC maps and leaflets on the many walkways around the Marlborough Sounds and environs. The centre is open daily from 8.30 am to 6.30 pm in summer and shorter hours in winter (closed on Sunday). The AA office (☎ 578 3399) is at 23 Maxwell Rd on the corner of Seymour St.

Things to See

The 5.5-hectare **Brayshaw Museum Park**, off New Renwick Rd, has several attractions including a reconstructed village of buildings designed to recreate colonial Blenheim. There's also some early farming equipment, a miniature railway, a model-boating pond, and the Museum & Archives Building. The park is open during daylight hours and admission is free.

Pollard Park & Waterlea Gardens, off Parker St, have a children's playground and a fitness trail; flowers bloom all year here.

Near Seymour Square are relics of Blenheim's violent early history, including **Blenkinsopp's cannon** which is on the corner of High and Seymour Sts. Originally part of the equipment of the whaling ship *Caroline* which Blenkinsopp captained, this is reputedly the cannon for which Te Rauparaha was persuaded to sign over the Wairau Plains, and was, therefore, one of the causes of the subsequent massacre at Tuamarina.

Recreation Areas There are many areas of public land where you can get away from the bustle of the larger towns. These places are outlined in DOC's pamphlet *Central Marlborough Recreation Areas*, and have a variety of different flora and landforms. The Robertson Range and Whites Bay near Port Underwood are to the north of Blenheim – there are great vistas of Cloudy Bay from here. At the **Wairau Lagoons**, to the east of Blenheim, you can see some of the more than 70 bird species which frequent this area. Many of the areas have been set aside to preserve flora, such as native broom or prostrate kowhai.

The coastal road from Blenheim to Picton requires a good two hours to drive but if you have the time then it is well worthwhile for the spectacular coastal views and remnants of early European history. Good spots for picnics are Robin Hood Bay, Ocean Bay and at the head of Port Underwood (Hakahaka Bay). From the narrow winding road from Waikawa to Rarangi there are superb views of the North Island silhouetted on the horizon.

Activities

There is **skiing** at the Rainbow Valley ski area (☎ 521 1861), 130 km (1½ hours) west of Blenheim. Back Country Safaris (☎ 575 7525) and JJs Ski Transport (☎ 544 7081) buses go right to the ski field.

The more adventurous could try **white-water rafting** in some of the nearby rivers. Action in Marlborough (☎ 578 4531) at 59 Lakings Rd, Blenheim, can get you wet anytime. The costs range from about $60 for a half-day trip to over $400 for three-day expeditions. A number of their trips focus on the Buller and Gowan rivers.

Tours

Deluxe Coachlines (☎ 578 5467) has a six-hour 'Scenic Wine Trail' tour of local wineries which costs $34 (children $17). Highlight Tours (☎ 578 9904) offer personalised tours for between $35 and $45 per person. If you have your own wheels you can construct your own wine trail tour – pick up a copy of the *Marlborough Winemakers Wine Trail Guide* from the information centre, showing the location of over 20 wineries around the Blenheim district. Most are open over the weekend and many serve food.

Places to Stay

Camping & Cabins The *Blenheim A1 Holiday Park* (☎ 578 3667), at the northern end of town at 78 Grove Rd (SH1), is the pick of the camping places. It has sites for $16 for two, cabins from $26 to $35 for two and tourist flats from $45. The *Blenheim Motor Camp* (☎ 578 7419) at 27 Budge St is one km from the town centre off SH1. Tent/powered sites are $15/16, cabins are available from $25 to $32, and tourist flats cost $45; all prices are for two.

Camping grounds further out include

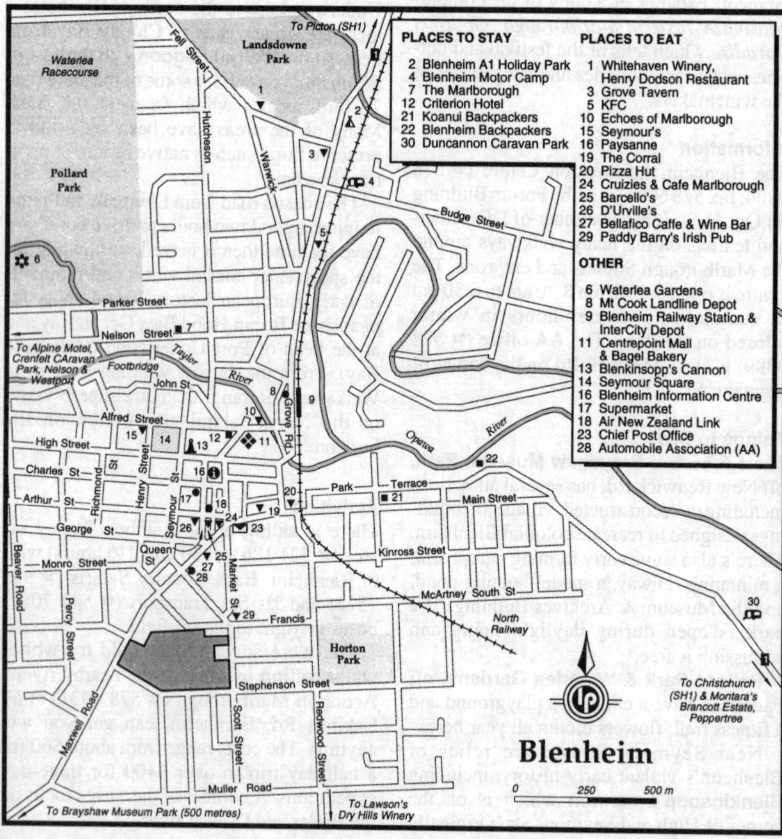

Top: Shantytown, Greymouth, West Coast (TW)
Bottom Left: Truck Home, Nelson (JW)
Bottom Right: Toilet entrance (lava-tory) at the Volcano, Lyttleton, Canterbury (JW)

Top: View from the Treble Cone Ski Area, Otago (RS)
Bottom: West Coast Express Bus, Nelson (JW)

Duncannon Caravan Park (☎ 578 8193), two km south of the town centre, where powered sites cost $13 for two and on-site caravans $22 for two. *Grenfelt Caravan Park* (☎ 578 1259) at 173 Middle Renwick Rd charges $14 for two for powered sites and $24 for two for backpackers' accommodation. The *Spring Creek Holiday Park* (☎ 570 5893), on Rapaura Rd six km out towards Picton and about 500 metres off SH1, has camp sites and cabins. It is nice and quiet out here and is located near a good fishing creek.

Hostels *Blenheim Backpackers* (☎ 578 6062) is at 29 Park Terrace, Blenheim, in an old maternity home. Doubles are $30 and share rooms $13.50 per person. The Opawa River runs behind the house and you can borrow canoes. At 33 Main St you will find *Koanui Backpackers* (☎ 578 7487). Here bunks are $13.50 per person, and twins/doubles are $30/34. This is a friendly place where a number of itinerant fruit pickers base themselves. It has a laundry, bikes, pool table, TV and video, and electric blankets on all the beds.

Hotels, Motels & Guesthouses Rooms at the *Criterion Hotel* (☎ 578 3299) on Market St cost $50/66 for singles/twins.

Reasonably priced motels include the *Raymar Motor Inn* (☎ 578 5104) at 164 High St, where double rooms cost $55, and the similarly priced *Alpine Motel* (☎ 578 1604) at 148 Middle Renwick Rd. At most other motels, doubles cost from about $65.

The most upmarket place in town is *The Marlborough* (☎ 577 7333) at 20 Nelson St, close to Pollard Park. Rooms are from $150 to $180 for a double (GST not included).

Two homestays that are thoroughly recommended are *Peppertree* (☎ 578 7009) on SH1 south of town in its beautiful garden setting, and *Stonehaven* (☎ 572 9730), on Rapaura Rd north west of town. The price range is $65 to $85 for B&B; Stonehaven has a swimming pool, air conditioning, open fireplaces and central heating. For directions and a comprehensive listing see the information centre.

Places to Eat

Snacks & Fast Food There are plenty of takeaways and cafes around the centre. *McDonald's* is in Main St, *KFC* on the northern side of town and *Pizza Hut* on Main St near the town centre.

Barcello's at 67 Queen St, is a small cafe and bar with ambience. Here you can get a good cup of real coffee – cappuccino and espresso. Try their great hot chocolate which is served in a huge cup.

For classy fast food, try the *Bagel Bakery*, a tiny place with a big, successful product. You choose the filling for your bagel for about $3 – a touch of New York in a provincial town. At *Cruizies*, 10 Maxwell Rd, you can buy filled rolls, bagels and giant muffins.

For self-caterers, the supermarket at Charles and Queen Sts is open daily.

Restaurants For pub food there is the *Criterion*, corner of Market and Alfred Sts, which has a large carvery. *Paddy Barry's* is an Irish-style place on Scott St with Guinness on tap; enjoy this with seafood and steaks. The *Echoes of Marlborough* at 22a Alfred St specialises in pizza and sandwiches but its great plus is that it is a good place to try out some Marlborough wines.

Those looking for spicy Tex-Mex food should try *The Corral* at 3 Main St, which is open for dinner every day. Chinese cuisine lovers should head to the *Bamboo Garden* at 53 Maxwell Rd, where there is a large selection of seafoods and Cantonese dishes.

At the top of the dining tree are *D'Urville's* at 52 Queen St, serving international cuisine (mains are about $22); the award-winning *Seymour's* on the corner of Henry and Alfred Sts where the Captain Cook seafood platter for $29.50 and the Sunday evening smorgasbord at $22 are great value; *Bellafico Caffe & Wine Bar* at 17 Maxwell Place has a really interesting, varied menu; and *Paysanne* upstairs in the new Forum building, has a blackboard express menu, a selection of pizzas, and mains from $21.

Wineries Several of the wineries around Blenheim also serve meals. The *Henry*

Dodson Restaurant in the Whitehaven Winery north of town in Dodson St, off Grove Rd, has tasty food. The *Hunters* and *Merlen* wineries on Rapaura Rd also serve food; at Hunters you can barbecue your own meal. At Merlen's you can enjoy your German-style meal and wine in the Weingarten. Also recommended by a noted bon(ne) vivant is the *Twelve Trees Restaurant* at Allan Scott's winery in Jacksons Rd. *Lawson's Dry Hills* also serve meals, usually enjoyed after a wine tour.

Out in Renwick, 10 km west of Blenheim, is the *Cork & Keg*, an 'olde English' pub where you can lunch and relax with a beer if you have tired of wine.

Getting There & Away

Air New Zealand Link (☎ 578 4059), at 29 Queen St, has direct flights to Wellington with connections to other centres. Ansett (☎ 578 7333) has flights to and from Wellington from Blenheim. The Blenheim airport is on Middle Renwick Rd, about six km west of town. Soundsair and Float Air also operate from Koromiko, about halfway between Blenheim and Picton.

Deluxe Coachlines (☎ 578 5467) at 45 Main St has regular services between Blenheim and Picton. Both main companies, Mt Cook Landline and InterCity, pass through Blenheim on their way to Christchurch and Nelson. Mt Cook Landline (☎ (0800) 800 827) picks up and drops off at the railway station in Sinclair St and has a Picton-Blenheim-Christchurch service with connections to Dunedin and Invercargill.

InterCity (☎ 577 2890) buses also operate from the railway station with services from Picton through Blenheim to Christchurch, Dunedin and Invercargill. West-bound InterCity buses from Picton stop at Blenheim on their way to Havelock, Nelson, Greymouth and the West Coast glaciers. See the Picton Getting There & Away section for details of bus services. There are a number of shuttle buses to both Nelson, Christchurch and the West Coast; inquire at the information centre in town about prices and routes.

The daily *Coastal Pacific* Picton-Christchurch train stops at Blenheim. The reservations number is ☎ (0800) 802 802.

You can get a taxi to Blenheim airport from the town centre for about $8. You can also hire mountain bikes for $25 per day in town from the information centre and Spokesman Cycles on Queen St.

HAVELOCK

Heading west from Picton or Blenheim, the first town you'll come to of any size (yet with a population a mere 400) is Havelock. Founded around 1860 and named after Sir Henry Havelock of Indian Mutiny fame, this attractive town is situated at the confluence of the Pelorus and Kaiuma rivers, 43 km from Blenheim.

Havelock was once the hub of the timber milling and export trade, and later became the service centre for gold-mining activities in the area. Today it's a thriving small-boat harbour and a pleasant place to drop off the planet for a while. Havelock is proud to be the 'green-shelled [*sic*] mussel capital of the world'.

Information

The Marlborough Travel Centre/Havelock Information Centre (☎ 574 2532; fax 574 2774) is on the main street not far into town. You can do bookings and get information on the Sounds here. It is open daily from 8 am to 8 pm in summer, 8 am to 4.30 pm in winter.

Glenmore Cruises (☎ 574 2532) on the foreshore also provides some information but it is only open half an hour prior to their cruises. The DOC (☎ 574 2019) has a small office on Mahakipawa Rd.

The tiny **museum** on the main street, across from the information centre, is a good source of information on local history. It is open all day from 8 am to 5 pm; admission is free.

Activities

Walks There's not much to do in the town itself but there are a number of good walks, including the four-hour return walk to **Takorika Summit** behind the township, and the half-hour walk to Cullen Point from where there are good views of Havelock and the sunset. The YHA supplies information on these and other walks.

There are a number of extended walks in the area of Havelock. The **Mt Stokes** walk takes you to the 1204-metre summit, the highest point in the Marlborough Sounds. From here you can see the Kaikouras, Tararuas (in the North Island) and the Sounds below. Another walk is the three-day **Pelorus Track** to Nelson. This follows the Pelorus River, then heads over Dun Saddle via a historic railway line. Mountain bikers can test their pedal strength on the **Maungatapu Track** which passes through scenic Maitai Reserve.

The **Nydia Track** commences at Kaiuma and ends at Duncan Bay. The suggested walking time is two days or 10½ hours. There is accommodation at Murray's Place ($10) about halfway and a couple of *DOC camping grounds*. Nydia Bay was originally the site of a Maori pa and its Maori name meant 'place of sadness' – the DOC pamphlet explains why. The walk passes through different habitats of various species of birds.

It is best to get dropped off at Shag Point by water taxi (Wilderness Express ☎ 574 2532; $10 per person) as it is only a five-minute trip past the mudflats. Glenmore Cruises provide boat access to the track on Tuesday only. At the other end, Sounds Detours (☎ 574 2104) can pick you up. The minimum cost is about $60 so it pays to go with a few people. You can attempt the track in either direction; there is a phone at Murray's Place where you can contact either the water taxi or shuttle service.

Sea Kayaking If you wish to go sea kayaking in this part of Marlborough Sounds try Te Hoiere Sea Kayaks (☎ 574 2610) for daily or weekly rentals. Their trips leave from Havelock and go to Jacobs Bay, taking in bird and bush life; note that there is a four-person minimum. They rent all equipment for two days at $70, four days at $130. Sea Kayaking Adventure Tours (☎ 574 2765) operate from Anakiwa at the end of the Queen Charlotte Walkway; they hire kayaks, mountain bikes ($25 per day) and have one-day guided kayak tours for $55 per person.

Tours

Glenmore Cruises take passengers on the **mail-run boat**, stopping at isolated homesteads to deliver mail and supplies. Tea and coffee are available free on board. If you want to camp or tramp anywhere along the way you can get dropped off and collected again on a specified day. Once on land you're on your own, so take what you need. Fresh water is available in some places; ask the locals whether you need to take any.

The trips depart at 9.30 am on Tuesday, Wednesday and Thursday, and then return between 5 and 6 pm. Between Christmas and Easter, Glenmore Cruises have various other trips every day except Monday, including an additional Friday sailing of the mail-run boat. The round-trip mail-run fare is $45 (children $20).

The **Mussel Run** (☎ 574 2532) visits the mussel farms and you get the opportunity to sample the product. The boat departs from Havelock wharf at 8 am on Tuesday (Pelorus and Kenepuru Sounds) and on Wednesday (D'Urville Island, French Pass, Okiwi Bay). On Monday it operates in the Queen Charlotte Sound and Port Underwood areas. The cost of $55 includes tea and coffee.

There is a daily scenic adventure cruise operated by Wilderness Express which departs daily at 10 am and costs $68. It includes a bush walk at Putanui Point, an insight into the mussel industry, lunch, a 4WD trip to the Crail Bay lookout and a return cruise, reaching Havelock at 4 pm.

There are a number of water taxis operating out of Havelock. Inquire about the hire of MVs *Reliance, Kanona* and *Ariki-Tai*. In particular, each January there are five nature cruises to Maud Island, abode of the takahe, kakapo and Hamilton frog.

Places to Stay

The *Havelock Motor Camp* (☎ 574 2339) on Inglis St has tent/powered sites for $13/15 for two, and cabins for $25 for two. The *Chartridge Park* (☎ 574 2129), six km south of Havelock at Kaiuma Bridge on SH6, has camp sites at $16 for two and budget beds at $10 per person in a basic bunk room. It has a swimming pool, six-hole golf course and a river runs through it.

The *Havelock YHA Hostel* (☎ 574 2104) is on the corner of Lawrence St and Main Rd. The cost is $14 per person in dorms, and twin rooms are $32. The hostel occupies an 1881 schoolhouse once attended by Lord Ernest Rutherford, who discovered the atomic nucleus. The manager has information on walks and other local activities including fishing, farmstays, explorations around the sounds, and more. The hostel is well equipped with bicycles, billiards, volleyball, piano, guitar and so on.

Havelock has a couple of small motels, both on the main road through town. The *Havelock Garden Motel* (☎ 574 2387) has units at $50 to $60 for two, with low-season discounts available. The *Pelorus Tavern* (☎ 574 2412), which has a restaurant and pub, has motel units for about $55.

Places to Eat

The *Pelorus Jack Tearooms* on the main road has snacks and light meals. The more upmarket *Sounds Cafe* has good quality evening meals in which mussels feature heavily (mains are from $12 to $25). You can get counter or restaurant meals at the *Pelorus Tavern* and dine overlooking the Havelock marina.

Getting There & Away

Mt Cook Landline and InterCity buses have Picton-Blenheim-Nelson buses that stop at the information centre at least once each day. Barry's Bus passes through town at least four times a day; the cost to Blenheim is $8, Picton $11 and to Nelson is also $11.

HAVELOCK TO NELSON

The SH6 from Havelock to Nelson is 75 km of scenic highway, passing the Wakamarina Valley, Pinedale (also known as Canvastown), the Pelorus Bridge Scenic Reserve and Rai Valley.

Pinedale

The tiny township of Pinedale, in the Wakamarina Valley eight km west of Havelock, got the nickname Canvastown back in the 1860s when gold was discovered in the river. By 1864 thousands of canvas tents had sprung up as miners flocked to the prosperous working goldfield, one of the richest in the country. By 1865 the boom was over. Nevertheless gold is still found in the area and in 1986 a tourist panned a five-gram nugget from the river.

Visits to the interesting indoor-outdoor gold-mining museum, gold panning, horse trekking, bushwalking and trout fishing are all popular activities. The **Wakamarina Track**, an old gold-miners trail which passes through the Mt Richmond State Forest Park, begins from Butchers Flat, 15 km into the Wakamarina Valley on the metalled road from Pinedale.

The *Trout Hotel* at the entrance to the Wakamarina Valley (☎ 574 2120) has singles/doubles at $25/40 and motel units at $50 for two. The *Pinedale Motor Camp* (☎ 574 2349) has tent/powered sites for $14/16 for two, and cabins from $25 to $35 for two; you can hire gold pans and other equipment here and they have half-hour lessons for $10 and two-hour tours for $60 for a group of up to 20 people. You can hire a pan for $3 and do it yourself. The *Wakavale Backpackers* is another cheapie along the Wakamarina road, and Butchers Flat, Roadend, Wakamarina Valley is a local *DOC camping ground.*

Pelorus Bridge

The Pelorus Bridge Scenic Reserve, 18 km west of Havelock, has interesting walks of between 30 minutes and three hours on the Pelorus and Rai rivers, with waterfalls, a suspension bridge and the Pelorus Bridge itself. Within the reserve are tearooms, tent/caravan sites are $12/16 for two, and cabins are $22 for two. Ask for the ranger at the Rai Valley Tearoom (☎ 571 6019).

The *Lord Lionel* (☎ 574 2770) is on SH6 near the Pelorus Bridge Scenic Reserve; the

German-speaking owners offer single/ double B&B for $35/70.

Rai Valley
At Carluke, 1.5 km from the Rai Valley township on the road leading to Tennyson Inlet, is the Rai Valley Pioneer Cottage, built in 1881 when the area was still virgin bush. The cottage served as a home to its owner for 28 years and had been used as a sheep shed and chicken house before being restored in 1969 and given to the Historic Places Trust in 1980. There's no charge to see the cottage, but donations are appreciated.

South Marlborough

Many travellers head west or north-west from Picton to the walking tracks or the West Coast glaciers, but there are also a number of points of interest along the route south from the Marlborough district across the Seaward Kaikoura foothills to Christchurch.

KAIKOURA

Kaikoura is a Mecca for wildlife enthusiasts. It is a small place – with a population of 2400 – on SH1, 133 km south of Blenheim. Just south of Kaikoura the road splits: SH1 continues along the coast, while the very windy SH70 branches off inland and later merges with SH7 crossing over from the west coast.

Until early 1988 the sleepy little seaside town was noted mainly for its fishing and its fine setting on an incredibly beautiful bay backed by the steeply rising foothills of the Seaward Kaikouras, snowcapped in winter. It was also known for its crayfish (lobster) – Kaikoura means 'to eat crayfish' in Maori.

At Christmas 1987, Nature Watch Charters began whale-watching trips – the first such commercial operation in NZ. The tours quickly became famous and put Kaikoura on the tourist map.

One whale-watch and two dolphin swimming companies are now operating very successfully. The host of other things to do in the area and the simple beauty of the town keep visitors around for days after they've gone to see the whales and dolphins.

History
In Maori legend, the tiny Kaikoura Peninsula (Taumanu-o-te-waka-a-Maui) was the seat upon which the demigod Maui sat when he fished the North Island up from the depths of the sea. The area was heavily settled before Europeans came – at least 14 Maori pa (fortified village) sites have been identified.

Excavations near the Fyffe House show that the area was a moa-hunter settlement about 800 to 1000 years ago. In 1857 George Fyffe came upon an early moa-hunter burial site near the present Fyffe House and among other things he found an almost complete moa egg shell, the largest moa egg ever found (240 mm long, 178 mm in diameter).

In 1828 the beachfront of Kaikoura, now the site of the Garden of Memories, was the scene of a tremendous battle when a Ngati Toa war party led by the chief Te Rauparaha from Kapiti Island in the south of the North Island, bore down on Kaikoura armed with muskets, killing or capturing several hundred of the local Ngai Tahu tribe.

Captain Cook passed by here on 15 February 1770, but did not land. His journal states that 57 Maoris in four double-hulled canoes came out from shore towards the *Endeavour*, but 'would not be prevail'd upon to put along side'. Cook called the peninsula 'Lookers on', a name which was later mistakenly ascribed to the Seaward Kaikouras.

The first European to settle in Kaikoura was Robert Fyffe, who established a whaling station in 1842. Kaikoura was a whaling centre from 1843 until 1922. Meanwhile the land had been discovered to be rich for settlement and sheep-farming; after whaling ended, the sea and the farmland continued to support the community.

Information
The Kaikoura Visitor Information Centre (☎ 319 5641; fax 319 6819), on The Esplanade by the car park (on the beach side), is open from 8 am to 7 pm every day in summer, and from 9 am to 5 pm in winter.

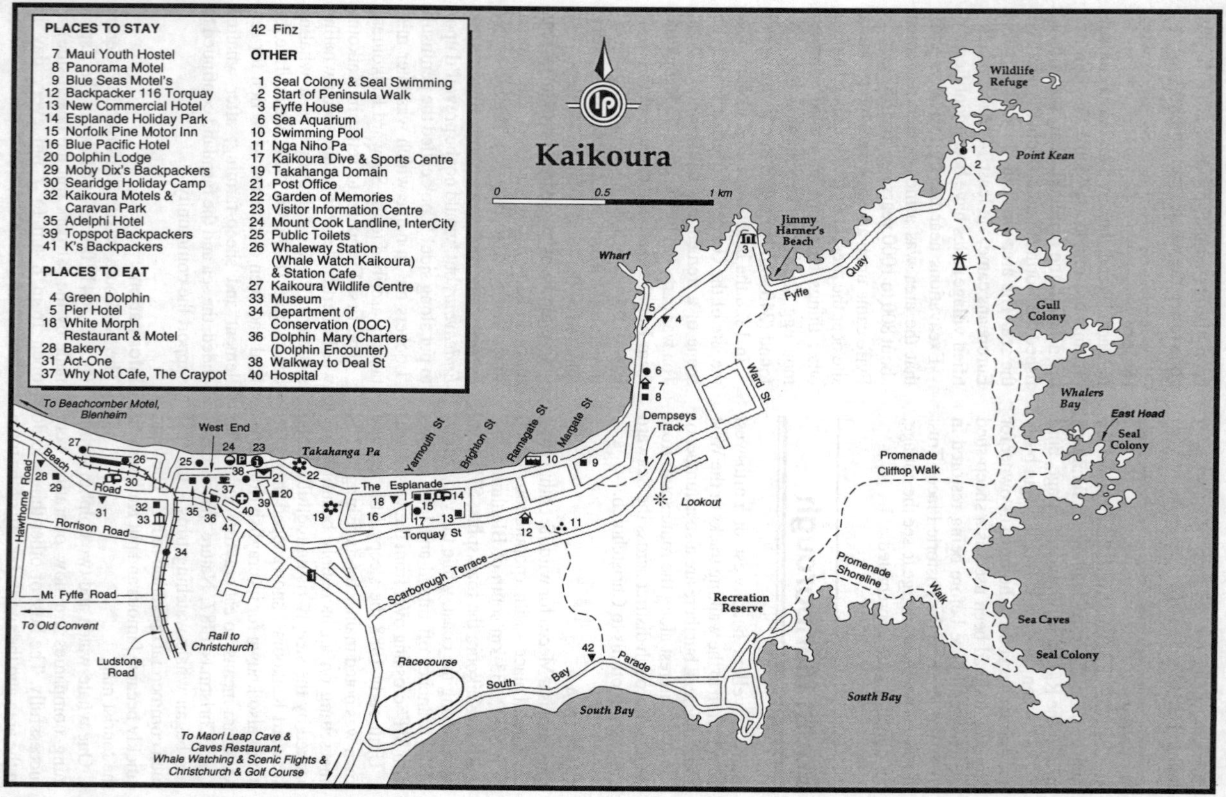
Kaikoura
0
0.5
1 km
PLACES TO STAY
7 Maui Youth Hostel
8 Panorama Motel
9 Blue Seas Motel's
12 Backpacker 116 Torquay
13 New Commercial Hotel
14 Esplanade Holiday Park
15 Norfolk Pine Motor Inn
16 Blue Pacific Hotel
20 Dolphin Lodge
29 Moby Dix's Backpackers
30 Searidge Holiday Camp
32 Kaikoura Motels & Caravan Park
35 Adelphi Hotel
39 Topspot Backpackers
41 K's Backpackers
PLACES TO EAT
4 Green Dolphin
5 Pier Hotel
18 White Morph Restaurant & Motel
28 Bakery
31 Act-One
37 Why Not Cafe, The Craypot
42 Finz
OTHER
1 Seal Colony & Seal Swimming
2 Start of Peninsula Walk
3 Fyffe House
6 Sea Aquarium
10 Swimming Pool
11 Nga Niho Pa
17 Kaikoura Dive & Sports Centre
19 Takahanga Domain
21 Post Office
22 Garden of Memories
23 Visitor Information Centre
24 Mount Cook Landline, InterCity
25 Public Toilets
26 Whaleway Station (Whale Watch Kaikoura) & Station Cafe
27 Kaikoura Wildlife Centre
33 Museum
34 Department of Conservation (DOC)
36 Dolphin Mary Charters (Dolphin Encounter)
38 Walkway to Deal St
40 Hospital
Wildlife Refuge
Point Kean
Jimmy Harmer's Beach
Wharf
Fyffe Quay
Gull Colony
Whalers Bay
East Head
Seal Colony
Ward St
Dempseys Track
Promenade Clifftop Walk
Lookout
Margate St
Ramsgate St
Brighton St
Yarmouth St
Takahanga Pa
The Esplanade
Torquay St
West End
To Beachcomber Motel, Blenheim
Beach Road
Hawthorne Road
Rorrison Road
Mt Fyffe Road
To Old Convent
Ludstone Road
Rail to Christchurch
Scarborough Terrace
Racecourse
South Bay Parade
South Bay
Recreation Reserve
Promenade Shoreline Walk
Sea Caves
Seal Colony
South Bay
To Maori Leap Cave & Caves Restaurant, Whale Watching & Scenic Flights & Christchurch & Golf Course

The staff are very helpful and can make bookings for any tour. They screen an excellent 20-minute audiovisual on all the attractions around Kaikoura; the cost is $2 per person.

The DOC office (☎ 319 5714) is on Ludstone Rd. Get information on walks, camping and so on at the information centre.

Fyffe House

George Fyffe, cousin of NZ's first European settler, Robert Fyffe, came to Kaikoura from Scotland in 1854 and built Fyffe House around 1860. It is the only building remaining from the whaling days and is now under the protection of the Historic Places Trust. The house, on The Esplanade about two km east of the town centre, is open from 10 am to 5 pm daily. The curator conducts tours for $3.50 (children free).

Other Attractions

The **museum** on Ludstone Rd is not as small as it looks; it has several big sections out the back, including the old town jail, built in 1910. There are also many historical photographs, Maori and colonial artefacts, and an exhibit on the region's whaling era. The museum is open daily from 2 to 4 pm in summer and during school holidays in winter. Admission is $1 (children 50c).

There's a tiny **Sea Aquarium** beside the YHA hostel on The Esplanade, with a single tank of sea animals and a video presentation on Kaikoura's ocean wildlife. It's run by the University of Canterbury Research Centre and is open most days; admission is free.

Tours of **Maori Leap Cave**, a limestone cave formed by the sea and discovered in 1958, take place several times daily and depart from the Caves Restaurant, three km south of the town on SH1 (no bus to the restaurant, unfortunately). The 40-minute tour costs $7.50 (children $3.50). Report 15 minutes before the tour times – 10.30 and 11.30 am, and 12.30, 1.45, 2.30 and 3.30 pm.

On The Esplanade beachfront is the **Garden of Memories**, a pleasant garden with a walk-way arched by whalebones.

Up on the hill at the eastern end of town there's a water tower which is a great **lookout**; you can see both sides of the peninsula and all down the coast. Take the walking track up to the tower from The Esplanade or drive up Scarborough Terrace.

Wildlife Viewing & Tours

This is the reason for most people coming to Kaikoura and the town is now geared up for the many international visitors it receives.

Whale-Watching Only one company now operates daily whale-watch tours: Whale Watch Kaikoura (☎ 319 5045) whose office is in the old railway (Whaleway) station. Most of the year the tours start at 5.30 am and continue through to 1.30 pm every day. Whale Watch has a free phone for reservations, ☎ (0800) 655 121. It is usually necessary to book three to four days in

advance. Their boats, equipped with hydrophones (underwater microphones) to pick up the sounds of whales below the surface, set out to sea in search of the whales and other wildlife. They have three rigid-hulled, six-metre inflatables (Naiads), a 12.4-metre Naiad and a much larger 13-metre catamaran (45 passengers); the latter is best for those after comfort and warmth.

The cost is $95 for a three-hour sea tour, and there's a children's' rate of $60. (The trips are not suitable for children under five.)

For most people the tour is a thrilling experience – the main attraction is the sperm whale; and it just happens that Kaikoura is the most accessible spot on the planet for seeing them (for more information see the Flora & Fauna section).

There are frequent sightings of other types of whales on these trips including the killer (orca), minke, humpback and southern right. You may also see shearwaters, fulmars, petrels, and royal and wandering albatross.

There is one really bad hitch to the whole whale-watch experience – the weather. Nothing is more dismal than heading to a place for a special encounter with nature, then to have it stopped by the intervention of the uncontrollable. As Whale Watch depends on its spotter planes to locate the whales out at sea, they can't usually find them in foggy or wet conditions. The booking clerk at the Whale Watch office then cancels line after line of disappointed customers. The town benefits each time this happens as many people stay on to try the next day. If this trip is a *must* for you, allow a few days.

You can also see whales from the air by aircraft or helicopter. Air Tours Kaikoura (☎ 319 5986) and Whale Watch Air (☎ 358 8334) charge about $80 each (two minimum, $50 children) for a half-hour flight. Kaikoura Helicopters (☎ 319 6622) also offer flights out over the whales; the flight is 25 minutes and the cost is $120. They also guarantee that you see the 'whole whale'.

To know more before you go out whale watching (or even dolphin swimming), get a copy of the excellent publication *Whales & Dolphins of Kaikoura, NZ* by Barbara Todd.

Dolphin Swimming The original operators, Dolphin Mary Charters (Dolphin Encounter, ☎ 319 6777) at 58 West End, offer you the opportunity to swim with huge pods of dusky dolphins. They also provide wetsuits (essential in this water), masks and snorkels for $80 for a three-hour 'dolphin encounter' ($55 if you are just a spectator). The Kaikoura Wildlife Centre (☎ 319 6622), near the railway station, also operate dolphin swimming trips for the same price.

Seal Swimming Seals may appear threatening if approached on land but underwater, in their element, they are completely passive. Graeme's Seal Swim (☎ 319 6182) arranges snorkelling with NZ fur seals. These two-hour 'off-the-shore' guided tours, which give you a great opportunity to view your mammalian cousins at close hand, commence at 10 am and 1.30 pm; sometimes there is a 4.30 pm trip. The cost is $35 (children $15). Dave at Topspot Backpackers also arranges similar trips.

You can also snorkel with the seals from a boat. From September to May, the Kaikoura Wildlife Centre (☎ 319 6622), next to the railway station, organise seal swimming and supply all equipment; the cost is $50, less if you are watching from the boat.

Other Wildlife There's a lot of other wildlife to be seen. The 'Big Five' most likely to be seen are the sperm whale, Hector's dolphin (smallest and rarest of dolphins), the dusky dolphin (found only in the southern hemisphere), the NZ fur seal, and the bottlenose dolphin. Other animals frequently seen include the orca, common dolphins, pilot whales, blue penguins, and many sea birds including the royal albatross.

There's no guarantee of seeing any specific animal on any one tour, but it's fairly certain that something of interest will be out there any time you go. Sperm whales are most likely to be seen from October to August, and orcas from December to March. Most of the other fauna is seen all year round.

There is a reason why all these animals are found at Kaikoura. It is here that the

Dolphin Swimming

I didn't quite know what to expect when I went dolphin swimming. At the Dolphin Encounter office I was fitted out with a good-quality wetsuit, flippers, face mask and snorkel. The early hour added to the confusion and the only hint of what I was about to experience was given by the numerous photographs and postcards scattered around the office.

We headed out in a powered catamaran to an area between Oaro and Goose Bay, the preferred feeding ground of the pods of dusky dolphins. There was no guarantee that the dolphins would be there but the skipper had successfully located many in the previous days. When the first pod was sighted, the atmosphere on board the boat was electric. The skipper manoeuvred in front of the pod, which was feeding on squid, and advised us to enter the water. The eight of us donned our masks and flippers and jumped into the cold water. The initial shock was quickly overcome as streaks of quicksilver flashed by. Before I knew it, a curious dusky circled below me and I gasped for air through my snorkel: I was witness to one of the most beautiful, streamlined creatures of the sea. I raised my head out of the water to see another dolphin performing, circus-like, back flip after back flip – not one or two, but 10, 11, 12...

I dived down to show more of me to the curious dolphins and for a brief instant I was an interloper in their underwater world. I now had a better view of their graceful forms as they darted by. It made me feel that there really is some inexplicable spiritual communication between human and dolphin.

Three pods of dusky dolphins – numbering some 450 in total – had joined together for mass feeding on that day. Later they were joined by a pod of common dolphins, and on the way back to Kaikoura, a lone bottlenose dolphin, Maui, came up to the boat. Three dolphin species in one day. The encounter was over and my satisfaction complete. I don't think I have ever experienced anything quite like it before.

Jeff Williams

continental shelf comes closest to land, just about 800 metres off the coast. From land, the shelf slopes gradually to a depth of about 90 metres and then drops abruptly to a depth of over 800 metres. Warm and cold currents converge here, and when the southerly current hits the continental shelf it creates an upwelling current, bringing nutrients up from the ocean floor and into the light zone. The nutrients attract small marine animals, which in turn attract larger fish and squid – the sperm whale's favourite food!

Walks

There are a number of good walkways around the Kaikoura Peninsula. There are two promenade **walkways** around the tip of the peninsula, one along the seashore and one above it along the cliff top. If you go on the seashore trail, check the tides beforehand! Both walks afford excellent views of the NZ fur seal and red-billed seagull colonies. A walks pamphlet is available from the information centre and DOC.

Other good walks in the area are at Mt Fyffe Forest, nine km from Kaikoura; the Puhi Puhi Scenic Reserve, 18 km from town; and the Omihi Lookout, 19 km from town.

The **Mt Fyffe Walking Track** centres on Mt Fyffe (1602 metres), an outlier of the Seaward Kaikoura Range, which dominates the narrow Kaikoura plain and the town. The eastern face of Fyffe is cloaked in forest and there's an enjoyable forest walk here. Information about history, vegetation, birds and the walking tracks is found in *Mt Fyffe Forest: Kaikoura*, available from DOC.

A popular day or overnight walk is to the summit of Fyffe and the hut of the same name. From here there are impressive views of the peninsula and plains; on a clear day you can see Banks Peninsula to the south and Cape Palliser in the North Island.

There are two access routes to the forest. The first is from the end of Mt Fyffe Rd, which leads to the short forest walk, and the second is from the western end of Postmans Rd, the access route to the Hinau Picnic area.

The **Kaikoura Coast Track** is a three-day walk through private farmland and along the Amuri coast, 50 km south of Kaikoura. The walk has spectacular coastal views and each night you stay in comfortable farm cottages – the Staging Post at Hawkswood (☎ 319 2708), where you get information on the walk), Ngaroma near the sea, and Medina on the Conway River Flats. You can get a shuttle from Kaikoura and the cost is $60. You have to bring your own sleeping bag and food.

Other Activities

In winter there's **skiing** at Mt Lyford ski area. The daily charges for the lifts are quite reasonable. Transport is available from Kaikoura with Sea to Summit Safaris (☎ 319 6182; or book through the information centre or a backpackers) for $20 return; this leaves in winter only at 8 am and returns about 6.30 pm.

Golf is also very popular here. Clubs can be hired from the information centre at $10 per set; green fees are $15 for 18 holes.

There's safe **swimming** along the stretch of beach in front of The Esplanade, at beaches on the peninsula's north east (eg Jimmy Harmers) and at South Bay. The whole coastline, with its rocky formations and abundant marine life, makes for worthwhile snorkelling and diving. Mangamanu Beach, about 15 km north of Kaikoura, has good surfing.

Fishing is popular off the new and old wharves, at the Kahutara river mouth, or by surfcasting on the many beaches.

The Kaikoura Dive & Sports Centre (☎ 319 6444) on Yarmouth St is the place to ask about **diving** – it does diving trips, hires tanks, and has an air-filling station.

Tours

Kaikoura Four Wheeler Safaris (☎ (025) 362 120) operate four-wheeler **motorbike rides** on and around Mt Fyffe and the Kowhai River where you drive through rivers, hill country and bush. The cost for a three-hour trip is $85, a half-day $100 and a full-day trip along the coast $130, lunch included.

You can go **horse trekking** with Fyffe View Horse Treks (☎ 319 5069), which runs half-day guided horse treks for $35.

Lake Rotorua Bird-Watch Cruises (☎ 319 5985) have **birdwatching** tours for the avid twitcher. They show you the hide-outs of the pied shag, an inland nesting colony of little black cormorants and, occasionally, groups of royal spoonbills. The two-hour trip includes a one-hour boat ride across the lake, and views of the farm and Maori pa sites. The cost is $60; there is a maximum of 10 people. All pick up from the information centre.

Places to Stay

Camping & Cabins *Kaikoura Motels & Caravan Park* (☎ 319 5999) at 11 Beach Rd, near the railway overpass, has tent/powered sites for $14/19, cabins from $20 to $40, tourist flats from 445 to $50 ($11 each extra adult); all prices are for two. A double or twin in their lodge cum bunkroom is $28.

The *Searidge Holiday Park* (☎ 319 5362), on Beach Rd beside the railway station, has tent/powered sites for $15/18, and a standard two-berth cabin is $30. The *Esplanade Holiday Park* (☎ 319 5947), 126 The Esplanade, also has sites and cabins.

DOC has two seaside camping grounds near Kaikoura: *Peketa Camping Ground* (☎ 319 6299), eight km south, with 100 tent sites, 100 power points, 10 cabins and a camp shop; and *Goose Bay Camping Ground* (☎ 319 5348), 18 km south, with 100 tent sites, 90 power points, and five cabins. The Goose Bay camp is actually several camping areas spread over a five-km stretch of coastline. Generally, the sites at each camping ground cost $6 per adult (an extra $4 for power), and the cabins cost around $24 for two.

The *Waitane Cabins* (☎ 319 5494) at Oaro, 22 km south of Kaikoura off SH1, has two self-contained cabins (you only need to bring linen), each costing $35 for two. Also at Oaro is the *Ocean View Motel* (☎ 319 5454), where powered sites are $14 and motel units $50; costs are also for two.

Hostels The *Maui YHA Hostel* (☎ 319 5931), at 270 The Esplanade, is an attractive, modern hostel beside the sea about 1.5 km from the town centre. The common room is open all day and has a superb view along the bay to the mountains beyond. The cost is $14 per person in dorms and twin rooms are $36. Mt Cook Landline buses drop off and pick up passengers at the door. The hostel will send someone to pick you up from the railway station if you arrange it in advance.

The *Topspot Backpackers* (☎ 319 5540) at 22 Deal St has plenty of accommodation space and is a non-smokers' haven. There is a BBQ and sundeck here, they have a courtesy van, and the clean and tidy share rooms are $15 per person, and double units with ensuites are from $35. There's a sign near the post office indicating the path to this place.

K's Backpackers (☎ 319 5538), 11 Churchill St, is a small homely place a small walk from town. The comfortable beds are a change from the old sleeping bag and there is a nice lounge and kitchen with tea and coffee-making facilities. The cost is $17.50 per person in twin or double rooms. *Dolphin Lodge* (☎ 319 5842) at 15 Deal St, almost directly across the road from the Topspot, is a homely place which gets good comments from readers. It has recently been extended and dorm beds are $14 per person, and twins and doubles about $33.

Across the road from the whale-watching operations, at 65 Beach Rd, you'll find *Moby Dix's Backpackers* (☎ 319 6699) where dorms are $14.50 per person, and twins and doubles are $33. It has all the necessary facilities, volleyball court, sundeck with a BBQ and a creek at the back.

Hotels & Motels The *Adelphi Hotel* (☎ 319 5141) on West End has twins and doubles from $44 to $48 for two; not all rooms have private facilities. There's also the *Blue Pacific Hotel* (☎ 319 5017) at 114 The Esplanade, where backpackers beds are $15 and budget rooms are $20 per person (it is assumed that backpackers will probably have their own sleeping bag).

There are plenty of motels in Kaikoura, especially along The Esplanade. Most charge at least $65 to $80 per night for two, including the *Kaikoura Motels & Caravan Park* mentioned under Camping & Cabins ($55 to $70). *Panorama Motel* (☎ 319 5053) at 266 The Esplanade, *Blue Seas Motels* (☎ 319 5441) at 222 The Esplanade, and *Beachcomber* (☎ 319 5623) at 169 Beach Rd are all similarly priced.

The *Norfolk Pine Motor Inn* (☎ 319 5120), 124 The Esplanade, has studio units for $60 and two-bedroom units for $80 for two ($14 for an extra adult, $11 for a child).

The *White Morph Motor Inn* (☎ 319 5014) at 92-94 The Esplanade is the best place in town, and it is in a really great position across from the beach and next to the restaurant of the same name. A studio unit is $100, a two-bedroom apartment $120 and one of the luxury units is $160 (all prices are for two, it is $15 for an extra adult, $11 for a child).

The *Old Convent* (☎ 319 6603), out on Mt Fyffe Rd (near the junction with Mill Rd) and about three minutes from the town, is neither a motel nor a convent. It is a highly regarded B&B where singles/doubles or twins are $35/50, respectively. Their advertising: 'Get in the habit ... nun can compare'.

Places to Eat

When in season, crayfish (lobster) are often featured in Kaikoura restaurants; you even find them in the local takeaways. Before the whale-watching boom, the crayfish alone made Kaikoura a worthwhile stop!

There are many takeaways and coffee shops around town. The *Why Not Cafe* in the town centre specialises in home-made food, with takeaways, pizza, sandwiches, salads and some health food selections.

Other places include *Wong's*, near the Adelphi Hotel on West End, for Chinese; the *Station Cafe* for snacks while booking trips, although the breakfasts are overpriced – a case of captive market syndrome; and *Act-One* for pizzas from $9, including the Shaftesbury special with chicken, brie and cranberries. The *bakery* out on Beach Rd (on the corner of Hawthorne Rd) is a good place to pick up a quick snack before eco-touring.

Various hotels serve standard pub fare including the *Pier Hotel* near the wharf,

Adelphi Hotel, *Blue Pacific* and *New Commercial Hotel*. To give you an idea, the roast of the day at the Adelphi costs $14.

The Craypot on West End has been here for as long as we remember and maintains its consistency. You can always be guaranteed a good feed of crayfish; a half crayfish is about $27 but you can help yourself to as much salad and vegetables as you can eat. The *White Morph* at 94 The Esplanade is housed in a stately old home and has both indoor and outdoor garden tables. With local seafood so plentiful, what better place is there to try a paella ($24)?

The *Green Dolphin* is at 12 Avoca St opposite the Pier Hotel near the wharf. The food is continental and delicious and the owners (the people who started whale-watching here) share a wealth of knowledge on the marine mammals of the area. Soup of the day with bread is $4.50, a main course pasta is $12.50, other mains such as steak are around $16, and desserts are $6.50. It is open at night, every day in the summer.

Out at South Bay is *Finz*, a predominantly seafood place with a bar; it is open every evening from 6 pm until late.

Getting There & Away

There are no commercial airlines serving Kaikoura. The daily InterCity and Mt Cook Landline bus services operating between Picton and Christchurch all stop at Kaikoura. InterCity and Mount Cook Landline buses arrive and depart from the town car park (by the information centre); tickets for both are sold at the information centre.

Several shuttle buses pass through Kaikoura – Compass Coachlines, South Island Connections, Southern Link, Ko-op, Catch-a-Bus and Nationwide. Expect to pay about $15 to get to Christchurch; for more details contact the information centre. Kaikoura Shuttles (☎ 319 5846) has a daily door-to-door service, to/from Christchurch, for $20.

One northbound and one southbound *Coastal Pacific* train between Picton and Christchurch stops at Kaikoura every day. The northbound arrives at about 10.20 am and the southbound at about 3.45 pm.

Getting Around

The Maui Youth Hostel hires bicycles to guests. The West End (Shell), and the Mobil garage on Beach Rd also hire out bikes.

Nelson Province

The Nelson region is one of the top destinations for travellers to NZ. In addition to its equable climate, it is home to some of the best and most popular national parks in the country – Kahurangi, Nelson Lakes and the Abel Tasman. In these parks there is a wealth of walking possibilities, and a host of other outdoor activities. The city of Nelson and the towns of Motueka, Takaka and Collingwood are great places to 'lay back' for a while.

NELSON

The city of Nelson is a pleasant, bright and active place. The surrounding area has some of the finest beaches in New Zealand and more sunshine than any other part of the country so it's not surprising that it's a popular holiday area. Apart from beaches and bays, Nelson is noted for its fruit-growing industry and its very energetic local arts & crafts community.

Nelson stages many noteworthy events throughout the year. One of the most interesting of all, the Wearable Art Award is held in September. In early March there is the Taste Nelson Festival featuring locally produced food and beverages. There is a regional population of 76,000.

History

The Maoris began to migrate to the South Island during the 16th century, and among the first to arrive in Nelson were the Ngati Tumatakokiri. By 1550 this tribe occupied most of the province, as Abel Tasman was to find out to his cost when he turned up at the place he later named Murderers' Bay. Other tribes followed the Tumatakokiri, settling at the mouth of the Waimea River. The Tumatakokiri remained supreme in Tasman Bay until the 18th century, when the Ngati-apa from Wanganui and the Ngai Tahu – the largest tribe in the South Island – got together in a devastating attack on the Tumatakokiri, who virtually ceased to exist as an independent tribe after 1800.

The Ngati-apa's victory was short-lived, because between 1828 and 1830 they were practically annihilated by armed tribes from Taranaki and Wellington who sailed into the bay in the largest fleet of canoes ever assembled in New Zealand.

By the time the European settlers arrived there were no Maoris living at Te Wakatu – the nearest pa being at Motueka – and the population of those that remained in the area was so decimated they put up no resistance. The first Pakeha settlers sailed in response to advertisements by the New Zealand Company, which was set up by Edward Gibbon Wakefield to colonise the country systematically. His grandiose scheme was to transplant a complete slice of English life from all social classes. In reality 'too few gentlemen with too little money' took up the challenge and the new colony almost foundered in its infancy from lack of money.

The settlement was planned to comprise small but workable farms grouped around central towns. However, the New Zealand Company's entitlement to the land was disputed and it was almost a year before this problem was sorted out. So while the land around the town had been distributed early, the farmland was not available for such a long time that landowners and labourers forced to live in town had whittled away their capital simply to survive.

The Wairau Massacre (described in the Marlborough Provence History section) resulted in the deaths of 22 of Nelson's most able citizens, including Captain Wakefield whose leadership was irreplaceable, and plunged the colony into deep gloom. To make matters worse the New Zealand Company was declared bankrupt in April 1844 and, since nearly three-quarters of the population were dependent on it in some way or another, particularly for sustenance, the situation was so grim as to be near famine. Only the later arrival of hard-working German immigrants saved the region from economic ruin.

Information

The Nelson Visitor Information Centre (☎ 548 2304; fax 546 9008), on the corner of Trafalgar and Halifax Sts, is open daily from 7.30 am to 6 pm in summer (from 8.30 am to 5.30 pm in winter). It also serves as Nelson's Transit Centre – all buses serving Nelson arrive and depart from this office. Trafalgar St, which crosses the river just before the information centre and runs straight up to the cathedral, is the main street in Nelson. Get *Your Guide to Nelson City* from the information centre.

General inquiries about national parks and walks are fielded at the visitor information centre by DOC officials. The DOC office (☎ 546 9335) is a couple of blocks away in the Monroe Building at 186 Bridge St. They have good topographical maps on the Nelson and Marlborough area, the Abel Tasman, Heaphy and Wangapeka tracks in Kahurangi National Park, and Nelson Lakes National Park. The office is open from 8 am to 4.35 pm Monday to Friday. The AA office is nearby at 45 Halifax St.

Camping gear can be hired in Nelson from many, in fact most, of the hostels, or from Alp Sports at 220 Hardy St (☎ 546 8536). Basecamp (☎ 548 1710) at 295 Trafalgar St sell good equipment. Bruce Rollo BBQ & Camping (☎ 548 2363) at 12 Bridge St also has a more limited selection of gear for hire. Prices are usually reasonable, around $5 a day for packs and boots, $8 a day for tents.

If you are on a working holiday there's fruit picking and other agricultural work from February to May, and there may be some casual daily work at fish processors down at the port. Contact the Employment NZ office or individual growers about picking work.

Historic Buildings

The focal point of Nelson is its **cathedral**, at the top of Trafalgar St. The present building has had a somewhat chequered career. The foundation stone for the cathedral was laid

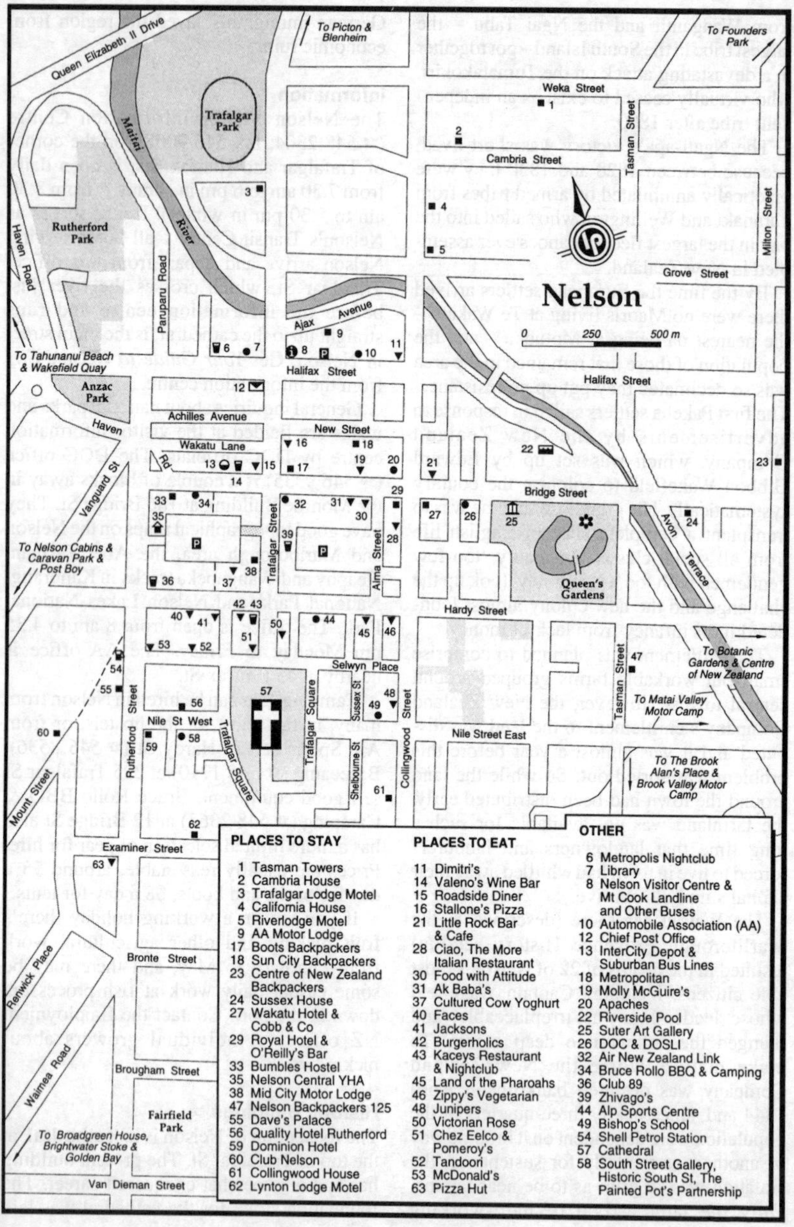
Nelson
0
250
500 m
Queen Elizabeth II Drive
To Picton & Blenheim
To Founders Park
Trafalgar Park
Maitai River
Weka Street
Cambria Street
Tasman Street
Milton Street
Grove Street
Rutherford Park
Haven Road
Paruparu Road
Ajax Avenue
To Tahunanui Beach & Wakefield Quay
Halifax Street
Anzac Park
Achilles Avenue
Haven Rd
New Street
Wakatu Lane
Vanguard St
Bridge Street
Trafalgar Street
Alma Street
To Nelson Cabins & Caravan Park & Post Boy
Queen's Gardens
Avon Terrace
Hardy Street
Selwyn Place
To Botanic Gardens & Centre of New Zealand
To Matai Valley Motor Camp
Nile St West
Nile Street East
Rutherford Street
Trafalgar Square
Sussex St
Shelbourne St
Collingwood Street
To The Brook Alan's Place & Brook Valley Motor Camp
Mount Street
Examiner Street
Bronte Street
Renwick Place
Waimea Road
Brougham Street
Fairfield Park
To Broadgreen House, Brightwater Stoke & Golden Bay
Van Dieman Street
PLACES TO STAY
1 Tasman Towers
2 Cambria House
3 Trafalgar Lodge Motel
4 California House
5 Riverlodge Motel
9 AA Motor Lodge
17 Boots Backpackers
18 Sun City Backpackers
23 Centre of New Zealand Backpackers
24 Sussex House
27 Wakatu Hotel & Cobb & Co
29 Royal Hotel & O'Reilly's Bar
33 Bumbles Hostel
35 Nelson Central YHA
38 Mid City Motor Lodge
47 Nelson Backpackers 125
55 Dave's Palace
56 Quality Hotel Rutherford
59 Dominion Hotel
60 Club Nelson
61 Collingwood House
62 Lynton Lodge Motel
PLACES TO EAT
11 Dimitri's
14 Valeno's Wine Bar
15 Roadside Diner
16 Stallone's Pizza
21 Little Rock Bar & Cafe
28 Ciao, The More Italian Restaurant
30 Food with Attitude
31 Ak Baba's
37 Cultured Cow Yoghurt
40 Faces
41 Jacksons
42 Burgerholics
43 Kaceys Restaurant & Nightclub
45 Land of the Pharoahs
46 Zippy's Vegetarian
48 Junipers
50 Victorian Rose
51 Chez Eelco & Pomeroy's
52 Tandoori
53 McDonald's
63 Pizza Hut
OTHER
6 Metropolis Nightclub
7 Library
8 Nelson Visitor Centre & Mt Cook Landline and Other Buses
10 Automobile Association (AA)
12 Chief Post Office
13 InterCity Depot & Suburban Bus Lines
18 Metropolitan
19 Molly McGuire's
20 Apaches
22 Riverside Pool
25 Suter Art Gallery
26 DOC & DOSLI
32 Air New Zealand Link
34 Bruce Rollo BBQ & Camping
36 Club 89
39 Zhivago's
44 Alp Sports Centre
49 Bishop's School
54 Shell Petrol Station
57 Cathedral
58 South Street Gallery, Historic South St, The Painted Pot's Partnership

in 1925 but construction dragged on for many years and in the 1950s arguments raged over whether the building should be completed to its original design. Eventually construction recommenced to a modified design in the 1960s and was completed in 1967. When the cathedral was finally consecrated in 1972, 47 years had passed since the foundation stone was laid! The cathedral is open from 8 am to 7 pm daily.

For about 90 years from 1840, **Bishop's School** served Nelson as a school. On display are the notes and textbooks used in the old days. It's on Nile St East and is open from 2 to 4 pm on Sunday, and on Tuesday and Thursday during holidays. If you don't find it open, ask at 28 Nile St.

Broadgreen House on Nayland Rd is another historic two-storey cob house built about 1855. It is open daily in the summer except on Monday. Entry is $3 (50c for kids).

Museums & Galleries

The **Founders Park**, at 87 Atawhai Drive, is a collection of old Nelson buildings, reflecting the town's early history. It's open from 10 am to 4.30 pm daily and admission is $5 (children $2).

The **Nelson Provincial Museum**, at Isel Park in the nearby town of Stoke, has New Zealand's largest photographic collection, and exhibits on local and Maori history. It's open from 10 am to 4 pm Tuesday to Friday, and from 2 to 5 pm on weekends and holidays; it's closed on Monday. Admission is $2 for adults, $1 for children.

Also in Isel Park is the historic **Isel House**, open from 2 to 4 pm on Saturday and Sunday, but only from late October to Easter; admission is $1 for adults and 50c for children. You can get there on the bus to Stoke.

The **Suter Art Gallery** adjoins Queen's Gardens on Bridge St and is open from 10.30 am to 4.30 pm every day; entry is $1 (children 20c). As well as having a permanent art collection it has art exhibitions, musical and theatrical performances, films and craft displays. The gallery takes its name from Bishop Suter, founder of the Bishopdale Sketching Club in 1889.

If you're interested in pottery, visit the **South St Gallery**, close to the Cathedral on Nile St West. It's open from 10 am to 5 pm Monday to Thursday, 10 am to 7 pm Friday, and 10 am to 4 pm weekends and holidays.

There are numerous other galleries in the area. Nelson's artistic reputation is partly due to the local clay which attracted many potters. The Nelson Potters' Association has a leaflet showing where to find the potters around Nelson – get it from the visitor centre.

Gardens

Nelson has some fine gardens, including the beautiful Botanic Gardens and Queens Gardens. In the **Botanic Gardens** there's a good lookout at the top of Botanical Hill, with a spire proclaiming it NZ's exact geographical centre.

Activities

Beaches & Swimming The best-known beach near Nelson is Tahunanui, five km from the town centre. At Tahunanui Beach, windsurfers, wave skis and body boards can be hired, and there's also a windsurfing school. You can reach Tahunanui on a Nelson Suburban bus. Rabbit Island is another popular beach, with 13 km of undeveloped beach backed by forest. There's road access to the island but it's closed off after 9 pm daily, and camping is not allowed; hours depend on the fire risk.

White-Water Rafting The Rapid River Adventure Company (☎ 542 3110) and Ultimate Descents (☎ 546 6212) both do white-water rafting on the Buller and Gowan rivers. It costs about $55 for a half-day trip and $90 for the full day.

Parapenting & Parachuting You can go parapenting with Airborn (☎ 543 2669) or Active Air Paragliding (☎ 544 1182). For those with a little extra spending money try a tandem parachute jump with Tandem Skydive Nelson (☎ 548 7652). It costs $170 per person and this includes transport, 10 minutes' instruction, the free fall and parachute descent (what you came for) and, importantly, a certificate. The Nelson Visitor Centre has information on these and many other activities around Nelson.

Walks The riverside footpath makes a pleasant stroll through the city, and there are many other fine walks and tramps. The Maitai Valley is particularly restful and beautiful.

Tours

There are many tours around Nelson, all of which can be booked through the Nelson Visitor Centre. Some of the more popular tours are Wine Trail tours ($30 to $35), Craft & Scenic Tours (from $25), and the Motueka Horticultural Tour (from $25) which visits a number of unusual agricultural operations including hop, green tea, kiwi fruit, nashi pear and other fruit farms, with their accompanying hop harvesters and packing houses.

A less sedate way to see the surrounding countryside is with a Happy Valley 4x4 Motorbike Tours (☎ 545 0304); it costs from $45 for a two-hour trip.

During the summer, day trips from Nelson to the Abel Tasman National Park are popular and good value. See Abel Tasman National Park in the Nelson to Golden Bay section in this chapter for details.

Places to Stay

Camping & Cabins There are plenty of camping grounds around Nelson, including the *Tahuna Beach Holiday Park* (☎ 548 5159) near the airport – the largest motor camp in Australasia! It can accommodate 4500 people and there are lots of tent and powered sites at $16, cabins and lodges from $25 to $38, and tourist flats from $43 (prices are for two). Linen can be hired. The site is five km from the city centre and just a couple of minutes from the beach – but light sleepers, beware! It's also very near the airport. The convenient camp supermarket is open to campers and to the public daily.

The *Brook Valley Motor Camp* (☎ 548 0399) in the upper Brook Valley is situated in a superb position near a stream and surrounded by rolling pastures and forested hills. It's about the same distance from the centre as Tahunanui, but rather smaller and more personal. Tent/powered sites are $13/14, and the cabins range from very basic two-bunk ones at $20 up to more luxurious ones at around $36; all prices are for two. The camp is a long way uphill if you're walking.

The city council's *Maitai Valley Motor Camp* (☎ 548 7729), Maitai Valley Rd, is on the riverbank, six km from the centre; tent/powered sites are $13/14 for two.

The *Nelson Cabins & Caravan Park* (☎ 548 1445) at 230 Vanguard St has cabins at $33.50 for two with cutlery and cooking utensils supplied, and you can hire linen. Tourist flats are $45 for two. It's very central but there are no tent sites; powered sites are $14.50 for two.

Other sites in the area include the *Richmond Holiday Park* (☎ 544 7323), 13 km from Nelson at Richmond, and the *Waimea Town & Country Club* (☎ 544 6476), also in Richmond, on Lower Queen St.

Hostels Hostels have been popping up like the proverbial mushrooms around Nelson, and the number has reached double figures – plenty of choice in this not-so-large town!

The new purpose-built *Nelson Central YHA* (☎ 548 8817) at 57 Rutherford St has room for about 80 people. The hostel has been designed so that large groups can be accommodated without interfering with smaller groups. It has several areas where you can get away from it all in a soundproofed environment, the kitchens and other facilities are expansive. There is an integrated outdoor area that opens into the food preparation areas and lounges. A dorm bed is $15 per person, and singles/doubles are $20/32. There are full paraplegic facilities in this complex.

The new *Dave's Palace* (☎ 548 4691) at 114 Rutherford St is still run by Dave. It is in the impressive Baigent Villa, a turn-of-the-century edifice which has great views out over the city. It is only 400 metres from the bus station and well worth the walk but more than likely Dave himself will pick you up (he is wearing the hat). The house is surrounded by expansive gardens and there are plenty of areas where you can sit down and relax. There is a book exchange, mountain bike hire and heaps of local information is provided. The shared rooms are $16, doubles and twins are $36 for two.

The *Tasman Towers* (☎ 548 7950) at 10 Weka St is a spacious, purpose-built hostel. The cost is $15 per person in dorms and share rooms, and twins and doubles are $34 (there is a surcharge on credit card payments!) and there are good kitchen and lounge facilities. Also in Weka St, at No 42, is the old YHA hostel, now renovated and under new management and a new name *Paradiso Backpackers* (☎ 546 6703). It is a lovely old building with spacious grounds. The cost is $15 per person in bunkrooms, and $34 for twins and doubles.

You can't miss the brightly coloured *Boots Backpackers* (☎ 548 9001), right in the centre of town on the corner of Trafalgar and Bridge Sts. There are very ordinary, basic dorm, double and twin rooms – select carefully as some of them were very unkempt when we checked (stained mattresses etc). Dorms are $14 per person and the other rooms cost $32 for two. There's a special sound-proofed 'Party Room' where parties take place several times weekly. There is a climbing wall out the back for the really adventurous and it costs $7 a go.

Not far away from here is *Sun City Backpackers* (☎ 548 9905) at 131 Bridge St (enter from New St pub on Bridge St) in the former Metropolitan Hotel. They charge $14 per person in dorms, and doubles or twins are $32 (most with their own shower). A big drawback is the location above one of Nelson's less salubrious pubs, so quite often it is noisy.

In the centre of town, at 8 Bridge St, is *Bumbles* (☎ 548 2771), a former hotel now with a backpacker feel. Dorm beds are $14 per person, and twin and doubles/triples are $38/51. It has recycling facilities, a big common room, plenty of information, gas BBQ, video and helpful staff.

A little bit of an uphill walk away is a rambling building called *Club Nelson* (☎ 548 3466) at 18 Mount St. Beds in dorm rooms are $15 per person, and twin or double rooms are $39. Be an orphan for the night in a single room from $18. Phone for free pick-up from the bus stop and railway station.

There are also two smaller hostels – Alan's Place and Nelson Backpackers 125. *Alan's Place* (☎ 548 4854) at 42 Westbrook Terrace is a bit further out, but still a reasonable walk from town, and offers dorm beds for $14 per person, and twins or doubles are $32 ($12/28 each night after the first), plus welcoming scones and all the free tea you can drink. Alan, one of the 'originals' in the backpacker industry, may even take you for a free tour of town when you arrive. There are free mountain bikes and stoves are rented for those doing tramping tracks. *Nelson Backpackers 125* (☎ 548 7576), 125 Tasman St, is conveniently located and has dorms for $13 per person, and doubles are $30.

The *Centre of New Zealand Backpackers* (☎ 546 6667), at 193 Milton St, is centrally situated near the Queen's Gardens and the swimming pool. It occupies a beautiful large historic manor house, built in 1881, with ample space both inside and out around the grounds. The cost is $15 per person in share and dorm rooms, and single/twin/double rooms are $20/34/36.

The *Beach Hostel* (☎ 548 6817) has recently moved to 25 Muritai St, Tahunanui Beach. It's an enjoyable hostel, with free bicycles and luggage storage, and although it's four km from the town centre it's not inconvenient. Local and long-distance buses stop just around the corner, it's an easy hitch to town, and the friendly owner Colin takes people along in the van whenever he goes to town. Phone for free pick-up when you arrive. Dorm beds are $15 per person, and doubles and twin rooms are $32. It is the closest hostel to the airport and there is a pub just across the road.

B&Bs, Guesthouses & Homestays Nelson has plenty of B&B places, but you might still have difficulty finding somewhere to stay in the high season. Best known and probably most expensive is *Cambria House* (☎ 548 4681) at 7 Cambria St. It is the top of the range and costs from $125/165 for a single/double. *California House* (☎ 548 4173), at 29 Collingwood St, is just across the river from the town centre. The owners provide a real Californian breakfast that might include orange juice, fresh berries and cream, ham and sour cream omelettes, apricot nut bread, apple and cheese blintzes, and pancakes with maple syrup and coffee. The cost is $125 to $150 for two including the hearty breakfast. There are only double rooms; if you're alone it's going to cost $95. California is only open September to May.

Further south along the same street, at No 174, is *Collingwood House* (☎ 548 4481) where singles/doubles are $50/70. *Sussex House* (☎ 548 9972), at 238 Bridge St, costs $50 per person or $75/85 a double without/with ensuite.

The *Harbour House* (☎ 548 7430) at 371 Wakefield Quay charge $50/70 for singles/doubles. There are many others including the *Willowbank* (☎ 548 5041) at 71 Golf Rd, Tahunanui Beach; *Aloha Lodge* (☎ 546 4000), at 19 Beach Rd, Tahunanui Beach; and *Pepper Tree Place* (☎ 542 3376), 126 Lord Rutherford Rd, in Brightwater.

Nelsonians are a friendly lot, and a number of private homes in the area offer accommodation for a maximum of four guests at a time, with rates usually about the same as the hostels. Ask for a réferral at the visitor centre. For real Kiwi hospitality stay with *Kay Cederman* (☎ 548 7993) at 81 Cleveland Terrace, on the east side of town, a 10-minute walk from the centre. There's rooms set aside for guests for $15 per person, and great views out to Tasman Bay.

Hotels & Motels There are plenty of regular hotels around Nelson. They include the *Dominion* (☎ 548 4984) at 2 Nile St West where singles cost from $28.50 to $31.50 and doubles cost $43 to $47; and the *Wakatu Hotel* (☎ 548 4299) at 83 Collingwood St with singles/doubles at $39/59.50. The expensive 115-room *Quality Hotel Rutherford* (☎ 548 2299) is on Nile St West and has everything from a sauna and swimming pool to a spa and gym. The cheapest rooms cost about $130, with discounts on weekends.

There are a great number of motels in Nelson, many of them near the airport at Tahunanui. Motels that are both fairly central and reasonably priced include the *Lynton Lodge Motel* (☎ 548 7112) at 25 Examiner St with double rooms for $62 to $73. The *Riverlodge Motel* (☎ 548 3094) is at 31 Collingwood St, on the Grove St corner; double rooms cost $65 to $85. At the *Trafalgar Lodge Motel* (☎ 548 3980), 46 Trafalgar St, units cost $60 to $70 for doubles (less in winter) while B&B is $35/55.

The *Mid City Motor Lodge* (☎ 546 9063), in the centre of town at 218 Trafalgar St, has rooms priced from $70 to $88 for doubles. By the river at 8 Ajax Ave the *AA Motor Lodge* (☎ 548 8214) is conveniently located with rooms around $88 for two people.

Places to Eat

It is the wealth of local produce that makes dining out in Nelson such a pleasure. Seafood is the main menu item as over 70% of the country's fishing quota is owned by Nelson businesses. Deep sea fish such as orange roughy and hoki, scallops from Tasman and Golden Bays, and mussels and oysters harvested commercially are all available in the town's restaurants. These are complemented by a wide range of locally produced wines and beers.

Snacks & Fast Food There are plenty of sandwich specialists around the centre and, a little further out, a *Pizza Hut* and a *KFC*. *McDonald's* has also appeared in the centre of Nelson – it's on Rutherford St on the Selwyn Place corner. The *Roadside Diner* is a big white pie cart that has been serving moe fast foods in Nelson since 1933. It's reputed to have the 'biggest burgers in NZ'. You can find it parked on Trafalgar St near Bridge St after 6 pm every day except Sunday. It's open until late most nights, until 3.30 am on Friday and Saturday!

Food with Attitude on Bridge St serves greasy burgers to alleviate the late-night hunger horrors. On Hardy St is *Burgerholics*, described by a traveller as 'fantastic'. Above their door is the sentence: 'World! The not yet famous Burgerholics'. Try the delicious char-grilled beef and bacon burger with whole grained mustard. Sadly for 'holics, both places are closed on Monday.

The cafe at the *Suter Art Gallery* is worth considering for a more expensive but pleasant lunch – it's open daily.

Pub Food There's a *Cobb & Co* in the Wakatu Hotel on the corner of Collingwood and Bridge Sts, with the usual Cobb & Co menu and opening hours – 7.30 am to 10 pm daily. *Kaceys*, on the corner of Trafalgar and Hardy Sts, also has a fairly standard pub-style menu. The *Post Boy* on the corner of Vanguard and Gloucester St has real cheap home-cooked roasts for $7 with desserts included.

At 281 Trafalgar St is the *Victorian Rose*, a pastiche of English/Irish pub styles in airy premises. The Guinness is served with care and there is a varied selection of beers.

Cafes & Restaurants Nelson is a town suited to the cafe. The *Chez Eelco*, near the cathedral at 296 Trafalgar St, is a Nelson institution and still the place to go to find out about the 'alternative' scene. It's a relaxed coffee bar and restaurant which is open from 6 am to 11 pm, daily. They serve everything from strong coffee, croissants, sandwiches and fruit juices to regular restaurant meals. It's a popular meeting place and the front window is an equally popular local notice board. Give it a try. Next door, at 276 Trafalgar St, the place with a pervasive smell of fresh roasted coffee is *Pomeroys*, where you can get cakes, croissants and coffee.

Zippy's Vegetarian at 276 Hardy St, with its decor based on the 1970s cartoon character, and the very popular *Broccoli Row* at 5 Buxton Square, are the best choices for vegetarian meals. At the latter, bookings are essential and meals are less than $20 for a main course.

The *Land of the Pharaohs* at 270 Hardy St is appropriately run by a real Egyptian who knows how to serve a bevy of Middle eastern delights for under $15. *Ak Baba's* at 130 Bridge St is run by Turks and you dine at low tables surrounded by Turkish rugs and carpets; three courses will set you back $15. Both of these Middle Eastern places do takeaways. *Dimitri's* Greek restaurant is on the corner of Collingwood and Halifax Sts, is. It is quite expensive but is difficult to pass up the mezedes Meraklis-style (with a glass of ouzo) for $13.50. The *Tandoori* on Selwyn Place has takeaways but you can sit down to a three-course meal from the tandoori oven for around $20.

Quayside, *Coasters* and *The Boatshed* are at Wakefield Quay on the road to Tahunanui. The Boatshed is an excellent restaurant and serves chilli crab out of the shell for a mere $18 or a full plate of sashimi for $13.50. If you are lucky get a table outside and look out over the sea watching the boats plying past in the harbour. A touch of the Cote d' Azur in sunny Nelson.

Across the road from the Wakatu Hotel is the *Little Rock Bar & Cafe* where you will meet some of Nelson's well to do enjoying pizza and budget meals while listening to good music. The cost of the original wrought iron sculpture is added to the wide range of cocktails. *Jacksons*, at 142 Hardy St, is a glossy modern restaurant with a decidedly international menu including Greek, Californian, Mexican and Chinese influences.

Ciao, The More Italian Restaurant, at 94 Collingwood St, is a BYO place open for lunch and dinner, Monday to Saturday. *Faces* on Hardy St is a bit more raunchy. Here you will get a plate of good Italian food for around $15. They have a good selection of local and international wines, and also have the cleverly named 'Live Poets Society' on the third Wednesday of every month. *Valeno's Wine Bar* on Bridge St is good place for cheap food and meals are less than $15.

Entertainment

Various pubs have entertainment including the *Ocean Lodge Hotel* at Tahunanui with a disco. *O'Reilly's Bar* at the Royal Hotel and *Kaceys* in the central city have entertainment on Wednesday. Beware, the latter is one of those places where humungous bouncers flex their 'pill-popped' muscles.

At the time of writing a Nelson music fan summed up the current scene thus: for blues go to *Apaches* on Bridge St; the *Metropolitan*, also on Bridge St, for hard rock; *Molly McGuire's* for Irish, folk and country; the *Victorian Rose* for blues and pop; and *O'Reilly's* for pop, blues and dance music.

Nelson also has several nightclubs. There's the *Metropolis* in Halifax St near the CPO; *Zhivago's* in the City Centre shopping arcade is clean, tidy and safe; and *Club 89*, on Hardy St, which looks a bit of a dive from outside, surprises once you are inside. Most nightclubs in town have one night during the week when they offer a special deal and become packed out with locals out for a good time. The *Metropolitan* underneath Sun City Backpackers is safe enough as long as you maintain your best social distancing skills.

Also worth a mention is the evening entertainment at the Suter Art Gallery. Besides the theatre, music, dance and so on, they have the Stage Two theatre with a top selection of popular and international art films.

Wherever you're dining in Nelson make a point of trying the local beer. Mac's beer is Nelson's own, brewed by an independent brewer; the appropriately named Pink Elephant – reminiscent of some Belgian Trappist varieties – is also worth a try; and Bay's beer is the latest of the local brews.

Getting There & Away

Air The Air New Zealand Link (Air Nelson Ltd) office (☎ 546 6242) is on the corner of Trafalgar and Bridge Sts. Air New Zealand Link have direct flights to Wellington, Auckland, Christchurch, Westport and New Plymouth, with connections to other cities. Ansett New Zealand (Tranzair; ☎ 547 7560) have direct flights to Wellington, with connections to other centres. Flight Corporation (☎ 547 8175) fly from Nelson to Wellington daily except Saturday for $70; book with the visitor centre.

Bus All buses serving Nelson arrive and depart from the Nelson Visitor Centre (☎ 548 2304) on the corner of Trafalgar and Halifax Sts. The office sells tickets for all bus lines. The InterCity Travel Centre (☎ 548 1539) is at 27 Bridge St.

InterCity buses run daily to Picton and Christchurch and to Greymouth via Murchison and Westport, with connections to the Franz Josef and Fox glaciers. The latter is an interesting route to Greymouth as it goes via the Buller Gorge and the scenic Coast Road, with a stop at Punakaiki's Pancake Rocks.

Mt Cook Landline (☎ 548 2304) also has daily buses from Nelson to Picton, which continue on to Christchurch, and buses to Christchurch via Lewis Pass (summer only).

Besides these two major bus lines, Nelson has a surprising number of more local operators. White Star (☎ 546 8687) operate between Nelson and Picton daily except Saturday, and Nelson to Christchurch via the Lewis Pass daily. White Star go through Springs Junction and Reefton to the 'Coast' so the trip is an hour shorter. Catch-a-Bus have an on-demand service between Blenheim, Picton and Nelson, with one service taking scenic Queen Charlotte Drive.

Heading west to Motueka and Golden Bay there's quite a variety of transport. Abel Tasman National Park Enterprises (☎ 548 7801) provide transport from Nelson, Motueka and Takaka to the Abel Tasman Track (see the Abel Tasman National Park section later in this chapter for details) and to the Heaphy Track. Barry's Buses (☎ (0800) 802 300) operate between Nelson and Blenheim, and Nelson and Hokitika daily. In summer they also operate the Abel Tasman Express (☎ 528 7014) to Marahau at the start of the Abel Tasman Coastal Track ($10) and to Motueka ($6); a return trip from Nelson to Marahau is $18. Bayways Book-a-Bus (☎ 525 9864) have daily services to Collingwood ($35), Takaka ($20) and Motueka ($9).

Several local companies have buses to the Nelson Lakes National Park (see that section in this chapter for more information). Wadsworths Motors (☎ 522 4248) has buses from Nelson to Lake Rotoiti and Tadmor on Monday, Wednesday and Friday, plus buses to Tapawera on weekdays. For trampers heading to the Heaphy and Wangapeka tracks, the Mt Arthur Tablelands, Cobb Valley and Mt Richmond forest park there is Transport for Trampers; phone ☎ 545 1055 for costs, timetable and minimum numbers.

A backpackers bus, the West Coast Express, departs from Nelson for six-day trips down the 'Coast' to Queenstown, with plenty of stops along the way. Since hitching is notoriously slow and seeing all the sights can be difficult travelling by public bus, this is a good way to see the West Coast. See the Getting Around chapter for details.

Getting out of Nelson is not easy as the city sprawls so far. It's best to take a bus to the outskirts. Hitching to the West Coast can be hard going.

Getting Around

Super Shuttle Nelson (☎ 547 5782) offers door-to-door service to and from the airport for $6; it operates daily. A taxi to the airport costs about $12. The Super Shuttle Nelson was set up to provide airport transport, but since it makes continuous return trips from Nelson to Tahunanui and on to the airport, many people use it to go just between Nelson and Tahunanui. Catch it from the visitor centre or the Quality Hotel Rutherford.

Nelson Suburban Bus Lines (☎ 548 3290) operates local services from its terminal on Lower Bridge St. They run out to Richmond via Tahunanui and Stoke, and also to Wakefield. Buses operate during the day until about 5 or 6 pm on weekdays, with one later bus at about 7 pm on Friday night. On Saturday buses run in the morning; there are no buses on Sunday.

Bicycles can be hired from Stewart Cycle City (☎ 548 1666) at 114 Hardy St, by the half-day, day, week or month, or from Fraine Cycles Ltd (☎ 548 3877) at 105 Bridge St. Thunderbike Engineering (☎ 548 7888) on Achilles Ave hire out touring motorbikes.

AROUND NELSON

Brightwater & Wakefield

The small town of Brightwater, the birthplace of Lord Rutherford, is a pleasant place to stay. Brightwater is nine km south of Richmond on the SH6, and there are farmstays and homestays in the region. Also south of Nelson, at Pigeon Valley, Wakefield, is the **Waimea Steam Museum**, with an interesting collection of vintage steam-driven machinery. It's open daily from 9 am to 4.30 pm.

Wineries

There are a number of vineyards on the Nelson Wine Trail which you can follow by doing a loop from Nelson through Richmond to Motueka, following the SH60 coast road in one direction and the inland Moutere River road in the other. Wineries open for visitors include Ruby Bay Wines, Neudorf Vineyards, Weingut Seifried, Redwood Cellars, Pelorus Vineyard, Robinson Brothers, Glover's Vineyard and Laska Cellars. McCashin's Brewery & Malthouse is also nearby if you wish to sample the legendary Black Mac. You can get a Wine Trail map from the information centres in Nelson or Motueka.

NELSON LAKES NATIONAL PARK

Nelson Lakes National Park is 118 km southwest of Nelson. Two beautiful glacial lakes are fringed by beech forest and flax, with a backdrop of forested mountains. There's good tramping, walking, lake scenery and also skiing (in winter) at the Rainbow Valley and Mt Robert ski fields. Information on the park is available at the Park Visitors Centre (☎ 521 1806) in St Arnaud or at the Lake Rotoroa Ranger Station (☎ 523 9369) near the northern end of Lake Rotoroa.

The park is accessible from two different areas, lakes Rotoiti and Rotoroa. St Arnaud village, at Lake Rotoiti, is the main centre and Rotoroa receives far fewer visitors (mainly trampers and fishing groups). An excellent three-day tramp from St Arnaud takes you south along the eastern shore of Lake Rotoiti to Sabine Hut, across the Travers River and up the Cascade Track to Angelus Hut on beautiful alpine Lake Angelus. The trip back to St Arnaud takes you along Roberts Ridge to the Mt Robert ski field. On a clear day this ridge walk affords magnificent alpine views all along its length. The track descends steeply to the Mt Roberts car park, from where it's a seven-km road walk back to St Arnaud. Other walks at Rotoiti include Peninsula Nature walk (1½ hours), Black Hill track (1½ hours return), Mt Robert Lookout (20 minutes), St Arnaud Range Track (five hours), Loop Track (1½ hours return) and Lakehead Track around the Lake (six hours).

There are a number of walks around Lake Rotoroa. Two short ones are the Short Loop Track (20 minutes) and the Flower Walk (10 minutes). Medium ones include Porika Lookout (two to three hours), Lakeside Track (six hours) and Braeburn Walk (two hours). The track along the eastern shore of the lake connects with the Sabine, Blue Lake and Lake Constance area of the walk described under Lake Rotoiti. For more information get a copy of the publications *Lake Rotoroa, Lake Rotoiti, Mt Robert* and *Peninsula Nature Walks* – these have condensed much of the information you need to know about NZ's forests into tiny, excellent volumes. For information on other walks in the Nelson Lakes region, ask at the ranger stations or refer to LP's *Tramping in New Zealand*.

Places to Stay & Eat

Lake Rotoiti There are *DOC Camping Grounds* (☎ 521 1806) at the edge of the lake in West and Kerr bays; the cost for tent/powered sites is $14/18 for two; there are toilets, coin-operated hot showers and a kitchen (the latter only at West Bay).

The *Yellow House* (☎ 521 1887) in St Arnaud has hostel-style accommodation for $15 per person in a dorm, share or twin, and a double is $32. It has a spa pool, laundry facilities, drying room and TV lounge, and is only a five-minute walk to Lake Rotoiti. Next door are the self-contained *St Arnaud Log Chalets* (☎ 521 1887), which are $75 for two.

The *Alpine Lodge* (☎ 521 1869), a 10-minute walk from the lake, has doubles for $95. The bar service here is abysmal. Across the car park is the *Alpine Chalet*, backpackers accommodation, which is booked at the lodge. This is a large, clean and very European-style 'alpine' building where it is $15/17 per person in dorms/share rooms, and $40 for a double. No-one seems to be running it however, and guests are left very much to themselves (there is a $5 key deposit).

There are also several camping grounds and lodges within the park itself – contact the Park Visitors Centre. There's a restaurant at the Alpine Lodge, and a snack bar at the petrol station, which also sells limited supplies of groceries. The *Tophouse* (☎ 521 1848), eight km from St Arnaud, dates from the 1880s when it was a hotel. It is now a comfortable (haunted?) farmstay where you can get dinner, bed and breakfast for $50.

Lake Rotoroa There is not much accommodation here. There is a basic *DOC camping ground* by the lake where the facilities only extend to a toilet and a water point; it costs a mere $2 per person. At the *Retreat Camping Ground*, towards Gowan Bridge, camp sites are $7 per night. The other two places, *Rotoroa Lodge* and *Braeburn Lodge*, are both very expensive. At the Rotoroa Lodge expect to pay about $250/500 for a single/double, full board.

Getting There & Away

Nelson Lakes Transport buses (☎ 548 6858) go from St Arnaud to Nelson daily at 8 am ($18), except on Sunday. Wadsworths Motors (☎ 522 4248) of Tapawera operate a service between Nelson and St Arnaud on Monday, Wednesday and Friday, leaving St Arnaud at 1 pm. In Nelson you catch this service at the Beaurepaires for Tyres car park, 72 Rutherford St. The Sounds to Coast Shuttle (☎ (0800) 802 225) passes through St Arnaud on Monday and Friday (also on Wednesday in summer) on its Picton to Greymouth service. The timetables for these services change all the time, so ring and check with the operators.

If you wish to get to Lake Rotoroa you will

usually have to hitch from Gowan Bridge. Nelson Lakes Transport will pick up but it is expensive unless in a group. The majority of visitors get here in their own cars. Nelson Lakes Shuttle (☎ 521 1887) operates in the region to Lake Rotoroa, Mt Roberts and Kawatiri; enquire at the Yellow House. JJ's Ski Transport (☎ 544 7081) operate from Nelson to the Rainbow Valley ski field and the Mt Robert car park in winter.

Water taxis operate on lakes Rotoiti and Rotoroa; these can be booked on (☎ 521 1894; Lake Rotoiti) or (☎ 523 9199; Lake Rotoroa). On Lake Rotoiti it is $10 from Kerr Bay to the lakehead (minimum of four). For the Lake Rotoroa run to the head of the lake from the village expect to pay $20 each if there are three passengers, $25 each if there are two.

NELSON TO MOTUEKA

From Richmond, south of Nelson, SH60 heads west to Motueka. The region fringing Tasman Bay is very popular with local holidaymakers. There is plenty of accommodation and many things to see and do such as arts & crafts, vineyards, yacht charters, fishing and swimming.

The picturesque Waimea Inlet and the twin villages of **Mapua** and **Ruby Bay** are at the mouth of the Waimea River. Facing them is Rabbit Island with great swimming beaches, boating, fishing and forest walks. *Naturesmoke*, right on Mapua wharf, is a great cafe, which dishes up delicious wood-smoked seafood such as groper, tarakihi, moki and snapper.

On the back road route along Wilson's Rd from Nelson to Motueka are the **tame eels** of the Moutere River. The eels are about 11 km from Upper Moutere village – look out for the signpost. Patient feeding over the years has made them so tame that they'll actually slither out of the water to take bits of meat from your hand. It's an unusual sight! Entry is $3 (children $1) and feeding times are supposedly 10 am to noon and 1 to 4 pm, but they're fairly flexible. The eels hibernate over winter, from late May to early August.

Places to Stay

The *Mapua Leisure Park* (☎ 540 2666) at 33 Toru St, Mapua, is 'NZ's first clothes-optional leisure park'! It has a private beach, nine-hole golf course, tennis and volleyball courts, swimming pool, sauna and spa, and a children's playground. Tent/powered sites are $18/20, cabins are from $29, on-site caravans are $42, or more expensive tourist flats are $57; all prices are for two persons (with off-season reductions).

The *McKee Memorial Reserve*, two km north of the leisure park, is a very basic camping ground right on the water's edge. Water, toilets and barbecue pits are the only amenities, but rates are cheap at $5 per camp site.

There is a backpackers in this region. The *Ruby Bay Backpackers Lodge* (☎ 540 3542) is on SH60, giving the impecunious a chance to explore the sights.

There are many homestays and farmstays in the region. Out at Thorpe, accessible from Motueka, Richmond or Mapua, you can stay at a rural retreat, *Rerenga Farm* (☎ 543 3825), on the Dovedale-Woodstock Rd. In this 80-year-old homestead B&B is $45/65 for singles/doubles and there is a self-contained cottage (maximum of three) for $40. Dinners with the hosts (one from Holland and the other from the USA) are $20 per person. Nearby is *Doone Cottage* (☎ 526 8740), Woodstock, which has singles/doubles with private bathrooms for $50/90; dinner is $25 extra. It is close to some great fishing spots.

Holton House (☎ 554 2269) is situated in an historic home at Ruby Bay, just to the north-west of Mapua. It costs $120/135 for singles/doubles, breakfast included; special diets are catered for. Also recommended is *Bronte Homestead* (☎ 540 2422) on Bronte Rd East, a turn-off from SH60. In this luxurious place, situated on the Waimea Inlet, single/double B&B is from $105/120; dinner is $30 extra. Other good places are *Wairepo* (☎ 526 6011) at Weka Rd, Mariri, off SH60, which has single/double B&B for $60/100; and the clay house *Mudcastle* (☎ 543 2113) on Neudorf Rd, Upper Moutere, with singles/doubles for $80/100.

MOTUEKA

Motueka is the centre of a green tea, hops and fruit-growing area. People often come here for the summer fruit-picking work and it's also a popular base for trampers en route to the walks in the Abel Tasman and Kahurangi national parks. The inhabitants are very cosmopolitan and include many craftspeople. In summer it's a bustling place, but in winter they say you could shoot a gun down the main street and not hit a thing!

Information

At the Motueka Visitor Information Centre (☎ 528 6543; fax 528 6563), 236 High St, you can get information, make bookings and buy tickets for most things happening around town, including tours, kayaks, launches and transport. It's open in summer from 8.30 am to 7 pm every day, in winter from 8.30 am to 5 pm. It is also the AA agent. The information centre provides the *Motueka Valley Craft Trail* guide which details the location of artists and craftspeople and, also, a *Wine Trail* map.

The DOC office (☎ 528 9117) is on the corner of High and King Edward Sts, and is open from 8 am to 4.30 pm on weekdays. The office is an excellent source of information on, and maps for, the Abel Tasman and Kahurangi national parks. Facilities Use Passes for the Abel Tasman Track can be bought in Motueka at either the information centre or DOC. Also check with the visitor centre and DOC for tidal information.

Coppins Great Outdoor (☎ 528 7296) at 255 High St, hires tents and backpacks for use on the tracks. Sleeping bags and cooking gear can be hired from the White Elephant and Motueka Backpacker hostels.

Activities

There are good **beaches** near Motueka at Kaiteriteri, Marahau, and the dress-optional Mapua Leisure Park. The best beach in the area is Kaiteriteri, north of Motueka on the road in to Abel Tasman National Park. The beaches along the Abel Tasman National Park coast can be easily reached on day launch trips; see the Abel Tasman National Park section in this chapter.

The Ultimate Descents (☎ 528 6363) is based in Motueka and does **white-water rafting** trips on the Buller and Gowan rivers. There's a half-day trip for $60 or an all-day trip for $95. There's also an easier 1½ hour trip on the Motueka River that's good for families, costing $30 (children $20).

You can hire **sea kayaks** from a number of places in the area. See also Sea Kayaking in Abel Tasman National Park.

Tours

Agriland Explorer Tours (☎ 527 8115) offer a horticulture tour around Motueka. They leave from the information centre and a tour costs $18 (children $10). They also have a wine tour for $22.50 (minimum numbers apply).

Launch trips off the Abel Tasman National Park coast are popular and good value; see Abel Tasman National Park in this section.

Places to Stay

Camping & Cabins The *Vineyard Tourist Units* (☎ 528 8550) are at 328 High St, near the centre of town. There's a variety of cabins and flats which are simple but good value, each with its own kitchen. Small cabins sleep up to four people for $32 to $38 for two; tourist units with private toilet facilities cost $44 to $50 for two.

The new *Fernwood Holiday Park* (☎ 528 7488) is sandwiched between SH60 and High St South at the south end of town. Tent/powered sites in this well-equipped park are $13/16 for two (children $3 extra).

Fearon's Bush Motor Camp (☎ 528 7189), at the northern end of town, has tent or powered sites at $17 for two, and cabins $26 for two.

Hostels The *White Elephant* (☎ 528 6208), a good backpackers, is at 55 Whakarewa St. It has room for 20 people in a big, comfortable old house set on almost one hectare of land. It costs $15 per person in dorm and share rooms, and $34 for doubles, including linen (there are a few tent sites). If it was full,

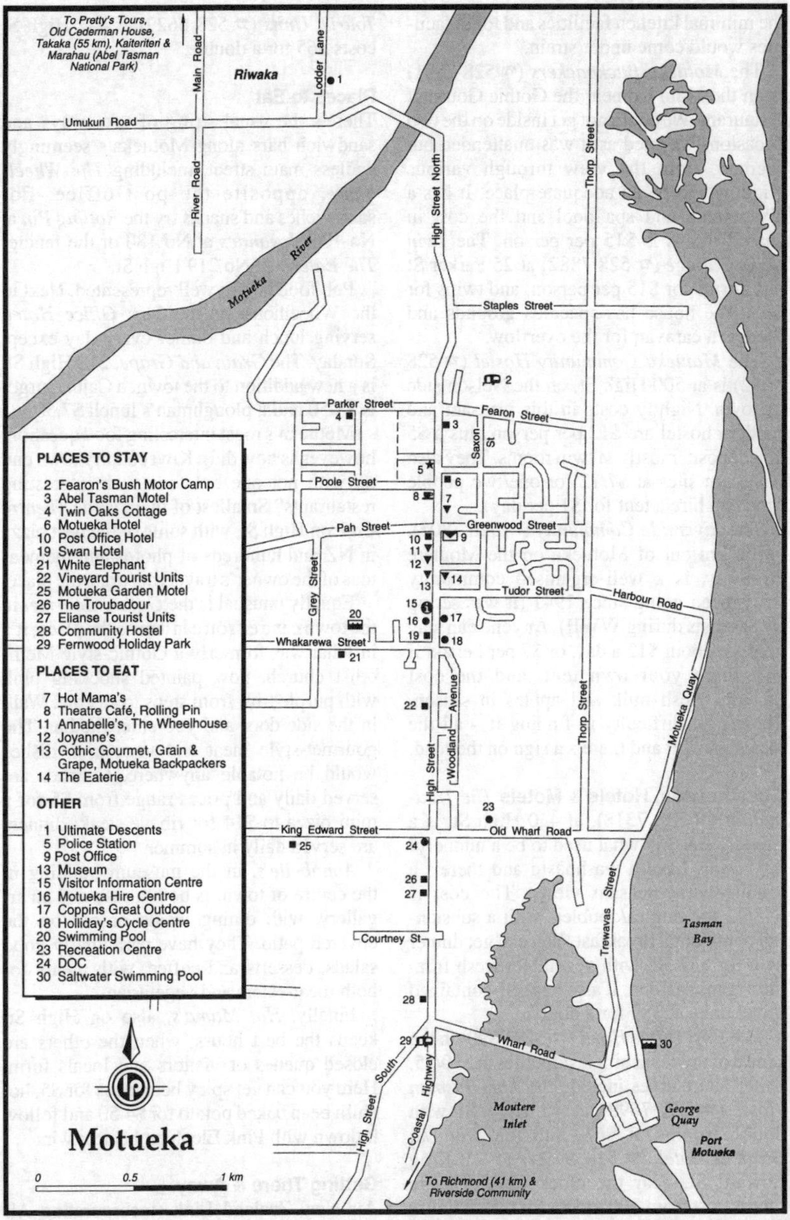
To Pretty's Tours, Old Cederman House, Takaka (55 km), Kaiteriteri & Marahau (Abel Tasman National Park)
Riwaka
Main Road
Lodder Lane
Umukuri Road
River Road
Motueka River
High Street North
Thorp Street
Staples Street
Parker Street
Fearon Street
Saxon St
Poole Street
Pah Street
Greenwood Street
Tudor Street
Harbour Road
Grey Street
Whakarewa Street
Woodland Avenue
High Street
Thorp Street
Motueka Quay
King Edward Street
Old Wharf Road
Trewavas Street
Courtney St
Tasman Bay
Wharf Road
High Street South
Coastal Highway
Moutere Inlet
George Quay
Port Motueka
To Richmond (41 km) & Riverside Community
PLACES TO STAY
2 Fearon's Bush Motor Camp
3 Abel Tasman Motel
4 Twin Oaks Cottage
6 Motueka Hotel
10 Post Office Hotel
19 Swan Hotel
21 White Elephant
22 Vineyard Tourist Units
25 Motueka Garden Motel
26 The Troubadour
27 Elianse Tourist Units
28 Community Hostel
29 Fernwood Holiday Park
PLACES TO EAT
7 Hot Mama's
8 Theatre Café, Rolling Pin
11 Annabelle's, The Wheelhouse
12 Joyanne's
13 Gothic Gourmet, Grain & Grape, Motueka Backpackers
14 The Eaterie
OTHER
1 Ultimate Descents
5 Police Station
9 Post Office
13 Museum
15 Visitor Information Centre
16 Motueka Hire Centre
17 Coppins Great Outdoor
18 Holliday's Cycle Centre
20 Swimming Pool
23 Recreation Centre
24 DOC
30 Saltwater Swimming Pool
Motueka
0
0.5
1 km

NELSON

the minimal kitchen facilities and toilet facilities would come under strain.

The *Motueka Backpackers* (☎ 528 7581) is on the Main Rd near the Gothic Gourmet restaurant. We could not get inside on the two occasions we tried as it was unattended but seemed, from the view through various windows, to be an adequate place. It has a TV lounge and spa pool and the cost in shared rooms is $15 per person. The *Twin Oaks Cottage* (☎ 528 7882) at 25 Parker St has dorms for $15 per person, and twins for $32. The house has spacious grounds and there is a caravan for the overflow.

The *Motueka Community Hostel* (☎ 528 8652) is at 500 High St, on the Nelson side of town. Nightly costs in this pleasant and modern hostel are $12 per person plus a $5 key deposit, mostly in twin rooms. They also have tent sites at $7/12 for one/two people (you can hire a tent for $1 per day).

The *Riverside Community* (☎ 526 7805), seven km out of Motueka on the Moutere Highway, is a well-organised community that's been going since 1941 (it was set up by pacifists during WWII). Anyone can stay here for about $12 a day, or $7 per person if you pitch your own tent, and the cost includes fresh milk and apples in season. There's no difficulty in finding it – all the locals know it and there's a sign on the road.

Guesthouses, Hotels & Motels *The Troubadour* (☎ 528 7318), at 430 High St, is a friendly B&B in what used to be a nunnery! All rooms have a washbasin and there's a lounge with pleasant views. The cost is $48/72 for singles/doubles, with a substantial continental breakfast. You can get dinner here for $22.50, with vegetables fresh from the organic garden. It also has self-contained motel units at $89 for a double.

The *Post Office Hotel* (☎ 528 9890) in the centre of town has singles/doubles at $30/45. Other alternatives include the *Abel Tasman Motel* (☎ 528 7699) at 45 High St with double rooms at $63, and the *Motueka Garden Motel* (☎ 528 9299) at 71 King Edward St, near the clock tower, where rooms cost from $60 to $85 for two. *Elianse Tourist Units* (☎ 528 6629) at 432 High St costs $65 for a double.

Places to Eat

There's the usual string of takeaways and sandwich bars along Motueka's seemingly endless main street, including *The Wheelhouse*, opposite the post office. For sandwiches and snacks try the *Rolling Pin* at No 105, *Joyannes* at No 180 or the fancier *The Eaterie* at No 219 High St.

Pub food is also well represented. Next to the Wheelhouse is the *Post Office Hotel*, serving lunch and dinner every day except Sunday. The *Grain and Grape*, 218 High St, is a new addition to the town; a Cajun burger is $8.50 and a ploughman's lunch $7.50.

Motueka's most interesting food question, however, is how did a Kiwi country town end up with not one but four such interesting restaurants? Smallest of them is the *Theatre Cafe* on High St, with some of the best pizza in NZ and hundreds of photos and mementoes of the owner's travels decorate the place.

Equally unusual is the *Gothic Gourmet* in the town centre. You can't miss the place; it's in what was formerly a Gothic-style Methodist church, now painted shocking pink with purple trim from steps to steeple. Walk in the side door and you enter the bar. The gourmet-style meat and vegetarian dishes would be notable anywhere. Lunches are served daily and prices range from $5 for a mini pizza to $14 for ribeye steak; dinners are served daily in summer.

Annabelle's, in the museum building in the centre of town, is both a cafe and an art gallery, with dining inside or out on the covered patio. They have particularly good salads, desserts and coffee, with plenty for both meat-eaters and vegetarians.

Finally, *Hot Mama's*, also on High St, keeps the best hours; when the others are closed queues of visitors and locals form. Here you can get spicy beef tacos for $5, hot chilli bean baked potato for $4.50 and follow it down with Pink Elephant beer or wine.

Getting There & Away

Air New Zealand Link (incorporating Air

Nelson; ☎ 528 6766) has direct flights to Takaka and Wellington, with many connections to other centres.

Abel Tasman National Park Enterprises (☎ 528 7801) operate from the information centre at 236 High St. They have services from Motueka to Nelson, Takaka, Collingwood and the Abel Tasman National Park (both ends of the track all year round). They also operate a daily bus service into the Heaphy Track in summer. Also during the summer they have buses linking Motueka with Nelson and Kaiteriteri, connecting in Kaiteriteri with their launch going up and down the coast following the Abel Tasman Track – but you *must* book ahead.

Bayways Book-a-Bus (☎ 525 9864) has daily buses from Takaka to Nelson which pass through Motueka; you can catch them at the visitor centre. They also operate to and from Totaranui by arrangement. See the Abel Tasman National Park entry in this section for more information on transport to and from the track.

Holliday's Cycle Centre at 227 High St hires mountain bicycles. The White Elephant and Motueka Backpackers hostels also hire bicycles. This area is ideal to explore on bike, especially if you are going to the wineries or craft places. Think twice, however, about cycling up Takaka Hill to get the views.

MOTUEKA TO TAKAKA

From Motueka, SH60 continues over Takaka Hill to Takaka and Collingwood. Before ascending Takaka Hill you pass a turn-off on your right to Kaiteriteri and the southern end of Abel Tasman National Park, then a turn-off on your left to Riwaka Valley, a good area for picnicking, swimming in river pools, and walks. You can walk to the spring that is the source of the Riwaka River.

Takaka Hill, 791 metres high, separates Tasman Bay from Golden Bay. Near the summit are the **Ngarua Caves** (☎ 528 8093) where you can see moa bones. Just before the Ngarua Caves there is the Hawkes Lookout from where there are great views of the source of the Riwaka River. The caves are open from 10 am to 4 pm daily except Friday but are closed from mid-June to August.

Also in the area is the biggest tomo (entrance or cave) in the southern hemisphere, **Harwood's Hole**. It is 400 metres deep and 70 metres wide. It will take you a full half day to get there from Motueka, as it is a half-hour walk one way from the car park at the end of Canaan Rd, off SH60. Exercise caution as you approach the lip of the hole – accidents have occurred here.

There are many homestays and farmstays in the region. On the way up Takaka Hill, 17 km north-west of Motueka, is a comfortable homestay, *Kairuru* (☎ 528 8091), where it is $100 for two with breakfast. Their cottages sleep four so a group is charged $20 each for their use, and dinner is $25 per person. A little further up the road and nestled amid the karst formations is *Marble Park* (☎ 528 8061); here single/double B&B costs from $55/75; dinner is $25 extra.

As you cross the crest of the hill there are fine views from Harwood Lookout down the Takaka River Valley to Takaka and Golden Bay. There's an interesting explanation of the geography and geology of the area at the lookout. The view extends from the North-west Nelson peneplain to the Anatoki Ranges. A peneplain, you ask? It is an area worn almost flat by erosion.

From the lookout you wind down through the beautiful Takaka Hill Scenic Reserve to the river valley, through Upper Takaka and on to Takaka itself.

Kaiteriteri Beach

This is one of the most popular beaches in the area, and it is just 13 km from Motueka on a sealed road. This beach has genuine golden sand. All water sports are available here as well as a great kids' playground complete with mini golf! Behind the camping ground you can try **Withells Walk**, a 45-minute excursion into native bush from where there are great views out across the bay. Otherwise walk to Kaka Pah Point at the end of the beach and find some of the secluded little coves and hideaways.

Places to Stay & Eat Summer brings many holidaymakers to Kaiteriteri, mainly locals. Despite its popularity there is not a great deal of accommodation available.

The *Kimi Ora Holiday & Health Resort* (☎ 527 8027), Martin Farm Rd, has a number of choices. The time of year affects pricing markedly with about a 10% add-on for Christmas holidays. Twin/double rooms range from $55 to $79 (or $95 with kitchen), and six-person units are from $100 to $160. The *Kaiteriteri Motor Camp* (☎ 527 8010), adjacent to the beach, has facilities for over 450 caravans. There are, however, cabins that cost from $22 and $30 for two, and on-site caravans for $26 (plus camp charges of $17 for two).

Apart from the *Vegetarian Restaurant* at Kimi Ora and the *Seafarers* near the beach there are not many dining choices here.

Getting There & Away With sufficient numbers the hire of a water taxi can be economical. Water-Taxi Charter (☎ 528 7497) at Kaiteriteri Beach can drop off at various parts of the national park or even provide transport for diving trips.

ABEL TASMAN NATIONAL PARK

The coastal Abel Tasman National Park is a popular tramping area and the various walks include one around the coast – but beware of the sandflies. The park is at the northern end of a range of marble and limestone hills extending from Kahurangi National Park, and the interior is honeycombed with caves and potholes. There are other tracks in the park, including an inland track, but the coastal track is the popular one.

Abel Tasman Coastal Track

This three to four-day track is one of the most beautiful in the country, passing through pleasant bush overlooking beaches of golden sand lapped by bright blue water. The numerous bays, small and large, make it like a travel brochure come to life.

Once little known outside the immediate area, this track has now been 'discovered' and in summer hundreds of backpackers may be on the track at any one time – far more than can be accommodated in the huts, so bringing a tent is a good idea. At other times of the year it's not so crowded.

Information The track operates on a Great Walks Pass system – the cost is $6 per night on the track (children $3) whether you stay in the huts or camp. You can obtain the pass from DOC or information centres in Nelson, Motueka and Takaka. All these DOC offices are sources of track information, and there's also a National Park Visitors Centre at Totaranui, open seasonally from late November to February. The huts (Anchorage, Awaroa, Bark Bay and Whariwharangi Homestead have bunks for 20 or more people and are equipped with wood stoves. (Or see LP's *Tramping in New Zealand*.)

Walking the Track Several sections of the main track are tidal, with long deviations during high tides, particularly at Awaroa. As the tidal stretches are all just on the northern side of huts, it is important to do the track in a southerly direction if the low tides are in the afternoons, and from south to north if they are in the mornings. Check the newspaper, subtracting 20 minutes from the Nelson tidal times. Tide tables and advice are available at the DOC office in Motueka.

If you have the time, take additional food so that you can stay longer should you have the inclination. Bays around all the huts are beautiful but the sandflies are a problem, except at the tiny, picturesque beach of Te Puketea near the Anchorage Hut.

Excess luggage can be sent very cheaply by the various buses between Nelson, Motueka and Takaka. There are four-day guided walks on the track for around $525 (children $465). Or you could parallel the track in a sea kayak. Estimated walking times are as follows, south to north:

Marahau to Anchorage Hut or Torrent Bay Hut	three to four hours
Torrent Bay to Bark Bay Hut	three hours
Bark Bay to Awaroa Hut	three hours
Awaroa to Totaranui	1½ hours

Activities

Sea Kayaking Some people prefer to follow the track around the coast by sea kayak. A traveller from Denmark, Steen Rasmussen, wrote to say:

> I did the Abel Tasman National Park kayaking instead of walking, and can definitely recommend it. No overfilled tracks or huts, and you're alone with nature all the time. There are plenty of secluded beaches where trampers can't get access. No tiring hills, and possibility of bringing all you want. The beauty and the silence of the sea beats everything, and the seals playing below and around your boat are just amazing.

The Ocean River Adventure Company (☎ 527 8266) on Main Rd, Marahau, rents sea kayaks for $90 per person for two days (two-day, two-person minimum). It also has one, two, three and four-day trips that vary in price from $85 to $370 per person, depending on duration. Another operator out of Marahau is Abel Tasman Kayaks (☎ 527 8022), whose prices are similar to Ocean River.

Seal Swimming Abel Tasman Seal Swim (☎ 527 8136) organise swimming trips with seals off Tonga Island; they have the DOC licence for this activity. They supply snorkel, mask, flippers and a snack for $65. If you prefer to just watch as the swimmers frolic with the seals it only costs $40.

Tours

Abel Tasman National Park Enterprises (☎ 528 7801) has 6½-hour launch services departing from Kaiteriteri at 9 am, dropping off trampers in Totaranui (the northern end of the track) at 12.15 pm and picking up returning trampers, and arriving back at Kaiteriteri at about 3.30 or 4 pm.

The launch service doubles as trampers transport and also a pleasant day cruise. Along the way it stops at Tonga Bay, Bark Bay, Torrent Bay and Tinline Bay. You can easily combine a walk along part of the Abel Tasman track with the cruise, being dropped off at one bay and picked up later at another.

Sea Kayaking in Abel Tasman National Park

A lot of people choose to sea kayak around the relatively safe and definitely very scenic waters of Abel Tasman National Park. A popular starting-point is Marahau at the southern end of the Abel Tasman Track. The peak season is from November to Easter but you can paddle all year round. Winter is a really good time as you will see more birdlife. Instruction is given to first-timers. For those going on a day trip, enough guidance is provided – ie basic strokes – for you to manage a day's paddling. If renting, you will be given a couple of hours' briefing on tides, weather and basic strokes.

Firstly, you could try a day trip. Typically, from Marahau you are on the water by 9.30 am (depending on the tides). You can hope to get to Fisherman and Adele islands in about one hour of paddling. On the way you will see lagoons, an important wildlife habitat, and several species of wading birds. If you are lucky, when you head into the open sea you will spot penguins, black shags, Australasian gannets, black-backed gulls, crested and white-fronted terns, and sometimes black-fronted and Caspian terns. Often, a delicious lunch is caught – mussels, pipis and scallops – complemented with pitta bread, salad, kebabs, orange juice, tea, coffee, and cake from the Park Cafe.

Longer trips, operated by the two main companies at Marahau, are typically two nights and three days; the cost is around $250. It may be a base-camp trip returning to the same camp each night, say North Head or Bark Bay. From the base you will paddle out to Tonga Island to see fur seals and, tide permitting, into the lagoons. It would not be unusual to see a dolphin. The other type of trip would cover a set distance, eg Marahau to Onetahuti Beach, with two overnight stops at Te Puketea Bay/Anchorage and then Mosquito Bay/Tonga Quarry. Return is by water taxi to Marahau. Again, the paddlers see Tonga Island and fern-lined lagoons.

Save your feet for the bigger walks down south and paddle Abel Tasman National Park. ■

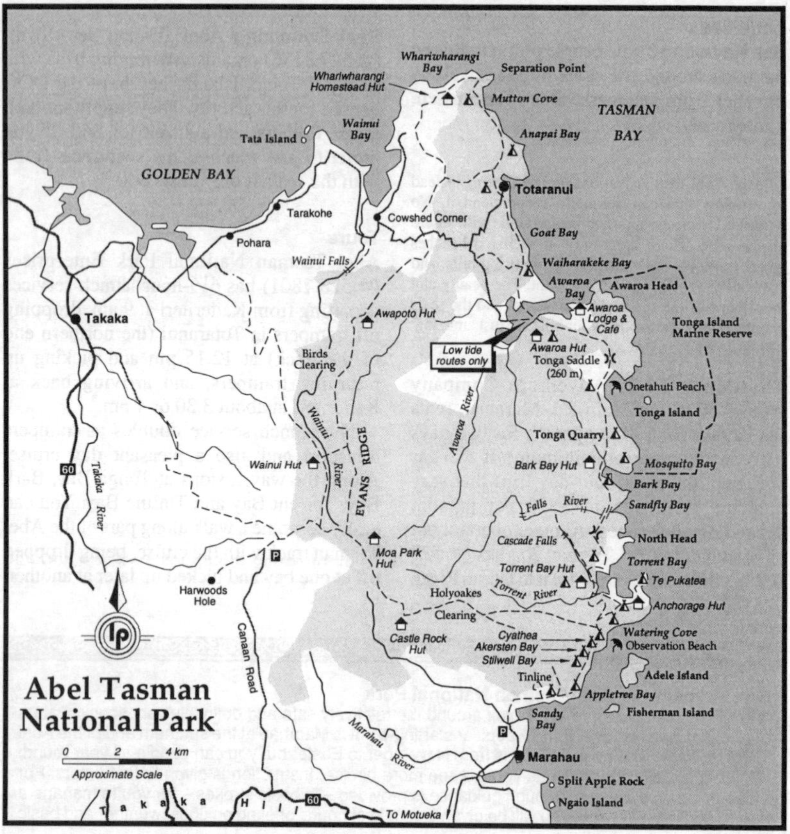

Abel Tasman National Park

There are several such options, the most popular being to disembark at Bark Bay, walk the track 2½ hours to Torrent Bay, have time on the beach for swimming, and be picked up there. The cost for either the full day cruise or walk/cruise option is $42 (children $14).

The launch service operates on a scheduled route from 1 September to 11 June each year, but will go at any time of the year if it has enough bookings. All launch trips must be booked in advance, either directly with Abel Tasman National Park Enterprises or at the information centres in Nelson or Motueka. The same company operates a bus service from Nelson and Motueka which connects with the launch, making it an easy day trip from either town.

Christopher Grey Adventure Cruises (☎ (03) 546 9885) run overnight cruises in the *Christopher Grey* from Nelson to the Abel Tasman National Park all year round; the cost is $138 with all meals ($45 for the lift only, no meals or beds).

Places to Stay & Eat

At Awaroa Bay you can stay at the *Awaroa Lodge & Cafe* (☎ (025) 433 135) which is only 300 metres from the water. At this place, 200 metres off the track, share accommodation is from $15 to $19 per person, and singles/doubles are $40/$60. Their cafe offers a range of health food, and the proprietors will also pack lunches. Stay a while to look at the birds – white faced herons, pied stilts, Caspian terns, tuis, bellbirds and moreporks are all found here. You have three ways of getting to Awaroa Lodge: by water taxi, walking part of the Abel Tasman Track from Totaranui, or driving to the Awaroa car park and then walking. The *Marahau Beach Camp* (☎ 527 8176) at Marahau, 18 km north of Motueka, has tent/powered sites for $16/26, cabins for $35 and a self-contained flat for $50; all prices are for two.

There is also *The Barn* hostel and camping ground (☎ 527 8043) on Harvey Rd, Marahau, at the entrance to the national park, where dorm beds are $14 per person, and doubles are $35; there are 15 camp sites at $8 per person. They offer a range of supplies and activities including sea kayaking and horse trekking. The bus service from Nelson drops you off at The Barn. We get many readers' recommendations for this place.

Also at Marahau are the self-contained *Ocean View Chalets* (☎ 527 8232) on Sandy Bay Rd, the comfortable *Marahau Lodge* (☎ 527 8250), *Old MacDonald's Farm* (☎ 527 8288) on Harveys Rd, and the homestay *Abel Tasman Stables* (☎ 527 8181). At the latter, single/ double B&B with a continental breakfast is $30/55; dinner is $15 extra.

Nearby is the *Park Cafe* which has good food and a great atmosphere; gorge on cakes, muffins, blueberry crumble and milkshakes before heading out on the track.

The *Totaranui Beach Camp* (☎ 525 8026) at Totaranui, 33 km from Takaka in the northern part of the national park, is administered by DOC, with campsites at $6.50 per person. Sites for the Christmas holidays can be reserved from July onwards.

Getting There & Away

Abel Tasman National Park Enterprises (☎ 528 7801) operates buses from Motueka and Nelson to Kaiteriteri, from where its launch departs. You can take either the bus or the launch separately, but you must book this bus, as well as the launch, in advance. In summer the bus departs from Nelson daily at 7.35 am and arrives at Marahau at 9 am and at Totaranui at 11.15 am. The launch departs from Kaiteriteri at 9 am reaching Torrent Bay at 10.25 am ($17), Bark Bay at 11 am ($20), Awaroa at 11.30 am ($28) and Totaranui at 12.30 pm ($28); there is an express service in summer.

Bayways Book-a-Bus (☎ 525 9864) operates buses between Takaka and Totaranui by arrangement. Barry's Buses (☎ 546 2300) have a summertime Abel Tasman Express, three times daily, from Nelson to Marahau ($10).

The catamaran *Spirit of Golden Bay* (☎ 525 9135) commutes between Golden Bay and Nelson, picking up and dropping off trampers anywhere in the park. It departs from Tarakohe in Golden Bay at 9 am, and arrives in Nelson at the Akersten St boat ramp at 12.30 pm, before departing for the return journey at 1.30 pm.

In summer Abel Tasman Seafaris (☎ 527 8083) also do a morning and afternoon trip from Marahau to Awaroa Lodge; in winter the morning trip is by arrangement only.

TAKAKA

The small centre of Takaka is the last town of any size as you head towards the northwest corner of the South Island. It's the main centre for the beautiful Golden Bay area. It's also quite a hip little community – lots of children of the 60s and artistic types have settled here. Pohara Beach is a popular summer resort near the town.

Information

Just about everything in Takaka is found along Commercial St, which is the main road through town, only a few blocks long. On the Motueka side of town there's a helpful information centre (☎ 525 9136) open daily from 9 am to 5 pm in summer and 10 am to 4 pm in winter. Pick up a copy of their promotional booklet *Golden Bay Visitors Guide* (in return for a small donation) which has interesting articles about the many points of interest around Golden Bay.

There's a DOC office (☎ 525 8026) with information on the Abel Tasman and Kahurangi national parks, the Heaphy and Kaituna tracks, Farewell Spit, Cobb Valley, the Aorere goldfield and the Pupu Springs Scenic Reserve. It's open from 8.30 am to noon and 1 to 4 pm, Monday to Friday.

Facilities Use Passes for the Abel Tasman track are available in Takaka from the DOC office, Tickets & Trips at 49 Commercial St and the Shady Rest Hostel. There's an AA agent in the centre of town.

Windsurfing is a popular activity on Golden Bay – all the local beaches are excellent – and windsurfers are available at the Shady Rest and the Pohara Beach Camp.

Pupu Springs

These springs (the full Maori name is Waikoropupu, but everyone calls it simply Pupu) are the largest freshwater springs in NZ. Many springs are dotted around the Pupu Springs Scenic Reserve, including one with 'dancing boulders' thrown upwards by the great volume of incredibly clear water emerging from the ground.

Walking tracks through the reserve take you to the springs, passing by gold-mining works from last century – gold was discovered in Golden Bay in 1865, four years after the first NZ discovery in the Coromandel. DOC has an excellent leaflet about the reserve. To reach Pupu from Takaka, go four km north-west on SH60, turn inland at Waitapu Bridge and continue for three km.

Other Attractions

Takaka has a small **museum**, open daily (adults $1, children 50c). The **Begonia House** in Clifton, eight km east of town, is open in summer to show off its colourful flowers.

Many artists and craftspeople are based in the Golden Bay area, including painters, potters, blacksmiths, screen printers, silversmiths and knitwear designers. In town, a cooperative of the Golden Bay craftspeople has established the large **Artisans' Shop** in Commercial St, next to the Village Theatre, to display their wares. Many other artists and craftspeople are tucked away all around the bay. The *Golden Bay Craft Trail* leaflet gives directions to the galleries and workshops. The Whole Meal Trading Company and the Golden Bay Gallery (in the old post office) also have local art on display.

The **Rawhiti Caves** (☎ 525 9061) near Takaka have the largest entrance of any cave in NZ, well worth a look (*ra* is the Maori sun god and *whiti* is the morning sun). A three-hour return guided tour of the caves costs $12 (children $5). To reach the caves you walk for 45 minutes through stands of 400-year-old totara. It's an enjoyable and popular tour that's good value.

Places to Stay

Camping & Cabins The *Pohara Beach Camp* (☎ 525 9500) is 10 km from Takaka, right on the beach. Tent/powered sites are $13.50/14.50 for two, and there are cabins at $24 and $34 for two. On Tukurua Beach, 18 km north of Takaka and eight km south of Collingwood, the *Golden Bay Holiday Park* (☎ 525 9742) has powered sites at $16, on-site caravans for $25 and cabins at $28; all prices are for two.

Hostels The *Shady Rest Hostel* is a hospitable and relaxed hostel in a big historic home on the main road (141 Commercial St), 400 metres from the town centre on the Collingwood side. The twins and doubles are listed at $20 per person, although you may get them for less. The hostel has windsurfers for hire, and you can spend some time feeding the tame eels, pukekos and ducks in the creek behind the house. It is 'Telecom-free'.

The *Sans Souci Inn* (☎ 525 8663) at Pohara Beach is a rammed-earth building with grass growing out of the roof. They provide set meals or you can cook your own. The cost here is $17 per person in dorms or twins.

About 15 km west of Takaka you will find the *Shambhala Beach Farm Hostel* (☎ 525 8463), spectacularly set overlooking the beach at Onekaka. Here the emphasis is on alternative energy, renewable resources etc. You just get off the Bayway Book-a-Bus at the Mussel Inn at Onekaka or if driving take the right turn 50 metres before the Inn (coming from Takaka). It is only $15 per person in share rooms, and $35 in twins and doubles. In this area there is snorkelling, windsurfing, swimming, boating, and party nights at the Mussel Inn. There is a great German-language book exchange and much of the owner's artwork adorns the walls.

B&Bs, Hotels & Motels There are far too many B&B places in this region to mention them all. They are listed in the pamphlet *Bed & Breakfast: Golden Bay Directory*, available free from information centres.

The rudimentary *Junction Hotel* (☎ 525 9207), on the main street, has singles/doubles for $34/50. The *River Inn* (☎ 525 9425) is three km north of town on Waitapu rd, just off SH60. It has recently been modernised and has a good restaurant and a lively bar; singles/doubles are $25/50.

There are a number of motels in or around Takaka, particularly at Pohara Beach, all charging around $60 to $70 for two. The *Golden Bay Motel* (☎ 525 9428) is on the main road in Takaka, and there's the *Tata Beach Motel* (☎ 525 9712) on Tata Beach. At Pohara, the *Pohara Beachfront Motel* (☎ 525 9660) has units at $57 to $80 for two (an $85 minimum applies in the peak Christmas season). Also on Pohara Beach, and slightly cheaper at $48 for two, is the *Sunflower Motel* (☎ 525 9075).

Places to Eat

The *Whole Meal Trading Company* in the town centre is a local institution, an enjoyable wholefoods cafe, restaurant and art gallery which also sells bulk natural foods, has a bulletin board, and sometimes has live music in the evenings.

Milliways further down the main road is another good spot with a relaxed atmosphere; it is licensed and open daily in the summer. The *Takaka Tearooms* is next to an inexpensive Chinese and fish & chip takeaway. If you haven't already eaten enough pasta on the Abel Tasman Track then pop into *Pasta Place* in Commercial St.

Getting There & Away

Air New Zealand Link (incorporating Air Nelson) has direct flights to Motueka, with connecting flights to Wellington; inquire at the information centre for schedules. Takaka Valley Air Service (☎ 525 8613) fly to Nelson and Wellington, Friday and Sunday.

The Bayways Book-a-Bus service (☎ 525 9864) goes from Takaka to Collingwood and to Nelson daily, and return. To get from Pohara to Takaka call Bayways Book-a-Bus. The Abel Tasman Park Enterprises bus also operates from Nelson to Takaka ($20) and Takaka to Collingwood ($12) daily.

The catamaran *Spirit of Golden Bay* operates from Nelson to Pohara Beach near Takaka daily in the summer; the one-way fare is $50 (return $100).

KAHURANGI NATIONAL PARK

Formerly the North-West Nelson Forest Park, this is the newest and second largest of NZ's national parks and, undoubtedly, one of the greatest. Within its 500,000 hectares is an ecological wonderland – over 100 bird species, 50% of all NZ's plant species, 80% of its alpine plant species, a karst landscape and the largest known cave system in the southern hemisphere. Kahurangi means 'treasured possession'. Few keen trampers will disagree, as the many fine tracks and the rugged country attracts them in droves, most coming to walk the Heaphy Track.

Information

Detailed information, park maps and Great Walks Passes for the Heaphy Track are obtainable from these DOC offices:

Nelson Conservancy: Munro State Building, 186 Bridge St (☎ 546 9335)
Nelson Visitor Information Centre: corner of Trafalgar & Halifax Sts (☎ 548 2304)
Motueka Field Centre: corner of King Edward & High Sts (☎ 528 9117)
Takaka Field Centre: 1 Commercial St (☎ 525 8026)
Karamea Field Centre: Main Rd (☎ 782 6852)

For those who require the services of a guide in this region, there is Bush & Beyond (☎ 526 6093). Parties have a maximum of six people and two guides; the cost is about $250/350 for two/three days.

Heaphy Track

The four to six-day Heaphy Track is one of the best known tracks in NZ. The track doesn't have the spectacular scenery of the Routeburn, but it still has its own beauty. Surprisingly, some people find it a disappointment if done immediately after the nearby Abel Tasman Coastal Track.

The track lies almost entirely within the Kahurangi National Park. Highlights include the view from the summit of Mt Perry (two-hour walk, return, from Perry Saddle Hut) and the coast, especially around the Heaphy Hut. It's worth spending a day or two resting at the Heaphy Hut, something which is appreciated by those travelling south from Collingwood. It is possible to cross the Heaphy River at its mouth at low tide.

Huts are geared for 20 or more people. They all have gas stoves, except Heaphy and Gouland Downs which have wood stoves, and nightly hut fees are $8 (children $4); camping is permitted and is $6 per person.

Walking the Track Most people travel west from Collingwood to Karamea. From Brown Hut the track passes through beech forest to Perry Saddle (but don't take the shortcut uphill, unless you are fit). The country then opens up to the swampy Gouland Downs, then closes in with sparse bush all the way to Mackay Hut. The bush becomes more dense towards the Heaphy Hut with the beautiful nikau palm growing at lower levels.

The final section is along the coast through heavy bush and partly along the beach. Unfortunately, the sandflies are unbearable along this, the most beautiful part of the track. The climate here is surprisingly mild but do not swim in the sea as the undertows and currents are vicious. The lagoon at Heaphy Hut is good for swimming though, and fishing is possible in the Heaphy River.

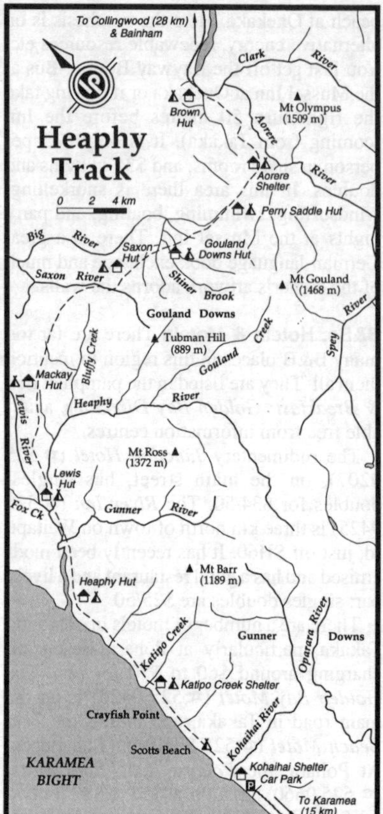

The Heaphy now has km markers along its length; the zero marker is at the start of the track at the Kohaihai River near Karamea and the total length is 76 km.

Estimated walking times are as follows:

Brown Hut to Perry Saddle Hut	five hours
Perry Saddle to Gouland Downs Hut	two hours
Gouland Downs to Saxon Hut	1½ hours
Saxon to Mackay Hut	three hours
Mackay to Lewis Hut	three to four hours
Lewis to Heaphy Hut	two to three hours
Heaphy Hut to Kohaihai River	five hours

Wangapeka & Leslie-Karamea Tracks

It is possible to return to the Nelson/Golden Bay region by the more scenic, if harder, **Wangapeka Track** (about five days) starting just south of Karamea. Although not as well known as the Heaphy, the Wangapeka, also in Kahurangi National Park, is thought by many to be a more enjoyable walk. The track starts some 25 km south of Karamea at Little Wanganui (on the West Coast side) and runs 56 km east to the Rolling River near Tapawera. It takes about five days and there is a good chain of huts ($4 to $8 per night, children $2 to $4) along the track.

The 90-km **Leslie-Karamea Track** is a medium to hard tramp of five to seven days. It connects the Cobb Valley near Takaka with Little Wanganui, south of Karamea, on the West Coast (thus including part of the Wangapeka Track on the final two days).

Cobb Valley & Mt Arthur Tablelands

In particular the areas outlined in the DOC pamphlets, *Cobb Valley* and *Mt Arthur Tablelands Walks*, offer plenty of scope. The Cobb Valley is 28 km from the Upper Takaka turn-off. You first drive up to the power station and from here it is another 13 km drive to the valley. Once in the valley there are a number of walks to choose from. These range from the 45-minute Mytton's Forest Walk to others of a few hours' duration, eg Cobb Ridge to Peat Flat and Trilobite Hut to Chaffey Hut. Chaffey Hut, built in 1954, is constructed of split beech slabs.

To get to the Mt Arthur Tablelands you drive from Motueka south to Pokororo. From here take the Graham Rd into the Flora car park. From here there are a great number of walking possibilities. Walks include Mt Arthur Hut (three km, one hour), Mt Arthur (eight km, three hours), Mt Lodestone (five km, two hours) and Flora Hut (two km, 30 minutes).

Kaituna Track

This track is situated west of Collingwood and the user is provided with two choices: a return walk of two to three hours through the old gold workings and bush scenery, and a longer track (five to seven hours, 12 km) which takes you to the West Coast at Whanganui Inlet. The pamphlet *Kaituna Track* is most informative, outlining in detail flora & fauna to be seen along the way. Included is the nikau, the world's most southerly occurring palm, and the crown fern.

Aorere Adventure Tramps, Walks & Kayaks (☎ 524 8040), run by the people from the Inn-let, guide a one-day walk through the beautiful Wakamarama Range for $65.

Aorere Goldfield

The Aorere goldfield was the first major goldfield in New Zealand. In February 1857, five ounces (142 grams) of Collingwood gold were auctioned in Nelson, precipitating a gold rush which lasted three years, although various companies continued to wrest gold from the soil by sluicing and stamping batteries right up until WWI. The old gold fields are now overgrown but the more durable features such as terraces, water races and mine shafts can still be seen.

The DOC office in Takaka has an excellent publication, *Aorere Goldfields/Caves Walk*, detailing the history of the goldfield and guiding you on a historical walk, with directions beginning from Collingwood. The walk takes most of the day to complete. You can learn more about the local history at the small museum in town.

Getting There & Away

Hitchhiking to either the Karamea or Bainham end of the Heaphy Track is very difficult. Collingwood Safari Tours (☎ 524 8257), in Collingwood, provide transport to the track on demand. Abel Tasman National Park Enterprises (☎ 528 7801; 525 9443) have a service from Collingwood and Takaka to the track entrance in summer ($15 and $20 respectively); in winter it is on demand and expensive. Bayways Book-a-Bus (☎ 525 9864) will transport you to the start of the Heaphy Track from Takaka for $22.50 (minimum of four). There's a phone at the trailhead so you can call for one of the many buses. For details at the Karamea end of the track (and also for the Wangapeka and Leslie-Karamea tracks) see Karamea in the Westland chapter.

Transport for Trampers (☎ 545 1055), Nelson, specialise in providing transport to and from other walking tracks in Kahurangi National Park. The cost of a ride from Nelson to Cobb Valley is $30, to the Mt Arthur Tablelands $23, to the Wangapeka Track $25 and to the Heaphy Track $35 (minimum of four for all trailheads).

COLLINGWOOD

The tiny township of Collingwood is almost at the end of the line, which is one of its main attractions. For many it's simply one jumping-off point for the Heaphy Track in the Kahurangi National Park. For others who wish to explore, there are many rewards such as the natural wonderland of Farewell Spit.

As befits a frontier town, there is a place where you can get a horse. Cape Farewell Horse Treks (☎ 524 8031) are based in Puponga; a one-hour ride is $15 and a three-hour trip to Wharariki is $50. And a kayak? A full-day trip in Whanganui Inlet with Aorere Adventure Tramps, Walks & Kayaks (☎ 524 8040) is $70 if there are five people, $80 if there are only three.

Farewell Spit

Farewell Spit is a wetland of international importance and a renowned bird sanctuary. It's the summer home to thousands of migratory waders from the Arctic tundra. On the 26-km beach run there are huge crescent-shaped sand dunes from where you get panoramic views of the Spit, Golden Bay, and at low tide, the vast salt marsh.

At the Puponga car park (before the restricted section of road) there are bones from a sperm whale that beached here. You can look out over the eel grass flats and see many waders and seabirds such as pied and variable oystercatchers, turnstones, Caspian terns, eastern bar-tailed godwits, black and white-fronted terns, and big black shags. The Puponga visitors centre provides information as well as refreshments, and powerful binoculars are set up to view the wetlands and the many species of wading birds.

From here the crossing to the north side of the Spit is made by the tour companies. The trucks grind up over the beach to about a km from Cape Farewell. Down towards the start of the sand are a number of fossilised shellfish. From this point it is 27 km to the end of the sandy spit. Again many species of birds are seen along the way and, often, a stranded pilot whale carcass. The normal trip ends at the old lighthouse compound. The 100-year-old metal lighthouse has an eight-sided light which flashes every 15 seconds.

Further east, up on the blown shell banks which comprise the far extremity of the Spit are colonies of Caspian terns and Australasian gannets.

There are two guided tours to the remarkable Farewell Spit region. This is the only way you can visit the Spit, as it's a protected wildlife sanctuary and only licensed tour operators have permission to go onto it.

The original company that pioneered travel up the sandy beach to the lighthouse was Collingwood Safari Tours (☎ 524 8257). The five-hour Farewell Spit Safari Tour costs $45 (children $25), and you go up the beach in a 4WD vehicle. Tours leave daily on demand, timed to the tides. Collingwood Bus Services (☎ 524 8188) also conduct a tour to the lighthouse under the name Farewell Spit Nature Tours; it costs $50 and lunch is included.

If you want to visit the gannet colony, Collingwood Safari Tours are licensed by DOC to conduct two trips for 20 persons weekly. The trip involves a km walk from the lighthouse to the colony, where various features are pointed out. The 5½-hour tour costs $55. Collingwood Safari Tours also operate a wader-watch tour on the inside of the sandy spit (the estuarine side), travelling about a third of the way along the inside beach three to four times per week; again it is a five-hour tour which is limited to 10 people – a must for twitchers.

In addition to a Farewell Spit tour, Collingwood Bus Service offers a couple of other good tours. The Scenic Mail Run tour visits isolated farming settlements and communities around Cape Farewell and the west coast. The driver points out many points of historical and contemporary interest along the way. The tour lasts five hours, departing from the Collingwood post office at 9.30 am Monday to Friday, and the cost of $35 ($20 for children under 12) includes a picnic lunch on a 1000-hectare farm.

Wharariki Beach

This beach is 29 km to the north of Collingwood and involves a 20-minute walk to the beach from the car park. It is a wild introduction to the West Coast with unusual dune formations, two looming, rock islets just out from shore, and a seal colony at its eastern end. A special place to get away entirely from the 'rat race' of Collingwood.

Places to Stay

The *Collingwood Motor Camp* (☎ 524 8149), William St, near the centre of the tiny township has tent/powered sites for $12/14 for two, and cabins are from $24 to $40 for two. The *Pakawau Beach Motor Camp* (☎ 524 8327) is 13 km north of Collingwood, which means it's even closer to the end of the road. Tent/powered sites are $13.50/14.50 for two, and cabins from $30 to $35 for two.

The *Collingwood Motel* (☎ 524 8224) in Haven Rd has self-contained units for $65 for two. In Tasman St, the *Beachcomber Chalets* (☎ 524 8499) has units at $45 for two ($10 for each extra adult).

An upmarket B&B place 10 km south of Collingwood is the *Northwest Lodge* (☎ 524 8108); singles/doubles are from $60 to $80/ $80 to $120, and all have ensuite facilities.

There is a really friendly 'organic' accommodation house, *The Inn-let* (☎ 524 8040), on the way to Pakawau and about five km from Collingwood. Jonathan and Katie are really attuned to their environment and are full of details about the surrounding area. They recently received a liquor licence. Comfortable beds in renovated rooms are from $16 upwards; make sure that you phone in advance. There are twin and double rooms for $38, and a cabin for $45. The owners pick up from Collingwood and also arrange excursions (with a difference) to nearby attractions. Incidentally, Opua means 'terrace', so sit on theirs above the river of that name, have a BBQ and relax in native bush surroundings.

Places to Eat

If you're not fixing your own food there's a pub opposite the post office, or the *Collingwood Cafe*, a dairy and cafe that's open from 7.30 am to 8 or 9 pm every day. The *bistro* at the tavern serves passable food, but check to see that your meal has not been left in the bain-marie.

About halfway between Takaka (15 km) and Collingwood there is a new (modelled on a turn-of-the-century) alehouse, the *Mussel Inn*. Good meals are available eg pan-fried fish and salad or steak with mushroom sauce for $10. Although they only serve local boutique beers it seems a huge selection. You can also get meals at the visitor centre at Puponga.

Getting There & Away

Bayways Book-a-Bus (☎ 524 8188) has a bus service from Collingwood to Takaka then to Nelson on Tuesday and Friday only. In summer, Abel Tasman National Park

Enterprises (☎ 528 7801) has daily services from Nelson to Motueka connecting with services to Takaka and Collingwood.

Collingwood Bus Services also provides transport to and from the Browns Hut end of the Heaphy Track, 35 km from Collingwood. These services only run on demand; the cost is about $60 per trip for the minibus, or $12 per person if there are more than five people.

The West Coast

The best thing about the West Coast (Westland) is its ruggedness – the narrow coastal strip is still very much untamed. The pebbled and rocky beaches are wild, and from them the bush-clad hills sweep up to towering icy peaks. Often the narrow strip of land is *pakihi* (dried-up) swamp or second-class farmland, and the whole region is studded by jewel-like lakes which mirror the peaks above.

Here and there are patches of native forest that have escaped the axe and fire. Scattered throughout the bush and by the rivers is the rusted debris of 100 years of exploitative industry – gold and coal mining, and timber milling. The two glaciers, Fox and Franz Josef, are perhaps the major drawcards to the West Coast, but visitors soon find that the whole stretch from Karamea to Jackson Bay is worth exploring.

The road hugs the coastline most of the way from Westport in the north to Hokitika, then runs inland until it finally joins the coast again between Knights Point and Haast, before turning east and heading over the Haast Pass. Not far inland from the coast, but a long way by road, are Mts Cook and Tasman.

Most visitors come to the West Coast in summer, and the area is heavily visited from December to January. From May to September the days can often be warm and clear, with views of snow-capped peaks; there are no crowds and you can often get off-peak accommodation rates. The West Coast is definitely worth a visit at any time of the year.

HIGHLIGHTS

- White-water and black-water rafting in the rivers and caves near Westport
- Any foray into the remote stands of indigenous forest which are alive with birdlife, especially in the World Heritage areas near Moeraki and Haast
- Walking on or aerial flightseeing over the Franz Josef and Fox glaciers
- Adventuring (jet-boating, flying and walking) in Mt Aspiring National Park near Makarora
- Driving the coast road from Westport to Greymouth
- Visiting the kotuku (white heron) colony near Whataroa (Waitangi-Toana)
- Relaxing in one of the coast's remote fishing settlements or small towns for a few days

Climate

Westland could aptly be called 'Wetland'. It rains a lot here, five metres (200 inches) or more a year. This said, the West Coast receives as many sunshine hours as the Christchurch region. An early and poetically inspired visitor to Hokitika summed up the West Coast weather situation pretty well:

It rained and rained and rained
The average fall was well maintained
And when the tracks were simply bogs
It started raining cats and dogs
After a drought of half an hour
We had a most refreshing shower
And then the most curious thing of all
A gentle rain began to fall
Next day also was fairly dry
Save for a deluge from the sky
Which wetted the party to the skin
And after that the rain set in

TO THE COAST VIA BULLER GORGE

The road across from Nelson to the coast via the Buller Gorge is interesting and scenic. The Buller area is still scarred from the 1929

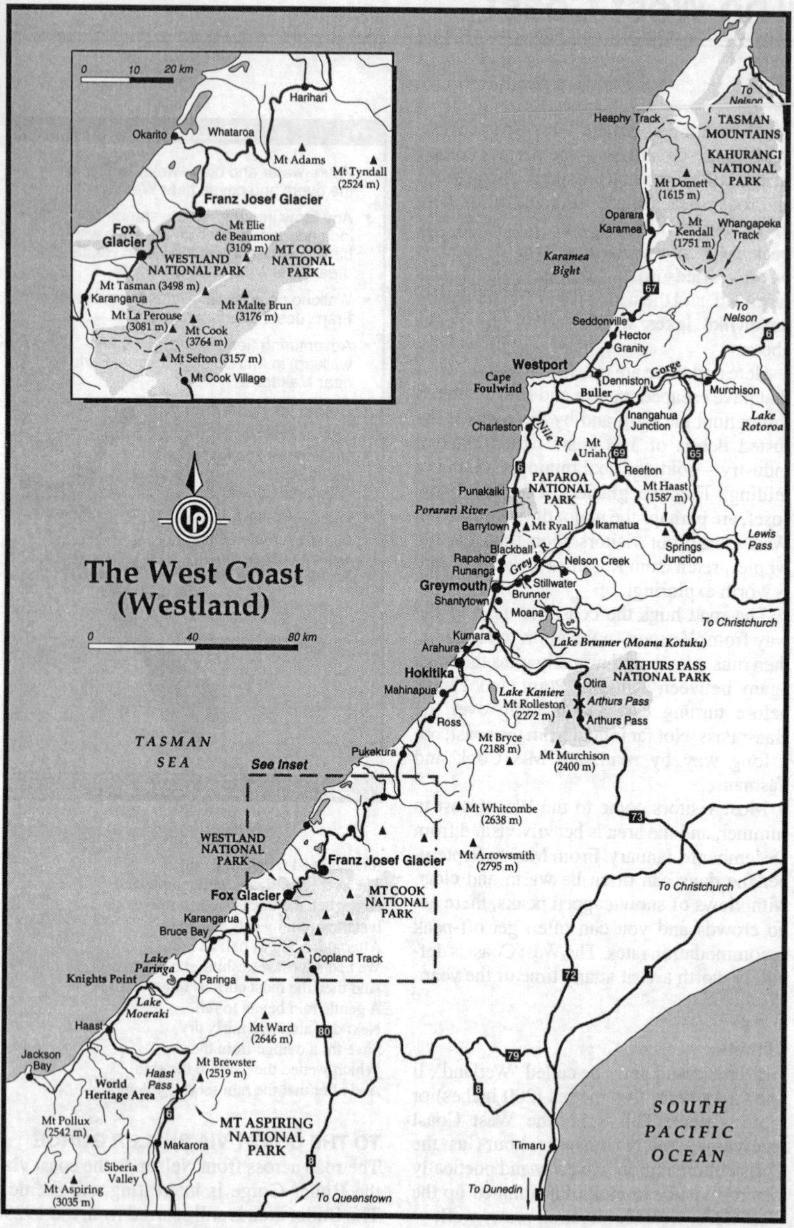
The West Coast
(Westland)
0
40
80 km
TASMAN
SEA
SOUTH
PACIFIC
OCEAN
See Inset
0
10
20 km
Harihari
Okarito
Whataroa
Mt Adams
Mt Tyndall
(2524 m)
Franz Josef Glacier
Fox
Glacier
Mt Elie
de Beaumont
(3109 m)
MT COOK
NATIONAL
PARK
WESTLAND
NATIONAL PARK
Mt Tasman (3498 m)
Karangarua
Mt Malte Brun
(3176 m)
Mt La Perouse
(3081 m)
Mt Cook
(3764 m)
Mt Sefton (3157 m)
Mt Cook Village
To
Nelson
Heaphy Track
TASMAN
MOUNTAINS
KAHURANGI
NATIONAL
PARK
Mt Domett
(1615 m)
Oparara
Karamea
Mt
Kendall
(1751 m)
Whangapeka
Track
Karamea
Bight
67
Seddonville
Hector
Granity
To
Nelson
6
Westport
Cape
Foulwind
Denniston
Gorge
Buller
Murchison
Inangahua
Junction
Lake
Rotoroa
Charleston
Nile R
Mt
Uriah
69
65
6
Reefton
Mt Haast
(1587 m)
Punakaiki
PAPAROA
NATIONAL
PARK
Porarari River
Barrytown
Mt Ryall
Ikamatua
Lewis
Pass
Springs
Junction
Blackball
Rapahoe
Runanga
Grey R
Nelson Creek
Greymouth
Stillwater
Brunner
Shantytown
Moana
To Christchurch
Kumara
Arahura
Lake Brunner (Moana Kotuku)
Hokitika
ARTHURS PASS
NATIONAL PARK
Otira
Mahinapua
Lake Kaniere
Arthurs Pass
Mt Rolleston
(2272 m)
Arthurs Pass
Ross
Mt Bryce
(2188 m)
Mt Murchison
(2400 m)
Pukekura
Mt Whitcombe
(2638 m)
73
WESTLAND
NATIONAL
PARK
Mt Arrowsmith
(2795 m)
Franz Josef Glacier
Fox Glacier
MT COOK
NATIONAL
PARK
To Christchurch
Karangarua
Bruce Bay
Copland Track
Lake
Paringa
Knights Point
Paringa
72
1
Lake
Moeraki
Haast
Mt Ward
(2646 m)
80
79
Jackson
Bay
Mt Brewster
(2519 m)
Haast
Pass
World
Heritage Area
8
6
Mt Pollux
(2542 m)
MT ASPIRING
NATIONAL
PARK
Makarora
Timaru
Siberia
Valley
8
Mt Aspiring
(3035 m)
To Queenstown
To Dunedin
1

Murchison and 1968 Inangahua earthquakes. From Inangahua Junction you can head through the lower Buller Gorge to the coast, or you can go on to Greymouth via Reefton on the inland route. The coastal route has more to offer but is a fair bit longer. Before you have to make the choice, the first town of any size that you will come to is Murchison.

Murchison

Murchison is on the Buller Gorge Heritage Highway, some 125 km south of Nelson. With a population of 600, 'Murch' is an important service centre for the surrounding region and the starting point for a number of adventure activities. It is actually in the Nelson region but is included here as it is very much the gateway for travellers coming from the north to the West Coast.

The Murchison information centre (☎ 523 9350) in Waller St is open from October to April daily from 10 am to 5 pm, and opens occasionally in winter. There's a small **museum**, open daily from 10 am to 4 pm.

Activities A great variety of recreational activities can be enjoyed in the Murchison area including fishing, rafting, kayaking, tramping, gold-panning, boating, mountain biking, caving and rock climbing.

Go West Rafting (☎ 523 9315), based at the Riverview Motor Camp, offers a number of exciting **white-water rafting** options. These include a Fun Run on the Gowan and Buller (two to three hours, $65 for adults).

Buller Experience (☎ 523 9696) offers **jet-boating** on the Matakitaki, Mangles and Buller rivers; the cost of a 25-minute trip is $40 for adults, $20 for children or $120 for two adults and four kids.

There are a number of **mountain-bike trails** in the area and popular rides include the west bank of the Matakitaki (16 km return) and the Upper Matakitaki (the return trip is 76 km). There is also good **horse trekking** in the Tutaki Valley. Tiraumea Horse Treks (☎ 523 9341) runs trips from one hour to a full day. The **fishing** in nearby rivers is rightly said to be 'unbelievable', but a guided day out to hook a trout is not cheap – it costs up to $650. Still interested? Contact guides on ☎ 523 9525.

Places to Stay There is a seasonal *YHA Hostel* (☎ 523 9416) in the Aorangi Hall at the Domain. It's open from December to March and costs $9 per person ($13 for non-members). *Kiwi Park* (☎ 523 9248), 170 Fairfax St, has standard cabins for $25, and self-contained units at $45 for two ($10.50 for each extra adult). The *Riverview Motor Camp & Cabins* (☎ 523 9315), two km north of the town, has tent sites at $15, cabins at $28, and self-contained tourist flats at $42; all prices are for two ($11 each extra adult). There are two motels in town: the *Murchison* (☎ 523 9026) and the *Mataki* (☎ 523 9088); expect to pay from $60 for two. The *Hampden Hotel* (☎ 523 9008) on Fairfax St has singles/doubles for $25/40.

There's a Department of Conservation (DOC) *camping ground* at Lyell, Upper Buller Gorge, 10 km north of Inangahua.

Places to Eat There are two of the ubiquitous tearooms – *Collins* and the *Murchison*. The *Hampden* and *Commercial* serve pub meals such as steak and fish for about $15 a main. There is a new restaurant, *Beechwoods*, on the south edge of town; it is open from 6 am until about 11 pm. A feast at the luxury *Moonlight Lodge*, 32 km south of Murchison on SH65, will set you back about $50 (per person).

Getting There & Away A number of bus services pass through Murchison. These include Nelson Lakes Transport, Barry's Bus, White Star, Blenheim Taxis, InterCity and Mt Cook Landline (only in summer). These buses stop either at Collins Tearooms on Fairfax St, or outside Beechwoods on SH6.

Buller Gorge

Travelling from Murchison to Westport takes about 1½ hours. To get on to the Buller Gorge road you turn off at Sullivan's Bridge (the road straight ahead goes to Maruia

Springs and the Lewis Pass). Just past the bridge, look up the valley to the left to see **Old Man Mountain**. With imagination you see a pot-bellied supine fellow – the cloud above is smoke from his hidden pipe. Further on is New Zealand's longest swing bridge.

The road winds through the gorge to Inangahua Junction. This was the epicentre of a major earthquake in 1968 – over seven on the Richter scale. The scarred hillsides still bear testimony to the power of nature.

The Buller Gorge itself is dark and forbidding, especially on a murky day – primeval ferns and cabbage trees cling to steep cliffs, and toi toi flanks the road between gorge and river. A drive through the gorge's scenic reserve is picturesque in any weather.

At **Hawks Crag** the road has been literally hacked out of the rock. Buses pass through it very slowly as the rock overhang comes extremely close to the top of the vehicle. It is named not after the birds but a goldminer, Robert Hawks, who prospected in the area.

WESTPORT

Westport, the major town at the northern end of the West Coast, has a population of 4590 and is developing a reputation for outdoor activities. Its prosperity is based on coal mining although the mining activity takes place some distance from town. Westport is five km north from the turn-off for Greymouth on the main coast road, SH6. The SH67 passes through Westport and ends beyond Karamea at the start of the Heaphy Track.

Information

The Buller Visitor & Information Centre (☎ & fax 789 6658) is in Brougham St, a couple of doors off Palmerston St. It's open daily from 9 am to 5 pm except on Friday when the hours are 9 am to 5.30 pm. On winter weekends, it is open from 10 am to 4 pm. It has information on the seal colony and the many tracks and walkways in the area. It also operates the laundrette on Brougham St. The DOC office (☎ 789 7742) on Russell St is open on weekdays from 9 am to noon. The AA agency (☎ 789 8002) is on Marine Parade, Carters Beach. The post office is on the corner of Brougham and Palmerston Sts.

Seal Colony

There's a seal colony at Tauranga Bay, 12 km from Westport. It is on the southern end of the Cape Foulwind Walkway, which follows the coastline for four km from Cape Foulwind to Tauranga Bay (see Other Activities in this section). If you have wheels you can drive to the car park and take the five-minute walk to the viewing deck above the seal colony.

Depending on the time of the year there may be anything from 20 to over 100 seals down on the rocks. Pups are born from late November to early December and for about a month afterwards the mothers stay on the rocks to tend the young before setting off to sea on feeding forays. Don't venture past the marked areas as the cliffs can be dangerous.

Karaka Tours (☎ 789 5080) runs trips to the seal colony for $15 per person. These take about two hours and include a scenic drive. Karaka Tours also provides a range of tours ranging from one hour to a full day.

Coaltown

This well laid out museum in Queen St reconstructs aspects of coal-mining life, including a walk through a simulated mine complete with authentic sound effects. There are also two audiovisual presentations, coal-mining artefacts and some excellent photographic exhibits. In winter it's open every day from 9 am to 4.30 pm and in summer daily from 8.30 am to 5 pm; admission is $6 (children $3). The locally owned Miner's Brewery near the clocktower is a good place to quench your thirst after a mine tour.

Activities

'Underworld' rafting has really caught on in New Zealand. In the Westport area, Norwest Adventures Ltd (☎ 789 6686) runs a number of trips into a place that could easily be the legendary reaches of Xanadu. For $70 you'll be taken down Coleridge's sacred river (the

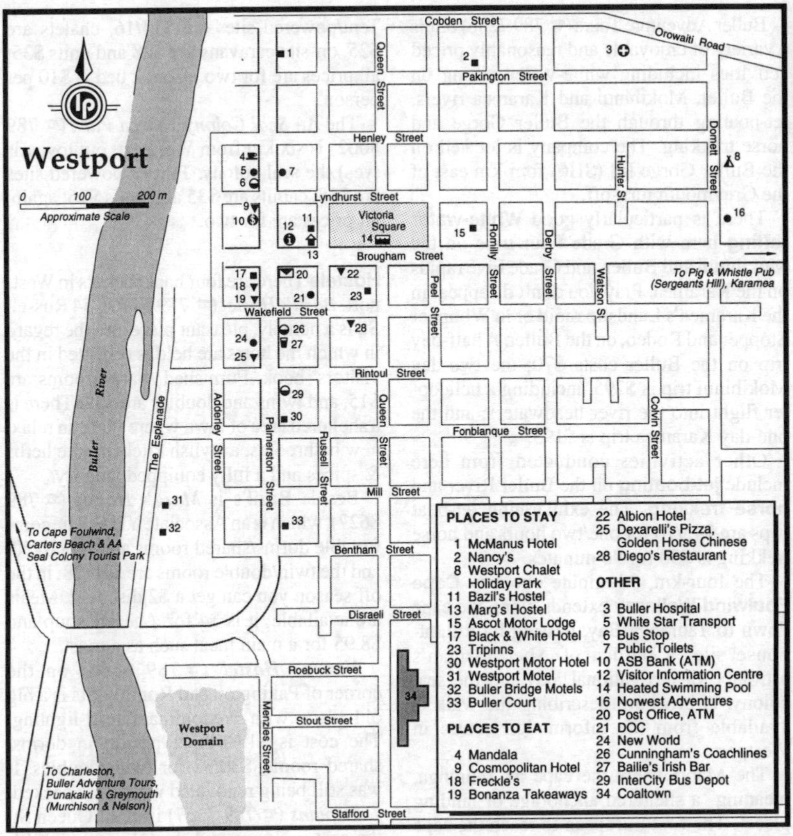

Nile actually). In the lower, active levels of Metro Cave you sit in rubber rafts and paddle through spectacular glow-worm-filled caverns. The trip ends in the rapids of the larger Nile River – definitely not a trip for the air-conditioned bus set. You can take along any child over 10 who can walk for three hours. Get in touch with them at Charleston or at 41 Dommett St, Westport.

There are two trips daily, departing Westport at 8.30 am and 2 pm; there is a limit of 36 passengers and four guides on any one trip.

Another adventure activity started here by Norwest Adventures is **adventure caving**. This is a thrilling four-hour experience which starts with a 30-metre abseil into the Te Tahi *tomo* (hole), also near the Nile River. You then worm your way through rock squeezes and waterfalls, exploring prehistoric fossils and formations as you go (stalactites, stalagmites, straws and columns). In this cave system there is an embedded whale skeleton – it once used to span the full width of the cave. The cost of this trip is $120. There is even an option for those not keen on abseiling; you creep into the system via another entrance.

Buller Adventure Tours (☎ 789 7286) offers a variety of enjoyable and reasonably priced activities including white-water rafting on the Buller, Mokihinui and Karamea rivers, jet-boating through the Buller Gorge and horse trekking. The company is located on the Buller Gorge Rd (SH6) four km east of the Greymouth turn-off.

There is particularly good **White-water rafting** here with Grade Four trips on the Mokihinui and Buller, and Grade Five rapids on the Karamea. Pray you don't disappear in the Karamea's Landslip rapid or in Whopper Stopper and Rodeo, on the Buller. A half-day trip on the Buller costs $70; the two-day Mokihinui trip is $295, including a helicopter flight into the river headwaters; and the one-day Karamea trip is $195.

Other activities conducted from here include **jet-boating** on the Buller River and **horse trekking**. The exhilarating jet-boat trips are $45/70 for one/two hours and horse trekking is $30 for 90 minutes.

The four-km, 90-minute one-way **Cape Foulwind Walkway** extends along the cape down to Tauranga Bay, passing by a lighthouse site, a replica of Abel Tasman's astrolabe (a navigational aid) and the seal colony. A brochure describing the walk is available from the information centre in Westport.

The Maori knew the cape as Tauranga, meaning 'a sheltered anchorage or landing place'. The first European to reach the cape was Abel Tasman, who sighted it in December 1642 and named it Glyphaygen Hock or Rocky Point. When Captain Cook anchored here in March 1770 his ship, the *Endeavour*, was rocked by a furious storm, so he gave it the apt name it retains today.

The information centre has many brochures on other **bush walks** in the region, many of which pass through old gold and coal-mining areas. For those keen on walking this is an ideal place to come to.

Places to Stay

Camping & Cabins The *Westport Chalet Holiday Park* (☎ 789 7043) is on Domett St only one km from the post office. Tent/powered sites are $14/16, chalets are $25, on-site caravans are $28 and units $35; all prices are for two. A bunk bed is $10 per person.

The *AA Seal Colony Tourist Park* (☎ 789 8002) is six km from Westport, out towards (yes) the seal colony. Tent or powered sites are $18, cabins are $35 and units $76; again, all prices are for two.

Hostels There are four backpackers in Westport. *Bazil's Hostel* (☎ 789 6410), 54 Russell St, is a homely, pleasant place and the regard in which the hosts are held is reflected in the visitors' book. Furnished shared rooms are $15, and twins and doubles are $32. There is a sheltered area of lawn where you can relax, new bathrooms, a stylish kitchen, free herbs & spices and a fully equipped laundry.

Beside Bazil's is *Marg's Hostel* (☎ 789 8627), which is an Associate YHA. The comfortable dorms/shared rooms are $16/16.50, and the twin/double rooms are $36/38; in the off season you can get a $2 discount. Meals are available; it is $4 for a hearty soup and $8.95 for a main meal such as a roast.

Nancy's Hostel (☎ 789 6565) on the corner of Pakington and Romilly Sts is a big old place with predominant lead-lighting. The cost is $13/14 per person in dorms/shared rooms, $30/32 for twins/doubles. It was still being renovated when we checked.

Tripinns (☎ 789 7367) is at 72 Queen St; the cost in dorms and shared rooms is $14, and twins and doubles are $34.

Hotels & Motels There are a number of hotels along Palmerston St. The *McManus Hotel* (☎ 789 6304) has singles/twins for $25/43. Also on Palmerston St, opposite the post office, the *Black & White Hotel* (☎ 789 7959) is $25/50 for a single/double.

Westport Motel (☎ 789 7575) on the Esplanade has self-contained units at $68 for two and, at this price, they are as good as anywhere. Another reasonable place is the *A1 Motels* (☎ 789 9808) at 63 Queen St with doubles for $70. The *Westport Motor Hotel* (☎ 789 7889) at 75 Palmerston St has double rooms from $75 and a restaurant; the *Buller Bridge* (☎ 789 7519) on the Esplanade – recommended by 'Coasters' – has singles/doubles for $67.50/75; the *Buller Court* (☎ 789 7979) at 235 Palmerston St costs from $70 for two; and the *Ascot Motor Lodge* (☎ 789 7832), 74 Romilly St, is top of the list with rooms at about $80 for two.

Places to Eat

There are a number of takeaways and sandwich places along Palmerston St including *Bonanza Takeaways* near the Wakefield St corner; you can take food away or sit down and eat there. *Freckle's* on Palmerston St is a quaint little cafe serving homemade food. Pub food is available in the evenings, Thursday to Sunday, at the *McManus*, *Black & White, Pig & Whistle* and *Cosmopolitan*.

The *Mandala* on Palmerston St is a coffee house. Open from 7 am until late, it has lost the touch which once made it the culinary oasis in this town. *Diego's* at 18 Wakefield St now assumes that mantle with its innovative menu, eg tempura seafood kebabs, chilli mussels, turbot fillets with ginger and mushroom sauce. In summer it is open every evening from 5 pm until late.

The party scene centres on *Bailie's Irish Pub* in Palmerston St. There's live Irish music on Friday night and an indoor BBQ costs $10.95. This is where most travellers will gravitate after bush walks or rafting trips. A small nachos ($4) should read 'huge' as it easily feeds two – only the brave fortified with Guinness should try a large ($8). A Mr Spud with either salsa, savoury toppings or chilli con carne is $4.

Getting There & Around

Air New Zealand Link (☎ 789 7209) has daily direct flights to Wellington, with connections to many other centres including Auckland, Christchurch and Dunedin. A taxi to the airport costs around $12.

InterCity buses make return trips between Westport and Greymouth (two hours) with a rest stop at the Pancake Rocks (Punakaiki) every day. From Westport they have connecting buses heading north to Nelson and south to the glaciers.

White Star has a Nelson-Westport-Christchurch service (via Springs Junction). This bus leaves for Springs Junction at 10.05 am every day except Saturday; the cost to Christchurch is $33, to Nelson $27.

East-West Express has a shuttle to Christchurch ($39 adult, $30 child). It leaves Craddock Service Station on Palmerston St at 8 am and arrives in Christchurch at the railway station at 12.30 pm. It leaves from the Christchurch station at 2 pm and returns to Westport at 6.30 pm.

Heading north to Karamea for the Heaphy Track, Cunningham's buses make the return trip Monday to Friday, leaving Karamea in the morning and returning from Westport in the afternoon at 3.10 pm (the cost is $15).

Barry's Buses depart from the information centre at 10.45 am for Nelson and Picton and connect with the 6.30 pm Interislander sailing from Picton to Wellington; they return to Westport the same day arriving at 7.25 pm.

For getting around Westport, you can hire bicycles from Beckers Cycles & Sports and Anderson Sports on Palmerston St, and also from Bazil's and other hostels.

WESTPORT TO KARAMEA

This trip north along SH67 passes through a number of interesting towns. The first reached is Waimangaroa and the turn-off to **Denniston**. This town was once the largest producer of coal in NZ and can be reached by the Denniston Walkway. The track follows the original path to the town and from it you get great views of the Denniston Incline. In its day this was acclaimed as a feat of engineering, as empty coal trucks were hauled back up the incline by the weight of the descending loaded trucks, sometimes at a gradient of one in one. Four km north of Waimangaroa is the **Britannia Track**, a six-hour return walk to the Britannia battery and other remnants of the gold-mining era.

At Granity head uphill for five km to the ghost towns of Millerton and Stockton. The **Millerton Incline Walk** is 40 minutes return and takes in the old railway, a tunnel and an old dam. Just near Granity there is another interesting walk at **Charming Creek**. This all-weather track follows an old coal line through the picturesque Ngakawau River Gorge; allow five hours return for this walk.

You could continue along the Charming Creek Walkway all the way to **Seddonville**, a town on the Mohikinui River about halfway between Westport and Karamea. This town is surrounded by hills covered in bush. You could choose either the *Motor Camp* (☎ 782 1816) or *Motor Hotel* (☎ 782 1828) to stay in – the hotel is $50 for two and the camp's bunkrooms are $12 for two.

There is a charming little restaurant, the *Cowshed Cafe*, near Gentle Annie Beach at the mouth of the Mohikinui. Muffins, salads and steaks are the specialities of this place. It's NZ's only cowshed restaurant – 'No shit!'

Between Mohikinui and Little Wanganui you pass over the **Karamea Bluff**, a magnificent scenic drive through rata and matai forest with views of the Tasman Sea below. The *Northern Buller Bay See & Do Guide* ($1.50) outlines other attractions of this region.

KARAMEA

From Westport, SH67 continues 100 km north to Karamea, an 'end of the road' town near the Heaphy and the Wangapeka tracks. Information is available at the Karamea information centre (☎ & fax 782 6652), the DOC office (☎ 782 6852) or the Last Resort (☎ 782 6617).

Oparara Basin & Honeycomb Caves

Several spectacular limestone arch formations are found in the Karamea area, 15 km from the North Beach turn-off – of particular interest are the Oparara Arch and Moria Gate in the Oparara River valley. You can actually canoe up to another arch, the Honeycomb (in fact canoeing provides the only means of access). The cost of the bus trip to the Oparara Basin is $20 and a one-day exploration of the river by canoe is $120 per person, transport included.

The Honeycomb Caves are magnificent, with a collection of bones of moa and other extinct species. On a visit through these caves you will see bones of three of the five moa species found – slender, small and giant moas (*Megalapteryx didinus*, *Pachyornis elephantopus* and *Dinornis giganteus*). This is the cave where bones of the now extinct giant Haast eagle, the world's largest, were discovered. This eagle, with a three to four-metre wingspan, preyed on the moa.

The cave is also home to the cave-dwelling spider, *gradungula*, unique to this area; it has a body length of 2.5 cm (about an inch)

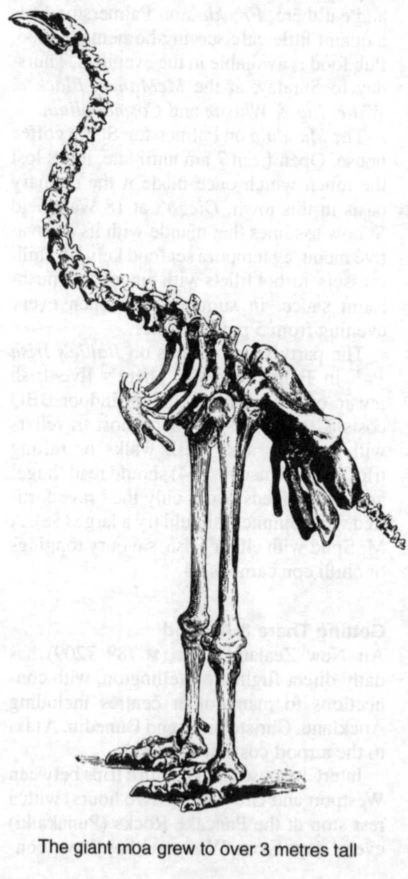

The giant moa grew to over 3 metres tall

and leg span of 10 cm. If you're lucky you will also see the carnivorous snail *(Powelliphanta hochstetteri)*, favourite food of the weka. Understandably, access to the cave is restricted, but you can go through them on a tour ($50); inquire at the Last Resort.

Perhaps the greatest feature of the Honeycomb area is the primitive rainforest which has grown over the karst landscape. Moss-laden trees droop over a golden river illuminated by light filtering through the dense forest canopy.

Activities

The Karamea River offers good swimming, fishing and canoeing. There are also good **swimming** holes on the Wanganui, Oparara and Kohaihai rivers. Swimming is dangerous in the open sea but there are tidal lagoons one km north and three km south of Karamea where swimming is good at high tide. There are lots of beautiful beaches around but the only drawback is the millions of sandflies. A long-running local saying is that 'sandflies work in pairs – one pulls back the sheets, while the other eats you alive'.

Fishing is now popular with visitors, and the Last Resort will advise of places to check out along the Karamea River (the locals have known about them for ages!).

Many good day **walks** are found in this area, including the five-hour Fenian Track into Adams Flat and the eight-hour return trek to the 1084-metre Mt Stormy. There's another walk to Lake Hanlon and the first leg of the Wangapeka Track also makes a good day walk. Those not keen on walking the whole Heaphy Track may walk as far as Heaphy Hut and then return the same way. This walk includes what is considered by many to be the best part, the walk along the beach. One loop of the **Nikau Walkway** has wheelchair access – it takes about an hour. For more information on the Heaphy and Wangapeka tracks, see LP's *Tramping in New Zealand* and the Kahurangi National Park section in the Marlborough & Nelson chapter.

Places to Stay & Eat

The *Karamea Holiday Park* (☎ 782 6758) has sites for $13, cabins at $25 and units at $47; all prices are for two. At Kohaihai, 15 km north of Karamea, is a *DOC camping ground*.

Bravely, the local backpackers place here has the appellation *The Last Resort* (☎ 782 6617); it certainly isn't that, as it has been designed specifically for the budget traveller and incorporates many features of communal living. A single budget room is $15 per person ($20 with linen), and a double is $40 ($75 with an ensuite). You can cook for yourself or there is a fully licensed restaurant; a light/full breakfast is $5/12.

The *Township Motel* (☎ 782 6838) on High St is $48 for two and $12 for each extra adult. The *Arapito Valley B&B* (☎ 782 6643), on the Arapito Rd on the south bank of the Karamea River, has singles/doubles for $35/50.

The food at the *Karamea Tavern* is excellent; a whitebait patty with chips is about $5.

Getting There & Away

A Cunningham's bus (☎ 782 6750) departs from Karamea at 8.30 am, arriving in Westport at 10 am. The bus to Karamea departs from Cunningham's depot in Palmerston St at 3.10 pm; it is $15 either way.

WESTPORT TO PUNAKAIKI

This is an interesting stretch of road. Nowadays the towns along the way are extremely small – 10 or so inhabitants. It was a different story 130 years ago when the gold rush was in full swing. **Charleston** was a booming town with shanties all along the pack route and gold-diggers moving out to their claims on the Nile River. Today, the raucous pubs are all closed but you may find sanctuary in the *Charleston Motel* (☎ 728 7599) or *Motor Camp* (☎ 728 6773) – it costs from $55 to $65 for two in the motel and $27 in the motor camp cabins. Norwest Adventures run their 'Underworld' rafting and tomo exploring trips from here. **Constant Bay**, once the busy port for the mining settlement, is a pleasant picnic area nearby.

The coast from Fox River to Runanga is rugged and the road will remind west coast Americans of California's Big Sur – with similar spectacular views. Woodpecker Bay, Tiromoana, Punakaiki, Barrytown, 14-mile, Motukiekie, 10-mile, Nine-mile and Seven-mile are all beaches sculpted by the relentless fury of the Roaring Forties.

Paparoa National Park & Punakaiki
Almost midway between Westport and Greymouth is Punakaiki and the Paparoa National Park, centred around the area better known as the **Pancake Rocks & Blowholes**. These limestone rocks at Dolomite Point have formed into what looks like stacks of pancakes, through a weathering process known as stylobedding. If there's a good tide running here, the water surges into caverns below the rocks and squirts out in impressive geyser-like blowholes.

There's a 15-minute walk from the road, around the rocks and blowholes, and back again. It's best to go there at high or king tide when the blowholes perform. Heed the signs warning you to keep on the track.

There was pressure for years to have this area declared a national park and this was finally accomplished in December 1987, when the 30,000-hectare Paparoa National Park became NZ's 12th national park.

In addition to the rocks at Punakaiki, the park has many other natural attractions: mountains (the Paparoa Range), rivers, wilderness areas, limestone formations including cliffs and caves, diverse vegetation, and a Westland black petrel colony – the only nesting area of this rare sea bird.

The park has a number of interesting walks including the 25-km **Inland Pack Track**. This is a two-day track along a route established by miners around 1867 to circumvent the more rugged coastal walk. Also notable is the **Croesus Track**, a full-day or two-day tramp over the Paparoa Range from Blackball to Barrytown, passing through historic gold-mining areas. There are also many shorter river and coast walks. If you're planning on walking, register your intentions at the park's visitor centre. Many of the tracks were closed after the Cave Creek tragedy in 1995 when several visitors were killed after a viewing platform collapsed; check the status of tracks at the park's visitor centre.

The Punakaiki Visitor Centre (☎ 731 1895; fax 731 1888) is next to the highway and in summer is open every day from 8.30 am to 6 pm (sometimes it stays open until late). In winter it is open daily from 9 am to 4 pm. It has interesting displays including an audiovisual, pamphlets and maps on all the park's walks and attractions, and can supply information on tides and current conditions throughout the park. Many of the inland walks are subject to river flooding and other conditions, so check here before setting out.

Tours There are tours to the world's only breeding colony of the **Westland black petrel** *(Procellaria westlandica)*, the largest burrowing petrel. Contact Paparoa Nature Tours (☎ 731 1826) for details of their tours which commence 30 minutes before sunset; the cost is $15 per person.

Ra Clay's **Kiwa Sea Adventures** (☎ 731 1893) are a combination of natural history, history, geology and an adrenaline-inducing boat ride. Hector's dolphins, seals and spotted shags may be seen. A two-hour trip to Seal Island is $55 (children $30) and a 30-minute trip to Dolomite Point, $25 ($15).

Paparoa Horse Treks (☎ 731 1839) organises horse trekking; it is $40 for a half day.

Places to Stay & Eat The *Punakaiki Camping Ground* (☎ 731 1894) has tent/powered sites at $14/15, cabins from $26 to $30 (prices are for two), and bunkroom accommodation at $10 per person. The *Punakaiki Cottages* (☎ 731 1008) has studio and family units from $75 to $80 for two.

The *Te Nikau Retreat* (☎ 731 1111) is a magnificent place, replete with 'bush' character in its thick forest setting. The cost is $12.50 in dorms and $30 for twin and double rooms. There is a sleep out, the *Tui*, which is $40 per couple. Te Nikau is three km north of Punakaiki on the seaward side of the road, 200 metres past the entry to the Truman

Track. Follow the rough no-exit drive for 450 metres.

The comfortable *Punakaiki Beach Hostel* (☎ 731 1852), on Webb Terrace, is in a converted motel near the village, one km from the visitor centre. A shared room is $15 per person and singles and doubles are $35; there are facilities for the disabled. Only a stone's throw from the beach, it is close to walking tracks and a picturesque river.

The *Pancake Tearooms* opposite the Pancake Rocks are open all year round from 9 am. Also here is the very pleasant *Nikau Palms Cafe*, which is open 'most of the time' and serves natural food.

Getting There & Around InterCity buses between Westport and Greymouth stop at Punakaiki every day except Sunday. Barry's Buses (☎ (0800) 802 300) operate daily between Nelson and Hokitika. Kea West Coast Tours (☎ 768 9292) has an 18-seater bus which goes from Greymouth to Punakaiki for $30 per person return.

There are a few options for getting around this beautiful region. Perhaps the most tranquil are by horse, bicycle or canoe. Bikes and canoes can be hired in Punakaiki from Pororari Canoe & Cycle Hire (☎ 731 1870).

THE COAST ROAD

The coast road from Punakaiki to Greymouth is scenic. There are white-capped breakers and rugged rocks out at sea and the steep, bush-clad Paparoa Ranges force you to drive almost on the precipice. If you're looking for solitude, you'll find a number of accommodation possibilities along this coastline.

At **Barrytown**, 16 km south of Punakaiki, the *All Nations (Barrytown) Tavern* (☎ 731 1812) has double and twin rooms at $40/50 for two/three persons. There's a fully equipped kitchen for guests, or takeaways and bistro meals. It's a good option for those who have just finished the Croesus Track.

Motukiekie, about 20 km north of Greymouth, is a very scenic spot. There is a B&B in an old miner's cottage, *Tiggers House* (☎ 731 1654), where singles/doubles are $30/55 nightly. The view from this small place is memorable and there are peaceful sunset walks along Motukiekie Beach. The *Motukiekie B&B* (☎ 731 1886) is also good value. Not far north, at 16-Mile, is *Sandie's Vegetarian B&B* (☎ 731 1889) where the rate is $25/45 for one/two persons. The backpackers' rate is $14 for a bed only, and vegetarian meals are $12.

Whitebait

Whitebait is a translucent, elongated small fish, which is the imago (immature) stage of the river smelt. They swarm up the West Coast rivers in dense schools and are caught in set seine-net traps or large, round scoop nets. Many an argument has been had along a riverbank or near a river mouth as to the best rock to position yourself on for catching the biggest haul. The season has been limited in recent years in an attempt to allow the declining stocks to breed. Usually it is September to mid-November, but may vary from year to year. Cooked in batter, these small fish are delicious and highly prized by locals.

One of the West Coast's doyennes of culinary expertise provided this perfect recipe for whitebait patties:

> Take a pint of whitebait (about half a litre – yes, the fish are measured as a liquid rather than a solid as they used to be loaded into glass pint milk bottles for sale) and pour it into a bowl. For the batter take one egg, about three tablespoons of flour, a pinch of salt and a little milk to make a smooth paste. Mix this and then pour over the whitebait; cook in smoking hot fat until golden brown and serve straight away with mint sauce and hot potato chips. Pickled onions are a fine accompaniment. ■

The township of **Runanga**, about seven km north of Greymouth, is an archetypal mining village. It is not far from Rapahoe (Seven-Mile) Beach and there is a 90-minute return walk to nearby Coal Creek falls.

The windswept *Rapahoe Hotel* (☎ 762 7701) is two km north of Runanga at the northern terminus of the Point Elizabeth Track. A creek choked in flax is out one door, the looming Paparoa's can be seen out the back and there is a driftwood-covered beach in front. It's good value at $60 for two, breakfast included. Also at Rapahoe, the *Rapahoe Motor Camp* (☎ 762 7337) has tent and caravan sites, and cabins.

THE GREY VALLEY

After passing through Murchison you can reach the West Coast via the Buller Gorge route, Westport and the coast road, or you can turn off at Inangahua Junction and go inland via Reefton and the Grey Valley. You can almost smell the sea as soon as you enter the Grey Valley. Despite the best efforts of a century of plunderers the green-cloaked hills have re-established themselves and the paddocks have fast become overgrown. Fuelled with an abundant rainfall the bush has grown back and the small towns provide a reminder of those futile attempts to tame the land.

Reefton

If you choose the inland route to the West Coast you will pass through Reefton, a pleasant little town in the heart of great walking country. Reefton's name comes from the gold-bearing quartz reefs in the region. As early as 1888 Reefton had its own electricity supply and street lighting, beating all other towns in NZ and many fashionable suburbs in places such as London and New York.

Two old buildings worth exploring are the **School of Mines** and **Blacks Point Museum**; the museum is open in summer daily (except Monday) from 9 am to noon and 1 to 4 pm.

The Reefton Visitor Centre (☎ 732 8391; fax 732 8616) at 67 Broadway is run by enthusiastic, helpful staff who give out lots of information on the many walks in the region. The DOC office is in the same building. Exhibits in the visitor centre include one on beech forests, a restored working winding engine, and the replica Quartzopolis Mine.

In the surrounding area there are a number of interesting **walks** and great possibilities for mountain biking. The walks include short ones around town such as the Powerhouse Walk, Reefton Walkway and the historic Reefton Walk.

There is a wealth of walking in **Victoria Forest Park**, the second largest such park in the country. The two-day Big River and three-day Kirwans, Blue Grey River and Robinson Valley tracks are all exciting possibilities. Reefton is close to the Lewis Pass and more excellent walking tracks (and superb trout fishing along the way).

Places to Stay & Eat The *Reefton Domain Camp* (☎ 732 8477), Main St, has tent/powered sites for $10/12 and cabins at $25 for two. The *Bellbird Motel* (☎ 732 8444) on Broadway has singles/doubles for $50/62 and the *Reefton Motel* (☎ 732 8574), Central Broadway, charges $48 for two.

There is a proliferation of *takeaways* and *tearooms* on Broadway and the *Electric Light Cafe* in the Dawson. The *Al Fresco* on Broadway is, as its name suggests, an outdoor eatery with _ la carte and takeaway pizzas (a small is $7 and a large is $13).

The *DOC camping ground* is nearby at Slab Hut Creek, 10 km south of Reefton. There is a basic backpackers house, *Inwoods Farm* (☎ 789 0205), at Inangahua Junction, 35 km north of Reefton; it is $11 per person.

Getting There & Away White Star operates a Westport-Springs Junction-Christchurch bus service and East West Express a Christchurch to Westport service – both pass through Reefton. The Sounds to Coast Shuttle (Picton to Greymouth) passes through Reefton on Monday and Friday only.

SH7 to Greymouth

From Reefton, SH7 heads east via Springs Junction and the Lewis Pass to Christchurch and south-west to Greymouth. For those heading towards Christchurch, there are two *DOC camping grounds* in the area: Marble Hill, 6.5 km east of Springs Junction (start of the Lake Daniells walk); and Deer Valley, Lewis Pass, 25 km east of Springs Junction

At Hukarere, 21 km south of Reefton, you can turn east to visit **Waiuta**, now a ghost town but once the focus of a rich gold mine. Get the excellent DOC pamphlet *Waiuta: Victoria Forest Park* for help with your search through the past. The drive through beech forest to Waiuta is scenic and the views from the ghost town are well worth the time spent travelling there; watch out for cars coming in the other direction on the narrow dirt road. The *Waiuta Lodge* is a 30-bunk facility; it's fully equipped and heated but you must bring your own linen. It costs $12 for adults and $6 for children; book at the Reefton Visitor Centre.

If you choose the inland route via Reefton you could stay at **Ikamatua**. The *Station* (☎ 732 3555), behind the pub, has bunk beds for $13.50 per person. Why Ikamatua? Just pop in and find out – there's no better introduction to the hidden delights of the Grey Valley. It is 50 km from Greymouth and a world away from anywhere.

Just before Ngahere, and 32 km from Greymouth, you can turn off to beautiful **Nelson Creek** and a great swimming hole. This area is full of reminders of the gold-mining era, with a number of walks including Callaghans which heads to a lookout. Nelson Creek has a *DOC camping ground* and a *pub* cheekily advertised as 'the only pub in Nelson Creek'.

Blackball This town, 25 km north of Greymouth on the road to Reefton, was established in 1866 as a centre where gold diggers purchased provisions. It was then a coal-mining centre from the late 1880s until 1964, and the town in which the national Federation of Labour (organisation of trade unions) was born after two cataclysmic strikes in 1908 and 1931.

The *formerly the Blackball Hilton* (☎ 732 4705) is a hostel which offers dorm and share rooms for $14, and double or twin rooms for $32. The 'formerly' has been added as this humble backpackers was such a threat to a giant hotel chain that it mounted a challenge to force the place to change its name. The former has been designated a New Zealand Historic Place.

The owners are friendly and have lots of information on the history of the hotel, the town, and things to do around Blackball. The *ftBH* is full of character and has a TV lounge and spa pool; it is also non-smoking. If you ring from Greymouth they can usually organise transport out to here with locals.

Activities you can participate in from here include tramping over the Croesus Track, gold panning ($12 for two hours), horse riding (one hour is $20, and a half-day is $45) and a historic walk ($5 for two hours).

After passing through the sawmilling town of Stillwater, the former coal-mining town of Dobson and pastoral Kaiata, you arrive at the mouth of the Grey River near the Cobden Bridge and the Cobden Gap.

Lake Brunner At Stillwater you can make a detour to Lake Brunner (also known as Moana Kotuku, 'Lake Heron'). The other points of access to the lake are near Jacksons on the Arthur's Pass road or near Kumara on the same road. If you have never baited a hook or gaffed an eel, then Lake Brunner offers you the big chance. They say that the trout here die of old age – that is probably an age-old adage! Fishing guides can be hired at Lake Brunner Lodge to show you the spots where the big ones shouldn't get away.

There is a wildlife park in the **Moana Reserve** with a large area devoted to indigenous species which can be viewed in their natural surroundings from the walkways. You are likely to see kereru (native pigeon), tui, bellbirds, fantails, and sometimes white heron (kotuku). The nearby Velenski Walk, which starts near the camping ground, leads through a remarkable tract of native bush consisting of totara, rimu and kahikatea.

The *Moana Camping Ground* (☎ 337 0572) is in the township on the shores of Lake Brunner; a tent/powered site is $10/14 and cabins are $24, both for two (each extra adult is $10). The *Moana Hotel* (☎ 738 0083) has singles/doubles for $25/45 (with ensuite $85 for a double) and cabins from $15 per person; they serve meals here.

The *BYO Station House Cafe* on the lake shore comes recommended. Across the lake is the upmarket *Lake Brunner Lodge* at Mitchells where meals are available.

GREYMOUTH

Greymouth was once the site of a Maori pa and was known to its inhabitants as Mawhera, meaning 'widespread river mouth'. To the Ngai Tahu people, the Cobden Gap to the north of the town is where their ancestor Tuterakiwhanoa broke the side of Te Waaka o Aoraki (the canoe of Aoraki), releasing trapped rainwaters out to sea.

Greymouth is also a town with a long gold-mining history, and it still has a hint of gold-town flavour today. Despite its small population (7030), it's the largest town on the West Coast. It's located at the mouth of the Grey River – hence its name – and despite the high protective wall along the Mawhera Quay the river still manages to flood the town after periods of heavy rain. The Grey River meets the sea at the 'bar' (an accumulation of sand just below the waterline) between Cobden and Blaketown headlands.

The seascapes here are phenomenal: to the south you can see a large sweep of beach which culminates in the faint outlines of Mts Cook and Tasman and, to the north, the rocky promontory of Point Elizabeth and Big Rock at the far end of Cobden Beach.

Information

The Greymouth Information Centre (☎ 768 5101; fax 768 0317) is in the Art Deco Regent Theatre, on the corner of Herbert and Mackay Sts. In summer it's open daily from 9 am to 6 pm and in winter it's open on weekdays from 9 am to 5 pm and on weekends from 10 am to 4 pm. It organises free tours of Westland Breweries, which must be booked in advance. The AA office (☎ 768 4300) is at 84 Tainui St.

Things to See

At the **Jade Boulder Gallery**, on the corner of Guinness and Tainui Sts, original jade sculpture and jewellery is crafted. The gallery is open daily from 8.30 am to 5 pm, and in summer until 9 pm.

Less aesthetic (but to the 'beer-o-phile', more intrinsically interesting) are the free tours of **Westland Breweries**, home of Monteith's Extra Bitter Brown. The tours, conducted Monday to Friday at 10.30 am and 2 pm, are much better than the ones you pay for in larger cities, and you get a free beer!

The quay walk from Cobden Bridge towards Blaketown is well worth doing; get a copy of the informative *Great Wall of Greymouth* from the visitor centre.

Interesting nearby **mining** areas include the Brunner Mine Site, the Rewanui Mine Site near Runanga and Nelson Creek. The information centre can give directions and historical information on all these sites, and on good spots where you might try panning for gold.

Activities

There are a number of good walks in the region. The five-hour **Point Elizabeth Track**, which passes through the Rapahoe Range Scenic Reserve, is six km north of Greymouth. This track passes through interesting old gold-mining areas.

Wild West Adventures (☎ (0800) 223 456) has designed a subterranean adventure which is not for the faint-hearted. You're taken into the **Taniwha Cave** either by abseiling or climbing down a ladder. The trip begins with a 30-minute walk through native beech forest. You then float on inflated tubes down through a subterranean glow-worm gallery, and end the trip by sliding down a 30-metre natural hydroslide. The cost of this five-hour trip is $85.

The exhilarating **jet-boat rides** offered by Scenicland Ocean Jets (☎ 768 9770) in their 6.8-metre *Wavebaron* are a welcome tourist attraction. The tours go up the Grey River to the Brunner Mine site (45 minutes, $35), out to sea to Point Elizabeth (one hour, $35) and

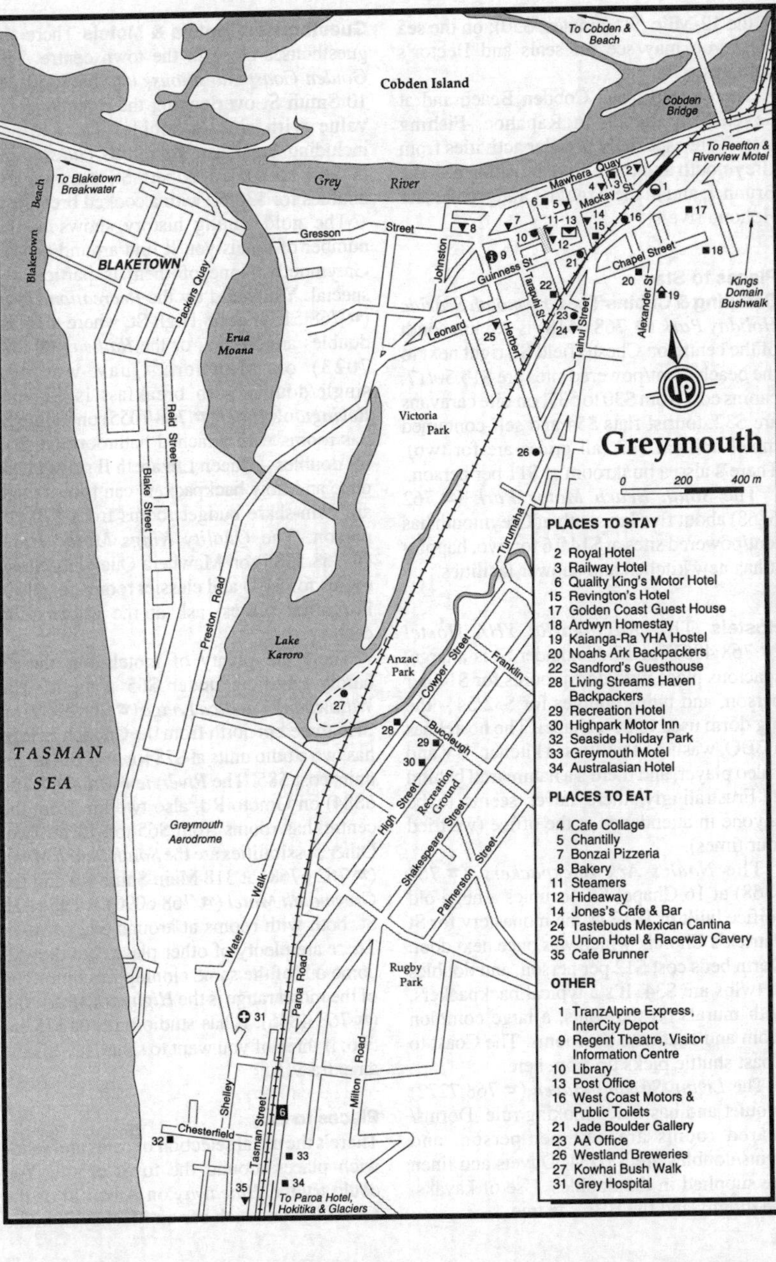

Greymouth
0
200
400 m
To Cobden & Beach
Cobden Island
Cobden Bridge
To Reefton & Riverview Motel
Grey
River
To Blaketown Breakwater
Blaketown Beach
BLAKETOWN
Packers Quay
Gresson Street
Mawhera Quay
Mackay St
Johnston
Guinness St
Tarapuhi St
Chapel Street
Alexander St
Kings Domain Bushwalk
Leonard
Herbert
Tainui Street
Erua Moana
Victoria Park
Reid Street
Blake Street
Preston Road
Tumuaha
Lake Karoro
Anzac Park
Cowper Street
Franklin
Buccleugh
Recreation Ground
High Street
Shakespeare Street
Palmerston Street
TASMAN SEA
Greymouth Aerodrome
Water Walk
Paroa Road
Milton Road
Rugby Park
Shelley
Tasman Street
Chesterfield
To Paroa Hotel, Hokitika & Glaciers
PLACES TO STAY
2 Royal Hotel
3 Railway Hotel
6 Quality King's Motor Hotel
15 Revington's Hotel
17 Golden Coast Guest House
18 Ardwyn Homestay
19 Kaianga-Ra YHA Hostel
20 Noahs Ark Backpackers
22 Sandford's Guesthouse
28 Living Streams Haven Backpackers
29 Recreation Hotel
30 Highpark Motor Inn
32 Seaside Holiday Park
33 Greymouth Motel
34 Australasian Hotel
PLACES TO EAT
4 Cafe Collage
5 Chantilly
7 Bonzai Pizzeria
8 Bakery
11 Steamers
12 Hideaway
14 Jones's Cafe & Bar
24 Tastebuds Mexican Cantina
25 Union Hotel & Raceway Cavery
35 Cafe Brunner
OTHER
1 TranzAlpine Express, InterCity Depot
9 Regent Theatre, Visitor Information Centre
10 Library
13 Post Office
16 West Coast Motors & Public Toilets
21 Jade Boulder Gallery
23 AA Office
26 Westland Breweries
27 Kowhai Bush Walk
31 Grey Hospital

to the 12-Mile (90 minutes, $50); on the sea tours you may see fur seals and Hector's dolphins.

There's surfing at Cobden Beach and at Seven-Mile Beach in Rapahoe. Fishing safaris are especially popular activities from Greymouth and there's good fishing at Lake Brunner, and in the Arnold, Orangepuke and Hohonu rivers.

Places to Stay

Camping & Cabins The *Greymouth Seaside Holiday Park* (☎ 768 6618) is 2.5 km south of the centre on Chesterfield St, right next to the beach. Tent/powered sites are $15.50/17, cabins cost from $30 to $37, on-site caravans are $32, tourist flats $54 and self-contained motel units at $62 (all prices are for two). There's also a bunkroom at $11 per person.

The *South Beach Motor Park* (☎ 762 6768) about five km south of Greymouth has tent/powered sites at $14/16 for two; happily it has new kitchen and shower facilities.

Hostels The *Kaianga-Ra YHA Hostel* (☎ 768 4951) at 15 Alexander St is a large, spacious place with dorm rooms for $14 per person, and twins/doubles for $32/34 – the big dorm used to be a chapel. The hostel has a BBQ, washing facilities, a kitchen, TV and video player, and there's a nature trail behind it. Frustratingly, there never seems to be anyone in attendance at the office (we tried four times).

The *Noah's Ark Backpackers* (☎ 768 4868) at 16 Chapel St, occupies a huge old edifice built in 1912 as the monastery for St Patrick's Church, which was once next door. Dorm beds cost $12 per person, and doubles or twins are $34. It's a typical backpackers, with murals on the walls, a large common room and adequate bedrooms. The Coast to Coast shuttle picks up from here.

The *Living Streams Haven* (☎ 768 7272) is quiet and has a no-smoking rule. Dorms/shared rooms are $13 per person, and twins/doubles are $32/34. Duvets and linen are supplied in the doubles. Use of kayaks, the dinghy and the BBQs is free.

Guesthouses, Hotels & Motels There are guesthouses close to the town centre. The *Golden Coast Guesthouse* (☎ 768 7839), at 10 Smith St overlooking the river, is good value with singles/doubles for $45/66, including breakfast. *Sandfords Guesthouse* (☎ 768 5605), 62 Albert St, has singles/doubles for $30/60 with a cooked breakfast.

The gold-mining history shows in the number of hotels you'll find around central Greymouth. None of them is particularly special. You could try the *Recreation Hotel* (☎ 768 5154) at 68 High St, where singles/doubles are $42/52, or the *Railway* (☎ 768 7023) on Mawhera Quay where a single/double with breakfast is $27/54. *Revington's Hotel* (☎ 768 7055) on Tainui St has rooms with attached bathroom for $65 for doubles – Queen Elizabeth II stayed here once and now backpackers can too as there are twin-share budget rooms from $20 per person. The *Quality Kings Motor Hotel* (☎ 768 5085) on Mawhera Quay has classy rooms for $105 and classier rooms for $130. For other places, ask at the information centre.

There are plenty of motels but there's hardly anything under $65 a night! The *Willowbank Pacifica Lodge* (☎ 768 5339) on SH6 three km north from the Cobden Bridge has two studio units at $78 for two, but larger units cost $85. The *Riverview Motel* (☎ 768 6884) on Omoto Rd, also two km from the centre, has rooms from $65 to $73 for two. Other possibilities are the *South Beach Motel* (☎ 762 6768) at 318 Main South Rd and the *Greymouth Motel* (☎ 768 6090) at 195 High St, both with rooms at around $72 for two. There are plenty of other places but they all come out of the same cloning machine. Top of the motel range is the *Highpark Motor Inn* (☎ 768 4846). It has studio units at $75 for two; if three of you want to share, it will cost an extra $15.

Places to Eat

There's the usual selection of cafes and sandwich places around the town centre. You could try the *Hideaway* on Albert St or the *Chantilly* sandwich bar on Mackay St in the

Mall. The *Bonzai Pizzeria* at 29 Mackay St is a pleasant little place with 16 varieties of pizza. It opens at 9 am weekdays and stays open until late. Greymouth also has a *Tastebuds Mexican Cantina* (about time!) serving delicious enchiladas, burritos and guacamole; a meal averages $6. Travellers may write on the walls – add your mark.

At the Union Hotel on Herbert St, near the railway line, the *Raceway Carvery* is something of a local institution, and it is open daily. The front is very unpromising but it's quite reasonable inside. The accent here is on low prices and big quantities; cuisine highlights are a definite second. Quite a few other pubs offer food, including the *Royal Hotel* on Mawhera Quay and *Ham's* at the Paroa Hotel. Two other good places are the *Cafe Brunner* in the Ashley Motor Inn on Tasman St, Karoro, and *Steamers* in Mackay St near the library. At the Brunner main meals cost about $14. Steamers, housed in a former shipping company office, is a pleasant cafe and bar. It's licensed and has a good selection of beers.

For a fancier night out try *Cafe Collage* on Mackay St. This is a BYO, quite expensive at $18 to $25 for a main course, but it offers a good range of international cuisine; recommended is the whitebait (in season).

Greymouth's 'glitterati' head to *Jones's Cafe & Bar* at 37 Tainui St for fish of the day ($17), steaks ($17.50) and kebabs ($16).

Getting There & Away

Air New Zealand Link flights operate only from Hokitika, 40 km from Greymouth. Greymouth Taxis (☎ 768 7078) go to Hokitika airport for $15.

Barry's Buses (☎ 768 5101) leave the information centre in Greymouth for Nelson at 9.10 am daily, arriving in Nelson at 2.30 pm and in Picton at 5.40 pm ($62). Sounds to Coast operates on Monday and Friday; their buses leave Greymouth at 1.15 pm and arrive at Picton at 6.30 pm ($49).

InterCity/Mount Cook Landline buses depart from the railway station (☎ 768 1435). They have daily services to Westport and Nelson and south to the glaciers.

The Coast to Coast Shuttle (☎ (0800) 800 847) operates between Christchurch and Greymouth via Arthur's Pass. Buses arrive at Greymouth at 12.30 pm and depart for Christchurch at 1 pm. Christchurch to Arthur's Pass is $25 and Arthur's Pass to Greymouth is $15, one way. If you travel and return within four days from Christchurch to Greymouth, the discount fare is $60.

The TranzAlpine Express operates daily between Christchurch and Greymouth. The trip, which currently costs an exorbitant $69 ($97 for a return day trip), takes about five hours and is notable for its spectacular scenery – it crosses some remarkable gorges on its climb through the Southern Alps, passing over numerous viaducts and bridges and through 19 tunnels, including the 8.5-km Otira Tunnel. Between Arthur's Pass and Greymouth the road and railway line take quite different routes. For bookings contact NZ Rail (☎ (0800) 802 802). Various combination packages are offered. If you can get it (numbers are limited), a Super Saver will cost $35 one way.

Getting Around

You can hire a car from Value Rentals (☎ 762 7503) from $40 per day all inclusive of kms (there is a $100 bond); car hire sometimes works out cheaper than some of the tours. Tracy Mann (☎ 768 0255), 173 Tainui St, and Graeme Peters Cycle & Sport (☎ 768 6559), 37 Mackay St, rent bicycles ($25 per day), stock a full range of components and carry out repairs.

SHANTYTOWN & PAROA BEACH

From Greymouth to Hokitika you get great views of the wild West Coast. If you deviate from the main road towards the beach you will see miles of salt spray and endless lines of driftwood.

The model village of Shantytown is 8 km south of Greymouth and three km inland from the main road. Advertised as 'NZ's most unique tourist attraction', it is hardly that – Shantytown is a reconstruction of West Coast life in the gold rush era, and has period buildings. For many the prime attraction will be the two 1897 steam locomotives.

You can also try gold panning; there's an old fellow who'll give you pointers. Everyone is assured of coming up with at least a few flakes of gold to take away.

Shantytown is open daily from 8.30 am to 5 pm (until 7 pm in summer) and entry, including train rides and gold panning, costs $10 (children $5).

You can't go past the *Paroa Hotel & Motel* (☎ 762 6860) for good old-fashioned West Coast hospitality. It is on the beach and the new Wintergarten offers a respite from the sandflies. Self-contained motel units cost $70 for two; there is budget accommodation available at $25 per person, and good hearty meals are available from *Ham's* restaurant. It's worth staying just for an evening stroll along unspoilt Paroa Beach, 100 metres away.

HOKITIKA

Hokitika, or Hoki as it is affectionately known to the locals, is 40 km south of Greymouth. It was settled in the 1860s after the discovery of gold in the region. It became a very busy port and ships often lay four abreast in the river by the wharf. In one busy five-day period, 42 vessels entered the river.

Hokitika is now a major centre for the working of greenstone and, for a while, its tourism resurgence was based on this. There is, however, far more to do in the region than look at stone being mass-produced into bookends, tikis and taniwha. Hoki is the centre of a region that is rich in history and nearby are a wealth of native forests, lakes and rivers.

Trivia? Hoki was the first place in NZ to have a scheduled air service. Air Travel (NZ) started flying de Havilland Fox Moths to airstrips in South Westland 60 years ago and continued doing so in biplanes until 1967.

Information

The Westland Visitor Information Centre (☎ 755 8322; fax 755 8026), at the corner of Weld and Sewell Sts, is open on weekdays from 9 am to 5 pm. From mid-December to March it's also open on Saturday and Sunday, from 9 am to 6 pm. It acts as the AA agent.

Hokitika has several banks and, except for one branch of the Westland Bank in Harihari and a few EFTPOS facilities, there are no banks further south until you reach Wanaka.

Things to See

Take the time to do the historical walk which is outlined in the museum pamphlet *Hokitika Historic Walk*. The **Custom House** and **Gibson Quay** are well worth looking at

Greenstone

Greenstone is big in Hoki. Historically, greenstone – or jade – was much treasured by the Maori who used it for decorative jewellery (tikis) and for carving their lethal weapons (the flat war clubs known as meres). Since greenstone is found predominantly on the West Coast, expeditions undertaken by the Maori to collect it not only took months but were also dangerous. Working the stone with their primitive equipment was no easy task either, but they managed to produce some exquisite items.

The legend of Tamatea explains why there are differing types of greenstone in the South Island. Tamatea's three wives were either abducted by Poutini (a taniwha) or they deserted him. At Anita Bay he found one wife, Hinetangiwai, turned into greenstone, and when he wept his tears entered it, giving it its flecked appearance, hence the name of *tangiwai* ('water of weeping') given to the stone. When travelling north he heard voices in the Arahura Valley and went to investigate. His companion, Tumuaki, breached *tapu* (sacred law) by putting his burnt fingers in his mouth while cooking, so Tamatea was not able to find his other wives. Like Hinetangiwai, the other wives were turned into greenstone – *auhanga* and *pounamu*. ■

– it is not hard to imagine the river and wharf choked with sailing ships many years ago.

The **West Coast Historical Museum**, on Tancred St, has many gold-mining relics. Medal collectors will revel in the wealth of items here. It's open daily from 9.30 am to 5 pm. Admission is $2.55 (children $1) including an audiovisual presentation about the gold rush. You can pan for gold at the museum for $5.

The Heritage Hokitika group has renovated the historic wharf along Gibson Quay.

There's a **glow-worm dell** right beside the road on the northern edge of the town.

Phelp's Goldmine is two km south of Hoki on SH6. Open-cast methods are used and visitors can pan for gold; it's $5 entry plus $4 to pan.

Activities

Alpine Rafts (☎ 755 8156) offers various **white-water rafting** trips including all-day 'thrill seeker' trips down some of NZ's steepest rafting rivers. Helicopters are used for access to the upper parts of the rivers, making the experience doubly exciting. A full day trip down the Whanganui River includes a dip in the hot pools on the riverbank and a

BBQ at the end; the cost is $185 per person. A half-day trip on the Taipo is $155 (including a helicopter ride). Alpine Rafts used to go out to the Frisco Canyon – inquire as to whether or not they still do this great piece of white water.

WestAir (☎ mobile (025) 330 969) runs return **scenic flights** from Hokitika or Greymouth to the glaciers ($155); a minimum of two passengers is required. Wilderness Wings (☎ 755 8118) also operates scenic flights to many destinations, including the glaciers.

There are many **walks** in the area and detailed brochures outlining these are available from the information centre or the DOC office. A number of walks are near Lake Kaniere. Dorothy Falls, Kahikatea Forest and Canoe Cove are all short walks, but the Lake Kaniere Walkway is 13 km and takes about four hours. Longer walks include Mt Tahua and Mt Brown, both of seven hours duration. The Mahinapua Walkway, which takes you through the scenic reserve to a swamp teeming with wildlife and to sand dunes, takes two hours, covering 5.5 km. For the more sedentary, the *Takutai Belle*, a **paddle steamer**, operates on Mahinapua Creek taking visitors up to the lake and back.

Places to Stay

Camping, Cabins & Hostels The *Hokitika Holiday Park* (☎ 755 8172), at 242 Stafford St, has a variety of accommodation possibilities. Tent/powered sites are $14/16, a selection of cabins are priced from $22 to $36, and tourist flats are $46 (all for two) and bunkroom beds cost $9 per person.

Nearly on the beach, at 137 Revell St, you'll find the *Beach House Backpackers* (☎ 755 6859). Dorm beds are $14 per person, and twins and doubles are $30. This place has a great atmosphere – there are beach views from the back and mountain views from the front verandah. It is being upgraded bit by bit and the friendly owners make you feel welcome.

The *Blue Spur Lodge* (☎ 755 8445) is five km east from town on the Cement Lead Rd and is reached via the Hau Hau Rd. It is a new place with shared rooms for $14 per person, and twins and doubles for $32. Contact the information centre for details about a free lift. There are pleasant walks nearby and the owners arrange transport to them; free bikes are also available. If both backpackers are full, try *Pete's Place* (☎ 755 8845), 40 Fitzherbert St.

There are *DOC camping grounds* at Goldsborough (17 km); Shanghai Bay, Lake Mahinapua (16 km) and Hans Bay, Lake Kaniere (18 km) – distances are from Hoki.

Hotels & Motels There are several hotels around the town centre. The big *Westland Hotel* (☎ 755 8411), on the corner of Weld and Revell Sts, has twins from $40 to $60. The *Club Hotel* (☎ 755 8170) at 131 Revell St has rooms for $30/52. The *Southland Hotel* (☎ 755 8334), also on Revell St (No 111), has budget singles/doubles at about $32/42, in addition to more expensive 'deluxe' rooms at $72/82. The *Pioneer Hotel* (☎ 755 8641), on the corner of Gibson Quay and Bealey St, has budget rooms and a reasonable B&B.

Hokitika has a number of motels and the *Jade Court Motor Lodge* (☎ 755 8855) at 85 Fitzherbert St comes recommended; a room here costs from $65 to $80 for two. The pleasant *Teichelmann's B&B* (☎ 755 8232) at 20 Hamilton St is a cosy place with singles from $54 to $76 and doubles from $68 to $86; prices include a big continental breakfast. The visitor information centre has listings for farmstays in Hokitika and South Westland.

Places to Eat

For snacks and sandwiches you can try *Preston's Bakery* on Revell St, *Millie's Place* at 135 Weld St and *PR's Coffee Shop* in Tancred St. Millie's Place has a Beijing chef who prepares an all-you-can-eat, four-course carvery for $20; they have a menu of over 70 items. *Porky's Takeaway* on Weld St does fish & chips.

Overlooking Hokitika's windswept and grey beach (the attraction for a lot of diners) is the *Tasman View* à la carte restaurant; they have a smorgasbord on Friday which is popular with locals. The French-style food at the *Cafe de Paris*, in Tancred St near the corner of Hamilton St, is recommended – venison, lamb, mussels, whitebait with just a little hint of 'la rive gauche'.

Trappers at 79 Revell St is open from 11 am to 11 pm and serves feral venison, buffalo, wild pig, rabbit, duck and even kangaroo; main meals are from $16 to $23.

Things to Buy

There are a great number of arts & craft outlets in Hoki, most of them open daily from 8 am to 5 pm. You can buy jewellery, tikis of course, and other greenstone ornaments from Westland Greenstone on Tancred St. Whether you're buying or not you can visit the workshop and see greenstone being carved. Even with modern tools and electric power, working greenstone is not simple and good greenstone pieces will not be cheap. Mountain Jade in Weld St specialises in jade sculpture as well as jewellery.

There are several other craft outlets including the House of Wood and the Hokitika Craft Gallery, both almost opposite Westland Greenstone. Next door, the Gold Room sells handcrafted gold jewellery made from locally mined gold; there are many specimens of the distinctively flat gold nuggets found in the region. Also in Tancred St is the Hokitika Glass Studio. In Weld St is Revelations and Ocean Paua. Seaside Jade, in Revell St, is another of the many art & craft establishments in this area. The Sheep Station in Sewell St has a most unusual entrance – be engorged by a giant ram before you buy its outer coat.

Getting There & Away

Air New Zealand Link (☎ 755 8134) has three daily direct flights to Christchurch, with connections to other centres.

The InterCity/Mount Cook Landline services travelling from Greymouth to Fox Glacier pass through Hokitika daily. Travel time is 40 minutes to Greymouth, and four hours to Fox Glacier. The InterCity/Mount Cook agent is Hokitika Travel Centre at 65 Tancred St. The Coast to Coast Shuttle, servicing Arthur's Pass and Christchurch, also calls into Hoki; book at the visitor centre.

SOUTH FROM HOKITIKA

It's about 140 km south from Hokitika to the Franz Josef Glacier but you can make a few stops on the way. Hitching along this coast is notoriously bad, so go by bus – the InterCity/Mount Cook Landline buses from Greymouth to the glaciers will stop anywhere along the highway. The *Mahinapua Hotel* is a bit of a local institution – and very much a typical West Coast pub. The *Mahinapua Backpackers* (☎ 755 8500) is popular with backpacker bus companies like the Kiwi Experience; as a guide a package of dinner, bed & breakfast is $45 to $50; budget accommodation costing $15/36 for singles/doubles is available for backpackers who hitch here and get waylaid by the Hooker Ale.

Ross

Ross, 30 km south of Hokitika, is a small, historic gold-mining township; in fact gold is still mined there today. It was the place where NZ's largest gold nugget, the 99-ounce 'Honourable Roddy', was found in 1907. Grimmond House – in the gold rush era home to the Bank of New Zealand – is now the information centre. There's also a small museum in a **Miner's Cottage**. It's supposed to be open daily from 8 am to 4 pm, but if it's closed just ask around town and someone will open it.

The cottage stands at the beginning of two historic goldfield **walkways**, the Jones Flat Walk and the Water Race Walk. Each takes about one to two hours and passes by interesting features from the gold rush era.

Near the car park in front of the cottage is a new working gold mine – you can look down on the operations. In the centre of town is a display of old gold-mining equipment and buildings.

The atmospheric *Empire Hotel* (☎ 755 4005), 19 Aylmer St, has tent sites at $16, cabins at $28, and share/ensuite rooms at $40/50; all prices are for two. Around the corner the *Ross Motel* (☎ 755 4022) has motel units at $58 a double; ask about them at the Manera Store. The *Empire Hotel* has bar meals, the *City Hotel* has a dining room and there's also the *Nicada Tearooms*.

Pukekura to Okarito

From Ross it's another 109 km to Franz Josef, but there are plenty of bush tracks and lakes along the way if you want to break the journey and can cope with the sandflies. Heading southwards the rainforest becomes more dense, and in many parts it looks as if it would be easier to walk over the top of it than to find a way through!

Many places along here provide low-cost accommodation. About 20 km south of Ross, *Lake Ianthe Cabins* (☎ 755 4032) near Pukekura has cabins at $27 for two, with activities including boating, sailing and fishing. About 100 metres south of the lake on the eastern side of the road is a giant matai tree. The short track to it is marked. There is also a *DOC camping ground* here.

South Westland Saddle Safaris (☎ 755 4144) conducts horse treks from the Bushmen's Centre at Pukekura; full-day treks cost $75. The **Bushmen's Centre**, by its very name, may seem to exclude women, but they take money from anyone. The centre has a *restaurant* which serves up West Coast wild foods – this effectively excludes vegetarians. Entry to the West Coast's Castle Machismo costs $5 ($2 for bush-children).

On a more pleasing note, there are several interesting **walks** in the region. About two hours from Greens Beach is a seal colony, and the adventurous can head down to Saltwater Lagoon, a truly beautiful and remote place. The **Coastal Pack Track** goes to the end of La Fontaine Creek; get details from the 'Bush-persons' Centre.

Harihari

The small town of Harihari is 22.5 km south of Lake Ianthe. Harihari made world headlines in 1931 when Aussie Guy Menzies completed the first solo flight across the Tasman Sea from Sydney, Australia. The landing was anything but smooth as he crash-landed *Southern Cross Junior* in the La Fontaine swamp. The aircraft turned over and when he undid his safety straps he fell head-first into the mud. He had made the trip in 11¾ hours, 2½ hours less than fellow Australian Charles Kingsford Smith and his crew in 1928.

There are several interesting things to do around Harihari. The two to three-hour **Harihari Coastal Walkway** (also called the Doughboy Walk) is a popular local attraction, with a lookout over the coastline, forest and mountains. You can also walk up into the Wilberg Range near the town (20 minutes return). Other possibilities are an old goldminers pack track, river mouth fishing for trout and salmon, or exploring the estuaries and wetlands of the Poerua and Wanganui rivers. Go **birdwatching** and try to spot native parakeets, herons, penguins, kakas and a number of migratory wading birds; get more information from the Hokitika Visitor Centre.

The *Harihari Motor Inn* (☎ 753 3026) has motel units at $58 for two, and bunk beds at $15 per person, with free use of the hot spa pool. Across the road, *Tomasi's Motel* (☎ 753 3116) has cabins with private bathroom at $30 for two, and motel units at $50 a double. Neither offers kitchen facilities for backpackers, but there are several places in town where you can get inexpensive meals, including a *tearoom*, a *fish & chip shop*, and the Motor Inn, which has pub meals and takeaways plus a restaurant and two bars.

If you want to stay on a farm try the *Wapiti Park Homestead* (☎ 753 3074) at Harihari; B&B is from $100 to $120 for two.

Whataroa & the Kotuku Sanctuary

Near Whataroa, 35 km south of Harihari, is a sanctuary for the kotuku (white heron), which nest here from November to February; it is the only NZ nesting site of this species. The herons then fly off individually to spend winter throughout the country.

White Heron Sanctuary Tours (☎ 753 4120) at Whataroa operates jet-boat tours to see the birds in their colony beside the Waitangi-Taona River. Don't panic, bird lovers – the jet-boat doesn't actually enter the nesting area. You walk along a boardwalk to the hide and are accompanied by a DOC officer. The cost is $60 (children $30) for the two-hour return trip. You can go in on your own but you must first obtain permission from the DOC and then check with the warden at the sanctuary.

There is a motel behind the sanctuary tours office. *White Heron Sanctuary Tours Motel & Cabins* (☎ 753 4120) – part of this operation is called Whataroa Backpackers – has cabins for $15 per person (BYO linen) and motel-style doubles for $55. The *Whataroa Hotel* (☎ 753 4076) charges $36 for two in twins. It also serves meals. Across the road from the tours office *Country Fare* dishes up good West Coast tucker.

Okarito

Another 15 km south of Whataroa is the Forks. From here it's just 17 km to Franz Josef, but if you turn off here you will find peaceful Okarito, 13 km away on the coast. Much of Keri Hulme's best seller *The Bone People* is set in this region.

There are lots of walks along the coast from Okarito – get hold of leaflets from the visitor centres in Hokitika or Franz Josef. Note that the kotuku sanctuary tours depart from Whataroa.

Okarito Nature Tours (☎ 753 4014), The Strand, organises kayaking trips into the beautiful **Okarito Lagoon**. The lagoon is New Zealand's largest unmodified wetland and consists of shallow open water and tidal flats. Okarito Lagoon is the feeding ground for the kotuku and it's a good place for watching all kinds of birds in their natural habitat, including kiwis. The lake is surrounded by rimu and kahikatea rainforest. Nature tour operators provide species lists.

The small, recently electrified *Okarito YHA Hostel* (☎ 753 4082) costs $10 per night. Hot showers are available from the nearby caravan park for multiples of 50c. Originally the hostel was a schoolhouse, built in the 1870s when Okarito was a thriving gold town. Opposite the hostel is a very basic *camping ground* with BBQs and toilets. It's a pleasant location and the price is right: just give whatever you care to donate to the camp's upkeep. If you plan to stay at Okarito, bring your own food and sleeping bag, as supplies out there are limited. There's also a *DOC camping ground* here.

Okarito to the Glaciers

Back towards the Forks turn-off, three km in from the highway, the *Forks Lodge* (☎ 753 4122) is an attractive little lodge with shared rooms for about $12 per person. It has all you need – fully equipped kitchen, showers etc – but bring your own bedding and food. It also has powered sites at $12 for two.

Soon after the Forks you'll reach Franz Josef, Westland National Park and the lofty peaks of the Southern Alps.

THE GLACIERS

The two most famous glaciers in the Westland National Park – the Fox and the Franz Josef – are among the most interesting sights in New Zealand. Nowhere else in the world, at this latitude, have glaciers advanced so close to the sea. Unlike the Tasman Glacier, on the other side of the dividing range in Mt Cook National Park, these two are just what glaciers should be – mighty rivers of ice, tumbling down a valley towards the sea.

The reason for the glaciers' development is threefold. The West Coast is subject to the prevailing westerlies which often bring rain. Much of this falls as snow high up in the névés. The snow crystals fuse to form clear ice at a depth of about 20 metres. Secondly, the zones where the ice accumulates on the glacier are very large, so there's a lot of ice to push down the valley.

Finally, they're very steep glaciers – the ice can get a long way before it finally melts. The rate of descent is staggering: a plane that crashed on the Franz Josef in 1943, 3.5 km from the terminal face, made it down to the bottom 6½ years later – a speed of 1.5 metres per day. At times the glacier can move at up to five metres a day, over 10 times as fast as glaciers in the Swiss Alps. Generally, though, it moves at the rate of about one metre a day.

Advance & Retreat

Glaciers always advance, they never really retreat. Sometimes, however, the ice melts even faster than it advances, and in that case the terminal, or end, face of the glacier moves back up the mountain, and appears to be retreating.

The great mass of ice higher up the mountain pushes the ice down the Fox and Franz Josef valleys at prodigious speeds but – like most glaciers in the world – this past century has been a story of steady retreat and only the odd short advance.

The last great ice age of 15,000 to 20,000 years ago saw the glaciers reach right down to the sea. Then warmer weather came and they may have retreated even further back than their current position. In the 14th century a new 'mini ice age' started and for centuries the glaciers advanced, reaching their greatest extent around 1750. At both Fox and Franz Josef, the terminal moraines from that last major advance can be clearly seen. In the nearly 250 years since then, the glaciers have steadily retreated and the terminal face is now several km back from its first recorded position in the late 19th century or even from its position in the 1930s.

From 1965 to 1968 the Fox and Franz Josef glaciers made brief advances of about 180 metres, and in 1985 they once again started to advance and have been moving forward steadily and fairly dramatically ever since. Nobody is quite sure why this advance is taking place. It could be cooler or more overcast summers or it could be the result of heavy snowfalls 10 or 15 years ago, which are now working their way down to the bottom of the glacier.

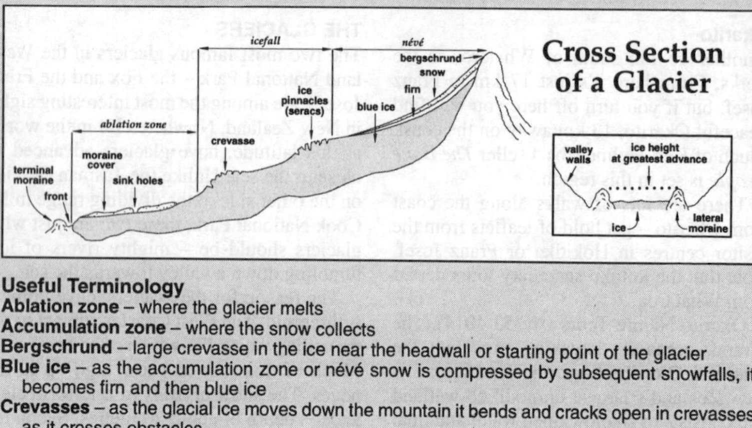

Useful Terminology

Ablation zone – where the glacier melts
Accumulation zone – where the snow collects
Bergschrund – large crevasse in the ice near the headwall or starting point of the glacier
Blue ice – as the accumulation zone or névé snow is compressed by subsequent snowfalls, it becomes firn and then blue ice
Crevasses – as the glacial ice moves down the mountain it bends and cracks open in crevasses as it crosses obstacles
Dead ice – as a glacier retreats, isolated chunks of ice may be left behind. Sometimes these can remain for many years
Firn – partly compressed snow on the way to becoming glacial ice
Glacial flour – the river of melted ice that flows off glaciers is a milky colour from the suspension of finely ground rocks
Icefall – when a glacier descends so steeply that the upper ice breaks up in a jumble of iceblocks
Kettle lake – lake formed by the melt of an area of isolated dead ice
Lateral moraine – walls of debris formed at the sides of the glacier
Névé – snowfield area where firn is formed
Seracs – ice pinnacles formed, like crevasses, by the glacier passing over obstacles
Terminal – the final ice face at the end of the glacier
Terminal moraine – mass of boulders and rocks marking the end point of the glacier, its final push down the valley ■

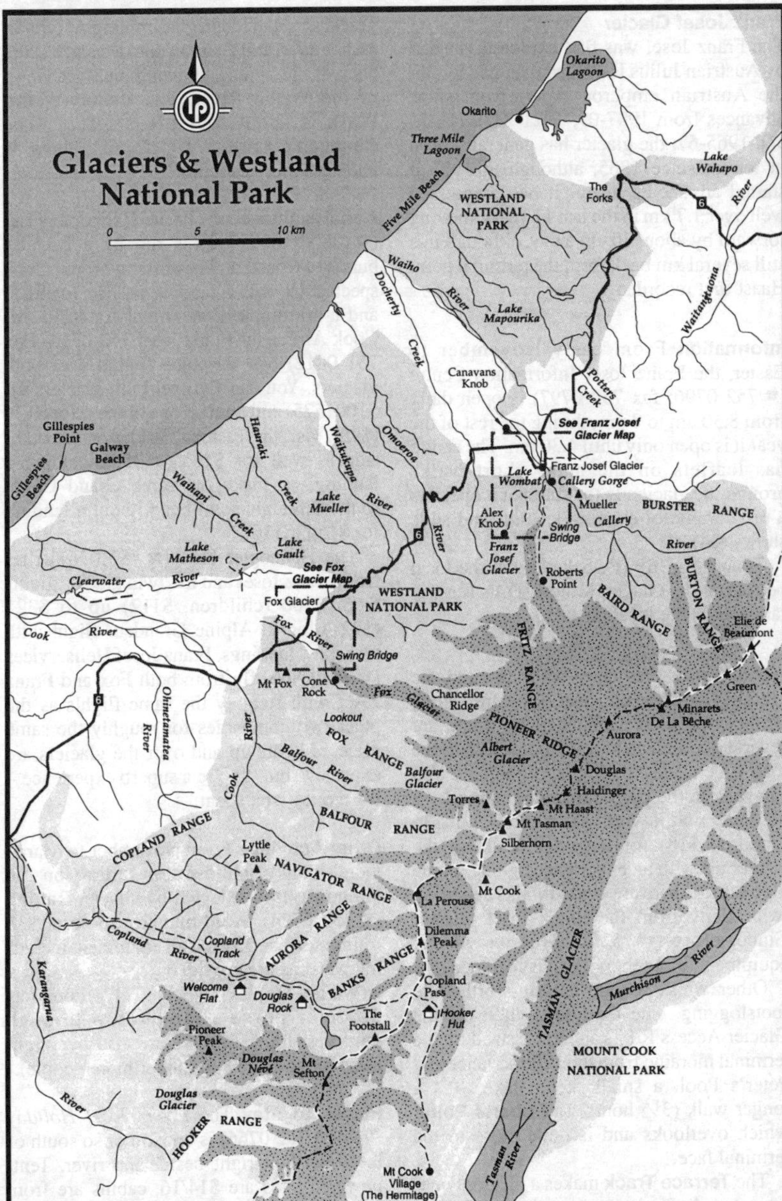
Glaciers & Westland National Park
0 5 10 km
Okarito Lagoon
Okarito
Three Mile Lagoon
Lake Wahapo
The Forks
Five Mile Beach
WESTLAND NATIONAL PARK
Waiho River
Docherty Creek
Lake Mapourika
Waitangitaona
Canavans Knob
Potters Creek
See Franz Josef Glacier Map
Franz Josef Glacier
Lake Wombat
Callery Gorge
Mueller
BURSTER RANGE
Callery River
Alex Knob
Swing Bridge
Franz Josef Glacier
Roberts Point
Gillespies Point
Galway Beach
Gillespies Beach
Hauraki Creek
Waikukupa River
Omoeroa River
Waihapi Creek
Lake Mueller
Lake Matheson
Lake Gault
See Fox Glacier Map
Clearwater River
Fox Glacier
WESTLAND NATIONAL PARK
Cook River
Fox River
Swing Bridge
Mt Fox
Cone Rock
Fox Glacier
Chancellor Ridge
Lookout
FOX RANGE
Balfour River
Balfour Glacier
Ohinetamatea River
Cook River
FRITZ RANGE
BAIRD RANGE
BURTON RANGE
Elie de Beaumont
Green
Minarets
De La Bêche
Aurora
PIONEER RIDGE
Albert Glacier
Douglas
Haidinger
Torres
Mt Haast
Mt Tasman
Silberhorn
BALFOUR RANGE
COPLAND RANGE
Lyttle Peak
NAVIGATOR RANGE
Mt Cook
La Perouse
AURORA RANGE
Dilemma Peak
Copland River
Copland Track
BANKS RANGE
Copland Pass
Welcome Flat
Douglas Rock
Hooker Hut
The Footstall
Karangarua River
Pioneer Peak
Douglas Névé
Mt Sefton
TASMAN GLACIER
Murchison River
MOUNT COOK NATIONAL PARK
Douglas Glacier
HOOKER RANGE
Tasman River
Mt Cook Village (The Hermitage)
6

Franz Josef Glacier
The Franz Josef was first explored in 1865 by Austrian Julius Haast, who named it after the Austrian emperor. Apart from short advances from 1907-09, 1921-34, 1946-59 and 1965-67, the glacier has generally been in retreat since 1865, although in 1985 it started advancing again. It has progressed well over 1.7 km in the last 11 years, moving forward by about 70 cm a day, although it is still several km back from the terminal point Haast first recorded.

Information From early November to Easter, the Franz Josef Information Centre (☎ 752 0796; fax 752 0797) is open daily from 8.30 am to 8 pm; during the rest of the year it is open only until 4.30 pm. The centre has leaflets on the many short walks around the glacier. In the summer it operates a programme of evening lectures and slide shows ($4).

There is an EFTPOS facility at the local petrol station, Glacier Motors. DA's Restaurant acts as the local postal agency.

Walks There are many walks around the glacier. Ask at the information centre for one of their excellent walk leaflets. There are several good glacier viewpoints close to the road which leads to the glacier car park. You can walk to the glacier from the car park, or you may find it worthwhile to fork out $36 (children $18) for a guided walk on the glacier ice with an experienced guide. In the high season there are guided walks departing twice daily from the Franz Josef Glacier Guides office (☎ 752 0763) in the village; equipment, including boots, is included.

Other walks require a little worthwhile footslogging. The **Douglas Walk**, off the Glacier Access Rd, is an hour's stroll by the terminal moraine from the 1750 advance and Peter's Pool, a small 'kettle lake'. It's a longer walk (3½ hours) to **Roberts Point**, which overlooks and is quite close to the terminal face.

The **Terrace Track** makes a pleasant one-hour round trip. It starts on the old Callery Track, scene of much gold-mining activity in earlier days, and leads up onto a terrace at the back of the village, showing pleasant views of the Waiho River. The **Callery-Waiho Walk** is about four hours return. The **Canavan's Knob Walk**, closer to town, is about 40 minutes return.

Aerial Sightseeing Glacier Helicopters Ltd (☎ (0800) 800 732) is run by a friendly bunch of Coasters. They offer a Mount Cook spectacular with a landing on Fox for $100 and a 40-minute Cook flight for $230. Mt Cook Airline (☎ Franz Josef 752 0714; Fox 751 0812) has ski-plane flights over both glaciers. You can fly over both glaciers for $100 ($75) and land on one of them for $130 ($98), visit the Tasman Glacier on the other side as well for $180 ($135) including a landing, or make the same Grand Circle route (three glaciers) but without a landing for $155 ($116).

The Helicopter Line (☎ 752 0767) flies from Franz Josef and has twin glacier flights from $160 (children, $112) up to $325 ($227) for an Alpine Grandeur flight with two snow landings. Franz Josef Heliservices (☎ 751 0866) fly from both Fox and Franz Josef with roughly the same flights as the other two companies for roughly the same prices. Flights up and over the glaciers are expensive but they're a superb experience – it's money well spent.

Other Activities From November to March there's milky **white-water rafting** on the Waiho River, conducted by Glacier Rafting (☎ 752 0704). A 90-minute trip costs $38 (minimum age 13) and all equipment including wetsuits are provided.

Waiho Stables (☎ 752 0747) conducts 2½-hour **horse riding tours** through rainforest for $35; there are also overnight treks for an extra $30 (six or more people).

Places to Stay The *Franz Josef Holiday Park* (☎ 752 0766) is one km or so south of the township, right beside the river. Tent/powered sites are $14/16, cabins are from $22 to $36, or tourist flats are $46; all prices

Top: Cathedral Square, Christchurch (TW)
Bottom: The Wizard, Cathedral Square, Christchurch (JW)

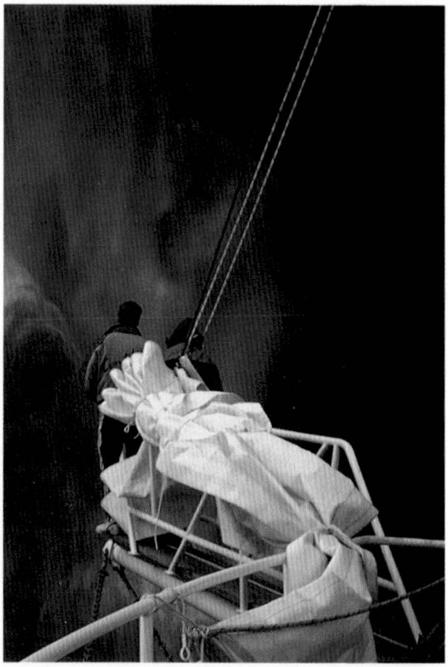

Top Left: Dune Formation, Farewell Spit, Nelson (JW)
Top Right: Collecting water from Stirling Falls, the *Wanderer*, Milford Sound, Southland (JW
Bottom: Fox Glacier, West Coast (HL)

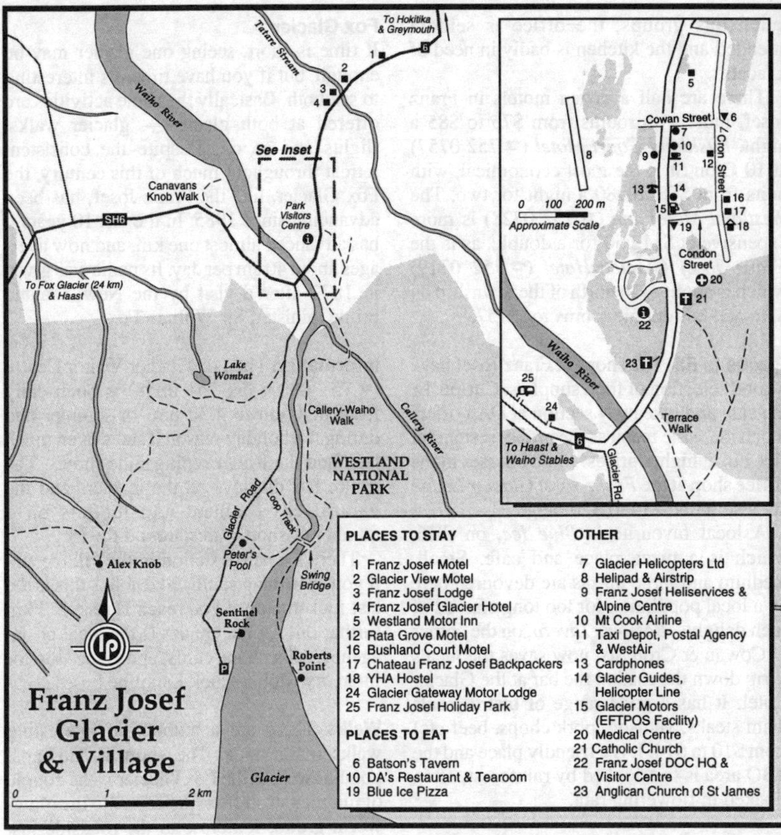

are for two. Letters to Lonely Planet have described the atmosphere as 'grumpy' – the place needs a genuine KiwiHost overhaul. For a great *DOC camping ground*, try McDonalds Creek, Lake Mapourika, 10 km north of Franz Josef.

The *Franz Josef Glacier YHA Hostel* (☎ 752 0754) is at 2-4 Cron St, just off the main road. It's a pleasant hostel with friendly managers, and costs $15 per person in dorms and $34 for doubles or twins. All rooms are centrally heated. There are family rooms available, and the hostel is open all day. It has a small shop, pool table, videos in the evenings, and a budget-priced meal service from September to April.

Next door is the *Chateau Franz Josef Backpackers* (☎ 752 0738) where shared rooms are $15.50 per person and doubles and twins are $35. There are a number of facilities at this pleasant place, including laundry, dryer, video library and bicycle hire.

On SH6 is *Franz Josef Lodge* (☎ 752 0712), a backpackers with centrally heated rooms and a drying room. The rooms, $15.50 per person in shared, twins and doubles and $25 in singles, are close to the Franz Josef public bar/bistro. It is now inundated with jaded bus groups, the office is seldom attended and the kitchen is badly in need of a facelift.

There are half a dozen motels in Franz Josef, most with rooms from $75 to $85 a night. *Bushland Court Motel* (☎ 752 0757) at 10 Cron St is the most economical, with units from $68 to $80 a night for two. The *Westland Motor Inn* (☎ 752 0728) is more expensive at $112.50 for a double, as is the *Franz Josef Glacier Hotel* (☎ 752 0719) which is about a km north of the township on SH6 and has double rooms for $157.

Places to Eat The shops at Franz Josef have a good selection of food supplies. Curiously, the cafe and takeaway section at *DA's* offers much the same menu as the proper restaurant side but at higher prices! Main courses in the coffee shop at the *Franz Josef Glacier Lodge* are also in the $14 to $20 range.

A local favourite is *Blue Ice*, on SH6, which is a pizza place and cafe. Small, medium and large pizzas are devoured here by a local population for too long starved of such delights. *Batson's Tavern*, on the corner of Cowan & Cron Sts, now saves the locals a trip down the road to the bar at the Glacier Hotel. It has a good range of bistro meals (ham steaks, venison, pork chops, beef etc) from $10 to $14. It is a friendly place and the BBQ area is overlooked by rainforest, often cloaked in flowering rata.

Getting There & Away North and southbound InterCity/Mt Cook Landline buses cross between the two glaciers, with daily buses south to Fox Glacier and Queenstown and north to Greymouth. The connections are such that Nelson to Queenstown (or vice versa) by bus along the West Coast takes a minimum of two days. In the high season (in summer) these buses can be heavily booked, so plan well ahead or be prepared to wait until there's space.

Along the West Coast, hitching prospects can be very bleak. If you're lucky you might do Greymouth to Queenstown in three days – if you're not you could well stand on the same spot for a couple of days.

Fox Glacier

If time is short, seeing one glacier may be enough, but if you have time it's interesting to see both. Basically the same activities are offered at both glaciers – glacier walks, flights and so on. Despite the consistent retreat throughout much of this century, the Fox Glacier, like the Franz Josef, has been advancing since 1985. In the last 10 years it has advanced almost one km, and now averages about 40 cm per day. Its name was given in 1872 after a visit by the New Zealand prime minister, Sir William Fox.

Information The Fox Glacier Visitor Centre (☎ 751 0807; fax 751 0858) is open daily from 8.30 am to 4.30 pm. In summer and during the holiday season it stays open much later and there are evening slide shows. The centre has displays on the glaciers and the natural environment and leaflets on a number of short walks around the ice.

There's a petrol station in the village and if you're driving south, take note – this is the last fuel stop until you reach Haast, 120 km further on. Alpine Guides is the local postal agency, sells phone cards, and is the stop for InterCity/Mount Cook Landline buses.

Walks There are a number of interesting walks in the area. The shortest and most popular walk at the Fox Glacier is the couple of minutes stroll from the centre to the glowworm grotto. It's close to the roadside just opposite the garage. Of course, you have to go at night to see them glowing.

Head towards the coast from the township for a lookout with a superb vista of the glacier and the Southern Alps. Before this lookout is the turn-off to **Lake Matheson** and one of the most famous panoramas in NZ. It's an hour's walk around the lake and at the far end you'll get an unforgettable view of the mountains and their reflection in the lake. The best time to see the famed reflection is very early in the morning, when the lake is at its most mirror-like calm.

An almost equally famous viewpoint can be found off Glacier View Rd, by making the short climb up to **Cone Rock**, or the easier

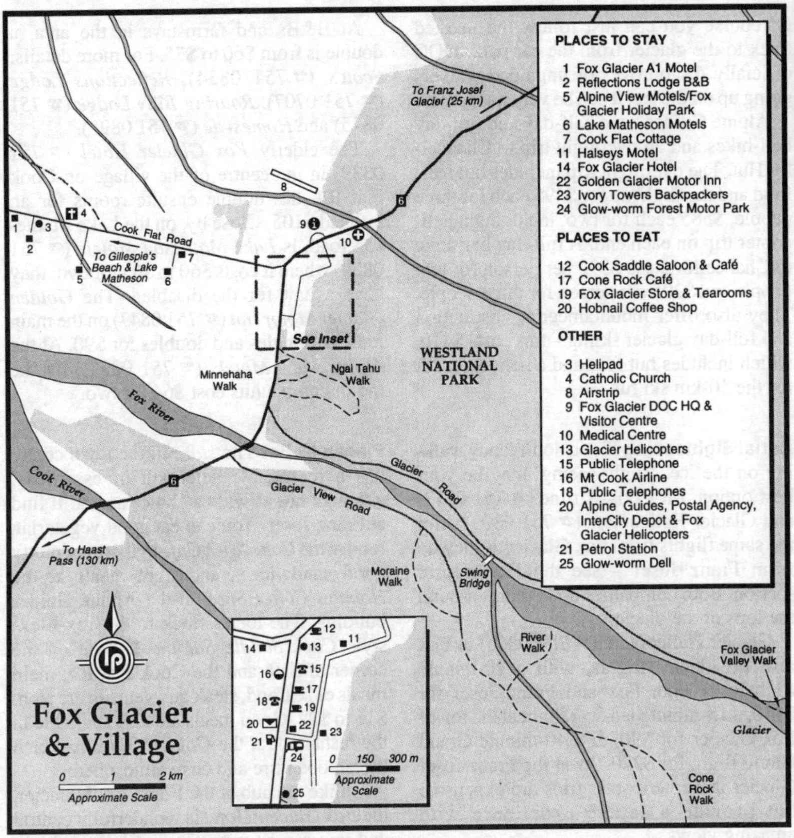

walk to Chalet lookout. **Mt Fox**, off SH6 to Haast, is another excellent viewpoint – a three-hour walk one way.

There are many other interesting walks around the glacier, including the short moraine walk over the advance of 200 years ago, or forest walks on the Ngai Tahu Track, the short Minnehaha Walk or the River Walk. It takes something over an hour to walk from the village to the glacier – it's 1.5 km from Fox to the turn-off, and the glacier is another five km back from the main road.

A particularly interesting walk is the two-hour coastal walk to the seal colony at **Gillespie's Beach**. Up to 1500 seals can be seen here and the walk also passes an old miners' cemetery and the remains of gold dredges. It is quite hazardous in places and not a suitable walk for children.

Guided Walks & Other Glacier Trips As at Franz Josef you can take guided walks up onto the glacier ice with Alpine Guides (☎ 751 0825). Tours leave at 9.30 am and 2 pm daily from the village, and boots and other equipment are included in the $34 (children $22) cost. From December to April they also have full-day guided glacier walks.

Of course you can just follow the marked track to the glacier from the car park. DOC officially disapproves of unguided walkers going up on the ice; it can be very dangerous.

Alpine Guides have half-day and full-day heli-hikes and an overnight trip to Chancellor Hut. The overnight trip includes hut fees, food and the flight up for $495 each for three people, $585 each for two, including a helicopter trip on each end. A full-day heli-hike to Chancellor costs $390 per person for two people and $295 per person for three people. They also offer mountaineering instruction and full-day glacier skiing – this costs $410, which includes hut fees and a helicopter lift for the 10-km ski run.

Aerial Sightseeing If you don't fancy walking on the ice, 'flight-seeing' may be your best option. Mt Cook Airline (☎ 751 0812) and Glacier Helicopters (☎ 751 0803) offer the same flights from Fox Glacier as they do from Franz Josef – see the Franz Josef section. Both companies do landings around the tops of the glaciers.

Glacier Helicopters (☎ 751 0866) at Fox also do glacier flights, with a 20-minute flight over both Fox and Franz Josef for $140, a 15-minute landing flight at the top of Fox Glacier for $90, or a 40-minute Grand Circle flight for $220. As at the Franz Josef Glacier these helicopter trips are expensive but provide a superb experience with amazing views.

Places to Stay The *Fox Glacier Holiday Park* (☎ 751 0821) is a motor camp 400 metres down the Lake Matheson road from the township. Tent/powered sites cost $16.50/18 for two, bunkroom accommodation is $11 per person, cabins are $34 for two, and tourist cabins are $50 for two.

The *Ivory Towers* (☎ 751 0838), on Sullivans Rd, behind the Golden Glacier Motor Inn, is tidy and well equipped; its rates are $15 a night in rooms sleeping four, or $36 for a twin or double. As one of the management said, it is the *only* backpackers in town, so, unfortunately, there is no alternative.

At B&Bs and farmstays in the area, a double is from $60 to $75. For more details: *Scott's* (☎ 751 0834), *Reflections Lodge* (☎ 751 0707), *Roaring Billy Lodge* (☎ 751 0815) and *Homestyle* (☎ 751 0895).

The elderly *Fox Glacier Hotel* (☎ 751 0839) in the centre of the village on Cook Flat Rd, has double ensuite rooms for an inflated $105. Close by, on the Lake Matheson road, is *Lake Matheson Motels* (☎ 751 0830) where it costs $60 to $65 for two; they have a unit for the disabled. The *Golden Glacier Motor Inn* (☎ 751 0847) on the main road has singles and doubles for $90. At the *Alpine View Motels* (☎ 751 0821), by the motor camp, units cost $64 for two.

Places to Eat The *store* in the town centre has a reasonable selection of essentials, although not as wide a choice as you'll find at Franz Josef. You can eat good vegetarian food at the *Cone Rock Cafe* or there are pretty good sandwiches and light meals at the *Hobnail Coffee Shop* in the Alpine Guides building. The locals flock to the Tex-Mex-style *Cook Saddle Saloon & Cafe* on the corner of SH6 and the Cook Flat Rd; main meals of seafood, steak and venison are from $16 to $22. Good meals are also available in the restaurant at the *Golden Glacier*, which has an open fire and cosy atmosphere.

Unlike the pub at the Franz Josef Glacier, the *Fox Glacier Hotel* is wonderfully central and you can sit with a jug of beer and talk about the day's activities. The *Cook Saddle Cafe* hums most nights and if you want a more expensive, intimate evening try the bar at the *Golden Glacier*.

Getting There & Away The InterCity/Mount Cook Landline bus services overlap – southbound services from Greymouth start and finish at Fox Glacier, northbound ones from Queenstown continue on to Franz Josef. Buses run every day to and from Greymouth (four hours) and Queenstown (eight hours). From Greymouth there are onward connections to Westport, Nelson, Picton and Christchurch.

See the Franz Josef section for the sad news on hitchhiking and a warning about the heavily booked bus services.

SOUTH TO HAAST

South of the glaciers the road (SH6) eventually departs from the West Coast and climbs over the Haast Pass and on down to Wanaka. Another road splits from the SH6 at Haast and heads further down the West Coast to Jackson Bay and the mighty Cascade River. Heading south from the glaciers, the rainforest is so dense on both sides of the road that you can barely see a couple of metres into it. Further on, it opens up to reveal broad sweeps of coastline.

Just 26 km south of Fox Glacier is the **Copland Valley**. This is at the end of the Copland Track, coming over from Mt Cook. It's a very pleasant six-hour walk up the valley from the highway here to the last hut at Welcome Flat, where there are hot springs. A sign on the road marks the entrance to the valley and the track. The excellent modern hut at Welcome Flat sleeps 40 and costs $8 per night. There's transport from Fox Glacier to the Copland Valley entrance by InterCity/Mount Cook Landline, but for the short length of journey it is expensive.

There are a few places to stay on the stretch of road between Fox Glacier and Haast if you wish to break up the journey. The *Pinegrove Motels* (☎ 751 0898), 35 km south of Fox Glacier, has a variety of accommodation including powered sites at $16, basic cabins at $30, and units at $50; all prices are for two persons.

Lake Paringa

Lake Paringa, about 70 km south of Fox Glacier and 50 km north of Haast, is a tranquil little trout-filled lake surrounded by forest, right beside the road. The *Lake Paringa Heritage Lodge* (☎ 751 0894) is on the lake shore and has boats and canoes for hire. Rates are $40 for two in self-contained cabins if you supply your own bedding, or $70 for two in the larger motel units. About one km further south, still on the lakefront, is a free DOC camping area with just basic facilities – toilets and picnic areas. The *Lake Paringa Cafe* is a quaint little place where toasted sandwiches with three fillings are $3 and main meals are from $16 to $18.

The historic **Haast-Paringa Cattle Track** begins from the main road 43 km north of Haast, and comes out at the coast by the Waita River, just a few km north of Haast. Before the Haast Pass road was opened in 1965, this trail was the only link between Otago/Southland and the West Coast. The first leg of the track makes a pleasant day hike. Information on the track is available from the World Heritage Visitor Centre in Haast.

Lake Moeraki

Lake Moeraki, 31 km north of Haast, not far off the highway, is another peaceful forest lake with good fishing. It's also not far from the coast – just a 40-minute walk along a stream brings you to **Monro Beach**, where there's a breeding colony of Fiordland crested penguins; they can be found there from July to November. Also at Monro Beach are fur seals and good snorkelling. There are many other good short and long walks around the lake and the Moeraki River which runs from the lake to the sea.

The *Wilderness Lodge Lake Moeraki* (☎ 750 0881), right on the highway and just 20 metres from the lakeside, is a very special place where visitors can fully enjoy a wilderness experience. It has rooms at $140/175 per person in low/high season for dinner, bed & breakfast. Daily outdoor and nature activities, such as walks to Fiordland crested penguin colonies and canoe safaris, are organised; short activities up to 90 minutes' duration are free for guests and half-day trips cost $48. The *Riverside Restaurant*, with its superb views of the massive trees growing outside, specialises in fish and game dishes. The canoe safaris are also open to the public.

Just beyond Moeraki is the much photographed **Knight's Point** where the Haast road was eventually opened in 1965; there is an information shelter here. And Knight? He was a surveyor's dog.

THE HAAST REGION

The Haast region is the centre of a major wildlife refuge where some of the biggest stands of rainforest survive alongside some of the most extensive wetlands. The kahikatea swamp forests, sand dune forests, seal and penguin colonies, the kaka, Red Hills and vast sweeps of beach have ensured the listing of this hauntingly beautiful place as a World Heritage area.

In the forests you will see the flaming red rimu in flower, and kahikatea thriving in swampy lagoons. Birdlife abounds and the observant twitcher might see fantail, bellbird, native pigeon (kereru), falcon, kaka, kiwi and morepork. On the beaches you are likely to see blue penguins and Fiordland crested penguins. This is the home turf of the legendary Arawata Bill who roamed this domain as a self-styled prospector and explorer. Walk through his incredible country and take a trip back hundreds of years – raupo, ferns and cabbage trees inhibit progress if you stray off the beaten track.

Haast

The tiny community of Haast is on the coast where the wide Haast River meets the sea, 120 km south of Fox Glacier. There's really not much to the town, although this is an area which has been targeted for tourist development; it is now a World Heritage area. Probably in the very near future there will be more activities including white-water rafting, jet-boating, horse trekking and so on, and more options in places to stay.

A series of tracks has been developed, including the **Hapuka Estuary Walk** leading from the motor camp, and a rainforest, seacoast and wetland walk along **Ship Creek**, halfway between Haast and Lake Moeraki.

The South West New Zealand World Heritage Visitor Centre (☎ 750 0809; fax 750 0832), at the junction of SH6 and Jackson Bay Rd on the southern bank of the Haast River, has information on the area and on nature-related activities.

Places to Stay & Eat The *Haast Motor Camp* (☎ 750 0860) is at Okuru, 11 km south of Haast township on the road to Jackson Bay. Tent/powered sites cost $14/15.50 for two, and there are various cabins at $33 or $40 for two, with linen for hire if needed. In the township is the newly-opened *Wilderness Backpackers* (☎ 0800 750 029) in Pauareka Rd. It has beds from $15 per person – write and tell us what you think.

Also in town is the oddly administered *Haast Highway Accommodation* (☎ 750 0703), at Marks Rd, three km east of the Visitor Centre and 200 metres from SH6. Here tent sites are $8 per person, a backpackers bed is $14.50 and units are from $50 to $68 for two. The rarest things in the backpackers section are items of crockery – there aren't any! It seems you have to pay a bond of $12 to get some and this is refunded in the morning. If you arrive after the shop closes drink directly from the sink, eat with your fingers or share the one cooking pot left in the kitchen for all the backpackers. The lights are off at 11 pm. This place *could* be a great backpackers but it isn't. Vote with your feet!

The *World Heritage Haast Hotel* (☎ 750 0828) has single/double rooms from $75/85 and two-bedroom suites from $130. Two of their units are set up for disabled travellers. There is a public bar nearby, a house bar and a good restaurant with a good selection of à la carte dishes. The pub meals are really good value and $9 will see you well satisfied.

Haast to Jackson Bay & the Cascade

A road heads south from the SH6 at Haast to the Arawata River. Near Okuru is the walk to the tidal Hapuka Estuary. On the south side of the Arawata bridge there is a junction; both roads leading off from it are worth driving.

The road due south is gravel but in generally good condition. It follows the Jackson River and soon reaches the track to **Lake Ellery**, a one-hour return walk. Continue to Martyr Saddle where there are views of the incredible Red Hills and the Cascade River valley. The **Red Hills** are examples of ultramafic rock, so called because of the high concentrations of magnesium and iron which give them their distinctive colour. This unusual occurrence is explained by the fact that the Australo and Pacific tectonic plates meet at this point and some millions of years ago forced up these concentrations of rock. Continue on from Martyr Saddle to the flats of the Cascade River, a true wilderness region.

The road west emerges at the Tasman Sea at the scenic fishing hamlet of **Jackson Bay**. The views north to the Southern Alps are memorable and there are colonies of Fiordland crested penguins close to the road. In 1875, an ambitious scheme to set up a large port and town here were doomed to failure. A Royal Commission set up in 1878 found malpractice charges against the then Resident Agent were unfounded but it did not rule out the possibility of sabotage from other quarters.

There are a number of interesting short **walks** here including the three-hour Smoothwater Bay Track, the 15-minute Jackson Viewpoint Walk and the 30-minute Wharekai Te Kau Walk. Keener trampers can walk to Stafford Bay Hut; it can be made a long day walk or an easier two-day walk with an overnight stop at the hut. Check tidal information with the visitor centre in Haast.

HAAST PASS

Turning inland at Haast, snaking along beside the wide Haast River and climbing up the pass, you soon enter the Mt Aspiring National Park and the scenery changes again – the vegetation becomes much more sparse the further inland you proceed, until beyond the 563-metre summit you reach snow country covered only in tussock and scrub. Along the Haast Pass are many picturesque waterfalls, most of them just a couple of minutes walk off the road.

The roadway over Haast Pass was opened in 1965. Prior to that the only southern link to the West Coast was by the Haast-Paringa Cattle Track, walking or on horseback! En route to Wanaka you can see two sets of waterfalls close to the road – **Fantail** and **Thunder Creek falls**. See the DOC booklet *Haast Pass Highway: Short Walks*.

Heading south, the next town of any size you come to after Haast is Wanaka, a distance of 145 km, about 3½ hours by road (see the Otago chapter). If you're driving north, check your fuel gauge – the petrol station at Haast is the last one you'll come to until you reach Fox Glacier, 120 km north.

Makarora & the Siberia Valley

When you reach Makarora you have left the West Coast. It has been included in this chapter as it still has a frontier feel about it, akin to the general atmosphere of the West Coast, and it is the gateway to the Haast Pass and the West Coast for traffic heading up north.

Don't be put off by the misleading names of places in this region given to them by an early traveller. He called one of the world's most beautiful valleys Siberia and nearby Matterhornesque peaks Dreadful and Awful – he is not to be believed. In the Siberia valley you can walk in one of the last refuges of the blue duck and the rare orange-wattled South Island kokako (thought to be nearly extinct).

Makarora's permanent population is around 30. You really can't see the cluster of A-frame units from the road but they are capable of accommodating about 140 people, which can be useful from time to time when adventure-seekers arrive in town. Apart from these, there isn't much in this township – and that is part of its charm.

'Siberia Experience' Makarora is the base for one of NZ's great outdoor adventures – the Siberia Experience. This is one of those Kiwi extravaganzas that combines sundry thrill-seeking activities – in this case a small-plane flight (half an hour), a three-hour bush walk through a remote mountain valley, and a jet-boat trip (45 minutes) down a river valley. Make sure you follow the markers as you descend from Siberia; people have got lost and have had to spend the night out here!

Southern Alps Air (☎ 443 8372) operates the 'experience' from mid-October to mid-April and it costs $122 (minimum of three passengers). It also has 40-minute trips over

Mt Aspiring ($100 per person), 70-minute trips to Mt Cook and the glaciers ($185) and landings at Milford Sound ($195).

Other Activities There are plenty of **jet-boating** trips. A 50-km, one-hour return trip into Mt Aspiring National Park costs $42 with a minimum of four people. Compare this with the 20-minute Shotover jet trip at $65. There is a transport service for trampers wishing to reach the top of the Wilkin River and a ferry service across from the Young River mouth when the Makarora is in flood (about $10 per person). For booking details, inquire on ☎ 443 8351 or at the Makarora Tourist Service.

There are many **walks** in the area. Shorter ones include the Old Bridal Track (1½ hours) which heads from the top of the Haast pass to Davis Flat; a 20-minute nature walk around Makarora; and the Blue Pools River Walk where you can see huge rainbow trout.

Two longer walks are the three-day Gillespies Pass tramp and the walk from the head of the Wilkin River to Lake Castalia. The **Gillespies Pass** tramp goes via the Young, Siberia and Wilkin rivers (hopefully this will be further developed to take some of the heat off the Routeburn). With a jet-boat ride down the Wilkin to complete it, this surely could rate alongside the Milford Track as one of the great tramps. The **Wilkin Valley Track** heads off from Kerin Forks Hut (where you can be dropped by jet-boat). It leads to Top Forks Hut, then the north branch of the Wilkin. Here you will see the picturesque lakes Diana, Lucidus and Castalia. These are one hour, 1½ hours and three to four hours respectively from Top Forks Hut.

For further information about this region take a look at the Mt Aspiring National Park Service's *Makarora Region*.

Places to Stay & Eat The Makarora Tourist Service operates the *A-Frame Motels & Cabins* (☎ 443 8372), in a bush setting. The cost is $60 for two people in the self-contained chalets, $34 for two in the A-frame cabins, and $7.50 for a tent site.

A new place, the *Larrivee Homestead* (☎ 443 9177), is not far from the Makarora Tourist Service. To get to it you take the road closest to the DOC office and drive up until you reach the octagonal masterpiece at the end of the drive. The cost for homestay B&B is $40 per person and there is cheaper accommodation in a cottage (which many would find more comfortable than their own homes); the cost is $50 for two and $12 for each extra person (maximum of five). The house and cottage are made of stone and hand-split cedar. Dinners are prepared for $25 per person.

There are DOC *camping grounds* at Cameron Flat, on SH6, and Davis Flat, on SH6, 11 and 14 km north of Makarora respectively.

If you want to stay in the Siberia Valley there is a 10-bed *hut* available; fees are payable at the ranger station at Makarora.

The *tearooms* open from 8.30 am to 6 pm for lunch and snacks only, but the grocery stocks basic supplies.

Getting There & Away West Coast Express, Magic Bus and Kiwi Experience buses regularly stop here. InterCity/Mount Cook Landline have one northbound (to the glaciers) and one southbound (to Hawea, Wanaka and Queenstown) bus per day.

Canterbury

Canterbury is the hub of the South Island. The large Canterbury region extends from near Kaikoura in the north to near Oamaru in the south, and from the Pacific to Arthur's Pass and Mt Cook in the Southern Alps.

This is one of the driest and flattest areas of NZ. The moisture-laden westerlies blowing in from the Tasman Sea are swept upwards by the Southern Alps, causing heavy rainfall on the West Coast – over five metres a year! When the winds continue east over Canterbury, they have lost most of their moisture, and the Canterbury region, though not so far from the West Coast, has a markedly different climate, with an annual rainfall of only around 75 cm.

The predominant feature of the region is the Canterbury Plains, a large, flat area primarily devoted to farming and agriculture, which lies between the coast and the mountain foothills. Canterbury, however, contains the highest of New Zealand's mountains – Mts Cook (Aoraki), Tasman, Sefton etc – so presents much more of a geographical contrast than any other part of NZ. This is perhaps the New Zealand – the blend of the rural and rugged – that is most often depicted to the overseas traveller.

HIGHLIGHTS

- The beautiful City of Christchurch (and in particular the fascinating Canterbury Museum – one of the best regional museums anywhere)
- The charming settlement of Akaroa – a great place for relaxing or starting the Banks Peninsula Walk
- Arthur's Pass National Park – all types of walking opportunities and fabulous mountainscapes
- Exploring the Port Hills and Banks Peninsula region by car or on foot
- Mt Cook National Park – the grandeur of Aoraki (Mt Cook) and the glaciers
- The Lewis Pass region and the getaway town of Hanmer with its hot springs
- Lake Tekapo – an azure blue lake surrounded by mountains

Christchurch Region & the North

Christchurch is the focal point of Canterbury, centrally located on the coast midway between Kaikoura and Timaru. It is a large, ordered city with a population of 308,200. To the west, beyond the extensive alluvial plain, are the imposing Southern Alps and Arthur's Pass National Park; to the north, beyond the rolling hills, are Hanmer and more forest parks; and to the south-east is the absorbing Banks Peninsula.

CHRISTCHURCH

At the base of the hills of Banks Peninsula, Christchurch is often described as the most English of New Zealand's cities. The city, nestled beneath the Southern Alps, exists as a great South Pacific incongruity. Many statues honour persons with English names; and trams rattle past streets with oh-so English names (Oxford, Worcester etc). It is easy to forget that this epitome of Englishness is the capital of Te Wahipounamu, long-time ancestral home of the Ngai Tahu.

The first Europeans in Christchurch began building huts along the Avon in 1851, but it was not until March 1862 that it was

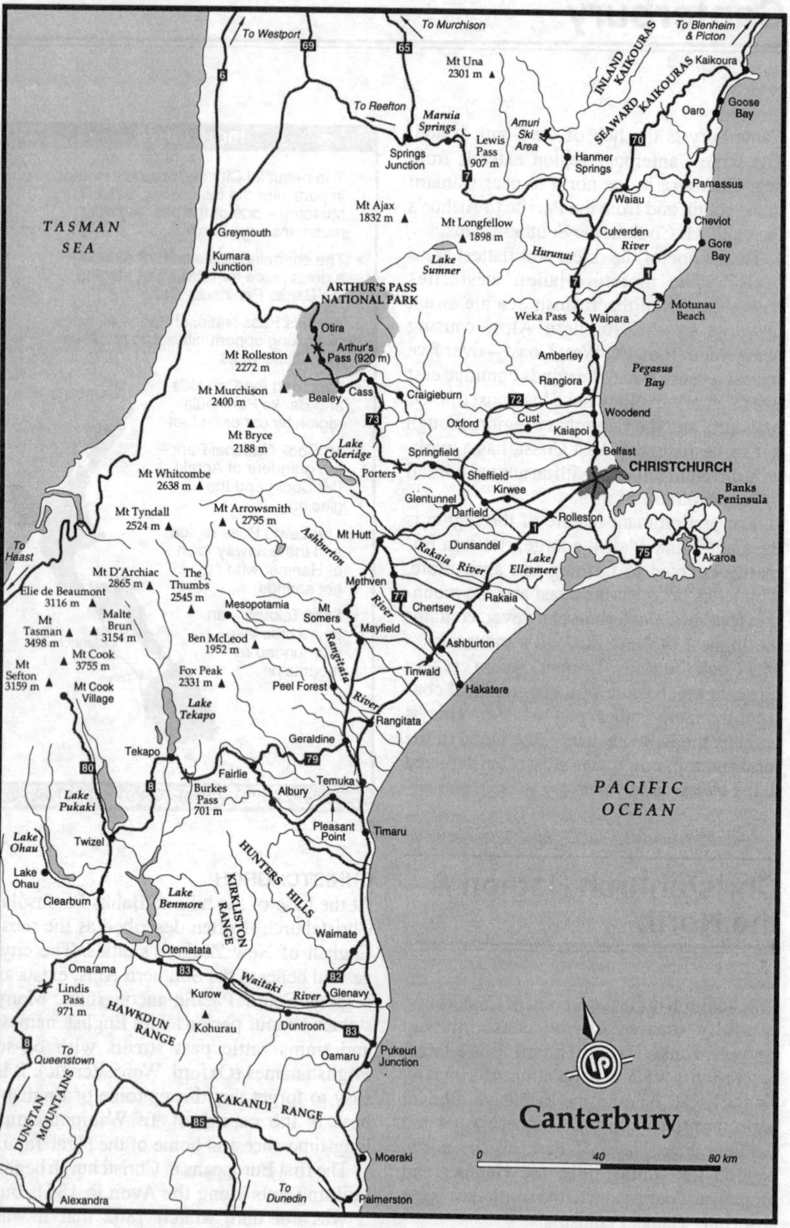
Canterbury
0
40
80 km
To Westport
To Murchison
To Blenheim & Picton
To Reefton
INLAND KAIKOURAS
SEAWARD KAIKOURAS
Kaikoura
Goose Bay
Oaro
Mt Una 2301 m
Maruia Springs
Springs Junction
Amuri Ski Area
Lewis Pass 907 m
Hanmer Springs
Parnassus
Waiau
Cheviot
Mt Ajax 1832 m
Mt Longfellow 1898 m
Culverden
River
Gore Bay
Hurunui
Lake Sumner
TASMAN SEA
Greymouth
Kumara Junction
ARTHUR'S PASS NATIONAL PARK
Weka Pass
Waipara
Motunau Beach
Otira
Arthur's Pass (920 m)
Mt Rolleston 2272 m
Amberley
Pegasus Bay
Rangiora
Mt Murchison 2400 m
Bealey
Cass
Craigieburn
Woodend
Cust
Oxford
Kaiapoi
Mt Bryce 2188 m
Lake Coleridge
Springfield
Belfast
CHRISTCHURCH
Porters
Sheffield
Mt Whitcombe 2638 m
Kirwee
Banks Peninsula
Glentunnel
Darfield
Mt Tyndall 2524 m
Mt Arrowsmith 2795 m
Rolleston
Ashburton
Mt Hutt
To Haast
Rakaia River
Dunsandel
Lake Ellesmere
Akaroa
Mt D'Archiac 2865 m
The Thumbs 2545 m
Methven
Elie de Beaumont 3116 m
River
Rakaia
Mesopotamia
Chertsey
Mt Tasman 3498 m
Malte Brun 3154 m
Mt Somers
Mayfield
Ben McLeod 1952 m
Ashburton
Mt Cook 3755 m
Mt Sefton 3159 m
Fox Peak 2331 m
Rangitata
Tinwald
Mt Cook Village
Peel Forest
Hakatere
Lake Tekapo
River
Rangitata
Geraldine
Tekapo
Fairlie
Temuka
PACIFIC OCEAN
Lake Pukaki
Burkes Pass 701 m
Albury
Pleasant Point
Timaru
Lake Ohau
Twizel
HUNTERS HILLS
Lake Ohau
KIRKLISTON RANGE
Lake Benmore
Clearburn
Waimate
Otematata
Omarama
Lindis Pass 971 m
Kurow
Waitaki River
Glenavy
HAWKDUN RANGE
Kohurau
Duntroon
To Queenstown
Oamaru
Pukeuri Junction
DUNSTAN MOUNTAINS
KAKANUI RANGE
Moeraki
To Dunedin
Alexandra
Palmerston
69
65
6
7
70
1
72
73
1
75
77
79
80
8
83
82
83
8
85

incorporated as a city. The name Christchurch comes from Christ Church College at Oxford, as one of the leaders of the early settlers was educated there. The Avon River which flows through Christchurch is named after a stream in Ayrshire, Scotland.

Even the central square is dominated by a neogothic cathedral in the fashion of English towns. Get away from the centre, out to the western suburbs such as Fendalton, Avonhead, Bryndwr, Burnside and Ilam, and you'll be struck by the tranquil atmosphere. Here are the exquisite gardens Christchurch is famous for, gardens of geraniums, chrysanthemums and carefully edged lawns where not a blade of grass is out of place.

Orientation & Information

The Cathedral Square is very much the centre of town. To find it, just look for the spire, and once there, climb to the top to get your orientation. Christchurch is a compact city and walking around is easy, although slightly complicated by the river which twists and winds through the centre and crosses your path in disconcertingly varied directions. The network of one-way streets adds even more excitement if you're driving. Colombo St, running north-south through the Square, is the main shopping street. You will find the post office and payphones in the south-west corner of the Square.

Tourist Offices Walk down Worcester St from the Square to the Christchurch/Canterbury Visitor Centre (☎ 379 9629; fax 377 2424) by the river, on the corner of Oxford Terrace. It's open from 8.30 am to 5 pm, Monday to Friday and from 8.30 am to 4 pm on weekends; it stays open later in the summer. This is the best bet for local information. Adventure Canterbury, where you can get information on all manner of outdoor pursuits, is in the same building and uses the same phone number. There are branches of the information centre at both Christchurch domestic (☎ 353 7774) and international (☎ 353 7783) airports. A good free publication is the monthly *In and Around Christchurch*. Note that bus numbers refer to Canride buses unless indicated otherwise.

The DOC (☎ 379 9758) at 133 Victoria St has leaflets and information on most national parks, walkways and other outdoor attractions around the South Island. It is open from 8 am to 4.30 pm, Monday to Friday.

The Automobile Association (☎ 379 1280) is at 210 Hereford St. If Christchurch is your point of entry to New Zealand and you intend buying a car, you can have an AA inspection carried out in this city.

The YHA national headquarters is in Christchurch. The Travel Centre (☎ 379 9970), on the corner of Gloucester and Manchester Sts, handles membership and makes domestic and international bookings.

The Disabilities Service (☎ 366 6189), 314 Worcester St, open from 9 am to 5 pm Monday to Friday, has information on accessible facilities and equipment for hire.

Money You will have no problem changing travellers cheques or foreign currency in Christchurch; however, it's wise to shop around, as rates vary wildly.

Foreign Consulates Consulates in Christchurch include:

Belgium	☎ 348 0969	Malaysia	☎ 338 9059
Denmark	☎ 389 5086	Netherlands	☎ 366 9280
France	☎ 351 6259	Sweden	☎ 365 0000
Germany	☎ 379 3193	UK	☎ 365 5440
Italy	☎ 359 7372	USA	☎ 379 004
Japan	☎ 366 56800		

Bookshops Christchurch has numerous bookstores. Bennetts GP Book Shop at 147 Hereford St carries government publications, DOSLI maps and specialised NZ guidebooks. Scorpio Books, corner of Hereford St and Oxford Terrace, and Arnold Books at 11 New Regent St also has a wide range of books. Smith's Bookshop, at 133 Manchester St, is a classic secondhand bookshop – one room is devoted to books on New Zealand, including Maori culture and art, and poetry and fiction by NZ authors. The Epicentre in the Arts Centre, Hereford St, the place for environmental books, is open daily

CANTERBURY

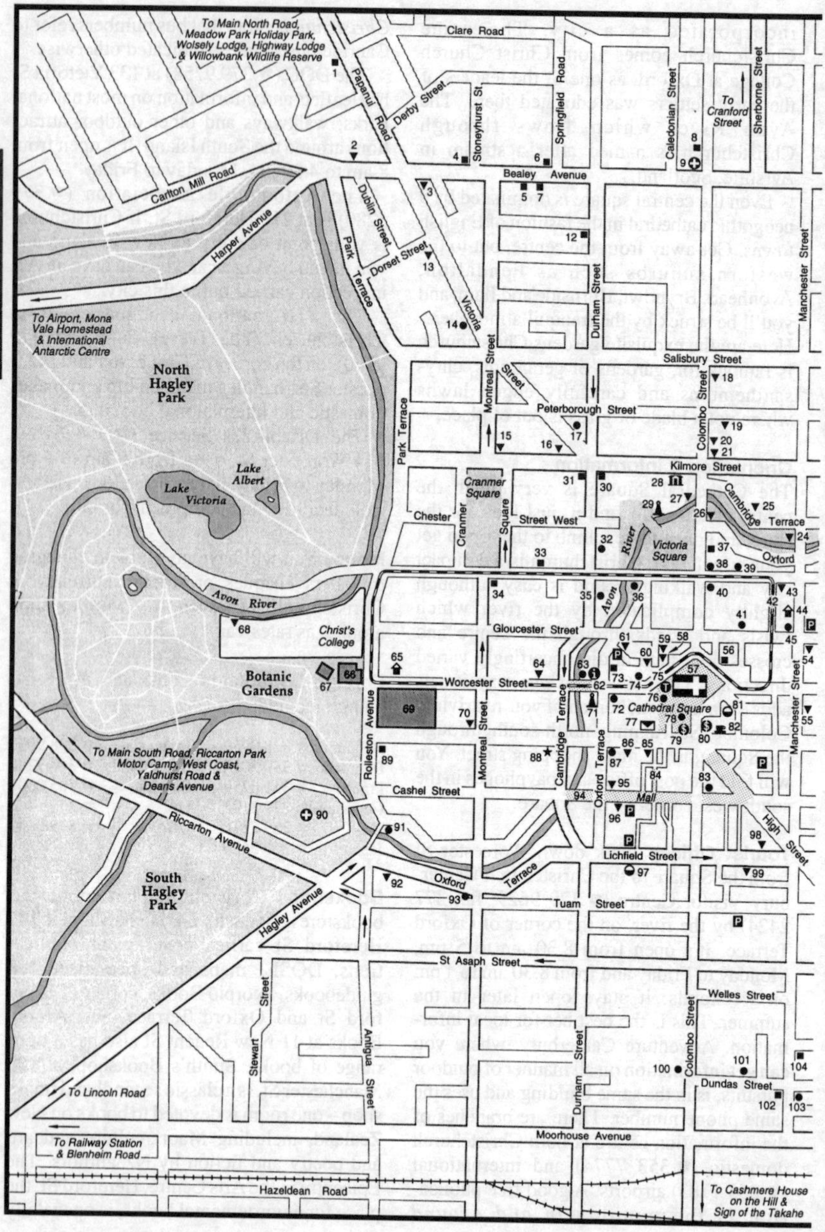
To Main North Road, Meadow Park Holiday Park, Wolsely Lodge, Highway Lodge & Willowbank Wildlife Reserve
Clare Road
Papanui Road
Derby Street
Stoneyhurst St
Springfield Road
Caledonian Street
To Cranford Street
Sherborne Street
Carlton Mill Road
Bealey Avenue
Dublin Street
Harper Avenue
Park Terrace
Dorset Street
Victoria
Durham Street
Manchester Street
To Airport, Mona Vale Homestead & International Antarctic Centre
North Hagley Park
Montreal Street
Salisbury Street
Peterborough Street
Colombo Street
Kilmore Street
Lake Albert
Lake Victoria
Cranmer Square
Cambridge Terrace
Chester
Street West
Avon River
Victoria Square
Oxford
Christ's College
Gloucester Street
Botanic Gardens
Worcester Street
Cathedral Square
Rolleston Avenue
To Main South Road, Riccarton Park Motor Camp, West Coast, Yaldhurst Road & Deans Avenue
Oxford Terrace
Mall
Cashel Street
High Street
Riccarton Avenue
Lichfield Street
South Hagley Park
Hagley Avenue
Tuam Street
St Asaph Street
Welles Street
Stewart Street
Antigua Street
To Lincoln Road
Dundas Street
Moorhouse Avenue
To Railway Station & Blenheim Road
Hazeldean Road
To Cashmere House on the Hill & Sign of the Takahe

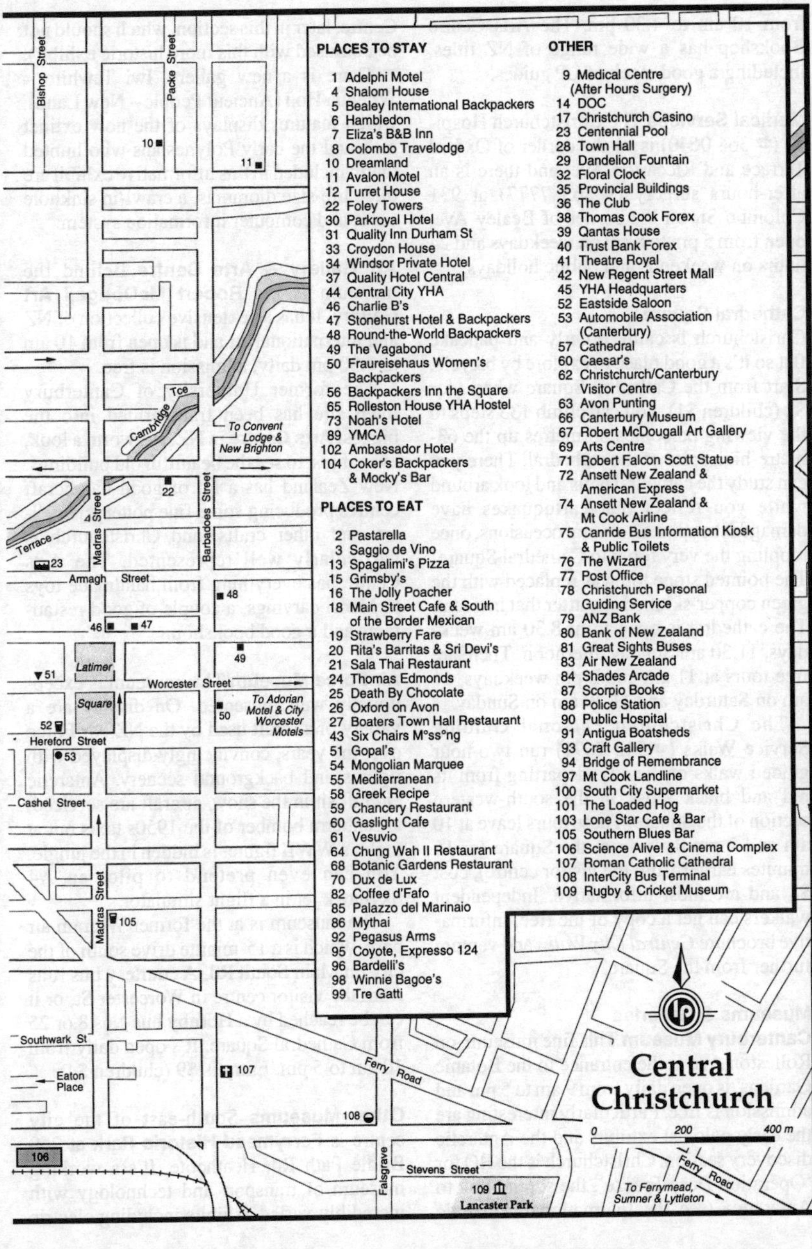
PLACES TO STAY
1 Adelphi Motel
4 Shalom House
5 Bealey International Backpackers
6 Hambledon
7 Eliza's B&B Inn
8 Colombo Travelodge
10 Dreamland
11 Avalon Motel
12 Turret House
22 Foley Towers
30 Parkroyal Hotel
31 Quality Inn Durham St
33 Croydon House
34 Windsor Private Hotel
37 Quality Hotel Central
44 Central City YHA
46 Charlie B's
47 Stonehurst Hotel & Backpackers
48 Round-the-World Backpackers
49 The Vagabond
50 Fraureisehaus Women's Backpackers
56 Backpackers Inn the Square
65 Rolleston House YHA Hostel
73 Noah's Hotel
89 YMCA
102 Ambassador Hotel
104 Coker's Backpackers & Mocky's Bar
PLACES TO EAT
2 Pastarella
3 Saggio de Vino
13 Spagalimi's Pizza
15 Grimsby's
16 The Jolly Poacher
18 Main Street Cafe & South of the Border Mexican
19 Strawberry Fare
20 Rita's Barritas & Sri Devi's
21 Sala Thai Restaurant
24 Thomas Edmonds
25 Death By Chocolate
26 Oxford on Avon
27 Boaters Town Hall Restaurant
43 Six Chairs M°ss°ng
51 Gopal's
54 Mongolian Marquee
55 Mediterranean
58 Greek Recipe
59 Chancery Restaurant
60 Gaslight Cafe
61 Vesuvio
64 Chung Wah II Restaurant
68 Botanic Gardens Restaurant
70 Dux de Lux
82 Coffee d'Fafo
85 Palazzo del Marinaio
86 Mythai
92 Pegasus Arms
95 Coyote, Expresso 124
96 Bardelli's
98 Winnie Bagoe's
99 Tre Gatti
OTHER
9 Medical Centre (After Hours Surgery)
14 DOC
17 Christchurch Casino
23 Centennial Pool
28 Town Hall
29 Dandelion Fountain
32 Floral Clock
35 Provincial Buildings
36 The Club
38 Thomas Cook Forex
39 Qantas House
40 Trust Bank Forex
41 Theatre Royal
42 New Regent Street Mall
45 YHA Headquarters
52 Eastside Saloon
53 Automobile Association (Canterbury)
57 Cathedral
60 Caesar's
62 Christchurch/Canterbury Visitor Centre
63 Avon Punting
66 Canterbury Museum
67 Robert McDougall Art Gallery
69 Arts Centre
71 Robert Falcon Scott Statue
72 Ansett New Zealand & American Express
74 Ansett New Zealand & Mt Cook Airline
75 Canride Bus Information Kiosk & Public Toilets
76 The Wizard
77 Post Office
78 Christchurch Personal Guiding Service
79 ANZ Bank
80 Bank of New Zealand
81 Great Sights Buses
83 Air New Zealand
84 Shades Arcade
87 Scorpio Books
88 Police Station
90 Public Hospital
91 Antigua Boatsheds
93 Craft Gallery
94 Bridge of Remembrance
97 Mt Cook Landline
100 South City Supermarket
101 The Loaded Hog
103 Lone Star Cafe & Bar
105 Southern Blues Bar
106 Science Alive! & Cinema Complex
107 Roman Catholic Cathedral
108 InterCity Bus Terminal
109 Rugby & Cricket Museum
Bishop Street
Packe Street
Cambridge Tce
Terrace
Madras Street
Barbadoes Street
To Convent Lodge & New Brighton
Armagh Street
Latimer Square
Worcester Street
To Adorian Motel & City Worcester Motels
Hereford Street
Cashel Street
Southwark St
Eaton Place
Ferry Road
Falsgrave Street
Stevens Street
Lancaster Park
To Ferrymead, Sumner & Lyttleton
Central Christchurch
0
200
400 m

from 10 am to 4.30 pm. The Arts Centre Bookshop has a wide range of NZ titles, including a good stock of LP guides.

Medical Services The Christchurch Hospital (☎ 364 0640) is on the corner of Oxford Terrace and Riccarton Ave, and there is an after-hours surgery (☎ 365 7777) at 931 Colombo St, on the corner of Bealey Ave, open from 5 pm to 8 am on weekdays and 24 hours on weekends and public holidays.

Cathedral Square

Christchurch is calm, orderly and pancake flat so it's a good place to explore by bicycle. Start from the Cathedral Square where, for $2 (children $1), you can climb 133 steps to the viewing balconies 30 metres up the 63-metre-high spire of the cathedral. There you can study the cathedral bells and look around while you reflect that earthquakes have damaged the spire on several occasions, once toppling the very top into Cathedral Square! The pointed stone top was replaced with the green copper-skinned one after that incident. The cathedral is open from 8.30 am weekdays, 11.30 am Sunday afternoon. There are free tours at 11 am and 2 pm weekdays, 11 am on Saturday and 11.30 am on Sunday.

The Christchurch Personal Guiding Service Walks (☎ 342 7691) run two-hour guided walks of the city, departing from its red and black kiosk in the south-western section of the Square. These tours leave at 10 am and 2 pm daily from the Square (or 15 minutes earlier from the visitor centre), cost $8 and are most informative. Independent walkers can get a copy of the free, informative brochure *Central City Walks* and venture further from the Square.

Museums & Galleries

Canterbury Museum This fine museum, on Rolleston Ave at the entrance to the Botanic Gardens, is open daily from 9 am to 5 pm and admission is free. Particularly interesting are the early colonist exhibits and the Antarctic discovery section. Christchurch is the HQ for 'Operation Deep Freeze', the supply link to Antarctica (see the International Antarctic Centre, later in this section, which should not be confused with this more historic exhibit).

There is a new gallery, Iwi Tawhito – Whenua Hou (Ancient People – New Land), which features displays of the now extinct moa and the early Polynesians who hunted them; included in this informative exhibit are three life-size dioramas, a crawl-in sinkhole cave, and computer information system.

Art Gallery & Arts Centre Behind the museum is the **Robert McDougall Art Gallery**. It has an extensive collection of NZ and international art and is open from 10 am to 4.30 pm daily; admission is free.

The former University of Canterbury town site has been transformed into the biggest **Arts Centre** in NZ. It's worth a look, even if just to see the beautiful old buildings. New Zealand has a lot of good handicraft centres producing some fine pottery, jewellery and other crafts, and Christchurch is particularly well represented. The Arts Centre has everything from handmade toys to Maori carvings, a couple of good restaurants and a good bookshop.

Air Force Museum This museum is exceptionally well presented. On display are a variety of aircraft used by the NZ Air Force over the years, convincingly displayed with figures and background scenery. Antarctic aircraft sit in the snow, aircraft are serviced, a Canberra bomber of the 1950s taxis out at night, a WWII fighter is hidden in the jungle. You can even pretend to pilot an A4 Skyhawk jet in a flight simulator.

The museum is at the former Wigram air base, which is a 15-minute drive south of the city on Main South Rd. A courtesy bus runs from the visitor centre in Worcester St, or it can be reached by a Hornby bus Nos 8 or 25 from Cathedral Square. It's open daily from 10 am to 5 pm. Entry is $9 (children $4).

Other Museums South-east of the city centre is **Ferrymead Historic Park** at 269 Bridle Path Rd, Heathcote. It's a working museum of transport and technology with incredibly varied exhibits including electric and steam locomotives, household appliances, cars and machinery of all types, plus hundreds of mechanical musical instruments. It's open from 10 am to 4.30 pm daily. Entry is $7 for adults (children $3.50) including a ride on a steam train or tram. Catch Canride bus No 3 bus from the Square.

The **Yaldhurst Transport Museum**, opposite the Yaldhurst Hotel on the Main West Rd, 11 km from the city centre, is open daily between 10 am and 5 pm. Displayed on the grounds of an attractive 1876 homestead is some of NZ's earliest transport, including horse-drawn vehicles, vintage cars, racing cars, motorcycles, steam engines and aircraft; admission is $6.50 (children $2.50).

In the old railway station, on Moorhouse Avenue, you will find **Science Alive!**, an interesting hands-on science exhibit featuring 50 interactive stations. Open daily from 9 am to 5 pm. Its slogan is: 'If I wasn't meant to touch anything, what are these things on the end of my arms for?' A great place for kids. Entry is $8 for adults, children $4.

Out at the Lancaster Park sports complex, three km from the Square, is the **Rugby & Cricket Museum**. Not every traveller's cup of tea, but for cricket and rugby fanatics it is an absolute shrine. On display is a 130-year-old cricket bat used by the New South Wales (Australia) Natives team against the World and much memorabilia of Sir Richard Hadlee, taker of 431 test wickets and a regular at Lancaster Park, is on display. It's open daily from 10 am to 4 pm; admission is $3 for adults and $1 for children.

The Wizard

This latter-day Merlin attempts to conquer gravity through levity, and can be seen and heard spouting in Cathedral Square at 1 pm from Monday to Friday. One of NZ's more amusing eccentrics, he dresses the part – long black velvet robes and cape in winter and white robes in summer – and plays it to the hilt. An extremely eloquent man, the Wizard has a line of glib patter – pet subjects are bureaucracy, the weakness of the male gender, Americans, priests, insurance companies and feminism – and a skilful way of playing with the hecklers. Whether you like what he has to say or not, it's a production you shouldn't miss.

Christchurch Casino

Las Vegas comes to sleepy hollow but the slogan is cosmic: 'Odds on for a great time'! NZ's premier casino is located right in the heart of town on Victoria and Kilmore Sts. It is open from 11 am to 3 am Monday to Wednesday then continuously from 11 am Thursday to 3 am Monday. All the traditional methods of losing your money are provided and draconian dress standards (ie no jeans) apply. So, forget that your 501s were quadruple the price of a St Vinnie suit.

Christchurch Tramway

Trams, first introduced to Christchurch streets in 1905, only lasted as a means of transport for 60 years. Restored green and cream trams have been reintroduced as part of a 2.5-km inner-city loop which takes in many of the city's best features and shopping areas. The trams operate every day from 8 am to 11 pm. Ticket costs are $3 for one hour, $5 for four hours and $10 for a full day (children $2/3/7). It's probably quicker (and certainly cheaper) to walk! One plus is the fact that it passes through the historic precinct of **New Regent St**, where there are many examples of Spanish architecture.

The Banks of the Avon

Beside the museum off Rolleston Ave the **Botanic Gardens**, open from 7 am to sunset, are 30 hectares of greenery beside the Avon River. The many floral-show houses and the popular fern house are open daily from 10.15 am to 4 pm. Tours leave from the cafe between 11 am and 4 pm when the weather is fine. The garden restaurant serves smorgasbord lunches from noon to 2 pm.

That invitingly calm, picturesque **Avon River** obviously requires canoes, so head to the Antigua Boatsheds by the footbridge at the southern end of Rolleston Ave. One-person canoes are $4 and two-person canoes $8 an hour, and paddle boats are $8 a half-hour. The boatsheds are open from 9.30 am to 4 pm daily and there's a good sandwich bar right by it.

If paddling a canoe sounds like too much effort you can relax and be punted along the river. **Punts** depart from behind the visitor centre, with departures and landings also available opposite the Town Hall Restaurant and the Thomas Edmonds Restaurant. For a 20-minute trip it's $10 per person, for 30 minutes $12, and for 45 minutes it's $15 (children under 12 half price). The punts ply the river daily from 10 am, stopping at 6 pm from October to March, 5 pm in April and September, and 4 pm from May to August.

Enchanting **Mona Vale**, an Elizabethan-style riverside homestead with 5.5 hectares of richly landscaped gardens, ponds and fountains, is open every day from 8 am to 7.30 pm October to March, and from 8.30 am to 5.30 pm April to September. It's 1.5 km from the city on Fendalton Rd (bus No 9).

International Antarctic Centre

This centre is near the airport, on Orchard Rd. It is part of a huge complex built for the administration and warehousing for the NZ, US and Italian Antarctic programmes.

The centre has hands-on exhibits, video presentations and the 'sights and sounds' of the vast continent. The first room you enter is the introductory 'Antarctic experience' which allows visitors to experience the four seasons, an aurora, changes in weather, and a penguin rookery, with the aid of special lighting, sound effects and holograms. The *Great White South* video is marvellous.

The centre is open October to March from 9.30 am to 8.30 pm; and April to September from 9.30 am to 5.30 pm. Entry is $10 per adult, $6 per child. To get there catch a bus bound for the airport; ask at the visitors centre. To return, catch an airport bus heading for the city. The centre has a luggage room for storage of backpacks, and there are bicycle stands. There is a well-stocked souvenir shop and the 60° South Cafe & Bar.

Christchurch Gondola

For a cost of $12 for adults ($9 after 5 pm), $5 for children and $25 for families you can be whisked up from the Heathcote Valley terminal on a 4½-minute ride to a point somewhere above the Lyttelton Rd tunnel. There are great views at the top (Mt Cavendish, 945 metres).

The gondola whisks from 10 am daily, and the free Gondola bus leaves regularly from the city centre and major hotels, or you can reach it on bus No 12. Once up there, you can mountain-bike down with The Mountain Bike Adventure Company (☎ 329 9699) for $38 or paraglide down with Nimbus Paragliding (☎ 332 2233).

National Marae

The largest marae in New Zealand is at 250 Pages Rd, six km north-east of the city. Nga Hau e Wha ('The Four Winds') is a multicultural facility open to all people – 'Nau mai haere mai' (all are welcome). You get the opportunity to see the carvings, weavings and paintings in the whare nui ('meeting house') and whare whananga ('house of learning').

Tours (☎ 388 7685) are $5.50 (children $3.50) and the powhiri (welcome ritual) is $2.50 per head by arrangement. You can reach the marae on bus No 5. The times for tours are 9 and 11 am and 1 and 3 pm Monday to Friday, weekends by arrangement.

Wildlife Reserves

The **Orana Park Wildlife Trust** has an excellent nocturnal kiwi house and lots of other animals including tigers, rhino, camels, water buffalo and the rare scimitar-horned oryx. Feeding times for the various animals are scheduled daily. There is now a walk-through lion enclosure where you can see cubs at close hand. It's open from 10 am to 5.30 pm daily (last admission at 4.30 pm) and entry is $10 per adult (children $5). It's on McLeans Island Rd, Harewood, beyond the airport, and about 20 minutes from the city. There's no public bus but tour buses and the City Circuit bus do come here.

The **Willowbank Wildlife Reserve** has exotic and local animals including a variety of domestic animals. There's also a model of a traditional Maori village and a nocturnal kiwi house. The reserve is open daily from 10 am to 10 pm and entry is $8 (children $3.50). The reserve is on Hussey Rd. The City Circuit bus runs there from outside the visitor centre daily.

Other Attractions

A must for the kids is **Queen Elizabeth II Park** near New Brighton, eight km north-east from the centre of town. This huge sports complex, with four indoor pools, two water-slides and seven squash courts was the venue for the 1974 Commonwealth Games. The fun park has a variety of amusement park attractions and is open from 10 am to 5 pm in summer and 11 am to 4 pm in winter. The recreation centre is open from 9 am till late. To get there take Canride bus Nos 10 or 19 from the square.

South-east of the city centre and just over the Ferrymead Bridge on the main road to Sumner, **Cob Cottage** is a restored sod hut from the 1860s. **Riccarton House**, an imposing Victorian mansion, is near the eponymous bush on Kahu Rd. Nearby, **Dean's Cottage**, built in 1843, is the oldest building in the province and is now a private museum, standing in a native bush reserve.

Activities

Swimming & Surfing The closest beaches to the city are North Beach (10 km, bus No 19), South Brighton beach (10 km, bus No 5), Sumner (11 km, bus No 3), Waimairi (10 km, bus No 19), New Brighton (eight km, bus No 5) and Taylors Mistake – a pleasant sheltered beach further out from Sumner, popular for surfing.

Walks See Adventure Canterbury in the Christchurch/Canterbury Visitor Centre for details and leaflets about walks around Christchurch. The bus information kiosk has a leaflet on bus access to the various walks.

Starting in the city are the **Riverside Walk** – the leaflet on this is packed with information – and various historical walks. For great views of the city, there is a walkway from the **Sign of the Takahe**. The various 'Sign of the ...' places in this area were originally roadhouses built during the depression as rest stops. Now they vary from the impressive tearooms at the Sign of the Takahe to a simple shelter at the Sign of the Bellbird, and are referred to primarily as landmarks. This walk leads up to the **Sign of the Kiwi** through Victoria Park, and then along near the Summit Rd to Scott Reserve – there are several lookout points along the way. The walk is accessible by bus No 2 from Victoria Square near the Town Hall.

How about walking one way to Lyttelton on the **Bridle Path**? It leads from Heathcote Valley to Lyttelton and takes one to 1½ hours at an easy pace. To get to Heathcote Valley, take Canride bus No 28 or the free Gondola shuttle. The **Godley Head Walkway** is a two-hour round trip from Taylors Mistake, crossing then recrossing Summit Rd with beautiful views on a clear day. The **Rapaki Track** is an excellent walk taking just a couple of hours and offering fine views of the whole city and of Lyttelton.

The **Crater Rim Walkway** around Lyttelton Harbour goes some 14 km from the Bridle Path to the Ahuriri Scenic Reserve, passing through a number of scenic reserves along the way, plus the Sign of the Bellbird and the Sign of the Kiwi. The walkway can easily be done in several short stages.

There are a number of shorter walks in and around **Nicholson Park & Sumner Head**, about 25 minutes by car from the Square, or catch a No 3 bus. Here you'll see many inshore birds, such as the eastern bar-tailed godwit, gulls, shags and black swans.

Skiing There are several ski areas within a two-hour drive of Christchurch. For more information see Skiing in the Outdoor Activities chapter and individual entries for each of the resorts in this chapter. Information on all ski areas is available from the Christchurch/Canterbury Information Centre.

Tours

The City Circuit bus departs on the hour from the visitor centre (see Getting Around in this section). Unique Tours (☎ 366 1661) operates a number of tours which are good value. There's a 9.30 am three-hour tour of the city which costs $39, and a three-hour afternoon tour of the hills, coast and harbour for $44. It also has full-day tours to Akaroa ($84) and to Kaikoura ($187); the latter includes a whale-watch trip.

Gray Line (☎ 343 3874) has a three-hour morning highlights tour which includes Mona Vale and the Port Hills ($26, children half-price), an afternoon sights tour to Sumner, Lyttelton Harbour (launch cruise) and the Port Hills ($32, children half-price); an afternoon sights tour with the gondola ride thrown in ($44, children half-price).

Travel Pioneer (☎ 388 2042) has interesting trips (described by travellers as 'gorgeous, outstanding, brilliant and enjoyable') which offer activities that other bus trips don't. Akaroa via the coastal back roads is $58; Arthur's Pass and the Otira Gorge $78; and Hanmer Springs via the Waipara Gorge back road is $58. All trips depart at about 8.30 am and return about 6 pm. There's courtesy pick-up from inner city hostels.

Christchurch Sightseeing Tours (☎ 366 9660) offer half-day city tours ($23) and three-hour garden tours to the city's leading gardens on Tuesday, Thursday and Saturday from November to March ($20).

Canterbury Leisure Tours (☎ 351 0551) has half and full-day golfing tours (equipment, fees and transport included) for $85/120. A number of readers recommend Canterbury Trails (☎ 337 1185) who offer personalised tours to various parts of the province in a 4WD vehicle; an all inclusive three-day tour is $295.

Places to Stay

Christchurch is the major city and the only international arrival point on the South Island. As a result it has many accommodation choices. (Distances quoted are taken from Cathedral Square.)

Camping & Cabins There are plenty of camping grounds, some very conveniently located. The *Showground Motor Camp* (☎ 338 9770), at 47-51 Whiteleigh Rd off Lincoln Rd, is only three km south-west of the city centre and has tent/powered sites at $12.70/14.65 for two. It also has a variety of cabins from as little as $23 for two. Other cabins are $43 with fully equipped kitchens, private shower and toilet. It's conveniently located, comfortable and cheap – but closed for two weeks during the show in early November. Get there on bus No 7.

The *Meadow Park Holiday Park* (☎ 352 9176) at 39 Meadow St off the Main North Rd, is five km north. Camping, with power, costs $10 per person, cabins are from $33 to $50 for two, tourist flats are $57 for two and a lodge with 22 units which sleep two to five is $43 for two, each extra adult $11. The camping ground has a covered, heated swimming pool, a spa, children's playground and a recreation hall. Take bus No 4.

Russley Park Motor Camp (☎ 342 7021) is at 372 Yaldhurst Rd, opposite Riccarton Racecourse about 10 km north-west of the Square or five km from the airport. Tent/powered sites cost $16/19, on-site vans are from $30 to $35, chalet cabins from $30 to $39 and some fancier tourist flats are from $50; all prices are for two. Take bus No 8.

South New Brighton Park (☎ 388 9844), in Halsey St off Estuary Rd, 10 km north-east, is another attractive park. Tent/powered sites are $15/17 for two and cabins are $25. Take bus No 5. The *All Seasons Holiday Park* (☎ 384 9490) is at 5 Kidbrooke St, Linwood, about 4 km east of the city. In this park tent/powered sites are $14/18.50, on-site vans are $25, cabins are $37 and tourist flats $55; again, all prices are for two.

Amber Park Caravan Park (☎ 348 3327) is conveniently located at 308 Blenheim Rd, only five km south of the Square. Tent/powered sites cost $16/19, and tourist flats, which share the camp kitchen facilities but have their own showers and toilets, are from $44 to $52; prices are for two. Take bus No 25 to get there. The *North South Airport Holiday Park* (☎ 359 5993), is at the corner of Johns and Sawyers Arms Rds, on the North-South Bypass, 2.5 km from the airport. Here tent/powered sites are $12/16, basic cabins $25 and tourist cabins $35; all prices are for two.

Out-of-town parks include the *Prebbleton Holiday Park* (☎ 349 7861), 18 Blakes Rd, Prebbleton, 12 km south of the city; and *Spencer Park Holiday Camp* (☎ 329 8721) Heyders Rd, Spencerville, 14 km north.

Hostels Christchurch has three YHA hostels and some popular backpackers. *Rolleston House YHA Hostel* (☎ 366 6564) at 5 Worcester St is opposite the Canterbury Museum near the Arts Centre, and only 700 metres from the Square (about eight minutes walk) so it's very conveniently located. A dorm bed is $16 per person, and twins are $36. Close by is the Dux if you need a beer.

Another YHA hostel, *Cora Wilding* (☎ 389 9199), is at 9 Eveleyn Couzins Ave, Richmond, five km north-east from the city centre. To get there catch bus No 10 from the Square to Tweed St. The cost here is $14 per person and the place is quite elegant, being a former mansion in a well-cared-for city park. The office shuts during the day but the rest of the hostel remains open.

There is a new, large and centrally located YHA on the 1st floor at 273 Manchester St; the *Central City YHA* (☎ 379 9535) has four-bed rooms for $17 per person, and twins and doubles for $38. It has a spacious common room, excellent kitchen facilities and quiet, tidy rooms with heating. Better still it has 24-hour access for guests, no duties or restrictive rules.

The ever popular *Foley Towers* (☎ 366 9720) is at 208 Kilmore St near Madras St. It's a straightforward travellers hostel with plenty of space. There's a pleasant little garden at the back and the usual kitchen and laundry facilities. A dorm or share room costs $14 per person, and the twin and double rooms are $28/35 without/with ensuite. It's run by the organiser of the NZ Backpackers 'Blue Book', who knows travellers' needs.

Bealey International Backpackers (☎ & fax 366 6760) at 70 Bealey Ave (between Montreal and Durham Sts), is a smaller place with a friendly atmosphere, an outdoor garden and BBQ area, and a cosy log fire in winter. It offers luggage storage and will book a range of activities. Rates are $15 for a share room, or $17 per person for a twin or double.

The *Backpackers Inn the Square* (☎ 366 5158), right in Cathedral Square, is one of Christchurch's once famous hotels now fallen on hard times. Its share rooms are $12.50 per person, and its twin and double rooms with ensuite are $32 (some include bed linen). The hostel is open 24 hours but there is no off-street parking. As it is part of the now soggy Pavlova chain, there is no visitor book. Perhaps the management feel your comments aren't worthwhile.

Down towards the Moorhouse Avenue end of Manchester St is the large and well-equipped *Coker's Backpackers* (☎ 379 8580). It is an extremely large, labyrinthine place but even boasts a dishwasher and walk-in refrigerator and three spacious rest areas including a library, common room and dining room. There are dorms for $16 per person, and twins and doubles for $39 (each of the rooms has ensuite facilities and telephone); TVs are made available in the rooms if there is group agreement.

Dreamland (☎ 366 3519), 21 Packe St, is basically two houses on adjoining blocks. (It was still being converted when we called.) The cost for share rooms is $13.50 per person, $32 for twins or doubles. Marcus, the owner, is a keen cyclist and he maintains visitors' bikes in his own workshop. It is a homely little place with open fireplaces, lots of information and a nice atmosphere. It is often closed in winter, so ring beforehand.

The *YMCA* (☎ 366 0689) at 12 Hereford St, is a few steps from the Arts Centre and Canterbury Museum. Here twins and doubles are from $45 to $90, and apartments are $85 (sleep two to three) or $100 (sleep four to six). There's a cafeteria serving cheap meals, a hostellers kitchen and paraplegic toilets and showers. During the school terms most of the single and double plain rooms may be full of students, but there should always be room for casuals. The hostel, open 24 hours, takes both men and women. The *YWCA* (☎ 355 4903) at 93 Harewood Rd is a fair way from the Square, about five km from the airport; it takes women only. Bus Nos 1 and 4 run frequently from the Square; ring in advance to find out if rooms are free.

Charlie B's (☎ 379 8429) is centrally located on the corner of Madras and Gloucester Sts. Prices have gone down in a war to lure backpackers through the door of this, in parts, shabby establishment. The cheapest dorm rooms (one has 35 beds) are $10 and you get exactly what you pay for – no frills! It is $13 per person in triples/quads, and $28 for doubles/twins ($18 for a single). There's a courtesy van and drop-off, cooking, laundry and ironing facilities, a games room, SkyTV, videos, BBQ and off-street parking. A number of LP informants believe this place epitomises true travellers 'digs' and love it; others loath it.

Fraureisehaus – The Homestead (☎ 366 2585), located at 272 Barbadoes St, only five minutes walk from the central city, is a women-only backpackers representing the very best of this European idea. It has a full kitchen and laundry, TV and video, games room, library and free linen. Bikes are available and there is a vegetable and herb garden. Tastefully furnished double, twin and bunk (four-bed) rooms are only $10 per person. Phone beforehand or just turn up.

Further north, at 314 Barbadoes St is the new, modern *Round-the-World Backpackers* (☎ 365 4363). It is purpose built, extremely well set up and all the fixtures and fittings are brand new. A dorm is $15 per person, and twins or doubles are $34. This is really good value as each clean room has a heater, strategically placed lights and beds with duvets.

Several places provide good accommodation at hostel rates in addition to their regular rooms. *Shalom House* (☎ 366 6770) is at 69 Bealey Ave near the corner of Stoneyhurst St. It's a small guesthouse with rooms at $30/52 but if you bring your own bedding it's just $15 per person in twin rooms.

Thistle Guesthouse (☎ 348 1499) at 21 Main South Rd is near the junction of Riccarton and Yaldhurst Rds, about 6 km from the city square. with frequent buses to town. Singles/doubles are $30/40, but if you provide your own bedding it's $17/30. Breakfast is available and there's a kitchen, laundry and off-street parking.

The *Stonehurst Hotel* (☎ 379 4620) at 241 Gloucester St is very close to the city centre. It has a sadly neglected separate building with the usual hostel facilities (kitchen, laundry, etc). Four-bed bunkroom beds are $16 per person (provide your own bedding) or there are singles/doubles (linen provided) at $25/36. Hostellers are welcome to use the bars, TV and billiards rooms of the hotel next door. Room rates in the hotel, also suffering from neglect, are $67.50 for doubles, and breakfast is from $5.

The *Ambassador Hotel* (☎ 366 7808) at 19 Manchester St is a ten-minute walk south of the city centre. It's quite a flash old hotel, with leadlight windows, a lovely lounge area and deep velvety carpets. The backpacker rate is $20 and upstairs the B&B rates are $55/65 for singles/doubles. There's no kitchen although continental or cooked breakfasts are served.

At the time of writing a new place was opening up – *Vagabond* (☎ 379 9677) at 232 Worcester St is a small place with full kitchen and laundry facilities, disabled facilities, BBQ and sunny outdoor garden. A bunk is $12.50, shared rooms are from $14 per person, and singles/doubles are $17/28.

Guesthouses & B&Bs The *Windsor Private Hotel* (☎ 366 1503) at 52 Armagh St is just five to 10 minutes walk from the city centre. It's meticulously clean and orderly and rooms with private bath cost $50/78. Two km north-west of the Square, the *Wolseley Lodge* (☎ 355 6202) at 107 Papanui Rd is an old-fashioned place in a quiet setting with rooms at $25/50 with breakfast. A few doors down at No 121 the *Highway Lodge* (☎ 355 5418) has rooms at $60 for two and a continental breakfast is available. You can get to both these lodges on a No 1 bus.

Built in 1885, *Turret House* (☎ 365 3900), 435 Durham St (Nth), has been elegantly restored. The $85 room charge for two includes a continental breakfast, and private bathroom. At 82 Bealey Ave is the elegantly restored *Eliza's B&B Inn* (☎ 366 8584) with bedrooms from $75 to $130. It has a fully licensed restaurant, a bar and provides hot chocolate (yum) at any time. *Hambledon* (☎ 379 0723) at 103 Bealey Ave is, as it says in its literature, a 'gracious' old place; singles are from $65 to $90 and doubles from $85 to $110. The gardens are delightful.

At 141 Hackthorne Rd, at the foot of the hills of the same name, is *Cashmere House on the Hill* (☎ 332 7864), an elegantly restored mansion on Cashmere Hill. It has an acre of gardens and views over the city. Singles/doubles cost from $110/140.

For those who elect to stay near the beach there is *Convent Lodge* (☎ 388 3388) at 97 Lonsdale St, New Brighton; singles/doubles are $40/60 or there are budget beds for $14 per person. The host of the backpackers section is an A-grade mechanic who will assist those looking for a car to find a sound and reliable vehicle. It's worth staying here just for that level of free advice.

Motels Christchurch is well endowed with motels, most of them costing from $70 to $90 a double. The *Christchurch Motel Guide* lists most motels and has a map of their locations. Better priced motels include:

Achilles Motel, 118 Sherbourne St, St Albans, on SH1 (☎ 379 9688), doubles $69 to $88
Adelphi Motel, 49 Papanui Rd (☎ 355 6037), doubles $75 to $85
Adorian Motel, 347 Worcester St, Linwood (☎ 366 7626) singles/doubles $69/79
Airport Lodge Motel, 105 Roydvale Ave, Burnside, (☎ 358 5119), doubles $78 to $84
Avalon Motel, corner Bealey Ave and Geraldine St (☎ 379 9680), doubles $69 to $75
Avon City Motel, 402 Main North Rd (☎ 352 6079), doubles/triples $65/75
Avonhead Lodge Motel, 168 Yaldhurst Rd (☎ 348 1309), doubles $69 to $89 during holidays
Belle Bonne Motel, 95 Yaldhurst Rd, Riccarton (☎ 348 8458) singles/doubles $68/77
Canterbury Court Motel, 140 Lincoln Rd, Addington (☎ 338 8351), doubles/triples $75/90
Cashel Court Motel, 457 Cashel St (☎ 389 2768), doubles $60 to $70 with kitchen
City Worcester Motels, 336 Worcester St (☎ 366 4491), doubles from $69
Colombo Travelodge, 965 Colombo St (☎ 366 3029), singles/doubles $55/60
Cranford Court Motel, 63 Cranford St, St Albans (☎ 379 2406), doubles $74 to $98
Earnslaw Motel, 288 Blenheim Rd, Riccarton (☎ 348 6387), single/double $60/70
Golden Mile Motor Lodge, Main South Rd, Riccarton (☎ 349 6153), doubles $50 to $88
Golden Sands Beach Motel, 121 Estuary Rd, New Brighton (☎ 388 7996), double $68
Hagley Motel, 13 Darvel St, Riccarton (☎ 348 7683), singles/doubles $70/81
Holiday Lodge Motel, 862 Colombo St (☎ 366 6584), doubles $63
Middlepark Motel, 120 Main South Rd (☎ 348 7320), Upper Riccarton, doubles $58 to $72
Riccarton Motel, 92 Main South Rd, Upper Riccarton (☎ 348 7127), doubles $64.50
Tall Trees Motel, 454 Papanui Rd, Papanui (☎ 352 6681), doubles $59 to $79

Hotels Top-bracket Christchurch hotels include the *Christchurch City Travelodge* (☎ 379 1180) at 356 Oxford Terrace, the *Chateau on the Park* (☎ 348 8999) on the corner of Deans Ave and Kilmarnock St, the *Quality Hotel Durham* (☎ 365 4699) on the corner of Durham and Kilmore Sts, the *Quality Hotel Central* (☎ 379 5880) at 776 Colombo St, *Noah's* (☎ 379 4700) on the corner of Worcester St and Oxford Terrace, and out at the airport the *Airport Plaza* (☎ 358 3139). In these hotels doubles are from $140 to $160 (and up).

Right at the top of the price scale is the imaginatively designed and wonderfully situated *Parkroyal Hotel* (☎ 365 7799), corner of Durham and Kilmore Sts, where a double costs nearly $340, with great views.

Places to Eat

It is unbelievable how the food choices have improved in this town in recent years. You can find whatever you want, and you can eat in Christchurch every day and at all hours. The *Classic Canterbury Dining Out Guide* ($9.95) dodges any critique of its advertisers but is a good reference for opening hours, locations and precis of menus. Many restaurants supply their own 'dodgers' to the tourist centres; let their glossy photos tempt you.

Fast Food & Cafes If you would like to sit at the base of one of the statues, or on a bench in the square then go to one of the many nearby takeaway food stalls which sell a variety of international cuisine. The *Greek Recipe* at 55 Cathedral Square, beside the West End Theatre, has authentic, inexpensive Greek takeaways and is open from 10 am to 10 pm every day but Sunday. Only a block from the square at 176A Manchester St, the *Mediterranean* has that eastern Mediterranean blend of Turkish/ Greek/Lebanese food, such as doner kebabs.

A reader, describing himself as one of 'the fussiest and most hopelessly addicted drinkers of gourmet speciality coffees' recommends *Coffee d'Fafo*, 137 Hereford St, for its authentic products. Just as good is *Expresso 124* at 124 Oxford Terrace, open until 11 pm; and the *Coffee House*, 290 Montreal St, open until the witching hour.

There's an economically priced cafeteria at the *YMCA*, opposite the Arts Centre on Hereford St. The coffee bar in the foyer of the *Town Hall* is open every day and in the evening whenever there's a concert. As wearers of jeans we were unable to try out the coffee in the *Grand Cafe* in the Casino. The *Vesuvio* at 182 Oxford Terrace is another street-front cafe which is popular with locals. It has a small Japanese restaurant attached.

Pub Food On Colombo St by the river, the conveniently located *Oxford on Avon* has a family restaurant. It's open daily from 11 am to 10 pm. Main courses, which span the pub-food universe from family roasts to T-bone steaks, are in the $8 to $15 range, and there's also a cheaper children's menu. A favourite is *Nancy's at the Park*, corner of Deans Ave and Riccarton Rd, and it is good to see that it pays attention to old-fashioned NZ fare as well as innovative new dishes.

There are *Cobb & Co's* at the Caledonian Hotel, 101 Caledonian Rd, north of the Square, and at McKenzies Hotel, 51 Pages Rd, Linwood. Cobb & Co's are open every day until 10 pm and have standard and consistent pub food.

Other possibilities include the *Carlton Hotel* on the corner of Papanui Rd and Bealey Ave; the *Coachman Inn*, at 144 Gloucester St, with a theatre restaurant set-up; *Churchills*, an English-style pub at 441 Colombo St, Sydenham; the *Pegasus Arms*, 14 Oxford Terrace near the hospital, for a bistro lunch and a view out over the 1886 topsail cutter *Pastime*; and the *Chancery* in Chancery Lane, which features roasts and steaks at around $12 a main.

Restaurants The *Botanic Gardens Restaurant* in the wonderful Botanic Gardens is renowned for excellent smorgasbords which cost $12.50 including coffee; it's served from noon to 2 pm daily. The restaurant is open from 10 am to 4.30 pm for snacks and other light meals.

The riverside setting of the *Boaters Town Hall Restaurant* restaurant in the town hall makes it a popular place to eat. There's a weekday lunch-time buffet for $20, a Sunday smorgasbord lunch or dinner for $22, and a regular à la carte menu for dinner or late supper, with main courses from $19 to $25. Across the plaza at the ultra-modern, ultra-expensive Parkroyal Hotel, the inner courtyard is given over to a rather elegant *Victoria Street Cafe* which is not as expensive as it looks – main courses, both meat and vegetarian, cost around $20, and there's an attractive salad bar. The wine list is extensive. Also in the Parkroyal are the *Yamagen*, an expensive Japanese place, and the very upmarket and award-winning *Canterbury Tales* (mains from $25 to $32).

The riverside *Thomas Edmonds* is housed in what used to be a band rotunda by the river on Cambridge Terrace. It's a great position and you could complement the romantic atmosphere by arriving by punt! It's reasonably priced with light main courses for lunch at around $10, for dinner from $20, with both meat and vegetarian selections It's open for lunch Monday to Friday and on Sunday; in the evening from Monday to Saturday.

A number of locals recommended the very chic *Expresso 124* (see Fast Food & Cafes), 124 Oxford Terrace, for breakfast, lunch and dinner – it is open daily. Next door is *Coyotes* where you will not necessarily have your arm bitten off but you can try some pumpkin and poppy seed nachos or just people-watch.

The restaurant areas off Colombo St offer good dining possibilities. These include the Oxford on Avon just south of the river (see Pub Food) and the *Main Street Cafe*, with its smoke-free bar, further north. Or try *Sri Devi's Marco Polo* at No 812 with an interesting mix of Indian and South-east Asian dishes. It's open daily for lunch and dinner, with main courses from $11 to $15.

Cafe Valentino's at 813 Colombo St is a casual place with spacious wooden beam-and-brick décor. It serves Italian food, is open daily from noon until late and dinner mains are from $11 to $23. At No 818, try nachos or burritos at *Rita's Burritas*, open daily.

Strawberry Fare at 114 Peterborough St is a restaurant famed for its desserts, such as the ubiquitous Death by Chocolate. It also serves great breakfasts including a Parisian special; meals are served from 7 am to midnight daily, except weekends when it opens at the more respectable hour of 8 am.

On the subject of cocoa-ingested demise, *Death by Chocolate* tempts in Faustian fashion at 209 Cambridge Terrace; a death certificate is written for a mere $15.50.

There is a good representation of quality Italian restaurants in Christchurch, in addition to Valentino mentioned earlier. *Spagalimi's Pizza* at 155 Victoria St is a very popular place that also does takeaways. At 76 Lichfield St, just south of the city centre, *Tre Gatti* has Italian dishes of a reasonable standard and is open, commendably, until late at night. Close by at 83 Lichfield St is *Winnie Bagoe's*, a lively hostelry which is also open until late serving pizza until 3 am. An upmarket place is *Saggio di Vino*, at 185 Victoria St (corner of Bealey Ave), which has a great wine selection; more than 50 are available by the glass and light meals are also served. Popular with locals is *Bardelli's*, in the city centre at 98 Cashel St. Specialising in Mediterranean and Asian food, it has blackboard and à la carte menus.

There are plenty of Asian restaurants including the imposing *Chung Wah II* at 63 Worcester St. At the *Mongolian Marquee*,on the corner of Manchester and Gloucester Sts, you can eat as much barbecued food as you like for the set price of $22. It is open daily from 5.30 pm until late. The *Jade Garden*, 109 Cambridge Terrace, is a good choice for Cantonese and Szechuan styles; and the *Shangri-La*, corner of Kilmore and Victoria Sts, specialises in good Chinese beef dishes.

Chinese is well represented but so are other Asian flavours. Plenty of letters have arrived at LP extolling the virtues of the satays and roti chanai at *Khadijah's*, a Malaysian place at 82 Cashel Mall. Fans of Thai food will not be disappointed with the authentic cuisine at *Mythai*, 84 Hereford St; *Kannigai's Thai Foods*, 18A Carlton Courts in the city; and the *Sala Thai*, corner of Colombo and Kilmore Sts. Skip the Singha!

The *Sign of the Takahe*, south of the city at Cashmere Hills, is in an impressive old stone building, with fine views of the city, a great setting, careful service, a top chef and quite high prices to go with the pluses. It's open daily for Devonshire teas, buffet lunches and dinner. You can get there on bus No 2.

Grimsby's, opposite Cranmer Square, on the corner of Kilmore and Montreal Sts, is considered by many to be the pinnacle of dining in this town, but is definitely not in the budget category. It's open daily from 6.30 pm until late.

Twisted Fork Best Name category goes to ... *Six Chairs M°ss°ng* at 36 New Regent St; sounds like best movie candidate at Cannes but *La Grand Bouffe*, *Like Water for Chocolate* and *Babette's Feast* it is not. Instead, lunches are $9 and dinners (Wednesday to Sunday) are from $22.

Vegetarian Vegetarians are well catered for in all price categories. *Gopal's* at 143 Worcester St is another of the Hare Krishna-run restaurants. It's open for lunch on weekdays, on Friday night and even budget travellers can afford to dine here.

Exceptionally good vegetarian food can be found at the *Main Street Cafe* at 840 Colombo St. This is a relaxed and very popular place with an open-air courtyard at the back. Imaginative main courses are from $8 to $14 or you could have bread and salad for $5. The salads are good and the desserts, particularly the varied selection of cheesecakes, are mouthwatering. It's open from 10 am to late daily.

Dux de Lux is another very popular place for gourmet vegetarian taste treats. It's close to the Arts Centre, on Montreal St near Hereford St. There's a green outdoor courtyard and service is counter style, with main courses around $10 for lunch or $14 for dinner. It's licensed, with its own bar and brewery, and live music several nights a week. Dux de Lux is open from around 10 am until midnight, every day.

Entertainment

Dance & Music There are several pubs with rock music at night, particularly on the weekends. Popular ones include *Dux de Lux* with its own brewery and bar (see Vegetarian Restaurants) and *Bush Inn* at 364 Riccarton Rd, which has a small cover charge. The *Carlton*, on the corner of Bealey Ave and Papanui Rd, also has weekend entertainment. Or there's the *Star & Garter* at 332 Oxford Terrace, the *Imperial* on the corner of St Asaph and Barbadoes Sts, the *Ferrymead Tavern*, the *Bishopdale Tavern*, the *Eastside Tavern*, the *Lancaster Park Hotel* and plenty of others.

An old favourite is *Bailies* at Backpackers Inn the Square. In here smoke fills the room, the Guinness is carefully decanted into pint glasses, and boiled eggs and salt are left on the bar for patrons.

There's rock all week at *The Playroom* on the corner of Cuffs and Pages Rds. *Caesars* in Chancery Arcade is a quintessential nightclub. Other nightclubs are the *Palladium* on Gloucester St, and *Warners*, in Cathedral Square, which has rock music and Baillie's which has Irish and folk music.

The best place for aficionados of good blues music is the *Southern Blues Bar*, firmly ensconced in the red-light/bathhouse enclave at the corner of Madras and Tuam Sts. Here 'workers' mix with the city's elite. For a good old-fashioned night out that lingers well into the 'wee' hours there is the *Jolly Poacher* opposite the Casino on Victoria St.

Two other places in the south part of town, down towards the old railway station are *The Loaded Hog*, at 39 Dundas St off Manchester St, with its own brewery and excellent Weiss Beer; and *The Lone Star Cafe & Bar*, on the corner of Manchester and Eaton Sts. The latter is one of those Tex-Mex saloons with a great 'Wild West' atmosphere. *Coyotes* at Oxford Terrace seems to go off after dark, and *The Club* at 88 Armagh St has been recommended for those who really think a lot of themselves.

Other Entertainment Christchurch is the cultural centre of the South Island. The focus is the Town Hall (☎ 366 8899) on Kilmore St by the riverside. This is where you are likely to see a chamber or symphony orchestra. The James Hay Theatre in the town hall and the Theatre Royal in Gloucester St are the centres of live theatre. There is a big cinema complex in the old railway station.

Getting There & Away

Air Christchurch is the South Island's only international arrival and departure point. Qantas, Air New Zealand, Air Pacific, Singapore and Korean Airlines all fly here.

Air New Zealand has its Christchurch office (☎ 379 5200; 353 4899) at the Triangle Centre, 702 Colombo St. There are daily direct flights between Christchurch and many destinations including Auckland, Dunedin, Invercargill, Mount Cook, Nelson, Queenstown, Timaru and Wellington, with connections to most other centres. A number of these flights are run in conjunction with Mount Cook Airline and Air Nelson as part of Air New Zealand Link. Mt Cook Airline (☎ 379 0690), 47 Riccarton Rd, flies between Christchurch and the Chatham Islands.

Ansett New Zealand (☎ 371 1146), 78 Worcester St, also has direct flights to Auckland, Dunedin, Invercargill, Queenstown, Rotorua and Wellington.

Smaller airlines operating out of Christchurch include Associated Air which fly to Blenheim and on to Paraparaumu near Wellington. Wairarapa Airlines fly between Christchurch and Nelson or Masterton.

The airport is modern and has an information centre (☎ 358 5029) open every day. There are luggage lockers at 50c for eight hours, $1.50 for 24 hours. Ask about storing luggage for longer periods. Don't forget your $20 departure tax on international flights.

Other overseas airlines with offices in Christchurch are:

Qantas Airways
119 Armagh St (☎ (0800) 808 767)
Singapore Airlines
AMP Bldg, Cathedral Square (☎ 366 8003)
United Airlines
152 Hereford St (☎ 366 1736)

Bus InterCity buses (☎ 379 9020) depart from the corner of Moorhouse and Fitzgerald Avenues. Mt Cook Landline buses (☎ (0800) 800 287; 379 0690) go from 40 Lichfield St, near Cathedral Square, and pick up from its depot at 47 Riccarton Rd.

Christchurch to Picton is a trip of about five to six hours, with Kaikoura an interesting midway stopping point. Both InterCity and Mt Cook Landline do this route. Both also operate south to Dunedin and continue south from there to Invercargill. Mt Cook has a Christchurch to Nelson service (via either Lewis Pass or Picton) with connections through to Westport and Greymouth on the West Coast, or another route to Westport running more directly across the island.

InterCity also has daily services from Greymouth south to the glaciers. The trip from Christchurch across the South Island via Arthur's Pass is not serviced by the major companies but rather by a smaller operator, Coast to Coast Shuttle (☎ (0800) 800 847; see Getting There & Away for Greymouth for more details). This route is a stunningly beautiful journey, not to be missed.

InterCity and Mt Cook Landline also have daily bus services to Mt Cook and Queenstown. The quickest is with Mt Cook if you are going direct to Queenstown. If you wish to go to the Mt Cook village with Mt Cook Landline you would change at Twizel. From November to April Mt Cook Landline has an additional daily Christchurch-Queenstown excursion bus which makes an extended stopover at Mt Cook. InterCity buses take the same route daily all year round (to Queenstown via Mt Cook) but with a 40-minute stop at Mt Cook.

Other InterCity services from Christchurch include buses to Akaroa, Hanmer Springs, Lake Tekapo and Wanaka.

The Kiwi Experience and Magic Bus services pass through Christchurch, and the Flying Kiwi bus can also be picked up here as well as from Picton. In addition a number of shuttle operators pass through. For example Atomic Shuttles (☎ 322 8883) has return services from Picton, Dunedin and Queenstown. See the Getting Around chapter for details on the 'backpacker' buses.

Train The railway station (☎ (0800) 802 802) is on Clarence St in Addington, some way out of the city and there is a free morning bus service; ask at the visitor centre.

Trains run daily each way between Christchurch and Picton, connecting with the 1.30 pm *Interislander* ferry and the 9.10 pm *Lynx* Express across to Wellington. There's also a weekday *Southerner* service each way between Christchurch and Invercargill via Dunedin (during holiday periods there are scheduled weekend services). The *TranzAlpine* Express train runs daily between Christchurch and Greymouth via Arthur's Pass. Crossing over to the west coast the section of railway through the Waimakariri Gorge (above Springfield) has interesting scenery, but the road follows a different and even more spectacular route.

Car & Motorcycle From Christchurch it's 340 km north to Picton, 362 km south to Dunedin, about four or five hours drive in either direction. Westbound it's 150 km to Arthur's Pass, 248 km to Greymouth, 331 km to Mt Cook or 486 km to Queenstown, all on sealed roads.

CANTERBURY

Hitching It's pretty good hitching on the whole but Christchurch to Dunedin can be a long day. Generally it gets harder the further south you go, then easier as you approach Dunedin. Catch a Templeton bus (Nos 25 or 8) to get out of the city. It's also possible to hitch between Christchurch and Picton in a day, although there can be long waits. If you're hitching north take a Christchurch bus to Woodend to get you on your way.

To hitch west take bus No 8 (Yaldhurst) – then keep your fingers crossed; it can be a long, hard haul, as much as two days. Pick up the train along the way if you become despondent. The first part is easily hitched, but once you leave SH1 it gets harder to find a lift.

Getting Around

To/From the Airport The public bus service to the airport is operated by Canride from Cathedral Square. Buses depart about every half-hour from around 6 am to nearly 6 pm, then less frequently until the last at 9.45 pm on weekdays; they're also less frequent on Saturday and Sunday. The cost is $2.40 (children $1.20).

There are several door-to-door airport shuttle buses. Super Shuttle (☎ 365 5655) operates 24 hours a day, serving not only the airport ($8) but also the bus and railway stations. A taxi to or from the airport will cost about $14 to $18 depending on the time you go, so it can work out cheaper than the shuttles with several people.

Bus Most city buses are operated by Canride and run from Cathedral Square. Unlike most NZ urban bus services, Christchurch's is good, cheap and well organised. For bus information phone Bus Info (☎ 366 8855). Fares start at 50c and step up 50c for each additional section, to $2.50. Note the Christchurch tradition of hanging baby strollers and pushchairs (but not babies!) off the back of buses.

The Double Decker Bus (☎ 377 1644) passes more than 100 points of interest in the city in a 90-minute circuit; the cost is $22 (children $10). The City Circuit bus (☎ 385 5386) has two circuits (Plains and Port), both leaving from the visitor centre hourly from 9 am to 6 pm; it costs $25 for eight hours of travel.

Taxi There are plenty of taxis in Christchurch but, as with other places in NZ, they don't cruise. You find them on taxi ranks, or phone: Blue Star (☎ 379 9799), First Direct (☎ 377 5555) and Gold Band (☎ 379 5795).

Car The major operators all have offices in Christchurch, as do numerous smaller local companies. With the smaller operators, unlimited km rates start from around $50 a day plus about $12 per day for insurance, for rental periods of three days or more.

Avis
  Lichfield St (☎ 379 6133)
Avon Freedom Rent-a-Car
  corner of Tuam & Antigua Sts (☎ 379 3822)
Budget Rent-a-Car
  corner of Oxford Terrace & Lichfield St (☎ 366 0072)
Economy Rental Cars
  518 Wairakei Rd, Burnside (☎ 359 7410)
Hertz
  48-50 Lichfield St (☎ 366 0549)
Pegasus Rental Cars
  127 Peterborough St (☎ 365 1100)
Renny Rentals
  156 Tuam St (☎ 366 6790)
Shoestring Rentals
  17 Wise St (☎ 338 6636)

Wheels ChCh – Sales (☎ 366 4855), 20 Manchester St, hires cars at about $250 per week, everything included, but they also have a programme whereby they sell you a car and buy it back at a pre-agreed price.

For wheels with panache contact Kampa South Rentals (☎ 384 4751) at 1013 Ferry Rd; its genuine fully equipped kombis (VWs) are from $69 per day (2-berth) including unlimited kms and insurance – get 'konverted'. A 4-berth van is $109 per day.

Motorcycles can be hired from Phil Payne's Cycletreads (☎ 379 7382) at 50 Tuam St, Eric Wood Suzuki (☎ 366 0129) at 35 Manchester St, or from Greentours

(☎ 388 8351), 244 Pine Ave, Harald. At the latter a 600 cc bikes is $75 and a 750 cc bike is $80 per day, with 300 free km daily.

Bicycles are ideal for Christchurch as it is nice and flat. There are cycling lanes on many roads, and Hagley Park, which encompasses the Botanical Gardens, has many cycling paths. You can pedal away on a mountain bike from Summit Cycles (☎ 355 7017) in St Albans, or the Mountain Bike Adventure Co (☎ 384 0006) in Lyttelton; both hiring companies also conduct guided trips of the Port Hills and Banks Peninsula.

BANKS PENINSULA

Near Christchurch, Banks Peninsula makes an interesting side trip. A change from the flat area around the city itself, this hilly peninsula was formed by two giant volcanic eruptions in the distant past. Small harbours such as Le Bons, Pigeon and Little Akaroa bays radiate out from the peninsula's centre giving it a cog-wheel shape.

The peninsula has a chequered history of settlement. Captain Cook first sighted the peninsula in 1770, although he thought it was an island. He named it after naturalist Sir

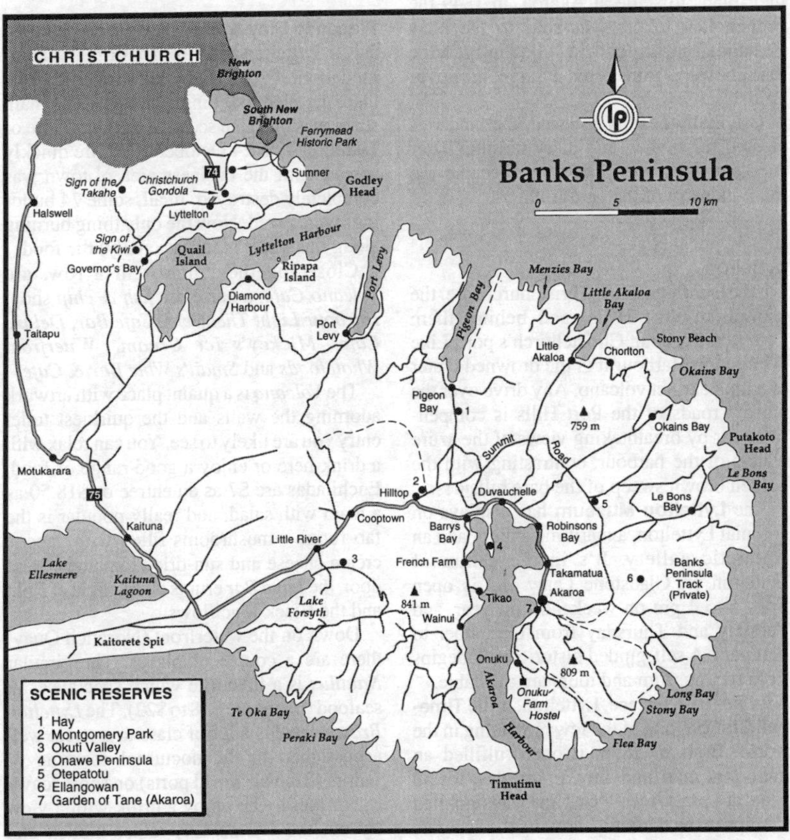

Joseph Banks. The Maori Ngai Tahu tribe, who then occupied the peninsula, were attacked by Te Rauparaha in 1831 and suffered a severe decline in numbers.

A few years later, in 1836, the British established a whaling station at Peraki. In 1838 the French captain Jean Langlois chose the site of Akaroa as an attractive spot for French settlement. He returned to France and in 1840 a group of 63 French settlers set out in the *Comte de Paris* from Rochefort. Meanwhile, also in 1840, the Treaty of Waitangi was signed, bringing all New Zealand under British sovereignty.

The French, however, did go ahead with their plans to settle at Akaroa. In 1849 the French land claim was sold to the New Zealand Company and the following year the French were joined by a large group of British settlers.

Originally heavily forested, the land was cleared for timber, and dairy farming, later supplanted by sheep farming, became the main industry of the peninsula.

Lyttelton

To the south-east of Christchurch are the prominent Port Hills, and behind them Lyttelton Harbour, Christchurch's port. Like Wellington Harbour it is the drowned crater of a long extinct volcano. Any drive over the narrow roads of the Port Hills is compensated for by breathtaking views of the azure waters of the harbour, contrasting with the golden brown sweep of the bare hillsides.

The **Lyttelton Museum** has displays on colonial Lyttelton, a maritime gallery and an Antarctic gallery. It's in the centre of Lyttelton on Gladstone Quay and is open from 2 to 4 pm on weekends, all year, and Tuesday and Thursday from December to February. A self-guided historic walk begins from the museum and tours are available.

In Reserve Terrace, Lyttelton, is the **Timeball Station**, one of the few remaining in the world. Built in 1876, it once fulfilled an important maritime duty. Every day, for 58 years at 1 pm, Greenwich Time was signalled to ships in the harbour, allowing the accurate calculation of longitude. Open from 10 am to 5 pm daily, entry is $3 (children $1).

Harbour Trips There are all sorts of boat trips on Lyttelton Harbour, starting from as low as $4 (children $2) for the one-way trip to Diamond Harbour and Quail Island. The turn-of-the-century steam tug *Lyttelton* does two-hour harbour cruises from January to April every Sunday at 2 pm. It departs from No 2 Wharf and the cost is about $12 (children $6). Lyttelton Harbour Cruises (☎ 328 8368) also cruise every day at 2 pm from Jetty B to Ripapa Island Historic Reserve, also for about $12 (children $6).

Places to Stay & Eat There are no places to stay in Lyttelton apart from basic pub accommodation. If you visit Lyttelton at lunch time there are plenty of dining choices. The main street was once the scene of the Great Fire of Lyttelton – on 24 October 1870 fire quickly spread until the business area of town was completely destroyed. In all, some 74 buildings were razed. Now the only thing burning along this street is (occasionally) the food.

Close together, almost in a row, are *Volcano Cafe*, a nameless *fish & chip* shop, *Harbour Light Theatre & Cafe Bar*, *Deluxe Cafe*, *Mickey's Ice Cream*, *Waterfront Wholefoods* and *Smail's Wine Bar & Cafe*.

The *Volcano* is a quaint place with artwork adorning the walls and the quirkiest toilet entry you are likely to see. You can relax with a drink here or enjoy a good range of food. Enchiladas are $7 as an entree or $18.50 as a main with salad, and really popular is the fab fungi – mushrooms filled with capers, cream cheese and sun-dried tomatoes. Next door, the *Lava Bar* erupts every night at 5 pm and the Black Mac flows.

Down on the waterfront (Norwich Quay) there are a couple of places. The circular *Nautilus* is a favourite which specialises in seafood (mains are $18 to $22). The *Lyttelton Brasserie* adds a bit of class to a street well accustomed to the nocturnal roaming of sailors (from all world ports) on shore leave.

For those who enjoy a drink with a view try out the *Wunderbar*, rather hidden and with a convoluted stairway entry. From the Volcano head downhill towards the waterfront and take the first turn left into a car park, from where you should hear the bar rocking. There is a new music venue a couple of fire escapes away; the Wunder-barbarians will direct you there.

Getting There & Away Bus No 28 from Cathedral Square takes you to Lyttelton. If travelling by car from Christchurch, there are three roads to choose from. The quickest way is through the road tunnel (12 km). Alternatively, you can go via Sumner and Evans Pass (19 km) or head straight down Colombo St from the Square, and continue up over Dyers Pass (22 km).

Akaroa

Akaroa, meaning 'long harbour' in Maori, is 82 km from Christchurch on the Banks Peninsula. It's good value for day trips – there are boats for rent, horse riding and a number of good dining choices. The best way to get around this intriguing village is on foot.

The original group of French colonists have clearly stamped their mark on this place. Streets (rues Lavaud, Balguerie, Jolie) and houses (Langlois-Eteveneaux) have French names, and descendants of the original French settlers reside in the town.

Information Most of the places of interest are concentrated along the waterfront from where SH75 enters the township in the north, to the lighthouse at the south end of town. SH75 merges into Rue Lavaud which then becomes Beach Rd. The Akaroa Information Centre (☎ 304 8600) is in the council office (post office building) on the corner of rues Lavaud and Balguerie.

Walking Tour The Akaroa Civic Trust produces an excellent pamphlet: *Akaroa Historic Village Walk*. The tour starts at Waeckerle Cottage at the northern end of town, follows Rue Lavaud then Rue Brittan up to L'Aube Hill Reserve, the first consecrated Pakeha burial ground in Canterbury. It then returns to Rue Lavaud to take in such fine buildings as the Town Hall, Courthouse, St Peter's Anglican Church, Langlois-Eteveneaux Cottage, the Custom House and the Church of St Patrick. Continue along Rue Jolie as there are a number of interesting houses in this main wharf locality, such as Glencarrig, built in 1852 for Akaroa's first Anglican vicar. Return to the start of the walk via the waterfront and wander out to Daly's wharf to get a different aspect of the town.

Things to See The **Akaroa Museum**, also on the corner of rues Lavaud and Balguerie, has a 20-minute audio-visual presentation on the Maori history of Banks Peninsula, exhibits on the whaling industry which attracted the French to settle Akaroa in 1840 and the British settlers who came along in 1850. The cocksfoot grass display ('What?' you ask) is particularly interesting – go in and find out.

The **Langlois-Eteveneaux Cottage** in front of the museum also contains exhibits – it's one of the oldest houses in New Zealand and was partly prefabricated in France. The Customs House by Daly's Wharf has been restored and is also part of the museum. The museum is open daily from 10.30 am to 4.30 pm; admission is $3 (children $1).

Activities Daily **harbour cruises** are operated on the *Canterbury Cat* (☎ 304 7641), departing from the Main Wharf at 11 am and 1.30 pm, except from April to November when only the 1.30-pm trip departs. The cost is $23 (children $10). You can buy tickets from the office on the wharf (☎ 304 7641).

The *Canterbury Clipper* (☎ 304 7641), an inflatable naiad, does an outer bays' tour where you may see Hector's dolphins, little blue penguins and NZ fur seals. It departs at 1.15 pm – the cost is $35 (children $20).

A quiet, peaceful way to cruise the waters around Akaroa is in a **sea kayak** with Sea Kayak Banks Peninsula (☎ 304 8776), 114 Rue Jolie. A one-day guided harbour paddle costs a reasonable $70 per person, lunch included. Rental costs $35 per day, but kayaks are not rented out to solo kayakers.

Advertised as 'Four nights, four days, four beaches, four bays', the **Banks Peninsula Walking Track** allows you to make a two to four-day walk across private farmland and then around the dramatic coastline of Banks Peninsula. It starts at the Onuku Farm Hostel and ends at the Mt Vernon Lodge – the convenient place for pick-up is the Akaroa post office. A package tour which includes transport from Akaroa to the first hut, four nights' hut accommodation, landowners' fees, track registration and a booklet which describes features of the track and the history, is $100 (the standby rate for four days is $85). The two-day option is $60 (no standby rate). Phone ☎ 304 7612 for information as prior booking is essential.

The exhausting Southern Bays Walkway (☎ 329 0007) begins and ends at Little River; a four-day option is $112, the two-day $79.

Places to Stay – Akaroa The *Akaroa Holiday Park* (☎ 304 7471) on Morgans Rd, off Old Coach Rd, has sites at $18, on-site caravans at $32, cabins from $42 and tourist flats at $56; all prices are for two.

At the one backpackers, *Chez la Mer* (☎ 304 7024), Rue Lavaud, share and dorm rooms are $14 per person, doubles and twins are $32. Beautiful lavender and jasmine gardens have been established at the back of the house, there are washing and ironing facilities, a common room and kitchen and, importantly, children are welcome.

The *Mt Vernon Lodge & Stables* (☎ 304 7180), PO Box 51, on Rue Balguerie is a combination hostel and guest lodge (it is an Associate YHA). Rates are $45 ($5 each extra adult) for two in a four-bed unit if you supply your own bedding. The rooms have a mezzanine floor over the main area and there are share-kitchen facilities. There's a swimming pool, BBQ and a large comfortable common room with an open fire, and you can ride the horses from the stables. In the hostel section dorm beds are $13 per person, and doubles or twins are $30.

The *Grand Hotel* (☎ 304 7011) at 6 Rue Lavaud has singles/doubles at $22.50/45. The *Hotel Madeira* (☎ 304 7009) at 48 Rue Lavaud has rooms at $45 for two, with a one-night only surcharge of $5.

Cheaper motels include *La Rive Motel* (☎ 304 7651) at 1 Rue Lavaud and the *Waiiti Motel* (☎ 304 7292) at 64 Rue Jolie, with rooms from $60 to $75. *L'Hotel Motel* (☎ 304 7559) at 75 Beach Rd has doubles at $92; there's a disabled-equipped unit.

The *Oinako Lodge* (☎ 304 8787), 99 Beach Rd, is a fabulous retreat in a grand old building near the beach. The rooms all have private facilities (some have spas) and B&B is from $135 to $180 for two. Another good spotless B&B is *Lavaud House* (☎ 304 7121), 83 Rue Lavaud; singles/doubles are $40/70. It is run by Francis and Frances!

The *Akaroa Village Inn* (☎ 304 7421), Beach Rd, is a NZ honeymooners' destination. It has a number of units which sleep a maximum of eight. These are $90 for two ($15 for each extra adult); full board is $79 per person, with a minimum of two.

Places to Stay – Banks Peninsula Most of the places to stay on the Banks Peninsula are in or near Akaroa but a few other possibilities are scattered around the various bays.

At the *Duvauchelle Reserve Camping Ground* (☎ 304 5777), eight km from Akaroa off SH75, tent sites are $6 per person. The *Le Bons Bay Motor Camp* (☎ 304 8533), on Le Bons Bay Valley Rd about 22 km from Akaroa, has tent/powered sites at $14/16 for two, and on-site caravans are $30 for two. The *Okains Bay Domain* also has tent sites for $5 ($3 for children), a new kitchen and shower cubicles. The nearby Okains Bay museum has a sacred god stick from the 1400s, an Akaroa hei tiki and a war canoe; admission is $4 adults, $1 for children.

Six km south of Akaroa at Onuku, the *Onuku Farm Hostel* (☎ 304 7612) is beside the bay on a 400-hectare sheep farm. It's a friendly and relaxed place but badly in need of a good library. Nightly costs are $14 in the house, $10 in summer huts, or $7 for camp sites. It is close to the start of the Banks Peninsula Walk and a good place to be if you want to get away from it all.

The *Kukupa Hostel* (☎ 304 6888) at

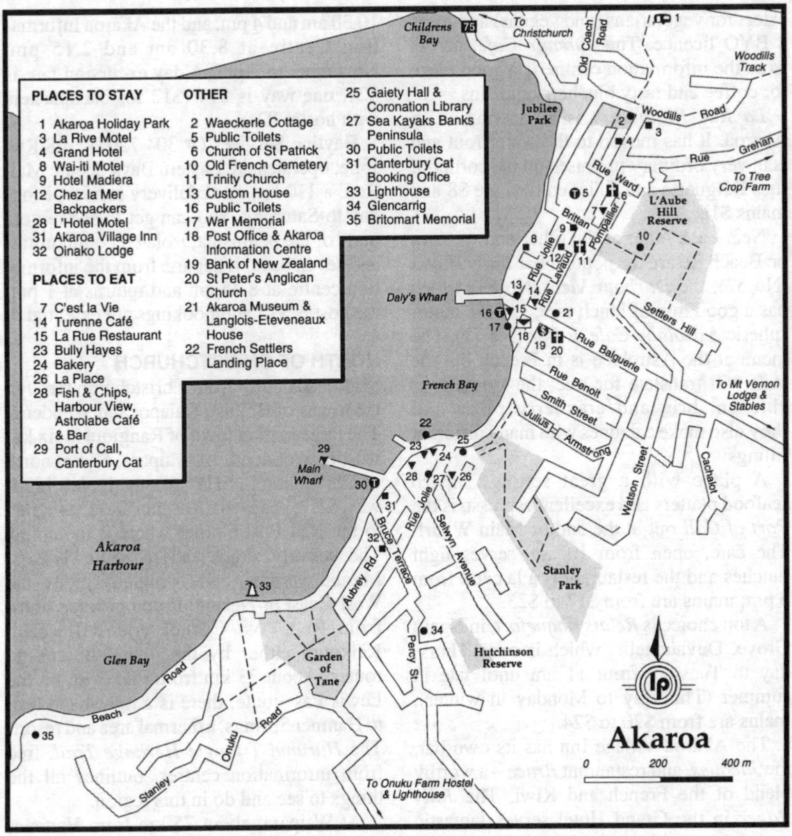

Pettigrew's Rd, Pigeon Bay, has just two bunkrooms; the cost is $9 for members, $10 for others and $30 for families. Set in magnificent bush, it's a bit far from everything if you don't have your own car – Pigeon Bay is about 35 km from Akaroa and very remote. The nonresident manager lives in the second house on the left up Starvation Gully Rd.

Le Bons Bay Backpackers (☎ 304 8582), is quite out of the way – it is on the right-hand side of the hill about six km before Le Bons Bay. The cost here is $12 per person, and doubles are $30, both including breakfast. The farm house is in a great location with commanding views down the valley. An evening meal costs $8 and you can choose from the menu. It is a suitable place for people with cars but the proprietors do pick up from Akaroa; ring in advance as places are limited. Fishing trips on secluded Le Bons Bay can be organised from here.

Places to Eat Sit outside the *Bakery* on Beach Rd at the far end of town under the shadow of one of the few 'tricolors' flying in NZ and enjoy a hearty filled roll with egg, salad and ham and a bottomless cup of coffee. The *C'est La Vie* on Rue Lavaud, caters for vegetarians (and vegans) and it has a BYO licence. The *Turenne Cafe*, across from the information centre, is a good place for coffee and tasty blueberry muffins.

La Rue Restaurant is an institution in Akaroa. It has moved to the waterfront and is in very ordinary premises on the corner of rues Balguerie and Jolie; entrees are $8 and mains $16.

Near each other at the other end of town on Beach Rd are the popular bar *Bully Hayes* (No 57); the *Harbour View* (No 69) which has a good mix of lunch fare; and the atmospheric *Astrolabe Cafe & Bar* (No 71). The menu at the Astrolabe is in French but the staff will translate for free; the specialty is chicken, brie and cranberry pizza and they also make calzones with many different fillings.

A place with a great setting, superb seafood platters and excellent espresso is the *Port of Call* out at the end of Main Wharf. The cafe, open from 10 am, serves light lunches and the restaurant is à la carte from 6 pm; mains are from $17 to $23.

A top choice is *Relais Roquefort*, in Ngaio Grove, Duvauchelle, which is open Thursday to Tuesday from 11 am until late in summer (Thursday to Monday in winter); mains are from $20 to $24.

The Akaroa Village Inn has its own bar, the *Jacques*, and restaurant *Bruce* – a worthy blend of the French and Kiwi. The *Jolly Roger* in the Grand Hotel serves fantastic seafood crepes for $12 with salad and chips.

At the end of the Woodills track is *Tree Crop Farm*, 'hip' with yuppie BMW and 4WD day trippers escaping from Christchurch.

Getting There & Away Akaroa is only 82 km from Christchurch and there are regular buses, as well as daily excursions available through the French Connection; book with InterCity (☎ 377 0951). The bus leaves the InterCity Centre at 8.30 am, the Christchurch Information Centre at 8.50 am, returns from Akaroa at 3.40 pm and the cost is $15/30 for a one-way/return fare.

The Akaroa Shuttle (☎ (0800) 500 929) departs from Christchurch Visitor Centre at 10.30 am and 4 pm, and the Akaroa Information Centre at 8.30 am and 2.15 pm, November to April. A day excursion fare is $24, one-way is $14 ($12 for backpackers with hostel IDs).

Bayline Services (☎ 304 7207), 108 Rue Jolie, operates the Eastern Bays Scenic Mail Run, a 110-km rural delivery service, Monday to Saturday. You can get to see remote parts of the peninsula, isolated communities and seven bays. It departs from the information centre at 8.45 am and returns at 1 pm; the cost is $15 and bookings are essential.

NORTH OF CHRISTCHURCH

SH1 heads north from Christchurch through the towns of Belfast, Kaiapoi and Woodend. The large market town of Rangiora is six km west of Woodend. At Waipara, 57 km north of Christchurch, SH1 splits – the left highway, SH7, heads via Hurunui and Culverden to the Red Post Corner where it too splits. The westerly choice leads to the Lewis Pass, Maruia Springs, and eventually either the West Coast or Nelson. If you proceed north from Red Post Corner you will reach Kaikoura either by the inland or coastal routes. About 23 km from Red Post, on the Lewis Pass route, there is a right-hand turn to Hanmer Springs, a thermal area and resort. The *Hurunui Triangle Heritage Trail*, free from information centres, outlines all the things to see and do in this region.

At Waipara, about 75 km from Hanmer, the *Waipara Sleepers* (☎ 314 6708) has novel accommodation; the 'fare' in the four-bed guard's vans is $15/30 for one/two, a railway hut with wheelchair access is $20 for a single and tent/unpowered sites are also available for $16/20 for two.

Kaiapoi

This town, on the coast 20 km north of Christchurch, takes its name from a famous pa site of the Ngai Tahu tribe. It is now noted for its wool mills. The **museum** in the Old Courthouse on Williams St has exhibits on local history. It's open from 2 to 4 pm on Sunday and Thursday; entry is $1 (kids 20c).

From Kaiapoi you can make trips on the

Top: Queenstown and the Remarkables, Otago (RS)
Bottom Left: TSS *Earnslaw*, Queenstown, Otago (TW)
Bottom Right: Bungy jumping near Queenstown, Otago (TC)

Top: Lake Tekapo, Canterbury (TW)
Bottom Left: Mt Cook, Canterbury (TW)
Bottom Right: Copland River, West Coast (VB)

Tuhoe, an old steamer, which sails most Sundays to Kairaki and back (just over an hour). It doesn't sail every Sunday so check on ☎ 327 5665; sailings are subject to weather conditions. Tickets, sold an hour before sailing, cost $8 (children $4).

There's fishing for trout, salmon and whitebait on the Kaiapoi River. You can reach Kaiapoi from Christchurch on Kaiapoi bus Nos 1 or 4, Waikuku bus Nos 1 or 4, or Rangiora bus No 4; it's a 35-minute trip. For times and points of departure, phone Bus Info (☎ 366 8855).

Places to Stay & Eat There are a couple of places to stay in Kaiapoi. *Pineacres Holiday Park* (☎ 327 5022) is two km north of town. tent/powered sites are $17/19, cabins $27.50, tourist flats $55 and motel units $60; all prices are for two. The *Blueskies* (☎ 327 8007) is at 12 Williams Rd; hostel beds are $7 per person and tent/powered sites are $10/16 for two. Heading further north, past Woodend, is a *DOC camping ground* at Mt Thomas, Hayland Rd, 30 km north of Rangiora.

As far as food goes there is not a great selection here; drive to Christchurch. If your car breaks down then try the *Taurus*, 134 Williams St, which serves good old favourites for $11 to $18. Dinner is served every evening from about 5.30 to 8.30 pm, and it stays open later on weekend nights.

Hanmer Springs

This, the main thermal resort in the South Island, is about 10 km off SH7, the highway to the West Coast. It's popular for a variety of outdoor activities including forest walks, horse treks, river and lake fishing, jet-boating, rafting, bungy jumping from the Waiau ferry bridge, skiing in winter and golfing at the 18-hole course. And of course, the hot pools! It is a small place with a permanent population of 1100.

Information The Hurunui Visitor Information Centre (☎ 315 7128) is on the corner of Amuri Rd and Jacks Pass Rd. It's open from 9 am to 6 pm daily in summer. In winter the hours are 10 am to 4.30 pm weekdays, 10 am to 5 pm on weekends. You can also get information from The Log Cabin (☎ 315 7192) on Amuri Rd. The BNZ is in the Mall on Conical Hill Rd and the Price Cutter Supermarket has an EFTPOS facility.

Thermal Reserve For over a hundred years, maybe more, Hanmer Springs has been renowned for its thermal waters. The springs are part of the legend of the fires of Tamatea. It is said that they are a piece of the fire dropped from the sky after an eruption of Mt Ngauruhoe's volcanic ridge. Centuries later it has metamorphosised into the Hanmer Springs Thermal Reserve (☎ 315 7511). It is open daily from 10 am to 9 pm, and a far cry from the grubby appearance of a few years ago. There are three 'relaxer' pools (temperatures range from 37° to 40°C); four rock pools connected by a rock stream; private pools (39°C); a fresh-water 25-metre pool; sauna and steam room and a toddlers' pool (34°C). Admission is $6 for adults, $3 for children and a day pass is $8 (come and go as much as you like).

Activities There are three **skiing** areas near Hanmer Springs. Amuri is the closest as it is only 27 km from Hanmer, and Lyford, a new area, is 75 km away. They are not nearly as expensive as the larger resorts. (See Skiing in the Outdoor Activities chapter for more details.)

At Thrillseekers Canyon **bungy jumping** takes place where the Waiau ferry bridge crosses the river of the same name. It costs $89 to hurl yourself from this bridge (37 metres high), money better saved for the more aesthetic surrounds of the Kawarau or Shotover rivers. If it's your only chance however, being the closest to Christchurch, the reservation number is ☎ 315 7046; it operates from 9 am to 5.30 pm.

There are two companies operating **jet-boat trips** through the Waiau Gorge. They are Thrillseekers Jet (☎ 315 7046) and Amuri Jet (☎ 315 7323). Thrillseekers charge $49 for adults and $25 for children; Amuri $55 and $20. You can raft the gorge

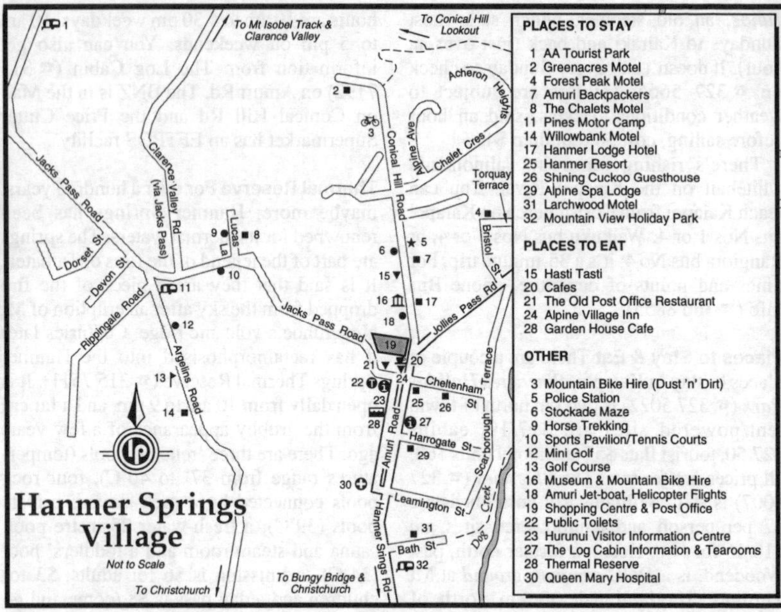

with four different companies (enquire at the visitor centre). The three-hour raft trip departs at 9.30 am and 1 pm in summer, and costs from $45 to $49 per person.

Rainbow Adventures (☎ 315 7444) at The Stables, Jacks Pass Rd, take **horse treks** around Hanmer; a one-hour ride is $25, a half day is $45 and a full day is $90. For longer treks Alpine Horse Safaris (☎ 314 4293) at Waitohi Downs, Hawarden, has a good reputation; a two-day ride into the Mandamus River valley is $205 and an exciting 10-day ride in the valleys near Lewis Pass is $1200.

This region is very popular for **mountain biking**. Dust and Dirt (☎ 315 7233) operates two-hour guided trips for $19 and a full-day Molesworth Station ride for $69 (lunch included). You can hire bikes from $7 for one hour and $25 for a whole day; a map of all the tracks is provided.

Tours There is a company providing safaris to Molesworth Station, the largest in New Zealand's high country. Tours with Trailways Safaris (☎ 315 7401) are $45 for a half-day, and $89 for a full-day tour (lunch is provided on the latter). You can also do a flight-seeing tour over Molesworth Station in a helicopter or light plane – get advice and prices from the Hurunui Visitor Information Centre.

Places to Stay The *Mountain View Holiday Park* (☎ 315 7113), on the south edge of town, has tent/powered sites at $16/18, a variety of cabins at $31 to $40 and fully equipped tourist flats at $52 to $59; prices are for two. The *AA Tourist Park* (☎ 315 7112) is on Jacks Pass Rd, three km from the town centre, with tent/powered sites at $14/18, cabins at $37 and tourist flats at $55; again, prices are for two, with a discount for AA members. Also on Jacks Pass Rd, adjacent to the golf course, is the *Pines Motor Camp* (☎ 315 7152) where tent/powered sites are $11/13, and cabins $30 for two. At the *Hanmer River Holiday Park* (☎ 315 7111), six km south, cabins are $30 for two.

Backpackers can get a comfortable bed for $15 per night at *Amuri Backpackers* (☎ 315 7196), a small, comfortable wooden chalet (a winter ski lodge) on Conical Hill Rd.

The *Hanmer Lodge Hotel* (☎ 315 7021) is a fine old, but extremely cold, hotel right in the centre of town. Rooms cost $40/60 for singles/doubles or twin; some with private bathroom facilities. Tiny electric heaters are provided but really, the management should turn on the central heating!

There are numerous motels, most costing at least $65 per night. The *Willowbank* (☎ 315 7211) on Argelins Rd is less expensive; units cost from $49 to $59 for two. The zenith of motel luxury are the tower units in the *Alpine Spa Lodge* (☎ 315 7311), on the corner of Amuri Rd and Harrogate St, where some units have circular beds and spa baths, for a cool $180. It has other older units from $66 for two.

Other good places are *Greenacres* (☎ 315 7125), Conical Hill Rd; and *Larchwood* (☎ 315 7281), 12 Bath St. Units in both places are from $75 for two persons. At the *Forest Peak* (☎ 315 7132) on Torquay Terrace rooms cost $55 to $75 for two. The *Hanmer Resort* (☎ 315 7362) on the corner of Amuri Rd and Cheltenham St has apartments and good family-sized units. The *Hanmer Springs Forest Camp* (☎ 315 7202), three km from the village up Jollies Pass Rd, has facilities for the disabled and comes highly recommended.

Places to Eat The *Village Plus* is a good place for a cup of coffee and *Hasti Tasti* is great for takeaways; both are on Conical Hill Rd. Also on Conical Hill Rd is the more up-market *Jaywalk Cafe* which has expensive main meals. The *Garden House Cafe* is in the hot pools complex; by day it is a cafe and from 6 pm daily is open for meals.

The Old Post Office is quite expensive but the dishes are tasty NZ fare. Entrées are about $9.50, mains are from $19.50 and it is open from 6 pm for dinner, Monday to Saturday. The *Regency*, in the Hanmer Lodge, is a good old-fashioned place where an à la carte four-course meal is $25.

The *Alpine Village Inn*, near the Mall on Conical Hill Rd, has bistro meals for under $13.50 from 5.30 to 8 pm every night. This is where the locals go for a beer.

Getting There & Away Hanmer Connection (☎ 315 7575) run daily between Hanmer Springs and Christchurch; it's a two-hour trip. Mt Cook Landline and White Star buses go from Christchurch to the Hanmer turn-off, Monday to Saturday. Remember, these buses, unlike Hanmer Connection, just drop you at the junction and you have to make your own way into the town, 10 km away.

West of Hanmer Springs

SH7 continues west from the Hanmer Springs turn-off to Lewis Pass, Maruia Springs and Springs Junction. From Lewis Pass (907 metres) there are a number of interesting walks – these are outlined in the pamphlet *Lewis Pass Walks*. Most of the tracks pass through beech forest, snow-capped mountains form the backdrop and there are lakes, alpine tarns and mountain rivers.

Maruia Springs is 69 km from the Hanmer turn-off. The natural thermal springs have been redeveloped and we have received good reports from travellers. You can stay at the *Maruia Springs Thermal Resort* (☎ 523 8840) where camping is $11, backpacker beds are $15 per person and units are $80 for two.

From Maruia the road continues to Springs Junction where it splits. SH65 heads north to the Buller Gorge and SH6 to Nelson. SH7 continues west from here to Reefton, then down the Grey Valley to Greymouth and the 'Coast'. The informative pamphlet *Hanmer Springs to the West Coast: A guide to the Lewis Pass Highway* outlines points of interest along the way.

The forest near Lewis Pass is mainly red and silver beech. The kawhais which grow along the river terraces are spectacular in spring.

WEST OF CHRISTCHURCH

Heading west from Christchurch on SH73, it's about a two-hour trip to Arthur's Pass and the Arthur's Pass National Park. The crossing from Christchurch to Greymouth, over the pass, is a very scenic covered by both bus and the TranzAlpine Express train.

Nowhere in New Zealand do you get a better picture of the climb from the sea to the mountains than on SH73 to the West Coast via Arthur's Pass. From Christchurch and almost at sea level, the road cuts through the flat Canterbury Plains, through rural towns such as Kirwee, Darfield, Racecourse Hill, Sheffield and Springfield. The road then winds up into the skiing areas of Porters Heights and Craigieburn before following the Waimakariri and Bealey rivers to Arthur's Pass. Picturesque lakes are passed on the way, including lakes Pearson and Grassmere.

To the south west of Christchurch and reached by SH73 and SH77 is the Mt Hutt ski resort and the adventure centre, Methven.

Craigieburn Forest Park

This forest park is 110 km north-west of Christchurch and 42 km south of Arthur's Pass, on SH73. There is a good system of walking tracks in the park, and in the valleys west of the Craigieburn Range longer tramps are possible. The nearby country is suitable for rock climbing and skiing. The predominant vegetation types are beech, alpine tussock, snow totara, mountain toatoa and turpentine scrub. If you are lucky you may see patches of South Island edelweiss *Leucogenes grandiceps*. Get a copy of the DOC pamphlet *Craigieburn Forest Park Walks* for details.

The *Flock Hill Lodge* (☎ 318 8196) is a high-country sheep station 35 km east of Arthur's Pass on SH73, adjacent to Lake Pearson and the Craigieburn Forest Park. It can accommodate 36 people in twin rooms or bunkrooms for $22 per person and there's a fully equipped communal kitchen. Activities include tramping and forest walks, canoeing, windsurfing, swimming, fishing, horse riding, skiing and ice skating.

Craigieburn is one of the best **skiing** areas in the country, as it has a rise of 503 metres. It is set in wild country and suits the advanced skier (see also Broken River, Porters Heights and Mount Cheeseman under Skiing in the Outdoor Activities chapter).

About 16 km east of Arthur's Pass at **Bealey** is the now legendary *Bealey Hotel* (☎ 318 9277) with rooms for $70 a double. This is the location of a recent hoax, which led people across the nation to believe that a live moa (that large and long-extinct bird) had been sighted in the area. The publican at this hotel had his sighting confirmed by two German tourists ... and business is booming.

Arthur's Pass

The small settlement of Arthur's Pass is four km from the pass of the same name. The 924-metre pass was on the route used by the Maori to reach Westland, but its European discovery was made by Arthur Dobson in 1864, when the Westland gold rush created enormous pressure to find a crossing over the Southern Alps from Christchurch. A coach road was completed within a year of Dobson's discovery. Later on, the coal and timber trade demanded a railway, which was completed in 1923.

The town is a fine base for walks, climbs, views and winter-time skiing (at Temple Basin) in Arthur's Pass National Park, and you can go there on a day trip from Greymouth or Christchurch.

Information The Arthur's Pass Visitor Centre (☎ 318 9211; fax 318 9271) in the town is open from 8 am to 5 pm every day. It has information on all the park walks, with pamphlets on many good day walks as well as topographical maps and route guides for a dozen longer tramps with huts. The staff can also offer valuable advice on the park's often savagely changeable weather conditions – check here before you go on any walk, and fill out an intentions card. Be sure to sign out again when you leave, otherwise they'll send a search party to find you!

The visitors centre is also a park museum,

with excellent displays, an audiovisual presentation, and a three-dimensional model of the park. In January there's a summer programme of guided walks and evening talks, discussions, films and slide shows.

Arthur's Pass National Park There are day walks in the park which offer 360° views of the snow-capped peaks. Many of these peaks are over 2000 metres, the highest being Mt Murchison at 2400 metres. One of the most spectacular views to be had from the road is of the Bealey Face of Mt Rolleston.

The park has huts on the tramping tracks and also several areas suitable for camping. The day walks leaflet from the visitor centre lists half-day walks of one to four hours and day walks of five to eight hours. The two-hour (one-way) walk to Temple Basin provides superb views of the surrounding peaks. There's skiing at Temple Basin (see Skiing in the Outdoor Activities chapter).

Places to Stay From November to March all the accommodation is in demand; it is advisable to book ahead. The *Sir Arthur Dudley Dobson Memorial YHA Hostel* (☎ 318 9230) has bunkroom accommodation at $15 per night for members ($19 for non-members). Across the road is *Mountain House* (☎ 318 9258), a good backpackers which has share and dorm rooms for $15 – from June to August (the best time to be here) stay three nights for the price of two.

The *Alpine Motel* (☎ 318 9233) has doubles at $65 and some simpler rooms from $50. The *Chalet Guesthouse* (☎ 318 9236) offers B&B for $75 for a double with shared facilities, $85 a double with private facilities. One small place is the *Snow Grass Cabin* which has one unit: a double and two bunks, bathroom, kitchen and TV; it costs $50 for two and $5 each additional person

You can camp at the *Public Shelter* for $3 per night; the facilities at this price are understandably basic, cold water and a flush toilet. Another place to try is Maori Flat, east out of the village, which is free.

Outside town, the *Otira Hotel* (☎ 738 2802) in the township of Otira, 14.5 km west

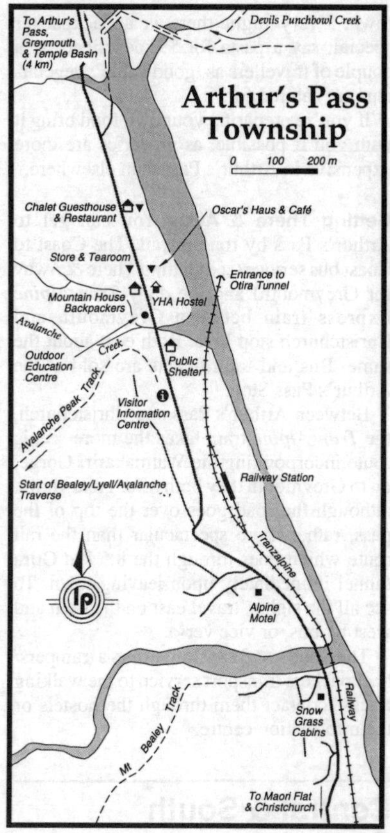

of, and over the other side of Arthur's Pass, has singles from $25, backpacker accommodation from $12 and meals are served. There are some great walks in the area including the Goat Pass trip which forms part of the Coast to Coast endurance race. Also nearby is the start of the Harpers Pass Track.

Places to Eat You can eat in the *Arthur's Pass Store & Tearoom* or in the *Chalet Restaurant*, which has a cheaper coffee bar beyond its restaurant area. *Oscar's Haus Alpine Crafts* has built a new cafe and bar which has fast become the social focus of the town. Every night there is a backpacker special, say a pasta for $9, described by a couple of travellers as 'good value'; vegetarians are catered for.

If you're preparing your own food bring it with you if possible, as groceries are more expensive in Arthur's Pass than elsewhere.

Getting There & Away You can get to Arthur's Pass by road or rail. The Coast to Coast bus service (see Getting There & Away for Greymouth) and the daily *TranzAlpine* Express train between Greymouth and Christchurch stop here. Both cost about the same. Bus and train tickets are sold at the Arthur's Pass Store.

Between Arthur's Pass and Christchurch, the *TranzAlpine* train takes the more scenic route incorporating the Waimakariri Gorge; on to Greymouth they both offer great views, although the road goes over the top of the pass, rather more spectacular than the rail route which goes through the 8.5 km Otira tunnel immediately upon leaving town. To see all the sights, travel east on the train and west by bus, or vice versa.

The South (☎ 318 9266) offers a trampers/backpackers transport service to the walking tracks; contact them through the hostels or the information centre.

Central & South Canterbury

If you head south from Christchurch there are two routes through the South Canterbury region. Taking SH1 south along the coast you come to Ashburton, Timaru, Oamaru and then Dunedin. Or you can head inland, crossing the Mackenzie Country to reach the spectacular lakes and the Southern Alps.

CHRISTCHURCH TO OTAGO

The SH1, south of Christchurch, is very flat and boring as you cross the Canterbury Plains. Being in a bus, makes all the difference to your view, allowing you to see over the nearby hedges and obstructions. In clear weather there are some magnificent views to be seen of the distant Southern Alps and their foothills.

South of Christchurch you drive through plantation forests that were flattened by a storm some years ago. There are many wide, glacial-fed rivers to be crossed – quite a sight in flood, though you don't see much water at other times. The Rakaia River Bridge is about two km long and this river is popular for jet-boating; the Rangitata River attracts white-water rafters; and salmon fishing is possible in many streams in South Canterbury. The first sizeable town that you come to is Ashburton.

Ashburton

Ashburton (population 14,200) is very much the service centre for the surrounding district. It is about 85 km south of Christchurch and lies between the Rakaia and Rangitata rivers. There are six **museums** in or around this town – the Plains Museum in nearby Tinwald, the Station Museum, an Aviation Museum, Museum of Woodwork & Ornamental Turning, Vintage Car Club Museum and the Ashburton Museum.

The Ashburton Walkway is an easy walk of 19 km from the town to the coast at Hakatere; there is a free camping ground along the way. For information on other activities in the area contact the Ashburton Information Centre (☎ & fax 308 1064) on the corner of East and Burnett Sts. The AA area office (☎ 308 7128) is at 119 Tancred St.

Places to Stay & Eat There is a full range of accommodation in Ashburton. The *Coronation Holiday Park* (☎ 308 6603), 780 East St, has tent/powered sites for $12/14, on-site caravans for $26, cabins for $40 and motel units from $50; all costs are for two people. Next door is the *Academy Lodge Motel* (☎ 308 5503) for $65 for two. There are at least seven other motels typically charging from $55 to $70 for a unit; inquire at the information centre. The information centre also has a list of farmstays that are available in the mid Canterbury region.

There is a *KFC* in Ashburton for fast-food freaks. Other dining possibilities are *Cactus Jack's* for Mexican in Wills St, open daily from 5 pm; *Tuscany Cafe & Bar* on the corner of East and Burnett Sts; the *Royal Oak*, a good old-fashioned family restaurant on West St which is open daily; the *100 Pipers Bakery* in The Arcade for cakes and takeaways which make your journey south more tolerable; and *The Stables*, one km south in the Tinwald Tavern, has meals for kids. Don't expect gourmet food – this town is just discovering that there's more to life than mutton and lamb.

Getting There & Away Both InterCity and Mt Cook Landline pass via Ashburton on their way to Dunedin or Christchurch. InterCity's depot is Ashburton Station Souvenirs (☎ 308 5178), East St, and Mt Cook's is Farmers Corner Tearooms, 208 Havelock St (☎ 308 8332). In winter, Mountain Transport (☎ 302 8443) operates a bus to Mt Hutt.

Methven

Inland from Ashburton on SH77 is Methven (population 920), a good centre for the Canterbury Plains or the mountains. A small town, Methven is quiet for most of the year, coming alive in winter when it fills up with skiers using it as a base for Mt Hutt and other ski areas. There is a world-class 18-hole golf course nearby.

Information The Methven Information Centre (☎ & fax 302 8955) is on Mt Hutt Rd next to the Mt Hutt Ski Area office. The staff make bookings for accommodation, skiing packages and other activities in this area. They don't work on holidays, it seems, just when travellers needs them most!

A number of the restaurants and services are concentrated around the Mall and the adjacent shopping centre at the intersection of Chertsey and Mt Hutt Rds and Forest Drive. There are two banks near the Mall and the medical centre is opposite, on the corner of Chertsey and Mt Hutt Rds.

Activities The Mt Hutt Forest, an area of predominantly mountain beech, is located 14 km west of Methven. It is adjoined by two reserves, the Awa Awa Rata Reserve and the Pudding Hill Scenic Reserve. There are two access roads, Pudding Hill Rd which leads to foot access for Pudding Hill Stream; and McLennan's Bush Rd to Pudding Hill Reserve and Awa Awa Rata Reserve. There are many **walking trails**: the Pudding Hill Stream Route, which requires many stream crossings, takes 2½ hours, and the Awa Awa Rata Reserve Loop Track takes 1½ hours. In the rata reserve there are many short walks set up to show the diverse vegetation within the surrounding forest.

It is **skiing** that has really set Methven on an upward growth curve. Mt Hutt is nearby and, offering six months of skiing, it has perhaps the longest ski season of any resort in NZ. The skiable area is 365 hectares and snow-making facilities ensure there is an adequate cover for the whole season. All levels of alpine skiing, snow-boarding, telemarking and recreational racing are catered for. *Beaches Restaurant* on the mountain is the highest dining establishment in Australasia. (See Skiing in the Outdoor Activities chapter for more details.)

There are two **jet-boat** operators in this area. White Water Jets (☎ 318 6574) and Rakaia Gorge Scenic Jet (☎ 318 6515) zip up to the Rakaia Gorge, every day or on demand. As you can only see the gorge from the river, a jet-boat is the best means of transport in this braided river system.

If you want to see what the Canterbury Plains look like while you are looping the loop, barrel rolling and stall turning in a Pitts Special **aerobatic aircraft**, ring Four Season Tours (☎ 308 8787). Flights over other parts of Canterbury that you are unlikely to see from the ground are also organised.

If **free-fall parachuting** is your bag then visit the Parachute Centre (☎ mobile (025) 321 135) which is based at Pudding Hill, five km from Methven. You leap out of a plane attached to a competent instructor and free-fall before engaging a special tandem parachute. More sedate is a **balloon flight** organised through Aoraki Balloon Safaris

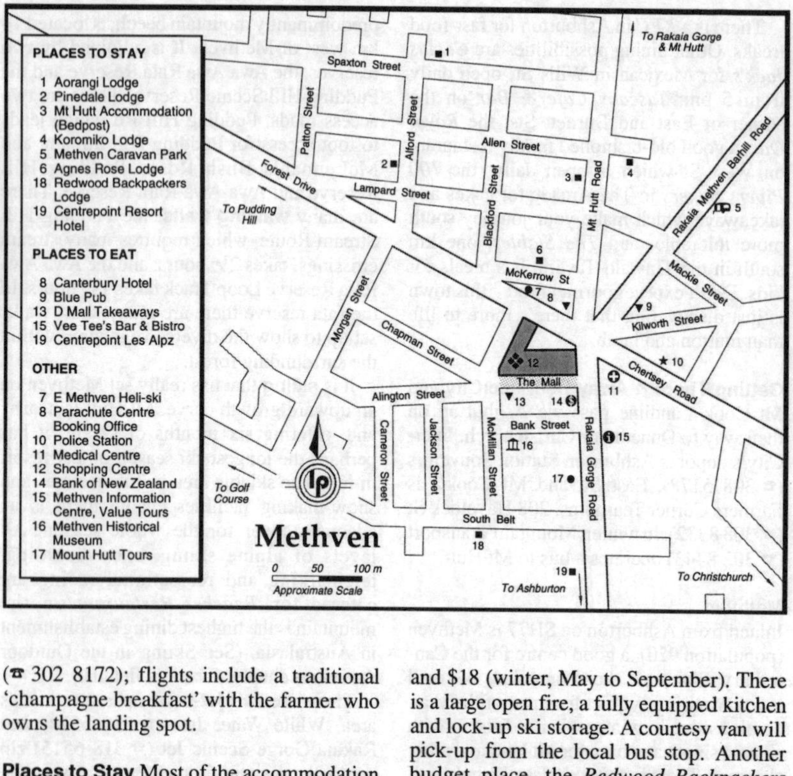

(☎ 302 8172); flights include a traditional 'champagne breakfast' with the farmer who owns the landing spot.

Places to Stay Most of the accommodation places are geared for winter tourists who are here to ski on Mt Hutt. There is, nevertheless, a full range of accommodation, from budget places to international quality resorts.

Methven Caravan Park (☎ 302 8005) on the Rakaia-Methven Barhill Rd has tent/powered sites at $10/15 for two, and basic cabins at $12 per person. You can hire bedding and cooking utensils if you don't have your own. The *Mt Hutt Accommodation (Bedpost)* (☎ 302 8508) near the corner of Mt Hutt Rd and Lampard St in central Methven has hostel-style accommodation from $16 to $18 in winter. You can hire bedding for $2.

On the corner of Alford and Allen Sts is *Pinedale Lodge* (☎ 302 8621) where share rooms are $12 (summer, October to April) and $18 (winter, May to September). There is a large open fire, a fully equipped kitchen and lock-up ski storage. A courtesy van will pick-up from the local bus stop. Another budget place, the *Redwood Backpackers Lodge* (☎ 302 8287), is near the corner of South Belt Rd and McMillan St. It has a well-equipped kitchen, log fire, stereo and TV, and linen is supplied. In summer it costs a very reasonable $10 (winter is $20) per person in share rooms; storage is available. The *Agnes Rose Lodge* (☎ 302 8556), 10 McKerrow St, is a comfortable little backpackers with a ski-gear storage room. A dorm bed with linen and duvets supplied costs about $15.

Pudding Hill Chalets, (☎ 302 8416) five km from town on SH72, has tent/powered sites at $14/18 for two, and chalets where B&B is $33 per person in twin rooms, $42 per person in larger rooms. There are lots of extras including sauna, spa pool, swimming pool, children's play area, billiards, a ski room and drying room. This is also the base for the Parachute Centre and tandem free-fall parachuting.

Aorangi Lodge (☎ 302 8482), 38 Spaxton St, has B&B for $35 per person during the ski season, and for $25 in summer. *Mt Hutt Homestead* (☎ 302 8130) is part of a high country sheep and deer station just outside Methven. B&B is not cheap at $90/115 for singles/doubles, but the food is excellent and it's an interesting place to stay. There are other motels and hotels, such as the comfortable *Koromiko Lodge* (☎ 302 8165) on SH77 (Mt Hutt Rd), where a twin is $94 in winter. Readers have recommended the *Chelsea Lodge* (☎ 318 2700) near Glentunnel, on SH77, some 40 km north of Methven.

The *Centrepoint Resort Hotel* (☎ 302 8724) on Rakaia Gorge is the flashest place in town; a double is about $170. There are many more places; enquire for a list from the visitor centre.

Places to Eat In the main shopping centre there are a number of takeaways including *Uncle Dominic's*, *Munchies* and *Woodsey's*. Additionally, there are a number of good restaurants. *Vee Tees Bar & Bistro*, above the information centre on Mt Hutt Rd serves good family meals. There are two pubs, the *Canterbury Hotel*, on the corner of Mt Hutt Rd and Forest Drive, and the famous *Blue Pub* across from it. The latter is very popular with ski bums during winter, but both serve good pub meals. Good seafood meals are served at the *Centrepoint Les Alpz* on Rakaia Gorge Rd. There is lots of entertainment in winter when skiers converge on the town after a day's skiing.

Getting There & Away There is an InterCity bus service, summer and winter, to Methven; the cost to Christchurch Airport return is about $40. Also Value Tours (☎ 302 8112) and Allan's Bus (☎ 359 3199) will pick you up from the Christchurch airport and will drop you off at your accommodation. Value Tours and Guthreys usually include ski hire, transport and accommodation in a package.

Getting Around As it is such a compact town most people walk to get around. Many accommodation places have courtesy vehicles; ask when you book in. A village shuttle operates in winter from May to October. Mount Hutt Tours (☎ 302 8611) run a daily service from Ashburton, Methven and Toll Gate to Mt Hutt.

CANTERBURY

Temuka

In 1853 William Hornbrook settled on his run Arowhenua, on the south bank of the Temuka River. His wife, who settled there a year later, was the first Pakeha female pioneer in South Canterbury. Arowhenua had long been a pa site of the Ngai Tahu people. Their earth ovens, *te umu kaha* or 'fierce strong ovens', gave Tumukaha, later Temuka, its name. A number of relics of early settlement survive, including middens, Old Hope Cottage, Mendelssohn House and the magnificent redwood trees on the corner of King St and Wilmhurst Rd. The site of pioneer aviator Richard Pearse's first attempted flight is out on Main Waitohi Rd, 13.5 km from Temuka towards Hanging Rock Bridge. He took off from the road but crashed into a nearby hedge, which has long since been removed. The District Council Service Centre (☎ 615 9537), Domain Avenue, acts as an information centre.

Places to Stay & Eat The *Temuka Holiday Park* (☎ 615 7241), 2 Fergusson Drive, has tent/powered sites for $14/15, and cabins for $26 for two. Temuka has five hotels and four motels. The *Royal Hotel* (☎ 615 7507) has B&B for $27 and the *A & A Motel* (☎ 615 8004), 54 King St, has reasonable singles/doubles for $36/45.

Along King St there are pubs serving meals, a number of takeaways and the omnipresent tearooms. The local cheeses – edam, cheddar, colby, gouda and high cream cheddar – are superb.

Timaru

Timaru is a pleasant little port roughly halfway between Christchurch and Dunedin; it is a convenient stopping point with an

Three Great Champions

The Timaru region has produced three great sporting champions – two human, the third a horse.

In the centre of Timaru, next to the ANZ Bank, is a statue of Robert Fitzsimmons, three times world boxing champion with a record barely matched today. Fitzsimmons was born in 1862 and developed his impressive physique at his father's blacksmith's forge. He defeated Jack Dempsey (the Irish Jack Dempsey, not the illustrious 1920s American boxer of the same name) in 1891 to take the world middleweight crown, Jim Corbett in 1897 in 14 rounds to win the heavyweight crown (held until 1899) and, four years later, took the world light-heavyweight championship. He died in 1917, three years after the last of his 350 or so professional bouts.

Dr John Edward ('Jack') Lovelock, born in 1910, was the world record-holder for the one mile. In 1936, in front of a crowd of 120,000 at the Berlin Olympics, he broke the record for the 1500 metres and took the gold medal. Hitler presented him with an oak tree, which is still growing today in the grounds of Timaru Boys' High School, North St.

The racecourse at Washdyke is named after New Zealand's most famous galloper, Phar Lap, who was born at nearby Seadown. In the late 1920s and early 1930s Phar Lap swept all challengers before him. After winning the Melbourne Cup in 1930, he was later taken to the USA where he continued his winning streak. Here he died, apparently poisoned, soon after winning the richest race in the world, the Agua Caliente Handicap in Mexico. Despite racing in the Depression years, Phar Lap was for many years the greatest stakes winner in the world. Today, Phar Lap's stuffed skin is on display in the National Museum of Victoria (Australia), his skeleton is in the Auckland Museum and his heart is preserved at the Institute of Anatomy in Canberra (also in Australia). ■

especially attractive beach at Caroline Bay. The Caroline Bay Christmas Carnival, beginning on 26 December and continuing for about 10 days, is a lot of fun.

Timaru comes from the Maori name Te Maru, meaning 'the place of shelter', but there was no permanent Maori settlement here when the first Europeans, the Weller brothers of Sydney, set up a whaling station in 1839. The *Caroline*, one of the sailing ships which picked up whale oil, gave the picturesque bay its name.

The town really began to boom when a landing service was established at the foot of Strathallan St. Later a better landing service building was established in 1868 in George St and is still there, now renovated into a boutique brewery. After about 30 vessels were wrecked between the mid-1860s and 1880s attempting to berth near Timaru, the decision was made to establish an artificial harbour. The end result is the excellent port which stands there today and Caroline Bay's beach which has resulted from the construction of breakwaters. Declared a city in 1948, it now has a population of 27,300.

Information Timaru's main road, SH1, is a road of many names – the Hilton Highway north of town, Evans St as it enters town and Stafford St as it goes through the town centre. Most businesses are on or near Stafford St. Continuing south, it becomes King St and then SH1 as it emerges from town heading south.

The Timaru Visitor Information Centre (☎ 688 6163; fax 688 6162) at 14 George St, diagonally across from the railway station, is minded by zealous staff. It's open from 8.30 am to 5 pm Monday to Friday, and on weekends from 10 am to 3 pm. The AA is on the corner of Church and Bank Sts. A street map and the interesting pamphlet *Timaru City Historic Walk* are available from the information centre. The public library on Sophia St is open Monday to Saturday (check the varying daily hours).

Things to See One of the few safe, sheltered beaches along the east coast is **Caroline Bay**. The park along the beach has a walk-through aviary, a maze, a pleasant walkway and other attractions. A pleasant walk heads north from

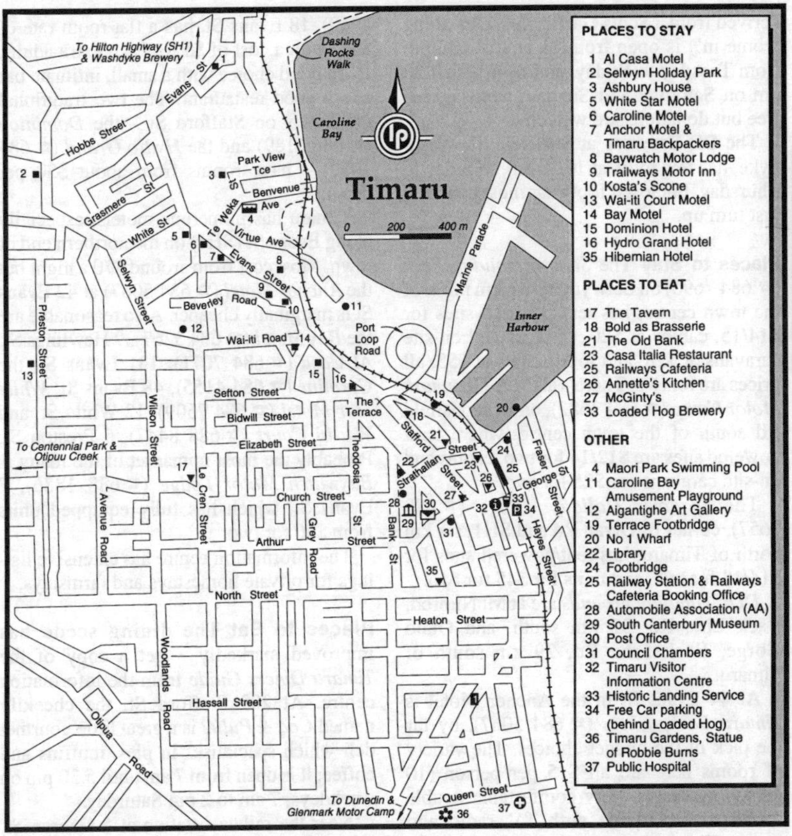

town along Caroline Bay, past the Benvenue Cliffs and on to the Dashing Rocks and rock pools at the north end of the bay. Caroline Bay is sheltered and calm but there's good surfing south of town. There is an easy 45-minute walk around the bay outlined in an old Timaru City Council pamphlet; it should still be available from the information centre.

Timaru has other good parks including Centennial Park along the Otipua Creek with a pleasant 3.5 km walkway along the stream bed. The information centre has leaflets outlining a scenic drive.

The **South Canterbury Museum**, in the Pioneer Hall on Perth St, is the main regional museum, with exhibits on the whalers and early settlers. Admission is free and it's open daily from 1.30 to 4.30 pm except Monday. One fascinating exhibit is a replica of the aeroplane designed and flown by early South Canterbury aviator, Richard Pearse, in 1903 (some nine months before Orville Wright in the USA). Pearse died in a psychiatric hospital in Christchurch in 1953, virtually unknown to the outside world.

Over 900 works of art, plus changing exhibits, feature at the **Aigantighe Art Gallery** at 49 Wai-iti Rd. The gallery (Aigantighe is derived from a Scots Gaelic phrase meaning 'come in') is open from 11 am to 4.30 pm from Tuesday to Friday, and from 2 to 4.30 pm on Saturday and Sunday; admission is free but donations are welcome.

The **DB Brewery** at Sheffield St, Washdyke, has free tours at 10.30 am, Monday to Thursday. Enclosed footwear must be worn; just turn up.

Places to Stay The *Selwyn Holiday Park* (☎ 684 7690) on Selwyn St, two km north of the town centre, has tent/powered sites for $14/15, cabins at $20, cottages and on-site caravans at $28, and tourist flats at $55; all prices are for two. There's also the *Glenmark Motor Camp* (☎ 684 3682), on Beaconsfield Rd south of the town centre, where tent/powered sites are $12/14 for two, cabins and on-site caravans are $25 for two.

The *Seadown Holiday Village* (☎ 688 2657), corner of Divan Rd and SH1, six km north of Timaru, has tent/powered sites for $14/18 for two, and units for $45 for two.

DOC camping grounds are at Mt Nimrod, Back Line Rd, 32 km south, and Otaio Gorge, Back Line Rd, 29 km south of Timaru.

At 44 Evans St in the Anchor Motel is *Timaru Backpackers* (☎ 684 5067), by far the pick of the budget choices. The variety of rooms here are all $15 per person (10 person capacity). Very comfortable double rooms are available with TV, radio and toaster. The management go out of their way to look after you. *Jan's Place* (☎ 688 4589) at 4A Rose St offers B&B at $27 per person; there are also backpackers beds for $15 per person. *Kosta's Scone* (☎ 688 0871) at 24 Evans St almost never made it into this edition as management decided whether or not they would stay as a backpackers. They decided in favour of the pack-bedecked traveller and now offer dorm and share rooms for $12 per person, doubles for $28.

Ashbury House (☎ 684 3396) at 30 Te Weka St has rooms at $30/55 including a big cooked breakfast. The *Hibernian Hotel* (☎ 688 8124), 6 Latter St, has rooms at $70 for two. The *Trailways Motor Inn* (☎ 688 4049), 18 Evans St, has a flat room rate of $81 (with a cost of $5 for each extra adult). It is a good choice with a small, intimate bar and a good restaurant. The two traditional old hotels on Stafford St – the *Dominion* (☎ 688 6189) and the *Hydro Grand* (☎ 684 7059) – have rooms from about $30 per person.

Timaru has numerous motels, especially along Evans St (SH1) on the northern end of town. Most cost from around $70 a night but the *Anchor Motel* (☎ 684 5067) at 42 Evans St is marginally cheaper. Also reasonable are the *Bay Motel* (☎ 684 3267), 9 Hewlings St; *Al Casa* (☎ 684 7071), 131 Evans St; the *Caroline* (☎ 684 4155), 48 Evans St; *White Star Motel* (☎ 684 7509), 12 White St, and *Wai-iti Court* (☎ 688 8447), 5 Preston St. Probably the most upmarket of the many is *Baywatch Motor Lodge* (☎ 688 1886), 7 Evans St, which has fully equipped units from $80 for two.

The information centre has extensive listings for private homestays and farmstays.

Places to Eat The dining scene has improved markedly – get a copy of the *Timaru Diners Guide* from the information centre. At 209 Stafford St, the cheekily named *Coq & Pullet* is a great little gourmet deli which specialises in pies, muffins and coffee; it is open from 7 am until 5.30 pm on weekdays, 7 am to 2 pm Saturday.

Near the railway station at 5 George St, *Annette's Kitchen* is a licensed place with main courses from $7 (lunch) and $12.50 (dinner); it's open daily. A welcome addition to the international line-up is *Casa Italia*, Strathallan St. It is housed in a beautiful building, has an excellent wine list and serves authentic Italian food – bellissimo. What's more, it is open daily.

The pick of the town's eateries is the *Bold as Brasserie*, upstairs at 335 Stafford St on the corner of Sefton St. There is an innovative menu as the chef likes to introduce the timid local diners to exotic tastes. There are excellent breads (eg blue-cheese brioche), hearty soups and a great wine selection.

A boutique brewery is housed in the

former Landing Service building in George St – the *Loaded Hog Brewery* has a veritable trough of selections for the beer lover – Hog Gold lager, Hogs Head dark and Weiss beer.

Two other popular night venues where you can also get a meal are the *Old Bank*, near the corner of Strathallan St and The Terrace, and *McGinty's*, near the corner of George and Stafford Sts.

Getting There & Away Air New Zealand Link (☎ (0800) 652 881) has daily flights to Christchurch and Wellington.

The InterCity depot is at the Travellers Rest & Booking Centre (☎ 688 3597) at the railway station; InterCity has buses passing through Timaru on the Christchurch-Invercargill route at least twice daily. Mt Cook Landline (☎ 684 3597), also at the station, has daily Picton-Invercargill and Christchurch-Lake Tekapo-Mt Cook routes. Several shuttle buses pass through Timaru such as Catch-a-Bus (☎ 477 7900), Atomic (☎ 322 8883) and Ko-op Shuttles (☎ (0800) 805 505).

The *Southerner* train (Christchurch-Invercargill) passes through Timaru daily; at 10.35 am going south, 3.09 pm going north.

For hitching north get a Canride Grantlea bus to Jellicoe St and save yourself a walk. For a taxi to Timaru airport, contact Call-a-Cab (☎ 688 8811); it costs about $10.

Waimate

This town, 45 km south of Timaru, is reached by a deviation off SH1 onto SH82. It is possible to do a loop and rejoin SH1 near the Waitaki River. Tourist literature neglects to mention that the town's name translates as 'stagnant water' although there is little hint of it today. Here you will find instead the historic **Cuddy**, a thatched cottage constructed from a single totara tree. For a tour, which includes the woolshed (☎ 689 8737). You can obtain information from the Waimate Information Centre (☎ 689 8079), Queen St.

Don't be surprised if you see wallabies in the nearby hills, as they have bred like rabbits since they were introduced here from Australia.

At the *Waimate Motor Camp* (☎ 689 7387), Victoria Park, a tent/powered site is $10/14 for two, and basic cabins are $8 per person. A room in the *New Criterion* (☎ 689 8069), corner of Mill Rd and Queen St, will cost $35/60 for a single/double. The *Lochiel Motel* (☎ 689 7570), 100 Shearman St, charges $25 for B&B in simple rooms, and its units are $52 for two.

There are plenty of places where you can get a meal along Queen St. Tearooms and the inevitable *Country Fare* opens its doors to the weary traveller.

TO THE MACKENZIE COUNTRY

Those heading to Queenstown and the lakes from Christchurch will probably turn off SH1 onto SH79. This scenic route passes through the towns of Geraldine and Fairlie before joining with SH8 which heads over Burkes Pass to Lake Tekapo.

Geraldine

On the road inland to Mt Cook is Geraldine, a picturesque town with a country village atmosphere. Geraldine was not settled until 1854 when Samuel Hewlings built the first bark hut in Talbot St; a totara tree planted at that time still survives today. There are a number of early settlers' cottages still remaining. The information centre (☎ 693 8597) is on Talbot St, opposite the police station.

The **Vintage Car & Machinery Museum**, on Lower Talbot St, includes a De Dion Bouton (1907), an International Motor Buggy (1908), a couple of 1910 Model Ts and lots of cars from the 1900s, 20s and 30s. The huge shed at the back houses about 60 tractors, dating back to the 1920s; the tractors are entered in the annual Geraldine tractor races and competitions. The museum is open from 10 am to 4.30 pm on weekends all year, by arrangement through the information centre and daily during school holidays; entry is $2 (children free).

Barker's Wines (☎ 693 8969) specialising in elderberry and other berry wines, is eight

CANTERBURY

km out of Geraldine, off SH79 towards Mt Cook. It is open for tasting Monday to Saturday until 6 pm.

Places to Stay & Eat The *Geraldine Motor Camp* (☎ 693 8860), Hislop Rd, has tent sites for $8, cabins for $15 per person. At the *Farmyard Holiday Park* (☎ 693 9355), seven km from Geraldine, you can get cabins for $23 for two. There is now a backpackers here: *The Olde Presbytery* (☎ 693 9644) at 13 Jollie St. A bed here costs $15 per person with everything supplied. There are limited beds but the place is neat and tidy and it has friendly, concerned owners.

The Crossing (☎ 693 9689), Woodbury Rd, is a pretty B&B with a licensed restaurant. Standard rooms are $62/84 for doubles/twins with ensuite. On Talbot St there is the *Crown Hotel* (☎ 693 8458) where B&B is $30/50 for singles/doubles or twins; this hotel has a restaurant. There are two motels: the *Geraldine* (☎ 693 8501), 97 Talbot St, costs $60 for two; and the *Andorra* (☎ 693 8622), 16 McKenzie St, is between $70 and $80 for a unit.

For a good breakfast go to *Robbie's Tearooms & Restaurant* in Talbot St. *The Oaks*, unashamedly established to entice the bus trade, is on the corner of Talbot and Cox Sts – all the usual travellers' delights are found here, from greasies to restaurant fare.

Peel Forest & Mt Somers

The Peel Forest, 19 km north of Geraldine, is one of NZ's most important areas of indigenous podocarp forest. Mt Peel station is nearby, and the road from it leads to Mesopotamia, once the run of the English writer Samuel Butler in the 1860s. Before heading into the park stop at the Peel Forest Park DOC office (☎ 696 3826) and obtain more information including *Peel Forest Park: Track Information*. The DOC also take bookings for the excellent *camping ground* on the banks of the Rangitata River; $6.50 each adult, and an extra $2.50 for power. Other *DOC camping grounds* in this region are found at Orari Gorge, Yates Rd, 12 km north of Geraldine; Waihi Gorge, Waihi Gorge Rd, 14 km north of Geraldine; and Pioneer Park, Home Bush Rd, 14 km west of Geraldine.

You are only minutes away from a magnificent native podocarp (conifer) forest of totara, kahikatea and matai. One fine example of totara can be seen on the **Big Tree Walk** – it is nine metres in circumference and over 1000 years old. The birdlife attracted to this forest includes the rifleman, kereru (native pigeon), bellbird, fantail and grey warbler. There are nesting New Zealand falcons on the higher reaches of Mt Peel. There are also picturesque waterfalls in the park – Emily Falls (1½ hour), Rata Falls (two hours) and Acland Falls (20 minutes).

The 10-hour **Mt Somers Subalpine Walkway** traverses the northern face of Mt Somers, linking the Sharplin Falls with Woolshed Creek. The highlight of this trip is the several altitudinal plant sequences which walkers pass through, although there is also plenty of regenerating beech forest. Two huts, the Pinnacles and Mt Somers, are available on the walk; $4 each adult. Be warned that this route is subject to sudden changes in weather and all normal tramping precautions should be taken.

A **white-water rafting** company operates in the nearby Rangitata River – Mt Peel-based Rangitata Rafts (☎ (0800) 251 251); it has budget accommodation at Mt Peel where you can get a basic bunk bed for $10. Rafters who have done a number of trips say that the Rangitata Gorge is one of the best, because of the exhilarating Grade Five rapids at all water levels. Rangitata Rafts charge $105 per person for the Rangitata Gorge; this includes lunch and a BBQ dinner. The trips depart from Christchurch between 9 and 9.30 am and arrive at the river base at 11.30 am. The trip on the river is about three hours and return to Christchurch is about 7 to 8 pm. Rangitata Rafts are 10 minutes past Peel Forest and about three km is on dirt; drive carefully.

Fairlie

This town is often described as 'the gateway to the Mackenzie' because, just west of here, the landscape changes dramatically as the road mounts Burkes Pass to the open spaces of the Mackenzie Country. It was named after the town of Fairlie in Ayrshire, Scotland, the birthplace of the first hotel owner to set up in the New Zealand Fairlie in 1865.

One legacy of the early residents is the tree-lined avenues. The colonial **Mabel Binney cottage** and **Vintage Machinery Museum** are on the main highway, just west of the town centre. There is a horse-drawn covered wagon and traction engine at the museum. A few minutes drive west of Fairlie is the historic limestone **woolshed** of the Three Springs Sheep Station, which once had space on its floor for nine blade shearers.

There is a good scenic drive of 1½ hours just out from Fairlie which takes in the spectacular Opihi Gorge. The drive takes you to Allandale, then along Middle Valley Rd and Spur Rd to Opihi, and back to Fairlie – it is 38 km in length. You can get information on Fairlie and the surrounding area from the Sunflower Centre (☎ 685 8258), 31 Main St.

There are two **skiing** areas near Fairlie. Fox Peak (☎ 685 8539), located in the Two Thumb Range north-west of Fairlie, is a club ski area which offers skiers a vertical run of 680 metres top to bottom. Mt Dobson (☎ 685 8039), also north-west (26 km) of Fairlie, is situated in a basin three km wide, accessed from the highest car park in NZ (1692 metres). Mt Cook and the Southern Alps are clearly viewed while skiing here. Daily transport is offered from the ski shop in Fairlie. For more information see the Skiing section in the Outdoor Activities chapter.

Places to Stay & Eat The *Fairlie Motor Camp* (☎ 685 8375), Allandale Rd, has tent/powered sites for $12/14, and cabins for $23 for two. One of the local hotels acts as a backpackers with cheap rates; inquire at the Sunflower Centre. The *Tallyho Backpackers* (☎ 685 8723), 7 School Rd, is close to town and bus stops; the cost is $14 per person in share rooms, or $30 for twins and doubles. There are free spas in the evening, an indoor pool and tennis court next door. The *Allandale Lodge*, 10 Allandale Rd, is predominantly a B&B place but it also has dorm beds for $10 per person in a fully equipped backpackers lodge.

The *Aorangi Motel* (☎ 685 8340), 26 Denmark St, and the *Rimuwhare Country Retreat* (☎ 685 8058), 53 Mt Cook Rd, has units for between $65 and $75 for two; there is a restaurant in the latter which is open for breakfast, lunch and dinner.

The *Sunflower Centre* serves good wholefood meals; *Fairlie Stores* and *Tom's*, both on Main St, cater for the fast food and fish & chip cravers; and the hotels have pub food.

Getting There & Around Both InterCity and Mt Cook Landline have depots in Fairlie. InterCity's depot is the BB Stop (☎ 685 8139), 81 Main St and Mt Cook Landline's (☎ 685 8311) depot is on Main St as well.

One unusual way of getting around is in a horse-drawn wagon. The horse power comes from two Clydesdales. The route follows a mountain stream to a camp site near Mackenzie Pass. The evening meal is cooked for you before you turn in to a comfortable bed in one of the wagons. Contact Fairlie Creek Waggon Company (☎ 685 8336); the cost for a two to three-hour trip is $25 per person with lunch included. An overnight trip is

$100 per adult (minimum of four) and bedding and meals are provided.

MACKENZIE COUNTRY

The high country from which the Mt Cook park rises is known as the Mackenzie country after a legendary sheep rustler, Jock Mackenzie, who is said to have run his stolen flocks in that uninhabited region around 1843. When he was finally caught other settlers realised the potential of the land and followed in his footsteps. The first people to traverse the Mackenzie were the Maori who used to trek from Banks Peninsula to Otago hundreds of years ago.

Lake Tekapo

At the southern end of Lake Tekapo the small settlement of Lake Tekapo is a popular rest stop for buses heading to or from Mt Cook or Queenstown. It derives its name from *taka* ('sleeping mat') and *po* ('night').

There's a little cluster of businesses by the main road, from where there are sweeping views across the lake with the hills and mountains as a backdrop. It is a place to avoid when the buses arrive at meal times and, fortunately, it does not take much to get away from that scene.

The turquoise colour of the lake is created by 'rock flour', which is finely ground particles of rock held in suspension in the glacial melt water.

The picturesque little **Church of the Good Shepherd** beside the lake was built of stone and oak in 1935. Further along is a statue of a collie dog, a touching tribute to the sheep dogs which made the development of the Mackenzie country possible. It is not, as a lot of people believe, the infamous dog

The Legend of Jock Mackenzie

A legend this rightly is – many subsequent investigations have only helped cloud or confuse the truth. It is thought that James (Jock) Mackenzie was born in 1820 in Scotland. In his short time in this country (date of arrival unknown), possibly only two years, he achieved great notoriety. In March 1855 he was caught near present-day Mackenzie Pass in possession of 1000 sheep which had been stolen from the Levels run, north-west of Timaru.

It was believed at the time that he had stolen the sheep to stock a run he had purchased in Otago, and that he was aided only by his remarkable dog, Friday. He was captured near the pass by the Levels overseer and two Maori shepherds. He escaped and made his way to Lyttleton where, while hiding in a loft, he was recaptured by a police sergeant. He was then tried for sheep stealing and sentenced to five years' imprisonment. Throughout the trial Mackenzie had pleaded not guilty and nine months after the trial was granted a pardon. He had escaped from prison three times, it is reputed, during his nine-month incarceration, always proclaiming his innocence. Even the then Superintendent of Canterbury, James Fitzgerald, added: 'I am inclined to believe his story'. Popular myth has it that he was then ordered to leave the country, but there is no evidence to back this up.

Lyttleton's town clock now covers the foundations of the gaol that once held Mackenzie; he was interned here after the only Supreme Court trial ever held in the town. It is believed by some that James Mackenzie's 'treasure' – well, his savings anyway – are concealed in a bush near Edendale, 39 km north of Invercargill. He supposedly selected the bush as it was tapu to the local Maoris. As legend has it, Mackenzie was only pardoned on the condition that he leave New Zealand for ever – so he never returned to pick up his savings.

If you're heading to Timaru via Mackenzie Pass you will see a monument erected near the spot where Mackenzie was apprehended, although no one really knows the exact spot. The pass is said to be named after Mackenzie as the discoverer, but it is now believed that it had appeared on an earlier map in the late 1840s. Similarly there is no proof that he had ever purchased land in Otago to stock with either stolen or bought sheep. Little is known of his later life, and the date of his death is a mystery. ■

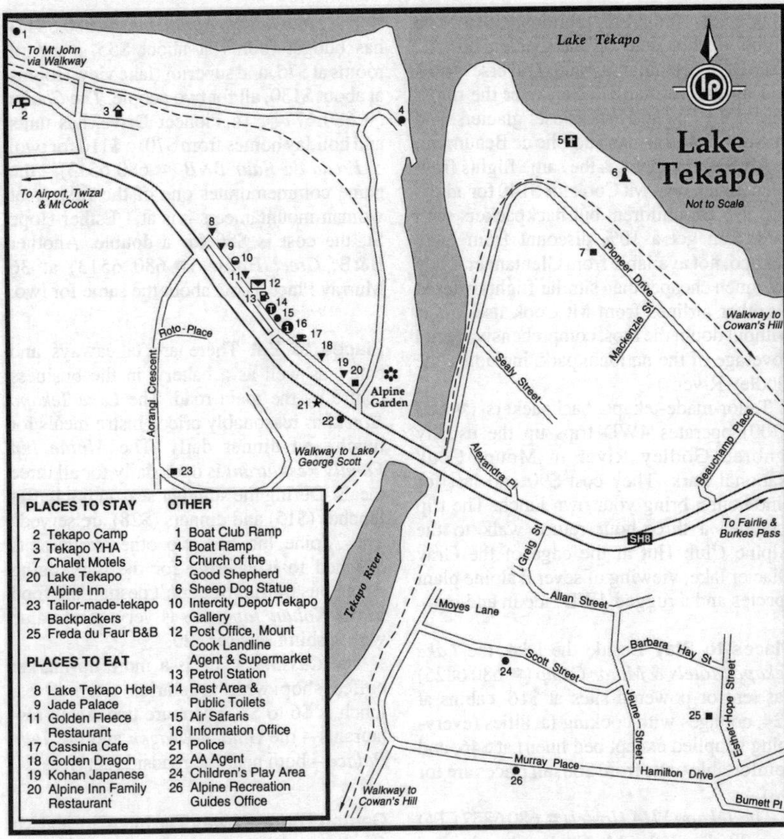

Friday of James Mackenzie. Again, walk down here when the last bus departs. It is a peaceful place and probably just as its founders intended. If they build an information centre they must keep it well away from the Church of the Good Shepherd.

Other popular activities around Lake Tekapo include fishing, boating, kayaking and bicycle touring, horse trekking and hang-gliding. In winter, Lake Tekapo is the base for downhill skiing at Mt Dobson, or cross-country skiing on Two Thumb Range. There's ski area transport and ski hire in season. Lake Tekapo also has an open-air ice skating rink which is open from June to September from 10 am to 10 pm; skate hire is $5 and the rink fee is $5.

There are a number of good **walks** in the region. It's an hour's walk to the top of Mt John and you can continue on to lakes Alexandrina and McGregor, an all day walk. Other walks are along the eastern side of the lake to the ski area road: the one-hour return walk to the Tekapo Lookout and 1½ hours to the power station.

Tours Air Safaris (☎ 680 6880) operates flights from Lake Tekapo over Mt Cook and its glaciers for $135 (children $90). The flights do not land on the glacier, but Air Safari's spectacular 'Grand Traverse' takes you up the Tasman Glacier, over the upper part of the Fox and Franz Josef glaciers, and by Mts Cook, Tasman and Elie de Beaumont.

Air Safaris operates the same flights from Glentanner, near Mt Cook for $140 for adults and $95 for children, but backpackers with cards can get a 10% discount from Lake Tekapo, not available from Glentanner. They are much cheaper than similar flights offered by other airlines from Mt Cook itself. It is without doubt the most comprehensive aerial coverage of the national park, including the Godley River.

Tailor-made-tekapo backpackers (☎ 680 6700) operates 4WD trips up the usually ignored Godley River in Mount Cook National Park. They cost $90 and last for nine hours; bring your own lunch. The trip includes a three-hour return walk to the Alpine Club Hut at the edge of the Gray Glacier lake, viewing of several alpine plant species and a rugged 4WD ride in and out.

Places to Stay Beside the lake, the *Lake Tekapo Motels & Motor Camp* (☎ 680 6825) has tent or powered sites at $16, cabins at $24, cottages with cooking facilities (everything supplied except bed linen) at $46, and comfortable units from $68; all prices are for two.

The *Tekapo YHA Hostel* (☎ 680 6857), PO Box 38, is on the Mt Cook side of town, beyond the post office and shops, down towards the water. It's a well-equipped, friendly little hostel with great views across the lake to the mountains beyond. It's open all day and the dorm cost is $14 per person, twins are $32 or there are limited tent sites beside it for about $7.50 per person.

Wilma and Michael, who advertise themselves as 'can do' people, run *tailor-made-tekapo backpackers* (☎ 680 6700) where their rooms all cost $15 per person (duvets are supplied). It has full kitchen facilities, a laundry and, importantly, caring owners. It is in Aorangi Crescent, not far from the highway where all the buses stop.

The *Lake Tekapo Alpine Inn* (☎ 680 6848) has budget rooms at about $55, standard rooms at $75, and superior (lake view) rooms at about $130, all for two people. *The Chalet* (☎ 680 6774), 14 Pioneer Drive, has units and holiday homes from $70 to $110 for two.

Freda du Faur B&B (☎ 680 6513) – the name commemorates one of the first great woman mountaineers – is at 1 Esther Hope St; the cost is $80 for a double. Another B&B, *Creel House* (☎ 680 6513) at 36 Murray Place, costs about the same for two.

Places to Eat There are takeaways and cafes, as well as a bakery, in the business centre by the main road. The *Lake Tekapo Hotel* has reasonably priced bistro meals for lunch and dinner daily. The *Alpine Inn Family Restaurant* is open daily for all three meals. During the summer season hot buffet lunches ($15) and dinners ($28) are served. The Alpine Inn has two other restaurants attached to it catering for the burgeoning Asian bus traffic. But don't despair the food in the *Kohan Japanese* is very good value with sashimi sets for $20.

The *Cassinia Cafe* is a more up-market coffee shop with vegetarian alternatives; lunch is $6 to $8. There are two Asian restaurants – the *Golden Dragon* and the *Jade Palace* – both near the roadside services.

Getting There & Away The InterCity and Mt Cook Landline southbound services to Queenstown, Wanaka and Mt Cook come through every day, as do the northbound services to Christchurch. The InterCity (☎ 680 6870) depot is at the Tekapo Gallery on Main St and the Mount Cook Landline agent is Tekapo Services (☎ 680 6809).

Nationwide, Catch-a-Bus, Southern Link, Kiwi Discovery (takes bikes for free) and Atomic Shuttles include Lake Tekapo on their route; it is $25 to Christchurch and $25 to Queenstown. All shuttles pick up at the Kiwi Treasures Craft Shop, tailor-made-tekapo backpackers or the YHA.

Hitching in or out of Lake Tekapo can sometimes be difficult as there is not much traffic; but once you've got a ride it will probably be going a fair way.

Twizel

Slightly south of Lake Pukaki, Twizel (population 2000) is a convenient base for the surrounding area. By car it's only about 30 minutes from Mt Cook. Nearby Lake Ruataniwha has an international rowing centre, fishing, boating and windsurfing. In the Ben Ohau ranges there is heli-skiing in winter. And there's a huge hydroelectric power station; you can arrange a free tour at the town's information centre.

There is a black stilt captive breeding centre near Twizel. The black stilt is the rarest wader species in the world (see the Flora & Fauna section).

Information The Twizel Information & Display Centre (☎ 435 0802; fax 435 0852) on Wairepo Rd is open from 9 am to 4 pm on weekdays and 10 am to 3 pm on the weekends. It also houses the DOC and is the headquarters of the very important black stilt breeding programme. Informative tours to the black stilt hide leave from here at 10.30 am and 2 pm on weekdays and 3 pm on weekends; the cost is $5 for adults (children $1, the minimum charge for a tour is $10).

Places to Stay The *High Country Holiday Lodge* (☎ 435 0671), formerly Basil's, has all sorts of accommodation starting with hostel-style bunks (only two beds to a room, though) at $12 per person, and singles/doubles and twins at $27/39. Linen is provided in all rooms except the backpackers. Another cheap alternative is *Mountain Chalets* (☎ 435 0785), Wairepo Rd; twin rooms in the 12-person lodge are $13 per person. This is a very comfortable place and would work out cheaply for a group. The lodge is in an A-frame building and kitchen facilities, lounge area with TV and bathrooms are available. Separate motel units (in the A-frame style) are $75 per double; an extra adult is $14.

The *Colonial Motels* (☎ 435 0100), on Mackenzie Drive near the service station, have been recommended. At the edge of town the *MacKenzie Country Inn* (☎ 435 0869) has rooms at $110 a double. Right beside the lake, four km out of town, the *Ruataniwha Motor Camp* (☎ 435 0613) has powered sites at $17 for two and cheap, although fairly basic, cabins at $12.50 per person.

Glenbrook Station (☎ 438 9407) is a high-country sheep station between Twizel and Omarama on SH8, eight km south of Twizel and 22 km north of Omarama. Dinner, bed and breakfast is $96/152 for singles/doubles, but there are also some budget beds available in a bunkhouse ($14 per person). It's an interesting place to stay, with horse riding, cross-country trail riding and bush walks.

There's homestead accommodation on the 72-sq-km *Rhoborough Downs Sheep Station*, 15 km from Twizel near the SH8 and SH80 junction. There's just one twin room and one double room, and the rate, including breakfast and dinner, is $120 for two.

There's a *DOC camping ground* in Temple Forest, Lake Ohau Rd, 50 km west of Twizel.

Places to Eat The plain *Black Stilt Cafe* offers takeaways, burgers at $3.50 to $5, cooked breakfast at $7 and meals at around $10. Also in the shopping centre, the *Lunch Box* has takeaways and outdoor tables. The *Hunter's Bar & Cafe*, 2 Market Place, is open from 11 am until late and has a blackboard menu in the evening from 6 pm.

At 13 Tasman Rd is the *Top Hut*, a cafe and bar which is open daily from 10 am; there is a sit-down bistro and also takeaways. For higher class dining there's the restaurant at the *Mackenzie Country Inn*, which also serves less expensive bistro meals; it is open for breakfast, and for dinner from 6.30 to 9 pm.

Getting There & Away The InterCity and Mt Cook Landline buses serving Mt Cook all stop at Twizel, with additional buses shuttling between Twizel and Mt Cook; it's about a 50-minute bus ride. The Mount Cook depot is at the High Country Holiday Inn.

Lake Ohau & Ohau Forest

There are six forests in the Lake Ohau area – Dobson, Hopkins, Huxley, Temple, Ohau and Ahuriri, all administered by the DOC. The walks in this vast area are too numerous to mention but you will find them outlined in the DOC pamphlet *Ohau Forests Recreation Guide*. There are many huts scattered throughout the region for the more adventurous trampers.

The less adventurous can stay in the *Lake Ohau Lodge* (☎ 438 9885) on the western shore of Lake Ohau. Powered camp sites cost $14 for two, beds in the Huxley wing are $15 per person, doubles in the Maitland wing are $52 and in the Temple wing $68; there is a tennis court for guests. The Temple wing has views of the lake and mountains. This is a great base for tramping.

MT COOK NATIONAL PARK

Mt Cook National Park, along with Fiordland, Aspiring and Westland national parks, has been incorporated into a World Heritage area which extends from the Cook River in Westland down to the base of Fiordland. The Mt Cook National Park is 700 sq km in size and one of the most spectacular parks in a country famous for its parks. Encompassed by the main divide, the Two Thumb, Liebig and Ben Ohau ranges, more than one third of the park is in permanent snow and glacial ice.

Of the 27 New Zealand mountains over 3050 metres, 22 are in this park including the mighty Mt Cook – at 3755 metres the highest peak in New Zealand and Australasia.

Known to the Maori as Aoraki, after a deity from Maori mythology, the tent-shaped Mt Cook was named after Captain James Cook by Captain Stokes of the survey ship HMS *Acheron*. It was first climbed on Christmas Day 1894 (by local mountaineers Jack Clarke, Tom Fyfe and George Graham) and many famous climbers, including Sir Edmund Hillary, have sharpened their skills on this formidable peak. Dominating the park, it is the centrepiece of the vista from the Hermitage.

In the early hours of 14 December 1991, a substantial piece of the east face (around 14 million cubic metres) fell away in a massive landslide. Debris spewed out over the surrounding glaciers for 7.3 kilometres, following a path down the Grand Plateau and Hochstetter Icefall and reaching as far as the Tasman Glacier.

Information

The National Park Visitor Centre (☎ 435 1818; fax 435 1895), open daily from 8 am to 5 pm (extended to 7 pm in summer), will advise you on what guided tours are available and on tramping routes. For information before you arrive write to: The Field Centre Manager, PO Box 5, Mt Cook. They screen a dated but excellent audiovisual on the history, mountaineering and human occupation in the Mt Cook region at 8.30 and 10.30 am and 1.30 and 3.30 pm; the cost is $2.

A post office and general store are not far from the visitor centre. Travellers' cheques can be cashed at the Hermitage or, if in NZ dollars, at the visitor centre.

The Alpine Guides Mountain Shop (☎ 435 1834) sells equipment for skiing and mountaineering, or you can rent a variety of equipment including boots, parkas, ice axes, crampons, packs, rain pants, day packs and gaiters. Importantly, the staff guide over the Copland Pass (see Copland Pass Route in this section). The shop is open daily from 8 am to 5.30 pm (extended hours in summer).

The best introduction to this park is the beautifully illustrated *The Alpine World of Mount Cook National Park* by Andy Dennis and Craig Potton. It has details of flora & fauna, walks and the park's history ($16).

The Hermitage

Skiing on the Tasman Glacier, and the crossing to Westland via the Copland Pass Track are two of the energetic attractions of the park, but one of the park's chief attractions is rather more sedentary. The Hermitage is the most famous hotel in New Zealand – principally for its location and the fantastic views out to Mt Cook. Originally constructed in 1884, when the trip up here from Christchurch took several days, the first hotel was destroyed in a flash flood in 1913.

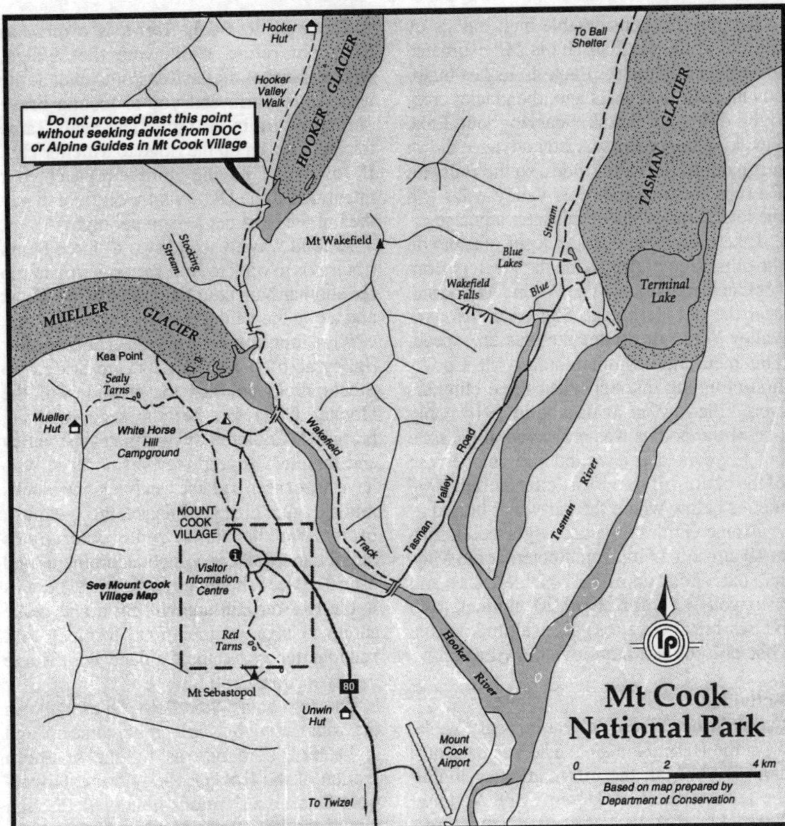

You can see the foundations about a km from the current Hermitage. Rebuilt, it survived until 1957 when it totally burnt out; the present Hermitage was built on the same site.

Even if your budget is not up to staying here, make sure you come in for a beer so you can relax and look out the huge windows straight up to Mt Cook.

Tasman Glacier

Higher up, the Tasman Glacier is a spectacular sweep of ice just like a glacier should be, but further down it's ugly. Glaciers in New Zealand (and elsewhere in the world) have generally been retreating all this century, although they are advancing now. Normally as a glacier retreats it melts back up the mountain, but the Tasman is unusual because its last few km are almost horizontal. In the process of melting over the last 75-or-so years it has contracted vertically rather than horizontally: the stones, rocks and boulders it carried down the mountain are left on top as the ice around them melts. So the Tasman in its 'ablation zone' (the region it melts in) is covered in a more or less solid mass of debris – which slows down its melting rate and makes it look pretty unpleasant.

Despite this considerable melt the ice by the site of the old Ball Hut is still estimated to be over 600 metres thick. In its last major advance, 17,000 years ago, the glacier crept right down to Pukaki, carving out Lake Pukaki in the process. A later advance didn't reach out to the valley sides, so the Ball Hut Rd runs between the outer valley walls and the lateral moraines of this later advance.

Like the Fox and Franz Josef glaciers on the other side of the divide the glaciers from Mt Cook move fast. The Alpine Memorial, near the old Hermitage Site on the Hooker Valley Walk, illustrates the glaciers' speed. The memorial commemorates Mt Cook's first climbing disaster when three climbers were killed by an avalanche in 1914. Only one of the bodies was recovered at the time but 12 years later a second body melted out of the bottom of the Hochstetter Icefall, 2000 metres below where the party was buried.

Alpine Guides organises sightseeing trips at 10 am and 2 pm, from September to May. Its coach goes up as far as Blue Lakes and then you walk for about 20 minutes (500 metres, but 100 metres gain in altitude) to the Glacier Lookout; inquire in the village.

Activities

Valley Walks There are various easy walks from the Hermitage area. The visitor centre can give you all the information including the leaflet *Walks in Mount Cook National Park* ($1) that lists the main attractions, describes the degree of difficulty and tells you about the flora & fauna in the area. If you're there in the summer keep a look out for the large mountain buttercup, often called the Mt Cook lily. There are also mountain daisies, gentians and edelweiss. Among the animals you may see are the thar, a goat-like mammal and excellent climber; the chamois, smaller and of lighter build than the thar but an agile climber; and red deer.

The trail to **Kea Point** is an easy two to three-hour (return) walk with much native plant life and fine views of Cook, the Hooker Valley and the ice faces of Mt Sefton and the Footstool. You will probably see several cheeky keas on this walk.

The walk to **Sealy Tarns** is a three to four-hour return walk from the village, which branches off the Kea Point track. If the weather is warm and you're feeling brave you can swim in the tarns. The Sealy Tarns track continues up the ridge to Mueller Hut. If you intend staying up here register your intentions at the DOC visitor centre and pay the hut fee ($14 per person per night).

A good way to spend two to three hours (return) is to walk to **Red Tarns**. If you climb for another half-hour the views of Mt Cook and along the valley are spectacular.

It is a four-hour return walk up the **Hooker Valley** across a couple of swing bridges to Stocking Stream and the terminus of the Hooker Glacier. After the second swing bridge Mt Cook totally dominates the valley and there are superb views. For those who have never seen a glacier 'calving' ice blocks into the azure blue glacial lake, this is a must. From here the alpine route deteriorates rapidly and walkers without equipment (and sound advice) should go no further. Hut fees in the Hooker Hut are $14 per night; make sure you sign an intentions form at park headquarters. (See the Copland Pass Route in this section.)

The two-hour **Wakefield Track** follows the route used by early mountaineers and sightseers, then returns by the southern section of the Hooker Valley track. **Governors Bush** is a short one-hour walk through one of the last stands of silver beech in the park. A brochure on the native plants found in Governors Bush is available at the visitor centre.

Shorter walks include the 10-minute **Bowen Bush Walk** through a small patch of totara trees near the Alpine Guides shop. The 15-minute **Glencoe Walk**, beginning from the rear of the Hermitage, ascends through totara forest to a lookout point facing Mt Cook and the Hooker Valley.

A number of short tracks branch off from the **Tasman Valley Rd** including a track to view the Wakefield Falls, another to overlook the five Blue Lakes, and various tracks providing viewpoints of the Tasman Glacier. All are signposted from the road.

Copland Pass Route This well-known three to four-day route crosses from the Hermitage right over the Southern Alps and down to the West Coast road (SH6), 26 km south of Fox Glacier. The crossing is only for those with alpine experience in ice or snow and with the right equipment. Once over the pass, however, the descent down to the road past the Douglas Rock and Welcome Flat huts is not too difficult. The hot springs near Welcome Flat Hut is the highlight for many.

The most favourable time of year to attempt the Copland Pass Route is from early December to mid-March, although the crossing is always dependent on weather and snow conditions.

On no account attempt this route before checking with Alpine Guides or at the DOC headquarters, where you *must* register your intentions. Heed their advice carefully, especially if they tell you that they feel you are not suitably equipped or that you lack the necessary experience – this route is not one to take lightly as it has killed many people!

If you do not have the equipment and experience, it is possible to hire a guide who will take your party up and over the pass and then leave you to follow the trail down to the West Coast. With Alpine Guides in Mt Cook this costs $400 for a one-person party, $500 for two people, $600 for three. Estimated walking times are as follows:

Hermitage to Hooker Hut	half a day
Hooker Hut over the Copland to Douglas Rock Hut	full day (10 hours)
Douglas Rock to Welcome Flat Hut	three hours
Welcome Flat to SH6	six hours

Guided Walks Alpine Recreation Canterbury (☎ 680 6736) offer two high altitude guided walks in the area. The Ball Pass trip is a two to three-day crossing over Ball Pass (2130 metres) from the Tasman to the Hooker valleys; it allows you to get close to Mt Cook without requiring mountaineering experience (with a group of six to eight people it would cost $400 each). The Mackenzie High Country walk is an easy three-day trip through alpine tussock country (with a group of four it is $245 per person).

Mountaineering There is unlimited scope here for climbing for the experienced, but beware, there have been over 170 people killed in climbing accidents in the park, with an average of five deaths each year! The Copland Pass Route is a particularly problematic track, as it is well known and is too often attempted by people who are not sufficiently experienced to handle it safely.

The highly changeable weather is an important factor around here – Mt Cook is only 44 km from the Tasman coast, catching the weather conditions blowing in over the Tasman Sea. The weather can change abruptly and you can suddenly find yourself in a storm. Unless you are experienced in such conditions, don't attempt to climb anywhere without a guide.

It's important to check with the park rangers before attempting any climb, and not only to check with them, but to heed their advice! Fill in a climber's intentions card before starting out on any climb, so they can check on you if you are overdue coming out.

Alpine Guides has ski-touring and mountaineering courses but they are costly; they also provide guides for the Copland (see Mountaineering in the Outdoor Activities chapter).

Heli-Skiing & Heli-Hiking A smaller guiding operation is Charlie Hobb's Southern Alps Guiding Mt Cook (☎ 435 1890) that runs winter ski-touring trips and ski-mountaineering courses. The specialty is heli-skiing. Day-trips on the Tasman Glacier are $395 (two skiplane flights) and 3000 metres of vertical in the Ben Ohaus will cost $550 (lunch is thrown in). An overnight ski adventure on the Tasman is $550, with two skiplane flights provided.

A really interesting combination is the heli-hike. The cost of $180 includes two helicopter flights over the superb Ben Ohaus with great views out over the Southern Alps. Included is a two-hour walk downhill on snow, a good introduction to this spectacular alpine environment.

Tours

Aerial Sightseeing The skies above Mt Cook are alive with the sound of aircraft. This is almost the antipodean equivalent of the Grand Canyon in the USA. The views are superb and glacier landings are a great experience – a must on any NZ adventure.

Air trips are operated by Mt Cook Airlines from Mt Cook, or by Air Safaris from Lake Tekapo (see Lake Tekapo in this chapter) and Glentanner, and The Helicopter Line from Glentanner. Backpackers get a 10% discount on the Air Safaris flights if taken from Lake Tekapo, a saving not offered from Glentanner.

The Mt Cook skiplane landing flights are the most expensive but still worthwhile. The 30-minute Skiplane flight is $143; the 40-minute Glacier Highlights flight is $199; and a 55-minute Grand Circle flight is $283.

The Helicopter Line (☎ 435 1801) has a 30-minute Trans-Glacier flight at $120; an exhilarating 30-minute flight over the Richardson Glacier with a landing at $200; and a 45-minute Mountains High flight over the Tasman Glacier and by Mt Cook with a glacier landing for $275. These flights depart from Glentanner Park.

Air Safaris flights are great value although they do not actually land on the glacier. Air Safaris' Grand Traverse takes you up the Tasman Glacier, over the upper part of the Fox and Franz Josef glaciers, by Mt Cook and Mt Tasman and generally gives you your fill of mountain scenery (see the Lake Tekapo section in this chapter).

Glacier Helicopters (☎ 435 0268) fly from Twizel; the 50-minute flight is $273.

Land Tours The interesting (but at $24, rather expensive) two-hour Tasman Glacier Guided Coach Tour is operated two or three times a day in season – check at the Hermitage about bookings and tour times. The rocky road follows the lateral moraines of the Tasman Glacier and the bus stops several times to see this mighty river of ice. Part of the tour involves an optional 15-minute walk to view the glacier.

If you actually want to boat on a glacial lake then contact the Hermitage booking desk. You go out in a small motorised inflatable with about six people. You can see the glacier calving into the water; trips are over two hours and cost $65 (children $30).

From Glentanner (☎ 435 1855) you can go on horse treks over this high-country station from $25 for half an hour to $120 for three hours. There are 4WD trips for $25 per person ($15 for children), lasting about 90 minutes, which climb up to the highest point of the station at about 1500 metres. You can also do guided fishing safaris with the quarry being brown and rainbow trout; these are quite expensive costing $200 for a half day or $350 for a full day.

Another good 4WD trip is Alan's Tasman Glacier Tours (☎ 435 1809) where it is guaranteed that all '...will rub knees, shoulders and bums' as the vehicle climbs up to Husky Flat above the glacier. Here, the driver points out interesting alpine flora. The cost of this 2½-hour trip is $55.

Places to Stay

Camping is allowed at the White Horse Hill *camping ground* at the old Hermitage site, the starting point for the Hooker Valley track, 1.8 km from Mt Cook Village. There's running water and toilets but no electricity, showers or other luxuries you find at motor camps. It's run by the DOC on a first-come, first-served basis (no advance bookings) and the cost is $3 per night for each adult (children $1). For more information contact the visitor centre.

The nearest motor camp to the park is 23 km down the valley on the shores of Lake Pukaki at *Glentanner Park* (☎ 435 1855). Facilities are good and powered sites are $13 for two, on-site vans at $12 per person, basic cabins are $30 and deluxe cabins $55 for two. There is a restaurant but no longer a store at the park. You can still buy milk, bread and basics at the restaurant from 8 am to 9 pm. Otherwise you have to head up to Mt Cook Village. There is a booking service in the complex for Air Safaris, The Helicopter Line, and Glentanner 4WD Tours & Safaris.

About 3.5 km before the village is the NZ Alpine Club's *Unwin Hut* (☎ 435 1890). Members get preference but there are usually beds or bed space available for intrepid travellers who wish to meet spider-person ascensionists. It's basic bunk accommodation but there is a big common room with open fireplace, showers, well-equipped kitchen and excellent views up the Tasman Glacier to the Minarets and Elie de Beaumont and also of the Hooker Glacier. Feel privileged and stay here for a mere $15 per person!

The excellent *Mt Cook YHA Hostel* (☎ 435 1820), on the corner of Bowen and Kitchener Drives, sadly often suffers from indifferent service. Nevertheless it can still get crowded in the high season, from December to April, so try to book at least four days in advance. It's well equipped, with a sauna, BBQ, and disabled facilities. It's also conveniently located and is open all day. The cost in dorm rooms is $18 per person, and twins/doubles are $42/50.

Apart from the YHA all accommodation in the village itself is booked by phoning ☎ 435 1809. At the bottom of the price range are the *Mt Cook Chalets* which cost $107 for up to four persons. It has two mini bedrooms and a fold-out double sofabed, so between four it can be reasonably economical. Well-equipped kitchens and a dining table add to the convenience. It may be closed in the winter season though.

Above this, the prices become expensive. The *Travelodge (Mt Cook)*, open only during the summer season from September to April, costs $186 for doubles; the rooms have no cooking facilities but the price includes breakfast. The *Hermitage* has prices and services in line with its fame – from about $214 to $290 for a double or twin.

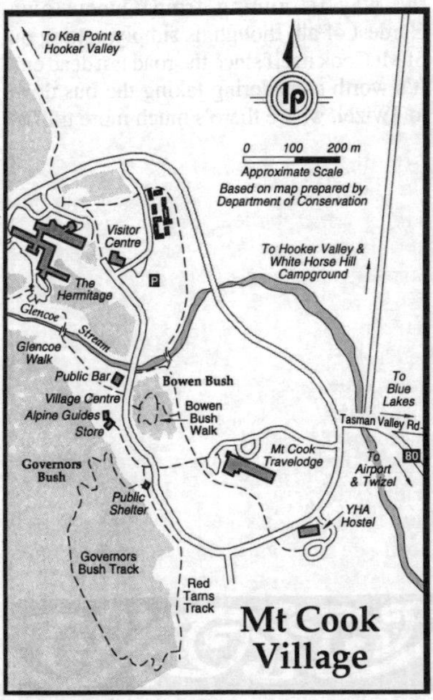

Places to Eat

The only way to eat economically at Mt Cook is to prepare your own food or voluntarily fast. There's a small, but well-stocked, store and prices aren't too out of line, although you'll save a bit by bringing food up with you. There is a *cafe* at Glentanner and a little *coffee shop* at the Mt Cook airport.

Otherwise you have three choices at the Hermitage and one at the Travelodge. The Hermitage base line is the *coffee shop* which is usually open from 9 am to 5 pm but sometimes closes earlier. It does very unexciting sandwiches and pies. Then there is the *Alpine Room* where main courses are around $15 to $19 (but if you want vegetables or a salad, then expect to pay a few dollars extra) and desserts are around $6. For breakfast and lunch the Alpine Room does buffets – $17 for breakfast, $25 for lunch. A la carte prices are $8.50 for appetisers, mains from $19 to $25 and desserts for $7.50. The *Travelodge (Mt Cook)* has a similarly priced restaurant but it's open only for dinner in the evening.

Finally, there's the Hermitage's *Panorama Room* where two people can spend well over $100 but the surroundings and the view must be amongst the best in the world – Sefton to your left, Cook in the centre and the Ben Ohau's, brown dark and forbidding to your right.

For entertainment, there's a *village tavern* where you can drink, sit around and talk, or rave at the occasional disco held here on Friday nights during the busy season. The Hermitage sometimes has a pianist. On magical moonlit nights wander out and look upwards to your majestic mountain voyeurs.

Getting There & Away

Air Mt Cook Airlines (☎ 435 1848) has daily direct flights to/from Queenstown and Christchurch, with connections to other centres. At certain times of the year it also has daily flights to/from Te Anau. Mt Cook provides bus services to and from the airport.

There's no scheduled air service to Fox or Franz Josef but you can fly over one way if you like. It's a way of combining transport with a scenic flight and means you can avoid the difficult Haast route if hitching. But you can't rely on the weather and may get held up at Mt Cook for quite a while waiting for suitable conditions to get across.

Bus Mt Cook Landline (☎ 435 1849) has daily buses to Queenstown, Te Anau and Christchurch. Most of the services connect with the longer routes through Twizel, 70 km (a 45-minute drive) from Mt Cook. There are year round daily buses, but in summer extra, more direct services are added, making travel time quicker. From November to April special excursion buses are run between Christchurch and Queenstown, and day trips out of Christchurch, allowing time at Mt Cook to take a scenic flight.

InterCity also has a daily Queenstown-Christchurch route with a one-hour stop at Mt Cook. The InterCity buses stop at the Youth Hostel and at the Hermitage. Mount Cook Landline buses stop at the Hermitage.

Hitching Hitching is hard – expect long waits once you leave SH1, if coming from Christchurch or Dunedin, and long waits all the way if coming from Queenstown. Hardest of all, though, is simply getting out of Mt Cook itself since the road is a dead end. It's worth considering taking the bus down to Twizel, where there's much more traffic.

Otago

Otago has come of age. A number of pearls have developed in this once hoary oyster – Queenstown and Wanaka and their adrenaline activities, and the Otago Peninsula, which is New Zealand's first real foray into ecotourism. Otago is a must for any visitor to New Zealand. Dunedin, the capital of the region, is a town of great surprises – its architecture, nightlife, band scene and eco-activities should not be missed.

There are several sides to this fascinating region and none more interesting than the history of the gold rushes. Many aspects of the region's geography hark back to an era of prosperity when the rivers and creeks swarmed with prospectors in search of gold.

As Otago occupies a central position in the South Island it can be approached from a number of directions. The main route is SH1 from Christchurch to Dunedin along the east coast. From Southland you can approach Otago via the southern scenic route, through the Catlins or via SH1 from Invercargill. The most scenic way, however, is via the West Coast (SH6) and across Haast Pass.

HIGHLIGHTS

- Pristine Lake Wanaka and surrounds offer myriad activities on water, land and in the air
- Queenstown and Lake Wakatipu – the hub of the South Island's adventure activities
- Glenorchy, the Rees-Dart & Routeburn tracks – a must for all serious adventurers in spectacular mountain scenery
- Skiing in any of the ranges near Queenstown (The Remarkables and Coronet Peak), Wanaka (Treble Cone) and Cardrona
- The historic towns of the Manuherikia and Maniototo valleys and the goldfields of Central Otago
- Dunedin – an architecturally rich city with plenty of activities and the best nightlife in the South Island
- The Otago Peninsula – a rich ecotourist destination with the chance to see albatross, rare penguins, and sea lions

Dunedin & the Otago Peninsula

Otago Harbour, a long fiord-like inlet, has become the hub for many ecotourism activities, especially on the Otago Peninsula and in nearby coastal areas. The fauna-rich peninsula is close to Otago's main centre – Dunedin, a quaint city with a great many historic buildings and a convenient base for trips further afield to Central Otago and the Catlins.

DUNEDIN

Dunedin is predominantly a student town and there are about 12,000 attending the tertiary institutions here; this represents about 10% of Dunedin's population of 113,680. The local entertainment scene, cafe and pub life, and arts are a consequence of this. Another very evident feature is Dunedin's distinct Scottishness – not surprising considering the name is Celtic for Edinburgh. It's a solid, no nonsense sort of place – second city of the South Island, home of NZ's first university and at one time (during the gold rush days) the largest city in the country.

As mentioned earlier there are many historic buildings in this town and careful efforts have been made to preserve its architectural heritage.

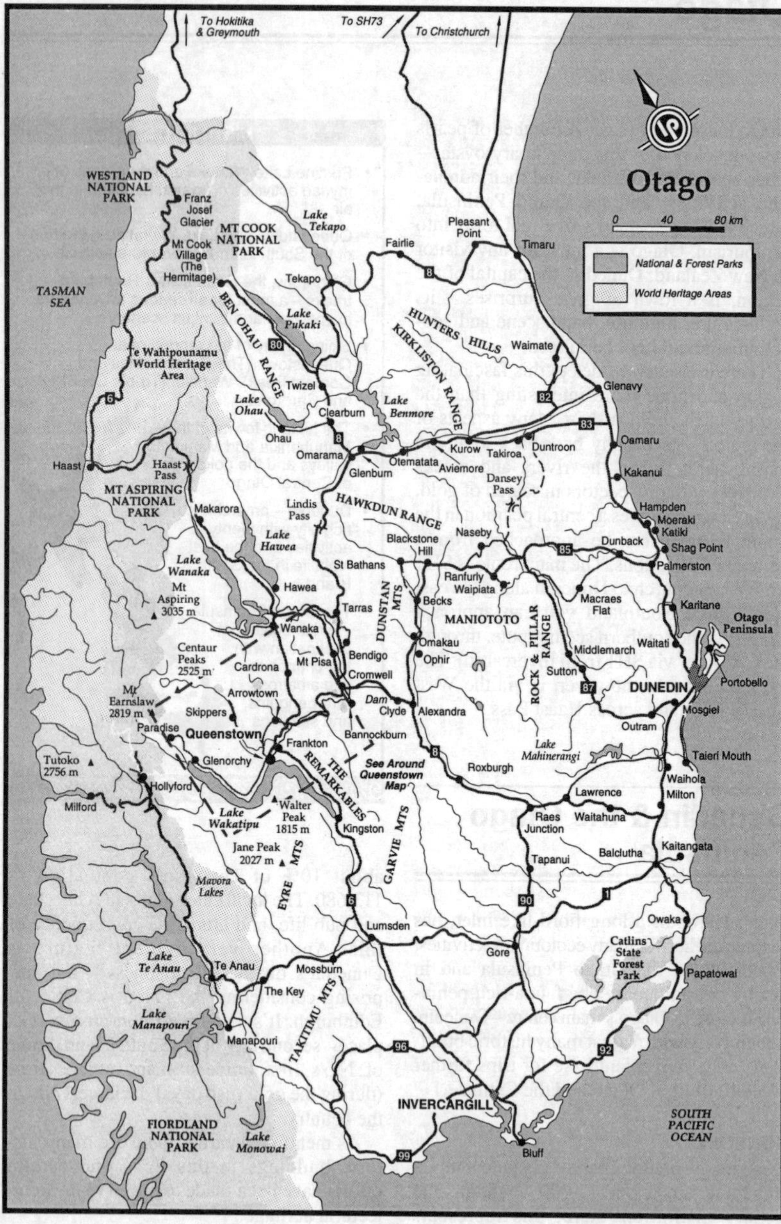
Otago
0
40
80 km
National & Forest Parks
World Heritage Areas
To Hokitika & Greymouth
To SH73
To Christchurch
WESTLAND NATIONAL PARK
Franz Josef Glacier
MT COOK NATIONAL PARK
Mt Cook Village (The Hermitage)
Lake Tekapo
Tekapo
Fairlie
Pleasant Point
Timaru
TASMAN SEA
BEN OHAU RANGE
Lake Pukaki
HUNTERS HILLS
KIRKLISTON RANGE
Waimate
Te Wahipounamu World Heritage Area
Twizel
Lake Ohau
Clearburn
Lake Benmore
Glenavy
Ohau
Omarama
Otematata
Kurow
Takiroa
Duntroon
Oamaru
Haast
Haast Pass
Glenburn
Aviemore
Dansey Pass
Kakanui
MT ASPIRING NATIONAL PARK
Makarora
Lindis Pass
HAWKDUN RANGE
Hampden
Moeraki
Katiki
Naseby
Lake Hawea
Blackstone Hill
Dunback
Shag Point
Lake Wanaka
St Bathans
Ranfurly
Palmerston
Hawea
Waipiata
Mt Aspiring 3035 m
DUNSTAN MTS
Becks
Macraes Flat
Karitane
Tarras
MANIOTOTO
ROCK & PILLAR RANGE
Otago Peninsula
Wanaka
Waitati
Centaur Peaks 2525 m
Omakau
Middlemarch
Ophir
Bendigo
Cardrona
Mt Pisa
Sutton
Portobello
Cromwell
DUNEDIN
Mt Earnslaw 2819 m
Arrowtown
Dam
Mosgiel
Skippers
Clyde
Alexandra
Outram
Paradise
Queenstown
Bannockburn
Frankton
Tutoko 2756 m
Glenorchy
THE REMARKABLES
See Around Queenstown Map
Lake Mahinerangi
Taieri Mouth
Roxburgh
Hollyford
Waihola
Milford
Walter Peak 1815 m
Lawrence
Milton
Lake Wakatipu
Raes Junction
Waitahuna
Kingston
GARVIE MTS
Jane Peak 2027 m
EYRE MTS
Balclutha
Kaitangata
Tapanui
Mavora Lakes
Owaka
Lumsden
Catlins State Forest Park
Gore
Lake Te Anau
Te Anau
Mossburn
Papatowai
The Key
TAKITIMU MTS
Lake Manapouri
Manapouri
INVERCARGILL
SOUTH PACIFIC OCEAN
FIORDLAND NATIONAL PARK
Lake Monowai
Bluff
6
8
80
82
83
85
87
90
1
92
96
99

History

The early Maori history of the Dunedin area was particularly bloody, with a three-way feud between tribes occupying the Otago Peninsula. *Utu* (revenge) followed attack as the feud between the Ngai Tahu and the Ngatimamoe tribes escalated at the end of the 1800s. With the advent of sealing and whaling along the coast the Maori population was ravaged by disease. By 1848 the once considerable population of Otakau Pa was just over 100.

The first permanent European settlers arrived at Port Chalmers in March 1848, six years after the plan for a Presbyterian settlement on the east coast of the South Island was initially mooted. Not long after the settlers' arrival in Dunedin, gold was discovered in Otago and the province quickly became the richest and most influential in the colony. In 1879 it was the first city outside the USA to have its own tram system, and this remained working until the last one was phased out in 1957.

Orientation & Information

The eight-sided Octagon – really more of a circle – marks the centre of Dunedin. The main street runs through it, changing name from Princes St on the southern side to George St on the northern side.

The well-organised and extremely helpful Dunedin Visitor Centre (☎ 474 3300; fax 474 3311) is at 48 The Octagon, in the magnificently restored municipal chambers. It's open from 8.30 am to 5 pm on weekdays and from 9 am to 5 pm on weekends, with extended hours in summer. As well as providing a great deal of information and advice, the centre takes bookings for tours.

The DOC Shop (☎ 477 0677), at 77 Lower Stuart St, has pamphlets and information on walking tracks. The AA (☎ 477 5945), at 450 Moray Place just east of Princes St, is open from 8.30 am to 5 pm, Monday to Friday.

The informative, free *Focus on Dunedin* is widely available. The visitor centre has other helpful pamphlets including *Historic Dunedin*, the recreational guide *Dunedin Outdoors* ($1), and *Accessibility for People with Disabilities*.

Things to See

Olveston This is a fine old turn-of-the-century house at 42 Royal Terrace, preserved as it was when lived in by the wealthy Theomin family of the early 1900s. Olveston was designed by a London architect and built between 1904 and 1906. It is lavishly furnished, especially with decorative art from East Asia, collected by David Theomin on his extensive travels. The guided tour is a real education. There are six tours daily – phone ahead (☎ 477 3320) to reserve a place; admission is $10 (children $3).

Chocolate, Whisky & Beer A tour of the Cadbury's **chocolate factory** is a major attraction – in fact it's so popular that you have to book well in advance and you can give up all hope during school holidays! The one-hour tour shows you how all the chocolates are made and concludes with a free sample of the delicious stuff. Tours are held twice daily from Monday to Thursday and can be booked at the visitor centre or by phoning ☎ 467 7800. The entrance to the factory is on Cumberland St. The factory is closed over the Christmas holiday period.

Wilson's (☎ 474 3300 for bookings) on George St, is New Zealand's only 'legal' **whisky distillery** and the southernmost distillery in the world. All aspects of distillation are covered in the informative 1½-hour guided tour ($5). An excellent video is screened and, importantly, the product is sampled. The whisky is made entirely from local products – pure water piped from the Lammerlaw range, and local malting barley. Tours run at 1 and 2.45 pm, Monday to Friday, and you book at the visitor centre. Enjoy your 'wee dram'.

When you've overdosed on chocolate (but hopefully not whisky) you can head to **Speight's Brewery** in Rattray St for a tour (10.30 am Monday to Thursday). It costs $5 (children free), and you must book in advance (☎ 477 9480). Tours start from the brewery's visitors centre. The brewery is one

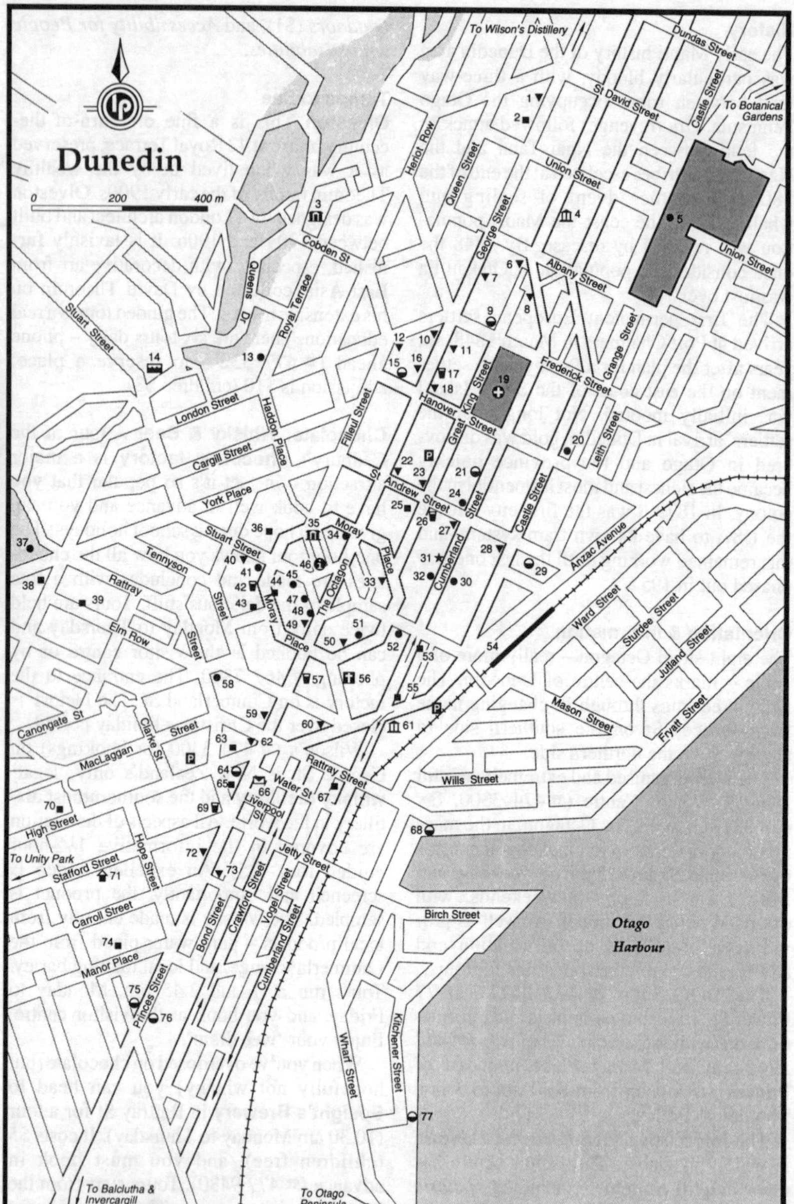
Dunedin
0
200
400 m
To Wilson's Distillery
To Botanical Gardens
Dundas Street
St David Street
Castle Street
Heriot Row
Union Street
Queen Street
George Street
Albany Street
Union Street
Cobden St
Queens Dr
Royal Terrace
Stuart Street
Frederick Street
Grange Street
Great King Street
Hanover Street
Leith Street
London Street
Haddon Place
Filleul Street
Cargill Street
York Place
St Andrew Street
Castle Street
Cumberland Street
Anzac Avenue
Stuart Street
Moray Place
Tennyson
Rattray
Elm Row
Street
The Octagon
Moray Place
Ward Street
Sturdee Street
Jutland Street
Mason Street
Fryatt Street
Canongate St
Clarke St
MacLaggan
Street
Rattray Street
Water St
Liverpool St
Wills Street
High Street
Hope Street
To Unity Park
Stafford Street
Jetty Street
Carroll Street
Bond Street
Crawford Street
Vogel Street
Cumberland Street
Birch Street
Otago Harbour
Manor Place
Princes Street
Kitchener Street
Wharf Street
To Balclutha & Invercargill
To Otago Peninsula
1
2
3
4
5
6
7
8
9
10
11
12
13
14
15
16
17
18
19
20
21
22
23
24
25
26
27
28
29
30
31
32
33
34
35
36
37
38
39
40
41
42
43
44
45
46
47
48
49
50
51
52
53
54
55
56
57
58
59
60
61
62
63
64
65
66
67
68
69
70
71
72
73
74
75
76
77

PLACES TO STAY

- 2 Sahara Guesthouse
- 25 The Statesman
- 36 Quality Hotel Dunedin
- 38 Elm Lodge Too
- 39 Elm Lodge
- 43 Next Stop Dunedin Backpackers
- 44 YMCA
- 53 Law Courts Hotel
- 55 Leviathan Hotel
- 63 Southern Cross Hotel
- 65 Wains Boutique Hotel
- 67 Penguin Palace Backpackers
- 70 Chalet Backpackers
- 71 Stafford Gables YHA Hostel
- 74 Manor House Backpackers

PLACES TO EAT

- 1 Santa Fe
- 6 Captain Cook Hotel
- 7 Blades
- 8 Governor's
- 10 Albert Arms Tavern
- 11 Mega Bite, Robbie Burns Hotel & Planet Foxy's
- 12 Blue Note Café
- 16 Huntsman Chargrill Steak House
- 18 Abalone's
- 22 McDonald's
- 23 Little India
- 27 Bentleys
- 33 Parisettes
- 40 Smithies Pizza
- 49 Etrusco at the Savoy (upstairs)
- 50 Café Zambezi
- 52 Potpourri
- 59 New Canton
- 60 Palms Café
- 62 Ports o' Call
- 69 Provincial Hotel
- 72 Rogano's Seafood
- 73 Lone Star

OTHER

- 3 Olveston
- 4 Otago Museum
- 5 University & Hocken Library
- 9 Taxi Stand
- 13 Royal Terrace
- 14 Moana Pool
- 15 Taxi Stand
- 17 Planet Foxy's
- 19 Public Hospital
- 20 Emerson's Bakery
- 21 Suburban Bus Lines
- 24 Supermarket
- 26 Crossroads
- 28 Rosie O'Grady's
- 29 Mt Cook Landline
- 30 Cadbury's Chocolate Factory
- 31 Police Station
- 32 Supermarket (New World)
- 34 Library
- 35 Town Hall
- 37 Beverley Begg Observatory
- 41 Fortune Theatre
- 42 Abbey Road
- 45 Stuart Street Terrace Houses
- 46 Dunedin Visitor Centre
- 47 Dunedin Public Art Gallery
- 48 Air New Zealand
- 51 Automobile Association (AA)
- 52 DOC
- 54 Railway Station & Taieri Gorge Railway
- 56 First Church
- 57 Bailey's 109
- 58 Speight's Brewery
- 61 Early Settlers Museum
- 64 Taxi Stand
- 66 Central Post Office
- 68 MV *Monarch* Harbour Cruises
- 69 Provincial Hotel
- 75 Newton's Tours
- 76 InterCity Buses
- 77 Harbour Cruise (Blue Waves)

of the smallest in the country and the 1¾-hour tour concludes with a glass of beer in the board room. Unfortunately, the commentary is delivered in an unpalatable monotone.

Another good brewery tour is held at **Emerson's Brewery** (☎ 477 1812), at 4 Grange St, one of those boutique places which produces good German dark malt beers. The best times to go are from noon to 2 pm, and 4 to 6 pm, Monday to Friday, and Saturday from 11 am to 6 pm.

Museums The **Otago Museum**, on the corner of Great King and Union Sts, has a large and varied collection including Maori and South Pacific exhibits; items from ancient Egypt, Greece, Rome, Japan, China, Tibet, South-East Asia; a marine and maritime hall; and a lot more. Particularly good are the natural history displays featuring penguins and moas. There is a hands-on science centre (Discovery World) for children. Admission is free and it's open from 10 am to 5 pm on weekdays, 1 to 5 pm on weekends. There is also a cafe and craft shop.

The **Early Settlers Museum**, at 220 Cumberland St near the railway station, has a fine collection relating to the early settlement of the region. At the railway station end of the museum there are a couple of old steam locomotives in glassed-in display rooms. These include *Josephine*, the first engine to run between Dunedin and Port Chalmers. The museum is open from 10 am to 5 pm on weekdays, and 1 to 5 pm on weekends; admission is $4 (children free).

The **Dunedin Public Art Gallery**, in Logan Park, near the university at the northern end of Anzac Ave, is soon to be shifted to new premises near the information centre in the Octagon. It's open from 10 am to 5 pm on weekdays and 2 to 5 pm on weekends;

admission is by donation. It's the oldest art gallery in NZ and has an extensive local and international collection.

The **Geology Museum** of the University of Otago has displays illustrating mineral types and NZ fossils. Admission is free and it's open from 9 am to 5 pm on weekdays during teaching time, and by arrangement at other times (☎ 479 1100).

Also in the university is the **Hocken Library** (☎ 479 1100), founded by Dr TM Hocken (1836-1910). It has an extensive collection of books, manuscripts, paintings and photographs relating to New Zealand and the Pacific. This library is open from 9.30 am to 5 pm, Monday to Friday, and 9 am to noon on Saturday. On Tuesday the library is open until 9 pm.

The university itself is worth a walk around. It was founded in 1869, 25 years after the settlement of Otago, with 81 students. There's a wide variety of old and new styles of architecture on the campus.

Other Attractions Dunedin has plenty of parks, including the **Botanical Gardens** at the northern end of the city on the lower slopes of Signal Hill. The hothouse is open from 10 am to 4.30 pm. There is also an aviary, with keas and other native birds.

If the night is clear it's possible to do a little stargazing at the **Beverly Begg Observatory** (☎ 477 7683), in the Robin Hood Ground – it's off to your left across the lawn when you reach the top (western end) of Rattray St. There's usually viewing on clear Sunday nights at around 7.30 pm, but this may be later or not at all during summer when it gets dark as late as 10 pm. The cost is only around $2.

A short but definitely strenuous walk is that up **Baldwin St**. It is listed in the *Guinness Book of Records* as the steepest street in the world with a gradient of 1 in 1.266; get directions from the visitor centre.

Activities

Surf Rafting Surf Rafting Wildlife Tours (☎ 478 0046) has devised an exhilarating and educational trip. They operate their motorised rigid-hulled inflatable surf craft from beach-side premises at Wellers Rock, just before the albatross colony.

The boat powers out to Taiaroa Head and stops beneath the albatross observatory where NZ fur seals, including many pups, can be spotted. Nearby is the almost palatial estate of a colony of pied shags. Bottlenose dolphins can be seen frolicking in the water from time to time.

After viewing a host of fauna at a safe and not intrusive range the driver turns the raft towards Aramoana Beach where the thrill section of the ride begins. The inflatable darts in and out of the surf breaking on the beach and the passengers hang on in fear. The boat follows the waves in at a speed greater than the break and as quickly turns to face the oncoming breakers and then leaps into the air. Kaikai Beach and Murderers Bay are passed and sometimes landed on to allow grimacing riders to rest.

The trip can be undertaken by all except young children. All safety matters are attended to and the drivers cut their teeth as surf lifesavers, using similar equipment. There are back-up boats and the rafts are in radio contact with base. The cost is $60 for 90 minutes and this includes transport to and from town. They surf raft all summer, and from May to October on demand.

Beaches & Walks On the headland at the end of St Clair Beach is a heated outdoor saltwater pool. It's open only in the summer – catch bus No 7. St Clair and St Kilda are good beaches to walk along or, if you happen to be there on the shortest day (the middle of the winter), you can join the famous Shortest Day Swim (in the sea, not the heated pool!).

There is a 1.5-km walkway to **Tunnel Beach**, south-west of the city centre. Catch a Corstorphine bus from the Octagon to Stenhope Crescent and walk along Blackhead Rd until you reach a 'no exit' road leading towards the coast. Head towards the triangular promontory, where you'll find a hand-hewn stone tunnel leading towards a secluded beach. The walkway is closed in

September and October for the lambing season.

If you catch a Normandy Citibus from the Octagon to the start of Norwood Rd, you can walk up the road to the **Mt Cargill-Bethunes Gully Walkway**, north-east of town. It takes two hours uphill, and 90 minutes down. The highlight is the view from Mt Cargill, which is accessible by car. In Maori legend the three peaks of Cargill represent the petrified head and feet of a princess of an early Otakau tribe. 'Cargill' comes from Captain William Cargill, a leader of the early Otago colonists. Take warm clothes as it gets very windy at the top.

The walkway continues from Mt Cargill to the Organ Pipes (1½ hours return). These formations are about 10 million years old and were formed during the cooling of lavas which flowed across here.

North of Dunedin is the five-km **Pineapple Flagstaff Walk**, which is not accessible by public transport. There are great views of the harbour, coastline and inland ranges from here. You can get leaflets and directions to all of these walks from the visitor centre.

Other Activities There are plenty of other activities around Dunedin including golf (there are three 18-hole golf courses), tennis and 10-pin bowling. There are three **flightseeing** companies: Otago Aero Club (☎ 489 6158), Beck Aviation – Helicopters (☎ 489 3540), Helicopters Otago (☎ 486 1784) and Mainland Air Services (☎ 486 2200).

The Otago Tramping & Mountaineering Club has regular meetings at their clubrooms at 3 Young St, St Kilda; you can get information on these activities from the Wilderness Shop (☎ 477 3679), 101 Stuart St.

If you wish to go **horse trekking** there are a number of choices: from Broad Bay to Larnach Castle with Castle Discovery Horse Treks (☎ 478 0592) at 9.30 am and 1.30 pm daily; Trojan Horseriding (☎ 465 7013) has rides along the beach north of Dunedin from $25 to $75; and Westwood Stables (☎ 481 1348) is based south of Dunedin.

Tours

Taieri Gorge Railway There are four-hour train excursions on this railway from October to April, departing from Dunedin Station on various days at 2.30 pm and returning by 6.30 pm; in winter (May to August) it leaves at 1.30 pm. Some visitors have rated this as one of the great train journeys of the world, similar to the Silverton to Durango line in Colorado. The return cost to Pukerangi is $43 ($47 to Middlemarch) (student ID cardholders $34.50) and one child can ride for free with each paying adult. Phone ☎ 477 4449 for a schedule and reservations. The operators publish the excellent pamphlet *Your Guide to the Taieri Railway*.

Cruises You can take one to five-hour cruises with Otago Harbour Cruises (☎ 477 4276) on the MV *Monarch* from Rattray St Wharf. Among the *Monarch* cruises is one out along Otago Harbour, passing fur seal, shag and gull colonies and the royal albatross colony at Taiaroa Head. This half-day full harbour cruise costs $43 (children half-price). Their hour-plus cruise to Wellers Rock, which takes in Taiaroa Head, is $20, and the six-hour cruise/coach option is $69. They also run evening supper cruises and the smorgasbord is, by all reports, quite good.

The 57-foot (17½-metre) *Southern Spirit* (☎ 477 1031) sails daily on a similar five-hour harbour cruise to Taiaroa Head, departing from the Harbour Board Basin Marina in Birch St; the cost is $40. There are two-hour ($45) and four-hour ($75) salmon-fishing trips. This is a participatory activity as you have a hand in sailing the yacht.

Also available are Otago Harbour Jet (☎ 456 0227) 45-minute adventure cruises ($25) and nature trips ($50). Blue Wave Cruise (☎ 472 7056) has a two-hour wildlife trip to Taiaroa Head ($35) and a three-hour fishing trip ($45).

Bus Tours There are numerous tours to choose from. (See also the bus tours detailed in the Otago Peninsula section.) Silverpeaks Tours (☎ 489 6167) has jet-boating and white-water rafting trips on the Taieri River.

Gold Trail Mini Tours (☎ 455 3139) take visitors via the Pig Root to the Macraes gold mine and the historic Golden Point Battery. Lunch is at Stanleys Hotel in Macraes Flat. The tour connects with the Taieri Gorge train for the return trip to Dunedin, and the cost of this trip is $71.50.

Wildlife Tracking A highly recommended tour with a difference is Catlins Wildlife Trackers (☎ 415 8163; 474 3300). They offer a 'total' unified eco-experience. Natural history, landforms and geology are interwoven with recent history; the secrets of the sea, littoral, rainforest, wetlands and sky are all gathered together, dissected and meticulously explained; and nature's rare, timid creatures are revealed. Now, NZ's ex-best kept secret!

The operators organise food, transport (on both land and water) and a bed in their superbly located crib (holiday home) overlooking the estuary of the Tahakopa River and the sweep of Tahakopa Bay, at Papatowai. From here you can observe many species of birds, see Hooker's sea lions, and watch the changing moods of the southern ocean. Most importantly they supply binoculars, torches (flashlights) and snorkels, masks, flippers and wet suits.

The meals, including picnic lunches, are the best you are likely to taste in the region. The cost of this tour is $180 for two days, ex Balclutha; they will pick you up from here, arrange car storage and onward transport if needed.

Places to Stay

Camping & Cabins The *Tahuna Park Seaside Camp* (☎ 455 4690) is near the showgrounds and beach at St Kilda. You can get there on a St Kilda bus from Cumberland St. Tent/powered sites cost $16/18, cabins start at $28 and tourist flats at $51 (prices are for two).

At the *Aaron Lodge Motor Camp* (☎ 476 4725), at 162 Kaikorai Valley Rd, tent/powered sites cost $15.50/17, cabins are $28 to $31, and tourist flats are $55 (again, for two). Get there on a Bradford bus from Cumberland St; the Brockville bus goes nearby on some runs.

The *Leith Valley Touring Park* (☎ 467 9936) at 103 Malvern St, Woodhaugh, has tent and powered sites at $18 for two, and on-site caravans at $30 for two.

The *Farmlands Caravan Park* (☎ 482 2730) is on Waitati Valley Rd, 13 km north of Dunedin off SH1. There are no tent sites, caravan sites are $17, and on-site caravans cost from $26 to $35 for two. There's an adventure playground with pony rides, a flying fox, and farm animals.

The *Brighton Motor Camp* (☎ 481 1404) is at 1044 Brighton Rd, Brighton, about 10 km south of Dunedin. The cost is $15 for tent or powered sites for two, on-site caravans are $27 for two, and there are boats for hire.

Hostels The *Stafford Gables YHA Hostel* (☎ 474 1919) is at 71 Stafford St, only about a five-minute walk from the Central Post Office. It's a very elegant and sprawling old building, once used as a private hotel. The cost is $15 per person in dorm/share rooms, $35/25 for twins and doubles/singles. There are good laundry facilities here.

At 296 High St is *Chalet Backpackers* (☎ 479 2075) where share rooms are $15 per person, singles $25, and twins and doubles $35. It is both centrally heated and centrally located, which is a big plus. It was purpose-built in the 1930s as a hospital but with a great deal of effort from its new owners it now exudes a rejuvenated charm. There is plenty of information and some comfortable spots in the building's nooks and crannies where you can get away from it all.

Elm Lodge (☎ 474 1872), at 74 Elm Row, 10 minutes uphill (five back down) from the Octagon, is situated in a fine old family home with a cosy atmosphere. It costs $13/14 per person in dorm/share rooms and twins and doubles are $32. There's free pick-up from central locations, and the lodge rents out bicycles. Despite its central location, Elm Lodge has fantastic harbour views. This is a great backpackers, made a success by Brian, Lesley and staff. They pick up and drop off visitors (within reason) and often look for another hostel if theirs is full. They have an overflow building, *Elm Lodge Too*, on Arthur St, almost directly up from the main building, where prices are the same.

In one of Dunedin's old stately homes is *Manor House Backpackers* (☎ 477 0484) at 28 Manor Place; dorm/shared rooms are $13/14 per person, and twins/singles are $30/17.50. The helpful management operate a courtesy vehicle. It has all facilities and a comfortable common room.

Right in the centre of Dunedin *Penguin Palace Backpackers* (☎ 479 2175), on the corner of Rattray and Vogel Sts, is a city-style hostel with beds for $13 per person in cramped dorms ($14 to $15 in not-so-cramped shared rooms) and a single, when available, is $22. You can't miss it – the outside is painted bright lavender and green! It now has a decent common area in an upstairs mezzanine.

Also close to the Octagon at 2 View St, a very steep street, is *Next Stop Dunedin Backpackers* (☎ 477 0447). This hostel is in a converted church hall which still retains a lot of original features. There are dorm/share rooms for $13.50/15 per person, and twins and doubles are $36. It is still being developed but the bathroom facilities are new and the kitchen is fully equipped.

B&Bs, Guesthouses & Motels At the *Sahara Guesthouse & Motel* (☎ 477 6662), 619 George St, quite close to the university, singles/doubles are $45/69, including breakfast; there are motel units for $69 for two.

One place recommended by readers is *Alvand House* (☎ 477 7379) at 3 Union St (off George St). All rooms have colour TV, tea and coffee-making facilities, electric blankets and a clock radio, and cost $48/68 for singles/doubles ($17 for each extra person). The *Baldwin St B&B* (☎ 473 0215) is for those who like to be close to the record books – it is on the steepest street in the world. The cost is as steep as the street at $55 per person per night. The *Albatross Inn* (☎ 477 2727), 770 George St, is another place worth checking out and a double here costs from $80 to $95.

There is a good farmstay in East Taieri on SH1, 18 km from Dunedin. The *Silverpeaks Lodge* (☎ 489 6167) is a working farm with sheep, cattle and goats. The price per person is $50 for B&B.

There are a number of moderately priced motels along Musselburgh Rise, on the Otago Peninsula side of town. They include the *Arcadian Motel* (☎ 455 0992) at Nos 85-89, the *Chequers Motel* (☎ 455 0778) at No 119, and the *Bayfield Motel* (☎ 455 0756) at No 210. Double rooms cost between $60 and $65 at each of these places.

The *Dunedin Motel* and *Academy Court Motel* (☎ 477 7692), both at 624 George St, have double rooms from $70 to $85. The *Argyle Court Motel* (☎ 477 5129), on the corner of Duke and George Sts, is slightly cheaper, as is the *St Kilda Motel* (☎ 455 1151) on the corner of Victoria Rd and Queens Drive. (See the *Focus on Dunedin* brochure, available at the visitor centre, for a fuller listing of motels.)

Hotels Hotels in the relatively cheap bracket include the small *Statesman* (☎ 477 8411) at 91 St Andrew St. Singles/doubles cost $30/60, although they may sometimes have special deals; breakfast is an extra $5 (continental) or $10 (cooked). The really central *Law Courts Hotel* (☎ 477 8036), at 65 Stewart St, has budget rooms for $45/68 for single/doubles ($14 for an extra adult); cheaper 'pub-bed' rates are available.

The *Beach Hotel* (☎ 455 4642), at 134 Prince Albert Rd in St Kilda, has singles/doubles with private facilities for $40/60. *Wains Boutique Hotel* (☎ 477 9283), at 310 Princes St, is a great-looking old place close to the town centre with B&B at $95 for doubles. Out at Port Chalmers, *Chicks Hotel* (☎ 472 8736), at 2 Mount St, is a classic old stone building with B&B for $25 per person.

The solid, reliable, old-fashioned and central *Leviathan Hotel* (☎ 477 3160), on the corner of Cumberland and High Sts, is a Dunedin landmark. Its budget twin rooms are $55, the standard rate is $78, and studio units are $88 for one or two people.

At the top of the Dunedin hotel listings are

the *Quality Hotel Dunedin* (☎ 477 6784) on Upper Moray Place and the *Southern Cross* (☎ 477 0752), with its excellent DeliCafe, at 118 High St. Prices at both start on the high side of $130. Costing a bit less is *Cargill's Motor Inn* (☎ 477 7983), 678 George St.

Places to Eat

Dunedin's a surprisingly good place for eating out in just about all categories. There is plenty of information on restaurants and dining out available from the visitor centre.

Fast Food & Cafes Dunedin has an excellent selection of places for a sandwich or for lunch, many located along George St and around Moray Place. You might first try the BYO *Cafe Zambezi* (once the Sidewalk Cafe) at 480 Moray Place. It's open from 10 am to 4 pm daily and for dinner from Wednesday to Saturday. The cafe has an excellent selection of sandwiches and light meals. *Potpourri*, at 97 Lower Stuart St, is another good wholefood place open Monday to Friday from 9 am to 8 pm, and on Saturday from 11 am to 3 pm. It has salads, vegetarian burritos ($5), quiche ($4) and other light meals. The sister cafe to Potpourri is *Mega Bite* at 388 George St. Its menu is similar, especially the desserts topped with Vitari soft serve and Colombo frozen yoghurt.

At 119 Lower Stuart St is the *Coffee Shop on Stuart St* which has a comprehensive lunch-time menu and fine coffee; try a 'pav' or lemon meringue pie. *Stewarts Coffee House* (Dunedin's first), downstairs at 12 Lower Octagon, has cheap sandwiches and excellent coffee.

The superb *DeliCafe* in the Southern Cross Hotel is open until late but get there early for a sumptuous breakfast for $9.50 or great value lunches from $5.50. Top of the cafe tree is *Parisettes*, 368 Moray Place, where they seem to have got the cafe/eatery mix just right; they have a full blackboard menu. *Botanica*, in the botanical gardens, open from 10 am to 4 pm daily, receives good comments about its service and food.

For a good-value student-type meal (eg baked beans on toast) try the *Governor's*, at the top end of Great King St, before Albany St. A filling baked potato with 'the works' is $3 to $4. The burgers at *Burgers Wisconsin*, 392 Princes St, come recommended; eg the Jamaican with honey and ginger sauce for $5.90 or a quarter-pounder with marinated venison strips for $8.

The Dunedin 'cheap, greasy spoon' goes to *Galata Kebab House*, 126 Princes St, for reheating their doner in a pot of boiling water instead of slicing it from a revolving spit! Yucky, and hardly authentic Turkish cuisine.

Pub Food The *Albert Arms Tavern*, on the corner of George and London Sts, is open every day for excellent bistro meals – steak and seafood – for under $10. The *Ports o'Call* in the Southern Cross Hotel has fish, chicken, seafood and vegetarian dishes; expect to pay $15 upwards for a main meal. The brasserie, open from 11 am to 10 pm, is very popular with the office crowd.

At 65-69 Lower High St, the *Leadlight Room* in the Leviathan Hotel has mains from $17 to $20 including the Leviathan's Choice, a special dish of the day which combines the freshest of local produce. The *Captain Cook Hotel* is a popular student pub and has good food upstairs – if you can get in the door – and also a beer garden. It's at the intersection of Albany and Great King Sts.

Restaurants *Palms Cafe*, at the corner of Dowling and Lower High Sts, is a very pleasant and deservedly popular place, open from 5 pm onwards, Monday to Friday, and from 6 pm on weekends. It has entrees from $8.50, mains from $18 and desserts for $6.50.

At the *Santa Fe*, 629 George St, you can get great Mexican and Cajun food – Aunt Belle's chicken, barbequed pork ribs, mixed pot gumbo stew, enchiladas and tacos. The restaurant is open from 6 pm, Wednesday to Monday. Main courses cost from $16 up and fresh clam bakes with onions are $11.

For Italian food go to *Casa Italia Ristorante*, in the municipal building on the Octagon (west of the visitor centre), an elegant restaurant with fine cuisine, and priced accordingly. The *Etrusco at the*

Savoy, at 8A Moray Place, is fully licensed and open from 5.30 pm, Tuesday to Sunday. Try their Tuscan garlic bread topped with tomato (fett'unta con pomodori) for $4. Italian in name but not necessarily in style, is *Rogano's Seafood*, upstairs at 388 Princes St, where the 'early bird' special of three courses will set you back $20.

A great Indian eatery is the tandoori *Little India* at 82 St Andrew St; try the vegetarian banquet for $19.50 per person or the 'practically everything' banquet for $26.50.

Steak-lovers head to the *Huntsman Chargrill Steak House*, 311 George St – you can't go wrong with 20 steak dishes to choose from as well as a fantastic selection of salads. More steak (and other dishes) are on offer at *Bentley's*, near the corner of Cumberland and St Andrew Sts. The *Miners Steak & Seafood*, in Vogel St near the Penguin Palace, is one of those 'select and then cook it yourself' places; expect to pay around $25 for a full meal. But beware, burn it and you eat it!

If you're looking for an expensive night out at the best Dunedin has to offer then two places to try are *Blades*, way up at 450 George St, where all entrees are $7.50 and all mains are $18.50; or the *Blue Note Cafe* at 95 Filleul St – try an entree of green lipped mussels in spicy sauce for $6.50, or a main of ratatouille and potato gnocchi for $17.50.

Entertainment

Pubs Dunedin is a drinkers' town and there are plenty of places to slake that thirst. They include several places already mentioned under Pub Food, such as the *Albert Arms* and the *Captain Cook*. The 'Cook', on the corner of Albany and Great King Sts near the university, is a popular student pub. It gets so crowded that you can hardly get in the door.

Prepare yourself for an inner city pub crawl. Put your car keys down then start off at *Abbey Road* at 110 Moray Place where John, Paul, George and Ringo scatter their ambience in speakeasy fashion. Head into the Octagon for a quick drink at *Bogart's*

OTAGO

The Dunedin Sound

Dunedin was once the most active place in the New Zealand music scene. In the past dozen or so years it has produced a number of successful bands, many of which have achieved international recognition. A lot of this has had to do with the success of the Flying Nun (FN) record label and its successful overseas promotion. Although the label has now moved to Auckland, it has been replaced with the Port Chalmers-based Xpressway label.

In fact, so many of the Dunedin 'gig goers' have affiliations with musicians that it led one American observer to say of Dunedin that 'it's just a town full of band members'. A lot of really good bands evolve in this town, make an album which receives a small local following, perhaps get recognition overseas, then disband. As soon as they have gone, the vast resource pool of student musicians and songwriters in town throws up another band to fill the void.

Some North Americans equate Dunedin, a relatively small city, with Athens, Georgia, home of the B-52s and mega band REM. Bands from Dunedin which have been or are popular on the college airwaves in the USA include the Verlaines, Straitjacket Fits, the Clean and, perhaps most popular of all, the Chills.

Ten years of Flying Nun and a large chunk of the Dunedin band scene was celebrated with the release of *Getting Older*, which featured the four bands mentioned earlier, along with other well-known acts such as the Able Tasmans, the Bats and the Headless Chickens. Another compilation album, *Pink Flying Saucers over the Southern Alps*, covered a more recent selection and included Dunedin's 3Ds, which in the early 90s were getting good press overseas.

So, while in Dunedin, head out to one of the pubs where a band is playing – there are a number of them. Maybe one of next year's supergroups will be playing, and you will have seen them for the price of a couple of beers. ■

where shirts, ties and shoulder pads are all the go. The *Bank*, corner of the Octagon and Stewart St, is another yuppie place which borrows from a pastiche of English decor. Saunter to the *Statesman* on the corner of St Andrew and Great King Sts; just another typical bar but at this stage who cares. Opposite is the *Crossroads* where blues and jazz, the influence of the spirits of Abbey Road, are played on weekend nights.

Almost staggering, roll to *Rosie O'Grady's*, at the corner of Castle and St Andrew Sts, where the Irish music inspires you to push on to yet another destination, the immortal *Captain Cook* – be prepared for the crush. Backtrack to the Albert Arms, Planet Foxy's, the Bowling Green and the Robbie Burns if you still have the energy or inclination. If you would prefer NZ or imported wine by the glass, try the *Bacchus Winebar* on the 1st floor, 12 The Octagon.

Pubs which feature music, particularly in the evenings, include the *Beach Hotel* in St Kilda, the Albert Arms, Planet Foxy's, Captain Cook, Abbey Road, Rosie O'Grady's, Crossroads, the Lone Star, Port O'Call in the Southern Cross, Bailey's 109, and a great many others.

Several locals recommended *Abalone's* on the corner of George and Hanover Sts. It attracts the after-work crowd then fills up with an equally well-heeled crowd and the workers who decide to linger. Another recommended place is *Cassidy's Saloon Bar* at 116 Albany St where there are Tex-Mex meals.

Other Entertainment Dunedin has a number of theatres including the professional Fortune Theatre and several amateur companies. The New Edinburgh Folk Club meets at 6 Carroll St at 8 pm on Friday. Dunedin is an important part of NZ's live music scene and a number of pubs specialise in featuring new as well as proven acts. Check the *Otago Daily Times* on Sunday or the free monthly *Otago Happenings* for what's on.

Getting There & Away

Air Air New Zealand (☎ 477 5769) is on the corner of Princes St and the Upper Octagon. There are daily direct flights to Auckland, Christchurch, Invercargill and Wellington, with connections to other centres. Ansett New Zealand (☎ (0800) 800 146) at 1 George St (on the Octagon) has flights to Auckland, Christchurch, Wellington and Invercargill. Queenstown Air (☎ (0800) 838 828) has flights to Queenstown on Monday, Wednesday and Saturday at 10.45 am and on Tuesday and Wednesday at 4 pm ($130).

Bus InterCity buses (☎ (0800) 731 711) depart from 599 Princes St. They have services to Christchurch, Invercargill, Queenstown, Te Anau, Milford, Wanaka and the 'Coast'. There are several buses daily to Christchurch and Invercargill.

Mt Cook Landline (☎ (0800) 800 287) at 205 St Andrew St, has daily services up and down the east coast of the South Island, all the way from Picton to Invercargill via Christchurch and Dunedin; it takes about 15 hours from end to end.

Catch-a-Bus (☎ 477 7900) provides door-to-door services from Dunedin to Christchurch, Invercargill, Queenstown, Te Anau and Wanaka. There are daily Nationwide and Atomic shuttles, Dunedin to Christchurch; for both phone ☎ 474 3300. The cost to Christchurch is from $27 to $30.

Train Stuart St, which runs through the Octagon, continues down to the railway station on Anzac Ave. The *Southerner* (Christchurch-Invercargill) train passes through in both directions every day except Saturday. Tickets for the *Southerner* (and the *Interislander*) are sold at the railway station and at the visitor centre.

Hitching To hitch northwards you can get a Pinehill bus to the beginning of the motorway or a Normandy bus to the botanical gardens from the Octagon, or walk there in about 30 or 40 minutes. Hitching south, you can take an Otago Road Services bus from Lower High St (opposite Queens Gardens) to Fairfield. Alternatively take an InterCity

OTAGO

bus to Mosgiel, alighting at the turn-off or, if it's a long-distance bus, at East Taieri.

Getting Around

Five companies offer door-to-door services to and from the airport: Dunedin Airport (☎ 477 7777), Gold Star Super (☎ 489 5184), Johnson's Express (☎ 476 2519), City Airport (☎ 477 1771) and Ritchies Airport (☎ 477 9238). Shuttles cost around $10 per person (children $5) and the 27-km trip to the airport takes 40 minutes.

Citibus buses leave from the Octagon area and suburban buses leave from Cumberland St. Unlike most places in NZ, they run every day, although buses are more frequent during the week. Get timetables from the visitor centre. The average trip costs about $1.80.

You can rent bicycles from Browns for Bikes (☎ 477 7259), 109 Lower Stuart St, and Penguin Palace (☎ 479 2175), Vogel St.

OTAGO PENINSULA

The Otago Peninsula is one of the most significant wildlife areas in the South Island. You can spend a pleasant afternoon, or longer, tripping around this peninsula. Stops can be made at Glenfalloch Woodland Gardens, the Portobello Aquarium, and Otakou Marae where there's a Maori church and meeting house with a small museum. There are many other historical sites, walkways, natural formations and so on dotted around the peninsula, making for an interesting trip. The *Otago Peninsula* brochure and map, published by the Otago Peninsula Trust and available at the visitor centre ($2), lists over 40 sights and activities on the peninsula.

Peninsula Wildlife

A wealth of interesting fauna is to be found on the Otago Peninsula, and for many people it is the main reason for visiting.

Albatrosses At the end of the peninsula is Taiaroa Head where the only northern royal albatross colony in the world close to human habitation can be seen (see Flora & Fauna chapter). Public access is allowed only by purchasing a permit for $25 (children $10) from the visitor centre in Dunedin, entitling you to a one-hour conducted visit. It is open from 8.30 am to 5 pm daily except on weekends, when it's open from 9 am to 5 pm. The viewing platform closes from 16 September to 24 November, but this varies.

To get to the albatross colony, catch a Portobello bus, then hitch the remaining 11 km through beautiful scenery to the colony. Otherwise you can come on any of several tours from Dunedin (see Tours in this section). There is an element of chance involved in what you will see – in calm weather it's unlikely you'll see an albatross flying. The later you get there the more likely you are to see them fly as there's usually more wind later in the day.

The birds arrive at the nesting site in September, court and mate in October, lay eggs in November, then incubate the eggs until January, when the chicks hatch. Between March and September the chicks are left alone at the colony while their parents collect food for them, returning only for feeding. By September the fledged chicks depart.

The albatross tour is extremely popular and bus tour operators often snap up places in advance, leaving independent travellers (many who have hitched out here) to be turned away. The moral: book in advance (☎ 478 0499; 474 3300). The *Monarch* cruise and surf-rafting trips are good alternative ways of seeing these birds.

Penguins The yellow-eyed penguin (Maori: hoiho), one of the rarest penguin species on earth, can be seen at close quarters on the peninsula. To visit the yellow-eyed penguin colonies you have a few options.

At the Penguin Place, just off the Portobello Rd, you can obtain entry to a unique hoiho wildlife conservation project. The 1½-hour tour includes a 20-minute talk on penguins and their conservation ($25); check at the Dunedin Visitor Centre for tour times. The project is funded entirely through profits from these tours including a longer, more informative seven-hour tour operated from November to May ($46). You can photograph the penguins from a range of five

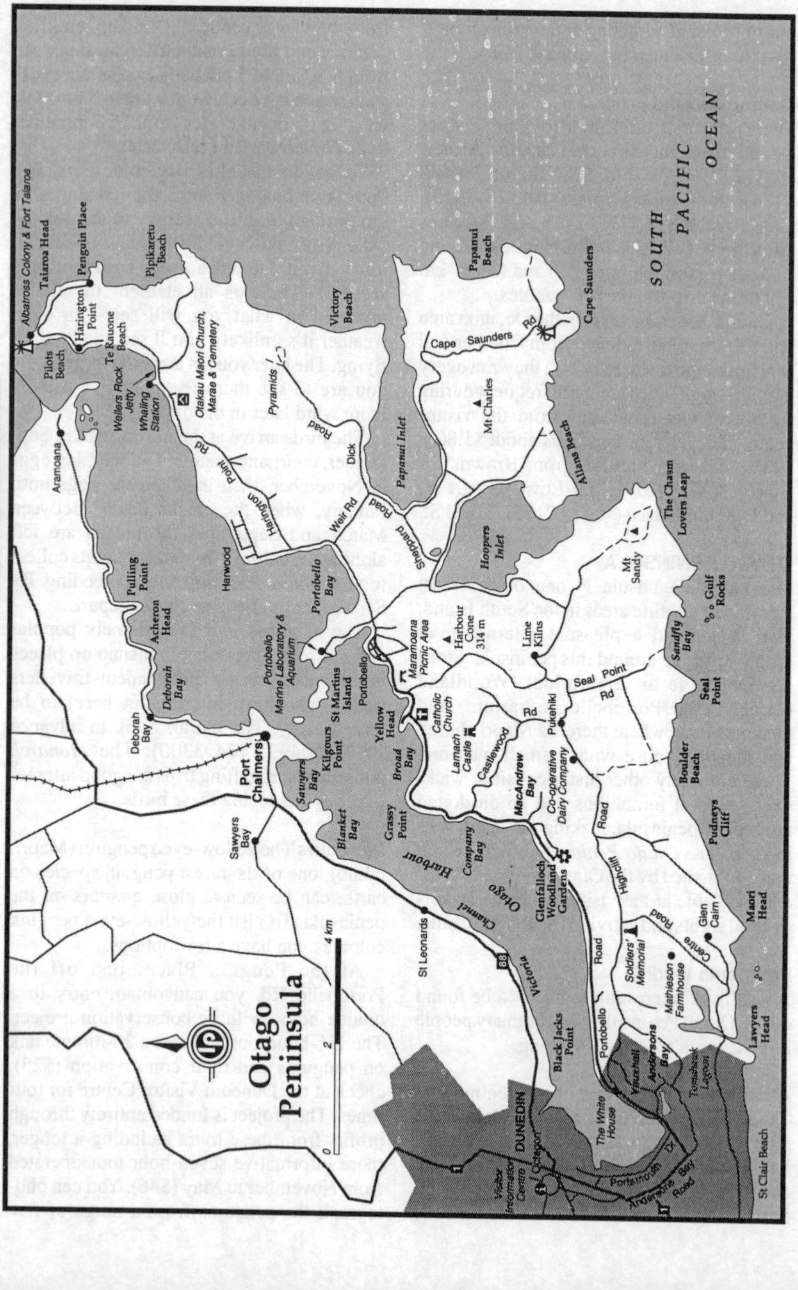
Otago Peninsula
0
2
4 km
SOUTH PACIFIC OCEAN
Albatross Colony & Fort Taiaroa
Taiaroa Head
Penguin Place
Pilots Beach
Harington Point
Te Rauone Beach
Pipikaretu Beach
Victory Beach
Papanui Beach
Cape Saunders
Cape Saunders Rd
Wellers Rock Jetty
Whaling Station
Otakau Maori Church, Marae & Cemetery
Pyramids
Dick Road
Harington Point Rd
Aramoana
Papanui Inlet
Mt Charles
Allans Beach
Weir Rd
Shepherd Road
Harwood
Pulling Point
Acheron Head
Deborah Bay
Deborah Bay
Portobello Bay
Portobello Marine Laboratory & Aquarium
Hoopers Inlet
The Chasm
Lovers Leap
Mt Sandy
Gulf Rocks
Sandfly Bay
Seal Point
Seal Point Rd
Harbour Cone 314 m
Lime Kilns
Maramoana Picnic Area
Portobello
St Martins Island
Yellow Head
Kilgours Point
Port Chalmers
Sawyers Bay
Sawyers Bay
Catholic Church
Larnach Castle
Castlewood Rd
Pukehiki
Broad Bay
MacAndrew Bay
Co-operative Dairy Company
Grassy Point
Blanket Bay
Company Bay
Otago Harbour
Highcliff Road
Boulder Beach
Pudneys Cliff
Glenfalloch Woodland Gardens
Victoria Channel
St Leonards
88
Glen Cairn
Centre Road
Maori Head
Soldiers' Memorial
Portobello Road
Mathieson Farmhouse
Lawyers Head
Black Jacks Point
Vauxhall
Andersons Bay
Tomahawk Lagoon
The White House
DUNEDIN
Octagon
Visitor Information Centre
Portsmouth Dr
Andersons Bay Road
St Clair Beach
1

metres. For more information, phone the Yellow Eyed Penguin Conservation Reserve (☎ 478 0286) or the Dunedin Visitor Centre (☎ 474 3300).

The operators of Penguin Place have replanted the breeding habitat, built nesting sites, cared for sick and injured birds and, importantly, trapped predators. The hoiho's greatest threat is loss of habitat, especially the low-lying coastal vegetation in which they nest. Sadly, many farmers in Southland and Otago allow cattle to trample remaining patches of vegetation favoured by the hoiho.

You can also view the penguins at Southlight Wildlife (☎ 478 0287) on Harington Point Rd, off Portobello Rd, 2.5 km before the albatross colony. You need to obtain a key to the gate ($5 adults, $2.50 children; it is well signposted). This leads to a colony of yellow-eyed penguins which you view from a distance; bring some binoculars. A number of tour operators go to other beaches where there are hoiho (see Tours in this section).

Little blue penguins and fur seals can be seen easily in a number of locations on the peninsula; ask at the Dunedin Visitor Centre.

Conservation efforts focus on restoring the nesting habitat of the rare yellow-eyed penguin on the Otago Peninsula

Hooker's Sea Lions The Hooker's sea lions can only be seen on a tour to a 'secret' beach. It is likely that at any one time you will see six or more animals. It was at this beach that the first pup was born on the New Zealand mainland after a breeding absence of 700 years. The sea lions, visitors from Campbell Island and the Auckland Islands, are predominantly bachelor males.

Tours to the sea lions are only operated by Elm Lodge Wildlife Tours and South Coast Nature Tours (see Tours in this section).

Things to See

Approximately nine km from Dunedin, the **Glenfalloch Woodland Gardens** are noted for their rhododendrons and azaleas and for the domestic birds which wander freely in the grounds. The gardens are open from 9.30 am until dusk every day. There's a restaurant (open from Tuesday to Saturday) and tearoom there too. You can get to Glenfalloch on a Portobello bus.

The built highlight of the peninsula is probably **Larnach Castle** (☎ 476 1616), a conglomeration of architectural styles and fantasies on the highest point of the peninsula. It's open to the public from 9 am to 5 pm (longer from December to May). Built by JWM Larnach in 1871, its construction cost over $10 million by today's standards. It's hardly the Loire Valley, however, and foreigners may prefer to spend their money looking at the peninsula's unique wildlife.

You can get to Larnach Castle, 15 km from central Dunedin, by taking the Portobello bus to Company Bay, from where it's a four km uphill walk, or you can take a tour from Dunedin. Entry to the castle and gardens is a steep $9.50 (children $3.50), or $4 (children $1) to visit only the gardens, stable and ballroom. There is a cafe in the castle ballroom. Accommodation is also available (see Places to Stay in this section).

The **Portobello Aquarium**, run by the University of Otago, sits at the end of a small peninsula near Portobello. It has a small room with displays of fish and invertebrates from a variety of local marine habitats, and also a number of 'touch tanks' where you can

OTAGO

touch the animals and plants found in shallow waters and rock pools. They also have a tuatara (see Flora & Fauna chapter) and natural-history videos. The aquarium is open all year from noon to 4.30 pm on weekends. It's also open every day from November to February and during school holidays. Admission is $3 (children $1, family $6).

A tour to the historic 150-mm **Armstrong Disappearing Gun** can be combined with the visit to the albatross colony (included if you have a ticket to the albatross colony). The gun was installed in the late 19th century to counter the threat of attack from Tsarist Russia – the 'Russian scare'. It is the only Armstrong Disappearing Gun in working order left in the world.

Tours

Several companies do full-day minibus tours of the Otago Peninsula. Citibus Newton's Tours (☎ 477 5577), at 595 Princes St, has a number of tours in the region. Their Tour No 2 ($25) goes to the high part of the peninsula (Larnach Castle, Glenfalloch), and Tour No 3 ($62) features the peninsula's wildlife. Citisights (☎ 477 2224) operates a scheduled service to the main sights and stop at Olveston, Glenfalloch, Larnach Castle and the Octagon. A half-day ticket is $20 (children $15), a full-day ticket $30 (children $20) and a single circuit $10 (children $6).

Two really interesting tours which feature all the wildlife highlights of the peninsula are run by Elm Lodge Wildlife Tours (☎ 474 1872) for $36 and South Coast Nature Tours (☎ (025) 345 076) for $42. Wildlife seen usually includes the royal albatross, little blue penguins, fur seals, yellow-eyed penguins (hoiho) and Hooker's sea lions. The hoiho are at Sandfly Bay and access is limited to tour operators. Many other species of birds are spotted on the way, especially waders in the peninsula's eastern estuaries.

One recommended operation for small group ecotours is Wings of Kotuku (☎ 473 0077), with a German-speaking guide. They have trips to see the yellow-eyed penguins at Sandfly Bay.

Places to Stay & Eat

There are a few places where you can stay on the peninsula. The *Portobello Village Tourist Park* (☎ 478 0359) is at 27 Hereweka St in Portobello township; tent/powered sites are $15/16 for two. The *Penguin Place Lodge* (☎ 478 0286), at McGrouther's Farm on Harington Point Rd, has a lounge, fully equipped kitchen and laundry; you need only supply your bedding and food. The cost is $15 per person (linen is $5 extra).

The *Larnach Lodge* (☎ 476 1616) is in the grounds of the famous castle. Bedrooms in the historic stable building cost $30 for two, and hotel-style rooms in the lodge cost $49 for two with shared bathroom (or $74 with private facilities).

One restaurant consistently recommended by happy readers is Portobello's *1908 Cafe & Bar*. It serves a variety of seafood – blue cod, bay clams, mussels and many other delights.

Wanaka Region

If you choose to enter Otago via the Haast Pass, the first sizeable towns you'll reach are Hawea and Wanaka, after passing between lakes Wanaka and Hawea at the Neck. The central feature of this region is Mt Aspiring, surrounded by the national park of the same name.

WANAKA

Wanaka is nirvana for those seeking to combine an adrenaline buzz with fine living while overdosing on scenery and the outdoors. Just over 100 km from Queenstown, at the southern end of Lake Wanaka, Wanaka with a town population of 1200, is the gateway to the Mt Aspiring National Park and the Treble Cone, Cardrona, Harris Mountains and Pisa Range ski areas. It is a laid-back town and very much a sharp contrast to the hype of Queenstown.

In December 1964 around 200 hectares in north-western Otago and southern Westland were earmarked as national park. The park,

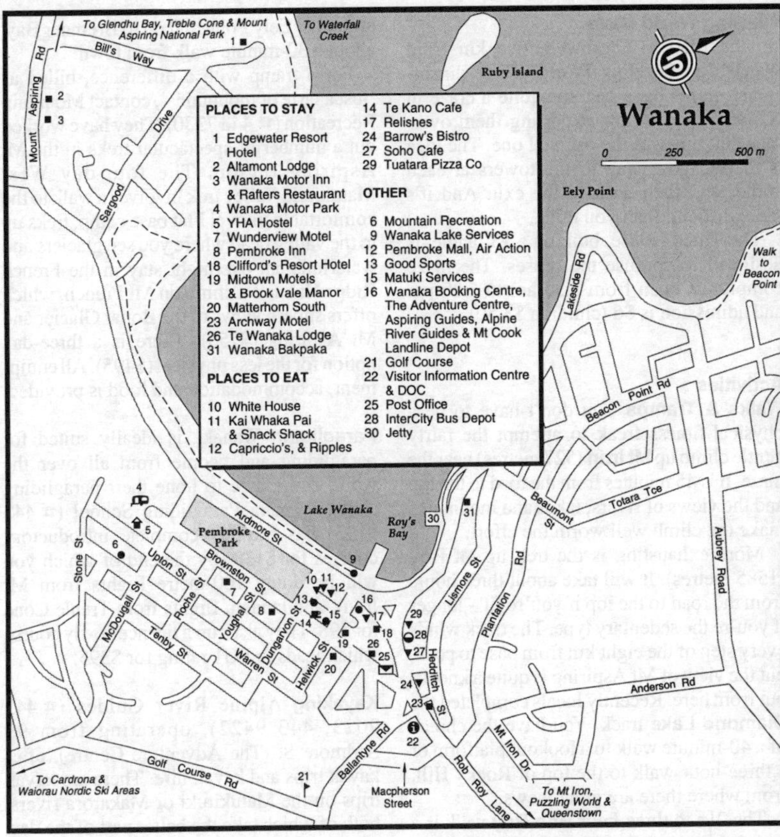

named after its highest peak, 3027-metre Mt Aspiring, now extends over 2900 sq km along the Southern Alps between the Haast and Te Anau highways.

Information

The Wanaka Visitor Information Centre (☎ 443 1233; fax 443 9238) is located in the Mt Aspiring National Park Visitor Centre (☎ 443 7660) in Ardmore St. It is open from 8 am to 4.45 pm from Monday to Friday, and on weekends from 9 am to 4.30 pm throughout the year. It has displays and audiovisuals on the park.

The Adventure Centre (☎ 443 9422) at 99 Ardmore St has lots of information on a whole range of adventurous activities including kayaking, parapenting, rock climbing, white-water sledging and rafting, skiing and canyoning. It is open from 9 am to 6 pm in summer and in winter it changes its name to Harris Mountain Heli-Ski & Treble Cone Ski Field and is open daily from 6 am to 6.30 pm.

Wanaka Lake Services (☎ 443 7495), in the small building beside the jetty, has information about things to do on the lake. It's open from 8.30 am to 6 pm daily.

Puzzling World Maze

On the road to Cromwell, two km from Wanaka, is Puzzling World. Three-dimensional mazes have become quite a craze in NZ and they're now exporting them overseas, but this was the original one. The idea is to find your way to the towers at each corner and then back to the exit. And it's more difficult than you think.

The Tilted House, built on a 15° angle, is designed to confuse the senses. The maze complex is open from 8.30 am to 5.30 pm and admission is $6 (children $3.50).

Activities

Walks & Tramps You don't have to be a physical-fitness freak to attempt the fairly gentle climb up **Mt Iron** (527 metres) near the maze. It is 45 minutes from the road to the top and the views of rivers, lakes and mountains make the climb well worth the effort.

More exhausting is the trek up **Mt Roy** (1585 metres). It will take about three hours from the road to the top if you're fit – longer if you're the sedentary type. The track winds every step of the eight km from base to peak, but the view of Mt Aspiring is quite a knockout from here. Recently locals completed the **Diamond Lake** track. You have the choice of a 40-minute walk to a lookout platform or a three-hour walk to the top of Rocky Hill, from where there are great views.

The 2½ to three-hour **Rob Roy** walk is a popular bush walk with good views. It's a one-hour drive up the Matukituki Valley (in summer you can bus up there with Matuki Services), from where the walk goes up the Rob Roy Stream to a point below the Rob Roy Glacier.

There are lots of places to go tramping in Mt Aspiring National Park and the Matukituki, Motatapu, Makarora, Blue and Wilkin valleys. You can get all the information you need for these walks and tramps from the National Park Information Centre. Get hold of their *Wanaka Walks*; it has a rough map and outlines eleven walks. Easiest of all is the lakeside walk which starts along the grassy lakefront in town and runs around to Eely Point and on to Bremner Bay, about a 30-minute walk from town.

For a tramp with a difference, billed as 'just a taste of mountains', contact Mountain Recreation (☎ 443 7330). They have worked out a number of spectacular treks in the Mt Aspiring region. The four-day West Matukituki Valley trek involves a walk to the comfortable Shovel Flat base camp, treks up to the valley head where you see glaciers and waterfalls, an overnight stay in the French Ridge Hut and a climb on Mt French, which offers superb views of the Bonar Glacier and Mt Aspiring ($750). There is a three-day option for the less physical ($495). All equipment, accommodation and food is provided.

Paragliding Wanaka is ideally suited for paragliding and people from all over the world come here to hone their paragliding skills. Wanaka Paragliding School (☎ 443 9193) has full-day complete introductory courses for $138 (by the end of which you will be doing 100-metre flights from Mt Iron); and tandem flights from Treble Cone for $98. They also run a licence-to-fly course which leads to PG1 rating for $395.

Kayaking Alpine River Guides (☎ 443 9023; 443 9422), operating from 99 Ardmore St (The Adventure Centre), offer kayak trips and kayak hire. There are kayak trips on the Matukituki or Makarora rivers, both of which take the better part of the day. The Matukituki trip starts at the put-in point at Raspberry Creek, after the guides have gone through the rudiments of kayaking. All of these trips have been tested by Lonely Planet and come highly recommended. A full day out (well, about seven hours) costs $95 and is well worth it. The main guide, Graeme Kayak, is one of NZ's true characters or 'dudes'. Be at the Adventure Centre at 10 am.

Canyoning Those with a sense of adventure and a smattering of 'daring-do' will love this summertime-only activity. It is not a sport for claustrophobics, however, as it involves tobogganing, swimming and abseiling through confined, steep and wild gorges.

Transport to the canyon, a picnic lunch, instruction and equipment are included in the price of $145. The Deep Canyon Experience (☎ 443 7922) trips start from the Adventure Centre at 9.30 am and return at 4.30 pm.

Other Activities The Wanaka and Hawea lakes are good for trout and salmon **fishing**. Hawea is about 16 km from Wanaka. Guided fishing trips cost $168 for two hours. They're not too bad if you get four people together ($42 each). Alternatively, you can hire a boat and go fishing on your own.

NZ Backcountry Saddle Expeditions (☎ 443 8151), based 26 km from Wanaka on the Cardrona Valley Rd (SH 89), offers two-hour **horse treks** for $45 (children $30) and overnight wilderness trips from $130.

Wanaka is a good place to learn the skills required to reach some of the spectacular peaks in the area (see Mountaineering in the Outdoor Activities chapter). There are two **mountaineering** schools in town.

Out on a Thread (☎ 443 9418), 155 Tenby St, offers a full day of **rock climbing** instruction (including the essential skills of belaying and protection placement) for $75. Wack in a 'Friend' and go for it!

Wanaka is near several good **skiing** areas: Treble Cone, Cardrona, the Pisa Range Nordic Ski Area (for cross-country skiing), and Harris Mountain for heli-skiing (see Skiing in the Outdoor Activities chapter.)

There are plenty of other seasonal activities on the lake in summer, including windsurfing, water-skiing, jet-skiing, and so on. Good Sports (☎ 443 7966), on Dunmore St, hires out a vast array of sports equipment.

Tours

On the Lake Wanaka offers lots of activities on its beautiful lake. Check with Wanaka Lake Services by the waterfront. A hovercraft makes trips on the lake twice daily. It's $20 (children $10) for a 15-minute trip or $48 (children $25) for 45 minutes. The Wanaka Riverjet does 50-minute jet-boat trips on the lake for $45 (children $22). Or take lake cruises from one to four hours on the MV *Paranui* – trips to Pigeon Island (four hours) and Glendhu Bay (two hours) are popular.

Edgewater Adventures (☎ 443 8422) has jet-boat trips on the Clutha River for $45 (children $28).

Aerial Sightseeing Aspiring Air (☎ 443 7943) and Wanaka Aviation (☎ 443 1385), both located at the airport, have scenic flights ranging from a 45-minute flight over Mt Aspiring, the glacier and alpine country for $115 to a flight to Mt Cook for about $215 or Milford Sound for around $190. With a launch trip on Milford Sound added, the cost all up is $240. Children travel for half-price on all these trips.

For those who want to see the scenery from an upside-down vantage point there are joyrides in either Tiger Moths or a Pitts Special stunt plane. These are operated by Biplane Adventures (☎ 443 1000), also at Wanaka Airport. Near their office is the New Zealand Fighter Pilots Museum; entry costs $5 (children $2.50).

Places to Stay

Camping & Cabins The *Wanaka Motor Park* (☎ 443 7883) is at 212 Brownston St, about one km from the town centre. A powered site costs $16 for two, a bunkroom costs $11.50 per person, cabins are $28 and tourist flats $48 for two people. The *Pleasant Lodge Holiday Park* (☎ 443 7360), three km from Wanaka on Glendhu Bay Rd, has cabins and tourist flats at similar prices.

Adjacent to Lake Wanaka, 13 km from town on the Treble Cone road, is the *Glendhu Bay Camp* (☎ 443 7243), again with camping for $13 and cabins from $25 to $30; prices are for two.

There are *DOC camping grounds* at Wharf Creek Reserve, adjacent to SH6, at the head of Lake Wanaka; at Kidds Bush Reserve, Hunter Valley Rd, west of the Neck between lakes Hawea and Wanaka; and at Albert Town reserve, adjacent to SH6, five km north of Wanaka.

Hostels At 56 Brownston St, *Matterhorn South* (☎ 443 1119), is a small homely

OTAGO

20-bed hostel with a cosy log fire. Dorm and share rooms here are $14.50 per person, and double and twins are $33. The owners, Marleen and Rudy, are friendly and informative. They have recently extended their accommodation facilities and the new ultramodern section has four-bed rooms with en suite for $16.50 per person, and smart, comfortable doubles for $55 (plus $14 per extra person). There is a great new kitchen in this complex.

The *Wanaka YHA Hostel* (☎ 443 7405), at 181 Upton St, has a relaxed, friendly atmosphere and its facilities are open all day. The cost is $15 per person in dorms and doubles are $36. Mountain bikes are available from the hostel, which also sponsors many other activities.

The friendly *Wanaka Bakpaka* (☎ 443 7837) at 117 Lakeside Rd is opposite the jetty on the northern side of Roy's Bay, just a few metres from the lake. It's on a hill with a great view of the lake, town and mountains. There's a hot spa pool (only open during the ski season) and you can hire mountain bikes, kayaks or a canoe. The cost per person is $14.50 in dorm and share rooms, and twins/doubles are $33/35.

B&Bs & Guesthouses The *Altamont Lodge* (☎ 443 8864), on Mt Aspiring Rd, is good value, offering very comfortable accommodation. The rooms are $22 per person and linen is supplied for an extra $2.50. It has a fully equipped modern kitchen, private tennis court, TV/video room, reading room, playground, BBQ, spa pool, and is only 25 minutes from Treble Cone. As it is over a km from town it only suits those with transport.

Perhaps the most exciting accommodation in the area is at the *Minaret Mountain Resort* (☎ 443 7590) on the western edge of the lake. But you have to be rich – the transport cost is a minimum of $100 per person, the B&B budget singles/doubles are $100/125 and the executive suites are $300 per double, with all meals.

There are least 20 B&B-style places in and around Wanaka; get a list of their rates from the visitor information centre. As a rule, singles/doubles start from $45/70.

Hotels & Motels There are plenty of places in this category in Wanaka. At *Midtown Motels* (☎ 443 8333), 51 Brownston St, you can get a single/double with a private bathroom, fridge and tea and coffee-making facilities for $45/55. The *Brook Vale Manor* (☎ 443 8333), 31 Brownston St, has rooms from $78 for two. The attractive *Te Wanaka Lodge* (☎ 433 9224) at 23 Brownston St hasn't been open long but Lonely Planet is already receiving lots of mail very much in it's favour. Rooms cost $70 to $90 and there are two guest lounges, open wood fires and cooking facilities; the price includes breakfast.

Cheaper motels include the *Archway Motel* (☎ 433 7968), 64 Hedditch St, which has double rooms for $60. More centrally located are the similarly priced *Wunderview Motel* (☎ 433 7480) and the *Pembroke Inn* (☎ 433 7296), both on Brownston St.

The excellent *Bayview Motel* (☎ 433 7766) is three km from town on the Glendhu Bay Rd. There are great views from all of the rooms which cost from $80 to $95 for two and the whole complex is surrounded by beautiful, spacious gardens (one of which has been set up for the disabled). They will set and light your open fire for $5. Note that rates escalate in the high season.

Clifford's Resort Hotel (☎ 433 7826), on Ardmore St, has double rooms from $75 to $95 and the *Edgewater Resort Hotel* (☎ 433 8311), on Sargood Drive, has rooms from $145 to $225. The *Wanaka Motor Inn* (☎ 443 8216), on Mt Aspiring Rd, is also a very swish establishment with double rooms for $108.

Places to Eat

The *Snack Shack* on Ardmore St, by the mall, has pizzas and the usual takeaway food. Next door is the highly recommended *Kai Whaka Pai*, a pleasant cafe where good cheap food, such as doner kebabs, are served. In the mall are the indifferent *Munchies* and the *Doughbin* for bread and baked food. *Barrow's Bistro*, in the tavern of the same name on Ardmore St, also serves good pub fare – hoki & chips, for instance.

Wanaka is surprisingly well equipped with restaurants, including the *Te Kano Cafe* on Brownston St. This little cottage has well-prepared, imaginative, filling and delicious vegetarian food and pizzas. Soup costs $4.50, entrees around $7.50, and main courses $13.50 to $17.50. In winter you can get gluhwein (hot spiced red wine) and superb desserts (often bearing the flag of your country of origin) for about $6.50.

The *Tuatara Pizza Co*, on Ardmore St, is an interesting little place with friendly owners. Pizzas range from $15 to $25 and all toppings are fresh. Indulge in a heated game of table soccer whilst enduring pre-eating salivation.

Prize-winning *Relishes*, on Ardmore St, is the pick of the town's cafes. They have dinner mains for around $15 and lunches are cheaper. It is a great place to chill out with a piece of country-style baked cake, muffins and a frothy cappuccino.

In the mall, the up-market BYO *Ripples* offers alfresco dining on the verandah, with good views of the lake and mountains. *Capriccio's* is an Italian restaurant, also in the mall, which sometimes has intriguingly un-Italian 'Chinese nights'! It has several award-winning specialities but it's not cheap – main courses are in the $22 to $30 range.

Just around the corner the *White House*, in Dungarvon St, is an interesting place for a meal and comes with a swag of recommendations. For a late-night drink head upstairs to the licensed *Soho Cafe*, across the road from Clifford's on Ardmore St, where there is a good selection of beers on tap.

Getting There & Away

Aspiring Air (☎ 443 7943) has flights to Queenstown up to three times daily ($80), connecting with Mt Cook Airline and Ansett New Zealand flights to other centres.

The InterCity bus depot is at the Paper Place, 84 Ardmore St, opposite Clifford's. Daily buses from Queenstown stop at Wanaka on the way to the glaciers via Haast Pass, as does a bus from Tarras on InterCity's daily service from Queenstown to Christchurch via Mt Cook. InterCity also has a connecting bus from Cromwell on the Queenstown to Dunedin route every day.

Mt Cook Landline buses operate from the Wanaka Travel Centre (☎ 443 7414) on Ardmore St in the town centre. Buses run every day to Christchurch, Dunedin and Mt Cook and Queenstown.

The Catch-a-Bus (☎ (0800) 508 000) shuttle travels to Dunedin ($35), Christchurch ($50) and Invercargill via Queenstown ($15).

Car Although the Cardrona road to Queenstown looks much shorter on the map than the route via Cromwell, it's a winding, climbing, unsealed mountain road so travel is unlikely to be quicker. Rental cars and campervans are banned from this road, and a large sign at each end announces that caravans are also banned.

Hitching If you're heading out of Queenstown to the Haast Pass and glacier country you could try hitching to Wanaka, but you will have to be very patient. Hitching out of Queenstown is difficult and hitching through the Haast Pass to Fox or Franz Josef is almost impossible because of the light traffic. The Haast Pass road branches off the Cromwell road about two km from Wanaka, just beyond the Maze. Hitchhikers have written, on stones by the roadside, the sorry stories of their long waits.

Getting Around

Mt Aspiring Express (☎ 443 7414) offers regular transport to track entrances along the Matukituki River; expect to pay about $35 return ($90 to charter the vehicle). Matuki Services (☎ 443 7980) offers charter bus trips also; for example, $100 for 10 people to the Matukituki road end. Wanaka Taxis (☎ 443 7999) also provide transport to various tramping destinations. Edgewater Resort Adventures (☎ 443 8311) does two-day 4WD trips in the area for around $300.

A few years ago somebody got the idea of hiring mountain bikes in Wanaka and now there are about as many mountain bikes for hire as there are people in the town! You can hire them from the YHA hostel (whether or not you're staying there) for $10 per day or $5 for half a day. Good Sports and Wanaka Lake Services also hire bikes. Cyclists passing through town may want to check Mountain Bikes Unlimited (☎ 443 7882) at 99 Ardmore St for spares, repairs and advice.

HAWEA

Lake Hawea, which is separated from Lake Wanaka by a narrow isthmus, is 35 km long and plunges to a depth of 410 metres. The lake was raised 20 metres in 1958 to provide those important cusecs for power stations downriver. Trout and landlocked salmon can be caught in its waters.

Hawea has a hotel, motel and motor camp. At the *Lake Hawea Motor Camp* (☎ 443 1767), on the lake shore, tent/powered sites are $14/16 and cabins cost $27; prices are for two people. At the *Lake Hawea Hotel* (☎ 443 1224) there is a poorly equipped hostel where a bed in a four-bed dorm costs $18; their hotel rooms are $75 for a double. At the *Glenruth Lakeview Motel* (☎ 443 1440) a room is $70 for two. The pub puts on a good meal, or you can arrange to have the fish you caught earlier cooked for you.

Central Otago

Most of the towns in Central Otago owe their origin to about 40 years of gold-mining last century. The goldfields heritage area extends from Wanaka down to Queenstown and Glenorchy, east through Alexandra to the coast at Palmerston, and south-east from Alexandra to Milton. There are several interpretative pamphlets which show towns and gold-mining areas, such as *Goldfields: Heritage Trail.*

Throughout this area you will stumble across the impedimenta of the gold rush – stone buildings, equipment and machinery, and miles of tailings (waste left over from mining). Queenstown, an important town during Otago's golden days, maintains its glory in the modern gold rush – tourism.

CROMWELL

This pleasant little town of 3400 people, on the main route between Wanaka and Queenstown, is a good place for a short pause. The Cromwell & Districts Information Centre (☎ 445 0212; fax 445 1649) in the Cromwell Mall, has some excellent displays and slide presentations on the hydroelectric projects in the Clutha Valley. It's open daily from 10 am to 4 pm. Get a copy of *Cromwell and Districts: A Historical Guide* here.

Cromwell has a **museum** with artefacts of local mining, including a section on the Chinese miners. It's open from 10 am to 4 pm daily. In Melmore Terrace several historic buildings, some made of stone, have been restored to recreate a main street of Old Cromwell. They were painstakingly removed from the original Cromwell, now covered by the waters of the Dunstan Dam.

Cromwell is the heart of stone fruit country. There are a number of roadside stalls here where you can buy apricots, peaches, nectarines, plums, cherries, apples and pears. Try some – you'll probably be tempted after seeing the giant Carmen Miranda's hat display in front of the town.

The Kawarau Gorge between here and Queenstown is spectacular and you can pause to watch the bungy jumping at the interesting old Kawarau suspension bridge. Built in 1880 for access to the Wakatipu goldfields, it was used until 1963.

There are a number of gold-mining sites around Cromwell – Bannockburn, Bendigo and the Kawarau. You can see a working exhibition of gold-mining technology at the Kawarau Mining Centre (Hidden Valley Goldmine). Access is across a footbridge spanning the Kawarau.

Bendigo, 18 km from Cromwell on the Bendigo Loop Rd, is a classic ghost town. If you hunt around in the scrub you'll find the ruins of stone cottages. There are also many deep mine shafts so stick to obvious tracks when exploring.

Places to Stay & Eat

The *Sunhaven Motor Camp* (☎ 445 0164) on Alpha St, about two km from the town

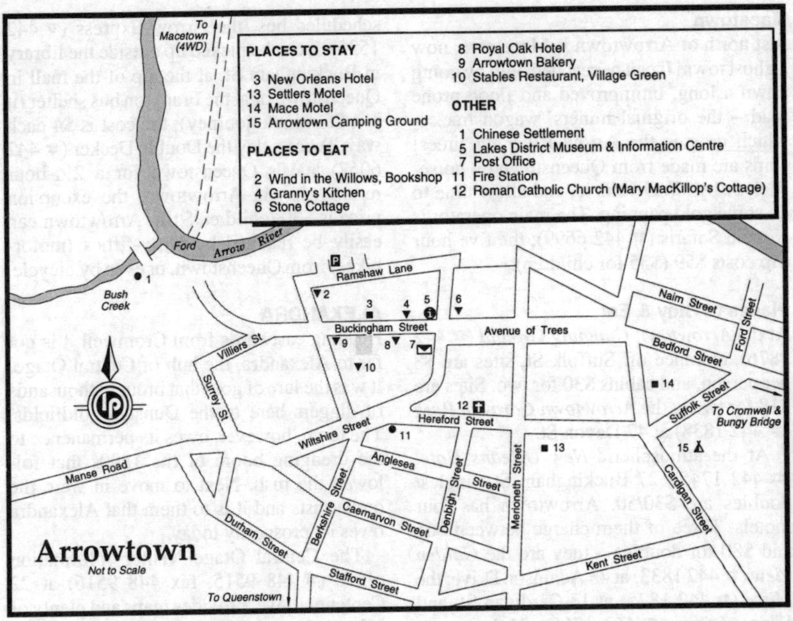

centre, has tent and powered sites for $16 for two and cabins from $22 to $34 for two. The *Backpackers Chalet* (☎ 445 1893) is at the bottom of Barry Ave; a bed in a twin with a washbasin is $15 per person. There are also hotels and motels, including the *Golden Gate Lodge* (☎ 445 1777) on Barry Ave with restaurant, lounge and public bars; doubles are $95 here. The *Twin Rivers Motel* (☎ 445 0035) at 69 Inniscort St has singles/doubles for $55/68.

There are a number of sandwich places in the Cromwell Mall. Try the *Gold Mine*, which has good food, or the pricier *Daniel's*.

ARROWTOWN

Between Cromwell and Queenstown (not far past the bungy bridge) is the loop road turn-off to Arrowtown. Arrowtown, with a population of 1200, is a faithfully restored early gold-mining settlement with a beautiful avenue of deciduous trees.

The **Lake District Museum**, which also acts as the local information office, has displays on gold mining and local history. It's open from 9 am to 5 pm and admission is $3 (children 50c). Get a copy of *Historic Arrowtown* and *Arrowtown Walks* from the museum – the latter has information about getting to Macetown as well as historic notes about the area.

Perhaps the best remaining example of a gold-era **Chinese settlement** in NZ is near Bush Creek, at the top end of Buckingham St. A store and two huts have been restored as a reminder of the role played by many Chinese 'diggers' during and after the gold rush. The Chinese were subjected to prejudice, especially during the economic depression of the 1880s. More often than not they did not seek new gold claims but worked through the tailings looking for the fine gold which had been undetected by earlier miners. The museum sells a brochure, *Arrowtown Chinese Settlement* for $2.50.

Macetown

Just north of Arrowtown is Macetown, now a ghost town. It can be reached only by going down a long, unimproved and flood-prone road – the original miners' wagon track – which crosses the Arrow River 44 times! Trips are made from Queenstown on horseback or by 4WD vehicle, and allow time to do some gold panning. The main operator is Nomad Safaris (☎ 442 6699); the five-hour trip costs $59 ($35 for children).

Places to Stay & Eat

At the *Arrowtown Camping Ground* (☎ 442 1876), entrance off Suffolk St, sites are $8 per person, and cabins $30 for two. Sites are $18 for two at the *Arrowtown Caravan Park* (☎ 442 1838) at 47 Devon St.

At the atmospheric *New Orleans Hotel* (☎ 442 1745), 27 Buckingham St, singles/doubles are $30/50. Arrowtown has four motels. Three of them charge between $65 and $80 for doubles – they are the *Golden View* (☎ 442 1833) at 48 Adamson Drive; the *Mace* (☎ 442 1825) at 13 Cardigan St; and *Viking Lodge* (☎ 442 1765), 21 Inverness Crescent. Top of the range is the *Settlers Motel* (☎ 442 1734) at 20-22 Hereford St, where doubles are $85 to $100.

Most places to eat are along Buckingham St. Best value is the *Arrowtown Bakery*, purveyors of excellent Bolognese mince pies, rolls, and German-style bread. Both the *New Orleans* and *Royal Oak* hotels have bistros where you can get the usual pub fare.

Three restaurants, housed in gold-era houses are *Granny's Kitchen*, the *Stables* and the *Stone Cottage*. The *Wind in the Willows*, on Ramshaw Lane behind the New Orleans, serves lunches and good coffee ($2.50); a ploughman's lunch is $7.50.

About 400 metres from the Kawarau Bridge is the *Gibbston Valley Winery* which has a cellar restaurant and outdoor courtyard set amongst the vines. The blackboard menu is changed daily and the food receives rave reviews. Dine here *after* your bungy jump.

Getting There & Away

Arrowtown is served from Queenstown by a scheduled bus, the Arrow Express (☎ 442 1535). It can be picked up outside the library in Buckingham St, at the top of the mall in Queenstown or at the Frankton bus shelter (it is a 25-minute journey); the cost is $4 each way. Twice a day the Double Decker (☎ 442 6067) leaves Queenstown for a 2½-hour return trip via Arrowtown; the excursion price is $30 (children $10). Arrowtown can easily be reached by Nifty-fifties (motorbikes) from Queenstown, or even by bicycle.

ALEXANDRA

Heading eastwards from Cromwell it is not far to Alexandra, the hub of Central Otago. It was the lure of gold that brought thousands of diggers here to the Dunstan goldfields. The town, however, owes its permanence to the dredging boom of the 1890s that followed the rush. Next to move in were the orchardists and it is to them that Alexandra owes its prosperity today.

The Central Otago Visitor Information office (☎ 448 9515; fax 448 9516) at 22 Centennial Ave, provides maps and plenty of information on things to see and do in the region. Look out for their excellent *Walk – Central Otago*, a series of eight free pamphlets which outline interesting walks in the town and the nearby region. The DOC office (☎ 448 8874) is at 45 Centennial Ave.

The **Sir William Bodkin Museum** (☎ 448 7077), on the corner of Thompson and Walton Sts, houses a comprehensive collection of mining and pioneering relics; it is open Monday to Friday from 11 am to 4 pm.

There are many other attractions in the area including a plethora of **vineyards**, the southernmost in the world. The free *Central Otago Vineyards* map indicates the location of a dozen vineyards.

Those who get off on four-wheel driving can attempt the **Dunstan Trail**, a magnificent rugged mountain road from Alexandra to SH87 near Outram, an hours' drive from Dunedin. The trail leaves you in awe of the tenacity of the early gold prospectors who stumbled across muddy sections and over steep hills with their bullock wagons and horse-drawn drays. Check with the DOC office in Alexandra before you begin the trail and remember to leave all gates as you found them. With time spent for stops at Paerau (Styx), Serpentine Flat and the Great Moss Swamp the trip will take five to six hours.

Clyde

This former gold town, only 10 km west of Alexandra, has a very colourful history. It was once the centre of the Dunstan Goldfields, and historic stone buildings still line the streets. Clyde has two **museums**: the Clyde Museum, in Blythe St in the historic Magistrate's Court House, features exhibits depicting domestic life on the early goldfields; and the Stationary Engine Display, Upper Fraser St, includes all sorts of rural machinery. The Clyde Lookout Point, reached from a signposted road, gives great views out over the once bustling goldfields. At 1 pm daily there are tours of the Clyde Dam project from the Clyde information office (☎ 448 9642); bookings are essential.

Mountain Biking

Alexandra is known as mountain bike heaven as there are numerous old gold trails which can be followed through the Old Man, Dunstan, Raggedy and Knobby ranges. A highlight for keen bikers would be the Dunstan Trail, mentioned earlier.

You can hire bikes from two places in town – Henderson Cycles in Limerick St and MCS Services in Shannon St – both have bikes for about $22 per day. And there is one touring company, Central Outdoor Adventures (☎ 448 6360). The pamphlet *Mountain Biking* details five exhilarating rides.

Places to Stay & Eat

Alexandra has a full range of accommodation options. There are two camping grounds in town and one in nearby Clyde. The *Alexandra Holiday Camp* (☎ 448 8297), at Manuherikia Rd, has sites for $14 for two and basic cabins from $20 to $28 for two. The *Pine Lodge Holiday Camp* (☎ 448 8861), at Ngapara St, has sites for $16, basic units for $26, and cabins for $30 (all prices for two). In nearby Clyde, the *Clyde Holiday Park* (☎ 449 2713) has tent/powered sites for $11/13, and on-site vans and cabins for $26.

There is one budget hostel in town – the *Alexandra Riverside Associate YHA Hostel* (☎ 448 8152) at 4 Dunorling St. At this hostel, which overlooks the Clutha River, a bed in a dorm/twin room will cost $12/14 per person. The *Willows Guest House* (☎ 449 2231) at 3 Young Lane (off SH8 to Clyde), has singles/doubles for $35/60. In Clyde, *Oliver's Lodge* (☎ 449 2860) at Main St, has rooms in the stables for $106 and in the lodge for $151.

The two motels in Alexandra and four in Clyde each charge from $60 to $70 per room.

There are a few bakeries such as the *Avenue* and *The Bakery* on Centennial Ave, and the *Kiwi Milk Bar* in the Centrepoint Mall. In Tarbert St there are a number of takeaway and sandwich places. Pub food is served at the *Bendigo Hotel*, Tarbert St. The award-winning *Oliver's Restaurant*, 34 Sunderland St, Clyde, is open for lunch and dinner daily.

Getting There & Away

InterCity, Mt Cook Landline, Catch-a-Bus and the ICE buses all have services which pass through Alexandra. The InterCity and Mt Cook Landline agent is Travel for Less (☎ 448 8198) at 56 Centennial Ave. Southern Link Shuttles (☎ (0800) 502 522) operates directly through to Christchurch ($50).

ALEXANDRA TO PALMERSTON

To the north-east of Alexandra lies the Manuherikia Valley, which is rich in evidence of Otago's golden age. At Blackstone Hill the road, SH85, swings south-east to the Maniototo plain and out, via the Pig Root, to the sea and Palmerston.

About 27 km north of Alexandra, and a small sidetrip from Omakau on the main highway, is the small township of **Ophir**. Today peacefulness belies its once bustling past. There is a restored post and telegraph building, dating from 1886, in the town. The Manuherikia River is spanned by the **Dan O'Connell bridge**, built in the 1870s and still in use today. The town has the widest temperature range of any in NZ; from -20°C in winter to 35°C in summer.

At the town of Becks, where there is a great old pub, the road forks. The left fork leads to **St Bathans**, also once a thriving gold-mining town with a population of 2000 – today there are less than 20 inhabitants. This is a real get-away sort of place and the visitor is able to enjoy a peaceful stroll through a town which retains a number of original buildings. The 'haunted' *Vulcan Hotel* (☎ 447 3629) is a quaint living museum, and is the only remainder of the town's 14 hotels. Here B&B is $30/50 for singles/doubles (dinner is $20 extra). In winter the curling teams compete on frozen ponds near the town. The **Blue Lake**, formed entirely by sluicing activity, is a popular picnic spot close to town.

Back on SH85, past Blackstone Hill and heading east, the next main town is **Naseby**, once the largest gold-mining town on the Maniototo. There's a museum here, and the surrounding area is great walking country. From May to September the Maniototo Ice Rink (☎ 444 9270) is used for skating, curling and ice hockey. The *Ancient Briton Hotel & Motel* (☎ 444 9992) in Lever St has rooms for $22 per person and motel rooms for $68 for two. There is a *backpackers* (☎ 444 9904) which will pick up travellers (and their bikes) from Ranfurly; the cost is $12 per person.

Some 39 km north of Naseby is **Dansey Pass**, another goldfields town with a great old pub dating from the 1860s. Apparently the stonemason was paid a pint of beer for each stone laid! The *Danseys Pass Coach Inn* (☎ 444 9048), strategically located on the route between the Maniototo and the Waitaki Valley, has been extensively refurbished; a double with en suite costs $86 for two.

Ranfurly

This small town is the hub of the Maniototo. Nearby Naseby with its goldfields, and the more luckless Hamiltons goldfields near Waipiata, were the original reasons for Europeans coming to this part of New Zealand. The vast inland plain is now referred to as the Maniototo and is the site of a number of stud farms.

Tent/powered sites at the *Ranfurly Motor Camp* (☎ 444 9144) in Reade St, are $9.50/12, and cabins are $20 for two. You can actually stay on a farm in the Maniototo and not ransom your own station to do it. *Peter's Farm Hostel* (☎ 444 9083) is in a 100-year-old homestead, three km from Waipiata and 12 km from Ranfurly. The farm offers kitchen and bathroom facilities, open log fire, and a number of activities – all for $13 per night (there are tent sites at $8 per person). A pool (eight ball) room has been built 100 metres from the main house so that the noise will not disturb those who are sleeping. If you ring in advance Peter may be able to help with transport from Dunedin. If you head out this way, do so for a couple of days or more to make the trip worthwhile.

The *Ranfurly Lion* (☎ 444 9140) at Charlemont St East, has doubles for $60. The *Lion's Restaurant* is the best of the town's eateries, with chicken, steak and fish dishes.

ALEXANDRA TO DUNEDIN

If you head south-east from Alexandra via SH8 to Dunedin you get the opportunity to see more evidence of last century's gold seekers as well as spectacular scenery. **Fruitlands** is the first place of interest and there is a restored pub, dating from 1866, where food and crafts are sold. One km away, via Symes Rd, is the restored **Mitchells Cottage**, a fine example of the Shetland Island stonemasons' building skills.

The next town of any size is **Roxburgh**, in an area known for fruit growing. Sales begin in early December, continuing until early winter. There is a motor camp and a couple of motels in this town of 900 people. The *Villa Rose Backpackers* (☎ 485 9101), 79 Scotland St, is a tidy converted house with all facilities; a dorm or share room is $14, and twin and double rooms (if not taken up by itinerant fruit pickers) are $32.

Between Roxburgh and Milton, near the town of Lawrence, is **Gabriels Gully**, the site of a frenzied stampede for gold by 10,000 miners in July 1861, after Gabriel

OTAGO

Read discovered gold in the Tuapeka River. In Lawrence, you can get cheap accommodation at *Oban Guest House – Backpackers*, 1 Oban St, (☎ 485 9600) for $15 in share or dorm rooms, and $34 for twins and doubles.

There is a *takeaway*, and bistro in the *Coach & Horses Tavern*, both in Ross Place. There are also a number of interesting walks in the vicinity of the town, including that up Gabriels Gully to Jacobs Ladder.

At Lawrence the road splits and you have the choice of reaching the coast and SH1 to Dunedin by one of two ways: either to Milton on SH1 or by Lake Mahinerangi and the Waipori goldfield (and Waipori Falls) where there are more relics of the gold rushes. Dunedin is 55 km north of Milton or about half that distance from where the Waipori Falls road meets SH1.

THE CLUTHA DISTRICT

The Clutha district is a collection of small communities around the mighty Clutha River, not NZ's longest but the one with the greatest volume of discharge. (It is 16 km shorter than the Waikato.) Clutha is Gaelic for Clyde, alluding to that river in Scotland; to the Maori it is Mata-au ('surface current').

The Clutha drains a huge area including lakes Hawea, Wanaka and Wakitipu. In a number of places the river has been dammed to feed hydroelectric power stations – the most recent project is the Clyde Dam, which holds back the waters of Lake Dunstan. Such development has not been without controversy. Any future damming of the Clutha will be opposed by locals who have too often witnessed the drowning of areas of natural beauty.

The towns of Clinton, Lawrence, Milton, Waihola, Owaka, Tapanui and Balclutha are all part of the region. Owaka is covered in the Catlins (see the Southland chapter).

Balclutha

The largest town in the South Otago region, Balclutha, is dominated by an impressive arched concrete bridge across the Clutha River. The Clutha Information Centre (☎ 418 0388; fax 418 1877) at 63 Clyde St is sometimes open (but not on the day we sought information).

Fortunately, the **museum** at 1 Renfrew St will probably provide the information you need; it is open from 10 am to 4 pm Monday to Friday and 1 to 4 pm Sunday. Particularly interesting is the scattered collection of old farming and household implements (among some 10,000 items) which indicate how much things have changed over the years.

The *Naish Park Camping Ground* (☎ 418 0088) in Charlotte St has sites for $12, cabins for $22 for two. The flashiest place in town is the *Rosebank Lodge* (☎ 418 1490) at 265 Clyde St; a double or twin costs $80. The information centre has a list of motels, homestays and farmstays in the region.

The *265 Restaurant* in the Rosebank Lodge is the place to eat (it has a menu featuring locally caught salmon and trout) or there is the *Hotel South Otago* and a string of takeaways along the main street.

Lake Wakatipu

Most people coming to this region make a beeline for Queenstown, the self-styled 'adventure capital of the world'. When the party ends and the recovery begins the Wakatipu region, with its stunning lake and surrounding mountain scenery, materialises as the real attraction. The aptly monikered Remarkables and the Eyre Mountains form a breath-taking backdrop. Words hardly do the Remarkables justice – capped with snow, at sunrise or in the afterglow of dusk, pure magic!

QUEENSTOWN

Queenstown, right on the shores of Lake Wakatipu, is nestled in what is surely one of the most scenic spots in the world. Or was! Developers have blocked out some of the unforgettable views by building along the waterfront. Imagine painting advertising graffiti over the ceiling of the Sistine Chapel for similar short-term gain. Such a travesty is indicative of the malaise that has pervaded

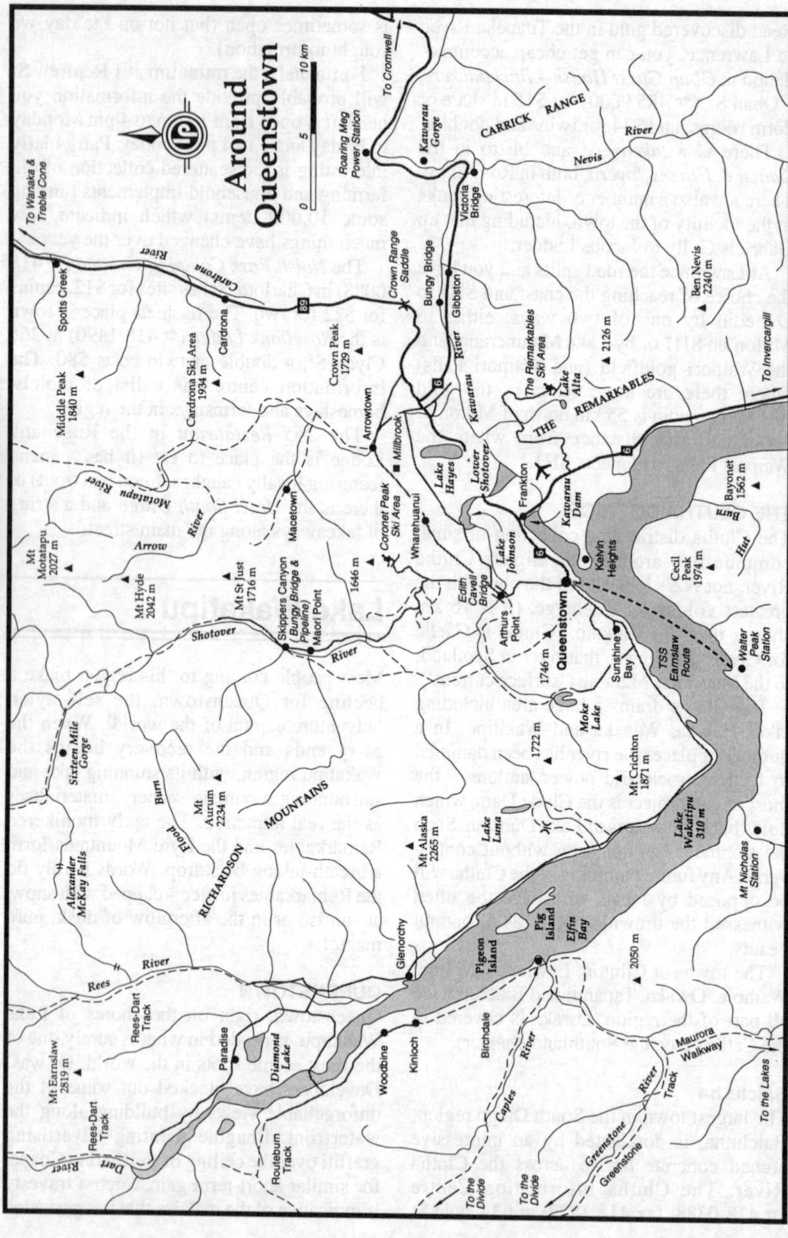
Around Queenstown
0
5
10 km
To Cromwell
To Wanaka & Treble Cone
Roaring Meg Power Station
Kawarau Gorge
CARRICK RANGE
Nevis
River
Victoria Bridge
Ben Nevis 2240 m
Crown Range Saddle
Bungy Bridge
Gibbston
Kawarau
River
Cardrona
River
Spotts Creek
Cardrona
89
Cardrona Ski Area 1934 m
Crown Peak 1729 m
Middle Peak 1840 m
Arrowtown
Millbrook
The Remarkables Ski Area
Lake Alta
2126 m
THE REMARKABLES
To Invercargill
6
Lake Hayes
Lower Shotover
Frankton
Kawarau Dam
Bayonet 1562 m
Hut
Burn
Motatapu River
Macetown
Coronet Peak Ski Area
Wharehuanui
Lake Johnson
Kelvin Heights
Cecil Peak 1974 m
Mt Motatapu 2027 m
Arrow
River
Mt Hyde 2042 m
Mt St Just 1716 m
Skippers Canyon (Bungy Bridge & Pipeline)
Maori Point
1646 m
Edith Cavell Bridge
Arthurs Point
Queenstown
1746 m
Sunshine Bay
TSS Earnslaw Route
Walter Peak Station
Shotover
River
Sixteen Mile Gorge
Moke Lake
1722 m
Mt Crichton 1871 m
Mt Aurum 2234 m
Flood
Burn
RICHARDSON
MOUNTAINS
Lake Luna
Lake Wakatipu 310 m
Alexander McKay Falls
Mt Alaska 2265 m
Mt Nicholas Station
Glenorchy
Pigeon Island
Pig Island
Elfin Bay
2050 m
Rees
River
Rees-Dart Track
Birchdale
Kinloch
Woodbine
Caples
River
Maurora Walkway
To the Lakes
Mt Earnslaw 2819 m
Paradise
Diamond Lake
Routeburn Track
To the Divide
To the Divide
Greenstone
River
Track
Greenstone
Dart
River
Rees-Dart Track

this town in recent times – its famous pleasantness and charm is quickly being traded for the 'fast buck'.

However, there is still great skiing in winter and plenty of substitute adrenaline activities to compensate for the lack of snow in summer. Most activities are centred around the lake and many rivers nearby, especially the Dart, Shotover and Kawarau. White-water rafting and sledging, jet-boating and boogey boarding are all great ways to get wet. Bungy jumping, heli-bungy, tandem parachuting, hang-gliding and parapenting are similarly exciting ways to fly. You will always find some exhilarating activity to suit you.

Those wishing to relax and move at a much more leisurely pace are also catered for. Take a trip on the TSS *Earnslaw* to Walter Peak Station, stroll through golden Arrowtown in autumn, play golf on beautiful Millbrook, or shop in Queenstown's many (expensive) boutiques.

It's extremely easy to go through a lot of money here but Queenstown is a 'doing' place and sometimes you just have to forget the cost and 'do' it. So relax and enjoy the fantastic setting; here there's lots to do, many foreign travellers and more nightlife than most places in NZ.

History

There is evidence that Queenstown was once the site of a Maori settlement. However, when the Pakeha began arriving in the mid-1850s the region was deserted. The first settlers in the area were sheep farmers, but in 1862 two shearers, Thomas Arthur and Harry Redfern, discovered gold on the banks of the Shotover River, precipitating a rush of prospectors to the area. Queenstown fast developed into a mining town and by early 1863 streets had been laid out and permanent buildings established. Then the gold petered out and by 1900 the population had dropped from several thousand to a mere 190 people.

During this era the lake was the principal means of communication and at the height of the mining boom there were four paddle steamers and about 30 other craft plying the waters. The road skirting the lake between Queenstown and Glenorchy was only completed in 1962.

Orientation & Information

Queenstown, a compact town of 2500 people is arrayed around the shores of the lake and backed by steep hills. The main streets are the pedestrian-only mall and Shotover St, where a number of activity booking offices are located. There are a great number of places offering information, most designed to remove money from your pocket. You will continually ask yourself 'Who do I believe?'

The visitor information centre (☎ 442 4100; fax 442 8907), close to the lake in the Clocktower Centre on the corner of Shotover and Camp Sts, is open from 7 am to 7 pm in summer, and 7 am to 6 pm in winter.

Directly across the road is the Station (☎ 442 5252), a video jungle which is perhaps the most useful of the town's information places. When you walk in, however, prepare to dig deep into your pockets to splurge on adventure measured in dollars per second and 'red badge of courage' T-shirts. They take bookings for almost every activity imaginable (and some unimaginable).

The Backpacking Specialists (☎ 442 8178), at 18b Shotover St, is open seven days a week for bookings. The emphasis is on saving you money, eg cheap buses and activities.

Fiordland Travel (☎ (0800) 656 501) has an office near the steamer wharf where they take bookings for their trips on the lake, and for trips to Doubtful and Milford Sounds.

Dane's Queenstown Information Centre (☎ 442 7318), also on a corner of Shotover and Camp Sts, takes bookings for local activities including white-water sledging. The office is open in winter from 7.30 am to 8 pm and in summer from 7.30 am to 10 pm daily.

Also on Shotover St is the Information & Track Walking Centre (☎ 442 9708). They do bookings for the Routeburn, Greenstone-Caples, Kepler, Milford and Rees-Dart tracks. They know all the transport options to the trail heads. They are open in summer from 8 am to 8 pm, and in winter until 7 pm.

The DOC (☎ 442 7933) is on Shotover St opposite the Trust Bank; there's also one in Ballarat St. It has information on the many natural attractions of the area, and on long and short drives and walks. It's open from 9 am to 4.30 pm, Monday to Friday all year round, and also from 10 am to 3 pm on weekends during Christmas holidays.

There is a 24-hour free information service, Infophone (☎ 442 5024), which lists a variety of activities. There's a useful notice board right in the middle of the mall. The AA centre (☎ 442 5155) is at 37 Stanley St, next to the library.

And oh, the post office in Camp St (with poste restante facilities) is open from 9 am to 5 pm, Monday to Friday.

Things to See

Try starting at, literally, the top of the town. Catch the Skyline Gondola to the summit of the hill overlooking the town for incredible *views* over the lake – the only drawback is the hefty return fee of $12 (children $4). If the view isn't enough then look at *Kiwi Magic*, a hi-tech film which screens on the hour from 10 am to 8 pm. It's a chance to get rid of more change from your pocket – $7 for adults ($3 for children). If you're more energetic you can walk up the vehicle track to Skyline from Lomond Crescent, but the ride is worth experiencing. The gondola operates in summer from 10 am to 10 pm and in winter from 10 am to 9 pm daily.

If you want to get views in the other direction you can drive up to the back of the ski field. A short track leads past Lake Alta to a viewpoint at the top of the Remarkables. From here you look down over the lake back to a diminutive Queenstown.

The **motor museum** just below the lower gondola terminal has a fine collection of cars, all well restored and in running order. There's also a motorcycle collection upstairs and a fine old Tiger Moth suspended overhead. The museum is open from 9 am to 5.30 pm daily; admission is $6 (children $3).

Also below the gondola terminal is the **kiwi & birdlife park**. It has what is becoming a NZ standard – the nocturnal kiwi house. The park is open from 9 am to 5 pm daily and admission is $6 (children $2.50).

On the pier at the end of the mall, near the centre of Queenstown, is **Underwater World**, a submerged observation gallery where you can see eels and trout in the clear waters of the lake. The agile little scaup or 'diving' ducks also make periodic appearances outside the windows. The cost of entry is $5 (children $2.50) – avoid this by just peering into the water from the jetty.

There are also **garden tours** which include the Speight Gardens ($48), escorted tours, Farm Scene for the kids, a Maori concert and hangi-style feast and more. Enquire at the many information offices.

Activities

Bungy Jumping Of all the things to do around Queenstown, probably the one that sparks the most interest is bungy jumping. These days there is no shortage of 'jumping' options. AJ Hackett's Action Culture (☎ 442 7100) is in the Station on the corner of Shotover and Camp Sts. AJ Hackett became world famous when he bungy jumped off the Eiffel Tower in 1986. He began operating at Queenstown in November 1988.

The historic **Kawarau Suspension Bridge**, 23 km from Queenstown on SH6, attracts the most jumpers; it's 43 metres from the special bungy platform to the Kawarau River below. Observation platforms have been built to accommodate all the viewers, and even if you don't jump yourself, you can watch others do it. The jump at Kawarau costs $99, including a bungy T-shirt which you can only get if you've jumped. If you include a video the package will cost $129.

The **Skippers Canyon Bridge**, towering 71 metres over a narrow gorge above the Shotover River, is a more spectacular site. It's also more difficult to reach, about an hour's ride down a tortuous road from Queenstown.

Neither of these high enough? Then throw yourself from the **Pipeline**, the latest of the adrenaline 'highs'. Pipeline Bungy (☎ 442 5455) has built a bridge across Skippers – the largest single-span suspension bridge in the

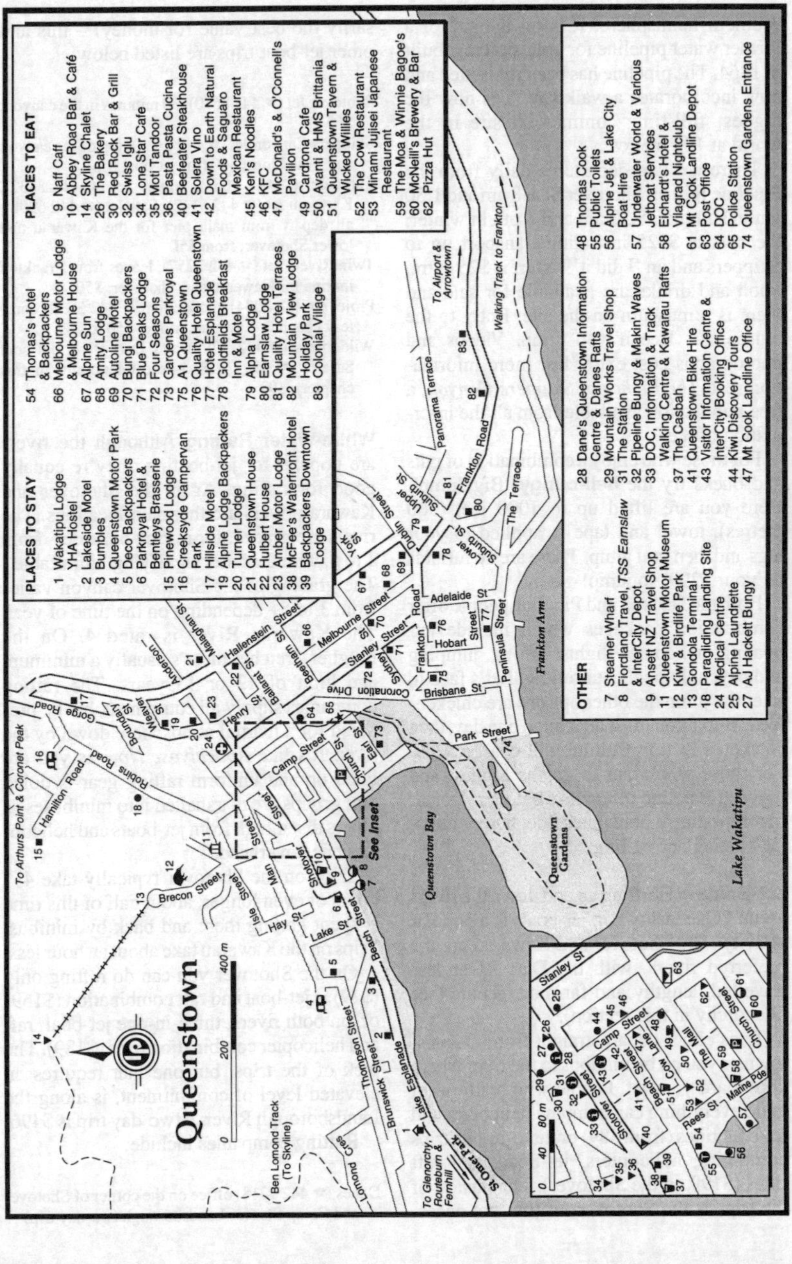
Queenstown
PLACES TO STAY
1 Wakatipu Lodge
YHA Hostel
2 Lakeside Motel
3 Bumbles
4 Queenstown Motor Park
5 Deco Backpackers
6 Parkroyal Hotel & Bentleys Brasserie
15 Pinewood Lodge
16 Creeksyde Campervan Park
17 Hillside Motel
19 Alpine Lodge Backpackers
20 Turner Lodge
21 Queenstown House
22 Hulbert House
23 Amber Motor Lodge
38 McFee's Waterfront Hotel
39 Backpackers Downtown Lodge
54 Thomas's Hotel & Backpackers
66 Melbourne Motor Lodge & Melbourne House
67 Alpine Sun
68 Amity Lodge
69 Autoline Motel
70 Bungi Backpackers
71 Blue Peaks Lodge
72 Four Seasons
73 Gardens Parkroyal
75 A1 Queenstown
76 Quality Hotel Queenstown
77 Hotel Esplanade
78 Goldfields Breakfast Inn & Motel
79 Alpha Lodge
80 Earnslaw Lodge
81 Quality Hotel Terraces
82 Mountain View Lodge
83 Colonial Village Holiday Park
PLACES TO EAT
9 Naff Caff
10 Abbey Road Bar & Café
14 Skyline Chalet
26 The Bakery
30 Red Rock Bar & Grill
32 Swiss Iglu
34 Lone Star Cafe
35 Moti Tandoor
36 Pasta Pasta Cucina
40 Beefeater Steakhouse
41 Solera Vino
42 Down to Earth Natural Foods & Saguaro Mexican Restaurant
45 Ken's Noodles
46 KFC
47 McDonald's & O'Connell's Pavilion
49 Cardrona Cafe
50 Avanti & HMS Brittania
51 Queenstown Tavern & Wicked Willies
52 The Cow Restaurant
53 Minami Jujisei Japanese Restaurant
59 The Moa & Winnie Bagoe's
60 McNeill's Brewery & Bar
62 Pizza Hut
OTHER
7 Steamer Wharf
8 Fiordland Travel, TSS Earnslaw & InterCity Depot
9 Ansett NZ Travel Shop
11 Queenstown Motor Museum
12 Kiwi & Birdlife Park
13 Gondola Terminal
18 Paragliding Landing Site
24 Medical Centre
25 Alpine Laundrette
27 AJ Hackett Bungy
28 Dane's Queenstown Information Centre & Danes Rafts
29 Mountain Works Travel Shop
31 The Station
32 Pipeline Bungy & Makin' Waves
33 DOC, Information & Track Walking Centre & Kawarau Rafts
37 The Casbah
41 Queenstown Bike Hire
43 Visitor Information Centre & InterCity Booking Office
44 Kiwi Discovery Tours
47 Mt Cook Landline Office
48 Thomas Cook
55 Public Toilets
56 Alpine Jet & Lake City Boat Hire
57 Underwater World & Various Jetboat Services
58 Eichardt's Hotel & Vilagrad Nightclub
61 Mt Cook Landline Depot
63 Post Office
64 DOC
65 Police Station
74 Queenstown Gardens Entrance
To Arthurs Point & Coronet Peak
Ben Lomond Track (To Skyline)
To Glenorchy, Routeburn & Fernhill
To Airport & Arrowtown
Walking Track to Frankton
See Inset
Queenstown Bay
Queenstown Gardens
Frankton Arm
Lake Wakatipu
0 200 400 m
0 40 80 m

southern hemisphere. It is on the site of a former water pipeline for gold sluicing, built in 1864. The pipeline has been reinstated and now incorporates a walkway. It is now the highest full-time commercial site in the world at 102 metres.

There are two departures daily from the Pipeline Iglu on Shotover St at 8 am and 1.30 pm in summer, 8.30 am and 1 pm in winter; the cost is $125 including transport up to Skippers and an 'I did it' T-shirt is $25 extra. Food and drinks are available for sale and there is a museum on the site. Entry to the museum is free if you jump. Videos and photographs cost extra. For more information read *The Riches of Skippers Canyon*, a free publication available from all the information offices.

For those who enjoy a combination of guts and bucks try the **heli-bungy** 'Big Jump'. Here you are lifted up to 1000 feet (300 metres), towel and tape is applied to your legs and then you jump. There are no refunds on your $299, so jump!

Both the Hackett and Pipeline people offer combination packages which include jet-boating, helicopter flights, rafting, jumping and psychological counselling. Let's face it, after the jump the other options are chickenfeed. But if you must do it all in one day, then Hackett's Action Culture will charge $289. For those who want to do the highest and biggest, Pipeline offers its Shotover Assault incorporating a helicopter ride, bungy jump, jet-boating and rafting.

Jet-Boating Hurtling up and down the rivers around Queenstown in jet-boats is a popular activity. The Shotover and Kawarau are the preferred rivers, with the Dart River less travelled, lengthy and far more scenic (see Glenorchy in this section).

Trips either depart straight from Queenstown or you go by minibus to the river where you board your jet. People who really want to do everything can combine helicopter and jet-boat rides (from $89) or three-in-one trips combining helicopters, jet-boats and raft rides ($199 on the Shotover). The busiest of the trips is the Shotover Jet (but not necessarily the best value for money) – this and other jet-boat trips are listed below:

Shotover Jet (☎ 442 8570); 30 minutes in the canyon; $65

Skippers Canyon Jet (☎ 442 9434); top of the canyon and a land tour; $40 (for jet-boat trip)

Turbo-Jet (☎ 442 9667), Alpine Jet (☎ 442 8832), Kawarau Jet (☎ 442 6142), Lets Jet (☎ 442 6908); all depart from main pier for the Kawarau and lower Shotover; from $50

Twin Rivers Jet (☎ 442 3257); leaves from Frankton marina for Kawarau and Shotover; $50

Projet (☎ 442 3034) and Helijet (☎ 442 3034) courtesy coach to Kawarau bridge; $50 to $89

Wilderness (☎ 442 9792) and Dart River Jet-boat Safaris (☎ 442 7318) – see Glenorchy in this chapter); $99

White-Water Rafting Although the rivers are popular for jet-boating, they're equally good for rafting. Again the Shotover and Kawarau rivers are the main locations. The rivers are graded, for rafting purposes, from 1 to 6, with the latter signifying 'unraftable'. The grading of the Shotover canyon varies from 3 to 5+ depending on the time of year. The Kawarau River is rated 4. On the rougher stretches there's usually a minimum age limit of 12 or 13 years. The rafting companies supply all equipment, but be prepared for a martial atmosphere down by the river. It's like *Apocalypse Now* as you are lined up and uniform rafting gear is doled out; groups are marshalled into minibuses as others disembark from jet-boats and helicopters buzz overhead.

Trips on the Shotover typically take 4½ hours or even longer; about half of this time is spent getting there and back by minibus. Trips on the Kawarau take about an hour less.

On the Shotover you can do rafting only ($79), a jet-boat and raft combination ($159) or, on both rivers, three-in-one jet-boat, raft and helicopter combination trips ($189). The pick of the trips, but one that requires an elevated level of commitment, is along the Landsborough River; a two-day trip is $496.

Rafting companies include:

Danes (☎ 442 7318) office on the corner of Shotover and Camp Sts (for Landsborough two-day trip)

Extreme Green Adventure Co (☎ 442 7100), attached to the Hackett empire (involves bungy jumps)
Kawarau Raft Expeditions (☎ 442 9792), based at the Information & Track Walking Centre
Kiwi Discovery Tours (☎ 442 7340), on Camp St
Makin' Waves The Rafting Co (☎ 442 8636), 27 Shotover St (trips on the upper Shotover usually in combination with heli-jet-bungy options)

White-Water Sledging & River Surfing Perhaps the most exciting things you can do in the water near Queenstown are white-water sledging or river surfing in the Kawarau River (near the Bungy Bridge).

Frogz Have More Fun (mobile ☎ (0800) 338 737 or (025) 388 737) and Danes (☎ 442 7318) take sledge trips through the churning Chinese Dogleg rapid. The great thing about this trip is that you actually get to steer the highly manoeuvrable polystyrene sleds through the rapids; the cost is $89 for the best adrenaline buzz in town.

You can also surf the same seven-km section of the Kawarau with Serious Fun (☎ 442 6207) using modified boogey boards. The first trip costs $89 and includes a T-shirt.

Parapenting & Parachuting If you are up to it, let yourself be tempted into a tandem aerial parapente jump from Bob's Peak. Operators are Max Air (☎ 442 9792), Queenstown Tandems (☎ 442 7318), Renegade Tandems (☎ 442 7640) and Flying Cow (☎ 442 8636); all charge $110 for a tandem flight. The Freeflight Parapenting School (☎ 442 6311) has a one-day introductory course for $180 and a three-day PG1 course for $390. For those who prefer a delta wing there is Skytrek Hanggliding (☎ 442 6311); their flights cost $125.

Pardon the pun, but why not take the Ultimate Jump (mobile ☎ (025) 325 961)? For $245 you can tandem freefall at your 'terminal' velocity before your parachute is opened and you are nursed safely to ground. The sign on their loo declares: 'The Ultimate Dump!'

Paraflying on the lake is another active way to see the sights from the air. Contact Paraflying (☎ 442 8507); an eight-minute flight behind their boat is $65.

Skiing The Remarkables and Coronet Peak ski fields operate from Queenstown. For those who prefer motorised mobility to skis you can churn up the white stuff with Summit Snowmobiling (☎ 442 9757) for $95; this is a winter only activity. See Skiing in the Outdoor Activities chapter for more details or tune into 92 MHz FM for ski information.

Mountain Biking The Queenstown region is great terrain for mountain bikes. A good way to do this activity, if you are not that fit, is to get an operator with a vehicle to cover the strenuous uphill pedalling by taking you and your bike to a suitable high point. Gravity Action (☎ 442 8178) has a 'mega' trip into Skippers Canyon ($48). You can also mountain bike in and raft out for $125.

Motorcycling The region around Queenstown is the perfect environment for bikers who enjoy riding on off-road bikes, bigger touring bikes or four-wheelers on wild country tracks. Europeans find the freedom of these tracks a pleasant change from the restricted roads in their countries.

The rides combine thrills with a real chance to see inaccessible historical areas amid the canyons and hills of Central Otago. You are looking at about $160 for three hours of the best biking you are ever likely to experience. Contact Dennis at Guided Motorcycle Adventure Tours (☎ 442 7858) for more information, prices and (especially) ideas.

Walks Many of Queenstown's activities are decidedly expensive but the walks cost nothing. Stroll along the waterfront through town and keep going to the park on the peninsula. It's a peaceful place. There's now a lake shore walkway from Queenstown beginning at the end of Peninsula St; it takes just over an hour each way.

One of the shortest climbs around Queenstown is up Queenstown Hill, overlooking the town. It's 900 metres high, and a comfortable climb with good views – two to three hours return. For a more spectacular view, climb Ben Lomond (1746 metres) – it is a difficult walk requiring a good level of fitness as it takes six hours return. Follow the Skyline vehicle track for half an hour until you get to a small rock cairn, which marks a turn-off on your left. When you reach the saddle, head west to the top of Ben Lomond.

There are many other walks in the area, especially from Arthurs Point and Arrowtown, areas rich in history – consult the DOC office for information.

If you're planning to go on longer walks there are several places in town where you can hire camping equipment: Mountain Works (☎ 442 7329) in Camp St; R&R Sports (☎ 442 7791) in the mall, and Kiwi Discovery (☎ 442 7340) in Camp St.

Other Activities Still not enough activities in Queenstown? Well, you can go fishing, water-skiing, windsurfing, charter a yacht, hire a catamaran or a horse, try a space shuttle simulator, ride a water-bike, visit an amusement park or underwater observatory, hire a moped or collapse in a heap.

Tours

Lake Cruises The stately old coal-burning TSS (Twin Screw Steamer) *Earnslaw* is the most famous of the lake's many cruise boats. The steel-hulled *Earnslaw* churns across the lake at 13 knots full speed, burning a tonne of coal an hour. Measuring 51 metres in length and 7.3 metres across the beam, it is licensed to carry 810 passengers and at one time was the major means of transport on the lake. The development of modern roads ended its career with NZ Railways. Since 1969 it has been used for lake cruises and it now it works harder than ever – check this schedule:

Walter Peak Sheep Station morning tour: departs 9 am, October to April; three hours. At the station you will see sheep dogs in action and sheep shearing; the cost is $41 (children $10).

Walter Peak afternoon tour: departs 2 pm all year except June (when the boat is being refitted), cost as for the morning tour.

Short lunch-time cruise: departs at 12.30 pm all year except June, costs $21 ($10), not including lunch, which is available on board for an additional $5 to $10.

Evening dinner cruise: departs at 5.30 pm, cost is $26 ($10) for the 1½ hour cruise. The main dining excursion includes a buffet meal at Walter Peak (adult $62, children $31).

Four-hour horse-riding option at Walter Peak run in conjunction with Moonlight Stables. You head over on the *Earnslaw* at 9 am or 2 pm and, after a farm tour, can undertake a very scenic one-hour horse ride before returning on a jet-boat ($85, children $42.50).

The *City of Dunedin* was the sole NZ craft in the 1982 single-handed round-the-world yacht race. She was one of only a few vessels to complete the 43,470 km (27,000 mile) voyage, taking nine months to reach the finish line, with many adventures along the way. The *City* does two-hour sailings in which every passenger (maximum 19) can become part of the crew and participate. The yacht sails at 10.30 am, 1 and 4 pm daily from the water-taxi jetty opposite the Parkroyal Hotel; the cost is $45 (children $20) and food is $10 extra.

There are other lake cruises including an opportunity to match race in a yacht for two to three hours. Sail South (☎ 442 6946) conducts these trips all week and you act as part of the crew; the cost is $65 and the owner is none other than Graeme Hull! Sail South departs from the pier at the end of the mall.

Bus Tours There are all sorts of bus trips from Queenstown. The red Double Decker bus makes a 2½-hour trip to Arrowtown at 10 am and 2 pm daily; the cost is $16 (children $8). It leaves from several points around town, including near the mall. There is also the Arrow Express (☎ 442 1535) scheduled service. Long-distance InterCity and Mt Cook buses from Queenstown also stop at Arrowtown (see Arrowtown, Getting There & Away, earlier in this chapter).

Nomad Safaris (☎ 442 6699), Outback Tours (☎ 442 7386) and Great Sights Gray Line (☎ 442 4640) all do 4½-hour bus trips up the winding road above the Shotover River. The scenery is spectacular, the road is hair-raising, and there's plenty of historical interest as well. The cost is about $45 (children $22), including a stop to try your luck panning for gold. For $69 you also see the museum and have a jet-boat ride.

Day trips via Te Anau to Milford Sound are operated by Fiordland Travel, Mt Cook, Great Sights and InterCity. They take 12 to 13 hours and cost from $99 (children about half-price) including a two-hour launch cruise on the sound. The Queenstown-Milford Sound trip makes a very long day, so if you're going to Te Anau it makes a lot more sense to make the trip from there. The same is true for trips to Doubtful Sound, which cost $170 (children $74) from Queenstown or $140 ($70) from Manapouri.

From October to March Fiordland Travel has a 'backpackers alternative' trip to Milford which takes two days and costs $194. The first day you go from Queenstown to Walter Peak on the MV *Walter Peak*, then a bus takes you to Te Anau via the back road; you stay there overnight on the *Milford Wanderer*. On the second day the bus takes you from Milford back to Queenstown via the back road. You board the TSS *Earnslaw* for the return trip across Lake Wakatipu.

Aerial Sightseeing No possibility is ignored in Queenstown – if you can't boat up it, down it or cross it, walk around it, or get a chairlift over it, then you can fly over it. There are all sorts of options from short helicopter flights over The Remarkables with a landing (from $120) to flights to Milford Sound (from $166). More expensive flights to Milford include a brief landing, or a one or two-hour launch cruise on the sound. Mt Cook Airline, Fiordland Travel, Air Fiordland and Air Wakatipu all fly this route (from $195 to $265).

Places to Stay

Despite the fact that Queenstown has some 15,000 beds you will probably have trouble finding a room at peak periods. Prices vary with the season; they go sky high during the peak summer period and in the middle of the ski season, then drop in between (high-season prices for Queenstown are given here). Try the Queenstown reservation service (☎ (0800) 804 111) for instant bookings.

Camping & Cabins There are plenty of camping grounds in and around Queenstown, all with cabins. The closest in is the *Queenstown Motor Park* (☎ 442 7252), less than one km from the town centre at the end of Man St. A tent/powered site is $18/20, cabins cost from $30 and tourist flats from $56 (all prices are for two). As well as being so conveniently located, the camp is very well equipped – good kitchen, coin-operated laundry, TV room and so on.

The *Creeksyde Campervan Park* (☎ 442 9447) on Robins Rd is a modern, comfortable place. It has campervan sites for $20, and a self-contained cottage for $50 for two ($10 for each extra adult). Tenters, forget it.

The *Mountain View Lodge Holiday Park* (☎ 442 8246) is on Frankton Rd, just over one km from the town centre on the Frankton side. Camping costs $11 per night for two, and there's a lodge with 10 rooms, each sleeping two to four people, that cost $40 for two. You need your own cooking equipment for the communal kitchens.

At *Frankton Motor Camp* (☎ 442 2079), six km from town, tent/powered sites are $15/17 for two, and cabins are from $32 to $34 for two. The *Kawarau Falls Lodge & Motor Camp* (☎ 442 3510) is also at Frankton; it has a hostel-style lodge which charges $15.50 per person. *Arthurs Point Camping Ground* (☎ 442 9306) at Arthurs Point, has tent sites for $16 and cabins for $30 (prices are for two).

The *Closeburn Alpine Park* (☎ 442 6073) is about eight km south of town in a particularly peaceful and attractive forest setting overlooking the lake. It has tent/powered sites at $12/17 for two (or $20 for two with private facilities), and on-site caravans with attached bathrooms cost $35 for two people.

The *DOC camping ground* at 12-Mile Creek Reserve, Glenorchy Rd, is just five km from Queenstown.

Hostels The *Wakatipu Lodge YHA Hostel* (☎ 442 8413) is right by the lake at 80 Lake Esplanade. It's a large hostel with beds for 100 people; the cost is $17 per person in dorms and $39 for twins and doubles. The night-time curfew at the hostel has been extended until 3 am and you can also get tasty food here – a huge lasagne is about $8. In winter the hostel can get hopelessly booked out due to all the skiers and the office gets clogged up, probably as a result of the restricted hours of opening.

Also along Lake Esplanade are two other places. *Bumbles* (☎ 442 6298) on the corner of Brunswick St, has dorm/twin bunkrooms for $16/18 per person, twins and doubles for $40 and 'supurb' [*sic*] views. The main hostel is comfortable but there is a less salubrious overflow house. Make sure you know where you are being put when you ring. People either love or hate this place.

In the town itself, there is *Thomas's Hotel & Backpackers* (☎ 442 7180) at 50 Beach St, no more expensive than other similar places but extras are offered that you don't get elsewhere. It has a first-floor kitchen and lounge with views of Lake Wakatipu. All rooms are heated and have their own bathrooms. Share rooms here are $17.50 ($22 with linen) and budget doubles are $49 with TV. *McFee's Waterfront Hotel* (☎ 442 7400) at 48a Shotover St, has ordinary dorm and share rooms for $16 per person, and twins/doubles for $36/40; all have en suite bathrooms. *Backpackers Downtown Lodge* (☎ 442 6395) at 48 Shotover St, in addition to its extremely cramped reception area, has dorm beds for $16 per person, and twins/doubles for $36/40. The Downtown also has a laundry, kitchen and dining area with a TV.

A few minutes (the management boast one minute) from town is *Deco Backpackers* (☎ 442 7384) at 52 Man St. It is in a restored Art Deco building (hence its name), and has share rooms for $16 per person, and twins and doubles for $36. We get letters of praise and letters of loathing about this place.

Bungi Backpackers (☎ 442 8725), on the corner of Sydney and Melbourne Sts, has share rooms for $16 per person and double/twins for $40. This place is slated to be pulled down. Probably not such a bad idea as it is an unkempt, tired-looking place.

Alpine Lodge Backpackers (☎ 442 7220), 13 Gorge Rd, a solid sort of place with all facilities including an outdoor area. It costs $16 per person in dorm and share rooms; twins and doubles are $36, or a group can take over the complete upstairs area for $120 (really good value). The only drawback is that it is close to a busy road. The office is closed from 1 to 3 pm.

The *Pinewood Lodge* (☎ 442 8273) is a little further from the centre at 48 Hamilton Rd. If you supply your own bedding the cost in dorm/share rooms is $16 per person or it's $36 for a twin or double room; you can hire linen and blankets if needed. There's a free pick-up service from all transport terminals.

Just a bit further out and south of the centre, *Alpha Lodge* (☎ 442 6095) – once known as FAB – at 42 Frankton Rd is also a former motel; in fact it still has some motel units, costing $50 for doubles. Shared accommodation is $14 in dorms (up to five people) or $30 for a twin room. Each room has its own kitchen and bathroom with shower and tub.

Another possibility is the *Queenstown Lodge* (☎ 442 7107) on Sainsbury Rd in Fernhill, about two km east of the centre, with a magnificent view of the lake. Rooms (with linen service and bathroom en suite) are $35 per person, and rooms without en suite bathrooms are $25 per person; the basic backpackers rate is $15 per person. The lodge has budget meals, a licensed restaurant and bar, games and various activities including party nights.

Guesthouses The upmarket *Queenstown House* (☎ 442 9043) at 69 Hallenstein St, on the corner of Malaghan St, has B&B singles/doubles from $95/125. There are good views over the town and lake from the balcony and it's close to the town centre. Nearby, *Melbourne House* (☎ 442 9043), Melbourne St, has B&B singles/twins for $50/77. Just off Gorge Rd at 2 Turner St is the *Turner Lodge* (☎ 442 9432) where single/double B&B is $50/80, and serviced rooms are $30 per person.

Between Melbourne House and Queenstown House is the wonderful old *Hulbert House* (☎ 442 8767) at 68 Ballarat St. This is upper-class B&B; just a handful of very gracious rooms, wonderful views. It will cost you $90 to $125 for a single and $125 to $145 for a double. It has its own restaurant, Tutulia.

Similar to the above is the *Stone House* (☎ 442 9812) at 47 Hallenstein St, a great B&B in a historic building; singles/doubles are $102/154.

The *Goldfields Breakfast Inn* (☎ 442 7211) is at 41 Frankton Rd; B&B is $48/62 for one/two people. The *Adelaide St Guesthouse* (☎ 442 6207) is a B&B place not far from town; expect to pay from $50 to $60.

Not a guesthouse, but reasonably priced, is *Wakatipu View & Sydney St Apartments* (☎ 442 7180) at 8 and 14 Frankton Rd; a studio is $75 for two and a two-bedroom apartment costs from $105 ($10 for each extra adult).

Motels Motel prices in Queenstown are not cheap but tend to fluctuate with the seasons. The *Mountain View Lodge* (☎ 442 8246) on Frankton Rd is a good example – there are cabins and motel-style rooms as well as adjoining camping facilities. The main building is known as the bottle house – nearly 15,000 bottles (none of them beer bottles!) are set into the walls. Rooms here cost $75/85 for singles/doubles.

At *Melbourne Motor Lodge* (☎ 442 8431; see also Melbourne House), 35 Melbourne St, rooms are from $95 to $106 for two. It's a friendly and well-organised place with laundry facilities and a guest lounge, and it's conveniently close to the town centre.

There are quite a few other motels in and around Queenstown, generally costing from $65 to $85 for two. Reasonable ones are:

A1 Queenstown (☎ 442 7289), 13 Frankton Rd
Alpine Sun (☎ 442 8482), 14 Hallenstein St
Alpha Lodge (☎ 442 6095), 42 Frankton Rd
Amber Motor Lodge (☎ 442 8480), corner of Shotover St & Gorge Rd
Autoline (☎ 442 8734), corner of Frankton Rd & Dublin St
Blue Peaks Lodge (☎ 442 9224), corner of Stanley & Sydney Sts
Colonial Village (☎ 442 7629), 100 Frankton Rd
Goldfields (☎ 442 7211), 41 Frankton Rd
Hillside (☎ 442 9280), 35 Gorge Rd
Lakeside (☎ 442 8976), 18 Lake Esplanade

Hotels At the *Hotel Esplanade* (☎ 442 8611), overlooking the lake at 32 Peninsula St, singles/doubles with bath cost $39/59. Breakfast is available for $6 (continental) or $8 (cooked) and there's an indoor pool and sauna. In addition to backpackers beds, *Thomas's* (☎ 442 7180), 50 Beach St, has singles/doubles for $55/75. The *Old Ferry Hotel* (☎ 442 2194), about ten minutes' drive from town on Spence Rd, Lower Shotover, has B&B doubles for $60. The *Sherwood Manor Motor Inn* (☎ 442 8032), Goldfield Heights on Frankton Rd, comes recommended; doubles are $99 to $180.

Some other top-range establishments are the *Earnslaw Lodge* (☎ 442 8728) at 53 Frankton Rd; *Holiday Inn Queenstown* (☎ (0800) 655 557) on Sainsbury Rd, Fernhill; the *Quality Hotel Queenstown* (☎ 442 8123) at 27 Frankton Rd; the *Lodges* (☎ 442 7552) at 8 Lake Esplanade; *Quality Hotel Terraces* (☎ 442 7950), 48 Frankton Rd; and an old favourite which has cheaper weekend rates, the *Queenstown Parkroyal* (☎ 442 7800) on Beach St.

Pick of the crop is the magnificent *Millbrook* (☎ 442 1563), on Malaghans Rd between Queenstown and Arrowtown. It has beautiful scenery, luxurious accommodation, restored historic buildings and there are myriad things to do in the vicinity. The golf course here is superlative. But this luxury costs – from $290 to $320 a double.

Places to Eat

The Queenstown dining scene, advertised as '...a triumph of taste sensations' (yeech!), has its share of pricey restaurants but there are plenty of places with reasonably priced good-value food.

Fast Food & Cafes The *Bakery*, at 11 Shotover St just beyond Camp St, has baked items, sandwiches and pizzas. For a good fish meal go to the *Fishbone Grill* at 7 (Upper) Beach St – the fish is fresh and they will cook fish that you have caught. The tiny *Habebe's Lebanese* is near the waterfront in the arcade on the corner of Rees and Beach Sts (opposite McFee's Waterfront Hotel).

Three American fast-food giants have set up their predictable outlets in Queenstown. *Pizza Hut* and *KFC* are on Camp St, and *McDonald's* is in O'Connell's Pavilion. The *Gourmet Express*, on Shotover St towards the waterfront in the Bay Centre, looks very American but it's popular for breakfast (the miner's special is worth the $8.25). The menu features a variety of tasty-looking burgers for $4 to $7.50. Burger freaks will be seen gorging the char-grilled product at the oxymoronic *Berkels Gourmet Burgere*, Shop 5, 19 Shotover St.

O'Connell's Food Hall, in O'Connell's Pavilion, Beach St, is the place to go for a wide range of snacks. There is a Thai takeaway with $5 satays; a Mexican place with fruit burritos for $5; *Nature's Pantry*, for, naturally, really healthy food; a sandwich bar; and place to buy sweets. The food hall is open from 9 am to 9 pm daily.

Ken's Noodles, on Camp St near Kiwi Discovery, is a local favourite where the hungry go for all types of udon (noodles) and sushi at reasonable prices.

If you want the definitive cup of coffee, go to *Naff Caff* at 62 Shotover St. They have their own coffee roaster; fresh croissants make the perfect accompaniment. Not since Coffee d'Fafo in Christchurch will you have spaced out so well on pure caffeine.

Restaurants The *Cow Restaurant* in Cow Lane is something of a Queenstown institution. Unfortunately, you are almost prised out of your seat when you have finished your meal. Turnover is obviously more important than the pizzas and pasta served. These are good – if only you were allowed to digest them. At 6 Brecon St, just down from the Lone Star, is a place that is receiving rave reviews: *Pasta Pasta Cucina*. It makes all its own pastas and sauces daily and serves delicious Italian flat bread, delectable Florentines, gelato and a range of coffees. In the mall is *Avanti*, a straightforward Italian BYO with pizzas from $7 to $28, pastas and Italian main courses from $9.50 to $12.50, and desserts for $5 – nothing special but good value and with a pleasant courtyard at the back.

Directly opposite, the *Stonewall Cafe* is a pleasant place for snacks, lunch, dinner, desserts and cappuccino. Tasty food with a variety of international dishes is served at tables inside, out on the mall, and in the cosy courtyard – a good spot for people-watching.

Another mall establishment is *HMS Britannia*, set up nautically as an English galleon. The emphasis is on seafood but there are plenty of other items on the menu. Also in the centre of town is the tiny *Jazz Bar* where food is, in the words of a reader, '...healthy, good value and nicely presented'. Next door to Eichardt's is the *Moa* where the blackboard menu features fresh seafood, pasta dishes and good salads. At the *Pot au Feu* (☎ 442 8333), on Camp St, the food is consistently good and because of abundant local support, reservations are essential.

There are two spicy Indian restaurants in town and, with a little imagination, the Remarkables will take on the appearance of the Hindu Kush or Himalaya. The *Little India*, with starters from $4.50 and vegetarian/meat mains from $7.50/13.50, is upstairs at 11 Shotover St. The *Moti Tandoor*, at 10 Brecon St, specialises in Mughlai and tandoori dishes. You can choose from mild, medium, hot or very hot! Mutton and vegetable curries are about $12 and a full tandoori chicken is $17.

The *Lone Star Cafe*, at 14 Brecon St, is a great place to dine and enjoy a drink. The food is Tex-Mex in style. A plate of nachos here is large enough for two people. It is a rowdy place, both upstairs and downstairs, as it brings out the nocturnal twitchings of the town's vast battalions of adrenaline junkies. Upstairs in the Trust Bank Arcade in Beach St, *Saguaro* has scrumptious Mexican

Top: Lake Hawea, Otago (RS)
Bottom: Dart River, Otago (JW)

Top: Moeraki Boulders, South of Oamaru, Canterbury (TC)
Bottom: Hot air ballooning, near Queenstown, Otago (RS)

food – enchiladas, tacos, burritos and fajitas. A platter costs $17.90 and a larger combo is $25. It's open until late every night.

There are plenty of more expensive restaurants. *Roaring Megs*, in an old miner's cottage at 57 Shotover St, is one of the town's better and pricier BYO eating places with main courses in the $18 to $25 range. For those who can stomach the damage done to the view by the steamer wharf, there are a couple of eateries here. The *Boardwalk* is open for seafood lunches and dinners and the *Lagos* has a Mediterranean menu and alfresco dining.

If you can afford a sushi/sashimi feast try *Minami Jujisei* on Rees St. It is expensive with mains from $20 and sets (miso, pickles, rice and tea) for an extra $10. Steak-lovers will be seen at the *Beefeater*, 40 Shotover St, which has been around for over 20 years. A variety of steaks are available from $20 and are served with a baked potato; there is a free salad bar for diners and no corkage.

A number of the more swish hotels have their own restaurants. The Lakeland Hotel, at 14 Lake Esplanade, has the award-winning *Clancy's*; the Queenstown Parkroyal the superb and reasonably priced *Bentleys Brasserie*; and the Quality Hotel has *Peppers*. The *Treetops of Queenstown* (☎ 442 7328), on Arawata Terrace at Sunshine Bay, provides a courtesy vehicle which delivers you right to the door of this Japanese-style teahouse – dining in this style does not come cheaply.

For those lucky enough to be staying at Millbrook there are two excellent restaurants to choose from. Their *Italian Cafe* has pizza and mains from $14 and at the *Clubhouse* mains cost around $26, eg Chateaubriand is $52 for two.

Entertainment

Queenstown is a small place but there's a reasonable variety of night-time activities. In the mall near the waterfront is *Eichardt's Hotel*, which has been around for a long time – during the 1879 floods, hard-drinking miners are said to have paddled up to the bar in rowing boats! During the Franco-Prussian war, 1870 to 1871, Herr Eichardt, being a good Prussian nationalist, ran the Prussian flag up the flagpole after every Prussian victory. Meanwhile, down the road at Monsieur Francois St Omer's bakery, the tricolour flew every time the French won. The public bar is a popular local meeting and drinking place. Upstairs you'll find activity until late at night in the very time-warped *Vilagrad* nightclub. Around the corner on Church St is *McNeill's Brewery & Bar*. The beer here is good and costs between $2 and $3 for a half-pint; try the dark McNeill's Classic or savour the Moonlight or Wakatipu Gold.

On Upper Camp St is the *Red Rock Bar & Grill*, where the locals sip aperitifs before going out for dinner or home to the TV. They also serve generous lunches and dinners. A little later, 'stayers' will have gravitated to *Solera Vino*, a tapas bar, at 25 Beach St. They serve 40 wines by the glass or bottle and open from 4 pm until late. *Wicked Willies* on Beach St has recently had a major rebuild and is one of the few places in town with genuine pub 'cred'.

At *Abbey Road*, opposite The Lofts on Shotover St, the emphasis is on boozing and this is the spot where bus-bound backpackers congregate. Further down Shotover St is the *Casbah* where chic sheik espies potential harem. It's a great place and as noisy, smelly, smoky, bustling, boozy and colourful as befits a real kasbah.

If you threw yourself off the Pipeline you may wish to head back to where your day of 'daring-do' started – the *Swiss Iglu*, 27 Shotover St, is a great place for an after-dinner cocktail, a late meal, desserts, coffee and Schweitzerdeutsch-speaking Eskimos.

The rich can ride the gondola to the *Skyline Chalet* where there's entertainment with dinner each night and impressive views back down to the lights of Queenstown. The meal is overpriced but you are up here for the view – price is directly proportional to height!

Getting There & Away

Air Air New Zealand/Mt Cook Airline and Ansett New Zealand all fly into Queenstown.

OTAGO

Air New Zealand/Mt Cook Airline (☎ (0800) 800 737) has daily direct flights to Auckland, Christchurch, Rotorua, Te Anau, Milford Sound, Wanaka and Mt Cook, with a number of connecting flights from Christchurch. The Mt Cook office is in Rees St next to the pier at the end of the mall.

Ansett New Zealand (☎ (0800) 800 146), out at the airport, has daily direct flights to Christchurch, Palmerston North, Wanaka, Rotorua and Auckland with connections to Wellington. Tranzair fly on their behalf to Te Anau and Milford.

Bus The InterCity booking office (☎ 442 8238) is on the corner of Shotover and Camp Sts, part of the visitor information centre. InterCity buses have several daily routes to and from Queenstown. The route to Christchurch goes via Mt Cook. The other routes are to Te Anau and Milford Sound, Invercargill and Dunedin. InterCity also has a daily West Coast service to the glaciers via Wanaka and the Haast Pass. If you want to continue up the coast from the glaciers you have to overnight at Fox or Franz Josef. It takes a minimum of two days (longer if you want to see more than a bus window) to Nelson.

If you want to go up the coast to Nelson by bus, the West Coast Express, Kiwi Experience or the Flying Kiwi are probably the best alternatives, particularly if you have a bit of time and want to get out and see things. See the Getting Around chapter for details on these 'alternative' bus lines.

Mt Cook Landline (☎ (0800) 800 287) also has several bus routes from Queenstown, with daily buses to Christchurch, Invercargill (operated by Cityline), Dunedin, Wanaka, Mt Cook, Te Anau and Milford. From November to April daily buses to Christchurch include a stopover at Mt Cook with enough time for you to take a scenic flight with a glacier landing. Mt Cook buses leave from the depot on Church St. There is a combined InterCity/Mt Cook Landline service up the West Coast.

Magic Bus picks up passengers from nearly all of the backpackers; enquire at the Backpacking Specialists (☎ 442 8178) in Shotover St.

Several companies have buses to Milford via Te Anau, including InterCity and Fiordland Travel. An InterCity coach/cruise option is $135 (children $89) but if you have kids then the Mt Cook Landline package will be cheaper as they charge $67.50 for the 'littlies'.

A good way of getting around this region is in the 16-seater bus Southern Explorer (☎ 249 7820). It has a fixed weekly itinerary and departs Queenstown each Wednesday, returning Sunday. You can do all of it or just a one-day section: Queenstown-Dunedin is $120; and a full circuit is $150. One-day sections are: Queenstown-Te Anau via the back road $35 (direct $25); Te Anau-Milford return $35; Te Anau-Invercargill and Bluff $35; Invercargill-Dunedin via the Catlins $35; and Dunedin through the Central Otago goldfields to Queenstown (or Te Anau) $35.

Tramping Transport Backpackers Express (☎ 442 9939) runs to and from the Routeburn, Greenstone, Caples, and Rees-Dart tracks, all via Glenorchy. Kiwi Discovery (☎ 442 7340) services the Routeburn and Greenstone from the east and the Routeburn and Milford from west of the Divide via Te Anau. The Backpackers Express departs from the Track Walking Centre on Shotover St, and Kiwi Discovery from their office in Camp St. Approximate prices are:

Queenstown to the Routeburn	$20
Queenstown to the Greenstone-Caples	$25
Glenorchy to the Rees	$12
Glenorchy to the Greenstone-Caples	$15
Queenstown to the Rees	$22
Queenstown to Glenorchy	$10
Dart to Glenorchy	$12
Greenstone-Caples to Glenorchy	$15

The services between Queenstown and Milford via Te Anau can be used for track transport or simply as a way to get to or from Milford. Buses generally run two or three times weekly but the schedule varies according to demand, with extra trips in summer and possibly none at all in winter.

Hitching Hitching into Queenstown is usually relatively easy, but getting out may require real patience. Big wet backpacks are a real deterrent.

Getting Around

To/From the Airport The Super Shuttle (☎ 442 9803) and Johnson's Shuttle (☎ 442 3639) meet most incoming and outgoing flights and cost $5 each way per person, picking you up and dropping you off wherever you wish. A taxi, either Economy Taxis (☎ 442 6666) or Queenstown Taxis (☎ 442 7788), is just as good a deal for two people and even better for a larger group (about $15 for up to four people).

Bicycle & Moped You can rent bicycles and mopeds at Queenstown Bike Hire, 23 Beach St. They have single-speed and 10-speed bikes, tandems, triples, side-by-side bikes, and 10, 12 and 18-speed mountain bikes, and mopeds. Mountain bikes can also be hired from Replay Sports in the Windsurf Mania house at 27 Shotover St. NZ Rent-a-Car, on Camp St near the corner of Shotover St, also hires out mopeds.

GLENORCHY

The picturesque tiny hamlet of Glenorchy, which lies at the head of Lake Wakatipu, is 47 km (a 40-minute drive) from Queenstown. If you are looking for some tranquillity after Queenstown, then Glenorchy may well be what you are after. A great many pass through briefly in their rush to knock off the Routeburn Track, and thus bypass perhaps one of the greatest tramping opportunities – the Rees and Dart river valleys. Glenorchy was once the terminus for the TSS *Earnslaw* – now a stream of buses, a high-speed boat and helicopters make the trip.

For information and bookings go to the Chocolate Fish (Glenorchy General Store; ☎ 442 9906); they also stock tramping food and equipment.

Activities

Jet-Boating The Dart River jet-boat trip is one of the best value-for-money rides in NZ. It, along with those in the Makarora region, offers a scenic trip into the heart of the wilderness. The Dart River must be one of NZ's most beautiful places. Savour the grandeur of the slopes of Mt Earnslaw and the bush that cascades down from the mountain walls on both sides of the river. You are in this breathtaking scenery for 2½ hours, and the driver even stops to let you take a walk through the beech forest at Beansburn, downriver from the turnaround point. Sure, the driver will spin the boat and pretend to almost crash into river obstacles, but this is only a small portion of the experience.

Dart River Jet-boat Safaris (☎ 442 9992 anytime) depart from Queenstown at 8 and 11 am, and 2 pm in summer; check departure times in winter. If coming from Queenstown it costs $99 (for what is essentially a five-hour trip).

Wilderness Jet (☎ 442 9792) also operates trips on the Dart but as they depart from the Dart River bridge they miss a deal of scenery.

Kayaking A novel way to finish the Rees-Dart Track is to kayak the last day of the walk. Eric Billoud gets you to the start of the Rees (saving you normal transport costs), you then walk independently for three days through the scenery of the Rees and Upper Dart valleys. On the fourth day you are met at Sandy Bluff and from there you travel in an inflatable canoe down the Dart to the Dart River bridge near Glenorchy, where you are taken by courtesy vehicle back to Queenstown. Book with Danes (☎ 442 7318), corner of Shotover & Camp Sts; the cost is $79 from Queenstown, $69 from Glenorchy.

There is also a day trip – jet-boat up with Dart River Jet-boat Safaris and canoe down with Eric. You get the opportunity to canoe through the Rockburn Chasm. No experience is necessary and the return cost from Queenstown is $149.

Other Activities A good way to see this spectacular country is on a **horse trek**. Dart Stables (☎ 442 9968) has two-hour trips daily at 9 am and 1 pm ($45). The Glenorchy

Cafe (☎ 442 9915) hires out horses by the hour ($10) or by the day ($50).

Glenorchy Air (☎ 442 2207) has a local **flight-seeing** trip around Mt Earnslaw and the Routeburn; the cost is $80 for 20 minutes. If Mt Aspiring and the Olivine Ice Plateau are included, the cost is $149 (45 minutes).

Places to Stay & Eat

Glenorchy is small and there is a limited range of places to stay. The *Glenorchy Holiday Park* (☎ 442 9939) at 2 Oban St has camp sites for $7 per person, cabins and hostel beds for $12 per person, and twins and doubles are $28. It is really well set up for those doing the Greenstone, Caples, Rees-Dart and Routeburn tracks.

Next door to the Glenorchy Hotel (and part of it) is *Glenorchy Backpackers Retreat* (☎ 442 9902) where a bed costs between $13 and $16 per night depending on whether or not you need linen. The *Glenorchy Hotel* (☎ 442 9902) has B&B for $55/75 a single/double. The hotel has a restaurant and two bars. Close by is the *Glen Roydon Outdoor Lodge* (☎ 442 9968), with doubles for $70.

The comfy *Glenorchy Cafe* is the local hang-out. It has freshly baked rye bread ($3.50 a loaf), strudel ($3), organic salads and vegetables, and home-cooked meals. For a fuller meal try the Glenorchy Hotel where seafood features in the specialities; a hearty chowder is $5.50.

Getting There & Away

There are a number of ways of getting to Glenorchy. In summer there are almost daily trampers' buses such as Backpackers Express and Kiwi Discovery (see Tramping Transport in the Queenstown section). You can catch the 'Bladerunner-esque' MV *Queenstown Explorer* (☎ 442 8665) for a speedy boat journey. It leaves from opposite the Parkroyal and a return trip costs $40 (children $35).

LAKE WAKATIPU REGION TRAMPS

The mountainous region at the northern head of Lake Wakatipu combines some of the greatest scenery in NZ with a number of the best tramping tracks – the famous Routeburn and lesser known Greenstone, Caples and Rees-Dart tracks are all found here. Glenorchy is a convenient base, with excellent facilities, from which to do all of these tramps. See also Tramping Transport in Getting There & Away, Queenstown.

Track Information

For all details on accommodation either side of the tracks, transport to and from all trailheads (including the Rees-Dart) and the location of DOC information offices and ranger stations, see the Queenstown and Glenorchy sections in this chapter and Te Anau in the Southland chapter.

The DOC staff will advise on the best maps to use, outline track conditions and sell hut and Great Walk passes. For more detailed information on the tracks mentioned here see Lonely Planet's *Tramping in New Zealand*.

The Routeburn Track

The great variety of country and scenery makes the three to four-day Routeburn Track one of the best rainforest/subalpine tracks in the country. Unfortunately, it has become the surrogate for those that miss out on the Milford Track and pressures on the track have necessitated the introduction of a booking system, along the lines of that in operation on the Milford.

Now, no one is allowed to commence the Routeburn until they have arranged their accommodation. In summer, huts (Routeburn Flats, Routeburn Falls, Mackenzie and Howden) are $25, camp sites are $12.50 per person and must be booked in advance. From May to the end of September both huts and camp sites are $4.

The Routeburn Track is often closed by snow in the winter and note that it is extremely popular in January. A stretch of the track between Harris Saddle and Lake Mackenzie is very exposed and dangerous in bad weather. This section has even been closed by snow in the middle of summer, so check with the wardens if the weather looks dicey.

There is a guided four-day walk on the Routeburn (including return transport,

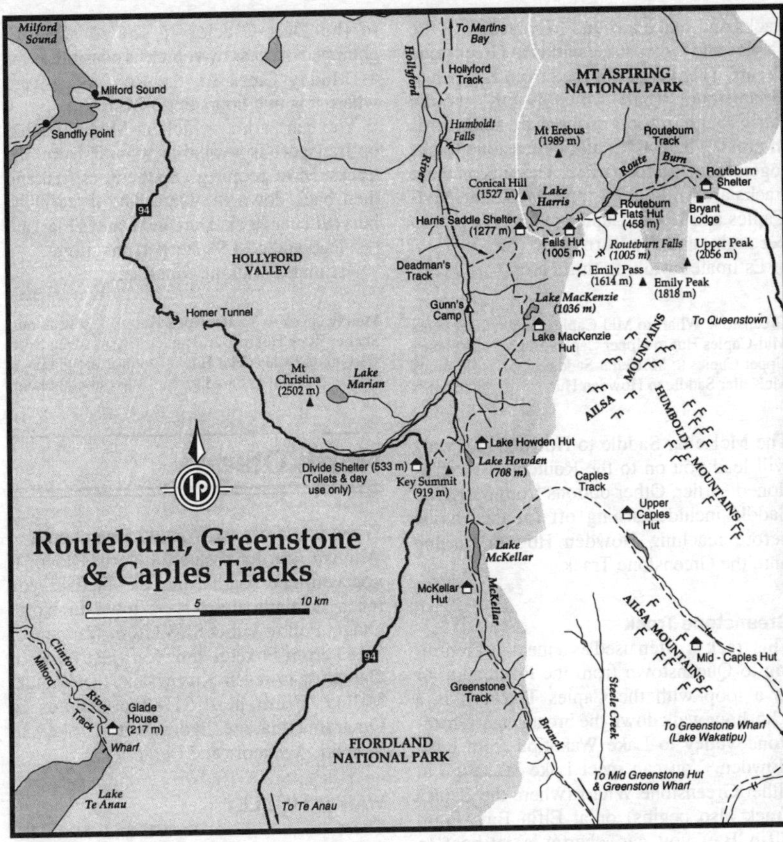

accommodation, meals and guiding); enquire at the visitor information centres.

Walking the Track The track can be started from either end. Many people travelling from the Queenstown end attempt to reach the Divide in time to catch the bus to Milford, connecting with the launch trip across Milford Sound. The highlight of the track is the view from the Harris Saddle, or more especially from the top of nearby Conical Hill. You can see the waves breaking on the West Coast beach at Martins Bay. The view is almost as good as the view from Key Summit, which offers a panorama not only of the Hollyford Valley but also of the Eglinton and Greenstone River valleys.

Estimated walking times are:

Routeburn Shelter to Flats Hut	2½ hours
Flats Hut to Falls Hut	one hour
Falls Hut to Harris Saddle	1½ hours
Harris Saddle to Mackenzie Hut	3½ hours
Mackenzie Hut to Howden Hut	three hours
Howden Hut to the Divide	one hour

Routeburn-Greenstone & Caples Tracks An option on the Routeburn tramp is to combine it with the Caples or Greenstone tracks and make a round trip. Access at the Caples and Greenstone end is at Greenstone Wharf. There is now a road from Kinloch to Greenstone Wharf which is OK, though fairly rough in spots as there are some fords to cross. The Caples and Greenstone tracks together form a loop track. The huts on these tracks are Mid-Greenstone, McKellar, Mid-Caples and Upper Caples (all $8 per person per night) and Sly Burn ($4).

Estimated walking times are:

Greenstone Wharf to Mid-Caples Hut	three hours
Mid-Caples Hut to Upper Caples Hut	2½ hours
Upper Caples to McKellar Saddle	3½ hours
McKellar Saddle to Howden Hut	three hours

The McKellar Saddle to Howden Hut walk will lead you on to the Routeburn as mentioned earlier. Other options from McKellar Saddle include turning off for the Divide before reaching Howden Hut, or turning onto the Greenstone Track.

Greenstone Track

This track is often used as a means of returning to Queenstown from the Routeburn, or as a loop with the Caples Track. It is a 13.5-hour walk down the broad, easy Greenstone Valley to Lake Wakatipu from Lake Howden. You can meet Lake Wakatipu at either Greenstone Wharf (where the Caples Track also begins) or at Elfin Bay. From Elfin Bay you can charter a jet-boat to Queenstown, and from Greenstone Wharf there are minibuses to and from Glenorchy. There is only a shelter at Elfin Bay.

Estimated walking times are:

Greenstone Wharf to Slip Flat Bivvy	three hours
Slip Flat Bivvy to Mid-Greenstone Hut	3½ hours
Mid-Greenstone Hut to McKellar Hut	five hours
McKellar Hut to Howden Hut	two hours

Rees-Dart Track

This is a difficult four to five-day circular route from the head of Lake Wakatipu by way of the Dart River, Rees Saddle and Rees River valley, with the possibility of a side trip to the Dart Glacier if you're suitably equipped. Access by vehicle is possible as far as Muddy Creek on the Rees side, from where it is two hours to 25-Mile Hut.

You can park a vehicle at Muddy Creek, or transport is available to and from the tracks. Most people go up the Rees first and then back down the Dart. The three DOC huts (Shelter Rock, Dart and Daleys Flat) are serviced and cost $8 per person a night.

Estimated walking times are:

Muddy Creek to Shelter Rock Hut	seven hours
Shelter Rock Hut to Dart Hut	five to seven hours
Dart hut to Daleys Flat Hut	six to eight hours
Daleys Flat Hut to Paradise	six to eight hours

North Otago

When you cross the Waitaki River south of Waimate you have entered North Otago. If you continue south from the Waitaki you reach Oamaru, the largest town in North Otago. Follow either SH82 from Waimate or SH83 from Pukeuri Junction (just north of Oamaru), to reach Kurow and the Waitaki Valley. From here SH83 continues to Omarama via the hydroelectric lakes of Waitaki, Aviemore and Benmore.

WAITAKI VALLEY

There is quite a lot to see and do in the Waitaki Valley and there are a number of interesting towns between the turn-offs on SH1 and Omarama: Glenavy, Duntroon, Kurow and Otematata. **Duntroon** was established in 1859 by Robert Campbell, owner of Otekaieke Station, as a village for his workers. It was named after Duntroon Castle in Scotland. In addition to an authentic blacksmith shop in the town, there is trout and salmon fishing nearby and jet-boating in the Waitaki. Accommodation is available at the motor camps (including Dansey Pass) and food is served at the Duntroon tavern.

There are Maori rock drawings at **Takiroa**, 50 km west of Oamaru on SH83. The sandstone cliff drawings were done with red ochre and charcoal and may date back to the moa-hunting period (between 1000 and 1500 AD). Other rock art sites in the region portray humans, moas, dogs, birds and fish as well as unrecognisable or simple geometrical shapes. Most of the sites are on private land and can only be visited with permission from the owners but there are several on public land, in addition to the ones at Takiroa. The Oamaru Visitor Information Centre can give directions; or contact the NZ Historic Places Trust in Wellington (☎ (04) 472 4341).

Kurow is at the junction of the Waitaki and Hakataramea rivers. Loosely translated the name means a 'hundred mists' as nearby Mt Bitterness is often covered with fog. From 1928, when the Waitaki power station was built, Kurow has been a service centre for hydroelectric schemes in the Waitaki. Benmore power station was constructed from 1956 to 1965 and Aviemore in 1968. There is fishing, boating and snow skiing all within a relatively short distance. For accommodation there are motels in the town and nearby farm stays; check with the Kurow Community Centre (☎ 436 0812).

Omarama is at the head of the Waitaki Valley, 119 km north-west of Oamaru, at the junction of SH8 and SH83. Not far from Omarama are the Paritea or **Clay Cliffs**, formed by the active Osler fault line which continually exposes clay and gravel cliffs. These clay pinnacles change colour during the day and are quite spectacular.

Omarama has a world-wide reputation for gliding due to the area's north-west thermals – the world championships were held here. Omarama has hotels, a motel and two motor camps (including Glenburn, seven km away) and food is available at a few tearooms.

Comfortable rooms at the *Omarama Hotel* (☎ 438 9713) are $25 per person and they have a small cabin at the back of the hotel for $15. Eight km north of Omarama is *Buscot Station* (☎ 438 9646) – backpackers' accommodation on a merino sheep and Hereford cattle farm. You can stay here for as little as $12 per person (an extra $2 for linen); it is closed from May to August.

Fishing

No coverage of the Waitaki would be complete without mention of the fishing possibilities in the river, hydro lakes and tributaries. The season is usually from 1 October to 30 April but lasts all year in some rivers.

Rainbow and brown trout are caught in the Waitaki, Hakataramea, Otematata and Maerewhenua rivers, Deep Stream and Waitaki, Aviemore and Benmore lakes; and quinnat salmon are taken from the Waitaki. Anglers, stop drooling and toss in a Tylo, a Pheasant tail nymph, a Royal Wulff or Craig's Nighttime and wait for that elusive bite. At night, a caddis imitation will be just the ticket. The locals may reveal some of their secrets (for a few cans of beer).

OAMARU

Visitors to Oamaru are in for a surprise – this is an extremely pretty town of 13,000 people centred in a region where there is a lot to do. Oamaru was first settled by Europeans in 1853. By the 1870s and early 1880s it was the seventh largest town in New Zealand. The Otago goldfields had a lot to do with its early prosperity, and this factor, allied with the availability of sandstone in the area, resulted in the erection of a number of imposing and enduring buildings. In addition, Oamaru has fine public gardens, and colonies of the rare yellow-eyed and little blue penguins.

The Oamaru Information Centre (☎ 434 1656; fax 434 1657), on the corner of Thames and Itchen Sts, is open from 9 am to 5 pm Monday to Friday and 10 am to 4 pm on the weekend. The extremely helpful staff vigorously promote their area. There's an AA agent on the corner of Thames and Usk Sts.

The **public gardens** date back to 1876 and have been improved upon since. There is a red Japanese bridge which crosses Oamaru Creek, an Oriental Garden, Fragrant Garden, Rhododendron Dell, Cactus House, Azalea Lawn and so on. Floraphiles will adore this place. The main entrance gates are on Severn St where SH1 crosses the railway line. On the weekend, October through March, you can go on a Clydesdale & Wagon Tour for $2.50 (children $1.50).

Harbour-Tyne Historic Precinct

Oamaru boasts the best preserved collection of historic commercial buildings in New Zealand. Nowhere better is this seen than in the Harbour-Tyne Street Precinct; in all, 22 buildings have been classified for preservation. Oamaru's architecture, as in many NZ towns, is a mosaic of styles. Expect to find Gothic revival alongside neo-classical (Italianate and Greek) styles. The local limestone could be sawn (it hardened later when it was exposed to the air) so it was readily accepted as the most convenient building material.

The excellent brochure *Historic Oamaru*, available free from the information centre, describes the historic precinct.

Penguin Watching

Both the yellow-eyed penguin (Maori: hoiho) and little blue penguin (Maori: koroa) are found in close proximity to Oamaru. It is probably one of the few towns where you can actually walk out to the colonies from the town centre. The yellow-eyed is one of the world's rarest penguins and the reason for their decline is thought to be the loss of coastal forest where they breed. Bushy Beach, close to Oamaru, has good natural vegetation and efforts are being made to extend it.

Importantly, a hide has been constructed so these beautiful birds can be observed without being disturbed. The yellow-eyeds are shy and easily upset, so on no account disturb them either with your presence or loud noises. The best time to view them is in the late afternoon when they come ashore to feed their chicks.

The little blue penguins nest right around the Oamaru Harbour area; they couldn't be closer to human habitation. One area of the foreshore is now a penguin refuge. Native shrubs have been planted in the nesting area and nesting boxes have been provided. The best viewing of their return from fishing at sea, usually around dusk, is from the car park at the end of Waterfront Rd. Again, in no way disturb these birds and keep the most deadly of predators, dogs, well away from the area. Cameras with a flash are an absolute no-no; while binoculars can be useful even in dull light. Oamaru has a great natural asset here so enjoy it. There is a small entry fee.

Places to Stay & Eat

The *Oamaru Gardens Holiday Park* (☎ 434 7666) is in Chelmer St, adjacent to the large public gardens. Tent or powered sites cost $8.50 per person and there are various cabins for $25 to $39 for two. At the south side of the Waitaki bridge, on SH1, is the *Waitaki Mouth Motor Camp* (☎ 431 3880). Tent/powered sites are $12/14 for two, and cabins are $15/25 for one/two people. There's a *DOC camping ground* at Glencoe Reserve, adjacent to SH1, two km south of Herbert.

The *Red Kettle YHA Seasonal Hostel* (☎ 434 5008), on the of corner of Reed and Cross Sts, is open from mid-October to mid-May. Dorm beds are $13 per person, and twins are $30.

The *Alpine Motel* (☎ 434 5038), at 285 Thames St, is conveniently located and has units sleeping one to seven people for $65 to $72 for two. The *Thames Court Motel* (☎ 434 6963), at 252 Thames St, is similarly priced ($59 for two); the *Avenue Motel* (☎ 437 0091), 473 Thames Highway, has rooms for $52 to $62 for two; and *Tui Motels* (☎ 437 1443), 469 Thames Highway, has doubles from $49.

The information centre has the *Farm & Homestay Guide: Waitaki District* which lists 20 or so homestay and country farmstay places in and around Oamaru; typically the cost per person is $25 to $35.

Oamaru's restaurants, tearooms and takeaways are mostly concentrated along Thames St and the Thames Highway. There are about a dozen *tearooms*, two-thirds of which are on Thames St. There are also about a dozen takeaways, including *McDonald's* and *KFC*.

The *Woolstore Cafe*, near the harbour in

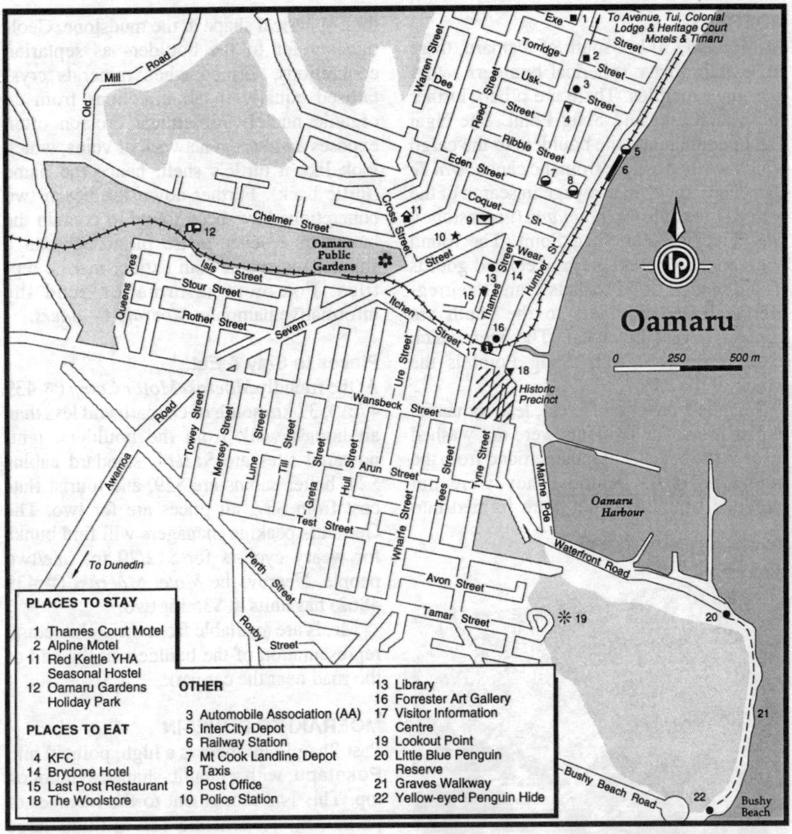

the historic precinct, has a good range of light meals and serves proper coffee. Good meals are also served at the *Brydone Hotel* on the corner of Wear and Thames Sts. On Thames St is the town's first post office now revived as the *Last Post*. Main courses here are about $19 and sweets $6; the filo parcel mixes chicken, brie, peach and peach schnapps in a really exciting way.

Getting There & Away

There is no air service to Oamaru. The InterCity and Mt Cook Landline bus services between Christchurch and Dunedin all stop at Oamaru. Shuttles which pass through are generally cheaper but not as reliable. Nationwide (☎ 474 3300), Atomic (☎ (0800) 322 888) and Catch-a-Bus (☎ (0800) 508 000) charge about $15 one way to Dunedin. To Christchurch it costs $24 for pick-up only and $35 for door to door.

The Christchurch-Invercargill rail service also stops at Oamaru, with a train in each direction every day except Saturday and Sunday. Trains depart for Invercargill at 11.35 am and for Christchurch at 2.09 pm.

There is a taxi service (☎ 434 8790). The best way to see the old part of town is on foot.

MOERAKI

At Moeraki, 30 km south of Oamaru, there are extraordinary spherical boulders rather like giant marbles. There are others further south at Katiki and Shag Point. The Ngai Tahu people relate the boulders to the cargo which washed ashore from the canoe *Arai Te Uru*. The canoe, on a voyage in search of the prized stone of *te wai pounamu* (greenstone), was wrecked near Shag Point. The round boulders at Moeraki are baskets and gourds (*te kai hinaki*, 'food baskets'), and the irregularly shaped boulders to the south are kumara (sweet potatoes). The reef which extends seaward from Shag Point is the wreck of the canoe.

Scientists have a different, less romantic, explanation. The boulders were not washed up onto the beach, but rather eroded from the mudstone cliffs behind. They were not moulded by the surf but were formed into their spherical shape in the mudstone. Geologists refer to the boulders as septarian concretions, formed when minerals crystallised equally in all directions from an organic nuclei. Subsequent erosion often exposes an internal network of veins, which look like a turtle's shell, hence the name 'turtle back'. Further down the beach two concretions have been found to contain the bones of a seven-metre plesiosaur and a smaller mosasaur, both extinct marine reptiles. For more information read the informative pamphlet *Moeraki Boulders*.

Moeraki boulders

Places to Stay & Eat

At the friendly *Moeraki Motor Camp* (☎ 439 4759), 37 km south of Oamaru and less than an hour's walk from the boulders, tent/powered sites are $13/14, standard cabins $24, better cabins are $29, and tourist flats cost from $37; all prices are for two. The German-speaking managers will find bunks for weary cyclists for $12/20 for one/two people. Nearby, the *Motel Moeraki* (☎ 439 4862) has units at $35 for two.

Meals are available from the architectural representation of the boulders at the end of the road near the car park.

MOERAKI TO DUNEDIN

Past Shag Point there is a high, pointed hill, **Puketapu**, with a phallic-shaped symbol on top. This is a monument to the member of parliament responsible for splitting large farms into smaller holdings. There's a track to the top signposted from the northern end of **Palmerston**. This town has places where you can get food for the road, such as *Locomotion No 1* at the railway station and *McGregor's Bakery* at 126 Ronaldsay St.

From Palmerston the **Pig Root** to Central Otago leaves SH1, the name probably having to do with the early road's condition. Gold miners preferred this route into the Maniototo as it was far more sheltered than the Old Dunstan Trail. The much improved road makes a great scenic trip into Central Otago (see Central Otago in this chapter).

About 34 km north of Dunedin is the town of **Karitane**, which overlooks part of the

Waikouaiti estuary. Up on the cliff is the two-storey house, King's Cliff, where in 1907 Sir Truby King founded the Plunket Society, whose nurses continue today to care for the country's babies. King revolutionised child care and in his lifetime saw infant mortality in NZ drop by two-thirds from about 90 to 30 deaths per thousand births.

Southland

Southland is a captivating place, with eye-catching scenery and an abundance of flora & fauna, which is too often left out of travellers' itineraries. Many make it to Milford Sound and Te Anau in two-day trips from Queenstown and get no further into this mountainous, frontier province.

Southland has a predominantly Scottish heritage and many of its inhabitants speak with a distinctive rolling of their 'r's. There is also a considerable Maori population, and their maraes are being re-established.

The weather is a bit of a deterrent, but if you come prepared for it you'll enjoy the experience much more.

There are three main routes into Southland: via Queenstown to Fiordland; from Queenstown down SH6 to Invercargill; or from Dunedin to Invercargill on SH1. All three, however, miss spectacular scenery, so some local routes with much to see along the way have been described in this chapter.

HIGHLIGHTS

- Cruises on lakes Te Anau and Manapouri – to the head of the lake, Te-Ana Au Caves and Doubtful Sound
- Walking in the Fiordland National Park, especially the famed Milford and Kepler tracks
- Sea kayaking on magnificent Milford Sound (or cruises and flightseeing for the less adventurous)
- Driving from Te Anau to Milford via Lake Te Anau, the Eglinton Valley, Homer Tunnel and Cleddau Canyon
- The Southern Scenic Route from Manapouri to Invercargill
- The displays at the Southland Museum & Art Gallery in Invercargill, especially the ancient tuataras
- The fauna-rich Catlins, where there are many surprises – ancient fossilised forests, native bushland, Hector's dolphins, penguins, and rare birds

Fiordland

The spectacular Fiordland National Park and World Heritage area includes some of NZ's most famous walks, including the best known of the lot, the Milford Track. The tracks, however, barely penetrate this raw, powerful region. The immensity of it all can only really be appreciated from the air or from a boat or kayak out on the sounds.

TE ANAU

Lake Te Anau, and its three arms that penetrate into the mountainous forested shore, was gouged out by a huge glacier. It is 417 metres at its deepest, and 53 km long and 10 km across at its widest, making it NZ's second largest lake after Taupo in the North Island. The lake takes its name from the caves discovered on its western shore, Te Ana-au or 'cave of rushing water'.

The township of 1500 people is beautifully situated on the lake shore, and is a bit like a smaller, low-key version of Queenstown. There are all manner of activities and trips here to keep you busy, although for many visitors the town is just a jumping-off point for trips to Milford and the Milford Track.

Information

Most of the activities and businesses in Te Anau are found along two streets – Te Anau

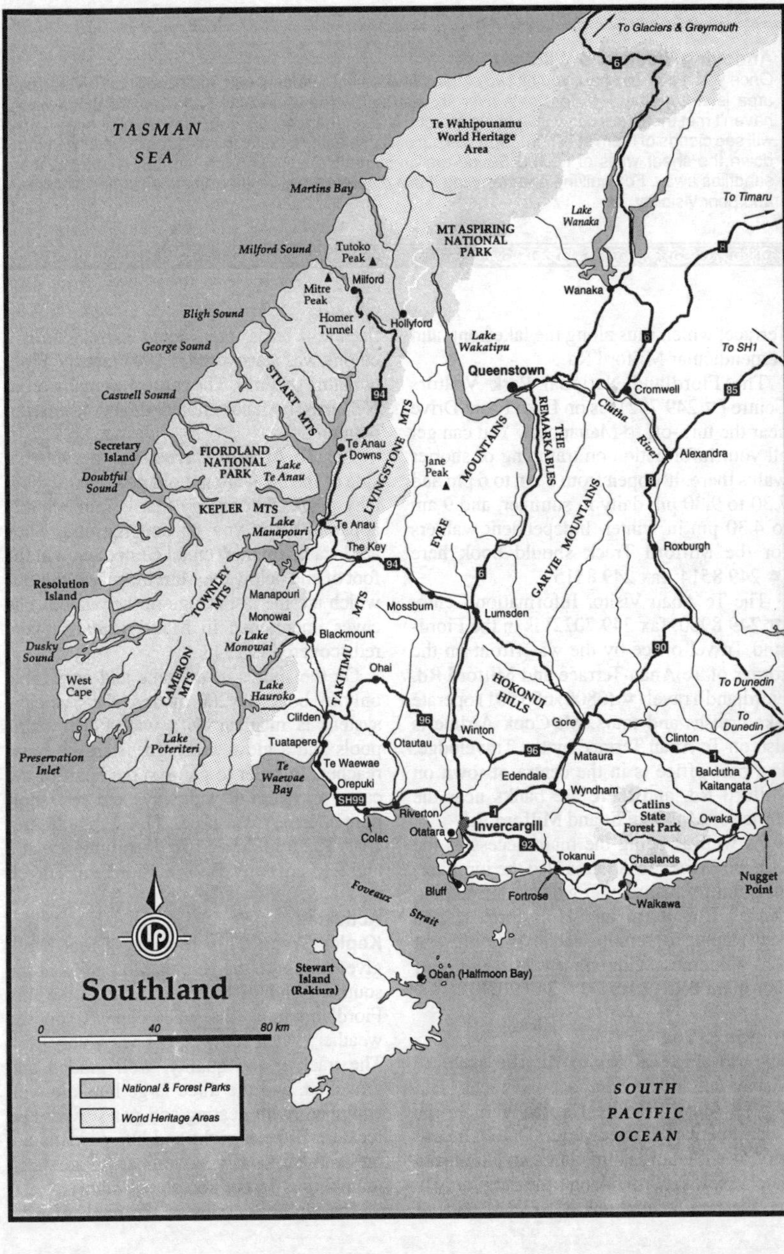
To Glaciers & Greymouth
6
TASMAN
SEA
Te Wahipounamu
World Heritage
Area
Martins Bay
Lake
Wanaka
To Timaru
8
MT ASPIRING
NATIONAL
PARK
Milford Sound
Tutoko
Peak
Mitre
Peak
Milford
Wanaka
Bligh Sound
Homer
Tunnel
Hollyford
6
Lake
Wakatipu
To SH1
George Sound
STUART MTS
Queenstown
Cromwell
Caswell Sound
94
REMARKABLES
THE
85
Clutha
River
Secretary
Island
Te Anau
Downs
LIVINGSTONE MTS
EYRE MOUNTAINS
GARVIE MOUNTAINS
Alexandra
FIORDLAND
NATIONAL
PARK
Lake
Te Anau
Jane
Peak
Doubtful
Sound
8
KEPLER MTS
Lake
Manapouri
Te Anau
The Key
Roxburgh
94
6
Resolution
Island
TOWNLEY MTS
Manapouri
Mossburn
Lumsden
Monowai
TAKITIMU MTS
Lake
Monowai
Blackmount
90
Dusky
Sound
CAMERON MTS
Ohai
HOKONUI
HILLS
West
Cape
To Dunedin
Lake
Hauroko
Clifden
96
Winton
Gore
To
Dunedin
Tuatapere
Otautau
96
Mataura
Clinton
Lake
Poteriteri
1
Preservation
Inlet
Te Waewae
Te
Waewae
Bay
Edendale
Wyndham
Balclutha
Orepuki
Kaitangata
SH99
Riverton
1
Catlins
State
Forest Park
Owaka
Colac
Invercargill
Otatara
92
Tokanui
Chaslands
Nugget
Point
Bluff
Fortrose
Waikawa
Foveaux
Strait
Stewart
Island
(Rakiura)
Oban (Halfmoon Bay)
Southland
0
40
80 km
National & Forest Parks
World Heritage Areas
SOUTH
PACIFIC
OCEAN

Annoying Weather & Wildlife

Once you leave Te Anau, you hit two of the menaces of Fiordland: rain and sandflies. Rain in this area is very heavy – Milford gets over six metres (20 feet) annually! Sandflies, for those who haven't met them, are nasty little biting insects, smaller than mosquitoes, with a similar bite – you will see clouds of them at Milford. Don't be put off sightseeing by rain; the masses of water hurtling down the sheer walls of Milford Sound are an incredible sight and the rain tends to keep the sandflies away. For walking and tramping it is a different story, as the rain means flooded rivers and poor visibility. ■

Terrace, which runs along the lakefront, and perpendicular Milford Rd.

The Fiordland National Park Visitors Centre (☎ 249 7921) is on Lake Front Drive near the turn-off to Manapouri. You can get all your information on tramping or shorter walks there. It's open from 8 am to 6 pm and 7.30 to 9.30 pm daily in summer, and 9 am to 4.30 pm in winter. Independent walkers for the Milford Track should book here (☎ 249 8514; fax 249 8515).

The Te Anau Visitor Information Centre (☎ 249 8900; fax 249 7022) is in the Fiordland Travel office by the waterfront on the corner of Te Anau Terrace and Milford Rd. Fiordland Travel (☎ (0800) 656 501) operate lake cruises and tours. Mt Cook Airline is also on Te Anau Terrace by the Travelodge. The post office is in the centre of town on Milford Rd, and there are banks near the corner of Mokonui St and Milford Rd.

As well as being the main access to the Milford Track, Te Anau is also the jumping-off point for many other walks – the Kepler, Dusky, Routeburn and Hollyford. If you need a guide for remote walks, try Southwest NZ Wilderness Guiding (☎ 249 7832) or Fiordland Bird & Bush (☎ 249 7078).

Things to See

Just outside Te Anau, on the road to Manapouri, is the compact and nicely laid out **Te Anau Wildlife Centre**, run by the Department of Conservation (DOC). It concentrates on native birds but also has a trout hatchery. It's worth taking time out if only to see the rare takahe, one of NZ's species of flightless birds, considered extinct until a colony was discovered in 1948 (see the Flora & Fauna section). The centre has many other NZ birds, both common and rare; admission is free.

The **Te Ana-au Caves**, on the western side of the lake, are not old geologically, but they possess an energy that is immediately apparent when you go underground. They are located on the Tunnel Burn stream at the foot of and below the Murchison Mountains, which are the last refuge of the takahe. The caves, mentioned in Maori legends, were rediscovered in 1948.

On the shores of the lake and accessible only by boat, the 200 metres of active cave system is magical with waterfalls, whirlpools and a glow-worm grotto in the inner reaches. In order to get into the heart of the caves a system of walkways and two short punt journeys are used. The 2½-hour trip costs $32 (children $10); departures are at 2 and 8.15 pm daily. Book at Fiordland Travel.

Activities

Kepler Track This four-day Great Walk gives access to the Kepler Mountains at the southern end of Lake Te Anau. Like any Fiordland track the walk depends on the weather; when it's wet, it's very, very wet. The track is top quality, well graded and gravelled, and the three large huts are well equipped, with heating and gas stoves. Hut fees are $15 per night and hut wardens are on hand from early November to late April (camping is $6 per person per night).

The alpine sections of the track may be

closed in winter due to weather conditions (the cost in winter is $4 per night); these sections also require a good level of fitness. Other sections are much easier.

Walking the Track The walk can be done over four days and features a variety of vegetation and terrain including lakeside and riverside sections (good trout fishing), then climbing up out of the beech forest to the treeline, where there are panoramic views. The alpine stretch between Iris Burn Hut and Mt Luxmore Hut goes along a high ridge line, well above the bush with fantastic views when it's clear. Other sections cross U-shaped glacier-carved valleys. It's recommended that the track be done in the Mt Luxmore-Iris Burn-Moturau direction. Estimated walking times are as follows:

Park Visitor Centre to control gates	45 minutes
Control gates to Brod Bay	1½ hours
Brod Bay to Mt Luxmore Hut	3½ to 4½ hours
Mt Luxmore to Iris Burn Hut	five to six hours
Iris Burn to Moturau Hut	five to six hours
Moturau to Rainbow Reach	1½ hours
Rainbow Reach to control gates	2½ to 3½ hours

There are plenty of other walks to choose from in the Te Anau area; they are outlined in the DOC pamphlet *Te Anau Walks* and are all less than a day in duration. Fiordland Bird & Bush (☎ 249 7078) has a range of guided walks, tailor-made to suit your requirements. They specialise in the remote George Sound Track (four days, $540 per person, minimum of six).

Sea Kayaking Two companies offer sea-kayaking trips in this enthralling natural environment. Fiordland Wilderness Experiences – Sea & Lake Kayaking (☎ 249 7700) at 66 Quintin Drive, Te Anau, and Fiordland Kayaks (☎ 249 8275), also in Te Anau, offer either guided trips or independent rentals. All trips are in the World Heritage area and could

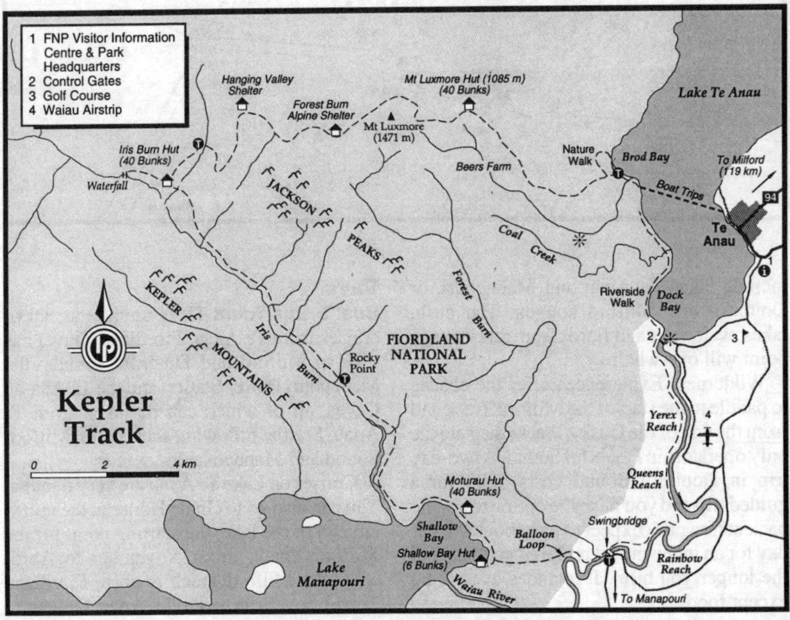

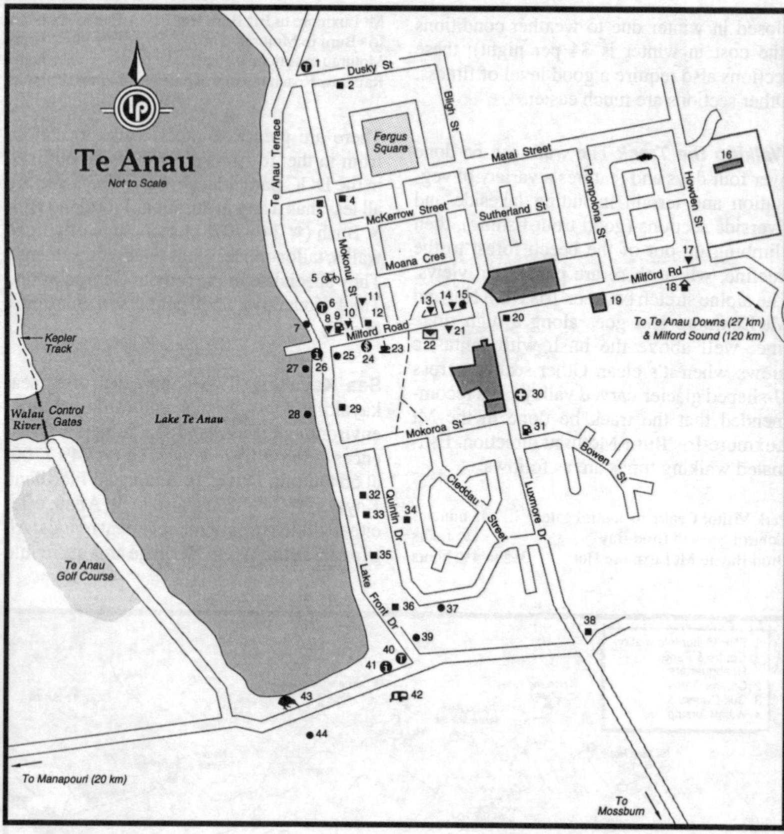

include lakes Te Anau and Manapouri, or Doubtful and Milford sounds. The bush, lakes, waterfalls and fiords from this vantage point will overwhelm you.

Wilderness Experiences offer the chance to paddle to the start of the Milford Track and from the end of the Dusky Track; they are the only operators in Doubtful Sound. A two-day trip in Doubtful Sound costs $200 for a guided trip and you have the option to paddle back at hire rate. Expect to pay about $40 per day for an independent rental (it gets cheaper the longer you hire). It includes everything except food.

Tours

Boat & Bus Tours There are all manner of cruises from Te Anau. Fiordland Travel has trips to Milford and Doubtful sounds, the Manapouri Power Station and the Te Ana-au Caves, all of which can be taken from Te Anau. See the following sections on Milford Sound and Manapouri for details.

Cruises on Lake Te Anau are very popular. You can also go to Glade House at the northern end of the lake, the starting point for the Milford Track. From November to April, when the Milford Track is open, Fiordland Travel boats run from Te Anau Downs to

PLACES TO STAY

2 Shakespeare House
3 Mountain View Holiday Park
4 Matai Lodge
11 Luxmore Resort
17 Te Anau YHA Hostel
19 Lynwood Lodge
29 Te Anau Travelodge
32 Edgewater XL Motel
33 Te Anau Backpackers
34 Anchorage Motel
35 Lakeside Motel
36 Quality Hotel
38 Fiordland Motor Lodge & Te Anau Club
42 Te Anau Motor Park

PLACES TO EAT

8 Pop Inn
10 Redcliff Café
11 Baileys & Luxmore Bistro
12 Ming Gardens Restaurant
13 The Ranch
16 Takeaway, Dairy
20 Keplers
21 La Toscana
23 Jailhouse Café
29 Henry's

OTHER

1 Public Toilets
5 Bicycle Hire
6 Public Toilets
7 Lakeland Boat Hire
9 Petrol Station
12 InterCity Depot/Air Fiordland
14 Library
15 Swimming Pool
18 Police Station
22 Post Office
24 Bank of New Zealand
25 Mt Cook Lines Booking Office
26 Te Anau Visitor Information Centre, Fiordland Travel & *Manuska*
27 Southern Lakes Helicopters
28 Waterwings Airways
30 Medical Centre
31 Petrol Station
37 Fiordland Wilderness Experiences
39 Trout Observatory
40 Public Toilets
41 Fiordland National Park Visitors Centre & DOC
43 Wildlife Centre (Takahe Display)
44 Ivon Wilson Park

Glade House for the Milford Track trampers. They run at 2 pm every day during the season, and at 8.30 am during school holidays. You can go on the 2 pm boat only if there is extra space, and you'll have to come straight back if you're not doing the track. However, going on the morning boat gives you about a five-hour stopover – enough time to walk to Clinton Forks (the first independent hut on the Milford Track), and back to meet the afternoon boat on its homeward trip. InterCity buses to Te Anau Downs connect with the 2 pm boat trip but not with the morning trip. The boat trip costs $38 (children $10).

Yacht charters and scenic cruises on the lake are also made by Sinbad Cruises (☎ 249 7106) on the gaff ketch *Manuska*, sailing to Glade House for $50 or Brod Bay for $15 ($30 return). Lakeland Boat Hire (☎ 249 8364) rents out rowing boats, outboard motors, pedal boats, catamarans, canoes or jet skis from a little caravan beside the lake. Trips 'n' Tramps (☎ 249 7081) offers a variety of things to do around Te Anau, including half-day and all-day guided walks.

Aerial Sightseeing Waterwings Airways (☎ 249 7405) has floatplane flights from right off Te Anau Terrace in the town centre. There's a quick zip around the area for $36, a flight to Dusky and Doubtful sounds for $195, one over the Kepler Track for $66 and to Doubtful Sound for $131. Waterwings also has a variety of Milford flights including morning and afternoon Milford Sound Overheads for $165. Children's fares are 60% of adult fares. All the flights can be made either by floatplane or normal plane.

Air Fiordland (☎ 249 7505) has short scenic flights from Milford for $48, flights to Milford Sound from Te Anau for $146 and to Doubtful Sound for $115, or a 1½-hour tour over both sounds and the Fiordland National Park for $242. The trips to Milford include fly/cruise/fly ($244) and coach/cruise/fly options ($217). The fly/cruise/coach option is $145 from Te Anau. Why is it cheaper? Because they need to fill seats on the way in. Children's fares are 60% of adult fares. The flight to Milford Sound goes over the Milford Track, with views of the amazing drop of the Sutherland Falls and Lake Quill.

They can do cheaper scenic flights from Milford as they have a plane based there in summer. There is a big range of flights available; Sutherland Falls, for instance, is $72 for a 25-minute flight. Charters are also available – Milford or Hollyford to Martins Bay would be $265 for charter of a plane (four people with packs).

Southern Lakes Helicopters (☎ 249 7167) also has flights around the area. On one combination trip, similar but not as good as the Siberia Experience (see Makarora in the Westland chapter), you can 'heli-trek-sail' for $85. Southern Lakes take you up to Mt Luxmore, then you walk to Brod Bay (about three hours) and then sail back to Te Anau on the *Manuska*.

Places to Stay

Camping & Cabins The *Te Anau Motor Park* (☎ 249 7457), opposite the lake just one km from Te Anau on the road to Manapouri, has tent/powered sites for $17/20, standard cabins at $30, tourist cabins at $40, tourist flats from $55 (all prices are for two) and there's also a bunkhouse with beds for $13. It's a large, well-equipped camping ground with attractive surroundings and a very pleasant atmosphere. Car, van and gear storage is available for trampers. If you're lucky you may see the Southern Lights (Aurora Australis) from this camping ground.

Mountain View Holiday Park (☎ 249 7462) on Mokonui St has tent sites for $20 for two, and cabins and on-site caravans from $40 for two. About 1.5 km north of town on the Milford Rd is the *Fiordland Holiday Park* (☎ 249 7059). Camp sites are $14 for two (power is $1 extra), the bunkroom is $20 per person and on-site caravans are $28.

There are over a dozen basic *DOC camping grounds* in this region, all adjacent to SH94 (see The Road to Milford).

Hostels At the friendly *Te Anau Backpackers* (☎ 249 7713) at 48 Lake Front Drive, dorm/share rooms are $13 per person and twins and doubles are $36. They help arrange transport to the Kepler Track, and have complimentary bikes and gear storage, dinghies for hire and a garden to relax in. There is a summer-only pool here also. The upstairs dorm room has an excellent view, and there are also kitchen facilities, a small lounge and radio up there; book ahead if you intend staying.

The *Te Anau YHA Hostel* (☎ 249 7847), about 800 metres out of town on Milford Rd, has dorm beds for $15 per person, and twins and doubles for $34. You can hire camping equipment, and store gear here while you're away tramping. There is a takeaway and small shop across the road.

Guesthouses Te Anau has a couple of well-kept B&B places. *Shakespeare House* (☎ 249 7349) at 10 Dusky St offers B&B accommodation 'as you like it' but the prices have risen considerably. The quiet and pleasant rooms are off a bright, covered-in verandah and the breakfast is substantial. Rooms cost $76 for a single and $96 to $112 for doubles from December to March.

At *Matai Lodge* (☎ 249 7360) on the corner of Matai and Mokonui Sts, B&B costs $54/72 for singles/doubles in the high season and a bit less during the rest of the year. The *Rainbow Downs Country Lodge* (☎ 249 8006) on Mt York Rd off the Te Anau-Manapouri road has B&B doubles for $75/80 with continental/cooked breakfast.

Hotels & Motels The *Lynwood Lodge* (☎ 249 8538), on the corner of Luxmore Drive and Milford Rd, is the former O Tapara Lodge (once located near Cascade Creek on the Milford Rd); doubles are $80 and it is $20 for each extra person. The *Edgewater XL Motel* (☎ 249 7258) at 52 Te Anau Terrace has singles/doubles for $65/77 per night. There's a small one-night surcharge and lower off-season rates. The *Lakeside Motel* (☎ 249 7435) at 36 Lake Front Drive is slightly more expensive than the Edgewater.

Another moderately priced motel is the *Anchorage* (☎ 249 7256) at 47 Quintin Drive with rooms for $80 for a double. There are numerous other motels at similar or higher prices. If you're aiming for the top, the *Te Anau Travelodge* (☎ 249 7411) is on Te Anau Terrace in the town centre; rooms are from $115. The *Luxmore Resort* (☎ 249 7526), on Milford Rd near the corner of Mokonui St, and *Quality Hotel* (☎ 249 7421), Te Anau Terrace, are other up-market options.

Places to Eat

The *Pop Inn* near the lakefront has light snacks and sandwiches; as it is often crammed with forlorn and starved bus travellers, the service seldom extends beyond mediocre. Several places along Milford Rd and in Jailhouse Mall in the town centre serve snacks and takeaways – try the *Jailhouse Café*, which has good sandwiches, the popular *Te Anau Dairy* or the *Fiordland Bakery*. *Bailey's,* on the corner of Mokonui St, serves breakfast all day, bistro lunches, and morning and afternoon teas.

Just off Milford Rd, on Mokonui St, is the atmospheric *Redcliff Café*, which has pleasant outdoor and indoor bar areas and an intimate restaurant where they serve hearty food (try the huge serves of nachos). It seems that the bar and catering staff from Te Anau's hotels come here when they need a change from their own hotel food.

Henry's at the Te Anau Travelodge has a Sunday evening buffet for $17.50 (children $8); it is open for lunch, and for dinner from 5.30 to 9 pm. *Keplers* on Milford Rd features venison and seafood on its menu, with main courses from $15 to $23. The *Settlers Steak House*, Milford Rd, is the local hunting ground for carnivores.

On the main street in the town centre is *La Toscana*, a BYO place that has Italian food, eg ravioli di oggi (pasta of the day) for about $8.50. Pizzas range from $12.50 to $19.50 and all sweets are $4.50.

The *Village Inn* on Mokoroa St serves continental food, including a range of vegetarian dishes; try 'magic mushrooms' for $7.50/15.25 for entrees/mains.

The *Ming Gardens*, on Milford Crescent, is one local Chinese place and another is the licensed *China City*, next to the library. Directly behind China City, *The Ranch* has a variety of family-style mains from $13 to $16, and kids' meals for $9.50.

Getting There & Away

Air Mt Cook Airline (☎ 249 7516) has daily flights to Queenstown and Mt Cook, with connections to other centres. Waterwings Airways (☎ 249 7405), an agent for Ansett New Zealand, has flights to Queenstown and Milford. Air Fiordland (☎ 249 7505) also has flights from Milford to Te Anau and Queenstown (both $146).

Bus InterCity (☎ 249 7559) has daily bus services between Queenstown and Milford via Te Anau, taking 2½ hours from Te Anau to either Queenstown or Milford. There's also a daily service to Invercargill (three hours) and Dunedin (six hours), involving a half-hour transfer stop in Lumsden. Buses arrive at and depart from the InterCity depot on Milford Rd. Mt Cook Landline (☎ 249 8059) also has daily buses between Queenstown and Te Anau, Milford and Invercargill.

Topline Tours (☎ 249 8059), 80 Quintin Drive, operate a daily service between Te Anau and Queenstown ($33, discounted $23). It departs from Te Anau at 10 am and Queenstown at 2 pm. Spitfire Shuttle (☎ (0800) 737 002) depart Te Anau daily for Invercargill at 8.30 am, returning at 1 pm; the fare is $40 (discount $34).

Fiordland Travel (☎ 249 7419) on the lakefront has buses to Queenstown and Milford. See Queenstown in the Otago chapter for details on the Southern Explorer, a good way for backpackers to get around this region.

Hitching Hitching in and out is a bit easier than to Milford, though still fairly hard. Hitching between Manapouri and Te Anau is good if you go there for a day trip.

Getting Around

For trampers doing the Kepler Track there is a shuttle service operating from the Te Anau Motor Park (☎ 249 7457). The Kepler Track Shuttle costs $4 to the control gates and $8 to the swing bridge. Kiwi Discovery (☎ 442 7340), who provide trampers' transport, pass through Te Anau at 10 am on the way to Milford and 6 pm returning to Queenstown.

You can hire bicycles from Little Golf & Bike Hire (☎ 249 7959) just off Milford Rd, on Mokonui St; and the Te Anau Motor Park ($10 for two hours and $20 for a day).

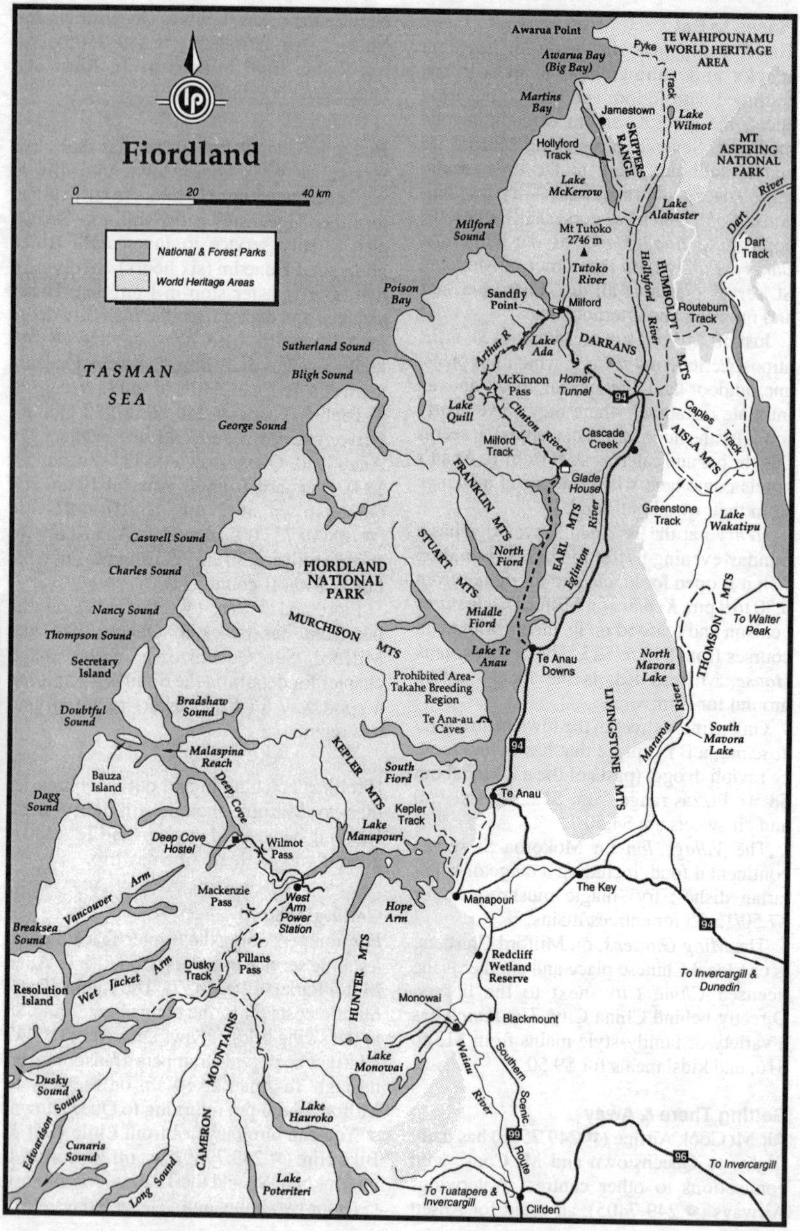
Fiordland
0
20
40 km
National & Forest Parks
World Heritage Areas
TASMAN SEA
Awarua Point
Awarua Bay (Big Bay)
TE WAHIPOUNAMU WORLD HERITAGE AREA
Pyke
Track
Martins Bay
Jamestown
SKIPPERS RANGE
Lake Wilmot
Hollyford Track
Lake McKerrow
MT ASPIRING NATIONAL PARK
Lake Alabaster
Dart River
Milford Sound
Mt Tutoko 2746 m
Dart Track
Tutoko River
Poison Bay
Sandfly Point
Milford
Hollyford River
HUMBOLDT MTS
Routeburn Track
Sutherland Sound
Arthur R
Lake Ada
DARRANS
Bligh Sound
McKinnon Pass
Homer Tunnel
94
Lake Quill
Clinton River
Caples Track
AISLA MTS
George Sound
Milford Track
Cascade Creek
Glade House
FRANKLIN MTS
Greenstone Track
EARL MTS
Eglinton River
Lake Wakatipu
Caswell Sound
Charles Sound
FIORDLAND NATIONAL PARK
STUART MTS
North Fiord
Nancy Sound
Middle Fiord
THOMSON MTS
To Walter Peak
Thompson Sound
MURCHISON MTS
Lake Te Anau
Te Anau Downs
North Mavora Lake
Secretary Island
Prohibited Area-Takahe Breeding Region
LIVINGSTONE MTS
Bradshaw Sound
Doubtful Sound
Te Ana-au Caves
Mararoa River
South Mavora Lake
Malaspina Reach
Bauza Island
KEPLER MTS
South Fiord
Deep Cove
Dagg Sound
Te Anau
Kepler Track
Lake Manapouri
Deep Cove Hostel
Wilmot Pass
Vancouver Arm
Mackenzie Pass
West Arm Power Station
Manapouri
The Key
Hope Arm
Breaksea Sound
Pillans Pass
Redcliff Wetland Reserve
Dusky Track
Resolution Island
Wet Jacket Arm
HUNTER MTS
To Invercargill & Dunedin
Monowai
Blackmount
Lake Monowai
Waiau River
Southern Scenic Route
Dusky Sound
CAMERON MOUNTAINS
Edwardson Sound
Lake Hauroko
99
Cunaris Sound
96
To Invercargill
Long Sound
Lake Poteriteri
To Tuatapere & Invercargill
Clifden

SOUTHLAND

MANAPOURI

Just 19 km south of Te Anau, on the shores of the lake of the same name, Manapouri is a popular centre for trips, cruises and walking expeditions into the Fiordland area. The lake is in a spectacular setting, surrounded by mountains which are, in their lower reaches, covered by native bush. The town exists on a combination of hydroelectricity generation and tourism, an incongruous and volatile mix at the best of times. Now greenies work hand in hand with rednecks – the damage has been done and all are attempting to preserve their livelihoods.

Orientation & Information

Fiordland Travel (☎ (0800) 656 502; fax 249 6603) is the main information and tour centre here – the office at Pearl Harbour organises most of the trips. Pick your times, as they won't have time to help you just prior to a boat leaving. Although the Manapouri Power Station and Doubtful Sound trips depart from Manapouri, there are connecting buses from Te Anau for these trips.

Tours

Doubtful Sound A popular cruise out of Manapouri is Fiordland Travel's trip to Doubtful Sound. The cruise across the lake from Manapouri is followed by a bus trip down a two-km spiral tunnel to the West Arm Power Station machine hall, about two-km underground – a long way! From the power station, water is passed through a 10-km-long tailrace to Deep Cove in Doubtful Sound.

The power station on West Arm was built primarily to provide power for an aluminium smelter near Bluff. Not surprisingly, the project was the focus of intense environmental battles in the 1970s. At one time it was planned to considerably raise the level of the lake but this plan was defeated by the Save Manapouri Petition – the longest petition in NZ history. When you see the beauty of what has been described as 'New Zealand's loveliest lake' it's hard to imagine that anyone would want to destroy it. Manapouri is the second deepest lake in NZ after Hauroko.

The road from West Arm over the Wilmot Pass to Doubtful Sound, built during the construction of the powerhouse, is totally isolated from the rest of the NZ road system. Before the road was built in 1959 only the most intrepid tramper or sailor entered the inner reaches of Doubtful Sound. Even Captain Cook, who named it, did not enter it – when he observed it from off the coast in 1770, he was 'doubtful' whether the winds in the sound would be sufficient to blow the ship back out to sea. He consequently named the place Doubtful Sound and continued sailing up the coast. In 1793 the Spanish entered the sound, and Malsapina Reach is named after one of the leaders of this expedition, Bauza Island after another.

Today, Doubtful Sound is an exquisitely peaceful place. Bottlenose and dusky dolphins can be seen in its waters, and there's also a small colony of fur seals. The Fiordland crested penguin nests in the sound for about six to eight weeks in October and November. Life is also abundant below the surface, with black coral growing at an unusually shallow depth due to the fresh water on the surface, brought down by the power station and darkening the water.

The power station visit takes nearly four hours and costs $41 (children $10); book at Fiordland Travel. If you want to continue to Deep Cove and go on the Doubtful Sound cruise it'll cost you $140 (children $70) for the all-day excursion. You can order lunch when you book or take your own.

Ecology Holiday Fiordland Ecology Holidays (☎ 249 6600), at 1 Home St, set out to offer a completely different type of experience to a small number of clients. These tours are run by Lance and Ruth Shaw, both very familiar with the flora and fauna of the area. They sail their yacht into parts of the World Heritage area that are only now being discovered. You will have the chance to dive in the fiords, as many visiting marine biologists do, plunging into a 40-metre depth of fresh water that reveals deep-water species you couldn't hope to see elsewhere.

Their onshore B&B accommodation is

$40/60 for singles/doubles; there are reduced rates for stays of more than two nights. Take the opportunity to stay with them and discuss more exciting possibilities in Fiordland; it will always be less expensive in a manageable group of six or so people, and over a period of three to five days. There is every chance that you will then sit amidst fur seals and swim with the resident pod of dolphins.

Places to Stay & Eat

The *Lakeview Motor Park* (☎ 249 6624), one km from the post office on the Te Anau road, has tent/powered sites at $15/17 for two, and cabins from $28 for two. The motor park has a sauna and spa pool.

The *Manapouri Glade Motor Park* (☎ 249 6623), on a stunning site adjacent to the river and lake, has sites at $15 for two, and cabins at $26 for two. There's a spa pool here, and it's only a 400-metre walk to Doubtful Sound cruise departures.

There are no hostels in Manapouri but you can stay at the *Deep Cove Hostel* (☎ 216 1340) on Doubtful Sound for $17 per person. The hostel has dinghies, fishing lines, lifejackets and wet-weather gear for hire, and there are a number of good walks in the vicinity. For most of the year it also hosts school groups. Independent arrangements must be made through the hostel and travel arrangements through Fiordland Travel at Pearl Harbour.

SOUTHLAND

The fine old *Murrell's Grand View House* (☎ 249 6642), built in 1889, has four comfortable double/twin en suite rooms. B&B is $120/145 for singles/doubles and 'gourmet' dinners are available for $50.

There are motels attached to both camping grounds. At the *Lakeview* units are from $58, and at the *Manapouri Glade* they're $60.

The *Pearl Harbour Coffee Bar* has good sandwiches and other snacks. If you're going on a day trip it's cheaper putting something together here (or before you arrive) rather than paying $9/21 for a lunch pack/deluxe picnic. Meals are available at the *Lakeview Motor Inn*; the ordinary service is compensated for by great views.

Getting There & Away

Fiordland Travel has lots of people going from Manapouri to Te Anau to hook up with their Te Anau trips and vice versa, so they operate a Te Anau-Manapouri bus service for $5 (children $2.50) one way.

You can rent rowing boats from Manapouri Motors (☎ 249 6644) at Waiau St, for $4 per person per day, plus $2 a night if you keep it overnight, while you go on the walking tracks across the river. The hitching between Te Anau and Manapouri is OK if you don't rely on it to make a connection with the Doubtful Sound cruises.

TE ANAU TO MILFORD

It is 119 km from Te Anau to Milford on one of the most scenic roads you could hope to travel along. The first part of the road is through relatively undulating farmland which sits atop the lateral moraine of the glacier that once gouged out the lake. At 16 km the road enters a patch of mountain beech forest, passes the **Te Anau Downs Harbour** at 29 km and heads towards the entrance of Fiordland National Park and the Eglinton Valley. Again, patches of beech – red, silver and mountain – are passed through, as well as alluvial flats and meadows.

Two interesting sights on the way are the **Avenue of the Disappearing Mountain** and the **Mirror Lakes**; the latter are 58 km from Te Anau, about halfway to Milford.

At the 77-km mark is the locale now referred to as O Tapara, but known more commonly as **Cascade Creek**. O Tapara is the original name for nearby Lake Gunn, and refers to a Ngai Tahu ancestor, Tapara. The lake was a stopover for parties heading to Anita Bay in search of greenstone. A 40-minute walking track passes through tall red beech forest that shelters a variety of birdlife such as fantails, tomtits, bellbirds, parakeets, kereru and riflemen. On the lake, paradise ducks and New Zealand scaup are often seen. Lake Gunn is the largest of the Eglinton Valley lakes but Fergus and Lochie are higher. The forest floor is an array of mosses, ferns and lichens. In Cascade Creek you may see long-tail bats, NZ's only native land mammal.

The vegetation alters significantly as **the Divide** is approached. The size of the bush is reduced and ribbonwood and fuchsia are prominent. The Divide is the lowest east-west pass in the Southern Alps, and there is a good shelter here for walkers either finishing or commencing the Routeburn and Greenstone tracks. About a 1½-hour walk along the Routeburn brings you to **Key Summit**, where there are numerous tarns and patches of alpine bog. Three river systems – the Hollyford, Greenstone/Clutha and Eglinton/Waiau – start from the sides of this feature and radiate out to the west, east and south coasts of the island.

From the Divide, the road falls into the beech forest of the **Hollyford Valley** and there is an interesting turn-off to Hollyford (Gunn's) Camp and the start of the Hollyford Track to Martins Bay. The views either side of the road are stupendous. One km down the Lower Hollyford road from Marian Corner, where the avalanche barriers are, is a track leading to **Lake Marian** with splendid views; it's four hours return and a hard tramp.

From the corner, the road rises up to the east portal of the **Homer Tunnel**, 101 km from Te Anau. The tunnel is named after Harry Homer who discovered the Homer Saddle in 1889; however, work on the tunnel didn't begin until 1935 (to provide relief work for the unemployed after the Depression), and it wasn't finished until 1952. Rough-hewn, it has a steep east to west gradient of one in 11, but emerges into the spectacular **Cleddau Canyon** on the Milford side. At the portals are short nature walks, describing alpine species found here.

The road is normally open all year, but may be closed in winter by avalanches.

About 10 km before Milford is the **Chasm Walk**. The Cleddau River plunges through eroded boulders in a narrow chasm, the Upper Fall, which is 22 metres deep. About 16 metres lower it cascades under a natural rock bridge to another waterfall.

There are views of **Mt Tutoko**, Fiordland's proudest and highest peak, glimpsed above the beech forest just before you arrive in Milford. In this area lie the majestic Darrans and proud Mt Tutoko. A track leads off from the western side of the bridge over Tutoko River. After a two-hour walk through bush, the scenery here is overpowering. Don't venture any further unless you are a competent tramper and very well equipped. There is no development in this region – nature, swarms of gigantic sandflies and abundant rainfall seem to retort 'Just you try'.

Hollyford Track (to Martins Bay)

This is a well-known track along the broad Hollyford Valley through rainforest to the Tasman Sea at Martins Bay. Because of its length (five days one way) it should not be undertaken lightly. Check at Fiordland Park headquarters, Te Anau, for detailed information and the latest on track conditions.

There are guided walks on the Hollyford which include the flight out and a jet-boat trip on Lake McKerrow, which avoids the hardest and most tedious part of the walk, Demon Trail. For transport information contact the Hollyford Tourist & Travel Company (☎ 442 3760). The five DOC huts – Hidden Falls, Alabaster, McKerrow Island, Demon Trail and Hokuri – are all $4 per person and the private hut at Martins Bay $6.

Estimated walking times are as follows:

Hollyford Camp to Hidden Falls	2½ to three hours
Hidden Falls to Lake Alabaster	3½ to four hours
Lake Alabaster to Lake McKerrow	three hours
Lake McKerrow to Demon Trail	1½ hours
Demon Trail to Hokuri River	five hours
Hokuri River to Martins Bay	five hours

Places to Stay & Eat

There are a number of *DOC camping grounds* along the Milford road (distances given are from Te Anau):

Location	*Km*	*Location*	*Km*
Ten Mile Bush	17	Deer Flat	62
Henry Creek	25	Kiosk Creek	65
Boyd Creek	45	Smithy Creek	67
Walker Creek	49	Upper Eglinton	71
McKay Creek	53	Cascade Creek	78
Totara Creek	53	Lake Gunn	81
East Branch Eglinton	56		

SOUTHLAND

At Te Anau Downs, 27 km on the road to Milford, is the *Te Anau Downs Motor Inn* (☎ 249 7811). Here B&B costs $85 for two, and the self-contained units are from $97.50 to $112.50 for two.

You can also camp at *Hollyford Camp*, formerly Gunn's Camp, in the Hollyford Valley for $8 for two. The camp has rustic cabins (innersprung mattresses, wood and coal-burning stoves, separate kitchen, hand basins; you supply the rest) at $14/24 for one/two people. The camp also has a shop with basic trampers' supplies (sorted into 'pack-friendly' bags), and an interesting little museum, the very personal creation of owner Murray Gunn, who has been finding things in the hills around here for nearly 40 years and saving mementoes of the area's history; entry is free if you stay in his cabins.

Just before the Homer Tunnel is a turn-off to the hidden *Homer Hut*, the property of the NZ Alpine Club. They take casual guests during the week for a minimal fee; check with the caretaker at the hut – if there is one!

SOUTHLAND

MILFORD SOUND

Whether or not you walk the Milford Track, you should make a visit to Milford Sound, the 22-km-long fiord that marks the end of the walk and beside which rises the beautiful, 1695-metre-high Mitre Peak. The fiord is really breathtaking. The water, usually calm, mirrors the sheer peaks that rise all around.

There's a small display on the history of Milford in the foyer of the Milford Sound Hotel, with photographs and stories relating to the geology and the glacial formation of the fiords. There are also photographs and stories of Donald Sutherland, 'the Hermit of Milford' (1843-1919), who ran the first accommodation place at Milford Sound. The Sutherland Falls are named after him. You can see his grave behind the hotel.

Activities

Milford Track Described by some as 'the finest walk in the world', this four-day walk is along a very scenic track. It is the country's best known walk and one that most Kiwis dream of doing, even if it's the *only* track they ever walk. Many overseas visitors also make a special effort to do the track though, sadly, they often leave NZ without realising that many other great tracks exist.

For some walkers who have done other tracks, Milford generates a lot of bitterness because of the way it is run. This is partly because of the enforced regulation of numbers on the track. However, the benefits of regulating the numbers of walkers outweigh the inconvenience it may cause. Firstly, keeping the number of people going through to a reasonable level and making sure everyone is accommodated in the huts (ie no camping) means that the environment is better protected. Secondly, whilst it is a hassle to book yourself on it, you are guaranteed that the track won't be overcrowded.

The track is subject to a booking system from late October to mid April, and in the off season it is still possible to walk the track if it is not closed by snow.

Milford is synonymous with rain: 5.5 metres of it a year is only average. However, the number of rainy days is not exceptionally high, so when it does rain in this country of granite the effect is an experience not to be missed. Water cascades *everywhere* and small streams become raging torrents within minutes. Remember your raincoat and pack your belongings in an extra plastic bag.

Information & Costs You can walk the track as an independent 'freedom walker' or as part of a guided tour. The track can only be done in one direction, from Lake Te Anau to Milford, and you need a permit from the Track Walking Office at the national park headquarters in Te Anau. This allows you to enter the track on a particular day and no other. As bookings can be heavy it pays to book as far ahead as possible – even several months in advance, especially for December-January. Independent bookings are made through the DOC office in Te Anau (☎ 249 8514; fax 249 8515). Milford Track Guided Walk (☎ (0800) 659 255) takes bookings for the guided option.

For independent walkers the cost of doing the walk is made up of an $85 permit fee ($55 for children), which covers three nights in the huts, plus the costs for the launch from the end of the track to Milford Sound ($19, children $11.50), the bus to Te Anau Downs ($11, children $7), the boat from there to the track ($38, children $10) and the bus back to Te Anau ($35, children $21). All this will probably come to around $190 per person (children $140). There are 30% family discounts for two adults and children.

In addition to independent trampers, organised parties are taken through by guides and they stay at a different chain of huts. These huts are usually an hour before the 'freedom walkers' huts so there is little mingling of the two. The guided walk costs around $1350, somewhat less for children (around $850). Children under 10 are not accepted.

Walking the Track The track follows the fairly flat Clinton River valley up to the Mintaro Hut, passing through rainforest. From Mintaro it passes over the scenic Mackinnon Pass, down to the Quintin Hut and through the rainforest in the Arthur River valley to Milford Sound. You can leave your pack at the Quintin Hut while you make the return walk to Sutherland Falls, NZ's highest. If the pass appears clear on arrival at Mintaro Hut make the effort to climb it, after a hot drink, as it may not be clear the next day. The highlights of Milford are the beautiful views from the Mackinnon Pass, the 630-metre Sutherland Falls, the rainforest and the crystal-clear streams, swarming with clever trout and eels.

Estimated walking times are as follows:

Glade House to Clinton Forks Hut	two hours
Clinton Forks to Mintaro Hut	4½ hours
Mintaro to Dumpling Hut	six hours
Side trip to Sutherland Falls	1½ hours return
Dumpling to Sandfly Point	5½ hours

Guided walkers stop at their own huts – Glade House, Pompolona and Quintin. And for their money they have a longer walk than independent walkers on the last day (from Quintin out to Sandfly Point).

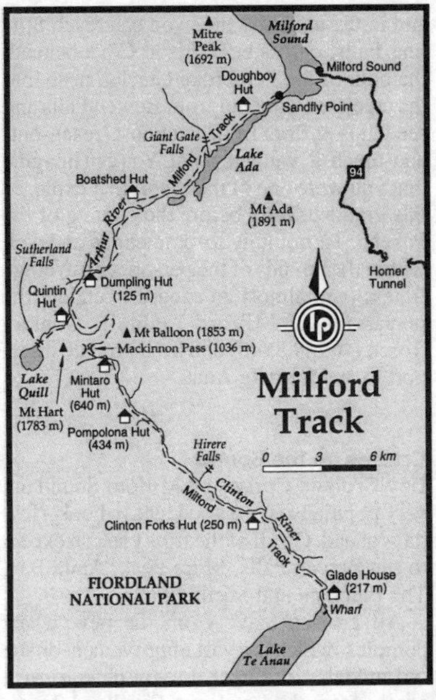

Getting There & Away InterCity has a bus from Te Anau to Te Anau Downs, connecting with the Fiordland Travel boat to the head of Lake Te Anau, where the Milford Track begins. Other, smaller operators offer the boat trip cheaper. See the Te Anau section in this chapter for details. At the end of the track, the ferry to Milford departs from Sandfly Point at 2 pm.

Sea Kayaking The most spectacular way to see Milford Sound is at water level in a sea kayak. Here in your plastic shell you fully realise your insignificance in the sound's huge natural amphitheatre. Whatever the weather, the feeling you get as you look up to the towering bulk of the bush-clad mountains is nothing short of awesome!

Rosco Gaudin, a Kiwi of proportions reflecting the sound's natural immensity, operates summer sea-kayak trips of about six hours duration. These are great value at $69, and in the paddling time you can reach Stirling Falls, egress at Harrison Cove beneath the bulk of the Pembroke Glacier, nose into the creek spewing out from Bowen Falls and see fauna & flora from an almost 'reach-out-and-touch-it' vantage point. You can imagine that you were one of the Maori that explored this grandeur long before the coming of the Pakeha. Thoroughly recommended and well within the bounds of the person with average fitness (and almost an excuse to endure the privations of Milford Lodge!). Contact Rosco (☎ 249 8840) and he'll arrange transport to and from Te Anau.

Cruises on the Sound

Day Cruises Cruises on Milford Sound are very popular so it's a good idea to book a few days ahead. On all of the trips you can expect to see Bowen Falls, Mitre Peak, Anita Bay, The Elephant and Stirling Falls.

All cruises leave from the new wharf complex, which is a vast improvement on the old model. No longer do you have to rush across from the hotel in a Fiordland downpour to get on the boats; there is a covered and elevated walkway through a patch of Fiordland bush from the overnight car park to the wharf.

Fiordland Travel (☎ 249 7419) offers cruises on the *Milford Haven* and *Milford Monarch* which last a little over 1½ hours and cost $38 (children $10). You can have a buffet lunch for $21 (children $10) or you can get a packed lunch for $9, otherwise bring your own. Tea and coffee are served on all cruises.

The Milford Sound Hotel (☎ (0800) 657 444) also operates cruise boats on the sound in their Red Boats. They take basically the same route as the Fiordland Travel boats and cost the same. Red Boats operate the *Lady of the Sounds*, an 85-foot (26-metre) catamaran, and MVs *Mitre Peak II* and *Lady Bowen.*

The prices quoted in this section are for a simple cruise. Various packages involving busing or flying into and out of Milford are available; see Queenstown in the Otago chapter and Te Anau in this chapter.

Overnight Cruises Fiordland Travel's *Milford Wanderer*, modelled on an old trading scow, is designed to carry 150 passengers on daytime cruises and 70 passengers overnight. The overnight cruise gives you the opportunity to take in the awesome views from the sound at a time when there is very little water traffic and definitely no flightseers, which are omnipresent during the day. If you are extra lucky you will probably see a pod of dolphins while the *Wanderer* is moored in Harrison Cove. The *Wanderer* is impressive when the sails are unfurled as it heaves its way through the Tasman swell out from Milford Sound. The small crew of four perform miracles when feeding all of the passengers. The overnight cost is $194 from Queenstown or $150 from Te Anau.

The owners of the MV *Pembroke* (☎ 249 8833), operating as Fiordland Fish 'n' Dive, offer tours with a difference. They concentrate on the natural history of the sound, and offer swimming with dolphins and seals, scuba diving with experienced guides to view red and black corals, fishing outside the sound, and walking at Anita Bay beach and to St Ann's lighthouse.

Places to Stay & Eat

Accommodation at Milford Sound is very limited, so it's a good idea to book ahead if you want to stay there. Over the last four years the hostel-style *Milford Lodge* (☎ 249 8071) has often been one of the most abysmal places to stay on earth. Various changes of management have done nothing to improve the place and promises of a 'clean-up' remain unfulfilled. The owners should be ashamed to present this to trampers after the beauty and purity of the Milford Track. If you do get stuck, take a deep breath; tent/powered sites are $16/18 for two, lifeless dorm and share rooms are $16 per person and doubles are $45 for two. Don't let the slime escape from the bottom of the fridge and remember, lights out at 10.30 pm. Yuck! Catch the bus to Te Anau rather than stay here.

The other accommodation option at

Milford is the *Milford Sound Hotel* (☎ 249 7926), where standard rooms are from $135 to $200 for two. The hotel is attractively situated at the tip of the sound and has great views, but it's becoming rather elderly and frayed. The booking offices for many scenic flight-seeing operations are in the hotel foyer. The hotel has a restaurant and the bar serves basic pub food – well, only pies at the last check. Breakfast in the restaurant is good value and you can fill up for the day for $9.50. Those staying overnight on the *Wanderer* are treated to a sumptuous dinner.

Getting There & Away

You can reach Milford Sound by four methods, all interesting: hike, fly, bus or drive. Probably the most spectacular way to go is to fly there. Flights operate from Queenstown and Te Anau; see those sections for details. A good combination trip is to go to Milford by bus and return by air.

You can do the return trip by bus from Te Anau or further afield. Making the return trip from Queenstown in one day involves a lot of bus travel (about 10 hours). Te Anau is a better jumping-off point as it's only about five hours return. The 120-km trip by road is spectacular, and InterCity, Mt Cook Landline and Fiordland Travel all run daily bus services from Te Anau.

The one-day Fiordland Travel coach/cruise/coach excursion, leaving Te Anau at 8 am and returning at 5 pm, costs $80 (children $40). From Queenstown it departs at 7.15 am and returns at 7.45 pm. InterCity has basically the same excursion at the same price, except the cruise is on the THC Red Boats. It's essential to book in advance for the Milford excursions during the high season. If going to Milford Sound by bus pay a little extra for Fiordland Travel's glass-roofed coaches so that you can fully appreciate the scenery on both sides of the Homer Tunnel.

If you go by car the drive itself should take about 2½ hours, but make sure you allow extra time to stop off on the way, especially if you're planning to take photographs.

Hitching on the Milford road is possible but hard going. There's little traffic and nearly all of it is tourist traffic which is unlikely to stop.

THE SOUTHERN SCENIC ROUTE

The Southern Scenic Route is only now being discovered and appreciated by travellers. It starts in Te Anau and goes via Manapouri, Blackmount and Clifden to Tuatapere. At Tuatapere SH99 is followed to Invercargill via Colac Bay and Riverton. From Invercargill to Dunedin the road hugs the south-east coast. Many of the attractions in the Invercargill-Dunedin portion of the scenic route are covered in the Catlins section of this chapter.

From Te Anau to Invercargill there are a number of interesting features along the way. Between Manapouri and Blackmount watch out for the one sign indicating the **Redcliff Wetland Reserve** – birdwatchers will be particularly pleased as they observe a predatory bush falcon in action. Just before Blackmount there is a turn-off to the right to **Lake Monowai** and Borland Lodge. Monowai stands today as testament to blunder – it was flooded in 1925 for a very small power station and the lake is still unsightly all these years later.

The town of **Clifden** has a cave system nearby and the Clifden Suspension Bridge, built in 1902. The mystical Clifden (Waiau) Caves can be explored without guides but heed all the warnings. You will need at least two torches. The caves are 17 km from Tuatapere; turn left towards Eastern Bush at Lime Works and continue one km up the road. Ladders are provided in steep sections.

About 16 km from Clifden there is a walk to 1000-year-old totara trees. From Clifden you can drive out on 30 km of unsealed road to **Lake Hauroko**, the deepest in NZ. Hauroko lies in a beautiful bush setting, with precipitous slopes on its sides. In 1967, out on Mary Island, a good example of a Maori cave burial was discovered. In this tapu place a woman of high rank was buried, sitting upright, in about 1660.

The three-day tramp to Supper Cove on Dusky Sound starts at Hauroko Burn. For more information see LP's *Tramping in New*

Zealand. Lake Hauroko Tours (☎ 226 6681) organise four and eight-day tramps from Hauroko to Lake Manapouri.

The Southern Coastal Track and the Hump Track are described in the DOC pamphlet *Waitutu Tracks*; both commence at Te Waewae Bay. The coastal track goes via Port Craig (where there is an old schoolhouse) to Lake Hakapoua, and the Hump to Teal Bay at the base of Hauroko, and then via the lake's eastern shore to the Hauroko roadhead.

Tuatapere

Once a timber milling town, Tuatapere (population 860) is now a farming centre on the banks of the Waiau River. More recently it has become infamous as the 'sausage capital' of NZ. It is a good base for trips to Hauroko or Te Waewae Bay and beyond. To check out how effective the woodchoppers were, look at the small remnant of native forest in the town's domain – once most of the area looked like this!

About 10 km south of Tuatapere the scenic route reaches the cliffs above **Te Waewae Bay**, where Hector's dolphins and southern right whales are sometimes seen. In this bay, at the eastern end, is Monkey Island or Te Poka a Takatimu (anchor stone of the *Takatimu* canoe). Nearby is **Orepuki**, where the strong southerlies have had a dramatic effect on the growth of macrocarpas, trees windblown so that they grow in a direction away from the shore. A little further on, the next point on the coast reached is **Colac Bay**, an old Maori settlement and now a popular holiday spot for Southlanders.

For more information on the myriad activities in the region contact the Tuatapere information centre (☎ 226 6186) on the main road in town. They provide a map to the Clifden Caves.

Three jet-boats operate on the Wairaurahiri River, considered by many to be one of the more adventurous rivers in NZ. The cost is $100 per head (minimum of four persons) for about a 90-minute trip. There are also helicopter tours to The Hump, Percy Burn viaduct and the Waitutu Forest. For jet-boating and helicopter flights see the Tuatapere information centre. For trampers' transport, contact Tuatapere Taxis & Minibus Tours (☎ 226 6700).

Places to Stay & Eat The *Mickaela Motor Camp* (☎ 226 6626), on Peace St just off SH96, has a limited number of camp sites at $12 for two; their cabin is a bargain at $32 for four persons. At the very ordinary *Five Mountains Backpackers Lodge* (☎ 226 6418) at 14 Clifden Rd, twin units are $24. Bedrooms at the *Waiau Hotel* (☎ 226 6409), at 47 Main St, are $45/75 for singles/doubles, and the *Tuatapere Motel* (☎ 226 6593) at 41 Orawia Rd has rooms for two at $60. For information on B&Bs and farmstays contact the information centre.

Good solid country fare is to be had at the Waiau Hotel or from one of the other places on Main St. If you must sample one of the great Tuatap sausages try *L & L Butchery* in town or the hotel (if you want someone else to cook them up as your breakfast).

Riverton

Riverton, 38 km west of Invercargill and at the mouths of the Aparima and Pourakino rivers, is considered to be one of the oldest settlements in NZ, dating from the sealing and whaling days. With a small population of just over 1700, this is a very pretty village. There is an Early Settlers Museum on Palmerston St open daily in the afternoon; and, in the town of Thornbury, close by, there is a Vintage Machinery Museum. The Riverton Rocks area is a popular local beach, and Taramea Bay is a safe place to swim.

Places to Stay & Eat At the *Riverton Motor Camp* (☎ 234 8526), off Roy and Hamlet Sts, tent/powered sites are $12/14 for two, cabins are $20 for two and the cottages $40 for four. The *Riverton Beach Motel* (☎ 234 8181) at 4 Marne St, has singles/doubles for $50/55.

Readers have recommended *Hillcrest* (☎ 234 5129) at Pahia, near Monkey Island (25 km west of Riverton). Campers and backpackers are welcome on this working sheep farm; beds in an adjoining house are a very reasonable $8 per person.

Riverton now has a really modern backpackers, the type of building desperately needed in Queenstown. The *Riverton Rock* (☎ (0800) 248 886) was still being built when we visited but the results were impressive. The backpackers area has modern facilities and comfortable dorm rooms and there is guesthouse-style accommodation upstairs. There is a large reception area where you can read lots of information on the area. The cost of the dorm and share rooms is $17 per person, and the doubles are from $38 to $68 for two.

On Palmerston St you will find the town's eateries, including *Ricardo's Pizzeria* at No 135 and the *Pioneer Food Bar* at No 118.

Central Southland

SH1, from Invercargill to Gore, in effect cuts the province into two. To the west is Fiordland and to the south-east the Catlins. Most of Southland's population is concentrated in the centre of the province along SH1 and in the city of Invercargill.

INVERCARGILL

This is the southernmost city in NZ, very much a farm-service community but with a surprising amount of wealth. It is often claimed to be the southernmost city in the world but has probably been eclipsed by Ushuaia in Argentina. In fact, relative to South America it's at the northern end of Patagonia rather than the southern end.

To many travellers coming here it's just a jumping-off point for the tramping tracks of Stewart Island. As the main city of Southland, with a population of 48,100, however, it offers a great deal of other possibilities including the nearby Catlins and the wild areas of southern Fiordland. It is a remarkably ordered city based on a grid pattern. Its biggest drawback is the lack of any break in the geometricity of its surroundings. Built on a plain, it is 'flat as a tack'.

The locals staunchly defend their city, despite snide comments from the rest of NZ about its backwardness and its ennui.

History

When the Chief Surveyor of Otago, JT Thomson, travelled south to settle on a site for Invercargill, the region was uninhabited and covered in a dense forest known as Taurakitewaru Wood, which stretched from the Otepuni Stream (then known as the Otarewa) in the south to the Waihopai River in the north. Realising that ships of 500 tons could sail up the estuary to the mouth of the Otepuni Stream, Thomson chose Taurakitewaru Wood as the best site for the new town. It was laid out over 'a mile square' with four reserves just inside its boundaries and a fifth one running down the banks of the Otepuni Stream. Originally, Queens Park was just over the northern boundary and 200 acres (80 hectares) of forest was set aside for it. Today the only part of the forest that remains is a small area known as Thomsons Bush.

Information

The Invercargill Visitor Information Centre (☎ & fax 218 9753) is in the museum building near the entrance to Queen's Park. For most of the year it's only open from 9 am to 5 pm on weekdays and from 1 to 5 pm on Saturday and Sunday. The chief post office is in Don St and is open from 8.30 am to 5 pm Monday to Friday.

The AA Southland office (☎ 218 9033) is at 47-51 Gala St and the DOC office (☎ 214 4589) is on the 7th floor of the State Insurance Building on Don St. If you're going to Stewart Island it's a good idea to drop in at the DOC office to pick up all the details on walks.

Invercargill's beach is Oreti, 9.5 km west of the city. It's a long, sweeping beach and the water is much milder than in most of the South Island beaches because a warm current sweeps across from Australia.

Things to See

Southland Museum & Art Gallery Invercargill's two main attractions are near the entrance to Queens Park. Part of the museum

SOUTHLAND

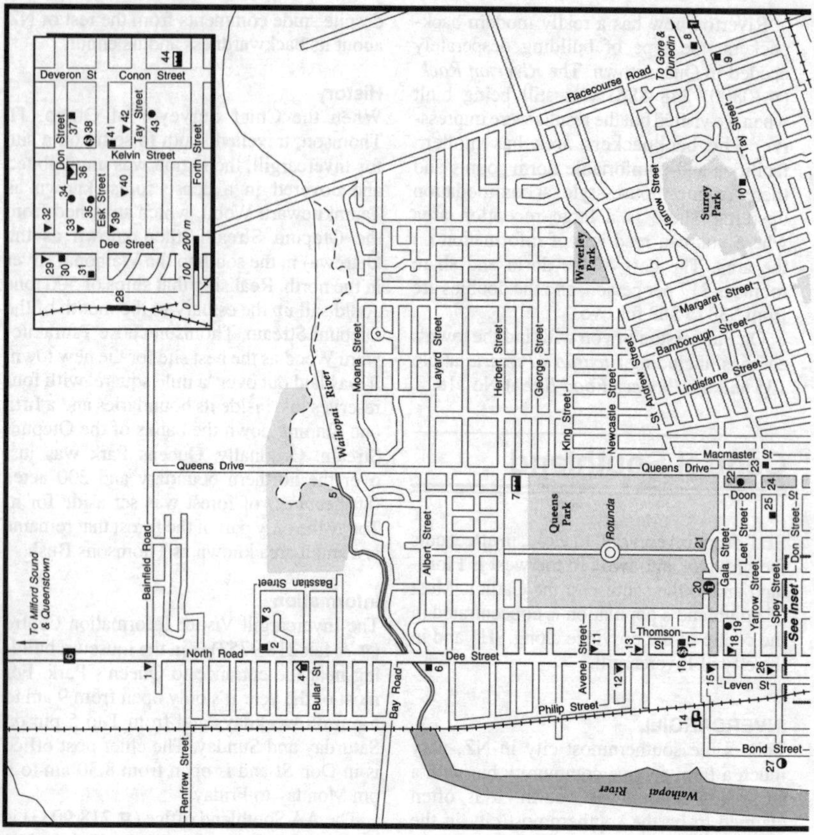

has been developed as an interpretation centre for the Subantarctic. The Roaring Forties gallery, a major part of the Subantarctic centre, is expected to be open sometime in 1996. The Roaring Forties Experience audiovisual takes you on a 25-minute journey to the Subantarctic islands between New Zealand and the Antarctic. As you watch, you can feel the chill wind, thunderstorms and horizontal rain that has shaped these islands. Walk amidst the rookeries, dodge elephant seals and climb up to the exposed nests of shy mollymawks. Andris Apse's photography captures the remote and surreal atmosphere of the last stands of the great untouched. It is well worth the $2 (50c for children) entrance fee.

There's also a tuatara house, where several of the ancient and rare NZ reptiles are on display. One, Henry, is about 100 years old (they can live to about 150 years in captivity), and new ones are being born here – some of the young ones are on display. Other features include a Maori gallery, a natural history gallery, a gallery on the history and technology of Southland, and three art galleries that have a number of temporary and touring exhibitions.

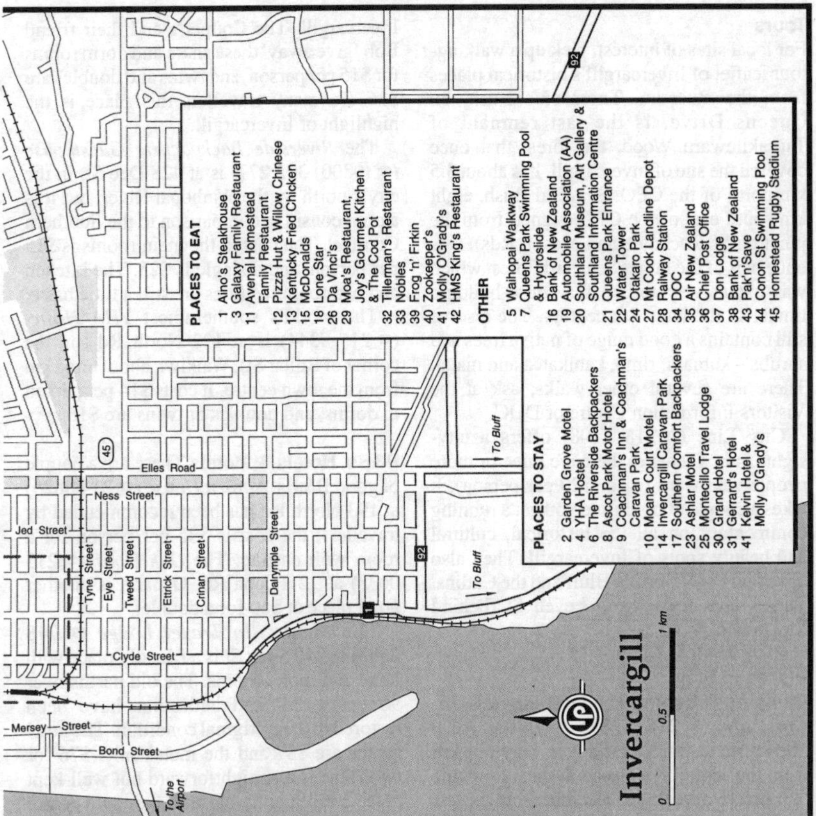

The museum itself is open from 9 am to 5 pm Monday to Friday and from 1 to 5 pm on weekends; admission is free.

Other Attractions The **Anderson Park Art Gallery** (☎ 215 7432) is seven km north of town. Turn off the main road to Queenstown onto McIvor Rd and drive down it for three km; it is signposted. It's open from 2 to 4.30 pm every day except Friday; afternoon tea is available at this elegant Georgian house.

Queens Park is the town's principal park and the absolute essence of Englishness. If there was a river running through it you would see punts and punters in straw boaters. Among its attractions are various animals, an aviary, duck ponds, rose gardens, a tea kiosk open daily from 10 am to 5 pm, and a swimming pool and waterslide complex, in addition to the Museum & Art Gallery mentioned earlier. The Queens Park Golf Course is good value at $22 for club hire, 18 holes of golf and green fees.

The curious **water tower** at the bottom of Leet St was built in 1889. Climb to the top for a bird's-eye view of the town's flatness; go next door to fetch a key ($1).

Tours

For local sites of interest, pick up a walking-tour leaflet of Invercargill's historical places from the museum. Thomson's Bush, on Queens Drive, is the last remnant of Taurakitewaru Wood, the forest that once covered the site of Invercargill. It is about 3.5 km north of the CPO. Seaward Bush, eight km south-east of the CPO (signed from the junction of Rockdale and Mason Rds), was once part of the larger Seaward Forest which was extensively milled for house-building timber in the late 19th century. The reserve still contains a good range of native trees and shrubs – kamahi, rimu, kahikatea and matai. There are several other walks; ask at the Visitors Information Centre or DOC.

City Line (☎ 218 7108) offers a city-sights tour whenever there are three or more people who want to go ($20 per person). It takes a couple of hours and you get a running commentary on all the historical, cultural and beauty spots of Invercargill. They also have tours of Riverton, Bluff and the Catlins. These tours leave from Leven St (behind McDonald's).

SOUTHLAND

Places to Stay

Camping & Cabins The *Invercargill Caravan Park* (☎ 218 8787) is at the A&P Showgrounds on Victoria Ave, only one km from the centre. It's closed during showtime (the first two weeks in December) but the rest of the year tent/powered sites are $14/16 for two, and cabins are from $22 to $26 for two.

The *Coachman's Caravan Park* (☎ 217 6046) at 705 Tay St has tent/powered sites for $13/16 for two, and cabins at $27.50 for two.

Hostels The *Southern Comfort Backpackers* (☎ 218 3838) at 30 Thomson St, consistently rated one of the best in the country, is housed in a turn-of-the-century Art Nouveau villa, with beautifully manicured gardens and pleasant, clean dorms. The kitchen is modern, the dining room grandiose and there are free bikes for guests to use. If you ring well in advance you might get to sleep in the outdoor playhouse, the most serene spot in Invercargill. The Couper's and their friend Bob 'give away' these share and dorm rooms for $15 per person, and twins and doubles are $36. To many travellers this place is the highlight of Invercargill.

The *Riverside Backpackers Guesthouse* (☎ (0800) 302 277) is at 428 Dee St, in the city's north by the Waihopai River, but it is a poor cousin in comparison to the Southern Comfort. The cost in the main rooms is $15 per person, and a single is $25. The kitchen and bathroom facilities are still a little basic.

The world's southernmost *YHA Hostel* (☎ 215 9344) is at 122 North Rd (on the corner of Bullar St), Waikiwi, about three km from the town centre. It costs $14 per person in dorms, and doubles or twins are $16.

B&Bs, Hotels & Motels There are a couple of good B&Bs. *Aarden House* (☎ 214 8825) at 193 North Rd has been recommended by travellers; the cost is $35 per person for a room with ensuite. The *Oak Door* (☎ 213 0633) at 22 Taiepa Rd, Otatara, is another good place at $60 for a double.

The *Montecillo Travel Lodge* (☎ 218 2503) at 240 Spey St is a friendly place with hotel and motel rooms. The old part is over 90 years old, and bedrooms have been restored to their original condition. The hotel rooms are $87 and the motel units $76 for two. This is a straightforward but well-kept place conveniently close to the town centre (about a 10-minute walk).

At the *Coachman's Inn* (☎ 217 6046) tourist flats are $73 for two. Other reasonably cheap motels include the *Ashlar Motel* (☎ 217 9093) at 81 Queens Drive, where doubles are $78 to $82; *Garden Grove Motel* (☎ 215 9555) at 161 North Rd, with doubles for $65; and *Moana Court Motel* (☎ 217 8443) at 554 Tay St, at about $70 for two. There are numerous other motels, typically from around $70. The *Queens Park* (☎ 214 4504), 85 Alice St, and the *Tower Lodge* (☎ 217 6729), 119 Queens Drive, have been recommended by readers; both are about $75 for two.

Gerrard's Hotel (☎ 218 3406) is on the corner of Esk and Leven Sts, opposite the

Top: Lake Manapouri, Southland (TW)
Middle: Skiing at Treble Cone above Lake Wanaka, Otago (RN)
Bottom: Lake Wanaka, Otago (RN)

Top: Otago University, Dunedin (RS)
Bottom: Little Mangere Island, Chatham Islands (JW)

railway station. It's an ornate 1896 building (with additions in 1907), which has been renovated. It also houses one of the town's best licensed restaurants. Twin/double rooms with private facilities cost $85 to $90.

On Dee St, opposite the end of Don St, is the imposing old *Grand Hotel* (☎ 218 8059) where doubles cost $50 to $70, depending on their size. The restaurant there is open every day. The pretty ordinary *Kelvin Hotel* (☎ 218 2829) on Kelvin St in the town centre is the largest of its ilk in Invercargill. It's well kept but bland and costs a hefty $100/105 for singles/doubles. The best place in town is the *Ascot Park Motor Hotel* (☎ 217 6195), corner of Tay St and Racecourse Rd (it's next to the racecourse), which has a rate of $88 per motel room. Breakfast, extra o' course, is porridge made o' oats!

Places to Eat

Fast Food & Pub Food Along Dee St and around the town centre there's the usual collection of fast-food and sandwich places. *Nobles* at 47 Dee St serves good 'mousetraps' (onion, cheese and bacon on toast) but also the wateriest cappuccino around. *Joy's Gourmet Kitchen* at 122 Dee St (and another branch on Esk St) has a good selection of salads, sandwiches, wholemeal pizzas and budget hot roast meals. You can eat in or take away. The *Cod Pot* on Dee St turns out a consistently good feed of fish & chips.

Despite its plain appearance, *Moa's Restaurant* at 142 Dee St is something of a local institution and is open commendably long hours. *Da Vinci's* at 300 Dee St is the pick of the pizza places in town; a large pizza will cost about $16 and an extra large $18. Further north up Dee St, there's a *Pizza Hut*, *McDonald's*, *KFC* and several other big drive-in takeaways.

As in Dunedin, there are plenty of pubs here and most of them serve food as well. *Molly O'Grady's* in the Kelvin Hotel has value smorgasbords at lunch time. The *Avenal Homestead Family Restaurant*, on the corner of Dee and Avenal Sts, Avenal, has the usual bars and a good restaurant. It is a modern, pleasant place with standard pub food (roast of the day, fresh fish) from $12 to $17. It's open for dinner every day except Saturday, after the bars open at 4.30 pm. The licensed *Galaxy Family Restaurant* at the Waikiwi Family Inn has, for those with kids in tow, a good children's menu for about $5.

Restaurants Most of the restaurants in Invercargill are pretty mundane. An exception and a good vegetarian, wholemeal food place is *Tillerman's*, at 16 Don St. It's quite a local gathering spot and is open in the evening from Tuesday to Saturday until late for meals. There is also an Art Deco bar.

The *Willow* at 232 Dee St, next to the Pizza Hut, is an attractive licensed Chinese restaurant with six-course meals for $13 at lunch time and around $20 to $24 in the evening. On Sunday there's a six-course 'family special' for $18 (children half-price).

If you want to sample some of the local fish, try *HMS King's Restaurant* at 83 Tay St, home of the 'famous fisherman's platter' (who was he?). It is decked out like an old sailing ship, and oysters, whitebait, blue cod and crayfish all feature on the menu. A crayfish and prawn (or scallops) mornay costs $35. It is open Monday to Saturday, from 11.30 am to 2.30 pm, and 5 to 9.30 pm.

The *Lone Star*, on the corner of Dee and Leet St, is open from 4.30 pm until late. It has two parts, a back bar and dining area. A huge plate of nachos is about $12 and will release the thirst that they want you to quench in the adjoining bar. The other meals are hearty and reasonable value. The *Frog 'n' Firkin* is next to the cinema complex at 31 Dee St. It is open for lunch then stays open until quite late. There is a restaurant and bar and you can pick up a meal for under $10. Their fiery potato wedges make the perfect accompaniment to the fine selection of ales. Just around the corner in Tay St is *Zookeeper's*, also another late-night place, good for a meal.

You could try the simple and straightforward *Ainos Steakhouse* on Dee St in Waikiwi, seven blocks north of the YHA hostel. It's open for dinner every day except Sunday, from 6 to 10 pm.

The pick of the town's (and probably Southland's) dining is the licensed *Strathern Inn* at 200 Elles Rd; entrees are from $6 to $10 and mains from $12 to $18.

Entertainment

Although the town centre closes with a bang after 9 pm, there *is* entertainment if you are willing to search it out. The odd nightclub buzzes until the early hours, and a lot is happening out in the suburbs, but you need to ask around.

One place with an intimate atmosphere is *Zookeeper's* at 50 Tay St. It is the sort of place you go to, if for no other reason, to buy the establishment's T-shirt. The Zoo has really good value meals, laid-back staff, some of Invercargill's brighter (read 'party animal') patrons and corrugated iron statuary. Folksy *Tillerman's*, the Tex/Mex *Lone Star* and the 'hits & memories' *Frog 'n' Firkin* are of a similar ilk to the Zoo.

The *Waikiwi Tavern*, on Gimblett St just off Dee St, is at least handy to the YHA hostel. Their nightclub, *Lazers*, in the rear of the same large building, is your worst 'small town' nightmare come true with punch-drunk bouncers, check-shirted red-necks, marauding firebrands, wall-to-wall hatred and the sorriest looking bunch of hangers-on you are ever likely to see. Sisters, unite and close this place down. If you want to stoop to something twice as bad, try the *Don Lodge*, 77 Don St, after dark.

The *Rafters Bar* at the Whitehouse Hotel is possibly the best place to go to for music, but it's right out at Lorneville, eight km north of Waikiwi (a left turn towards Riverton). There's a cover charge. The weekend editions of the *Southland Times* will indicate what's on elsewhere. In Invercargill for Labour weekend? Get out fast – the Trucking & Country Music Convention is on.

Getting There & Away

Air Air New Zealand (☎ 214 4737) has an office at 46 Esk St. It has daily direct flights to Dunedin, Christchurch, Auckland and Wellington, although not all flights to Auckland and Wellington are direct. From these four cities there are connections to many other centres. Ansett New Zealand (☎ 214 4644), at Invercargill Airport, has daily flights to and from Christchurch, Wellington, Palmerston North and Auckland, also with connections to other centres.

Flights to Stewart Island are made with Southern Air (☎ 218 9129). Charter flights to remote parts such as Mason's Bay can be made with Southeast Air (SEA, ☎ 214 5522). See the Stewart Island section for details. The airport is spacious and very much the transport hub of this city.

Bus InterCity buses are based at the railway station (☎ 218 1837, 214 0598). Daily buses run from Invercargill to Te Anau, Queenstown and Christchurch, with more frequent buses to Dunedin.

The Mt Cook Landline bus depot (☎ 218 2419) is at the west end of Spey St. It has daily buses up the coast through Dunedin, Christchurch and on to Picton to connect with the Interislander. Other services include buses to and from Queenstown every day except Saturday, and to Te Anau and Wanaka, Monday to Friday.

Catch-a-Bus (☎ 214 6243) has a scheduled service between Invercargill and Dunedin, which leaves Invercargill at 1.30 pm and Dunedin at 7.30 am, going via Gore and Balclutha ($31 with a discount). You can arrange to go to Christchurch and Picton on connecting services. Spitfire Shuttle (☎ 214 1851) operate from Invercargill to Te Anau and return (see Te Anau for details).

There are two services that pass through the Catlins; see that section for details.

Train The *Southerner* Christchurch to Invercargill train operates every weekday, departing from each end at around 8.50 am and arriving at the other end around 6.30 pm. Phone ☎ (0800) 802 802 for bookings and information.

Hitching Hitching between Dunedin and Invercargill is usually fairly simple and should only take about half a day. If you're

SOUTHLAND

on your way to Queenstown or Te Anau it gets steadily harder the further you go, and many people get stuck overnight in Lumsden. Without transport the coastal route between Dunedin and Invercargill is pretty hard – public transport is almost non-existent and there's little traffic for hitching. The same is true for the coast road heading west towards Te Anau.

Getting Around

The airport is 2.5 km from the centre and you can get there by taxi for around $8 or with Spitfire Shuttle for $3 (they pick up from your accommodation). There are two taxi companies: Taxi Co (☎ 214 4478) and Blue Star (☎ 218 6079).

City Line buses (☎ 218 7108) run only from around 7 am to 6 pm Monday to Friday, or until around 9 or 10 pm on late shopping nights. There are no city buses on weekends and local bus trips cost $1.20. City Line also has two daily services to Queenstown via Lumsden. Campbelltown Bus (☎ 212 7404) offer a Stewart Island ferry connection and will pick up from backpackers etc, for $6 per person ($10 same day return).

Wensley's Cycles (☎ 218 6206), corner of Tay and With Sts, hires out bicycles.

BLUFF

Invercargill's port, and the departure point for the Stewart Island catamaran, is Bluff, 27 km to the south. A small place of 2600 people, its Maori name is Motupohue ('Motu' because it looks like an island, 'pohue' from white convolvulus flower).

There's an observation point at the top of 265-metre **Bluff Hill** – you can drive all the way to the top, or walk it in half an hour or so – from where you can see the Island Harbour, Foveaux Strait, Stewart Island and the Tiwai Point aluminium smelter. Hills being quite a rare physical feature in this area, it's one of the better vantage spots.

Also at Bluff is **Fred & Myrtle's Paua Shell House**, at 258 Marine Parade. It has an amazing array of kitsch statuary (check out the fountain) and shells collected from all over the world. Visitors are welcome from 9 am to 5 pm every day; there's no admission fee, but you could make a donation. The nonagenarian couple secretly enjoy their macabre celebrity status.

Further on past the Paua Shell House is an ocean lookout with a **signpost** indicating your distance to the South Pole, the equator and many other places around the world.

Across the harbour from Bluff is the **Tiwai aluminium smelter**, the eighth largest in the world and a major source of employment for Invercargill's citizens – around 1600 jobs – and they get mighty sensitive to any hint of criticism about it. Aluminium is NZ's fifth ranked principal export, after meat, wool, dairy and forest products. Free tours can be arranged by phoning ☎ 218 5494 in advance. The tours are at 10 am Monday to Friday, and daily during holidays; you need your own car to get out there.

Foveaux Walk is a 6.6-km walkway from the southern end of SH1 to Ocean Beach, where it emerges at a bus stop. It takes about 2½ hours. Don't be misled by the name 'Ocean Beach' – what you will find there is a smelly freezing works.

Places to Stay & Eat

The four budget options are *Flynn's Club Hotel* (☎ 212 8124), 100 Gore St, with beds for $25 per person; *Bayview* (☎ 212 8615) at Gore St, where singles/doubles are $25/50; the *Bluff Motor Camp* (☎ 212 8704), Gregory St; and *Property Arcade Backpackers* (☎ 212 8074) at 120 Gore St. At the latter, untidy share and dorm rooms are $12 per person. This rambling backpackers, in an ongoing but seemingly never-ending process of restoration, is 100 metres from the wharf.

The *Land's End* (☎ 212 7575), a B&B at the end of SH1 near the signpost, is the pick of the local accommodation.

The Land's End opens from 11 am for meals and they specialise in smorgasbords; reflect, as you eat, on the distance to Scandinavia from here. Nearby is the *Stirling Point* restaurant/tearooms, open all day during the week and for dinner on weekends from 6 pm until late.

Getting There & Away

See the Stewart Island section in the Stewart, Chathams & Other Islands chapter for details on getting to and from Stewart Island.

INVERCARGILL TO DUNEDIN

There are two ways of getting from Invercargill to Dunedin: either by SH1 via Gore and Balclutha, or by the continuation of the Southern Scenic Route, SH92, via the coastal road through the Catlins. The state highway passes through rural scenery, which you may just have had enough of by now. If so, read about the Catlins and plan to spend some extra time there – you won't regret it. The three sizeable towns on the SH1 route are Mataura, site of a huge freezing works; Gore, home of the Big Brown Trout and country music; and Balclutha (in Otago), with a good little regional museum.

Gore

This farming-community service town is actually not in such a bad locale. Southland's second largest town spans the Mataura River, and the Hokonui Hills are a great backdrop. In June, Gore hosts the NZ Gold Guitars, an annual country & western festival. The place is booked out at this time, so lovers of country & western music should plan well ahead.

Find the trout and you will find the Gore Information Centre (☎ & fax 208 9908), on Ordsal St near the Mataura River. In summer it is open Monday to Friday from 9 am to 7 pm and weekends 10 am to 7 pm. In winter it is open from 9 am to 5 pm.

The **Eastern Southland Museum & Art Gallery** is on Hokonui Drive, and is open Monday to Friday from 10 am to 5 pm, and Sunday from 2 to 4.30 pm.

Hopefully you will catch a trout the size of the 'big one' in one of the many (40 or so) excellent streams, including the Pomahaka, Mataura, Waimea, Otamita and Waipahi. If the anglers are drinking more Hokonui moonshine than the trout you never know what stories you will hear. For further information see the Southland Fish & Game Council's pamphlet *Anglers' Access*; this is free from the information centre.

SOUTHLAND

Places to Stay & Eat

At the south end of town at 35 Broughton St you will find the *Gore Motor Camp* (☎ 208 4919) where sites are $9 per person, and cabins are $30 for two. The *Charlton Motel* (☎ 208 9733) at 9 Charlton Rd and the *Oakleigh Motel* (☎ 208 4863) at 70 Hokonui Drive both have rooms for $72 a double. The *Croydon Lodge* (☎ 208 9029), Main Queenstown Highway (Waimea St), has rooms for $90 for two and a nine-hole par-three golf course. The *O Te Ika Rama Marae* at McNab, a short drive north of Gore on SH1, is a special place to stay because travellers get a chance to experience Maori culture first-hand.

There are a number of places that help you keep the wolf from the door along Main St. They range from the *Gore Pie Cart*, next to the United Video shop, the *Guangzhou Chinese*, and the very successful *Table Talk Cafe* and the BYO *Cafe 1901*. The Croydon Lodge has two dining rooms and two bars.

The Catlins

If you've got your own transport and you're travelling between Invercargill and Dunedin, take the longer Catlins coastal route allowing a couple of days for stopovers. The distance is pretty similar to the inland route although it's somewhat slower since some of the road is unsealed. The route goes through the region known as the Catlins, which stretches from Waipapa Point in Southland to Nugget Point in South Otago. It includes the Western Catlins Forest (22,250 hectares) and a number of other forests and scenic reserves. The Catlins is a totally absorbing area.

History

The area was once inhabited by the moa hunters and evidence of their camp sites and middens have been found at Papatowai. Between 1600 and 1800 the Maori population thinned out, attributable to the decline of the moa, the lack of kumara cultivation,

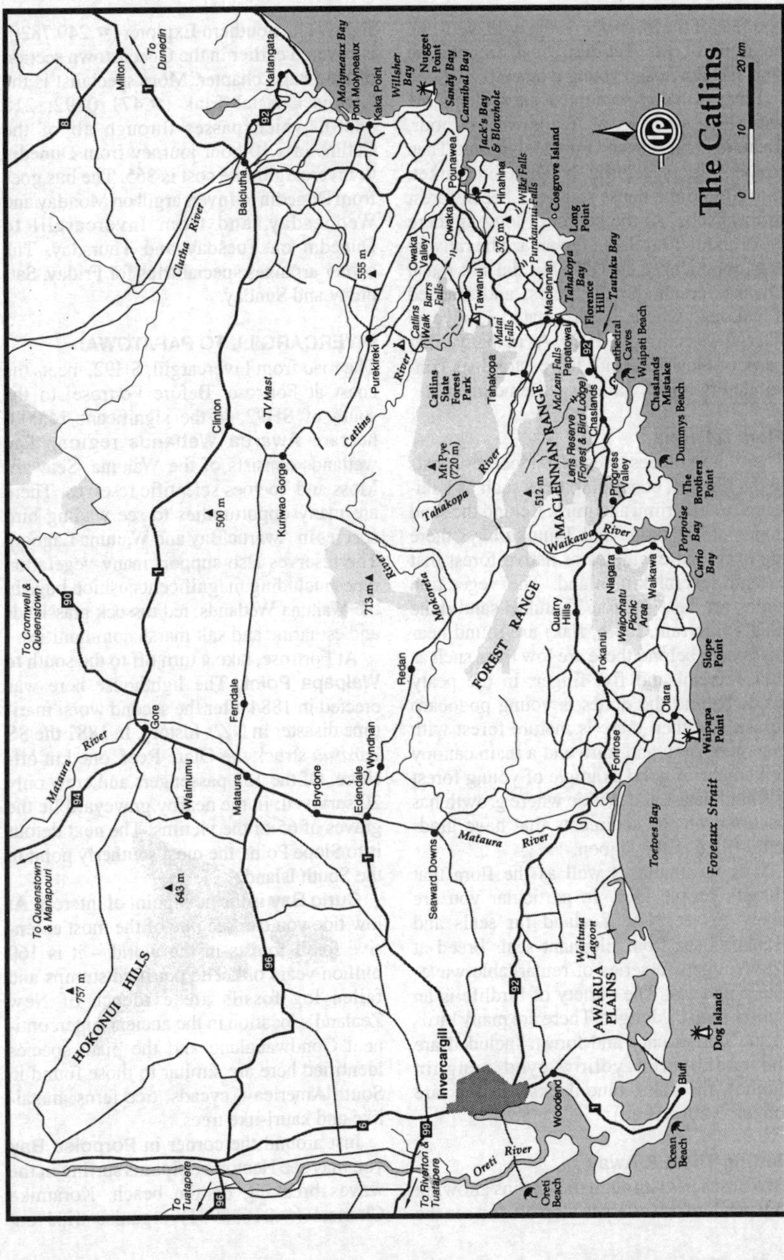
The Catlins
0
10
20 km
To Dunedin
Milton
Kaitangata
Molyneaux Bay
Port Molyneaux
Kaka Point
Willsher Bay
Nugget Point
Sandy Bay
Cannibal Bay
Jack's Bay & Blowhole
Pounawea
Owaka
Owaka Valley
Hinahina
Wilkie Falls
Purakaunui Falls
Cosgrove Island
Long Point
Tautuku Bay
Tahakopa Bay
Florence Hill
Maclennan
376 m
Tawanui
Barrs Falls
Catlins Walk
Matai Falls
Purekireki
Catlins River
Catlins State Forest Park
Tahakopa
McLean Falls
Papatowai
Cathedral Caves
Waipati Beach
Chaslands Mistake
Chaslands
Lens Reserve (Forest & Bird Lodge)
MACLENNAN RANGE
Mt Pye (720 m)
Tahakopa River
512 m
Progress Valley
Dummys Beach
The Brothers Point
Porpoise Bay
Curio Bay
Waikawa River
Waikawa
Niagara
Waipohatu Picnic Area
Quarry Hills
Tokanui
FOREST RANGE
Mokoreta River
713 m
Slope Point
Otara
Waipapa Point
Fortrose
Toetoes Bay
Foveaux Strait
Waituna Lagoon
AWARUA PLAINS
Dog Island
Bluff
Ocean Beach
Woodend
Oreti Beach
Oreti River
Invercargill
To Riverton & Tuatapere
To Tuatapere
HOKONUI HILLS
757 m
643 m
To Queenstown & Manapouri
Seaward Downs
Mataura River
Edendale
Wyndham
Brydone
Mataura
Waimumu
Gore
Ferndale
Redan
Mataura River
To Cromwell & Queenstown
Kuriwao Gorge
500 m
Clinton
TV Mast
555 m
Clutha River
Balclutha

SOUTHLAND

and fear of the *Maeroero* – the wild, yeti-like creature of the Tautuku bush, reputed to snatch children and young women.

Later, whalers occupied sites along the shoreline such as at Waikawa Harbour, Tautuku Peninsula and Port Molyneaux. Then timber millers, serving the Dunedin market, moved into the dense stands of beech forest in the 1860s. At the height of logging there were about 30 mills in the area. The railway was commenced in 1879 but did not reach Owaka for another 25 years, and reached Tahakopa, where it terminated, 36 years later; it was closed in 1971. As in many other parts of New Zealand, the pastoralists constituted the final wave of settlement.

Flora & Fauna

There are still reserves of podocarp forests in the Catlins, containing trees such as kahikatea, totara, rimu and miro. Behind the sand dunes of Tahakopa and Tautuku bays there are excellent examples of native forest that extend several km inland. The vegetation zones are best seen at Tautuku: sand-dune plants (marram, lupin, flax) are found near the beach; behind these are low trees such as rata, kamahi and five-finger; in the peaty sands behind the dunes is young podocarp forest; and then there is mature forest with emergent rimu and miro and a main canopy of kamahi. A good example of young forest is found near Lake Wilkie where growth has occurred on the sediments that have gradually filled in the lagoon.

It is the fauna as well as the flora that attracts people here. In particular you are likely to see New Zealand fur seals and Hooker's sea lion. Elephant seals breed at The Nuggets, a series of remarkable wave-like pinnacles. The variety of birdlife is an ornithologist's delight. There are many birds of the sea, estuary and forest. Included are the endangered yellow-eyed penguin (hoiho), the kaka, blue ducks and the rare mohua (yellowhead).

Getting There & Away

Two buses pass through the Catlins allowing independent travellers to stop off and see the sights. The Southern Explorer (☎ 249 7820) is covered earlier in the Queenstown section of the Otago chapter. More specialist is the Catlins Coastal Link (☎ 471 0292; 218 3838), which passes through all of the Catlins in a 10-hour journey from Dunedin to Invercargill; the cost is $65. The bus goes from Dunedin to Invercargill on Monday and Wednesday, and from Invercargill to Dunedin on Tuesday and Thursday. The owner arranges special trips for Friday, Saturday and Sunday.

INVERCARGILL TO PAPATOWAI

The road from Invercargill, SH92, meets the coast at Fortrose. Before Fortrose, to the south of SH92, is the significant 14,000-hectare **Awarua Wetlands** region. The wetlands consists of the Waituna, Seaward Moss and Toetoes scientific reserves. There are many opportunities to see wading bird species in Awarua Bay and Waituna Lagoon. The reserves also support many vegetation types including magnificent cushion bogs in the Waituna Wetlands, red tussock grasslands and estuarine and salt marsh communities.

At Fortrose, take a turn off to the south to **Waipapa Point**. The lighthouse here was erected in 1884 after the second worst maritime disaster in NZ's history. In 1881 the SS *Tararua* struck the Otara Reef, one km offshore. Of the 151 passengers and crew only 20 survived; in the nearby graveyard lie the graves of 65 of the victims. The next detour is to Slope Point, the most southerly point in the South Island.

Curio Bay is the next point of interest. At low tide you can see one of the most extensive fossil forests in the world – it is 160 million years old. The petrified stumps and fallen log fossils are evidence of New Zealand's location in the ancient supercontinent Gondwanaland and the plant species identified here are similar to those found in South America – cycads, tree ferns, matai-like and kauri-like trees.

Just around the corner in **Porpoise Bay** you may see Hector's dolphins surfing in the waves breaking on the beach. Koramika Charters (☎ 216 5931) organise trips out from Waikawa Harbour to see the dolphins, which come close into shore over summer to rear their young. Their two cruises are $35 and $45; the latter price includes a trip to the Brothers Point, where NZ fur seals and Hooker's sea lions are often seen and an absolute must is a swim with the Hector's dolphins. The seals and sea lions are a friendly bunch of residents – must be the vibes emanating from the dolphins.

There is now a **dolphin information centre** and shop in the old church at Waikawa. Ask to see their video of a live dolphin stranded on the beach at Porpoise Bay. A study is being conducted on the effect of human contact on the dolphins. In Waikawa harbour you are also likely to see yellow-eyed penguins.

The **Cathedral Caves**, on Waipati Beach, so named for their resemblance to an English cathedral, are only accessible at low tide (tide-tables are posted at the turn-off from SH92). The caves are about a 40-minute walk from the road, but part of the walk is through beautiful native forest. At **Tautuku Bay** there is a 15-minute walk to the beach, a stunning sweep of sand punctuated by drifts of seaweed, and a five-minute walk to **Lake Wilkie**, where there are some unique forms of plant life. Just past Tautuku there is a good vantage point at **Florence Hill** from where you can distinguish the different vegetation types and other points of interest.

Papatowai, at the mouth of the Tahakopa River, is the next town reached. This is the base for Catlins Wildlife Trackers and some amazing forays into the close forests (see Wildlife Tracking in the Dunedin section of the Otago chapter).

Places to Stay & Eat

You have a few choices of places to stay along this route. There is a *camping ground* (☎ 246 8897) at Curio Bay and *camp sites* at Waipohatu. At the *Papatowai Motor Camp* (☎ 415 8500) a tent/powered site is $5/7, and there is one on-site caravan for $12/16 for one/two persons. There is one motel along the route, the *Chaslands Farm Motor Lodge* (☎ 415 8501) at Waipati Rd, Chaslands, which has ordinary but spacious units for $50 for two ($10 each extra adult).

Probably the pick of the places to stay is the *Catlins Farmstay* (☎ 246 8843) in Progress Valley near Tokanui. A great B&B costs $35 per person in a very comfortable house. It is $15 per person in their secluded bush sleep-out (a must for those who wish to be alone). They provide breakfast for $8.50 for those out in the bush hut and dinners for those on the farm which include paua, local fish, meat and vegetables for $20. Not far east is the *Egilshay Farmstay* (☎ 246 8703) and to the south, at the southernmost point of the South Island, is *Pope's Place* (☎ 246 8420), a farmstay that welcomes backpackers and costs $14 per person.

One really out of the way place to go – if you can organise your accommodation – is the *Tautuku Lodge* (☎ 415 8034), six km south of Papatowai in the Lenz Reserve. It is owned by the Royal Forest & Bird Protection Society and they charge $20 for non-members in the six-bed lodge or four-bed cabin, and $15 per person in the A-frame cabin.

A place with fantastic views is *Hilltop* (☎ 415 8028), a backpackers reached on the Tahakopa Rd just before the bridge near Papatowai. It is a little over one km from the main road and then another 500 metres up a steep hill and through two gates. You will probably be greeted by the dogs. At the moment it is only a small place with six beds but will most likely be enlarged. Judging by the visitors' book this is a place that people continually return to.

The *Papatowai Trading Post* organises meals, sandwiches and cups of tea or coffee.

PAPATOWAI TO BALCLUTHA

Between Papatowai and the regional centre of Owaka there are many interesting places to visit. First, follow SH92 east to **Matai Falls** on the Maclennan River. After looking at these, head south on the signposted road to the more scenic **Purakaunui Falls**. It is only a short walk through bush to these tiered falls, best viewed from a platform at their base.

In the **Catlins State Forest Park** you can do the river walk, a good day trip out of Owaka. There is a track to Tawanui from the Wisp camping area – observant walkers may see the rare mohua (yellowhead) here. Out near the mouth of the Catlins River, on the western side, is **Jack's Blowhole**, a 55-metre-deep hole in the middle of paddocks. It is 200 metres from the sea but connected by a subterranean cavern.

On the eastern side of the river, south of Owaka, is the **Pounawea Nature Walk**, a 45-minute loop through kahikatea, ferns, kamahi, rimu, totara and southern rata. There is a salt marsh near the Catlins River estuary.

To the east of Owaka at **Tunnel Hill** there is a short track that leads to NZ's most southerly railway tunnel, excavated by hand in 1893 as part of the Catlins Branch Railway.

The road leading south from Tunnel Hill heads to **Cannibal Bay**, where Hooker's sea lions sometimes beach themselves; if you are extra lucky you may see a grey-coated female. The bay gets its name from the fact that the surveyor Hector discovered human bones in a midden here, and assumed it was part of a feast. Te Rauparaha also popped up here and exacted revenge which may have included acts of cannibalism.

Further around the coast, on a not-to-be-missed sidetrack from the Kaka Point road, is **Nugget Point**. This is one of NZ's special places. The islands sitting out from the lighthouse promontory seem to lead off to the very edge of the world. Fur seals bask below on the rocks, as do Hooker's sea lions and elephant seals on occasions, the only place on the NZ mainland where these species coexist. There is a wealth of birdlife; yellow-eyed and little blue penguins, gannets, shags and sooty shearwaters breed here, and many other pelagic species such as the cape pigeon pass by. The lighthouse, constructed of stone, was built in 1869.

Avoid the temptation to leave the track – observe only from above with binoculars so as not to disturb the birds. Look down on the huge bladderkelp forests in the water that fringe the Nuggets' reefs.

From Nugget Point the road loops back around through Kaka Point and Port Molyneaux to SH92. Balclutha, not far up the road, is covered in the Otago chapter.

Owaka

Owaka, the main town of the Catlins area, has a population of 380. The DOC office (☎ 415 8341), on the corner of Ryley and Campbell Sts, has information about the area. The Catlins information centre (☎ 415 8392) is next to the Catlins Diner at Main Rd. The Owaka Museum (☎ 415 8136) is open from 1.30 to 4 pm on Thursday or by appointment.

Places to Stay & Eat

Close to Owaka are the *Pounawea Motor Camp* (☎ 415 8483) with tent/powered sites for $12/14 for two, and cabins for $30 for two; and the *Kaka Point Camping Ground* (☎ 412 8814) with sites for $6 per person and one cabin at $18 for two.

The *Catlins Backpackers* (☎ 415 8392) is on Main Rd near the information centre. It is an adequate place with a cosy fire and provides a good base from which to explore the Catlins; the cost is $12.50 per person. The *Candy Cone Backpackers* (☎ 415 8636) is basic and unfinished with few facilities; dorm beds are $12 and doubles are $40.

There are two motels in town: the *High-view Motels* (☎ 415 8686) at 23 Royal Terrace; and *Owaka Lodge* (☎ 415 8728) on the corner of Ryley and Campbell Sts. At the latter it costs about $60 for two. You can eat out at the *Catlins Diner* on Main St or at the *Catlins Inn*, 21 Ryley St.

Down near the Nuggets is the *Nuggets Accommodation* (☎ 412 8783), which has a self-contained flat for $35 for two (when serviced it is $55) and homestay B&B at $60 for a double. From here it is only two km to the lighthouse.

There are *DOC camping grounds* at the following areas in the Catlins, all in SE Otago: Tawanui, Catlins State Forest Park; Purakaunui Bay; and Papatowai, 24 km from Owaka (fully serviced).

Stewart, Chathams & Other Islands

New Zealand is often mistakenly considered to consist of just the two islands, North and South. There are a number of island groups off its shores and these contain fascinating culture, unique flora and fauna, magnificent scenery and, importantly, isolation and solitude for those who want to escape.

HIGHLIGHTS

- Kiwi spotting on Ocean Beach, Stewart Island
- Any of Stewart Island's walking tracks – truly a remote walking experience
- The isolation and peace of the getaway centre of Halfmoon Bay, Stewart Island
- The rich birdlife of Paterson Inlet, Stewart and Ulva islands
- Exploring Chatham Island, its isolated lagoons, ramshackle fishing settlements and wild landscapes
- Tracing Moriori culture on Chatham Island, especially the dendroglyphs at Hapupu

Information

All telephone numbers in Stewart Island and the Chatham Islands have an 03 prefix if you are calling them from the North or South Island.

Stewart Island

Called Rakiura by the Maoris, New Zealand's third largest island is often not even considered by travellers as a potential destination – it should be! Rakiura means 'land of the glowing skies' in Maori, perhaps referring to the aurora australis which is often seen in this southern sky, or the spectacular blood red sunrises and sunsets that are witnessed here. The island is thought of as being isolated and suffering the battering of harsh southern winds. Actually Stewart Island is not as inhospitable as that, but it most definitely is an unspoilt, get-away-from-it-all place.

The minuscule population of 400 is congregated in the one town of any size, Oban, on Halfmoon Bay. Half an hour's walk from there and you enter a sanctuary of forest, beaches and hills. The hardy and independent people have a healthy suspicion of the law and bureaucracy. The weather is incredibly changeable – brilliant sunshine one minute, pouring rain the next. Conditions can be very muddy underfoot and you will need boots and waterproof clothing, but the temperature is much milder than you would expect. As one islander has pointed out: the island's rainforest *is*, after all, more beautiful in the rain – and mud is 'great character-building stuff'!

History

There is evidence that parts of Rakiura were occupied by moa hunters as early as the 13th century AD. According to Polynesian mythology New Zealand was hauled up from the depths of the South Pacific Ocean by Maui who said 'Let us go out of sight of land and when we have quite lost sight of it, then let the anchor be dropped; but let it be very far off – quite out in the open sea'. One interpretation of this myth is that the North Island was a great flat fish caught by Maui; the South Island his canoe and Rakiura the anchor – 'Te Punga o te Waka a Maui' being the legendary name for the latter.

The first Pakeha to come across Stewart Island was good old Captain Cook in 1770,

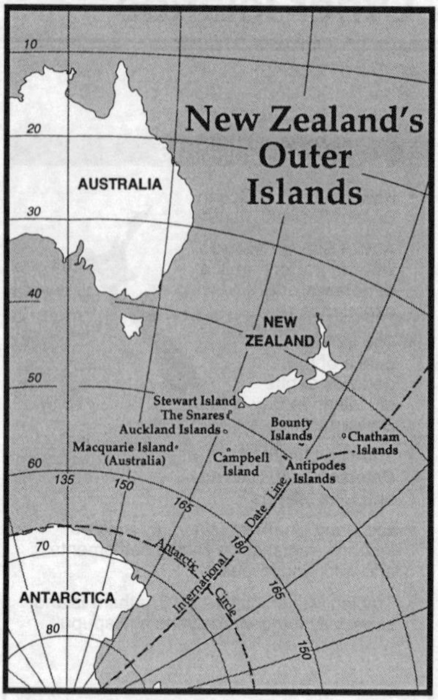

who sailed around the eastern, southern and western coasts but could not make up his mind whether it was an island or a peninsula. Deciding it was part of the South Island mainland he called it Cape South. Several decades later his theory was disproved when the sealing vessel *Pegasus*, under the command of Captain Chase, circumnavigated Stewart Island – presumably becoming the first European ship to do so. The island was named after William Stewart, first officer of the *Pegasus*, who charted the southern coast of the island in detail.

In June 1864 Stewart and the adjacent islands were bought from the Maoris for the sum of £6000. Early industries consisted of sealing, timber milling, fish curing and ship building. The discovery of gold and tin towards the end of the 19th century also led to an increase in settlement but the rush didn't last long and today the island's economy is based on fishing – crayfish, paua (abalone), salmon and cod – and tourism.

Flora & Fauna

If you know anything about trees the first thing you'll notice is that, unlike the North and South islands, there is no beech forest on Stewart Island. The predominant lowland vegetation is hardwood but there are also lots of tree ferns, a variety of ground ferns and several different kinds of orchid, including a lady's slipper orchid, two earinas and a number of spider orchids. Along the coast the vegetation consists of muttonbird scrub, grass tree, tree daisies, supplejack and leatherwood. You are warned, however, not to go tramping off the beaten track, as the bush is impenetrable in most places.

Stewart Island is an ornithologist's delight. Apart from the many seabirds that breed here, bush birds such as tuis, parakeets, kakas, bellbirds, fernbirds, robins (the last two are seen near Freshwater Flats) dotterels and kiwis abound. The weka can sometimes be spotted, and the Fiordland crested, yellow-eyed and the little blue penguins are also seen (see Ulva Island in this section).

Two species of deer were introduced to the island early in the 20th century. They are the red deer found mainly around Mt Anglem, in the Freshwater and Rakeahua valleys and at Toi Toi Flat in the south-east, and the Virginia (whitetail) deer which inhabits the coastal areas of the island. Also introduced were brush-tailed possums, which are very

New Zealand fur seal

numerous in the northern half of the island and rather destructive to the native bush. Stewart Island has lots of NZ fur seals too.

Around the shores there are clusters of bull kelp, common kelp, fine red weeds, delicate green thallus and bladders of all shapes and sizes.

Orientation & Information

Stewart Island is 64 km long and 40 km across at its widest, has less than 20 km of roads and its rocky coastline is incised by numerous inlets, the largest of these being Paterson. The highest point on the island is Mt Anglem at 980 metres. The principal settlement is Oban, which takes its name from a place in Scotland, on the shores of Halfmoon Bay, with roads extending a few km further out from there.

For information on tracks and tramping you can contact the DOC (☎ 214 4589) on Don St, Invercargill, before you take off for the island. On the island, the Stewart Island Visitor Information Centre (☎ 219 1218; fax 219 1555) is at the DOC Visitors Centre just a few minutes walk from the wharf. It's very close to both the Stewart Island Travel office (where you'll be taken to if you come by plane). In addition to practical information on the island it has good displays on flora, fauna, walks and so on, and a summer activities programme in January. The friendly staff have many ideas on how you could spend your time on the island.

Several handy, cheap pamphlets on tramps on the island, including *Halfmoon Bay Walks*; *Rakiura Track* and *North West Circuit* (all $1 each) can be purchased here. You can store gear at the DOC centre while you're walking ($2.50 small locker, $5 large).

The Adventure Centre (☎ 219 1134) at the end of the wharf is a booking agency for activities on the island and The Agency

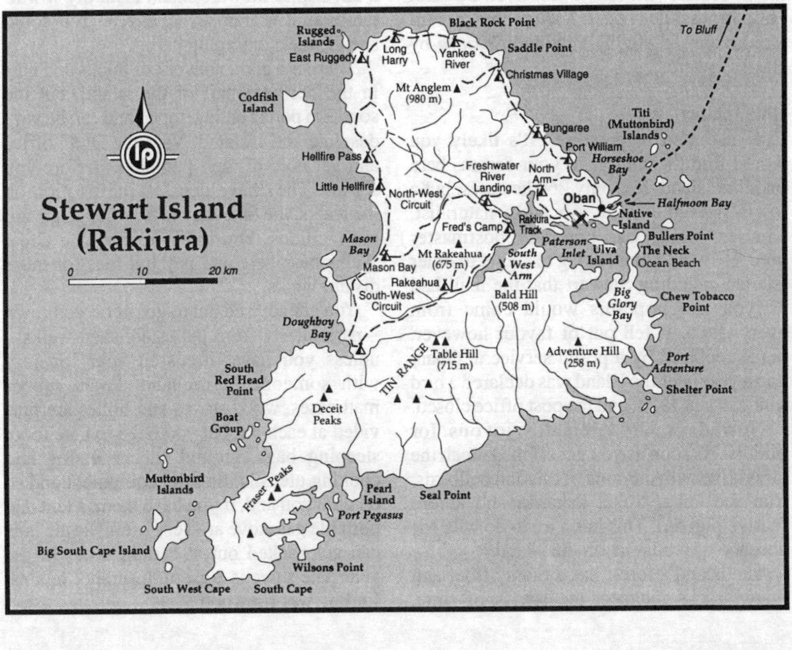

(☎ 219 1171), also near the wharf, has information on a wide range of accommodation.

There is a general store, Ship to Shore, at Halfmoon Bay which is open from 8 am to 6.30 pm during the week, 9 am until 4.30 pm on weekends in summer. There is a wide variety of supplies such as dried foods, gas canisters, fresh fruit and vegetables and hardware, etc. It has EFTPOS. The Lettuce Inn sells fruit and vegetables, sweets, films, ice creams and fresh fish. Stewart Island Travel has EFTPOS, fax and photocopying facilities.

There is a postal agency on Elgin Terrace, Halfmoon Bay, about five minutes walk from the wharf. Stewart Island is a local (not long-distance) phone call from Invercargill. There are cardphones outside Stewart Island Travel, at the Shearwater Inn and coinphones in the hotel foyer and, after hours, on the wharf at the Adventure Centre. There are public toilets at DOC, the South Sea Hotel, the wharf and the public hall.

Essential companions (if you can get them) are *Stewart Island Explored* by John Hall-Jones, *The Last Refuge* by Erwin Brinkmann & Neville Peat and *Rakiura* by Basil Howard.

Ulva Island

Ever dreamed of paradise? It's likely you would find the subject of your dreams here on Ulva Island. It is only 260 hectares, but a lot is packed into it. An early naturalist, Charles Traill, was honorary postmaster here. He would hoist a flag to signal to other islands including Stewart that the mail had arrived and hopefuls would come from everywhere. It fell out of favour however, being replaced by a postal service at Oban, and a year later the island was declared a bird sanctuary in 1922, and the post office closed.

Nowadays Ulva remains joyous for birders. As soon as you get off the launch the air is alive with the song of tuis and bellbirds. You see kaka, weka, kakariki and kereru (native pigeon). This has a lot to do with the absence of predators on the island.

The island's forest has a mossy floor and many tracks intersect the stands of rimu, miro, totara and rata – all of which, added to the delight of the birdsong, create a setting you won't forget. The birds come so close that you don't even need a telephoto lens.

A number of tour operators pass here on their way to view salmon farms. If you would rather follow tracks to quiet, private beaches than visit a commercial salmon farm in Big Glory Bay, alight here while the launch excursion visits the farms. They will pick you up when they stop on the return trip to let the other passengers briefly explore the island.

You can get to Ulva using a water taxi from Golden Bay wharf; expect to pay about $15 for a return trip. You can arrange the length of your stay with booking agencies.

Walks

If you want to visit Stewart Island, plan on spending a few days so you can enjoy the beaches, seals and rare bird and plant life. There are many walks on the island; although some take only a couple of hours, a day trip to Stewart Island is hardly worthwhile as it is tramper's heaven. You could spend weeks tramping here.

There is a good network of tracks and huts in the northern part of the island, but the southern part is undeveloped and can be very desolate and isolated. Visit the DOC office and get hold of their pamphlets before you set off. They have detailed information on the walks, the time they take, when to go and hut facilities. You can purchase you Great Walks pass here and pay hut fees for more distant walks.

You are advised not to go off on your own – particularly from the established walks – unless you have discussed your itinerary with someone beforehand. Foam rubber mattresses, wood stoves and billies are provided at each hut but you need to take food, sleeping bags, ground sheets, eating and cooking utensils, first-aid equipment and so on with you and, if you have them, a tent and portable gas stove are very useful as the huts can get packed out at certain times of the year. The stove is a useful insurance against finding wet firewood.

The **Rakiura Track**, starting from Oban makes an interesting three-day circular tramp. Huts at Port William and North Arm have space for 30 trampers, and access to the huts costs $8 per night; camping is $6 per person. (There's a maximum stay of two nights in a hut.) This is one of the Great Walks for which you require a pass. The track is well defined (as it has been extensively boardwalked) and it's an easy walk, the major drawback being that it gets very crowded in the summer.

The northern portion of the island has the **North-West Circuit Track** but it is long, some eight to 10 days. Fees for most of the North-West Circuit huts are $4 (children $2). The tracks further away from Halfmoon Bay can be very muddy and quite steep in places. These two longer walks are detailed in LP's *Tramping in New Zealand* by Jim DuFresne & Jeff Williams.

Around Halfmoon Bay there are a number of shorter walks. Take the 15-minute walk to Observation Rock which affords good views over Paterson Inlet. You can continue past the Stone House at Harrold Bay to Ackers Point, where there are good views of Foveaux Strait. Seals and penguins can be seen near the rocks and this is the site of a shearwater colony. There are many other possible walks outlined in DOC's *Halfmoon Bay Walks*.

Other Attractions

The **Rakiura Museum** on Ayr St is no Victoria & Albert but it's worth a visit if you're interested in the history of the island – it features whaling, sealing, tin mining, timber milling and fishing. In the collection of shipping memorabilia there is scrimshaw and photographs of the many ferries that plied across Foveaux Strait. Particularly interesting is the section dealing with the Maori heritage. It is believed that Maoris have lived on Rakiura for 800 years or more. The muttonbirds (titi) on the islands adjacent to Rakiura were an important seasonal food source for the southern Maori. Today's southern Maori population is predominantly Ngai Tahu, with earlier lineages to Kati Mamoe and Waitaho. There is a dolphin teeth necklace on display, alongside a collection of adzes and barter goods traded between Maoris and whalers, such as pipes from The Neck.

The museum is open from 10 am to noon on Monday to Saturday, noon to 2 pm on Sunday. Entry costs $1 (children 50c).

Also on Ayr St is a **library** which is open for even less time, from 2 to 3.15 pm on Wednesday, Friday and Saturday from 11 am to noon. There is a craft shop & gallery, **The Fernery** (☎ 219 1453), about 400 metres south from town in a bush setting, and housed in a new building designed to look like an original island cottage. Here, tiny fernlets from the hen-and-chicken fern, *Aplenium bulbiferum*, are placed in small egg-shaped containers and grow, ultimately to four or five feet tall. There are a number of other tasteful items for sale.

At Harrold Bay, about three km north-east of town, is an **old stone house** built by Lewis Acker around 1835. It's one of the oldest stone buildings in New Zealand.

Tours

In summer there are minibus tours around Halfmoon Bay, Horseshoe Bay and various other places. They are zippy little trips because there really isn't very far you can drive on Stewart Island! A one-hour trip costs $14 and the other 90-minute trip is $14.50. Check with Stewart Island Travel (☎ 219 1269), or check the notice boards next to the store, for more information.

Bravo Adventure Cruises (☎ 219 1144) has daily trips to Ulva Island and salmon farms for $40. Moana Charters (☎ 219 1202) take half-day fishing and sightseeing trips for up to 21 persons for $40 a head. Thorfinn Charters (☎ 219 1210) have a 30-foot (nine-metre) launch available for half-day and full-day cruises; nature tours are their speciality. The *Southern Isle* (☎ 219 1133) may be chartered for fishing trips. The water taxi *Flyer* (☎ 219 1394) is available for travel within Paterson Inlet and as far up the coast as Christmas Bay.

Kayaks can be rented for independent

exploring of Paterson Inlet; see the visitor centre for information. The inlet is 100 sq km of bush-clad sheltered waterways, with 20 islands, DOC huts and two navigable rivers. A popular trip is a paddle to Freshwater River Landing (seven km upriver from the inlet) followed by a three to four-hour walk to Mason Bay to see kiwis in the wild.

Kiwi Spotting This is one of the best eco-activities of New Zealand. The search for *Apteryx australis lawryi* would be a difficult one if you did not know where to look. The Stewart Island kiwi is a distinct sub-species of the brown kiwi, with larger legs and beak than its northern cousins. These kiwis are common over much of the island, particularly around beaches where they forage for sandhoppers under washed-up kelp. Unusually, *A. australis lawryi* is active during the day as well as night, as they are forced to forage for longer to attain breeding condition. Many trampers on the North-West Circuit spot them, especially at Mason Bay.

On any one night in summer you will probably see about three to five kiwis on Ocean Beach. Nowadays, they are quite used to human voyeurs and they even let people close enough to take video footage.

There is one complicating factor to this whole exercise, and some far-sighted official has implemented it for the kiwis' protection. Only 15 humans, on any consecutive night, can travel to Ocean Beach on the MV *Volantis* to view this flightless marvel. Demand outstrips supply, so book ahead with Bravo Adventure Cruises (☎ 249 1144) to avoid disappointment. The tours are $50, but in actuality are priceless.

Places to Stay

The DOC Stewart Island Visitors Centre (☎ 219 1218) has information on all accommodation options. There is a free *camping*

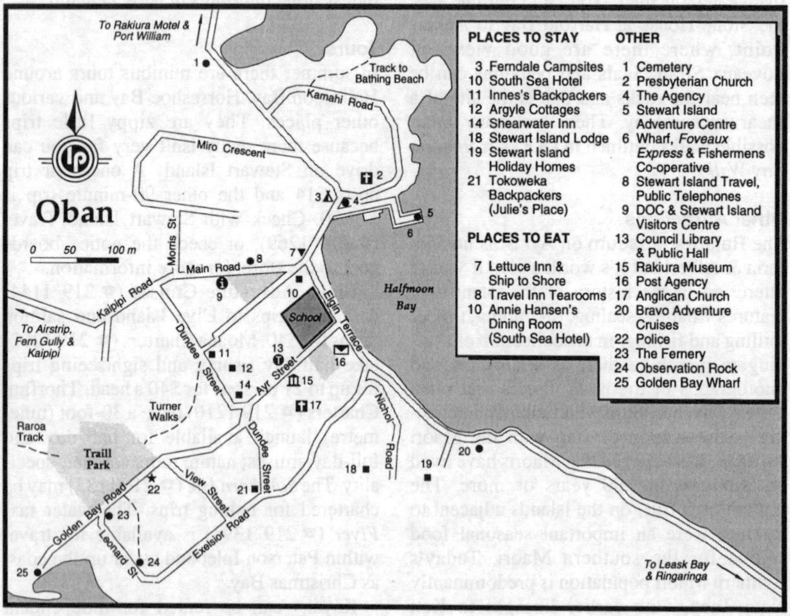

ground at Apple Bridge and Kaipipi Rd, but it's definitely basic, with a fireplace, wood and water supply and pit toilets only. It's about a half-hour walk from the wharf along Main Rd.

The *Ferndale Campsites* (☎ 219 1176) at Halfmoon Bay has tent sites for $5 – it has an ablution block with coin-operated showers ($2 for six minutes), toilets, picnic tables and rubbish collection.

Ann Pullen of *Ann's Place* (☎ 219 1065) offers tramping-style accommodation in a small house behind the main house for $10 per night. It's very basic, but then the price is basic too, and it's a supremely friendly place to stay. Bring your own sleeping bag and food. *Tokoweka Backpackers* (☎ 219 1568), more commonly known as Julie's Place after the friendly owner, has five or so beds for $15 each. There is a beautiful view from the verandah and dining room and a very clean, comfortable bathroom. For women wishing for a safe, secure place, this is your choice.

An excellent alternative is to stay in one of the several homes on the island offering hostel-style accommodation at hostel (or lower) rates. Ask at the visitor centre for the latest information. *Andy & Jo's B&B* (☎ 219 1230), on the corner of Main Rd and Morris St, have basic beds for $15 or $18 if linen is provided. Heti Atkins (☎ 219 1274), who enjoys the company of travellers, has a self-contained flat which costs $15 per person (maximum of five); *Joy's Place* (☎ 219 1376) has bunkroom beds for $15, but there is definitely no drinking or smoking here; *Iris & Mick Gibb* (☎ 219 1575) also have a flat for five for $12 each ($60 per night).

There are a number of converted bachelor pads on the island. Michael Squires (☎ 219 1425) can accommodate up to six people in his *'house hostel'* at the start of the Golden Bay Rd. The cost is $15; bring your own sleeping bag and food. *David's* (☎ 219 1078) is another place at $15. *Innes' Backpackers* (☎ 219 1080), also $15, is another possibility. The visitors centre will show you photos of all these places and direct you to them.

The *Shearwater Inn* (☎ 219 1114) on Ayr St, in the centre of the township, has singles/doubles (linen included) at $34/56, or $22 per person in larger shared rooms (three or four people). The inn has a restaurant serving breakfast ($12 cooked) and dinner. You can cook your own meals here but be warned the facilities are really limited.

The *South Sea Hotel* (☎ 219 1059), close to the wharf, costs $40/78 for singles/ twins, or $95 for a room with a sea view. A room at the *Rakiura Motel* (☎ 219 1096), 1.5 km from the township, costs $70 for two ($15 each extra adult). The glamorous *Stewart Island Lodge* (☎ 219 1085) is much more expensive. Its four rooms all have private facilities and cost about $197 per person in twin share rooms (or $237 for a single), including all meals.

Another option on Stewart Island is to hire a holiday home. There are several available. Jeanette and Peter Goomes (☎ 217 6585; 219 1057) of *Stewart Island Holiday Homes* have two, each sleeping up to 10 people, about a five-minute walk from the town. The cost is $75 for two plus $15 for an extra adult (children $7.50). The Goomes also have the pick of the B&B options at $50 per person.

Argyle Cottages (☎ 219 1269) has a couple of places at $46 for two, plus $14 each extra adult; families are especially welcome. For other rental houses contact The Agency (☎ 219 1171); their range includes places which are from $60 to $80 for two persons ($15 each extra adult).

Places to Eat

There's not much choice of eating places on Stewart Island. The South Sea Hotel has *Annie Hansen's* which features local seafood on the menu. The *Shearwater Inn* has a blackboard menu every night and is open from September until April. Stewart Island is still screaming out for a cafe which serves decent coffee, muffins, etc. Those familiar with courteous service and haute cuisine are unlikely to find either at the *Travel Inn Tearooms.*

You can get basic necessities from the *general store*, fruit and vegetables from the *Lettuce Inn*, buy fresh fish and crayfish from the locals, catch your own fish or bring food

A Paua Recipe

First things first – what is a paua? It is quite a large shellfish with a green-black body and a concave shell which is rough on the outside and rather beautiful on the inside. In other countries it is called abalone.

There are parts of New Zealand where you can pick up unprepared paua quite cheaply. It is then up to you to prepare it in a fashion that would set you back by about $45 for two in a restaurant.

Try the following recipe (provided by the Goomes family of Oban, Rakiura).

> First, stir-fry the onion rings from one brown onion with one minced clove of garlic and a dab (teaspoon) of butter. Cut the skirt off the paua then beat the flesh until tender (with a meat mallet) – the shell can be cleaned later and used as a receptacle for knick-knacks. Slice the paua into five-mm thick slices and cook with the onion rings for exactly three minutes. Serve on a lettuce leaf with lemon and tomato wedges. Voilà! ■

across from Invercargill and prepare meals yourself. Often the Fishermen's Coop on the Halfmoon Bay wharf, Southern Seafoods at Horseshoe Bay or the Lettuce Inn have fresh fish and crayfish for sale – yum!

The only place to go for any nightlife here is the pub – there is only one. If you're tired of conversation, escape to the TV room with takeaways and local ale. Return to the bar when you can't stand the video any more and observe the evening life cycle of the endangered, white-gumbooted Stewart Islander again.

Getting There & Away

Air Southern Air (☎ 218 9129) flies from Invercargill to Stewart Island for $67.50 one way and $118 return (children half price). The student/YHA standby fare is $33.75 (return $67.50); you must present either a YHA or a student card. Be at the airport 30 minutes before departure; it's a good idea to telephone ahead to see if any discounted seats are available before going out to the airport. Flights go three or four times a day and take 20 minutes to hop over the narrow strait.

The bus from the Ryans Creek airstrip to 'town' on Stewart Island is included in the airfare. Baggage allowance is only 15 kg per person, which is small if you have tramping gear – exceed it and you'll be charged extra.

Ferry Stewart Island Marine's (☎ 212 7660) *Foveaux Express* runs from Bluff to Stewart Island for $37/74 one-way/return (children 15 and under half price). There are departures twice daily at 9.30 am and 5 pm in summer (once on Sunday). In winter the ferry sails once daily on Monday, Wednesday, Friday and Sunday. There are often extra sailings on public holidays. It's wise to book at least a few days ahead, especially in summer but in winter it's not so busy. The crossing takes one hour across Foveaux Strait, noted for its often stormy weather – it can be a rough trip, so take some seasickness pills with you.

Campbelltown Passenger (☎ 212 7404) connects with the ferry and picks up from anywhere in Invercargill. In the past, the ferry operator offered discounts or standby fares but now they don't – if you go standby on the plane it works out cheaper. Fly!

Getting Around

Stewart Island Travel (☎ 219 1269) arranges bus tours, taxis and accommodation, and is an agent for Southern Air. Go there for travel advice, especially air and boat charters. With a lack of roads, a boat trip is a good option to get a feel for the island.

Oban Taxis & Tours (☎ 219 1456) near the wharf provides a 24-hour taxi service and runs a 90-minute scenic bus tour. There are rental cars available from Stewart Island Travel ($70 for a full day). A couple of places on the island have mountain bikes for hire.

A number of charter boats are available for picks-ups and drop-offs on remote parts of the island. The Stewart Island Water Taxi (☎ 219 1394) takes six passengers; to Ulva Island costs $15 per person and a half-day trip sightseeing would cost about $80 per person (both have a minimum of two).

Chatham Islands

The Chathams are an isolated, mysterious and wild group of islands, very much off the beaten track. Given the name Rekohu (Misty Sun) by the Moriori, they are out in the Pacific, about 770 km east of Christchurch. There are 10 islands in the group but apart from the 50 or so people on Pitt Island, only Chatham Island, with 700 people, is significantly populated. The islands offer a world of contrast – rugged coastlines and towering cliffs, volcanic peaks, lagoons and peat bogs, sweeping beaches devoid of human habitation, isolated farms, wind-stunted vegetation and dense patches of forest. Apart from farming and tourism, the other main industry is crayfish processing and there are plants at Waitangi, Kaingaroa, Owenga and Port Hutt. These four towns look like neglected junk heaps choking in the flotsam and jetsam of their raison d'être. They may not be flash but exude a nuggety, dilapidated charm.

History

Chatham Island is renowned for being the last home of the Moriori, an isolated group of Polynesians. They were here before the Maori settlement of New Zealand, but with the arrival of Europeans things rapidly began to go wrong.

A British expedition commanded by Lieutenant Broughton first arrived at the island in 1791 and even that initial visit resulted in a clash, at aptly named Skirmish Bay (now Kaingaroa), and one Moriori was killed. There are two memorials at this spot to this day. In the 1820s and 1830s European and American whalers and sealers began to arrive and then, in 1835, a Maori tribe, the Ngati-awa, was resettled in the Chathams. The impact on the peaceable Morioris was dramatic as the Ngati-awa, under Chief Pomare, established themselves by right of conquest; the Moriori population crashed from around 2000 at the time of the first European arrival in 1791 to only about 100 in the 1860s. By the beginning of the 20th century there were just 12 full-blooded Morioris left.

The Maori leader and prophet Te Kooti was imprisoned here last century, after he had eluded the British troops and officials on the mainland for many years. He turned to peace and established the Ringatu faith while incarcerated here.

Fauna

There are 18 species of bird unique to the islands, and because of the isolation there is a large degree of endemism, as with the local tomtit, pigeon and robin. Entry to the sanctuaries, such as those near Pitt, and Rangatira (South East) Island, is prohibited but many species can still be seen. DOC staff will outline the best viewing spots for birdwatchers. There are numerous rare and unusual birds to be seen. The birds include the endangered black robin, which at one stage was perilously close to extinction in its last refuge, Little Mangere Island near Pitt Island (read more about the Black Robin story in the Flora & Fauna section). The rare taiko *(Pterodroma magentae)* was recently rediscovered nesting in the Tuku River region of the south coast of Chatham. Black swans, pukekos, wekas and many species of ducks are common.

There is a fur seal colony near Kaingaroa in the north-east of Chatham Island.

Information

Waitangi is the only sizeable town on the islands. There are a couple of shops, a hotel, motel, tourist lodge and a post office with savings bank facilities. The free fortnightly *Chatham Islander* carries the local news. They also have their own radio station, Radio Weka, and TV station (Chathams Television) run in conjunction with TVNZ. There is an

The Last Moriori?

One of the most fascinating aspects of the Chathams is the cultural legacy of the Moriori. There are still Moriori descendants on the islands and there are a few remnants of the once flourishing culture.

There has been much speculation as to where the Moriori came from. It is now generally accepted that they were Polynesians, like the Maori, who sailed to the Chathams from New Zealand. The date of their arrival is in dispute, however, as there is little archaeological evidence, but it was some time between 900 AD and 1500 AD.

Once in the Chathams they began to develop a separate identity from the mainland Maori. They did not have rigid social divisions, they forbade tribal warfare and settled disputes on a one-to-one basis with hand-to-hand combat, and their language developed subtle differences. Most importantly, they carved their symbols into trees (dendroglyphs) and into the rocks which fringe Te Whanga Lagoon (petroglyphs). When the HMS *Chatham* visited the island in 1791 there were believed to be about 2000 Moriori on the islands.

From about November 1835 groups of Maori began to arrive in the Chathams and soon there were about 900 new residents made up of the Ngati Tama and Ngati Mutunga of the Taranaki Ati Awa. They began to occupy the land in a process known as *takahi* and killed about 300 Moriori who resisted, and enslaved others. By 1841 there were believed to be only 160 Moriori and over 400 Maori and it was not until two years later that the Maori released the last of the Moriori slaves. In 1870 the Native Land Court Hearings recognised that the Maori had sovereignty over 97% of the Chathams by right of conquest; small reserves were created for the surviving 90 Moriori. The Moriori and Maori intermarried in time and slowly the unique identity of the Moriori faded. Their language died with the last great Moriori scholar, Hirawanu Tapu, in 1900. There were only 12 full blood Morioris left at this stage.

The last full blood Moriori was Tommy Solomon, who died in 1933. His passing was seen at the time as the extinction of a particular race but it was far from that. His three sons and two daughters are identified as Moriori and there were many other families on the island who claimed Moriori ancestry.

There are now believed to be over 300 Moriori descendants and there has been a revival of Moriori consciousness, particularly strong after the building of the Solomon monument at Manakau near Owenga in the south-east of the island. Today Moriori, Pakeha and Maori live side by side as Chatham Islanders. ■

STD and facsimile link with the mainland. The signposted DOC office is in Te One; ring before you go as it is likely to be unattended.

Information on the islands is available from Air New Zealand or, more particularly, from Mt Cook Airlines. *A Land Apart*, by Michael King & Robin Morrison provides a wealth of information about the islands.

The Chatham Islands, because of their location, are very exposed but they have a temperate climate. Average daily temperatures vary from 12°C to 18°C in February and 6°C to 10°C in July. The best time to visit is in December and January; often the temperatures then reach 23°C to 24°C.

Chatham Islands time is 45 minutes ahead of mainland New Zealand time.

Things to See

The islands have plenty of fine beaches and they're a popular place for fishing and particularly for catching crayfish. Crayfish are a major industry in the Chatham Islands, and they're exported to North America and Japan. Six crayfish can be caught per person per day and 10 paua are allowed each person; check with the DOC in Te One. Scuba divers can explore the shipwrecks around the islands while trampers will also find interesting country to explore, particularly at the southern end of Chatham Island. The DOC have set up six formal reserves, developed with walking tracks of anything from an hour to full day in duration. The northern end of Chatham is flat and windswept. There's a small museum with Moriori artefacts in the council offices.

Three unusual attractions to be seen are the tree carvings, rock engravings and fossilised black sharks' teeth. The 200-year-old Moriori **tree carvings** (dendroglyphs) can be found in a grove adjacent to the old Te Hapupu aerodrome, in a signposted and fenced-off area. These mysterious carvings are gradually disappearing. The **rock engravings** (petroglyphs) are found on the shores of Te Whanga Lagoon, not far from the airstrip. The **fossilised sharks' teeth** can be found at Blind Jim's Creek, also on the shores of Te Whanga Lagoon. The teeth are about 40 million years old and a local heritage – please leave them where you see them. Their appearance here, pushed up by the waves of the lagoon, has not yet been fully explained.

The waters to the Chatham Islands are home to succulent crayfish

One unusual sight is the **statue** of the 'last Moriori', Tommy Solomon, at Manukau Point. Tommy's eyes seem to follow you as you scramble around the rocks below (see the aside earlier in this section).

Manukau Point will host a special party on 31 December 1999. Because of the kink in the International Datelaine it will be the first land to see in the year 2000.

Places to Stay & Eat

The *Hotel Chathams* (☎ 305 0048), Waterfront Rd, Waitangi, has singles/doubles for $45/50, or $35 per person for twin share rooms. The hotel also has a small souvenir shop (where you can get the highly sought-after Chathams T-shirt). They hire cars and organise trips. Meals are served and breakfast is $10, lunch $15 and an excellent three-course dinner is $25. Note that GST is *not* included.

The newer and more up-market *Chatham Lodge*, north of the Kaingaroa and Airport Roads junction and well signposted, (☎ 305 0196) has singles/doubles for $130/190 including all meals. There are package tour rates available and a self-contained cottage for $100 per day for four people. The lodge hires out 4WDs and boats and can arrange a variety of activities including diving, fishing, boating, horse-riding, tramping in nearby Henga Reserve and the world's most easterly windsurfing. Meals are $15 for breakfast and $25 for dinner.

Rooms at the *Tuanui Motel*, about 500 metres south of Waitangi, (☎ 305 0157) cost $45 for singles and a self-contained unit is $65 for two. Unlike the hotel and the lodge, there are kitchens here where you can prepare your own meals. Otherwise breakfast is $6 and dinner is $20.

Homestays with locals are also possible, especially when all other accommodation is booked up. The Smith family farmstay *Te Matarae* (☎ 305 0144), near the shores of Te Whanga Lagoon, is surrounded by natural bush. They have double rooms for $65 per person and prepare great dinners for $15.

Ask permission from the locals before camping anywhere. The Norm Kirk Centre, just north of Waitangi on the road to the airport, has basic camp sites for $10 for two and there are showers and cooking facilities.

You can buy crayfish and blue cod at the packaging factory in Waitangi. Flounder and whitebait can be caught in the lagoon, and paua and kina gathered just offshore. For the true gourmets there are swan egg omelettes and roast weka – yes the weka is consumed here as it is not native to the islands. Entertainment – bring your own or head to the Hotel Chathams, the local, to listen to a few yarns and trade friendly jibes.

Getting There & Away

Apart from a periodic freight-only cargo ship, the only transport to the islands is by air – Mt Cook Airlines (whose agents are Air New Zealand) using HS748 aircraft or Air Chathams (fax 305 0209) using a Metroliner. Mt Cook goes from Wellington and Christchurch, and the Air Chathams flight from Napier; the fare is $344 one way (children $228). There are also Super Thrifty fares of $185 one way ($370 return), which put the Chathams within reach of many more travellers. The flight takes three hours and

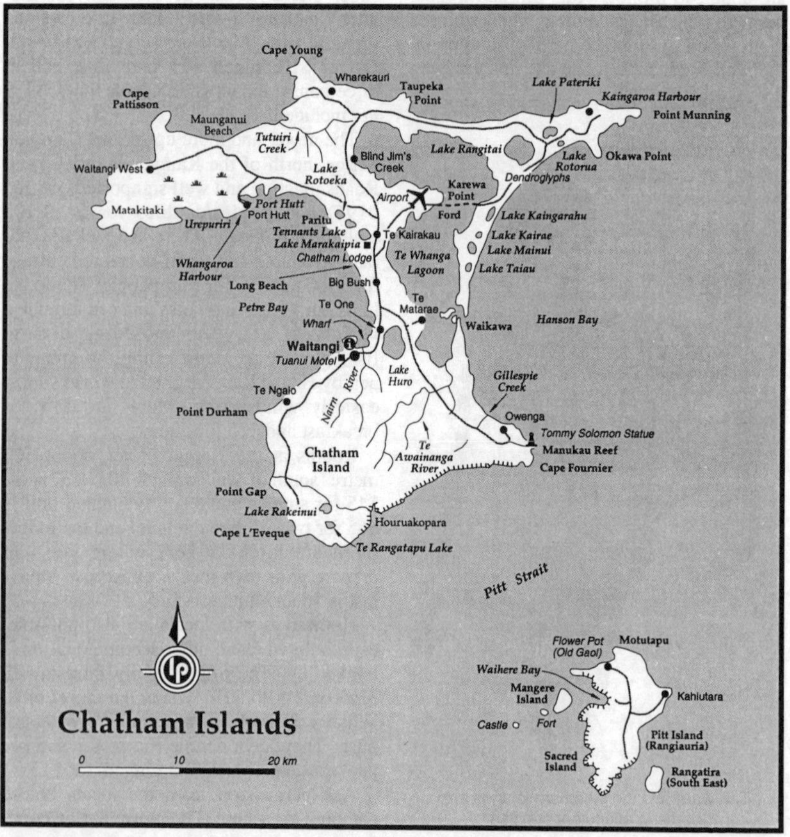

since there are only minimal seats available it's wise to book well ahead. Bookings for Air Chathams are handled through Ansett.

Getting Around

Beyond Waitangi most roads are unsealed and there is no public transport. The staff of the Hotel Chathams and the Chathams Lodge will pick you up from Karewa Airport if they know of your arrival, otherwise on occasion visitors have been left stranded at the airport. Chatham Motors (☎ 305 0093) hires small 4WDs for $60 per day plus 21c per km, or larger ones for $82 per day plus 26c per km. Chathams Lodge has Mazda station wagons for $70 and Nissan station wagons for $5 more; you pay for fuel. There are two other operators – Black Robin Rentals and the Hotel Chathams – hiring vehicles. Black Robin are particularly good and very helpful. It's also quite easy to hitch around the island.

Air Chathams (☎ 305 0126) operates a light aircraft (five-seat Cessna) for flightseeing and for trips to Pitt Island. It may be possible to hitch a ride with fishing vessels across to Pitt Island, but the seas are very rough, often with mountainous waves.

Tours are available from Chathams Lodge; prices are on application. It is relatively easy to hire a car and see most of the island's sights by yourself. Walking is a popular form of transport but check with DOC about access across private land.

Subantarctic Islands

New Zealand administers a number of subantarctic islands – the Snares, Campbell, Auckland, Bounty and Antipodes islands – where there are established nature reserves. Entry is restricted to three of the five island groups and is by permit only. To get some idea of this wild environment go to the Southland Museum & Art Gallery in Invercargill and watch the *Roaring Forties Experience* audiovisual.

The islands have a colourful human history – sealing, ship wrecks and forlorn attempts at farming. Now the islands are important as a reserve for remaining areas of vegetation unmodified by humans and breeding grounds for seabirds, penguins and mammals such as the elephant seal.

Few are fortunate enough to visit these remote islands but increasing eco-tourism possibilities, well-managed and guided, are being created. At the moment the only way of getting to the Subantarctic Islands is by boat on an expensive tour. A 15-day cruise, which takes in all the islands, will cost you about US$4500, all inclusive. One tour operator is Southern Heritage Expeditions (☎ (03) 314 4393; fax 314 4137). If you have the money you will consider it well spent, because of the rich variety of flora & fauna encountered.

SNARES ISLANDS

The Snares are famous for the incredible number of sooty shearwaters (muttonbirds) which breed there. It has been estimated that on any one evening during the season there will be six million in the air before they crash land to find their burrows. Other birds found here are the endemic Snares crested penguin, cape pigeon and Bullers mollymawks.

AUCKLAND ISLANDS

These are probably the most accessible of the islands, especially Enderby Island. At Sandy Bay on Enderby you will be able to see the Hooker's sea lion. Many species of birds also make Enderby their home (either temporary or permanent), including endemic shags, the flightless teal and the royal albatross. Skuas (gull-like birds) are ever present in the skies above the sea lion colony. Settlement was attempted in Erebus Cove, and it was not until 1992 that the last introduced cattle were destroyed. On Disappointment Island there are some 50,000 white-capped mollymawks.

CAMPBELL ISLAND

This is the only inhabited island in the New Zealand subantarctic islands, as there is a contingent from the NZ meteorological service stationed here. Apart from a few humans it is the true domain of pelagic bird species. It is estimated that there are over 7500 pairs of southern royal albatross here, as well as colonies of greyheaded and black-browed mollymawks.

ANTIPODES ISLANDS

These islands get their name from the fact that they are opposite latitude 0° at Greenwich, England. The real treat on this island is the endemic Antipodes Island parakeet, which is found with, but does not breed with, the red-crowned parakeet (similar to the NZ species of parakeet). In the short grass at the top of the islands, wandering albatross nest.

BOUNTY ISLANDS

Landing is not permitted on any of the 13 Bounty Islands – there is a good chance that you would step on the wildlife anyway, as the 135 hectares of land that makes up these granite islands is covered with mammals or birds. There are literally thousands of erect crested penguins, fulmar prions and salvins mollymawks clustered in crevices, near the lower slopes and on all other available pieces of real estate.

Index

Abbreviations

North Island – NI
South Island – SI
Outer Islands – OI

MAPS

TEXT

Map references are in **bold** type

Thanks

Thanks to the following travellers (apologies if we've missspelt your name) who took the time to write to us about their experiences in New Zealand:

Kelly Adams, Julia Alabaster, Lucy Appleton, Nick Archer, Jean Arnold, Elizabeth Ashley, John Ayers

Georgina Bade, Jens Baranowski, Marg Barr-Brown, Cynthia Bartholomew, Stefan Bartling, Sharron Beh, John Behle, Bryan Bell, J R & H F Bellaney, Paolo Bellino, Joachim Bender, Steve Best, Joanne Bina, Anthony Birtwistle, N Blaton & P De Clerck, Vera & Reto Blazar, Roy Bourne, Maria Bowers, John & Vera Boxall, Caprice Bradley, Brian Brakenridge, Frank Brandes, Gottlieb Braun-Elwert, Tom & Chris Brayton, Alan Breen, Kathy Brierley, Tim Brill, Mary Brogan, Louise Brooks, Graham Brown, Jean Buckle, Lee Bumsted, Barabra Burger, Robyn Burgess, John Burns, Gabrielle Busch

David Cambra, Christine Cameron, M D & J R Cann, Daniel Carey, Roy Carter, S Casanova & M Petruzzi, Fredric Chanania, Ryan & Danielle Chapman, Anna Chipchase, John Chislett, Glenn Churchill, Joyce Clarke, Birgit & Monty Claxton, Simon Clegg, Richard Colbey, W S Collins, Anne Conrady, Paul E Cowan, Grang & Julia Craig, J M Crapper, Heather Crookes, Barry Cuthbertson

Glen Davenport, Ruth & Rob Davies, Kim Dellaco, Jessie Dennett, J Deschepper, Paul & Fran Dickson, Susan Dixon, Leeza Dobson, Jochen Domscheit, D & J Downes, Nick Doyle, Colin & Amber Draper, Mrs A Draper, Jan Duker, Joy Durighello, Paul Dyer, Leonie & John Dymock

John & Mavis Earnshaw, Barry & Pam Eaton, Ron Ebert, John Eidschun, Rebecca Elder, Alicia Eppler, Ingela Eriksson, Liz Evans

Zoya Fansler, Zoya Fansler, David Farnham, Alex Farrell, Denis Farrelly, P & T Ferris, Rex & Karen Finlayson, Rosemary Fleming, Nigel Foster, Bill Fox, Helene Frankel, Hugh Fraser, Lucille Frauenstein, Jean & John Frazier, Elizabeth Friedman, Caroline Friedman

Siobhan Gallagher, Dominic Galvin, James Garrett, Bill Glass, Jon Glosser, Patricia Goddard, P Gordon, Robyn Gorton, David Green, David Griffiths, Roger Guillaume, Mary Gutmann

Elisabeth von Haacke, Karen Hales, Bobbe Hall, Gavin Hall, Carol Handin, Henrik Hansen, Denis Hansen, Robin Harrington, Alison Harris, Sandra Harrison, Nina Harrison, Steve Harrison, C A Healey, Arthur Heathfield, Ingrid Hecht, Raymond Hector, Dena Henderson, Mary Higinbottom, King Hang Ho, Dawn & John Hoare, Martina Holmgren, M & P van Hoogstralen, Jennifer Horner, Adrian Huber, T Bradford Hunter, Rosemary Hunter, David Hurst, Lynn Hurton

Michael Ibbotson, Anne Ingram, J & B Irwin, Takanobu Iwamatsa

Paul Jacobs, Mrs Erika Jarvis, Chris Jathom, JeffMcCaull, Sussi & Claus Jensen, Nikola Jeschke, Julia Johns, Dee Johns, Mandy Johnson, Tom Johnson, Jane Johnston, Chris Jones, John Jones, Connie Jones, Jean Luc Jourdan, A Juno

Paul Kane, A Kapelus, P Kavanagh, Siobhan Kelly, Mrs M J Kilgour, P J Killick, Nils & Lois King, Priska King, Jeffrey Knorr, I van Kokorn, Sam & Pam Kopecky, Andy Kost, Herman van der Kuil

Yvonne Lambert, Stuart Landsborough, Jacqul Lane, Jody Lawson, Adam Leavesley, Cheryl Lee, Jonathan Lightman, Klaus & Lilian, Heather Lindauer, Helga & Tony van der Lisdonk, Brigitte Liuduer, Elke Lohlein, Elke Lorenzen, Gabriele Losch

Hamish MacDonald, James Maffei, Annie Manfredi, H Manson, M Massey-Chase, Elizabeth McAusland, Gael McConachy, Jessica McDonald, Eliz & Howard McGrouther, Ellis McIntyre, Linda & Ian McMillan, Stuart Meadows, Pauline Menzies, Alberto & Franca Meotti, John Mernick, Manfred Meyer, Sharon Michelle, O Middleton, Tina Moe, Miss Annette Montague, Joanne Mower, Beth Moyle, Charles Mulner

Lynnette Nestor, Steve Nichols, Judy Nickels, Ole Nissen, Elizabeth Nolan

Bruce O'Halloran, Carley Olley, Jane Osmond, Claire-Lise Ourdouillie

Ellen Paanakker, Lisa Pachmayer, Jennie Page, Joan & Robert Panzer, A Duflos & A Parienty, Kurt Salloux & N Partamian, Gordon & Janet Pearce, Morten Pedersen, Mr CJ Penny, Nicholas Perugino, S Peter, Nikki Pitman & Rob Dixon, Marg Popovitch, Doug Powell, Debbie Price, Rainer Prigge, Steven Proctor, Erica & Richard Proposch, C R T Puckle, Mark & Tracy Purkiss

R Raderstorf & C McPherson, Keith Rakow, Raymond Ravinsky, Ian Read, J Redfern, Beatrice Reichmutter, Kay Reynard, Andy Rigby, Daniel Roberts, Sian Roberts, Cynthia Roberts, P Barclay & E Robinson, S & P Robinson, Andreas Rogall, M & M Rolli, Marita Ros, Jane Ross, Claire Rowsell, Alister Runge, Wendee de Ryke

Jill Salvin, H Whidden Sankarsingh, Britta Sannel, Lex & Sarah, Carsten Sauter, Kay Savage, Peter Schaefer, Angela Schorah, John Scott, Hazel Seeto, Noeline & Keith Sellar, Pamela Shebs, Helen & Lakpa Sherpa, R & E Siegrist, Stella Sims, Rob Sintes, Francese Sirno, Nicola Skudder, Jo-Ann Smiley, Kathleen Smith, Michael Smith, Dick Smith, Rory Smith, Morten Snaprud, John Soar, Joan Sokolich, George Spark, Richard Sparn, Sue Spear, Yvonne Spreckelmeyer, S & J Stavenson, Yvonne Steggall, Anton Steltenpohl, Kerstin Stevert, Uyken Stewart, Dr Alison Stirland, Antony Stockwell, June Stratford, Leon Strauss, Robert Strenski, S Susino & J Du Bois, Joan & George Sutherland

Ann Taylor, Mrs A Tebutt, Jean & John Telfour, Hila Tene, Dr Barry Teperman, Simon Thomas, Helen & Roger Thomas, C Thompson & M Stephens, Mr & Mrs A & E Thompson, Richard & Jenny Thomson, Toni-ann & Gary Thurlby, Stephen & Lois Tonnison, Jesus Ayuso Toral, P & C Treadwell, Gaye & Murray Tremlett, Doug Tuckett, Peter Tuohy, Nicola Turner, Roger Turner, Askild Tveit

Heike Ulrich

Claudio Valente, Kirsty Vickerstaff, Joyce Voit, Martin Volkening, Fay Vollmer

ET Wainwright, Theres Waldersbuhl, Janet & Richard Walker, Louise Walls, Philip Walters, Nick Ward, A Wason, Dominic Watters, Joanne Way, Geoff Wayatt, Andrew Welch, Alison Welch, Karin Wernstrom, Diana Whitwell, Uls Widmer, Miss E Wilding, Lindsay Williams, C Williams, Tanya Williams, Sue & Dick Williman, Tim Willment, N Wilson & A Heitsch, Melanie Winkelmann, Helen Wright, Anne Wright

Elihu York

Stefanie Zaug, Tony Zimmerman

LONELY PLANET JOURNEYS

JOURNEYS is a unique collection of travellers' tales – published by the company that understands travel better than anyone else. It is a series for anyone who has ever experienced – or dreamed of – the magical moment when they encountered a strange culture or saw a place for the first time. They are tales to read while you're planning a trip, while you're on the road or while you're in an armchair, in front of a fire.

JOURNEYS books will catch the spirit of a place, illuminate a culture, recount a crazy adventure, or introduce a fascinating way of life. They will always entertain, and always enrich the experience of travel.

ISLANDS IN THE CLOUDS
Travels in the Highlands of New Guinea
Isabella Tree

This is the fascinating account of a journey to the remote and beautiful Highlands of Papua New Guinea and Irian Jaya. The author travels with a PNG Highlander who introduces her to his intriguing and complex world. *Islands in the Clouds* is a thoughtful, moving book, full of insights into a region that is rarely noticed by the rest of the world.

'One of the most accomplished travel writers to appear on the horizon for many years . . . the dialogue is brilliant' **– Eric Newby**

LOST JAPAN
Alex Kerr

Lost Japan draws on the author's personal experiences of Japan over a period of 30 years. Alex Kerr takes his readers on a backstage tour: friendships with Kabuki actors, buying and selling art, studying calligraphy, exploring rarely visited temples and shrines . . . The Japanese edition of this book was awarded the 1994 Shincho Gakugei Literature Prize for the best work of non-fiction.

'This deeply personal witness to Japan's wilful loss of its traditional culture is at the same time an immensely valuable evaluation of just what that culture was'
– Donald Richie of the Japan Times

THE GATES OF DAMASCUS
Lieve Joris
Translated by Sam Garrett

This best-selling book is a beautifully drawn portrait of day-to-day life in modern Syria. Through her intimate contact with local people, Lieve Joris draws us into the fascinating world that lies behind the gates of Damascus.

'A brilliant book . . . Not since Naguib Mahfouz has the everyday life of the modern Arab world been so intimately described' **– William Dalrymple**

SEAN & DAVID'S LONG DRIVE
Sean Condon

Sean and David are young townies who have rarely strayed beyond city limits. One day, for no good reason, they set out to discover their homeland, and what follows is a wildly entertaining adventure that covers half of Australia. Sean Condon has written a hilarious, offbeat road book that mixes sharp insights with deadpan humour and outright lies.

'Funny, pithy, kitsch and surreal . . . This book will do for Australia what Chernobyl did for Kiev, but hey you'll laugh as the stereotypes go boom' **– Andrew Tuck, Time Out**

LONELY PLANET TRAVEL ATLASES

Lonely Planet has long been famous for the number and quality of its guidebook maps. Now we've gone one step further and in conjunction with Steinhart Katzir Publishers produced a handy companion series: Lonely Planet travel atlases – maps of a country produced in book form.

Unlike other maps, which look good but lead travellers astray, our travel atlases have been researched on the road by Lonely Planet's experienced team of writers. All details are carefully checked to ensure the atlas corresponds with the equivalent Lonely Planet guidebook.

The handy atlas format means no holes, wrinkles, torn sections or constant folding and unfolding. These atlases can survive long periods on the road, unlike cumbersome fold-out maps. The comprehensive index ensures easy reference.

- full-colour throughout
- maps researched and checked by Lonely Planet authors
- place names correspond with Lonely Planet guidebooks – no confusing spelling differences
- legend and travelling information in English, French, German, Japanese and Spanish
- size: 230 x 160 mm

Available now:
Thailand; India & Bangladesh; Vietnam; Zimbabwe, Botswana & Namibia

Coming soon:
Chile; Egypt; Israel; Laos; Turkey

LONELY PLANET TV SERIES & VIDEOS

Lonely Planet travel guides have been brought to life on television screens around the world. Like our guides, the programmes are based on the joy of independent travel, and look honestly at some of the most exciting, picturesque and frustrating places in the world. Each show is presented by one of three travellers from Australia, England or the USA and combines an innovative mixture of video, Super-8 film, atmospheric soundscapes and original music.

Videos of each episode – containing additional footage not shown on television – are available from good book and video shops, but the availability of individual videos varies with regional screening schedules.

Video destinations include: Alaska; Australia (Southeast); Brazil; Ecuador & the Galápagos Islands; Indonesia; Israel & the Sinai Desert; Japan; La Ruta Maya (Yucatán, Guatemala & Belize); Morocco; North India (Varanasi to the Himalaya); Pacific Islands; Vietnam; Zimbabwe, Botswana & Namibia.

Coming soon: The Arctic (Norway & Finland); Baja California; Chile & Easter Island; China (Southeast); Costa Rica; East Africa (Tanzania & Zanzibar); Great Barrier Reef (Australia); Jamaica; Papua New Guinea; the Rockies (USA); Syria & Jordan; Turkey.

The Lonely Planet TV series is produced by:
Pilot Productions
Duke of Sussex Studios
44 Uxbridge St
London W8 7TG UK

Lonely Planet videos are distributed by:
IVN Communications Inc
2246 Camino Ramon
California 94583, USA

107 Power Road, Chiswick
London W4 5PL UK

Music from the TV series is available on CD & cassette.
For ordering information contact your nearest Lonely Planet office.

PLANET TALK

Lonely Planet's FREE quarterly newsletter

We love hearing from you and think you'd like to hear from us.

When... is the right time to see reindeer in Finland?
Where... can you hear the best palm-wine music in Ghana?
How... do you get from Asunción to Areguá by steam train?
What... is the best way to see India?

For the answer to these and many other questions read PLANET TALK.

Every issue is packed with up-to-date travel news and advice including:

- a letter from Lonely Planet co-founders Tony and Maureen Wheeler
- go behind the scenes on the road with a Lonely Planet author
- feature article on an important and topical travel issue
- a selection of recent letters from travellers
- details on forthcoming Lonely Planet promotions
- complete list of Lonely Planet products

To join our mailing list contact any Lonely Planet office.

Also available: Lonely Planet T-shirts. 100% heavyweight cotton..

LONELY PLANET ONLINE

Get the latest travel information before you leave or while you're on the road

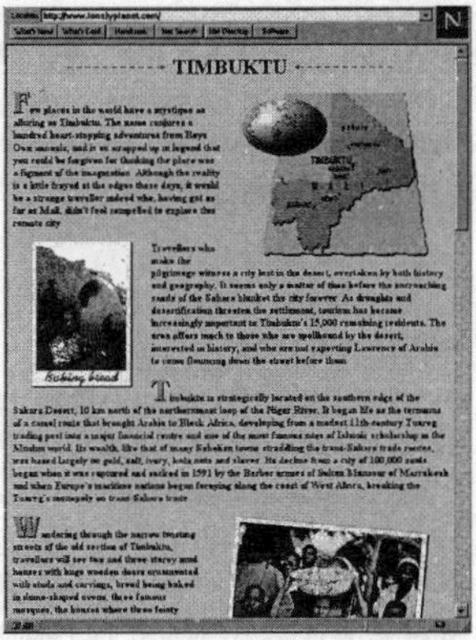

Whether you've just begun planning your next trip, or you're chasing down specific info on currency regulations or visa requirements, check out the Lonely Planet World Wide Web site for up-to-the-minute travel information.

As well as travel profiles of your favourite destinations (including interactive maps and full-colour photos), you'll find current reports from our army of researchers and other travellers, updates on health and visas, travel advisories, and the ecological and political issues you need to be aware of as you travel.

There's an online travellers' forum (the Thorn Tree) where you can share your experiences of life on the road, meet travel companions and ask other travellers for their recommendations and advice. We also have plenty of links to other Web sites useful to independent travellers.

With tens of thousands of visitors a month, the Lonely Planet Web site is one of the most popular on the Internet and has won a number of awards including GNN's Best of the Net travel award.

http://www.lonelyplanet.com

LONELY PLANET PRODUCTS

Lonely Planet is known worldwide for publishing practical, reliable and no-nonsense travel information in our guides and on our web site. The Lonely Planet list covers just about every accessible part of the world. Currently there are eight series: *travel guides*, *shoestring guides*, *walking guides*, *city guides*, *phrasebooks*, *audio packs*, *travel atlases* and *Journeys* – a unique collection of travellers' tales.

EUROPE

Austria • Baltic States & Kaliningrad • Baltic States phrasebook • Britain • Central Europe on a shoestring • Central Europe phrasebook • Czech & Slovak Republics • Dublin city guide • Eastern Europe on a shoestring • Eastern Europe phrasebook • Finland • France • Greece • Greek phrasebook • Hungary • Iceland, Greenland & the Faroe Islands • Ireland • Italy • Mediterranean Europe on a shoestring • Mediterranean Europe phrasebook • Poland • Prague city guide • Russia, Ukraine & Belarus • Russian phrasebook • Scandinavian & Baltic Europe on a shoestring • Scandinavian Europe phrasebook • Slovenia • St Petersburg city guide • Switzerland • Trekking in Greece • Trekking in Spain • Vienna city guide • Walking in Switzerland • Western Europe on a shoestring • Western Europe phrasebook

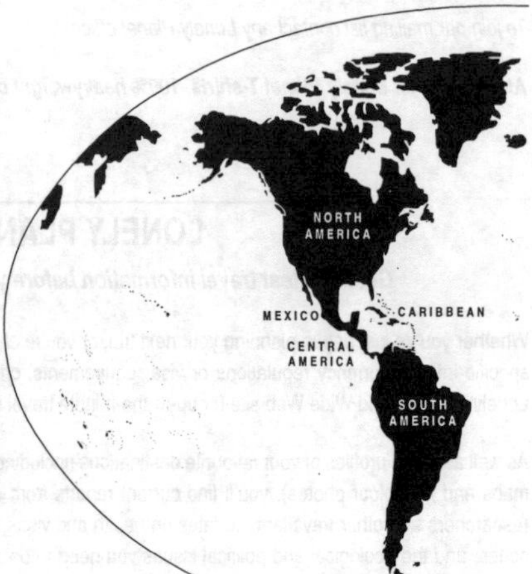

NORTH AMERICA & MEXICO

Alaska • Backpacking in Alaska • California & Nevada • Canada • Hawaii • Honolulu city guide • Los Angeles city guide • Pacific Northwest USA • Rocky Mountain States • San Francisco city guide • Southwest USA • USA phrasebook

CENTRAL AMERICA & THE CARIBBEAN

Baja California • Central America on a shoestring • Costa Rica • Eastern Caribbean • Guatemala, Belize & Yucatán: La Ruta Maya • Mexico

SOUTH AMERICA

Argentina, Uruguay & Paraguay • Bolivia • Brazil • Brazilian phrasebook • Buenos Aires city guide • Chile & Easter Island • Colombia • Ecuador & the Galápagos Islands • Latin American Spanish phrasebook • Peru • Quechua phrasebook • Rio de Janeiro city guide • South America on a shoestring • Trekking in the Patagonian Andes • Venezuela

ALSO AVAILABLE:

Travel with Children • Traveller's Tales

AFRICA

Arabic (Moroccan) phrasebook • Africa on a shoestring • Cape Town city guide • Central Africa • East Africa • Egypt & the Sudan • Ethiopian (Amharic) phrasebook • Kenya • Morocco • North Africa • South Africa, Lesotho & Swaziland • Swahili phrasebook • Trekking in East Africa • West Africa • Zimbabwe, Botswana & Namibia • Zimbabwe, Botswana & Namibia travel atlas

MAIL ORDER

Lonely Planet products are distributed worldwide. They are also available by mail order from Lonely Planet, so if you have difficulty finding a title please write to us. North American and South American residents should write to Embarcadero West, 155 Filbert St, Suite 251, Oakland CA 94607, USA; European and African residents should write to 10 Barley Mow Passage, Chiswick, London W4 4PH; and residents of other countries to PO Box 617, Hawthorn, Victoria 3122, Australia.

NORTH-EAST ASIA

Beijing city guide • Cantonese phrasebook • China • Hong Kong, Macau & Canton • Japan • Japanese phrasebook • Japanese audio pack • Korea • Korean phrasebook • Mandarin phrasebook • Mongolia • Mongolian phrasebook • North-East Asia on a shoestring • Seoul city guide • Taiwan • Tibet • Tibet phrasebook • Tokyo city guide

Travel Literature: Lost Japan

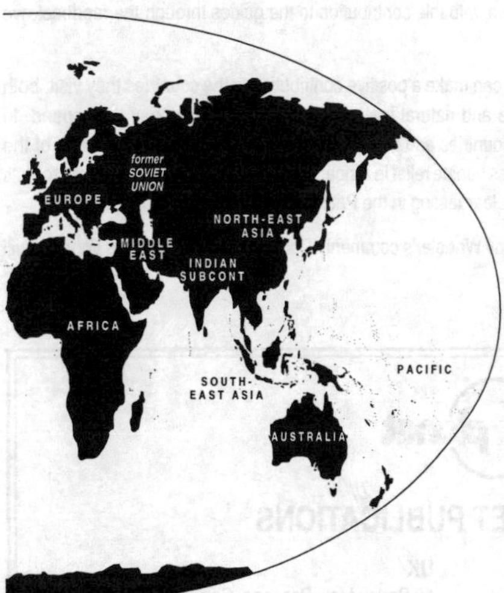

MIDDLE EAST & CENTRAL ASIA

Arab Gulf States • Arabic (Egyptian) phrasebook • Central Asia • Iran • Israel • Jordan & Syria • Middle East • Turkey • Turkish phrasebook • Trekking in Turkey • Yemen

Travel Literature: The Gates of Damascus

ISLANDS OF THE INDIAN OCEAN

Madagascar & Comoros • Maldives & Islands of the East Indian Ocean • Mauritius, Réunion & Seychelles

INDIAN SUBCONTINENT

Bengali phrasebook • Bangladesh • Delhi city guide • Hindi/Urdu phrasebook • India • India & Bangladesh travel atlas • Karakoram Highway • Kashmir, Ladakh & Zanskar • Nepal • Nepali phrasebook • Pakistan • Sri Lanka • Sri Lanka phrasebook • Trekking in the Indian Himalaya • Trekking in the Nepal Himalaya

SOUTH-EAST ASIA

Bali & Lombok • Bangkok city guide • Burmese phrasebook • Cambodia • Ho Chi Minh city guide • Indonesia • Indonesian phrasebook • Indonesian audio pack • Jakarta city guide • Java • Laos • Lao phrasebook • Malaysia, Singapore & Brunei • Myanmar (Burma) • Philippines • Pilipino phrasebook • Singapore city guide • South-East Asia on a shoestring • Thailand • Thailand travel atlas • Thai phrasebook • Thai audio pack • Thai Hill Tribes phrasebook • Vietnam • Vietnamese phrasebook • Vietnam travel atlas

AUSTRALIA & THE PACIFIC

Australia • Australian phrasebook • Bushwalking in Australia • Bushwalking in Papua New Guinea • Fiji • Fijian phrasebook • Islands of Australia's Great Barrier Reef • Melbourne city guide • Micronesia • New Caledonia • New South Wales & the ACT • New Zealand • Outback Australia • Papua New Guinea • Papua New Guinea phrasebook • Queensland • Rarotonga & the Cook Islands • Samoa • Solomon Islands • Sydney city guide • Tahiti & French Polynesia • Tonga • Tramping in New Zealand • Vanuatu • Victoria • Western Australia

Travel Literature: Islands in the Clouds • Sean & David's Long Drive

THE LONELY PLANET STORY

Lonely Planet published its first book in 1973 in response to the numerous 'How did you do it?' questions Maureen and Tony Wheeler were asked after driving, bussing, hitching, sailing and railing their way from England to Australia.

Written at a kitchen table and hand collated, trimmed and stapled, *Across Asia on the Cheap* became an instant local bestseller, inspiring thoughts of another book.

Eighteen months in South-East Asia resulted in their second guide, *South-East Asia on a shoestring*, which they put together in a backstreet Chinese hotel in Singapore in 1975. The 'yellow bible', as it quickly became known to backpackers around the world, soon became *the* guide to the region. It has sold well over half a million copies and is now in its 8th edition, still retaining its familiar yellow cover.

Today there are over 180 titles, including travel guides, walking guides, language kits & phrasebooks, travel atlases and travel literature. The company is one of the largest travel publishers in the world. Although Lonely Planet initially specialised in guides to Asia, we now cover most regions of the world, including the Pacific, North America, South America, Africa, the Middle East and Europe.

The emphasis continues to be on travel for independent travellers. Tony and Maureen still travel for several months of each year and play an active part in the writing, updating and quality control of Lonely Planet's guides.

They have been joined by over 70 authors and 170 staff at our offices in Melbourne (Australia), Oakland (USA), London (UK) and Paris (France). Travellers themselves also make a valuable contribution to the guides through the feedback we receive in thousands of letters each year.

The people at Lonely Planet strongly believe that travellers can make a positive contribution to the countries they visit, both through their appreciation of the countries' culture, wildlife and natural features, and through the money they spend. In addition, the company makes a direct contribution to the countries and regions it covers. Since 1986 a percentage of the income from each book has been donated to ventures such as famine relief in Africa; aid projects in India; agricultural projects in Central America; Greenpeace's efforts to halt French nuclear testing in the Pacific; and Amnesty International.

Lonely Planet's basic travel philosophy is summed up in Tony Wheeler's comment, 'Don't worry about whether your trip will work out. Just go!'

LONELY PLANET PUBLICATIONS

Australia
PO Box 617, Hawthorn 3122, Victoria
tel: (03) 9819 1877 fax: (03) 9819 6459
e-mail: talk2us@lonelyplanet.com.au

USA
Embarcadero West, 155 Filbert St, Suite 251,
Oakland, CA 94607
tel: (510) 893 8555 TOLL FREE: 800 275-8555
fax: (510) 893 8563
e-mail: info@lonelyplanet.com

UK
10 Barley Mow Passage, Chiswick,
London W4 4PH
tel: (0181) 742 3161 fax: (0181) 742 2772
e-mail: 100413.3551@compuserve.com

France:
71 bis rue du Cardinal Lemoine, 75005 Paris
tel: 1 44 32 06 20 fax: 1 46 34 72 55
e-mail: 100560.415@compuserve.com

World Wide Web: http://www.lonelyplanet.com